T0214576

Lecture Notes in Computer Science　11274

Commenced Publication in 1973
Founding and Former Series Editors:
Gerhard Goos, Juris Hartmanis, and Jan van Leeuwen

More information about this series at http://www.springer.com/series/7410

Thomas Peyrin · Steven Galbraith (Eds.)

Advances in Cryptology – ASIACRYPT 2018

24th International Conference on the Theory
and Application of Cryptology and Information Security
Brisbane, QLD, Australia, December 2–6, 2018
Proceedings, Part III

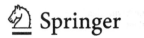 Springer

Editors
Thomas Peyrin ⓘ
Nanyang Technological University
Singapore, Singapore

Steven Galbraith
University of Auckland
Auckland, New Zealand

ISSN 0302-9743   ISSN 1611-3349 (electronic)
Lecture Notes in Computer Science
ISBN 978-3-030-03331-6   ISBN 978-3-030-03332-3 (eBook)
https://doi.org/10.1007/978-3-030-03332-3

Library of Congress Control Number: 2018959424

LNCS Sublibrary: SL4 – Security and Cryptology

This Springer imprint is published by the registered company Springer Nature Switzerland AG
The registered company address is: Gewerbestrasse 11, 6330 Cham, Switzerland

Preface

ASIACRYPT 2018, the 24th Annual International Conference on Theory and Application of Cryptology and Information Security, was held in Brisbane, Australia, during December 2–6, 2018.

The conference focused on all technical aspects of cryptology, and was sponsored by the International Association for Cryptologic Research (IACR).

Asiacrypt 2018 received a total of 234 submissions from all over the world. The Program Committee selected 65 papers for publication in the proceedings of this conference. The review process was made by the usual double-blind peer review by the Program Committee, which consisted of 47 leading experts of the field. Each submission was reviewed by at least three reviewers and five reviewers were assigned to submissions co-authored by Program Committee members. This year, the conference operated a two-round review system with rebuttal phase. In the first-round review the Program Committee selected the 145 submissions that were considered of value for proceeding to the second round. In the second-round phase the Program Committee further reviewed the submissions by taking into account their rebuttal letter from the authors. The selection process was assisted by a total of 347 external reviewers. These three-volume proceedings contain the revised versions of the papers that were selected. The revised versions were not reviewed again and the authors are responsible for their contents.

The program of Asiacrypt 2018 featured three excellent invited talks by Mitsuru Matsui, Melissa Chase, and Vanessa Teague. The conference also featured a traditional rump session that contained short presentations on the latest research results of the field. The Program Committee selected the work "Block Cipher Invariants as Eigenvectors of Correlation Matrices" by Tim Beyne for the Best Paper Award of Asiacrypt 2018. Two more papers, "Learning Strikes Again: the Case of the DRS Signature Scheme" by Yang Yu and Léo Ducas, and "Tighter Security Proofs for GPV-IBE in the Quantum Random Oracle Model" by Shuichi Katsumata, Shota Yamada, and Takashi Yamakawa, were solicited to submit the full versions to the *Journal of Cryptology*. The program chairs selected Chris Brzuska and Bart Mennink for the Best PC Member Award.

Many people contributed to the success of Asiacrypt 2018. We would like to thank the authors for submitting their research results to the conference. We are very grateful to all of the PC members as well as the external reviewers for their fruitful comments and discussions on their areas of expertise. We are greatly indebted to Josef Pieprzyk, the general chair, for his efforts and overall organization. We would also like to thank Waleed Alkalabi, Niluka Arasinghe, Mir Ali Rezazadeh Baee, Lynn Batten, Xavier Boyen, Ed Dawson, Ernest Foo, Mukhtar Hassan, Udyani Herath, Qingyi Li, Georg Lippold, Matthew McKague, Basker Palaniswamy, Anisur Rahman, Leonie Simpson, Shriparen Sriskandarajah, Gabrielle Stephens, and Chathurika Don Wickramage, the local Organizing Committee for their continuous support. We thank Craig Costello, Léo Ducas, and Pierre Karpman for expertly organizing and chairing the rump session.

Finally we thank Shai Halevi for letting us use his nice software for the paper submission and review process. We also thank Alfred Hofmann, Anna Kramer, and their colleagues for handling the editorial process of the proceedings published in Springer's LNCS series.

December 2018

Thomas Peyrin
Steven Galbraith

ASIACRYPT 2018

**The 24th Annual International Conference on Theory
and Application of Cryptology and Information Security**

Sponsored by the International Association for Cryptologic Research (IACR)

December 2–6, 2018, Brisbane, Australia

General Chair

Josef Pieprzyk   CSIRO, Data61, Australia

Program Co-chairs

Thomas Peyrin   Nanyang Technological University, Singapore
Steven Galbraith   University of Auckland, New Zealand

Program Committee

Martin Albrecht   Royal Holloway University of London, UK
Prabhanjan Ananth   MIT, USA
Lejla Batina   Radboud University, The Netherlands
Sonia Belaïd   CryptoExperts, France
Daniel J. Bernstein   University of Illinois at Chicago, USA
Chris Brzuska   Aalto University, Finland
Bernardo David   Tokyo Institute of Technology, Japan
Nico Döttling   Friedrich-Alexander University Erlangen-Nürnberg, Germany
Léo Ducas   CWI, The Netherlands
Jens Groth   University College London, UK
Dawu Gu   Shanghai Jiao Tong University, China
Goichiro Hanaoka   AIST, Japan
Viet Tung Hoang   Florida State University, USA
Takanori Isobe   University of Hyogo, Japan
Jérémy Jean   ANSSI, France
Stefan Kölbl   Technical University of Denmark, Denmark
Ilan Komargodski   Cornell Tech, USA
Kaoru Kurosawa   Ibaraki University, Japan
Virginie Lallemand   Ruhr-Universität Bochum, Germany
Gaëtan Leurent   Inria, France
Benoît Libert   CNRS and ENS de Lyon, France
Helger Lipmaa   University of Tartu, Estonia

Atul Luykx   Visa Research, USA
Stefan Mangard   TU Graz, Austria
Bart Mennink   Radboud University, The Netherlands
Brice Minaud   Royal Holloway University of London, UK
Mridul Nandi   Indian Statistical Institute, India
Khoa Nguyen   Nanyang Technological University, Singapore
Svetla Nikova   KU Leuven, Belgium
Elisabeth Oswald   University of Bristol, UK
Arpita Patra   Indian Institute of Science, India
Giuseppe Persiano   Università di Salerno, Italy and Google, USA
Carla Ràfols   Universitat Pompeu Fabra, Spain
Amin Sakzad   Monash University, Australia
Jae Hong Seo   Hanyang University, Korea
Ling Song   Institute of Information Engineering, Chinese Academy
                              of Sciences, China
                            Nanyang Technological University, Singapore
Douglas Stebila   University of Waterloo, Canada
Marc Stevens   CWI, The Netherlands
Qiang Tang   New Jersey Institute of Technology, USA
Mehdi Tibouchi   NTT laboratories, Japan
Yosuke Todo   NTT Secure Platform Laboratories, Japan
Dominique Unruh   University of Tartu, Estonia
Gilles Van Assche   STMicroelectronics, Belgium
Frederik Vercauteren   KU Leuven, Belgium
Bo-Yin Yang   Academia Sinica, Taiwan
Yu Yu   Shanghai Jiao Tong University, China
Aaram Yun   UNIST, Korea

External Reviewers

Behzad Abdolmaleki   Paulo Barreto
Aysajan Abidin   Gilles Barthe
Shweta Agrawal   Hridam Basu
Estuardo Alpirez Bock   Aurélie Bauer
Joël Alwen   Carsten Baum
Abdelrahaman Aly   Christof Beierle
Andris Ambainis   Adi Ben-Zvi
Elena Andreeva   Ela Berners-Lee
Jan-Pieter d'Anvers   David Bernhard
Kazumaro Aoki   Pauline Bert
Nuttapong Attrapadung   Ward Beullens
Karim Baghery   Rishiraj Bhattacharyya
Shi Bai   Jean-Francois Biasse
Gustavo Banegas   Nina Bindel
Subhadeep Banik   Bruno Blanchet

Olivier Blazy
Xavier Bonnetain
Charlotte Bonte
Carl Bootland
Jonathan Bootle
Cecilia Boschini
Raphael Bost
Christina Boura
Florian Bourse
Dusan Bozilov
Andreas Brasen Kidmose
Jacqueline Brendel
Ignacio Cascudo
Dario Catalano
Andrea Cerulli
Avik Chakraborty
Debrup Chakraborty
Long Chen
Yu Chen
Yu Long Chen
Wonhee Cho
Ashish Choudhury
Chitchanok Chuengsatiansup
Michele Ciampi
Sandro Coretti
Alain Couvreur
Ben Curtis
Dana Dachman-Soled
Joan Daemen
Nilanjan Datta
Pratish Datta
Alex Davidson
Thomas De Cnudde
Luca De Feo
Lauren De Meyer
Gabrielle de Micheli
Fabrizio De Santis
Rafael Del Pino
Cyprien Delpech de Saint Guilhem
Yi Deng
Amit Deo
David Derler
Apoorvaa Deshpande
Lin Ding
Ning Ding
Christoph Dobraunig

Rafael Dowsley
Alexandre Duc
Avijit Dutta
Ratna Dutta
Sébastien Duval
Edward Eaton
Maria Eichlseder
Ali El Kaafarani
Keita Emura
Naomi Ephraim
Muhammed Esgin
Thomas Espitau
Martianus Frederic Ezerman
Leo (Xiong) Fan
Antonio Faonio
Oriol Farràs
Prastudy Fauzi
Serge Fehr
Dario Fiore
Tore Frederiksen
Thomas Fuhr
Eiichiro Fujisaki
Benjamin Fuller
Philippe Gaborit
Clemente Galdi
Nicolas Gama
Chaya Ganesh
Si Gao
Luke Garratt
Romain Gay
Nicholas Genise
Rosario Gennaro
Essam Ghadafi
Anirban Ghatak
Satrajit Ghosh
Junqing Gong
Alonso González
Hannes Gross
Paul Grubbs
Charles Guillemet
Siyao Guo
Qian Guo
Kyoohyung Han
Javier Herranz
Julia Hesse
Harunaga Hiwatari

Thang Hoang
Dennis Hofheinz
Seungwan Hong
Akinori Hosoyamada
Kathrin Hövelmanns
James Howe
Andreas Huelsing
Ilia Iliashenko
Ai Ishida
Masahito Ishizaka
Mitsugu Iwamoto
Tetsu Iwata
Håkon Jacobsen
Christian Janson
Dirmanto Jap
Jinhyuck Jeong
Ashwin Jha
Luke Johnson
Antoine Joux
Pierre Karpman
Shuichi Katsumata
Andrey Kim
Dongwoo Kim
Duhyeong Kim
Jeongsu Kim
Jihye Kim
Jiseung Kim
Myungsun Kim
Elena Kirshanova
Fuyuki Kitagawa
Susumu Kiyoshima
Yashvanth Kondi
Ben Kreuter
Toomas Krips
Veronika Kuchta
Marie-Sarah Lacharite
Junzuo Lai
Esteban Landerreche
Tanja Lange
Joohee Lee
Iraklis Leontiadis
Tancrède Lepoint
Jie Li
Qinyi Li
Shun Li
Wei Li

Xiangyu Li
Fuchun Lin
Donxi Liu
Fukang Liu
Hanlin Liu
Junrong Liu
Shengli Liu
Ya Liu
Zhen Liu
Zhiqiang Liu
Victor Lomne
Yu Long
Xianhui Lu
Yuan Lu
Chen Lv
Shunli Ma
Xuecheng Ma
Rusydi Makarim
Giulio Malavolta
Mary Maller
Alex Malozemoff
Yoshifumi Manabe
Avradip Mandal
Mark Manulis
Marco Martinoli
Daniel Masny
Pedro Maat Costa Massolino
Takahiro Matsuda
Alexander May
Sogol Mazaheri
Patrick McCorry
Florian Mendel
Peihan Miao
Vincent Migliore
Kazuhiko Minematsu
Matthias Minihold
Takaaki Mizuki
Andrew Morgan
Paz Morillo
Fabrice Mouhartem
Pratyay Mukherjee
Alireza Naghipour
Yusuke Naito
Maria Naya-Plasencia
Ryo Nishimaki
Ariel Nof

Wakaha Ogata
Emmanuela Orsini
Rafail Ostrovsky
Carles Padró
Tapas Pandit
Louiza Papachristodoulou
Alain Passelègue
Kenny Paterson
Goutam Paul
Michaël Peeters
Chris Peikert
Massimo Perillo
Léo Perrin
Edoardo Persichetti
Peter Pessl
Thomas Peters
Christophe Petit
Stjepan Picek
Zaira Pindado
Bertram Poettering
Eamonn Postlethwaite
Thomas Prest
Emmanuel Prouff
Elizabeth Quaglia
Adrián Ranea
Shahram Rasoolzadeh
Divya Ravi
Ling Ren
Guénaël Renault
Joost Renes
Joost Rijneveld
Thomas Roche
Paul Rösler
Mélissa Rossi
Dragos Rotaru
Yann Rotella
Arnab Roy
Sujoy Sinha Roy
Sylvain Ruhault
Mohammad Sabt
Mohammad Reza Sadeghi
Yusuke Sakai
Simona Samardzijska
Olivier Sanders
John Schanck
Peter Scholl

André Schrottenloher
Jacob Schuldt
Peter Schwabe
Danping Shi
Kyoji Shibutani
SeongHan Shin
Ferdinand Sibleyras
Janno Siim
Javier Silva
Thierry Simon
Luisa Siniscalchi
Kit Smeets
Yongha Son
Gabriele Spini
Christoph Sprenger
Martijn Stam
Damien Stehle
Ron Steinfeld
Joshua Stock
Ko Stoffelen
Shifeng Sun
Siwei Sun
Moon Sung Lee
Koutarou Suzuki
Alan Szepieniec
Akira Takahashi
Katsuyuki Takashima
Benjamin Tan
Adrian Thillard
Jean-Pierre Tillich
Elmar Tischhauser
Radu Titiu
Junichi Tomida
Ni Trieu
Boaz Tsaban
Thomas Unterluggauer
Christine Van Vredendaal
Prashant Vasudevan
Serge Vaudenay
Philip Vejre
Muthuramakrishnan
   Venkitasubramaniam
Daniele Venturi
Benoît Viguier
Jorge L. Villar
Srinivas Vivek

Antonia Wachter-Zeh
Alexandre Wallet
Michael Walter
Peng Wang
Ping Wang
Yuyu Wang
Man Wei
Zihao Wei
Friedrich Wiemer
Tim Wood
Joanne Woodage
Thomas Wunderer
Keita Xagawa
Haiyang Xue
Shota Yamada
Takashi Yamakawa
Avishay Yanai
Kang Yang
Qianqian Yang
Kan Yasuda
Kevin Yeo

Scott Yilek
Kazuki Yoneyama
Jingyue Yu
Yang Yu
Xingliang Yuan
Thomas Zacharias
Michal Zajac
Rina Zeitoun
Mark Zhandry
Bin Zhang
Cong Zhang
Fan Zhang
Jiang Zhang
Juanyang Zhang
Ren Zhang
Yingjie Zhang
Raymond K. Zhao
Shuoyao Zhao
Linfeng Zhou
Vincent Zucca

Local Organizing Committee

General Chair

Josef Pieprzyk   CSIRO, Data61, Australia

Advisors

Lynn Batten   Deakin University, Australia
Ed Dawson   QUT, Australia

Members

Waleed Alkalabi   QUT, Australia
Niluka Arasinghe   QUT, Australia
Mir Ali Rezazadeh   QUT, Australia
  Baee
Xavier Boyen   QUT, Australia
Ernest Foo   QUT, Australia
Mukhtar Hassan   QUT, Australia
Udyani Herath   QUT, Australia
Qingyi Li   QUT, Australia
Georg Lippold   Mastercard, Australia
Matthew McKague   QUT, Australia
Basker Palaniswamy   QUT, Australia
Anisur Rahman   QUT, Australia

Leonie Simpson   QUT, Australia
Shriparen   QUT, Australia
  Sriskandarajah
Gabrielle Stephens   QUT, Australia
Chathurika Don   QUT, Australia
  Wickramage

Contents – Part III

Multi-Party Computation

On Multiparty Garbling of Arithmetic Circuits

Aner Ben-Efraim[1,2(✉)]

[1] Department of Computer Science, Ben Gurion University of the Negev,
Be'er Sheva, Israel
anermosh@post.bgu.ac.il
[2] Department of Computer Science, Ariel University, Ariel, Israel

Abstract. We initiate a study of garbled circuits that contain both Boolean and arithmetic gates in secure *multiparty* computation. In particular, we incorporate the garbling gadgets for arithmetic circuits recently presented by Ball, Malkin, and Rosulek (ACM CCS 2016) into the multiparty garbling paradigm initially introduced by Beaver, Micali, and Rogaway (STOC '90). This is the first work that studies arithmetic garbled circuits in the *multiparty* setting. Using mixed Boolean-arithmetic circuits allows more efficient secure computation of functions that naturally combine Boolean and arithmetic computations. Our garbled circuits are secure in the semi-honest model, under the same hardness assumptions as Ball et al., and can be efficiently and securely computed in constant rounds assuming an honest majority.

We first extend free addition and multiplication by a constant to the multiparty setting. We then extend to the multiparty setting efficient garbled multiplication gates. The garbled multiplication gate construction we show was previously achieved only in the two-party setting and assuming a random oracle.

We further present a new garbling technique, and show how this technique can improve efficiency in garbling selector gates. Selector gates compute a simple "if statement" in the arithmetic setting: the gate selects the output value from two input integer values, according to a Boolean selector bit; if the bit is 0 the output equals the first value, and if the bit is 1 the output equals the second value. Using our new technique, we show a new and designated garbled selector gate that reduces by approximately 33% the evaluation time, for any number of parties, from the best previously known constructions that use existing techniques and are secure based on the same hardness assumptions.

On the downside, we find that testing equality and computing exponentiation by a constant are significantly more complex to garble in the multiparty setting than in the two-party setting.

Keywords: Arithmetic garbled circuits · Constant round MPC
Multiparty garbling

Research supported by ISF grant 152/17, by the Frankel Center for Computer Science, and by the BGU Cyber Security Research Center.

T. Peyrin and S. Galbraith (Eds.): ASIACRYPT 2018, LNCS 11274, pp. 3–33, 2018.
https://doi.org/10.1007/978-3-030-03332-3_1

1   Introduction

Garbled circuits are a fundamental cryptographic primitive, introduced by Yao in the 1980s [33]. They are used in one-time programs, key-dependent message security, homomorphic computation, verifiable computation, and more. The original motivation of garbled circuits, and to date still their main use, is for secure computation. The most practical approaches of secure two-party computation are based on garbled circuits.

Since their introduction, garbled circuits have been significantly optimized in a series of works, [5,21,25,26,29–31,34] being a very partial list. These works reduced the size of the garbled gates and concretely improved the efficiency of garbling protocols. For example, using the free-XOR technique introduced by Kolesnikov and Schneider [25], XOR gates are "for free", meaning they incur no communication or cryptographic operations.

Due to efficiency reasons, garbled circuits were almost exclusively considered for Boolean circuits. However, there have been a few attempts to efficiently extend the ideas of garbled circuits to arithmetic circuits (in the two-party setting), e.g., [1,2,28]. The works of Ball et al. [2] and Malkin et al. [28] showed how to extend free-XOR to free addition and multiplication by a constant. They further showed how to efficiently garble multiplication in $\mathbb{F}_p$, for small p. Ball et al. also showed how to efficiently garble exponentiation by a constant. By combining CRT representations in a primorial modulus, Ball et al. showed that the above results extend to efficient garbling of arithmetic circuits over the *integers*.

Garbled circuits are important also for secure *multiparty* computation. The multiparty garbling paradigm was introduced by Beaver et al. [4] in the first constant round secure multiparty protocol. The first implementation of secure multiparty computation, FairplayMP [6], followed this multiparty garbling paradigm. Recently, experimental results in [8,32] suggested that concretely efficient implementations following the multiparty garbling paradigm, such as [8] in the semi-honest model and [22,32] in the malicious model, are more suited for secure multiparty computations over networks with high latency, such as the internet.

The adversarial model. We assume throughout that the adversary is semi-honest, i.e., follows the protocol but might try to learn private information from the messages it receives. A more realistic adversarial model is the malicious adversary, which can deviate from the protocol arbitrarily. Nevertheless, advances in semi-honest secure computation, and garbled circuits in particular, have often proved to be a significant stepping stone for later advances in the malicious model. Aside from numerous examples in the two-party setting, this was recently demonstrated also in the multiparty setting: the concretely efficient semi-honest protocols of [8] have been efficiently extended to maliciously secure protocols in [22] and [7].

We also assume an honest majority, i.e., the adversary corrupts only a strict minority of the parties. We do so in order to use the efficient constant round protocol for unbounded fan-in multiplication of Bar-Ilan and Beaver [3], which is needed in several of our constructions. Note that this is only needed for gates with mixed Boolean-arithmetic inputs/output. Thus, arithmetic circuits can also be garbled efficiently in the *dishonest majority* setting, assuming oblivious transfer. Due to space constraints, this is explained in the full version.

The hardness assumption we rely on is the existence of a mixed-modulus circular correlation robust (MMCCR) hash function, introduced by Ball et al. [2]; see Definition 1. The definition of MMCCR hash functions is similar to the definition of circular 2-correlation robust hash functions, introduced by Choi et al. [12] to prove the security of free-XOR [25]. Ball et al. [2] conjecture that one could use AES to construct a MMCCR hash function. Using AES is known to be extremely fast in practice using AES-NI instructions.

Our results and techniques. We study garbled circuits containing both a Boolean part and an arithmetic part in secure *multiparty* computation. We show both how to compute efficient arithmetic garbled circuits, and also how the Boolean and arithmetic parts of the circuit can efficiently affect each other. This allows for more efficient secure multiparty computation of functions that naturally combine Boolean and arithmetic computations, see our motivating example below.

We begin by extending known results for garbled arithmetic circuits from the two-party setting to the multiparty setting. In the *two-party* setting, Ball et al. [2] and Malkin et al. [28] showed that the free-XOR idea of Kolesnikov and Schneider [25] can be extended to free addition and multiplication by a constant in $\mathbb{F}_p$. We show that these results naturally extend to the multiparty setting. This follows similar lines to the extension of free-XOR to the multiparty setting by Ben-Efraim et al. [8].

We further efficiently extend the half-gates construction of Zahur et al. [34] (which efficiently compute AND gates in the 2-party setting) to efficient multiplication gates in the multiparty setting. There are three challenges we overcome in this extension: **(1)** Since there is no single garbler, the parties perform the computation using their shares. This requires understanding the values computed in each half gate, which were not explicitly written (only implicitly used) in previous works. **(2)** Since the evaluating parties also participate in the garbling (and thus have additional knowledge), the output wire's permutation element and keys are partitioned to avoid revealing secret information. **(3)** Extending from Boolean to $\mathbb{F}_p$ requires extending the technique of [34], by showing that the correct way to look at the solution of [34] is to multiply the external value of one wire with the key of the other. Proving this extended technique based on MMCCR also requires an additional step in the proof that was not needed in previous similar proofs (e.g., in [2,34]).

Using the half-gate extension, we manage to garble multiplication gates in $\mathbb{F}_p$, in the multiparty setting, with only $2p$ garbled rows. By representing numbers in a primorial modulos and using the Chinese Remainder Theorem, as suggested by Ball et al. [2], we obtain efficient arithmetic computations over the integers. In the two-party setting, efficient garbled multiplication gates were previously suggested by Malkin et al. [28] and by Ball et al. [2], see Table 1.

We then show how the Boolean and arithmetic parts of the circuit efficiently affect each other. In the multiparty setting, this requires a simple primitive that we call a multifield-shared bit, in which the same bit is secret shared in multiple fields of different characteristics. We show an efficient protocol for constructing this primitive in the semi-honest model with an honest majority. Furthermore, we explain that this primitive can be precomputed before the circuit is known.

To show how the Boolean part can efficiently affect the arithmetic part, we look at selector gates, which compute a simple "if statement": A selector gate has 3 input wires, x, y, and w_0. The wires x, y hold values in $\mathbb{F}_p$ and the wire w_0 holds a Boolean value representing the selection bit. The output wire z should equal either x or y, according to the value of the selection bit. I.e., denote the value on wire ω by v_ω, then a selector gate computes the following simple if statement: If ($v_{w_0} == 0$) then $v_z = v_x$ else $v_z = v_y$.

We show two constructions for garbled selector gates: the first is an extension of known techniques to the multiparty setting, using projection gates from Boolean to $\mathbb{F}_p$. To the best of our knowledge, this is the best construction of selector gates using existing techniques that relies only on MMCCR hash functions.[1] Our second construction is a designated construction, using new techniques described below. This construction reduces the evaluation time by approx. 33% from the construction using projection gates.

We give an informal overview of the main ideas in the designated selector gate construction: The gate contains two components. Using the first component, the evaluator tries to compute the multiplication between the Boolean value and the values in $\mathbb{F}_p$. But since the Boolean value seen by the evaluator is not the real value on the wire, this computation possibly inserts an error. To solve this, the second component is "corrector gates". The result from the corrector gate is (freely) added in order to correct the values from the first component. However, the (possibly) inserted error depends on the value seen by the evaluator on the Boolean wire. Thus, there are in fact 2 corrector gates, and the evaluator decrypts only one of them, according to the value it sees. This raises a question of security, as a corrupt evaluator can also decrypt the "wrong" corrector gate. This issue is solved by double partitioning of the keys and permutation elements, ensuring the decrypted keys and external values on the "wrong" corrector gate leak no information, even given the correctly decrypted keys and values. To the best of our knowledge, the technique of using a double partition of the keys and permutation elements is new in this setting.

To show how the arithmetic part can affect the Boolean part, we extend to the multiparty setting the construction of Ball et al. [2] of gates that test equality. These equality gates use free subtraction and projection gates. Unfortunately, we find that garbling general projection gates, and garbling equality gates in particular, is significantly more complicated in the multiparty setting. To explain

---

[1] In the 2-party setting there is a more efficient construction based on *stronger assumptions* by Ball et al. [2], see Remark 5. Nevertheless, since these stronger assumptions are currently not needed to optimize any other garbled gate, we believe it is of interest also to optimize selector gates which are secure based on MMCCR.

this, we note that the equations for equality gates require exponentiation. In the multiparty setting, the values needed for the offline computation are secret shared, and so this exponentiation is computed using MPC. We optimize these computations using the constant round protocol of [3]. However, this still implies that the offline time for computing equality gates is significantly slower. On the positive side, the size of garbled projection gates and their evaluation time are not affected by this, and therefore the difference in the online phase from the two-party setting is similar to the Boolean case.

A motivating example. Many real-world applications naturally use a mixture of Boolean and arithmetic computations. To illustrate the importance of mixed Boolean-arithmetic circuits, we look at a simple natural problem, the problem of conditional summation. Of course, it is possible to encode the problem as a Boolean circuit or as an arithmetic circuit. However, notice that encoding the conditions in arithmetic $0/1$ would be very inefficient when the conditions are complex. On the other hand, the summation could be expensive in Boolean, while free in an arithmetic circuit (using free addition). Therefore, a more efficient manner to perform the computation would be to compute the conditions in a Boolean circuit, then use selector gates, and finally compute the summation in an arithmetic circuit. Possibly, the conditions (which are Boolean) could decide multiplication constants instead of only $0, 1$, (i.e., weighted conditional summation) in which case multiplication gates are also required.

Comparison with previous works and techniques. Garbled multiplication gates were previously considered in the two-party setting by Malkin et al. [28] and by Ball et al. [2]. In Table 1 we compare our garbled multiplication gates with those of [2] and [28]. We compare only with 2-party garbling protocols, because previous multiparty garbling protocols did not handle arithmetic gates.[2] For sake of comparison, we also include the values of our garbled multiplication gate in the 2-party setting. The difference is that in the 2-party setting, the number of rows in each half-gate can be reduced by one, using the row reduction technique [29]. Furthermore, in the multiparty setting, each row requires n ciphertexts, and "decrypting" a row requires n^2 decryptions (hash function calls), whereas in the two-party setting each row is a single ciphertext and requires a single decryption.

In Table 2 we compare garbled selector gates using known techniques (projection gates) and the new designated construction.

Other related works. Most protocols for securely computing arithmetic circuits follow the secret-sharing paradigm, e.g., [10,11,14–16,23] to name but a few. In the secret-sharing paradigm, the parties share their inputs. Then, for each layer of the circuit, the parties interact in order to compute shares for the next layer. Thus, the number of rounds depends on the depth of the circuit. This could potentially lead to very slow online times when the circuit is very deep and the latency is high (for example over the internet), as demonstrated

---

[2] One could of course use an encoding of arithmetic into Boolean, e.g. the CRT encoding in [1], and then apply any Boolean multiparty garbling protocol. For a comparison between encoding into Boolean and arithmetic gates as discussed here, see [2].

Table 1. Comparison of our garbled multiplication gates with those of [2, 28] in number of parties, number of garbled rows, total size of garbled gate, security assumption, and number of decryptions (hash function calls needed in the online phase). For high fan-in multiplication, the construction of [2] scales differently than ours, but still seems to have more rows.

Garbled Multiplication Gate					
	Parties	Rows	Size	Sec. Ass.	# Dec.
[28]	2	$2p - 2$	$(2p - 2)\kappa$	Random Oracle[a]	2
[2]	2	$6p - 5$	$(6p - 5)\kappa$	MMCCR	6
New	2	$2p - 2$	$(2p - 2)\kappa$	MMCCR	2
New	n	$2p$	$(2p)\kappa \cdot n$	MMCCR	$2 \cdot n^2$

[a]Possibly, this construction, which is also based on extending half-gates, could be proven secure based on MMCCR, using techniques later developed in [2]. However, we note that proving the extension of half-gates to multiplication gates based on MMCCR requires an additional step that was not needed in previous proofs, see Sect. 6.

in [8]. On the other hand, using garbled circuits breaks the dependency of the round complexity on the depth of the underlying circuit. Furthermore, garbled circuits are an important primitive that proved worth investigating even outside the context of secure computation.

Hence, these works in the secret-sharing paradigm are incomparable with our work. In addition, the recent works of Damgård et al. [17] and Keller et al. [24] in the secret-sharing paradigm use gate-scrambling, which shares many ideas with garbling. Advances in garbling techniques could potentially aid these protocols.

Apart from the works of Ball el al. [2] and Malkin et al. [28], another notable work that studied arithmetic garbled circuits in the two-party setting is the work of Applebaum et al. [1]. The main result of [1] relies on LWE and is quite complex. It is unclear if their result can be efficiently extended to the multiparty setting – one of the main difficulties seems to be that their construction requires preprocessing the circuit layer by layer. Thus, it does not seem to naturally lend itself to an efficient constant round multiparty protocol, since a natural protocol for this preprocessing would require rounds corresponding to the depth of the

Table 2. Comparison of garbled selector gates using known techniques (projection gates) and the new designated construction.

Garbled Selector Gate					
	Parties	Rows	Size	Sec. Ass.	# Dec.
New – Known Techniques	n	$2p + 2$	$(2p + 2)\kappa n$	MMCCR	$3 \cdot n^2$
New Technique	n	$2p + 2$	$(2p + 2)\kappa n$	MMCCR	$2 \cdot n^2$

circuit. The secondary result of [1] using CRT has been surpassed by the results of Ball et al. [2].

There have also been several other works that dealt with mixed Boolean-arithmetic computations in secure computation, most notably the ABY framework by Demmler et al. [18]. This work deals with mixed Boolean-arithmetic computations in the 2-party setting by efficiently converting between arithmetic secret-sharing, Boolean secret-sharing (for GMW), and Yao garbled circuits. Their protocol is for 2 parties and not constant round. It is an interesting question if the ABY framework can be extended to the multiparty setting (replacing Yao with a BMR garbled circuit) and, in this case, how it would compare with our constant-round protocol.

Organization. In Sect. 2 we review the basics of multiparty garbling and garbling of arithmetic circuits. In Sects. 3 and 4 we explain how to efficiently garble multiplication gates and selector gates, respectively.[3] In Sect. 5 we describe our constant-round secure multiparty protocol for mixed Boolean-arithmetic circuits. In Sect. 6 we prove the security of our protocols.

2 Preliminaries

We assume that the reader is familiar with the BGW protocol and its improvement [9,19]. Sections 2.4 and 4 also use the constant round protocol for unbounded fan-in multiplication of Bar-Ilan and Beaver [3]. This protocol is nicely explained in [13, Sect. 4].

2.1 Security Model

We follow the standard definition of secure multiparty computation for semi-honest adversaries, as it appears in "Foundations of Cryptography" by Oded Goldreich [20].[4] To prove semi-honest security according to this definition, we present a simulator for the ideal world that receives the output from the trusted party and internally interacts with the real-world adversary. Informally, the protocol is secure if the view of the adversary (input, randomness, messages received) in the ideal world is computationally indistinguishable from the view of the adversary in the real world, given any fixing of the inputs of the honest parties.

2.2 Notation, Conventions, and Security Assumption

We list some of the conventions and notations that we use throughout this paper. We consider a static semi-honest adversary $\mathcal{A}$ corrupting a strict minority of the

---

[3] The garbling of equality testing gates and exponentiation by a public constant are explained in the full version.

[4] These security definitions are for the stand-alone model. There appears to be no obstruction to prove also for the stronger UC model, but this has not been done in this work.

parties. The circuit of the function to be computed is denoted by C, and $g \in C$ denotes both the gate and its index. The set of all wires is denoted by W, and $\mathcal{W}$ denotes the wires that are *not* outputs of "free gates" (e.g., XOR, addition, and multiplication by a constant gates). The respective sets of wires with values in $\mathbb{F}_p$ are denoted W_p and $\mathcal{W}_p$ respectively. The number of parties in the protocol is n, and $t = \lfloor \frac{n-1}{2} \rfloor$ is the bound on the number of corrupt parties. We denote the security parameter by κ. For binary fields, the keys are therefore in $\mathbb{F}_{2^\kappa}$. Notice that for characteristic p fields, keys should be in $\mathbb{F}_{p^{\kappa_p}}$, with $\kappa_p \geq \lceil \kappa / \log p \rceil$; see also Remark 1. We often abuse notation, writing $p^\kappa \stackrel{\text{def}}{=} p^{\kappa_p}$.

Throughout the paper we have computations in several fields. We often avoid mentioning the field in which the computations are carried out when this can be inferred from the equation. For example, if $\lambda \in \mathbb{F}_p$ and $\Delta_p^i \in \mathbb{F}_{p^\kappa}$ then the multiplication $\lambda \Delta_p^i$ is computed in $\mathbb{F}_{p^\kappa}$. Observe that $\mathbb{F}_p \subset \mathbb{F}_{p^\kappa}$ is a field extension, so this is well defined. We also ensure that the computation is well defined for the shares of λ and Δ_p^i; see Remark 1.

We sometimes use vector notation for the keys of the parties. For example, if each party P_i has a key $k_x^i \in \mathbb{F}_{p^\kappa}$ then we write $k_x \stackrel{\text{def}}{=} (k_x^1, \ldots, k_x^n) \in \mathbb{F}_{p^\kappa}^n$. Addition of vectors and multiplication by a constant are the standard linear algebra operations.

The hardness assumption we rely on, which we define next, is the existence of a mixed-modulus circular correlation robust hash function that we denote by H. This is the exact same assumption used by Ball et al. [2] in the two-party setting. Ball et al. conjectured that it is secure to construct H using AES.

Definition 1. *Let H be a hash function, and for each p in some set of primes P let $\Delta_p \in \mathbb{F}_{p^\kappa}$. We define an oracle $\mathcal{O}_P^H$ that acts as follows:*

$$\mathcal{O}_P^H(\rho, a, b, k, \gamma, \delta) = H(k + \gamma \Delta_{p_a}, \rho) + \delta \Delta_{p_b} \tag{1}$$

where $\rho \in \mathbb{N}$, $p_a, p_b \in P$, $\gamma \in \mathbb{F}_{p_a}$, $\delta \in \mathbb{F}_{p_b}$, $k \in \mathbb{F}_{p_a^\kappa}$, and the output of H is interpreted as in $\mathbb{F}_{p_b^\kappa}$. Note that $\gamma \Delta_{p_a}$ is the inner offset and $\delta \Delta_{p_b}$ is the outer offset. Legal queries to the oracle have inputs in the correct domains and satisfy:

1. *The oracle is never queried with $\gamma = 0$,*
2. *For each ρ, all the queries have the same p_a, p_b, and each $\gamma \in \mathbb{F}_{p_a} \setminus 0$ is used in at most one query.*

We say that H is mixed-modulus circular correlation robust if for all polynomial time adversaries making only legal queries to the oracle, the oracle $\mathcal{O}_P^H$, for random $\Delta_p s$, is indistinguishable from a random function (with the same input/output domains).

We use the shortened notation $\mathcal{F}_k(\rho) \stackrel{\text{def}}{=} H(k, \rho)$ ($\mathcal{F}$ can be thought of as a PRF). In our garbled gates, we use $\rho = g \| j$ (formally, $\rho = ng + j$), where g is the index of the gate we garble and $j \in [n]$. In most gates, the key of each party is "encrypted", using $\mathcal{F}$, by all parties, see for example Eqs. (2) and (3).[5] We therefore use the shortened notation $Enc_{k_x}\left[\,k_z^j\,\right] \stackrel{\text{def}}{=} \left(\Sigma_{i=1}^n \mathcal{F}_{k_x^i}(g\|j)\right) + k_z^j$. The outputs of the $\mathcal{F}_{k_x^i}(g\|j)$'s are, in this case, assumed to be in the same field as k_z^j. "Decryption" of the above ciphertext is by subtracting $\Sigma_{i=1}^n \mathcal{F}_{k_x^i}(g\|j)$.

Remark 1. In our offline protocols, the parties share both "small" field elements $\lambda \in \mathbb{F}_p$ and "large" keys/offsets $k_x^i, \Delta_p^i \in \mathbb{F}_{p^\kappa}$, with $\kappa_p \geq \lceil \kappa / \log p \rceil$. These are shared using Shamir secret-sharing scheme in fields of characteristic p (to allow linear combinations). Apart from the characteristic, there are three other requirements of the fields in which the elements, keys, and offsets are shared. The first two are always required by Shamir secret-sharing schemes.

1. The field must contain at least $n + 1$ elements.
2. The size of the field is at least the size of the domain of the secret.
3. We need to be able to multiply shares of the field element $\lambda \in \mathbb{F}_p$ with the shares of the offset $\Delta_p^i \in \mathbb{F}_{p^\kappa}$.

In order to satisfy the first requirement, the parties share λ in a field extension $\mathbb{F}_{p^{m_p}}$ with $p^{m_p} > n$. In order to satisfy the second requirement, k_x^i and Δ_p^i are shared in $\mathbb{F}_{p^\kappa}$, as they cannot be shared in a smaller field. In order to satisfy the third requirement, it must hold also that $m_p | \kappa_p$, so that $\mathbb{F}_{p^{m_p}} \subseteq \mathbb{F}_{p^{\kappa_p}}$. One way to ensure all the requirements are met is to set $m_p = \kappa_p = \lceil \kappa / \log p \rceil$. This is not always the most efficient solution – any implementation should optimize the choice of m_p and κ_p for each p, in correspondence with the bound on the number of parties, such that they satisfy all the above requirements.

2.3   Multiparty Garbling

In the multiparty setting, the first proposal for constructing a multiparty garbled circuit was given in [4]. We extend a simplified description for the semi-honest model given in [8] to the arithmetic setting (in the field $\mathbb{F}_p$), by applying the ideas of [2,28]. The construction of [8] allows the free-XOR ideas of [25]. In the two-party setting, Malkin et al. [28] and Ball et al. [2] showed that free-XOR extends to free addition, subtraction, and multiplication by a public constant in the field $\mathbb{F}_p$. As we shall see, this is also the case in the multiparty setting.

The multiparty garbling paradigm consists of two phases. In the first phase, often called the offline or garbling phase, the parties collaboratively construct a garbled circuit. Then, in the second phase, called the online or evaluation phase, the parties exchange masked input values and the corresponding keys. After that, each party (or a designated evaluating party) locally computes the outputs of the function. Our secure computation protocol that follows this paradigm is given in Sect. 5. We next recall the basics of the multiparty garbling paradigm.

---

[5] As we explain later, it is more efficient to garble Boolean gates regularly than using half-gates in the multiparty setting. However, this requires assuming also the existence of a circular *two*-correlation robust hash function (as defined in [12]), which we denote, using shortened notation, by $\mathcal{F}_{k_1,k_2}^2$. If we garble AND gates using the half-gates construction in Sect. 3, this extra assumption is not needed.

Boolean Circuits. For constructing the garbled circuit, each party P_i chooses, for each wire $\omega \in \mathcal{W}$, two random keys, $k_{\omega,0}^i$ and $k_{\omega,1}^i$. To enable the free-XOR technique [25], the parties need to choose the keys such that $k_{\omega,1}^i = k_{\omega,0}^i \oplus \Delta^i$ for some global offset Δ^i.

Each wire ω in the circuit is assigned a random secret permutation bit λ_ω. This bit masks the real values of the wires during the online phase. For an AND gate with input wires x, y and output wire z, the garbled gate is the encryptions $g_{\alpha,\beta} = \left(g_{\alpha,\beta}^1, \ldots, g_{\alpha,\beta}^n \right)$ for $(\alpha,\beta) \in \{0,1\}^2$, where

$$g_{\alpha,\beta}^j = \left(\bigoplus_{i=1}^n \mathcal{F}_{k_{x,\alpha}^i, k_{y,\beta}^i}^2 (g\|j) \right) \oplus k_{z,0}^j \oplus \left([(\lambda_x \oplus \alpha) \cdot (\lambda_y \oplus \beta) \oplus \lambda_z] \Delta^j \right). \quad (2)$$

Notice that all the values are "encrypted" by *all* the parties. XOR gates are computed using the free-XOR technique of Kolesnikov and Schneider [25], which was extended to the multiparty setting in [8] – the permutation bit and keys on the output wire are set to be the XOR of those on the input wires; they require no cryptographic operations or communication. For the circuit output wires, the permutation bits are revealed. For input wires of party P_i, the corresponding permutation bits are disclosed to party P_i.

During the evaluation phase, an evaluating party learns at each wire ω a bit e_ω, called the *external* or *public* value, and the corresponding keys. The keys on the output wire of a garbled gate are recovered by decrypting the row g_{e_x, e_y} using the keys on the input wires. As was first pointed out in [27], if the evaluating party participates in the garbling (which we generally assume), the external value can be extracted from the decrypted key – an evaluating party P_i can compare the ith key with the keys it used for the garbling, and thus learn the external value. I.e., if the key is $k_{z,0}^i$ then $e_z = 0$ and if it is $k_{z,1}^i$ then $e_z = 1$.

The external value e_ω is the XOR of the real value v_ω with the random permutation bit λ_ω. Since the permutation bit is random and secret, the external value reveals nothing about the real value to the evaluating party. The evaluating party uses the external value and keys to continue the evaluation of the proceeding garbled gates. For the output wires of the circuit, the permutation bit values are revealed, and thus the output is learnt by XORing with the external values.

Extension to $\mathbb{F}_p$ Arithmetic. The above generalizes naturally to arithmetics in the field $\mathbb{F}_p$. We explain this briefly; see [2] for a detailed explanation (in the two-party setting). Instead of each wire having a permutation bit λ, now each wire has a random secret permutation field element $\lambda \in \mathbb{F}_p$. The external value on wire ω is similarly defined $e_\omega \stackrel{\text{def}}{=} v_\omega + \lambda_\omega$. The permutation field elements are shared, using a linear secret-sharing scheme, in a field of characteristic p. Furthermore, each party P_i has a global random secret offset $\Delta_p^i \in \mathbb{F}_{p^\kappa}$. For each wire ω, each party P_i has a random key $k_\omega^i \in \mathbb{F}_{p^\kappa}$. The p keys of each party

P_i that relate to the p possible external values, are set to be $k^i_{\omega,\alpha} \overset{\text{def}}{=} k^i_\omega + \alpha\Delta^i_p$ for each $\alpha \in \mathbb{F}_p$.[6]

Thus, addition and subtraction are "free": The zero keys of the output of an addition/subtraction gate are chosen to be the sum/difference of the keys of the input wires. The permutation field element of the output wire is set to be the sum/difference of the permutation elements of the input wires. Since the keys and permutation elements are shared using a linear secret-sharing scheme in a field of characteristic p, the shares of the addition/subtraction can be computed locally by the parties (by performing local additions on their shares). Similarly, multiplication by a public constant c is also free: if $c \neq 0$, the zero keys and permutation element of the output wire are set to be the multiplication by c. Again, all the necessary computations can be performed locally by the parties, both at the garbling phase and the evaluation phase. The case of $c = 0$ is dealt using a global 0 wire.

A straightforward method for garbling multiplication gates is to extend Eq. 2 from Boolean to characteristic p. I.e., for a multiplication gate with input wires x, y and output wire z, the garbled gate is the encryptions

$$g^j_{\alpha,\beta} = \left(\Sigma^n_{i=1} \mathcal{F}^2_{k^i_{x,\alpha}, k^i_{y,\beta}} (g\|j) \right) + k^j_{z,0} + \left([(\alpha - \lambda_x) \cdot (\beta - \lambda_y) + \lambda_z] \Delta^j_p \right) \quad (3)$$

for every $\alpha, \beta \in \mathbb{F}_p$ and $j \in [n]$. The summations and multiplications in the above equation are carried out in $\mathbb{F}_{p^\kappa}$. Observe that for this equation to make sense, the output of $\mathcal{F}^2$ must also be in $\mathbb{F}_{p^\kappa}$. At the online phase, the evaluator recovers the output keys by decrypting row (e_x, e_y).

The above straightforward method requires p^2 garbled rows. In Sect. 3 we describe a more efficient way to garble multiplication gates in the multiparty setting that requires only $2p$ garbled rows, by extending the half-gates idea of Zahur et al. [34]. Extension of half-gates to $\mathbb{F}_p$ was shown in the two-party setting by Malkin et al. [28], but their techniques are quite different from ours. Also, in the two-party setting, Ball et al. [2] suggested a different solution to garble multiplication gates in $O(p)$ garbled rows. However, their solution relies heavily on projection gates. Unfortunately, projection gates are relatively expensive to garble in the multiparty setting, as we explain in Sect. 2.3.2.

2.3.1   CRT Representation and Application to Arithmetic Garbled Circuits

We briefly explain the idea presented by Ball et al. [2] for constructing efficient arithmetic garbled circuits over *the integers*; see [2] for a more detailed explanation. The idea is to use the Chinese Remainder Theorem (CRT), along with efficient garbling in the field $\mathbb{F}_p$, for small p.

The computations are done in the primorial modulus $Q_k = 2 \cdot 3 \cdots p_k$, the product of the first k primes. The number of primes k is chosen such that $Q_k > Z$, where Z is the bound on the possible intemediate values of the computation. Each number is represented by a bundle of wires, one for each of the k primes.

---

[6] Note that $\mathbb{F}_p \subset \mathbb{F}_{p^\kappa}$ is a field extension so $\alpha \cdot \Delta^i_p$ is well defined.

We call such a representation a CRT bundle representation. Adding two numbers is free, because the sum can be carried out in each prime separately (and addition in $\mathbb{F}_p$ is free), and similarly multiplication by a constant. Multiplication and exponentiation by a constant are also computed separately for each prime. Thus, the total number of computations and garbled rows is the sum of the computations/garbled rows in the different primes. Correctness of computing this way follows from the Chinese Remainder Theorem.

2.3.2   General Projection Gates

One of the main garbling gadgets used by Ball et al. [2] is projection gates. A projection gate is a gate which has one input wire and one output wire. For example, an exponentiation gate that computes $x \mapsto x^c$, where c is a public constant. In addition to gates $g \colon \mathbb{Z}_N \to \mathbb{Z}_N$, there are also useful projection gates in which the domain of the input wire differs from the domain of the output wire. Ball et al. [2] showed in the two party setting that any projection gate $g \colon \mathbb{Z}_{N_1} \to \mathbb{Z}_{N_2}$ can be garbled using at most $N_1 - 1$ garbled rows, where the -1 comes from the row reduction technique [29]. Furthermore, they showed that, in the two-party setting, it is not difficult to compute these garbled projection gates, because the garbler knows all the information for constructing the gate. In particular, the garbler knows all the permutation bits/elements.

In contrast, in the multiparty setting, the parties only hold shares of the permutation bits/elements. Therefore, the garbled gates are computed via an MPC subprotocol with these shares. In general, garbling a projection gate might require computing a very complex equation in MPC. Projection gates in which the output domain differs from the input domain are potentially even more complex.

We discuss three types of projection gates: a projection identity gate from Boolean to $\mathbb{F}_p$, an equality testing gate from $\mathbb{F}_p$ to Boolean, and an exponentiation by a (public) constant gate from $\mathbb{F}_p$ to $\mathbb{F}_p$ (the latter two are explained in the full version). The first gate can be computed very efficiently. On the other hand, the equality and exponentiation gates, while significantly more efficient than general projection gates, do still seem to be quite expensive. This is because there are exponentiations in the gate equations, and computing exponentiation in MPC is expensive, even using the protocols suggested in [3] or [13].

On the positive side, the number of garbled rows in our projection gates is only one row more than the respective garbled gates in the two-party construction of [2]. Thus, the size of the garbled projection gates is only slightly more than n times of the respective gate in the two-party setting. Furthermore, at the evaluation phase only a single row is decrypted. Therefore, the online computation is only about n^2 times than the two-party setting. This matches the Boolean case.

2.4   Multifield-Shared Bits

In this section we introduce a new primitive that we use in some of our constructions. Note that garbling multiplication gates does not require this primitive; the primitive is necessary only for garbling mixed Boolean-arithmetic gates. The primitive is a random bit $b \in \{0,1\}$ that is shared multiple times in different fields, of different characteristics. That is, each party holds multiple shares of the same secret random bit, where each share is in a different field with a different characteristic.

In the semi-honest model with an honest majority, it is quite simple to construct this primitive. First, each party P_i chooses a random bit b_i. The secret random bit will be $b = \bigoplus_{i=1}^{n} b_i$. Note that if there is an additional requirement that $b_z = b_x \oplus b_y$ (as needed in some of our constructions to allow free XOR), then party P_i sets $(b_z)_i := (b_x)_i \oplus (b_y)_i$ instead of randomly choosing it – permutation bits/elements are chosen only for the input wires of the circuit and for output wires of garbled gates/components. Next, the parties run protocols to share b in each field; these protocols are run in parallel.

We next explain the bit-sharing protocols. The sharing we describe is of Shamir shares, which is the type of shares used in our constructions. The sharing protocol depends on the characteristic of the field. See Remark 1 regarding the fields in which the shares should be generated.

1. In characteristic 2 fields, each party P_i shares its bit b_i amongst all the parties in a $(t + 1)$-out-of-n Shamir sharing. The parties sum (XOR) their received shares to obtain shares of the bit b.
2. In characteristic $p \neq 2$ fields, each party P_i shares the value $b_i' = \begin{cases} -1, b_i = 1 \\ 1, b_i = 0 \end{cases}$ amongst all the parties in a $t + 1$-out-of-n Shamir sharing. Then, the parties use an MPC protocol to compute shares of $b = \frac{1 - \left(\Pi_{i=1}^{n} b_i' \right)}{2}$. This is computed in constant rounds by combining the protocol of Bar-Ilan and Beaver [3] for unbounded fan-in multiplication (to compute shares of $\Pi_{i=1}^{n} b_i'$) and then linear operations on the shares (note that 2 is invertible in $\mathbb{F}_p$ and the inverse is easily computable).

Observe that b computed in both protocols is the same: $b = 0$ if and only if an even number of b_is is 1. This happens if and only if an even number of b_i's is -1, which is if and only if $\Pi_{i=1}^{n} b_i' = 1$, so if and only if $\frac{1 - \Pi_{i=1}^{n} b_i'}{2} = 0$. The case of $b = 1$ is similar.

Remark 2. In our description of the protocol, we assume the parties know the circuit when computing the multifield-shared bits. However, it is possible to compute all the multifield-shared bits even before the function is known, at almost no extra cost. This is explained in the full version.

3   Multiparty Multiplication Gates

In this section we show how to extend the notion of half-gates, introduced by Zahur et al. [34], to multiplication gates in the multiparty setting. The multiplication gates are in the finite field $\mathbb{F}_p$ (note that regular half-gates, i.e. AND gates, are multiplication in $\mathbb{F}_2$). The total cost of a multiplication gate in $\mathbb{F}_p$ will be $2p$ garbled rows, in comparison with p^2 garbled rows of the naïve construction. In particular, the Boolean AND gate will cost $4 = 2 * 2 = 2^2$ garbled rows using both the half-gates and the regular construction.

Remark 3. In the two party case, row reduction allows to reduce 2 garbled rows using half-gates, while other methods either allow only a single row reduction or are not compatible with the free-XOR technique. This is the main reason to use half-gates also in the two-party Boolean case. However, no *efficient* row reduction technique is yet known for the general multiparty case. Therefore, half-gates does not seem to be suitable for the multiparty Boolean case.[7]

Remark 4. In [2], multiplication gates in $\mathbb{F}_p$ are constructed differently, mainly using projection gates. As explained, projection gates seem to be considerably more expensive in the multiparty case than in the two-party case. Therefore, multiplication using an extension of the half-gates idea, as explained here, should be preferred in the multiparty setting. In fact, the garbled multiplication gate of [2] require slightly more rows and more decryptions, so possibly using the half-gates extension should be considered also for the two-party setting.

We follow the convention of [34], describing the two half gates as the "Garbler Half Gate" and "Evaluator Half Gate", because these gates are somewhat similar to the 2-party components of [34]. However, note that in our scenario all parties perform the garbling collaboratively (i.e., there is no single garbler), and each party can perform the evaluation.

Before going into the details of each half-gate, we give an informal overview of the idea. Assume we have a multiplication gate with input wires x, y and output wire z. During evaluation, the evaluating party learns on the input wires the external values bits $e_x = v_x + \lambda_x$ and $e_y = v_y + \lambda_y$, where v and λ are the real value and the permutation element on the wires respectively. The evaluating party also learns the keys corresponding to these external values. Using this, the evaluating party should be able to recover the output external value

$$e_z = v_z + \lambda_z = v_x v_y + \lambda_z \tag{4}$$

and corresponding keys.[8] In the naïve construction, this is done by decrypting the row (e_x, e_y), see Sect. 2.3.

In the half-gates construction, the computation is split into two distinct half-gates, each performing a different computation. Informally, the first gate computes $-\lambda_y v_x$ and the second half-gate computes $v_x(v_y + \lambda_y)$. Then, adding the two outputs, which is free, results in $v_z = v_x v_y$.

To securely compute a multiplication gate using these two half gates in the *multiparty* setting, two adjustments have to be made. The necessity of these adjustments will become apparent when we discuss security. The first adjustment

---

[7] Using half gates requires double the amount of decryptions during evaluation and is therefore inferior in this case despite having the same number of garbled rows.

[8] As explained in Sect. 2.3, it is enough to learn the keys; the evaluating party learns the external value by comparing with its local key used for the garbling.

is that the permutation element on the output wire, λ_z, must be partitioned $\lambda_z = \widetilde{\lambda_z} + \widehat{\lambda_z}$, where $\widetilde{\lambda_z}, \widehat{\lambda_z} \in \mathbb{F}_p$ are random elements under the constraint that they sum to λ_z (which is the random permutation element of the output wire). This is because the outputs of both half gates must be hidden, otherwise information might be leaked on some of the values.[9]

The second adjustment is that the zero keys k_z^i on the output wire also need to be partitioned $k_z^i = \widehat{k_z}^i + \widetilde{k_z}^i$, where $\widehat{k_z}^i, \widetilde{k_z}^i \in \mathbb{F}_{p^\kappa}$ are random under the constraint that they sum to k_z^i. The main idea of this partition is that the output keys of an honest party P_i on both half gates do not leak information on the global offset Δ_p^i. The permutation elements and keys $\widetilde{\lambda_z}, \widetilde{k_z}^i$ are used in the Garbler half gate, and $\widehat{\lambda_z}, \widehat{k_z}^i$ are used in the Evaluator half gate.

To conclude, informally the half gates construction computes the output using the following equation:

$$e_z = v_x v_y + \lambda_z = \overbrace{\left(-\lambda_y v_x + \widetilde{\lambda_z}\right)}^{\text{"Garbler Half Gate"}} + \overbrace{\left(v_x (v_y + \lambda_y) + \widehat{\lambda_z}\right)}^{\text{"Evaluator Half-Gate"}}, \tag{5}$$

The true construction and resulting equations are more involved, and we next explain them in detail.

3.1 Garbler Half Gate

In the original description of this half gate in [34], the idea is described that the garbler can take advantage that it knows the permutation bit (or color bit in the terminology of [34]). In the multiparty case, no unauthorized subset (i.e., a subset that could be controlled by the adversary) is allowed to know the permutation element on any wire that it should not learn. However, we can use the fact that the permutation elements are secret-shared to do the necessary computations. The computed gate is slightly more complicated than in the two-party case because the garbling parties also participate in the evaluation, and thus have additional information.

As already stated, the garbler half gate should compute the value $-\lambda_y v_x + \widetilde{\lambda_z}$. Note that v_x is the real value on the wire x (in an ungarbled computation) and is therefore never known – neither during garbling nor during the evaluation phase. Thus, we cannot hope to use it directly.

To overcome this, the value is computed using the equation $-\lambda_y v_x + \widetilde{\lambda_z} = -\lambda_y (v_x + \lambda_x) + \lambda_y \lambda_x + \widetilde{\lambda_z}$. The value $v_x + \lambda_x$ is the external value on wire x and thus revealed during evaluation. For garbling, the rows are computed for all p values, using the BGW protocol with the shares of permutation bits, and with $v_x + \lambda_x$ treated as a constant (as α in the αth row). The final garbled garbler half gate is the set of encryptions

$$\tilde{g}_\alpha^i = Enc_{k_{y,\alpha}} \left[\widetilde{k_z}^i + \left(-\alpha \lambda_y + \lambda_y \lambda_x + \widetilde{\lambda_z}\right) \Delta_p^i \right] \tag{6}$$

---

[9] This is different than the two-party case, where the evaluator half gate can be handled differently, cf. [34].

for every $\alpha \in \mathbb{F}_p$ and $i \in [n]$. Note that α is a constant and all other values are secret-shared. Since the multiplicative depth of this equation is 2, computing this half gate (Eq. (6)) requires two BGW degree-reduction rounds.

To verify that the correct output key is recovered, we observe that if the input external value is e_x, then the encryptions $\tilde{g}^i_{e_x}$ are decrypted for all i. Thus, the recovered output keys are

$$\tilde{k}^i_z + \left(-e_x \lambda_y + \lambda_y \lambda_x + \widetilde{\lambda_z}\right) \Delta^i_p$$

$$= \tilde{k}^i_z + \left(-(v_x + \lambda_x)\lambda_y + \lambda_y \lambda_x + \widetilde{\lambda_z}\right) \Delta^i_p$$

$$= \tilde{k}^i_z + \left(-\lambda_y v_x + \widetilde{\lambda_z}\right) \Delta^i_p = \tilde{k}^i_{z, -\lambda_y v_x + \widetilde{\lambda_z}}$$

matching the expected value of the keys corresponding to $-\lambda_y v_x + \widetilde{\lambda_z}$.

3.2   Evaluator Half Gate

As in the two-party case, the main idea of this half gate is that the evaluating party learns at the evaluation phase the external values of the wires, and can use this information for the computation. As we shall see more clearly when we extend the half gates to $\mathbb{F}_p$, the operation done by the evaluating party is to multiply by this external value.

The evaluator half gate should compute the value $v_x(v_y + \lambda_y) + \widehat{\lambda_z}$. The value $v_y + \lambda_y$ is the external value e_y on input wire y, and therefore known at evaluation time. On the other hand, the value v_x is the true value on wire x, and thus generally should never be learnt by any subset of parties. Therefore, to compute the gate we use the equation:

$$v_x(v_y + \lambda_y) + \widehat{\lambda_z} = (v_x + \lambda_x)(v_y + \lambda_y) + \lambda_x(v_y + \lambda_y) + \widehat{\lambda_z}. \tag{7}$$

The computation of the value $\lambda_x(v_y + \lambda_y) + \widehat{\lambda_z}$ is similar to the computations in the Garbler Half Gate. Thus, the main addition in this half gate is the computation of the value $(v_x + \lambda_x)(v_y + \lambda_y)$. Naïvely, it would seem that this requires p^2 rows in order to garble for each combination of $(v_x + \lambda_x, v_y + \lambda_y) \in (\mathbb{F}_p)^2$. However, in the two party Boolean case, [34] observed that this computation can be obtained practically for free. We first explain the observation of [34], and then extend it to the multiparty $\mathbb{F}_p$ case.

In the Boolean case, the external values are $(v_x \oplus \lambda_x)$ and $(v_y \oplus \lambda_y)$. Note first that $(v_x \oplus \lambda_x)(v_y \oplus \lambda_y)$ can be computed at evaluation time as both external values are known. This is still insufficient, because the evaluating party needs to recover some key that corresponds to this value. The "trick" performed by [34] is to XOR with the key on the wire x if $v_y \oplus \lambda_y = 1$ and to ignore it if $v_y \oplus \lambda_y = 0$. We next describe this slightly differently for the $\mathbb{F}_p$ case, but the descriptions in fact coincide for $p = 2$.

To extend the technique of [34], during evaluation, each evaluating party multiplies the key on wire x by the external value $v_y + \lambda_y$ and adds it to the decrypted key. Notice that this completely coincides with the Boolean case when $p = 2$ (since multiplying the key by 0 is the same as ignoring the key). The only subtlety is that now the corresponding multiplication of the zero key must be subtracted from the encrypted key during the garbling. However, the proof for this extended technique is slightly trickier, as we shall see in Sect. 6.

The garbled evaluator half gate is the set of encryptions

$$\tilde{g}^j_\beta = Enc_{k_{y,\beta}} \left[\widehat{k}^i_z - \beta k^i_x + \left(-\beta\lambda_x + \widehat{\lambda}_z \right) \Delta^i_p \right] \tag{8}$$

for every $\beta \in \mathbb{F}_p$ and $i \in [n]$. Since the multiplicative depth is 1, computing this half gate (Eq. 8) requires one BGW degree-reduction round.

Now during evaluation, the evaluating party multiplies the key on the x wire by the external value $e_y = v_y + \lambda_y$. This is then added to the key decrypted at row e_y. We next verify that the recovered output keys indeed corresponds to the correct value: the recovered output keys are the sum (for each $i \in [n]$) of $e_y(k^i_x + e_x\Delta^i_p)$ and $\widehat{k}^i_z - e_y k^i_x + \left(-e_y\lambda_x + \widehat{\lambda}_z \right) \Delta^i_p$. Simplifying,

$$e_y(k^i_x + e_x\Delta^i_p) + \widehat{k}^i_z - e_y k^i_x + \left(-e_y\lambda_x + \widehat{\lambda}_z \right) \Delta^i_p$$

$$= e_y k^i_x + e_y(v_x + \lambda_x)\Delta^i_p + \widehat{k}^i_z - e_y k^i_x + \left(-e_y\lambda_x + \widehat{\lambda}_z \right) \Delta_p$$

$$= \widehat{k}^i_z + \left(e_y v_x + \widehat{\lambda}^i_z \right) \Delta^i_p = \widehat{k}^i_{z, e_y v_x + \widehat{\lambda}_z}$$

matching the expected key value of $v_x (v_y + \lambda_y) + \widehat{\lambda}_z$.

3.3 Summing the Two Half Gates

Recall that $\lambda_z = \widetilde{\lambda}_z + \widehat{\lambda}_z$ and $k^i_z = \widetilde{k}^i_z + \widehat{k}^i_z$. At the evaluation phase, once both half gates are evaluated as above, each evaluating party computes for each $i \in [n]$ the output keys of the gate, by summing the two keys it recovered from the two half gates, i.e.,

$$k^i_{z, e_z} = \left(\widetilde{k}^i_z + \left(-\lambda_y v_x + \widetilde{\lambda}_z \right) \Delta^i_p \right) + \left(\widehat{k}^i_z + \left(e_y v_x + \widehat{\lambda}_z \right) \Delta^i_p \right)$$

$$= (\widetilde{k}^i_z + \widehat{k}^i_z) + \left(-\lambda_y v_x + \widetilde{\lambda}_z + (v_y + \lambda_y)v_x + \widehat{\lambda}_z \right) \Delta^i_p$$

$$= k^i_z + (v_x v_y + \lambda_z) \Delta^i_p = k^i_{z, v_x v_y + \lambda_z}.$$

Next, evaluating party P_j recovers the external value $e_z = v_x v_y + \lambda_z$, by comparing the recovered key k^j_z with its local keys.

4   Selector Gates

One of the more challenging tasks of performing an arbitrary computation using arithmetic circuits is to perform conditional statements. In this section, we discuss a gate computing a simple if statement. Namely, we build a "selector" gate, which chooses between two input wires in $\mathbb{F}_p$, according to a Boolean "selection bit". I.e., the gate has three input wires x, y, and w_0, and an output wire z. The values on the input wires x, y are from $\mathbb{F}_p$ and the value on w_0 is the selection bit. The selector gate computes the following if statement: If ($v_{w_0} == 0$) then $v_z = v_x$ else $v_z = v_y$. Note that by applying this to each wire in the CRT representation, we get a selector gate for integers.

We show two constructions for a selector gate. The first construction is using known techniques. The gate is constructed by first projecting the value of w_0 into $\mathbb{F}_p$ using a projection gate, and then using a multiplication gate. That is, the gate is computed using the equation:

$$v_z = \varphi(v_{w_0}) \cdot v_x + \varphi(v_{w_0} \oplus 1) \cdot v_y = \varphi(v_{w_0}) \cdot v_x + (1 - \varphi(v_{w_0})) \cdot v_y$$
$$= \varphi(v_{w_0}) \cdot (v_x - v_y) + v_y \qquad (9)$$

where φ denotes the projection of the bit into $\mathbb{F}_p$. There is one projection and one $\mathbb{F}_p$ multiplication in Eq. 9, costing 2 and $2p$ garbled rows respectively. Thus, a selector gate using the above construction has $2p+2$ garbled rows. However, note that the evaluator has to decrypt 3 rows using this method: 1 for the projection gate, and 2 for the multiplication gate (1 in each half gate). To the best of our knowledge, this is the best selector gate construction using existing techniques and relying only on the existence of MMCCR PRFs; see Remark 5.

Our second construction will be a new and designated construction of a garbled selector gate. The cost of the designated garbled selector gate will be also $2p + 2$ garbled rows. However, the number of rows the evaluator will have to decrypt will be only 2. Thus, we expect evaluation of this designated selector gate to be approx. 33% faster.

Remark 5. If w_0 is in $\mathbb{F}_p$ then a selector gate can be garbled with $2p$ rows and only 2 decryptions at evaluation (since projection is not needed). However, we argue that it is important to consider the case of Boolean w_0 for two reasons: the first is that when computing over the integers using CRT, we would like the same bit to select in all the characteristics. The second is that w_0 could be determined by a complex set of conditions, so it would make sense that w_0 is the output or intermediate value of a Boolean sub-circuit.

If we do not restrict the security assumption to only MMCCR hash functions, then in the 2-party setting, Ball et al. [2] showed a direct construction of a selector gate that has $2p - 1$ rows and requires only 1 decryption, which can be proved secure based on a random oracle (or possibly also on some extension of Definition 1 to allow correlation and circularity on two input keys). Note that in the 2-party setting, also the new designated construction and the construction using a projection gate have $2p - 1$ rows (this is because row-reduction [29] reduces 1 row from every garbled *component*). However, they require 2 and 3 decryptions, respectively. Nevertheless, since in the two-party setting this is the only garbled gate which an optimization is known using a stronger assumption, we feel it is important also to optimize constructions that are based only on MMCCR.

4.1   Charateristic 2 to Characteristic p Projection Gates

In this section we explain how to construct a projection gate that maps a bit value on a Boolean wire to the same value on a wire in $\mathbb{F}_p$. The projection gate has a single input wire w_0 containing a Boolean value, and an output wire z, containing the same value in $\mathbb{F}_p$. I.e., if $v_{w_0} = 0$ then $v_z = 0$ and if $v_{w_0} = 1$ then $v_z = 1$ (note that $v_{w_0} \in \mathbb{F}_2$ and $v_z \in \mathbb{F}_p$). This projection gate is needed if one wishes to multiply the bit value by a value in $\mathbb{F}_p$, as in the first selector gate construction described above.

The projection gate takes advantage of the following observation: Suppose that $v_{w_0}, \lambda_{w_0} \in \{0, 1\}$. Then,

$$v_{w_0} \oplus \lambda_{w_0} = \begin{cases} v_{w_0} - \lambda_{w_0}, & v_{w_0} \oplus \lambda_{w_0} = 0 \\ v_{w_0} + \lambda_{w_0}, & v_{w_0} \oplus \lambda_{w_0} = 1, \end{cases} \tag{10}$$

where the computations on the left and right are in $\mathbb{F}_2$, the computation in middle is in $\mathbb{F}_p$, and equality signifies that the value is the same value in $\{0, 1\}$ (whether in $\mathbb{F}_2$ or $\mathbb{F}_p$). I.e., if $v_{w_0} = \lambda_{w_0}$ then $v_{w_0} - \lambda_{w_0} = 0 = v_{w_0} \oplus \lambda_{w_0}$ and if $v_{w_0} \neq \lambda_{w_0}$ then $v_{w_0} + \lambda_{w_0} = 1 = v_{w_0} \oplus \lambda_{w_0}$.

To use Eq. (10), we will assume that λ_{w_0} is a multifield-shared bit, shared in both a field of characteristic 2 and a field of characteristic p. Note that although the output value is known to be a bit, it is masked using a random permutation element in $\mathbb{F}_p$ to avoid leaking information. Thus, the equation of the gate will be

$$e_z = v_z + \lambda_z = v_{w_0} + \lambda_z = \begin{cases} (v_{w_0} \oplus \lambda_{w_0}) + \lambda_{w_0} + \lambda_z, & v_{w_0} \oplus \lambda_{w_0} = 0 \\ (v_{w_0} \oplus \lambda_{w_0}) - \lambda_{w_0} + \lambda_z, & v_{w_0} \oplus \lambda_{w_0} = 1. \end{cases} \tag{11}$$

Hence, the garbled projection gate is the following encryptions for every $i \in [n]$:

$$Enc_{k_{w_0,0}} \left[\widehat{k}_z^i + (\lambda_{w_0} + \lambda_z) \Delta_p^i \right], \tag{12}$$

$$Enc_{k_{w_0,1}} \left[\widehat{k}_z^i + (1 - \lambda_{w_0} + \lambda_z) \Delta_p^i \right]. \tag{13}$$

As explained in Sect. 2, although $k_{w_0,0}, k_{w_0,1} \in \mathbb{F}_{2^\kappa}$, the output of the PRF in this case is in $\mathbb{F}_{p^\kappa}$. Assuming we have λ_{w_0} as a multifield-shared bit, i.e., the parties already posses Shamir shares of the the bit λ_{w_0} in the correct field of characteristic p, Eqs. (12), (13) can be computed using one additional BGW degree-reduction round. Using Eq. (11), it is not difficult to verify that for both values of e_{w_0} the decrypted key corresponds to e_z.

4.2   Designated Selector Gate Construction

In this section we explain a designated construction for a selector gate. The gate contains three components. The first component, which we call the chooser partial gate, has 2 garbled rows. The other two components, which we call the corrector partial gates, contain p garbled rows each. Thus, this construction of a selector gate will require $2p + 2$ garbled rows, same as the previous construction. However, this construction requires less decryptions at the evaluation phase, as we explain next.

The main idea we use in our construction can be seen as an extension of the half-gate technique – the evaluating party uses the key of one of the input wires, according to the external value on the selection wire. Furthermore, the evaluating party decodes only one of the two corrector partial gates according to the external value on the selection wire. Therefore, only two rows are decrypted when evaluating the gate (one in the chooser gate and one in the corrector gate), 1 less than the previous construction.

Note that since the external values are known only at the evaluation phase, we cannot prevent a corrupt evaluating party from decrypting also the other corrector partial gate. Thus, we must ensure that the decrypted key from this does not leak any extra information. This is achieved using a double partitioning of the output zero keys and permutation bit. I.e.,

$$\lambda_z = \widehat{\lambda_z} + \widetilde{\lambda_z} = \widehat{\widehat{\lambda}}_z + \widetilde{\widetilde{\lambda}}_z, \tag{14}$$

$$k_z^i = \widehat{k_z^i} + \widetilde{k_z^i} = \widehat{\widehat{k}}_z^i + \widetilde{\widetilde{k}}_z^i, \tag{15}$$

where $\widehat{\lambda_z}, \widetilde{\lambda_z}, \widehat{\widehat{\lambda}}_z, \widetilde{\widetilde{\lambda}}_z \in \mathbb{F}_p$ are random such that they satisfy Eq. (14) and likewise $\widehat{k}_z^i, \widetilde{k}_z^i, \widehat{\widehat{k}}_z^i, \widetilde{\widetilde{k}}_z^i \in \mathbb{F}_{p^\kappa}$ are random such that they satisfy Eq. (15). Note for example that $\widetilde{\widetilde{\lambda}}_z$ is random even given $\widehat{\lambda_z}, \widetilde{\lambda_z}$. Such observations are crucial for security, as we later explain. Otherwise, a corrupt evaluator could learn secret information by decrypting the "wrong" corrector gate. This idea of double partition of the keys and permutation elements appears to have not been used before in garbled circuits.

4.2.1   Half-Selector Gate

We now show the construction of a half selector gate that receives only two input wires, x and w_0, and outputs either x or 0 according to w_0. This easily extends to a full selector gate, using the equation

$$v_z = v_{w_0} \cdot v_x + (v_{w_0} \oplus 1) \cdot v_y = v_{w_0} \cdot (v_x - v_y) + v_y. \tag{16}$$

I.e., computing the value of $x - y$ using free subtraction, then using a half-selector, and then freely adding the value of y. It is also possible to construct a full selector gate directly. This is explained in the full version. The construction of the half-selector gate is significantly simpler, but contains most of the main ideas.

Informally, the half-selector gate is computed using the following equation:

$$v_x v_{w_0} + \lambda_z = \begin{cases} \overbrace{v_x(v_{w_0} \oplus \lambda_{w_0}) + \widehat{\lambda_z}}^{\text{``Chooser Gate''}} \quad \overbrace{+\lambda_{w_0} v_x + \widehat{\lambda_z}}^{\text{``Corrector Gate''}} & v_{w_0} \oplus \lambda_{w_0} = 0 \\[2em] v_x(v_{w_0} \oplus \lambda_{w_0}) + \widetilde{\lambda_z} \quad -\lambda_{w_0} v_x + \widetilde{\lambda_z} & v_{w_0} \oplus \lambda_{w_0} = 1. \end{cases} \tag{17}$$

This equation works because $v_x(v_{w_0} \oplus \lambda_{w_0}) = \begin{cases} v_x v_{w_0} - \lambda_{w_0} v_x & v_{w_0} \oplus \lambda_{w_0} = 0 \\ v_x v_{w_0} + \lambda_{w_0} v_x & v_{w_0} \oplus \lambda_{w_0} = 1, \end{cases}$
as one can readily verify for the 4 combinations of $v_{w_0}, \lambda_{w_0} \in \{0, 1\}$. Note also that the equations of the chooser gate in the first and second row simplify to $\widehat{\lambda_z}$ and $v_x + \widehat{\lambda_z}$ respectively, since the value of $v_{w_0} \oplus \lambda_{w_0}$ is already fixed. The reason why we need to use different partitions of λ_z in the two rows will become clear when we discuss the corrector partial gates in detail. In short, the reason is to ensure that decrypting the "wrong" corrector gate does not leak any information.

Chooser Partial Gate for Half Selector. The chooser partial gate is somewhat similar to the evaluator half gate. The first garbled row, which is decrypted when $v_{w_0} \oplus \lambda_{w_0} = 0$, should output a key corresponding to $v_x(v_{w_0} \oplus \lambda_{w_0}) + \widehat{\lambda_z} = \widehat{\lambda_z}$ if decrypted. The $\widehat{\lambda_z}$ is secret-shared, so this computation is done in a straightforward manner.

The second garbled row is decrypted when $v_{w_0} \oplus \lambda_{w_0} = 1$, and the output keys should correspond to the value $v_x(v_{w_0} \oplus \lambda_{w_0}) + \widehat{\lambda_z} = v_x + \widehat{\lambda_z}$. Here we use a similar trick as in the evaluator half-gate, i.e., the equation $v_x + \widehat{\lambda_z} = (v_x + \lambda_x) - \lambda_x + \widehat{\lambda_z}$, where for the value $v_x + \lambda_x$ the evaluator will add the key on the input wire x, as in the evaluator half gate. To conclude, the chooser partial gate for a half selector gate has the following encryptions for every $i \in [n]$:

$$Enc_{k_{w_0},0}\left[\widehat{k}_z^i + \widehat{\lambda_z}\Delta_p^i \right], \tag{18}$$

$$Enc_{k_{w_0},1}\left[\widehat{\widehat{k}}_z^i - k_x^i + \left(-\lambda_x + \widehat{\lambda_z}\right)\Delta_p^i \right]. \tag{19}$$

At the garbling phase, these equations require one BGW degree-reduction round. At the evaluation phase, if the external value e_{w_0} is 1, the evaluating party also adds the key on wire x after decryption.

We verify that the decrypted keys indeed correspond to the values $v_x(v_{w_0} \oplus \lambda_{w_0}) + \widehat{\lambda_z}$ and $v_x(v_{w_0} \oplus \lambda_{w_0}) + \widehat{\lambda_z}$:

1. If $e_{w_0} = 0$ the decrypted keys are $\widehat{k}_z^i + \widehat{\lambda_z}\Delta_p^i = \widehat{k}_{z,\widehat{\lambda_z}}^i = \widehat{k}_{z,v_x(v_{w_0} \oplus \lambda_{w_0}) + \widehat{\lambda_z}}^i$,

2. If $e_{w_0} = 1$ the output is the sum of $k_x^i + e_x\Delta_p^i$ and $\widehat{\widehat{k}}_z^i - k_x^i + \left(-\lambda_x + \widehat{\lambda_z}\right)\Delta_p^i$.

   Simplifying:

$$[k_x^i + e_x\Delta_p^i] + \left[\widehat{\widehat{k}}_z^i - k_x^i + \left(-\lambda_x + \widehat{\lambda_z}\right)\Delta_p^i\right] = \widehat{\widehat{k}}_z^i + \left(v_x + \widehat{\lambda_z}\right)\Delta_p^i$$

$$= \widehat{\widehat{k}}_{z,v_x+\widehat{\lambda_z}}^i = \widehat{\widehat{k}}_{z,v_x(v_{w_0} \oplus \lambda_{w_0}) + \widehat{\lambda_z}}^i.$$

Corrector Partial Gate for Half Selector. The computation of each corrector partial gate is similar to the garbler half gate. The interesting point is that there are two corrector gates for every selector gate, and only one value is used at evaluation. However, since which of the two is used is known only at the evaluation phase, both corrector gates need to be computed at the garbling phase.

The garbled rows of the first corrector gate, which correspond to the value $\lambda_{w_0}v_x + \widetilde{\lambda_z} = \lambda_{w_0}(v_x + \lambda_x) - \lambda_{w_0}\lambda_x + \widetilde{\lambda_z}$, are the following encryptions for each $\alpha \in \mathbb{F}_p$ and $i \in [n]$:

$$Enc_{k_{x,\alpha}}\left[\widetilde{k}_z^i + \left(\alpha\lambda_{w_0} - \lambda_{w_0}\lambda_x + \widetilde{\lambda_z}\right)\Delta_p^i\right]. \tag{20}$$

The garbled rows of the second corrector gate, which correspond to the value $-\lambda_{w_0}v_x + \widetilde{\widetilde{\lambda_z}} = -\lambda_{w_0}(v_x + \lambda_x) + \lambda_{w_0}\lambda_x + \widetilde{\widetilde{\lambda_z}}$, are the following encryptions for each $\alpha \in \mathbb{F}_p$ and $i \in [n]$:

$$Enc_{k_{x,\alpha}}\left[\widetilde{\widetilde{k}}_z^i + \left(-\alpha\lambda_{w_0} + \lambda_{w_0}\lambda_x + \widetilde{\widetilde{\lambda_z}}\right)\Delta_p^i\right]. \tag{21}$$

Assuming λ_{w_0} is a multifield-shared bit, computing these gates requires two BGW degree-reduction rounds. Verification is slightly tedious and hence omitted.

Combining the above components results in the half-selector gate: At the evaluation phase, an honest evaluating party decrypts the chooser partial gate and only one of the corrector gates, according to the external value on the selector wire w_0. By summing the values, the evaluating party recovers the key corresponding to $v_x v_{w_0} + \lambda_z$.

Observe that the same key is used to decrypt both corrector gates. Thus, a corrupt evaluating party can recover the decrypted keys on both corrector gates, regardless of the external value on wire w_0. Therefore, we must ensure that the unused decrypted value does not leak any information. We explain the intuition for the case $e_{w_0} = 0$; the case of $e_{w_0} = 1$ is similar. Notice that the keys decrypted from the inactive corrector gate are $\widetilde{\widetilde{k}}_z^i + \left(-e_x\lambda_{w_0} + \lambda_{w_0}\lambda_x + \widetilde{\widetilde{\lambda_z}}\right)\Delta_p^i$ for $i \in [n]$. There are 2 key observations:

- Clearly, a corrupt evaluating party P_i can learn the value $-e_x\lambda_{w_0} + \lambda_{w_0}\lambda_x + \widetilde{\widetilde{\lambda_z}}$ by subtracting $\widetilde{\widetilde{k}}_z^i$ and dividing by Δ_p^i. Furthermore, $e_x, e_{w_0}, \widehat{\lambda_z}$, and $\lambda_{w_0}v_x + \widetilde{\lambda_z}$ are known to the evaluator from the protocol.[10] Nevertheless, $\widetilde{\widetilde{\lambda_z}} \in \mathbb{F}_p$ is random even given these values. Thus, the value $-e_x\lambda_{w_0} + \lambda_{w_0}\lambda_x + \widetilde{\widetilde{\lambda_z}}$ leaks no information on λ_{w_0} and λ_x.

- A corrupt evaluating party learns $\widetilde{\widetilde{k}}_z^j + \left(-e_x\lambda_{w_0} + \lambda_{w_0}\lambda_x + \widetilde{\widetilde{\lambda_z}}\right)\Delta_p^j$ also for every honest party P_j. However, $\widetilde{\widetilde{k}}_z^j \in \mathbb{F}_{p^\kappa}$ is random even given the keys

---

[10] Usually, the permutation bits must remain secret as they hide the value on the wire. However, in this specific case, the value on the wire corresponding to $v_x e_{w_0} = 0$ is publicly known. Thus, there is no need to hide $\widehat{\lambda_z}$ in this specific case. However, $\widehat{\lambda_z}$ is crucial for security, otherwise $\lambda_z = \widehat{\lambda_z}$ and this would be insecure when $e_{w_0} = 1$.

party P_i recovers from following the protocol. Thus, this does not leak any information on Δ_p^j.

The proof of security in Sect. 6 formalizes the above intuition.

5   Protocol for Secure Computation

In this section we give the details of our secure multiparty computation protocol. The protocol is an extension of the semi-honest BMR protocol, e.g. [8], to the arithmetic case. The details of the garbled gates are explained in Sects. 3 and 4.[11] The proofs of correctness and security appear at Sect. 6.

The garbling phase of protocols following the multiparty garbling paradigm is often abstracted as a functionality that outputs the garbled circuit and the necessary permutation bits to the respective parties. This functionality, which we term F_{GC}, is described in Fig. 1. We next sketch out a straightforward protocol for securely computing F_{GC} in constant rounds, using a combination of the BGW protocol [9,19] and the constant round protocol for unbounded fan-in multiplication of Bar-Ilan and Beaver [3].

Step 1, Setup: For each prime p in the primorial modulus, each party P_i does the following:
- For each wire $\omega \in W_p$ (i.e., input wires of the circuit and output wires of garbled gates/components), randomly chooses a random element $(\lambda_\omega)_i \in \mathbb{F}_p$ and (zero) key $k_\omega^i \in \mathbb{F}_{p^\kappa}$.[12] The random permutation element on the wire is $\lambda_\omega \overset{\text{def}}{=} \Sigma_{i=1}^n [(\lambda_\omega)_i]$.
- In topological order on the circuit, computes $(\lambda_\omega)_i$ and k_ω^i for each wire $\omega \notin W_p$, by summing/multiplying by a constant (according to gate type), by using λ_i and k^i on the input wires – see Sect. 2.3 on "free" gates.
- Each party randomly chooses a random global offset $\Delta_p^i \in \mathbb{F}_{p^\kappa}$.
- For each garbled component $g \in C$, compute $\mathcal{F}_{k_{x,\alpha}^i}(g,j)$ for each $j \in [n]$ and $\alpha \in \mathbb{F}_p$, where p is according to the gate/component type.

Step 2, Sharing: Each party P_i shares all the keys, elements, and outputs of $\mathcal{F}$ in Step 1 using $(t+1)$-out-of-n Shamir secret-sharing scheme. Multifield-shared bits are also shared using Protocol 2 in Sect. 2.4 for each p. The parties obtain shares of λ_ω for each wire by locally summing their shares of $\{(\lambda_\omega)_i\}_{i=1}^n$.

Step 3, Computing the garbled gates: Shares of the garbled rows of each garbled gate/component are computed using their respective equation (e.g., Eqs. 6, 8, 12, 13), where in each equation
- Addition and multiplication by a constant are computed locally,
- Multiplication is computed using a BGW degree-reduction round,

---

[11] Due to lack of space, some of the constructions are deferred to the full version.
[12] In the designated selector gates, this choice is slightly more involved – P_i randomly chooses $(\widehat{\lambda_\omega})_i, (\widehat{\overline{\lambda_\omega}})_i, (\widetilde{\lambda_\omega})_i, (\widetilde{\overline{\lambda_\omega}})_i$ such that $(\widehat{\lambda_\omega})_i + (\widetilde{\lambda_\omega})_i = (\widehat{\overline{\lambda_\omega}})_i + (\widetilde{\overline{\lambda_\omega}})_i$. The keys are similarly partitioned; see Sect. 4.

- Exponentiation is computed using the protocol of [3].

More details can be found in the respective section.

Step 4, Reconstructing the outputs: The parties exchange the shares (of the outputs of F_{GC}) and reconstruct the outputs of F_{GC}, namely the garbled gates/components and the output permutation elements. Furthermore, each party receives the shares and reconstructs the permutation elements on its input wires.

Remark 6. The above protocol is constant round since all gates are computed in parallel and each step is constant round (Step 1 is local). However, the protocol can be considerably optimized using techniques described in [7], such as share-conversion and masking by additive shares of zeros. Due to space limitations, the optimized protocol is deferred to the full version. An alternative protocol for arithmetic garbled circuits that does not require an honest majority, which is based on oblivious transfer, is also given in the full version.

Next, in Fig. 2 we give the details of our MPC protocol, in the F_{GC}-hybrid model (i.e., F_{GC} can be executed securely as a black-box). The protocol is similar to other protocols following the multiparty garbling paradigm, e.g., [8]. The only major difference is the external values are not exclusively Boolean, and the size of the garbled gates/components varies according to the gate type. The evaluation of the various gates (Step 3b in Fig. 2) is explained in the respective section. Correctness and security of the protocol are shown in Sect. 6.

6   Correctness and Security

In this section we state the correctness and security of our protocol. Due to lack of space, we only give sketches of the proofs. The full proof of security, as well as the straightforward proof of Claim 1, will be given in the full version.

Correctness. We briefly explain the correctness of the protocol. To show that the outputs received by the parties in Π_{online} (Fig. 2) corresponds to the correct output, we show the following statement: for each wire, the evaluating parties recover at evaluation the correct external value $e_z = v_z + \lambda_z$, and the corresponding keys. For input wires, this statement follows from Step 2. The statement is then proved by induction on the topological ordering of the gates. For output wires of each gate type, this is shown in the respective section. Using the induction argument, the statement holds also for the output wires of the circuit. Thus, in Step 4, the value recovered by the parties at wire z is $e_z - \lambda_z = v_z$.

Security. We now show the security of our protocol. We assume a semi-honest adversary corrupting a strict minority of the parties. We begin with the following lemma:

Lemma 1. *Protocol Π_{GC} securely computes F_{GC} in the presence of a static semi-honest adversary controlling a strict minority of the parties.*

Functionality F_{GC}

Computation Course:

1. For every prime p in the mixed modulos, the functionality assigns a random global offset $\Delta_p^i \in \mathbb{F}_{p^\kappa}$ to each party P_i.
2. For each wire $\omega \in \mathcal{W}_p$, the functionality assigns
   - A random permutation element $\lambda_\omega \in \mathbb{F}_p$.
   - For each party P_i, a random zero key $k_\omega^i \in \mathbb{F}_{p^\kappa}$. The keys associated with the p external values are set to be $k_{\omega,\alpha}^i = k_\omega^i + \alpha k_\omega^i$ for $\alpha \in \mathbb{F}_p$.
3. For each addition gate or multiplication by a constant $c \neq 0$ gate, with output wire $z \in \mathcal{W}_p$ and input wires x, y (or just x), the functionality computes
   - The permutation element of the output wire $\lambda_z = \lambda_x + \lambda_y$ or $\lambda_z = c\lambda_x$ respectively.
   - The zero keys of the output wire, $k_z^i = k_x^i + k_y^i$ or $k_z^i = ck_x^i$ respectively for each party P_i.
   The computations are in the fields $\mathbb{F}_p$ and $\mathbb{F}_{p^\kappa}$ respectively.
4. The functionality computes the garbled circuit GC, i.e., computes the garbled rows for each garbled gate/component. For non-Boolean gates, this is computed according to the gate equations in Sections 3 and 4.

Outputs:

1. The functionality outputs the garbled gates to the evaluating parties.
2. For output wires of the circuit, the functionality outputs the permutation bits to the evaluating parties.
3. The functionality outputs to each party its global offsets, its zero key for each wire $w \in \mathcal{W}$, and the permutation bit of each of its input wires.

Fig. 1. Functionality F_{GC} for Constructing a Multiparty Garbled Circuit

Proof Sketch. Protocol Π_{GC} computes F_{GC} using only Shamir secret sharing, the BGW protocol, and the constant round protocol for unbounded fan-in multiplication of [3]. These are secure and composable with each other (the protocol of [3] can be based on BGW) in the semi-honest model with an honest majority. The intermediate messages the adversary sees throughout the protocol (Steps 2 and 3) are only Shamir shares, which appear random in the information theoretic sense. Thus, they are easily simulated. The messages of the last round (Step 4) are computed by the simulator using the output (given from the trusted party) and the messages already given to the adversary in previous rounds.   □

Before stating our main security theorem, we state the following claim that follows from Definition 1:

Claim 1. *Let $B \subset [n]$. If H is mixed-modulus circular correlation robust, then for all polynomial time adversaries making only legal queries to the oracle, the oracle*

$$\mathcal{O}_P^{H,B}\left(\rho, a, b, \left(k^i\right)_{i \in B}, \gamma, (\delta_i)_{i \in B}\right) \stackrel{def}{=} \Sigma_{i \in B}\left[\mathcal{O}_P^{H,i}\left(\rho, a, b, k^i, \gamma, \delta_i\right)\right], \qquad (22)$$

where each $\mathcal{O}_P^{H,i}$ is equal to $\mathcal{O}_P^H$ with random and independent $\Delta_p^i s$ for each $p \in P$ and $i \in B$, is indistinguishable from a random function (with the same input/output domains).

Claim 1 is proved from Definition 1 by a reduction. The proof is deferred to the full version. Informally, the importance of Claim 1 is to use the claim with B as the set of honest parties, so $\mathcal{O}_P^{H,B}$ mimics "encryption" by all the honest parties. Further, the oracle adds offsets, corresponding to $\delta_i \Delta_p^i s$, to the encrypted keys of the honest parties.

To give some intuition, this allows the distinguisher to change the values to which the encrypted keys correspond to, without knowing the $\Delta_p^i s$. For example, let e_x and e_z be the external values on the input and output wires of the gate. If the distinguisher wants to encrypt row $e_x + 1$ with the key corresponding to $e_z + 2$, then for the jth part it uses $\gamma = 1$ and $\delta_i = \begin{cases} 2 & i = j \\ 0 & i \neq j \end{cases}$ for each $i \in B$ (the computation of δ_j for the evaluator half gate and designated selector gates

---

Protocol Π_{online}

1. **Offline phase:** The parties execute functionality F_{GC} to receive the garbled circuit, the output wires' permutation elements, and the input permutation elements on their respective input wires.

2. **Exchange garbled keys associated with inputs:** For every circuit-input wire w:
   (a) Let P_i be the party whose input is associated with wire w and let x_{i_w} be P_i's input value associated with the wire. Then, P_i sends $e_w = x_{i_w} + \lambda_w$ to all parties.
   (b) Each party P_j sends its part k_{w,e_w}^j of the garbled label on w to the evaluating parties.
   (c) At this point, the evaluating parties hold $k_{w,e_w}^1, \ldots, k_{w,e_w}^n$ for every circuit-input wire.

3. **Local circuit computation:** Each evaluating party locally evaluates the garbled circuit by traversing the circuit in a topological order, computing gate by gate. Let g be the current gate with output wire z and input wires x, y (or just x). Let e_x and e_y be the *extrenal values* on wires x and y, respectively.
   (a) If g is an addition or multiplication by $c \neq 0$ gate, then P_0 sets $e_z = e_x + e_y$ or $e_z = c e_x$ respectively. In addition, for every $j = 1, \ldots, n$, it computes $k_{z,e_z}^j = k_{in1,e_{in1}}^j + k_{in2,e_{in2}}^j$ or $k_{z,e_z}^j = c \cdot k_{in1,e_{in1}}^j$.
   (b) If g is a non-free gate, then the evaluating party recovers the output keys and external value by evaluating the gate. This is explained, according to the gate type, in Sections 3 and 4.

4. **Output determination:** For every output wire w, the evaluating party computes the *real* output value of wire w to be $e_w - \lambda_w$, where e_w is the external value on wire w and λ_w is as received from the output of F_{GC}.

Fig. 2. The online phase – circuit evaluation

is slightly more complex, as explained in the proof). This way, the distinguisher only uses the keys k^i_{x,e_x}, k^i_{z,e_z} of the honest parties. Next, we state our main security theorem:

Theorem 2. *If H is a mixed-modulus correlation robust hash function then Protocol Π_{online} in Fig. 2 securely computes f_C in the F_{GC}-hybrid model, in the presence of a static semi-honest adversary.*

The proof follows the general ideas used in [12], with the extended assumption. The main difficulty of the proof, on which we focus, is to show how the simulator simulates the output of F_{GC}, and in particular a fake garbled circuit, such that no polynomial time distinguisher can distinguish this fake garbled circuit from a real garbled circuit. To show this, we describe a distinguisher that uses H and legal queries to an oracle $\mathcal{O} \in \left\{\mathcal{O}^{H,B}_P, Rand\right\}$ in order to construct a circuit that distributes either as a real garbled circuit or as a fake garbled circuit, according to the oracle. Thus, distinguishing between the two types of circuits breaks the mixed-modulus correlation robustness of H. See the full version for more details.

There are two main differences from similar proofs: the first appears in multiplication gates, and specifically in the evaluator half gate. The second appears in the designated selector gates. Therefore, we split the proof sketch into two parts. In the first, we give an overview of the general proof structure and ideas, i.e., the construction of the fake circuit by the simulator, and the construction of the circuit by the distinguisher (which distributes as a real or fake circuit according to the oracle). In the second part, we explain the difficulties and necessary changes for evaluator half gates, and give a more detailed explanation on the subtleties of selector gates.

Proof Sketch. **Simulator:** The simulator chooses a random path on the circuit, i.e., for each wire $\omega \in \mathcal{W}$ selects a random *external value*. For each wire $\omega \in \mathcal{W}$ and for each honest party, the simulator chooses random keys corresponding to these external values. Then, the simulator computes the external values and corresponding keys of free gates. Using these values, the simulator computes a single encrypted row for each non-free gate/component – this row corresponds to the external value on the input wire. The other rows are sent as completely random strings (or more precisely as a random vector in $\mathbb{F}^n_{p^\kappa}$ for the appropriate p). There are slight differences in the designated selector gates, and these are explained later in the proof.

Distinguisher: The distinguisher starts by following the simulator construction for computing the first encrypted row. The other rows are computed differently, by using the oracle. The key observation is that the distinguisher can compute the γ's it needs tosupply the oracle in order to, in the case $\mathcal{O} = \mathcal{O}^{H,B}_P$, encrypt the rows correctly *and* can compute the δ_i's in order to, if necessary, change the keys of the honest parties that are encrypted in that case.[13]

Computing γ is simply by the difference in the rows – this part is unchanged in the different gate types. Note that this ensures that $\gamma \neq 0$ and that each $\gamma \in \mathbb{F}_{p_a}$ is used only once for each gate and party index. Thus, the distinguisher makes only legal queries to the oracle.

To compute the δ_i's, the distinguisher uses the inputs to compute the real values on the wires. Using the real and external values, the distinguisher extracts the permutation elements, which are used to compute δ_i for each row and each $i \in B$. In the computation of the δ_i's there are differences and subtleties from similar proofs in both the evaluator half-gate and the designated selector gate, and we address these next.

Evaluator Half Gates: The simulator computes the evaluator half gates exactly the same. I.e., the simulator chooses an "external value" $\widehat{e}_z$ and corresponding random key $\widehat{k}^i_{z,\widehat{e}_z}$. However, note that the "external value" of output wire of the evaluator half gate represents $\widehat{e}_z = v_x(v_y + \lambda_y) + \widehat{\lambda_z}$, but the key $\widehat{k}^i_{z,\widehat{e}_z}$ represents $\widehat{k}^i_z - e_y k^i_x + \left(-e_y \lambda_x + \widehat{\lambda_z}\right) \Delta^i_p$. This is because the evaluator should add $e_y k^i_{x,e_x}$ after decrypting row e_y.

This poses an extra challenge to the distinguisher when trying to compute the other rows, because they require deducting different multiplications of k^i_x, but the distinguisher does not know k^i_x.[14] However, the distinguisher does know $k^i_{x,e_x} = k^i_x + e_x \Delta^i_p$. Therefore, to deduct βk^i_x, the distinguisher computes $\beta(k^i_x + e_x \Delta^i_p) = \beta k^i_x + \beta e_x \Delta^i_p$. Then, this is deducted, and the βe_x is aggregated to the computation of the δ_i of that row. Thus, the simulator calls the oracle with these aggregated δ_i's. The technical details are given in the full version.

Designated Selector Gates: First note that in the designate selector gates the simulator chooses three random external values and corresponding keys, although one of the corrector gates should not be decrypted. Furthermore, the simulator knows which corrector gate should not be decrypted. Nevertheless, the simulator constructs this gate as usual (one row correctly encrypted, and the other rows are random).

As for the distinguisher, the construction of the two corrector gates is similar to regular gates. The distinguisher builds both corrector gates, despite knowing which one should be decrypted. For the unused row in the chooser gate, the distinguisher uses the technique described for the evaluator half gate.

Conclusion: The proof concludes with the following key observation: If $\mathcal{O} = Rand$ then the circuit created by the distinguisher distributes as a fake garbled

---

[13] All the keys of the corrupt parties are known to the distinguisher. For the honest parties, the distinguisher knows the keys corresponding to the external values (chose them randomly), but does not know the Δ^i_p's. Therefore, in order to change which value the honest parties' encrypted keys correspond to, it must use the oracle $\mathcal{O}^{H,B}_P$.

[14] The random Δ^i_ps of $i \in B$ are an internal part of $\mathcal{O}^{H,B}_P$. The Δ^i_ps of the adversary $(i \notin B)$ are known to both the simulator and the distinguisher.

circuit created by the simulator, while if $\mathcal{O} = \mathcal{O}_P^{H,B}$ the circuit distributes as a real garbled circuit, created by a real execution of the protocol. Thus, distinguishing between the two cases breaks the mixed-modulus circular correlation robustness. $\qquad\square$

At first sight, it might not be obvious where in the proof we required the double partition of the keys and permutation bits. However, a closer inspection shows that by the simulator and distinguisher choosing the external values and keys of the two corrector gates randomly and independently, this fact is implicitly used. Otherwise (without the double partition), in a real garbled circuit the two external values are dependent and similarly the two keys, and would not match the distinguisher's construction. Furthermore, in a real execution of the protocol, if the λ's are not double partitioned, by subtraction of the two external values, a corrupt evaluator learns $2\lambda_{w_0} v_x$ (here λ_{w_0} is treated as an $\mathbb{F}_p$ element), violating security. If the keys are not double partitioned, then a corrupt evaluator can subtract the decrypted keys of an honest party P_i and recover a multiplication of Δ_p^i. Thus, this double partition is crucial.

Acknowledgements. I would like to thank Amos Beimel, Eran Omri, and Yehuda Lindell for the many ideas and helpful discussions. Special thanks to the anonymous referees for their remarks and suggestions, and to abhi shelat and Mike Rosulek for helping me to better understand their papers.

References

1. Applebaum, B., Ishai, Y., Kushilevitz, E.: How to garble arithmetic circuits. In: Proceedings of the 2011 IEEE 52nd Annual Symposium on Foundations of Computer Science, FOCS 2011, pp. 120–129. IEEE Computer Society (2011)
2. Ball, M., Malkin, T., Rosulek, M.: Garbling gadgets for Boolean and arithmetic circuits. In: Proceedings of the 23rd Conference on Computer and Communications Security, ACM CCS, pp. 565–577 (2016)
3. Bar-Ilan, J., Beaver, D.: Non-cryptographic fault-tolerant computing in constant number of rounds of interaction. In: PODC (1989)
4. Beaver, D., Micali, S., Rogaway, P.: The round complexity of secure protocols. In: Proceedings of the Twenty-Second Annual ACM Symposium on Theory of Computing, STOC 1990, pp. 503–513 (1990)
5. Bellare, M., Hoang, V.T., Keelveedhi, S., Rogaway, P.: Efficient garbling from a fixed-key blockcipher. In: 2013 IEEE Symposium on Security and Privacy, SP 2013, Berkeley, CA, USA, 19–22 May 2013, pp. 478–492 (2013)
6. Ben-David, A., Nisan, N., Pinkas, B.: FairplayMP: a system for secure multi-party computation. In: Proceedings of the 15th ACM Conference on Computer and Communications Security, ACM CCS, pp. 257–266 (2008)
7. Ben-Efraim, A., Omri, E.: Concrete efficiency improvements for multiparty garbling with an honest majority. In: Proceedings of the 5th International Conference on Progress in Cryptology, LATINCRYPT (2017, to appear)
8. Ben-Efraim, A., Lindell, Y., Omri, E.: Optimizing semi-honest secure multiparty computation for the internet. In: Proceedings of the 23rd ACM Conference on Computer and Communications Security, ACM CCS, pp. 578–590 (2016)

9. Ben-Or, M., Goldwasser, S., Wigderson, A.: Completeness theorems for noncryptographic fault-tolerant distributed computations. In: Proceedings of the 20th ACM Symposium on the Theory of Computing, pp. 1–10 (1988)
10. Bogdanov, D., Laur, S., Willemson, J.: Sharemind: a framework for fast privacy-preserving computations. In: Jajodia, S., Lopez, J. (eds.) ESORICS 2008. LNCS, vol. 5283, pp. 192–206. Springer, Heidelberg (2008). https://doi.org/10.1007/978-3-540-88313-5_13
11. Burkhart, M., Strasser, M., Many, D., Dimitropoulos, X.: SEPIA: privacy-preserving aggregation of multi-domain network events and statistics. Network (2010)
12. Choi, S.G., Katz, J., Kumaresan, R., Zhou, H.-S.: On the security of the "Free-XOR" technique. In: Cramer, R. (ed.) TCC 2012. LNCS, vol. 7194, pp. 39–53. Springer, Heidelberg (2012). https://doi.org/10.1007/978-3-642-28914-9_3
13. Cramer, R., Damgård, I.: Secure distributed linear algebra in a constant number of rounds. In: Kilian, J. (ed.) CRYPTO 2001. LNCS, vol. 2139, pp. 119–136. Springer, Heidelberg (2001). https://doi.org/10.1007/3-540-44647-8_7
14. Damgård, I., Geisler, M., Krøigaard, M., Nielsen, J.B.: Asynchronous multiparty computation: theory and implementation. In: Jarecki, S., Tsudik, G. (eds.) PKC 2009. LNCS, vol. 5443, pp. 160–179. Springer, Heidelberg (2009). https://doi.org/10.1007/978-3-642-00468-1_10
15. Damgård, I., Pastro, V., Smart, N.P., Zakarias, S.: Multiparty computation from somewhat homomorphic encryption. In: Safavi-Naini, R., Canetti, R. (eds.) CRYPTO 2012. LNCS, vol. 7417, pp. 643–662. Springer, Heidelberg (2012). https://doi.org/10.1007/978-3-642-32009-5_38
16. Damgård, I., Keller, M., Larraia, E., Pastro, V., Scholl, P., Smart, N.P.: Practical covertly secure MPC for dishonest majority – or: breaking the SPDZ limits. In: Crampton, J., Jajodia, S., Mayes, K. (eds.) ESORICS 2013. LNCS, vol. 8134, pp. 1–18. Springer, Heidelberg (2013). https://doi.org/10.1007/978-3-642-40203-6_1
17. Damgård, I., Nielsen, J.B., Nielsen, M., Ranellucci, S.: The tinytable protocol for 2-party secure computation, or: gate-scrambling revisited. In: Katz, J., Shacham, H. (eds.) CRYPTO 2017. LNCS, vol. 10401, pp. 167–187. Springer, Cham (2017). https://doi.org/10.1007/978-3-319-63688-7_6
18. Demmler, D., Schneider, T., Zohner, M.: ABY-A framework for efficient mixed-protocol secure two-party computation. In: NDSS (2015)
19. Gennaro, R., Rabin, M.O., Rabin, T.: Simplified VSS and fast-track multiparty computations with applications to threshold cryptography. In: Proceedings of the Seventeenth Annual ACM Symposium on Principles of Distributed Computing, PODC 1998, pp. 101–111. ACM (1998)
20. Goldreich, O.: Foundations of Cryptography: Volume 2, Basic Applications. Cambridge University Press, Cambridge (2009)
21. Gueron, S., Lindell, Y., Nof, A., Pinkas, B.: Fast garbling of circuits under standard assumptions. In: Proceedings of the 22nd ACM Conference on Computer and Communications Security, ACM CCS, pp. 567–578 (2015)
22. Hazay, C., Scholl, P., Soria-Vazquez, E.: Low cost constant round MPC combining BMR and oblivious transfer. In: Takagi, T., Peyrin, T. (eds.) ASIACRYPT 2017. LNCS, vol. 10624, pp. 598–628. Springer, Cham (2017). https://doi.org/10.1007/978-3-319-70694-8_21
23. Keller, M., Orsini, E., Scholl, P.: Mascot: faster malicious arithmetic secure computation with oblivious transfer. In: Proceedings of the 23rd ACM Conference on Computer and Communications Security (ACM CCS), pp. 830–842 (2016)

24. Keller, M., Orsini, E., Rotaru, D., Scholl, P., Soria-Vazquez, E., Vivek, S.: Faster secure multi-party computation of AES and DES using lookup tables. In: Gollmann, D., Miyaji, A., Kikuchi, H. (eds.) ACNS 2017. LNCS, vol. 10355, pp. 229–249. Springer, Cham (2017). https://doi.org/10.1007/978-3-319-61204-1_12
25. Kolesnikov, V., Schneider, T.: Improved garbled circuit: free XOR gates and applications. In: Aceto, L., Damgård, I., Goldberg, L.A., Halldórsson, M.M., Ingólfsdóttir, A., Walukiewicz, I. (eds.) ICALP 2008. LNCS, vol. 5126, pp. 486–498. Springer, Heidelberg (2008). https://doi.org/10.1007/978-3-540-70583-3_40
26. Kreuter, B., Shelat, A., Shen, C.-H.: Billion-gate secure computation with malicious adversaries. In: USENIX Security Symposium, pp. 285–300 (2012)
27. Lindell, Y., Pinkas, B., Smart, N.P., Yanai, A.: Efficient constant round multiparty computation combining BMR and SPDZ. In: Gennaro, R., Robshaw, M. (eds.) CRYPTO 2015. LNCS, vol. 9216, pp. 319–338. Springer, Heidelberg (2015). https://doi.org/10.1007/978-3-662-48000-7_16
28. Malkin, T., Pastero, V., Shelat, A.: An algebraic approach to garbling. Unpublished manuscript
29. Naor, M., Pinkas, B., Sumner, R.: Privacy preserving auctions and mechanism design. In: Proceedings of the 1st ACM Conference on Electronic Commerce, EC 1999, pp. 129–139. ACM (1999)
30. Nielsen, J.B., Orlandi, C.: LEGO for two-party secure computation. In: Reingold, O. (ed.) TCC 2009. LNCS, vol. 5444, pp. 368–386. Springer, Heidelberg (2009). https://doi.org/10.1007/978-3-642-00457-5_22
31. Pinkas, B., Schneider, T., Smart, N.P., Williams, S.C.: Secure two-party computation is practical. In: Matsui, M. (ed.) ASIACRYPT 2009. LNCS, vol. 5912, pp. 250–267. Springer, Heidelberg (2009). https://doi.org/10.1007/978-3-642-10366-7_15
32. Wang, X., Ranellucci, S., Katz, J.: Global-scale secure multiparty computation. In: Proceedings of the 24th ACM Conference on Computer and Communications Security, ACM CCS, pp. 39–56 (2017)
33. Yao, A.C.: Protocols for secure computations. In: Proceedings of the 23rd IEEE Symposium on Foundations of Computer Science, pp. 160–164 (1982)
34. Zahur, S., Rosulek, M., Evans, D.: Two halves make a whole. In: Oswald, E., Fischlin, M. (eds.) EUROCRYPT 2015. LNCS, vol. 9057, pp. 220–250. Springer, Heidelberg (2015). https://doi.org/10.1007/978-3-662-46803-6_8

Free IF: How to Omit Inactive Branches and Implement $\mathcal{S}$-Universal Garbled Circuit (Almost) for Free

Vladimir Kolesnikov[(✉)]

School of Computer Science, Georgia Institute of Technology, Atlanta, USA
kolesnikov@gatech.edu

Abstract. Two-party Secure Function Evaluation (SFE) allows two parties to evaluate a function known to both parties on their private inputs. In some settings, the input of one of the parties *is* the definition of the computed function, and requires protection as well. The standard solution for SFE of private functions (PF-SFE) is to rely on Universal Circuits (UC), which can be programmed to implement *any* circuit of size s. Recent UC optimizations report the cost of UC for s-gate Boolean circuits is $\approx 5s \log s$.

Instead, we consider garbling that allows evaluating one of a given *set* $\mathcal{S}$ of circuits. We show how to evaluate one of the circuits in $\mathcal{S}$ at the communication cost comparable to that of evaluating the largest circuit in $\mathcal{S}$. In other words, we show how to *omit* generating and sending inactive GC branches. Our main insight is that a garbled circuit is just a collection of garbled tables, and as such can be reused to emulate the throw-away computation of an inactive execution branch without revealing to the Evaluator whether it evaluates active or inactive branch.

This cannot be proven within the standard BHR garbled circuits framework because the function description is inseparable from the garbling by definition. We carefully extend BHR in a general way, introducing *topology-decoupling circuit garbling*. We preserve all existing constructions and proofs of the BHR framework, while allowing this and other future constructions which may treat garbled tables separately from function description.

Our construction is presented in the semi-honest model.

1 Introduction

Using circuit representation of the evaluated function brings a significant disadvantage in the SFE world. Indeed, in contrast with the Random-Access Machine (RAM) model, circuits introduce expensive, often crippling, redundancies to SFE by requiring to generate, send and evaluate *all conditional branches*, even if one of the players knows the branch taken. Circuits require unrolling loops, incur linear costs when accessing an array element, etc. Yet, circuit-based SFE is currently the highest-performing technique in most settings, due to extremely high efficiency of the private evaluation of circuit gates.

T. Peyrin and S. Galbraith (Eds.): ASIACRYPT 2018, LNCS 11274, pp. 34–58, 2018.
https://doi.org/10.1007/978-3-030-03332-3_2

Addressing the limitations of the circuit-based representation has focused mainly on improving random access to memory. A celebrated line of work on Oblivious RAM (ORAM), started by [GO96], resulted in ORAM being a standard ingredient in MPC.

Our work. We address the need to pay for inactive throw-away conditional branches. We propose an *extremely simple* technique, Free IF, to **fully eliminate inactive GC branches** in scenarios where one of the players knows the executed branch. This is a natural scenario frequently occurring in practice, as we will argue next.

We extend the BHR framework [BHR12] to introduce *topology-decoupling circuit garbling* and present the construction in general terms. The extended BHR framework, which treats garbled circuits as strings, is a contribution of independent interest.

To our knowledge, this is the first such circuit-based technique. We discuss previous work in Sect. 1.2; most well-known prior work on circuit size reduction is generic universal circuit (UC) constructions.

1.1   Motivating Applications

We list several practical applications where our approach can be applied.

Evaluating one of several policy options. In Blind Seer [PKV+14, FVK+15], a GC-based private database (DB) system, private DB search is achieved by two players jointly securely evaluating the query match function on the search tree of the data. Blind Seer does not fully protect query privacy: it leaks the query circuit topology as the full universal circuit is not practical, as admitted by the authors. Applying our solution to that work would hide this important information, *at (almost) no extra cost*. Indeed, say, by policy the DB client is allowed to execute one of several (say, 50) types of queries. The privately executed SQL query can then be a represented as a switch of the number of clauses selected by the querier, each corresponding to an allowed query type. With our technique, only a GC corresponding to a single branch will need to be sent instead of the 50 required today. Most of the cost of the Blind Seer DB system is in running SFE of the query match function at a large scale, so improvement to the query circuit will directly translate to overall improvement. We note that the core of the Blind Seer system is in the semi-honest model, but a malicious client is considered in [FVK+15].

Our work can be viewed as secure evaluation of a circuit universal for a set of functions $\mathcal{S} = \{\mathcal{C}_1, ..., \mathcal{C}_k\}$ ($\mathcal{S}$-universal circuit, or $\mathcal{S}$-UC) at the cost similar to that of a single function. The next motivating example provides another illustration of how our work may improve applications where we want to evaluate and hide which function/query was chosen by a player (say, which one of several functions allowed by policy or known because of auxiliary information).

SFE of semi-private functions (SPF-SFE) (see additional discussion in Sect. 1.2) is a notion introduced in [PSS09], bridging the gap between expensive private function SFE (PF-SFE) based on Universal Circuit [Val76, KS08b, KS16, LMS16], and regular SFE (via GC) that does not hide the evaluated function. SPF-SFE partially hides the evaluated function; namely, given a set of functions, the evaluator will not learn which specific function was evaluated. (The GC Generator does know the evaluated function.) Indeed, often only specific subroutines are sensitive, and it is they that might be sufficiently protected by S-universal circuit for an appropriate set of circuits S. [PSS09] presents a convincing example of privacy-preserving credit checking, where the check function itself needs to be protected, and shows that using S-universal circuits as building blocks is an effective way of approaching this. Further, [PSS09] builds a compiler which assembles GC from the S-universal building blocks (which they call PPB, Privately Programmable Blocks). While [PSS09] provides only a few very simple hand-designed blocks (see our discussion in Sect. 1.2), our work can be viewed as an efficient general way of constructing such blocks.

CPU/ALU emulation. Extending the idea of SPF-SFE, one can imagine a general approach where the players privately emulate a CPU evaluating a *fixed* sequence of complex instructions from a fixed instruction set (instruction choice implemented as a GC `switch`). Additionally, if desired, instructions' inputs can be protected by employing the selection blocks of [KS08b]. Such an approach can be built within a suitable framework (e.g., that of [PSS09]) from S-universal circuits provided by this work. We note that circuit design and optimization is tedious, and not likely to be performed by hand except for very simple instances, such as those considered in [PSS09]. Instead, our approach will result in immediate performance improvement, reducing the cost of the ALU step implementation by a large factor.

For example, in a recent work [WGMK16], a secure and practically efficient MIPS ALU is proposed, where the ALU is implemented as a `switch` over 37 currently supported ALU instructions evaluated on ORAM-stored data. Tiny-Garble [SHS+15] also design and realize a garbled processor, using the MIPS I instruction set, for private function evaluation. Our constructions would work with [WGMK16, SHS+15] in a drop-in replacement manner, for implementing straight-line functions known to one party. The ALU step will be correspondingly reduced from containing implementations of *all* ALU instructions per step (37 in [WGMK16], of which the output of 36 of them is discarded), to a single instruction with our approach!

The client-server setting. Our approach is particularly attractive in the client-server setting. Indeed, the cost of the GC generator for the S-UC of n circuits, while proportional to n, only involves a simple operation per circuit of S. The bulk of the cost of the GC generator is in garbling and sending (only) the active branch. Because of this, the set S of the circuits can be very large and still scale well allowing the server being able to service many clients. This is because (essentially) the sole cost of adding more circuits to S is *the evaluator* having to evaluate each circuit in S. This allows for a variety of trade-offs between efficiency and the level of hiding of the evaluated function.

1.2 Background and Related Work

Garbled Circuit, OT and Universal Circuit. Significant part of SFE research focuses on minimizing the size of the basic GC of Yao [Yao86,LP09], such as garbled row reduction techniques Free-XOR [KS08a] and its enhancements FleXOR [KMR14] and half-gates [ZRE15]. In contrast, in this work, we eliminate the need for evaluation (i.e. sending) of all but one subcircuits in a switch.

Asymptotically, Valiant's Universal Circuit [Val76,LMS16,KS16,GKS17] is the optimal underlying technique to fully protect the evaluated function in MPC. Respectively, for sub-circuits of size n, the size of the universal circuit generated by [Val76,KS08b] is $\approx 19n \log n$, and $\approx 1.5n \log^2 n + 2.5n \log n$. Recent works [LMS16,KS16,GKS17] polish and implement Valiant's construction. They report a precise estimate of the cost (in universal gates) of Valiant's UC of $\approx 5n \log n$. We note that UC-based constructions cannot take advantage of Free-XOR (other than gates on permutation subcircuits), since Free-XOR of course identifies positions of XOR gates. Thus, the classical universal circuit approach becomes competitive for a number of clauses far larger than a typical switch.

Another technique for Private Function Evaluation (PFE) was proposed by Mohassel and Sadeghian [MS13]. They propose an alternative (to the universal circuit) framework of SFE of a function whose definition is private to one of the players. Their approach is to map each gate outputs to next gate outputs by considering a mapping from all circuit inputs to all outputs, and evaluate it obliviously. For GC, they achieve a factor 2 improvement as compared to Valiant [Val76] and a factor 3–6 improvement as compared to Kolesnikov and Schneider [KS08b]. Similarly to [Val76,KS08b], [MS13] will not be cost-effective for a small number of clauses.

We also mention, but do not discuss in detail, that hardware design considers circuit minimization problems as well. However, their typical goal is to minimize chip area while allowing multiple executions of the same (sub)circuit. Current state-of-the-art in applying to MPC the powerful tool chains from hardware design is producing 10–20% circuit (garble table) reduction [SHS+15,DDK+15, DKS+17], while our approach will achieve large factor performance improvement for the setting it can operate in).

Semi-private function SFE (SPF-SFE) [PSS09]. As discussed above, SPF-SFE is a convincing trade-off between efficiency and the privacy of the evaluated function. Our work on construction of container circuits corresponds to that of privately programmable blocks (PPB) of [PSS09], which were hand-optimized in that work. In our view, the main contribution of [PSS09] is in identifying and motivating the problem of SPF-SFE and building a framework capable of integrating PPBs into a complete solutions. They provide a number of very simple (but nevertheless useful) PPBs, such as $\mathcal{S}_{COMP} = \{<, >, \leq, \geq, \neq\}$. Each of these PPB sets only consists of functions with already identical or near-identical topology; this is what enabled hand-optimization and optimal sizes of the containers. Other than the universal circuit PPB, no attempt was made to investigate construction PPBs of circuits of *a priori* differing topology.

In contrast, we can work with *any set* $\mathcal{S}$ of circuits for $\mathcal{S}$-universal circuit and achieve large factor performance improvement stemming from not having to transmit inactive branches.

Circuit overlay heuristic [KKW17]. Finally, a recent work of Kennedy et al. [KKW17] explored a *heuristic* approach to $\mathcal{S}$-UC circuit generation, based on alignment and overlay of underlying graphs. The authors were able to demonstrate significant reduction in the size of a circuit implementing a `switch` of 32 small circuits. Specifically, for their `switch` of 32 small chosen circuits of total size of $\approx 20,000$ gates, they were able to achieve the $\mathcal{S}$-UC of size $\approx 3,000$ gates, achieving $\approx 6\times$ circuit size reduction.

In contrast, our approach is *much* simpler and is readily implementable. It is *not* a heuristic, and has clean and understandable performance, which will nearly always beat [KKW17] (often by a significant factor!) in our setting where the GC generator knows the evaluated function. This is because of the following. In this case both our and [KKW17] cost consists of GC generator Gen generating and sending a single GC. However, in our case, this circuit size is equal to $\max|C_i|, C_i \in \mathcal{S}$, while the [KKW17] circuit size is $|C_0|$, where C_0 is the circuit universal for all $C_i \in \mathcal{S}$. Clearly, $|C_0| \geq \max|C_i|$, but it is difficult to give a precise comparison since [KKW17] is a heuristic. As reported in [KKW16], the full version of [KKW17], while overlay algorithm performed well on certain pairs (groups) of circuits, it did not do well on others. For example, expansion metric for circuits 29 and 30 (computing functions $B \cdot A + 555$ and $B^2 + A^2 > 1$ respectively on 32 bit values) is reported to be 1.00 (Table 3 in [KKW16]), which means that heuristic did not improve on simple circuit concatenation. In contract, our approach will immediately work for these circuits.

The BHR framework [BHR12]. We present our generic protocol in the terminology of BHR, which we extend to allow formal discussion of our work. We explain the very useful BHR framework at length in Sect. 5.

2   Our Contributions

We present Free IF, an extremely simple (and hence easy-to-implement and to adopt) method of eliminating the generation and transmission of *all* inactive branches in a GC computation, when branch is selected by the GC generator. An additional OT round, transferring secrets of size independent of the circuit sizes and concretely small, is required.

Our approach works with state-of-the-art garbling schemes, including half-gates [ZRE15].

We believe that our main idea — viewing GC as a collection of garbled tables and separating the circuit topology from GC thus hiding the computed function — will have other exciting applications, such as improved GC constructions.

Our result in very natural in retrospect; it is surprising it was not discovered earlier, given a substantial body of work on private function evaluation. One explanation is that we challenge "obvious facts" such as that GC is not reusable or that "GC is a structure, not a string". Both are widely accepted and are at the core of very general BHR framework. Both are challenged in our approach.

As a contribution of independent interest, we carefully extend the BHR framework to support a separation of circuit topology from the cryptographic material (such as garbled tables), and to provide convenient formalization for manipulating output encodings at wire granularity.

3   Technical Overview of Our Approach

Recall, garbled circuit (GC) can be viewed simply as a collection of garbled (encrypted) gate tables. Specifically, it need not include the specification of the evaluation topology (i.e. wire connections among the gates). While topology is needed for the evaluation, it may be conveyed to the evaluator Ev separately from the garbled tables, or by implicit agreement among the participants Gen and Ev. Further, GC may, but need not, provide confirmation to Ev that the obtained garbled label is a valid label.

Let $\mathcal{S} = \{\mathcal{C}_1, \mathcal{C}_2, ..., \mathcal{C}_n\}$ be a set of Boolean circuits. We assume that all circuits consist of fan-in-2 gates and have the same number of inputs and outputs. Let the Generator Gen have $n_{\text{in-x}}$ input bits, and the Evaluator Ev have $n_{\text{in-y}}$ input bits (total $n_{\text{in}} = n_{\text{in-x}} + n_{\text{in-y}}$). Without loss of generality, let players receive the same output consisting of n_{out} bits. This is a standard and natural setting for GC and universal circuits.

Recall, in our setting, (only) Gen knows which of the circuits in $\mathcal{S} = \{\mathcal{C}_1, \mathcal{C}_2, ..., \mathcal{C}_n\}$ is being evaluated. Let's imagine for now that all the circuits in $\mathcal{S}$ are of the same size s (i.e. consisting of the same total number of gates); we will later show this easily generalizes. We *do not* place any other restrictions on the topologies of the circuits. Suppose Gen wishes to evaluate its target circuit $\mathcal{C}_t \in \mathcal{S}$. Our underlying idea is to have Gen generate a *single* GC $\widehat{\mathcal{C}}$ implementing $\mathcal{C}_t$ and send it to Ev. Ev knows $\mathcal{S}$, but it will not know which of the circuits in $\mathcal{S}$ is the target circuit. Now, for each $\mathcal{C}_i \in \mathcal{S}$, Ev will interpret $\widehat{\mathcal{C}}$ as garbling of $\mathcal{C}_i$ and evaluate it as such, obtaining the garbled output. With a little care in GC design, it is possible to ensure that Ev will not be able to distinguish which of the circuits in $\mathcal{S}$ is the target circuit $\mathcal{C}_t$. We stress that the fact that circuts in $\mathcal{S}$ have varying topologies is not an issue since GCs only contain garbled tables which can be used with any topology.

The next step is for Ev to obliviously discard the wire labels which belong to non-target circuits and to propagate the (encrypted) output of the target circuit. To be more precise, Gen and Ev will run an *output selection* (OS) protocol. Ev will provide as input to the protocol all (active) output labels it obtained in evaluating $|\mathcal{S}|$ circuits, and Gen will provide the indices of the labels corresponding to the target circuit $\mathcal{C}_t$, as well as $\mathcal{C}_t$'s zero labels on output wires. The OS protocol will output (re-encoded) labels corresponding to the output of $\mathcal{C}_t$.

This step is efficiently implemented via GC. We further observe that providing full-length output labels (i.e of length of the computational security parameter κ) as input to OS is not needed; statistical security is sufficient and the labels can be truncated to σ bits for OS input, improving performance. Even further improvement is possible simply by having Gen ensure the labels on each output wire of $\mathcal{C}_t$ differ in the last bit. Then Ev and Gen can submit only the last bits of the labels they obtain. Note that it does not affect correctness or security if the last bits on the active and inactive wires of circuits other than $\mathcal{C}_t$ are the same, since selection is done based on the index t provided by Gen, and further Ev will not obtain both labels of any wire (and hence won't detect the mismatch between $\widehat{\mathcal{C}}$ and the interpreted evaluation of $\mathcal{C}_i$).

Free XOR and half-gates. Our construction works with the Free XOR garbling [KS08a].

Using half-gates [ZRE15] also works. Intuitively, this is because its garbled tables also look like random strings. We show this in Sects. 6 and 6.1. We note that using half-gates is concretely efficient, since the LSB of labels `true` and `false` is different and hence the garbled output can be cheaply fed into output selection protocol.

Addressing different circuit sizes in $\mathcal{S}$. It is easy to see that our approach does not limit us to considering $\mathcal{S}$ consisting only of the circuits of the same size. Indeed, let $s_{\max} = \max_i |\mathcal{C}_i|$ be the maximum circuit size in $\mathcal{S}$. It is sufficient[1] for Gen to garble the target circuit $\widehat{\mathcal{C}}_t$ *and pad it with randomly generated garbled tables* to obtain $\widehat{\mathcal{C}}_t'$, so as the total number of garbled tables in the produced circuit $\widehat{\mathcal{C}}_t'$ is equal to $s_{\max}$. Then, a simple convention can be easily designed to allow Ev to use only the garbled tables of needed in evaluating each circuit $\mathcal{C}_i$ by appropriately interpreting $\widehat{\mathcal{C}}_t'$.

On the cost of SFE and OT rounds. Our $\mathcal{S}$-UC GC protocol adds a round of communication for each switch statement. We argue that the associated latency cost is negligible in many practical scenarios. This is because often the latency-related idling will be productively used for computation and communication in the same or another SFE instance. This is the case, e.g., in larger-scale SFE deployments, where many instances will be run in parallel, and where SFE throughput is a far more important parameter than latency.

Composing our protocol with GC. We note that we additionally design a secret-shared-output functionality, where the output of the computation is not reconstructed, but remains shared GC-style. Hence, it can be privately plugged into another GC.

Nesting switch *clauses.* Our protocol naturally works for the nested clauses. One way to implement a nested clause is to bring all choice variables to the same level, placing us in the non-nested setting.

Figure 1 illustrates how a nested clause (left) can be rewritten to a single-level branching (right). Again, we note that Gen must know the selection choices.

---

[1] This holds for main schemes, such as classical Yao, Free-XOR and half-gates, as we show in Sect. 6.1. It is possible to craft garbling schemes where this specific technique won't work. See Sect. 5.3 for a formal discussion.

• if a = 1 then 　• if b = 1 then run F_{11} 　• if b = 2 then run F_{12} • if a = 2 then 　• if b = 1 then run F_{21} 　• if b = 2 then run F_{22}	• if a = 1 and b = 1 then run F_{11} • if a = 1 and b = 2 then run F_{12} • if a = 2 and b = 1 then run F_{21} • if a = 2 and b = 2 then run F_{21}

Fig. 1. switch nesting rewriting. Left: nested. Right: flat.

We note that this nesting management results in no additional communication rounds due to nesting. In most cases, the nesting would not be deep/wide enough to overwhelm the computational resource. Indeed, the computation cost would be less than implementing the same circuit using standard Yao GC.

To illustrate the costs, consider the above example and let's suppose all functions are of the same size $s_{\max}$, and Gen's choice variables are $a = 2$ and $b = 1$. Then our protocol will require Gen to generate and send a single GC $\widehat{C}$ implementing F_{21}, and Ev to evaluate the received $\widehat{C}$ four times. Standard GC will require Gen to generate and send four GCs, and Ev to evaluate four GCs.

3.1 Extending the BHR Framework: Decoupling the Topology

An important conceptual contribution of this work is the departure from thinking of garbled circuits as monolithic objects, but rather, emphasizing that they are strings representing (separately) the computed function and the cryptographic material, such as garbled tables. We formalize this approach by extending the BHR framework to support this vision. We are able to change some of the most fundamental concepts of the framework while preserving it completely and not requiring redefining any of its functions. This allows to reuse all existing body of work in the popular and very useful BHR framework.

Specifically, our main change to BHR is a restriction that the garbled circuit F must consist of two components, the function topology T and cryptographic material E. This adjustment does not affect any of the existing BHR functions, constructions and proofs, but allows us to introduce a new security property related to obliviousness, which formalizes indistinguishability of GC evaluation under different topologies.

We state our main result, Free IF, in the new extended BHR framework.

3.2 Outline of the Presentation

We already described at a high level the technical details of our contribution in Sect. 3. Next, we introduce preliminary notation and definitions. In Sect. 5, we review the relevant aspects of the BHR framework and introduce its extension that allows to reason about circuit garblings separately from the function encoding. We present our GC construction in the above extended framework, prove security and formally discuss suitable garbling schemes, including half-gates, in Sect. 6. Finally, in Sect. 7, we discuss the performance of our improvement.

4   Preliminaries

4.1   Notation

Throughout the paper we use the following notation: the computational and statistical security parameters are denoted by κ and σ, respectively. We will denote circuits by $\mathcal{C}$ and garbled circuits by $\widehat{\mathcal{C}}$. We denote a circuit's gate by $\mathcal{G}_i$ and a garbled gate by $\widehat{G}_i$. We denote by $\mathcal{S}$ the set $\mathcal{S} = \{\mathcal{C}_1, \mathcal{C}_2, ..., \mathcal{C}_n\}$ of circuits with respect to which we design our universal circuit. We denote size of $\mathcal{S}$ by $s = |\mathcal{S}|$. NOT gates are implemented in the standard way by switching the wire label semantics and we don't discuss them further. We count the number of non-XOR gates in a circuit as its size $s_{\mathcal{C}_i} = |\mathcal{C}_i|$. We denote the maximal circuit size in $\mathcal{S}$ by $s_{\max} = \max_{\mathcal{C}_i \in \mathcal{S}} |\mathcal{C}_i|$. We denote by $s_{\mathcal{C}_i}^{\mathsf{Total}} = |\mathcal{C}_i|^{\mathsf{Total}}$ the size of the circuit $\mathcal{C}_i$, *including/counting XOR gates*. We use the notation $\overset{c}{=}$ to denote computational indistinguishability of ensembles of random variables.

4.2   Defining $\mathcal{S}$-Universal GC

We introduce security definitions with which we operate in this work. We are interested in efficient $\mathcal{S}$-Universal GC evaluation. In Fig. 2 we formalize the functionality $\mathcal{F}^{\mathcal{S}\text{-UC}}$ which will serve as the basic definition.

Intuitively, our goal is simple: we wish to evaluate a function chosen by one of the players P_1 among the known set of functions $\mathcal{S}$.

We additionally define a more convenient functionality $\mathcal{F}^{\mathcal{S}\text{-UC-s}}$ for shared-output $\mathcal{F}^{\mathcal{S}\text{-UC}}$. $\mathcal{F}^{\mathcal{S}\text{-UC-s}}$ requires that the players don't get the output of the function $\mathcal{C}_t$ directly, but rather a GC-style secret sharing of the computed value. The functionality $\mathcal{F}^{\mathcal{S}\text{-UC-s}}$ is presented in Fig. 3. We will present our construction for the simpler $\mathcal{F}^{\mathcal{S}\text{-UC}}$ functionality; extension to the more convenient $\mathcal{F}^{\mathcal{S}\text{-UC-s}}$ functionality is simple, and we briefly discuss it in Sect. 6.

5   Extending the BHR Framework

It is beneficial to present the work in the terminology of garbling schemes [BHR12], introduced by Bellare, Hoang and Rogaway (BHR). In our abstraction approach, we aim to find a balance between generality and simplicity, while maximizing the reuse of the thoughtfully designed BHR framework.

We start by reminding the reader of the relevant details of the BHR framework.

5.1   BHR Garbling Schemes

Bellare, Hoang, and Rogaway [BHR12] introduce the notion of a garbling scheme as a cryptographic primitive. We refer the reader to their work for a complete treatment and give a brief summary of relevant aspects here. We note that their definitions apply to any kind of garbling, such as decision trees, automata, etc.

PARAMETERS:

1. Let $\mathcal{S} = \{\mathcal{C}_1, \mathcal{C}_2, ..., \mathcal{C}_n\}$ be a set of Boolean circuits. All circuits $\mathcal{C}_i$ have the same number n_{in} of input wires (with the same number $n_{in\text{-}x}$ and $n_{in\text{-}y}$ wires provided by P_1 and P_2 respectively) and the same number n_{out} of output wires.
2. Two players P_1 and P_2 have inputs $x \in \{0,1\}^{n_{in\text{-}x}}$ and $y \in \{0,1\}^{n_{in\text{-}y}}$.
3. P_1 provides additional input: index $t \in [1..n]$ of the target circuit $\mathcal{C}_t$ to be evaluated.

FUNCTIONALITY:

Both players obtain the output $\mathcal{C}_t$ (x,y).

Fig. 2. $\mathcal{S}$-UC functionality $\mathcal{F}^{\mathcal{S}\text{-UC}}$

PARAMETERS:

1. Let $\mathcal{S} = \{\mathcal{C}_1, \mathcal{C}_2, ..., \mathcal{C}_n\}$ be a set of Boolean circuits. All circuits $\mathcal{C}_i$ have the same number n_{in} of input wires (with the same number $n_{in\text{-}x}$ and $n_{in\text{-}y}$ wires provided by P_1 and P_2 respectively) and the same number n_{out} of output wires.
2. Two players P_1 and P_2 have inputs $x \in \{0,1\}^{n_{in\text{-}x}}$ and $y \in \{0,1\}^{n_{in\text{-}y}}$.
3. P_1 provides additional input: index $t \in [1..n]$ of the target circuit $\mathcal{C}_t$ to be evaluated.

FUNCTIONALITY $\mathcal{F}^{\mathcal{S}\text{-UC-s}}$ PROCEEDS AS FOLLOWS:

1. Compute the n_{out}-bit plaintext output $out = \mathcal{C}_t(x, y)$.
2. Randomly sample $2 \cdot n_{out}$ bit strings of size κ each: $\ell_i^0, \ell_i^1 \in_R \{0,1\}^\kappa$, where $i \in [1..n_{out}]$.
3. Send all labels ℓ_i^0, ℓ_i^1 to P_1.
4. For each $i \in [1..n_{out}]$:
   • Designate label $\ell_i^{out[i]}$ to be sent to P_2.
5. Send all designated labels to P_2.

Fig. 3. $\mathcal{S}$-UC-s functionality $\mathcal{F}^{\mathcal{S}\text{-UC-s}}$

We focus the notation on circuits and *circuit* garbling, which BHR consider as a special case, by requiring certain constraints on syntax and semantics of general object in their framework. A circuit garbling scheme consists of the following algorithms: Garble takes a circuit f as input and outputs (F, e, d) where F is a garbled circuit, e is encoding information, and d is decoding information. Encode takes an input x and encoding information e and outputs a garbled input X. Eval takes a garbled circuit F and garbled input X and outputs a garbled output Y. Finally, Decode takes a garbled output Y and decoding information d and outputs a plain circuit-output (or an error $\bot$).

Most relevant in our context are the prv.sim (privacy) and obv.sim (obliviousness) security definitions from [BHR12], which we state below. In the prv.sim and obv.sim games, the Initialize procedure chooses $\beta \leftarrow \{0,1\}$, and the Finalize(β') procedure returns $\beta \stackrel{?}{=} \beta'$. In both games, the adversary can make a single call to the Garble procedure, which is defined below. Additionally, the function Φ

denotes the information about the circuit that is allowed to be leaked by the garbling scheme; the function $\mathcal{S}$ is a simulator, and G denotes a garbling scheme.

prv.sim$_{G,\Phi,\mathcal{S}}$:	obv.sim$_{G,\Phi,\mathcal{S}}$:
Garble(f,x): if $\beta = 0$ $\quad (F,e,d) \leftarrow$ Garble$(1^\kappa, f)$ $\quad X \leftarrow$ Encode(e,x) else $(F,X,d) \leftarrow \mathcal{S}(1^\kappa, f(x), \Phi(f))$ return (F,X,d)	Garble(f,x): if $\beta = 0$ $\quad (F,e,d) \leftarrow$ Garble$(1^\kappa, f)$ $\quad X \leftarrow$ Encode(e,x) else $(F,X) \leftarrow \mathcal{S}(1^\kappa, \Phi(f))$ return (F,X)

We then define the advantage of the adversary in the security games:

$$\mathsf{Advtg}^{\mathsf{prv.sim}}_{G,\Phi,\mathcal{S}}(\mathsf{Adv}, \kappa) := \left| \Pr[\mathsf{prv.sim}^{\mathsf{Adv}}_{G,\Phi,\mathcal{S}}(\kappa) = 1] - \frac{1}{2} \right|;$$

$$\mathsf{Advtg}^{\mathsf{obv.sim}}_{G,\Phi,\mathcal{S}}(\mathsf{Adv}, \kappa) := \left| \Pr[\mathsf{obv.sim}^{\mathsf{Adv}}_{G,\Phi,\mathcal{S}}(\kappa) = 1] - \frac{1}{2} \right|.$$

We say that a garbling scheme satisfies privacy (resp. obliviousness) if for any polytime adversary Adv, the corresponding advantage Advtg is negligible. We omit restating here the remainder of the BHR framework, and refer the reader to the original work.

5.2 Intuition for Topology Decoupling and Composition

Ability to decouple the topology of evaluated GC, highlighted and used in this work, is related to the standard obliviousness property formalized by BHR. Intuitively, BHR obliviousness means that a party acquiring F and X, but not d, shouldn't learn anything about f, x, or y beyond that is explicitly allowed in the leakage function Φ. This is roughly the property we require as well, but with a different formalization, requiring careful handling.

The following are the technical issues that need to be addressed to enable discussion of our protocols in the (extended) BHR framework.

1. Let F be a string representing a garbled circuit. Firstly, we need to syntactically separate the function encoding (e.g., topology) T from the cryptographic material E included in F, such as garbled tables. That is, we wish to explicitly write $F = (T, E)$, thus enabling consideration of a GC (T', E). We note that in the BHR framework, the function description T is either implicit in Eval or is included in F in an unspecified manner.
2. Secondly, once this syntactic convention is adopted, we need to adjust the definitions to support evaluation under a "wrong" function encoding, and further, to require that Eval will not detect whether it operates with a "right" or "wrong" encoding.
3. Thirdly, the BHR framework naturally treats circuits as "the whole thing," and does not provide for a clean interface to discuss shared output (e.g.

undecoded wire labels which may later be used as encrypted input in another computation). In particular, the BHR decoding function Decode is required to output the correct plaintext value of the computation.

We now sketch a suitable formalization approach addressing the above issues for natural circuit representations. We take the BHR framework as the basis and adjust it as described next. The formal definitions are presented in Sect. 5.3.

We stress that for concreteness and convenience we next discuss specific ways to encode a circuit in GC. We note that that the definitions of Sect. 5.3 are more general, and may use arbitrary encodings.

Topological encoding in GC F. In BHR, $Y = \mathsf{Eval}(F, X)$ takes as input the garbled circuit F and garbled input X. The BHR framework does not discuss how garbled function F encodes information which allows Eval to proceed with the evaluation. In BHR, conventional Boolean circuits are viewed as a tuple (n, m, q, A, B, G). Here $n \geq 2$ is the number of inputs, $m \geq 1$ is the number of outputs, and $q \geq 1$ is the number of gates. A (resp. B) is a function identifying a gate's first (resp. second) incoming wire, and G is a function identifying the gate function of the gate. BHR introduces the notation of *topological circuit* f^-, which is defined to be a conventional circuit f without the gate function component. That is, for a circuit $f = (n, m, q, A, B, G)$, the topological circuit f^- is defined as (n, m, q, A, B).

Let's consider the question of evaluating a GC, given a list of garbled tables. It is easy to see that f^- contains sufficient topological information to evaluate classical Yao's GC, assuming an implicit correspondence between gate id and the garbled table associated with it. Such a correspondence is typically implemented by enforcing a canonical ordering of the gates and garbled tables.

At the same time, f^- does not have sufficient information to evaluate circuits garbled with Free-XOR [KS08a]. This is because the ids of XOR gates are not included in f^- and cannot be inferred from a bare list of garbled tables. To generalize this, we will consider *type-topological* circuits:

Definition 1. *Following the BHR notation, we say that f^* is a conventional type-topological* circuit, *if $f^* = (n, m, q, A, B, G^*)$, where G^* specifies the gate type of each gate. We will often simply say* topological circuit *or* topology *instead of* type-topological circuit *when clear from the context.*

We stress that the topological circuit must provide sufficient information to the Eval function to enable GC evaluation.

A typical example of gate types referred by G^* is the set {XOR, non-XOR}. Topology f^* with G^* defined over this type set allows evaluation of Free-XOR and half-gate garbled circuits. We note that other natural definitions of circuit topology are possible. One example is to include pointers to the garbled tables implementing gates. We choose the representation of Definition 1 as a balance of generality and simplicity which may be convenient to use for known GC schemes.

Topology Decoupling and Evaluation with Different topology. We need to enable parsing and evaluation of GC F with varying topology. As outlined above, for this we need to syntactically decouple the (implicit and deterministically computed) GC topology from the (generated using randomness) cryptographic material, such as encrypted tables. Without loss of generality, we *require* parsing the garbled circuit F as $F = (T, E)$, where T is the type-topological circuit f^* and E is the cryptographic material, such as a set of encrypted tables. We set $f^* = (n, m, q, A, B, G^*)$. We thus require Garble to produce F in the above format, and Eval(F, X) to accept this format $F = (T, E)$ of garbled circuit.

By extracting the type-topology T out of the GC F we enable evaluating F with an arbitrary topology T'. As a security feature of a circuit garbling scheme, we will require that evaluator is unable to tell whether it is evaluating with the intended topology T or an arbitrary different one T'. This will be ensured by requiring that the ensembles $\{(T, E), X\}$ and $\{(T', E), X\}$ are indistinguishable, where X are the (encoded) input labels, T is the matching topology, and T' is any admissible topology. In Sect. 5.3, we define the intuitive notion of admissible topology (by considering classes of mutually admissible functions) and formalize the above indistinguishability property.

Again, we stress that different topology representations are possible. While the type-topology described above is convenient for known GC schemes, our definitions in Sect. 5.3 do not restrict to using above representation.

Shared Output and Composition in Garbled Circuits. As noted above, the BHR framework does not naturally handle in generality the composition of garbled functions. It has the concept of garbled output, which, together with the decoding information can be seen as the secret-sharing of the function output. However, this representation is too general, and as one consequence, does not support discussing manipulation of the undecoded or partial output and feeding such output into a subsequent execution. In [BHR12], the authors sometimes handle over-generality by parsing standard BHR objects in a certain way. For example, faced with the need to discuss circuit input labels and their use in OT, the authors simply say "parse $(X_1^0, X_1^1, ..., X_n^0, X_n^1) \leftarrow e$." This, of course, assumes a specific garbling scheme, and represents a trade off between simplicity, generality and formalism.

One way of formalizing the required secret-shared output bits is by introducing restrictions on the format of the decoding information Y [2].

It would be convenient to formalize this restriction *as an option* for circuit garbling scheme, by requiring that the garbled output $Y = (Y_1, ... Y_{n_{\mathrm{out}}})$ is a vector of garbled wire outputs and allows for syntactic access to any particular component. Similarly, we require that the decoding information $d = (d_1, ..., d_{n_{\mathrm{out}}})$

---

[2] Indeed, BHR allows arbitrary representation options, including exotic ones such as $Y = \mathrm{AES}_k(y)$ being an AES encryption of the multi-bit output y, and $d = k$ being the AES decryption key. Clearly such a representation, while secure, is inconvenient for revealing a partial output or providing the unencrypted output for further GC evaluation.

is a vector of output wire decodings, such that d_i allows to decode the garbled output Y_i. We will overload the standard BHR Decode function to take as input any subsets of garbled wire labels and corresponding decoding information.

5.3 Definition of Topology-Decoupling Circuit Garbling

We now formalize the intuition described in Sect. 5.2.

Recall, in the BHR framework [BHR12], the garbling scheme is a five-tuple of algorithms GS = (Garble, Encode, Decode, Eval, eval). A BHR circuit garbling scheme CGS = (Garble, Encode, Decode, Eval, eval) is a garbling scheme with certain natural syntactic restrictions. To reason about our protocol in generality, we introduce a further syntactic restriction on the BHR garbled circuits. Namely, syntactically, we will require the garbled circuit to be specified as $F = (T, E)$. Here T is a function encoding, such as the *conventional type-topologic circuit* (cf. Definition 1), and E is cryptographic material, such as garbled tables. We keep the syntax of all BHR functions Garble, Encode, Decode, Eval, eval.

In the following we use the standard BHR notation, and we only present notions and objects different from standard BHR.

Definition 2 (Circuit Garbling Scheme (CGS)). *We consider Circuit Garbling Scheme as defined by BHR, with the following difference:*

Garbled circuit. We require the garbled circuit $F = (T, E)$ to explicitly define the function encoding component T. T is implicit in and deterministically obtained from the computed plaintext circuit f. We will often say topology *instead of function encoding when clear from the context.*

Garble. *On input $(1^\kappa, f)$, Garble will output (F, e, d), where $F = (T, E)$. Here $T = T(f)$ is deterministic and hence can be computed by any party, including the GC evaluator.*

Eval. *The garbled evaluation function Eval takes garbled input X and $F = (T', E)$ as input. Eval outputs garbled output labels Y or a special failure symbol $\bot$.*

Reusing BHR machinery. With the above syntactic restriction, we are able to reuse the existing BHR garbling machinery in defining a generalization of BHR circuit garbling. Importantly, our notion is a *special case* of BHR garbling scheme, and thus we can keep the BHR function definitions and correctness and security requirements as is. This is because we (so far, with a single exception) restricted the syntax of the BHR notions. Our only generalization (allowing to evaluate under different topology), is not exercised in BHR definitions. Therefore, all BHR notation and definitions retain their meaning and are reused.

In other words, the BHR framework (which we retain in full as the foundation!) is sufficient to handle the case of evaluating a circuit with correct topology. We only need to define the behavior of circuit garbling in the generalized case of evaluation under different topology.

Specifically, we only need to define the security properties ensuring that evaluation under an admissible topology is indistinguishable from correct evaluation.

Topology-decoupling circuit garbling schemes. There are several approaches to defining indistinguishability of garbled circuits with matching ("right") and non-matching ("wrong") topology.

In one approach, we could require the Garble function to take an additional parameter s, specifying the size of the maximal circuit. Garble then would produce a garbled circuit implementing the given function f, but which has extra garbled tables, suitable for implementing any circuit of size up to s. Then we would require that the output (T, E) of such Garble function is such that ensembles (T, E) and (T', E) are indistinguishable. This general approach requires either overloading syntax of a standard BHR function, or introducing a new function. In turn, BHR definitions stipulating security guarantees of standard functions will need to be rephrased and stated second time for the new function.

Another approach could be to define a small-family garbling scheme w.r.t. a fixed set of circuits which we intend to use as conditional clauses, and then define generalized obliviousness. This is a natural approach, but it requires showing the security of the garbling scheme for each set of circuits that might be required.

Our approach. Instead, we will take a cleaner and more general definitional approach. We consider classes of mutually topologically admissible circuits. Such a class would be defined by a canonical (for the class) circuit f_{can}. (For example, in known schemes, such as Free-XOR and half-gates, the class of circuits will be defined by the maximal number s of non-XOR gates, and f_{can}^s could be a circuit consisting of s AND gates.) We stress that multiple circuits could be canonical for the same class C.

For convenience, we first introduce the following notation.

Definition 3 (Embedding of cryptographic material). *We denote by* Embed *the procedure of introducing the cryptographic material E of a function f into the cryptographic material E_{can} of the canonical circuit f_{can}. We will write* Embed(E, E_{can}) *to denote the output of this procedure.*

The idea of the Embed procedure and its use, formalized in the definitions next, is that the cryptographic material Embed(E, E_{can}) can be used to evaluate f, but is indistinguishable from embeddings of cryptographic material Embed(E', E_{can}) of any other function f', where f and f' belong to the same class of mutually admissible circuits. The indistinguishability must hold even if the encoded input is given. Embed will be defined as part of garbling scheme description.

We stress that circuit encoding details, such as wiring, number of inputs and outputs, etc., need not be explicitly specified and discussed in the definition. Instead, this is handled by considering a class C of circuits for which the garblings are compatible or mutually admissible (defined below).

We now formally define the indistinguishability requirement.

Definition 4 (Topology-decoupling circuit garbling). *Let* CGS $=$ (Garble, Encode, Decode, Eval, eval, Embed) *be a circuit garbling scheme as discussed above (Definition 2), with the added* Embed *function. Let f_{can} be a circuit,*

$$\boxed{\begin{array}{l}
\mathsf{topo}_{\mathsf{CGS},C,f_{\mathsf{can}}}: \\[4pt]
\hline
\underline{\mathsf{Garble}(f, f', x):} \\
\text{if } f \notin C \text{ or } f' \notin C, \text{ abort.} \\
(F_{\mathsf{can}}, e_{\mathsf{can}}, d_{\mathsf{can}}) \leftarrow \mathsf{Garble}(1^\kappa, f_{\mathsf{can}}), \text{ where } F_{\mathsf{can}} = (T_{\mathsf{can}}, E_{\mathsf{can}}) \\
(F, e, d) \leftarrow \mathsf{Garble}(1^\kappa, f), \text{ where } F = (T, E) \\
(F', e', d') \leftarrow \mathsf{Garble}(1^\kappa, f'), \text{ where } F' = (T', E') \\
X \leftarrow \mathsf{Encode}(e, x) \\
\text{if } \beta = 1 \\
\quad\quad \text{return } ((T, \mathsf{Embed}(E, E_{\mathsf{can}})), X) \\
\text{else} \\
\quad\quad \text{return } ((T', \mathsf{Embed}(E', E_{\mathsf{can}})), X)
\end{array}}$$

Fig. 4. Game $\mathsf{topo}_{\mathsf{CGS},C,f_{\mathsf{can}}}$.

and let $C = Class(f_{\mathsf{can}})$ be a set (or class) of circuits. Consider the distinguishing advantage of the adversary winning the game topo of Fig. 4 (cast in the BHR setup with Initialize() and Finalize() procedures as in BHR).

We say that CGS is topology-decoupling within C and that f_{can} is canonical for C, if for every polytime adversary Adv, the following is negligible:

$$\mathsf{Advtg}_{\mathsf{CGS}}^{\mathsf{topo}, f_{\mathsf{can}}}(\mathsf{Adv}, \kappa) = |Pr[\mathsf{topo}_{\mathsf{CGS},C,f_{\mathsf{can}}}^{\mathsf{Adv}}(\kappa) = 1] - \frac{1}{2}| \tag{1}$$

We note that the topo game of Definition 4 exactly corresponds to our proposed construction, where the circuit's cryptographic material is evaluated under different function encodings/topologies with the same garbled input.

Finally, we need to require correct evaluation of a circuit $(T, \mathsf{Embed}(E, E'))$, where T, E are matching, i.e. produced by $F \leftarrow \mathsf{Garble}(\kappa)$. Formally:

Definition 5 (Extended correctness). *Let* CGS *be a circuit garbling scheme (Definition 2). Let* $((T, E), e, d) = \mathsf{Garble}(1^\kappa, f)$ *and* $((T_{\mathsf{can}}, E_{\mathsf{can}}), e_{\mathsf{can}}, d_{\mathsf{can}}) = \mathsf{Garble}(1^\kappa, f_{\mathsf{can}})$, *where* f *belongs to a class defined by a canonical function* f_{can}. *We say that* CGS *has extended correctness, if it always holds that:* $\mathsf{Decode}(d, \mathsf{Eval}[(T, \mathsf{Embed}(E, E_{\mathsf{can}})), \mathsf{Encode}(e, x)]) = \mathsf{eval}(f, x)$.

We note that topology-decoupling does not imply extended correctness, since the experiment in the topology decoupling definition does not have access to output encoding.

Notation. Extended correctness is an obvious and default requirement. Therefore, for convenience of notation, we will say *topology-decoupling circuit garbling* to mean "topology-decoupling circuit garbling with extended correctness."

We will use topology-decoupling circuit garbling schemes. To use them in constructing S-UC protocols, one will need to first design a topology-decoupling garbling scheme and then apply the generic construction presented in the next section. Designing a required garbling scheme can be simply done by starting with an existing scheme, such as half-gates, and showing that it meets the additional requirements (Definitions 4 and 5) or adjust it so that it does. This approach relies on and reuses the existing body of work of proving security in the BHR framework.

5.4 Output Manipulation Extension

We introduce the notation for bitwise output manipulation with the goal of keeping the standard BHR notation intact, while at the same time allowing formalizations and use in generic protocols.

Definition 6 (Topology-decoupling circuit garbling with bitwise decoding). *Let* CGS = (Garble, Encode, Decode, Eval, eval, Embed) *be a topology-decoupling circuit garbling scheme.*

We say that a topology-decoupling circuit garbling scheme CGS *supports bitwise decoding if the following holds:*

1. *The garbled output* Y *is a vector of garbled wire outputs* $Y = (Y_1, ... Y_{n_{\text{out}}})$ *and allows for syntactic access to any particular component by index* Y_i.
2. *The decoding information* d *is a vector of output wire decodings* $d = (d_1, ..., d_{n_{\text{out}}})$ *and allows syntactic access to any particular component by index* d_i.
3. *Extended correctness of decoding holds per wire. That is, let* $((T, E), e, d) =$ Garble$(1^\kappa, f)$ *and* $((T_{\text{can}}, E_{\text{can}}), e_{\text{can}}, d_{\text{can}}) =$ Garble$(1^\kappa, f_{\text{can}})$, *where* f *belongs to a class defined by a canonical function* f_{can}. *Let* $Y =$ Eval$[(T, \text{Embed}(E, E_{\text{can}})), \text{Encode}(e, x)]$. *Then we require* Decode$(d_i, Y_i) =$ eval$(f, x)|_i$.

A similar definition is easily constructed for standard BHR framework.

6 $\mathcal{S}$-UC Construction from Topology-Decoupling Circuit Garbling

We now show a generic $\mathcal{S}$-UC construction built from the generic notion of topology-decoupling circuit garbling schemes with extended correctness, introduced above. In this section, we exclusively work with such schemes. For convenience, we may refer to them in this section simply as circuit garbling, when clear from context.

Let CGS = (Garble, Encode, Decode, Eval, eval, Embed) be a circuit-garbling scheme with topology-decoupling garbling (Definition 4) and extended correctness (Definition 5). The construction of Fig. 7 is presented in the generic terms of such circuit garbling. In reviewing the construction, it may be instructive to think in terms of a specific garbling scheme, such as the half-gates scheme or classical Yao, and the class of admissible circuits as all circuits with up to s non-XOR gates, where the canonical circuit is the s-gate circuit consisting of AND gates.

We start with presenting a generalized output selection functionality (Fig. 5). Here, instead of the specific way of feeding the shared input into the functionality, we tailor it to work with generic BHR-style sharing, where one party will hold garbled output, and the other will hold the decoding information. We note that protocol $\Pi^{\text{gen-out}}$ of Fig. 6 implementing $\mathcal{F}^{\text{gen-out}}$ can be refined if circuit garbling supports bitwise decoding (Definition 6). In the formal construction (Fig. 7), we omit this and other natural enhancements (such as considering specific bits of the output labels or producing shared output $a\text{-}la$ functionality $\mathcal{F}^{\text{out-s}}$) for simplicity of presentation.

PARAMETERS:

- Two parties: P_1 and P_2. Circuit garbling scheme CGS.

  P_1's first input $j \in [1..n]$ denotes the selection index. P_1's second input is the decoding information for a circuit with n_{out} output wires.

  P_2's input is a vector of vectors $\text{out} = \text{out}_1, ..., \text{out}_n$, where each out_i is a string representing garbled output Y_i.

FUNCTIONALITY:

Players submit their inputs to $\mathcal{F}^{\text{gen-out}}$.
$\mathcal{F}^{\text{gen-out}}$ outputs $\text{Decode}(d, Y_j)$.

Fig. 5. Generalized output selection functionality $\mathcal{F}^{\text{gen-out}}$

Theorem 1. *Let* CGS $=$ (Garble, Encode, Decode, Eval, eval, Embed) *be a topology-decoupling circuit garbling scheme (Definitions 4 and 5) with respect to a class C and a canonical circuit $\mathcal{C}_{\text{can}}$. Then the construction of Fig. 7 securely implements the $\mathcal{S}$-UC functionality of Fig. 2.*

Proof. **Security against corrupt** Gen. This part of the security proof closely follows the standard Yao GC proof and is omitted. Indeed, the view of Gen only includes the messages sent by the OT executions and the messages received as part of the output selection functionality $\mathcal{F}^{\text{gen-out}}$, and is easily simulated (in part) by plugging in the output of the corresponding simulators.

Security against corrupt Ev. Intuitively, we need to argue that Ev does not gain additional information from evaluating the *same* GC $\hat{\mathcal{C}}$ when interpreted as garblings of different circuits $\mathcal{C}_i$. We exhibit a simulator Sim_{Ev} and prove that its output is indistinguishable from the real execution. We will rely on the topology decoupling property of circuit garbling, as formalized by Definition 4.

Constructing Sim_{Ev}. Recall, the simulator $\text{Sim}_{\text{Ev}}(y, z)$ knows the set of circuits $\mathcal{S} = \{\mathcal{C}_1, \mathcal{C}_2, ..., \mathcal{C}_n\}$, where each $\mathcal{C}_i \in C(\mathcal{C}_{\text{can}})$. $\text{Sim}_{\text{Ev}}(y, z)$ takes as input the true input and the output of the real execution and outputs the simulated view $\text{View}_{\text{Sim}_{\text{Ev}}}$.

PARAMETERS:

1. Two parties: P_1 and P_2.

   P_1's first input $j \in [1..n]$ denotes the selection index. P_1's second input is the decoding information for a circuit with n_{out} output wires.

   P_2's input is a vector of vectors $\mathsf{out} = \mathsf{out}_1, ..., \mathsf{out}_n$, where each out_i is a string representing garbled output Y_i.

PROTOCOL:

1. Let C be the output selection circuit, computing (non-shared) Generalized Output Selection Functionality $\mathcal{F}^{\mathsf{gen\text{-}out}}$ of Figure 5.
2. Players P_1 and P_2 execute Yao's GC protocol evaluating C using classical GC protocol of [LP04], and using the OT extension protocol of [IKNP03].

Fig. 6. Generalized output selection protocol $\Pi^{\mathsf{gen\text{-}out}}$ realizing $\mathcal{F}^{\mathsf{gen\text{-}out}}$ of Fig. 5.

PARAMETERS:

Parties Gen and Ev with inputs $x \in \{0,1\}^{n_{\mathsf{in\text{-}x}}}$ and $y \in \{0,1\}^{n_{\mathsf{in\text{-}y}}}$ respectively. A set of Boolean circuits $\mathcal{S} = \{C_1, C_2, ..., C_n\}$, where each $C_i \in C(C_{\mathsf{can}})$. All circuits C_i have the same number of input wires n_{in}, $n_{\mathsf{in\text{-}x}}$, $n_{\mathsf{in\text{-}y}}$, and the same number of output wires. Let $C_t \in \mathcal{S}$ be the circuit Gen wishes to evaluate.

PROTOCOL:

1. Gen runs $((T_{\mathsf{can}}, E_{\mathsf{can}}), e_{\mathsf{can}}, d_{\mathsf{can}}) \leftarrow \mathsf{Garble}(1^\kappa, C_{\mathsf{can}})$ and $((T, E), e, d) \leftarrow \mathsf{Garble}(1^\kappa, C_t)$. Gen sends $E' = \mathsf{Embed}(E, E_{\mathsf{can}})$ to Ev.
2. Given encoding information e, Gen sends to Ev active wire labels for the wires on which Gen provides input.
3. For i-th input bit of Ev, Gen and Ev execute Oblivious Transfer (OT), where Gen plays the role of the Sender, and Ev plays the role of the Receiver.
   (a) Gen's two input secrets are the two labels of the target GC $\widehat{C}_t$ for the wire corresponding to Ev's i-th input. Ev's choice-bit input is its input on that wire.
   (b) Upon completion of OT, Ev receives active wire label on the wire. This label will be used as active wire in each of the circuits in $\mathcal{S}$.
4. Ev had received input encoding X by executing Steps 2 and 3. For each circuit $C_j \in \mathcal{S}$, Ev obtains its topology T_j by running $((T_j, E_j), e_j, d_j) \leftarrow \mathsf{Garble}(1^\kappa, C_j)$ and discarding all but T_j. For each T_j, Ev computes output labels $Y_j = \mathsf{Eval}((T_j, E'), X)$.
5. Gen and Ev execute a Generalized Output Selection protocol $\Pi^{\mathsf{gen\text{-}out}}$ of Figure 6. Ev provides as input n candidate garbled outputs Y_j obtained in Step 4. Gen provides as input the index t of the target circuit, as well as the decoding information d.
6. Players output whatever $\Pi^{\mathsf{gen\text{-}out}}$ outputs.

Fig. 7. $\mathcal{S}$-universal garbled circuit protocol

$\mathsf{Sim}_{\mathsf{Ev}}$ starts by emulating the GC $\widehat{C}$ received in Step 1 of Fig. 7. To do so, $\mathsf{Sim}_{\mathsf{Ev}}$ simply runs $((T, E), e, d) \leftarrow \mathsf{Garble}(1^\kappa, C_{\mathsf{can}})$ and adds E to the view $\mathsf{View}_{\mathsf{Sim}_{\mathsf{Ev}}}$.

$\mathsf{Sim}_{\mathsf{Ev}}$ proceeds to emulate Step 2 by parsing $(X_1^0, X_1^1, ..., X_{n_{in}}^0, X_{n_{in}}^0) \leftarrow e^3$. For each index i of the wire provided by Gen, $\mathsf{Sim}_{\mathsf{Ev}}$ adds X_i^0, to the view $\mathsf{View}_{\mathsf{Sim}_{\mathsf{Ev}}}$.

$\mathsf{Sim}_{\mathsf{Ev}}$ emulates the receiver's view of OT (Step 3) by calling the provided OT simulator $\mathsf{Sim}_{\mathsf{OT}}$. $\mathsf{Sim}_{\mathsf{Ev}}$ provides input y to $\mathsf{Sim}_{\mathsf{OT}}$ as well as the corresponding input wire labels X_i^j generated by Garble above. This is intended to simulate the labels that are output as the result of OT. $\mathsf{Sim}_{\mathsf{Ev}}$ appends the Receiver view generated by $\mathsf{Sim}_{\mathsf{OT}}$ to the view $\mathsf{View}_{\mathsf{Sim}_{\mathsf{Ev}}}$.

$\mathsf{Sim}_{\mathsf{Ev}}$ emulates the evaluation of all n circuits of Step 4 by honestly executing Step 4 n times as prescribed in the protocol of Fig. 7. As a result, $\mathsf{Sim}_{\mathsf{Ev}}$ obtains n garbled outputs Y_j. These Y_j are implicit in the already-generated view and hence are not formally included in $\mathsf{View}_{\mathsf{Sim}_{\mathsf{Ev}}}$.

Next $\mathsf{Sim}_{\mathsf{Ev}}$ simulates Step 5 by calling the simulator $\mathsf{Sim}_{\Pi^{\mathsf{gen\text{-}out}}}$ for the protocol $\Pi^{\mathsf{gen\text{-}out}}$ realizing $\mathcal{F}^{\mathsf{gen\text{-}out}}$. For this, $\mathsf{Sim}_{\mathsf{Ev}}$ calls the simulator with input n garbled outputs Y_j, as well as the vector of the output labels received as $\mathsf{Sim}_{\mathsf{Ev}}$ input. $\mathsf{Sim}_{\mathsf{Ev}}$ appends the output of the simulator to its view $\mathsf{View}_{\mathsf{Sim}_{\mathsf{Ev}}}$, outputs its view and terminates.

Indistinguishability of the simulation. It is easy to verify that the simulation is indistinguishable from the real execution.

Firstly, garbled circuits and the input encoding obtained in Steps 1–3 of the real protocol are indistinguishable from the corresponding simulated view. This is because the circuit garbling scheme CGS is topology-decoupling (cf. Definition 4). Indeed, the real view is $((T, \mathsf{Embed}(E, E_{\mathsf{can}})), X)$, and the simulated view is $((T_{\mathsf{can}}, E_{\mathsf{can}}), X_{\mathsf{can}})$. The game $\mathsf{topo}_{\mathsf{CGS}, f_{\mathsf{can}}}$ of Definition 4 immediately implies that the above distributions are indistinguishable.

As a result, the view $\mathsf{View}_{\mathsf{Sim}_{\mathsf{Ev}}}$ up until the call to a realization $\Pi^{\mathsf{gen\text{-}out}}$ of $\mathcal{F}^{\mathsf{gen\text{-}out}}$ is indistinguishable.

Simulation of $\Pi^{\mathsf{gen\text{-}out}}$ step is done by referring to the $\Pi^{\mathsf{gen\text{-}out}}$ simulator $\mathsf{Sim}_{\Pi^{\mathsf{gen\text{-}out}}}$. We need to take care of two details:

1. ensure that input-output relationship of the call to $\Pi^{\mathsf{gen\text{-}out}}$ is consistent with the $\mathsf{View}_{\mathsf{Sim}_{\mathsf{Ev}}}$ generated so far. Indeed, this is consistent. $\mathsf{Sim}_{\mathsf{Ev}}$ will provide to $\mathsf{Sim}_{\Pi^{\mathsf{gen\text{-}out}}}$ the output labels it ($\mathsf{Sim}_{\mathsf{Ev}}$) received as input, as well as the collection of the candidate garbled labels Y_j that $\mathsf{Sim}_{\mathsf{Ev}}$ had computed.
2. ensure that simulation provided by $\mathsf{Sim}_{\Pi^{\mathsf{gen\text{-}out}}}$ is good, despite the fact that the P_2 input provided to $\mathsf{Sim}_{\Pi^{\mathsf{gen\text{-}out}}}$ *different* from the input provided to $\Pi^{\mathsf{gen\text{-}out}}$ in the real execution.

   This is slightly more involved, and will require looking inside how the standard simulators work for GC-based secure computation. We show that there exists a simulator of P_2 which works with our proof. Intuitively, this is possible because Receiver's real input is only used in the OT component of the simulation of $\Pi^{\mathsf{gen\text{-}out}}$, where it is not used in an essential manner.

   Consider the standard simulators of GC evaluator $\mathsf{Sim}_{\mathsf{Ev\text{-}LP}}$ of [LP04] and

---

[3] While BHR do not formally require that such a parsing is possible, it is quite unnatural to not permit it, and all current garbling schemes allow it. Futher, in their examples BHR implicitly assume existence of such parsing.

of the OT Receiver Sim_{R-IKNP} of [IKNP03]. Sim_{Ev-LP} accepts as input the player's input y and the function output $f(x, y)$; it uses y only to pass it (together with the needed OT output) to the OT Receiver simulator Sim_{R-IKNP}. "Inside" Sim_{R-IKNP} of [IKNP03], the simulation succeeds independently of what y is.

Finally, even though the input provided to $Sim_{\Pi^{gen-out}}$ *is not the same* as the input provided to $\Pi^{gen-out}$ in the real execution, this is not a problem, as they are still computationally indistinguishable when considered as part of the probability ensemble $\{f_1(x, y), S_2(y, f_2(x, y))\}$, as argued above.

$\square$

Achieving shared-output functionality $\mathcal{F}^{S-UC-s}$. The protocol of Fig. 7 can be naturally extended to implement $\mathcal{F}^{S-UC-s}$ of Fig. 3. This is achieved, e.g., by running a shared-output version $\Pi^{gen-out-s}$ of the output selection protocol $\Pi^{gen-out}$. In turn, $\Pi^{gen-out-s}$ is derived from $\Pi^{gen-out}$ by not sending the GC decoding information to the other player and not reconstructing the plaintext output in the last stage of $\Pi^{gen-out}$.

6.1 Standard Garbling Schemes are Topology-Decoupling with Extended Correctness

It is easy to verify that standard GC schemes (classical Yao, Free-XOR and half-gates) satisfy the required notion. For classic Yao, the topology decoupling is with respect to the class C of circuits with maximal circuit size s. For the Free-XOR [KS08a] and half-gates [ZRE15] schemes, C is the set of circuits of $\leq s$ non-XOR gates. In all three cases, the canonical circuit is the circuit consisting of s AND gates and can have any number of inputs and outputs.

In our generic treatment of circuit garbling schemes, we ask the scheme to define the Embed procedure. For the above standard schemes, we define the Embed procedure as follows:

Construction 1 (Embedfor standard schemes). *For classic Yao, Free-XOR and half-gates, we define Embed to be the syntactic procedure of replacing the prefix of the cryptographic material E_2 with another cryptographic material E_1. For $|E_1| \leq |E_2|$, we say $E = \mathsf{Embed}(E_1, E_2)$, if E is the string equal to E_2 whose first $|E_1|$ bits are set to be to be the string E_1.*

Theorem 2 (Half-gates garbling is topology-decoupling with extended correctness). *Assuming hashing functions used in the half-gates construction are modeled as a random oracle, the half-gates garbling of [ZRE15] with the above Embed satisfies Definition 4 with respect to the class C of circuits with the same number of input and output wires, and with number of non-XOR gates less or equal to s, where canonical circuit is the circuit consisting of s AND gates. The half-gates garbling also satisfies Definition 5.*

Proof. We first observe that syntactically the functions defined by the half-gates scheme will work with switched topology. In particular, the Eval procedure of the half-gates scheme *does not* check that there are leftover garbled tables after completion. We defined the Embed procedure above. No additional syntactic changes are needed to consider the scheme.

Extended correctness is immediate. Evaluation of the embedded half-gates GC will proceed identically to the standard half-gates evaluation.

Topology-decoupling. Recall, in the half-gates scheme, the insight is for the generator Gen to generate a uniformly random bit r, and to transform the original AND gate $v_c = v_a \wedge v_c$ into two half gates involving r:

$$v_c = (v_a \wedge r) \oplus (v_a \wedge (r \oplus v_b))$$

This has the same value as $v_a \wedge v_b$ since it distributes to $v_a \wedge (r \oplus r \oplus v_b)$. Observe that in the first conjunction $(v_a \wedge r)$ the generator Gen knows r, and in the second conjunction $(v_a \wedge (r \oplus v_b))$, the evaluator Ev is allowed to learn $(r \oplus v_b)$. In both conjunctions one of the players knows one of the inputs in plaintext. ZRE call them half-gates, a generator half-gate and an evaluator half-gate.

ZRE [ZRE15] then use a standard construction of two-row tables for each of the half-gates. Further, a standard garbled-row reduction technique is applied to reduce size of each to a single row. Finally, the $v_c = v_a \wedge v_c$ is computed via the Free-XOR technique. Importantly for our proof, the garbled rows look random and do not contain any redundant information allowing evaluator to verify that it is evaluating a correctly garbled circuit.

Specifically, let p_a, p_b be the random permutation bits selected by Gen, and Δ is the Free-XOR offset also selected by Gen. The generator half-table row T_{Gen} is set to: $T_{\mathsf{Gen}} \leftarrow H(W_a^0) \oplus H(W_a^1) \oplus p_b\Delta$. The evaluator half-table row T_{Ev} is set to $T_{\mathsf{Ev}} \leftarrow H(W_b^0) \oplus H(W_b^1) \oplus W_a^0$. The garbled output wire W_c^0 is set to be $W_c^0 \leftarrow H(W_a^0) \oplus p_a T_{\mathsf{Gen}} \oplus H(W_b^0) \oplus p_b(T_{\mathsf{Ev}} \oplus W_a^0)$, and the other output label is set $W_c^1 = W_c^0 \oplus \Delta$. It is easy to trace this and to verify that the garbled tables output by the half-gates Gen are random-looking, assuming H is a random oracle, even given an input encoding X. That is, given input encoding X, a circuit consisting from randomly generated garbled tables is indistinguishable from the correctly generated half-gates GC corresponding to X. This immediately implies the theorem statement.   □

Similar theorems can be easily proven for Free-XOR, classical Yao, and many standard constructions. The proof relies on the property that the garbled circuit generated by Gen looks random, even given an input encoding.

Theorem 3. *Assuming hashing functions used in the Free-XOR construction are modeled as a random oracle, the Free-XOR garbling of [KS08a] with the above Embed satisfies Definition 4 with respect to the class C of circuits with the same number of input and output wires, and with number of non-XOR gates less or equal to s, where canonical circuit is the circuit consisting of s AND gates. The half-gates garbling also satisfies Definition 5.*

Theorem 4. *Assuming hashing function used in the classical Yao construction are modeled as a random oracle, the standard 4-row Yao garbling of [LP09] with the above* Embed *satisfies Definition 4 with respect to the class C of circuits with maximal circuit size s and with the same number of input and output wires, where canonical circuit is the circuit consisting of s AND gates. This garbling also satisfies Definition 5.*

7   Performance Calculation and Comparison

It is easy to evaluate performance of our $\mathcal{S}$-UC scheme. For a set $\mathcal{S}$ of n circuits of (non-XOR gate) sizes $s_{\mathcal{C}_i}$, our communication consists of transmitting *a single* GC of size $s_{\max} = \max s_{\mathcal{C}_i}$, plus the communication needed for $\Pi^{\text{gen-out}}$. $\Pi^{\text{gen-out}}$ requires $n_{\text{in}} \cdot n$ OTs and sending a circuit implementing $\Pi^{\text{gen-out}}$, which is a simple multiplexer and has approximately $n_{\text{out}} \cdot n$ gates.

The multiplexer circuit can process each of n_{out} wires at cost n non-XOR gates, e.g. as follows. The selector boolean input can be a vector of zeros except with a 1 in target position t. Then, the multiplexer computes XOR of all n_{out} conjunctions (of the selector bit and branch bit).

In contrast, the standard approach involves evaluating *all* n circuits, and the total communication cost will consist of sending $\sum_{i=1}^{n} |\mathcal{C}_i|$. We note that a recent heuristic circuit overlay approach [KKW17] can reduce this cost, sometimes significantly. As discussed in Sect. 1.2, our approach is more efficient and much simpler than [KKW17] in the case considered in this work (where the evaluated function is known to Gen).

For the special and representative case where all circuits are of the same size, our approach will require sending approximately $\max |\mathcal{C}_i|$ gates, while prior work required sending $n \cdot |\mathcal{C}_i|$ gates. (The cost of [KKW17] varies depending on the effectiveness of the heuristic and is between $\max |\mathcal{C}_i|$ and $n \cdot |\mathcal{C}_i|$ gates sent.) The auxiliary costs we incur (extra OTs and evaluating $\Pi^{\text{gen-out}}$ circuit) can often be ignored, e.g. when $\mathcal{C}_i$ is large relative to the auxiliary costs.

We note that if the branch clauses are very small circuits, then the cost of output selection may overweigh the benefit of Free IF. Precise determination of the break-even point mainly depends on the relative cost of the extra round of communication we require. Beyond the cost of the extra round, there is little we pay. Our output selection algorithm involves a circuit size similar to the multiplexer that would be used in regular GC; because we use OT as input, our multiplexer requires approximately twice the number of bits as the regular GC multiplexer.

Computation costs. We stress that the computation cost is reduced for the Generator (it would generate a single branch). However it remains the same as in the standard GC for the Evaluator. This is because the Evaluator must evaluate all branches of the circuit. We stress that in typical GC deployments communication is by far the most significant bottleneck, and runtime will usually be proportional to the amount of communication required.

Acknowledgements. I would like to thank anonymous reviewers of this paper and Viet Tung Hoang for valuable suggestions on presentation.

References

[BHR12] Bellare, M., Hoang, V.T., Rogaway, P.: Foundations of garbled circuits. In: Yu, T., Danezis, G., Gligor, V.D. (eds.) ACM CCS 12, pp. 784–796. ACM Press, October 2012

[DDK+15] Demmler, D., Dessouky, G., Koushanfar, F., Sadeghi, A.-R., Schneider, T., Zeitouni, S.: Automated synthesis of optimized circuits for secure computation. In: Ray, I., Li, N., Kruegel, C. (eds.) ACM CCS 15, pp. 1504–1517. ACM Press, October 2015

[DKS+17] Dessouky, G., Koushanfar, F., Sadeghi, A.-R., Schneider, T., Zeitouni, S., Zohner, M.: Pushing the communication barrier in secure computation using lookup tables. In: 24 Annual Network and Distributed System Security Symposium (NDSS 2017). The Internet Society, February 26-March 1, 2017. To appear

[FVK+15] Fisch, B.A., et al.: Malicious-client security in blind seer: a scalable private DBMS. In: 2015 IEEE Symposium on Security and Privacy, pp. 395–410. IEEE Computer Society Press, May 2015

[GKS17] Günther, D., Kiss, Á., Schneider, T.: More efficient universal circuit constructions. In: Takagi, T., Peyrin, T. (eds.) ASIACRYPT 2017. LNCS, vol. 10625, pp. 443–470. Springer, Cham (2017). https://doi.org/10.1007/978-3-319-70697-9_16

[GO96] Goldreich, O., Ostrovsky, R.: Software protection and simulation on oblivious RAMs. J. ACM **43**(3), 431–473 (1996)

[IKNP03] Ishai, Y., Kilian, J., Nissim, K., Petrank, E.: Extending oblivious transfers efficiently. In: Boneh, D. (ed.) CRYPTO 2003. LNCS, vol. 2729, pp. 145–161. Springer, Heidelberg (2003). https://doi.org/10.1007/978-3-540-45146-4_9

[KKW16] Kennedy, W.S., Kolesnikov, V., Wilfong, G.: Overlaying circuit clauses for secure computation. Cryptology ePrint Archive, Report 2016/685 (2016). http://eprint.iacr.org/2016/685

[KKW17] Kennedy, W.S., Kolesnikov, V., Wilfong, G.: Overlaying conditional circuit clauses for secure computation. In: Takagi, T., Peyrin, T. (eds.) ASIACRYPT 2017. LNCS, vol. 10625, pp. 499–528. Springer, Cham (2017). https://doi.org/10.1007/978-3-319-70697-9_18

[KMR14] Kolesnikov, V., Mohassel, P., Rosulek, M.: FleXOR: flexible garbling for XOR gates that beats free-XOR. In: Garay, J.A., Gennaro, R. (eds.) CRYPTO 2014. LNCS, vol. 8617, pp. 440–457. Springer, Heidelberg (2014). https://doi.org/10.1007/978-3-662-44381-1_25

[KS08a] Kolesnikov, V., Schneider, T.: Improved garbled circuit: free XOR gates and applications. In: Aceto, L., Damgård, I., Goldberg, L.A., Halldórsson, M.M., Ingólfsdóttir, A., Walukiewicz, I. (eds.) ICALP 2008. LNCS, vol. 5126, pp. 486–498. Springer, Heidelberg (2008). https://doi.org/10.1007/978-3-540-70583-3_40

[KS08b] Kolesnikov, V., Schneider, T.: A practical universal circuit construction and secure evaluation of private functions. In: Tsudik, G. (ed.) FC 2008. LNCS, vol. 5143, pp. 83–97. Springer, Heidelberg (2008). https://doi.org/10.1007/978-3-540-85230-8_7

[KS16] Kiss, Á., Schneider, T.: Valiant's universal circuit is practical. In: Fischlin, M., Coron, J.-S. (eds.) EUROCRYPT 2016. LNCS, vol. 9665, pp. 699–728. Springer, Heidelberg (2016). https://doi.org/10.1007/978-3-662-49890-3_27

[LMS16] Lipmaa, H., Mohassel, P., Sadeghian, S.: Valiant's universal circuit: improvements, implementation, and applications. Cryptology ePrint Archive, Report 2016/017 (2016). http://eprint.iacr.org/2016/017

[LP04] Lindell, Y., Pinkas, B.: A proof of Yao's protocol for secure two-party computation. Cryptology ePrint Archive, Report 2004/175 (2004). http://eprint.iacr.org/2004/175

[LP09] Lindell, Y., Pinkas, B.: A proof of security of Yao's protocol for two-party computation. J. Cryptol. **22**(2), 161–188 (2009)

[MS13] Mohassel, P., Sadeghian, S.: How to hide circuits in MPC an efficient framework for private function evaluation. In: Johansson, T., Nguyen, P.Q. (eds.) EUROCRYPT 2013. LNCS, vol. 7881, pp. 557–574. Springer, Heidelberg (2013). https://doi.org/10.1007/978-3-642-38348-9_33

[PKV+14] Pappas, V., et al.: Blind seer: a scalable private DBMS. In: 2014 IEEE Symposium on Security and Privacy, pp. 359–374. IEEE Computer Society Press, May 2014

[PSS09] Paus, A., Sadeghi, A.-R., Schneider, T.: Practical secure evaluation of semi-private functions. In: Abdalla, M., Pointcheval, D., Fouque, P.-A., Vergnaud, D. (eds.) ACNS 2009. LNCS, vol. 5536, pp. 89–106. Springer, Heidelberg (2009). https://doi.org/10.1007/978-3-642-01957-9_6

[SHS+15] Songhori, E.M., Hussain, S.U., Sadeghi, A.-R., Schneider, T., Koushanfar, F.: TinyGarble: highly compressed and scalable sequential garbled circuits. In: 2015 IEEE Symposium on Security and Privacy, pp. 411–428. IEEE Computer Society Press, May 2015

[Val76] Valiant, L.G.: Universal circuits (preliminary report). In: STOC, pp. 196–203. ACM Press, New York (1976)

[WGMK16] Wang, X., Gordon, S.D., McIntosh, A., Katz, J.: Secure computation of MIPS machine code. In: Askoxylakis, I., Ioannidis, S., Katsikas, S., Meadows, C. (eds.) ESORICS 2016. LNCS, vol. 9879, pp. 99–117. Springer, Cham (2016). https://doi.org/10.1007/978-3-319-45741-3_6

[Yao86] Yao, A.C.-C.: How to generate and exchange secrets (extended abstract). In: 27th FOCS, pp. 162–167. IEEE Computer Society Press, October 1986

[ZRE15] Zahur, S., Rosulek, M., Evans, D.: Two halves make a whole - reducing data transfer in garbled circuits using half gates. In: Oswald, E., Fischlin, M. (eds.) EUROCRYPT 2015. LNCS, vol. 9057, pp. 220–250. Springer, Heidelberg (2015). https://doi.org/10.1007/978-3-662-46803-6_8

Secure Computation with Low Communication from Cross-Checking

S. Dov Gordon[1(✉)], Samuel Ranellucci[2], and Xiao Wang[3]

[1] George Mason University, Fairfax, USA
gordon@gmu.edu
[2] Unbound Tech, Petach Tikva, Israel
samuel_ran@hotmail.com
[3] University of Maryland, College Park, USA
wangxiao@cs.umd.edu

Abstract. We construct new four-party protocols for secure computation that are secure against a single malicious corruption. Our protocols can perform computations over a binary ring, and require sending just 1.5 ring elements per party, per gate. In the special case of Boolean circuits, this amounts to sending 1.5 bits per party, per gate. One of our protocols is robust, yet requires almost no additional communication. Our key technique can be viewed as a variant of the "dual execution" approach, but, because we rely on four parties instead of two, we can avoid any leakage, achieving the standard notion of security.

1 Introduction

As secure multi-party computation (MPC) is transitioning to practice, one setting that has motivated multiple deployments is that of outsourced computation, in which hundreds of thousands, or millions of users secret share their input among some small number of computational servers. In this setting, the datasets can be extremely large, while the number of computing parties is small. The use of secure computation in such settings is often viewed as a safeguard that helps to reduce risk and liability. While companies and government agencies are increasingly choosing to deploy this safeguard, it is a security/performance tradeoff that many are not yet willing to make.

One important notion related to the security of an MPC protocol is the choice of adversarial threshold: a higher threshold means that the protocol can tolerate more corrupted parties. However, requiring a higher threshold usually results in feasibility and efficiency obstacles. For example, the earliest results in the field demonstrated key distinctions between $t \geq n/2$, $t < n/2$, and $t < n/3$ corruptions [3,5,22,32], including whether fairness could be guaranteed ($t < n/2$), whether a broadcast channel is needed ($t > n/3$), and whether cryptographic assumptions are necessary ($t > n/3$). More recently, when $t > n/2$, there are results showing how to reduce the bandwidth to just a constant number of field elements per party, per gate [13,14,18]. In contrast, when $t \geq n/2$, our best

© International Association for Cryptologic Research 2018
T. Peyrin and S. Galbraith (Eds.): ASIACRYPT 2018, LNCS 11274, pp. 59–85, 2018.
https://doi.org/10.1007/978-3-030-03332-3_3

protocols require expensive preprocessing, with communication cost that grows quadratically in n.

In this work, we develop a new protocol in the honest majority setting, tailored to the case where $n = 4$. Our protocol is secure against a single malicious corruption, consistent with the requirement that $t < n/2$. Focusing on this domain, we are able to construct extremely efficient protocols.

Looking at concrete costs, the most efficient secure two-party computation protocol (in terms of communication) requires roughly 290 bytes of communication per party per gate [31,33]. If we are willing to relax the setting by assuming that a malicious adversary can only corrupt one out of three parties, then we can further reduce the cost to 7 bits per party per gate [1]. Our protocol further reduces the cost significantly: our four-party protocol requires only 1.5-bits of communication per party. Furthermore, the results just cited for the two-party and three-party settings are for 40-bit statistical security, and their costs per gate increase for higher statistical security. Our protocol has no dependence on a statistical security parameter, and has only an additive $O(\kappa)$ term (where κ is a computational security parameter).

We also note that we can achieve 1-bit communication per party in the six-party setting. For these previous works as well as the protocol in this paper, all computation can be hardware accelerated and thus communication complexity is the most suitable indicator of real performance.

Contributions. We now summarize our contributions. Our main result is summarized in the theorem below. The construction and proof of security appear in Sects. 3 and 4. An additional improvement appears in Sect. 5.

Theorem 1. *In the four party setting, it is possible to construct a protocol for securely computing a circuit of size $|C|$ over a finite field F whose total communication complexity is $6|C| \log |F| + O(\kappa)$. In particular, for a Boolean circuit, this amounts to 1.5 bits per player, per gate.*

Binary Rings. An interesting result of our work is that we can securely evaluate an arithmetic function over binary rings, such as $(\mathbb{Z}_{2^{32}}, +, *)$, where $(+, *)$ denotes modular addition and multiplication. Note that most MPC protocols do not work over rings that are not fields. In particular, MAC-based protocols based on SPDZ [17] do not work over $\mathbb{Z}_{2^{32}}$, as the multiplicative inverse is necessary for constructing linear MAC schemes. The security of our protocol only relies on additive maskings, so we do not need a multiplicative inverse. The correctness of our protocol when computing over a binary ring follows from the distributivity property of rings. The distributivity property allows us to use beaver triples. A similar observation, in the semi-honest setting, was recently made by Mohassel and Zhang [30].

Robustness. We construct a robust variant of our protocol, guaranteeing that the honest parties always receive correct output. The cost of adding robustness is free if all the players act honestly, and only requires an additional $O(\kappa \log |C| \log |\mathbb{F}|)$ overhead when a player misbehaves (Sect. 6).

1.1 Technical Overview

From a high-level view, the construction of our protocol starts with a semi-honest protocol, π_1, for two-party computation in the preprocessing model. We would like two participants in the protocol to execute π_1. There are two main tasks towards our final goal:

1. Generating the preprocessing data for π_1 with malicious security.
2. Strengthening the security of π_1 in the online phase from semi-honest to malicious security.

Our solutions to these challenges rely heavily on the fact that we work in the four-party setting with only one corruption. In order to generate maliciously secure preprocessing, we ask the other two parties to locally emulate the preprocessing ideal functionality, both using the same randomness. To ensure that the computation of the preprocessing is done correctly, each of the parties executing π_1 verifies that he was sent two identical copies of the preprocessing.

The second challenge is trickier. Existing work that compiles semi-honest security to malicious security are not suitable for our use. The techniques can be broadly described as follows: (1) Using generic zero-knowledge proof, which is impractical for most cases; (2) Using certain forms of MACs on each party's share to ensure honest behavior. This approach has been made practical, but it requires preprocessing data of size (at least) $\Omega(\rho)$ bits per gate, to achieve $2^{-\rho}$ statistical security. (3) In the honest majority setting, one can use Shamir secret sharing, but our π_1 is a two-party protocol, where one can be malicious. Instead, our approach is based on a technique called "dual-execution" [24,28], which is known to have one-bit leakage in general. However, we show that in the four-party setting, by performing a special cross-checking protocol at the end, we are able to eliminate the leakage without any penalty to the performance. Details follow below.

Dual execution without leakage. In order to accommodate dual execution, we require that π_1 has certain special properties. Intuitively, the outcome of π_1 should leave both parties with "masked wire values" for all wires in the circuit, together with a secret sharing of the masks. This property can be satisfied by many protocols, e.g. the modified Beaver triple protocol [2] that we use in this paper, as well as the semi-honest version of TinyTable [15].

Now we are in the setting, where, say, P_1 and P_2 have generated the preprocessing, and each hold the full set of wire masks, namely λ^1. P_3 and P_4 have executed π_1, and recovered masked values, namely m^1. Our dual execution is done by letting P_1 and P_3 switch roles with P_2 and P_4. As a result, P_1 and P_2 will obtain m^2, while P_3 and P_4 will obtain λ^2 in the second execution. Conceptually, our cross-checking compares, for all wire values in the circuit, whether

$$\lambda^1 + \mathsf{m}^2 = \lambda^2 + \mathsf{m}^1.$$

Note that the above holds if both executions are honest, since both sides of the equation are equal to the true wire values, masked by both masks (λ^1 and λ^2). For details of the protocol, see Sect. 3.

Readers that are familiar with the dual execution paradigm in the two-party setting, from garbled circuits, might wonder how we remove the bit of leakage. There are two key insights here. First, when using garbled circuits, it seems difficult to check the consistency of internal wires, whereas the masked wires of the form just described allows us to easily check the consistency of *all* wires in the two evaluations. This eliminates the possibility of input inconsistency, and also prevents the adversary from flipping a wire value to see if it has any impact on the output. Second, in a garbled circuit implementation, the adversary can fix the output of a particular gate arbitrarily, creating a "selective failure attack": the change goes undetected if the output he chooses is consistent with the true output on that wire, and would otherwise cause an abort. With these masked wire evaluations, the adversary cannot fix a wire value arbitrarily; he is limited to adding some value to the wire, changing it in all cases, and always causing an abort. In particular, then, whether he is caught cheating no longer depends on any private value. By exploiting the structure of masks and masked values, checking for inconsistencies requires only $O(\kappa)$ bits of communication.

Reducing communication. The protocol described until this point is already extremely efficient, but we further reduce the communication in several interesting ways. In the preprocessing, we do this in a fairly straightforward way, using PRG seeds and hash functions to compress the material. In the cross checking, recall that we need the parties to verify, twice, whether $\lambda^1 + m^2 = \lambda^2 + m^1$, where these values have size $|C|$. (They verify twice because each member of one evaluation compares with one member of the other evaluation.) A naive way here would be to twice compare the hash of these values, but this is in fact insecure. If an adversary changes a value on one of the wires in his evaluation, as we have already noted, he will always be caught, because his partner will compare the hash of his modified masked wire values with an honest party from the other evaluation. However, the adversary can still learn sensitive information from the result of his *own* comparison with a member of the other evaluation. Instead, we can use any honest-majority, four-party protocol for comparing these two hash values. The circuit for this comparison has only $O(\kappa)$ gates, so this introduces very little overhead. Nevertheless, in Sect. 5 we show how to bootstrap this comparison, removing the reliance on other protocols.

Related work. Maliciously secure protocols, tailored for the three-party setting, have been studied in many works. Choi et al. [8] studied the dishonest majority setting based on garbled circuits. Araki et al. [1], Mohassel et al. [29], Furukawa et al. [19] studied the honest majority setting. However, we are not aware of any MPC protocol tailored for the four-party setting.

Other protocols that work in the four-party setting include honest majority protocols [4,10–12,16,26] and dishonest majority protocols [6,17,25,27,31,34]. These protocols can be used for MPC with more parties, but when applied in the four-party setting, their concrete performances are worse than our protocol. In particular, Damgård et al. [16] designed an efficient protocol in the honest majority setting. Their techniques appear to be different from ours and can be extended to more parties; however, our protocol is much more efficient in terms of the total cost than theirs in the four-party setting.

2   Preliminaries

In this paper, we mainly consider arithmetic circuits C with addition gates and multiplication gates. Each gate in the circuit is represented as (a, b, c, T), where $T \in \{+, \times\}$ is the operation; a and b are the input wire indices; and c is the output wire index.

We denote the set of wires as $\mathcal{W}$, the set of input wires as $\mathcal{W}_{\texttt{input}}$, the set of output wires of all addition gates as $\mathcal{W}_{\texttt{plus}}$, the set of output wires of all multiplication gates as $\mathcal{W}_{\texttt{mult}}$.

Masked evaluation. One important concept that we use in the paper is masked evaluation. Intuitively, every wire w in the circuit, including each input and output wire, is associated with a random mask, namely λ_w. The masked evaluation procedure works in a way such that for each gate two parties, holding masked input and some helper information, are able to obtain the masked output. All parties hold only secret shares of λ_w, namely $\langle \lambda_w \rangle$, therefore obtaining masked wire values does not reveal any information. We will use m_w to denote the masked wire value on wire w. That is, $\mathsf{m}_w = \lambda_w + x$, assuming that the underlying wire value on wire w is x.

Secure evaluation-masking two-party protocol. A secure two-party protocol for computing circuit C is an evaluation-masking scheme if (1) the protocol uses preprocessing, (2) the preprocessing assigns to the circuit C a masking λ (3) the players evaluate the gates of the circuit layer by layer; if a gate g is in layer L, then the evaluation of L allows both players to learn the masked values for the given layer, (4) if an adversary starts deviating from the protocol, the adversary should not learn any information about the computation unless the output is revealed. (5) any misbehavior from the adversary for a given wire is equivalent to him adding a fixed value to the wire that can be computed from his misbehavior. This type of attack is described as an additive attack in the work of [20]. They showed that certain MPC protocols have this property.

In this paper, we build upon a variant of Beaver's scheme [2] which is an evaluation-masking scheme. The main modification of Beaver is that the players will hold for each wire, secret shares of masks and both players will learn the sum of the mask and the actual underlying value. We denote the sum of a mask and a value as either a masking or a masked value.

Committing encryption. A public-key encryption scheme is committing if the ciphertexts serve as commitments.

- **Completeness.** A person who encrypts a message m resulting in a ciphertext c needs to be able to prove that c is indeed an encryption of m.
- **Soundness.** If the player who generated c can prove that c is an encryption of m then $\mathsf{dec}(sk, c) = m$.

– **Verifiability.** Given the public-key, it is easy to determine if a ciphertext is valid.

ElGammal encryption is committing due to the fact that (1) every element of the ciphertext space is a valid ciphertext, (2) it is easy to check that an element is in the ciphertext space, and (3) a player can unambiguously prove that a ciphertext maps to a particular plaintext by simply providing the randomness that was used to encrypt a message m.

Theorem 2. *(Informal) From any secure evaluation-masking two-party protocol π_1, secure against a semi-honest adversary, we can construct a protocol π_2 for four parties that is secure against a malicious adversary corrupting at most one player.*

Security definitions. We us the standard security definition for stand-alone security, as defined, for example, in Goldreich's textbook [21]. In Sect. 4, we claim *security with abort*, in which the ideal-world adversary receives output first, and then dictates whether the functionality should provide output to the honest parties. In our protocol of Sect. 6, we achieve security with *robustness*, or guaranteed output delivery, as defined by Goldwasser and Lindell [23]. Under this definition, the honest parties always receive output, regardless of how the adversary behaves.[1]

As is standard, we prove security in a modular way. We start by proving security of our preprocessing protocol, and we assume we have a secure protocol for comparing two strings. We then prove security of our main protocol in a *hybrid model* in which the participants in the real-world protocol are assumed to have access to the ideal functionalities achieved by these protocols. The seminal work of Canetti proves that this suffices for achieving standard, stand-alone security; the functionalities used in the hybrid world can be instantiated using any protocols that securely realize them [7].

3   Our Main Construction

A quick summary of our idea is that we run two executions of a two-party, semi-honest protocol in the preprocessing model, and verify consistency between these two executions through a strategy that we call cross-checking. We start by partitioning the players into two evaluation groups with two players in each group. Each group prepares preprocessing for the other. They leverage the fact that there is at most one corruption to verify that the preprocessing was done correctly. Then, each group evaluates the circuit using that preprocessing. As the outcome of the evaluation, each party holds masked wire values for all wires in the circuit. Finally, the two groups check the consistency of the two evaluations using

---

[1] Of course, if the adversary refuses to participate, we cannot hope to include his input in the computation. In this case, some default value can be used, or his input can be excluded entirely if the computation is well defined over 3 inputs.

their masked wire values and masks. Since one of the evaluations is guaranteed to be correct, any cheating will be caught in this step. Below we provide the details of each of these steps as well as why it is secure. A formal description of the protocol appears in Fig. 1, and in the other figures referenced from there.

The main protocol takes input from all 4 parties, and outputs the evaluation of C on those inputs. It makes use of the 3 components: $\mathcal{F}_{\text{pre}}$, π_{eval}, and π_{cross}.

Pre-processing
1. The four parties make two calls to $\mathcal{F}_{\text{pre}}$ (Fig. 2). In the first call, P_1 and P_2 receive the output $\langle \lambda^2 \rangle, \langle \gamma^2 \rangle$ for E_1 and E_2 respectively, while P_3 and P_4 receive λ^2, the output of D_1, D_2. In the second call, they reverse their roles, with P_1 and P_2 receiving λ^1, the output of D_1 and D_2, and P_3 and P_4 receive $\langle \lambda^1 \rangle, \langle \gamma^1 \rangle$, the output of E_1 and E_2.

Evaluation
1. The four parties run two instances of π_{eval} (Fig. 4). In the first instance, the players P_1 and P_2 take the role of evaluators E_1 and E_2 using $\langle \lambda^2 \rangle, \langle \gamma^2 \rangle$. Let m^1 denote the resulting masked wire values. In the second instance P_3 and P_4 take the role of evaluators E_1 and E_2 using $\langle \lambda^1 \rangle, \langle \gamma^1 \rangle$. Let m^2 denote the resulting masked evaluation.

Cross Checking
1. The four parties run π_{cross} (Fig. 5) where P_1, P_2 each input m^1, λ^2 while P_3, P_4 both input m^2, λ^1.
2. If π_{cross} outputs 0, then abort.
3. We define λ^1_{out} to be output masks for the first evaluation.
4. We define m^1_{out} to be the masked output wires for the first evaluation.
5. Player P_1, P_2 broadcast m^1_{out}, if their broadcasts disagree then all players abort.
6. Player P_3, P_4 broadcast λ^1_{out}, if their broadcasts disagree then all players abort.
7. Players compute the output by using m^1_{out} and λ^1_{out}.

Fig. 1. Main protocol in the hybrid model

Preprocessing. Recall that we partition four parties into two equal-sized groups. We first let one group create preprocessing material, and distribute the preprocessing to the other group. This procedure is then repeated with the roles reversed; we describe it only for one group. We will often refer to the group that is performing the preprocessing step as D_1 and D_2, and to the group that uses the preprocessing in the evaluation phase as E_1 and E_2, recognizing that one party plays the role of (say) D_1 in one execution while playing E_1 in the other execution. An ideal functionality for the preprocessing appears in Fig. 2.

To generate the preprocessing material, D_2 chooses a random string and sends it to D_1. They then each use this randomness to locally generate preprocessing, choosing mask values for every wire in the circuit as follows. They select a random field element for every wire $w \in \mathcal{W}_{\text{input}} \cup \mathcal{W}_{\text{mult}}$ (that is, for every input wire, and every wire that is the output of a multiplication gate). We refer

---

This 4-party, randomized functionality is called by two distributors and two evaluators. No parties contribute any input. The functionality generates a vector of random masks as output for the distributors, and a secret-sharing of these masks for the evaluators.

Input: None.
Computation
  1. Sample seed_1 and seed_2 uniformly at random. If the adversary corrupts D_2, allow him to specify the seeds.
  2. For each wire $w \in \mathcal{W}_{\mathsf{input}} \cup \mathcal{W}_{\mathsf{mult}}$:
      (a) $\Lambda_{1,w} \leftarrow \mathsf{G}(\mathsf{seed}_1)$,
      (b) $\Lambda_{2,w} \leftarrow \mathsf{G}(\mathsf{seed}_2)$
      (c) $\lambda_w \leftarrow \Lambda_{1,w} + \Lambda_{2,w}$.
  3. For each addition gate $(a, b, c, +)$: compute $\lambda_c \leftarrow \lambda_a + \lambda_b$.
  4. For each multiplication gate $(a, b, c, \times)$
      (a) $\gamma_c \leftarrow \lambda_a \cdot \lambda_b$
      (b) $\Gamma_{1,c} \leftarrow \mathsf{G}(\mathsf{seed}_1)$
      (c) $\Gamma_{2,c} = \gamma_c + \Gamma_{1,c}$
Output
  1. Output $\langle \gamma \rangle, \langle \lambda \rangle$ to E_1, E_2 (by sending seed_1 to E_1 and $(\mathsf{seed}_2, \{\Gamma_{2,w}\}_{w \in \mathcal{W}_{\mathsf{mult}}})$ to E_2)
  2. Output both seed_1 and seed_2 to both D_1, D_2
Malicious party: A malicious D_2 can choose the randomness.

Fig. 2. $\mathcal{F}_{\mathsf{pre}}$: Ideal functionality for preprocessing

to these mask values as λ^1, and the ones generated by the other 2 parties, in the second preprocessing execution, are denoted by λ^2. For the output wire of addition gate $(a, b, c, +)$, suppose the input wires a and b have already been assigned mask values λ_a and λ_b. Then the output wire of the gate is assigned the mask value $\lambda_a + \lambda_b$. Note that all circuit wires now have well defined masks. For each multiplication gate $(a, b, c, \times)$, the two parties additionally compute $\gamma_c = \lambda_a \cdot \lambda_b$. We let $\gamma^1 = \{\gamma_c\}_{c \in \mathcal{W}_{\mathsf{mult}}}$. D_1 and D_2 use their shared random string to construct secret sharings $\lambda^1 = \Lambda_1 + \Lambda_2$ and $\gamma^1 = \Gamma_1 + \Gamma_2$. That is, they create two identical copies of the secret sharing. They both send Λ_1 and Γ_1 to E_1, and they both send Λ_2 and Γ_2 to E_2. E_1 and E_2 each verify the equality of the two values he received before proceeding to the evaluation phase. Note that after agreeing on the random string at the beginning of the procedure described above, D_1 and D_2 require no further communication with each other. Because one of the parties must be honest, the equality checks performed by E_1 and E_2 suffice to catch any malicious behavior. Note that this idea shares some similarity with the one by Mohassel et al. [29] in the three-party setting based on garbled circuit.

We do not present the preprocessing protocol in quite the way that was just described. Instead, an optimized variant with reduced communication complexity is presented in Fig. 3. First, instead of choosing and sending random strings of length $O(|C|)$, the two parties choose two short seeds for a PRG: we

---

Two distributors D_1, D_2 want to generate preprocessing for players E_1, E_2.

Creation

1. D_2 chooses two random seeds, $\mathbf{seed}_1$ and $\mathbf{seed}_2$, and sends them to D_1.
2. For each wire $w \in \mathcal{W}_{\text{input}} \cup \mathcal{W}_{\text{mult}}$:
   (a) $\Lambda_{1,w} \leftarrow G(\mathbf{seed}_1)$,
   (b) $\Lambda_{2,w} \leftarrow G(\mathbf{seed}_2)$
   (c) $\lambda_w \leftarrow \Lambda_{1,w} + \Lambda_{2,w}$.
3. For each addition gate $(a, b, c, +)$: compute $\lambda_c \leftarrow \lambda_a + \lambda_b$.
4. For each multiplication gate $(a, b, c, \times)$
   (a) $\gamma_c \leftarrow \lambda_a \cdot \lambda_b$
   (b) $\Gamma_{1,c} \leftarrow G(\mathbf{seed}_1)$
   (c) $\Gamma_{2,c} = \gamma_c + \Gamma_{1,c}$

Distribution

1. D_1 sends $\mathbf{seed}_1$ to E_1 and $(\mathbf{seed}_2, \Gamma_2)$ to E_2.
2. D_2 sends $\mathbf{seed}_1$ to E_1 and $H(\mathbf{seed}_2 \| \Gamma_2)$ to E_2.
3. D_1 and D_2 output λ

E_1 Reconstruction

1. Receive $\mathbf{seed}_1$ from D_1 and D_2 and check they are the same. If not, abort.
2. $\{\Lambda_{1,w}\}_{w \in \mathcal{W}_{\text{input}} \cup \mathcal{W}_{\text{mult}}}, \{\Gamma_{1,w}\}_{w \in \mathcal{W}_{\text{mult}}} \leftarrow G(\mathbf{seed}_1)$
3. Output $(\{\Lambda_{1,w}\}_{w \in \mathcal{W}_{\text{input}} \cup \mathcal{W}_{\text{mult}}}, \{\Gamma_{1,w}\}_{w \in \mathcal{W}_{\text{mult}}})$.

E_2 Reconstruction

1. Receive $(\mathbf{seed}_2, \Gamma_2)$ from D_1 and $H(\mathbf{seed}_2 \| \Gamma_2)$ from D_2 and check they are consistent. If not, abort.
2. $\{\Lambda_{2,w}\}_{w \in \mathcal{W}_{\text{input}} \cup \mathcal{W}_{\text{mult}}} \leftarrow G(\mathbf{seed}_2)$
3. Output $(\{\Lambda_{2,w}\}_{w \in \mathcal{W}_{\text{input}} \cup \mathcal{W}_{\text{mult}}}, \{\Gamma_{2,w}\}_{w \in \mathcal{W}_{\text{mult}}})$.

Notation

1. For each wire $w \in \mathcal{W}_{\text{input}} \cup \mathcal{W}_{\text{mult}}$: $\langle \lambda_w \rangle \leftarrow (\Lambda_{1,w}, \Lambda_{2,w})$
2. For each multiplication gate $(a, b, c, \times) : \langle \gamma_c \rangle \leftarrow (\Gamma_{1,c}, \Gamma_{2,c})$

Fig. 3. Distributed preprocessing of masked beaver triples

let $\Lambda_1 = G(\mathbf{seed}_1)$, and $\Lambda_2 = G(\mathbf{seed}_2)$. As before, $\lambda^1 = \Lambda_1 + \Lambda_2$. Since the value of γ^1 depends on λ^1, we cannot do the same thing there, but we can generate the shares Γ_1 from the same $\mathbf{seed}_1$, and then fix Γ_2 appropriately, using $O(|\mathcal{W}_{\text{mult}}|)$ bits. This reduces the communication cost for each of the parties from $(2|\mathbb{F}|+1) \cdot |\mathcal{W}_{\text{mult}}|$ to $2\kappa + |\mathbb{F}| \cdot |\mathcal{W}_{\text{mult}}|$. Recall that D_1 and D_2 send identical copies of these values to an evaluator; we further reduce the communication by having one party send only a single hash of the preprocessing, which suffices for allowing each evaluator to verify the consistency of what he has received. Finally, note that this last optimization causes the communication costs to become unbalanced. Although we do not present it, note that we can re-balance the cost by having one party send the first half of Γ_2 together with a hash of the second half, while the other party sends the second half of Γ_2 together with a hash of the first half.

Evaluation. After receiving and verifying the consistency of the preprocessing, E_1 and E_2 proceed to perform a mask-evaluation of the circuit, layer by layer.

There are two evaluators E_1, E_2 who want to evaluate a circuit C using preprocessing provided by distributors D_1, D_2. Each of the four players is assigned a set of input wires corresponding to his input to C.

Input
1. For each input wire w, one party holds input x_w.
2. For each input wire w, D_1 and D_2 hold λ_w.
3. For each $w \in \mathcal{W}$, E_1 and E_2 hold $\langle \lambda_w \rangle$.
4. For each multiplication gate $(a, b, c, \times)$, E_1 and E_2 hold $\langle \gamma_c \rangle \leftarrow \langle \lambda_a \cdot \lambda_b \rangle$.

Sharing Input Values
For each input wire w belonging to E_1 with value x_w:
1. D_1, D_2 both send λ_w to E_1. E_1 aborts if they are different.
2. E_1 sends $\lambda_w + x_w$ to E_2

For each input wire w belonging to D_1 with value x_w:
1. D_1 sends $\mathsf{m}_w \leftarrow x_w + \lambda_w$ to E_1 and E_2.
2. E_1 and E_2 verify that they each received the same value and abort if it is not the case.

The input of E_2 is processed similarly to the input of E_1.
The input of D_2 is processed similarly to the input of D_1.

Evaluation
For each gate (a, b, c, T) following topological order:
1. if $T = +$
   (a) $\mathsf{m}_c \leftarrow \mathsf{m}_a + \mathsf{m}_b$.
2. if $T = \times$
   (a) $\langle \mathsf{m}_c \rangle \leftarrow \mathsf{m}_a \cdot \mathsf{m}_b - \mathsf{m}_a \cdot \langle \lambda_b \rangle - \mathsf{m}_b \cdot \langle \lambda_a \rangle + \langle \lambda_c \rangle + \langle \lambda_a \cdot \lambda_b \rangle$
   (b) $\mathsf{m}_c \leftarrow \mathsf{open}(\langle \mathsf{m}_c \rangle)$

Fig. 4. π_{eval} : Two-party masked evaluation

To begin, they first need masked input values for every input wire; these are of the form $\mathsf{m}_w \leftarrow \lambda_w + x_w$. For an input wire w held by $E \in \{E_1, E_2\}$, D_1 and D_2 send λ_w to E. E verifies that they each sent the same value: if not, he aborts. Otherwise, he computes $\lambda_w + x_w$ and sends it to the other evaluator. For input wire w belonging to $D \in \{D_1, D_2\}$, D sends $\lambda_w + x_w$ to E_1 and E_2. The evaluators compare values and abort if they don't agree.

For every gate $(a, b, c, +)$, E_1 and E_2 both locally compute $\mathsf{m}_c = \mathsf{m}_a + \mathsf{m}_b$. For every gate $(a, b, c, \times)$, they locally compute $\langle \mathsf{m}_c \rangle \leftarrow \mathsf{m}_a \cdot \mathsf{m}_b - \mathsf{m}_a \cdot \langle \lambda_b \rangle - \mathsf{m}_b \cdot \langle \lambda_a \rangle + \langle \lambda_c \rangle + \langle \lambda_a \cdot \lambda_b \rangle$. (Recall, they can compute the last term using $\langle \gamma_c \rangle$.) They then compute $\mathsf{m}_c \leftarrow \mathsf{open}(\langle \mathsf{m}_c \rangle)$ by exchanging their shares of m_c. At the conclusion of evaluation phase, one set of evaluators holds m^1, which is the set of masked values of all wires in the circuit, and the other group of parties hold m^2 after their evaluation phase.

Cross-checking. Note that during the evaluation phase, a malicious evaluator can modify the value on any $w \in \mathcal{W}_{\mathtt{mult}}$ simply by changing his share of m_w before reconstructing the value. Therefore, before either group recovers output from their computation, they first compare their masking with the masking of

---

Input
 1. P_1 has input $(\mathsf{m}_1^1, \lambda_1^2)$.
 2. P_2 has input $(\mathsf{m}_2^1, \lambda_2^2)$.
 3. P_3 has input $(\mathsf{m}_3^2, \lambda_3^1)$.
 4. P_4 has input $(\mathsf{m}_4^2, \lambda_4^1)$.
Computation
 1. P_1 computes $h_1 = H(\mathsf{m}_1^1 + \lambda_1^2)$,
    P_2 computes $h_2 = H(\mathsf{m}_2^1 + \lambda_2^2)$,
    P_3 computes $h_3 = H(\mathsf{m}_3^2 + \lambda_3^1)$,
    P_4 computes $h_4 = H(\mathsf{m}_4^2 + \lambda_4^1)$.
 2. All players sends h_i to $\mathcal{F}_{\mathsf{eq}}$, which outputs 1 if and only if $h_1 = h_3$ and $h_2 = h_4$.

Fig. 5. π_{cross} : Cross checking

the other evaluation. Of course, they cannot reveal the values on any wires while doing this check. Instead, for wire w that carries value x, each set of evaluators uses the masking from their evaluation, together with the masks that they generated for the other group during preprocessing, to compute

$$x + \lambda_w^1 + \lambda_w^2 = \mathsf{m}_w^1 + \lambda_w^2 = \mathsf{m}_w^2 + \lambda_w^1.$$

They then compare these "doubly masked" values for consistency.

As in the case of preprocessing, we use a hash function where possible, in order to reduce the communication cost. Each party begins by computing a hash of the doubly masked wire values described above; for P_i, we denote this hash by h_i. The four parties then call an ideal functionality, $\mathcal{F}_{\mathsf{eq}}$, which takes input h_i, and outputs 1 if and only if $h_1 = h_3$, and $h_2 = h_4$.

Taking P_1 as example, he obtains m_1^1 during evaluation and λ_1^2 when acting as a D. He will then compute $h_1 = H(\mathsf{m}_1^1 + \lambda_1^2)$. For the other three parties, it is defined similarly as follows: superscripts denote the index of the masked evaluation and subscripts denote the identity of the party.

$$h_2 = H(\mathsf{m}_2^1 + \lambda_2^2), \qquad h_3 = H(\mathsf{m}_3^2 + \lambda_3^1), \qquad h_4 = H(\mathsf{m}_4^2 + \lambda_4^1)$$

To see why this suffices for providing security, suppose P_1 changes some masking during evaluation, effectively changing a wire value for him and P_2. In this case, the doubly masked evaluations of P_2 and P_4 are inconsistent, and $\mathcal{F}_{\mathsf{eq}}$ will return 0; intuitively, comparing these hash values is equivalent to checking the masked values wire by wire.

3.1 Concrete Performance

Here we briefly discuss the concrete performance of our protocol against the most related state-of-the-art protocol by Araki et al. [1]. As mentioned previously, our protocol requires 1.5 bits of communication per gate per party, a 4.5× improvement over their protocol. Let's see if the same applies to the computation cost.

Note that in the protocol by Araki et al., the heaviest part of the computation is random shuffling, due to the use of the random bucketing technique in their paper. The rest are AES and hash computation, which can be hardware accelerated or very fast. Compared to their protocol, our protocol is much simpler and more efficient in terms of computation cost. The bulk of our computation is in the evaluation phase, where we do not need any random shuffling. For each 128 AND gates, each party only needs 6 calls to fix-key AES to implement the PRG, and roughly one call to a hash function. Araki et al. have a higher computational cost than we do, because of their random shuffle; since they are able to fill a 10 Gbps LAN, our protocol will certainly have no problem filling the same pipe. We believe the computation cost will not be the bottleneck for any reasonable hardware configuration.

Our protocol for the cross checking appears in Fig. 5. It is in a hybrid world where the parties have access to a functionality, $\mathcal{F}_{eq}$. We note that this functionality can be realized using any secure four party computation. The circuit needed to realize this functionality is small: it only performs two equality computations on strings of length $O(\kappa)$. Nevertheless, in Sect. 5, we also demonstrate how we can bootstrap this functionality, communicating just a small constant number of bits, and using almost no computation.

3.2 Multiplayer Extensions

Achieving one bit of communication using six parties. We note that if we use six players, we can maintain of the overhead of 6 bits communicated in total, thereby requiring each player to communicate just one bit per wire (on average). The idea of the six-party computation protocol is fairly straightforward given the four-party protocol. Two people agree on randomness for the preprocessing, and then each communicates the preprocessing material to two of the remaining four players. Those four parties now carry out two identical evaluations, in parallel, and cross check them with one another at the end. The communication overhead is still six bits per gate, but it is now divided among all six players.

Efficient Multiparty Protocols via Log-Depth Threshold Formulae. We note that our result can be used to construct MPC protocols tolerating up to a third of players being corrupted via the result of [9]. At a high level, their protocol employs player emulation and works by recursively composing a protocol for a small number of parties with itself via a log-depth threshold formulae.

4   Security Proof

4.1   Proof of Security for Preprocessing

Lemma 1. *The protocol in Fig. 3 for distributed preprocessing securely realizes the functionality of Fig. 2, with abort.*

Proof. Due to symmetry, we only prove the lemma for the following two cases: (1) D_1 is corrupt and (2) E_1 is corrupt.

Corrupted D_1. We will first describe our simulator S.

1. S queries $\mathcal{F}_{\text{pre}}$ and obtains $\text{seed}_1, \text{seed}_2$. If the $\mathcal{A}$ chooses to input randomness, use $\mathcal{A}$'s choice.
2. S acts as honest D_2, E_1 and E_2 for the rest of the protocol using the seeds obtained above. If an honest E_1 or E_2 would abort, S sends abort to $\mathcal{F}_{\text{pre}}$.

Note that none of the parties in the protocol have input. Therefore the indistinguishability of the ideal-world protocol and the real-world protocol is immediate, given the observation that the protocol aborts in the real world protocol if and only if it aborts in the ideal world protocol.

Corrupted E_1. Note that E_1 performs only local computation after receiving messages from other parties. The simulator queries $\mathcal{F}_{\text{pre}}$ and receives the seeds. He then simulates honest D_1 and D_2, sending seed_1 on their behalf. If E_1 aborts, the simulator will send abort to $\mathcal{F}_{\text{pre}}$ and aborts. Indistinguishability from the real-world protocol is immediate.

4.2 Proof of Security of the Main Protocol

Theorem 3. *Assuming H is drawn from a family of collision resistant hash functions, our main protocol, in Fig. 1, securely realizes $\mathcal{F}_{\text{4pc}}$ in the $(\mathcal{F}_{\text{pre}}, \mathcal{F}_{\text{eq}})$-hybrid model.*

Proof. In the following, we will prove the security of our main protocol assuming that P_1 is corrupted by $\mathcal{A}$. The simulator is as follows:

1. S honestly simulates the execution of $\mathcal{F}_{\text{pre}}$. He sends P_1 his resulting output, and records the simulated mask values: λ^1, which will mask the wire values in the evaluation of P_3 and P_4, and λ^2, which will mask the wire values in the evaluation of P_1 and P_2.
2. S simulates the masking of input values 0 from P_2, P_3 and P_4 for use in P_1's evaluation with P_2, using mask values from λ^2. He receives three maskings of P_1's input: one for each of P_3 and P_4 for use in their evaluation, using mask values from λ^1, and one using values from λ^2, sent to P_2 for his own evaluation with P_1. If the values sent to P_3 and P_4 are not equal, S sends abort to $\mathcal{F}_{\text{4pc}}$ and terminates the simulation. Otherwise, S extracts the input sent to P_2, and the one sent to P_3 and P_4, using his knowledge of the masks; he notes if P_1 misbehaves by using inconsistent values in the two evaluations.
3. S acts honestly as P_2, P_3 and P_4 in both executions of the masked evaluations. S obtains m^1 by interacting honestly with P_1 on behalf of P_2 for the remainder of their evaluation. He obtains m^2 by simulating (internally) the remainder of the evaluation of P_3 and P_4.

4. $\mathcal{S}$ collects P_1's input to $\mathcal{F}_{eq}$, and calculates the inputs of P_2, P_3, and P_4 to $\mathcal{F}_{eq}$ according to the honest execution using input values of 0. $\mathcal{S}$ executes the code of $\mathcal{F}_{eq}$ locally on these 4 values, and outputs the resulting value.

Comment: In Sect. 5, we describe a more efficient, interactive protocol, π_{vcc}, which replaces the use of $\mathcal{F}_{eq}$. To simulate our protocol when using π_{vcc}, we would proceed as follows, in place of the previous step. If $\mathcal{S}$ noted that P_1 misbehaved during evaluation, or when sending his masked input, then $\mathcal{S}$ runs π_{vcc}, simulating the messages of P_2 and P_4 when using different (random) inputs from one another. Otherwise, he runs π_{vcc} as though P_2, P_3 and P_4 all use input $m^1 \oplus \lambda^2$. If π_{vcc} outputs 0, $\mathcal{S}$ sends abort to $\mathcal{F}_{4pc}$.

5. $\mathcal{S}$ uses the input extracted in Step 2 and sends it to $\mathcal{F}_{4pc}$. He receives y and computes $\lambda^* = m_{out}^1 + y$. $\mathcal{S}$ acts as P_3 and P_4 sending λ^* to $\mathcal{A}$.

Now we will show that the joint distribution of the output from $\mathcal{A}$ and honest parties in the ideal world are indistinguishable from these in the real world protocol.

1. Hybrid$_1$: Same as the hybrid protocol, with $\mathcal{S}$ playing the role of honest players, using their true input. That is, in this hybrid, we give the input of the honest players to the simulator. (The resulting distribution is equivalent to that of the real world execution.)

2. Hybrid$_2$: Same as Hybrid$_1$, with messages simulated based on the true inputs of the honest parties. However, now $\mathcal{S}$ uses m^1 and λ^1 to compute $x_1 = m_{in}^1 + \lambda_{in}^1$. $\mathcal{S}$ sends x_1 to $\mathcal{F}_{4pc}$, which returns y. In step 5, $\mathcal{S}$ acts as P_3 and P_4 and broadcasts $\lambda^* = m_{out}^1 + y$.

3. Hybrid$_3$: Same as the Hybrid$_2$ except that $\mathcal{S}$ uses input values of 0 for all honest parties, instead of their true input.

It is fairly easy to see that Hybrid$_1$ is indistinguishable from Hybrd$_2$, as long as the function H is drawn from a family of collision resistant hash functions. Up until the simulation of $\mathcal{F}_{eq}$, the view of the adversary is identically generated in the two hybrids. If H is collision resistant, then the output of $\mathcal{F}_{eq}$ is 1, if and only if the adversary behaves honestly in his execution. When he acts honestly, the output generated in Hybrid$_2$ by the ideal functionality is the same as the output computed by $\mathcal{S}$ in Hybrid$_1$. The distribution characterizing the adversarial view in Hybrid$_3$ is identical to that of Hybrid$_2$, by the one-time-pad security of the random masking. It is easy to verify that the joint distribution described by the adversarial view and the honest output is identical in these two hybrids as well.

5   Cross Check from Veto

In this section, we will demonstrate how to construct an efficient cross checking protocol based on a functionality for 4-party, logical OR, $\mathcal{F}_{or}$. We sometimes call this a *veto functionality*, as the parties use the OR to "veto" the execution, by submitting a value of 1 (veto). The cross checking protocol from Sect. 3 required a 4-party computation of $\mathcal{F}_{eq}$, which compared 2 pairs of strings, each κ bits long. The improved cross checking protocol based on veto requires each party to compare two hashes locally, and then input a single bit to the veto functionality. While the cost of either of these protocols is small compared to the evaluation phase, the simplicity of the protocol here makes it hard to pass up. We also describe how to bootstrap $\mathcal{F}_{or}$, using a variant of the protocol from Sect. 3, and requiring just 6 bytes of communication per party. Perhaps one of the nicest features of this bootstrapping, from a practical standpoint, is that it allows us to avoid any dependence on other MPC implementations (Fig. 6).

Naive implementation of cross checking. A naive way of implementing cross checking is to have the two verifiers exchange their doubly masked evaluations, and compare them for inconsistencies. Unfortunately, this approach fails because the adversary can modify the values carried on any of the wires in his own evaluation, and determine precisely how the change impacted the evaluation of the circuit by subtracting his doubly masked evaluation from the other. The differences between these two doubly masked evaluations reveals the differences in the values carried on each wire in the two evaluations of the circuit.

The protocol assumes access to an ideal functionality, $\mathcal{F}_{or}$, for computing the logical OR of 4 input bits, each provided by one of the parties.

Input
1. P_1 has input $d_1 = \mathsf{m}_1^1 + \lambda_1^2$.
2. P_2 has input $d_2 = \mathsf{m}_2^1 + \lambda_2^2$.
3. P_3 has input $d_3 = \mathsf{m}_3^2 + \lambda_3^1$.
4. P_4 has input $d_4 = \mathsf{m}_4^2 + \lambda_4^1$.

Checking
1. P_1 samples a random seed and sends it to P_3.
2. P_1 (resp. P_3) send $H(d_1\|\mathsf{seed})$ (resp. $H(d_3\|\mathsf{seed})$) to P_2 and P_4
3. P_2 (resp. P_4) determines if it received the same value from P_1 and P_3. If it did, it will provide 0 to the $\mathcal{F}_{or}$ functionality, and otherwise it will provide 1.
4. Repeat the previous instructions with the variable exchanged as follows: P_1 is switched with P_2, and P_3 is switched with P_4, d_1 is switched with d_3, and d_2 is switched with d_4.
5. Players call the $\mathcal{F}_{or}$ functionality with the input that they were instructed to use in step 3.

Fig. 6. Cross check protocol from veto

Achieving secure and efficient cross checking. Our main observation for simplifying the cross check protocol is that, in the attack just described, P_1 will always cause the verification run by P_2 and P_4 to fail. This is because the evaluation of P_2 was also modified on wire w, but he will not modify λ_w^1 the way P_1 did. If the output of the equality test between P_1 and P_3 were hidden from P_1, shown only to P_2 and P_4, and, symmetrically, if P_1 only saw the result of their verification (which he already knows), then we can remove the bit of leakage. Specifically, each P_i learns a single bit, b_i, indicating whether the *other* verifying set passed the equality test. The four parties then run a secure protocol that computes the logical OR of these 4 bits. They can do this using any existing 4-party protocol.

One verification group reveals the equality of their masked evaluations to the other verification group as follows. (1) They agree on a random seed, (2) they hash it together with their doubly masked evaluation, and (3) they send the hash output to the players of the other verification group. The players in the other verification group can compute equality by simply checking that the hashes they receive are the same.

Note that $\mathcal{F}_{or}$ is a constant size circuit, and it likely does not matter which four party secure computation we use to realize it. Still, it is interesting to note that we can actually bootstrap this computation with another variant of our own protocol. In the protocol just previously described, letting $d_{i,w}$ denote the doubly masked value held by P_i for wire w, the parties effectively compute $\bigvee_{w \in \mathcal{W}}(d_{1,w} \neq d_{3,w}) \vee \bigvee_{w \in \mathcal{W}}(d_{2,w} \neq d_{4,w})$, where the hash value received by P_1 and P_3 (resp. P_2 and P_4) reveals the first (resp. second) disjunction of size $|\mathcal{W}|$ to P_1 and P_3 (resp. P_2 and P_4). The disjunction in the middle is where we use $\mathcal{F}_{or}$. Following the same discussion above, the reader can verify that it is also secure to compute $\bigvee_{w \in \mathcal{W}}((d_{1,w} \neq d_{3,w}) \vee (d_{2,w} \neq d_{4,w}))$. This can be achieved by having the four parties check the equality of gates in topological order by immediately exchanging the results of every equality check, rather than "batching them" with a hash function at the end of the evaluation. Removing the hash function in this way increases the communication to $O(|C|)$, so we would not prefer to use this as our cross-checking protocol. However, since $\mathcal{F}_{or}$ only has three gates, it is inefficient to bootstrap $\mathcal{F}_{or}$ using a hash function.

Security of Veto Cross Check

(Sketch). Assuming H is a non-programmable random oracle, our main protocol is secure if we replace the cross checking in the main protocol with the cross checking described in this section.

If the adversary acted maliciously during the masked evaluation, then it is clear that the verification group that does not contain the corrupt player (i.e. the honest verification group) will have inconsistent evaluations. As a result, the simulator can run the cross checking on behalf of the honest players as though the player in the honest verification group had inconsistent evaluations. In this case, the honest player in the same validation group as the corrupt player will always provide a veto. As a result, the simulator can safely always provide a simulated output of veto from $\mathcal{F}_{or}$, sends abort to $\mathcal{F}_{4pc}$, and the result is indistinguishable from a real execution.

If instead the corrupt player only misbehaves in the cross checking, the only possible deviation is to send the wrong hash value. In this case, the simulator can compute whether the corrupt player misbehaved by analyzing the hash value that he sent, together with the seed. The simulator knows that both players in the honest verification group will veto. As a result, the simulator can simply provide a simulated output of veto from $\mathcal{F}_{or}$, submit abort to $\mathcal{F}_{4pc}$, and the result is indistinguishable from a real execution.

Finally, if the adversary never deviates from the protocol, the simulator accepts the adversary's input to $\mathcal{F}_{or}$ and sends it back to him as the output of $\mathcal{F}_{or}$. If this value is a veto, the simulator sends abort to $\mathcal{F}_{4pc}$, and otherwise, he submits the adversary's input to $\mathcal{F}_{4pc}$, and simulates the opening of the output just as in Sect. 4.

Two distributors D_1, D_2 want to generate preprocessing for players E_1, E_2. We assume D_1 holds a key pair for a public key, committing encryption scheme, and that both hold key pairs for a digital signature scheme. The 3 public keys are known by all parties. We let $(\mathsf{pk}, \mathsf{sk})$ denote the encryption/decryption keys of D_1, and $(\mathsf{vk}_i, \mathsf{sk}_i)$ denote the verifying/signing keys of D_i.

Protocol

1. D_2 chooses $(\mathsf{seed}_1, \mathsf{seed}_2, \mathsf{r_{com}})$ at random and broadcasts $\mathsf{enc}(\mathsf{pk}, \mathsf{seed}_1 \| \mathsf{seed}_2 \| \mathsf{r_{com}})$. The other players then verify that D_2 broadcasted a valid ciphertext (by using the verifiability property of the committing encryption scheme). If D_2 did not broadcast a ciphertext, or if the ciphertext was not valid, then the other 3 parties halt this protocol and instead run a semi-honest 3-party protocol amongst themselves.

2. D_1 recovers $(\mathsf{seed}_1, \mathsf{seed}_2, \mathsf{r_{com}})$.

3. Each D_i computes the preprocessing that was described in Fig. 3.

4. Each D_i computes $\mathsf{commit}(\{\lambda_w\}_{w \in \mathcal{W}_{output}}; \mathsf{r_{com}})$. He includes these commitments in the preprocessing material.

5. Each D_i signs the preprocessing material: $\sigma_{1,i} = \mathsf{sign}(\mathsf{sk}_i; \mathsf{seed}_1)$ and $\sigma_{2,i} = \mathsf{sign}(\mathsf{sk}_i; \mathsf{seed}_2 \| \Gamma_2)$. He sends $(\mathsf{seed}_1, \sigma_{1,i})$ to E_1, and $(\mathsf{seed}_2, \Gamma_2, \sigma_{2,i})$ to E_2.

6. E_j receives $(m_{j,1}, \sigma_{j,1})$ and $(m_{j,2}, \sigma_{j,2})$. He checks whether $\mathsf{vrfy}(\mathsf{pk}_1, \sigma_{j,1}) = \mathsf{vrfy}(\mathsf{pk}_2, \sigma_{j,2}) = 1$, and whether $m_{j,1} = m_{j,2}$.
   - If one of the signatures does not verify, E_j continues the protocol using only the preprocessing material that was validly signed.
   - If both signatures verify, but $m_{j,1} \neq m_{j,2}$,
     - E_j broadcasts the two signed messages.
     - D_2 broadcasts $(\mathsf{seed}_1, \mathsf{seed}_2)$, together with the encryption randomness used in Step 1. All honest parties can now determine whether D_1 or D_2 misbehaved. They eliminate the guilty party and execute a 3-party, semi-honest protocol.
   - E_j outputs $m_{j,1}$.

Fig. 7. Robust preprocessing

The view in the real and ideal world are indistinguishable since (1) the simulator can always determine if there is a veto or not based on the behavior of the adversary and (2) the random oracles hides inputs from the other verification group.

6   Adding Robustness

We can make our protocol robust against a single cheater. We note that it is quite simple to strengthen our original protocol so that it is *fair*. If the malicious party aborts before anyone sends the output wire masks, then nothing is learned, and all parties can safely abort. If the adversary aborts after learning the output masks, his partner can still reveal the output for the other two evaluators. The only necessary modification is to prevent the malicious distributor from changing his output masks, revealing output values that conflict with what his partner reveals. This is easily handled by having all parties commit to their output masks prior to the evaluation: if the two distributors use the same randomness in their commitments, the evaluators can verify that they have both committed to the same mask value.

The main challenge in achieving robustness is that we cannot simply abort when we detect improper behavior, even if the output has not been revealed yet. Instead, we have to ensure that all honest parties correctly identify a misbehaving party, or at least a pair of parties that contains the adversary. To facilitate this, we make several adjustments. First, we modify the preprocessing protocol so that it either allows everyone to identify the adversary, or it ensures that both evaluators receive good preprocessing material. The robust preprocessing appears in Fig. 7. We then modify the input sharing to make it robust; the input sharing in Sect. 3 would trigger an abort if any party used different inputs in the two executions, but it would not allow the others to determine who cheated. After receiving the preprocessing material and the masked inputs, the evaluators continue the evaluation protocol from Sect. 3 until each party has a masking of the circuit. They then perform a robust variant of the cross checking protocol. In this variant, the parties cross check gate by gate, and if they ever find an inconsistency, they run a sub-routine to identify a pair of parties that contains the adversary.[2] Input sharing, evaluation, and robust cross checking are fully described in Fig. 8. We give a detailed overview of these changes below.

We will employ a broadcast channel throughout our protocol. We note that unconditionally-secure broadcast is possible in the four player model with one corruption due to the fact that less than $n/3$ players are corrupt.

Robust preprocessing: To make the preprocessing robust, one of the two distributors, D_2, starts by committing to the randomness that will be used in the preprocessing. This commitment is constructed by broadcasting a committing encryption under the public key of D_1. The randomness used in the preprocessing is denoted by $(\mathsf{seed}_1, \mathsf{seed}_2, \mathsf{r_{com}})$: seed_1 and seed_2 are used to create masks,

---

[2] To reduce communication of the robust cross checking, we can iteratively apply our cross check protocol from Sect. 5, performing a binary search on the masked circuit layers until we find the problematic layer. We then repeat that, performing a binary search within the problematic layer to find the problematic gate. This would yield a worst-case communication cost of $O(\kappa \log |C|)$. For simplicity, we describe the protocol as operating gate per gate.

just as in Sect. 3. r_{com} is used to construct a commitment to the output masks, which is then included in the preprocessing output.

After generating the preprocessing material, D_1 and D_2 each sign a copy of the output before sending it to E_1 and E_2. If they send conflicting values to E_1, the signatures allow E_1 to convince the other honest parties that one of D_1 or D_2 is malicious. The honest one of the two can now be exonerated: D_2 broadcasts the randomness used to encrypt the preprocessing randomness. E_1 broadcasts their view, and the honest parties can check the validity of the messages sent by D_1 and D_2. After removing the malicious party, the remaining three parties can run a semi-honest protocol in which one party supplies the preprocessing, the other two perform the evaluation, and no checking needs to be performed.

One other case of note deserves mention: suppose E_1 receives nothing[3] from, say, D_1. In this case, because there is no signature, E_1 cannot prove that D_1 or D_2 is malicious: it is equally possible that E_1 is himself malicious, and that he made the problem up. In this case, though, E_1 does need to persuade anybody. Because E_1 knows that D_1 is malicious, E_1 can simply continue the protocol using the preprocessing he received from D_2.

Robust input sharing: Let P_1 and P_2 perform distribution for P_3, P_4, and vice versa. Recall that Sect. 3, P_1 shares input x_w on wire w with P_3, P_4 by using the mask λ_w^1 that he and P_2 generated together. He shares his input with P_1, for their own evaluation, by using λ_w^2, which he receives from P_3, P_4. As written, nothing prevents him from sharing inconsistent values among the parties, and nothing prevents those parties from pretending he did so. To fix this, we first require P_3, P_4 to each sign λ_w^2, which allows P_1 to broadcast a proof of inconsistency when necessary. Then, P_1 signs and broadcasts his doubly masked input: $m_w = x_w + \lambda_w^1 + \lambda_w^2$. P_2 computes $m_w - \lambda_w^1$ for use in his evaluation with P_2. P_3, P_4 each compute $m_w - m_w^2$ for use in their evaluation.

Robust cross checking: Instead of cross checking the hashes of the full circuit maskings, the parties instead cross check gate by gate, starting at the input layer, and proceeding topologically through the circuit. This protocol begins with a pass over the circuit, one layer at a time, with the parties comparing their doubly masked values to locate the first gate at which the two evaluations depart from one another. Consider the case where P_3 decides that the two masked evaluations of some gate are inconsistent, and initiates a complaint. This can be due to one of the following cases:

1. The masked evaluation performed by P_1 and P_2 is invalid.
2. The masked evaluation performed by P_3 and P_4 is invalid.
3. Both evaluations were executed correctly, but either P_1 modified his input to cross-checking (i.e. his reported masked evaluation), or P_3 complained for no valid reason.

If the honest players know that the first case holds, then the corrupt player is either P_1 or P_2. They can therefore use the evaluation of P_3 and P_4 to determine

---

[3] Equivalently, something that is not validly signed.

Input phase

1. For each input wire w
   (a) Suppose $P_1 = E_1$ is the player who provides input x_w for wire w (we can generalize this to the other parties)
   (b) E_1 awaits the mask λ_w^2 from D_1, D_2, as well as signatures on λ_w^2.
      i. If E_1 receives a value for λ_w^2 without a signature from D_i then he ignores the mask that D_i sent him.
      ii. Otherwise, he received inconsistent masks, E_1 broadcasts the signed masks (thus identifying which evaluation group contains a cheater). If the players receive two different masks with valid signatures, they run the protocol, using only the masked evaluation of E_1, E_2.
   (c) E_1 broadcasts $\mathsf{m}_w = x_w + \lambda_w^1 + \lambda_w^2$.
   (d) E_1, E_2 set $\mathsf{m}_w^1 = \mathsf{m}_w - \lambda_w^1$ while D_1, D_2 set $\mathsf{m}_w^2 = \mathsf{m}_w - \lambda_w^2$.

Evaluation

Each evaluation group, using their own masked evaluation, as well as the share of the masks they received from distributors do the following:

For each gate (a, b, c, T) following topological order:
   (a) if $T = +$
      i. $\mathsf{m}_c \leftarrow \mathsf{m}_a + \mathsf{m}_b$.
   (b) if $T = \times$
      i. $\langle \mathsf{m}_c \rangle \leftarrow \mathsf{m}_a \cdot \mathsf{m}_b - \mathsf{m}_a \cdot \langle \lambda_b \rangle - \mathsf{m}_b \cdot \langle \lambda_a \rangle + \langle \lambda_c \rangle + \langle \lambda_a \cdot \lambda_b \rangle$
      ii. $\mathsf{m}_c \leftarrow \mathsf{open}(\langle \mathsf{m}_c \rangle)$

Cross Check

For every wire $w \in \mathcal{W}_{\mathtt{mult}} \cup \mathcal{W}_{\mathtt{input}}$, ordered by depth in the circuit.

For each verification group $V \in \mathcal{V}$
   1. $(V_1, V_2) \leftarrow V$
   2. V_1 send $d \leftarrow \mathsf{m}_w^1 + \lambda_w^1$ to V_2.
   3. V_2 broadcasts (error) if $d \neq \mathsf{m}_w^2 + \lambda_w^2$.
   4. If a player in V broadcasts (error), run complaint(w).
      (a) If the complaint phase returns (corrupt, P_1, P_2), P_1, P_2 broadcast decommitments to λ_w^1 for each output wire w. P_3, P_4 compute $\mathsf{m}_w^2 - \lambda_w^1$, broadcast the result, and the protocol terminates.
      (b) If the complaint phase returns (corrupt, P_3, P_4), P_3, P_4 broadcast decommitments to λ_w^2 for each output wire w. P_1, P_2 compute $\mathsf{m}_w^1 - \lambda_w^2$, broadcast the result, and the protocol terminates.
      (c) If the complaint phase returns (corrupt, verifier), set $\mathcal{V} \leftarrow \mathcal{V} \setminus V$ and restart the protocol with the updated $\mathcal{V}$.

Output

For each output wire w,
   1. Players P_1, P_2 broadcast the decommitment to λ_w^1.
   2. Players P_3, P_4 broadcast the decommitment to λ_w^2.
   3. P_1 and P_2 broadcast $\mathsf{m}_w^1 - \lambda_w^2$. Denote these values by $(\mathsf{out}_1, \mathsf{out}_2)$.
   4. P_3 and P_4 broadcast $\mathsf{m}_w^2 - \lambda_w^1$. Denote these values by $(\mathsf{out}_3, \mathsf{out}_4)$.
   5. All parties output $\mathsf{Majority}(\mathsf{out}_1, \mathsf{out}_2, \mathsf{out}_3, \mathsf{out}_4)$.

Fig. 8. Robust evaluation

Complaint Subprotocol

The *complaint* subprotocol is initiated for output wire w for a multiplication gate g_w when a player C has complained that the two masked evaluations were inconsistent on that wire. We denote by $V \in \mathcal{V}$ the verification group that contains C. This subprotocol allows the parties to identify either an evaluation group or a verification group that contains a cheater.

Complaint
1. $\mathcal{E}_1 \leftarrow \{P_1, P_2\}$, $\mathcal{E}_2 \leftarrow \{P_3, P_4\}$, $\mathcal{D}_1 \leftarrow \{P_3, P_4\}$, $\mathcal{D}_2 \leftarrow \{P_1, P_2\}$
2. Players run the validation functionality for wire w using $\mathcal{E}_1$ as the evaluators and $\mathcal{D}_1$ as the distributors.
3. Players run the validation functionality for wire w using $\mathcal{E}_2$ as the evaluators and $\mathcal{D}_2$ as the distributors.
4. If any of the calls to the validation functionality results in the functionality returning (corrupt,P_i,P_j), return the same. Otherwise, return (corrupt, verifier).

Validation

E_1, E_2, D_1 and D_2 want to verify that the masked evaluation of E_1, E_2 was done correctly for the gate g_w with output wire w.

Input
1. E_1, E_2 each input their masked evaluation for the 3 wires of g_w: $(\mathsf{m}_a, \mathsf{m}_b, \mathsf{m}_c)$.
2. D_1, D_2 each input the masks that they generated g_w: $(\lambda_a, \lambda_b, \lambda_c)$.

Functionality
1. If E_1 and E_2 provided distinct inputs, return (corrupt,E_1,E_2) and halt.
2. If D_1 and D_2 provided distinct inputs, return (corrupt,D_1,D_2) and halt.
3. If $(\mathsf{m}_a - \lambda_a) \cdot (\mathsf{m}_b - \lambda_b) + \lambda_c = \mathsf{m}_c$, then output (valid). Otherwise output (corrupt,E_1,E_2).

Fig. 9. Complaint

their output. By the same argument, if the players know that the second case holds, they can all safely use the evaluation of P_1 and P_2 to produce the output. Finally, if the players know they are in the third case, they know that the malicious party is either P_1 or P_3. In this case, they do not dismiss either evaluation, but they continue the cross checking using only between P_2 and P_4; since P_2 and P_4 are honest, their cross-checking suffices for ensuring a valid computation.

When someone detects an inconsistency in the cross checking of a gate, the parties execute a *complaint* subprotocol (See Fig. 9) to determine which of the above cases hold. In this subprotocol, the parties use an ideal functionality, which can later be bootstrapped generically using any MPC with identifiable abort. We stress that the circuit implementing this functionality is small: it only needs to be executed on a single gate, and it used at most twice in a computation. The functionality is called once for each of the two evaluations. In each instance, the two evaluators provide their masked input and masked output for the gate, while the two distributors provide the masks that they created for the gate. If the evaluators do not provide the same masked values then the functionality indicates that the evaluation set contains the cheater. If the distributors do not provide the same masks then the functionality indicates that the cheater is in the distribution set. Otherwise, the functionality uses the masked wire values and the mask values to check whether the gate evaluation was performed correctly. If the masked evaluation was invalid, the ideal functionality indicates that the evaluation set contains the cheater. Finally, if no error is detected, then the functionality indicates this, and the parties conclude that either the party that raised the alarm is malicious, or his partner in the cross-checking is malicious (case 3 above).

6.1   Robust Evaluation Simulator

Theorem 4. *If the robust evaluation protocol is instantiated using a CCA-Secure public-key committing encryption scheme, and a EU-CMA signature scheme, then it securely realizes $\mathcal{F}_{4pc}$ in the random oracle model. In addition, the protocol is robust.*

Simulator for robust preprocessing when D_2 is corrupt.

1. Wait that D_2 broadcasts the ciphertext c. If the ciphertext is not valid (which can be efficiently checked by the verifiability property of committing encryption) then the simulator submits a default input value to $\mathcal{F}_{4pc}$ on behalf of the adversary, and terminates. (This corresponds to the honest parties removing the adversary from the computation, upon agreeing that he is malicious.)
2. Recover $(\mathsf{seed}_1 \| \mathsf{seed}_2 \| \mathsf{r_{com}}) \leftarrow Dec(sk, c)$.
3. The simulator computes the preprocessing and broadcasts $\mathsf{commit}(\{\lambda_w\}_{w \in \mathcal{W}_{\mathrm{output}}}; \mathsf{r_{com}})$ on behalf of D_1.
4. Simulator awaits that D_2 sends the preprocessing material and signatures on the preprocessing material to each player. Then,
   (a) For each evaluator, if D_2 sent an invalid signature to the given evaluator, the simulator ignores what D_2 sent.
   (b) Otherwise, if D_2 sent invalid preprocessing to either evaluator, then simulate the broadcast from the given evaluator of the signed preprocessing and determining that D_2 misbehaved. The simulator notes that D_2 was identified as a cheater.

Simulator for robust preprocessing when D_1 is corrupt. Same as the simulation for D_2 except that the simulator broadcasts the encryption of the randomness to D_1.

Simulator for robust preprocessing when an evaluator is corrupt. The simulator chooses randomness and simulates the three honest players. If an evaluator sends a message claiming he received inconsistent preprocessing, but the signed messages he forwards do not substantiate his claim, the simulator sends a default input to $\mathcal{F}_{4pc}$ and terminates. (Technically, we did not describe in our protocol that the other parties remove the evaluator when he does this, because we felt it would unnecessarily complicate the protocol description.)

Indistinguishability of robust preprocessing.

1. In the case where the distributor is corrupt, we claim the view in the real and ideal worlds are indistinguishable. If the distributor deviates from the protocol, it is either ignored (if it does not send a signature with the preprocessing it shares), or it is eliminated from the computation (if it sends bad preprocessing with a valid signature). The committing property of the encryption scheme guarantees that he gets caught if he signs and sends a wrong value.
2. The only message sent by an evaluator is (possibly) to complain about inconsistent preprocessing. If the evaluator is corrupt, then in both the ideal and real world, the complaint would be ignored (due to the unforgeability of the underlying signature scheme).

Claim. Let $x = (x_1, x_2, x_3, x_4)$. Let $\mathsf{view}[\mathsf{Input}]_{\pi,\mathcal{A}} = \{\mathsf{view}[\mathsf{Input}]_{\pi,\mathcal{A}}\}_{x,\kappa}$ denote the random variable describing real-world view of $\mathcal{A}$ for some fixed set of inputs, and some fixed security parameter. There exists a simulator $\mathcal{S}$ such that $\mathsf{view}[\mathsf{Input}]_{\mathcal{F},\mathcal{S}} \equiv$ denote the random variable resulting from the ideal world simulation described in the $\mathcal{F}_{4\mathsf{pc}}$ (described below). There in the input sharing phase, and

1. If the corrupt player is providing input as an evaluator,
   (a) The simulator provides the signed masks from the other distributors.
   (b) The simulator awaits that the corrupt player broadcasts a double masking m_w. The simulator then computes the input of the corrupt player from the masks that were produced in the preprocessing and the double masking that the corrupt player sent.
2. If the corrupt player is a distributor, and the input wire belongs to an evaluator,
   (a) The simulator awaits that the corrupt player sends out a mask to the evaluator. If the mask is signed with the corrupt player's signature, and is not the value produced in the preprocessing, then the simulator produces a broadcast of the conflicting, signed masks. The simulator provides the default value to $\mathcal{F}_{4\mathsf{pc}}$ on behalf of the corrupt player and terminates.
3. If the corrupt player is an evaluator, and the input wire belongs to the other evaluator, the simulator broadcasts the doubly masked input.

Indistinguishability of input phase. We argue that since the view until the end of the preprocessing phase in the ideal world is indistinguishable from the view until the end of the preprocessing phase in the real world, then the views are also indistinguishable up through the end of the input phase. In the real and ideal world, when the distributor is corrupt, any deviation would either be ignored, or would result in the dealer being caught and eliminated from the computation. If the evaluator is corrupt, and he broadcasts an invalid complaint, he is eliminated due to the unforgeability of the underlying signature scheme.

Simulator for evaluation. The simulator of the evaluation step follows the same steps as the simulator for the masked evaluation in the main protocol. In particular, the simulator stores if the corrupt player misbehaved during his evaluation. We argue that since the view until the end of the input phase in the ideal world is indistinguishable from the view until the end of the input phase in the real world, then the views are also indistinguishable up through the end of the evaluation phase.. This holds from the fact that our main protocol (in particular the masked evaluation part) is secure.

Simulator for cross check. For every multiplication wire $w \in \mathcal{W}_{\mathtt{mult}}$,

1. If the corrupt evaluator had previously sent a wrong value in the evaluation of wire w,
   (a) The simulator broadcasts (error) on behalf of the verifiers that are not in the same verification group as the corrupt player. (He might also do so with the player that is in the same verification group as him.)
   (b) The simulator receives $(\lambda_a, \lambda_b, \lambda_c)$ and (m_a, m_b, m_c) from the adversary, intended for the first and second calls to the validation functionality, respectively (and without loss of generality). If $(\lambda_a, \lambda_b, \lambda_c)$ are inconsistent with the values simulated during preprocessing, the simulator implicates the adversary (and his partner) when simulating the output of the first call to the validation functionality. In either case he implicates the adversary (and his partner) in the simulated output of the second call to the validation functionality.
   The simulator then runs the protocol on behalf of the honest players using the honest evaluation group's masked evaluation.
2. Otherwise:
   (a) if simulating V_1, the simulator checks to see if the adversary sends a wrong doubly masked value to his partner: $m_w^1 + \lambda_w^1$.
   (b) if simulating V_2, the simulator checks to see if the adversary broadcasts (error).
   The simulator receives $(\lambda_a, \lambda_b, \lambda_c)$ and (m_a, m_b, m_c) from the adversary, intended for the first and second calls to the validation functionality, respectively (and without loss of generality). If $(\lambda_a, \lambda_b, \lambda_c)$ are inconsistent with the values simulated during preprocessing, the simulator implicates the adversary (and his partner) when simulating the output of the first call to the validation functionality. If (m_a, m_b, m_c) are inconsistent with simulated masked values of the evaluation phase, the simulator implicates the adversary (and his partner) when simulating the output of the second call to the validation functionality. If he is not implicated in either instance, then any future messages he might send during cross checking are ignored.

Indistinguishability of cross check. We argue that since the view until the end of the evaluation phase in the ideal world is indistinguishable from the view until the end of the evaluation phase in the real world, then the views are also indistinguishable up through the end of the cross check. If the corrupt player's evaluation group is deemed corrupt, then the protocol in the real world would dictate that the corrupt player no longer receive messages during the cross check phase. Therefore, it is clear that after the elimination has taken place, the views in the real and ideal world are indistinguishable.

We now claim that the validation function eliminates the adversary's evaluation set in the real world, if and only if the simulator implicates the adversary's evaluation set in the ideal world. Note that the simulator can detect if the adversary has modified any wire in the evaluation, as well as whether his input to the validation function is inconsistent with his partner's input. The reader can verify by inspection that the claim holds. Since the complaint phase consists of just two calls to the validation functionality, it follows that the adversary's view in the complaint phase is identically distributed in the two worlds. By the previous note, after this point, the cross check in the real and ideal worlds would be indistinguishable.

To complete the argument that the adversary's view is correctly simulated through the end of the cross check phase, we argue that, prior to being eliminated, the simulated view in the cross check phase is sampled from the same distribution as his view in the real world. This follows because he only sees doubly masked wire values, which are computationally indistinguishable from uniformly distributed strings (because they are generated using a PRG).

Simulator for output phase. The output phase is the easiest to simulate.

1. First the simulator queries the ideal functionality with the adversary's input and receives an output.
2. The simulator selects masks for the honest evaluation group so that the sum of the output and the masks of the honest evaluation group is equal to the masked evaluation of the corrupt player. The simulator then "broadcasts" decommitments to the masks of the honest evaluation group.
3. The simulator selects masked evaluation for the honest evaluation group so that the sum of the output and the masks of the corrupt player add up to the masked evaluation. The simulator then "broadcasts" the masked evaluations.

Indistinguishability of output phase. We now argue that the output distribution, conditioned on the adversary's view, is indistinguishable in the two worlds. We have already argued that the adversary is caught if he ever manipulates his evaluation. The reader can verify that whenever a transcript results in the use of a default adversarial input in the real world, the simulator submits default input in the ideal world. If the adversary never changes the masked values, then the input used in both worlds is the one he committed to in the input sharing phase.

References

1. Araki, T., et al.: Optimized honest-majority MPC for malicious adversaries - breaking the 1 billion-gate per second barrier. In: 2017 IEEE Symposium on Security & Privacy, pp. 843–862, May 2017

2. Beaver, D.: Efficient multiparty protocols using circuit randomization. In: Feigenbaum, J. (ed.) CRYPTO 1991. LNCS, vol. 576, pp. 420–432. Springer, Heidelberg (1992). https://doi.org/10.1007/3-540-46766-1_34

3. Beaver, D., Micali, S., Rogaway, P.: The round complexity of secure protocols (extended abstract). In: ACM STOC, pp. 503–513, May 1990

4. Ben-David, A., Nisan, N., Pinkas, B.: FairplayMP: a system for secure multi-party computation. In: ACM CCS 2008, pp. 257–266, October 2008

5. Ben-Or, M., Goldwasser, S., Wigderson, A.: Completeness theorems for non-cryptographic fault-tolerant distributed computation (extended abstract). In: 20th ACM STOC, pp. 1–10, May 1988

6. Bendlin, R., Damgård, I., Orlandi, C., Zakarias, S.: Semi-homomorphic encryption and multiparty computation. In: Paterson, K.G. (ed.) EUROCRYPT 2011. LNCS, vol. 6632, pp. 169–188. Springer, Heidelberg (2011). https://doi.org/10.1007/978-3-642-20465-4_11

7. Canetti, R.: Security and composition of multiparty cryptographic protocols. J. Cryptol. **13**(1), 143–202 (2000)

8. Choi, S.G., Katz, J., Malozemoff, A.J., Zikas, V.: Efficient three-party computation from cut-and-choose. In: Garay, J.A., Gennaro, R. (eds.) CRYPTO 2014. LNCS, vol. 8617, pp. 513–530. Springer, Heidelberg (2014). https://doi.org/10.1007/978-3-662-44381-1_29

9. Cohen, G., et al.: Efficient multiparty protocols via log-depth threshold formulae. In: Canetti, R., Garay, J.A. (eds.) CRYPTO 2013. LNCS, vol. 8043, pp. 185–202. Springer, Heidelberg (2013). https://doi.org/10.1007/978-3-642-40084-1_11

10. Damgård, I., Geisler, M., Krøigaard, M., Nielsen, J.B.: Asynchronous multiparty computation: theory and implementation. In: Jarecki, S., Tsudik, G. (eds.) PKC 2009. LNCS, vol. 5443, pp. 160–179. Springer, Heidelberg (2009). https://doi.org/10.1007/978-3-642-00468-1_10

11. Damgård, I., Ishai, Y.: Constant-round multiparty computation using a black-box pseudorandom generator. In: Shoup, V. (ed.) CRYPTO 2005. LNCS, vol. 3621, pp. 378–394. Springer, Heidelberg (2005). https://doi.org/10.1007/11535218_23

12. Damgård, I., Ishai, Y.: Scalable secure multiparty computation. In: Dwork, C. (ed.) CRYPTO 2006. LNCS, vol. 4117, pp. 501–520. Springer, Heidelberg (2006). https://doi.org/10.1007/11818175_30

13. Damgård, I., Ishai, Y., Krøigaard, M.: Perfectly secure multiparty computation and the computational overhead of cryptography. In: Gilbert, H. (ed.) EUROCRYPT 2010. LNCS, vol. 6110, pp. 445–465. Springer, Heidelberg (2010). https://doi.org/10.1007/978-3-642-13190-5_23

14. Damgård, I., Ishai, Y., Krøigaard, M., Nielsen, J.B., Smith, A.: Scalable multiparty computation with nearly optimal work and resilience. In: Wagner, D. (ed.) CRYPTO 2008. LNCS, vol. 5157, pp. 241–261. Springer, Heidelberg (2008). https://doi.org/10.1007/978-3-540-85174-5_14

15. Damgård, I., Nielsen, J.B., Nielsen, M., Ranellucci, S.: The TinyTable protocol for 2-party secure computation, or: gate-scrambling revisited. In: Katz, J., Shacham, H. (eds.) CRYPTO 2017. LNCS, vol. 10401, pp. 167–187. Springer, Cham (2017). https://doi.org/10.1007/978-3-319-63688-7_6

16. Damgård, I., Orlandi, C., Simkin, M.: Yet another compiler for active security or: efficient MPC over arbitrary rings. Cryptology ePrint Archive, Report 2017/908 (2017). http://eprint.iacr.org/2017/908

17. Damgård, I., Pastro, V., Smart, N., Zakarias, S.: Multiparty computation from somewhat homomorphic encryption. In: Safavi-Naini, R., Canetti, R. (eds.) CRYPTO 2012. LNCS, vol. 7417, pp. 643–662. Springer, Heidelberg (2012). https://doi.org/10.1007/978-3-642-32009-5_38
18. Franklin, M.K., Yung, M.: Communication complexity of secure computation (extended abstract). In: 24th ACM STOC, pp. 699–710, May 1992
19. Furukawa, J., Lindell, Y., Nof, A., Weinstein, O.: High-throughput secure three-party computation for malicious adversaries and an honest majority. In: Coron, J.-S., Nielsen, J.B. (eds.) EUROCRYPT 2017. LNCS, vol. 10211, pp. 225–255. Springer, Cham (2017). https://doi.org/10.1007/978-3-319-56614-6_8
20. Genkin, D., Ishai, Y., Prabhakaran, M., Sahai, A., Tromer, E.: Circuits resilient to additive attacks with applications to secure computation. In: 46th ACM STOC, pp. 495–504, May/June 2014
21. Goldreich, O.: Foundations of Cryptography: Basic Applications, vol. 2. Cambridge University Press, Cambridge (2004)
22. Goldreich, O., Micali, S., Wigderson, A.: How to play any mental game or a completeness theorem for protocols with honest majority. In: 19th ACM STOC, pp. 218–229, May 1987
23. Goldwasser, S., Lindell, Y.: Secure multi-party computation without agreement. J. Cryptol. 18(3), 247–287 (2005)
24. Huang, Y., Katz, J., Evans, D.: Quid-Pro-Quo-tocols: strengthening semi-honest protocols with dual execution. In: 2012 IEEE Symposium on Security & Privacy, pp. 272–284, May 2012
25. Ishai, Y., Prabhakaran, M., Sahai, A.: Founding cryptography on oblivious transfer – efficiently. In: Wagner, D. (ed.) CRYPTO 2008. LNCS, vol. 5157, pp. 572–591. Springer, Heidelberg (2008). https://doi.org/10.1007/978-3-540-85174-5_32
26. Lindell, Y., Nof, A.: A framework for constructing fast MPC over arithmetic circuits with malicious adversaries and an honest-majority. In: ACM CCS 2017, pp. 259–276 (2017)
27. Lindell, Y., Pinkas, B., Smart, N.P., Yanai, A.: Efficient constant round multiparty computation combining BMR and SPDZ. In: Gennaro, R., Robshaw, M. (eds.) CRYPTO 2015. LNCS, vol. 9216, pp. 319–338. Springer, Heidelberg (2015). https://doi.org/10.1007/978-3-662-48000-7_16
28. Mohassel, P., Franklin, M.: Efficiency tradeoffs for malicious two-party computation. In: Yung, M., Dodis, Y., Kiayias, A., Malkin, T. (eds.) PKC 2006. LNCS, vol. 3958, pp. 458–473. Springer, Heidelberg (2006). https://doi.org/10.1007/11745853_30
29. Mohassel, P., Rosulek, M., Zhang, Y.: Fast and secure three-party computation: the garbled circuit approach. In: ACM CCS 2015, pp. 591–602, October 2015
30. Mohassel, P., Zhang, Y.: SecureML: a system for scalable privacy-preserving machine learning. In: 2017 IEEE Symposium on Security & Privacy, pp. 19–38, May 2017
31. Nielsen, J.B., Nordholt, P.S., Orlandi, C., Burra, S.S.: A new approach to practical active-secure two-party computation. In: Safavi-Naini, R., Canetti, R. (eds.) CRYPTO 2012. LNCS, vol. 7417, pp. 681–700. Springer, Heidelberg (2012). https://doi.org/10.1007/978-3-642-32009-5_40
32. Rabin, T., Ben-Or, M.: Verifiable secret sharing and multiparty protocols with honest majority (extended abstract). In: 21st ACM STOC, pp. 73–85, May 1989
33. Wang, X., Ranellucci, S., Katz, J.: Authenticated garbling and efficient maliciously secure two-party computation. In: ACM CCS 2017, pp. 21–37 (2017)
34. Wang, X., Ranellucci, S., Katz, J.: Global-scale secure multiparty computation. In: ACM CCS 2017, pp. 39–56 (2017)

Concretely Efficient Large-Scale MPC
with Active Security (or, TinyKeys
for TinyOT)

Carmit Hazay[1]([✉]), Emmanuela Orsini[2], Peter Scholl[3],
and Eduardo Soria-Vazquez[4]

[1] Bar-Ilan University, Ramat Gan, Israel
carmit.hazay@biu.ac.il
[2] KU Leuven, imec-COSIC, Leuven, Belgium
emmanuela.orsini@kuleuven.be
[3] Aarhus University, Aarhus, Denmark
peter.scholl@cs.au.dk
[4] University of Bristol, Bristol, UK
eduardo.soria-vazquez@bristol.ac.uk

Abstract. In this work we develop a new theory for concretely efficient, large-scale MPC with active security. Current practical techniques are mostly in the strong setting of all-but-one corruptions, which leads to protocols that scale badly with the number of parties. To work around this issue, we consider a large-scale scenario where a small minority out of many parties is honest and design scalable, more efficient MPC protocols for this setting. Our results are achieved by introducing new techniques for information-theoretic MACs with short keys and extending the work of Hazay et al. (CRYPTO 2018), which developed new passively secure MPC protocols in the same context. We further demonstrate the usefulness of this theory in practice by analyzing the concrete communication overhead of our protocols, which improve upon the most efficient previous works.

1 Introduction

Secure multi-party computation (MPC) protocols allow a group of n parties to compute some function f on the parties' private inputs, while preserving

C. Hazay—Supported by the European Research Council under the ERC consolidators grant agreement n. 615172 (HIPS), and by the BIU Center for Research in Applied Cryptography and Cyber Security in conjunction with the Israel National Cyber Bureau in the Prime Minister's Office.

E. Orsini—Supported in part by ERC Advanced Grant ERC-2015-AdG-IMPaCT.

P. Scholl—Supported by the European Union's Horizon 2020 research and innovation programme under grant agreement No 731583 (SODA), and the Danish Independent Research Council under Grant-ID DFF-6108-00169 (FoCC).

E. Soria-Vazquez—Supported by the European Union's Horizon 2020 research and innovation programme under the Marie Skłodowska-Curie grant agreement No. 643161, and by ERC Advanced Grant ERC-2015-AdG-IMPaCT.

T. Peyrin and S. Galbraith (Eds.): ASIACRYPT 2018, LNCS 11274, pp. 86–117, 2018.
https://doi.org/10.1007/978-3-030-03332-3_4

a number of security properties such as *privacy* and *correctness*. The former property implies data confidentiality, namely, nothing leaks from the protocol execution but the computed output. The latter requirement implies that the protocol enforces the integrity of the computations made by the parties, namely, honest parties are not led to accept a wrong output. Security is proven either in the presence of a passive adversary that follows the protocol specification but tries to learn more than allowed from its view of the protocol, or an active adversary that can arbitrarily deviate from the protocol specification in order to compromise the security of the other parties in the protocol.

The past decade has seen huge progress in making MPC protocols communication efficient and practical; see [KS08, DPSZ12, DKL+13, ZRE15, LPSY15, WMK17, HSS17] for just a few examples. In the two-party setting, actively secure protocols [WRK17a] by now reach within a constant overhead factor over the notable semi-honest construction by Yao [Yao86]. On the practical side, a Boolean circuit with around 30,000 gates (6,400 AND gates and the rest XOR) can be securely evaluated with active security in under 20 ms [WRK17a]. Moreover, current technology already supports protocols that securely evaluate circuits with more than a billion gates [KSS12]. On the other hand, secure *multi-party* computation with a larger number of parties and a dishonest majority is far more difficult due to scalability challenges regarding the number of parties. Here, the most efficient practical protocol with active security has a multiplicative factor of $O(\lambda/\log|C|)$ due to cut-and-choose [WRK17b] (where λ is a statistical security parameter and $|C|$ is the size of the computed circuit). On the practical side, the same Boolean circuit of 30,000 gates can be securely evaluated at best in 500 ms for 14 parties [WRK17b] in a local network where the latency is neglected, or in more than 20 s in a wide network. The problem is that current MPC protocols do not scale well with the number of parties, where the main bottleneck is a relatively high communication complexity, while the number of applications requiring large scale communication networks are constantly increasing, involving sometimes hundreds of parties.

An interesting example is safely measuring the Tor network [DMS04] which is among the most popular tools for digital privacy, consisting of more than 6000 relays that can opt-in for providing statistics about the use of the network. Nowadays and due to privacy risks, the statistics collected over Tor are generally poor: There is a reduced list of computed functions and only a minority of the relays provide data, which has to be obfuscated before publishing [DMS04]. Hence, the statistics provide an incomplete picture which is affected by a noise that scales with the number of relays.

In the context of securely computing the interdomain routing within the Border Gateway Protocol (BGP) which is performed at a large scale of thousands of nodes, a recent solution in the dishonest majority setting [ADS+17] centralizes BGP so that two parties run this computation for all Autonomous Systems. Large scale protocols would allow scaling to a large number of systems computing the interdomain routing themselves using MPC, hence further reducing the trust requirements.

Another important application that involves a massive number of parties is an auction with private bids, where the winning bid is either the first or the second price. Auctions have been widely studied by different communities improving different aspects and are central in the area of web electronic commerce. When considering privacy and correctness, multi-party computation offers a set of tools that allow to run the auction while preserving the privacy of the bidders (aka. passive security). MPC can also enforce independent of inputs between the corrupted and honest parties as well as correctness, in the sense that parties are not allowed to change their vote once they learn they lost. This type of security requires more complicated tools and is knows as active security. Designing secure solutions for auctions played an important role in the literature of MPC. In fact, the first MPC real-world implementation was for the sugar beet auction [BCD+09] with three parties and honest majority, where the actual number of parties was 1129. In a very recent work by Keller et al. [KPR18], the authors designed a new generic protocol based on semi-homomorphic encryption and lattice-based zero-knowledge proofs of knowledge, and implemented the second-price auction with 100 parties over a field of size 2^{40}. The running time of their offline phase for the SPDZ protocol is 98 s. The authors did not provide an analysis of their communication complexity.

Motivated by the fact that current techniques are insufficient to produce highly practical protocols for such scenarios, we investigate the design of protocols that can more efficiently handle large numbers of parties with *strong security* levels. In particular, we study the setting of active security with only a minority (around 10–30%) of honest participants. By relaxing the well-studied, very strong setting of all-but-one corruptions (or *full-threshold*), we hope to greatly improve performance. Our starting point is the recent work by Hazay et al. [HOSS18] which studied this corruption setting with passive security and presented a new technique based on "short keys" to improve the communication complexity and the running times of full-threshold MPC protocols. In this paper we extend their results to the active setting.

Technical background for [HOSS18]. Towards achieving their goal, Hazay et al. observed that instead of basing security on secret keys held by each party individually, they can base security on the *concatenation of all honest parties' keys*. Namely, a secure multi-party protocol with h honest parties can be built by distributing secret key material so that each party only holds a *small part of the key*. Formalizing this intuition is made possible by reducing the security of their protocols to the *Decisional Regular Syndrome Decoding (DRSD)* problem, which, given a random binary matrix $\mathbf{H}$, is to distinguish between the syndrome obtained by multiplying $\mathbf{H}$ with an error vector $e = (e_1 \| \cdots \| e_h)$ where each $e_i \in \{0,1\}^{2^\ell}$ has Hamming weight one, and the uniform distribution. This can equivalently be described as distinguishing $\bigoplus_{i=1}^{h} \mathsf{H}(i, k_i)$ from the uniform distribution, where H is a random function and each k_i is a random ℓ-bit key. A specified in [HOSS18], when h is large enough, the problem is *unconditionally hard* even for $\ell = 1$, which means for certain parameter choices 1-bit keys can be used *without introducing any additional assumptions*.

Our contribution. In this work we develop a new theory for concretely efficient, large-scale MPC in the presence of an active adversary. More concretely, we extend the short keys technique from [HOSS18] to the active setting. Adapting these ideas to the active setting is quite challenging and requires modifying information-theoretic MACs used in previous MPC protocols [BDOZ11, DPSZ12] to be usable with short MAC keys. As our first, main contribution, we present several new methods for constructing efficient, distributed, information-theoretic MACs with short keys, for the setting of a small, honest minority out of a large set of parties. Our schemes allow for much lower costs when creating MACs in a distributed manner compared with previous works, due to the use of short MAC keys. For our second contribution, we show how to use these efficient MAC schemes to construct actively secure MPC for binary circuits, based on the 'TinyOT' family of protocols [NNOB12, BLN+15, FKOS15, HSS17, WRK17b]. All previous protocols in that line of work supported $n-1$ out of n corruptions, so our protocol extends this to be more efficient for the setting of large-scale MPC with a few honest parties.

Concrete efficiency improvements. The efficiency of our protocols depends on the total number of parties, n, and the number of honest parties, h, so there is a large range of parameters to explore when comparing with other works. We discuss this in more detail in Sect. 8. Our protocol starts to concretely improve upon previous protocols when we reach $n = 30$ parties and $t = 18$ corruptions: here, our triple generation method requires less than *half the communication cost* of the fastest MPC protocol which is also based on TinyOT [WRK17b] (dubbed WRK) tolerating up to $n-1$ corruptions. For a fairer comparison, we also consider modifying WRK to run in a committee of size $t + 1$, to give a protocol with the same corruption threshold as ours. In this setting, we see a small improvement of around 10% over WRK, but at larger scales the impact of our protocol becomes much greater. For example, with $n = 200$ parties and $t = 160$ corruptions we have up to an 8 times improvement over WRK with full-threshold, and a 5 times improvement when WRK is modified to the threshold-t setting.

Technical Overview

In our protocols we assume that two committees, $\mathcal{P}_{(h)}$ and $\mathcal{P}_{(1)}$, have been selected out of all the n parties providing inputs in the MPC protocol, such that $\mathcal{P}_{(h)}$ contains at least h honest parties and $\mathcal{P}_{(1)}$ contains at least 1 honest party. These can be chosen deterministically, for instance, if there are h honest parties in total we let $\mathcal{P}_{(h)} = \{P_1, \dots, P_n\}$ and $\mathcal{P}_{(1)} = \{P_1, \dots, P_{n-h+1}\}$. We can also choose committees at random using coin-tossing, if we start with a very large group of parties from which $h' > h$ are honest. Since we have $|\mathcal{P}_{(h)}| > |\mathcal{P}_{(1)}|$, to avoid unnecessary interaction we take care to ensure that committee $\mathcal{P}_{(h)}$ is only used when needed, and when possible we will do operations in committee $\mathcal{P}_{(1)}$ only.

Section 3. We first show a method for authenticated secret-sharing based on information-theoretic MACs with short keys, where given a message x, a MAC m and a key k, verification consists of simply checking that s linear equations hold. Our construction guarantees that forging a MAC to all parties can only be done with probability $2^{-\lambda}$, *even when the key length ℓ is much smaller than λ*, by relying on the fact that at least h parties are honest. We note that the reason for taking this approach is *not* to obtain a more efficient MAC scheme, but to design a scheme allowing more efficient *creation* of the MACs. Setting up the MACs typically requires oblivious transfer, with a communication cost proportional to the key length, so a smaller ℓ gives us direct efficiency improvements to the preprocessing phase, which is by far the dominant cost in applications. Our basic MAC scheme requires all parties in both committees to take part, but to improve this we also present several optimizations, which can greatly reduce the storage overhead by "compressing" the MACs into a single, SPDZ-like sharing in *only* committee $\mathcal{P}_{(1)}$.

Sections 4 and 5. We next show how to efficiently create authenticated shares for our MAC scheme with short keys. As a building block, we need a protocol for random correlated oblivious transfer (or random Δ-OT) on short strings. We consider a variant of the OT extension protocol of Keller et al. [KOS15], modified to produce correlated OTs (as done in [NST17]) and with short strings. Our authentication protocol for creating distributed MACs improves upon the previous best-known approach for creating MACs (optimized to use h honest parties) by a factor of $h(n-h)/n$ times in terms of overall communication complexity. This gives performance improvements *for all $h > 1$*, with a maximum $n/4$-fold gain as h approaches $n/2$.

Section 7. Finally, we introduce our triple generation protocol, in two phases. Similarly to [WRK17b], we first show how to compute the cross terms in multiplication triples by computing so-called 'half-authenticated' triples. This protocol does not authenticate all terms and the result may yield an incorrect triple. Next, we run a standard cut-and-choose technique for verifying correctness and removing potential leakage. Our method for checking correctness does not follow the improved protocol from [WRK17b] due to a limitation introduced by our use of the DRSD assumption. The security of our protocol relies on a variant of the DRSD assumption that allows one bit of leakage, and for this reason the number of triples r generated by these protocols depends on the security of RSD. So, while we can produce an essentially unlimited number of random correlated OTs and random authenticated bits, if we were to produce 'half-authenticated' triples in a naive way, we would be bounded on the total number of triples and hence the size of the circuits we can evaluate. To fix this issue we show how to switch the MAC representation from using one key Δ to a representation under another independent key $\tilde{\Delta}$. This switch is performed every r triples.

Extension to Constant Rounds. Since Hazay et al. [HOSS18] also described a constant round protocol based on garbled circuits with passive security, it is natural to wonder if our approach with active security also extends to this setting. Unfortunately, it is not straightforward to extend our approach to multi-party garbled circuits with short keys and active security, since the adversary can flip a garbled circuit key with non-negligible probability, breaking correctness. Nevertheless, we can build an alternative, efficient solution based on the transformation from [HSS17], which shows how to turn any non-constant round, actively secure protocol for Boolean circuits into a constant round [BMR90]-based protocol. When applying [HSS17] to our protocol, we obtain a multi-party garbling protocol with full-length keys, but we still improve upon the naive (full-threshold) setting, since the preprocessing phase is more efficient due to our use of TinyOT with short keys. More details will be given in the full version.

2 Preliminaries

We denote the computational and statistical security parameter by κ and λ, respectively. We say that a function $\mu : \mathbb{N} \to \mathbb{N}$ is *negligible* if for every positive polynomial $p(\cdot)$ and all sufficiently large κ it holds that $\mu(\kappa) < \frac{1}{p(\kappa)}$. The function μ is *noticeable* (or non-negligible) if there exists a positive polynomial $p(\cdot)$ such that for all sufficiently large κ it holds that $\mu(\kappa) \geq \frac{1}{p(\kappa)}$. We use the abbreviation PPT to denote probabilistic polynomial-time. We further denote by $a \leftarrow A$ the uniform sampling of a from a set A, and by $[d]$ the set of elements $\{1, \ldots, d\}$. We often view bit-strings in $\{0,1\}^k$ as vectors in $\mathbb{F}_2^k$, depending on the context, and denote exclusive-or by "$\oplus$" or "$+$". If $a, b \in \mathbb{F}_2$ then $a \cdot b$ denotes multiplication (or AND), and if $c \in \mathbb{F}_2^\kappa$ then $a \cdot c \in \mathbb{F}_2^\kappa$ denotes the product of a with every component of c.

Security and Communication Models. We use the universal composability (UC) framework [Can01] to analyse the security of our protocols. We assume all parties are connected via secure, authenticated point-to-point channels, as well as a broadcast channel which is implemented using a standard 2-round echo-broadcast. The adversary model we consider is a static, active adversary who corrupts up to t out of n parties at the beginning of the protocol. We denote by A the set of corrupt parties, and $\bar{A}$ the set of honest parties.

Regular Syndrome Decoding Problem. We recall that the *regular syndrome decoding* (RSD) problem is to recover a secret error vector $e = (e_1 \| \cdots \| e_h)$, where each $e_i \in \{0,1\}^{m/h}$ has Hamming weight one, given only $(\mathbf{H}, \mathbf{H}e)$, for a randomly chosen binary $r \times m$ matrix $\mathbf{H}$. In [HOSS18] it was shown that the search and decisional versions of this problem are equivalent and even statistically secure when h is big enough compared to r. In this work we use an interactive variant of the problem, where the adversary is allowed to try to guess a few bits of information on the secret e before seeing the challenge; if the guess is incorrect, the game aborts. We conjecture that this 'leaky' version of the problem, defined below, is no easier than the standard problem. Note that on average the leakage only allows the adversary to learn 1 bit of information on e, since if the game does not abort he only learns that $\bigwedge P_i(e) = 1$.

The 'leaky' part of the assumption is introduced as a result of an efficient instantiation of random correlated OTs on short strings (Sect. 4). Once the adversary has tried to guess these short strings, which act as short MAC keys in the authentication protocol (Sect. 5), a DRSD challenge is presented to him during the protocol computing the cross terms of multiplication triples (Sect. 7.1). As in [HOSS18], the appearance of the DRSD instance is due to the fact of 'hashing' the short MAC keys of at least h honest parties during said multiplications.

Definition 2.1 (Decisional Regular Syndrome Decoding with Leakage). *Let $r, h, \ell \in \mathbb{N}$ and $m = h \cdot 2^\ell$. Consider the game $\mathcal{L}\text{-DRSD}^b_{r,h,\ell}$ for $b \in \{0,1\}$, defined between a challenger and an adversary:*

1. *Sample $\mathbf{H} \leftarrow \mathbb{F}_2^{r \times m}$ and a random, weight-h vector $e \in \mathbb{F}_2^m$.*
2. *Send $\mathbf{H}$ to the adversary and wait for the adversary to adaptively query up to h efficiently computable[1] predicates $P_i : \mathbb{F}_2^m \to \{0,1\}$. For each P_i queried, if $P_i(e) = 0$ then abort, otherwise wait for the next query.*
3. *If $b = 0$, sample $u \leftarrow \mathbb{F}_2^r$ and send $(\mathbf{H}, u)$ to the adversary. Otherwise if $b = 1$, send $(\mathbf{H}, \mathbf{H}e)$.*

The DRSD problem with leakage with parameters (r, h, ℓ) is to distinguish between $\mathcal{L}\text{-DRSD}^0_{r,h,\ell}$ and $\mathcal{L}\text{-DRSD}^1_{r,h,\ell}$ with noticeable advantage.

2.1 Resharing

At several points in our protocols, we have a value $x = \sum_{i \in X} x^i$ that is secret-shared between a subset of parties $\{P_i\}_{i \in X}$, and wish to re-distribute this to a fresh sharing amongst a different set of parties, say $\{P_j\}_{j \in Y}$. The naive method to do this is for every party P_i to generate a random sharing of x^i, and send one share to each P_j. This costs $|X| \cdot |Y| \cdot m$ bits of communication, where m is the bit length of x. When m is large, we can optimize this using a pseudorandom generator $G : \{0,1\}^\kappa \to \{0,1\}^m$, as follows:

1. For $i \in X$, party P_i does as follows:
   (a) Pick an index $j' \in Y^2$
   (b) Sample random keys $k^{i,j} \leftarrow \{0,1\}^\kappa$, for $j \in Y \setminus j'$
   (c) Send $k^{i,j}$ to party P_j, and send $x^{i,j'} = \sum_j G(k^{i,j}) + x^i$ to party $P_{j'}$
2. For $j \in Y$, party P_j does as follows:
   (a) Receive $k^{i,j}$ from each P_i who sends P_j a key, and a share $x^{i,j}$ from each P_i who sends P_j a share. For the keys, compute the expanded share $x^{i,j} = G(k^{i,j})$.
   (b) Output $x^j = \sum_{i \in X} x^{i,j}$.

Now each P_i only needs to send a single share of size m bits, since the rest are compressed down to κ bits using the PRG. This gives an overall communication complexity of $O(|X| \cdot |Y| \cdot \kappa + |X| \cdot m)$ bits.

---

[1] By efficiently computable, we mean that the adversary sends a description of a polynomially-sized circuit that computes P.

[2] This can be chosen at random, or in some pre-agreed deterministic manner to load-balance communication among the parties.

3   Information-Theoretic MACs with Short Keys

We now describe our method for authenticated secret-sharing based on information-theoretic MACs with short keys. Our starting point is the standard information-theoretic MAC scheme on a secret $x \in \{0, 1\}$ given by $m = k + x \cdot \Delta$, for a uniformly random key (k, Δ), where $k \in \{0, 1\}^\ell$ is only used once per message x, whilst $\Delta \in \{0, 1\}^\ell$ is fixed. Given the message x, the MAC m and the key k, verification consists of simply checking the linear equation holds. It is easy to see that, given x and m, forging a valid MAC for a message $x' \neq x$ is equivalent to guessing Δ. In a nutshell, we adapt this basic scheme for the multi-party, secret-shared setting, with the guarantee that forging a MAC to all parties can only be done with probability $2^{-\lambda}$, *even when the key length ℓ is much smaller than λ*, by relying on the fact that at least h parties are honest.

Our scheme requires choosing two (possibly overlapping) subsets of parties $\mathcal{P}_{(h)}, \mathcal{P}_{(1)} \subseteq \mathcal{P}$, such that $\mathcal{P}_{(h)}$ has at least h honest parties and $\mathcal{P}_{(1)}$ at least 1 honest party. To authenticate a secret value x, we first additively secret-share x between $\mathcal{P}_{(1)}$, and then give every party in $\mathcal{P}_{(1)}$ a MAC on its share under a random MAC key given to each party in $\mathcal{P}_{(h)}$, as follows:

$$P_i \in \mathcal{P}_{(h)} : \quad \Delta^i, \{k^{i,j}[x^j]\}_{j \in \mathcal{P}_{(1)}, j \neq i}$$

$$P_j \in \mathcal{P}_{(1)} : \quad x^j, \{m^{j,i}[x^j]\}_{i \in \mathcal{P}_{(h)}, i \neq j}$$

$$\text{such that } x = \sum_j x^j \quad \text{and} \quad m^{j,i}[x^j] = k^{i,j}[x^j] + x^j \cdot \Delta^i.$$

where $k^{i,j}[x^j]$ is a key chosen by P_i from $\{0, 1\}^\ell$ to authenticate the message x^j that is chosen by P_j whereas $m^{j,i}[x^j]$ is a MAC on a message x^j computed using the keys Δ^i and $k^{i,j}[x^j]$. We denote this representation by $[x]_\Delta^{\mathcal{P}_{(h)}, \mathcal{P}_{(1)}}$. Note that sometimes we use representations with a different set of global keys $\Delta = \{\Delta^i\}_{i \in \mathcal{P}_{(h)}}$, but when it is clear from context we omit Δ and write $[x]^{\mathcal{P}_{(h)}, \mathcal{P}_{(1)}}$.

We remark that a special case is when $\mathcal{P}_{(h)} = \mathcal{P}_{(1)} = \mathcal{P}$, which gives the usual n-party representation of an additively shared value $x = x^1 + \cdots + x^n$, as used in [BDOZ11, BLN+15]:

$$[x] = \{x^i, \Delta^i, \{m^{i,j}, k^{i,j}\}_{j \neq i}\}_{i \in [n]}, \quad m^{i,j} = k^{j,i} + x^i \cdot \Delta^j,$$

where each party P_i holds the $n - 1$ MACs $\{m^{i,j}\}$ on x^i, as well as the keys $k^{i,j}$ on each x^j, for $j \neq i$, and a global key Δ^i.

The idea behind our setup is that to cheat when opening x to all parties would require guessing at least h MAC keys of the honest parties in committee $\mathcal{P}_{(h)}$. In Figs. 1 and 2 we describe our protocols for opening values to a subset $\bar{\mathcal{P}} \subseteq \mathcal{P}$ and to a single party, respectively, and checking MACs. First each party in $\mathcal{P}_{(1)}$ broadcasts its share x^j to $\mathcal{P}_{(h)}$, and then later, when checking MACs, P_j sends the MAC $m^{j,i}$ to P_i for verification. To improve efficiency, we make two optimizations to this basic method: firstly, instead of sending the individual MACs, when opening a large batch of values P_j only sends a single, random linear combination of all the MACs. Secondly, the verifier P_i does not check every MAC equation from each P_j, but instead sums up all the MACs and performs a single check. This has the effect that we only verify the sum x was opened correctly, and not the individual shares x^j.

Overall, to open x to an incorrect value x' requires guessing the Δ^i keys of all honest parties in $\mathcal{P}_{(h)}$, so can only be done with probability $\leq 2^{-h\ell}$. This means we can choose $\ell = \lambda/h$ to ensure security. Note that it is crucial when opening $[x]^{\mathcal{P}_{(h)},\mathcal{P}_{(1)}}$ that the shares x^j are *broadcast* to all parties in $\mathcal{P}_{(h)}$, to ensure consistency. Without this, a corrupt P_j could open, for example, an incorrect value to a single party in $\mathcal{P}_{(h)}$ with probability $2^{-\ell}$, and the correct share to all other parties.

More details on the correctness and security of our open and MACCheck protocols are given in the full version of this paper.

Efficiency Savings From Short Keys. Note that the reason for taking this approach is *not* to obtain a more efficient MAC scheme, but to design a scheme allowing more efficient *creation* of the MACs. Setting up the MACs typically requires oblivious transfer, with a communication cost proportional to the key length, so a smaller ℓ gives us direct efficiency improvements to the preprocessing phase, which is by far the dominant cost in applications (see Sect. 5 for details). Regarding the scheme itself, notice that this is actually *less efficient*, in terms of storage and computation costs, than the distributed MAC scheme used in the SPDZ protocol [DKL+13], which only requires each party to store $\lambda + 1$ bits per authenticated Boolean value. However, it turns out that these overheads are less significant in practice compared with the communication cost of setting up the MACs, where we gain a lot.

Extension to Arithmetic Shares. The scheme presented above can easily be extended to the arithmetic setting, with shares in a larger field instead of just $\mathbb{F}_2$. To do this with short keys, we simply choose the MAC keys Δ^i to be from a small subset of the field. For example, over $\mathbb{F}_p$ for a large prime p, each party chooses $\Delta^i \in \{0, \ldots, 2^\ell - 1\}$, and will obtain MACs of the form $m^{j,i} = k^{i,j} + x^j \cdot \Delta^i$ over $\mathbb{F}_p$, where $k^{i,j}$ is a random element of $\mathbb{F}_p$. This allows for a reduced preprocessing cost when generating MACs with the MASCOT protocol [KOS16] based on oblivious transfer: instead of requiring k OTs on k-bit strings between all $n(n-1)$ pairs of parties, where $k = \lceil \log_2 p \rceil$, we can adapt our preprocessing protocol from Sect. 5 to $\mathbb{F}_p$ so that we only need to perform ℓ OTs on k-bit strings between $(n-1)(t+1)$ pairs of parties to set up each shared MAC.

3.1   Operations on $[\cdot]^{\mathcal{P}_{(h)},\mathcal{P}_{(1)}}$-Shared Values

Recall that $\mathcal{P}_{(h)} \cap \mathcal{P}_{(1)}$ is not necessarily the empty set.

Addition and multiplication with constant: We can define addition of $[x]_\Delta^{\mathcal{P}_{(h)},\mathcal{P}_{(1)}}$ with a public constant $c \in \{0,1\}$ by:

1. A designated $P_{i^*} \in \mathcal{P}_{(1)}$ replaces its share x^{i^*} with $x^{i^*} + c$.

Protocol $\Pi_{[\text{Open}]}^{\mathcal{P}_{(h)},\mathcal{P}_{(1)}}$

PARAMETERS: $\mathcal{P}_{(h)}, \mathcal{P}_{(1)}, \bar{\mathcal{P}} \subseteq \mathcal{P}$ three (possibly overlapping) subsets of parties, such that $\mathcal{P}_{(h)}$ has at least h honest parties and $\mathcal{P}_{(1)}$ has at least one honest party; ℓ = key length ; m = number of authenticated bits

Open: To open $[x]^{\mathcal{P}_{(h)},\mathcal{P}_{(1)}}$ to a set of parties $\bar{\mathcal{P}} \subseteq \mathcal{P}$:

1. Each party $P_j \in \mathcal{P}_{(1)}$ broadcasts its share x^j to $\bar{\mathcal{P}}$.
2. All parties in $\bar{\mathcal{P}}$ locally compute $x = \sum_{j \in \mathcal{P}_{(1)}} x^j$.

Single Check: To check the MAC on the opened value x:

1. Each $P_j \in \mathcal{P}_{(1)}$ sends $m^{j,i}[x]$ to every $P_i \in \mathcal{P}_{(h)} \setminus \{P_j\}$.
2. Each party in $\bar{\mathcal{P}}$ broadcasts the previously received x to $\mathcal{P}_{(h)}$.
3. Each $P_i \in \mathcal{P}_{(h)}$ checks that

$$\sum_{j \in \mathcal{P}_{(1)} \setminus P_i} \left(m^{j,i}[x] + k^{i,j}[x] \right) + (x + x^i) \cdot \Delta^i = 0$$

where $x^i = 0$ if $P_i \notin \mathcal{P}_{(1)}$. If any check fails, abort.

Batch Check: To check the MACs on a batch of opened values $x_1, \ldots, x_m$:

1. Parties in $\bar{\mathcal{P}}, \mathcal{P}_{(h)}, \mathcal{P}_{(1)}$ sample m random values $\chi_1, \ldots, \chi_m \leftarrow \mathcal{F}_{\text{Rand}}(\mathbb{F}_{2^\lambda})$.
2. Each party in $\bar{\mathcal{P}}$ locally computes $y = \sum_{k=1}^m \chi_k \cdot x_k \in \mathbb{F}_{2^\lambda}$ and broadcasts this to $\mathcal{P}_{(h)}$.
3. If parties in $\mathcal{P}_{(h)}$ receive inconsistent values, then abort.
4. Each $P_i \in \mathcal{P}_{(h)} \cap \mathcal{P}_{(1)}$ computes $y^i = \sum_{k=1}^m \chi_k \cdot x_k^i$.
5. Parties in $\mathcal{P}_{(h)} \cup \mathcal{P}_{(1)}$ locally compute $[y]^{\mathcal{P}_{(h)},\mathcal{P}_{(1)}} = \sum_{k=1}^m \chi_k \cdot [x_k]^{\mathcal{P}_{(h)},\mathcal{P}_{(1)}}$ (with multiplication over $\mathbb{F}_{2^\lambda}$).
6. Each $P_j \in \mathcal{P}_{(1)}$ sends $m^{j,i}[y]$ to every $P_i \in \mathcal{P}_{(h)} \setminus \{P_j\}$.
7. Each $P_i \in \mathcal{P}_{(h)}$ has received values $\{y\}$ and MACs $\{m^{j,i}[y]\}, j \in \mathcal{P}_{(1)} \setminus \{P_i\}$, and checks that

$$\sum_{j \in \mathcal{P}_{(1)} \setminus \{P_i\}} \left(m^{j,i}[y] + k^{i,j}[y] \right) + (y + y^i) \cdot \Delta^i = 0,$$

where $y^i = 0$ if $P_i \notin \mathcal{P}_{(1)}$. If any check fails, abort.

Fig. 1. Protocols for opening and MAC-checking on $(\mathcal{P}_{(h)}, \mathcal{P}_{(1)})$-authenticated secret shares

2. Each P_i (for $i \in \mathcal{P}_{(h)}, i \neq i^*$) replaces its key $k^{i,1}[x]$ with $k^{i,1}[x] + c \cdot \Delta^i$. (All other values are unchanged.)

We also define multiplication of $[x]_\Delta^{\mathcal{P}_{(h)},\mathcal{P}_{(1)}}$ by a public constant $c \in \{0,1\}$ (or in $\{0,1\}^\ell$) by multiplying every share x^i, MAC $m^{i,j}[x]$ and key $k^{i,j}[x]$ by c.

Addition of shared values: Addition (XOR) of two shared values $[x]_\Delta^{\mathcal{P}_{(h)},\mathcal{P}_{(1)}}$, $[y]_\Delta^{\mathcal{P}_{(h)},\mathcal{P}_{(1)}}$ is straightforward addition of the components. Note that it is possible

---

Protocol $\Pi_{\mathsf{PrivateOpen}}^{\mathcal{P}_{(h)},\mathcal{P}_{(1)},P_{i_0}}$

Private Open: To open a value $[x]^{\mathcal{P}_{(h)},\mathcal{P}_{(1)}}$ towards P_{i_0}:

1. Each $P_j \in \mathcal{P}_{(1)}$ sends their share x^j to P_{i_0}, who locally reconstructs $x = \sum_{j \in \mathcal{P}_{(1)}} x^j$.

Batch Check: To check the MACs on a batch of opened values $x_1, \dots, x_m$:

1. Parties in $\mathcal{P}_{(h)}, \mathcal{P}_{(1)}$ call $\mathcal{F}_{\mathsf{aBit}}^{\mathcal{P}_{(h)},\mathcal{P}_{(1)}}$ to obtain λ random authenticated values $[r_1]_\Delta^{\mathcal{P}_{(h)},\mathcal{P}_{(1)}}, \dots, [r_\lambda]_\Delta^{\mathcal{P}_{(h)},\mathcal{P}_{(1)}}$
2. Each $P_j \in \mathcal{P}_{(1)}$ sends $r_1^j, \dots, r_\lambda^j$ to P_{i_0}.
3. Sample λ random values $\chi_k \leftarrow \mathbb{F}_{2^\lambda}$ using $\mathcal{F}_{\mathsf{Rand}}$, $k \in [m]$
4. P_{i_0} locally computes

$$y = \sum_{k=1}^m \chi_k \cdot x_k + \sum_{k=1}^\lambda X^{k-1} \cdot r_k,$$

and broadcasts the result to $\mathcal{P}_{(h)}$.
5. Each $P_i \in \mathcal{P}_{(h)} \cap \mathcal{P}_{(1)}$ computes

$$y^i = \sum_{k=1}^m \chi_k \cdot x_k^i + \sum_{k=1}^\lambda X^{k-1} \cdot r_k^i$$

6. Parties in $\mathcal{P}_{(h)} \cup \mathcal{P}_{(1)}$ locally compute

$$[y]_\Delta^{\mathcal{P}_{(h)},\mathcal{P}_{(1)}} = \sum_{k=1}^m \chi_k \cdot [x_k]_\Delta^{\mathcal{P}_{(h)},\mathcal{P}_{(1)}} + \sum_{k=1}^l X^{k-1} \cdot [r_k]_\Delta^{\mathcal{P}_{(h)},\mathcal{P}_{(1)}},$$

where multiplication is performed over the finite field $\mathbb{F}_{2^\lambda}$.
7. Each $P_j \in \mathcal{P}_{(1)}$ privately sends $m_\Delta^{j,i}[y]$ to every $P_i \in \mathcal{P}_{(h)} \setminus P_j$.
8. Each $P_i \in \mathcal{P}_{(h)}$ has received MACs $\{m_\Delta^{j,i}[y]\}_{j \in \mathcal{P}_{(1)} \setminus P_i}$, and checks that

$$\sum_{j \in \mathcal{P}_{(1)} \setminus P_i} \left(m_\Delta^{j,i}[y] + k_\Delta^{i,j}[y] \right) + (y + y^i) \cdot \Delta^i = 0$$

where $y^i = 0$ if $P_i \notin \mathcal{P}_{(1)}$. If any check fails, abort and notify all parties in $\mathcal{P}$.

Fig. 2. Protocol for privately opening $(\mathcal{P}_{(h)}, \mathcal{P}_{(1)})$-party authenticated secret shares to a single party P_{i_0} and MAC-checking

to compute the sum $[x]_\Delta^{\mathcal{P}_{(h)},\mathcal{P}_{(1)}} + [y]_\Delta^{\mathcal{P}_{(h)},\mathcal{P}_{(h)}}$ of values shared within different committees in the same way, obtaining a $[x+y]_\Delta^{\mathcal{P}_{(h)},\mathcal{P}_{(h)} \cup \mathcal{P}_{(1)}}$ representation.

3.2   Converting to a More Compact Representation

We can greatly reduce the storage overhead in our scheme by "compressing" the MACs into a single, SPDZ-like sharing in *only* committee $\mathcal{P}_{(1)}$ with longer keys. Recall that the SPDZ protocol MAC representation [DPSZ12, DKL+13] of a secret bit x held by the parties in $\mathcal{P}_{(1)}$ is given by

$$[\![x]\!] = \{x^j, \boldsymbol{m}^j[x]\}_{j \in \mathcal{P}_{(1)}}$$

where each party P_j in $\mathcal{P}_{(1)}$ holds a share x^j, a MAC share $\boldsymbol{m}^j[x] \in \mathbb{F}_2^\lambda$ and a global MAC key share $\Delta^j \in \mathbb{F}_2^\lambda$, such that

$$x = \sum_{j \in \mathcal{P}_{(1)}} x^j, \quad \sum_{j \in \mathcal{P}_{(1)}} \boldsymbol{m}^j = \left(\sum_{j \in \mathcal{P}_{(1)}} x^j \right) \cdot \left(\sum_{j \in \mathcal{P}_{(1)}} \Delta^j \right)$$

Using this instead of the previous representation gives a much simpler and more efficient MAC scheme in the online phase of our MPC protocol, since each party only stores $\lambda + 1$ bits per value, instead of up to $|\mathcal{P}_{(h)}| \cdot \ell + 1$ bits with the scheme using short keys. Therefore, to obtain *both* the efficiency of *generating* MACs in the previous scheme, and *using* the MACs with SPDZ, below we show how to convert an inefficient, pairwise sharing $[x]^{\mathcal{P}_{(h)}, \mathcal{P}_{(1)}}$ into a more compact SPDZ sharing $[\![x]\!]$. This procedure is shown in Fig. 3.

Note that with the SPDZ representation, the parties in $\mathcal{P}_{(1)}$ can perform linear computations and openings (within $\mathcal{P}_{(1)}$) in just the same way. For completeness, we present the opening and MAC check protocols in the full version of this paper.

Protocol $\Pi_{\mathsf{MACCompact}}^{\mathcal{P}_{(h)}, \mathcal{P}_{(1)}, m, \ell}$

PARAMETERS: $\mathcal{P}_{(h)}, \mathcal{P}_{(1)} \subseteq \mathcal{P}$ two (possibly overlapping) subsets of parties, such that $\mathcal{P}_{(h)}$ has at least h honest parties and $\mathcal{P}_{(1)}$ has at least one honest party; $\ell = $ key length; $m = $ number of authenticated bits.
On input $[x_1]_\Delta^{\mathcal{P}_{(h)}, \mathcal{P}_{(1)}}, \ldots, [x_m]_\Delta^{\mathcal{P}_{(h)}, \mathcal{P}_{(1)}}$, do as follows:

1. Each $P_i \in \mathcal{P}_{(h)}$ samples and broadcasts $r^i \leftarrow \mathbb{F}_{2^\lambda}$.
2. For $\iota \in [m]$:
   (a) Each $P_i \in \mathcal{P}_{(h)}$ computes $r^i \cdot \sum_{j \in \mathcal{P}_{(1)}} k^{i,j}[x_\iota]$, then reshares the resulting value to the parties in $P_j \in \mathcal{P}_{(1)}$, each of which obtains random shares $\{\tilde{k}^{i,j}[x_\iota]\}_{i \in \mathcal{P}_{(h)}}$.
   (b) Each $P_i \in \mathcal{P}_{(h)}$ reshares $\Delta^i \cdot r^i \in \mathbb{F}_{2^\lambda}$ to the parties in $\mathcal{P}_{(1)}$, each of which obtains $\{\tilde{\Delta}^{i,j}\}_{i \in \mathcal{P}_{(h)}}$.
   (c) Each $P_j \in \mathcal{P}_{(1)}$ outputs its part of $[\![x_\iota]\!]$ by computing the MAC share

$$\tilde{\boldsymbol{m}}^j[x_\iota] = \sum_{i \in \mathcal{P}_{(h)}} (\tilde{k}^{i,j}[x_\iota] + \boldsymbol{m}^{j,i}[x_\iota] \cdot r^i) \in \mathbb{F}_{2^\lambda}$$

and key share $\tilde{\Delta}^j = \sum_{i \in \mathcal{P}_{(h)}} \tilde{\Delta}^{i,j} \in \mathbb{F}_{2^\lambda}$.

Fig. 3. Protocol for transforming $[x]^{\mathcal{P}_{(h)}, \mathcal{P}_{(1)}}$ representations to $[\![x]\!]$ representations

To see correctness, first notice that from step 2a, we have that $\sum_j \tilde{k}^{i,j} = r^i \cdot \sum_j k^{i,j}$. So each party in $\mathcal{P}_{(1)}$ holds a share x^j and a MAC share $\tilde{m}^j \in \mathbb{F}_{2^\lambda}$, which satisfy:

$$\sum_j \tilde{m}^j = \sum_j \sum_i (\tilde{k}^{i,j} + m^{j,i} \cdot r^i)$$
$$= \sum_{i,j} (k^{i,j} + m^{j,i}) \cdot r^i = \sum_{i,j} x^j \cdot \Delta^i \cdot r^i = x \cdot \tilde{\Delta}.$$

The security of this scheme now depends on the single, global MAC key $\tilde{\Delta} = \sum_i \Delta^i \cdot r^i$, instead of the concatenation of Δ^i for $i \in \mathcal{P}_{(h)}$. Since at least h of the short keys $\Delta^i \in \mathbb{F}_{2^\ell}$ are unknown and uniformly random, from the leftover hash lemma [ILL89] it holds that $\tilde{\Delta}$ is within statistical distance $2^{-\lambda}$ of the uniform distribution over $\{0,1\}^\lambda$ as long as $h\ell \geq 3\lambda$. This gives a slightly worse bound than the previous scheme, but allows for a much more efficient *online phase* of the MPC protocol since, once the SPDZ representations are produced, only parties in $\mathcal{P}_{(1)}$ need to interact, and they have much lower storage and local computation costs. Note that in our instantiation of this scheme for the overall MPC protocol, we also need to choose the parameters h, ℓ such that the $\mathcal{L}$-DRSD assumption is hard; it turns out that all of our parameter choices (see Sect. 8) for this already satisfy $h\ell \geq 3\lambda$, so in this case using more compact MACs does not incur any extra overheads.

Improved Analysis for 1-bit Keys. When the key length is 1, we can improve upon the previous bound from the leftover hash lemma with a more fine-grained analysis. Notice that we can write the new key $\tilde{\Delta}$ as $\tilde{\Delta} = \mathbf{R} \cdot \Delta$, where $\mathbf{R} \in \{0,1\}^{\lambda \times n}$ is a matrix with r^i as columns. Since at least h positions of Δ are uniformly random, from randomness extraction results for bit-fixing sources (as used in, e.g. [NST17, Theorem 1]) it holds that since every honestly sampled row of $\mathbf{R}$ is uniformly random, $\tilde{\Delta}$ is within statistical distance $2^{\lambda-h}$ of the uniform distribution. We therefore require $h \geq 2\lambda$, instead of $h \geq 3\lambda$ as previously.

Optimization with Vandermonde Matrices Over Small Fields. If we choose each of the Δ^i keys to come from a small finite field $\mathbb{F}$, with $|\mathbb{F}| \geq n$, then we can optimize the compact MAC scheme even further, so that there is *no overhead* on top of the previous pairwise scheme. The idea is to use a Vandermonde matrix to extract randomness from all parties' small MAC keys in a deterministic fashion, instead of using random vectors r^i as before. This technique is inspired by previous applications of hyper-invertible matrices to MPC in the honest majority setting [BTH08].

Let $v_1, \ldots, v_n$ be distinct points in $\mathbb{F}$, where $\mathbb{F}$ is such that $h \cdot |\mathbb{F}| \geq \lambda$. Now let $\mathbf{V} \in \mathbb{F}^{n \times h}$ be the Vandermonde matrix given by

$$\mathbf{V} = \begin{pmatrix} 1 & v_1 & \dots & v_1^{h-1} \\ 1 & v_2 & \dots & v_2^{h-1} \\ \vdots & \ddots & \ddots & \vdots \\ 1 & v_n & \dots & v_n^{h-1} \end{pmatrix}$$

Party P_i defines the new MAC key share $\tilde{\Delta}^i = \boldsymbol{v}_i \cdot \Delta^i$, where $\boldsymbol{v}_i$ is the i-th row of $\mathbf{V}$. This results in a new global key given by $\tilde{\Delta} = (\Delta^1, \dots, \Delta^n) \cdot \mathbf{V} \in \mathbb{F}^h$. From the fact that at least h components of Δ are uniformly random, and the property of the Vandermonde matrix that any square matrix formed by taking h rows of $\mathbf{V}$ is invertible, it follows that $\tilde{\Delta}$ is a uniformly random vector in $\mathbb{F}^h$. More formally, this means that if $n - h$ components of Δ are fixed and we define Δ_H to be the h honest MAC key components, then the mapping $\Delta_H \mapsto \Delta \cdot \mathbf{V}$ is a bijection, so $\tilde{\Delta}$ is uniformly random as long as Δ_H is. Therefore we can choose $h \geq \lambda/|\mathbb{F}|$ to obtain $\leq 2^{-\lambda}$ cheating probability in the resulting MAC scheme.

Allowing leakage on the MAC keys. In our subsequent protocol for generating MACs, to obtain an efficient protocol we need to allow some *leakage* on the individual MAC keys $\Delta^i \in \{0,1\}^\ell$, in the form of allowing the adversary to guess a single bit of information on each Δ^i. For both the pairwise MAC scheme and the compact, SPDZ-style MACs, this leakage does not affect an adversary's probability of forging MACs in our actual protocols, since the entire MAC key still needs to be guessed to break security — allowing guesses on smaller parts of the key does not help, as a single incorrect guess causes the protocol to abort. We analyse the security of this for our compact MAC representation in the full version.

4   Correlated OT on Short Strings

As a building block, we need a protocol for random correlated oblivious transfer (or random Δ-OT) on short strings. This is a 2-party protocol, where the receiver inputs bits $x_1, \dots, x_m$, the sender inputs a short string $\Delta \in \{0,1\}^\ell$, and the receiver obtains random strings $t_i \in \{0,1\}^\ell$, while the sender learns $q_i = t_i + x_i \cdot \Delta$. The ideal functionality for this is shown in Fig. 4.

The protocol we use to realise this (shown in the full version of this paper) is a variant of the OT extension protocol of Keller et al. [KOS15], modified to produce correlated OTs (as done in [NST17]) and with short strings. The security of the protocol can be shown similarly to the analysis of [KOS15]. That work showed that a corrupt party may attempt to guess a few bits of information about the sender's secret Δ, and will succeed with probability 2^{-c}, where c is the number of bits. In our case, since Δ is small, a corrupt receiver may actually guess *all of* Δ with some noticeable probability, in which case all security for the sender is lost. This is modelled in the functionality $\mathcal{F}_{\Delta\text{-ROT}}$, which allows a corrupt receiver to submit such a guess. This leakage does not cause a problem in our multi-party protocols, because an adversary would have to guess the keys of *all* honest parties to break security, and this can only occur with negligible probability.

Communication complexity. Recall that λ is the statistical security parameter and κ the computational security parameter. The initialization phase requires ℓ random OTs, which costs $\ell\kappa$ bits of communication when implemented using OT extension. The communication complexity of the **Extend** phase, to create m Δ-ROTs, is $\ell(m+\lambda)$ bits to create the OTs, and $\kappa+2\lambda$ bits for the consistency check (we assume P_S only sends a κ-bit seed used to generate the χ_i's). This gives an amortized cost of $\ell + (\kappa + 3\lambda)/m$ bits per Δ-ROT, which is less than $\ell + 4$ bits when $m > \kappa$.

Functionality $\mathcal{F}_{\Delta\text{-ROT}}^{\ell}$

Initialize: Upon receiving (Init, Δ), where $\Delta \in \{0,1\}^{\ell}$ from P_S and (Init) from P_R, store Δ. Ignore any subsequent (Init) commands.

Extend: Upon receiving $(\mathsf{extend}, x_1, \ldots, x_m)$ from P_R, where $x_i \in \{0,1\}$, and (extend) from P_S, do the following:

- Sample $t_i \in \{0,1\}^{\ell}$, for $i \in [m]$. If P_R is corrupted then wait for $\mathcal{A}$ to input t_i.
- Compute $q_i = t_i + x_i \cdot \Delta$, for $i \in [m]$.
- If P_S is corrupted then wait for $\mathcal{A}$ to input $q_i \in \{0,1\}^{\ell}$ and recompute $t_i = q_i + x_i \cdot \Delta$.
- Output t_i to P_R and q_i to P_S, for $i \in [m]$.

Key queries: If P_R is corrupt then on receiving an efficiently computable predicate $P : \{0,1\}^{\ell} \to \{0,1\}$ from the adversary, send 1 to the adversary if $P(\Delta) = 1$. If $P(\Delta) = 0$ then the functionality aborts.

Fig. 4. Functionality for oblivious transfer on random, correlated strings.

5   Bit Authentication with Short Keys

In this section we describe our protocols for authenticating bits with short MAC keys. To capture the short keys used for authentication we need to define a series of different functionalities.

5.1   Authenticated Bit Functionality $\mathcal{F}_{\mathsf{aBit}}$

We begin with the description of the ideal functionality $\mathcal{F}_{\mathsf{aBit}}$ described in Fig. 5 that formalises the MACs we create. Each party $P_i \in \mathcal{P}_{(h)}$ chooses a global $\Delta^i \in \{0,1\}^{\ell}$, then $\mathcal{F}_{\mathsf{aBit}}$ calls the subroutine $(\mathcal{P}_{(h)}, \mathcal{P}_{(1)})$-Bracket (Fig. 6) that uses these global MAC keys $\{\Delta^i\}_{i \in \mathcal{P}_{(h)}}$ stored by the functionality to create pairwise MACs of the same length, as illustrated in Sect. 3.

Functionality $\mathcal{F}_{\mathsf{aBit}}^{\mathcal{P}_{(h)},\mathcal{P}_{(1)},m,\ell}$

PARAMETERS: m number of authenticated bits; ℓ key length.

Initialize: On receiving $(\mathsf{Init}, \Delta^i)$ from $P_i \in \mathcal{P}_{(h)}$ and (Init) from $P_j \in \mathcal{P}_{(1)}$, store all $\Delta^i \in \{0,1\}^\ell$.

aBit: On receiving (aBit, m) from $P_i \in \mathcal{P}_{(h)}$ and $(\mathsf{aBit}, \boldsymbol{x}^j = (x_1^j, \ldots, x_m^j))$ from every $P_j \in \mathcal{P}_{(1)}$:

1. Run $(\mathcal{P}_{(h)}, \mathcal{P}_{(1)})$-$\mathsf{Bracket}(\{x_h^j\}_{j \in \mathcal{P}_{(1)}})$ (see below), for every $h \in [m]$.
2. Output $\Delta^i, \{\boldsymbol{k}^{i,j}[x_h^j]\}_{j \in \mathcal{P}_{(1)} \setminus \{i\}}$ to every $P_i \in \mathcal{P}_{(h)}$ and $x_h^j, \{\boldsymbol{m}^{j,i}[x_h^j]\}_{i \in \mathcal{P}_{(h)} \setminus \{j\}}$ to every $P_j \in \mathcal{P}_{(1)}$.

Key queries: Upon receiving (i, P) from the adversary, where P is an efficiently computable predicate $P : \{0,1\}^\ell \to \{0,1\}$ and $i \in \mathcal{P}_{(h)}$, output 1 to the adversary if $P(\Delta^i) = 1$. Otherwise, abort.

Fig. 5. Functionality for authenticated bits

5.2 Bit Authentication Protocol

We now present our bit authentication protocol Π_{aBit}, described in Fig. 7, implementing the functionality $\mathcal{F}_{\mathsf{aBit}}$ (Fig. 5). The protocol first runs the Δ-OT protocol with short keys between every pair of parties in $\mathcal{P}_{(h)} \times \mathcal{P}_{(1)}$ to authenticate the additively shared inputs, in a standard manner. We then need to adapt the consistency check from the TinyOT-style authentication protocol presented by Hazay et al. [HSS17] to our setting of MACs with short keys distributed between two committees, to ensure that all parties input consistent values in all the COT instances.

Taking a closer look at the consistency checks in Step 3f, the first check verifies the consistency of the Δ^i values, whereas in the second set of checks we test the consistency of the individual shares x^j. To see correctness when all parties are honest, notice that in the first check, for $i \in \mathcal{P}_{(h)}$ we have:

$$z^i + \sum_{j \in (\mathcal{P}_{(1)} \setminus \{P_i\})} z^{j,i} = 0$$

$$\iff (y^i + y) \cdot \Delta^i + \sum_{j \in (\mathcal{P}_{(1)} \setminus \{P_i\})} (\boldsymbol{k}^{i,j}[y] + \boldsymbol{m}^{j,i}[y]) = 0$$

$$\iff (y^i + y) \cdot \Delta^i + \sum_{j \in (\mathcal{P}_{(1)} \setminus \{P_i\})} (y^j \cdot \Delta^i) = 0 \iff y \cdot \Delta^i + y \cdot \Delta^i = 0.$$

Macro $(\mathcal{P}_{(h)}, \mathcal{P}_{(1)})$-Bracket

On input $\{x^j\}_{j \in \mathcal{P}_{(1)}}$, authenticate the share $x^j \in \{0,1\}$, for each $j \in \mathcal{P}_{(1)}$, as follows:

P_j CORRUPT: Receive a MAC $m^{j,i} \in \mathbb{F}_2^\ell$ from $\mathcal{A}$ and compute the keys $\{k^{i,j} = m^{j,i} + x^j \cdot \Delta^i\}_{i \in (\mathcal{P}_{(h)} \setminus \{P_j\})}$.

OTHERWISE:

1. Sample honest parties' keys $k^{i,j} \leftarrow \mathbb{F}_2^\ell$, for $P_i \in \mathcal{P}_{(h)} \setminus (\mathcal{A} \cup \{P_j\})$.
2. Receive keys $k^{i,j} \in \mathbb{F}_2^\ell$, for each $P_i \in \mathcal{A} \cap \mathcal{P}_{(h)}$, from the adversary.
3. Compute the MACs $m^{j,i} = k^{i,j} + x^j \cdot \Delta^i$, where $P_i \in \mathcal{P}_{(h)}$.

Output $[x]_\Delta^{\mathcal{P}_{(h)}, \mathcal{P}_{(1)}}$.

Fig. 6. Macro used by $\mathcal{F}_{\mathsf{aBit}}$ to authenticate bits

For a corrupt party who misbehaves during the protocol, there are two potential deviations:

1. A corrupt $P_i, i \in \mathcal{P}_{(h)}^{\mathcal{A}}$ provides an inconsistent $\Delta^{i,j}$ when acting as a sender in $\mathcal{F}_{\Delta\text{-ROT}}^{m,\ell}$ with different honest parties, i.e. $\Delta^i \neq \Delta^{i,j}$ for some $j \in \mathcal{P}_{(1)} \setminus \mathcal{A}$.
2. A corrupt $P_j, j \in \mathcal{P}_{(1)}^{\mathcal{A}}$ provides an inconsistent input $x_\iota^{i,j}$ when acting as a receiver in $\mathcal{F}_{\Delta\text{-ROT}}^{m,\ell}$ with different parties, i.e. $x_\iota^i \neq x_\iota^{i,j}$, for some $j \in \mathcal{P}_{(h)} \setminus \mathcal{A}$.

Note that in the above, the 'correct' inputs Δ^i, x^j for a corrupt $P_i \in \mathcal{P}_{(h)}$ or $P_j \in \mathcal{P}_{(1)}$ are defined to be those in the $\mathcal{F}_{\Delta\text{-ROT}}$ instance with some fixed, honest party $P_{i_1} \in \mathcal{P}_{(1)}$ or $P_{j_1} \in \mathcal{P}_{(h)}$, respectively. We now prove the following two claims.

Claim 5.1. *Assuming a non-abort execution, then for every corrupted party $P_i, i \in \mathcal{P}_{(h)}^{\mathcal{A}}$, all Δ^i are consistent.*

Proof. In order to ensure that all Δ^i are consistent we use the first check. More precisely, we fix $P_j \in \mathcal{P}_{(h)}^{\mathcal{A}}$ and check that $\sum_{i \in [n]} z^{i,j} = 0, \forall j$. Since we require that $y \in \{0,1\}^\lambda$, the probability to pass the check is $1/2^\lambda$. More formally, let us assume that a corrupt P_j^* uses inconsistent $\Delta^{j,i}$ in $\mathcal{F}_{\Delta\text{-ROT}}$ with some $i \notin \mathcal{P}_{(h)}^{\mathcal{A}}$, then to pass the check P_j^* can send adversarial values in step 3c, i.e. when it broadcasts values $\bar{y}^j$, or in step 3d, when committing to the values $z^{j,i}$. Let $e_y \in \{0,1\}^\lambda$ denote an additive error so that $\sum_{i \in [n]} \bar{y}^i = y + e_y$, and let $e_z \in \{0,1\}^\lambda$ denote an additive error so that $\sum_{j \in \mathcal{P}_{(h)}^{\mathcal{A}}} \hat{z}^{j,i} = \sum_{j \in \mathcal{P}_{(h)}^{\mathcal{A}}} z^{j,i} + e_z$. Finally, let $\delta^{j,i} = \Delta^j + \Delta^{j,i}$. Then if the check passes, it holds that:

$$0 = \sum_i z^{i,j} = e_z + z^j + \sum_{i \neq j} z^{i,j} = e_z + (y + e_y + y^j) \cdot \Delta^j + \sum_{i \neq j} y^i \cdot \Delta^{j,i}$$

$$\iff \quad e_z + e_y \cdot \Delta^j = \sum_{i \neq j} y^i \cdot \delta^{j,i},$$

which implies that the additive errors e_z and e_y, that make the above equation equal to zero, depend on the y^i values, and that the adversary has to guess at least one of them in order to pass the check. This event happens with probability $2^{-\lambda}$ since the only information the adversary has about these values is that they are uniform additive shares of y, due to the randomization in step 3c. $\qquad \square$

Claim 5.2. *Assuming a non-abort execution, then for every corrupted party $P_j, j \in \mathcal{P}_{(1)}^{\mathcal{A}}$, all $x_\iota^{i,j}$ are consistent.*

Proof. We need to check that a corrupt P_j^* cannot input inconsistent $x^{j,i}$ to different honest parties without being caught. For every ordered pair of parties (P_i, P_j), we can define P_j's MAC $m^{j,i}[y]$ and P_i's key $k^{i,j}[y]$ respectively as

$$\sum_{\iota=1}^{m} \chi_\iota \cdot m^{j,i}[x_\iota] + \sum_{k=1}^{\lambda} X^{k-1} \cdot m^{j,i}[r_k] \quad \text{and}$$

$$\sum_{\iota=1}^{m} \chi_\iota \cdot k^{i,j}[x_\iota] + \sum_{k=1}^{\lambda} X^{k-1} \cdot k^{i,j}[r_k].$$

A corrupt P_j can commit to incorrect MACs $\hat{z}^{j,i}$, so that $\hat{z}^{j,i} = z^{j,i} + e_z^{j,i}$ and $\hat{y}^j = y^{j,i} + e_y^{j,i}$. In order to have the check passed, we have:

$$z^{j,i} + e_z^{j,i} = k[y]^{i,j} + (y^{j,i} + e_y^j) \cdot \Delta^i,$$

Which happens if and only if:

$$e_z^{j,i} + (y^{j,i} + e_y^j) \cdot \Delta^i = m^{j,i}[y] + k^{i,j}[y]$$

$$= \left(\sum_{\iota=1}^{m} \chi_\iota \cdot (x_\iota^j + \delta_\iota^{j,i}) + \sum_{k=1}^{\lambda} X^{k-1} \cdot (r_k^j + \delta_k'^{j,i}) \right) \cdot \Delta^i$$

$$\iff e_z^{j,i} = \left(y^{j,i} + e_y^j + \sum_{\iota=1}^{m} \chi_\iota \cdot (x_\iota^j + \delta_\iota^{j,i}) + \sum_{k=1}^{\lambda} X^{k-1} \cdot (r_k^j + \delta_k'^{j,i}) \right) \cdot \Delta^i$$

$$= \left(e_y^j + \sum_{\iota=1}^{m} \chi_\iota \cdot \delta_\iota^{j,i} + \sum_{k=1}^{\lambda} X^{k-1} \cdot \delta_k'^{j,i} \right) \cdot \Delta^i.$$

Then there are two cases for which the adversary can pass the check:

1. In case $e_z^{j,i} = (e_y^j + \sum_{\iota=1}^{m} \chi_\iota \cdot \delta_\iota^{j,i} + \sum_{k=1}^{\lambda} X^{k-1} \cdot \delta_k'^{j,i}) \cdot \Delta^i \neq 0$ the adversary needs to guess Δ^i, which can only happen with probability $2^{-\ell}$. Note that in order to pass this check the adversary needs to guess all honest parties' keys.

This is due to the fact that a corrupted P_j opens the same $\hat{y}^j$ to all parties, so if it cheats and provides an inconsistent value then it must pass the above check with respect to all honest parties. Therefore, the overall probability of passing this check is $2^{-\ell h} \leq 2^{-\lambda}$.

2. In case $e_z^{j,i} = 0$ and $e_y^j = \sum_{\iota=1}^m \chi_\iota \cdot \delta_\iota^{j,i} + \sum_{k=1}^\lambda X^{k-1} \cdot \delta_k'^{j,i}, \forall i \notin \mathcal{P}_{(1)}^A$. Assuming that there is at least one $i \notin \mathcal{P}_{(h)}^A$ s.t. $\delta_\iota^{j,i} = \delta^i = 0$ (recall that we view the inputs of P_j in the interaction with party P_{j_1} as the 'correct' inputs, then there must be at least one party for which this condition holds). This implies that $e_y^j = 0$ as well. Thus, for every $i \notin \mathcal{P}_{(h)}^A \cup j_1$ it needs to holds that

$$0 = \sum_{\iota=1}^m \chi_\iota \cdot \delta_\iota^{j,i} + \sum_{k=1}^\lambda X^{k-1} \cdot \delta_k'^{j,i}.$$

Since each χ_ι is uniformly random in $\mathbb{F}_{2^\lambda}$ and independent of the $\delta^{j,i}, \delta'^{j,i}$ values, it is easy to see that this only holds with probability $2^{-\lambda}$ if any $\delta_\iota^{j,i}$ is non-zero. □

In the full version we prove the following theorem.

Theorem 5.1. *Protocol* $\Pi_{\mathsf{aBit}}^{\mathcal{P}_{(h)}, \mathcal{P}_{(1)}, m, \ell}$ *securely implements the functionality* $\mathcal{F}_{\mathsf{aBit}}^{\mathcal{P}_{(h)}, \mathcal{P}_{(1)}, m, \ell}$ *in the* $(\mathcal{F}_{\Delta\text{-ROT}}^{m,\ell}, \mathcal{F}_{\mathsf{Rand}}, \mathcal{F}_{\mathsf{Commit}})$-*hybrid model.*

5.3   Efficiency Analysis

We now analyse the efficiency of our protocol and compare it with the previous best known approach to secret-shared bit authentication. When there are n parties with h honest, the previous best approach would be to use the standard TinyOT-style MAC scheme (as in [WRK17b, HSS17]) inside a committee of size $n-h+1$ parties, to guarantee at least one honest party. Here, the MACs must be of length at least λ, and the amortized communication complexity can be around $\lambda(n-h+1)(n-h)$ bits per authenticated bit. In contrast, in our scheme we have two committees of sizes n_1 and n_2, with h and 1 honest party, respectively. If we suppose the committees are deterministically chosen from a set of n parties with h honest, then we get $n_1 = n$ and $n_2 = n - h + 1$. To ensure security of the MAC scheme we need MACs of length $\ell \geq \lambda/h$, for statistical security λ. This gives an amortized complexity for creating a MAC of around $\ell n_1 n_2 = \lambda n(n-h+1)/h$ bits. Compared with the TinyOT approach, this gives a reduction in communication of $h(n-h)/n$ times in our protocol. This is maximized when $h = n/2$, with a $n/4$ times reduction in communication cost over TinyOT, and for smaller h we still have savings for all $h > 1$.

Protocol $\Pi_{\mathsf{aBit}}^{\mathcal{P}_{(h)},\mathcal{P}_{(1)},m,\ell}$

PARAMETERS: m, number of authenticated bits; ℓ, key length.

Initialize: On input Δ^i from each $P_i \in \mathcal{P}_{(h)}$, every pair of parties $(P_i, P_j) \in \mathcal{P}_{(h)} \times \mathcal{P}_{(1)}$, $i \neq j$ calls $\mathcal{F}_{\Delta\text{-ROT}}^\ell$ functionality with input (Init, Δ^i) from P_i and (Init) from P_j.

aBit: On input $(x_1^j, \ldots, x_m^j) \in \{0,1\}^m$ from each $P_j \in \mathcal{P}_{(1)}$:

1. Each $P_j \in \mathcal{P}_{(1)}$ samples λ random bits r_k^j, $k \in [\lambda]$.
2. Call $\mathcal{F}_{\Delta\text{-ROT}}^\ell$ with inputs (x_ι^j, r_k^j) from P_j, so P_j gets $t^{j,i}$ and P_i gets $q^{i,j}$, such that for $\iota \in [m], k \in [\lambda]$,

$$t_\iota^{j,i} + q_\iota^{i,j} = x_\iota^j \cdot \Delta^i \qquad t_k^{j,i} + q_k^{i,j} = r_k^j \cdot \Delta^i$$

   For $\iota \in [m]$, define $[x_\iota]^{\mathcal{P}_{(h)},\mathcal{P}_{(1)}}$ as follows.
   Each $P_i \in \mathcal{P}_{(h)}$ sets $\boldsymbol{k}^{i,j}[x_\iota] = \boldsymbol{q}^{i,j}$ for $j \in (\mathcal{P}_{(1)} \setminus \{P_i\})$ and each $P_j \in \mathcal{P}_{(1)}$ sets $\boldsymbol{m}^{j,i}[x_\iota] = \boldsymbol{t}_\iota^{j,i}$ for $i \in (\mathcal{P}_{(h)} \setminus \{P_j\})$.
   For $k \in [s]$, the parties define $[r_k]^{\mathcal{P}_{(h)},\mathcal{P}_{(1)}}$: Each $P_i \in \mathcal{P}_{(h)}$ sets $\boldsymbol{k}^{i,j}[r_k] = \boldsymbol{q}_k^{i,j}$ for $j \in (\mathcal{P}_{(1)} \setminus \{P_i\})$ and each $P_j \in \mathcal{P}_{(1)}$ sets $\boldsymbol{m}^{j,i}[r_k] = \boldsymbol{t}_k^{j,i}$ for $i \in (\mathcal{P}_{(h)} \setminus \{P_j\})$.
3. Check consistency of the inputs as follows:
   (a) Call $\mathcal{F}_{\mathsf{Rand}}$ to obtain m field elements $\chi_\iota \in \mathbb{F}_2^\lambda, \iota \in [m]$.
   (b) Locally compute, over $\mathbb{F}_{2^\lambda}$, the shares

$$[y]^{\mathcal{P}_{(h)},\mathcal{P}_{(1)}} = \sum_{\iota=1}^{m} \chi_\iota \cdot [x_\iota]^{\mathcal{P}_{(h)},\mathcal{P}_{(1)}} + \sum_{k=1}^{\lambda} X^{k-1} \cdot [r_k]^{\mathcal{P}_{(h)},\mathcal{P}_{(1)}} \,,$$

   so that each $P_j \in \mathcal{P}_{(1)}$ holds a share $y^j \in \mathbb{F}_2^\lambda$, and MACs $\{\boldsymbol{m}^{j,i}[y]\}_{i \in \mathcal{P}_{(h)} \setminus P_j}$ and each $P_i \in \mathcal{P}_{(h)}$ holds keys $\{\boldsymbol{k}^{i,j}[y]\}_{j \in \mathcal{P}_{(1)} \setminus P_i}$.
   (c) The parties in $\mathcal{P}_{(1)}$ call $\mathcal{F}_{\mathsf{Zero}}^\ell$ so that each $P_j \in \mathcal{P}_{(1)}$ obtains a zero-share $\rho^j \in \{0,1\}^\ell$. P_j then broadcasts $\bar{y}^j := y^j + \rho^j$, and reconstructs $y = \sum_{j \in \mathcal{P}_{(1)}} \bar{y}^j$.
   (d) Each $P_i \in \mathcal{P}_{(h)}$ defines and commits, to all parties in $\mathcal{P}_{(h)}$, the following values. Note that $y^i = 0$ if $P_i \notin \mathcal{P}_{(1)}$:

$$z^i = (y^i + y) \cdot \Delta^i + \sum_{j \in \mathcal{P}_{(1)} \setminus P_i} \boldsymbol{k}^{i,j}[y].$$

   (e) Each $P_j \in \mathcal{P}_{(1)}$ defines and commits, to all parties in $\mathcal{P}_{(h)}$:

$$y^j, \quad \{z^{j,i} = \boldsymbol{m}^{j,i}[y]\}_{i \in \mathcal{P}_{(h)} \setminus P_j}.$$

   (f) Each party in $\mathcal{P}_{(h)} \cup \mathcal{P}_{(1)}$ opens its commitments and parties in $\mathcal{P}_{(h)}$ check that:

$$\forall i \in \mathcal{P}_{(h)}, \quad z^i + \sum_{j \in \mathcal{P}_{(1)} \setminus P_i} z^{j,i} = 0$$

   and

$$\forall j \in \mathcal{P}_{(1)}, i \in \mathcal{P}_{(h)} \setminus P_j, \quad z^{j,i} = \boldsymbol{k}^{i,j}[y] + y^j \cdot \Delta^i.$$

   If any of these checks fails, abort.
4. Output $[x_1], \ldots, [x_m]$.

Fig. 7. Protocol for authentication of random shared bits using committees

6 Actively Secure MPC Protocol with Short Keys

Similarly to prior constructions such as [DPSZ12, NNOB12, FKOS15, KOS16], our protocol is in the pre-processing model where the main difference is that the computation is carried out via two random committees $\mathcal{P}_{(h)}$ and $\mathcal{P}_{(1)}$. The preprocessing phase is function and input independent, and provides all the correlated randomness needed for the online phase where the function is securely evaluated.

6.1 The Online Phase

Our online protocol, shown in Fig. 8, runs mostly as that of [DPSZ12, DKL+13] within a small committee $\mathcal{P}_{(1)} \subseteq \mathcal{P}$ with at least 1 honest party. The main difference is that we need the help of the bigger $\mathcal{P}_{(h)} \subseteq \mathcal{P}$ committee with at least h honest parties to authenticate the inputs of any $P_i \in \mathcal{P}$ using the $[\cdot]^{\mathcal{P}_{(h)}, \mathcal{P}_{(1)}}$-representation before converting them to the more compact $\llbracket \cdot \rrbracket$-representation described in Sect. 3.2.

The Boolean MPC Protocol - Π_{BBB}

Prep: Parties call $\mathcal{F}_{\mathsf{Preprocessing}}$ with (Prep, m, M) to generate m random $[\cdot]^{\mathcal{P}_{(h)}, \mathcal{P}_{(1)}}$ bits and M random multiplication triples with compact MACs.

Input: To authenticate an input x of $P_i \in \mathcal{P}$:

    1. Call the **Private Open** command in $\Pi_{\mathsf{PrivateOpen}}^{\mathcal{P}_{(h)}, \mathcal{P}_{(1)}, P_i}$ on an unused bit $([r]^{\mathcal{P}_{(h)}, \mathcal{P}_{(1)}}, P_i)$ from **Prep**, so only P_i learns r.

    2. Call the **Batch Check** command in $\Pi_{\mathsf{PrivateOpen}}^{\mathcal{P}_{(h)}, \mathcal{P}_{(1)}, P_i}$ on all the privately opened values in the previous step. If the check fails, abort.

    3. P_i broadcasts $d = x + r$ to $\mathcal{P}_{(1)}$, who compute $[x]^{\mathcal{P}_{(h)}, \mathcal{P}_{(1)}} = [r]^{\mathcal{P}_{(h)}, \mathcal{P}_{(1)}} + d$.

    4. Call $\Pi_{\mathsf{MACCompact}}$ on input $[x]^{\mathcal{P}_{(h)}, \mathcal{P}_{(1)}}$ to obtain $\llbracket x \rrbracket$.

Add: On input $(\llbracket x \rrbracket, \llbracket y \rrbracket)$, locally compute $\llbracket x + y \rrbracket = \llbracket x \rrbracket + \llbracket y \rrbracket$.

Multiply: On input $\llbracket x \rrbracket$, $\llbracket y \rrbracket$, parties in $\mathcal{P}_{(1)}$ do the following:

    1. Pick an unused random multiplicative triple from **Prep** ($\llbracket a \rrbracket$, $\llbracket b \rrbracket$, $\llbracket c \rrbracket$).

    2. Compute $\llbracket \epsilon \rrbracket = \llbracket x \rrbracket + \llbracket a \rrbracket$, and $\llbracket \rho \rrbracket = \llbracket y \rrbracket + \llbracket b \rrbracket$ and call $\Pi_{\llbracket \mathsf{Open} \rrbracket}$ on these to reveal ϵ, ρ to $\mathcal{P}_{(1)}$.

    3. Parties set $\llbracket x \cdot y \rrbracket = \llbracket c \rrbracket + \epsilon \cdot \llbracket b \rrbracket + \rho \cdot \llbracket a \rrbracket + \epsilon \cdot \rho$.

Output: To output a value $\llbracket x \rrbracket$ to $\mathcal{P}$ or a subset of it, do the following:

    1. Call **BatchCheck** on $\Pi_{\llbracket \mathsf{Open} \rrbracket}$ for all $\llbracket \cdot \rrbracket$ values opened so far. If the check fails, abort.

    2. Call commands **Open** and **Single Check** of $\Pi_{\llbracket \mathsf{Open} \rrbracket}$ on input $\llbracket x \rrbracket$. If the check fails, abort, otherwise accept x as a valid output.

Fig. 8. The Boolean MPC protocol

6.2   The Preprocessing Phase

The task of $\mathcal{F}_{\text{Preprocessing}}$ is to create random authenticated bits under the $[\cdot]^{\mathcal{P}_{(h)}, \mathcal{P}_{(1)}}$-representation and random authenticated triples under the compact $[\![\cdot]\!]$-representation.

7   Triple Generation

Here we present our triple generation protocol implementing the functionality described in Fig. 9. First, protocol $\Pi_{\text{HalfAuthTriple}}$ (Fig. 11) implements the functionality $\mathcal{F}_{\text{HalfAuthTriple}}$ (Fig. 10) to compute cross terms in triples: each party $P_i \in \mathcal{P}_{(h)}$ inputs random shares $y_k^i, k \in [m]$, and committees $\mathcal{P}_{(h)}, \mathcal{P}_{(1)}$ obtain random representations $[x_k]_\Delta$ as well as shares of the cross terms defined by $\sum_{i \in \mathcal{P}_{(h)}} \sum_{j \neq \mathcal{P}_{(1)} \setminus \{P_i\}} x_k^j \cdot y_k^i, k \in [m]$.

Given this intermediate functionality, protocol Π_{Triple} (Fig. 12) implements $\mathcal{F}_{\text{Triple}}^{m,\ell}$ (Fig. 9) computing correct authenticated and non-leaky triples $([\![x_k]\!], [\![y_k]\!], [\![z_k]\!])$ such that $(\sum_{j \in \mathcal{P}_{(1)}} x_k^j) \cdot (\sum_{j \in \mathcal{P}_{(1)}} y_k^j) = \sum_{j \in \mathcal{P}_{(1)}} z_k^j$. Checking correctness and removing leakage is achieved using classic cut-and-choose and bucketing techniques. Note that even though the final triples are under the compact $[\![\cdot]\!]$-representation we produce them first using $[\cdot]^{\mathcal{P}_{(h)}, \mathcal{P}_{(1)}}$-representations in order to *generate* MACs more efficiently and having an efficient implementation of $\mathcal{F}_{\text{HalfAuthTriple}}$.

It is crucial to note that the security of $\Pi_{\text{HalfAuthTriple}}$ is based on the hardness of RSD, and for this reason the number of triples r generated by this protocol depends on the security RSD. So while essentially an unlimited number of random correlated OTs and random authenticated bits can be produced as described on previous sections, a naive use of short keys would actually result in an upper bound on the number of triples that can be produced securely. To fix this issue, during $\Pi_{\text{HalfAuthTriple}}$ we make the parties 'switch the correlation' on representations $[x]_\Delta$, so they output a new representation under an independent correlation $[x]_{\tilde{\Delta}}$, with $\Delta \neq \tilde{\Delta}$ being the relevant value for the RSD assumption. Finally, the fact that $\tilde{\Delta}$ is short combined with the adversarial possibility of querying some predicates about it requires the reduction to use an interactive version of RSD, which we denote by $\mathcal{L}$-DRSD as in Definition 2.1.

7.1   Half Authenticated Triples

Here we show how $\Pi_{\text{HalfAuthTriple}}^{\mathcal{P}_{(h)}, \mathcal{P}_{(1)}, r, \ell}$ securely computes cross terms in triples. The main difficulty arises from modelling the leakage due to using short keys in the real world, and proving that it cannot be distinguished from uniformly random. Looking at individual parties, security relies on the fact that on step 6a of the protocol $s_k^{i,j}$ is a fresh, random sharing of zero and hence $y_k^{i,j}$ is perfectly masked. Nevertheless, when considering the *joint* leakage from all honest parties, the $\mathcal{L}$-DRSD assumption kicks in and requires a more thoughtful consideration.

Security is showed in the following theorem, proved in the full version.

Functionality $\mathcal{F}_{\text{Triple}}^{m,\ell}$

PARAMETERS: m, number of multiplications; ℓ, key length.
This functionality runs in committee $\mathcal{P}_{(1)}$ only.

On input (Triples, m, ℓ) from all parties, generate m random authenticated triples as follows.
Initialize: Receive Δ^i from the adversary for each corrupt $P_i \in \mathcal{P}_{(1)}^{\mathcal{A}}$ and sample $\Delta^i \leftarrow \mathbb{F}_2^\lambda$ for each $P_i \in \mathcal{P}_{(1)} \setminus \mathcal{P}_{(1)}^{\mathcal{A}}$.
Honest parties:

1. Sample random sharings $[\![x_k]\!], [\![y_k]\!], [\![z_k]\!]$, with $x_k, y_k, z_k \leftarrow \{0,1\}$ such that $z_k = x_k \cdot y_k, k \in [m]$.

Corrupt parties: Corrupt parties choose their own randomness in the MAC shares.

Fig. 9. Functionality for triples generation.

Functionality for Half Authenticated Triples - $\mathcal{F}_{\text{HalfAuthTriple}}^{\mathcal{P}_{(h)}, \mathcal{P}_{(1)}, r, \ell}$

PARAMETERS: r, number of multiplications; ℓ, key length. The functionality runs between a set of parties $\mathcal{P} = \{P_1, \ldots, P_n\}$, containing two (possibly overlapping) subsets $\mathcal{P}_{(h)}, \mathcal{P}_{(1)}$, such that $\mathcal{P}_{(h)}$ has at least h honest parties and $\mathcal{P}_{(1)}$ has at least one honest party and an adversary $\mathcal{A}$.

1. The functionality receives correlations Δ^i from each $P_i \in \mathcal{P}_{(h)}$, picks random $[x_k]_\Delta^{\mathcal{P}_{(h)}, \mathcal{P}_{(1)}}$ for $k \in [r]$ and sends the relevant part of the representation to the relevant parties.
2. The functionality receives bits $\{y_k^{i,j}\}_{j \in (\mathcal{P}_{(1)} \setminus \{P_i\}), k \in [r]}$ from each $P_i \in \mathcal{P}_{(h)}$. Then it samples random bits $\{v_k^\tau\}_{\tau \in (\mathcal{P}_{(h)} \cup \mathcal{P}_{(1)}), k \in [r]}$, such that:

$$\sum_{\tau \in (\mathcal{P}_{(h)} \cup \mathcal{P}_{(1)})} v_k^\tau = \sum_{i \in \mathcal{P}_{(h)}} \sum_{j \in (\mathcal{P}_{(1)} \setminus \{P_i\})} x_k^j \cdot y_k^{i,j},$$

and sends $v_k^\tau, k \in [r]$, to $P_\tau \in (\mathcal{P}_{(h)} \cup \mathcal{P}_{(1)})$.

Global Key Queries: Upon receiving (i, P) from $\mathcal{A}$, where P is an efficiently computable predicate $P : \{0,1\}^\ell \to \{0,1\}$, output 1 to $\mathcal{A}$ if $P(\Delta^i) = 1$. Otherwise, output 0 to $\mathcal{A}$ and abort.

Fig. 10. Functionality for half authenticated triples

Theorem 7.1. *Protocol $\Pi_{\text{HalfAuthTriple}}^{\mathcal{P}_{(h)}, \mathcal{P}_{(1)}, r, \ell}$ securely implements $\mathcal{F}_{\text{HalfAuthTriple}}^{\mathcal{P}_{(h)}, \mathcal{P}_{(1)}, r, \ell}$ in the $(\mathcal{F}_{\text{aBit}}, \mathcal{F}_{\text{Zero}})$-hybrid model as long as $\mathcal{L}$-DRSD$_{r,h,\ell}$ is secure.*

Protocol $\Pi_{\text{HalfAuthTriple}}^{\mathcal{P}_{(h)},\mathcal{P}_{(1)},r,\ell}$

REQUIRE: r, number of multiplications; ℓ, key length. The protocol runs between a set of parties $\mathcal{P} = \{P_1, \ldots, P_n\}$, containing two (possibly overlapping) subsets $\mathcal{P}_{(h)}, \mathcal{P}_{(1)}$, such that $\mathcal{P}_{(h)}$ has at least h honest parties and $\mathcal{P}_{(1)}$ has at least one honest party.

INPUT: From all $P_i \in \mathcal{P}_{(h)}$: $\Delta^i \in \mathbb{F}_2^\ell$ and $\boldsymbol{y}^{i,j} = (y_1^{i,j}, \ldots, y_r^{i,j}) \in \mathbb{F}_2^m$, where j ranges for every $P_j \in \mathcal{P}_{(1)} \setminus \{P_i\}$.

COMMON INPUT: Random functions $\mathsf{H}_{i,j} : [r] \times \{0,1\} \times \{0,1\}^\ell \to \{0,1\}$ for $P_i \in \mathcal{P}_{(h)}, P_j \in \mathcal{P}_{(1)}$.

OUTPUT: Values $[x_1]_\Delta^{\mathcal{P}_{(h)},\mathcal{P}_{(1)}}, \ldots, [x_r]_\Delta^{\mathcal{P}_{(h)},\mathcal{P}_{(1)}}$ and shares $v_1^j, \ldots, v_r^j$ for $P_j \in \mathcal{P}_{(1)}$.

1. Parties call $\mathcal{F}_{\text{aBit}}^{\mathcal{P}_{(h)},\mathcal{P}_{(1)},m,\ell}$ on input random $\{x_k^j\}_{k\in[r]}$ from $P_j \in \mathcal{P}_{(1)}$ to obtain $[x_k]_\Delta^{\mathcal{P}_{(h)},\mathcal{P}_{(1)}}, k \in [r]$.

2. Parties initialize a new $\mathcal{F}_{\text{aBit}}^{\mathcal{P}_{(h)},\mathcal{P}_{(1)},r,\ell}$ instance with $\Delta^i + \tilde{\Delta}^i$, and then call this on input the shares $(x_1^j, \ldots, x_r^j)$ to obtain $[x_1]_{\Delta+\tilde{\Delta}}^{\mathcal{P}_{(h)},\mathcal{P}_{(1)}}, \ldots, [x_r]_{\Delta+\tilde{\Delta}}^{\mathcal{P}_{(h)},\mathcal{P}_{(1)}}$.

3. Each $P_i \in \mathcal{P}_{(h)}$ sets $\boldsymbol{k}_{\tilde{\Delta}}^{i,j}[x_k] = \boldsymbol{k}_\Delta^{i,j}[x_k] + \boldsymbol{k}_{\Delta+\tilde{\Delta}}^{i,j}[x_k]$ for $k \in [r], j \in \{\mathcal{P}_{(1)} \setminus P_i\}$.

4. Each $P_j \in \mathcal{P}_{(1)}$ sets $\boldsymbol{m}_{\tilde{\Delta}}^{j,i}[x_k] = \boldsymbol{m}_\Delta^{j,i}[x_k] + \boldsymbol{m}_{\Delta+\tilde{\Delta}}^{j,i}[x_k]$ for $k \in [r], i \in \{\mathcal{P}_{(h)} \setminus P_j\}$.

5. Parties $P_i \in \mathcal{P}_{(h)}$ call $\mathcal{F}_{\text{Zero}}$ so that each P_i obtains shares $\{(s_1^{i,j}, \ldots, s_r^{i,j})\}_{j\in\mathcal{P}_{(1)}}$ s.t. $\sum_{i\in\mathcal{P}_{(h)}} s_k^{i,j} = 0, \forall k \in [r]$.

6. For each $k \in [r]$, $P_i \in \mathcal{P}_{(h)}$ and $P_j \in \mathcal{P}_{(1)}$:
   (a) $P_i \in \mathcal{P}_{(h)}$ computes:
   $$d_k^{i,j} = \mathsf{H}_{i,j}(k, 0, \boldsymbol{k}_{\tilde{\Delta}}^{i,j}[x_k]) + \mathsf{H}_{i,j}(k, 1, \boldsymbol{k}_{\tilde{\Delta}}^{i,j}[x_k] + \tilde{\Delta}^i) + y_k^{i,j} + s_k^{i,j},$$
   and privately sends it to P_j, for each $P_j \in (\mathcal{P}_{(1)} \setminus \{P_i\})$.
   (b) Each $P_j \in \mathcal{P}_{(1)}$ computes, for $i \in (\mathcal{P}_{(h)} \setminus \{P_j\})$:
   $$t_k^{j,i} = \mathsf{H}_{i,j}(k, x_k^j, \boldsymbol{m}_{\tilde{\Delta}}^{j,i}[x_k]) + x_k^j \cdot d_k^{i,j}.$$
   (c) Each $P_i \in \mathcal{P}_{(h)}$ computes (where $x_k^i = s_k^{i,i} = 0$ if $P_i \notin \mathcal{P}_{(1)}$):
   $$t_k^{i,i} = \sum_{j\in(\mathcal{P}_{(1)}\setminus\{P_i\})} \mathsf{H}_{i,j}(k, 0, \boldsymbol{k}_{\tilde{\Delta}}^{i,j}[x_k]) + x_k^i \cdot s_k^{i,i}.$$

7. Parties in $\mathcal{P}_{(h)} \cup \mathcal{P}_{(1)}$ call $\mathcal{F}_{\text{Zero}}$ so that each P_τ obtains shares $(\rho_1^\tau, \ldots, \rho_r^\tau)$ such that $\sum_{\tau\in(\mathcal{P}_{(h)}\cup\mathcal{P}_{(1)})} \rho_k^\tau = 0, \forall k \in [r]$.

8. For $k \in [r]$, each $P_j \in \mathcal{P}_{(1)}$ computes $v_k^j = \sum_{i\in\mathcal{P}_{(h)}} t_k^{j,i} + \rho_k^j$ and each $P_i \in (\mathcal{P}_{(h)} \setminus \mathcal{P}_{(1)})$ sets $v_k^i = t_k^{i,i} + \rho_k^i$.

Fig. 11. Protocol for half authenticated triples

7.2 Correct Non-leaky Authenticated Triples

Here we describe the protocol Π_{Triple} (Fig. 12) to create m correct random authenticated triples with compact MACs $[\![x_k]\!], [\![y_k]\!], [\![z_k]\!], k \in [m]$.

First, parties in $\mathcal{P}_{(h)} \cup \mathcal{P}_{(1)}$ call $\mathcal{F}_{\mathsf{aBit}}$ obtaining $m' = m \cdot B^2 + c$ random authenticated bits $\{[y_k]^{\mathcal{P}_{(h)}, \mathcal{P}_{(1)}}\}_{k \in m'}$, where B and c are parameters of the sub-protocol $\Pi_{\mathsf{TripleBucketing}}$ (Fig. 13). Then, each $P_j \in \mathcal{P}_{(1)}$ reshares their values y_k^j to parties in $\mathcal{P}_{(h)}$ obtaining $[\hat{y}_k]_{k \in m'}^{\mathcal{P}_{(h)}, \mathcal{P}_{(h)}}$ such that $\sum_{i \in \mathcal{P}_{(h)}} \hat{y}_k^i = y_k, k \in [m]$. This allows $\mathcal{P}_{(h)} \cup \mathcal{P}_{(1)}$ to call $\mathcal{F}_{\mathsf{HalfAuthTriple}}^{\mathcal{P}_{(h)}, \mathcal{P}_{(1)}, r, \ell}$ $\hat{m} = m/r$ times, on inputs $\{\hat{y}_{(\iota-1) \cdot r + k}\}_{k \in [r]}$, for each $\iota \in \hat{m}$. The outputs of each of these calls are the sharings $v_{(\iota-1) \cdot r + k}^\tau$, $\tau \in \mathcal{P}_{(h)} \cup \mathcal{P}_{(1)}$ and $k \in [r]$, of r cross terms products, i.e.

$$\sum_{\tau \in \mathcal{P}_{(h)} \cup \mathcal{P}_{(1)}} v_{(\iota-1) \cdot r + k}^\tau = \sum_{i \in \mathcal{P}_{(h)}} \sum_{j \in \mathcal{P}_{(1)}} x_{(\iota-1) \cdot r + k}^j \cdot \hat{y}_{(\iota-1) \cdot r + k}^i.$$

Notice that the number r of cross terms computed by $\mathcal{F}_{\mathsf{HalfAuthTriple}}^{\mathcal{P}_{(h)}, \mathcal{P}_{(1)}, r, \ell}$ depends on the leaky DRSD problem, and for this reason the protocol needs to call the functionality $\hat{m}$ times to obtain all the m' outputs it needs.

After this, parties in $\mathcal{P}_{(h)}$ reshare all the v_k^i, $k \in m'$ to $\mathcal{P}_{(1)}$, so that each $P_j \in \mathcal{P}_{(1)}$ gets $\hat{v}_k^j$, $k \in [m']$, where

$$\sum_{j \in \mathcal{P}_{(1)}} \hat{v}_k^j = \sum_{j \in \mathcal{P}_{(1)}} x_k^j \sum_{i \in \mathcal{P}_{(1)} \backslash j} y_k^i = \sum_{\tau \in \mathcal{P}_{(h)} \cup \mathcal{P}_{(1)}} v_k^\tau, \tag{1}$$

so that parties in $\mathcal{P}_{(1)}$ can locally add shares $x_k^j \cdot y_k^j$ to $\hat{v}_k^j$ obtaining z_k^j, $k \in [m']$.

Finally, $\mathcal{P}_{(h)} \cup \mathcal{P}_{(1)}$ call $\mathcal{F}_{\mathsf{aBit}}$ to obtain $[z_k]^{\mathcal{P}_{(h)}, \mathcal{P}_{(1)}}$, and run the $\Pi_{\mathsf{TripleBucketing}}$ subprotocol. This subprotocol is similar to the bucket-based cut-and-choose technique introduced by Larraia et al. [LOS14] and optimized by Frederiksen et al. [FKOS15], but adapted to run with two committees. It takes as input $m' = B^2 \cdot m + c$ triples. First, in Step I and II, it ensures that all the triples are correctly generated sacrificing $B \cdot m \cdot (B - 1) + c$ triples, and then (Step III) it uses random bucketing technique to remove potential leakage on the x_k values obtaining m private and correct triples. All the MACs on previously opened values are eventually checked (Step IV) calling the **Batch Check** command in $\Pi_{[\mathsf{Open}]}$ (Fig. 1). Finally, on that last step, the remaining triples are converted to SPDZ-style triples in $\mathcal{P}_{(1)}$ using $\Pi_{\mathsf{MACCompact}}$.

Correctness easily follows form the discussion above:

$$\sum_{j \in \mathcal{P}_{(1)}} z_k^j = \sum_{j \in \mathcal{P}_{(1)}} x_k^j \cdot y_k^j + \hat{v}_k^j, \tag{2}$$

where $\hat{v}_k^j$ is the re-sharing inside $\mathcal{P}_{(1)}$ of $\mathcal{F}_{\mathsf{HalfAuthTriple}}^{\mathcal{P}_{(h)}, \mathcal{P}_{(1)}, r, \ell}$'s output. More precisely, using Eq. 1 we can rewrite Eq. 2 as follows:

$$\sum_{j \in \mathcal{P}_{(1)}} z_k^j = \sum_{j \in \mathcal{P}_{(1)}} x_k^j \cdot y_k^j + \sum_{j \in \mathcal{P}_{(1)}} x_k^j \cdot \sum_{i \in \mathcal{P}_{(1)} \backslash j} y_k^i$$

$$= \sum_{j \in \mathcal{P}_{(1)}} x_k^j \cdot \left(y_k^j + \sum_{i \in \mathcal{P}_{(1)} \backslash j} y_k^i \right) = \left(\sum_{j \in \mathcal{P}_{(1)}} x_k^j \right) \cdot \left(\sum_{j \in \mathcal{P}_{(1)}} y_k^j \right).$$

Security is showed in the following theorem, proved in the full version.

Protocol for triples generation - $\Pi_{\text{Triple}}^{m,r}$

PARAMETERS: Let B, c be parameters as needed for $\Pi_{\text{TripleBucketing}}$ and $m' = m \cdot B^2 + c$. Let r be as needed for the security of the leaky DRSD problem in $\mathcal{F}_{\text{HalfAuthTriple}}^{\mathcal{P}_{(h)}, \mathcal{P}_{(1)}, r, \ell}$.

Initialize: Parties initialize $\mathcal{F}_{\text{aBit}}$ which outputs Δ^i to each $P_i \in \mathcal{P}_{(h)}$.

Triple Computation:

1. Parties in $\mathcal{P}_{(h)} \cup \mathcal{P}_{(1)}$ call $\mathcal{F}_{\text{aBit}}^{\mathcal{P}_{(h)}, \mathcal{P}_{(1)}, m', \ell}$ on input random $\{y_k^j\}_{k \in [m']}$ from $P_j \in \mathcal{P}_{(1)}$ and obtains random authenticated shares $\{[y_k]^{\mathcal{P}_{(h)}, \mathcal{P}_{(1)}}\}_{k \in [m']}$.

2. Reshare $y_k, k \in [m']$ from $\mathcal{P}_{(1)}$ to $\mathcal{P}_{(h)}$ as follows:
   - Each $P_j \in \mathcal{P}_{(1)} \setminus \mathcal{P}_{(h)}$ secret shares $y_k^j = \sum_{i \in \mathcal{P}_{(h)}} y_k^{i,j}$ and sends $y_k^{i,j}$ to $P_i \in \mathcal{P}_{(h)}$.
   - Each $P_i \in \mathcal{P}_{(h)}$ sets $\hat{y}_k^i = y_k^i + \sum_{j \in \mathcal{P}_{(1)}} y_k^{i,j}$, where $y_k^i = 0$ if $P_i \notin \mathcal{P}_{(1)}$.

3. Let $\hat{m} = \lceil m'/r \rceil$. For $\iota \in [\hat{m}]$, the parties call $\mathcal{F}_{\text{HalfAuthTriple}}^{\mathcal{P}_{(h)}, \mathcal{P}_{(1)}, r, \ell}$ on input $\{\hat{y}_{(\iota-1) \cdot r + k}^{i,j}\}_{k \in [r], j \in \mathcal{P}_{(1)}}$ from $P_i \in \mathcal{P}_{(h)}$, where $\hat{y}_{(\iota-1) \cdot r + k}^{i,j} = \hat{y}_{(\iota-1) \cdot r + k}^i, \forall j \in \mathcal{P}_{(1)}$, to obtain random $\{[x_{(\iota-1) \cdot r + k}]^{\mathcal{P}_{(h)}, \mathcal{P}_{(1)}}\}_{k \in [r]}$, and $\{v_{(\iota-1) \cdot r + k}^\tau\}_{\tau \in \mathcal{P}_{(h)} \cup \mathcal{P}_{(1)}, k \in [r]}, \forall \iota \in [\hat{m}]$.

4. Reshare $v_k^\tau, k \in [m']$, from $\mathcal{P}_{(h)} \cup \mathcal{P}_{(1)}$ to $\mathcal{P}_{(1)}$ as follows:
   - Each $P_i \in \mathcal{P}_{(h)} \setminus \mathcal{P}_{(1)}$ secret shares $v_k^i = \sum_{j \in \mathcal{P}_{(1)}} v_k^{j,i}$ and sends $v_k^{j,i}$ to $P_j \in \mathcal{P}_{(1)}$.
   - Each $P_j \in \mathcal{P}_{(1)}$ sets $\hat{v}_k^j = v_k^j + \sum_{i \in \mathcal{P}_{(h)} \setminus \mathcal{P}_{(1)}} v_k^{j,i}$.

5. For $k \in [m']$ each $P_j \in \mathcal{P}_{(1)}$ computes $z_k^j = x_k^j \cdot y_k^j \oplus \hat{v}_k^j$, where $y_k^j = 0$ if $P_j \notin \mathcal{P}_{(h)}$. Parties in $\mathcal{P}_{(h)} \cup \mathcal{P}_{(1)}$ call $\mathcal{F}_{\text{aBit}}^{\mathcal{P}_{(h)}, \mathcal{P}_{(1)}, m', \ell}$ on input $\{z_k^j\}_{k \in [m']}$ from $P_j \in \mathcal{P}_{(1)}$ to obtain $\{[z_k]^{\mathcal{P}_{(h)}, \mathcal{P}_{(1)}}\}_{k \in [m']}$.

Triple Checking: Run $\Pi_{\text{TripleBucketing}}$ to output m correct and secure triples.

Fig. 12. Protocol for triples

Theorem 7.2. *Protocol Π_{Triple} securely implements $\mathcal{F}_{\text{Triple}}^{m,\ell}$ in the $(\mathcal{F}_{\text{Rand}}, \mathcal{F}_{\text{aBit}}, \mathcal{F}_{\text{HalfAuthTriple}}^{\mathcal{P}_{(h)}, \mathcal{P}_{(1)}, r, \ell})$-hybrid model.*

Parameters: Based on the analysis from previous works [FKOS15, FLNW17, WRK17a], we choose $B = 3$ and 4, to guarantee security except with probability 2^{-64} in our estimations. The additional cut-and-choose parameter c can be as low as 3, so is insignificant as we initially need $m' = B^2 m + c$ triples to produce m final triples.

Subprotocol $\Pi_{\mathsf{TripleBucketing}}$

The protocol takes as input $m' = B^2 m + c$ triples, which may be incorrect and/or have leakage on the x component, and produces m triples which are guaranteed to be correct and leakage-free.

B determines the bucket size, whilst c determines the amount of cut-and-choose to be performed.

Input: Start with the shared triples $\{[x_k]_\Delta^{\mathcal{P}_{(h)},\mathcal{P}_{(1)}}, [y_k]_\Delta^{\mathcal{P}_{(h)},\mathcal{P}_{(1)}}, [z_k]_\Delta^{\mathcal{P}_{(h)},\mathcal{P}_{(1)}}\}_{k\in[m']}$.

Output: Correct, leakage-free and SPDZ-style triples $\{[\![x_k]\!], [\![y_k]\!], [\![z_k]\!]\}_{k\in[m]}$.

I: Cut-and-choose: Using $\mathcal{F}_{\mathsf{Rand}}$, the parties select at random and open c triples using $\Pi_{[\mathsf{Open}]}^{\mathcal{P}_{(h)},\mathcal{P}_{(1)}}$ (Figure 1). If any triple is incorrect (i.e. if $x \cdot y \neq z$), abort.

II: Check correctness: The parties now have $B^2 m$ unopened triples.

1. Use $\mathcal{F}_{\mathsf{Rand}}$ to sample a random permutation on $\{1, \ldots, B^2 m\}$, and randomly assign the triples into mB buckets of size B, accordingly.
2. For each bucket, check correctness of the first triple in the bucket, say $T = ([x], [y], [z])$, by performing a pairwise sacrifice between T and every other triple in the bucket. Concretely, to check correctness of T by sacrificing $T' = ([x'], [y'], [z'])$:
   (a) Compute $[d] = [x] + [x']$ and $[e] = [y] + [y']$ and call $(\mathsf{Open}, [d], \mathcal{P}_{(h)} \cup \mathcal{P}_{(1)})$, $(\mathsf{Open}, [e], \mathcal{P}_{(h)} \cup \mathcal{P}_{(1)})$ in $\Pi_{[\mathsf{Open}]}^{\mathcal{P}_{(h)},\mathcal{P}_{(1)}}$.
   (b) Using the opened values, compute $[f] = [z] + [z'] + d \cdot [y] + e \cdot [x] + d \cdot e$.
   (c) Call $(\mathsf{Open}, [f], \mathcal{P}_{(1)})$ in $\Pi_{[\mathsf{Open}]}^{\mathcal{P}_{(h)},\mathcal{P}_{(1)}}$ and check that $f = 0$. Otherwise, the parties abort.

III: Remove leakage: Taking the first triple in each bucket from the previous step, the parties are left with Bm triples. They remove any potential leakage on the $[x]$ bits of these as follows:

1. Place the triples into m buckets of size B.
2. For each bucket, combine all B triples into a single triple. Specifically, combine the first triple $([x], [y], [z])$ with $T' = ([x'], [y'], [z'])$, for every other triple T' in the bucket:
   (a) Compute $[d] = [y] + [y']$ and call $(\mathsf{Open}, [d], \mathcal{P}_{(h)} \cup \mathcal{P}_{(1)})$ in $\Pi_{[\mathsf{Open}]}^{\mathcal{P}_{(h)},\mathcal{P}_{(1)}}$.
   (b) Compute $[z''] = d \cdot [x'] + [z] + [z']$ and $[x''] = [x] + [x']$.
   (c) Output the triple $[x'']_\Delta^{\mathcal{P}_{(h)},\mathcal{P}_{(1)}}, [y]_\Delta^{\mathcal{P}_{(h)},\mathcal{P}_{(1)}}, [z'']_\Delta^{\mathcal{P}_{(h)},\mathcal{P}_{(1)}}$.

IV: Check MACs and compact them: Call **Batch Check** in $\Pi_{[\mathsf{Open}]}^{\mathcal{P}_{(h)},\mathcal{P}_{(1)}}$ for every item that was opened in Steps I-III. If the batched MAC check fails, abort. Otherwise call $\Pi_{\mathsf{MACCompact}}$ on input the first triple from each of the m buckets in the previous stage, which are renamed and output as $\{[\![x_k]\!], [\![y_k]\!], [\![z_k]\!]\}_{k\in[m]}$.

Fig. 13. Checking correctness and removing leakage from triples with cut-and-choose

8   Complexity Analysis

We now analyse the complexity of our protocol and compare it with the state-of-the-art actively secure MPC protocols with dishonest majority. As our online phase is essentially the same (even better) than that of SPDZ and TinyOT mixed with committees, we focus on the preprocessing phase.

Furthermore, since the underlying computational primitives in our protocol are very simple, the communication cost in the triple generation algorithm will be the overall bottleneck. We compare the communication cost of our triple generation algorithm with that of the corresponding multiparty Tiny-OT protocol by Wang et al. [WRK17b].

The main cost for producing m triples in this work, is $3mB^2$ calls to $\mathcal{F}_{\mathsf{aBit}}$ using keys $\Delta^i \in \{0,1\}^\ell$, plus mB^2 calls to $\mathcal{F}_{\mathsf{aBit}}$ using new keys $\Delta^i + \tilde{\Delta}^i \in \{0,1\}^\ell$ every r triples. The latter calls under new keys are more expensive, as the setup costs that incurs is roughly $128 \cdot \ell \cdot |\mathcal{P}_{(h)}| \cdot |\mathcal{P}_{(1)}|$ bits and is amortized only across those r triples. Measuring the cost of $\mathcal{F}_{\mathsf{aBit}}$ after setup as $|\mathcal{P}_{(h)}| \cdot |\mathcal{P}_{(1)}| \cdot \ell$ bits, we obtain an amortized communication complexity of $B^2 \cdot |\mathcal{P}_{(h)}| \cdot |\mathcal{P}_{(1)}| \cdot \ell \cdot (3 + (r + 128)/r)$ bits per triple.

The main cost for producing m triples in [WRK17b] is $3mB$ calls to their long-key equivalent of $\mathcal{F}_{\mathsf{aBit}}$ with long keys, plus sending $2mB$ outputs of a hash function. On the other hand, all their communication is within the smaller committee $\mathcal{P}_{(1)}$. Their main (amortized) cost is then of $B \cdot |\mathcal{P}_{(1)}|^2 \cdot 128 \cdot (3 + 2)$ bits per triple. Define $\alpha = |\mathcal{P}_{(h)}|/|\mathcal{P}_{(1)}|$. We can then conclude that the improvement in communication complexity of our work w.r.t. WRK is roughly that of a multiplicative factor of:

$$\frac{128 \cdot 5}{\alpha \cdot B \cdot \ell \cdot (4 + 128/r)}$$

Table 1. Amortized communication cost (in kbit) of producing triples in our protocol and WRK.

# parties n (honest)	30 (12)	50 (20)	70 (20)	100 (30)	150 (30)	200 (40)
ℓ	16	16	16	8	(8, 300)	(7, 400)
WRK $B = 3$	656	1785	4896	9542	27878	49959
WRK $B = 4$	876	2381	6528	12723	37171	65946
Ours $B = 3$	**381**	**950**	**2188**	**2481**	**6342**	**9413**
Ours $B = 4$	**677**	**1689**	**3890**	**4411**	**11275**	**16733**

Given the total number of parties n and honest parties h, we first consider the case of two deterministic committees $\mathcal{P}_{(h)}$ and $\mathcal{P}_{(1)}$ such that $|\mathcal{P}_{(h)}| = n$ and $|\mathcal{P}_{(1)}| = n - h + 1$, respectively. To give a fair comparison, we have chosen the parameters in such a way that $n - h + 1$ in our protocol is equal to n in WRK. The estimated amortized costs in kbit of producing triples are given in Table 1. Notice that given n and h, the key lenght ℓ and the number of triples r are established according to the corresponding leaky-DRSD instance with κ bits of security. We consider $\kappa = 128$ and bucket size $B = 3$ and 4.

As we can see from the table, the improvement of our protocol over WRK becomes greater as (n, h) increase (and ℓ consequently decreases). The key lenght greatly influences the communication cost as a smaller ℓ reduces significantly the cost of computing the pairwise OTs needed both for triple generation and authentication.

When n is larger we can use random committees $\mathcal{P}_{(h)}$ and $\mathcal{P}_{(1)}$ such that, except with negligible probability $2^{-\lambda}$, $\mathcal{P}_{(h)}$ has at least $h_2 \leq h$ honest parties and $\mathcal{P}_{(1)}$ has at least 1 honest party. Let $|\mathcal{P}_{(h)}| = n_2$, $|\mathcal{P}_{(1)}| = n_1$ and $\lambda = 64$, Table 2 compares the communication cost of our triple generation protocol with random committees with WRK, where we take $n = n_1$.

Table 2. Amortized costs in kbit for triple generation with n parties and h honest parties using two random committees of sizes n_1, n_2 with 1 and h_2 honest parties.

$(n, h, |\mathcal{P}_{(1)}|)$	$(h_2, \ell) = (20, 11)$		$(h_2, \ell) = (50, 6)$		$(h_2, \ell) = (80, 1)$		$(h_2, \ell) = (110, 1)$		$(h_2, \ell) = (150, 1)$		WRK
	n_2	Ours	n_2	Ours	n_2	Ours	n_2	Ours	n_2	Ours	
(300, 100, 89)	167	7141	240	5270	280	4486					15037
(500, 150, 108)	211	10950	316	8420	396	7698	456	4240			50700
(800, 200, 139)	275	18366	417	14301	533	13335	630	7539	733	6397	36829
(1000, 200, 179)	351	30188	531	23451	675	21748	796	12266	922	10363	61175

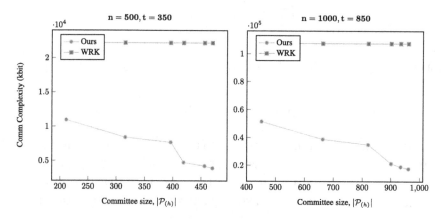

Fig. 14. Varying the larger committee size with total number of parties and corruptions $(n, t) = (500, 350)$ and $(1000, 850)$.

Varying the size of the committee $\mathcal{P}_{(h)}$, and the number h_2 of honest parties within $\mathcal{P}_{(h)}$, we obtain a tradeoff: with a larger committee we obtain a larger committee size n_2 and lower overall communication complexity, but on the other hand there are more parties interacting, which may introduce bottlenecks in the networking. Figure 14 illustrates this with 500 and 1000 parties in total and 350 and 850, respectively, corruptions.

References

[ADS+17]   Asharov, G., et al.: Privacy-preserving interdomain routing at Internet scale. PoPETs **2017**(3), 147 (2017)

[BCD+09]   Bogetoft, P., et al.: Secure multiparty computation goes live. In: Dingledine, R., Golle, P. (eds.) FC 2009. LNCS, vol. 5628, pp. 325–343. Springer, Heidelberg (2009). https://doi.org/10.1007/978-3-642-03549-4_20

[BDOZ11]   Bendlin, R., Damgård, I., Orlandi, C., Zakarias, S.: Semi-homomorphic encryption and multiparty computation. In: Paterson, K.G. (ed.) EUROCRYPT 2011. LNCS, vol. 6632, pp. 169–188. Springer, Heidelberg (2011). https://doi.org/10.1007/978-3-642-20465-4_11

[BLN+15]   Burra, S.S., et al.: High performance multi-party computation for binary circuits based on oblivious transfer. Cryptology ePrint Archive, Report 2015/472 (2015). http://eprint.iacr.org/2015/472

[BMR90]   Beaver, D., Micali, S., Rogaway, P.: The round complexity of secure protocols (extended abstract). In: 22nd ACM STOC, pp. 503–513. ACM Press, May 1990

[BTH08]   Beerliová-Trubíniová, Z., Hirt, M.: Perfectly-secure MPC with linear communication complexity. In: Canetti, R. (ed.) TCC 2008. LNCS, vol. 4948, pp. 213–230. Springer, Heidelberg (2008). https://doi.org/10.1007/978-3-540-78524-8_13

[Can01]   Canetti, R.: Universally composable security: a new paradigm for cryptographic protocols. In: 42nd FOCS, pp. 136–145. IEEE Computer Society Press, October 2001

[DKL+13]   Damgård, I., Keller, M., Larraia, E., Pastro, V., Scholl, P., Smart, N.P.: Practical covertly secure MPC for dishonest majority – or: breaking the SPDZ limits. In: Crampton, J., Jajodia, S., Mayes, K. (eds.) ESORICS 2013. LNCS, vol. 8134, pp. 1–18. Springer, Heidelberg (2013). https://doi.org/10.1007/978-3-642-40203-6_1

[DMS04]   Dingledine, R., Mathewson, N., Syverson, P.F.: Tor: the second-generation onion router. In: USENIX, pp. 303–320 (2004)

[DPSZ12]   Damgård, I., Pastro, V., Smart, N., Zakarias, S.: Multiparty computation from somewhat homomorphic encryption. In: Safavi-Naini, R., Canetti, R. (eds.) CRYPTO 2012. LNCS, vol. 7417, pp. 643–662. Springer, Heidelberg (2012). https://doi.org/10.1007/978-3-642-32009-5_38

[FKOS15]   Frederiksen, T.K., Keller, M., Orsini, E., Scholl, P.: A unified approach to MPC with preprocessing using OT. In: Iwata, T., Cheon, J.H. (eds.) ASIACRYPT 2015. LNCS, vol. 9452, pp. 711–735. Springer, Heidelberg (2015). https://doi.org/10.1007/978-3-662-48797-6_29

[FLNW17]   Furukawa, J., Lindell, Y., Nof, A., Weinstein, O.: High-throughput secure three-party computation for malicious adversaries and an honest majority. In: Coron, J.-S., Nielsen, J.B. (eds.) EUROCRYPT 2017. LNCS, vol. 10211, pp. 225–255. Springer, Cham (2017). https://doi.org/10.1007/978-3-319-56614-6_8

[HOSS18]   Hazay, C., Orsini, E., Scholl, P., Soria-Vazquez, E.: TinyKeys: a new approach to efficient multi-party computation. In: Shacham, H., Boldyreva, A. (eds.) CRYPTO 2018. LNCS, vol. 10993, pp. 3–33. Springer, Cham (2018). https://doi.org/10.1007/978-3-319-96878-0_1

[HSS17]   Hazay, C., Scholl, P., Soria-Vazquez, E.: Low cost constant round MPC combining BMR and oblivious transfer. In: Takagi, T., Peyrin, T. (eds.)

ASIACRYPT 2017. LNCS, vol. 10624, pp. 598–628. Springer, Cham (2017). https://doi.org/10.1007/978-3-319-70694-8_21

[ILL89] Impagliazzo, R., Levin, L.A., Luby, M.: Pseudo-random generation from one-way functions (extended abstracts). In: 21st ACM STOC, pp. 12–24. ACM Press, May 1989

[KOS15] Keller, M., Orsini, E., Scholl, P.: Actively secure OT extension with optimal overhead. In: Gennaro, R., Robshaw, M. (eds.) CRYPTO 2015. LNCS, vol. 9215, pp. 724–741. Springer, Heidelberg (2015). https://doi.org/10.1007/978-3-662-47989-6_35

[KOS16] Keller, M., Orsini, E., Scholl, P.: MASCOT: faster malicious arithmetic secure computation with oblivious transfer. In: Weippl, E.R., Katzenbeisser, S., Kruegel, C., Myers, A.C., Halevi, S. (eds.) ACM CCS 2016, pp. 830–842. ACM Press, October 2016

[KPR18] Keller, M., Pastro, V., Rotaru, D.: Overdrive: making SPDZ great again. In: Nielsen, J.B., Rijmen, V. (eds.) EUROCRYPT 2018. LNCS, vol. 10822, pp. 158–189. Springer, Cham (2018). https://doi.org/10.1007/978-3-319-78372-7_6

[KS08] Kolesnikov, V., Schneider, T.: Improved garbled circuit: free XOR gates and applications. In: Aceto, L., Damgård, I., Goldberg, L.A., Halldórsson, M.M., Ingólfsdóttir, A., Walukiewicz, I. (eds.) ICALP 2008. LNCS, vol. 5126, pp. 486–498. Springer, Heidelberg (2008). https://doi.org/10.1007/978-3-540-70583-3_40

[KSS12] Kreuter, B., Shelat, A., Shen, C.-H.: Billion-gate secure computation with malicious adversaries. In: USENIX, pp. 285–300 (2012)

[LOS14] Larraia, E., Orsini, E., Smart, N.P.: Dishonest majority multi-party computation for binary circuits. In: Garay, J.A., Gennaro, R. (eds.) CRYPTO 2014. LNCS, vol. 8617, pp. 495–512. Springer, Heidelberg (2014). https://doi.org/10.1007/978-3-662-44381-1_28

[LPSY15] Lindell, Y., Pinkas, B., Smart, N.P., Yanai, A.: Efficient constant round multi-party computation combining BMR and SPDZ. In: Gennaro, R., Robshaw, M. (eds.) CRYPTO 2015. LNCS, vol. 9216, pp. 319–338. Springer, Heidelberg (2015). https://doi.org/10.1007/978-3-662-48000-7_16

[NNOB12] Nielsen, J.B., Nordholt, P.S., Orlandi, C., Burra, S.S.: A new approach to practical active-secure two-party computation. In: Safavi-Naini, R., Canetti, R. (eds.) CRYPTO 2012. LNCS, vol. 7417, pp. 681–700. Springer, Heidelberg (2012). https://doi.org/10.1007/978-3-642-32009-5_40

[NST17] Nielsen, J.B., Schneider, T., Trifiletti, R.: Constant round maliciously secure 2PC with function-independent preprocessing using LEGO. In: NDSS 2017. The Internet Society, February/March 2017

[WMK17] Wang, X., Malozemoff, A.J., Katz, J.: Faster secure two-party computation in the single-execution setting. In: Coron, J.-S., Nielsen, J.B. (eds.) EUROCRYPT 2017. LNCS, vol. 10212, pp. 399–424. Springer, Cham (2017). https://doi.org/10.1007/978-3-319-56617-7_14

[WRK17a] Wang, X., Ranellucci, S., Katz, J.: Authenticated garbling and efficient maliciously secure two-party computation. In: Thuraisingham, B.M., Evans, D., Malkin, T., Xu, D. (eds.) ACM CCS 2017, pp. 21–37. ACM Press, October/November 2017

[WRK17b] Wang, X., Ranellucci, S., Katz, J.: Global-scale secure multiparty computation. In: Thuraisingham, B.M., Evans, D., Malkin, T., Xu, D. (eds.) ACM CCS 2017, pp. 39–56. ACM Press, October/November 2017

[Yao86] Yao, A.C.-C.: How to generate and exchange secrets (extended abstract). In: 27th FOCS, pp. 162–167. IEEE Computer Society Press, October 1986

[ZRE15] Zahur, S., Rosulek, M., Evans, D.: Two halves make a whole - reducing data transfer in garbled circuits using half gates. In: Oswald, E., Fischlin, M. (eds.) EUROCRYPT 2015. LNCS, vol. 9057, pp. 220–250. Springer, Heidelberg (2015). https://doi.org/10.1007/978-3-662-46803-6_8

Non-interactive Secure Computation
from One-Way Functions

Saikrishna Badrinarayanan[1]([✉]), Abhishek Jain[2], Rafail Ostrovsky[1],
and Ivan Visconti[3]

[1] UCLA, Los Angeles, USA
{saikrishna,rafail}@cs.ucla.edu
[2] JHU, Baltimore, USA
abhishek@cs.jhu.edu
[3] University of Salerno, Fisciano, Italy
visconti@unisa.it

Abstract. The notion of non-interactive secure computation (NISC) first introduced in the work of Ishai et al. [EUROCRYPT 2011] studies the following problem: Suppose a receiver R wishes to publish an encryption of her secret input y so that any sender S with input x can then send a message m that reveals $f(x,y)$ to R (for some function f). Here, m can be viewed as an encryption of $f(x,y)$ that can be decrypted by R. NISC requires security against both malicious senders and receivers, and also requires the receiver's message to be reusable across multiple computations (w.r.t. a fixed input of the receiver).

All previous solutions to this problem necessarily rely upon OT (or specific number-theoretic assumptions) even in the common reference string model or the random oracle model or to achieve weaker notions of security such as super-polynomial-time simulation.

In this work, we construct a NISC protocol based on the minimal assumption of one way functions, in the stateless hardware token model. Our construction achieves UC security and requires a single token sent by the receiver to the sender.

Keywords: Secure computation · Hardware tokens

A. Jain—This research was supported in part by a DARPA/ARL Safeware Grant W911NF-15-C-0213.

R. Ostrovsky—Research supported in part by NSF grant 1619348, DARPA SafeWare subcontract to Galois Inc., DARPA SPAWAR contract N66001-15-1C-4065, US-Israel BSF grant 2012366, OKAWA Foundation Research Award, IBM Faculty Research Award, Xerox Faculty Research Award, B. John Garrick Foundation Award, Teradata Research Award, and Lockheed-Martin Corporation Research Award. The views expressed are those of the authors and do not reflect position of the Department of Defense or the U.S. Government.

I. Visconti—Research supported in part by the European Union's Horizon 2020 research and innovation programme under grant agreement No. 780477 (project PRIViLEDGE) and in part by University of Salerno through a FARB grant.

T. Peyrin and S. Galbraith (Eds.): ASIACRYPT 2018, LNCS 11274, pp. 118–138, 2018.
https://doi.org/10.1007/978-3-030-03332-3_5

1   Introduction

A motivating scenario [1]. Suppose there is a public algorithm D that takes as input the DNA data of two individuals and determines whether or not they are related. Alice would like to use this algorithm to find family relatives, but does not want to publish her DNA data in the clear. Instead, she would like to publish an "encryption" of her DNA data b so that anyone else with DNA data a can send back a *single* message to Alice that reveals $D(a, b)$, i.e., whether or not Alice is related to that person. This process must be such that it prevents either party from influencing the output (beyond the choice of their respective inputs), while also ensuring the privacy of their DNA data.

Non-interactive Secure Computation. The notion of non-interactive secure computation (NISC), introduced by Ishai et al. [25], provides a solution to the above problem. In its general form, NISC allows a receiver party R to publish an encryption of her input y such that any sender party S with input x can then send a message m that reveals $f(x, y)$ to R (for some function f), where m can be viewed as an encryption of $f(x, y)$ that can be decrypted by R. NISC achieves security against malicious senders and receivers, and also allows the receiver's message to be reusable across multiple computations (w.r.t. a fixed input of the receiver).

Note that if malicious security was not required, then one could readily obtain a solution via Yao's secure computation protocol [33]. However, NISC guarantees malicious security, and is therefore impossible in the plain model w.r.t. polynomial-time simulation [20].

The work of Ishai et al. [25] gave the first solution for NISC in a hybrid model where the parties have access to the oblivious transfer (OT) functionality. Subsequently, efficient solutions for NISC based on cut-and-choose techniques were investigated in the common reference string (CRS) model [1,29], the global random oracle model [9], as well as the plain model with super-polynomial-time simulation [2].

Our Goal. All of these works, however, necessarily rely upon OT [2,25] (or specific number-theoretic assumptions, as in [1,9,29]). In this work, we ask whether it is possible to construct NISC protocols based on the minimal assumption of *one-way functions*?

Since OT is necessary for secure computation (even in CRS and random oracle model), we investigate the above question in the tamper-proof hardware token model, namely, where parties can send hardware tokens to each other.

Starting from the work of Katz [26], there is a large body of research work on constructing secure computation protocols in the hardware token model (see Sect. 3 for a detailed discussion). However, all known solutions require two or more rounds of interaction between the parties (after an initial token transfer phase) regardless of the assumptions and the number of tokens used in the protocol. Thus, so far, the problem of NISC in the hardware token model has remained open.

Our Result. In this work, we construct a UC-secure NISC protocol based on one-way functions that uses a single, stateless hardware token. Note that this is optimal both in terms of complexity assumption as well as the number of tokens.

Concretely, our solution uses the following template: first, a receiver R sends out a hardware token that has its input y hardwired. Upon communicating with the token, a sender S sends out a single message to R, who can then evaluate the output. Note that by using the transformation of [27] which involves adding a single message from R to S, we can also support the case where we want both parties to learn the output.

We remark that prior work on cryptography using hardware tokens has studied the use of both stateful and stateless hardware tokens. The latter is considered to be a more desirable model since it is more realistic, and places weaker requirements on the token manufacturer. Our protocol, therefore, only relies on a stateless hardware token. Moreover, following prior work, we do not make any assumptions on the token if R is malicious; in particular, in this case, the adversarial token may well be stateful.

2   Technical Overview

We now describe the techniques used in our non-interactive secure computation (NISC) protocol using one stateless token and assuming one way functions.

Token Direction. Recall that in a NISC protocol, the receiver R first sends her input y in some encrypted manner such that any sender S with input x computes on this encrypted input and sends back a message m that the receiver can then decrypt to recover the output $f(x, y)$. For different choices of the function f and input x, the sender can generate a fresh message m using the same encrypted input of the receiver. Therefore, to follow this paradigm, in the setting of stateless hardware tokens, we require that the receiver first sends a stateless token T (containing her input) which can be followed by a communication message from the sender. Another approach is to perhaps have the receiver first send a communication message followed by a token sent by the sender. However, such an approach has the drawback that to reuse the receiver's first message, each time, the sender has to generate and send a fresh token. Hence, we stick to the setting of the receiver first sending a token.

A natural first approach then is to start with the large body of secure computation protocols based on stateless tokens [11,18,23,24] and try to squish one of them into a protocol that comprises of just one token from the receiver and one communication message from the sender. However, in all these works, it is the sender who first sends a token to the receiver (as opposed to our setting where the direction of token transfer is reversed) and this is followed by at least two rounds of interaction between the two parties. As such, it is completely unclear how this could be done even if we were to rely on assumptions stronger than one-way functions.

Therefore, we significantly depart from the template followed in all prior works, and start from scratch for constructing NISC in the stateless hardware token model.

Input authentication. In the stateless hardware token model, an important desideratum is to prevent an adversary from gaining undue advantage by resetting the stateless token that it receives from the honest party. In all prior works, to prevent the adversary from resetting the token and changing its input in each interaction with the token and observing the output (which may potentially allow it learn more information), the token recipient's input encoding is first authenticated by the token creator before interaction with the token. However, such an approach necessarily requires at least two rounds of communication between S and R after the exchange of tokens which is not feasible in our setting. To overcome this issue, we in fact do allow S to potentially reset the token and interact with the token using different inputs! While this might seem strange at first, the key observation is that S performs only "encrypted" computation in its interaction with the token. Therefore, even if S resets and interacts with the token using different inputs, he learns no information whatsoever about R's input from his interaction with the token. Thus, resetting attacks are nullified even without authentication. We now describe how to perform such "encrypted" computation.

Protocol structure. At a very high level, our construction follows the garbled circuit based approach to secure computation [33]. That is, the sender S with input x sends a garbled version of a circuit C_x that computes $f(x, z)$ for any input z. Since we are in the setting of malicious adversaries, an immediate question is how does S prove correctness of the garbled circuit? Clearly, a proof of correctness to the receiver will require more than one message of interaction. Instead, we make S prove to the token T that the garbled circuit GC was correctly generated. At the end of the proof, T outputs a signature on GC which is sent by the sender S to the receiver R (along with GC) as authentication that this garbled circuit was indeed correctly generated.

To make this approach work, one question that naturally arises is how does R receive the labels corresponding to her input in order to evaluate the garbled circuit? Recall that we wish to rely on only one way functions and hence can't assume stronger primitives like oblivious transfer (OT). Also, previous stateless token based OT protocols rely on multiple rounds of interaction and in some cases, multiple tokens and stronger assumptions. We instead do the following: S sends the garbled circuit GC to T and additionally discloses the randomness rand used to generate the garbled circuit. The token can use this randomness to compute on its own the labels corresponding to R's input y. It then responds with a ciphertext CT of these labels, and further proves that this ciphertext was indeed correctly generated using the receiver's input y and the randomness rand. Then, if the proof verifies, S sends CT along with the garbled circuit GC and its signature to R. The receiver R decrypts the ciphertext CT to recover the labels and then evaluates the garbled circuit. To prevent S from tampering with the ciphertext in its message to R, we will additionally require that the token T signs the ciphertext as well. In fact, we require that the signature queries on GC and CT are performed *jointly* as a single query to prevent an adversarial sender from resetting the token and getting signatures from the token on a garbled circuit GC computed using randomness rand, and an encryption CT of the wire labels corresponding to R's input computed using different randomness rand' $\neq$ rand. Indeed, such an attack may allow the sender to force an incorrect output on R.

Selective Abort. One issue with the above protocol is that if R is malicious, the token could launch an aborting attack as follows: on being queried with the garbled circuit GC and randomness rand used for garbling, reconstruct the circuit C_x, thereby learning the sender's input x and output $\perp$ if x begins with 0 (for example). Now, if R received a valid message from S, she knows that S's input begins with 1. The observation is that it is crucial for the token T to not learn both the garbled circuit GC and the randomness rand used for garbling. Since it is necessary for T to know rand to generate the encrypted labels, we tweak the protocol to have S query the token only with a commitment to the garbled circuit (along with the randomness used for garbling) and prove that this commitment is correctly computed. T then produces a signature on this commitment. In his message to R, S now sends the commitment, the signature on it and the decommitment to help R recover the garbled circuit.

Subliminal Channel. Another attack that a malicious receiver could launch is by embedding information about the randomness rand in the ciphertext and signatures it generates. Note that even though the token proves that the signature and the ciphertext were correctly generated, a malicious token could still choose the randomness for generating the ciphertext/signature as a function of rand. Now, even though the proof verifies successfully, the receiver, using the knowledge of the encryption key/signing key, might be able to recover the randomness used for encrypting/signing and learn information about rand thus breaking the security of the garbled circuit GC (which, in turn, can reveal S's input). To prevent such an attack, it is necessary to enforce that the randomness used by the token to generate the ciphertext and signature is *independent of* rand, but unknown to the sender. We do this by making the token fix this randomness ahead of time (using a commitment) and proving that the randomness used to encrypt and sign was the one committed to before knowing rand. Additionally, we ensure (using pseudorandom functions) that a malicious sender, via resetting attacks, can not learn this randomness used for encrypting and signing.

Finally, note that to deal with resetting attacks in the proofs, we use a resettably sound zero-knowledge argument for the proof given by the sender to the token and a resettable zero-knowledge argument of knowledge for the proof from the token to the sender. Both these arguments are known assuming just one way functions [12–15]. Here, we need the argument of knowledge property in order to extract the receiver's input in the security proof. To extract the sender's input in the ideal world, the simulator uses knowledge of the garbled circuit (sent to the receiver) and the randomness for garbling (sent to the simulated token). We refer the reader to the main body for more details about our construction and other issues that we tackle.

3 Related Work

We briefly review prior work on cryptography using hardware tokens. The seminal work of Katz [26] initiated the study of secure computation protocols using tamper-proof hardware tokens and established the first feasibility results using *stateful* hardware tokens. Subsequently, this stateful token model has been extensively explored in several directions with the purpose of improving upon the complexity assumptions, round-complexity of protocols and the number of required tokens [16,17,21,28,30].

The study of secure computation protocols in the stateless hardware token model was initiated by Chandran et al. [10]. They constructed a polynomial round two-party computation protocol for general functions where each party exchanges one token with the other party, based on enhanced trapdoor permutations. Subsequent to their work, Goyal et al. [23] constructed constant-round protocols assuming collision-resistant hash functions (CRHFs). However, these improvements were achieved at the cost of requiring a polynomial number of tokens. Choi et al. [11] subsequently improved upon their result by decreasing the number of required tokens to only one, while still using only constant rounds and CRHFs. Recently, two independent works [18,24] obtained the first protocols for secure two party computation based on the minimal assumption of one-way functions. Specifically, Döttling et al. [18] construct a secure constant round protocol using only one token. Hazay et al. [24] construct two-round two-party computation in this model using a polynomial number of tokens.

All the above works, including ours, focus on achieving Universally Composable (UC) [6] security[1].

4 Preliminaries

UC-Secure Two Party Computation. We follow the standard real-ideal paradigm for defining secure two party computation. We include the formal definitions in Appendix A.

Non-interactive Secure Computation (NISC). A secure two party computation protocol in the stateless hardware token model between a sender S and a receiver R where only R learns the output is called a NISC protocol if it has the following structure: first, R sends a token to S and then the sender S sends a single message to R. We require security against both a malicious sender and a malicious receiver (who can create the token to be stateful). Further, note that we work in the stand-alone security model and don't consider composability.

Token functionality. We model a tamper-proof hardware token as an ideal functionality $\mathcal{F}_{\mathsf{WRAP}}$, following Katz [26]. A formal definition of this functionality can be found in Appendix A. Note that our ideal functionality models stateful

---

[1] Hazay et al. [24] study the stronger notion of Global UC security [7,9].

tokens. Although all our protocols use stateless tokens, an adversarially generated token may be stateful (Fig. 3).

Cryptographic primitives. In our constructions, we use the following cryptographic primitives all of which can be constructed from one way functions: pseudorandom functions, digital signatures, commitments, garbled circuits, private key encryption [19,31–33].

Additionally, we also use the following advanced primitives that were recently constructed based on one way functions: resettable zero knowledge argument of knowledge and resettably sound zero knowledge arguments. [3–5,8,12–15].

Interactive proofs for a "stateless" player. We consider the notion of an interactive proof system for a "stateless" prover/verifier. By "stateless", we mean that the verifier has no extra memory that can be used to remember the transcript of the proof so far. Consider a stateless verifier. To get around the issue of not knowing the transcript, the verifier signs the transcript at each step and sends it back to the prover. In the next round, the prover is required to send this signed transcript back to the verifier and the verifier first checks the signature and then uses the transcript to continue with the protocol execution. Without loss of generality, we can also include the statement to be proved as part of the transcript. It is easy to see that such a scenario arises in our setting if the stateless token acts as the verifier in an interactive proof with another party.

5   Construction

In this section, we construct a non-interactive secure computation (NISC) protocol based on one-way functions using only one stateless hardware token. Formally, we prove the following theorem:

Theorem 1. *Assuming one-way functions exist, there exists a non-interactive secure computation (NISC) protocol that is UC-secure in the stateless hardware token model using just one token.*

Notation. We first list some notation and the primitives used.

- Let λ denote the security parameter.
- Let's say the sender S has private input $x \in \{0,1\}^\lambda$ and receiver R has private input $y \in \{0,1\}^\lambda$ and they wish to evaluate a function f on their joint inputs.
- Let $PRF : \{0,1\}^\lambda \times \{0,1\}^{\lambda^2} \to \{0,1\}^\lambda$ be a pseudorandom function.
- Let Commit be a non-interactive[2] computationally hiding and statistically binding commitment scheme that uses n bits of randomness to commit to one bit.

---

[2] To ease the exposition, we use non-interactive commitments that are based on injective one-way functions. We describe later how the protocol can be modified to use a two-message commitment scheme that relies only on one-way functions without increasing the message complexity of the protocol.

- Let(Gen, Sign, Verify) be a signature scheme.
- Let (ske.setup, ske.enc, ske.dec) be a private key encryption scheme.
- Let RSZK = (RSZK.Prove, RSZK.Verify) be a resettably-sound zero-knowledge argument system for a "stateless verifier" and RZKAOK = (RZKAOK.Prove, RZKAOK.Verify) be a resettable zero knowledge argument of knowledge system for a "stateless prover" as defined in Sect. 4.
- Let (Garble, Garble.KeyGen, Eval) be a garbling scheme for poly sized circuits.

Note that all the primitives can be constructed assuming the existence of one-way functions.

NP languages. We will use the following NP languages in our protocol.

1. NP language L^T characterized by the following relation R^T.
   Statement : $\mathsf{st} = (c_{\mathcal{GC}}, \mathsf{ct}, \sigma, c_y, c_{ek}, c_{sk}, c_k, \mathsf{toss}, \mathsf{vk}, r_{\mathsf{ske.enc}}, r_{(c_{\mathcal{GC}}, \mathsf{ct})})$
   Witness : $\mathsf{w} = (y, r_y, \mathsf{ek}, r_{ek}, \mathsf{sk}, r_{sk}, \mathsf{k}, r_k, \ell_y, r_{\mathsf{Sign}})$
   $R_2^T(\mathsf{st}, \mathsf{w}) = 1$ if and only if :
   - $c_y = \mathsf{Commit}(y; r_y)$ (AND)
   - $c_{ek} = \mathsf{Commit}(\mathsf{ek}; r_{ek})$ (AND)
   - $c_{sk} = \mathsf{Commit}(\mathsf{sk}; r_{sk})$ (AND)
   - $c_k = \mathsf{Commit}(\mathsf{k}; r_k)$ (AND)
   - $\ell_y = \mathsf{Garble.KeyGen}(y; \mathsf{toss})$ (AND)
   - $\mathsf{ct} = \mathsf{ske.enc}(\mathsf{ek}, \ell_y; \mathsf{PRF}(\mathsf{k}, r_{\mathsf{ske.enc}}))$ (AND)
   - $(\mathsf{vk}, \mathsf{sk}) = \mathsf{Gen}(r_{\mathsf{Sign}})$ (AND)
   - $\sigma = \mathsf{Sign}(\mathsf{sk}, (c_{\mathcal{GC}}, \mathsf{ct}); \mathsf{PRF}(\mathsf{k}, r_{(c_{\mathcal{GC}}, \mathsf{ct})}))$.
2. NP language L characterized by the following relation R.
   Statement : $\mathsf{st} = (\mathsf{toss}, c_{\mathcal{GC}}, f)$
   Witness : $\mathsf{w} = (x, \mathcal{GC}, r_{gc})$
   $R(\mathsf{st}, \mathsf{w}) = 1$ if and only if :
   - $\mathcal{GC} = \mathsf{Garble}(\mathcal{C}; \mathsf{toss})$ (AND)
   - $\mathcal{C}(\cdot) = f(x, \cdot)$ (AND)
   - $c_{\mathcal{GC}} = \mathsf{Commit}(\mathcal{GC}; r_{gc})$

5.1 Protocol

The NISC protocol π is described below:

Token Transfer:
$\mathcal{R}$ does the following:

1. Pick a random key $\mathsf{k} \xleftarrow{\$} \{0,1\}^\lambda$ for the function PRF.
2. Pick random strings $r_y, r_{ek}, r_{sk}, r_k, r_{\mathsf{Sign}}$.
3. Compute $(\mathsf{sk}, \mathsf{vk}) \leftarrow \mathsf{Gen}(\lambda; r_{\mathsf{Sign}})$ and $\mathsf{ek} \leftarrow \mathsf{ske.setup}(\lambda)$.
4. Create a token $\mathbf{T}$ containing the code in Fig. 1.
5. Send token $\mathbf{T}$ to $\mathcal{S}$.

Communication Message:
The sender $\mathcal{S}$ does the following:

1. Query the token with input "Start" to receive $(c_y, c_{ek}, c_{sk}, c_k, vk)$.
2. Pick random strings $(toss, r_{ske.enc}, r_{(c_{\mathcal{GC}},ct)})$. Compute $\mathcal{GC} = \mathsf{Garble}(\mathcal{C}_x; toss)$ where toss is the randomness for garbling and $\mathcal{C}_x$ is a circuit that on input a string y, outputs $f(x, y)$. Then, compute $c_{\mathcal{GC}} = \mathsf{Commit}(\mathcal{GC}; r_{\mathcal{GC}})$.
3. Using the prover algorithm (RSZK.Prove), engage in an execution of an RSZK argument with $\mathbf{T}$ (who acts as the verifier) for the statement st $= (toss, c_{\mathcal{GC}}, f) \in L$ using witness w $= (x, \mathcal{GC}, r_{\mathcal{GC}})$. That is, as part of the RSZK, if the next message of the prover is msg, query $\mathbf{T}$ with input ("RSZK", $toss, c_{\mathcal{GC}}, r_{ske.enc}, r_{(c_{\mathcal{GC}},ct)}, msg).^3$
4. At the end of the above argument, receive $(ct, \sigma_{(c_{\mathcal{GC}},ct)})$ from $\mathbf{T}$.
5. Then, using the verifier algorithm (RZKAOK.Verify), engage in an execution of a RZKAOK with $\mathbf{T}$ (who acts as the prover) for the statement $st^{\mathbf{T}} = (c_{\mathcal{GC}}, ct, \sigma_{(c_{\mathcal{GC}},ct)}, c_y, c_{ek}, c_{sk}, c_k, toss, vk, r_{ske.enc}, r_{(c_{\mathcal{GC}},ct)}) \in L^{\mathbf{T}}$. That is, as part of the RZKAOK, if the next message of the verifier is msg, query $\mathbf{T}$ with input ("RZKAOK", $toss, r_{ske.enc}, r_{(c_{\mathcal{GC}},ct)}, msg)$. Output $\perp$ if the argument does not verify successfully.
6. Send $(c_{\mathcal{GC}}, \mathcal{GC}, r_{\mathcal{GC}}, ct, \sigma_{(c_{\mathcal{GC}},ct)})$ to the receiver $\mathcal{R}$.

Output Computation Phase:
$\mathcal{R}$ does the following to compute the output:

1. Abort if $\mathsf{Verify}_{vk}((c_{\mathcal{GC}}, ct), \sigma_{(c_{\mathcal{GC}},ct)}) = 0$.
2. Abort if $c_{\mathcal{GC}} \neq \mathsf{Commit}(\mathcal{GC}; r_{\mathcal{GC}})$.
3. Compute $\ell = \mathsf{ske.dec}(ek, ct)$.
4. Evaluate the garbled circuit $\mathcal{GC}$ using the labels ℓ to compute the output. That is, $out = \mathsf{Eval}(\mathcal{GC}, \ell)$.

Remark: In the above description, we were assuming non-interactive commitments (which require injective one way functions) to ease the exposition. In order to rely on just one way functions, we switch our commitment scheme to a two message protocol where the receiver of the commitment sends the first message. Now, we tweak our protocol as follows: after receiving the token, P_1 sends the first message of the commitment which is then used by the token $\mathbf{T}$ to compute c_y. Similarly, P_1 computes c_1 after receiving a first message receiver's commitment message from $\mathbf{T}$. Note that this doesn't affect the round complexity of the NISC protocol.

5.2   Correctness

The correctness of the protocol follows from the correctness of all the underlying primitives.

---

[3] Looking ahead, note that a malicious sender can't change the value of toss across different rounds of the RSZK argument because the token checks the signed copy of the transcript at each step.

Constants: $(k, vk, sk, ek, y, r_y, r_{ek}, r_{sk}, r_k, r_{Sign})$
Case 1: If Input $=$ "Start":

- Compute $c_y = \text{Commit}(y; r_y)$, $c_{ek} = \text{Commit}(ek; r_{ek})$, $c_{sk} = \text{Commit}(sk; r_{sk})$ and $c_k = \text{Commit}(k; r_k)$.
- Output $(c_y, c_{ek}, c_{sk}, c_k, vk)$.

Case 2: If Input $=$ ("RSZK", toss, $c_{\mathcal{GC}}$, $r_{ske.enc}$, $r_{(c_{\mathcal{GC}}, ct)}$, msg):

- Using a random tape defined by $\text{PRF}(k_{\mathcal{R}}, c_1)$ and the verifier algorithm (RSZK.Verify), engage in an execution of a RSZK argument with the querying party as the prover for the statement $st = (\text{toss}, c_{\mathcal{GC}}, f) \in L$.
- Output $\perp$ if the argument does not verify successfully.
- Compute $\ell_y = \text{Garble.KeyGen}(y; \text{toss})$, $ct = \text{ske.enc}(ek, \ell_y; \text{PRF}(k, r_{ske.enc}))$ and $\sigma_{(c_{\mathcal{GC}}, ct)} = \text{Sign}(sk, (c_{\mathcal{GC}}, ct); \text{PRF}(k, r_{(c_{\mathcal{GC}}, ct)}))$.
- Output $(ct, \sigma_{(c_{\mathcal{GC}}, ct)})$.

Case 3: If Input $=$ ("RZKAOK", toss, $r_{ske.enc}$, $r_{(c_{\mathcal{GC}}, ct)}$, msg):

- Using a random tape defined by $\text{PRF}(k_{\mathcal{R}}, 1^{\lambda^2})$ and the prover algorithm (RZKAOK.Prove), engage in an execution of a RZKAOK with the querying party as the verifier for the statement $st^T = (c_{\mathcal{GC}}, ct, \sigma_{(c_{\mathcal{GC}}, ct)}, c_y, c_{ek}, c_{sk}, c_k, \text{toss}, vk, r_{ske.enc}, r_{(c_{\mathcal{GC}}, ct)}) \in L^T$ using witness $w^T = (y, r_y, ek, r_{ek}, sk, r_{sk}, k, r_k, \ell_y, r_{Sign})$.

Fig. 1. Code of token **T**

6 Security Proof: Malicious Receiver

Let's first consider the case where the receiver $\mathcal{R}^*$ is malicious. Let the environment be denoted by $\mathcal{Z}$. Initially, the environment chooses an input $\{x\} \in \{0, 1\}^\lambda$ and sends it to the honest sender $\mathcal{S}$ as his input.

6.1 Simulator Description

The strategy for the simulator Sim against a malicious receiver $\mathcal{R}^*$ is described below:

Token Exchange Phase:
Receive token **T** from $\mathcal{R}^*$.

Token Interaction:

1. Query the token with input "Start" to receive $(c_y, c_{ek}, c_{sk}, c_k, vk)$.
2. Pick random strings (toss, $r_{ske.enc}$, $r_{(c_{\mathcal{GC}}, ct)}$). Compute $c_{\mathcal{GC}} = \text{Commit}(0^\lambda; r_{\mathcal{GC}})$.
3. Using the simulator Sim_{RSZK}, engage in an execution of an RSZK argument with **T** (who acts as the verifier) for the statement $st = (\text{toss}, c_{\mathcal{GC}}, f) \in L$. That is, as part of the RSZK, if the next message of Sim_{RSZK} is msg, query **T** with input ("RSZK", toss, $c_{\mathcal{GC}}$, $r_{ske.enc}$, $r_{(c_{\mathcal{GC}}, ct)}$, msg). Note that Sim forwards the code M of the token **T** that it received from $\mathcal{F}_{\text{WRAP}}$ to Sim_{RSZK}.

4. At the end of the above argument, receive $(\mathsf{ct}, \sigma_{(\mathsf{c}_{\mathsf{Sim}.\mathcal{GC}}, \mathsf{ct})})$ from $\mathbf{T}$.
5. Then, using the verifier algorithm (RZKAOK.Verify), engage in an execution of a RZKAOK with $\mathbf{T}$ (who acts as the prover) for the statement $\mathsf{st}^{\mathbf{T}} = (\mathsf{c}_{\mathcal{GC}}, \mathsf{ct}, \sigma_{(\mathsf{c}_{\mathcal{GC}}, \mathsf{ct})}, \mathsf{c}_{\mathsf{y}}, \mathsf{c}_{\mathsf{ek}}, \mathsf{c}_{\mathsf{sk}}, \mathsf{c}_{\mathsf{k}}, \mathsf{toss}, \mathsf{vk}, \mathsf{r}_{\mathsf{ske.enc}}, \mathsf{r}_{(\mathsf{c}_{\mathcal{GC}}, \mathsf{ct})}) \in L^{\mathbf{T}}$. That is, as part of the RZKAOK, if the next message of the verifier is msg, query $\mathbf{T}$ with input ("RZKAOK", toss, $\mathsf{r}_{\mathsf{ske.enc}}, \mathsf{r}_{(\mathsf{c}_{\mathcal{GC}}, \mathsf{ct})}$, msg). Output $\bot$ if the argument does not verify successfully.

Query to Ideal Functionality:

1. Run $\mathsf{Ext}_{\mathsf{RZKAOK}}$ on the transcript of the above argument to extract a witness $(\mathsf{y}, \mathsf{r}_{\mathsf{y}}, \mathsf{ek}, \mathsf{r}_{\mathsf{ek}}, \mathsf{sk}, \mathsf{r}_{\mathsf{sk}}, \mathsf{k}, \mathsf{r}_{\mathsf{k}}, \ell_{\mathsf{y}}, \mathsf{r}_{\mathsf{Sign}})$. Note that Sim forwards the code M of the token $\mathbf{T}$ that it received from $\mathcal{F}_{\mathsf{WRAP}}$ to $\mathsf{Ext}_{\mathsf{RZKAOK}}$.
2. Query the ideal functionality with input y to receive as output out. The honest sender does not receive any output from the ideal functionality.

Communication Message:

1. Using the output out, generate a simulated garbled circuit and simulated labels. That is, compute $(\mathsf{Sim}.\mathcal{GC}, \mathsf{Sim}.\ell_{\mathsf{y}}) \leftarrow \mathsf{Sim.GC}(\mathsf{out})$.
2. Compute a commitment to the garbled circuit. That is, compute $\mathsf{c}_{\mathsf{Sim}.\mathcal{GC}} = \mathsf{Commit}(\mathsf{Sim}.\mathcal{GC}; \mathsf{r}_{\mathsf{Sim}.\mathcal{GC}})$.
3. Recompute the ciphertext and the signature using the same keys and randomness as done by the token. That is, compute $\mathsf{ct} = \mathsf{ske.enc}(\mathsf{ek}, \mathsf{Sim}.\ell_{\mathsf{y}}; \mathsf{PRF}(\mathsf{k}, \mathsf{r}_{\mathsf{ske.enc}}))$, $\sigma_{(\mathsf{c}_{\mathsf{Sim}.\mathcal{GC}}, \mathsf{ct})} = \mathsf{Sign}(\mathsf{sk}, (\mathsf{c}_{\mathsf{Sim}.\mathcal{GC}}, \mathsf{ct}); \mathsf{PRF}(\mathsf{k}, \mathsf{r}_{(\mathsf{c}_{\mathcal{GC}}, \mathsf{ct})}))$.
4. Send $(\mathsf{c}_{\mathsf{Sim}.\mathcal{GC}}, \mathsf{Sim}.\mathcal{GC}, \mathsf{r}_{\mathsf{Sim}.\mathcal{GC}}, \mathsf{ct}, \sigma_{(\mathsf{c}_{\mathsf{Sim}.\mathcal{GC}}, \mathsf{ct})})$ to the receiver $\mathcal{R}^*$.

6.2   Hybrids

We now show that the real and ideal worlds are computationally indistinguishable via a sequence of hybrid experiments where Hyb_0 corresponds to the real world and Hyb_4 corresponds to the ideal world.

– Hyb_0 - **Real World:** Consider a simulator $\mathsf{Sim}_{\mathsf{Hyb}}$ that performs exactly as done by the honest sender $\mathcal{S}$ in the real world.
– Hyb_1 - **Extraction:** In this hybrid, $\mathsf{Sim}_{\mathsf{Hyb}}$ runs the "Query to Ideal Functionality" phase as in the ideal world. That is, run the algorithm $\mathsf{Ext}_{\mathsf{RZKAOK}}$ to extract $(\mathsf{y}, \mathsf{r}_{\mathsf{y}}, \mathsf{ek}, \mathsf{r}_{\mathsf{ek}}, \mathsf{sk}, \mathsf{r}_{\mathsf{sk}}, \mathsf{k}, \mathsf{r}_{\mathsf{k}}, \ell_{\mathsf{y}}, \mathsf{r}_{\mathsf{Sign}})$, then query the ideal functionality with the value y to receive output out.

  Note that $\mathsf{Sim}_{\mathsf{Hyb}}$ continues to use the honest circuit $\mathcal{GC}$ and its commitment $\mathsf{c}_{\mathcal{GC}}$ in its interaction with $\mathbf{T}$ and the receiver.
– Hyb_2 - **Simulate RSZK:** In this hybrid, in its interaction with the token $\mathbf{T}$, $\mathsf{Sim}_{\mathsf{Hyb}}$ computes the RSZK argument by running the simulator $\mathsf{Sim}_{\mathsf{RSZK}}$ instead of running the honest prover algorithm RSZK.Prove. Note that $\mathsf{Sim}_{\mathsf{Hyb}}$ forwards the code M of the token $\mathbf{T}$ that it received from $\mathcal{F}_{\mathsf{WRAP}}$ to $\mathsf{Sim}_{\mathsf{RSZK}}$.

- Hyb_3 - **Simulate Garbled Circuit:** In this hybrid, Sim_{Hyb} computes the message sent to the receiver as in the ideal world. That is, after interacting with the token, Sim_{Hyb} does the following:
  - Using the output out, generate a simulated garbled circuit and simulated labels. That is, compute $(Sim.\mathcal{GC}, Sim.\ell_y) \leftarrow Sim.GC(out)$.
  - Compute a commitment to the garbled circuit. That is, compute $c_{Sim.\mathcal{GC}} = Commit(Sim.\mathcal{GC}; r_{Sim.\mathcal{GC}})$.
  - Recompute the ciphertext and the signature using the same keys and randomness as done by the token. That is, compute $ct = ske.enc(ek, \ Sim.\ell_y; PRF(k, r_{ske.enc}))$, $\sigma_{(c_{Sim.\mathcal{GC}},ct)} = Sign(sk, (c_{Sim.\mathcal{GC}}, ct); PRF(k, r_{(c_{\mathcal{GC}},ct)}))$.
  - Send $(c_{Sim.\mathcal{GC}}, Sim.\mathcal{GC}, r_{Sim.\mathcal{GC}}, ct, \sigma_{(c_{Sim.\mathcal{GC}},ct)})$ to the receiver $\mathcal{R}^*$.

- Hyb_4 - **Switch Commitment:** In this hybrid, Sim_{Hyb} computes $c_{\mathcal{GC}} = Commit(0^\lambda; r_{\mathcal{GC}})$ and uses this in its interaction with the token. This hybrid corresponds to the ideal world.

We now prove that every pair of consecutive hybrids is computationally indistinguishable and this completes the proof.

Claim. Assuming the argument of knowledge property of the RZKAOK system, Hyb_0 is computationally indistinguishable from Hyb_1.

Proof. The only difference between the two hybrids is that in Hyb_1, Sim_{Hyb} also runs the extractor Ext_{RZKAOK} to extract the adversary's input y. Therefore, by the argument of knowledge property of the RZKAOK system, we know that the extractor Ext_{RZKAOK} is successful except with negligible probability given the transcript of the argument and the code of the prover (that is, the token's code M). Hence, the two hybrids are computationally indistinguishable.

Here, note that Sim_{Hyb} forwards the code M of the token **T** that it received from $\mathcal{F}_{WRAP}$ to the algorithm Ext_{RZKAOK}.

Claim. Assuming the zero knowledge property of the RSZK system, Hyb_1 is computationally indistinguishable from Hyb_2.

Proof. The only difference between the two hybrids is the way in which the RSZK argument is computed. In Hyb_1, Sim_{Hyb} computes the RSZK by running the honest prover algorithm RSZK.Prove, while in Hyb_2, Sim_{Hyb} computes the RSZK by running the simulator Sim_{RSZK}. Thus, it is easy to see that if there exists an adversary that can distinguish between these two hybrids with non-negligible probability, Sim can use that adversary to break the zero knowledge property of the RSZK argument system with non-negligible probability which is a contradiction.

Here, note that Sim_{Hyb} forwards the code M of the token **T** that it received from $\mathcal{F}_{WRAP}$ to the external challenger which it uses to run the algorithm Sim_{RSZK}.

Claim. Assuming the security of the garbling scheme (Garble, Eval) and the argument of knowledge property of the RZKAOK system, Hyb_2 is computationally indistinguishable from Hyb_3.

Proof. The only difference between the two hybrids is the way in which the garbled circuit and the labels that are sent to the receiver are computed. We show that if there exists an adversary $\mathcal{A}$ that can distinguish between the two hybrids, then there exists an adversary $\mathcal{A}_{\mathsf{GC}}$ that can break the security of the garbling scheme. The reduction is described below.

$\mathcal{A}_{\mathsf{GC}}$ interacts with the adversary $\mathcal{A}$ as done by $\mathsf{Sim}_{\mathsf{Hyb}}$ in Hyb_2 except for the changes below. $\mathcal{A}_{\mathsf{GC}}$ first runs the token interaction phase and the query to ideal functionality phase as done by $\mathsf{Sim}_{\mathsf{Hyb}}$ in Hyb_2. In particular, it picks a random string toss, computes $c_{\mathcal{GC}}$ as a commitment to an honest garbled circuit, generates a simulated RSZK argument, extracts the adversary's input y and learns the output out.

Then, $\mathcal{A}_{\mathsf{GC}}$ interacts with the challenger $\mathsf{Chall}_{\mathsf{GC}}$ of the garbling scheme and sends the tuple $(\mathcal{C}_{\mathsf{x}}, \mathsf{y}, \mathsf{out})$. Here, $\mathcal{C}_{\mathsf{x}}$ is a circuit that on input any string z outputs $f(x, z)$. $\mathsf{Chall}_{\mathsf{GC}}$ sends back a tuple $(\mathcal{C}^*, \ell_{\mathsf{y}}^*)$ which is a tuple of garbled circuit and labels that are either honestly generated or simulated. Then, $\mathcal{A}_{\mathsf{GC}}$ computes $\mathsf{c}^* = \mathsf{Commit}(\mathcal{C}^*; \mathsf{r}^*)$, $\mathsf{ct}^* = \mathsf{ske.enc}(\mathsf{ek}, \ell_{\mathsf{y}}^*; \mathsf{PRF}(\mathsf{k}, \mathsf{r}_{\mathsf{ske.enc}}))$, $\sigma_{(\mathsf{c}^*, \mathsf{ct}^*)} = \mathsf{Sign}(\mathsf{sk}, (\mathsf{c}^*, \mathsf{ct}^*); \mathsf{PRF}(\mathsf{k}, \mathsf{r}_{(c_{\mathcal{GC}}, \mathsf{ct}^*)}))$. Finally, $\mathcal{A}_{\mathsf{GC}}$ sends $(\mathsf{c}^*, \mathcal{C}^*, \mathsf{r}^*, \mathsf{ct}^*, \sigma_{(\mathsf{c}^*, \mathsf{ct}^*)})$ to the adversary $\mathcal{A}$ as the message from the sender.

Observe that when $\mathsf{Chall}_{\mathsf{GC}}$ computes the garbled circuit and keys honestly, the interaction between $\mathcal{A}_{\mathsf{GC}}$ and $\mathcal{A}$ corresponds exactly to Hyb_2. This is true because even though in Hyb_2, its the token that generates the ciphertext ct and the signature $\sigma_{(c_{\mathcal{GC}}, \mathsf{ct})}$, from the argument of knowledge property of the scheme RZKAOK, we know that except with negligible probability, they were generated using the message and randomness exactly as computed by $\mathcal{A}_{\mathsf{GC}}$. Then, when $\mathsf{Chall}_{\mathsf{GC}}$ simulates the garbled circuit and keys, the interaction between $\mathcal{A}_{\mathsf{GC}}$ and $\mathcal{A}$ corresponds exactly to Hyb_3. Now, note that the adversary $\mathcal{A}$ does not get access to the randomness toss or the commitment $c_{\mathcal{GC}}$ sent to the token $\mathbf{T}^*$ by the reduction $\mathcal{A}_{\mathsf{GC}}$. Also, crucially, the randomness used in either the ciphertext generation or the signature generation is completely independent of the message being encrypted or signed and hence they don't leak any subliminal information from the token $\mathbf{T}^*$ to the adversary $\mathcal{A}$. Finally, $\mathcal{A}_{\mathsf{GC}}$ does not require any of the randomness used by $\mathsf{Chall}_{\mathsf{GC}}$ to generate the garbled circuit and labels since $\mathcal{A}_{\mathsf{GC}}$ simulates the RSZK argument in its interaction with $\mathbf{T}^*$. Thus, if the adversary $\mathcal{A}$ can distinguish between these two hybrids with non-negligible probability, $\mathcal{A}_{\mathsf{GC}}$ can use the same guess to break the security of the garbling scheme with non-negligible probability which is a contradiction.

Claim. Assuming the hiding property of the commitment scheme Commit, Hyb_3 is computationally indistinguishable from Hyb_4.

Proof. The only difference between the two hybrids is the way in which the value $c_{\mathcal{GC}}$ is computed. In Hyb_3, it is computed as a commitment to the garbled circuit $\mathcal{GC}$ while in Hyb_4, it is computed as a commitment to 0^λ. Note that the value committed to or the randomness for commitment is not used anywhere else since the RSZK argument is now simulated. Thus, it is easy to see that if there exists an adversary that can distinguish between these two hybrids with non-negligible probability, Sim can use that adversary to break the hiding property of the commitment scheme Commit with non-negligible probability, which is a contradiction.

7 Security Proof: Malicious Sender

Consider a malicious sender $\mathcal{S}^*$. Let the environment be denoted by $\mathcal{Z}$. Initially, the environment chooses an input $\{y\} \in \{0,1\}^\lambda$ and sends it to the honest receiver $\mathcal{R}$ as his input.

7.1 Simulator Description

The strategy for the simulator Sim against a malicious sender $\mathcal{S}^*$ is described below:

Token Exchange Phase:
Sim does the following:

1. Pick a random key $k \xleftarrow{\$} \{0,1\}^\lambda$ for the function PRF.
2. Pick random strings $r_y, r_{ek}, r_{sk}, r_k, r_{Sign}$.
3. Compute $(sk, vk) \leftarrow Gen(\lambda; r_{Sign})$ and $ek \leftarrow ske.setup(\lambda)$.
4. Create a token $\mathbf{T}_{Sim}$ almost exactly as in the honest protocol execution with the only difference that instead of the honest receiver's input y, the token uses a random string y^* as input. For completeness, we describe the functionality of the simulated token's code in Fig. 2.
5. Send token $\mathbf{T}_{Sim}$ to $\mathcal{S}^*$.

Communication Message:
Receive $(c_{\mathcal{GC}}, \mathcal{GC}, r_{\mathcal{GC}}, ct, \sigma_{(c_{\mathcal{GC}},ct)})$ from the sender $\mathcal{S}^*$.

Query to Ideal Functionality:

1. Abort if $Verify_{vk}((c_{\mathcal{GC}}, ct), \sigma_{(c_{\mathcal{GC}},ct)}) = 0$.
2. Abort if $c_{\mathcal{GC}} \neq Commit(\mathcal{GC}; r_{\mathcal{GC}})$.
3. Amongst the queries made to the token $\mathbf{T}_{Sim}$, pick one containing the tuple $(c_{\mathcal{GC}}, toss)$ for which the RSZK argument verified. Note that the queries to the token are known to Sim by the observability property of the token.
4. Using this randomness toss from the above query and the garbled circuit $\mathcal{GC}$ sent by $\mathcal{S}^*$, recover $\mathcal{S}^*$'s input x. Recall that $\mathcal{GC} = Garble(\mathcal{C}_x; toss)$ where $\mathcal{C}_x(\cdot) = f(x, \cdot)$.
5. Send x to the ideal functionality and instruct it to deliver output to the honest receiver.

Constants: $(k, vk, sk, ek, y^*, r_y, r_{ek}, r_{sk}, r_k, r_{Sign})$

Case 1: If Input = "Start":

- Compute $c_y = \mathsf{Commit}(y^*; r_y)$, $c_{ek} = \mathsf{Commit}(ek; r_{ek})$, $c_{sk} = \mathsf{Commit}(sk; r_{sk})$ and $c_k = \mathsf{Commit}(k; r_k)$.
- Output $(c_y, c_{ek}, c_{sk}, c_k, vk)$.

Case 2: If Input = ("RSZK", toss, $c_{\mathcal{GC}}$, $r_{ske.enc}$, $r_{(c_{\mathcal{GC}}, ct)}$, msg):

- Using a random tape defined by $\mathsf{PRF}(k_{\mathcal{R}}, c_1)$ and the verifier algorithm (RZKAOK.Prove), engage in an execution of a RSZK argument with the querying party as the prover for the statement $st = (toss, c_{\mathcal{GC}}, f) \in L$.
- Output $\perp$ if the argument does not verify successfully.
- Compute $\ell_y = \mathsf{Garble.KeyGen}(y^*; toss)$, $ct = \mathsf{ske.enc}(ek, \ell_y; \mathsf{PRF}(k, r_{ske.enc}))$ and $\sigma_{(c_{\mathcal{GC}}, ct)} = \mathsf{Sign}(sk, (c_{\mathcal{GC}}, ct); \mathsf{PRF}(k, r_{(c_{\mathcal{GC}}, ct)}))$.
- Output $(ct, \sigma_{(c_{\mathcal{GC}}, ct)})$.

Case 3: If Input = ("RZKAOK", toss, $r_{ske.enc}$, $r_{(c_{\mathcal{GC}}, ct)}$, msg):

- Using a random tape defined by $\mathsf{PRF}(k_{\mathcal{R}}, 1^{\lambda^2})$ and the prover algorithm (RZKAOK.Prove), engage in an execution of a RZKAOK with the querying party as the verifier for the statement $st^T = (c_{\mathcal{GC}}, ct, \sigma_{(c_{\mathcal{GC}}, ct)}, c_y, c_{ek}, c_{sk}, c_k, toss, vk, r_{ske.enc}, r_{(c_{\mathcal{GC}}, ct)}) \in L^T$ using witness $w^T = (y^*, r_y, ek, r_{ek}, sk, r_{sk}, k, r_k, \ell_y, r_{Sign})$.

Fig. 2. Code of simulated token $\mathbf{T}_{\mathsf{Sim}}$. The difference from the honest token code is highlighted in red font. (Color figure online)

7.2 Hybrids

We now show that the real and ideal worlds are computationally indistinguishable via a sequence of hybrid experiments where Hyb_0 corresponds to the real world and Hyb_5 corresponds to the ideal world.

- Hyb_0 - **Real World:** Consider a simulator $\mathsf{Sim}_{\mathsf{Hyb}}$ that performs exactly as done by the honest receiver $\mathcal{R}$ in the real world.
- Hyb_1 - **Extraction:** In this hybrid, $\mathsf{Sim}_{\mathsf{Hyb}}$ also runs the "Query to Ideal Functionality" phase as in the ideal world. That is, $\mathsf{Sim}_{\mathsf{Hyb}}$ extracts the malicious sender's input, sends it to the ideal functionality and instructs it to deliver output to the honest party.
- Hyb_2 - **Simulate RZKAOK:** In this hybrid, in case 3 of the token's description, $\mathsf{Sim}_{\mathsf{Hyb}}$ computes the RZKAOK argument by using the simulator $\mathsf{Sim}_{\mathsf{RZKAOK}}$ instead of running the honest prover algorithm. Note that this happens only internally in the proof and not in the final simulator's description. Hence, the final simulator will not require the code of the environment or need to rewind it.
- Hyb_3 - **Switch Commitment:** In this hybrid, in case 1 of the token's description, $\mathsf{Sim}_{\mathsf{Hyb}}$ computes $c_y = \mathsf{Commit}(y^*; r_y)$.

- Hyb$_4$ - **Switch Ciphertext:** In this hybrid, in case 2 of the token's description, Sim$_{Hyb}$ sets $\ell_y =$ Garble.KeyGen(y^*; toss) and computes ct $=$ ske.enc(ek, ℓ_y ; $r_{ske.enc}$) as in the ideal world.
- Hyb$_5$ - **Honest RZKAOK:** In this hybrid, in case 3 of the token's description, Sim$_{Hyb}$ computes the RZKAOK argument by running the honest prover algorithm as in the ideal world. This hybrid corresponds to the ideal world.

We now prove that every pair of consecutive hybrids is computationally indistinguishable and this completes the proof.

Claim. Assuming the unforgeability property of the signature scheme (Gen, Sign, Verify), the binding property of the commitment scheme Commit, the soundness of the RSZK argument system, Hyb$_0$ is computationally indistinguishable from Hyb$_1$.

Proof. The only difference between the two hybrids is that in Hyb$_1$, Sim$_{Hyb}$ extracts the adversary's input x as in the ideal world. We now argue that this extraction is successful except with negligible probability and this completes the proof that the two hybrids are computationally indistinguishable.

First, from the soundness of the argument system RSZK, we know that except with negligible probability, in one of the arguments given by the malicious sender to the token containing the tuple ($c_{\mathcal{GC}}$, toss), there exists ($x, \mathcal{GC}, r_{\mathcal{GC}}$) such that $\mathcal{C}(\cdot) = f(x, \cdot)$, $\mathcal{GC} =$ Garble($\mathcal{C}$; toss) and $c_{\mathcal{GC}} =$ Commit($\mathcal{GC}$; $r_{\mathcal{GC}}$). Then, from the unforegability of the signature scheme, we know that except with negligible probability, the commitment $c_{\mathcal{GC}}$ sent by $\mathcal{S}^*$ in the first message is indeed the same as the one used in the above RSZK argument. Similarly, from the binding property of the commitment scheme, we know that except with negligible probability, the commitment $c_{\mathcal{GC}}$ sent by $\mathcal{S}^*$ in the first message is indeed a commitment to the same value $\mathcal{GC}$ that was used as witness in the above RSZK argument. Hence, the value x extracted by Sim$_{Hyb}$ is the adversary's input except with negligible probability. There is no difference in the adversary's view between the two hybrids. Thus the joint distribution of the adversary's view and honest party's input is indistinguishable between both the hybrids.

Claim. Assuming the resettable zero knowledge property of the RZKAOK system, Hyb$_1$ is computationally indistinguishable from Hyb$_2$.

Proof. The only difference between the two hybrids is the way in which the RZKAOK argument is computed. In Hyb$_1$, Sim$_{Hyb}$ computes the RZKAOK by running the honest prover algorithm RZKAOK.Prove, while in Hyb$_2$, Sim$_{Hyb}$ computes the RZKAOK by running the simulator Sim$_{RZKAOK}$. Thus, it is easy to see that if there exists an adversary that can distinguish between the joint distribution of the malicious sender's view and the honest party's output in these two hybrids with non-negligible probability, Sim can use that adversary to break the resettable zero knowledge property of the RZKAOK system with non-negligible probability, which is a contradiction.

Note: This is a non-black box reduction - that is, in this reduction, $\mathsf{Sim_{Hyb}}$ needs the adversary's code. However, this is only within this specific reduction. In particular, we stress again that the final simulator will not require the code of the environment or need to rewind it and hence the protocol achieves UC security.

Claim. Assuming the hiding property of the commitment scheme Commit, $\mathsf{Hyb_2}$ is computationally indistinguishable from $\mathsf{Hyb_3}$.

Proof. The only difference between the two hybrids is the way in which the value c_y is computed. In $\mathsf{Hyb_2}$, it is computed as a commitment to the string y while in $\mathsf{Hyb_3}$, it is computed as a commitment to 0^λ. Note that the value committed to or the randomness for commitment is not used as a witness in the RZKAOK since the argument is now simulated. We only need the value y to generate the ciphertext which is not a problem. Thus, it is easy to see that if there exists an adversary that can distinguish between the joint distribution of the malicious sender's view and the honest party's output in these two hybrids with non-negligible probability, Sim can use that adversary to break the hiding property of the commitment scheme Commit with non-negligible probability, which is a contradiction.

Claim. Assuming the semantic security of the encryption scheme (ske.setup, ske.enc, ske.dec), $\mathsf{Hyb_3}$ is computationally indistinguishable from $\mathsf{Hyb_4}$.

Proof. The only difference between the two hybrids is the way in which the ciphertext ct is computed. In $\mathsf{Hyb_3}$, it is computed as an encryption of the string $\ell_y = \mathsf{Garble.KeyGen}(y; \mathsf{toss})$ while in $\mathsf{Hyb_4}$, it is computed as an encryption of $\ell_y = \mathsf{Garble.KeyGen}(y^*; \mathsf{toss})$. Note that the message encrypted, the randomness for encryption or the secret key of the encryption scheme are not used as a witness in the RZKAOK since the argument is now simulated. We only need the value y^* to generate the ciphertext which is not a problem. Thus, it is easy to see that if there exists an adversary that can distinguish between the joint distribution of the malicious sender's view and the honest party's output in these two hybrids with non-negligible probability, Sim can use that adversary to break the semantic security of the encryption scheme with non-negligible probability which is a contradiction.

Claim. Assuming the resettable zero knowledge property of the RZKAOK system, $\mathsf{Hyb_4}$ is computationally indistinguishable from $\mathsf{Hyb_5}$.

Proof. This is identical to the proof of Subsect. 7.2.

8   Extension

Output for Both parties:
By using the transformation of [27] which involves the receiver's output also containing a signed copy of the sender's output that is then sent to the sender using an extra message from the receiver, we can get a two message protocol where both parties receive output. Formally:

Corollary 2. *Assuming one-way functions exist, there exists a two message UC-secure two party computation protocol in the stateless hardware token model using just one token, where both parties receive output.*

A   UC Framework and Ideal Functionalities

For simplicity, we define the two-party protocol syntax, and then informally review the two-party UC-framework, which can be extended to the multi-party case. For more details, see [6].

Protocol syntax. Following [22], a protocol is represented as a system of probabilistic interactive Turing machines (ITMs), where each ITM represents the program to be run within a different party. Specifically, the input and output tapes model inputs and outputs that are received from and given to other programs running on the same machine, and the communication tapes model messages sent to and received from the network. Adversarial entities are also modeled as ITMs.

The construction of a protocol in the UC-framework proceeds as follows: first, an *ideal functionality* is defined, which is a "trusted party" that is guaranteed to accurately capture the desired functionality. Then, the process of executing a protocol in the presence of an adversary and in a given computational environment is formalized. This is called the *real-life* model. Finally, an *ideal process* is considered, where the parties only interact with the ideal functionality, and not amongst themselves. Informally, a protocol realizes an ideal functionality if running of the protocol amounts to "emulating" the ideal process for that functionality.

Let $\Pi = (P_1, P_2)$ be a protocol, and $\mathcal{F}$ be the ideal-functionality. We describe the ideal and real world executions.

The real-life process. The real-life process consists of the two parties P_1 and P_2, the environment $\mathcal{Z}$, and the adversary $\mathcal{A}$. Adversary $\mathcal{A}$ can communicate with environment $\mathcal{Z}$ and can corrupt any party. When $\mathcal{A}$ corrupts party P_i, it learns P_i's entire internal state, and takes complete control of P_i's input/output behavior. The environment $\mathcal{Z}$ sets the parties' initial inputs. Let $\text{REAL}_{\Pi,\mathcal{A},\mathcal{Z}}$ be the distribution ensemble that describes the environment's output when protocol Π is run with adversary $\mathcal{A}$.

We also consider a $\mathcal{G}$-*hybrid model*, where the real-world parties are additionally given access to an ideal functionality $\mathcal{G}$. During the execution of the protocol, the parties can send inputs to, and receive outputs from, the functionality $\mathcal{G}$. We will use $\text{REAL}_{\Pi,\mathcal{A},\mathcal{Z}}^{\mathcal{G}}$ to denote the distribution of the environment's output in this hybrid execution.

The ideal process. The ideal process consists of two "dummy parties" $\hat{P}_1$ and $\hat{P}_2$, the ideal functionality $\mathcal{F}$, the environment $\mathcal{Z}$, and the ideal world adversary Sim, called the simulator. In the ideal world, the uncorrupted dummy parties obtain their inputs from environment $\mathcal{Z}$ and simply hand them over to $\mathcal{F}$. As in the real world, adversary Sim can corrupt any party. Once it corrupts party

$\hat{P}_i$, it learns $\hat{P}_i$'s input, and takes complete control of its input/output behavior. Let $\mathsf{IDEAL}^{\mathcal{F}}_{\mathsf{Sim},\mathcal{Z}}$ be the distribution ensemble that describes the environment's output in the ideal process.

Definition 1 *(UC-Realizing an Ideal Functionality)*. *Let $\mathcal{F}$ be an ideal functionality, and Π be a protocol. We say that Π **UC-realizes** $\mathcal{F}$ **in the $\mathcal{G}$-hybrid model** if for any hybrid-model PPT adversary $\mathcal{A}$, there exists an ideal process expected PPT adversary* Sim *such that for every PPT environment $\mathcal{Z}$:*

$$\{\mathsf{IDEAL}_{\mathcal{F},\mathsf{Sim},\mathcal{Z}}(n,z)\}_{n\in\mathbf{N},z\in\{0,1\}^*} \sim \{\mathsf{REAL}^{\mathcal{G}}_{\Pi,\mathcal{A},\mathcal{Z}}(n,z)\}_{n\in\mathbf{N},z\in\{0,1\}^*} \quad (1)$$

Note that the above equation, says that in the ideal world, the simulator Sim has no access to the ideal functionality $\mathcal{G}$. However, when $\mathcal{G}$ is a set-up assumption, this is not necessarily true and the simulator may have access to $\mathcal{G}$ even in the ideal world. Indeed, there exist different formulations of the UC framework, capturing different requirements on the set-assumptions (e.g., [7]). In [7] for example, the set-up assumption is global, which means that the environment has direct access to the set-up functionality $\mathcal{G}$. Hence, the simulator Sim needs to have oracle access to $\mathcal{G}$ as well.

The Ideal Token Functionality. We now describe the ideal token functionality. Note that our ideal functionality models stateful tokens. Although all our protocols use stateless tokens, an adversarially generated token may be stateful.

Functionality $\mathcal{F}_{\mathsf{WRAP}}$

The functionality is parameterized by a polynomial $\mathsf{p}(\cdot)$ and a security parameter n.

Create: Upon receiving an input $(\mathsf{CREATE}, \mathsf{sid}, \mathbf{C}, \mathbf{U}, \mathsf{M})$ from a party $\mathbf{C}$ (i.e., the token creator), where $\mathbf{U}$ is another party (i.e., the token user) and M is an interactive Turing machine, do:
If there is no tuple of the form $\langle \mathbf{C}, \mathbf{U}, \cdot, \cdot, \cdot \rangle$ stored, store $\langle \mathbf{C}, \mathbf{U}, \mathsf{M}, 0, \phi \rangle$. Send $(\mathsf{CREATE}, \langle \mathsf{sid}, \mathbf{C}, \mathbf{U} \rangle)$ to the adversary.
Deliver: Upon receiving $(\mathsf{READY}, \langle \mathsf{sid}, \mathbf{C}, \mathbf{U} \rangle)$ from the adversary, send $(\mathsf{READY}, \langle \mathsf{sid}, \mathbf{C}, \mathbf{U} \rangle)$ to $\mathbf{U}$.
Execute: Upon receiving an input $(\mathsf{RUN}, \langle \mathsf{sid}, \mathbf{C}, \mathbf{U} \rangle, \mathsf{msg})$ from $\mathbf{U}$, find the unique stored tuple $\langle \mathbf{C}, \mathbf{U}, \mathsf{M}, i, \mathsf{state} \rangle$. If no such tuple exists, do nothing. Otherwise, do:
If M has never been used yet, i.e, $i = 0$, then choose uniform $\mathsf{w} \in \{0,1\}^{\mathsf{p}(n)}$ and set $\mathsf{state} := \mathsf{w}$. Run $(\mathsf{out}, \mathsf{state}') := \mathsf{M}(\mathsf{msg}; \mathsf{state})$ for at most $\mathsf{p}(n)$ steps where out is the response and state' is the new state of M (set $\mathsf{out} := \perp$ and $\mathsf{state}' := \mathsf{state}$ if M does not respond in the allotted time). Send $(\mathsf{RESPONSE}, \langle \mathsf{sid}, \mathbf{C}, \mathbf{U} \rangle, \mathsf{out})$ to $\mathbf{U}$. Erase $\langle \mathbf{C}, \mathbf{U}, \mathsf{M}, i, \mathsf{state} \rangle$ and store $\langle \mathbf{C}, \mathbf{U}, \mathsf{M}, i+1, \mathsf{state}' \rangle$.

Fig. 3. The ideal token functionality $\mathcal{F}_{\mathsf{WRAP}}$ for stateful tokens.

References

1. Afshar, A., Mohassel, P., Pinkas, B., Riva, B.: Non-interactive secure computation based on cut-and-choose. In: Nguyen, P.Q., Oswald, E. (eds.) EUROCRYPT 2014. LNCS, vol. 8441, pp. 387–404. Springer, Heidelberg (2014). https://doi.org/10.1007/978-3-642-55220-5_22

2. Badrinarayanan, S., Garg, S., Ishai, Y., Sahai, A., Wadia, A.: Two-message witness indistinguishability and secure computation in the plain model from new assumptions. In: Takagi, T., Peyrin, T. (eds.) ASIACRYPT 2017. LNCS, vol. 10626, pp. 275–303. Springer, Cham (2017). https://doi.org/10.1007/978-3-319-70700-6_10

3. Barak, B., Goldreich, O., Goldwasser, S., Lindell, Y.: Resettably-sound zero-knowledge and its applications. In: FOCS (2001)

4. Bitansky, N., Paneth, O.: On the impossibility of approximate obfuscation and applications to resettable cryptography. In: STOC (2013)

5. Bitansky, N., Paneth, O.: On non-black-box simulation and the impossibility of approximate obfuscation. SIAM J. Comput. **1383**, 44–1325 (2015)

6. Canetti, R.: Universally composable security: a new paradigm for cryptographic protocols. In: FOCS (2001)

7. Canetti, R., Dodis, Y., Pass, R., Walfish, S.: Universally composable security with global setup. In: Vadhan, S.P. (ed.) TCC 2007. LNCS, vol. 4392, pp. 61–85. Springer, Heidelberg (2007). https://doi.org/10.1007/978-3-540-70936-7_4

8. Canetti, R., Goldreich, O., Goldwasser, S., Micali, S.: Resettable zero-knowledge (extended abstract). In: STOC (2000)

9. Canetti, R., Jain, A., Scafuro, A.: Practical UC security with a global random oracle. In: Proceedings of the 2014 ACM SIGSAC Conference on Computer and Communications Security, Scottsdale, AZ, USA, 3–7 November 2014, pp. 597–608 (2014)

10. Chandran, N., Goyal, V., Sahai, A.: New constructions for UC secure computation using tamper-proof hardware. In: Smart, N. (ed.) EUROCRYPT 2008. LNCS, vol. 4965, pp. 545–562. Springer, Heidelberg (2008). https://doi.org/10.1007/978-3-540-78967-3_31

11. Choi, S.G., Katz, J., Schröder, D., Yerukhimovich, A., Zhou, H.-S.: (Efficient) universally composable oblivious transfer using a minimal number of stateless tokens. In: Lindell, Y. (ed.) TCC 2014. LNCS, vol. 8349, pp. 638–662. Springer, Heidelberg (2014). https://doi.org/10.1007/978-3-642-54242-8_27

12. Chung, K.-M., Ostrovsky, R., Pass, R., Venkitasubramaniam, M., Visconti, I.: 4-round resettably-sound zero knowledge. In: Lindell, Y. (ed.) TCC 2014. LNCS, vol. 8349, pp. 192–216. Springer, Heidelberg (2014). https://doi.org/10.1007/978-3-642-54242-8_9

13. Chung, K., Ostrovsky, R., Pass, R., Visconti, I.: Simultaneous resettability from one-way functions. In: FOCS (2013)

14. Chung, K., Pass, R., Seth, K.: Non-black-box simulation from one-way functions and applications to resettable security. In: STOC (2013)

15. Chung, K., Pass, R., Seth, K.: Non-black-box simulation from one-way functions and applications to resettable security. SIAM J. Comput. **45**, 415–458 (2016)

16. Döttling, N., Kraschewski, D., Müller-Quade, J.: Unconditional and composable security using a single stateful tamper-proof hardware token. In: Ishai, Y. (ed.) TCC 2011. LNCS, vol. 6597, pp. 164–181. Springer, Heidelberg (2011). https://doi.org/10.1007/978-3-642-19571-6_11

17. Döttling, N., Kraschewski, D., Müller-Quade, J.: Statistically Secure linear-rate dimension extension for oblivious affine function evaluation. In: Smith, A. (ed.) ICITS 2012. LNCS, vol. 7412, pp. 111–128. Springer, Heidelberg (2012). https://doi.org/10.1007/978-3-642-32284-6_7
18. Döttling, N., Kraschewski, D., Müller-Quade, J., Nilges, T.: From stateful hardware to resettable hardware using symmetric assumptions. In: Au, M.-H., Miyaji, A. (eds.) ProvSec 2015. LNCS, vol. 9451, pp. 23–42. Springer, Cham (2015). https://doi.org/10.1007/978-3-319-26059-4_2
19. Goldreich, O., Goldwasser, S., Micali, S.: How to construct random functions. J. ACM (1986)
20. Goldreich, O., Oren, Y.: Definitions and properties of zero-knowledge proof systems. J. Cryptol. **7**(1), 1–32 (1994)
21. Goldwasser, S., Kalai, Y.T., Rothblum, G.N.: One-time programs. In: Wagner, D. (ed.) CRYPTO 2008. LNCS, vol. 5157, pp. 39–56. Springer, Heidelberg (2008). https://doi.org/10.1007/978-3-540-85174-5_3
22. Goldwasser, S., Micali, S., Rackoff, C.: The knowledge complexity of interactive proof systems. SIAM J. Comput. **18**, 186–208 (1989)
23. Goyal, V., Ishai, Y., Sahai, A., Venkatesan, R., Wadia, A.: Founding cryptography on tamper-proof hardware tokens. In: Micciancio, D. (ed.) TCC 2010. LNCS, vol. 5978, pp. 308–326. Springer, Heidelberg (2010). https://doi.org/10.1007/978-3-642-11799-2_19
24. Hazay, C., Polychroniadou, A., Venkitasubramaniam, M.: Composable security in the tamper-proof hardware model under minimal complexity. In: Hirt, M., Smith, A. (eds.) TCC 2016. LNCS, vol. 9985, pp. 367–399. Springer, Heidelberg (2016). https://doi.org/10.1007/978-3-662-53641-4_15
25. Ishai, Y., Kushilevitz, E., Ostrovsky, R., Prabhakaran, M., Sahai, A.: Efficient non-interactive secure computation. In: Paterson, K.G. (ed.) EUROCRYPT 2011. LNCS, vol. 6632, pp. 406–425. Springer, Heidelberg (2011). https://doi.org/10.1007/978-3-642-20465-4_23
26. Katz, J.: Universally composable multi-party computation using tamper-proof hardware. In: Naor, M. (ed.) EUROCRYPT 2007. LNCS, vol. 4515, pp. 115–128. Springer, Heidelberg (2007). https://doi.org/10.1007/978-3-540-72540-4_7
27. Katz, J., Ostrovsky, R.: Round-optimal secure two-party computation. In: Franklin, M. (ed.) CRYPTO 2004. LNCS, vol. 3152, pp. 335–354. Springer, Heidelberg (2004). https://doi.org/10.1007/978-3-540-28628-8_21
28. Kolesnikov, V.: Truly efficient string oblivious transfer using resettable tamper-proof tokens. In: Micciancio, D. (ed.) TCC 2010. LNCS, vol. 5978, pp. 327–342. Springer, Heidelberg (2010). https://doi.org/10.1007/978-3-642-11799-2_20
29. Mohassel, P., Rosulek, M.: Non-interactive secure 2PC in the Offline/online and batch settings. In: Coron, J.-S., Nielsen, J.B. (eds.) EUROCRYPT 2017. LNCS, vol. 10212, pp. 425–455. Springer, Cham (2017). https://doi.org/10.1007/978-3-319-56617-7_15
30. Moran, T., Segev, G.: David and goliath commitments: UC Computation for asymmetric parties using tamper-proof hardware. In: Smart, N. (ed.) EUROCRYPT 2008. LNCS, vol. 4965, pp. 527–544. Springer, Heidelberg (2008). https://doi.org/10.1007/978-3-540-78967-3_30
31. Naor, M.: Bit commitment using pseudorandomness. J. Cryptol. **4**, 151–158 (1991)
32. Rompel, J.: One-way functions are necessary and sufficient for secure signatures. In: Proceedings of the Twenty-Second Annual ACM Symposium on Theory of Computing, pp. 387–394. ACM (1990)
33. Yao, A.C.: How to generate and exchange secrets (extended abstract). In: FOCS (1986)

ORAM

Simple and Efficient Two-Server ORAM

S. Dov Gordon[1], Jonathan Katz[2], and Xiao Wang[2(✉)]

[1] George Mason University, Fairfax, USA
gordon@gmu.edu
[2] University of Maryland, College Park, USA
{jkatz,wangxiao}@cs.umd.edu

Abstract. We show a protocol for two-server oblivious RAM (ORAM) that is simpler and more efficient than the best prior work. Our construction combines any tree-based ORAM with an extension of a two-server private information retrieval scheme by Boyle et al., and is able to avoid recursion and thus use only one round of interaction. In addition, our scheme has a very cheap initialization phase, making it well suited for RAM-based secure computation. Although our scheme requires the servers to perform a linear scan over the entire data, the cryptographic computation involved consists only of block-cipher evaluations.

A practical instantiation of our protocol has excellent concrete parameters: for storing an N-element array of arbitrary size data blocks with statistical security parameter λ, the servers each store $4N$ encrypted blocks, the client stores $\lambda + 2 \log N$ blocks, and the total communication per logical access is roughly $10 \log N$ encrypted blocks.

1 Introduction

Protocols for *oblivious RAM* (ORAM) allow a client to outsource storage of an array to a server, and then read from/write to that array without revealing to the server anything about the data itself or the addresses of the data blocks being accessed (i.e., the client's *memory-access pattern*). Since the introduction of the problem by Goldreich and Ostrovsky [16], it has received a significant amount of attention [1,14,17,19,24,26–29,32–34]. The main parameters of interest are the storage at the client and server, as well as the number of communication rounds and the total client-server bandwidth needed to read or write one logical position of the array. In classical work on ORAM, the server was only required to physically read and write elements of some (encrypted) data array; more recent work [1,2,14,24,33] has considered solutions in which the server performs nontrivial computation as well. In that case, solutions relying on non-cryptographic computation, or symmetric-key cryptography alone, are preferable.

Lu and Ostrovsky [23] proposed exploring ORAM in a model where there are *two* non-colluding servers storing data on behalf of the client; the client interacts with the servers to read and write data, but the servers do not need to interact with (or even know about) each other. The solution by Lu and Ostrovsky achieves parameters that are asymptotically better than those realized by any

© International Association for Cryptologic Research 2018
T. Peyrin and S. Galbraith (Eds.): ASIACRYPT 2018, LNCS 11274, pp. 141–157, 2018.
https://doi.org/10.1007/978-3-030-03332-3_6

single-server solution: for accessing an N-element array of B-bit data blocks, the client in their protocol has storage independent of N and B, the servers each store $O(N)$ encrypted data blocks, and reading/writing has an amortized communication complexity of $O(\log N)$ encrypted data blocks. On the other hand, like most ORAM constructions with sublinear communication (with a few exceptions discussed below), the Lu-Ostrovsky protocol requires $O(\log N)$ rounds of interaction between the client and servers per logical memory access; since it is based on a hierarchical approach [16] and requires periodic reshuffling, their scheme is also relatively complex and does not offer good worst-case performance guarantees. A recent two-server ORAM scheme by Abraham et al. [1] improves the communication overhead to $O(\log N/\log\log N)$ when $B = \Omega(\lambda \log^2 N)$, but still requires $O(\log N)$ rounds.

1.1 Summary of Our Results

We show here a construction of a two-server ORAM protocol that improves on prior work both concretely and theoretically. Our scheme is also very simple to describe and implement, which we view as an added advantage especially when applying ORAM to RAM-based secure computation.

Concretely, our scheme is extremely efficient. In one instantiation of our scheme, the client stores $\lambda + 2\log N$ data blocks (where λ is a statistical security parameter), the servers each store $4N$ encrypted data blocks, and the total communication per logical read/write is only roughly $10 \log N$ encrypted blocks. This can be compared to the Lu-Ostrovsky scheme, which is estimated by the authors to have server storage $2N + O(\log^9 N)$ and an amortized bandwidth of more than $160 \log N$ encrypted data blocks per logical memory access. (Abraham et al. do not offer concrete estimates of the performance of their scheme, but we believe our protocol will have better communication overhead for practical parameters, especially for moderate B.) A drawback of our protocol is that it requires the servers to perform a linear scan of the entire data, and perform a linear number of symmetric-key operations.

In a theoretical sense, we improve upon prior work in several respects. Most importantly, our protocol requires only one round of communication per logical access; note that achieving logarithmic communication overhead with one round of interaction is a major open question for single-server ORAM.[1] Second, our communication bound holds *in the worst case*, in contrast to the Lu-Ostrovsky scheme for which it holds only in an amortized sense. Finally, in contrast to the scheme of Abraham et al., our protocol has good communication overhead regardless of the block size.

Applications to secure computation. Classical work on generic secure computation views the function being computed as a boolean or arithmetic circuit.

---

[1] Known single-server ORAM schemes with sublinear worst-case communication and one round of interaction [12,13] have communication complexity at least $\kappa B \log^2 N$ and would be prohibitively inefficient to implement. Other one-round schemes [11,33] have sublinear communication only in an amortized sense.

More recently, researchers have explored secure-computation protocols that work directly in the RAM model of computation [8–10,18,21,22,25,31,35]. A basic idea in these works is to leverage ORAM to ensure that the parties' accesses to (shared) memory are oblivious. These works all assume either that the shared memory is initially empty, or that initialization of the ORAM data structure is done during some trusted preprocessing phase, because initializing a non-empty ORAM as part of the protocol would be infeasible. For our ORAM protocol, initialization is essentially "for free" and can be done locally by the servers without any interaction with the client. (To the best of our knowledge, this is not true for any prior ORAM scheme with sublinear communication overhead.) This makes our protocol extremely well-suited for applications to RAM-based secure computation in both the two-party and multi-party settings.

Our scheme has the added advantage that reads from a public address can be done very efficiently, with communication of only $2 \log N$ encrypted blocks and negligible computation. This property is also very useful in applications to secure computation.

1.2   Overview of Our Construction

Our construction can be viewed as combining any tree-based ORAM protocol [27–30] with a two-server private information retrieval (PIR) scheme [7]. (Combining ORAM and PIR was suggested previously by Mayberry et al. [24] in the single-sever setting, and Abraham et al. [1] in the two-server setting.) We describe each of these primitives informally, and then provide an overview of our construction. Section 2 contains formal definitions; a detailed description of our protocol is given in Sect. 3.

Tree-based ORAM. At a somewhat informal level, which will be sufficient to understand the main ideas of our construction, a tree-based ORAM scheme—in the single-server setting—works in the following way.[2] Let D denote the client's data array with $D[i]$, for $0 \le i < N$, denoting the data block stored at address i of the array. The client maintains a function position (called a *position map*) that maps logical memory addresses to leaves in a binary tree of depth $L = O(\log N)$ stored by the server, where each node in the tree can store some bounded number of data blocks. It will be convenient for us to assume that every node in the tree stores the same (constant) number of data blocks, with the exception of the root that can store more items. Instead of being stored on the server, the root is stored on the client and is also called a *stash*.

At any point in time, the value $D[i]$ is stored at some node on the path from the root of the tree to the leaf at position(i) (we call this the *path to* position(i)). The client performs a logical read of address i by reading the entire path to position(i) and taking the value of $D[i]$ that is found closest to the root; a logical write to address i is done by storing the new value of $D[i]$ in the stash (replacing any old value of $D[i]$ found there).

---

[2] For simplicity, we ignore encryption of the data blocks in the description that follows.

Executions of an *eviction procedure* are interspersed with logical reads and writes. At a high level, during this procedure the client chooses a path $\mathcal{P}$ in the tree and then, for each data block $D[i]$ stored at some node in that path, pushes that block as far down in $\mathcal{P}$ as possible subject to the constraint that $D[i]$ must lie on the path to $\mathsf{position}(i)$. The updated values of the nodes on path $\mathcal{P}$ are then rewritten to the server. The purpose of the eviction procedure is to prevent nodes in the tree from overflowing.

Note that to ensure obliviousness, the position map must be random (so the server cannot correlate a particular path being read by the client with a logical address) and $\mathsf{position}(i)$ must be updated each time $D[i]$ is read (so the server cannot tell when the same logical address is accessed repeatedly). Since the position map itself has size $\Theta(N)$, the client must store the position map on the server in order to achieve client storage $o(N)$. The position map can be stored recursively using a tree-based ORAM; note, however, that this induces several rounds of interaction between the client and server for each logical memory access, and also increases the server-side storage.

Private information retrieval. Abstractly, a private information retrieval (PIR) scheme provides a way for a client to obliviously read a data block from an N-element array of B-bit items stored on a server using $o(BN)$ communication. For our purposes, the main distinction between PIR and ORAM is that PIR supports reads only. Historically, PIR schemes have also involved only one round of interaction.

PIR was first considered in the multi-server setting [7], where information-theoretic security is possible. Although PIR with computational security is possible in the single-server setting [6,15,20], constructions of (computationally secure) PIR in the two-server setting have much better computational efficiency. In particular, a recent construction of two-server PIR by Boyle et al. [3–5] requires only symmetric-key operations by both the client and the server, uses only one round, and has communication complexity $2B + O(\kappa \cdot \log N)$ for κ a computational security parameter. (In fact, they show that the communication can be reduced asymptotically to $2B + O(\kappa \cdot \log(N/\kappa))$ but for practical parameters this does not seem to yield a concrete improvement.)

Our construction. We show how to combine tree-based ORAM with PIR to obtain an efficient and conceptually simple protocol in the two-server setting.

In existing tree-based ORAM schemes the eviction procedure is already oblivious, as it involves either choosing a random eviction path [29] or choosing eviction paths according to a deterministic schedule [14,27]. Thus, only reads need to be made oblivious. As noted earlier, in prior work this is achieved using a random position map that is updated after each read. Our first conceptual insight is that we can instead have the client use (two-server) PIR to read the path associated with a particular data block. As a consequence, we can avoid ever having to update the position map (see below for why we need a position map at all) and so can use a pseudorandom position map, thereby avoiding recursion and allowing us to obtain a one-round protocol.

Obliviously reading a path in a tree of depth L can always be done using L parallel executions of a generic PIR protocol. Our second observation is that we can do better than this by adapting the specific (two-server) PIR scheme of Boyle et al. so as to natively support oblivious reading of a *path* in a tree with less than L times the communication. Details are given in Sect. 2.2.

Since a position map is no longer needed for obliviousness, it is tempting to think that we can avoid the position map altogether. Unfortunately this is not the case, as we still need a (pseudo)random mapping of addresses to leaves in order to ensure *correctness*—specifically, so that the probability of an overflow remains negligible. In our case, however, we show that it is sufficient to choose a random position map *once*, at the outset of the protocol, and then leave it fixed for the remainder of the execution. This also means that we can generate the pseudorandom position map based on a short key chosen at the beginning of the protocol. Finally, we observe that this allows for extremely efficient initialization (in settings where the data—perhaps in encrypted form—is initially held by the server), at least when the memory-access pattern is chosen non-adaptively; specifically, initialization can be done by sending the key defining the position map to the server, who then arranges the data blocks as needed.

2   Background

2.1   Oblivious RAM

We use the standard definitions of correctness and security for ORAM [16], repeated here for completeness. Readers familiar with these definitions can safely skip to the next section.

For fixed N, B, we define a *memory access* to be a tuple (op, i, v) where $\mathsf{op} \in \{\mathsf{read}, \mathsf{write}\}$, $i \in \{0, \dots, N-1\}$, and $v \in \{0,1\}^B$. Let D be an N-element array containing B-bit entries. The result of applying (read, i, v) to D is $D[i]$, and the array D is unchanged. The result of applying (write, i, v) is $\bot$, and D is updated to a new array D' that is identical to D except that $D'[i] = v$. Given an initial array D and a sequence of memory accesses $(\mathsf{op}_1, i_1, v_1)$, $\dots$, $(\mathsf{op}_M, i_M, v_M)$, we define correctness for the sequence of results $o_1, \dots, o_M$ in the natural way; namely, the sequence of results is correct iff, for all t, the result o_t is equal to the last value written to i_t (or is equal to $D[i_t]$ if there were no previous writes to i_t).

A two-server, one-round ORAM scheme is defined by a collection of four algorithms ORAM.Init, ORAM.C, ORAM.S, and ORAM.C′ with the following syntax:

- ORAM.Init takes as input 1^λ, 1^κ and elements $D[0], \dots, D[N-1] \in \{0,1\}^B$. It outputs state st and data T to be stored at the servers.
- ORAM.C takes as input st and a memory access (op, i, v). It outputs updated state st′ along with a pair of queries q_0, q_1.
- ORAM.S takes as input data T and a query q. It outputs updated data T' and a response r.

– ORAM.C' takes as input state st and a pair of responses r_0, r_1. It outputs updated state st' and a value o.

We define correctness and security via an experiment Expt. Given an array D (which defines the parameters N and B) and a sequence of memory accesses seq $= ((\mathsf{op}_1, i_1, v_1), \ldots, (\mathsf{op}_M, i_M, v_M))$, experiment $\mathsf{Expt}(1^\lambda, 1^\kappa, D, \mathsf{seq})$ first runs $(\mathsf{st}_0, T_0) \leftarrow \mathsf{ORAM.Init}(1^\lambda, 1^\kappa, D)$ and sets $T_{0,0} = T_{0,1} = T_0$. Then, for $t = 1$ to M it does:

1. Run $(\mathsf{st}'_{t-1}, q_{t,0}, q_{t,1}) \leftarrow \mathsf{ORAM.C}(\mathsf{st}_{t-1}, (\mathsf{op}_t, i_t, v_t))$.
2. Run $(T_{t,b}, r_{t,b}) \leftarrow \mathsf{ORAM.S}(T_{t-1,b}, q_{t,b})$ for $b \in \{0,1\}$.
3. Run $(\mathsf{st}_t, o_t) \leftarrow \mathsf{ORAM.C}'(\mathsf{st}'_{t-1}, r_{t,0}, r_{t,1})$.

Let $\mathsf{view}_b = (T_0, q_{1,b}, \ldots, q_{M,b})$. The output of the experiment is $(\mathsf{view}_0, \mathsf{view}_1, o_1, \ldots, o_M)$.

Correctness requires that for any polynomial M there is a negligible function negl such that for any λ, κ, D, and sequence of $M = M(\lambda)$ memory accesses seq $= ((\mathsf{op}_1, i_1, v_1), \ldots, (\mathsf{op}_M, i_M, v_M))$, if we compute $(\mathsf{view}_0, \mathsf{view}_1, o_1, \ldots, o_M) \leftarrow \mathsf{Expt}(1^\lambda, 1^\kappa, D, \mathsf{seq})$ then the sequence of results $o_1, \ldots, o_M$ is correct (for D and seq) except with probability $\mathsf{negl}(\lambda)$.

An ORAM protocol is secure if for any λ and PPT adversary A the following is negligible in κ:

$$\left| \Pr\left[\begin{array}{l} (D_0, \mathsf{seq}_0, D_1, \mathsf{seq}_1) \leftarrow A(1^\lambda, 1^\kappa); b \leftarrow \{0,1\}; \\ (\mathsf{view}_0, \mathsf{view}_1, o_1, \ldots, o_M) \leftarrow \mathsf{Expt}(1^\lambda, 1^\kappa, D_b, \mathsf{seq}_b) \end{array} : A(\mathsf{view}_0) = b \right] - \frac{1}{2} \right|$$

(and analogously for view_1), where D_0, D_1 have identical parameters N, B, and where $\mathsf{seq}_0, \mathsf{seq}_1$ have the same length. As usual, this notion of security assumes the servers are honest-but-curious.

We remark that, as is typical in this setting, both correctness and security are defined with respect to a non-adaptive selection of inputs (in terms of both the original data and the sequence of memory accesses). Our scheme remains secure even for adaptively chosen inputs, though in that case we cannot use the optimized initialization procedure discussed at the end of Sect. 3.1.

2.2 Private Path Retrieval

We review the notion of *private information retrieval (PIR)*, and propose an extension that we call *private path retrieval (PPR)*. We then describe an efficient construction of a two-server PPR scheme based on a two-server PIR scheme of Boyle et al.

Abstractly, a PIR scheme allows a client to obliviously learn one value out of an array of N values stored by a pair of servers. Specialized to XOR-based, one-round protocols in the two-server setting, we define a PIR scheme as a pair of algorithms (PIR.C, PIR.S) with the following syntax:

– PIR.C is a randomized algorithm that takes as input parameters $1^\kappa, B, N$, and an index $i \in \{0, \ldots, N-1\}$. It outputs a pair of queries q_0, q_1.

- PIR.S is an algorithm that takes as input $D[0], \ldots, D[N-1] \in \{0,1\}^B$, and a query q. It outputs a response r.

Correctness requires that for all κ, B, N, i, and D as above, we have

$$\Pr\left[\begin{array}{c}(q_0, q_1) \leftarrow \text{PIR.C}(1^\kappa, B, N, i); \\ \{r_b := \text{PIR.S}(D, q_b)\}_{b \in \{0,1\}} : r_0 \oplus r_1 = D[i]\end{array}\right] = 1.$$

A PIR scheme can be used by a client C and a pair of servers S_0, S_1 in the natural way. S_0 and S_1 each begin holding identical copies of an N-element array D of B-bit data blocks. When C wants to learn the element located at address i, it computes $(q_0, q_1) \leftarrow \text{PIR.C}(1^\kappa, B, N, i)$ and sends q_b to S_b. The servers compute their corresponding responses r_0, r_1, and send them to the client. The client can then recover $D[i]$ by computing $D[i] = r_0 \oplus r_1$.

Security requires that neither server learns anything about the client's desired address i. In other words, it is required that for all B, N, i, i', and $b \in \{0,1\}$ the following distributions are computationally indistinguishable (with security parameter κ):

$$\{(q_0, q_1) \leftarrow \text{PIR.C}(1^\kappa, B, N, i) : q_b\} \quad \text{and} \quad \{(q_0, q_1) \leftarrow \text{PIR.C}(1^\kappa, B, N, i') : q_b\}.$$

Private path retrieval. For our application, we extend PIR to a new primitive that we call *private path retrieval* (PPR). Here, we view the data stored by the servers as being organized in a depth-L binary tree with $N = 2^L$ leaves; the client wishes to obliviously obtain all the values stored on some *path* in that tree from the root to a leaf. (In fact, it will be convenient to omit the root itself.) Formally, and again specializing to XOR-based, one-round protocols in the two-server setting, we define a PPR scheme as a pair of algorithms (PPR.C, PPR.S) with the following syntax:

- PPR.C is a randomized algorithm that takes as input parameters $1^\kappa, B, N$, and an index $i \in \{0, \ldots, N-1\}$ corresponding to a leaf node. It outputs a pair of queries q_0, q_1.
- PPR.S is an algorithm that takes as input a tree T of elements $T[x] \in \{0,1\}^B$, for $x \in \{0,1\}^{\leq \log N}$, and a query q. It outputs a response vector $r^1, \ldots, r^L$.

Representing $i \in \{0, \ldots, N-1\}$ as an L-bit integer in the obvious way, we let $\langle i \rangle_t$ denote the t-bit prefix of i for $1 \leq t \leq L$. Correctness for a PPR scheme requires that for all κ, B, N, i, and T as above, and all $t \in \{1, \ldots, L\}$, we have

$$\Pr\left[\begin{array}{c}(q_0, q_1) \leftarrow \text{PPR.C}(1^\kappa, B, N, i); \\ \{(r_b^1, \ldots, r_b^L) := \text{PPR.S}(1^\kappa, T, q_b)\}_{b \in \{0,1\}} : r_0^t \oplus r_1^t = T[\langle i \rangle_t]\end{array}\right] = 1.$$

Security requires that neither server learns anything about the client's desired path. That is, we require that for all B, N, i, i', and $b \in \{0,1\}$ the following distributions are computationally indistinguishable (with security parameter κ):

$$\{(q_0, q_1) \leftarrow \text{PPR.C}(1^\kappa, B, N, i) : q_b\} \quad \text{and} \quad \{(q_0, q_1) \leftarrow \text{PPR.C}(1^\kappa, B, N, i') : q_b\}.$$

Constructing a PPR scheme. It is immediate that any PIR scheme can be used generically to construct a PPR scheme. Briefly: the servers view the the tree they store as a collection of L arrays, with the ith level of the tree corresponding to an array D_i containing 2^i elements. The client can then obliviously retrieve a path in the tree by running any underlying PIR protocol L times, once for each array $D_1, \ldots, D_L$. This increases both the client-to-server and the server-to-client communication by roughly a factor of L. This construction is "overkill," though, in the sense that it allows the client to retrieve an *arbitrary* data block at each level of the tree, whereas a PPR scheme only needs to support retrieval of data blocks along a *path*. This suggests that it may be possible to further optimize the construction.

Indeed, we show that by adapting the specific PIR scheme of Boyle et al. a better solution is possible. The communication complexity of their basic PIR scheme is $2B + O(\kappa \log N)$; thus, the generic construction sketched above would give a PPR scheme with communication complexity $2B \log N + O(\kappa \log^2 N)$. We show how to improve this to $2B \log N + O(\kappa \log N)$.

Rather than give the details of the PIR scheme of Boyle et al., we describe their scheme abstractly. To retrieve the ith element of an array D of length N, the client in their scheme sends each server S_b a query of length $\kappa + 1 + (\kappa + 2) \cdot \log N = O(\kappa \log N)$ bits; the query enables that server to compute a sequence of bits $\lambda_b[0], \ldots, \lambda_b[N-1]$ with the property that $\lambda_0[j] \oplus \lambda_1[j] = 1$ iff $j = i$. Server S_b then responds with $r_b = \bigoplus_{j=0}^{N-1} \lambda_b[j] \cdot D[j]$. It is easily verified that $r_0 \oplus r_1 = D[i]$.

To construct a PPR scheme, we leave the client algorithm unchanged. Let i denote the leaf corresponding to the path the client wishes to retrieve. As before, server S_b then computes a sequence of bits $\lambda_b[0], \ldots, \lambda_b[N-1]$ where $\lambda_0[j] \oplus \lambda_1[j] = 1$ iff $j = i$. Each server then constructs a logical binary tree of depth $L = \log N$ with the λ-values at the leaves, and recursively defines the values at each internal node of this logical tree to be the XOR of the values of its children. In this way, each server S_b obtains[3] a collection of bits $\{\lambda_b[x]\}_{x \in \{0,1\}^{\leq L}}$ with the property that $\lambda_0[x] \oplus \lambda_1[x] = 1$ iff x is a prefix of i (or, in other words, iff the node corresponding to x is on the path from the root to the ith leaf). Server S_b then computes the sequence of responses $r_b^t = \bigoplus_{x \,:\, |x|=t} \lambda_b[x] \cdot T[x]$ for $1 \leq t \leq L$. One can verify that $r_0^t \oplus r_1^t = T[\langle i \rangle_t]$ for all t. Note also that security of the PPR scheme is implied immediately by security of the original PIR scheme, which in turn is based on the existence of pseudorandom functions.

Summarizing, we have:

Theorem 1. *Assuming the existence of pseudorandom functions, there is a two-server PPR scheme in which the client sends each server a query of length $O(\kappa \log N)$, and each server sends back a response of length $B \cdot \log N$.*

---

[3] Readers familiar with the construction of Boyle et al. may observe that these values are already implicitly defined as part of their scheme; we explicitly describe the computation of these values for self-containment.

3 A Two-Server ORAM Scheme

We now present our two-server ORAM scheme, which can be viewed as being constructed by adapting the ring ORAM protocol [27] to the two-server setting and then combining it with the PPR scheme from Sect. 2.2. We build on ring ORAM for concreteness, but our general idea can also be applied to several other tree-based ORAM schemes from the literature (e.g., [28–30]).

3.1 Description of Our Scheme

Preliminaries. The client's data is viewed as a sequence of $N = 2^L$ data blocks $D[0], \ldots, D[N-1] \in \{0,1\}^B$. Each server stores identical copies of a depth-L, full binary tree T with N leaves numbered from 0 to $N-1$; we number the levels of the tree from the root at level 0 to the leaves at level L, and refer to each node of the tree (except the root) as a *bucket*. (The root will be treated differently from the other nodes; see further below.)

As in other tree-based ORAM schemes, the client maintains a position map that maps logical memory addresses to leaves in T. In our case, the position map will be static and we implement it by a pseudorandom function $F_K : [N] \to [N]$, with K chosen by the client. For $\mathsf{pos} \in \{0, \ldots, 2^L - 1\}$ denoting a leaf in T, we let $\mathcal{P}(\mathsf{pos})$ denote the path consisting of all buckets in the tree from the root to that leaf.

A *record* $(\mathsf{flag}, i, \mathsf{pos}, \mathsf{data}) \in \{0,1\} \times \{0,1\}^{\log N} \times \{0,1\}^{\log N} \times \{0,1\}^B$ contains four fixed-length fields, encrypted using a key held by the client. (For simplicity in what follows, we omit explicit mention of encrypting/decrypting these blocks.) If $\mathsf{flag} = 1$ then the record is *real* and we have $\mathsf{pos} = F_K(i)$ and $\mathsf{data} = D[i]$; if $\mathsf{flag} = 0$ then the record is a *dummy record* and $i, \mathsf{pos}, \mathsf{data}$ can be arbitrary (so long as they are the correct length). Each bucket in the binary tree stored by the servers contains Z records, where Z is a parameter we fix later.

As an optimization, we have the client store the root of the tree and refer to the root as the *stash*. (We stress, however, that when we refer to a path $\mathcal{P} = \mathcal{P}(\mathsf{pos})$ in the tree, that path always includes the root/stash.) All records in the stash are real, and we allow the stash to store more than Z records. Of course, the records in the stash do not need to be encrypted.

Invariant. In our scheme, the servers store identical copies of the tree T at all times. As in other tree-based ORAM schemes, we maintain the invariant that, for all i, there is always a (real) record $(1, i, \mathsf{pos}, D[i])$ located in some bucket on $\mathcal{P}(\mathsf{pos})$. It is possible that multiple real records with the same index appear in the tree at the same time; in this case, the one closest to the root is always the most up-to-date copy.

Accessing memory. To read logical address i of its array, the client simply needs to read the path $\mathcal{P}(F_K(i))$ and then find the corresponding record closest to the root. For obliviousness, reading this path is done using our PPR scheme. A logical write of the value v to address i of the array is done by storing the record $(1, i, F_K(i), v)$ in the stash (removing from the stash any outdated record with the same logical address, if necessary).

Eviction. As described, writing to the array will cause the number of records stored in the stash to grow without bound. We prevent this by performing an *eviction procedure* after every A memory accesses, where A is a configurable parameter. This eviction procedure reads a path $\mathcal{P}$ in the tree, updates the buckets in that path, and then writes the updated path $\mathcal{P}'$ back to the servers. To fully specify this process, we need to determine two things: (1) how the paths to be evicted are chosen and (2) how the chosen paths are updated.

- Following Gentry et al. [14], we choose paths to be evicted according to a deterministic schedule, namely, in reverse lexicographic order. This is also the schedule used in ring ORAM. Note that using a deterministic schedule ensures obliviousness.
- Our update procedure is similar (but not exactly identical) to the one used in path ORAM [29] and ring ORAM [27]. As in those schemes, we update a path $\mathcal{P}$ by pushing every real record $(1, i, \mathsf{pos}, v)$ in that path as far down the tree as possible, subject to the constraint that it must be located on $\mathcal{P}(\mathsf{pos})$ (and the constraint that each bucket holds at most Z records). In addition, prior to doing this, we also clear out any stale records in $\mathcal{P}$. That is, if for any i there are multiple records of the form $(1, i, \mathsf{pos}, \star)$ in $\mathcal{P}$, then only the one closest to the root is kept; the rest are replaced with dummy records.

We give a formal description of our scheme, assuming initialization of the tree has already been done, in Fig. 1. See below for a discussion of initialization.

Parameters. Each record has length exactly $1 + 2\log N + B$ bits before being encrypted.[4] Encryption adds at most κ additional bits; this can be reduced by using a global counter keeping track of how many records have been encrypted thus far. We let R denote the size, in bits, of a record (after encryption). If $\kappa = O(B)$ and $B \geq \log N$ (which is typical in practice), we have $R = O(B)$.

As described, the client's stash can grow arbitrarily large. We show in the next section that when $A = 1$ (i.e., eviction is done after every access) and $Z = 3$ the client's stash contains at most λ records except with probability negligible in λ. The servers each hold fewer than $2N$ buckets, with each bucket containing Z records; thus, for the parameter settings discussed above, each server's storage is at most $2ZNR = O(BN)$ bits.

The total communication for a logical memory access can be computed as follows:

1. As part of the PPR scheme, the client sends $O(\kappa \log N)$ bits to each server, and each server responds with $RZ \log N$ bits.
2. For eviction, one server sends $RZ \log N$ bits to the client, and then the client sends $RZ \log N$ bits to each server.

---

[4] As a small optimization, $F_K(i)$ need not be stored in a record, as the client can recompute it when needed.

The state of the client includes the stash, a key K, and a counter ctr initialized to 0 that indicates the next eviction path. The servers store ctr and identical copies of a tree T. The parameter A determines how often eviction is done.

On input (op, i, v) do:

1. Let pos $:= F_K(i)$.
2. The client uses PPR to read $\mathcal{P}(\text{pos})$ from T.
3. If op = read then scan through $\mathcal{P}(\text{pos})$ to find the real record $(1, i, \text{pos}, v_i)$ closest to the root, and output v_i.
4. If op = write then (1) remove any records of the form $(1, i, \text{pos}, \star)$ from the stash, and (2) add the record $(1, i, \text{pos}, v)$ to the stash.
5. Set ctr $=$ ctr $+ 1 \bmod A \cdot N$. If ctr $= 0 \bmod A$ then run procedure Evict(ctr/A).

Evict(ctr):

1. Let $\mathcal{P}$ be the path corresponding to ctr under reverse lexicographic order. Request $\mathcal{P}$ from one of the servers.
2. If, for any i, there are multiple (real) records $(1, i, \text{pos}, \star)$ in $\mathcal{P}$, then only the one closest to the root is kept; the rest are replaced with dummy records.
3. Process the remaining real records one-by-one, starting from the root. For each such record record $= (1, i, \text{pos}, v)$, find the bucket in $\mathcal{P}$ furthest from the root that (1) is on $\mathcal{P}(\text{pos})$ and (2) contains fewer than Z real records. Put record in that bucket in place of a dummy block. (If no such bucket is found then keep record where it is.) Finally, (re-)encrypt all records in the updated buckets.
4. The updated path $\mathcal{P}'$ is then written back to both servers.

Fig. 1. Our two-server ORAM scheme.

Thus, for the parameter settings discussed above, the total communication complexity is $O(B \log N)$ even when $A = 1$. Importantly, the constants are small; the worst-case communication (for general parameters) is at most

$$\kappa + 1 + (\kappa + 2) \cdot \log N + 5Z \cdot (\kappa + 2 \log N + B) \cdot \log N$$

bits, and the amortized communication (in bits) is

$$\kappa + 1 + (\kappa + 2) \cdot \log N + \left(2Z + \frac{3Z}{A}\right) \cdot (\kappa + 2 \log N + B) \cdot \log N.$$

Thus, as in path ORAM, we can trade off Z and A to reduce communication.

As described (and taking $A = 1$), the protocol uses three messages if we piggyback the server's eviction message with its response in the PPR scheme. However, if we delay the client's eviction message until the next time the client initiates the PPR protocol (for the next memory access), then we obtain a one-round protocol. Since the client must now store the updated path $\mathcal{P}'$ between memory accesses, this increases the storage of the client by $ZR \log N$ bits.

Initialization. Initialization can be done locally at the client by starting with a tree consisting only of dummy records and then simulating the process of writing each data block of the original array; the resulting tree is then uploaded to each server. We additionally observe that in settings where the servers initially hold the array (in encrypted form), initialization can be done in essentially the same way—but locally at each server—by having the client simply send K to the servers.[5]

3.2   Analysis

Correctness of our protocol follows by inspection, and obliviousness follows from obliviousness of the PPR scheme and the fact that a deterministic eviction procedure is used. Thus, in the remainder of this section we focus on analyzing the efficiency of the scheme, specifically, the size of the stash stored by the client. Compared to the similar analysis done for ring ORAM and other tree-based schemes, there are two differences: first, in our scheme the tree may contain stale records (i.e., real records $(1, i, \mathsf{pos}, v)$ that have been superseded by a more up-to-date record stored closer to the root on the same path $\mathcal{P}(\mathsf{pos})$); second, in our scheme the position map is fixed once-and-for-all rather than being updated each time a memory access is done. Careful examination of the proofs for prior tree-based ORAM schemes, however, shows that both of these changes have no effect on the final bound. Nevertheless, we include details of the analysis (following [27]) for completeness.

Recall that we assume eviction is done after every A accesses. We define the size of the stash after the Mth memory access to be the size of the stash following the last invocation of the eviction procedure. (In our one-round scheme the eviction procedure following the Mth memory access is not completed until the $(M + 1)$st memory access takes place; this difference can only increase the size of the stash by a single record.)

During the execution of our ORAM scheme, the resulting tree stored by the servers can contain two types of real records. We call a real record $(1, i, \mathsf{pos}, v)$ *stale* if there is another real record $(1, i, \mathsf{pos}, \star)$ stored closer to the root (including at the root itself); otherwise, we call the record *fresh*. Note that there is exactly one fresh record stored in the tree at any point in time for each logical memory address i. An important observation is that *stale records have no impact on the stash*. More formally:

Lemma 1. *Consider modifying the ORAM protocol (Fig. 1), so that in step 4 of processing a write operation the client also marks any stale records corresponding*

---

[5] Revealing the key to the servers does not affect the security of our scheme since we do not rely on secrecy of K for obliviousness. Rather, we rely on pseudorandomness of F_K only for bounding the size of the stash. We remark, however, that our analysis of the stash size assumes that the client's sequence of memory accesses is chosen independently of K. Thus, the optimized initialization (in which the client sends K to the servers) is only applicable when the client's sequence of memory accesses is not under adaptive control of an adversarial server.

to logical address i as dummy records (without regard for obliviousness). This modification does not affect the size of the stash, regardless of the position map or the sequence of memory accesses.

Proof. The only time a stale record can possibly have any effect on the stash in an execution of the real protocol is if there is a stale record (corresponding to some logical address i) in a path $\mathcal{P}$ being processed in step 3 of the eviction subroutine. But then the fresh record corresponding to address i is also in $\mathcal{P}$ at that moment, and so the stale record would have been replaced with a dummy record in step 2 of the eviction subroutine.

$\square$

A consequence of the above is that we may treat stale records as dummy records in our analysis, and it suffices for us to keep track of the placement of fresh records.

Fix a memory-access sequence seq of length M. We assume the binary tree T stored by the servers is initially filled entirely with dummy records; we thus let seq include the memory accesses done as part of initialization. For the purposes of proving a bound on the size of the stash, we may assume that all operations in seq are writes; moreover, the data values being written are irrelevant, and so we can simply focus on the sequence of logical memory addresses being accessed. If τ is a subtree of T, then we let $n(\tau)$ denote the number of nodes in τ. A subtree is *rooted* if it contains the root, and root denotes the root node (which is itself a rooted subtree).

We treat the position map as a random function $f : [N] \to [N]$ chosen independently of the memory-access sequence. For a subtree τ we let τ_Z be a random variable denoting the number of fresh records stored in each node of τ after our ORAM scheme (with bucket size Z) is used to carry out the sequence of memory accesses in seq. As in prior work [27,29], we let τ_∞ refer to the same random variable when buckets can hold an unbounded number of records. We let $X(\tau_Z)$ be a random variable denoting the total number of fresh records stored in τ_Z. (Using this notation, we are interested in bounding $X(\text{root}_Z)$.) We let $X_i(\tau_Z)$ be a random variable denoting the number of fresh records corresponding to logical address i that are in τ_Z; note that $X_i(\tau_Z) \in \{0, 1\}$.

We rely on the following result proved in prior work [27,29] for the same eviction procedure we use (when focusing on fresh blocks):

Lemma 2. *For any Z, S, it holds that*

$$\Pr[X(\text{root}_Z) > Z + S] \leq \sum_{n \geq 1} 4^n \cdot \max_{\tau : n(\tau)=n} \Pr[X(\tau_\infty) > Z \cdot n(\tau) + S],$$

where the maximum is over rooted subtrees τ of T.

The following result depends on the specifics of the eviction procedure and the position map. Nevertheless, the end result we obtain for our scheme is the same as what is shown in prior work.

Lemma 3. *Set $A = 1$ in our scheme. If b is a leaf node, $\mathbf{Exp}[X(b_\infty)] \leq 1$. If b is an internal node, $\mathbf{Exp}[X(b_\infty)] \leq 1/2$.*

Proof. If b is a leaf node, then a fresh record corresponding to logical address i can only possibly be stored in that node if i is mapped to b by the position map. Since there are N logical addresses, and each is mapped to b with probability $1/N$, the claimed bound follows.

Say b is a non-leaf node at level ℓ. If b is not on any of the first M eviction paths (note that this is independent of seq or the position map f), then b will contain no fresh records. Otherwise, let $1 \leq \mathsf{ctr}_1 \leq M$ denote the last time b was on an eviction path, and let $\mathsf{ctr}_0 < M$ denote the penultimate time b was on an eviction path (set $\mathsf{ctr}_0 = 0$ if there was no such time). By the properties of reverse lexicographic ordering, we have $\mathsf{ctr}_1 - \mathsf{ctr}_0 \leq 2^\ell$. The only possible fresh records that can be in b after all M instructions are executed are those corresponding to logical write addresses used in time steps $\mathsf{ctr}_0 + 1, \ldots, \mathsf{ctr}_1$. Moreover, each such address causes a fresh record to be placed in bucket b with probability exactly $2^{-(\ell+1)}$. Thus, the expected number of fresh records in b is at most $2^\ell \cdot 2^{-(\ell+1)} = 1/2$.

$\square$

A corollary is that if τ is a rooted subtree then $\mathbf{Exp}[X(\tau_\infty)] \leq 0.8 \cdot n(\tau)$ for all $N \geq 4$ (since in that case at most $N/(2N-1) \leq 4/7$ of the nodes in τ can be leaves). Following the analysis of Ren et al. [27, Sect. 4.3] (taking $a = 0.8$), we may then conclude that when $Z \geq 3$, the probability of overflow decreases exponentially in S. This implies that the stash will not exceed λ records except with probability negligible in λ.

In Table 1 we report concrete bounds on the number of blocks in the client's stash for different values of the bucket size Z and eviction parameter A. All values in the table are obtained from our theoretical analysis assuming N is sufficiently large. Simulations indicate that the stash size is even smaller than what the theoretical bounds indicate.

Table 1. Bounds on the number of blocks in the client's stash. These bounds hold except with probability 2^{-40} (per operation).

	$Z = 3$	$Z = 4$	$Z = 5$	$Z = 6$	$Z = 7$
$A = 1$	16	14	13	12	11
$A = 2$	-	21	18	16	15
$A = 3$	-	32	24	21	19
$A = 4$	-	-	33	26	23
$A = 5$	-	-	-	34	28

3.3   Optimizations

We briefly mention a few optimizations.

Heuristic parameters. As in the ring ORAM scheme, we experimentally observe that it suffices to set $A = 1$ and $Z = 2$ (giving the parameters mentioned in the abstract/introduction), or to set $A = 3$ and $Z = 3$ (giving slightly better communication at the expense of increased server storage).

A two-round variant. If we are willing to use one more round, the communication complexity can be further reduced by first having the client use PPR to read the indices in the records on the desired path, and then using an execution of PIR to read the single record of interest.

Acknowledgments. This material is based on work supported by NSF awards #1111599, #1563722, and #1564088.

References

1. Abraham, I., Fletcher, C.W., Nayak, K., Pinkas, B., Ren, L.: Asymptotically tight bounds for composing ORAM with PIR. In: Fehr, S. (ed.) PKC 2017. LNCS, vol. 10174, pp. 91–120. Springer, Heidelberg (2017). https://doi.org/10.1007/978-3-662-54365-8_5
2. Apon, D., Katz, J., Shi, E., Thiruvengadam, A.: Verifiable oblivious storage. In: Krawczyk, H. (ed.) PKC 2014. LNCS, vol. 8383, pp. 131–148. Springer, Heidelberg (2014). https://doi.org/10.1007/978-3-642-54631-0_8
3. Boyle, E., Couteau, G., Gilboa, N., Ishai, Y., Orrù, M.: Homomorphic secret sharing: optimizations and applications. In: 24th ACM Conference on Computer and Communications Security, pp. 2105–2122. ACM Press (2017)
4. Boyle, E., Gilboa, N., Ishai, Y.: Function secret sharing. In: Oswald, E., Fischlin, M. (eds.) EUROCRYPT 2015. LNCS, vol. 9057, pp. 337–367. Springer, Heidelberg (2015). https://doi.org/10.1007/978-3-662-46803-6_12
5. Boyle, E., Gilboa, N., Ishai, Y.: Function secret sharing: improvements and extensions. In: 23rd ACM Conference on Computer and Communications Security (CCS), pp. 1292–1303. ACM Press (2016)
6. Cachin, C., Micali, S., Stadler, M.: Computationally private information retrieval with polylogarithmic communication. In: Stern, J. (ed.) EUROCRYPT 1999. LNCS, vol. 1592, pp. 402–414. Springer, Heidelberg (1999). https://doi.org/10.1007/3-540-48910-X_28
7. Chor, B., Goldreich, O., Kushilevitz, E., Sudan, M.: Private information retrieval. In: 36th Annual Symposium on Foundations of Computer Science (FOCS), pp. 41–50. IEEE (1995)
8. Doerner, J., Evans, D., Shelat, A.: Secure stable matching at scale. In: 23rd ACM Conference on Computer and Communications Security (CCS), pp. 1602–1613. ACM Press (2016)
9. Doerner, J., Shelat, A.: Scaling ORAM for secure computation. In: 24th ACM Conference on Computer and Communications Security (CCS), pp. 523–535. ACM Press (2017)
10. Faber, S., Jarecki, S., Kentros, S., Wei, B.: Three-party ORAM for secure computation. In: Iwata, T., Cheon, J.H. (eds.) ASIACRYPT 2015. LNCS, vol. 9452, pp. 360–385. Springer, Heidelberg (2015). https://doi.org/10.1007/978-3-662-48797-6_16

11. Fletcher, C., Naveed, M., Ren, L., Shi, E., Stefanov, E.: Bucket ORAM: single online roundtrip, constant bandwidth oblivious RAM. Cryptology ePrint Archive, Report 2015/1065 (2015). http://eprint.iacr.org/2015/1065
12. Garg, S., Lu, S., Ostrovsky, R.: Black-Box Garbled RAM. In: 56th Annual Symposium on Foundations of Computer Science (FOCS), pp. 210–229. IEEE (2015)
13. Garg, S., Mohassel, P., Papamanthou, C.: TWORAM: efficient oblivious RAM in two rounds with applications to searchable encryption. In: Robshaw, M., Katz, J. (eds.) CRYPTO 2016. LNCS, vol. 9816, pp. 563–592. Springer, Heidelberg (2016). https://doi.org/10.1007/978-3-662-53015-3_20
14. Gentry, C., Goldman, K.A., Halevi, S., Julta, C., Raykova, M., Wichs, D.: Optimizing ORAM and using it efficiently for secure computation. In: De Cristofaro, E., Wright, M. (eds.) PETS 2013. LNCS, vol. 7981, pp. 1–18. Springer, Heidelberg (2013). https://doi.org/10.1007/978-3-642-39077-7_1
15. Gentry, C., Ramzan, Z.: Single-database private information retrieval with constant communication rate. In: Caires, L., Italiano, G.F., Monteiro, L., Palamidessi, C., Yung, M. (eds.) ICALP 2005. LNCS, vol. 3580, pp. 803–815. Springer, Heidelberg (2005). https://doi.org/10.1007/11523468_65
16. Goldreich, O., Ostrovsky, R.: Software protection and simulation on oblivious RAMs. J. ACM 43(3), 431–473 (1996)
17. Goodrich, M.T., Mitzenmacher, M.: Privacy-preserving access of outsourced data via oblivious RAM simulation. In: Aceto, L., Henzinger, M., Sgall, J. (eds.) ICALP 2011. LNCS, vol. 6756, pp. 576–587. Springer, Heidelberg (2011). https://doi.org/10.1007/978-3-642-22012-8_46
18. Gordon, S.D., et al.: Secure two-party computation in sublinear (amortized) time. In: 19th ACM Conference on Computer and Communications Security (CCS), pp. 513–524. ACM Press (2012)
19. Kushilevitz, E., Lu, S., Ostrovsky, R.: On the (in)security of hash-based oblivious RAM and a new balancing scheme. In: 23rd Annual ACM-SIAM Symposium on Discrete Algorithms (SODA), pp. 143–156. ACM-SIAM (2012)
20. Kushilevitz, E., Ostrovsky, R.: Replication is not needed: single database, computationally private information retrieval. In: 38th Annual Symposium on Foundations of Computer Science (FOCS), pp. 364–373. IEEE (1997)
21. Liu, C., Huang, Y., Shi, E., Katz, J., Hicks, M.W.: Automating efficient RAM-model secure computation. In: 2014 IEEE Symposium on Security and Privacy, pp. 623–638. IEEE (2014)
22. Liu, C., Wang, X.S., Nayak, K., Huang, Y., Shi, E.: ObliVM: a programming framework for secure computation. In: 2015 IEEE Symposium on Security and Privacy, pp. 359–376. IEEE (2015)
23. Lu, S., Ostrovsky, R.: Distributed oblivious RAM for secure two-party computation. In: Sahai, A. (ed.) TCC 2013. LNCS, vol. 7785, pp. 377–396. Springer, Heidelberg (2013). https://doi.org/10.1007/978-3-642-36594-2_22
24. Mayberry, T., Blass, E.O., Chan, A.H.: Efficient private file retrieval by combining ORAM and PIR. In: Network and Distributed System Security Symposium (NDSS) 2014. The Internet Society (2014)
25. Ostrovsky, R., Shoup, V.: Private information storage. In: 29th Annual ACM Symposium on Theory of Computing (STOC), pp. 294–303. ACM Press (1997)
26. Pinkas, B., Reinman, T.: Oblivious RAM revisited. In: Rabin, T. (ed.) CRYPTO 2010. LNCS, vol. 6223, pp. 502–519. Springer, Heidelberg (2010). https://doi.org/10.1007/978-3-642-14623-7_27
27. Ren, L., et al.: Constants count: practical improvements to oblivious RAM. In: USENIX Security Symposium, pp. 415–430. USENIX Association (2015)

28. Shi, E., Chan, T.-H.H., Stefanov, E., Li, M.: Oblivious RAM with $O((\log N)^3)$ worst-case cost. In: Lee, D.H., Wang, X. (eds.) ASIACRYPT 2011. LNCS, vol. 7073, pp. 197–214. Springer, Heidelberg (2011). https://doi.org/10.1007/978-3-642-25385-0_11

29. Stefanov, E., et al.: Path ORAM: an extremely simple oblivious RAM protocol. In: 20th ACM Conference on Computer and Communications Security (CCS), pp. 299–310. ACM Press (2013)

30. Wang, X., Chan, T.H.H., Shi, E.: Circuit ORAM: on tightness of the Goldreich-Ostrovsky lower bound. In: 22nd ACM Conference on Computer and Communications Security (CCS), pp. 850–861. ACM Press (2015)

31. Wang, X., Gordon, S.D., McIntosh, A., Katz, J.: Secure computation of MIPS machine code. In: Askoxylakis, I., Ioannidis, S., Katsikas, S., Meadows, C. (eds.) ESORICS 2016. LNCS, vol. 9879, pp. 99–117. Springer, Cham (2016). https://doi.org/10.1007/978-3-319-45741-3_6

32. Wang, X.S., Huang, Y., Chan, T.H.H., Shelat, A., Shi, E.: SCORAM: oblivious RAM for secure computation. In: 21st ACM Conference on Computer and Communications Security (CCS), pp. 191–202. ACM Press (2014)

33. Williams, P., Sion, R.: Single round access privacy on outsourced storage. In: 19th ACM Conference on Computer and Communications Security (CCS), pp. 293–304. ACM Press (2012)

34. Williams, P., Sion, R., Carbunar, B.: Building castles out of mud: practical access-pattern privacy and correctness on untrusted storage. In: 15th ACM Conference on Computer and Communications Security (CCS), pp. 139–148. ACM Press (2008)

35. Zahur, S., et al.: Revisiting square-root ORAM: efficient random access in multiparty computation. In: 2016 IEEE Symposium on Security and Privacy, pp. 218–234. IEEE (2016)

More is Less: Perfectly Secure Oblivious Algorithms in the Multi-server Setting

T.-H. Hubert Chan[1], Jonathan Katz[2], Kartik Nayak[2,3(✉)],
Antigoni Polychroniadou[4], and Elaine Shi[5]

[1] The University of Hong Kong, Pokfulam, Hong Kong
hubert@cs.hku.hk
[2] University of Maryland, College Park, USA
jkatz@cs.umd.edu
[3] VMware Research, Palo Alto, USA
nkartik@vmware.com
[4] Cornell Tech, New York, USA
antigoni@cornell.edu
[5] Cornell University, Ithaca, USA
runting@gmail.com

Abstract. The problem of Oblivious RAM (ORAM) has traditionally been studied in the single-server setting, but more recently the multi-server setting has also been considered. Yet it is still unclear whether the multi-server setting has any *inherent* advantages, e.g., whether the multi-server setting can be used to achieve stronger security goals or provably better efficiency than is possible in the single-server case.

In this work, we construct a perfectly secure 3-server ORAM scheme that outperforms the best known single-server scheme by a logarithmic factor. In the process we also show, for the first time, that there exist specific algorithms for which multiple servers can overcome known lower bounds in the single-server setting.

Keywords: Oblivious RAM · Perfect security

1 Introduction

Oblivious RAM (ORAM) protocols [12] allow a client to outsource storage of its data such that the client can continue to read/write its data while hiding both the data itself as well as the client's access pattern. ORAM was historically considered in the single-server setting, but has recently been considered in the multi-server setting [1,16,17,19,21,25] where the client can store its data on multiple, non-colluding servers. Current constructions of multi-server ORAM are more efficient than known protocols in the single-server setting; in particular, the best known protocols in the latter setting (when server-side computation is

An online full version of our paper [5] is available at http://arxiv.org/abs/1809.00825.

T. Peyrin and S. Galbraith (Eds.): ASIACRYPT 2018, LNCS 11274, pp. 158–188, 2018.
https://doi.org/10.1007/978-3-030-03332-3_7

not allowed) require bandwidth $O(\log^2 N/\log\log N)$ [3,7,15,18] for storing an array of length N, whereas multi-server ORAM schemes achieve logarithmic bandwidth[1] [21].

Nevertheless, there are several unanswered questions about the multi-server setting. First, all work thus far in the multi-server setting achieves either computational or statistical security, but not *perfect security* where correctness is required to hold with probability 1 and security must hold even against computationally unbounded attackers. Second, although (as noted above) we have examples of multi-server schemes that beat existing single-server constructions, it is unclear whether this reflects a limitation of existing single-server schemes or whether there are *inherent* advantages to the multi-server setting.

We address the above questions in this work. (Unless otherwise noted, our results hold for arbitrary block size B as long as it is large enough to store an address, i.e., $B = \Omega(\log N)$.) We construct a perfectly secure, multi-server ORAM scheme that improves upon the overhead of the best known construction in the single-server setting. Specifically, we show the following — henceforth if a multi-server ORAM scheme incurs, on average, $X(N)$ bandwidth (measured in terms of number of blocks transmitted) per logical memory access on a logical memory of length N, we say that the scheme has $X(N)$ *bandwidth blowup*.

Theorem 1. *There exists a 3-server ORAM scheme that is perfectly secure for any single semi-honest server corruption, and achieves $O(\log^2 N)$ bandwidth blowup. Further, our scheme does not rely on server-side computation or server-to-server communication.*

As a point of comparison, the best known *single-server*, perfectly secure ORAM schemes require $O(\log^3 N)$ bandwidth [6,9]. While Theorem 1 holds for any block size $B = \Omega(\log N)$, we show that for block sizes $B = \Omega(\log^2 N)$ our scheme achieves bandwidth blowup as small as $O(\log N)$.

As part of our construction, we introduce new building blocks that are of independent theoretical interest. Specifically, we show:

Theorem 2. *There exists a 3-server protocol for stable compaction that is perfectly secure for any single semi-honest server corruption, and achieves $O(n)$ bandwidth to compact an array of length n (that is secret-shared among the servers). The same result holds for merging two sorted arrays of length n.*

In the single-server setting, Lin, Shi, and Xie [20] recently proved a lower bound showing that any oblivious algorithm for stable compaction or merging in the balls-and-bins model must incur at least $\Omega(n\log n)$ bandwidth. The balls-and-bins model characterizes a wide class of natural algorithms where each element is treated as an atomic "ball" with a numeric label; the algorithm may perform arbitrary boolean computation on the labels, but is only allowed to

---

[1] Although Lu and Ostrovsky [21] describe their multi-server scheme using server-side computation, it is not difficult to see that it can be replaced with client-side computation instead.

move the balls around and not compute on their values. Our scheme works in the balls-and-bins model, and thus shows *for the first time* that the multi-server setting can overcome known lower bounds in the single-server setting for oblivious algorithms. Furthermore, for stable compaction and merging no previous multi-server scheme was known that is asymptotically faster than existing single-server algorithms, even in the weaker setting of computational security. We note finally that our protocols are asymptotically optimal since clearly any correct algorithm has to read the entire array.

1.1   Technical Roadmap

Oblivious sorting is an essential building block in hierarchical ORAM schemes. At a high level, our key idea is to replace oblivious sorting, which costs $O(n \log n)$ time on an array of length n, with cheaper, linear-time operations. Indeed, this was also the idea of Lu and Ostrovsky [21], but they apply it to a computationally secure hierarchical ORAM. Prior single-server ORAM schemes are built from logarithmically many cuckoo hash tables of doubling size. Every time a memory request has been served, one needs to merge multiple stale cuckoo hash tables into a newly constructed cuckoo hash table — this was previously accomplished by oblivious sorting [3,15,18]. Lu and Ostrovsky show how to avoid cuckoo hashing, by having one *permutation server* permute the data in linear time, and by having a separate *storage server*, that is unaware of the permutation, construct a cuckoo hash table from the permuted array in linear time (with the client's help). Unfortunately, Lu and Ostrovsky's technique fails for the perfect security context due to its intimate reliance on pseudorandom functions (PRFs) and cuckoo hashing — the former introduces computational assumptions and the latter leads to statistical failures (albeit with negligible probability).

We are, however, inspired by Lu and Ostrovsky's permutation-storage-separation paradigm (and a similar approach that was described independently by Stefanov and Shi [25]). The key concept here is to have one permutation-server that permutes the data; and have operations and accesses be performed by a separate storage server that is unaware of the permutation applied. One natural question is whether we can apply this technique to directly construct a linear-time multi-server oblivious sorting algorithm — unfortunately we are not aware of any way to achieve this. Chan et al. [4] and Tople et al. [27] show that assuming the data is already randomly permuted (where the permutation is hidden), one can simply apply any comparison-based sorting algorithm and it would retain obliviousness. Unfortunately, it is well-known that comparison-based sorting must incur $\Omega(n \log n)$ time, and this observation does not extend to non-comparison-based sorting techniques since in general RAM computations (on numeric keys) can leak information through access patterns.

New techniques at a glance. We propose two novel techniques that allow us to achieve the stated results, both of which rely on the permutation-storage-separation paradigm:

- Despite known lower bounds in the single-server setting [20], we show that with multiple servers, we can indeed achieve linear-time oblivious stable compaction and merging. As prior works [3,4,7,14] observe, merging and compaction are important building blocks in designing oblivious algorithms — we thus believe that our new building blocks are of independent interest.
- We use the linear-time oblivious stable compaction and merging algorithms to design a three-server ORAM. We adapt the single-server perfect ORAM scheme by Chan et al. [6] into a new multiserver variant to save a logarithmic factor. Specifically, in Chan et al. [6], the reshuffling operation was realized with oblivious sorting. This operation can now be expressed entirely with linear-time merging and stable compaction operations without relying on oblivious sorting.

Stable Compaction and Merging. We first explain the intuition behind our stable compaction algorithm. For simplicity, for the time being we will consider only 2 servers and assume perfectly secure encryption for free (this assumption can later be removed by using secret-sharing and by introducing one additional server). Imagine that we start out with an array of length n that is encrypted and resides on one server. The elements in the array are either real or dummy, and we would like to move all dummy elements to the end of the array while preserving the order of the real elements as they appear in the original array. For security, we would like that any single server's view in the protocol leaks no information about the array's contents.

Strawman scheme. An extremely simple strawman scheme is the following: the client makes a scan of the input array on one server; whenever it encounters a real element, it re-encrypts the element and writes it to the other server by appending it to the end of the output array (initially the output array is empty). When the entire input array has been consumed, the client pads the output array with an appropriate number of (encrypted) dummy elements.

At first sight, this algorithm seems to preserve security: each server basically observes a linear scan of either the input or the output array; and the perfectly-secure encryption hides array contents. However, upon careful examination, the second server can observe the time steps in which a write has happened to the output array — this leaks which elements are real in the original array. Correspondingly, in our formal modeling (Sect. 2), each server can not only observe each message sent and received by itself, but also the time steps in which these events occurred.

A second try. For simplicity we will describe our approach with server computation and server-to-server communication — but it is not hard to modify the scheme such that servers are completely passive. Roughly speaking, the idea is for the first server (called the *permutation server*) to randomly permute all elements and store the permuted array on the second server (called the *storage server*), such that the permutation is hidden from the storage server. Moreover, in this permuted array, we would like the elements to be tagged with pointers to form two linked lists: a real linked list and a dummy linked list. In both linked lists, the ordering of elements respects the ordering in the original array. If such a permuted array encoding two linked lists can be constructed, the client can simply traverse the real linked list first from the storage server, and then traverse the dummy linked list — writing down each element it encounters on the first server (we always assume re-encryption upon writes). Since the storage server does not know the random permutation and since every element is accessed exactly once, it observes a completely random access pattern; and thus it cannot gain any secret information.

The challenge remains as to how to tag each real (resp. dummy) element with the position of the next real (resp. dummy) element in the permuted array. This can be achieved in the following manner: the permutation server first creates a random permutation in linear time (e.g., by employing Fisher-Yates [11]), such that each element in the input array is now tagged with where it wants to be in the permuted array (henceforth called the position label). Now, the client makes a reverse scan of this input array. During this process, it remembers the position labels of the last real element seen and of the last dummy element seen so far — this takes $O(1)$ client-side storage. Whenever a real element is encountered, the client tags it with the position label of the last real seen. Similarly, whenever a dummy is encountered, the client tags it with the position label of the last dummy seen. Now, the permutation server can permute the array based on the predetermined permutation (which can also be done in linear time). At this moment, it sends the permuted, re-encrypted array to the storage server and the linked list can now be traversed from the storage server to read real elements followed by dummy elements.

It is not difficult to see that assuming that the encryption scheme is perfectly secure and every write involves re-encrypting the data, then the above scheme achieves perfect security against any single semi-honest corrupt server, and completes in linear time. Later we will replace the perfectly secure encryption with secret-sharing and this requires the introduction of one additional server.

Extending the idea for merging. We can extend the above idea to allow linear-time oblivious merging of two sorted arrays. The idea is to prepare both arrays such that they are in permuted form on the storage server and in a linked list format; and now the client can traverse the two linked lists on the storage server, merging them in the process. In each step of the merging, only one array is being consumed — since the storage server does not know the permutation, it sees random accesses and cannot tell which array is being consumed.

3-Server Perfectly Secure ORAM. We now explain the techniques for constructing a 3-server perfectly secure ORAM. A client, with $O(1)$ blocks of local cache, stores N blocks of data (secret-shared) on the 3 servers, one of which might be semi-honest corrupt. In every iteration, the client receives a memory request of the form (read, addr) or (write, addr, data), and it completes this request by interacting with the servers. We would like to achieve $O(\log^2 N)$ amortized bandwidth blowup per logical memory request.

Background on single-server perfect ORAM. We start out from a state-of-the-art single-server perfectly secure scheme by Chan et al. [6] that achieves $O(\log^3 N)$ amortized bandwidth per memory request. Their scheme extends from the original hierarchical ORAM framework of Goldreich and Ostrovsky [12, 13] where data blocks are stored in levels of geometrically increasing sizes. Recall that Goldreich and Ostrovsky [12, 13] achieve only computational security due to the use of a PRF; and thus one of the key ideas of Chan et al. [6] is how to remove the need for a PRF. More concretely, each level in Goldreich and Ostrovsky's hierarchical ORAM is an oblivious hash table capable of supporting non-recurrent requests (henceforth called one-time memory). Within each level, the position of a data block is determined by applying a PRF to the block's logical address. To achieve perfect security, the key requirement is to eliminate the use the PRF. Therefore, in Chan et al. [6], blocks within a level are secretly and randomly permuted using an oblivious sort. To access a block within a level, the client must first figure out the block's correct location within the level. To achieve this, a trivial method is for the client to locally store the entire mapping of the correct locations (henceforth called position labels), but this would consume linear client space. Instead Chan et al. recursively store the position labels in a smaller hierarchical ORAM, inspired by a standard recursion technique commonly adopted by tree-based ORAMs [24] (but Chan et al. show how to adapt it to the hierarchical ORAM setting). Thus, in Chan et al.'s construction, there are logarithmically many hierarchical ORAMs (also called position-based ORAMs), where the ORAM at depth d (called the parent depth) stores position labels for the ORAM at depth $d + 1$ (called the child depth); and finally, the ORAM at the maximum depth $D = O(\log N)$ stores the real data blocks.

Our multi-server perfect ORAM. We now explain how to build on top of Chan et al. [6]'s idea and obtain a multi-server ORAM that saves a logarithmic factor in bandwidth. The key to enabling this is a method for passing information between adjacent recursion depths, *without oblivious sort*. Below, we first explain how Chan et al. [6] passes information between adjacent recursion depths using oblivious sort, and then we explain our novel techniques to accomplish the same, but now relying only on *merging* and *compaction* in the multi-server setting.

As Chan et al. [6] point out, whenever a data block's location is updated at depth d through a shuffle operation, the position label at depth $d - 1$ needs to be updated to reflect the new location. This information passing between an ORAM at depth d to its parent ORAM at depth $d - 1$ is performed by using a coordinated shuffle between the logarithmically many ORAMs upon every memory request. This turns out to be the most intricate part of their scheme. During this shuffle, suppose that the parent and the child each has an array of logical addresses and a position label for each address. It is guaranteed by the ORAM construction that all addresses the child has must appear in the parent's array. Moreover, if some address appears in both the parent and child, then the child's version is fresher. We would like to combine the information held by the parent and the child by retaining the freshest copy of position label for every address. Chan et al. relied on oblivious sorting to achieve this goal: if some address is held by both the parent and child, they will appear adjacent to each other in the sorted array; and thus in a single linear scan one can easily cross out all stale copies.

To save a logarithmic factor, we must solve the above problem using only merging and compaction and not sorting. Notice that if both the parent's and the child's arrays are already sorted according to the addresses, then the afore-mentioned information propagation from child to parent can be accomplished through merging rather than sorting (in the full scheme we would also need stable compaction to remove dummy blocks in a timely fashion to avoid blowup of array sizes over time). But how can we make sure that these arrays are sorted in the first place without oblivious sorting? In particular, these arrays actually correspond to levels in a hierarchical ORAM in Chan et al. [6]'s scheme, and all blocks in a level must appear in randomly permuted order to allow safe (one-time) accesses — this seems to contradict our desire for sortedness. Fortunately, here we can rely again on the permutation-storage-separation paradigm — for simplicity again we describe our approach for 2 servers assuming perfectly secure (re-)encryption upon every write. The idea is the following: although the storage server is holding each array (i.e., level) in a randomly permuted order, the permutation server will remember an inverse permutation such that when this permutation is applied to the storage server's copy, sortedness is restored. Thus whenever shuffling is needed, the permutation server would first apply the inverse permutation to the storage server's copy to restore sortedness, and then we could rely on merging (and compaction) to propagate information between adjacent depths rather than sorting.

Outline. In Sect. 3, we explain our protocol for permuting and unpermuting a list of blocks under the permutation-storage-separation paradigm and build upon it to describe a protocol for oblivious stable compaction and merge. In Sect. 4, we show the protocol for a three-server oblivious one-time memory; this corresponds to a single level in position-based ORAM in Chan et al. [6]. In Sect. 5, we first show how a three-server position-based ORAM can be built using the one-time memory (Sect. 5.1), and then construct our final ORAM scheme consisting of logarithmic number of position-based ORAMs (Sect. 5.2).

1.2 Related Work

The notion of Oblivious RAM (ORAM) was introduced by the seminal work of Goldreich and Ostrovsky around three decades ago [12,13]. Their construction used a hierarchy of buffers of exponentially increasing size, which was later known as the hierarchical ORAM framework. Their construction achieved an amortized bandwidth blowup of $O(\log^3 N)$ and was secure against a computationally bounded adversary. Subsequently, several works have improved the bandwidth blowup from $O(\log^3 N)$ to $O(\log^2 N/\log\log N)$ [3,7,15,18] under the same adversarial model. Ajtai [2] was the first to consider the notion of a statistically secure oblivious RAM that achieves $O(\log^3 N)$ bandwidth blowup. This was followed by the statistically secure ORAM construction by Shi et al. [24], who introduced the tree-based paradigm. ORAM constructions in the tree-based paradigm have improved the bandwidth blowup from $O(\log^3 N)$ to $O(\log^2 N)$ [8,23,24,26,28]. Though the computational assumptions have been removed, the statistically secure ORAMs still fail with a failure probability that is negligibly small in the number of data blocks stored in the ORAM.

Perfectly secure ORAMs. Perfectly secure ORAM was first studied by Damgård et al. [9]. Perfect security requires that a computationally unbounded server does not learn anything other than the number of requests with probability 1. This implies that the oblivious program's memory access patterns should be *identically distributed* regardless of the inputs to the program; and thus with probability 1, no information can be leaked about the secret inputs to the program. Damgård et al. [9] achieve an *expected* $O(\log^3 N)$ simulation overhead and $O(\log N)$ space blowup relative to the original RAM program. Raskin et al. [22] and Demertzis et al. [10] achieve a *worst-case* bandwidth blowup of $O(\sqrt{N}\frac{\log N}{\log\log N})$ and $O(N^{1/3})$, respectively. Chan et al. [6] improve upon Damgård et al.'s result [9] by avoiding the $O(\log N)$ blowup in space, and by showing a construction that is conceptually simpler. Our construction builds upon Chan et al. and improves the bandwidth blowup to *worst-case* $O(\log^2 N)$ while assuming three non-colluding servers.

We note that since both Damgård et al. [9] and Chan et al. [6] employ perfectly oblivious random permutations, their schemes are Las Vegas algorithms and there is a negligibly small failure probability that the algorithm exceeds the stated runtime (however, perfect security is maintained nonetheless). Our multi-server ORAM avoids the need for oblivious random permutation and thus the algorithm's runtime is deterministic.

Multi-server ORAMs. ORAMs in this category assume multiple non-colluding servers to improve bandwidth blowup [1,16,17,19,21]. A comparison of the relevant schemes is presented in Table 1. Among these, the work that is closely related to ours is by Lu and Ostrovsky [21] which achieves a bandwidth blowup of $O(\log N)$ assuming two non-colluding servers. In their scheme, each server performs permutations for data that is stored by the other server. While their construction is computationally secure, we achieve perfect security for access patterns as well as the data itself. Moreover, our techniques can be used to perform an oblivious tight stable compaction and an oblivious merge operation in linear time; how to perform these operations in linear time were not known even for the computationally secure setting. On the other hand, our scheme achieves an $O(\log^2 N)$ bandwidth blowup and uses three servers. We remark that if we assume a perfectly secure encryption scheme, our construction can achieve perfectly secure access patterns using two servers. Abraham et al. [1], Gordon et al. [16] and Kushilevitz and Mour [19] construct multi-server ORAMs using PIR. Each of these constructions require the server to perform computation for using PIR operations. While Abraham et al. [1] achieve statistical security for access patterns, other work [16,19] is only computationally secure. While the work of Gordon et al. achieves a bandwidth blowup of $O(\log N)$, they require linear-time server computation. Abraham et al. and Kushilevitz and Mour, on the other hand, are poly-logarithmic and logarithmic respectively, both in computation and bandwidth blowup. In comparison, our construction achieves perfect security and requires a passive server (i.e., a server that does not perform any computation) at a bandwidth blowup of $O(\log^2 N)$.

Table 1. Comparison with existing multi-server Oblivious RAM schemes for block size $\Omega(\log N)$. All of the other schemes (including the statistically-secure schemes [1]) require two servers but assume the existence of an unconditionally secure encryption scheme. With a similar assumption, our work would indeed need only two servers too.

Construction	Bandwidth Blowup	Server Computation	Security
Lu-Ostrovsky [21]	$O(\log N)$	-	Computational
Gordon et al. [16]	$O(\log N)$	$O(N)$	Computational
Kushilevitz et al. [19]	$O(\log N \cdot \omega(1))$	$O(\log N \cdot \omega(1))$	Computational
Abraham et al. [1]	$O(\log^2 N \cdot \omega(1))$	$O(\log^2 N \cdot \omega(1))$	Statistical
Our work	$O(\log^2 N)$	-	Perfect

2 Definitions

In this section, we revisit how to define multi-server ORAM schemes for the case of semi-honest corruptions. Our definitions require that the adversary, controlling a subset of semi-honest corrupt servers, learns no secret information during the execution of the ORAM protocol. Specifically our adversary can observe all messages transmitted to and from corrupt servers, the rounds in which they were transmitted, as well as communication patterns between honest parties (including the client and honest servers). Our definition generalizes existing works [1] where they assume free encryption of data contents (even when statistical security is desired).

2.1 Execution Model

Protocol as a system of Interactive RAMs. We consider a protocol between multiple parties including a client, henceforth denoted by **C**, and k servers, denoted by $\mathbf{S}_0, \ldots, \mathbf{S}_{k-1}$, respectively. The client and all servers are Random Access Machines (RAMs) that interact with each other. Specifically, the client or each server has a CPU capable of computation and a memory that supports reads and writes; the CPU interacts with the memory to perform computation. The atomic unit of operation for memory is called a *block*. We assume that all RAMs can be *probabilistic*, i.e., they can read a random tape supplying a stream of random bits.

Communication and timing. We assume pairwise channels between all parties. There are two notions of time in our execution model, CPU cycles and communication rounds. Without loss of generality, henceforth we assume that it takes the same amount of time to compute each CPU instruction and to transmit each memory block over the network to another party (since we can always take the maximum of the two). Henceforth in this paper we often use the word *round* to denote the time that has elapsed since the beginning of the protocol.

Although we define RAMs on the servers as being capable of performing any arbitrary computation, all of our protocols require the servers to be passive, i.e., the server RAMs only perform read/write operations from the memory stored by it.

2.2   Perfect Security Under a Semi-Honest Adversary

We consider the client to be *trusted*. The adversary can corrupt a subset of the servers (but it cannot corrupt the client) — although our constructions are secure against any individual corrupt server, we present definitions for the more general case, i.e., when the adversary can control more than one corrupt server.

We consider a *semi-honest* adversary, i.e., the corrupt servers still honestly follow the protocol; however, we would like to ensure that no undesired information will leak. To formally define security, we need to first define what the adversary can observe in a protocol's execution.

View of adversary $\mathsf{view}^{\mathcal{A}}$. Suppose that the adversary $\mathcal{A}$ controls a subset of the servers — we abuse notation and use $\mathcal{A} \subset [k]$ to denote the set of corrupt servers. The view of the adversary, denoted by $\mathsf{view}^{\mathcal{A}}$ in a random run of the protocol consists of the following:

1. *Corrupt parties' views:* These views include (1) corrupt parties' inputs, (2) all randomness consumed by corrupt parties, and (3) an ordered sequence of all messages received by corrupt parties, including which party the message is received from, as well as the *round* in which each message is received. We assume that these messages are ordered by the round in which they are received, and then by the party from which it is received.
2. *Honest communication pattern:* when honest parties (including the client) exchange messages, the adversary observes their communication pattern, including which pairs of honest nodes exchange messages in which round.

We stress that in our model only one block can be exchanged between every pair in a round — thus the above $\mathsf{view}^{\mathcal{A}}$ definition effectively allows $\mathcal{A}$ to see the total length of messages exchanged between honest parties.

Remark 1. We remark that this definition captures a notion of timing patterns along with access patterns. For instance, suppose two servers store two sorted lists that needs to be merged. The client performs a regular merge operation to read from the two lists, reading the heads of the lists in each round. In such a scenario, depending on the rounds in which blocks are read from a server, an adversary that corrupts that server can compute the relative ordering of blocks between the two lists.

Defining security in the ideal-real paradigm. Consider an ideal functionality $\mathcal{F}$: upon receiving the input $\mathbf{I}_0$ from the client and inputs $\mathbf{I}_1, \ldots, \mathbf{I}_k$ from each of the k servers, respectively, and a random string ρ sampled from some distribution, $\mathcal{F}$ computes

$$(\mathbf{O}_0, \mathbf{O}_1, \ldots, \mathbf{O}_k) := \mathcal{F}(\mathbf{I}_0, \mathbf{I}_1, \ldots, \mathbf{I}_k; \rho)$$

where $\mathbf{O}_0$ is the client's output, and $\mathbf{O}_1, \ldots, \mathbf{O}_k$ denote the k servers' outputs, respectively.

Definition 1 (Perfect security in the presence of a semi-honest adversary). *We say that "a protocol Π perfectly securely realizes an ideal functionality $\mathcal{F}$ in the presence of a semi-honest adversary corrupting t servers" if and only if for every adversary $\mathcal{A}$ that controls up to t corrupt servers, there exists a simulator Sim such that for every input vector $(\mathbf{I}_0, \mathbf{I}_1, \ldots, \mathbf{I}_k)$, the following real- and ideal-world experiments output identical distributions:*

- *Ideal-world experiment. Sample ρ at random and compute $(\mathbf{O}_0, \mathbf{O}_1, \ldots, \mathbf{O}_k) := \mathcal{F}(\mathbf{I}_0, \mathbf{I}_1, \ldots, \mathbf{I}_k, \rho)$. Output the following tuple where we abuse notation and use $i \in \mathcal{A}$ to denote the fact that i is corrupt:*

$$\mathsf{Sim}(\{\mathbf{I}_i, \mathbf{O}_i\}_{i \in \mathcal{A}}), \quad \mathbf{O}_0, \{\mathbf{O}_i\}_{i \notin \mathcal{A}}$$

- *Real-world experiment. Execute the (possibly randomized) real-world protocol, and let $\mathbf{O}_0, \mathbf{O}_1, \ldots, \mathbf{O}_k$ be the outcome of the client and each of the k servers, respectively. Let $\mathsf{view}^{\mathcal{A}}$ denote the view of the adversary $\mathcal{A}$ in this run. Now, output the following:*

$$\mathsf{view}^{\mathcal{A}}, \quad \mathbf{O}_0, \{\mathbf{O}_i\}_{i \notin \mathcal{A}}$$

Note that throughout the paper, we will define various building blocks that realize different ideal functionalities. The security of all building blocks can be defined in a unified approach with this paradigm. When we compose these building blocks to construct our full protocol, we can prove perfect security of the full protocol in a composable manner. By modularly proving the security of each building block, we can now think of each building block as interacting with an ideal functionality. This enables us to prove the security of the full protocol in the ideal world assuming the existence of these ideal functionalities.

We note that while the definitions in this paper apply to both active-server protocols (where the server can perform arbitrary computation) as well as passive server protocols (where the server performs no computation), our scheme does not require server computation.

2.3 Definition of k-Server Oblivious RAM

Ideal logical memory. The ideal logical memory is defined in the most natural way. There is a memory array consisting of N blocks where each block is $\Omega(\log N)$ bits long, and each block is identified by its unique *address* which takes value in the range $\{0, 1, \ldots, N - 1\}$.

Initially all blocks are set to 0. Upon receiving (read, addr), the value of the block residing at address addr is returned. Upon receiving (write, addr, data), the block at address addr is overwritten with the data value data, and its old value (before being rewritten) is returned.

k-server ORAM. A k-server Oblivious RAM (ORAM) is a protocol between a client $\mathbf{C}$ and k servers $\mathbf{S}_1, \ldots, \mathbf{S}_k$ which realizes an ideal logical memory. The execution of this protocol proceeds in a sequence of iterations: in each interaction, the client $\mathbf{C}$ receives a logical memory request of the form (read, addr) or (write, addr, data). It then engages in some (possibly randomized) protocol with the servers, at the end of which it produces some output thus completing the current iteration.

We require perfect correctness and perfect security as defined below. We refer to a sequence of logical memory requests as a *request sequence* for short.

- *Perfect correctness.* For any request sequence, with probability 1, all of the client's outputs must be correct. In other words, we require that with probability 1, all of the client's outputs must match what an ideal logical memory would have output for the same request sequence.
- *Perfect security under a semi-honest adversary.* We say that a k-server ORAM scheme satisfies perfect security w.r.t. a semi-honest adversary corrupting t servers, if and only if for every $\mathcal{A}$ that controls up to t servers, and for every two request sequences $\mathbf{R}_0$ and $\mathbf{R}_1$ of equal length, the views $\mathsf{view}^{\mathcal{A}}(\mathbf{R}_0)$ and $\mathsf{view}^{\mathcal{A}}(\mathbf{R}_1)$ are identically distributed, where $\mathsf{view}^{\mathcal{A}}(\mathbf{R})$ denotes the view of $\mathcal{A}$ (as defined earlier in Sect. 2.2) under the request sequence $\mathbf{R}$.

Since we require perfect security (and is based on information-theoretic secret-sharing), our notion resists adaptive corruptions and is composable.

2.4 Resource Assumptions and Cost Metrics

We assume that the client can store $O(1)$ blocks while the servers can store $O(N)$ blocks. We will use the metric *bandwidth blowup* to characterize the performance of our protocols. Bandwidth blowup is the (amortized) number of blocks queried in the ORAM simulation to query a single virtual block. We also note that since the servers do not perform any computation, and the client always performs an $O(1)$ computation on its $O(1)$ storage, an $O(X)$ bandwidth blowup also corresponds to an $O(X)$ *runtime* for our protocol.

3   Core Building Blocks: Definitions and Constructions

Imagine that there are three servers denoted $\mathbf{S}_0$, $\mathbf{S}_1$, and $\mathbf{S}_2$, and a client denoted $\mathbf{C}$. We use $\mathbf{S}_b, b \in \mathbb{Z}_3$ to refer to a specific server. Arithmetic performed on the subscript b is done modulo 3.

3.1   Useful Definitions

Let T denote a list of blocks where each block is either a real block containing a payload string and a logical address; or a dummy block denoted $\perp$. We define *sorted* and *semi-sorted* as follows:

- *Sorted:* T is said to be sorted *iff* all real blocks appear before dummy ones; and all the real blocks appear in increasing order of their logical addresses. If multiple blocks have the same logical address, their relative order can be arbitrary.
- *Semi-sorted:* T is said to be semi-sorted *iff* all the real blocks appear in increasing order of their logical addresses, and ties may be broken arbitrarily. However, the real blocks are allowed to be interspersed by dummy blocks.

Array Notation. We assume each location of an array T stores a *block* which is a bit-string of length B. Given two arrays T_1 and T_2, we use $\mathsf{T}_1 \oplus \mathsf{T}_2$ to denote the resulting array after performing bitwise-XOR on the corresponding elements at each index of the two arrays; if the two arrays are of different lengths, we assume the shorter array is appended with a sufficient number of zero elements.

Permutation Notation. When a permutation $\pi : [n] \rightarrow [n]$ is applied to an array T indexed by $[n]$ to produce $\pi(\mathsf{T})$, we mean the element currently at location i will be moved to location $\pi(i)$. When we compose permutations, $\pi \circ \sigma$ means that π is applied *before* σ. We use $\mathfrak{e}$ to denote the identity permutation.

Layout. A layout is a way to store some data T on three servers such that the data can be recovered by combining information on the three servers. Recall that the client has only $O(1)$ blocks of space, and our protocol does not require that the client stores any persistent data.

Whenever some data T is stored on a server, informally speaking, we need to ensure two things: (1) The server does not learn the data T itself, and (2) The server does not learn *which* index i of the data is accessed. In order to ensure the prior, we XOR secret-share the data $\mathsf{T} := \mathsf{T}_0 \oplus \mathsf{T}_1 \oplus \mathsf{T}_2$ between three servers $\mathbf{S}_b, b \in \mathbb{Z}_3$ such that $\mathbf{S}_b$ stores T_b. For a server to not learn *which* index i in T is accessed, we ensure that the data is permuted, and the access happens to the permuted data. If the data is accessed on the same server that permutes the data, then the index i will still be revealed. Thus, for each share T_b, we ensure that one server permutes it and we access it from another server, i.e., we have two types of servers:

- Each server S_b acts as a *storage server* for the b-th share, and thus it knows T_b.
- Each server S_b also acts as the *permutation server* for the $(b + 1)$-th share, and thus it also knows T_{b+1} as well as π_{b+1}.

Throughout the paper, a layout is of the following form

$$3\text{-server layout}: \quad \{\pi_b, T_b\}_{b \in \mathbb{Z}_3}$$

where T_b and (π_{b+1}, T_{b+1}) are stored by server S_b. As mentioned, S_b not only knows its own share (T_b) but also the permutation and share of the next server (π_{b+1}, T_{b+1}).

Specifically, T_0, T_1, T_2 denote lists of blocks of equal length: we denote $n = |T_0| = |T_1| = |T_2|$. Further, $\pi_{b+1} : [n] \to [n]$ is a permutation stored by server S_b for the list T_{b+1}. Unless there is ambiguity, we use $\oplus_b$ to mean applying $\oplus_{b \in \mathbb{Z}_3}$ to three underlying arrays.

The above layout is supposed to store the array that can be recovered by:

$$\oplus_b \pi_b^{-1}(T_b).$$

Henceforth, given a layout $\{\pi_b, T_b\}_{b \in \mathbb{Z}_3}$, we say that the layout is *sorted* (or semi-sorted) iff $\oplus_b \pi_b^{-1}(T_b)$ is sorted (or semi-sorted).

Special Case. Sometimes the blocks secret-shared among S_0, S_1, S_2 may be unpermuted, i.e., for each $b \in \mathbb{Z}_3$, π_b is the identity permutation e. In this case, the layout is

$$\text{Unpermuted layout}: \quad \{e, T_b\}_{b \in \mathbb{Z}_3}$$

For brevity, the unpermuted layout $\{e, T_b\}_{b \in \mathbb{Z}_3}$ is also denoted by the abstract array T.

Definition 2 (Secret Write). *An* abstract *array* T *corresponds to some unpermuted layout* $\{e, T_b\}_{b \in \mathbb{Z}_3}$. *We say that the client secretly writes a value* B *to the array* T *at index* i, *when it does the following:*

- *Sample random values* B_0 *and* B_1 *independently, and compute* $B_2 := B \oplus B_0 \oplus B_1$.
- *For each* $b \in \mathbb{Z}_3$, *the client writes* $T_b[i] := B_b$ *on server* S_b *(and* S_{b-1}*).*

Definition 3 (Reconstruct). *Given some layout* $\{\pi_b, T_b\}_{b \in \mathbb{Z}_3}$, *the client reconstructs a value from using tuple* (i_0, i_1, i_2) *of indices, when it does the following:*

- *For each* $b \in \mathbb{Z}_3$, *the client reads* $T_b[i_b]$ *from server* S_b. *(It is important that the client reads* T_b *from* S_b, *even though* T_b *is stored in both* S_b *and* S_{b-1}.*)*
- *The reconstructed value is* $\oplus_b T_b[i_b]$.

Protocol Notation. All protocols are denoted as out $\leftarrow$ Prot(sin, cin). Here, sin and cin are respectively server and client inputs to the protocol Prot. Except for in an ORAM Lookup, all the outputs out are sent to the server.

3.2   Permute and Unpermute

Non-oblivious random permutation. Fisher and Yates [11] show how to generate a uniformly random permutation $\pi : [n] \to [n]$ in $O(n)$ time steps. This implies that the client can write a random permutation on a server with $O(n)$ bandwidth. The permutation is non-oblivious, i.e., the server *does* learn the permutation generated.

Definition of Permute. Permute is a protocol that realizes an ideal functionality $\mathcal{F}_{\mathrm{perm}}$ as defined below. Intuitively, this functionality takes some unpermuted input layout (i.e., unpermuted secret-shared inputs) and three additional permutations π_{b+1} from the three permutation servers $\mathbf{S}_b$. The functionality produces an output such that the three shares are secret-shared again, and the share received by storage server $\mathbf{S}_{b+1}$ is permuted using π_{b+1}. Secret-sharing the data again before applying the new permutations ensures that a storage server $\mathbf{S}_{b+1}$ does not learn the permutation π_{b+1} applied to its share.

- $\{\pi_b, \mathsf{T}'_b\}_{b \in \mathbb{Z}_3} \leftarrow \mathsf{Permute}((\{\mathbf{\mathsf{e}}, \mathsf{T}_b\}_{b \in \mathbb{Z}_3}, \{\pi_b\}_{b \in \mathbb{Z}_3}), \perp)$:
  - *Input*: Let $\{\mathbf{\mathsf{e}}, \mathsf{T}_b\}_{b \in \mathbb{Z}_3}$ be the unpermuted layout provided as input. (Recall that T_b and T_{b+1} are stored in server $\mathbf{S}_b$.)
    Moreover, for each $b \in \mathbb{Z}_3$, $\mathbf{S}_b$ has an additional permutation π_{b+1} as input (which could be generated by the client for instance).
    The arrays have the same length $|\mathsf{T}_0| = |\mathsf{T}_1| = |\mathsf{T}_2| = n$, for some n. The client obtains $\perp$ as the input.
  - *Ideal functionality* $\mathcal{F}_{\mathrm{perm}}$:
    Sample independently and uniformly random $\widehat{\mathsf{T}}_0, \widehat{\mathsf{T}}_1$ of length n.
    Now, define $\widehat{\mathsf{T}}_2 := \widehat{\mathsf{T}}_0 \oplus \widehat{\mathsf{T}}_1 \oplus (\oplus_b \mathsf{T}_b)$, i.e., $\oplus_b \widehat{\mathsf{T}}_b = \oplus_b \mathsf{T}_b$.
    For each $b \in \mathbb{Z}_3$, define $\mathsf{T}'_b := \pi_b(\widehat{\mathsf{T}}_b)$.
    The output layout is $\{\pi_b, \mathsf{T}'_b\}_{b \in \mathbb{Z}_3}$, and the client's output is $\perp$.

Protocol Permute. The implementation of $\mathcal{F}_{\mathrm{perm}}$ proceeds as follows:

1. *Mask shares.* For each data block, the client first generates block "masks" that sum up to *zero*, and then applies mask to T_{b+1} on server $\mathbf{S}_b$. Specifically, the client does the following, for each $i \in [n]$:
   - Generate block "masks" that sum up to *zero*, i.e., sample independent random blocks B_0^i and B_1^i, and compute $\mathsf{B}_2^i := \mathsf{B}_0^i \oplus \mathsf{B}_1^i$.
   - Apply mask B_{b+1}^i to $\mathsf{T}_{b+1}[i]$ stored on server $\mathbf{S}_b$, i.e., for each $i \in [b]$, the client writes $\widehat{\mathsf{T}}_{b+1}[i] \leftarrow \mathsf{T}_{b+1}[i] \oplus \mathsf{B}_{b+1}^i$ on server $\mathbf{S}_b$.
2. *Permute share of $\mathbf{S}_{b+1}$ and send result to $\mathbf{S}_{b+1}$.* The client uses π_{b+1} to permute a share on the permutation server and then sends this permuted share to the storage server, i.e., for each $b \in \mathbb{Z}_3$, the client computes computes $\mathsf{T}'_{b+1} := \pi_{b+1}(\widehat{\mathsf{T}}_{b+1})$ on server $\mathbf{S}_b$, and sends the result T'_{b+1} to $\mathbf{S}_{b+1}$. Each server $\mathbf{S}_b$ stores T'_b and $(\pi_{b+1}, \mathsf{T}'_{b+1})$; hence, the new layout $\{\pi_b, \mathsf{T}'_b\}_{b \in \mathbb{Z}_3}$ is achieved.

Theorem 3. *The* Permute *protocol perfectly securely realizes the ideal functionality* $\mathcal{F}_{\text{perm}}$ *(as per Definition 1) in the presence of a semi-honest adversary corrupting a single server with* $O(n)$ *bandwidth.*

Due to lack of space, the proof is in the full version of the paper [5].

Definition of Unpermute and Protocol Description. Similar to Permute, we also need a complementary Unpermute protocol. Its definition and protocol are described in the full version [5].

3.3 Stable Compaction

Definition of StableCompact. StableCompact is a protocol that realizes an ideal functionality $\mathcal{F}_{\text{compact}}$, as defined below:

- $\{\mathfrak{e}, T'_b\}_{b \in \mathbb{Z}_3} \leftarrow$ StableCompact($\{\mathfrak{e}, T_b\}_{b \in \mathbb{Z}_3}, \perp$):
  - *Input layout:* A *semi-sorted*, unpermuted layout denoted $\{\mathfrak{e}, T_b\}_{b \in \mathbb{Z}_3}$.
  - *Ideal functionality* $\mathcal{F}_{\text{compact}}$: $\mathcal{F}_{\text{compact}}$ computes $T^* := T_0 \oplus T_1 \oplus T_2$; it then moves all dummy blocks in T^* to the end of the array, while keeping the relative order of real blocks unchanged.

    Now, $\mathcal{F}_{\text{compact}}$ randomly samples T'_0, T'_1 of appropriate length and computes T'_2 such that $T^* = T'_0 \oplus T'_1 \oplus T'_2$. The output layout is a *sorted*, unpermuted layout $\{\mathfrak{e}, T'_b\}_{b \in \mathbb{Z}_3}$.

StableCompact Protocol. The input is a *semi-sorted*, unpermuted layout, and we would like to turn it into a *sorted*, unpermuted layout obliviously. The key idea is to permute each share of the list (stored on the 3 servers respectively), such that the storage server for each share does not know the permutation. Now, the client accesses all real elements in a sorted order, and then accesses all dummy elements, writing down the elements in a secret-shared manner as the accesses are made. We can achieve this if each real or dummy element is tagged with a pointer to its next element, and the pointer is in fact a 3-tuple that is also secret-shared on the 3 servers — each element in the 3-tuple indicates where the next element is in one of the 3 permutations.

Therefore, the crux of the algorithm is to tag each (secret-shared) element with a (secret-shared) position tuple, indicating where its next element is — this will effectively create two linked list structures (one for real and one for dummy): each element in the linked lists is secret-shared in to 3 shares, and each share resides on its storage server at an independent random location.

The detailed protocol is as follows:

1. First, each server $\mathbf{S}_b$ acts as the permutation server for $\mathbf{S}_{b+1}$. Thus, the client generates a random permutation π_{b+1} on the permutation server $\mathbf{S}_b$ using the Fisher-Yates algorithm described in Sect. 3.2. Basically, for each index i of the original list the client writes down, on each $\mathbf{S}_b$, that its $(b+1)$-th share (out of 3 shares), wants to be in position $\pi_{b+1}(i)$.

2. Next, the client makes a reverse scan of $(T_0, \pi_0), (T_1, \pi_1), (T_2, \pi_2)$ for $i = n$ down to 1. The client can access $(T_{b+1}[i], \pi_{b+1}(i))$ by talking to S_b. In this reverse scan, the client always locally remembers the position tuple of the last real element encountered (henceforth denoted $\mathfrak{p}_{real}$) and the position tuple of the last dummy element encountered (henceforth denoted $\mathfrak{p}_{dummy}$). Thus, if $T[k_{real}]$ is the last seen real element, then the client remembers $\mathfrak{p}_{real} = (\pi_b(k_{real}) : b \in \mathbb{Z}_3)$. $\mathfrak{p}_{dummy}$ is updated analogously. Initially, $\mathfrak{p}_{real}$ and $\mathfrak{p}_{dummy}$ are set to $\perp$.

   During this scan, whenever a real element $T[i]$ is encountered, the client secretly writes the link $L[i] := \mathfrak{p}_{real}$, i.e., $L[i]$ represents secret-shares of the next pointers for the real element and L itself represents an abstract linked list of real elements. The links for dummy elements are updated analogously using $\mathfrak{p}_{dummy}$.

   At the end of this reverse scan, the client remembers the position tuple for the first real of the linked list denoted $\mathfrak{p}_{real}^1$ and position tuple for the first dummy denoted $\mathfrak{p}_{dummy}^1$.

3. Next, we call Permute inputting (1) the original layout — but importantly, now each element is tagged with a position tuple (that is also secret-shared); and (2) the three permutations chosen by each S_b (acting as the permutation server for S_{b+1}). Thus, Permute is applied to the combined layout $\{\mathfrak{e}, (T_b, L_b)\}_{b \in \mathbb{Z}_3}$, where S_b has input permutation π_{b+1}. Let the output of Permute be denoted by $\{\pi_b, (T_b', L_b')\}_{b \in \mathbb{Z}_3}$.

4. Finally, the client traverses first the real linked list (whose start position tuple is $\mathfrak{p}_{real}^1$) and then the dummy linked list (whose start position tuple is $\mathfrak{p}_{dummy}^1$). During this traversal, the client secretly writes each element encountered to produce the sorted and unpermuted output layout.

   More precisely, the client secretly writes an abstract array T'' element by element. Start with $k \leftarrow 0$ and $\mathfrak{p} \leftarrow \mathfrak{p}_{real}^1$.

   The client reconstructs element $B := \oplus T_b'[\mathfrak{p}_b]$ and the next pointer of the linked list next $:= \oplus L_b'[\mathfrak{p}_b]$; the client secretly writes to the abstract array $T''[k] := B$.

   Then, it updates $k \leftarrow k+1$ and $\mathfrak{p} \leftarrow$ next, and continues to the next element; if the end of the real list is reached, then it sets $\mathfrak{p} \leftarrow \mathfrak{p}_{dummy}^1$. This continues until the whole (abstract) T'' is secretly written to the three servers.

5. The new layout $\{\mathfrak{e}, T_b''\}_{b \in \mathbb{Z}_3}$ is constructed.

Theorem 4. *The* StableCompact *protocol perfectly securely realizes the ideal functionality* $\mathcal{F}_{compact}$ *(as per Definition 1) in the presence of a semi-honest adversary corrupting a single server with* $O(n)$ *bandwidth.*

Due to lack of space, the proof is in the full version of the paper [5].

3.4   Merging

Definition of Merge. Merge is a protocol that realizes an ideal functionality $\mathcal{F}_{merge}$ as defined below:

- $\{\epsilon, U_b''\}_{b \in \mathbb{Z}_3} \leftarrow \mathsf{Merge}(\{\epsilon, (T_b, T_b')\}_{b \in \mathbb{Z}_3}, \perp)$:
  - *Input layout*: Two *semi-sorted*, unpermuted layouts denoted $\{\epsilon, T_b\}_{b \in \mathbb{Z}_3}$ and $\{\epsilon, T_b'\}_{b \in \mathbb{Z}_3}$ denoting abstract lists T and T', where all the arrays have the same length n.
  - *Ideal functionality* $\mathcal{F}_{\mathrm{merge}}$: First, $\mathcal{F}_{\mathrm{merge}}$ merges the two lists $T_0 \oplus T_1 \oplus T_2$ and $T_0' \oplus T_1' \oplus T_2'$, such that the resulting array is sorted with all dummy blocks at the end. Let U'' be this merged result. Now, $\mathcal{F}_{\mathrm{merge}}$ randomly samples U_0'' and U_1'' independently of appropriate length and computes U_2'' such that $U'' = U_0'' \oplus U_1'' \oplus U_2''$. The output layout is a *sorted*, unpermuted layout $\{\epsilon, U_b''\}_{b \in \mathbb{Z}_3}$.

Merge Protocol. The protocol receives as input, two semi-sorted, unpermuted layouts and produces a merged, sorted, unpermuted layout as the output. The key idea is to permute the concatenation of the two semi-sorted inputs such that the storage servers do not know the permutation. Now, the client accesses real elements in both lists in the sorted order using the storage servers to produce a merged output. Given that a *concatenation of the lists* is permuted together, elements from *which* list is accessed is not revealed during the merge operation, thereby allowing us to merge the two lists obliviously. In order to access the two lists in a sorted order, the client creates a linked list of real and dummy elements using the permutation servers, similar to the StableCompact protocol in Sect. 3.3.

The detailed protocol works as follows:

1. First, the client concatenates the two abstract lists T and T' to obtain an abstract list U of size $2n$, i.e., we interpret U_b as the concatenation of T_b and T_b' for each $b \in \mathbb{Z}_3$. Specifically, $U_b[0, n-1]$ corresponds to T_b and $U_b[n, 2n-1]$ corresponds to T_b'.
2. Now, each server $\mathbf{S}_b$ acts as the permutation server for $\mathbf{S}_{b+1}$. The client generates a random permutation $\pi_{b+1} : [2n] \to [2n]$ on server $\mathbf{S}_{b+1}$ using the Fisher-Yates algorithm described in Sect. 3.2. $\pi_{b+1}(i)$ represents the position of the $(b+1)$-th share and is stored on server $\mathbf{S}_b$.
3. The client now performs a reverse scan of $(U_0, \pi_0), (U_1, \pi_1), (U_2, \pi_2)$ for $i = n$ down to 1. During this reverse scan, the client always locally remembers the position tuples of the last real element and last dummy element encountered for both the lists. Let them be denoted by $\mathfrak{p}_{\mathrm{real}}, \mathfrak{p}_{\mathrm{real}}', \mathfrak{p}_{\mathrm{dummy}}$, and $\mathfrak{p}_{\mathrm{dummy}}'$. Thus, if $U[k_{\mathrm{real}}]$ is the last seen real element from the first list, the client remembers $\mathfrak{p}_{\mathrm{real}} = (\pi_b(k_{\mathrm{real}}) : b \in \mathbb{Z}_3)$. The other position tuples are updated analogously. Each of these tuples are initially set to $\perp$.

   During the reverse scan, the client maintains an abstract linked list L in the following manner. When $U[i]$ is processed, if it is a real element from the first list, then the client secretly writes the link $L[i] := \mathfrak{p}_{\mathrm{real}}$. $L[i]$ represents secret-shares of the next pointers for a real element from the first list. The cases for $\mathfrak{p}_{\mathrm{real}}', \mathfrak{p}_{\mathrm{dummy}}$, and $\mathfrak{p}_{\mathrm{dummy}}'$ are analogous.

   At the end of this reverse scan, the client remembers the position tuple for the first real and first dummy elements of both linked lists. They are denoted by $\mathfrak{p}_{\mathrm{real}}^1, \mathfrak{p}_{\mathrm{real}}'^1, \mathfrak{p}_{\mathrm{dummy}}^1$, and $\mathfrak{p}_{\mathrm{dummy}}'^1$.

4. We next call Permute to the combined layout $\{\mathfrak{e}, (U_b, L_b)\}_{b \in \mathbb{Z}_3}$, where each server $\mathbf{S}_b$ has input π_{b+1}, to produce $\{\pi_b, (U'_b, L'_b)\}_{b \in \mathbb{Z}_3}$ as output.

5. The linked lists can now be accessed using the four position tuples $\mathfrak{p}^1_{\text{real}}$, $\mathfrak{p}'^1_{\text{real}}$, $\mathfrak{p}^1_{\text{dummy}}$, and $\mathfrak{p}'^1_{\text{dummy}}$. The client first starts accessing real elements in the two lists using $\mathfrak{p}^1_{\text{real}}$ and $\mathfrak{p}'^1_{\text{real}}$ to merge them. When a real list ends, it starts accessing the corresponding dummy list.

   More precisely, the client secretly writes the merged result to the abstract output array U''.

   Start with $k \leftarrow 0$, $\mathfrak{p}^1 \leftarrow \mathfrak{p}^1_{\text{real}}$, $\mathfrak{p}^2 \leftarrow \mathfrak{p}^2_{\text{real}}$.

   For each $s \in \{1, 2\}$, the client reconstructs $B^s := \oplus_b U'_b[\mathfrak{p}^s_b]$ and $\text{next}^s :=$ $\oplus_b L'_b[\mathfrak{p}^s_b]$ at most once, i.e., if B^s and next^s have already been reconstructed once with the tuple $(\mathfrak{p}^p_b : b \in \mathbb{Z}_3)$, then they will not be reconstructed again. If B^1 should appear before B^2, then the client secretly writes $U''[k] \leftarrow B^1$ and updates $k \leftarrow k + 1$, $\mathfrak{p}^1 \leftarrow \text{next}^1$; if the end of the real list is reached, then it updates $\mathfrak{p}^1 \leftarrow \mathfrak{p}^1_{\text{dummy}}$. The case when B^2 should appear before B^1 is analogous.

   The next element is processed until the client has secretly constructed the whole abstract array U''.

6. The new merged layout $\{\mathfrak{e}, U''_b\}_{b \in \mathbb{Z}_3}$ is produced.

Theorem 5. *The* Merge *protocol perfectly securely realizes the ideal functionality $\mathcal{F}_{\text{merge}}$ (as per Definition 1) in the presence of a semi-honest adversary corrupting a single server with $O(n)$ bandwidth.*

Due to lack of space, the proof is in the full version of the paper [5].

4   Three-Server One-Time Oblivious Memory

We construct an abstract datatype to process non-recurrent memory lookup requests, i.e., between rebuilds of the data structure, each distinct address is requested at most once. Our abstraction is similar to the perfectly secure one-time oblivious memory by Chan et al. [6]. However, while Chan et al. only consider perfect security with respect to access pattern, our three-server one time memory in addition information-theoretically encrypts the data itself. Thus, in [6], since the algorithm does not provide guarantees for the data itself, it can modify the data structure while performing operations. In contrast, our one-time oblivious memory is a read-only data structure. In this data structure, we assume every request is tagged with a position label indicating which memory location to lookup in each of the servers. In this section, we assume that such a position is magically available during lookup; but in subsequent sections we show how this data structure can be maintained and provided during a lookup.

4.1   Definition: Three-Server One-Time Oblivious Memory

Our (three-server) one-time oblivious memory supports three operations: (1) Build, (2) Lookup, and (3) Getall. Build is called once upfront to create the data structure: it takes in a set of data blocks (tagged with its logical address), permutes shares of the data blocks at each of the servers to create a data structure that facilitates subsequent lookup from the servers. Once the data structure is built, lookup operations can be performed on it. Each lookup request consists of a logical address to lookup and a position label for each of the three servers, thereby enabling them to perform the lookup operation. The lookup can be performed for a real logical address, in which case the logical address and the position labels for each of the three servers are provided; or it can be a dummy request, in which case $\perp$ is provided. Finally, a Getall operation is called to obtain a list U of all the blocks that were provided during the Build operation. Later, in our ORAM scheme, the elements in the list U will be combined with those in other lists to construct a potentially larger one-time oblivious memory.

Our three-server one-time oblivious memory maintains obliviousness as long as (1) for each real block in the one-time memory, a lookup is performed at most once, (2) at most n total lookups (all of which could potentially be dummy lookups) are performed, and (3) no two servers collude with each other to learn the shares of the other server.

Formal Definition. Our three-server one-time oblivious memory scheme $\mathsf{OTM}[n]$ is parameterized by n, the number of memory lookup requests supported by the data structure. It is comprised of the following randomized, stateful algorithms:

- $\left(U, \left(\{\pi_b, (\widehat{\mathsf{T}_b}, \widehat{\mathsf{L}_b})\}_{b \in \mathbb{Z}_3}, \mathsf{dpos}\right)\right) \leftarrow \mathsf{Build}(\mathsf{T}, \perp)$:
  - *Input:* A sorted, unpermuted layout denoted $\{\mathfrak{e}, \mathsf{T}_b\}_{b \in \mathbb{Z}_3}$ representing an abstract sorted list T. $\mathsf{T}[i]$ represents a key-value pair (key_i, v_i) which are either real and contains a real address key_i and value v_i, or dummy and contains a $\perp$. The list T is sorted by the key key_i. The client's input is $\perp$.
  - *Functionality:* The Build algorithm creates a layout $\{\pi_b, (\widehat{\mathsf{T}_b}, \widehat{\mathsf{L}_b})\}_{b \in \mathbb{Z}_3}$ of size $2n$ that will facilitate subsequent lookup requests; intuitively, n extra dummy elements are added, and the $\widehat{\mathsf{L}_b}$'s maintain a singly-linked list for these n dummy elements. Moreover, the tuple of head positions is secret-shared $\oplus_b \mathsf{dpos}_b$ among the three servers.
  It also outputs a sorted list U of n key-value pairs $(\mathsf{key}, \mathsf{pos})$ sorted by key where each $\mathsf{pos} := (\mathsf{pos}_0, \mathsf{pos}_1, \mathsf{pos}_2)$; the invariant is that if $\mathsf{key} \neq \perp$, then the data for key is $\oplus_b \widehat{\mathsf{T}_b}[\mathsf{pos}_b]$.
  The output list U is stored as a sorted, unpermuted layout $\{\mathfrak{e}, U_b\}_{b \in \mathbb{Z}_3}$. Every real key from T appears exactly once in U and the remaining entries of U are $\perp$'s. The client's output is $\perp$.
  Later in our scheme, U will be propagated back to the corresponding data structure with preceding recursion depth during a coordinated rebuild. Hence, U does not need to carry the value v_i's.
- $v \leftarrow \mathsf{Lookup}\left(\left(\{\pi_b, (\widehat{\mathsf{T}_b}, \widehat{\mathsf{L}_b})\}_{b \in \mathbb{Z}_3}, \mathsf{dpos}\right), (\mathsf{key}, \mathsf{pos})\right)$:
  - *Input:* The client provides a key key and a position label tuple $\mathsf{pos} := (\mathsf{pos}_0, \mathsf{pos}_1, \mathsf{pos}_2)$. The servers input the data structure $\{\pi_b, (\widehat{\mathsf{T}_b}, \widehat{\mathsf{L}_b})\}_{b \in \mathbb{Z}_3}$ and dpos created during Build.

- *Functionality:* If key $\neq \perp$, return $\oplus_b \widehat{T_b}[\text{pos}_b]$ else, return $\perp$.
- $R \leftarrow \text{Getall}\left(\left\{\pi_b, (\widehat{T_b}, \widehat{L_b})\right\}_{b \in \mathbb{Z}_3}, \perp\right)$:
  - *Input:* The servers input the data structure $\{\pi_b, (\widehat{T_b}, \widehat{L_b})\}_{b \in \mathbb{Z}_3}$ created during Build.
  - *Functionality:* the Getall algorithm returns a sorted, unpermuted layout $\{\mathfrak{e}, R_b\}_{b \in \mathbb{Z}_3}$ of length n. This layout represents an abstract sorted list R of key-value pairs where each entry is either real and of the form (key, v) or dummy and of the form $(\perp, \perp)$. The list R contains all real elements inserted during Build including those that have been looked up, padded with $(\perp, \perp)$ to a length of n^2.

Valid request sequence. Our three-server one-time oblivious memory ensures obliviousness only if lookups are non-recurrent (i.e., the same real key is never looked up more than once); and the number of lookups is upper bounded by n, the size of the input list provided to Build. More formally, a sequence of operations is valid, iff the following holds:

- The sequence begins with a single call to Build, followed by a sequence of at most n Lookup calls, and finally the sequence ends with a call to Getall.
- All real keys in the input provided to Build have distinct keys.
- For every Lookup concerning a real element with client's input $(\text{key}, \text{pos} := (\text{pos}_0, \text{pos}_1, \text{pos}_2))$, the key should have existed in the input to Build. Moreover, the position label tuple $(\text{pos}_0, \text{pos}_1, \text{pos}_2)$ must be the correct position labels for each of the three servers.
- No two Lookup requests should request the same real key.

Correctness. Correctness requires that:

1. For any valid request sequence, with probability 1, every Lookup request must return the correct value v associated with key key that was supplied in the Build operation.
2. For any valid request sequence, with probability 1, Getall must return an array R containing every (key, v) pair that was supplied to Build, padded with dummies to have n entries.

Perfect obliviousness. Suppose the following sequence of operations are executed: the initial Build, followed by a valid request sequence of ℓ Lookup's, and the final Getall. Perfect obliviousness requires that for each $b \in \mathbb{Z}_3$, the joint distribution of the communication pattern (between the client and the servers) and the view[b] of $\mathbf{S}_b$ is fully determined by the parameters n and ℓ.

---

[2] The Getall function returns as output the unpermuted layout that was input to Build. It primarily exists for ease of exposition.

4.2   Construction

Intuition. The intuition is to store shares of the input list on storage servers such that each share is independently permuted and each server storing a share does not know its permutation (but some other server does). In order to lookup a real element, if a position label for all three shares are provided, then the client can directly access the shares. Since the shares are permuted and the server storing a share does not know the permutation, each lookup corresponds to accessing a completely random location and is thus perfectly oblivious. This is true so far as each element is accessed exactly once and the position label provided is correct; both of these constraints are satisfied by a valid request sequence. However, in an actual request sequence, some of the requests may be dummy and these requests do not carry a position label with them. To accommodate dummy requests, before permuting the shares, we first append shares of dummy elements to shares of the unpermuted input list. We add enough dummy elements to support all lookup requests before the one time memory is destroyed. Then we create a linked list of dummy elements so that a dummy element stores the position label of the location where the next dummy element is destined to be after permutation. The client maintains the head of this linked list, updating it every time a dummy request is made. To ensure obliviousness, the links (position labels) in the dummy linked list are also stored secret-shared and permuted along with the input list.

Protocol Build. Our oblivious Build algorithm proceeds as follows. Note that the input list T is stored as an unpermuted layout $\{\mathfrak{e}, \mathsf{T}_b\}_{b \in \mathbb{Z}_3}$ on the three servers.

1. *Initialize to add dummies.* Construct an extended abstract $\mathsf{T}'[0..2n-1]$ of length $2n$ such that the first n entries are key-value pairs copied from the input T (some of which may be dummies).
   The last n entries of T' contain *special* dummy keys. For each $i \in [1..n]$, the special dummy key i is stored in $\mathsf{T}'[n-1+i]$, and the entry has a key-value pair denoted by $\perp_i$. For each $i \in [1..n]$, the client secretly writes $\perp_i$ to $\mathsf{T}'[n-1+i]$.
2. *Generate permutations for* OTM. Each server S_b acts as the permutation server for S_{b+1}. For each $b \in \mathbb{Z}_3$, the client generates a random permutation $\pi_{b+1} : [2n] \to [2n]$ on permutation server S_b.
3. *Construct a dummy linked list.* Using the newly generated permutation π_{b+1} on server S_b, the client constructs a linked list of dummy blocks. This is to enable accessing the dummy blocks linearly, i.e., for each $i \in [1..n-1]$, after accessing dummy block $\perp_i$, the client should be able to access $\perp_{i+1}$.
   The client simply leverages $\pi_{b+1}(n..2n-1)$ stored on server S_b to achieve this. Specifically, for i from $n-1$ down to 1, to create a link between i-th and $(i+1)$-st dummy, the client reads $\pi_{b+1}(n+i)$ from server S_b and secretly writes the tuple $(\pi_{b+1}(n+i) : b \in \mathbb{Z}_3)$ to the abstract link $\mathsf{L}[n+i-1]$.
   There are no links between real elements, i.e., for $j \in [0..n-1]$, the client

secretly writes $(\perp, \perp, \perp)$ to (abstract) $\mathsf{L}[j]$.

Observe that these links are secret-shared and stored as an unpermuted layout $\{\mathfrak{e}, \mathsf{L}_b\}_{b \in \mathsf{S}_b}$.

Finally, the client records the positions of the head of the lists and secretly writes the tuple across the three servers, i.e., $\oplus_b \mathsf{dpos}_b := (\pi_b(n) : b \in \mathbb{Z}_3)$, where dpos_b is stored on server $\mathbf{S}_b$.

4. *Construct the key-position map U.* The client can construct the (abstract) key-position map $U[0..n-1]$ sorted by the key from the first n entries of T' and the π_b's. Specifically, for each $i \in [0..n-1]$, the client secretly writes $(\mathsf{key}_i, (\pi_b(i) : b \in \mathbb{Z}_3))$ to $U[i]$.

   Recall that U is stored as a sorted, unpermuted layout $\{\mathfrak{e}, U_b\}_{b \in \mathbb{Z}_3}$.

5. *Permute the lists along with the links.* Invoke Permute with input $\{\mathfrak{e}, (\mathsf{T}'_b, \mathsf{L}_b)\}_{b \in \mathbb{Z}_3}$, and permutation π_{b+1} as the input for $\mathbf{S}_b$. The Permute protocol returns a permuted output layout $\{\pi_b, (\widehat{\mathsf{T}_b}, \widehat{\mathsf{L}_b})\}_{b \in \mathbb{Z}_3}$.

6. As the data structure, each server $\mathbf{S}_b$ stores $(\widehat{\mathsf{T}_b}, \widehat{\mathsf{L}_b})$, $(\pi_{b+1}, (\widehat{\mathsf{T}_{b+1}}, \widehat{\mathsf{L}_{b+1}}))$, and dpos_{b+1}. The algorithm returns key-position map list U as output, which is stored as an unpermuted layout $\{\mathfrak{e}, U_b\}_{b \in \mathbb{Z}_3}$. This list will later be passed to the preceding recursion depth in the ORAM scheme during a coordinated rebuild operation.

Fact 6. *The* Build *algorithm for building an* OTM *supporting n lookups requires an $O(n)$ bandwidth.*

Protocol Lookup. Our oblivious $\mathsf{Lookup}\big(\big(\{\pi_b, (\widehat{\mathsf{T}_b}, \widehat{\mathsf{L}_b})\}_{b \in \mathbb{Z}_3}, \mathsf{dpos}\big), \big(\mathsf{key}, (\mathsf{pos}_0, \mathsf{pos}_1, \mathsf{pos}_2)\big)\big)$ algorithm proceeds as follows:

1. The client reconstructs $(\mathsf{pos}'_0, \mathsf{pos}'_1, \mathsf{pos}'_2) \leftarrow \oplus_b \mathsf{dpos}_b$.
2. *Decide position to fetch from.* If $\mathsf{key} \neq \perp$, set $\mathsf{pos} \leftarrow (\mathsf{pos}_0, \mathsf{pos}_1, \mathsf{pos}_2)$, i.e., we want to use the position map supplied from the input; if $\mathsf{key} = \perp$, set $\mathsf{pos} \leftarrow (\mathsf{pos}'_0, \mathsf{pos}'_1, \mathsf{pos}'_2)$, i.e., the dummy list will be used.
3. *Reconstruct data block.* Reconstruct $v \leftarrow \oplus \widehat{\mathsf{T}_b}[\mathsf{pos}_b]$ and $(\widehat{\mathsf{pos}}_0, \widehat{\mathsf{pos}}_1, \widehat{\mathsf{pos}}_2) \leftarrow \oplus \widehat{\mathsf{L}_b}[\mathsf{pos}_b]$.
4. *Update head of the dummy linked list.* If $\mathsf{key} \neq \perp$, the client re-shares the secrets $\oplus_b \mathsf{dpos}_b \leftarrow (\mathsf{pos}'_0, \mathsf{pos}'_1, \mathsf{pos}'_2)$ with the same head; if $\mathsf{key} = \perp$, the client secretly shares the updated head $\oplus_b \mathsf{dpos}_b \leftarrow (\widehat{\mathsf{pos}}_0, \widehat{\mathsf{pos}}_1, \widehat{\mathsf{pos}}_2)$.
5. *Read value and return.* Return v.

Fact 7. *The* OTM Lookup *algorithm requires $O(1)$ bandwidth.*

Protocol Getall. For Getall, the client simply invokes the Unpermute protocol on input layout $\{\pi_b, (\widehat{\mathsf{T}_b}, \widehat{\mathsf{L}_b})\}_{b \in \mathbb{Z}_3}$ and returns the first n entries of the sorted, unpermuted layout (and ignores the links created). This output is also stored as a sorted, unpermuted layout $\{\mathfrak{e}, \mathsf{T}_b\}_{b \in \mathbb{Z}_3}$. The data structure created on the servers during Build can now be destroyed.

Fact 8. *The* OTM Getall *algorithm requires an $O(n)$ bandwidth.*

Lemma 1. *The subroutines* Build, Lookup *and* Getall *are correct and perfectly oblivious in the presence of a semi-honest adversary corrupting a single server.*

Due to lack of space, the proofs for these statements are described in the full version of the paper [5].

5   3-Server ORAM with $O(\log^2 N)$ Simulation Overhead

Recall that Sect. 4 provided a construction for a three-server one-time memory that allows non-recurrent lookups so far as its position label is provided. In this section, we first extend this construction to create a hierarchy of one-time memories called position-based ORAM (similar to [6]) where each level acts as a "cache" for larger levels. We will first assume that position-labels are magically available in this position-based ORAM (Sect. 5.1). If a PRF could be used, the position labels could have been obtained using the PRF and this would indeed be an ORAM construction. However, to achieve perfect security, we instead maintain the position labels by recursively storing them in smaller hierarchies (Sect. 5.2).

Our ORAM scheme will consist of logarithmically many position-based ORAMs of geometrically increasing sizes, henceforth denoted ORAM_0, ORAM_1, ..., ORAM_D where $D := \log_2 N$. Specifically, ORAM_d stores $\Theta(2^d)$ blocks where $d \in \{0, 1, \ldots, D\}$. The actual data blocks are stored in ORAM_D whereas all other $\mathsf{ORAM}_d, d < D$ recursively store position labels for the next depth $d + 1$.

5.1   Position-Based ORAM

In this subsection, we focus on describing ORAM_d assuming the position labels are magically available. In the next subsection, we will describe how position labels are maintained across different depths.

Data Structure. For $0 \leq d \leq D$ each ORAM_d consists of $d + 1$ levels of three-server one-time oblivious memory that are geometrically increasing in size. We denote these one-time oblivious memories as $(\mathsf{OTM}_j : j = 0, \ldots, d)$ where $\mathsf{OTM}_j := \mathsf{OTM}[2^j]$ stores at most 2^j real blocks.

Every level j is marked as either *empty* (when the corresponding OTM_j has not been built) or *full* (when OTM_j is ready and in operation). Initially, all levels are empty.

Position label. To access a block stored in ORAM_d, its position label specifies (1) the level $l \in [0..d]$ such that the block resides in OTM_ℓ; and (2) the tuple $\mathsf{pos} := (\mathsf{pos}_0, \mathsf{pos}_1, \mathsf{pos}_2)$ to reconstruct the block from OTM_ℓ.

Operations. Each position-based ORAM supports two operations, Lookup and Shuffle.

Protocol <u>Lookup</u>:

- *Input:* The client provides $\big(\mathsf{key}, \mathsf{pos} := (l, (\mathsf{pos}_0, \mathsf{pos}_1, \mathsf{pos}_2))\big)$ as input, where key is the logical address for the lookup request, l represents the level such that the block is stored in OTM_l, and $(\mathsf{pos}_0, \mathsf{pos}_1, \mathsf{pos}_2)$ is used as an argument for $\mathsf{OTM}_l.\mathsf{Lookup}$.
  The servers store OTM_j for $0 \leq j \leq d$ where OTM stores layout $\big\{\pi_b, (\widehat{\mathsf{T}_b}, \widehat{\mathsf{L}_b})\big\}_{b \in \mathbb{Z}_3}$ and dpos for the level. Moreover, some of the OTMs may be empty.
- *Algorithm:* The lookup operation proceeds as follows:
  1. For each non-empty level $j = 0, \ldots, d$, perform the following:
     - The position label specifies that the block is stored at level OTM_l. For level $j = l$, set $\mathsf{key}' := \mathsf{key}$ and $\mathsf{pos}' := (\mathsf{pos}_0, \mathsf{pos}_1, \mathsf{pos}_2)$. For all other levels, set $\mathsf{key}' := \bot$, $\mathsf{pos}' := \bot$.
     - $v_j \leftarrow \mathsf{OTM}_j.\mathsf{Lookup}\Big(\big(\{\pi_b, (\widehat{\mathsf{T}_b}, \widehat{\mathsf{L}_b})\}_{b \in \mathbb{Z}_3}, \mathsf{dpos}\big), (\mathsf{key}', \mathsf{pos}')\Big)$.
  2. Return v_l.

Fact 9. *For* ORAM_d, *Lookup requires an* $O(d)$ *bandwidth.*

Protocol <u>Shuffle.</u> The shuffle operation is used in hierarchical ORAMs to shuffle data blocks in consecutive smaller levels and place them in the first empty level (or the largest level). Our shuffle operation, in addition, accepts another input U that is used to update the contents of data blocks stored in the position based ORAM. In the final ORAM scheme, the list U passed as an input to ORAM_d will contain the (new) position labels of blocks in ORAM_{d+1}. Similarly, the shuffle operation returns an output U' that will be passed as input to ORAM_{d-1}. More formally, our shuffle operation can be specified as follows:

$$(U', \widehat{\mathsf{T}}) \leftarrow \mathsf{Shuffle}_d\big((\mathsf{OTM}_0, \ldots, \mathsf{OTM}_l, U), l\big):$$

- *Input:* The shuffle operation for ORAM_d accepts as input from the client a level l in order to build OTM_l from data blocks currently in levels $0, \ldots, l$. In addition, ORAM_d consists of an extra OTM, denoted by OTM'_0, containing only a single element. Jumping ahead, this single element represents a freshly fetched block.
  The inputs of the servers consist of OTMs for levels up to level l, each of which is stored as a permuted layout $\{\pi_b, (\widehat{\mathsf{T}_b}, \widehat{\mathsf{L}_b})\}_{b \in \mathbb{Z}_3}$ and an array of key-value pairs U, stored as a sorted, unpermuted layout $\{\mathsf{e}, U_b\}_{b \in \mathbb{Z}_3}$. The array U is used to update the blocks during the shuffle operation.
  Throughout the shuffle operation we maintain the following invariant:
  - For every ORAM_d, $l \leq d$. Moreover, either level l is the smallest empty level of ORAM_d or l is the largest level, i.e., $l = d$.
  - Each logical address appears at most once in U.

- The input U contains a subset of logical addresses that appear in levels $0, \ldots, l$ of the ORAM_d (or OTM_0').
  Specifically, given a key-value pair (key, v), the corresponding block (key, v') should already appear in some level in $[0..l]$ or OTM_0'. An update rule will determine how v and v' are combined to produce a new value $\widehat{v}$ for key.

- The Shuffle algorithm proceeds as follows:

  1. **Retrieve key-value pairs from** $(\text{OTM}_0, \ldots, \text{OTM}_l)$. The client first retrieves the key-value pairs of real blocks from $(\text{OTM}_0, \ldots, \text{OTM}_l)$ and restore each array to its unpermuted form. More specifically, the client constructs the unpermuted sorted $\text{T}^j \leftarrow \text{OTM}_j.\text{Getall}(\{\pi_b, (\widehat{\text{T}}_b, \widehat{\text{L}}_b)\}_{b \in \mathbb{Z}_3}, \perp)$, for $0 \leq j \leq l$, and $\text{T}^0 \leftarrow \text{OTM}_0'.\text{Getall}(\{\pi_b, (\widehat{\text{T}}_b, \widehat{\text{L}}_b)\}_{b \in \mathbb{Z}_3}, \perp)^3$ Now, the old $\text{OTM}_0, \ldots, \text{OTM}_l$ instances can be destroyed.

  2. **Create a list for level** l. The client then creates a level l list of keys from $(\text{OTM}_0, \ldots, \text{OTM}_l)$.

     - *Merge lists from consecutive levels to form level l list.* The merge procedure proceeds as follows:
       For $j = 0, \ldots, l - 1$ do:
       $\widehat{\text{T}}^{j+1} \leftarrow \text{Merge}((\widehat{\text{T}}^j, \text{T}^j), \perp)$ where T^j and $\widehat{\text{T}}^j$ are of size 2^j
       Moreover, the lists are individually sorted but may contain blocks that have already been accessed. In the Merge protocol, for two elements with the same key and belonging to different OTM levels, we prefer the one at the smaller level first. For the case where $l = d$, perform another merge $\widehat{\text{T}}^d \leftarrow \text{Merge}((\widehat{\text{T}}^d, \text{T}^d), \perp)$ to produce an array of size 2^{d+1}; Jumping ahead, the size will be reduced back to 2^d in subsequent steps.
       At the end of this step, we obtain a merged sorted list $\widehat{\text{T}}^l$, stored as $\widehat{\text{T}}^l := \{\mathfrak{e}, \widehat{\text{T}}_b^l\}_{b \in \mathbb{Z}_3}$, containing duplicate keys that are stored multiple times (with potentially different values).

     - *Mark duplicate keys as dummy.* From the stored duplicate keys, we only need the value of the one that corresponds to the latest access. All other duplicate entries can be marked as dummies. At a high level, this can be performed in a single pass by the client by scanning consecutive elements of the unpermuted sorted layout $\widehat{\text{T}}^l$. The client keeps the most recent version, i.e., the version that appears first (and has come from the smallest OTM), and marks other versions as dummies. To maintain obliviousness, the secret-shares need to be re-distributed for each scanned entry.
       More specifically, suppose that there are λ duplicate keys. Then, the client scans through the unpermuted layout $\widehat{\text{T}}^l := \{\mathfrak{e}, \widehat{\text{T}}_b^l\}_{b \in \mathbb{Z}_3}$. For consecutive λ elements, $j, \ldots, j + \lambda - 1$ with the same key, the client re-distributes the secret for $\widehat{\text{T}}^l[j]$ for position j, and secretly writes $\perp$

---

[3] The layout inputs to the Getall operation are restricted to the ones stored in OTM_j for $0 \leq j \leq l$, respectively.

for positions $j + 1, \ldots, j + \lambda - 1$.

After this step, the resulting (abstract) $\widehat{T}^l$ is semi-sorted.

- *Compaction to remove dummies.* The client invokes the Stable-Compact protocol with input $\widehat{T}^l := \{\mathfrak{e}, \widehat{T}^l_b\}_{b \in \mathbb{Z}_3}$, i.e., $\widehat{T}^l \leftarrow$ StableCompact$(\widehat{T}^l, \perp)$ to obtain a sorted, unpermuted layout (where the dummies are at the end). We keep the first 2^l entries.

3. **Update $\widehat{T}^l$ with values from U.** The client updates $\widehat{T}^l$ so that it contains updated position values from U. Looking ahead, in our final scheme, U will contain the new position labels from an ORAM at a larger depth. Given that ORAM$_D$ is the largest depth and does not store position values, this step is skipped for ORAM$_D$.

We do this as follows:

- *Merge $\widehat{T}^l$ with U.* The client performs $A \leftarrow$ Merge$((\widehat{T}^l, U), \perp)$ to obtain a sorted, unpermuted layout. Ties on the same key break by choosing the blocks in $\widehat{T}^l$.
- *Scan and Update A.* In a single pass through the sorted, unpermuted layout A, it can operate on every adjacent pair of entries. If they share the same key, the following update rule is used to update both the values (the precise update rule is provided in the Convert subroutine in Sect. 5.2). In particular, in the final ORAM scheme, the keys in A correspond to logical addresses. Each address in a position-based ORAM at depth-d stores position labels for two children addresses at depth-$(d + 1)$. The entries in A that come from $\widehat{T}^l$ contain the old position labels for both children. For the entries from U, if children position labels exist, they correspond to the new labels. For each of the child addresses, if U contains a new position label, the update function chooses the new one; otherwise, it chooses the old label from $\widehat{T}^l$.
- *Compaction to remove dummies.* The client invokes the StableCompact protocol $A \leftarrow$ StableCompact$(A, \perp)$ to obtain an updated sorted, unpermuted layout A. We keep the first 2^l entries.

4. **Build OTM$_l$.** The client invokes $U' \leftarrow$ Build$(A, \perp)$ to generate a data structure OTM$_l$ and U'. Mark OTM$_l$ as *full* and OTM$_i$, for $i < l$, as *empty*.

We prove that the above position-based ORAM is correct and satisfies perfect obliviousness in the presence of a semi-honest adversary corrupting a single server in the full version of the paper [5].

5.2   ORAM Construction from Position-Based ORAM

Our ORAM scheme consists of $D + 1$ position-based ORAMs denoted as ORAM$_0$, $\ldots$, ORAM$_D$ where $D = \log_2 N$. ORAM$_D$ stores data blocks whereas ORAM$_d$ for $d < D$ stores a position map for ORAM$_{d+1}$. The previous section specified the construction of a position-based ORAM. However, it assumed that position labels are magically available at some ORAM$_d$. In this section, we show a full

ORAM scheme and specify (1) how these position labels for ORAM_d are obtained from ORAM_{d-1}, and (2) after a level of ORAM_d is built, how the position labels of blocks from the new level are updated at ORAM_{d-1}.

Format·of block address at depth d. Suppose that a block's logical address is a $\log_2 N$-bit string denoted by $\mathsf{addr}^{\langle D \rangle} := \mathsf{addr}[1..(\log_2 N)]$ (expressed in binary format), where $\mathsf{addr}[1]$ is the most significant bit. In general, at depth d, an address $\mathsf{addr}^{\langle d \rangle}$ is the length-d prefix of the full address $\mathsf{addr}^{\langle D \rangle}$. Henceforth, we refer to $\mathsf{addr}^{\langle d \rangle}$ as a depth-d address (or the depth-d truncation of addr).

When we look up a data block, we would look up the full address $\mathsf{addr}^{\langle D \rangle}$ in recursion depth D; we look up $\mathsf{addr}^{\langle D-1 \rangle}$ at depth $D - 1$, $\mathsf{addr}^{\langle D-2 \rangle}$ at depth $D - 2$, and so on. Finally at depth 0, only one block is stored at ORAM_0.

A block with the address $\mathsf{addr}^{\langle d \rangle}$ *in* ORAM_d *stores the position labels for two blocks in* ORAM_{d+1}, *at addresses* $\mathsf{addr}^{\langle d \rangle}\|0$ *and* $\mathsf{addr}^{\langle d \rangle}\|1$ *respectively.* Henceforth, we say that the two addresses $\mathsf{addr}^{\langle d \rangle}\|0$ and $\mathsf{addr}^{\langle d \rangle}\|1$ are *siblings* to each other; $\mathsf{addr}^{\langle d \rangle}\|0$ is called the left sibling and $\mathsf{addr}^{\langle d \rangle}\|1$ is called the right sibling. We say that $\mathsf{addr}^{\langle d \rangle}\|0$ is the left child of $\mathsf{addr}^{\langle d \rangle}$ and $\mathsf{addr}^{\langle d \rangle}\|1$ is the right child of $\mathsf{addr}^{\langle d \rangle}$.

An ORAM Lookup. An ORAM lookup request is denoted as $(\mathsf{op}, \mathsf{addr}, \mathsf{data})$ where $\mathsf{op} \in \{\mathsf{read}, \mathsf{write}\}$. If $\mathsf{op} = \mathsf{read}$ then $\mathsf{data} := \bot$. Here, addr denotes the address to lookup from the ORAM. The inputs are all provided by the client whereas the servers store position-based $\mathsf{ORAM}_0, \ldots, \mathsf{ORAM}_D$ as discussed in the previous section. We perform the following operations:

1. **Fetch.** For $d := 0$ to D, perform the following:
   - Let $\mathsf{addr}^{\langle d \rangle}$ denote the depth-d truncation of $\mathsf{addr}^{\langle D \rangle}$.
   - Call $\mathsf{ORAM}_d.\mathsf{Lookup}$ to lookup $\mathsf{addr}^{\langle d \rangle}$. Recall that the position labels for the block will be obtained from the lookup of ORAM_{d-1}. For ORAM_0, no position label is needed.
   - The block returned from Lookup is placed in a special OTM'_0 in ORAM_d. Jumping ahead, this will be merged with the rest of the data structure in the maintain phase.
   - If $d < D$, each lookup will return two positions for addresses $\mathsf{addr}^{\langle d \rangle}\|0$ and $\mathsf{addr}^{\langle d \rangle}\|1$. One of these will correspond to the position of $\mathsf{addr}^{\langle d+1 \rangle}$ which will be required in the lookup for ORAM_{d+1}.
   - If $d = D$, the outcome of Lookup will contain the data block fetched.
2. **Maintain.** We first consider depth D. Set depth-D's update array $U^D := \emptyset$. Suppose l^D is the smallest empty level in ORAM_D. We have the invariant that for all $0 \leq d < D$, if $l^D < d$, then l^D is also the smallest empty level in ORAM_d.
   For $d := D$ to 0, perform the following:
   (a) If $d < l^D$, set $l := d$; otherwise, set $l := l^D$.
   (b) Call $U \leftarrow \mathsf{ORAM}_d.\mathsf{Shuffle}((\mathsf{OTM}_0^d, \ldots, \mathsf{OTM}_l^d, U^d), l)$.
       Recall that to complete the description of $\mathsf{Shuffle}$, we need to specify

the update rule that determines how to combine the values of the same address that appears in both the current ORAM_d and U^d.

For $d < D$, in U^d and ORAM_d, each depth-d logical address $\text{addr}^{\langle d \rangle}$ stores the position labels for both children addresses $\text{addr}^{\langle d \rangle}||0$ and $\text{addr}^{\langle d \rangle}||1$ (in depth $d+1$). For each of the child addresses, if U^d contains a new position label, choose the new one; otherwise, choose the old label previously in ORAM_{d-1}.

(c) If $d \geq 1$, we need to send the updated positions involved in U to depth $d-1$. We use the Convert subroutine (detailed description below) to convert U into an update array for depth-$(d-1)$ addresses, where each entry may pack the position labels for up to two sibling depth-d addresses. Set $U^{d-1} \leftarrow \text{Convert}(U, d)$, which will be used in the next iteration for recursion depth $d-1$ to perform its shuffle.

The Convert subroutine. U is a sorted, unpermuted layout representing the abstract array $\{(\text{addr}_i^{\langle d \rangle}, \text{pos}_i) : i \in [|U|]\}$. The subroutine $\text{Convert}(U, d)$ proceeds as follows.

For $i := 0$ to $|U|$, the client reconstructs $(\text{addr}_{i-1}^{\langle d \rangle}, \text{pos}_{i-1}), (\text{addr}_i^{\langle d \rangle}, \text{pos}_i)$ and $(\text{addr}_{i+1}^{\langle d \rangle}, \text{pos}_{i+1})$, computes u_i' using the rules below and secretly writes u_i' to U^{d-1}.

- If $\text{addr}_i^{\langle d \rangle} = \text{addr}||0$ and $\text{addr}_{i+1}^{\langle d \rangle} = \text{addr}||1$ for some addr, i.e., if my right neighbor is my sibling, then write down $u_i' := (\text{addr}, (\text{pos}_i, \text{pos}_{i+1}))$, i.e., both siblings' positions need to be updated.
- If $\text{addr}_{i-1}^{\langle d \rangle} = \text{addr}||0$ and $\text{addr}_i^{\langle d \rangle} = \text{addr}||1$ for some addr, i.e., if my left neighbor is my sibling, then write down $u_i' := \perp$.
- Else if i does not have a neighboring sibling, parse $\text{addr}_i^{\langle d \rangle} = \text{addr}||b$ for some $b \in \{0, 1\}$, then write down $u_i' := (\text{addr}, (\text{pos}_i, *))$ if $b = 0$ or write down $u_i' := (\text{addr}, (*, \text{pos}_i))$ if $b = 1$. In these cases, only the position of one of the siblings needs to be updated in ORAM_{d-1}.
- Let $U^{d-1} := \{u_i' : i \in [|U|]\}$. Note here that each entry of U^{d-1} contains a depth-$(d-1)$ address of the form addr, as well as the update instructions for two position labels of the depth-d addresses $\text{addr}||0$ and $\text{addr}||1$ respectively. We emphasize that when $*$ appears, this means that the position of the corresponding depth-d address does not need to be updated in ORAM_{d-1}.
- Output U^{d-1}.

Lemma 2. *The above ORAM scheme is perfectly oblivious in the presence of a semi-honest adversary corrupting a single server.*

Fact 10. *Each ORAM access takes an amortized bandwidth blowup of $O(\log^2 N)$.*

Due to lack of space, the proofs are in the full version of the paper [5]. Summarizing the above, we arrive at the following main theorem:

Theorem 11 (Perfectly secure 3-server ORAM). *There exists a 3-server ORAM scheme that satisfies perfect correctness and perfect security (as per Sect. 2.3) against any single semi-honest server corruption with $O(\log^2 N)$ amortized bandwidth blowup (where N denotes the total number of logical blocks).*

Finally, similar to existing works that rely on the recursion technique [24,26], we can achieve better bandwidth blowup with larger block sizes: suppose each data block is at least $\Omega(\log^2 N)$ in size, and we still set the position map blocks to be $O(\log N)$ bits long, then our scheme achieves $O(\log N)$ bandwidth blowup.

Acknowledgments. T.-H. Hubert Chan was supported in part by the Hong Kong RGC under grant 17200418. Jonathan Katz was supported in part by NSF award #1563722. Kartik Nayak was supported by a Google Ph.D. fellowship. Antigoni Polychroniadou was supported by the Junior Simons Fellowship awarded by the Simons Society of Fellows. Elaine Shi was supported in part by NSF award CNS-1601879, a Packard Fellowship, and a DARPA Safeware grant (subcontractor under IBM).

References

1. Abraham, I., Fletcher, C.W., Nayak, K., Pinkas, B., Ren, L.: Asymptotically tight bounds for composing ORAM with PIR. In: Fehr, S. (ed.) PKC 2017. LNCS, vol. 10174, pp. 91–120. Springer, Heidelberg (2017). https://doi.org/10.1007/978-3-662-54365-8_5
2. Ajtai, M.: Oblivious RAMs without cryptographic assumptions. In: STOC (2010)
3. Chan, T.-H.H., Guo, Y., Lin, W.-K., Shi, E.: Oblivious hashing revisited, and applications to asymptotically efficient ORAM and OPRAM. In: Takagi, T., Peyrin, T. (eds.) ASIACRYPT 2017. LNCS, vol. 10624, pp. 660–690. Springer, Cham (2017). https://doi.org/10.1007/978-3-319-70694-8_23
4. Chan, T.-H.H., Guo, Y., Lin, W.K., Shi, E.: Cache-oblivious and data-oblivious sorting and applications. In: SODA (2018)
5. Chan, T.-H.H., Katz, J., Nayak, K., Polychroniadou, A., Shi, E.: More is less: Perfectly secure oblivious algorithms in the multi-server setting. CoRR, abs/1809.00825 (2018)
6. Chan, T.-H.H., Nayak, K., Shi, E.: Perfectly secure oblivious parallel RAM. In: TCC (2018)
7. Chan, T.-H.H., Shi, E.: Circuit OPRAM: a unifying framework for computationally and statistically secure ORAMs and OPRAMs. In: TCC (2017)
8. Chung, K.-M., Liu, Z., Pass, R.: Statistically-secure ORAM with $\tilde{O}(\log^2 n)$ overhead. In: Sarkar, P., Iwata, T. (eds.) ASIACRYPT 2014. LNCS, vol. 8874, pp. 62–81. Springer, Heidelberg (2014). https://doi.org/10.1007/978-3-662-45608-8_4
9. Damgård, I., Meldgaard, S., Nielsen, J.B.: Perfectly secure oblivious RAM without random oracles. In: Ishai, Y. (ed.) TCC 2011. LNCS, vol. 6597, pp. 144–163. Springer, Heidelberg (2011). https://doi.org/10.1007/978-3-642-19571-6_10
10. Demertzis, I., Papadopoulos, D., Papamanthou, C.: Searchable encryption with optimal locality: achieving sublogarithmic read efficiency. In: Shacham, H., Boldyreva, A. (eds.) CRYPTO 2018. LNCS, vol. 10991, pp. 371–406. Springer, Cham (2018). https://doi.org/10.1007/978-3-319-96884-1_13

11. Knuth, D.E.: The Art of Computer Programming, Volume 2 (3rd edn.): Seminumerical Algorithms. Addison-Wesley Longman Publishing Co., Inc., Boston (1997). ISBN: 0-201-89684-2
12. Goldreich, O.: Towards a theory of software protection and simulation by oblivious RAMs. In: STOC (1987)
13. Goldreich, O., Ostrovsky, R.: Software protection and simulation on oblivious RAMs. J. ACM **43**(3), 431–473 (1996). https://doi.org/10.1145/233551.233553. ISSN: 0004-5411
14. Goodrich, M.T.: Data-oblivious external-memory algorithms for the compaction, selection, and sorting of outsourced data. In: SPAA (2011)
15. Goodrich, M.T., Mitzenmacher, M.: Privacy-preserving access of outsourced data via oblivious RAM simulation. In: Aceto, L., Henzinger, M., Sgall, J. (eds.) ICALP 2011. LNCS, vol. 6756, pp. 576–587. Springer, Heidelberg (2011). https://doi.org/10.1007/978-3-642-22012-8_46
16. Gordon, D., Katz, J., Wang, X.: Simple and efficient two-server ORAM. In: Asiacrypt (2018)
17. Hoang, T., Ozkaptan, C.D., Yavuz, A.A., Guajardo, J., Nguyen, T.: S3ORAM: a computation-efficient and constant client bandwidth blowup ORAM with shamir secret sharing. In: CCS (2017)
18. Kushilevitz, E., Lu, S., Ostrovsky, R.: On the (in)security of hash-based oblivious RAM and a new balancing scheme. In: SODA (2012)
19. Kushilevitz, E., Mour, T.: Sub-logarithmic distributed oblivious RAM with small block size. CoRR, abs/1802.05145 (2018)
20. Lin, W.-K., Shi, E., Xie, T.: Can we overcome the $n \log n$ barrier for oblivious sorting? Cryptology ePrint Archive, Report 2018/227 (2018)
21. Lu, S., Ostrovsky, R.: Distributed oblivious RAM for secure two-party computation. In: Sahai, A. (ed.) TCC 2013. LNCS, vol. 7785, pp. 377–396. Springer, Heidelberg (2013). https://doi.org/10.1007/978-3-642-36594-2_22
22. Raskin, M., Simkin, M.: Oblivious RAM with small storage overhead. Cryptology ePrint Archive, Report 2018/268 (2018). https://eprint.iacr.org/2018/268
23. Ren, L., et al.: Constants count: practical improvements to oblivious RAM. In: USENIX Security Symposium, pp. 415–430 (2015)
24. Shi, E., Chan, T.-H.H., Stefanov, E., Li, M.: Oblivious RAM with $O((\log N)^3)$ worst-case cost. In: Lee, D.H., Wang, X. (eds.) ASIACRYPT 2011. LNCS, vol. 7073, pp. 197–214. Springer, Heidelberg (2011). https://doi.org/10.1007/978-3-642-25385-0_11
25. Stefanov, E., Shi, E.: Multi-cloud oblivious storage. In: CCS (2013)
26. Stefanov, E., et al.: Path ORAM - an extremely simple oblivious RAM protocol. In: CCS (2013)
27. Tople, S., Dang, H., Saxena, P., Chang, E.-C.: Permuteram: Optimizing oblivious computation for efficiency. Cryptology ePrint Archive, Report 2017/885 (2017)
28. Wang, X.S., Chan, T.-H.H., Shi, E.: Circuit ORAM: on tightness of the Goldreich-Ostrovsky lower bound. In: ACM CCS (2015)

Real World Protocols

A Universally Composable Framework for the Privacy of Email Ecosystems

Pyrros Chaidos[1(✉)], Olga Fourtounelli[1], Aggelos Kiayias[2,3],
and Thomas Zacharias[2]

[1] National and Kapodistrian University of Athens, Athens, Greece
{pchaidos,folga}@di.uoa.gr
[2] The University of Edinburgh, Edinburgh, UK
{akiayias,tzachari}@inf.ed.ac.uk
[3] IOHK, Edinburgh, UK

Abstract. Email communication is amongst the most prominent online activities, and as such, can put sensitive information at risk. It is thus of high importance that internet email applications are designed in a privacy-aware manner and analyzed under a rigorous threat model. The Snowden revelations (2013) suggest that such a model should feature a *global adversary*, in light of the observational tools available. Furthermore, the fact that protecting metadata can be of equal importance as protecting the communication context implies that end-to-end encryption may be necessary, but it is not sufficient.

With this in mind, we utilize the Universal Composability framework [Canetti, 2001] to introduce an expressive cryptographic model for email "ecosystems" that can formally and precisely capture various well-known privacy notions (unobservability, anonymity, unlinkability, etc.), by parameterizing the amount of leakage an ideal-world adversary (simulator) obtains from the email functionality.

Equipped with our framework, we present and analyze the security of two email constructions that follow different directions in terms of the efficiency vs. privacy tradeoff. The first one achieves optimal security (only the online/offline mode of the users is leaked), but it is mainly of theoretical interest; the second one is based on parallel mixing [Golle and Juels, 2004] and is more practical, while it achieves anonymity with respect to users that have similar amount of sending and receiving activity.

1 Introduction

During the last decade, internet users increasingly engage in interactions that put their sensitive information at risk. Social media, e-banking, e-mail, and e-government, are prominent cases where personal data are collected and processed in the web. To protect people's personal data, it is important that applications

This work was supported by the European Union's Horizon 2020 research and innovation programme under grant agreement No. 653497 (project PANORAMIX).

T. Peyrin and S. Galbraith (Eds.): ASIACRYPT 2018, LNCS 11274, pp. 191–221, 2018.
https://doi.org/10.1007/978-3-030-03332-3_8

intended for communication of such information over the internet are designed in a privacy-aware manner and analyzed under a rigorous threat model.

The recent revelations by Snowden (2013) on massive surveillance of citizens' internet interactions, confirmed researchers' views that current technology is sufficient to provide adversaries with the tools to monitor the entire network. This was a turning point in that, henceforth, treating internet security and privacy in a threat model that considers a *global adversary* seems not only desirable, but imperative for the design of state-of-the-art cryptographic protocols.

As far as standard security is concerned, i.e., hiding the context between communicating internet users, there have been significant advancements on the aforementioned matter, mainly to due to wide deployment of end-to-end (E2E) encryption tools, even for some of the world's most popular applications, such as WhatsApp, Viber, Facebook Messenger and Skype (over Signal). However, it is well understood that E2E encryption is not enough to protect the users' metadata (e.g. users' identities and location, or the communication time), that often can be of equal importance. The protection of metadata is studied in the context of *anonymous communications*, that were introduced by the seminal works of Chaum with the concept of mix-nets [10], followed by DC-nets a few years later [8]. A mix-net is a message transmission system that aims to decouple the relation of senders to receivers by using intermediate servers to re-encrypt and re-order messages. The operation of mix-nets relies on messages from A to B making intermediate stops in mix servers, with appropriate delay times so that multiple messages "meet" at each server. The server re-encrypts messages before forwarding them, thus breaking the link between incoming and outgoing messages. We will analyse a mix-based system in Sect. 6 and contrast its overhead to the more expensive broadcast solution in Sect. 5. Nowadays, the most scalable solutions of anonymous communications in the real-world rely on *onion-routing* [33], and mostly on the Tor anonymous browser [16]. Although very efficient and a major step forward for privacy-preserving technologies, it has been pointed out (e.g., [21,32,34]) that onion-routing can provide anonymity only against adversaries with local views with respect to the (three) relay routing nodes, whereas a global observer can easily derive the addresses of two entities that communicate over onion-routing applications. Towards the goal of communication anonymity against a global adversary [2,9,11–13,24–26,29,35], various schemes have been proposed, and several recent ones achieving reasonable latency [1,9,25,26,29,35].

Modeling privacy for email ecosystems. In this work, we focus on the study of privacy (as expressed via several anonymity-style notions cf. [27]) for email ecosystems. The reason why we choose to focus on the email case is threefold:

(i) Email is one of the most important aspects of internet communication, as email traffic is estimated to be in the order of $\sim 10^{11}$ messages per day, while there are approximately 2.5 billion accounts worldwide[1].

---

[1] https://www.radicati.com/wp/wp-content/uploads/2014/10/Email-Market-2014-2018-Executive-Summary.pdf.

(ii) The actual network infrastructure of an email ecosystem has some special features that encourage a separate study from the general case of private messaging. Namely, the users dynamically register, go online/offline, and communicate, in a client-friendly environment and the management of the protocol execution is mainly handled by their service providers (SPs) that manage their inboxes. In turn, the client interface allows the user to log in/log out and while online, submit send and fetch requests to their SP. Moreover, adding a subsystem of mix-nodes which, in principle, are functionally different than the clients and the SPs, stratifies the observational power of the global adversary into three layers (i) the client$\leftrightarrow$SP channels, (ii) the SP$\leftrightarrow$mix-node channels, and (iii) the channels within the mix-node system. Under this real-world setting, exploring the feasibility and the trade off between efficiency and privacy for anonymous email routing poses restrictions on the expected secrecy, that would not be present in a generic peer-to-peer setting (e.g. users jointly engaging in an MPC execution).

(iii) To the best of our knowledge, there is no prior work on general modeling of email privacy in a computational model, that captures protocol flow under a composition of individual email messaging executions. The *Universal Composability (UC)* framework [6] is the ideal tool for such a modeling.

Contributions. Our contributions are as follows:

(i) In Sect. 3, we introduce a framework for the formal study of email ecosystems in the real-ideal world paradigm of the UC model [6]. The real-world entities involved in our framework comprise the set of clients, the of SPs and the subsystem of mix-nodes; all entities are synchronized via a *global clock* functionality $\mathcal{G}_{clock}$ and communicate over an *authenticated channel functionality with bounded message delay* Δ_{net}, denoted by $\mathcal{F}_{auth}^{\Delta_{net}}$. In the ideal-world, an *email privacy functionality* $\mathcal{F}_{priv}^{Leak,\Delta_{net}}$ manages email traffic among dummy parties that forward their inputs. The functionality is parameterized by Δ_{net} and a *leakage function* Leak, defined over the history transcript, that formally expresses the underlying privacy notion the studied email ecosystem should satisfy. To illustrate the expressibility of our framework, in Sect. 4, we show how to formally capture intuitively well understood privacy notions by properly defining the leakage function. In particular, we express and study the relation of notions of anonymity, unlinkability, unobservability and pseudonymity defined in [27], as well as E2E encryption, and a notion we call *weak anonymity* that, although a relaxed version of standard anonymity (still stronger than E2E encryption), provides reasonable privacy guarantees given the setting.

(ii) In Sect. 5, we present and formally analyze a theoretical construction with quadratic communication overhead that we prove it achieves unobservability (i.e., only the online/offline mode of the clients is leaked), which we argue that it sets the optimal level of privacy that can be expected under the restrictions posed in our client-SP setting, even against a global adversary that only observes the network. As a result, the said construction shows that in principle, optimal privacy is feasible, while the challenge of every real-world email ecosystem is to balance the privacy vs. efficiency trade off.

(iii) In Sects. 6 and 7 we analyze a construction similar to the classical parallel mix of Golle and Juels [18], to illustrate the expressiveness of our model in a more practice-oriented protocol. We focus on the UC simulation in Sect. 6, and in Sect. 7, we use Håstad's matrix shuffle to model the permutation's distribution. This in turn makes our analysis relevant to Atom [25], a state of the art anonymity system using similar permutation strategies. At the same time, as we only assume an adversary that is a global passive observer, Atom's techniques to mitigate corruptions are complementary, even if orthogonal, to our work.

2   Background

2.1   Notation

We use λ as the security parameter and write $\mathsf{negl}(\lambda)$ to denote that some function $f(\cdot)$ is negligible in λ. We write $[n]$ to denote the set $\{1, \ldots, n\}$ and $[\![\cdot]\!]$ to denote a multiset. By $X \approx_\epsilon Y$, we denote that the random variable ensembles $\{X_\lambda\}_{\lambda \in \mathbb{N}}, \{Y_\lambda\}_{\lambda \in \mathbb{N}}$ are computationally indistinguishable with error $\epsilon(\cdot)$, i.e., for every probabilistic polynomial time (PPT) algorithm $\mathcal{A}$, it holds that

$$\big| \Pr[w \leftarrow X_\lambda : \mathcal{A}(w) = 1] - \Pr[w \leftarrow Y_\lambda : \mathcal{A}(w) = 1] < \epsilon(\lambda) \big|.$$

We simply write $X \approx Y$ when the error ϵ is $\mathsf{negl}(\lambda)$. The notation $x \xleftarrow{\$} S$ stands for x being sampled from the set S uniformly ar random.

2.2   IND-CPA Security of Public-Key Encryption Schemes

In our constructions, we utilize public-key encryption (PKE). We require that a PKE scheme $\mathsf{PKE} = (\mathsf{KeyGen}, \mathsf{Enc}, \mathsf{Dec})$ satisfies the property of *multiple challenge IND-CPA (m-IND-CPA) security*, which is equivalent to standard IND-CPA security (up to negligible error). We recall that m-IND-CPA with error $\epsilon(\lambda)$ dictates that any adversary $\mathcal{B}$ that (a) obtains the public key, and (b) sends (polynomially many) challenge queries of the form (M_0, M_1) to the challenger receiving encryption of M_b, where b is the random bit of the challenger, can not guess b with more than $1/2 + \epsilon(\lambda)$ probability.

2.3   Related Work

Early works treating anonymity followed the intuitive definition of Pfitzmann and Khöntopp [28] as "the state of not being identifiable within a set of subjects", and aimed to augment it by quantifying the degree of non-identifiability. One of the first efforts in that direction (predating [28]) was the concept of "k-anonymity" by Samarati and Sweeney [30], that (in the context of databases) attempts to identify an individual produce at least k candidates.

In [15,31], anonymity is quantified by measuring the probability that a message M was sent by a user U. Thus, we are no longer interested only in the size of the set of candidates, but also their relative probabilities. This definition improved upon the "folklore" metric of only measuring the size of the subject set, even if the probability distribution on that set was highly non-uniform –e.g. [23].

The seminal work of Dwork [17] on Differential Privacy, while originating in the realm of databases, highlights and formalizes the strength of combining different pieces of seemingly privacy-respecting information to arrive at a privacy-impacting conclusion. Influenced in part by Differential Privacy, AnoA [3] is a game-based privacy analysis framework that is flexible enough to model various privacy concepts. Their approach is based on games between a challenger and an adversary who has control of the execution of the game, apart from a challenge message representing the scenarios the adversary is trying to distinguish.

In a different direction, the Universal Composability (UC) framework, [6] models security as a simulation not against an adversary, but a malicious environment, given strong control over the inputs of each party as well as a complete view of the system. This rigorous approach produces strong and composable security guarantees but is quite demanding in that the simulation must operate with the bare minimum of data (i.e. what we assume the protocol leaks). This precision in both simulation and leakage is a key motivation of this work.

On the other hand, state of the art anonymous communication solutions such as Loopix [29] which aims for high performance while maintaining strong anonymity properties, as well as unobservability, are analyzed under a weaker adversary. Moreover, Atom [25] is engineered to provide statistical indistinguishable shuffling with strong safeguards against malicious servers, but lacks formal proofs. In our work, we analyze a construction that shares a similar design (namely Håstad's matrix shuffle), so that we are able to offer a suggested T value (i.e. mix length) as a side contribution in Sect. 7. A key difference between Loopix and Atom is that Loopix uses a free routing approach (i.e. a message's path is determined by its sender) as opposed to allowing mix nodes to route messages. The first approach is more agreeable with high-efficiency solution aiming for a practical level of resilience against active adversaries while the second approach is easier to reason about but requires a passive adversary or measures such as NIZKs or trap messages to ensure correct behavior.

Camenish and Lysyanskaya [5] offer a treatment of onion routing in the Universal Composability model. The defining characteristic of onion routing, is that routing is entirely determined by the initial sender and is not influenced by the intervening nodes. As such, their analysis focuses on defining security with regards to the encryption, padding, structuring and layering of onions rather than the routing strategy itself. This is orthogonal to our approach: we focus on evaluating the anonymity of different mixing strategies under what we view as realistic requirements about the message encapsulation.

Wikström [36] covers the UC-security of a specific mix construction. His analysis is well-suited to voting but is hard to generalize over other use cases and performance parameters. In contrast, our work, while focusing on email, is more general and flexible in regards to leakage, timings and network topology.

In the work of Alexopoulos *et al.* [1], anonymity is studied in the concept of messaging via a stand-alone simulation-based model. Even though formally treated, anonymity in [1] is defined under a framework that is weaker than UC.

3   A UC Framework for the Privacy of Email Ecosystems

In this section, we present our UC framework for email privacy. As in standard UC approach, privacy will be defined via the inability of an environment $\mathcal{Z}$, that schedules the execution and provides the inputs, to distinguish between (i) a real-world execution of an email ecosystem $\mathbb{E}$ in the presence of a (global passive) adversary $\mathcal{A}$ and (ii) an ideal-world execution handled by an email privacy functionality interacting with a PPT simulator Sim. More specifically, we adjust our definitions to the *global UC* setting [7], by incorporating a global clock functionality (cf. [4,22]) that facilitates synchronicity and is accessed by all parties, including the environment.

3.1   Entities and Protocols of an Email Ecosystem

The entities that are involved in a private email "ecosystem" $\mathbb{E}$ are the following:

- The *service providers (SPs)* $\mathsf{SP}_1, \ldots, \mathsf{SP}_N$ that register users and are responsible for mailbox management and email transfer.
- The *clients* $C_1, \ldots, C_n$ that wish to exchange email messages and are registered to the SPs. For simplicity, we assume that each client is linked with only one SP that manages her mailbox. We write $C_\ell @\mathsf{SP}_i$ to denote that C_ℓ is registered to SP_i, where registration is done dynamically. We define the set $\mathbf{C}_i := \{C_\ell \mid C_\ell @\mathsf{SP}_i\}$ of all clients whose mailboxes SP_i is managing.
- The *mix node* subsystem **MX** that consists of the mix nodes $\mathsf{MX}_1, \ldots, \mathsf{MX}_m$ and is the core of the anonymous email routing mechanism.

An email ecosystem $\mathbb{E}$ has the two following phases:

■ **Initialization** is a setup phase where all SPs and mix nodes generate any possible private and public data, and commune their public data to a subset of the ecosystem's entities.

■ **Execution** is a phase that comprises executions of the following protocols:

- The REGISTER protocol between client C_s and her service provider SP_i. For simplicity, we assume that registration can be done only once.
- The SEND protocol between client C_s and her service provider SP_i. In particular, C_s that wishes to send a message M to some client address $C_r @\mathsf{SP}_j$ authenticates to SP_i and provides her with an encoding $\mathsf{Encode}(M, C_r @\mathsf{SP}_j)$ of $(M, C_r @\mathsf{SP}_j)$ (that may not necessarily include information about the sender). At the end of the protocol, $\mathsf{Encode}(M, C_r @\mathsf{SP}_j)$ is at the outbox of $C_s @\mathsf{SP}_i$ managed by SP_i.

- The ROUTE protocol that is executed among $SP_1, \ldots, SP_N$ and $MX_1, \ldots, MX_m$. Namely, the encoded message $\mathsf{Encode}(M, C_r@SP_j)$ is forwarded to the $\mathbf{MX}$ subsystem, which in turn delivers it to SP_j that manages the inbox of C_r.
- The RECEIVE protocol between client C_r and her service provider SP_j, where C_r can retrieve the messages from the inbox of $C_r@SP_j$ via fetch requests.

Remark 1. In this work, we consider email solutions that follow the realistic client-side approach, where the client-side operations are relatively simple and do not include complex interaction with the other entities for the execution of heavy cryptographic primitives (e.g. pairwise secure MPC). As we will explain shortly, the client-friendly approach poses some limitations on the privacy level that the email ecosystem can achieve.

3.2   A Global Clock Functionality

In our setting, the protocol flow within the email ecosystem $\mathbb{E}$ advances in *time slots*, that could refer to any suitable time unit (e.g. ms). The entities of $\mathbb{E}$ are synchronized via a *global clock functionality* $\mathcal{G}_{\mathsf{clock}}$ that interacts with a set of parties $\mathbf{P}$, a set of functionalities $\mathbf{F}$, the UC environment $\mathcal{Z}$ and the adversary $\mathcal{A}$. In the spirit of [4,22], the functionality $\mathcal{G}_{\mathsf{clock}}$, presented in Fig. 1, advances when all entities in $\mathbf{P}$ and $\mathbf{F}$ declare completion of their activity within the current time slot, whereas all entities have read access to it.

The global clock functionality $\mathcal{G}_{\mathsf{clock}}(\mathbf{P}, \mathbf{F})$.

The functionality initializes the global clock variable as $\mathsf{Cl} \leftarrow 0$ and the set of advanced parties as $L_{\mathsf{adv}} \leftarrow \emptyset$.

- Upon receiving $(\mathsf{sid}, \text{ADVANCE\_CLOCK}, P)$ from $\mathcal{F} \in \mathbf{F}$ or $P \in \mathbf{P}$, if $P \notin L_{\mathsf{adv}}$, then it adds P to L_{adv} and sends the message $(\mathsf{sid}, \text{ADVANCE\_ACK}, P)$ to $\mathcal{F}$ or P, repsectively, and notifies $\mathcal{A}$ by forwarding $(\mathsf{sid}, \text{ADVANCE\_CLOCK}, P)$. If $L_{\mathsf{adv}} = \mathbf{P}$, then it updates as $\mathsf{Cl} \leftarrow \mathsf{Cl} + 1$ and resets $L_{\mathsf{adv}} \leftarrow \emptyset$.
- Upon receiving $(\mathsf{sid}, \text{READ\_CLOCK})$ from $X \in \mathbf{P} \cup \mathbf{F} \cup \{\mathcal{Z}, \mathcal{A}\}$, then it sends $(\mathsf{sid}, \text{READ\_CLOCK}, \mathsf{Cl})$ to X.

Fig. 1. The global clock functionality $\mathcal{G}_{\mathsf{clock}}(\mathbf{P}, \mathbf{F})$ interacting with the environment $\mathcal{Z}$ and the adversary $\mathcal{A}$.

3.3   A UC Definition of E-mail Privacy

Let $\mathbf{Ad}$ be the set of all valid email addresses linking the set of clients $\mathbf{C} = \{C_1, \ldots, C_n\}$ and with their corresponding providers in $\mathbf{SP} = \{SP_1, \ldots, SP_N\}$, i.e. $\mathbf{Ad} := \cup_{i \in [N]} \mathbf{C}_i$. We denote by $\mathbf{P}$ the union $\mathbf{C} \cup \mathbf{SP} \cup \mathbf{MX}$.

The *history* of an email ecosystem execution that involves the entities in $\mathbf{C}, \mathbf{SP}$ and $\mathbf{MX}$ is a transcript of actions expressed as a list H, where each action entry of H is associated with a unique pointer ptr to this action. The leakage in each execution step, is expressed via a *leakage function* $\mathsf{Leak}(\cdot, \cdot)$ that, when given as input (i) a pointer ptr and (ii) an execution history sequence H, outputs some leakage string z. Here, z could be $\perp$ indicating no leakage to the adversary. This leakage may depend on the entry indexed by ptr as well as on entries recorded previously (i.e. prior than ptr).

We require that during a time slot, the environment sends a message for every party, even when the party is idle (inactive) for this slot, so that the clock can be advanced as described in Fig. 1.

The ideal world execution. In the ideal world, the protocol execution is managed by the *email privacy functionality* $\mathcal{F}_{\mathsf{priv}}^{\mathsf{Leak}, \Delta_{\mathsf{net}}}(\mathbf{P})$, parameterized by the message delivery delay bound Δ_{net} and the leakage function $\mathsf{Leak}(\cdot, \cdot)$, with access to $\mathcal{G}_{\mathsf{clock}}$. The functionality $\mathcal{F}_{\mathsf{priv}}^{\mathsf{Leak}, \Delta_{\mathsf{net}}}(\mathbf{P})$ consists of the **Initialization, Execution**, and **Clock advancement** phases, that informally are run as follows:

- At the **Initialization** phase, all the SPs in **SP** and mix nodes in **MX** provide $\mathcal{F}_{\mathsf{priv}}^{\mathsf{Leak}, \Delta_{\mathsf{net}}}(\mathbf{P})$ with an initialization notification via public delayed output. The functionality proceeds to the **Execution** phase when all SPs and mix nodes are initialized. Note that in the ideal world, the SPs and the mix nodes remain idle after **Initialization** (besides messages intended for $\mathcal{G}_{\mathsf{clock}}$), as privacy-preserving email routing is done by $\mathcal{F}_{\mathsf{priv}}^{\mathsf{Leak}, \Delta_{\mathsf{net}}}(\mathbf{P})$. Their presence in the ideal setting is for consistency in terms of UC interface.
- At the **Execution** phase, $\mathcal{F}_{\mathsf{priv}}^{\mathsf{Leak}, \Delta_{\mathsf{net}}}(\mathbf{P})$ manages the email traffic, as scheduled per time slot by the environment. During this phase, the clients may (dynamically) provide $\mathcal{F}_{\mathsf{priv}}^{\mathsf{Leak}, \Delta_{\mathsf{net}}}(\mathbf{P})$ with registration, log in, log out, send or fetch requests. Upon receiving a request, $\mathcal{F}_{\mathsf{priv}}^{\mathsf{Leak}, \Delta_{\mathsf{net}}}(\mathbf{P})$ updates the history by adding the request as a new entry associated with a unique pointer ptr, in a 'pending' mode. Then, it notifies the simulator Sim by attaching the corresponding leakage. The execution of a pending request which record is indexed by a pointer ptr is completed when $\mathcal{F}_{\mathsf{priv}}^{\mathsf{Leak}, \Delta_{\mathsf{net}}}(\mathbf{P})$ receives an ALLOW_EXEC message paired with ptr from Sim.

Within a time slot T, each client may perform only one action that also implies a time advancement request to $\mathcal{G}_{\mathsf{clock}}$. In order for the clock to advance all the other parties that performed no action (i.e., the SPs, the mix nodes and the clients that remained idle during T), send an explicit time advancement request to $\mathcal{F}_{\mathsf{priv}}^{\mathsf{Leak}, \Delta_{\mathsf{net}}}(\mathbf{P})$. Besides, any party may submit clock reading requests arbitrarily. All the messages that are intended for $\mathcal{G}_{\mathsf{clock}}$ are forwarded to it by $\mathcal{F}_{\mathsf{priv}}^{\mathsf{Leak}, \Delta_{\mathsf{net}}}(\mathbf{P})$.

- At the **Clock advancement** phase, all parties have already submitted time advancement requests during time slot T, so $\mathcal{F}_{\mathsf{priv}}^{\mathsf{Leak}, \Delta_{\mathsf{net}}}(\mathbf{P})$ takes the necessary final steps before proceeding to $T + 1$. In particular, $\mathcal{F}_{\mathsf{priv}}^{\mathsf{Leak}, \Delta_{\mathsf{net}}}(\mathbf{P})$ completes the execution of all send and fetch requests that have been delayed for Δ_{net} steps (by Sim). This suggests that in the ideal-world, the delay in message delivery is upper bounded by Δ_{net}. Finally, $\mathcal{F}_{\mathsf{priv}}^{\mathsf{Leak}, \Delta_{\mathsf{net}}}(\mathbf{P})$ informs Sim of the leakage derived from the aforementioned executions, advances its local time by 1 and reenters the **Execution** phase for time slot $T + 1$.

Formally, the email privacy functionality $\mathcal{F}_{\mathsf{priv}}^{\mathsf{Leak}, \Delta_{\mathsf{net}}}(\mathbf{P})$ is described as follows:

Initialization on status 'init'.

- $\mathcal{F}_{\mathsf{priv}}^{\mathsf{Leak}, \Delta_{\mathsf{net}}}(\mathbf{P})$ sets its status to 'init'. It initializes the set of valid addresses **Ad**, the set of active entities L_{act}, the set of clock-advanced entities L_{adv}, the *history* list H, and the set of leaked entries L_{leak} as empty.
- Upon receiving $(\mathsf{sid}, \mathrm{INIT})$ from a party $P \in \mathbf{SP} \cup \mathbf{MX}$, if $L_{\mathsf{act}} \subsetneq \mathbf{SP} \cup \mathbf{MX}$, then it sends the message $(\mathsf{sid}, \mathrm{INIT}, P)$ to Sim.
- Upon receiving $(\mathsf{sid}, \mathrm{ALLOW\_INIT}, P)$ from Sim, if $P \in (\mathbf{SP} \cup \mathbf{MX}) \setminus L_{\mathsf{act}}$, then it adds P to L_{act}. If $L_{\mathsf{act}} = \mathbf{SP} \cup \mathbf{MX}$, then it sends $(\mathsf{sid}, \mathsf{ready})$ to Sim.
- Upon receiving $(\mathsf{sid}, \mathrm{EXECUTE})$ from Sim, it sends $(\mathsf{sid}, \mathrm{READ\_CLOCK})$ to $\mathcal{G}_{\mathsf{clock}}$.
- Upon receiving $(\mathsf{sid}, \mathrm{READ\_CLOCK}, \mathsf{Cl})$ from $\mathcal{G}_{\mathsf{clock}}$, it sets its clock as Cl and its status to 'execute', and sends the message $(\mathsf{sid}, \mathsf{start}, \mathsf{Cl})$ to Sim.

Execution on status 'execute'.

Registration:
- Upon receiving $(\mathsf{sid}, \mathrm{REGISTER}, @\mathsf{SP}_i)$ from C_ℓ, if for every $j \in [N] : C_\ell @\mathsf{SP}_j \notin$ **Ad** and $C_\ell \notin L_{\mathsf{adv}}$, then
    1. It sends the message $(\mathsf{sid}, \mathrm{ADVANCE\_CLOCK}, C_\ell)$ to $\mathcal{G}_{\mathsf{clock}}$.
    2. Upon receiving $(\mathsf{sid}, \mathrm{ADVANCE\_ACK}, C_\ell)$ from $\mathcal{G}_{\mathsf{clock}}$, it adds C_ℓ to L_{adv} and the entry $(\mathsf{ptr}, (\mathsf{sid}, \mathsf{Cl}, \mathrm{REGISTER}, C_\ell @\mathsf{SP}_i), \text{'pending'})$ to H.
    3. It sends the message $(\mathsf{sid}, \mathsf{ptr}, \mathsf{Leak}(\mathsf{ptr}, H))$ to Sim.
    4. Upon receiving $(\mathsf{sid}, \mathrm{ALLOW\_EXEC}, \mathsf{ptr})$ from Sim, if ptr refers to an entry of the form $(\mathsf{ptr}, (\mathsf{sid}, \mathsf{Cl}, \mathrm{REGISTER}, C_\ell @\mathsf{SP}_i), \text{'pending'})$, then
        (a) It adds $C_\ell @\mathsf{SP}_i$ to **Ad** and L_{act}, and initializes a list $\mathsf{Inbox}[C_\ell @\mathsf{SP}_i]$ as empty.
        (b) It updates the entry as $(\mathsf{ptr}, (\mathsf{sid}, \mathsf{Cl}', \mathrm{REGISTER}, C_\ell @\mathsf{SP}_i), \text{'(registered, Cl)'})$.
        (c) It sends the message $(\mathsf{sid}, \mathsf{ptr}, \mathsf{Leak}(\mathsf{ptr}, H))$ to Sim.

Log in:
- Upon receiving $(\mathsf{sid}, \mathrm{ACTIVE}, @\mathsf{SP}_i)$ from C_ℓ, if $C_\ell @\mathsf{SP}_i \in$ **Ad** and $C_\ell \notin L_{\mathsf{adv}}$,
    1. It sends the message $(\mathsf{sid}, \mathrm{ADVANCE\_CLOCK}, C_\ell)$ to $\mathcal{G}_{\mathsf{clock}}$.
    2. Upon receiving $(\mathsf{sid}, \mathrm{ADVANCE\_ACK}, C_\ell)$ from $\mathcal{G}_{\mathsf{clock}}$, it adds C_ℓ to L_{adv} and the entry $(\mathsf{ptr}, (\mathsf{sid}, \mathsf{Cl}, \mathrm{ACTIVE}, C_\ell @\mathsf{SP}_i), \text{'pending'})$ to H.
    3. It sends the message $(\mathsf{sid}, \mathsf{ptr}, \mathsf{Leak}(\mathsf{ptr}, H))$ to Sim.
    4. Upon receiving $(\mathsf{sid}, \mathrm{ALLOW\_EXEC}, \mathsf{ptr})$ from Sim, if ptr refers to an entry of the form $(\mathsf{ptr}, (\mathsf{sid}, \mathsf{Cl}', \mathrm{ACTIVE}, C_\ell @\mathsf{SP}_i), \text{'pending'})$, then
        (a) If $C_\ell @\mathsf{SP}_i \notin L_{\mathsf{act}}$, then it adds $C_\ell @\mathsf{SP}_i$ to L_{act}.
        (b) It updates the entry as $(\mathsf{ptr}, (\mathsf{sid}, \mathsf{Cl}', \mathrm{ACTIVE}, C_\ell @\mathsf{SP}_i), \text{'(logged in, Cl)'})$.
        (c) It sends the message $(\mathsf{sid}, \mathsf{ptr}, \mathsf{Leak}(\mathsf{ptr}, H))$ to Sim.

Log out:
– Upon receiving $(\text{sid}, \text{INACTIVE}, @\text{SP}_i)$ from C_ℓ, if $C_\ell @\text{SP}_i \in \mathbf{Ad}$ and $C_\ell \notin L_{\text{adv}}$, then

1. It sends the message $(\text{sid}, \text{ADVANCE\_CLOCK}, C_\ell)$ to $\mathcal{G}_{\text{clock}}$.
2. Upon receiving $(\text{sid}, \text{ADVANCE\_ACK}, C_\ell)$ from $\mathcal{G}_{\text{clock}}$, it adds C_ℓ to L_{adv} and the entry $(\text{ptr}, (\text{sid}, \text{CI}, \text{INACTIVE}, C_\ell @\text{SP}_i), \text{'pending'})$ to H.
3. It sends the message $(\text{sid}, \text{ptr}, \text{Leak}(\text{ptr}, H))$ to Sim.
4. Upon receiving $(\text{sid}, \text{ALLOW\_EXEC}, \text{ptr})$ from Sim, if ptr refers to an entry of the form $(\text{ptr}, (\text{sid}, \text{CI}', \text{INACTIVE}, C_\ell @\text{SP}_i), \text{'pending'})$, then
   (a) If $C_\ell @\text{SP}_i \in L_{\text{act}}$, then it deletes $C_\ell @\text{SP}_i$ from L_{act}.
   (b) It updates the entry as $(\text{ptr}, (\text{sid}, \text{CI}', \text{INACTIVE}, C_\ell @\text{SP}_i), \text{'(logged out, CI)'})$.
   (c) It sends the message $(\text{sid}, \text{ptr}, \text{Leak}(\text{ptr}, H))$ to Sim.

Send:
– Upon receiving $(\text{sid}, \text{SEND}, \langle C_s @\text{SP}_i, M, C_r @\text{SP}_j \rangle)$ from C_s, if $C_s @\text{SP}_i$, $C_r @\text{SP}_j \in \mathbf{Ad}$ and $C_s \in L_{\text{act}} \setminus L_{\text{adv}}$, then

1. It sends the message $(\text{sid}, \text{ADVANCE\_CLOCK}, C_s)$ to $\mathcal{G}_{\text{clock}}$.
2. Upon receiving $(\text{sid}, \text{ADVANCE\_ACK}, C_s)$ from $\mathcal{G}_{\text{clock}}$, it adds C_s in L_{adv} and the entry $(\text{ptr}, (\text{sid}, \text{CI}, \text{SEND}, \langle C_s @\text{SP}_i, M, C_r @\text{SP}_j \rangle), \text{'pending'})$ to H.
3. It sends the message $(\text{sid}, \text{ptr}, \text{Leak}(\text{ptr}, H))$ to Sim.
4. Upon receiving $(\text{sid}, \text{ALLOW\_EXEC}, \text{ptr})$ from Sim, if ptr refers to an entry $(\text{sid}, \text{CI}', \text{SEND}, \langle C_s @\text{SP}_i, M, C_r @\text{SP}_j \rangle)$ with status 'pending', then
   (a) It adds $(\text{sid}, \text{CI}', \text{SEND}, \langle C_s @\text{SP}_i, M, C_r @\text{SP}_j \rangle)$ to $\text{Inbox}[C_r @\text{SP}_j]$.
   (b) It updates as $(\text{ptr}, (\text{sid}, \text{CI}', \text{SEND}, \langle C_s @\text{SP}_i, M, C_r @\text{SP}_j \rangle), \text{'(sent, CI)'})$.
   (c) It sends the message $(\text{sid}, \text{ptr}, \text{Leak}(\text{ptr}, H))$ to Sim.

Fetch:
– Upon receiving $(\text{FETCH}, \text{sid}, C_r @\text{SP}_j)$ from C_r, if $C_r @\text{SP}_j \in \mathbf{Ad}$ and $C_r \in L_{\text{act}} \setminus L_{\text{adv}}$, then

1. It sends the message $(\text{sid}, \text{ADVANCE\_CLOCK}, C_r)$ to $\mathcal{G}_{\text{clock}}$.
2. Upon receiving $(\text{sid}, \text{ADVANCE\_ACK}, C_r)$ from $\mathcal{G}_{\text{clock}}$, it adds C_s in L_{adv} and the entry $(\text{ptr}, (\text{sid}, \text{CI}, \text{FETCH}, C_r @\text{SP}_j), \text{'pending'})$ to H.
3. It sends the message $(\text{sid}, \text{ptr}, \text{Leak}(\text{ptr}, H))$ to Sim.
4. Upon receiving $(\text{sid}, \text{ALLOW\_EXEC}, \text{ptr})$ from Sim, if ptr refers to an entry of the form $(\text{sid}, \text{CI}', \text{FETCH}, C_r @\text{SP}_j)$ with status 'pending', then
   (a) It sends the message $(\text{sid}, \text{Inbox}[C_r @\text{SP}_j])$ to C_r.
   (b) It updates the entry as $(\text{ptr}, (\text{sid}, \text{CI}', \text{FETCH}, C_r @\text{SP}_j), \text{'(fetched, CI)'})$.
   (c) It resets $\text{Inbox}[C_r @\text{SP}_j]$ as empty.
   (d) It sends the message $(\text{sid}, \text{ptr}, \text{Leak}(\text{ptr}, H))$ to Sim.

Clock reading:
– Upon receiving $(\text{sid}, \text{READ\_CLOCK})$ from a party $P \in \mathbf{P}$, then

1. It sends the message $(\text{sid}, \text{READ\_CLOCK})$ to $\mathcal{G}_{\text{clock}}$.
2. On receiving $(\text{sid}, \text{READ\_CLOCK}, \text{CI})$ from $\mathcal{G}_{\text{clock}}$ it adds $(\text{ptr}, (\text{sid}, \text{CI}, \text{READ\_CLOCK}, P))$ to H, sending $(\text{sid}, \text{READ\_CLOCK}, \text{CI})$ to P.

3. It sends the message $\big(\mathsf{sid}, \mathsf{ptr}, \mathsf{Leak}(\mathsf{ptr}, H)\big)$ to Sim.

Clock advance:
- Upon receiving $\big(\mathsf{sid}, \text{ADVANCE\_CLOCK}\big)$ from a party $P \in \mathbf{P} \setminus L_{\mathsf{adv}}$, then
  1. It sends the message $(\mathsf{sid}, \text{ADVANCE\_CLOCK}, P)$ to $\mathcal{G}_{\mathsf{clock}}$.
  2. Upon receiving $(\mathsf{sid}, \text{ADVANCE\_ACK}, P)$ from $\mathcal{G}_{\mathsf{clock}}$, it adds P in L_{adv} and $\big(\mathsf{ptr}, (\mathsf{sid}, \mathsf{Cl}, \text{ADVANCE\_CLOCK}, P)\big)$ to H.
  3. It sends the message $\big(\mathsf{sid}, \mathsf{ptr}, \mathsf{Leak}(\mathsf{ptr}, H)\big)$ to Sim.
  4. If $L_{\mathsf{adv}} = \mathbf{P}$, then it sets its status to 'advance' and proceeds to the **Clock advancement** phase below.

Clock advancement on status 'advance'.

- Upon setting its status to 'advance':
  1. For every history entry of the form $\big(\mathsf{sid}, \mathsf{Cl}', \text{SEND}, \langle C_s@\mathsf{SP}_i, M, C_r@\mathsf{SP}_j\rangle\big)$ with status 'pending' such that $\mathsf{Cl} - \mathsf{Cl}' = \Delta_{\mathsf{net}}$, it adds this entry to $\mathsf{Inbox}[C_r@\mathsf{SP}_j]$ and updates the entry's status to '(sent, Cl)'.
  2. For every history entry of the form $\big(\mathsf{sid}, \mathsf{Cl}', \text{FETCH}, C_r@\mathsf{SP}_j\big)$ with status 'pending' such that $\mathsf{Cl} - \mathsf{Cl}' = \Delta_{\mathsf{net}}$, it sends the message $(\mathsf{sid}, \mathsf{Inbox}[C_r@\mathsf{SP}_j])$ to C_r, resets the list $\mathsf{Inbox}[C_r@\mathsf{SP}_j]$ as input and updates the entry's status to '(fetched, Cl)'.
  3. It sends the message $\big(\mathsf{sid}, \mathsf{ptr}, \mathsf{Leak}(\mathsf{ptr}, H)\big)$ to Sim.
  4. It finalizes execution for the current slot as follows:
     (a) It advances its time by $\mathsf{Cl} \leftarrow \mathsf{Cl} + 1$.
     (b) It adds $\big(\mathsf{ptr}, (\mathsf{sid}, \text{CLOCK\_ADVANCED})\big)$ to H.
     (c) It reverts its status to 'execute' and resets L_{adv} to empty.
     (d) It sends the message $(\mathsf{sid}, \text{CLOCK\_ADVANCED})$ to Sim.

We denote by $\text{EXEC}^{\mathcal{F}_{\mathsf{priv}}^{\mathsf{Leak}, \Delta_{\mathsf{net}}}}_{\text{Sim}, \mathcal{Z}, \mathcal{G}_{\mathsf{clock}}}[\mathbf{P}](\lambda)$, the output of the environment $\mathcal{Z}$ in an ideal-world execution of $\mathcal{F}_{\mathsf{priv}}^{\mathsf{Leak}, \Delta_{\mathsf{net}}}(\mathbf{P})$ under the presence of Sim.

The $(\mathcal{G}_{\mathsf{clock}}, \mathcal{F}_{\mathsf{auth}}^{\Delta_{\mathsf{net}}})$-hybrid world execution. In the real world email ecosystem $\mathbb{E}$, the clients, the SPs and the mix nodes interact according to the protocols' guidelines and the environment's instructions. The message delivery is executed via the functionality $\mathcal{F}_{\mathsf{auth}}^{\Delta_{\mathsf{net}}}(\mathbf{P})$ described in Fig. 2 that captures the notion of an authenticated channel, upon which a maximum delivery delay Δ_{net} can be imposed. Clock advancement is done via calls to $\mathcal{G}_{\mathsf{clock}}$, which interacts with all entities and $\mathcal{F}_{\mathsf{auth}}^{\Delta_{\mathsf{net}}}$.

We denote by $\text{EXEC}^{\mathbb{E}^{\mathcal{G}_{\mathsf{clock}}, \mathcal{F}_{\mathsf{auth}}^{\Delta_{\mathsf{net}}}}}_{\mathcal{A}, \mathcal{Z}, \mathcal{G}_{\mathsf{clock}}}[\mathbf{P}](\lambda)$ the output of the environment $\mathcal{Z}$ in an execution of $\mathbb{E}^{\mathcal{G}_{\mathsf{clock}}, \mathcal{F}_{\mathsf{auth}}^{\Delta_{\mathsf{net}}}}$ under the presence of $\mathcal{A}$.

The UC definition of a private email ecosystem is provided below.

Definition 1 (UC Email Privacy). *Let $\Delta_{\mathsf{net}}, \epsilon$ be non-negative values. Let $\mathbb{E}$ be an email ecosystem with client set $\mathbf{C} = C_1, \ldots, C_n$, service provider set $\mathbf{SP} = \mathsf{SP}_1, \ldots, \mathsf{SP}_N$ and mix node set $\mathbf{MX} = \mathsf{MX}_1, \ldots, \mathsf{MX}_m$. Let $\mathbf{P} := \mathbf{C} \cup \mathbf{SP} \cup \mathbf{MX}$. We say that $\mathbb{E}^{\mathcal{G}_{\mathsf{clock}}, \mathcal{F}_{\mathsf{auth}}^{\Delta_{\mathsf{net}}}}$ achieves statistical (resp. computational) ϵ-privacy with respect to leakage (Leak) and message delay Δ_{net}, if for every unbounded (resp.*

The authenticated channel functionality $\mathcal{F}_{\text{auth}}^{\Delta_{\text{net}}}(\mathbf{P})$.

The functionality initializes a list of pending messages L_{pend} as empty.

- Upon receiving $(\text{sid}, \text{CHANNEL}, M, P')$ from $P \in \mathbf{P}$, then
  1. It sends the message $(\text{sid}, \text{READ\_CLOCK})$ to $\mathcal{G}_{\text{clock}}(\mathbf{P})$.
  2. Upon receiving $(\text{sid}, \text{READ\_CLOCK}, \text{Cl})$ to $\mathcal{G}_{\text{clock}}(\mathbf{P})$, it picks a unique pointer ptr and stores the entry $(\text{ptr}, (\text{sid}, \text{Cl}, \text{CHANNEL}, P, M, P'))$ to L_{pend}.
  3. It sends the message $(\text{ptr}, (\text{sid}, \text{CHANNEL}, P, M, P'))$ to $\mathcal{A}$.
- Upon receiving $(\text{sid}, \text{ALLOW\_CHANNEL}, \text{ptr}')$ from $\mathcal{A}$, if there is an entry $(\text{ptr}', (\text{sid}, \text{Cl}', \text{CHANNEL}, P, M, P'))$ in L_{pend}, then it sends the message (sid, M, P) to P' and deletes $(\text{ptr}', (\text{sid}, \text{Cl}', \text{CHANNEL}, P, M, P'))$ from L_{pend}.
- Upon any activation from a party $P \in \mathbf{P}$ or $\mathcal{A}$ as above,
  1. It sends the message $(\text{sid}, \text{READ\_CLOCK})$ to $\mathcal{G}_{\text{clock}}(\mathbf{P})$.
  2. Upon receiving $(\text{sid}, \text{READ\_CLOCK}, \text{Cl})$ to $\mathcal{G}_{\text{clock}}(\mathbf{P})$, it parses L_{pend}. For every entry $(\text{ptr}', (\text{sid}, \text{Cl}', \text{CHANNEL}, P, M, P'))$ s.t. $\text{Cl} - \text{Cl}' = \Delta_{\text{net}}$, it sends the message (sid, M, P) to P' and deletes $(\text{ptr}', (\text{sid}, \text{Cl}', \text{CHANNEL}, P, M, P'))$ from L_{pend}.

Fig. 2. The authenticated channel functionality $\mathcal{F}_{\text{auth}}^{\Delta_{\text{net}}}(\mathbf{P})$ interacting with the adversary $\mathcal{A}$.

PPT) global passive adversary $\mathcal{A}$, there is a PPT simulator Sim such that for every PPT environment $\mathcal{Z}$, it holds that

$$\text{EXEC}_{\text{Sim}, \mathcal{Z}, \mathcal{G}_{\text{clock}}}^{\mathcal{F}_{\text{priv}}^{\text{Leak}, \Delta_{\text{net}}}}[\mathbf{P}](\lambda) \approx_\epsilon \text{EXEC}_{\mathcal{A}, \mathcal{Z}, \mathcal{G}_{\text{clock}}}^{\mathbb{E}^{\mathcal{G}_{\text{clock}}}, \mathcal{F}_{\text{auth}}^{\Delta_{\text{net}}}}[\mathbf{P}](\lambda).$$

4 Formalizing Privacy Notions via Types of Leakage Functions

In [27], Pfitzmann and Hansen provide definitions for anonymity, unlinkability, unobservability and pseudonymity. Even though outside the context of a formal framework, the definitions in this seminal work have served as a reference point by researchers for the understanding of privacy notions. In this section, we formally express the said (yet not only these) notions by carefully specifying a corresponding leakage function.

Basic leakage sets. Below, we define some useful sets that will enable the succinct description of the various leakage functions that we will introduce. In our formalization, leakage will derive from the history entries that are in a 'pending' mode. This is due to technical reasons, as the ideal-world simulator Sim (cf. Sect. 3.3) must be aware of the actions to be taken by the email privacy functionality $\mathcal{F}_{\text{priv}}^{\text{Leak}, \Delta_{\text{net}}}(\mathbf{P})$ *before* allowing their execution, so that it can simulate the real-world run in an indistinguishable manner. In the following, the symbol $*$ denotes a wildcard, and $\text{ptr}' \leq \text{ptr}$ denotes that entry indexed with pointer ptr' was added earlier than the entry with pointer ptr.

– The *active address set for H by pointer* ptr:

$$\mathsf{Act}_{\mathsf{ptr}}[H] =: \Big\{ C_\ell @ \mathsf{SP}_i \ \Big| \ \exists \mathsf{ptr}' \leq \mathsf{ptr} : \Big[[(\mathsf{ptr}', (\mathsf{sid}, *, \mathrm{ACTIVE}, C_\ell @ \mathsf{SP}_i), \text{'pending'}) \in H] \vee$$

$$\vee \big[(\mathsf{ptr}', (\mathsf{sid}, *, \mathrm{REGISTER}, C_\ell @ \mathsf{SP}_i), \text{'pending'}) \in H \big] \Big] \wedge$$

$$\wedge \Big[\forall \mathsf{ptr}'' : \mathsf{ptr}' \leq \mathsf{ptr}'' \leq \mathsf{ptr} \Rightarrow (\mathsf{ptr}'', (\mathsf{sid}, *, \mathrm{INACTIVE}, C_\ell @ \mathsf{SP}_i), \text{'pending'}) \notin H \Big] \Big\}.$$

Note. To simplify the notation and terminology that follows, we consider as active all the addresses that are in a pending registration status.

– The *sender set for H by pointer* ptr:

$$\mathbf{S}_{\mathsf{ptr}}[H] := \Big\{ C_s @ \mathsf{SP}_i \ \Big| \ \exists \mathsf{ptr}' \leq \mathsf{ptr} : (\mathsf{ptr}', (\mathsf{sid}, *, \mathrm{SEND}, \langle C_s @ \mathsf{SP}_i, *, * \rangle), \text{'pending'}) \in H \Big\}.$$

– The *sender multiset for H by pointer* ptr, denoted by $[\![\mathbf{S}_{\mathsf{ptr}}]\!][H]$, is defined analogously. The difference with $\mathbf{S}_{\mathsf{ptr}}[H]$ is that the cardinality of the pending SEND messages provided by $C_s @ \mathsf{SP}_i$ is attached.

– The *message-sender set for H by pointer* ptr:

$$\mathbf{MS}_{\mathsf{ptr}}[H] := \Big\{ (M, C_s @ \mathsf{SP}_i) \ \Big| \ \exists \mathsf{ptr}' \leq \mathsf{ptr} :$$

$$(\mathsf{ptr}', (\mathsf{sid}, *, \mathrm{SEND}, \langle C_s @ \mathsf{SP}_i, M, * \rangle), \text{'pending'}) \in H \Big\}.$$

– The *recipient set for H by pointer* ptr:

$$\mathbf{R}_{\mathsf{ptr}}[H] := \Big\{ C_r @ \mathsf{SP}_j \ \Big| \ \exists \mathsf{ptr}' \leq \mathsf{ptr} :$$

$$(\mathsf{ptr}', (\mathsf{sid}, *, \mathrm{SEND}, \langle *, *, C_r @ \mathsf{SP}_j \rangle), \text{'pending'}) \in H \Big\}.$$

– The *recipient multiset for H at time slot* T, denoted by $[\![\mathbf{R}_{\mathsf{ptr}}]\!][H]$, is defined analogously. The difference with $\mathbf{R}_{\mathsf{ptr}}[H]$ is that the cardinality of the pending SEND messages intended for $C_r @ \mathsf{SP}_j$ is attached.

– The *message-recipient set for H by pointer* ptr:

$$\mathbf{MR}_{\mathsf{ptr}}[H] := \Big\{ (M, C_r @ \mathsf{SP}_j) \ \Big| \ \exists \mathsf{ptr}' \leq \mathsf{ptr} :$$

$$(\mathsf{ptr}', (\mathsf{sid}, *, \mathrm{SEND}, \langle *, M, C_r @ \mathsf{SP}_j \rangle), \text{'pending'}) \in H \Big\}.$$

– The *set of fetching clients for H by pointer* ptr

$$\mathbf{F}_{\mathsf{ptr}}[H] := \Big\{ C_r @ \mathsf{SP}_j \ \Big| \ \exists \mathsf{ptr}' \leq \mathsf{ptr} : (\mathsf{ptr}, (\mathsf{sid}, *, \mathrm{FETCH}, C_r @ \mathsf{SP}_j), \text{'pending'}) \Big\}.$$

Unobservability. Unobservability is the state where "the messages are not discernible from random noise". Here, we focus on the case of *relationship unobservability*, that we will refer to unobservability for brevity, where within the set of all possible sender-recipient-pairs, a message is exchanged in any relationship. Hence, in our setting the *unobservability set* is the set of the users that are online, i.e. only the "activity bit". As a result, we can define the *unobservability leakage function* $\mathsf{Leak}_{\mathsf{unob}}$ as the active address set:

$$\mathsf{Leak}_{\mathsf{unob}}(\mathsf{ptr}, H) := \mathsf{Act}_{\mathsf{ptr}}[H]. \tag{1}$$

Remark 2 (Unobservability a golden standard from email privacy). In our UC
formalization of e-mail ecosystems, we consider a dynamic scenario where the
clients register, go online/offline and make custom fetch requests, which is consistent with the real-world dynamics of email communication. It is easy to see
that in such a setting the clients' online/offline status may be leaked to a global
observer. E.g., the environment may provide send requests to offline clients and
notify the global adversary that provided the said requests, so that the latter
can check the activity of those clients. Hence, in our framework, unobservability
as defined in Eq. (1), sets a "golden standard" for optimal privacy. In Sect. 5,
we show that this golden standard is feasible in principle. Namely, we describe a
theoretical construction with quadratic communication complexity and we prove
it achieves unobservability. As a result, that construction sets one extreme point
in the privacy vs. efficiency trade off for the client-server email infrastructure, the
other being a simple and fast network with no security enhancements. Clearly,
the challenge of every email construction is to balance the said trade off between
these two extreme points.

We conclude our remark noting that a higher level privacy (e.g., no leakage
at all) could be possible if we considered an alternative setting where the email
addresses are a priori given, the clients are always online and mail delivery is via
continuous push by the SPs. However, we believe that such a setting is restrictive
for formally capturing what is an email ecosystem in general.

Anonymity. According to [27], *anonymity* "is the state of being not identifiable
within a set of subjects, the anonymity set". In the email scenario, a sender (resp.
recipient) should be anonymous within the set of potential senders (resp. recipients), i.e. the *sender* (resp. *recipient*) *anonymity set*. In addition, anonymity
sets may change over time, which in our framework is done via global clock
advancement and per slot. We recall from the discussion in Remark 2 that in
our setting, the anonymity sets are restricted within the set of online users.

We define the predicate $\mathsf{End}(\cdot, \cdot)$ over the pointers and history transcripts to
denote that a pointer ptr refers to the last history entry before the functionality enters the **Clock advancement** phase in order to finalize execution for
the running time slot. By the above, we define the *anonymity leakage function*,
$\mathsf{Leak}_{\mathsf{anon}}$, as follows:

$$\mathsf{Leak}_{\mathsf{anon}}(\mathsf{ptr}, H) := \begin{cases} (\mathbf{S}_{\mathsf{ptr}}[H], \mathbf{R}_{\mathsf{ptr}}[H], \mathsf{Act}_{\mathsf{ptr}}[H]), & \text{if } \mathsf{End}(\mathsf{ptr}, H) \\ \mathsf{Act}_{\mathsf{ptr}}[H], & \text{otherwise} \end{cases} \qquad (2)$$

Unlinkability. Unlinkability of items of interest (e.g. subjects, messages, etc.)
means that "the ability of the attacker to relate these items does not increase
by observing the system". Here, we provide an example of unlinkability from
the sender side, where the message and its intended recipient can not be related
to the original sender. We define the *sender-side unlinkability leakage function*
$\mathsf{Leak}_{\mathsf{s.unlink}}$ as follows:

$$\mathsf{Leak}_{\mathsf{s.unlink}}(\mathsf{ptr}, H) := \begin{cases} (\mathbf{S}_{\mathsf{ptr}}[H], \mathbf{MR}_{\mathsf{ptr}}[H], \mathsf{Act}_{\mathsf{ptr}}[H]), & \text{if } \mathsf{End}(\mathsf{ptr}, H) \\ \mathsf{Act}_{\mathsf{ptr}}[H], & \text{otherwise} \end{cases} \qquad (3)$$

Alternatively, we may define unlinkability from the recipient side via the function

$$\mathsf{Leak}_{\mathsf{r.unlink}}(\mathsf{ptr}, H) := \begin{cases} (\mathbf{MS}_{\mathsf{ptr}}[H], \mathbf{R}_{\mathsf{ptr}}[H], \mathsf{Act}_{\mathsf{ptr}}[H]), & \text{if End}(\mathsf{ptr}, H) \\ \mathsf{Act}_{\mathsf{ptr}}[H], & \text{otherwise} \end{cases}$$

Pseudonymity. According to [27] "being pseudonymous is the state of using a pseudonym as ID". To capture pseudonymity, we may slightly abuse definition and consider leakage as a randomized function (or program). Namely, the functionality initially chooses a random permutation π over the set of clients $\mathbf{C}$, and the pseudonym of each client C_ℓ is $\pi(C_\ell) \in [n]$. We denote by $\pi[H]$ the "pseudonymized history" w.r.t. to π, i.e. in every entry of H we replace C_ℓ by $\pi(C_\ell)$. Clearly, in our infrastructure, the clients remain pseudonymous among the set of clients that are registered to the same SP. We define the *pseudonymity leakage function* as follows:

$$\mathsf{Leak}_{\mathsf{pseudon}}(\mathsf{ptr}, H) := \pi[H], \quad \text{where } \pi \xleftarrow{\$} \{f \mid f : \mathbf{C} \longrightarrow [n]\}. \tag{4}$$

Besides anonymity, unlinkability, unobservability and pseudonymity defined in [27], other meaningful notions of privacy can be formally expressed in our framework. We present two such notions below.

Weak anonymity. We define *weak anonymity*, as the privacy notion where the number of messages that a client sends or receives and her fetching activity is leaked. In this weaker notion, the anonymity set for a sender (resp. recipient) consists of the subset of senders (resp. recipients) that are associated with the same number of pending messages. In addition, now the leakage for sender anonymity set is gradually released according to the protocol scheduling, whereas the recipient anonymity set still is leaked "per slot". The *weak anonymity leakage function*, $\mathsf{Leak}_{\mathsf{w.anon}}$, is defined via the sender and recipient multisets as follows:

$$\mathsf{Leak}_{\mathsf{w.anon}}(\mathsf{ptr}, H) := \begin{cases} ([\![\mathbf{S}_{\mathsf{ptr}}]\!][H], [\![\mathbf{R}_{\mathsf{ptr}}]\!][H], \mathbf{F}_{\mathsf{ptr}}[H], \mathsf{Act}_{\mathsf{ptr}}[H]), & \text{if End}(\mathsf{ptr}, H) \\ ([\![\mathbf{S}_{\mathsf{ptr}}]\!][H], \mathbf{F}_{\mathsf{ptr}}[H], \mathsf{Act}_{\mathsf{ptr}}[H]), & \text{otherwise} \end{cases}$$
$$\tag{5}$$

Remark 3. Even though not a very strong privacy notion, weak anonymity supports a reasonable level of privacy for email realizations that aim at a manageable overhead and practical use. Indeed, observe that if we can not tolerate to blow up the ecosystem's complexity by requiring some form of cover traffic (which is a plausible requirement in practical scenarios), then a global adversary monitoring the client-SP channel can easily infer the number of sent/received messages over this channel. Moreover, one may informally argue that in case the email users do not vary significantly in terms of their sending and fetching activity (or at least they can be grouped into large enough sets of similar activity), weak anonymity and standard anonymity are not far. In Sect. 6, we present an efficient weakly anonymous email construction based on parallel mixing [18,19].

End-to-end encryption. The standard notion of *end-to-end encryption*, now applied in many internet applications (e.g., Signal, WhatsApp, Viber, Facebook

Messenger, Skype), suggests context hiding of M in the communication of the end users (up to the message length $|M|$), in our case the sender and the recipient. Hence, we define the *end-to-end leakage function* $\mathsf{Leak_{e2e}}$ as shown below.

$$\mathsf{Leak_{e2e}} := \Big(\mathsf{Act_{ptr}}[H], \big\{ (C_s@\mathsf{SP}_i, |M|, C_r@\mathsf{SP}_j) \bigm| \exists \mathsf{ptr}' \le \mathsf{ptr} :$$
$$(\mathsf{ptr}', (\mathsf{sid}, *, \textsc{Send}, \langle C_s@\mathsf{SP}_i, M, C_r@\mathsf{SP}_j \rangle), \text{`pending'}) \in H \big\} \Big). \tag{6}$$

Relation between privacy notions. Observe that the relation between two privacy notions can be deduced via their corresponding leakage functions. Namely, if for every (ptr, H) a PPT adversary given the output of leakage function $\mathsf{Leak}_1(\mathsf{ptr}, H)$ can derive the output of some other leakage functions $\mathsf{Leak}_2(\mathsf{ptr}, H)$, then $\mathsf{Leak}_2(\cdot, \cdot)$ refers to a stronger notion of privacy than $\mathsf{Leak}_1(\cdot, \cdot)$. In Fig. 3, given the definitions of $\mathsf{Leak_{unob}}, \mathsf{Leak_{anon}}, \mathsf{Leak_{s.unlink}}/\mathsf{Leak_{r.unlink}}, \mathsf{Leak_{w.anon}}, \mathsf{Leak_{e2e}}$ above we relate the respective notions in an intuitively consistent way.

Unobservability $\Longrightarrow$ Anonymity $\Longrightarrow$ Sender/Recipient-side Unlinkability
$\Downarrow$
Weak anonymity $\Longrightarrow$ E2E encryption

Fig. 3. Relations between privacy notions. By $A \Longrightarrow B$, we denote that notion A is stronger than notion B.

Remark 4. We observe that pseudonymity can not be compared to any of the notions in Fig. 3. Indeed, even for the stronger notion of unobservability, having the set of active addresses is not enough information to derive the pseudonyms. Conversely, having the entire email activity pseudonymized, is not enough information to derive the active clients' real identities. In addition, we can combine pseudonymity with some other privacy notion and result in a new 'pseudonymized' version of the latter (e.g. pseudonymous unobservability/anonymity/etc.). It is easy to see that the new notions can also be expressed via suitable (randomized) leakage functions, by applying a random permutation on the clients' identities and then define leakage as in the original corresponding leakage function, up to this permutation. E.g., for $\pi \xleftarrow{\$} \{f \mid f : \mathbf{C} \longrightarrow \mathbf{C}\}$, "pseudonymized unobservability" could be expressed via the leakage function

$$\mathsf{Leak_{ps.unob}}(\mathsf{ptr}, H) := \big\{ \pi(C_\ell)@\mathsf{SP}_i \mid C_\ell@\mathsf{SP}_i \in \mathsf{Act_{ptr}}[H] \big\}.$$

Remark 5. As our E2E leakage does not cover fetch information, strictly speaking the implication from Weak anonymity to E2E encryption only holds if the fetch behavior is either known in advance (e.g. because of the system specification) or irrelevant. One could also opt to add the additional leakage to the E2E definition, but we believe there is little practical value in doing so.

5 An Email Ecosystem with Optimal Privacy

We present an email ecosystem, denoted by $\mathbb{E}_{comp}$, that achieves privacy at an optimal level at the cost of high (quadratic) communication complexity. Specifically, in each time slot all SPs in $\mathbb{E}_{comp}$ communicate with *complete connectivity* and always pad the right amount of dummy traffic, so that the activity of their registered clients is unobservable by a third party, leaking nothing more than that they are online (logged in). In addition, end-to-end communication between the clients is done via encryption layers by utilizing a public key encryption scheme $\mathsf{PKE} = (\mathsf{KeyGen}, \mathsf{Enc}, \mathsf{Dec})$. The encryption layers are structured according to the network route

$$Sender \longrightarrow Sender's\ SP \longrightarrow Receiver's\ SP \longrightarrow Receiver$$

To support unobservability, the online clients who do not send an actual message during some round provide their SPs with a dummy ciphertext.

Even though certainly impractical, $\mathbb{E}_{comp}$ sets a "golden standard" of privacy according to the discussion in Remark 2 that efficient constructions refer to in order to balance the privacy vs. efficiency trade off. **Description of $\mathbb{E}_{comp}$.** The email ecosystem $\mathbb{E}_{comp}$ operates under a known delay bound Δ_{net}. Throughout the description of $\mathbb{E}_{comp}$, we assume that the following simplifications: (a) all ciphertexts are of the same length. By $\mathsf{Enc}_{[P]}(M)$, we denote the encryption of M under P's public key, and (b) all computations require one time slot[2]:

The phases of $\mathbb{E}_{comp}$ are as follows:

∎ Initialization:

– On input $(\mathsf{sid}, \mathrm{INIT})$, a service provider SP_i that is not yet initialized, runs $\mathsf{KeyGen}(1^\lambda)$ to generate a private and a public key pair $(\mathsf{sk}_{\mathsf{SP}_i}, \mathsf{pk}_{\mathsf{SP}_i})$. Then, it initializes its list of setup entities, denoted by $L_{setup}^{\mathsf{SP}_i}$, as the pair $(\mathsf{pk}_{\mathsf{SP}_i}, \mathsf{SP}_i)$, implying that at first SP_i is only aware of itself. In addition, SP_i initializes its list of valid addresses, denoted by $\mathbf{Ad}_{\mathsf{SP}_i}$, as empty. Finally, it broadcasts the message $(\mathsf{sid}, \mathrm{CHANNEL}, (\mathsf{setup}, \mathsf{pk}_{\mathsf{SP}_i}), \mathsf{SP}_j)$ to $\mathcal{F}_{\mathsf{auth}}^{\Delta_{net}}(\mathbf{P})$ for every $j \in [N] \backslash \{i\}$, so that all other SPs receive its public key.
– Upon receiving $(\mathsf{sid}, (\mathsf{setup}, \mathsf{pk}_{\mathsf{SP}_j}), \mathsf{SP}_j)$ from $\mathcal{F}_{\mathsf{auth}}^{\Delta_{net}}(\mathbf{P})$, SP_i adds $((\mathsf{pk}_{\mathsf{SP}_j}, \mathsf{SP}_j))$ to $L_{setup}^{\mathsf{SP}_i}$. When $L_{setup}^{\mathsf{SP}_i}$ contains all SPs, the SP_i sets its status to 'execute', and only then it processes messages of the **Execution** phase described below.

∎ Execution:

Registration:
– On input $(\mathsf{sid}, \mathrm{REGISTER}, @\mathsf{SP}_i)$, if C_ℓ is not registered to any SP and has not yet sent a message $(\mathsf{sid}, \mathrm{ADVANCE\_CLOCK}, C_\ell)$, then:

---

[2] As it will become clear by the ecosystem's description, the above simplifications do not harm generality essentially. Namely,(a) can be reached via padding, while (b) leads to similar analysis as requiring a computational time upper bound.

1. C_ℓ sends the message (sid, ADVANCE_CLOCK, C_ℓ) to $\mathcal{G}_{\text{clock}}$.

2. Upon receiving (sid, ADVANCE_ACK, C_ℓ) from $\mathcal{G}_{\text{clock}}$, C_ℓ runs KeyGen(1^λ) to generate a private and a public key pair ($\text{sk}_\ell, \text{pk}_\ell$). It also initializes her list of setup entities, L^ℓ_{setup} as the pair (pk_ℓ, C_ℓ), and her list of valid addresses, $\mathbf{Ad}_\ell$ as empty. Then, she sends the message (sid, CHANNEL, (register, pk_ℓ), SP_i) to $\mathcal{F}^{\Delta_{\text{net}}}_{\text{auth}}(\mathbf{P})$.

3. Upon receiving (sid, (register, pk_ℓ), C_ℓ) from $\mathcal{F}^{\Delta_{\text{net}}}_{\text{auth}}(\mathbf{P})$, SP_i checks that $(C_\ell, \cdot) \notin L^{\text{SP}_i}_{\text{setup}}$ and that pk_ℓ is a valid public key, and if so, then it adds (pk_ℓ, C_ℓ) to $L^{\text{SP}_i}_{\text{setup}}$ and $C_\ell@\text{SP}_i$ to $\mathbf{Ad}_{\text{SP}_i}$. Next, it updates other SPs and its registered clients by broadcasting the message (sid, CHANNEL, (setup, $\text{pk}_{C_\ell}, C_\ell$), P) to $\mathcal{F}^{\Delta_{\text{net}}}_{\text{auth}}(\mathbf{P})$ for every $P \in (\mathbf{SP} \setminus \{\text{SP}_i\}) \cup \mathbf{C}_i$. It also sends the message (sid, CHANNEL, (setup, $\{\text{pk}_P, P\}_{P \in L^{\text{SP}_i}_{\text{setup}}}, \mathbf{Ad}_{\text{SP}_i}$), C_ℓ), updating C_ℓ with all the valid public keys and addresses it knows so far. Finally, it initializes the inbox Inbox[$C_\ell@\text{SP}_i$] of C_ℓ.

4. Upon receiving (sid, (setup, pk_ℓ, C_ℓ), SP_i) from $\mathcal{F}^{\Delta_{\text{net}}}_{\text{auth}}(\mathbf{P})$, SP_j checks that $(C_\ell, \cdot) \notin L^{\text{SP}_j}_{\text{setup}}$ and that pk_ℓ is a valid public key, and if so, then it, then it adds (pk_ℓ, C_ℓ) to $L^{\text{SP}_j}_{\text{setup}}$ and $C_\ell@\text{SP}_i$ to $\mathbf{Ad}_{\text{SP}_j}$. It also adds it adds C_ℓ to its set of active users, denoted by $L^{\text{SP}_i}_{\text{act}}$ and initialized as empty. Next, it updates its registered clients by broadcasting the message (sid, CHANNEL, (setup, $\text{pk}_{C_\ell}, C_\ell$), C) to $\mathcal{F}^{\Delta_{\text{net}}}_{\text{auth}}(\mathbf{P})$ for every $C \in \mathbf{C}_j$.

5. Upon receiving (sid, (setup, $\{\text{pk}_P, P\}_{P \in L^{\text{SP}_i}_{\text{setup}}}, \mathbf{Ad}_{\text{SP}_i}$), SP_i) from $\mathcal{F}^{\Delta_{\text{net}}}_{\text{auth}}(\mathbf{P})$, the client C_ℓ, newly registered to SP_i, checks that all public keys are valid. If the check is successful, then C_ℓ adds $\{\text{pk}_P, P\}_{P \in L^{\text{SP}_i}_{\text{setup}}}$ to L^i_{setup} and sets $\mathbf{Ad}_\ell \leftarrow \mathbf{Ad}_{\text{SP}_i}$. Thus, from this point, C_ℓ is aware of the public information of all SPs and all registered clients up to now. In addition, it sets its status as logged in to SP_i.

6. Upon receiving (sid, (setup, $\text{pk}_{C_t}, \text{SP}_j$), SP_i) from $\mathcal{F}^{\Delta_{\text{net}}}_{\text{auth}}(\mathbf{P})$, client C_ℓ (now already registered to SP_i) checks the validity of pk_{C_t}, and if so, then she adds (pk_t, C_t) to L^ℓ_{setup} and $C_t@\text{SP}_j$ to $\mathbf{Ad}_\ell$.

Log in:

– On input (sid, ACTIVE, @SP_i), if C_ℓ is not logged in, $C_\ell@\text{SP}_i$ is her valid address, and has not yet sent a message (sid, ADVANCE_CLOCK, C_ℓ), then:

1. C_ℓ sends the message (sid, ADVANCE_CLOCK, C_ℓ) to $\mathcal{G}_{\text{clock}}$.

2. Upon receiving (sid, ADVANCE_ACK, C_ℓ) from $\mathcal{G}_{\text{clock}}$, C_ℓ "logs in" by sending (sid, CHANNEL, $\text{Enc}_{[\text{SP}_i]}(\text{ACTIVE})$, SP_i) to $\mathcal{F}^{\Delta_{\text{net}}}_{\text{auth}}(\mathbf{P})$.

3. Upon receiving (sid, $\text{Enc}_{[\text{SP}_i]}(\text{ACTIVE})$, C_ℓ) from $\mathcal{F}^{\Delta_{\text{net}}}_{\text{auth}}(\mathbf{P})$, SP_i decrypts as (sid, ACTIVE, C_ℓ) and checks that $C_\ell@\text{SP}_i \in \mathbf{Ad}_{\text{SP}_i}$. If so, then it adds C_ℓ to $L^{\text{SP}_i}_{\text{act}}$.

Log out:

– On input (sid, INACTIVE, @SP_i), if C_ℓ is logged in, $C_\ell@\text{SP}_i$ is her valid address, and has not yet sent a message (sid, ADVANCE_CLOCK, C_ℓ), then:

1. C_ℓ sends the message (sid, ADVANCE_CLOCK, C_ℓ) to $\mathcal{G}_{\text{clock}}$.

A Universally Composable Framework for the Privacy of Email Ecosystems   209

2. Upon receiving $(\mathsf{sid}, \textsc{Advance\_Ack}, C_\ell)$ from $\mathcal{G}_{\mathsf{clock}}$, C_ℓ "logs out" by sending $(\mathsf{sid}, \textsc{Channel}, \mathsf{Enc}_{[\mathsf{SP}_i]}(\textsc{Inactive}), \mathsf{SP}_i)$ to $\mathcal{F}_{\mathsf{auth}}^{\Delta_{\mathsf{net}}}(\mathbf{P})$.

3. Upon receiving $(\mathsf{sid}, \mathsf{Enc}_{[\mathsf{SP}_i]}(\textsc{Inactive}), C_\ell)$ from $\mathcal{F}_{\mathsf{auth}}^{\Delta_{\mathsf{net}}}(\mathbf{P})$, SP_i decrypts as $(\mathsf{sid}, \textsc{Inactive}, C_\ell)$ and checks that $C_\ell@\mathsf{SP}_i \in \mathbf{Ad}_{\mathsf{SP}_i}$. If so, then it removes C_ℓ from $L_{\mathsf{act}}^{\mathsf{SP}_i}$.

Send:

– On input $(\mathsf{sid}, \textsc{Send}, \langle C_s@\mathsf{SP}_i, M, C_r@\mathsf{SP}_j\rangle)$, if C_s is logged in to SP_i and has not yet sent a message $(\mathsf{sid}, \textsc{Advance\_Clock}, C_s)$, then:

1. C_s sends the message $(\mathsf{sid}, \textsc{Advance\_Clock}, C_s)$ to $\mathcal{G}_{\mathsf{clock}}$.

2. Upon receiving $(\mathsf{sid}, \textsc{Advance\_Ack}, C_s)$ from $\mathcal{G}_{\mathsf{clock}}$, C_s encrypts the message M into layers and provides $\mathcal{F}_{\mathsf{auth}}^{\Delta_{\mathsf{net}}}(\mathbf{P})$ with the layered encryption

$$\left(\mathsf{sid}, \textsc{Channel}, \mathsf{Enc}_{[\mathsf{SP}_i]}\left(\mathsf{Enc}_{[\mathsf{SP}_j]}(C_r@\mathsf{SP}_j, \mathsf{Enc}_{[C_r]}(M))\right), \mathsf{SP}_i\right)$$

3. Upon receiving $(\mathsf{sid}, \mathsf{Enc}_{[\mathsf{SP}_i]}(\mathsf{Enc}_{[\mathsf{SP}_j]}(C_r@\mathsf{SP}_j, \mathsf{Enc}_{[C_r]}(M))), C_s)$ from $\mathcal{F}_{\mathsf{auth}}^{\Delta_{\mathsf{net}}}(\mathbf{P})$, SP_i checks that $C_s@\mathsf{SP}_i \in \mathbf{Ad}_{\mathsf{SP}_i}$. If so, then it decrypts the first layer with $\mathsf{sk}_{\mathsf{SP}_i}$ and adds $(\mathsf{sid}, C_s@\mathsf{SP}_i, \mathsf{Enc}_{[\mathsf{SP}_j]}(C_r@\mathsf{SP}_j, \mathsf{Enc}_{[C_r]}(M)))$ to its set of messages pending to be sent, denoted by $L_{\mathsf{send}}^{\mathsf{SP}_i}$ and initialized as empty.

Fetch:

– On input $(\mathsf{sid}, \textsc{Fetch}, C_r@\mathsf{SP}_j)$, if C_r is logged in to SP_j and has not yet sent a message $(\mathsf{sid}, \textsc{Advance\_Clock}, C_r)$:

1. C_r sends the message $(\mathsf{sid}, \textsc{Advance\_Clock}, C_\ell)$ to $\mathcal{G}_{\mathsf{clock}}$.

2. Upon receiving $(\mathsf{sid}, \textsc{Advance\_Ack}, C_r)$ from $\mathcal{G}_{\mathsf{clock}}$, C_r sends the message $(\mathsf{sid}, \textsc{Channel}, \mathsf{Enc}_{[\mathsf{SP}_j]}(\textsc{Fetch}), \mathsf{SP}_j)$ to $\mathcal{F}_{\mathsf{auth}}^{\Delta_{\mathsf{net}}}(\mathbf{P})$.

3. Upon receiving $(\mathsf{sid}, \mathsf{Enc}_{[\mathsf{SP}_j]}(\textsc{Fetch}), C_r)$ from $\mathcal{F}_{\mathsf{auth}}^{\Delta_{\mathsf{net}}}(\mathbf{P})$, C_r checks that $C_r@\mathsf{SP}_j \in \mathbf{Ad}_{\mathsf{SP}_j}$. If so, then she decrypts and adds $\mathsf{Inbox}[C_r@\mathsf{SP}_j]$ to her set of inboxes which messages are pending to be pushed, denoted by $L_{\mathsf{push}}^{\mathsf{SP}_j}$.

4. Upon receiving $(\mathsf{sid}, E_{r,1}, \ldots, E_{r,n}, \mathsf{SP}_j)$ from $\mathcal{F}_{\mathsf{auth}}^{\Delta_{\mathsf{net}}}(\mathbf{P})$ (see below), if C_r is registered to SP_j and has sent a $(\mathsf{sid}, \textsc{Fetch}, C_r@\mathsf{SP}_j)$ request, then she decrypts all ciphertexts and stores the ones that are not dummy, i.e. they correspond to actual mail messages with her as recipient. Otherwise, she discards $(\mathsf{sid}, E_{r,1}, \ldots, E_{r,n}, \mathsf{SP}_j)$.

Clock reading:

– On input $(\mathsf{sid}, \textsc{Read\_Clock})$, the entity $P \in \mathbf{C} \cup \mathbf{SP}$ sends the message $(\mathsf{sid}, \textsc{Read\_Clock})$ to $\mathcal{G}_{\mathsf{clock}}$. Upon receiving $(\mathsf{sid}, \textsc{Read\_Clock}, \mathsf{Cl})$ from $\mathcal{G}_{\mathsf{clock}}$, P stores Cl as its local time.

Clock advance (for clients):

– On input $(\mathsf{sid}, \textsc{Advance\_Clock})$, if the client C_ℓ is logged in to SP_i and has not yet sent a message $(\mathsf{sid}, \textsc{Advance\_Clock}, \mathsf{SP}_i)$, then she executes the following steps:

1. C_ℓ sends the message $(\mathsf{sid}, \textsc{Advance\_Clock}, C_\ell)$ to $\mathcal{G}_{\mathsf{clock}}$.

2. Upon receiving $(\mathsf{sid}, \textsc{Advance\_Ack}, C_\ell)$ from $\mathcal{G}_{\mathsf{clock}}$, then she sends a dummy message $(\mathsf{sid}, \mathsf{Enc}_{[\mathsf{SP}_i]}(\mathsf{null}))$ to SP_i via $\mathcal{F}_{\mathsf{auth}}^{\Delta_{\mathsf{net}}}(\mathbf{P})$ (in turn, SP_i will discard the received null upon decryption).

Clock advance (for SPs):

– On input $(\text{sid}, \text{ADVANCE\_CLOCK})$, if SP_i has not yet sent a message $(\text{sid}, \text{ADVANCE\_CLOCK}, \text{SP}_i)$, then it executes the following steps:

    1. SP_i sends the message $(\text{sid}, \text{ADVANCE\_CLOCK}, \text{SP}_i)$ to $\mathcal{G}_{\text{clock}}$.

    2. Upon receiving $(\text{sid}, \text{ADVANCE\_ACK}, \text{SP}_i)$ from $\mathcal{G}_{\text{clock}}$, for every address $C_s@\text{SP}_i \in \mathbf{Ad}_{\text{SP}_i}$:

       • If there is a message $\left(\text{sid}, C_s@\text{SP}_i, \text{Enc}_{[\text{SP}_j]}\left(C_r@\text{SP}_j, \text{Enc}_{[C_r]}(M)\right)\right)$ in $L_{\text{send}}^{\text{SP}_i}$, then SP_i broadcasts $\left(\text{sid}, \text{Enc}_{[\text{SP}_j]}\left(C_r@\text{SP}_j, \text{Enc}_{[C_r]}(M)\right)\right)$ to all SPs via $\mathcal{F}_{\text{auth}}^{\Delta_{\text{net}}}(\mathbf{P})$, and removes the message from $L_{\text{send}}^{\text{SP}_i}$.

       • If there is no such message for $C_s@\text{SP}_i$ but $C_s \in L_{\text{act}}^i$, then SP_i broadcasts a dummy message $\left(\text{sid}, \text{Enc}_{[\text{SP}_i]}(\text{null})\right)$ under its own key.

    3. Upon receiving a message $(\text{sid}, \tilde{E}, \text{SP}_i)$ from $\mathcal{F}_{\text{auth}}^{\Delta_{\text{net}}}(\mathbf{P})$, SP_j checks whether $\tilde{E}$ is a ciphertext under its public key that decrypts as a pair of a valid address $C_r@\text{SP}_j$ along with an (encrypted) message E. If so, then it adds E to $\text{Inbox}[C_r@\text{SP}_j]$.

    4. When $L_{\text{fin},k}^{\text{SP}_j}$ contains all SPs, then for every address $C_r@\text{SP}_j$:

       • If $\text{Inbox}[C_r@\text{SP}_j] \in L_{\text{push}}^{\text{SP}_j}$, then SP_j forwards all messages $E_{r,1}, \ldots E_{r,n_r}$ in $\text{Inbox}[C_r@\text{SP}_j]$ to C_r along with $n - n_r$ dummy ciphertexts under C_r's public key, empties $\text{Inbox}[C_r@\text{SP}_j]$ and removes it from $L_{\text{push}}^{\text{SP}_j}$.

       • If $\text{Inbox}[C_r@\text{SP}_j] \notin L_{\text{push}}^{\text{SP}_j}$ but $C_r \in L_{\text{act}}^{\text{SP}_j}$, then SP_j forwards n dummy encryptions of 'null' to C_r, under her public key.

Thus, in any case, if C_r is active, then SP_j sends a message of the form $(\text{sid}, E_{r,1}, \ldots, E_{r,n})$ to C_r via $\mathcal{F}_{\text{auth}}^{\Delta_{\text{net}}}(\mathbf{P})$.

Privacy of $\mathbb{E}_{\text{comp}}$. To prove the privacy of $\mathbb{E}_{\text{comp}}$, we require that the underlying public key encryption scheme $\text{PKE} = (\text{KeyGen}, \text{Enc}, \text{Dec})$ satisfies m-IND-CPA, as specified in Sect. 2.2. In the following theorem, we prove that $\mathbb{E}_{\text{comp}}$ only leaks the "activity bit" of the clients formally expressed by the leakage function $\text{Leak}_{\text{unob}}(\cdot, \cdot)$ defined in Eq. (1).

Theorem 1. *Let $\mathbb{E}_{\text{comp}}$ with clients $\mathbf{C} = \{C_1, \ldots, C_n\}$ and service providers $\mathbf{SP} = \text{SP}_1, \ldots, \text{SP}_N$ be implemented over the PKE scheme $\text{PKE} = (\text{KeyGen}, \text{Enc}, \text{Dec})$ that achieves m-IND-CPA security with error $\epsilon(\lambda)$. Then, $\mathbb{E}_{\text{comp}}^{\mathcal{G}_{\text{clock}}, \mathcal{F}_{\text{auth}}^{\Delta_{\text{net}}}}$ achieves computational $2(n + N)\epsilon(\lambda)$-privacy for message delay Δ_{net} with respect to the unobservability leakage function defined below*

$$\text{Leak}_{\text{unob}}(\text{ptr}, H) := \text{Act}_{\text{ptr}}[H].$$

Proof. Let $\mathcal{A}$ be a global passive PPT adversary against $\mathbb{E}_{\text{comp}}^{\mathcal{G}_{\text{clock}}, \mathcal{F}_{\text{auth}}^{\Delta_{\text{net}}}}$. We begin by constructing a simulator Sim for $\mathcal{A}$ as shown below.

Constructing a simulator for $\mathcal{A}$. The ideal adversary Sim for $\mathcal{A}$ that for any environment $\mathcal{Z}$, simulates an execution of $\mathbb{E}_{\text{comp}}$ as follows:

Simulating interaction between $\mathcal{Z}$ and $\mathcal{A}$.

- Upon receiving a message (sid, M) from $\mathcal{Z}$, it forwards (sid, M) to $\mathcal{A}$ playing the role of a simulated environment.
- Upon receiving a message (sid, M) from $\mathcal{A}$ intended for the environment, it forwards (sid, M) to $\mathcal{Z}$.

Achieving synchronicity.

- Upon receiving any message from $\mathcal{F}_{\text{priv}}^{\text{Leak}_{\text{unob}}, \Delta_{\text{net}}}(\mathbf{P})$, Sim sends the message $(\text{sid}, \text{READ\_CLOCK})$ to $\mathcal{G}_{\text{clock}}$. Upon receiving $(\text{sid}, \text{READ\_CLOCK}, \text{Cl})$ from $\mathcal{G}_{\text{clock}}$, it stores Cl as the global time of the real-world simulation. This way, Sim simulates an execution where the simulated entities are synchronized with respective actual ones in the ideal-world.

Simulating real − world message delivery.

- Upon receiving a leakage message of the form $(\text{sid}, (\text{ptr}, M))$ (possibly $M = \bot$) from $\mathcal{F}_{\text{priv}}^{\text{Leak}_{\text{unob}}, \Delta_{\text{net}}}(\mathbf{P})$, Sim knows that this message refers to some command (register/active/inactive/send/fetch) that in the real-world protocol is realized via communication between a client and her SP. Since in the simulation Sim also plays the role of $\mathcal{F}_{\text{auth}}^{\Delta_{\text{net}}}(\mathbf{P})$ in the eyes of $\mathcal{A}$, it must be consistent with the bounded delays (up to Δ_{net}) that $\mathcal{A}$ imposes on message communication. To achieve this consistency, Sim keeps record of the simulated message $\tilde{M}$ that sends to the simulated $\mathcal{F}_{\text{auth}}^{\Delta_{\text{net}}}(\mathbf{P})$ and is associated with ptr. Whenever the message delivery of $\tilde{M}$ is allowed, either by $\mathcal{A}$ or automatically when Δ_{net} delay has passed, Sim sends the message $(\text{sid}, \text{ALLOW\_EXEC}, \text{ptr})$ to $\mathcal{F}_{\text{priv}}^{\text{Leak}_{\text{unob}}, \Delta_{\text{net}}}(\mathbf{P})$.

Simulating Initialization.

- Upon receiving $(\text{sid}, \text{INIT}, \text{SP}_i)$ from $\mathcal{F}_{\text{priv}}^{\text{Leak}_{\text{unob}}, \Delta_{\text{net}}}(\mathbf{P})$, it runs $\text{Gen}(1^\lambda)$ on behalf of SP_i to generate a pair of a private and a public key pair $(\text{sk}_{\text{SP}_i}, \text{pk}_{\text{SP}_i})$. Then, it broadcasts the message $(\text{sid}, \text{CHANNEL}, (\text{setup}, \text{pk}_{\text{SP}_i}), \text{SP}_j)$ to every $j \in [N] \setminus \{i\}$, also simulating the role of $\mathcal{F}_{\text{auth}}^{\Delta_{\text{net}}}(\mathbf{P})$. Observe that since $\mathcal{A}$ is global and passive, the execution will always initiate upon $\mathcal{Z}$'s request. Then, Sim sends the message $(\text{sid}, \text{ALLOW\_INIT}, \text{SP}_i)$ to $\mathcal{F}_{\text{priv}}^{\text{Leak}_{\text{unob}}, \Delta_{\text{net}}}(\mathbf{P})$.
- Upon receiving $(\text{sid}, \text{ready})$ from $\mathcal{F}_{\text{priv}}^{\text{Leak}_{\text{unob}}, \Delta_{\text{net}}}(\mathbf{P})$, if all simulated SPs have initialized by generating and broadcasting their keys, then it sends $(\text{sid}, \text{EXECUTE})$ to $\mathcal{F}_{\text{priv}}^{\text{Leak}_{\text{unob}}, \Delta_{\text{net}}}(\mathbf{P})$. Otherwise, it aborts simulation.

Simulating Execution.

Whenever the environment sends a register/active/inactive/send/fetch/clock advance command to a dummy party P that forwards it to $\mathcal{F}_{\text{priv}}^{\text{Leak}_{\text{unob}}, \Delta_{\text{net}}}(\mathbf{P})$, Sim obtains (i) an $(\text{sid}, \text{ADVANCE\_CLOCK}, P)$ notification from $\mathcal{G}_{\text{clock}}$, and (ii) the leakage of the form $(\text{sid}, \text{ptr}, \text{Act}_{\text{ptr}}[H])$ from $\mathcal{F}_{\text{priv}}^{\text{Leak}_{\text{unob}}, \Delta_{\text{net}}}(\mathbf{P})$. Namely,

Sim obtains the sequence of clock advances and the transcript of activations/deactivations. We describe how using this information, Sim simulates execution:

- Upon receiving (sid, ADVANCE_CLOCK, C_ℓ) and (sid, ptr, $\mathsf{Act}_{\mathsf{ptr}}[H]$), then:
  - Playing the role of the global clock, Sim sends a simulated notification (sid, ADVANCE_CLOCK, C_ℓ) to $\mathcal{A}$.
  - If $C_\ell @ \mathsf{SP}_i$ is in $\mathsf{Act}_{\mathsf{ptr}}[H]$ and (sid, ptr, $\mathsf{Act}_{\mathsf{ptr}}[H]$) is the first entry that $C_\ell @ \mathsf{SP}_i$ is activated, then Sim deduces that this refers to a registration command (Recall that for simplicity we included the pending registration commands in the set of active addresses). In this case, Sim runs the registration protocol between C_ℓ and SP_i exactly as in the description of $\mathbb{E}_{\mathsf{comp}}$, except that it replaces the ciphertext contents with 'null' messages. When $\mathcal{F}_{\mathsf{auth}}^{\Delta_{\mathsf{net}}}$ delivers the message, Sim sends the message (sid, ALLOW_EXEC, ptr) to $\mathcal{F}_{\mathsf{priv}}^{\mathsf{Leak}_{\mathsf{unob}}, \Delta_{\mathsf{net}}}(\mathbf{P})$.
  - If $C_\ell @ \mathsf{SP}_i$ is in $\mathsf{Act}_{\mathsf{ptr}}[H]$ and is registered but not yet logged in, then Sim deduces that this refers to an active or a clock advance command. In either of these cases, Sim simulates execution by sending a dummy ciphertext (sid, CHANNEL, $\mathsf{Enc}_{[\mathsf{SP}_i]}(\mathsf{null}), \mathsf{SP}_i$) to the simulated $\mathcal{F}_{\mathsf{auth}}^{\Delta_{\mathsf{net}}}$. When $\mathcal{F}_{\mathsf{auth}}^{\Delta_{\mathsf{net}}}$ delivers the message, Sim sends the message (sid, ALLOW_EXEC, ptr) to $\mathcal{F}_{\mathsf{priv}}^{\mathsf{Leak}_{\mathsf{unob}}, \Delta_{\mathsf{net}}}(\mathbf{P})$.
  - If $C_\ell @ \mathsf{SP}_i$ is in $\mathsf{Act}_{\mathsf{ptr}}[H]$ and is registered and already logged in, then Sim deduces that this refers to either a inactive, send, fetch or a clock advance command. In either of these cases, Sim simulates execution by sending a dummy ciphertext (sid, CHANNEL, $\mathsf{Enc}_{[\mathsf{SP}_i]}(\mathsf{null}), \mathsf{SP}_i$) as above.
  - If $C_\ell @ \mathsf{SP}_i$ is not in $\mathsf{Act}_{\mathsf{ptr}}[H]$, then Sim deduces that $C_\ell @ \mathsf{SP}_i$ is inactive and takes no further action.
- Upon receiving (sid, ADVANCE_CLOCK, SP_i) and (sid, ptr, $\mathsf{Act}_{\mathsf{ptr}}[H]$):
  - Playing the role of the global clock, Sim sends a simulated notification (sid, ADVANCE_CLOCK, SP_i) to $\mathcal{A}$.
  - For every address $C_s @ \mathsf{SP}_i \in \mathbf{Ad}_{\mathsf{SP}_i}$, it broadcasts a dummy message (sid, CHANNEL, $\mathsf{Enc}_{[\mathsf{SP}_i]}(\mathsf{null}), \mathsf{SP}_i$) to all other SPs. Then, it sends the message (sid, ALLOW_EXEC, ptr) to $\mathcal{F}_{\mathsf{priv}}^{\mathsf{Leak}_{\mathsf{unob}}, \Delta_{\mathsf{net}}}(\mathbf{P})$.

Reducing privacy to m-IND-CPA security. We prove the privacy of $\mathbb{E}_{\mathsf{comp}}^{\mathcal{G}_{\mathsf{clock}}, \mathcal{F}_{\mathsf{auth}}^{\Delta_{\mathsf{net}}}}$ via a reduction to the m-IND-CPA security with error ϵ of the underlying public key encryption scheme $\mathsf{PKE} = (\mathsf{KeyGen}, \mathsf{Enc}, \mathsf{Dec})$, which is assumed in the theorem's statement. Our reduction works as follows: Let $\mathcal{A}$ be a real-world adversary and $\mathcal{Z}$ be an environment. First, we order the clients and servers as parties $P_1, \ldots, P_{n+N}$. Then, we construct a sequence of "hybrid" m-IND-CPA adversaries $\mathcal{B}_1, \ldots, \mathcal{B}_{n+N}$, where $\mathcal{B}_{j*}$ executes the following steps:

1. It receives a public key pk from the m-IND-CPA challenger.
2. It generates the parties $P_1, \ldots, P_{n+N}$ and simulates an execution of $\mathbb{E}_{\mathsf{comp}}^{\mathcal{G}_{\mathsf{clock}}, \mathcal{F}_{\mathsf{auth}}^{\Delta_{\mathsf{net}}}}$ conducted by $\mathcal{Z}$ and under the presence of $\mathcal{A}$, also playing the role of $\mathcal{G}_{\mathsf{clock}}, \mathcal{F}_{\mathsf{auth}}^{\Delta_{\mathsf{net}}}$. The simulation differs from an actual execution as shown below:

(a) Upon initialization of a party P_j: if $P_j \neq P_{j^*}$, then $\mathcal{B}_{j^*}$ honestly generates a fresh key pair $(\mathsf{sk}_j, \mathsf{pk}_j)$. If $P_j = P_{j^*}$, then it sets $\mathsf{pk}_{j^*} := \mathsf{pk}$.
(b) When a party P_i must send an encrypted message M under the public key of P_j (note it may be the case that $P_i = P_j$) via $\mathcal{F}_{\mathsf{auth}}^{\Delta_{\mathsf{net}}}$:
   – If $j < j^*$, then $\mathcal{B}_{j^*}$ sends an encryption of M under pk_j.
   – If $j = j^*$, then it sends a challenge pair $(M_0, M_1) := (\mathsf{null}, M)$ to the m-IND-CPA challenger. Upon receiving a ciphertext $\mathsf{Enc}_{[P_{j^*}]}(M_b)$, where b is the m-IND-CPA challenge bit, it sends $\mathsf{Enc}_{[P_{j^*}]}(M_b)$ to P_{j^*}.
   – If $j > j^*$, then it sends an encryption of null under pk_j.
(c) Since $\mathcal{A}$ is passive, all parties are honest, thus $\mathcal{B}_{j^*}$ is completely aware of the plaintext-ciphertext correspondence. Therefore, when P_i encrypts M under P_j's public key to a ciphertext $\mathsf{Enc}_{[P_j]}(M)$, $\mathcal{B}_{j^*}$ proceeds as if P_j had indeed decrypted this ciphertext to M.
3. It returns the output of $\mathcal{Z}$.

Given the description of $\mathcal{B}_{j^*}$, $j^* = 1, \ldots, n+N$, we make the following observations:

– *The limit case $j^* = 1$*: if $b = 0$, then $\mathcal{B}_1$ replaces all real-world communication with encryptions of 'null', exactly as Sim does in its simulation. Thus, we have that

$$\Pr\left[\mathcal{B}_1 = 1 \mid b = 0\right] = \mathrm{EXEC}_{\mathsf{Sim}, \mathcal{Z}, \mathcal{G}_{\mathsf{clock}}}^{\mathcal{F}_{\mathsf{priv}}^{\mathsf{Leak}_{\mathsf{unob}} \cdot \Delta_{\mathsf{net}}}}[\mathbf{P}](\lambda). \tag{7}$$

– *The hybrid step*: for every $1 \leq j^* < n+N$, the adversaries $\mathcal{B}_{j^*}$ and $\mathcal{B}_{j^*+1}$ have the same behavior regarding the parties P_j, where $j \neq j^*, j^*+1$. In addition, if the m-IND-CPA challenge bit b is 1, then $\mathcal{B}_{j^*}$ (i) respects the encryptions of P_j^* (hence, of every P_j, for $j \leq j^*$) and (ii) replaces with null any plaintext intended for P_j, for $j \geq j^* + 1$. Observe that this is exactly the behavior of $\mathcal{B}_{j^*+1}$, if $b = 0$. Therefore, it holds that

$$\Pr\left[\mathcal{B}_{j^*} = 1 \mid b = 1\right] = \Pr\left[\mathcal{B}_{j^*+1} = 1 \mid b = 0\right]. \tag{8}$$

– *The limit case $j^* = n + N$*: if $b = 1$, then $\mathcal{B}_{n+N}$ executes real-world communication respecting the environments' instructions and inputs. Thus, we have that

$$\Pr\left[\mathcal{B}_{n+N} = 1 \mid b = 1\right] = \mathrm{EXEC}_{\mathcal{A}, \mathcal{Z}, \mathcal{G}_{\mathsf{clock}}}^{\mathbb{E}^{\mathcal{G}_{\mathsf{clock}}, \mathcal{F}_{\mathsf{auth}}^{\Delta_{\mathsf{net}}}}}[\mathbf{P}](\lambda). \tag{9}$$

Consequently, by Eq. (7) and the m-IND-CPA security of PKE, we have that for every $j^* \in [n + N]$, it holds that

$$\left| \Pr\left[\mathcal{B}_{j^*} = 1 \mid b = 1\right] - \Pr\left[\mathcal{B}_{j^*} = 1 \mid b = 0\right] \right| =$$
$$= \left| \Pr\left[\mathcal{B}_{j^*} = 1 \mid b = 1\right] - \left(1 - \Pr\left[\mathcal{B}_{j^*} = 0 \mid b = 0\right]\right) \right| \leq$$
$$\leq \left| 2 \cdot \Pr\left[(\mathcal{B}_{j^*} = 1) \wedge (b = 1)\right] + 2 \cdot \Pr\left[(\mathcal{B}_{j^*} = 0) \wedge (b = 0)\right] - 1 \right| =$$
$$= \left| 2 \cdot \Pr\left[\mathcal{B}_{j^*}(1^\lambda) \text{ breaks } \mathsf{PKE}\right] - 1 \right| \leq \left| 2 \cdot \left(1/2 + \epsilon(\lambda)\right) - 1 \right| = 2\epsilon(\lambda). \tag{10}$$

Finally, by Eqs. (7), (8),(9), and (10), we get that

$$\left| \mathrm{EXEC}^{\mathcal{F}^{\mathsf{Leak}_{\mathsf{unob}}}_{\mathsf{priv}}, \Delta_{\mathsf{net}}}_{\mathsf{Sim}, \mathcal{Z}, \mathcal{G}_{\mathsf{clock}}} [\mathbf{P}](\lambda) - \mathrm{EXEC}^{\mathbb{E}^{\mathcal{G}_{\mathsf{clock}}}, \mathcal{F}^{\Delta_{\mathsf{net}}}_{\mathsf{auth}}}_{\mathcal{A}, \mathcal{Z}, \mathcal{G}_{\mathsf{clock}}} [\mathbf{P}](\lambda) \right| \leq 2(n+N)\epsilon(\lambda)$$

which completes the proof.   □

6   A Parallel Mix Email Ecosystem with t Strata

We will now describe a design to be used for routing messages between various users, based on parallel mixing [18,19]. A parallel mix is a design that borrows characteristics from stratified mixes i.e. mixes where servers are grouped in sets called *strata*, and routing is restricted so that each stratum except the first only receives messages from the previous one and each stratum except the last only forwards messages to the next (the first and last strata operate as the entry and exit points respectively). In parallel mixing routing is determined by the servers themselves in the interest of symmetry and predictability in performance and security. All t strata consist of σ nodes each. We use $\mathsf{MX}_{i,j}$ to indicate the j-th server in stratum i, and let $\mathbf{MX} = \{\mathsf{MX}_{i,j} | i \leq t, j \leq \sigma\}$. We use $\mathbf{P} = (\mathbf{C} \cup \mathbf{SP} \cup \mathbf{MX})$ to denote the set of all involved parties. We use a set of assumptions similar to those of Sect. 5, specifically: (a) all communication is executed via $\mathcal{F}^{\Delta_{\mathsf{net}}}_{\mathsf{auth}}(\mathbf{P})$ as described in Fig. 2; (b) all messages have the same size (i.e. messages are padded ahead of time); (c) all computations complete within one unit slot; (d) each client is assigned to exactly one address.

As we assume a passive adversary and no corruptions, we are able to use a simple layering of encryptions instead of a more complex onion scheme. In practice one may wish to use a scheme such as Sphinx [14] or a variant thereof.

■ **Initialization:** Nodes of the same stratum share stratum-specific keying material. In practice, because of the long structure of the mixnet, and the large number of nodes involved, we might have that the same entities will be running multiple servers across different strata. We can thus regain some robustness by excluding some entities from each stratum so that each entity is absent from at least one stratum. Alternatively, we may use per-node keys and allow free routing, at the cost of slower (in terms of rounds) convergence to a random permutation.

- On input $(\mathsf{sid}, \mathsf{INIT})$, a party $P \in \mathbf{P}$ that is not yet initialised, runs $\mathsf{Gen}(1^\lambda)$ to generate a pair of a private and a public key pair $(\mathsf{sk}_P, \mathsf{pk}_P)$. Then, it broadcasts the message $(\mathsf{sid}, (\mathsf{init}, \mathsf{pk}_P), P)$ to all clients and SPs by sending $(\mathsf{sid}, (\mathsf{init}, \mathsf{pk}_P), P')$ to $\mathcal{F}^{\Delta_{\mathsf{net}}}_{\mathsf{auth}}(\mathbf{G}[\mathbb{P}])$, for every $P' \in \mathbf{P} \setminus \{P\}$.
- When SP_i has received $(\mathsf{sid}, (\mathsf{init}, \mathsf{pk}_{\mathsf{SP}_j}), \mathsf{SP}_j)$ for every $i \in [N] \setminus \{j\}$, then begins the engagement in the email message exchange with its assigned clients and the other SPs.
- When $\mathsf{MX}_{i,1}$ has received $(\mathsf{sid}, (\mathsf{init}, \mathsf{pk}_S), S)$ for every $\mathsf{MX}_{i,j}, j > 1$, it runs $\mathsf{Gen}(1^\lambda)$ to generate stratum key pair $(\mathsf{sk}_i, \mathsf{pk}_i)$. Then, it broadcasts the

message $\left(\text{sid}, (\text{init}, \text{pk}_i), \text{MX}_{i,1}\right)$ to all parties P' outside stratum i by sending $\left(\text{sid}, (\text{init}, \text{pk}_i), P'\right)$ to $\mathcal{F}_{\text{auth}}^{\Delta_{\text{net}}}(\mathbf{G}[\mathbf{P}])$. For parties P'' in stratum i it sends $\left(\text{sid}, (\text{init}, (\text{pk}_i, \text{sk}_i)), P''\right)$ instead.

■ **Execution:** Our mixnet operates in rounds. A round consists of $t+2$ subrounds, each consisting of $t_{sub} \geq \Delta_{\text{net}} + 1$ timeslots. We assume timing information is publicly available. During each subround, messages are only sent during the first timeslot. The remaining timeslots exist to ensure that even delayed messages are delivered before the next subround. To simplify notation we will introduce three functions on the clock value CI:

Namely, we define (i) $round(\text{CI}) := \left\lfloor \frac{\text{CI}}{t_{sub}(t+2)} \right\rfloor$, (ii) $sub(\text{CI}) := \left\lfloor \frac{\text{CI}}{t_{sub}} \right\rfloor$, and (iii) $slot(\text{CI}) := \text{CI} \bmod t_{sub}$. Essentially, at clock CI we are in slot $slot(\text{CI})$ of subround $sub(\text{CI})$. We also assume that using the above functions use READ_CLOCK to determine the current value of CI.

Registration is handled as in Sect. 5. Messages are routed through the mixnet as follows:

- Messages from clients are queued by their SPs until the round begins.
- Once a round begins, in sub-round 0, clients send their messages to the SPs. In sub-round 1, each SP uniformly randomly selects a server in the first stratum to receive each message.
- In the sub-round 2 (3), first-stratum (second) servers tally up their incoming messages and pad them to a multiple of σ. They shuffle them and send $\frac{1}{\sigma}$ of them to each 2nd-stratum (3rd) server. No padding is required afterwards.
- In sub-round i, where $4 \leq i \leq t+1$, the servers of stratum $i-1$ shuffle their received messages and send $\frac{1}{\sigma}$ of them to each server in stratum i+1.
- At the end of sub-round $t+2$, the SPs move messages from their input buffers to user inboxes.

We will now formally describe our system. Note that some inputs will only have effect when given during particular sub-rounds or when given to certain parties (e.g. only Clients). As in the previous section, $\text{Enc}_{[X]}(Y)$ denotes the encryption of Y under X's public key. For brevity, we use $\text{Enc}_{[x,y]}(m)$ to denote $\text{Enc}_{[x]}\left(\text{Enc}_{[y]}(m)\right)$.

$C_s \in \mathbf{C}$. On input $\left(\text{sid}, \text{SEND}, \langle C_s @ \text{SP}_i, M, C_r @ \text{SP}_j \rangle\right)$, if C_s is not registered with an SP_i and $subround(\text{CI}) = 0$ and $slot(\text{CI}) = 0$, the client sets $reg = round(\text{CI})$ and runs the registration operation from Sect. 5.

$C_s \in \mathbf{C}$. On input $\left(\text{sid}, \text{SEND}, \langle C_s @ \text{SP}_i, M, C_r @ \text{SP}_j \rangle\right)$, if C_s is logged in to SP_i, she prepares the message $\left(\text{sid}, \text{Enc}_{[\text{SP}_i]}\left(C_s @ \text{SP}_i, \text{Enc}_{[\text{SP}_j]}\right.\right.$ $\left.\left.(C_r @ \text{SP}_j, \text{Enc}_{[C_r]}(M)))\right)\right)$ to be sent to SP_i. If, in addition the $sub(\text{CI})$ and $slot(\text{CI})$ are both 0 and $round(\text{CI}) > reg$, all prepared messages are sent to SP_i.

$C_r \in \mathbf{C}$. On input $\left(\text{sid}, \text{FETCH}, C_r @ \text{SP}_j\right)$, if C_r is logged in to SP_j, it sends the message $\left(\text{sid}, C_r @ \text{SP}_j, \text{Enc}_{[\text{SP}_j]}(\text{FETCH})\right)$ to SP_j which, if C_r@SP_j is a valid address, it decrypts and forwards all messages $E_{r,1}, \ldots E_{r,n_r}$ in $\mathsf{Inbox}[C_r@SP_j]$ to C_r, and empties $\mathsf{Inbox}[C_r@SP_j]$.

$C_r \in \mathbf{C}$. Upon receiving $(\mathsf{sid}, E_{r,1}, \ldots, E_{r,n})$ from SP_j and if C_r has sent a $(\mathsf{sid}, \textsc{Fetch}, C_r@SP_j)$ request, C_r decrypts all ciphertexts and stores the ones that are not 0, i.e. they correspond to non-dummy mail messages.

$P \in \mathbf{P}$. On input $(\mathsf{sid}, \textsc{Read\_Clock})$, the entity $P \in \mathbf{P}$ sends the message $(\mathsf{sid}, \textsc{Read\_Clock})$ to $\mathcal{G}_{\mathsf{clock}}$. Upon receiving $(\mathsf{sid}, \textsc{Read\_Clock}, \mathsf{Cl})$ from $\mathcal{G}_{\mathsf{clock}}$, P stores Cl as its local time and forwards the message $(\mathsf{sid}, \textsc{Read\_Clock}, \mathsf{Cl})$ to the environment.

$\mathsf{SP}_i \in \mathbf{SP}$. On input $\big(\mathsf{sid}, \mathsf{Enc}_{[SP_i]}\big(C_s@SP_i, \mathsf{Enc}_{[SP_j]}\big(C_r@SP_j, \mathsf{Enc}_{[C_r]}(M)\big)\big)\big)$, it checks that $C_s@SP_i \in \mathbf{Ad}$ and if so, then it decrypts and adds $\big(\mathsf{sid}, C_s@SP_i, \mathsf{Enc}_{[SP_j]}\big(C_r@SP_j, \mathsf{Enc}_{[C_r]}(M)\big)\big)$ to its set of messages pending to be sent, denoted by L_{send}^i.

$\mathsf{SP}_j \in \mathbf{SP}$. Upon receiving a message $(\mathsf{sid}, \mathsf{Enc}_{[SP_j]}(\cdot, \cdot))$ from some $\mathsf{MX}_{x,y}$, SP_j checks whether $x = t$, and if the content is a ciphertext under its public key that decrypts as a valid address $C_r@SP_j$ along with a ciphertext E. If so, then it adds E to $\mathsf{B}[C_r@SP_j]$.

$\mathsf{MX}_{1,j} \in \mathbf{S}$. On receiving $\big(\mathsf{sid}, \mathsf{Enc}_{[1,\ldots,t]}\big(C_r@SP_j, \mathsf{Enc}_{[C_r]}(M)\big), X\big)$, it checks that $X \in SP$ and if so, it decrypts it and adds $\big(\mathsf{sid}, \mathsf{Enc}_{[2,\ldots,t]}\big(C_r@SP_j, \mathsf{Enc}_{[C_r]}(M)\big)$ to its set of messages pending to be sent, denoted by L_{send}^i.

$\mathsf{MX}_{k+1,j} \in \mathbf{S}$. On receiving $\big(\mathsf{sid}, \mathsf{Enc}_{[k,\ldots,t]}\big(C_r@SP_j, \mathsf{Enc}_{[C_r]}(M)\big), X\big)$, it checks that $X = \mathsf{MX}_{k,x}$ for some x and if so, it decrypts it and adds $\big(\mathsf{sid}, \mathsf{Enc}_{[k+2,\ldots,t]}\big(C_r@SP_j, \mathsf{Enc}_{[C_r]}(M)\big)$ to its set of messages pending to be sent, denoted by L_{send}^i. If $k = t-1$, it instead adds $\big(\mathsf{sid}, \mathsf{Enc}_{[SP_j]}\big(C_r@SP_j, \mathsf{Enc}_{[C_r]}(M)\big)$ to the list.

$P \in \mathbf{P}$. On input $(\mathsf{sid}, \textsc{Advance\_Clock})$, the entity $P \in \mathbf{P}$ sends the message $(\mathsf{sid}, \textsc{Advance\_Clock})$ to $\mathcal{G}_{\mathsf{clock}}$.

$\mathsf{SP}_i \in \mathbf{SP}$. On input $(\mathsf{sid}, \textsc{Advance\_Clock})$, If $sub(\mathsf{Cl}) = 1$ and $slot(\mathsf{Cl}) = 0$, for each message $\big(\mathsf{sid}, C_s@SP_i, \mathsf{Enc}_{[SP_j]}\big(C_r@SP_j, \mathsf{Enc}_{[C_r]}(M)\big)\big)$ in L_{send}^i, then SP_i sends $\big(\mathsf{sid}, \mathsf{SP}_i, \mathsf{Enc}_{[1,\ldots,t]}\big(C_r@SP_j, \mathsf{Enc}_{[C_r]}(M)\big)\big)$ to a randomly selected $\mathsf{MX}_{1,j}$ and removes the message from L_{send}^i. Finally, it sends the message $(\mathsf{sid}, \textsc{Advance\_Clock})$ to $\mathcal{G}_{\mathsf{clock}}$.

$\mathsf{MX}_{k,j} \in \mathbf{S}$. On input $(\mathsf{sid}, \textsc{Advance\_Clock})$, If $sub(\mathsf{Cl}) \neq k+1$ or $slot(\mathsf{Cl}) \neq 0$, send the message $(\mathsf{sid}, \textsc{Advance\_Clock})$ to $\mathcal{G}_{\mathsf{clock}}$ and return. Otherwise, if $k = 1$ or $k = 2$, $\mathsf{MX}_{k,j}$ pads the list L_{send}^i with $(\mathsf{sid}, \mathsf{Enc}_{[k+1,\ldots,t]}(0))$ so that its length is a multiple of σ. The list is then shuffled randomly. For each message $\big(\mathsf{sid}, \mathsf{Enc}_{[k+1,\ldots,t]}\big(C_r@SP_j, \mathsf{Enc}_{[C_r]}(M)\big)\big)$ in L_{send}^i, then $\mathsf{MX}_{k,j}$ sends $\big(\mathsf{sid}, \mathsf{MX}_{k,j}, \mathsf{Enc}_{[k+1,\ldots,t]}\big(C_r@SP_j, \mathsf{Enc}_{[C_r]}(M)\big)\big)$ to server $\mathsf{MX}_{k+1,j \bmod \sigma}$, where j is the message's position on the list, and removes the message from L^i_{send}. Finally, it sends the message (sid, ADVANCE_CLOCK) to $\mathcal{G}_{\text{clock}}$.

$\mathsf{MX}_{t,j} \in \mathbf{S}$. On input (sid, ADVANCE_CLOCK), If $sub(\mathsf{Cl}) = t + 1$ and $slot(\mathsf{Cl}) = 0$, for each message (sid, $\mathsf{Enc}_{[\mathsf{SP}_j]}(C_r@\mathsf{SP}_j,$ $\mathsf{Enc}_{[C_r]}(M)))$ in L^i_{send}, $\mathsf{MX}_{t,j}$ forwards it to SP_j. Finally it sends the message (sid, ADVANCE_CLOCK) to $\mathcal{G}_{\text{clock}}$.

$\mathsf{SP}_j \in \mathbf{SP}$. On input (sid, ADVANCE_CLOCK), If $sub(\mathsf{Cl}) = t + 2$ and $slot(\mathsf{Cl}) = 0$, it moves the contents of every buffer $\mathsf{B}[C_r@\mathsf{SP}_j]$ to the corresponding inbox $\mathsf{Inbox}[C_r@\mathsf{SP}_j]$. Finally it sends the message (sid, ADVANCE_CLOCK) to $\mathcal{G}_{\text{clock}}$.

Efficiency & Delivery times. The overhead of the padding is an $O\left(\frac{\sigma^2}{m}\right)$ multiplicative increase in the messages sent, where m is the number of messages sent, which we expect to be low for typical use cases. Disregarding padding messages, the cost to deliver a single email, is $3 + t$ messages compared to 3 in the insecure case (sender to SP_s to SP_r to receiver) or $1 + s \cdot n$ for the "golden standard" solution of Sect. 5. While in principle this is identical to a cascade (i.e. single server per stratum) solution, in practice a parallel mix requires a larger t value. The load per mix server is $\frac{m}{\sigma}$ messages, compared to m in a cascade.

The encryption overhead depends on the specifics of the cryptosystem. While naive encryption might cause an exponential blow-up, solutions based on hybrid encryption, or onioning solutions such as Sphinx can reduce the overhead to a small linear factor. Delivery latency is also directly proportional to the length of the mixnet. We note that latency can be significantly reduced by pipelining (i.e. allowing messages to be sent at the end of every subround rather than at the end of the first round only), but we opt to describe the base version for clarity.

Security. Here, we will show that the system described above is secure under the weak anonymity definition and leakage function $\mathsf{Leak}_{\text{w.anon}}(\mathsf{ptr}, H)$, defined in Eq. (5). For convenience, we will assume that one timeslot maps to one round.

Theorem 2. *The parallel mix of Sect. 6, using t strata of σ servers to deliver m messages is $m^{1-\lfloor\frac{t-1}{2}\rfloor\frac{1}{4}}4^{\lfloor\frac{t-1}{2}\rfloor\frac{1}{2}}\log m^{\lfloor\frac{t-1}{2}\rfloor\frac{1}{4}}+2|\mathbf{P}|\epsilon_E$ weakly anonymous assuming Enc is ϵ_E m-IND-CPA secure.*

Proof. Due to space considerations, we postpone the proof to the full version of this work and sketch the main strategy to cover the difference between a real and simulated execution. We first utilize the m-IND-CPA security of the encryption and a series of hybrid games to replace message contents with dummies. To complete the proof, we use Theorem 3 (based on [20]) to show that replacing the final routing of messages with a random allocation that respects the leakage (i.e. messages per server) is statistically indistinguishable.

7   The Combinatorics of Parallel Mixing

Many of the works analysing parallel mixing investigate the probability distribution of a single message traversing the network. This is satisfactory for some definitions of anonymity but not for our modelling of a global adversary under universal composability. In our model, the environment determines the sender and receiver of each message, so it is not sufficient to argue that any one message is successfully shuffled (i.e. has a uniformly random exit point from the network).

To illustrate, assume messages are represented by a deck of n playing cards, and further assume that our mixnet operates by simply "cutting" the deck once, in secret (i.e. choosing $k \in \{0..n-1\}$, and placing the first k cards at the bottom of the deck in their original order). It is trivial to simulate drawing a single card from a deck shuffled this way, by sampling a random card. However, once a card has been drawn, subsequent draws are determined by the initial order. The environment knows the initial order because it set it, but the simulator does not, and the simulation fails.

Our approach will be to show that parallel mixing after a number of rounds produces a random permutation on the list of input messages, thus allowing the simulator to produce the list of output messages by sampling a random permutation of the recipients, independent of the senders (which is crucial as it does not know the relation between the two).

We will model parallel mixing as a generalisation of the square lattice shuffle of Håstad [20]. In a square lattice shuffle, $n = m^2$ cards are arranged in an $m \times m$ matrix, and shuffled as follows: in odd rounds each row is shuffled by an independently uniformly random sampled permutation. In even rounds, the same happens to columns. It is simple to check that t iterations of this process map directly to a t-stratum parallel mix with m servers per stratum, each with capacity m: we label odd strata as "rows" and even strata as "columns", where the i-th server corresponds to the i-th row (column). The mapping is then completed by noting the result of an odd round is that each row randomly contributes one of its elements to each column, and vice-versa for even rounds.

Thus Håstad's results are applicable to parallel mixing. A second observation is that because parties are assumed honest, we can assign multiple rows or columns to one party without invalidating the bounds. We thus reproduce Theorem 3.6 from [20] and explain how it applies in our construction.

Theorem 3 (Håstad [20], Theorem 3.6). *Let Π_t be the distribution defined by t iterrations of lattice shuffling on m objects. Then*

$$\Delta(\Pi_t, U_m) \leq O(m^{1-\lfloor \frac{t-1}{2} \rfloor \frac{1}{4}} \log m^{\lfloor \frac{t-1}{2} \rfloor \frac{1}{2}})$$

Closer examination of the proof, and assuming $m > 81$ enables us to dismiss the big-O and obtain:

$$\Delta(\Pi_t, U_m) \leq m^{1-\lfloor \frac{t-1}{2} \rfloor \frac{1}{4}} 1.5^{\lfloor \frac{t-1}{2} \rfloor} \log m^{\lfloor \frac{t-1}{2} \rfloor \frac{1}{2}}$$

This in turn implies

Corollary 1. *For $m > 10^6$, 31 rounds of lattice shuffling are statistically $\frac{1}{m}$ close to uniform.*

The theorem's proof also gives us insight in the effect of compromised servers in a stratum: as coupling takes place over 3 iterations (or 2 with the assumption that another honest iteration will follow), we must allow that a single compromised stratum essentially shortens our network by 3 strata at the worst case.

7.1 A Brief Discussion on Convergence Speed

The bounds stated above describe a parallel mix with many small servers. One would expect the situation to improve when examining fewer, larger servers. In that direction, we expect a generalization of Håstad's result to yield a tighter bound. That would be of value as there are few competing designs for random permutation networks suited to anonymous communication [25].

The core of Håstad's analysis is about the probability of "coupling" two permutations that start out differing by a single transposition, after 2 rounds of shuffling. A first observation is that with "large" servers, the probability that the transposition lies in one server (and thus the coupling is immediate) becomes significant, improving convergence. A second, is that the probability of a missed coupling is inversely proportional to the number of elements per server which again implies improved convergence. We believe that a bound of $m^{1-\lfloor\frac{t-1}{2}\rfloor}\frac{1}{2}^{\lfloor\frac{t-1}{2}\rfloor}1.5^{\lfloor\frac{t-1}{2}\rfloor}\log m^{\lfloor\frac{t-1}{2}\rfloor}\frac{\sigma-1}{\sqrt{\sigma}}^{\lfloor\frac{t-1}{2}\rfloor}$ is possible, which would approximately halve the rounds required for the bound to reach $\frac{1}{m}$, when σ is small, e.g. 17 rounds for $\sigma = 4$, $m > 300.000$. However, we consider the specifics outside the scope of this work, and leave the question of statistical bounds for parallel mixing open for further research.

References

1. Alexopoulos, N., Kiayias, A., Talviste, R., Zacharias, T.: MCMix: anonymous messaging via secure multiparty computation. In: USENIX (2017)
2. Angel, S., Setty, S.: Unobservable communication over fully untrusted infrastructure. In: OSDI (2016)
3. Backes, M., Kate, A., Manoharan, P., Meiser, S., Mohammadi, E.: AnoA: a framework for analyzing anonymous communication protocols. In: CSF (2013)
4. Badertscher, C., Maurer, U., Tschudi, D., Zikas, V.: Bitcoin as a transaction ledger: a composable treatment. In: Katz, J., Shacham, H. (eds.) CRYPTO 2017. LNCS, vol. 10401, pp. 324–356. Springer, Cham (2017). https://doi.org/10.1007/978-3-319-63688-7_11
5. Camenisch, J., Lysyanskaya, A.: A formal treatment of onion routing. In: Shoup, V. (ed.) CRYPTO 2005. LNCS, vol. 3621, pp. 169–187. Springer, Heidelberg (2005). https://doi.org/10.1007/11535218_11
6. Canetti, R.: Universally composable security: a new paradigm for cryptographic protocols. In: Foundations of Computer Science. IEEE (2001)

7. Canetti, R., Dodis, Y., Pass, R., Walfish, S.: Universally composable security with global setup. In: Vadhan, S.P. (ed.) TCC 2007. LNCS, vol. 4392, pp. 61–85. Springer, Heidelberg (2007). https://doi.org/10.1007/978-3-540-70936-7_4

8. Chaum, D.: The dining cryptographers problem: unconditional sender and recipient untraceability. J. Cryptol. 1(1), 65–75 (1988)

9. Chaum, D., et al.: cMix: mixing with minimal real-time asymmetric cryptographic operations. In: Gollmann, D., Miyaji, A., Kikuchi, H. (eds.) ACNS 2017. LNCS, vol. 10355, pp. 557–578. Springer, Cham (2017). https://doi.org/10.1007/978-3-319-61204-1_28

10. Chaum, D.L.: Untraceable electronic mail, return addresses, and digital pseudonyms. Commun. ACM 24(2), 84–90 (1981)

11. Corrigan-Gibbs, H., Boneh, D., Mazières, D.: Riposte: an anonymous messaging system handling millions of users. In: Security and Privacy (2015)

12. Corrigan-Gibbs, H., Ford, B.: Dissent: accountable anonymous group messaging. In: CCS, pp. 340–350 (2010)

13. Danezis, G., Dingledine, R., Mathewson, N.: Mixminion: design of a type III anonymous remailer protocol. In: Security and Privacy, pp. 2–15 (2003)

14. Danezis, G., Goldberg, I.: Sphinx: a compact and provably secure mix format. In: Security and Privacy (2009)

15. Díaz, C., Seys, S., Claessens, J., Preneel, B.: Towards measuring anonymity. In: Dingledine, R., Syverson, P. (eds.) PET 2002. LNCS, vol. 2482, pp. 54–68. Springer, Heidelberg (2003). https://doi.org/10.1007/3-540-36467-6_5

16. Dingledine, R., Mathewson, N., Syverson, P.: Tor: the second-generation onion router. Technical report, DTIC Document (2004)

17. Dwork, C.: Differential privacy. In: Automata, Languages and Programming, pp. 1–12 (2006)

18. Golle, P., Juels, A.: Parallel mixing. In: CCS, pp. 220–226. ACM (2004)

19. Goodrich, M.T., Mitzenmacher, M.: Anonymous card shuffling and its applications to parallel mixnets. In: Czumaj, A., Mehlhorn, K., Pitts, A., Wattenhofer, R. (eds.) ICALP 2012. LNCS, vol. 7392, pp. 549–560. Springer, Heidelberg (2012). https://doi.org/10.1007/978-3-642-31585-5_49

20. Håstad, J.: The square lattice shuffle. Random Struct. Algorithms 29(4), 466–474 (2006)

21. Johnson, A., Wacek, C., Jansen, R., Sherr, M., Syverson, P.: Users get routed: traffic correlation on tor by realistic adversaries. In: CCS, pp. 337–348 (2013)

22. Katz, J., Maurer, U., Tackmann, B., Zikas, V.: Universally composable synchronous computation. In: Sahai, A. (ed.) TCC 2013. LNCS, vol. 7785, pp. 477–498. Springer, Heidelberg (2013). https://doi.org/10.1007/978-3-642-36594-2_27

23. Kesdogan, D., Egner, J., Büschkes, R.: Stop-and-Go-MIXes providing probabilistic anonymity in an open system. In: Aucsmith, D. (ed.) IH 1998. LNCS, vol. 1525, pp. 83–98. Springer, Heidelberg (1998). https://doi.org/10.1007/3-540-49380-8_7

24. Kotzanikolaou, P., Chatzisofroniou, G., Burmester, M.: Broadcast anonymous routing (BAR): scalable real-time anonymous communication. Int. J. Inf. Sec. 16(3), 313–326 (2017)

25. Kwon, A., Corrigan-Gibbs, H., Devadas, S., Ford, B.: Atom: horizontally scaling strong anonymity. In: SOSP. ACM (2017)

26. Kwon, A., Lazar, D., Devadas, S., Ford, B.: Riffle: an efficient communication system with strong anonymity. PoPETS 2016(2), 115–134 (2015)

27. Pfitzmann, A., Hansen, M.: Anonymity, unlinkability, unobservability, pseudonymity, and identity management - a consolidated proposal for terminology. Version v0.25, December 2005

28. Pfitzmann, A., Köhntopp, M.: Anonymity, unobservability, and pseudonymity — a proposal for terminology. In: Federrath, H. (ed.) Designing Privacy Enhancing Technologies. LNCS, vol. 2009, pp. 1–9. Springer, Heidelberg (2001). https://doi.org/10.1007/3-540-44702-4_1
29. Piotrowska, A., Hayes, J., Elahi, T., Danezis, G., Meiser, S.: The loopix anonymity system. In: USENIX (2017)
30. Samarati, P., Sweeney, L.: Protecting privacy when disclosing information: k-anonymity and its enforcement through generalization and suppression. In: Security and Privacy (1998)
31. Serjantov, A., Danezis, G.: Towards an information theoretic metric for anonymity. In: Dingledine, R., Syverson, P. (eds.) PET 2002. LNCS, vol. 2482, pp. 41–53. Springer, Heidelberg (2003). https://doi.org/10.1007/3-540-36467-6_4
32. Shmatikov, V., Wang, M.-H.: Timing analysis in low-latency mix networks: attacks and defenses. In: Gollmann, D., Meier, J., Sabelfeld, A. (eds.) ESORICS 2006. LNCS, vol. 4189, pp. 18–33. Springer, Heidelberg (2006). https://doi.org/10.1007/11863908_2
33. Syverson, P.F., Goldschlag, D.M., Reed, M.G.: Anonymous connections and onion routing. In: Security and Privacy, pp. 44–54 (1997)
34. Syverson, P.F., Tsudik, G., Reed, M.G., Landwehr, C.E.: Towards an analysis of onion routing security. In: Federrath, H. (ed.) Designing Privacy Enhancing Technologies. LNCS, vol. 2009, pp. 96–114. Springer, Heidelberg (2001). https://doi.org/10.1007/3-540-44702-4_6
35. Van Den Hooff, J., Lazar, D., Zaharia, M., Zeldovich, N.: Vuvuzela: scalable private messaging resistant to traffic analysis. In: SOSP, pp. 137–152 (2015)
36. Wikström, D.: A universally composable mix-net. In: Naor, M. (ed.) TCC 2004. LNCS, vol. 2951, pp. 317–335. Springer, Heidelberg (2004). https://doi.org/10.1007/978-3-540-24638-1_18

State Separation for Code-Based Game-Playing Proofs

Chris Brzuska[1]([✉]), Antoine Delignat-Lavaud[2], Cédric Fournet[2],
Konrad Kohbrok[1], and Markulf Kohlweiss[2,3]

[1] Aalto University, Helsinki, Finland
chris.brzuska@gmail.com
[2] Microsoft Research, Redmond, USA
[3] University of Edinburgh, Edinburgh, UK

Abstract. The security analysis of real-world protocols involves reduction steps that are conceptually simple but still have to account for many protocol complications found in standards and implementations. Taking inspiration from universal composability, abstract cryptography, process algebras, and type-based verification frameworks, we propose a method to simplify large reductions, avoid mistakes in carrying them out, and obtain concise security statements.

Our method decomposes monolithic games into collections of stateful *packages* representing collections of oracles that call one another using well-defined interfaces. Every component scheme yields a pair of a real and an ideal package. In security proofs, we then successively replace each real package with its ideal counterpart, treating the other packages as the reduction. We build this reduction by applying a number of algebraic operations on packages justified by their state separation. Our method handles reductions that emulate the game perfectly, and leaves more complex arguments to existing game-based proof techniques such as the code-based analysis suggested by Bellare and Rogaway. It also facilitates computer-aided proofs, inasmuch as the perfect reductions steps can be automatically discharged by proof assistants.

We illustrate our method on two generic composition proofs: a proof of self-composition using a hybrid argument; and the composition of keying and keyed components. For concreteness, we apply them to the KEM-DEM proof of hybrid-encryption by Cramer and Shoup and to the composition of forward-secure game-based key exchange protocols with symmetric-key protocols.

1 Introduction

Code-based game-playing by Bellare and Rogaway [8] introduces pseudo-code as a precise tool for cryptographic reasoning. Following in their footsteps, we would like to reason about games using code, rather than interactive Turing machines [48]. Our code uses state variables and function calls, hiding the details of operating on local tapes and shared tapes. Function calls enable straightforward code composition, defined for instance by inlining, and enjoy standard but

© International Association for Cryptologic Research 2018
T. Peyrin and S. Galbraith (Eds.): ASIACRYPT 2018, LNCS 11274, pp. 222–249, 2018.
https://doi.org/10.1007/978-3-030-03332-3_9

useful properties, such as associativity. In the following, we refer to code units $\mathcal{A}$, R and G as *code packages*. If adversary $\mathcal{A}$ calls reduction R and R calls game G, we may see it either as code A-calling-R that calls code G, or as code $\mathcal{A}$ calling code R-calling-G. This form of associativity is used to define reductions, e.g., in abstract cryptography and in Rosulek's book *The Joy of Cryptography* [44].

As a first example, consider indistinguishability under chosen plaintext attacks, coded as a game $\mathtt{IND\text{-}CPA}^b$ with secret bit b, and let $\mathcal{A}$ be an adversary that interacts with this game by calling its encryption oracle, which we write $\mathcal{A} \circ \mathtt{IND\text{-}CPA}^b$. As a construction, consider a symmetric encryption scheme based on a pseudorandom function (PRF). We can decompose $\mathtt{IND\text{-}CPA}^b$ into some corresponding wrapper $\mathtt{MOD\text{-}CPA}$ that calls $\mathtt{PRF}^b$, where b now controls idealization of the PRF. The equality $\mathtt{IND\text{-}CPA}^b = \mathtt{MOD\text{-}CPA} \circ \mathtt{PRF}^b$ can be checked syntactically (and can be automatically discharged by proof assistants). IND-CPA security follows from PRF security using $\mathtt{MOD\text{-}CPA}$ as reduction:

$$\mathcal{A} \circ (\mathtt{MOD\text{-}CPA}) \circ \mathtt{PRF}^b = (\mathcal{A} \circ \mathtt{MOD\text{-}CPA}) \circ \mathtt{PRF}^b.$$

The extended version of this paper [15] presents this example in more details, including a discussion of our definitional choices. In particular, we encode all games as decisional games between a real game and an ideal game, following the tradition of [12,18,35].

KEM-DEM. Our second example, the composition of a key encapsulation mechanism (KEM) with a one-time deterministic encryption scheme (DEM), involves associativity and *interchange*, another form of code rearrangement (defined in Sect. 2). Cramer and Shoup [20] show that the composition of a KEM and a DEM that are both indistinguishable under chosen ciphertext attacks (IND-CCA) results in an IND-CCA public-key encryption scheme. We give a new formulation of their proof. While Cramer and Shoup consider standard IND-CCA security, we additionally require ciphertexts to be indistinguishable from random ($\$$-IND-CCA-security, defined in Sect. 4). As sampling random strings is a key-independent operation, this makes the ideal game behaviour closer to an ideal functionality.

We first reduce to the security of the KEM, replacing the encapsulated KEM key with a uniformly random key, then we reduce to the security of the DEM, which requires such a key. To facilitate these two reductions and analogously to the previous example, we decompose the PKE-CCA game for public-key encryption into a wrapper MOD-CCA that calls the games for KEM and DEM security. That is, we use a *parallel* composition of the KEM and the DEM game. As the KEM and the DEM share the encapsulated KEM key, we need to enable state-sharing between both games. We achieve this by also decomposing the KEM and DEM security games into two packages such that they both contain a so-called KEY package that stores the shared key.

The KEM Game. Figure 1a depicts the decomposed $\$$-IND-CCA KEM game using a KEY package (also see p. 16, Definition 9). The formal semantics of the graph-based notation of package composition is introduced in Sect. 2.2.

The $-IND-CCA KEM game allows the adversary to make a KEMGEN query to initialize the game as well as encapsulation queries ENCAP and decapsulation queries DECAP. Upon receiving an encapsulation query ENCAP, the KEM package makes a SET(k) query to KEY to store the real encapsulation key k, if the bit b is 0. In turn, if the bit b is 1, the KEM package makes a GEN query to the KEY package that samples a key uniformly at random.

In standard formulations of KEM security, the adversary not only receives an encapsulation, but also the encapsulated key (or a random key, if $b = 1$) as an answer to ENCAP. In our decomposed equivalent formulation, the adversary can access the encapsulated key (or a random key, if $b = 1$) via a GET query to the KEY package (also see p. 19, Definition 13 for the $-IND-CCA KEM game).

The DEM Game. Figure 1b depicts the decomposed $-IND-CCA DEM game that also contains a KEY package. Here, the adversary can ask a GEN query to the KEY package which induces the KEY package to sample a uniformly random key that the DEM package obtains via a GET query to the KEY package. Note that in the DEM game, the adversary only has access to the GEN oracle of the KEY package, but neither to SET nor to GET. Moreover, in the DEM game, the adversary can make encryption and decryption queries (see p. 19, Definition 14 for the definition of $-IND-CCA security for DEMs).

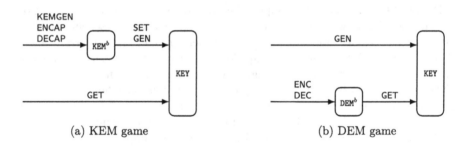

(a) KEM game   (b) DEM game

Fig. 1. Decomposed KEM and DEM games

KEM-DEM security. Recall that we prove that the KEM-DEM construction is a $-IND-CCA secure public-key encryption scheme. Using the packages KEM, DEM and KEY, we now write the $-IND-CCA security game for public-key encryption in a modular way, see Fig. 2. In the extended version of this paper [15] we prove via inlining, that the modular game in Fig. 2a, is equivalent to the monolithic $-IND-CCA game for public-key encryption with secret bit 0 and that the modular game in Fig. 2e, is equivalent to the monolithic $-IND-CCA game for public-key encryption with secret bit 1.

Thus, we first idealize the KEM package and then idealize the DEM package. Technically, this works as follows. Starting from the composition in Fig. 2a, we lengthen the edges of the graph such that the KEM^0 and KEY packages are on the right side of a vertical line (see Fig. 2b). Analogously to the first example, we use associativity (and additional rules, explained shortly) to reduce to the security of KEM by noticing that the packages on the left side of the vertical line call the packages on the right side of the vertical line, where the latter correspond to the KEM security game.

Reasoning on the graph corresponds to reasoning on compositions of packages, defined via the *sequential* operator ∘ and the *parallel* composition operator, see Sect. 2. The lengthening of edges corresponds to inserting forwarding packages, denoted *identity* ID. The aforementioned *interchange* rule then allows to formally interpret the vertical line in the graph as a sequential composition of the packages on the left side of the line with the packages on the right side. For a graphical depiction of the identity rule and the interchange rule, see Sect. 2.2.

After applying the KEM assumption (which modifies KEM^0 to KEM^1), we contract the graph which, again, corresponds to applying the interchange rule and then removing IDs, see Fig. 2c. Via the analogous mechanism, we stretch the graph edges such that the DEM^0 and KEY appear on the right side of a vertical line, see Fig. 2d. We apply the DEM assumption and then contract the graph to obtain Fig. 2e, as desired.

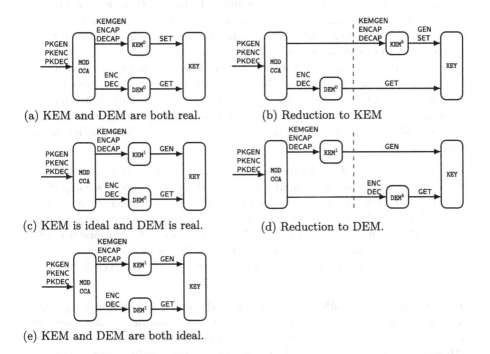

(a) KEM and DEM are both real.

(b) Reduction to KEM

(c) KEM is ideal and DEM is real.

(d) Reduction to DEM.

(e) KEM and DEM are both ideal.

Fig. 2. KEM-DEM proof.

Contents. §2 *Proof methodology.* In this section, we set up the underlying code framework and define sequential and parallel composition. We specify rules to operate on package compositions such as the aforementioned associativity, interchange and identity rules. Those rules enable the graphical interpretation as a call graph which we explain in Sect. 2.2.

§3 KEY *package composition.* We introduce keying games (such as the KEM game) and keyed games (such as the DEM game) which both contain a KEY package, introduced in this section. In a single key lemma we prove indistinguishability properties of composed keyed and keying packages. A core argument in the proof of the lemma is that the idealization of the keying game leads to only calling the GEN oracle. As keyed games rely on uniformly random keys, we model their security formally by inserting an identity package ID_{GEN} that only forwards the GEN oracle. Based on Sect. 2.2, we maintain a coherent mapping to the graphical notation in which accessible oracles are simply labels on edges.

§4 *KEM-DEM.* We provide the details of the KEM-DEM construction and proof discussed earlier. In particular, the security reduction is a straightforward application of the single key lemma.

§5 *Multi-Instance Packages and Composition.* In this section, we generalize to the multi-instance setting and carry out a multi-instance-to-single-instance composition proof. We then build on the multi-instance lemma to obtain multi-instance version of the single key lemma.

Avoiding multi-to-single instance reductions is one of the motivations of composition frameworks (see below). Hence, we see it as a sanity check that our proof methodology captures multi-to-single instance reductions. Note that also in the game-based setting, general multi-instance to single-instance reductions for classes of games have been provided before (see, e.g., Bellare, Boldyreva and Micali [5]).

§6 *Composition of forward-secure key exchange.* To showcase our key-composition techniques in the multi-instance setting, we re-prove a composition theorem for forward-secure game-based key exchange and arbitrary symmetric-key based protocols such as secure channels. This result was proven in Brzuska, Fischlin, Warinschi, and Williams [14,17] and becomes a straightforward application of the multi-instance key lemma. Our results are closely related to composition results very recently shown in the framework of CryptoVerif [13].

Limitations and Challenges. Our method considers distinguishing games for *single-stage* adversaries [42], that is, we do not consider games where the adversary is split into separate algorithms whose communications are restricted. Although suitable extensions might exist (e.g., by extending adversaries into packages that can call each other), we chose to restrict our current method to the simpler single-stage setting.

Another apparent restriction is that we encode all security properties via indistinguishability. Search problems such as strong unforgeability can also be encoded via indistinguishability. While the encoding might seem surprising when not used to it, at a second thought, an appropriate encoding of an unforgeability game also simplifies game-hopping: Imagine that we insert an abort condition whenever a message is accepted by verification that was not signed by the signer. This step corresponds to idealizing the verification of the signature scheme so that it only accepts messages that were actually signed before.[1]

A challenge that all cryptographic works on real-world protocols face is to decompose a protocol that does not inherently have a modular structure into cryptographic building blocks. As demonstrated by [11,30,32] this can be done even for archaic protocols such as TLS. Our method is influenced by the insights of the miTLS project to allow for the necessary flexibility.

Related Techniques. Our approach is inspired by important conceptual works from cryptography and programming language. In particular, we would like to acknowledge the influences of Canetti's universal composability framework (UC) [18], Renner's and Maurer's work on random systems and abstract cryptography [36,37], process algebras, such as the π-calculus of Milner, Parrow, and Walker [39], and type-based verification frameworks used, e.g., to verify the TLS protocol [10]. We now discuss these influences in detail.

Cryptographic Proof Frameworks. Composable proofs in the pen-and-paper world as pioneered by Backes, Pfitzmann, Waidner and by Canetti have a long history full of rich ideas [1,18,26,27,33,38,41,49], such as considering an environment that cannot distinguish a real protocol from an ideal variant with strong security guarantees.

Likewise, Maurer's and Renner's work on random systems, abstract cryptography and constructive cryptography [34–37] inspired and encouraged our view that a more abstract and algebraic approach to cryptographic proofs is possible and desirable. Several of our concepts have close constructive cryptography analogues: for instance, our use of associativity in this paper is similar to composition-order independence in Maurer's frameworks [35]. Sequential and parallel composition also appears in cryptographic algebras. An ambitious expression of the idea is found in [36, Sect. 6.2]. Abstract cryptography has an associativity law and neutral element for sequential composition and an interchange law for parallel composition. The same line of work [35,36] introduces a distinguishing advantage between composed systems and makes use of transformations that move part of the system being considered into and out of the distinguisher.

Our focus is not on definitions but on writing game-based security proofs. As such we are also influenced by game-based composition works, e.g., Brzuska, Fischlin, Warinschi, and Williams [17]. We aim to facilitate security proofs for full-fledged standardized protocols [19,23,28,32]. Such proofs typically involve large reductions relating a complex monolithic game to diverse cryptographic assumptions through an intricate simulation of the protocol.

---

[1] CryptoVerif [12] also encodes authentication properties as indistinguishability.

Language-Based Security and Cryptography. Algebraic reasoning is at the core of process calculi such as the π-calculus by Milner, Parrow and Walker [39]. They focus on concurrency with non-determinism, which is also adequate for symbolic reasoning about security protocols. Subsequently, probabilistic process algebras have been used to reason computationally about protocols, e.g., in the work of Mitchell, Ramanathan, Scedrov, and Teague [40] and the *computational indistinguishability logic* (CIL) of Barthe, Crespo, Lakhnech and Schmidt [3]. Packages can be seen as an improvement of CIL oracle systems, with oracle visibility and associativity corresponding to the context rules of CIL.

Monadic composition, a generalisation of function composition to effectful programs, is an central principle of functional languages such as Haskell, $F^\sharp$, and $F^\star$ [29,45,46]. Associativity is also used by Mike Rosulek in his rich undergraduate textbook draft *The Joy of Cryptography* to make the cryptographic reduction methodology accessible to undergraduate students with no background in complexity theory [44]. Our concept of packages is inspired by module systems in programming languages such as $F^\sharp$, OCaml, SML (see e.g. Tofte [47]). Our oracles similarly define a public interface for calling functions that may share private state.

Existing techniques for overcoming the crisis of rigour in provable security as formalised by Bellare and Rogaway [8] and mechanised in Easycrypt [4] have focused on the most intricate aspects of proofs. Easycrypt supports a rich module system similar to the ones found in functional programming languages [2] (including parametric modules, i.e. functors), but it has not yet been used to simplify reasoning about large reductions in standardized protocols.

The closest to our idea of package-based reductions is the modular code structure of miTLS, an cryptographically verified implementation of TLS coded in $F^\star$ [10,11,22,25]. Fournet, Kohlweiss and Strub [25] show that code-based game rewriting can be conducted on actual implementation code, one module at a time, with the rest of the program becoming the reduction for distinguishing the *ideal* from the *real* version of the module. Packages are simpler than $F^\star$ modules, with interfaces consisting just of sets of oracle names, whereas $F^\star$ provides a rich type system for specifying module interfaces and verifying their implementations.

Our method draws from both formal language techniques and pen-and-paper approaches for cryptographic proofs. We see facilitating the flow of information between the two research communities as an important contribution of our work. In this paper, we use pseudo-code, treating the concrete syntax and semantics of our language as a parameter. This simplifies our presentation and make it more accessible to the cryptographic community. Our method can be instantiated either purely as a pen-and-paper method or via using a full-fledged programming language, equipped with a formal syntax and operational semantics. The latter might also allow the development of tools for writing games and automating their proofs.

2   Proof Methodology

As discussed in the introduction, we suggest to work with *pseudo-code* instead of Turing machines as a model of computation and thus, this section will start by providing a definition of code. We then continue to define functions and function calls (to probabilistic and stateful functions), also known as oracles and oracle calls in the cryptographic literature. We will then collect several such functions (oracles) into a package, and when the package itself does not make any function calls, we call a package *closed* or a *game*. We then define sequential composition of 2 packages, where the first package calls functions (oracles) defined by the second package. Moreover, we define parallel composition which allows to take the functions defined by two packages and to take their union.

Then, we move to more advanced packages and algebraic rules that allow to implement the "moving to the right" operation that we hinted to in the introduction.

2.1   Composing Oracle Definitions

While we advocate to work with pseudo-code, we do not define a particular language, but rather *parametrize* our method by a language for writing algorithms, games, and adversaries. We specify below the properties of the syntax and semantics of any language capable of instantiating our approach. We first describe our pseudo-code and give a probabilistic semantics to whole programs, then we explain our use of functions for composing code.

Definition 1 (Pseudo-Code). *We assume given sets of values $v, \ldots$, local variables $x, y, \ldots$, expressions e, state variables a, T (uppercase denotes tables), $\ldots$, and commands c.*

Values provide support for booleans, numbers, and bitstrings. Expressions provide support for operations on them. Expressions may use local variables, but not state variables.

Commands include local-variable assignments $x \leftarrow e$, sampling from a distribution $x \leftarrow_\$ D$, state updates $T[x] \leftarrow e$, sequential compositions $c; c'$, and **return** e *for returning the value of e. We write $\mathsf{fv}(c)$ for the state variables accessed in c. We assume given default initial values for all state variables, e.g. $T \leftarrow \emptyset$.*

We write $\Pr[v \leftarrow c]$ for the probability that command c returns v. (We only consider programs that always terminate.) We assume this probability is stable under injective renamings of local variables and state variables.

For brevity, we often write commands with expressions that depend on the current state, as a shorthand for using intermediate local variables for reading the state, e.g. we write $T[x] \leftarrow T[x] + 1$ as a shorthand for $t \leftarrow T[x]; T[x] \leftarrow t + 1$.

Definition 2 (Functions). *We assume given a set of names $\mathsf{f}, \ldots$ for functions. We let O range over function definitions of the form $\mathsf{f}(x) \mapsto c$. and write $\Omega = \{\mathsf{f}_i(x_i) \mapsto c_i\}_{i=1..n}$ for a set of n function definitions with distinct function* names. We write $\mathsf{dom}(\Omega)$ for the set of names $\{f_1, \ldots, f_n\}$ defined in Ω and $\Sigma(\Omega)$ for the set of state variables accessed in their code.

We extend commands with function calls, written $y \leftarrow \mathsf{f}(e)$. We write $\mathsf{fn}(c)$ for the set of function names called in c, and similarly define $\mathsf{fn}(O)$ and $\mathsf{fn}(\Omega)$. We say that a term is closed when this set is empty.

We interpret all function calls by inlining, as follows: given the definition $\mathsf{f}(x) \mapsto c$; return e', the call $y \leftarrow \mathsf{f}(e)$ is replaced with $c; y \leftarrow e'$ after replacing x with e in the function body. We write $\mathsf{inline}(c, \Omega)$ for the code obtained by inlining all calls to the functions $f_1, \ldots f_n$ defined by Ω in the command c. Similarly, we write $\mathsf{inline}(\Omega', \Omega)$ for the set of definitions obtained by inlining all calls to functions in Ω into the code of the definitions of Ω'.

We consider function definitions up to injective renamings of their local variables.

Packages. We now introduce the general definition of *packages* as collections of oracles that subsume adversaries, games and reductions. Packages are sets of oracles Ωs defined above. Intuitively, we will treat the state variables of their oracles as private to the package, i.e., the rest of the code only get oracle access. Looking ahead to the composition of packages we endow each package with an *output* interface consisting of the oracles names that it defines and an *input* interface consisting of the oracles names that it queries.

Definition 3 (Packages). *A package* M *is a set of function definitions* Ω *(its oracles) up to injective renamings of its state variables* $\Sigma(\Omega)$.

We write $\mathsf{in}(\mathsf{M}) = \mathsf{fn}(\Omega)$ *for its* input interface *and* $\mathsf{out}(\mathsf{M}) = \mathsf{dom}(\Omega)$ *for its* output interface.

We disallow internal calls to prevent recursion. Technically, the disallowing of internal calls is captured (a) by the input interface of a package, since this input provides all oracles that are called by the oracles in Ω, and (b) by the Definition 4 of sequential composition that specifies that oracle calls are instantiated by the oracles of *another* package.

We often consider families of oracles O^Π and packages M^Π parametrized by Π, treating parameters as symbolic values in their code. We usually omit parameters and refer to oracles and packages by their name, unless context requires further clarification. In particular, we write $\mathsf{in}(\mathsf{M}^\Pi)$ only if the input interface differs for different parameters; $\mathsf{out}(\mathsf{M})$ never depends on the parameters.

Package composition. We say that M *matches* the output interface of M′ iff $\mathsf{in}(\mathsf{M}) \subseteq \mathsf{out}(\mathsf{M}')$. When composing two matching packages $\mathsf{M} \circ \mathsf{M}'$, we *inline* the code of all oracles of M′ called by oracles in M, as specified in Definition 2.

Definition 4 (Sequential Composition). *Given two packages* M *with oracles* Ω *and* M′ *with oracles* Ω' *such that* M *matches* M′ *and* $\Sigma(\Omega) \cap \Sigma(\Omega') = \emptyset$, *their sequential composition* $\mathsf{M} \circ \mathsf{M}'$ *has oracles* $\mathsf{inline}(\Omega, \Omega')$.

Thus, we have $\mathsf{out}(\mathsf{M} \circ \mathsf{M}') = \mathsf{out}(\mathsf{M})$ *and* $\mathsf{in}(\mathsf{M} \circ \mathsf{M}') = \mathsf{in}(\mathsf{M}')$.

Uniqueness. When describing a package composition, one cannot use the same package twice, e.g., it is not possible to have compositions such as $(M \circ M' \circ M)$. Note that this is a fundamental restriction, since it is unclear how to define the state of such a composition, since there would be copies of pointers to the same state (a.k.a. aliases).

Lemma 1 (Associativity). *Let* M_0, M_1, M_2 *such that* $\text{in}(M_0) \subseteq \text{out}(M_1)$ *and* $\text{in}(M_1) \subseteq \text{out}(M_2)$. *We have* $(M_0 \circ M_1) \circ M_2 = M_0 \circ (M_1 \circ M_2)$.

Proof outline. We rename the local variables and state variables of the three packages to prevent clashes, then unfold the definition of sequential compositions by inlining, and rely on the associativity of their substitutions of function code for function calls.

Identity packages. Some proofs and definitions make one or more oracles of a package unavailable to the adversary, which is captured by sequential composition with a package that forwards a subset of their oracle calls:

Definition 5 (Identity Packages). *The* identity package ID_X *for the names* X *has oracles* $\{f(x) \mapsto r \leftarrow f(x); \textbf{return } r\}_{f \in X}$.

Hence, for $X \subseteq \text{out}(M)$, the package $\text{ID}_X \circ M$ behaves as M after deleting the definitions of oracles outside X. In particular, the next lemma gives some identity compositions that do not affect a package.

Lemma 2 (Identity Rules). *For all packages* M, *we have* $M = \text{ID}_{\text{out}(M)} \circ M$ *and* $M = M \circ \text{ID}_{\text{in}(M)}$.

Proof outline. By definition of sequential composition and basic properties of substitutions, we obtain the following from $\text{ID}_{\text{out}(M)} \circ M$:
We substitute '$f(x) \mapsto c; \textbf{return } r$' in '$f(x) \mapsto r \leftarrow f(x); \textbf{return } r$' and yield '$f(x) \mapsto c; r \leftarrow r; \textbf{return } r$' which is equivalent to '$f(x) \mapsto c; \textbf{return } r$'. Analogously, for $M \circ \text{ID}_{\text{in}(M)}$:
We substitute '$f(x) \mapsto r \leftarrow f(x); \textbf{return } r$' in '$r' \leftarrow f(x)$' and yield '$r \leftarrow f(x); r' \leftarrow r$' which is equivalent to '$r' \leftarrow f(x)$'. □

We now define parallel composition, which is essentially a disjoint union operator that takes two packages and builds a new package that implements both of them in parallel. It is important to note that only the output interfaces of M and M' need to be disjoint, while they can potentially share input oracles. This feature allows for parallel composition of several packages that use the same input interface.

Definition 6 (Parallel Composition). *Given two packages* M *with oracles* Ω *and* M' *with oracles* Ω' *such that* $\text{out}(M) \cap \text{out}(M') = \emptyset$ *and* $\Sigma(\Omega) \cap \Sigma(\Omega') = \emptyset$, *their* parallel composition $\frac{M}{M'}$ *(alternatively* $(M|M')$) *has oracles* $\Omega \uplus \Omega'$. *Thus,* $\text{out}(\frac{M}{M'}) = \text{out}(M) \uplus \text{out}(M')$ *and* $\text{in}(\frac{M}{M'}) = \text{in}(M) \cup \text{in}(M')$.

(This composition may require preliminary renamings to prevent clashes between the state variables of M and M'.)

Lemma 3. *Parallel composition is commutative and associative.*

The proof of these properties directly follows from our definition of packages. Associativity enables us to write n-ary parallel compositions of packages. Next, we show that sequential composition distributes over parallel composition. (The conditions in the lemma guarantee that the statement is well defined.)

Lemma 4 (Interchange). *For all packages* M_0, M_1, M_0', M_1', *if* $\text{out}(M_0) \cap \text{out}(M_1) = \emptyset$, $\text{out}(M_0') \cap \text{out}(M_1') = \emptyset$, $\text{out}(M_0) \subseteq \text{in}(M_0')$ *and* $\text{out}(M_1) \subseteq \text{in}(M_1')$, *then*

$$\frac{M_0}{M_1} \circ \frac{M_0'}{M_1'} = \frac{M_0 \circ M_0'}{M_1 \circ M_1'}.$$

Proof outline. This equality follows from our definition, relying on the property that function-call inlining applies pointwise to each of the oracle definitions in the 3 sequential compositions above.

2.2   Graphical Representation of Package Composition

Writing fully-precise package compositions can be tedious. Recall the KEM-DEM proof of Fig. 2; the step from (a) to (b) corresponds to applying a mix of interchange and identity rules:

$$\text{CCA} \circ \left(\frac{\text{KEM}^0}{\text{DEM}^0} \circ \text{KEY} \right) = \text{CCA} \circ \left(\frac{\text{ID} \circ \text{KEM}^0}{\text{DEM}^0 \circ \text{ID}} \circ \text{KEY} \right) = \text{CCA} \circ \left(\left(\frac{\text{ID}}{\text{DEM}^0} \circ \frac{\text{KEM}^0}{\text{ID}} \right) \circ \text{KEY} \right)$$

Instead of writing such steps explicitly, we propose a graphical representation of package composition that allows us to reason about compositions "up to" applications of the interchange, identity and associativity rules.

From terms to graphs. Identity packages ID_S map to edges, one for each oracle in the set S. Other packages map to a node labelled with the package name. Each output oracle of the package maps to an incoming edge of the node, labelled with the oracle name. Similarly, input oracles map to outgoing edges.

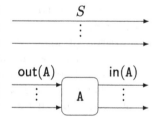

Sequential composition $A \circ B$ simply consists of merging the outgoing edges of A with the incoming edges of B with the same label. Note that in this process, some of the incoming edges of B may be dropped, i.e. A may not use all of the oracles exported by B.

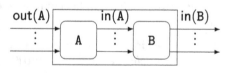

The parallel composition of A and B is simply the union of the graphs constructed from A and B. By definition of parallel composition, $\mathrm{out}(A) \cap \mathrm{out}(B) = \emptyset$, while *input* oracles may be used both by A and B. We merge shared input edges (i.e. unconnected outgoing edges) in the resulting graph to capture this sharing.

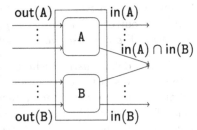

From graphs to terms. By inductive application of the above 3 rules, one can construct a graph representing any term. However, some information is lost in the process: most importantly, the order in which sequential and parallel compositions are applied. For instance, consider the left-hand side and right-hand side of the interchange rule both terms map to the same graph. This is by design, as we intend to represent terms modulo interchange. By drawing explicit boxes around parallel and sequential compositions, it is possible to ensure that a graph can be interpreted unambiguously as a term. For instance, the figure on the right shows how to depict the interchange rule on graphs with boxes.

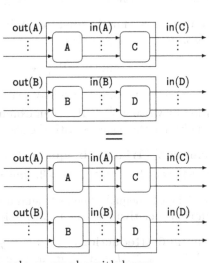

2.3   Games and Adversaries

Games. A *game* is a package with an empty input interface. We model security properties of a cryptographic scheme as indistinguishability between a *pair* of games, usually parameterized by a bit $b \in \{0, 1\}$ (which is equivalent to a single game that draws a bit and then runs one of the two games at random.).

Adversaries. An adversary $\mathcal{A}$ is a package with output interface {run} that returns a bit 0 or 1. We model the adversary as a package whose input interface is equal to the set of names of the oracles of the game that the adversary is meant to interact with.

Next, we define games and adversaries such that their composition $\mathcal{A} \circ G$ be a closed package of the form $R = \{\mathrm{run}() \mapsto c; \mathbf{return}\ g\}$.

Since Definition 1 defines our probabilistic semantics only on commands, we first extend it to such closed packages, defining $\Pr[1 \leftarrow R]$ as $\Pr[1 \leftarrow c; \mathbf{return}\ g]$. (The command $c; \mathbf{return}\ g$ is the 'top-level' code $g \leftarrow \mathrm{run}(); \mathbf{return}\ g$ after inlining the definition of run in R.)

Definition 7 (Games). *A game is a package* G *such that* $\mathrm{in}(G) = \emptyset$. *An adversary against* G *is a package* $\mathcal{A}$ *such that* $\mathrm{in}(\mathcal{A}) = \mathrm{out}(G)$ *and* $\mathrm{out}(\mathcal{A}) = \{\mathrm{run}\}$.

A game pair *consists of two games* G^0 *and* G^1 *that define the same oracles:* $\text{out}(G^0) = \text{out}(G^1)$. *Naturally, a game* G^b *with a binary parameter* b *defines a game pair. We thus use the two notions interchangeably.*

We now define distinguishing advantages. Note that we operate in the concrete security setting as it is more adequate for practice-oriented cryptography and therefore only define advantages rather than security in line with the critique of Rogaway [43], Bernstein and Lange [9]. Our ideas can be transferred analogously to the asymptotic setting.

Definition 8 (Distinguishing Advantage). *The advantage of an adversary* $\mathcal{A}$ *against a game pair* G *is*

$$\epsilon_G(\mathcal{A}) = \left| \Pr\left[1 \leftarrow \mathcal{A} \circ G^0\right] - \Pr\left[1 \leftarrow \mathcal{A} \circ G^1\right]\right|.$$

In the rest of the paper, we may refer to the advantage function ϵ_G in this definition by writing $G^0 \overset{\epsilon_G}{\approx} G^1$. As an example, we restate below the usual triangular equality for three games with the same oracles.

Lemma 5 (Triangle Inequality). *Let* F, G *and* H *be games such that* $\text{out}(F) = \text{out}(G) = \text{out}(H)$. *If* $F \overset{\epsilon_1}{\approx} G$, $G \overset{\epsilon_2}{\approx} H$, *and* $F \overset{\epsilon_3}{\approx} H$, *then* $\epsilon_3 \leq \epsilon_1 + \epsilon_2$.

The triangle inequality helps to sum up game-hops. Many game-hops will exploit simple associativity, as the following lemma illustrates.

Lemma 6 (Reduction). *Let* G *be a game pair and let* M *be a package such that* $\text{in}(M) \subseteq \text{out}(G)$. *Let* $\mathcal{A}$ *be an adversary that matches the output interface of* M, *then for both* $b \in \{0, 1\}$, *the adversary* $\mathcal{D} := \mathcal{A} \circ M$ *satisfies*

$$\Pr\left[1 \leftarrow \mathcal{A} \circ (M \circ G^b)\right] = \Pr\left[1 \leftarrow \mathcal{D} \circ G^b\right].$$

As a corollary, we obtain $\mathcal{A} \circ M \circ G^0 \overset{\epsilon(\mathcal{A})}{\approx} \mathcal{A} \circ M \circ G^1$ *for* $\epsilon(\mathcal{A}) = \epsilon_G(\mathcal{A} \circ M)$.

Proof. The proof follows by associativity of sequential composition, i.e., Lemma 1 yields $\mathcal{A} \circ (M \circ G^b) = (\mathcal{A} \circ M) \circ G^b = \mathcal{D} \circ G^b$.

3   KEY Package Composition

Many cryptographic constructions emerge as compositions of two cryptographic building blocks: The first building block generates the (symmetric) key(s) and the second building block uses the (symmetric) key(s). In the introduction, we already discussed the popular composition of key encapsulation mechanisms (KEM) with a deterministic encryption mechanism (DEM). Likewise, complex protocols such as TLS first execute a key exchange protocol to generate symmetric keys for a secure channel. In composition proofs, the keying building block and the keyed building block share the (symmetric) key(s). To capture this shared state, we introduce a key package KEY^λ that holds a single key k of length λ. (We handle multiple keys in Sect. 5.)

Definition 9 (Key Package). *For* $\lambda \in \mathbb{N}$, KEY$^\lambda$ *is the package that defines the three oracles below, i.e.,* out(KEY$^\lambda$) = {GEN, SET, GET}.

GEN()	SET(k')	GET()
assert $k = \bot$	**assert** $k = \bot$	**assert** $k \neq \bot$
$k \leftarrow_\$ \{0,1\}^\lambda$	$k \leftarrow k'$	**return** k

Hence, this package encapsulates the state variable k, initialized (once) by calling either GEN or SET, then accessed by calling GET. This usage restriction is captured using **asserts**, and all our definitions and theorems apply only to code that never violate assertions.

Definition 10 (Keying Games). *A* keying game K *is a game composed of a core keying package* CK *and the key package as follows:*

$$K^{b,\lambda} = \frac{CK^{b,\lambda}}{ID_{\{GET\}}} \circ KEY^\lambda.$$

where $b \in \{0,1\}$, in(CK$^{0,\lambda}$) = {SET}, *and* in(CK$^{1,\lambda}$) = {GEN}.

Definition 11 (Keyed Games). *A* keyed game D *is a game composed of a core keyed package* CD *and the key package as follows:*

$$D^{b,\lambda} = \frac{ID_{\{GEN\}}}{CD^{b,\lambda}} \circ KEY^\lambda.$$

where $b \in \{0,1\}$ *and* in(CD$^{b,\lambda}$) = {GET}.

Lemma 7 (Single Key). *Keying games* K *and keyed games* D *are compatible when they have the same key length* λ *and they define disjoint oracles, i.e.,* out(K)∩out(D) = ∅. *For all compatible keying and keyed games, with the notations above, we have*

$$(a) \quad \frac{CK^0}{CD^0} \circ KEY^\lambda \overset{\epsilon_a}{\approx} \frac{CK^1}{CD^1} \circ KEY^\lambda, \qquad (b) \quad \frac{CK^0}{CD^0} \circ KEY^\lambda \overset{\epsilon_b}{\approx} \frac{CK^0}{CD^1} \circ KEY^\lambda,$$

where, for all adversaries $\mathcal{A}$,

$$\epsilon_a(\mathcal{A}) \leq \epsilon_K \left(\mathcal{A} \circ \frac{ID_{out(CK)}}{CD^0} \right) + \epsilon_D \left(\mathcal{A} \circ \frac{CK^1}{ID_{out(CD)}} \right),$$

$$\epsilon_b(\mathcal{A}) \leq \epsilon_a(\mathcal{A}) + \epsilon_K \left(\mathcal{A} \circ \frac{ID_{out(CK)}}{CD^1} \right).$$

Proof. Figure 3 gives the proof outline using graphs: To show (a), we idealize the core keying package, switching from SET to GEN (left); we idealize the core keyed package (Fig. 3, right). To show (b), we also de-idealize the core keying package, switching back form GEN to SET (left).

We give a more detailed proof below, using the algebraic rules of Sect. 2 to rewrite packages in order to apply Definitions 10 and 11.

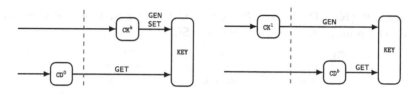

Fig. 3. Reduction to the keying game (left) and the keyed game (right).

(1) Idealizing the core keying package. The first intermediate goal is to bring the package into a shape where we can use Definition 10 to change CK^0 into CK^1. Below, for all adversaries $\mathcal{A}$, we have $\epsilon_1(\mathcal{A}) = \epsilon_K\left(\mathcal{A} \circ \frac{\text{ID}_{\text{out(CK)}}}{\text{CD}^0}\right)$.

$$\frac{\text{CK}^0}{\text{CD}^0} \circ \text{KEY}^\lambda = \frac{\text{ID}_{\text{out(CK)}}}{\text{CD}^0} \circ \frac{\text{CK}^0}{\text{ID}_{\{\text{GET}\}}} \circ \text{KEY}^\lambda \quad \text{(identity \& interchange)}$$

$$\overset{\epsilon_1}{\approx} \frac{\text{ID}_{\text{out(CK)}}}{\text{CD}^0} \circ \frac{\text{CK}^1}{\text{ID}_{\{\text{GET}\}}} \circ \text{KEY}^\lambda = \frac{\text{CK}^1}{\text{CD}^0} \circ \text{KEY}^\lambda$$

(2) Idealizing the core keyed package. As a second step, we want to use Definition 11 to move from CD^0 to CD^1 and thus need to make $\text{ID}_{\{\text{GEN}\}}$ appear. Note that we can use $\text{ID}_{\{\text{GEN}\}}$ because $\{\text{GEN}\}$ is equal to the input interface of CK^1. This was not possible before idealizing to CK^1, since $\text{in}(\text{CK}^0) = \{\text{SET}\}$. Below, for all adversaries $\mathcal{A}$, we have $\epsilon_2(\mathcal{A}) = \epsilon_D\left(\mathcal{A} \circ \frac{\text{CK}^1}{\text{ID}_{\text{out(CD)}}}\right)$.

$$\frac{\text{CK}^1}{\text{CD}^0} \circ \text{KEY}^\lambda = \frac{\text{CK}^1}{\text{ID}_{\text{out(CD)}}} \circ \frac{\text{ID}_{\{\text{GEN}\}}}{\text{CD}^0} \circ \text{KEY}^\lambda \quad \text{(identity \& interchange)}$$

$$\overset{\epsilon_2}{\approx} \frac{\text{CK}^1}{\text{ID}_{\text{out(CD)}}} \circ \frac{\text{ID}_{\{\text{GEN}\}}}{\text{CD}^1} \circ \text{KEY}^\lambda = \frac{\text{CK}^1}{\text{CD}^1} \circ \text{KEY}^\lambda$$

(3) De-idealizing the core keying package. Finally, we move back from CK^1 to CK^0, taking the inverse steps of idealizing the core keying package. We obtain $\epsilon_3(\mathcal{A}) = \epsilon_K\left(\mathcal{A} \circ \frac{\text{ID}_{\text{out(CK)}}}{\text{CD}^1}\right)$.

4   KEM-DEMs

Cramer and Shoup [20, Sect. 7] show that composing a CCA-secure key encapsulation mechanism (KEM) and a CCA-secure data encapsulation mechanism (DEM) yields a CCA-secure public-key encryption (PKE). Using the KEY package composition introduced in Sect. 3, we give a new formulation of their KEM-DEM proof.

Schemes are function definitions that do not employ state variables. We write M^β for a package calling functions of the scheme β in its parameters. Formally, for a package M with oracles Ω, M^β denotes the package with oracles $\text{inline}(\Omega, \beta)$.

We denote the set of functions defined by a PKE scheme with ciphertext expansion $clen(|m|)$ by $\zeta = \{kgen, enc, clen, dec\}$ with standard semantics. We denote the set of functions of a DEM scheme with key length λ and ciphertext expansion $clen(|m|)$ by $\theta = \{\lambda, enc, clen, dec\}$, where we recall that enc is a deterministic, one-time encryption algorithm. We prepend function names by ζ and θ for disambiguation. We denote a KEM scheme with output key length λ and encapsulation length $elen$ by $\eta = \{kgen, encap, elen, decap, \lambda\}$, where $kgen$ produces a key pair (pk, sk), $encap(pk)$ generates a symmetric key k of length $\eta.\lambda$ and a key encapsulation c of length $\eta.elen$, while $decap(sk, c)$ given sk and an encapsulation c returns a key k. For all three schemes, we consider perfect correctness. Throughout this section, we consider a single symmetric-key length λ that corresponds to the length of the symmetric key used by the DEM scheme as well as the length of the symmetric key produced by the encapsulation mechanism $\eta.encap$. We now turn to the security notions which are \$-IND-CCA security notions for all three primitives, i.e., we consider ciphertexts that are indistinguishable from random.

Definition 12 (PKE-CCA Security). *Let ζ be a PKE-scheme. We define its \$-IND-CCA advantage $\epsilon_{\mathrm{PKE-CCA}}^{\zeta}$, where $\mathrm{PKE-CCA}^{b,\zeta}$ defines the following oralces, i.e., $\mathrm{out}(\mathrm{PKE-CCA}^{\zeta}) = \{\mathrm{PKGEN}, \mathrm{PKENC}, \mathrm{PKDEC}\}$.*

PKGEN()	PKENC(m)	PKDEC(c')
assert $sk = \bot$	**assert** $pk \neq \bot$	**assert** $sk \neq \bot$
$pk, sk \leftarrow\!\!\text{\$}\; \zeta.kgen()$	**assert** $c = \bot$	**assert** $c' \neq c$
return pk	**if** $b = 0$ **then**	$m \leftarrow \zeta.dec(sk, c')$
	$\quad c \leftarrow\!\!\text{\$}\; \{0,1\}^{clen(|m|)}$	**return** m
	else	
	$\quad c \leftarrow\!\!\text{\$}\; \zeta.enc(pk, m)$	
	return c	

We model the KEM as a keying and the DEM as a keyed package. We will use the KEY^{λ} package as specified in Definition 9. Note that we additionally require that encapsulations are indistinguishable from random.

Definition 13 (KEM-CCA Security). *Let η be a KEM. We define its \$-IND-CCA advantage $\epsilon_{\mathrm{KEM-CCA}}^{\eta}$ using a keying game whose core keying package $\mathrm{KEM}^{b,\eta}$ defines the following oracles, so that $\mathrm{out}(\mathrm{KEM-CCA}^{\eta}) = \{\mathrm{KEMGEN}, \mathrm{ENCAP}, \mathrm{DECAP}, \mathrm{GET}\}$:*

KEMGEN()	ENCAP()	DECAP(c')
assert $sk = \perp$	**assert** $pk \neq \perp$	**assert** $sk \neq \perp$
$pk, sk \leftarrow_\$ \eta.kgen()$	**assert** $c = \perp$	**assert** $c' \neq c$
return pk	**if** $b = 0$ **then**	$k \leftarrow \eta.decap(sk, c')$
	$\quad k, c \leftarrow_\$ \eta.encap(pk)$	**return** k
	$\quad$ SET(k)	
	else	
	$\quad c \leftarrow_\$ \{0,1\}^{elen}$	
	$\quad$ GEN()	
	return c	

Note that the adversary queries GET to obtain the challenge key. Encoding the standard KEM notion in this way enables the following algebraic reasoning:

$$\text{KEM-CCA}^{0,\eta} = \frac{\text{KEM}^{0,\eta}}{\text{ID}_{\{\text{GET}\}}} \circ \text{KEY}^{\eta.\lambda} \overset{\epsilon^\eta_{\text{KEM-CCA}}}{\approx} \frac{\text{KEM}^{1,\eta}}{\text{ID}_{\{\text{GET}\}}} \circ \text{KEY}^{\eta.\lambda} = \text{KEM-CCA}^{1,\eta}$$

Definition 14 (DEM-CCA Security). *Let θ be a DEM. We define its $-IND-CCA$ advantage $\epsilon^\theta_{\text{DEM-CCA}}$ using a keying game with output interface* out(DEM $-$ CCA$^\theta$) = $\{\text{GEN}, \text{ENC}, \text{DEC}\}$*, where the oracles of the core keyed packages* DEM$^{b,\theta}$ *are defined as follows:*

ENC(m)	DEC(c')
assert $c = \perp$	**assert** $c \neq c'$
$k \leftarrow$ GET()	$k \leftarrow$ GET()
if $b = 0$ **then**	$m \leftarrow \theta.dec(k, c')$
$\quad c \leftarrow \theta.enc(k, m)$	**return** m
else	
$\quad c \leftarrow_\$ \{0,1\}^{clen(|m|)}$	
return c	

Note that DEM security justifies the following equational reasoning

$$\text{DEM-CCA}^{0,\theta} = \frac{\text{DEM}^{0,\theta}}{\text{ID}_{\{\text{GEN}\}}} \circ \text{KEY}^{\theta.\lambda} \overset{\epsilon^\theta_{\text{DEM-CCA}}}{\approx} \frac{\text{DEM}^{1,\theta}}{\text{ID}_{\{\text{GEN}\}}} \circ \text{KEY}^{\theta.\lambda} = \text{DEM-CCA}^{1,\theta}$$

4.1 Composition and Proof

We prove that the PKE scheme obtained by composing a KEM-CCA secure KEM and a DEM-CCA secure DEM is PKE-CCA secure.

Construction 1 (KEM-DEM Construction) *Let η be a KEM and θ be a DEM. We define the PKE scheme ζ with ciphertext expansion $\eta.elen + \theta.clen(|m|)$ as follows:*

$\zeta.kgen()$	$\zeta.enc(pk, m)$	$\zeta.dec(sk, c)$
return $\eta.gen()$	$k, c_1 \leftarrow_{\$} \eta.encap(pk)$	$c_1 \| c_2 \leftarrow c$
	$c_2 \leftarrow \theta.enc(k, m)$	$k \leftarrow \eta.decap(sk, c_1)$
	return $c_1 \| c_2$	$m \leftarrow \theta.dec(k, c_2)$
		return m

Theorem 1 (PKE Security of the KEM-DEM Construction). *Let ζ be the PKE scheme in Construction 1. For adversaries $\mathcal{A}$, we have that*

$$\epsilon_{\text{PKE-CCA}}^{\zeta}(\mathcal{A}) \leq \epsilon_{\text{KEM-CCA}}^{\eta}\left(\mathcal{A} \circ \text{MOD} - \text{CCA} \circ \frac{\text{ID}_{\text{out}(\text{KEM}^{\eta})}}{\text{DEM}^{0,\theta}}\right) +$$
$$\epsilon_{\text{DEM-CCA}}^{\theta}\left(\mathcal{A} \circ \text{MOD} - \text{CCA} \circ \frac{\text{KEM}^{1,\eta}}{\text{ID}_{\text{out}(\text{DEM}^{\theta})}}\right)$$

where the oracles of $\text{MOD} - \text{CCA}$ *are defined in Fig. 4.*

PKGEN()	PKENC(m)	PKDEC(c')
assert $pk = \bot$	**assert** $pk \neq \bot$	**assert** $pk \neq \bot$
$pk \leftarrow \text{KEMGEN}()$	**assert** $c = \bot$	**assert** $c \neq c'$
return pk	$c_1 \leftarrow \text{ENCAP}()$	$c_1' \| c_2' \leftarrow c'$
	$c_2 \leftarrow \text{ENC}(m)$	**if** $c_1' = c_1$ **then**
	$c \leftarrow c_1 \| c_2$	$m \leftarrow \text{DEC}(c_2')$
	return (c)	**else**
		$k' \leftarrow \text{DECAP}(c_1')$
		$m \leftarrow \theta.dec(k', c_2')$
		return m

Fig. 4. MOD-CCA construction.

In the extended version of this paper [15], we prove via code comparison that for $b \in \{0, 1\}$, PKE-CCA$^{b,\zeta}$ equals MOD-CCA $\circ \frac{\text{KEM}^{b,\eta}}{\text{DEM}^{b,\theta}} \circ \text{KEY}^{\lambda}$. Thus, for all adversaries $\mathcal{A}$, we can now apply Lemma 7a to the adversary $\mathcal{B} = \mathcal{A} \circ \text{MOD-CCA}$, as KEM-CCA$^{\eta}$ is a keying game, DEM-CCA$^{\theta}$ is a keyed game, and the two are compatible. Note that we do not de-idealize KEM$^{1,\eta}$ as PKE-CCA$^{1,\zeta}$ requires random ciphertexts. For all adversaries $\mathcal{B}$, we denote

$$\mathcal{B} \circ \frac{\text{KEM}^{\eta,0}}{\text{DEM}^{\theta,0}} \circ \text{KEY}^{\lambda} \overset{\epsilon(\mathcal{B})}{\approx} \mathcal{B} \circ \frac{\text{KEM}^{\eta,0}}{\text{DEM}^{\theta,1}} \circ \text{KEY}^{\lambda}.$$

and the value $\epsilon(\mathcal{B})$ is less or equal to

$$\epsilon_{\text{KEM-CCA}}^{\eta}\left(\mathcal{B} \circ \frac{\text{ID}_{\text{out}(\text{KEM}^{\eta})}}{\text{DEM}^{0,\theta}}\right) + \epsilon_{\text{DEM-CCA}}^{\theta}\left(\mathcal{B} \circ \frac{\text{KEM}^{1,\eta}}{\text{ID}_{\text{out}(\text{DEM}^{\theta})}}\right).$$

5   Multi-Instance Packages and Composition

Definition 15 (Indexed Packages). *For a command c with free names $\mathsf{fn}(c)$ we denote by c_i the command in which every function name $\mathsf{f} \in \mathsf{fn}(c)$ is replaced by a name f_i with the additional index i. For function definition $\mathsf{O} = \mathsf{f}(x) \mapsto c$, we denote by O_{i-} the definition $\mathsf{f}_i(x) \mapsto c$ and by O_i the definition $\mathsf{f}_i(x) \mapsto c_i$.*

Let D be a package with function definitions Ω. We denote by D_{i-} and D_i packages with definitions $\{\mathsf{O}_{i-} | \mathsf{O} \in \Omega\}$ and $\{\mathsf{O}_i | \mathsf{O} \in \Omega\}$ respectively. This means that $\mathsf{in}(\mathsf{D}_{i-}) = \mathsf{in}(\mathsf{D})$ and $\mathsf{in}(\mathsf{D}_i) = \{\mathsf{f}_i | \mathsf{f} \in \mathsf{in}(\mathsf{D})\}$.

Definition 16 (Multi-Instance Operator). *For a package D and $n \in \mathbb{N}$, we define $\prod_{i=1}^n \mathsf{D}_{i-} := (\mathsf{D}_{1-} | ... | \mathsf{D}_{n-})$ and $\prod_{i=1}^n \mathsf{D}_i := (\mathsf{D}_1 | ... | \mathsf{D}_n)$.*

Note that using a product sign $\prod_{i=1}^n \mathsf{D}_i$ to denote multi-instance parallel composition $(\mathsf{D}_1 | ... | \mathsf{D}_n)$ is convenient, since it allows to emphasize the multi-instance notation via a prefix which is more prominent than merely a special subscript or index, it reduces the number of brackets per expression, and it allows to avoid dots. While common in arithmetics and, notably, the π-calculus, product notation might be a bit unusual for cryptographers. Also note that including indices in oracle names assures that instances of the same package have disjoint output interfaces which is necessary for their parallel composition. The following lemma states that the multi-instance operator $\prod_{i=1}^n$ commutes with parallel composition, sequential composition and ID.

Lemma 8 (Multi-Instance Interchange). *Let M and N be packages such that M matches the output interface of N. Let P be a packages such that $\mathsf{out}(\mathsf{M})$ and $\mathsf{out}(\mathsf{P})$ are disjoint. Then, for any number n of instances, the following hold:*

$$\prod_{i=1}^n (\mathsf{M} \circ \mathsf{N})_i = \prod_{i=1}^n \mathsf{M}_i \circ \prod_{i=1}^n \mathsf{N}_i \qquad \mathsf{ID}_{\mathsf{out}(\prod_{i=1}^n \mathsf{M}_i)} = \prod_{i=1}^n (\mathsf{ID}_{\mathsf{out}(\mathsf{M})})_i$$

$$\prod_{i=1}^n \left(\frac{\mathsf{M}}{\mathsf{P}}\right)_i = \frac{\prod_{i=1}^n \mathsf{M}_i}{\prod_{i=1}^n \mathsf{P}_i} \qquad\qquad \mathsf{M}_{i-} = \mathsf{ID}_{\mathsf{out}(M),i-} \circ \mathsf{M}$$

Proof. Firstly, note that the package $\prod_{i=1}^n \mathsf{M}_i \circ \prod_{i=1}^n \mathsf{N}_i$ is well-defined, since $\prod_{i=1}^n \mathsf{M}_i$ matches the input interface of $\prod_{i=1}^n \mathsf{N}_i$ due to Definition 15. Using the interchange rule, we obtain that it is equal to $\prod_{i=1}^n (\mathsf{M} \circ \mathsf{N})_i$. Note that $\frac{\prod_{i=1}^n \mathsf{M}_i}{\prod_{i=1}^n \mathsf{P}_i}$ is well-defined due to the disjointness condition on the output interfaces. The term is equal to $\prod_{i=1}^n \left(\frac{\mathsf{M}}{\mathsf{P}}\right)_i$ by associativity of parallel composition. The last two equations follow by inspection of the ID definitions.

5.1   Multi-Instance Lemma

We introduce a multi-instance lemma that allows us to turn arbitrary games using symmetric keys into multi-instance games.

Lemma 9 (Multi-Instance). *Let* M *be a game pair with distinguishing advantage* ϵ_M. *Then for any number* n *of instances, adversaries* $\mathcal{A}$, *and reduction* $\mathcal{R}$ *that samples* $j \leftarrow_\$ \{1, \ldots, n\}$ *and runs*

$$\left(\prod_{i=1}^{j-1} M_i^0 \,\middle|\, ID_{out(M),j} - \,\middle|\, \prod_{i=j+1}^{n} M_i^1 \right)$$

we have that $MI^b = \prod_{i=1}^{n} M_i^b$ *is a game pair with* $\epsilon_{MI}(\mathcal{A}) \leq n \cdot \epsilon_M(\mathcal{A} \circ \mathcal{R})$.

In the extended version of this paper [15] we provide a systematic recipe for hybrid arguments and instantiate it for the proof of this lemma.

5.2   Multi-Instance Key Lemma

We now combine key composition and multi-instance lemmas. For this purpose, we use a multi-instance version of the following single-instance package CKEY. In contrast to the simpler KEY package, CKEY allows for corrupted keys (whence the name CKEY) and, consequently, needs to allow the symmetric-key protocol to check whether keys are honest.

Definition 17 (CKEY Package). *For* $\lambda \in \mathbb{N}$, CKEY *is the package that defines the oracles below, i.e.,* out(CKEY) = {GEN, SET, CSET, GET, HON}.

GEN()	SET(k')	CSET(k')	GET()	HON()
assert $k = \bot$	assert $k = \bot$	assert $k = \bot$	assert $k \neq \bot$	assert $h \neq \bot$
$k \leftarrow_\$ \{0,1\}^\lambda$	$k \leftarrow k'$	$k \leftarrow k'$		
$h \leftarrow 1$	$h \leftarrow 1$	$h \leftarrow 0$	**return** k	**return** h

A corruptible keying game is composed of a core keying package and the multi-instance version of CKEY$^\lambda$. The core keying package can set corrupt keys via the CSET oracle. A corruptible keyed game is single-instance but will be turned into a multi-instance game later. Its core keyed package can access the honesty status of keys via the HON oracle.

Definition 18 (Corruptible Keying Game). *A corruptible keying game* K *is composed of a core keying packages* CK *and the CKEY package as follows:*

$$K^{b,\lambda} = \frac{CK^{b,\lambda}}{\prod_{i=1}^{n} (ID_{\{GET, HON\}})_i} \circ \prod_{i=1}^{n} CKEY_i^\lambda.$$

where $n, \lambda \in \mathbb{N}$, $b \in \{0,1\}$, in($CK^{0,\lambda}$) = $\{SET_i, CSET_i\}_{i=1}^{n}$, *and* in($CK^{1,\lambda}$) = $\{GEN_i, CSET_i\}_{i=1}^{n}$.

Definition 19 (Corruptible Keyed Game). *A corruptible keyed game* D *is composed of a core keyed package* CD *and the CKEY package as follows:*

$$D^{b,\lambda} = \frac{ID_{\{GEN, CSET\}}}{CD^{b,\lambda}} \circ CKEY^\lambda.$$

where $\lambda \in \mathbb{N}$, $b \in \{0,1\}$, *and* in($CD^{0,\lambda}$) = in($CD^{1,\lambda}$) = {GET, HON}.

Lemma 10 (Multiple Keys). *Keying and keyed games* K *and* D *are compatible when they have the same key length* λ *and they define disjoint oracles* out(K) $\cap$ out($\prod_{i=1}^{n} D_i$). *For all compatible corruptible keying and keyed games, with the notation above, we have that*

$$\frac{\mathrm{CK}^0}{\prod_{i=1}^{n} \mathrm{CD}_i^0} \circ \prod_{i=1}^{n} \mathrm{CKEY}_i^\lambda \overset{\epsilon}{\approx} \frac{\mathrm{CK}^0}{\prod_{i=1}^{n} \mathrm{CD}_i^1} \circ \prod_{i=1}^{n} \mathrm{CKEY}_i^\lambda,$$

where for all adversaries $\mathcal{A}$, $\epsilon(\mathcal{A})$ *is less or equal to*

$$\epsilon_{\mathrm{K}}\left(\mathcal{A} \circ \frac{\mathrm{ID}_{\mathrm{out(CK)}}}{\prod_{i=1}^{n} \mathrm{CD}_i^0}\right) + n \cdot \epsilon_{\mathrm{D}}\left(\mathcal{A} \circ \frac{\mathrm{CK}^1}{\mathrm{ID}_{\mathrm{out}(\prod_{i=1}^{n} \mathrm{CD}_i)}} \circ \mathcal{R}\right) + \epsilon_{\mathrm{K}}\left(\mathcal{A} \circ \frac{\mathrm{ID}_{\mathrm{out(CK)}}}{\prod_{i=1}^{n} \mathrm{CD}_i^1}\right).$$

where reduction $\mathcal{R}$ *samples* $j \leftarrow_\$ \{1, \dots, n\}$ *and implements the package* $(\prod_{i=1}^{j-1} \mathtt{M}_i^0 | (\mathrm{ID}_{\mathrm{out(M)}})_{j-} | \prod_{i=j+1}^{n} \mathtt{M}_i^1)$, *where* $\mathtt{M}^b = \frac{\mathrm{ID}_{\{\mathrm{GEN},\mathrm{CSET}\}}}{\mathrm{CD}^b} \circ \mathrm{CKEY}^\lambda$.

Proof Outline. The proof proceeds analogously to the 3 steps in the proof of Lemma 7b, i.e., idealizing the corruptible keying game, then the corruptible keyed game and then de-idealizing the corruptible keying game. For the algebraic proof steps, we use the multi-instance variants of the identity rule and the interchange rule, as given in Lemma 8. We defer the details of the proof to the extended version [15] and here only include the multi-instance to single instance reduction involved in the idealization of the corruptible keyed game.

Multi-instance Lemma. We invoke Multi-instance Lemma 9 on game pair M with $\mathtt{M}^b = \frac{\mathrm{ID}_{\{\mathrm{GEN},\mathrm{CSET}\}}}{\mathrm{CD}^b} \circ \mathrm{CKEY}^\lambda$. By applying Lemma 9, we obtain that for all adversaries $\mathcal{B}$, we have

$$\epsilon_{\mathrm{MI}}(\mathcal{B}) \leq n \cdot \epsilon_{\mathrm{D}}(\mathcal{B} \circ \mathcal{R}), \tag{1}$$

where $\mathrm{MI}^b = \prod_{i=1}^{n} \mathtt{M}_i^b$ and reduction $\mathcal{R}$ samples $j \leftarrow_\$ \{1, \dots, n\}$ and implements the package $(\prod_{i=1}^{j-1} \mathtt{M}_i^0 | (\mathrm{ID}_{\mathrm{out(M)}})_{j-} | \prod_{i=j+1}^{n} \mathtt{M}_i^1)$.

6 Composition of Forward-Secure Key Exchange

We here give a short definition of authenticated key exchange (AKE) protocols with forward security based on the definition of forward security by Bellare, Rogaway and Pointcheval [6] adapted from password authentication to the setting with asymmetric long-term keys. Moreover, unlike [6], we do not encode security against passive adversaries via an Execute query but rather via require the existence of an origin-session, as suggested by Cremers and Feltz [21]. Brzuska, Fischlin, Warinschi and Williams [17] essentially use the same security definiting, except that they did not encode passivity and used session identifiers instead of partner functions. We explain our definitional choices at the end of this section.

Definition 20 (Key Exchange Protocol). *A key exchange protocol π consists of a key generation function $\pi.kgen$ and a protocol function $\pi.run$. $\pi.kgen$ returns a pair of keys, i.e., $(sk, pk) \leftarrow_\$ \pi.kgen$. $\pi.run$ takes as input a state and an incoming message and returns a state and an outgoing message, i.e., $(state', m') \leftarrow_\$ \pi.run(state, m)$.*

Each party holds several sessions and the function $\pi.run$ is executed locally on the *session* state. We use indices i for sessions and indices u, v for parties. For the ith session of party u, we denote the state by $\Pi[u, i].state$. The state contains at least the following variables. For a variable a, we denote by $\Pi[u, i].a$ the variable a stored in $\Pi[u, i].state$.

- (pk, sk): the party's own public-key and corresponding private key
- $peer$: the public-key of the intended peer for the session
- $role$: determines whether the session runs as an initiator or responder
- α: protocol state that is either *running* or *accepted*.
- k: the symmetric session key derived by the session

Upon initialization of each session, the session state is initialized with pair (pk, sk), the public-key $peer$ of the intended peer of a session, a value $role \in \{I, R\}$, $\alpha = running$ and $k = \bot$. The first three variables cannot be changed. The variables α and k can be set only once. We require that

$$\Pi[u, i].\alpha = accepted \implies \Pi[u, i].k \neq \bot.$$

The game that we will define soon will run $(state', m') \leftarrow_\$ \pi.run(state, \bot)$ on the initial state $state$ and an empty message $\bot$. For initiator roles, this first run returns $m' \neq \bot$, and for responder roles, it outputs $m' = \bot$.

Protocol correctness. For all pairs of sessions which are initialized with (pk_I, sk_I), pk_R, $role = I$, $\alpha = running$ and $k = \bot$ for one session, and (pk_R, sk_R), pk_I, $role = R$, $\alpha = running$ and $k = \bot$ for the other session, the following holds: When the messages produced by $\pi.run$ are faithfully transmitted to the other session, then eventually, both sessions have $\alpha = accepted$ and hold the same key $k \neq \bot$.

Partnering. As a partnering mechanism, we use sound partnering functions, one of the partnering mechanisms suggested by Bellare and Rogaway [7]. Discussing the specifics, advantages and disadvantages of partnering mechanisms is beyond the scope of this work, we provide a short discussion as well as a definition and the soundness requirement for partner functions in the extended version of this paper 15. For the sake of the AKE definition presented in this section, the reader may think of the partnering function $f(u, i)$ as indicating the (first) session (v, j) which derived the same key as (u, i), has a different role than (u, i), and is the intended peer of (u, i). On accepted sessions, it is a symmetric function, thus partners of sessions, if they exist, are unique.

Session key handles. Upon acceptance the SEND oracle returns the index of the CKEY package from which the session key can be retrieved using GET. This index is an administrative identifier that is set when the first of two partnered sessions accept. The second accepting session is then assigned the same identifier as its partner session.

Definition 21 (IND-AKE Security). *For a key exchange protocol $\pi = (kgen, run)$, a symmetric, monotonic, sound partnering function f, and a number of instances $n \in \mathbb{N}$, we define IND-AKE advantage $\epsilon_{IND-AKE}^{\pi,f,n}$ using*

NEWSESSION(u, i, r, v)

---

assert $PK[u] \neq \bot$, $PK[v] \neq \bot$, $\Pi[u,i] = \bot$

$\Pi[u,i] \leftarrow ($

    $(pk, sk) \leftarrow (PK[u], SK[u])$,

    $peer \leftarrow v$,

    $role \leftarrow r$,

    $\alpha \leftarrow running$,

    $k \leftarrow \bot)$

$(\Pi[u,i], m) \leftarrow\!\!\$\ \pi.run(\Pi[u,i], \bot)$

return m

SEND(u, i, m)

---

assert $\Pi[u,i].\alpha = running$

$(\Pi[u,i], m') \leftarrow\!\!\$\ \pi.run(\Pi[u,i], m)$

if $\Pi[u,i].\alpha \neq accepted$ **then**

    return $(m', \bot)$.

if $\Pi[f(u,i)].\alpha = accepted$ **then**

    return $(m', ID[f(u,i)])$

$ID[u,i] \leftarrow cntr$

if $H[\Pi[u,i].peer] = 1 \vee f(u,i) \neq \bot$ **then**

    if $b = 0$ **then**

        SET$_{cntr}(\Pi[u,i].k)$

    else

        GEN$_{cntr}()$

else

    CSET$_{cntr}(\Pi[u,i].k)$

$cntr \leftarrow cntr + 1$

return $(m', ID[u,i])$

NEWPARTY(u)

---

assert $PK[u] = \bot$

$(SK[u], PK[u]) \leftarrow\!\!\$\ \pi.kgen$

$H[u] \leftarrow 1$

return $PK[u]$

CORRUPT(u)

$H[u] \leftarrow 0$

return $SK[u]$

Fig. 5. Oracles of the core keying package AKE. *cntr* is initialized to 0.

a keying game IND − AKE$^{\pi,f,n}$ *with corruptible keying package* AKE$^{b,\pi,f}$ *whose oracles are defined in Fig. 5 yielding output interface* out(IND − AKE$^{\pi,f,n}$) = {NEWPARTY, NEWSESSION, SEND, CORRUPT, GET}.

Theorem 2 (BR-Secure Key Exchange is Composable). *Let* π *be a key exchange protocol with partnering function* f *such that for* $n, \lambda \in \mathbb{N}$, *their IND-AKE advantage is* $\epsilon_{\mathrm{IND-AKE}}^{\pi,f,n}$. *Let* D *be a corruptible keyed game that is compatible with the corruptible keying game* IND − AKE$^{\pi,f,n}$. *Then it holds that*

$$\frac{\mathrm{AKE}^{0,\pi,f}}{\prod_{i=1}^{n} \mathrm{CD}_i^0} \circ \prod_{i=1}^{n} \mathrm{CKEY}_i^\lambda \overset{\epsilon_{\mathrm{BR}}}{\approx} \frac{\mathrm{AKE}^{0,\pi,f}}{\prod_{i=1}^{n} \mathrm{CD}_i^1} \circ \prod_{i=1}^{n} \mathrm{CKEY}_i^\lambda,$$

where

$$\epsilon_{\mathrm{BR}}(\mathcal{A}) \leq \epsilon_{\mathrm{IND-AKE}}^{\pi,f,n}\left(\mathcal{A} \circ \frac{\mathrm{ID}_{\mathrm{out(AKE)}}}{\prod_{i=1}^{n} \mathrm{CD}_i^0}\right) + n \cdot \epsilon_{\mathrm{CD}}\left(\mathcal{A} \circ \frac{\mathrm{AKE}^{1,\pi,f}}{\mathrm{ID}_{\mathrm{out}(\prod_{i=1}^{n} \mathrm{CD}_i)}} \circ \mathcal{R}\right)$$

$$+ \epsilon_{\mathrm{IND-AKE}}^{\pi,f,n}\left(\mathcal{A} \circ \frac{\mathrm{ID}_{\mathrm{out(AKE)}}}{\prod_{i=1}^{n} \mathrm{CD}_i^1}\right),$$

and where reduction $\mathcal{R}$ *samples* $j \leftarrow_\$ \{1, \ldots, n\}$ *and implements the package* $\left(\prod_{i=1}^{j-1} \mathrm{M}_i^0 \,\middle|\, (\mathrm{ID}_{\mathrm{out(M)}})_{j-} \,\middle|\, \prod_{i=j+1}^{n} \mathrm{M}_i^1\right)$, *where* $\mathrm{M}^b = \frac{\mathrm{ID}_{\{\mathrm{GEN,CSET}\}}}{\mathrm{CD}^0} \circ \mathrm{CKEY}^\lambda$.

Proof. We observe that Theorem 2 is a direct application of the Multiple Key Lemma 10. Firstly, AKE is a corruptible core keying package as we have that in(AKE$^{0,\pi,f}$) = {SET, CSET} and in(AKE$^{1,\pi,f}$) = {GEN, CSET}. Also, by definition, D is a corruptible keyed game that is compatible with the corruptible keying game IND−AKE$^{\pi,f,n}$.

Discussion of definitional choices. Forward secrecy usually requires a notion of time that cryptographic games are not naturally endowed with and that we have no tools to handle in hand-written proofs. In the miTLS work and also in our notation of key exchange security, instead, it is decided *upon acceptance* whether a session shall be idealized or not. The advantage is that one can check *in the moment of acceptance* whether the preconditions for freshness are satisfied, and this check does not require a notion of time. In our encoding the CKEY package then stores either a real or a random key, and when the partner of the session accepts, the partner session inherits these idealization or non-idealization properties. A downside of this encoding is that it is only suitable for protocols with explicit entity authentication (See, e.g., Fischlin, Günther, Schmidt and Warinschi [24]), as in those, the first accepting session is already idealized. In particular, our model does not capture two-flow protocols such as HMQV [31].

Using partner functions instead of session identifiers or key partnering has the advantage that the *at most* condition of Match security defined by Brzuska, Fischlin, Smart, Warinschi and Williams [16] holds syntactically. Thus, one does not need to make probabilistic statements that are external to the games. Note that we made another simplification to the model: Currently, the CKEY module and thus CD does not receive information about the timing of acceptance. This can be integrated at the cost of a more complex CKEY module.

Acknowledgements. We are deeply indebted to Cas Cremers for extensive feedback on an early draft of our article. We are grateful to Simon Peyton Jones for pointing out the associativity of Monadic composition as a generalization of function composition to effectful programs. We thank Giorgia Azzurra Marson and Hoeteck Wee for feedback on the presentation of our IND-CPA toy example in the introduction. We thank Martijn Stam for suggesting to use KEM-DEM composition as one of our application cases. We are grateful to Håkon Jacobsen for feedback on our key exchange definition. We thank Ueli Maurer for an inspiring and helpful discussion on abstraction. We thank Sabine Oechsner, Frieder Steinmetz, Bogdan Warinschi, Jan Winkelmann, and Santiago Zanella-Béguelin for helpful suggestions and inspiration.

Chris Brzuska is grateful to NXP for the support of his previously held chair of IT Security Analysis at TU Hamburg. Much of the research was done while the first author was at Microsoft Research Cambridge and during internships and research visits supported by Microsoft and the EU COST framework. In particular, this work was supported by an STSM Grant from COST Action IC1306 "Cryptography for Secure Digital Interaction". This work was supported by Microsoft Research through its PhD Scholarship Programme. Markulf Kohlweiss is grateful for a fellowship from IOHK.

References

1. Backes, M., Pfitzmann, B., Waidner, M.: A general composition theorem for secure reactive systems. In: Naor, M. (ed.) TCC 2004. LNCS, vol. 2951, pp. 336–354. Springer, Heidelberg (2004). https://doi.org/10.1007/978-3-540-24638-1_19
2. Barthe, G., Crespo, J.M., Lakhnech, Y., Schmidt, B.: Mind the gap: modular machine-checked proofs of one-round key exchange protocols. In: Oswald, E., Fischlin, M. (eds.) EUROCRYPT 2015. LNCS, vol. 9057, pp. 689–718. Springer, Heidelberg (2015). https://doi.org/10.1007/978-3-662-46803-6_23
3. Barthe, G., Daubignard, M., Kapron, B.M., Lakhnech, Y.: Computational indistinguishability logic. In: ACM CCS, pp. 375–386 (2010)
4. Barthe, G., Grégoire, B., Heraud, S., Béguelin, S.Z.: Computer-aided security proofs for the working cryptographer. In: Rogaway, P. (ed.) CRYPTO 2011. LNCS, vol. 6841, pp. 71–90. Springer, Heidelberg (2011). https://doi.org/10.1007/978-3-642-22792-9_5
5. Bellare, M., Boldyreva, A., Micali, S.: Public-key encryption in a multi-user setting: security proofs and improvements. In: Preneel, B. (ed.) EUROCRYPT 2000. LNCS, vol. 1807, pp. 259–274. Springer, Heidelberg (2000). https://doi.org/10.1007/3-540-45539-6_18
6. Bellare, M., Pointcheval, D., Rogaway, P.: Authenticated key exchange secure against dictionary attacks. In: Preneel, B. (ed.) EUROCRYPT 2000. LNCS, vol. 1807, pp. 139–155. Springer, Heidelberg (2000). https://doi.org/10.1007/3-540-45539-6_11
7. Bellare, M., Rogaway, P.: Provably secure session key distribution: the three party case. In: STOC (1995)
8. Bellare, M., Rogaway, P.: The security of triple encryption and a framework for code-based game-playing proofs. In: Vaudenay, S. (ed.) EUROCRYPT 2006. LNCS, vol. 4004, pp. 409–426. Springer, Heidelberg (2006). https://doi.org/10.1007/11761679_25

9. Bernstein, D.J., Lange, T.: Non-uniform cracks in the concrete: the power of free precomputation. In: Sako, K., Sarkar, P. (eds.) ASIACRYPT 2013. LNCS, vol. 8270, pp. 321–340. Springer, Heidelberg (2013). https://doi.org/10.1007/978-3-642-42045-0_17

10. Bhargavan, K., Fournet, C., Kohlweiss, M., Pironti, A., Strub, P.-Y.: Implementing TLS with verified cryptographic security. In: Security and Privacy (2013)

11. Bhargavan, K., Fournet, C., Kohlweiss, M., Pironti, A., Strub, P.-Y., Zanella-Béguelin, S.: Proving the TLS handshake secure (As It Is). In: Garay, J.A., Gennaro, R. (eds.) CRYPTO 2014. LNCS, vol. 8617, pp. 235–255. Springer, Heidelberg (2014). https://doi.org/10.1007/978-3-662-44381-1_14

12. Blanchet, B.: A computationally sound mechanized prover for security protocols. IEEE Trans. Dependable Sec. Comput. 5(4), 193–207 (2008)

13. Blanchet, B.: Composition theorems for CryptoVerif and application to TLS 1.3. In: 31st IEEE Computer Security Foundations Symposium, CSF 2018, 9–12 July 2018, Oxford, United Kingdom, pp. 16–30 (2018)

14. Brzuska, C.: On the foundations of key exchange. Ph.D. thesis, Darmstadt University of Technology, Germany (2013)

15. Brzuska, C., Delignat-Lavaud, A., Fournet, C., Kohbrok, K., Kohlweiss, M.: State separation for code-based game-playing proofs. Cryptology ePrint Archive, Report 2018/306 (2018). http://eprint.iacr.org/2018/306

16. Brzuska, C., Fischlin, M., Smart, N.P., Warinschi, B., Williams, S.C.: Less is more: relaxed yet composable security notions for key exchange. Int. J. Inf. Sec. 12(4), 267–297 (2013)

17. Brzuska, C., Fischlin, M., Warinschi, B., Williams, S.C.: Composability of Bellare-Rogaway key exchange protocols. In: ACM CCS (2011)

18. Canetti, R.: Universally composable security: a new paradigm for cryptographic protocols. In: FOCS (2001)

19. Cohn-Gordon, K., Cremers, C.J.F., Dowling, B., Garratt, L., Stebila, D.: A formal security analysis of the signal messaging protocol. In: EuroS&P 2017 (2017)

20. Cramer, R., Shoup, V.: Design and analysis of practical public-key encryption schemes secure against adaptive chosen ciphertext attack. SIAM J. Comput. 33, 167–226 (2003)

21. Cremers, C.J.F., Feltz, M.: Beyond eCK: perfect forward secrecy under actor compromise and ephemeral-key reveal. Des. Codes Cryptography 74(1), 183–218 (2015)

22. Delignat-Lavaud, A., et al.: Implementing and proving the TLS 1.3 record layer. In: Security and Privacy (2017)

23. Dowling, B., Fischlin, M., Günther, F., Stebila, D.: A cryptographic analysis of the TLS 1.3 handshake protocol candidates. In: ACM CCS (2015)

24. Fischlin, M., Günther, F., Schmidt, B., Warinschi, B.: Key confirmation in key exchange: a formal treatment and implications for TLS 1.3. In: Security and Privacy (2016)

25. Fournet, C., Kohlweiss, M., Strub, P.-Y.: Modular code-based cryptographic verification. In: ACM CCS (2011)

26. Hofheinz, D., Shoup, V.: GNUC: a new universal composability framework. Cryptology ePrint Archive, Report 2011/303 (2011). http://eprint.iacr.org/2011/303

27. Hofheinz, D., Shoup, V.: GNUC: a new universal composability framework. J. Cryptol. 28(3), 423–508 (2015)

28. Jager, T., Kohlar, F., Schäge, S., Schwenk, J.: On the security of TLS-DHE in the standard model. In: Safavi-Naini, R., Canetti, R. (eds.) CRYPTO 2012. LNCS, vol. 7417, pp. 273–293. Springer, Heidelberg (2012). https://doi.org/10.1007/978-3-642-32009-5_17

29. Jones, S.P.: Haskell 98 language and libraries: the revised report (2003)

30. Kohlweiss, M., Maurer, U., Onete, C., Tackmann, B., Venturi, D.: (De-)Constructing TLS 1.3. In: Biryukov, A., Goyal, V. (eds.) INDOCRYPT 2015. LNCS, vol. 9462, pp. 85–102. Springer, Cham (2015). https://doi.org/10.1007/978-3-319-26617-6_5

31. Krawczyk, H.: HMQV: a high-performance secure Diffie-Hellman protocol. In: Shoup, V. (ed.) CRYPTO 2005. LNCS, vol. 3621, pp. 546–566. Springer, Heidelberg (2005). https://doi.org/10.1007/11535218_33

32. Krawczyk, H., Paterson, K.G., Wee, H.: On the security of the TLS protocol: a systematic analysis. In: Canetti, R., Garay, J.A. (eds.) CRYPTO 2013. LNCS, vol. 8042, pp. 429–448. Springer, Heidelberg (2013). https://doi.org/10.1007/978-3-642-40041-4_24

33. Kuesters, R., Tuengerthal, M.: The IITM model: a simple and expressive model for universal composability. Cryptology ePrint Archive 2013/025 (2013)

34. Maurer, U.: Constructive cryptography - a primer (invited paper). In: FC (2010)

35. Maurer, U.: Constructive cryptography - a new paradigm for security definitions and proofs. In: TOSCA (2011)

36. Maurer, U., Renner, R.: Abstract cryptography. In: ITCS (2011)

37. Maurer, U.: Indistinguishability of random systems. In: Knudsen, L.R. (ed.) EUROCRYPT 2002. LNCS, vol. 2332, pp. 110–132. Springer, Heidelberg (2002). https://doi.org/10.1007/3-540-46035-7_8

38. Micciancio, D., Tessaro, S.: An equational approach to secure multi-party computation. In: Innovations in Theoretical Computer Science, ITCS (2013)

39. Milner, R., Parrow, J., Walker, D.: A calculus of mobile processes. I. Inf. Comput. **100**(1) (1992)

40. Mitchell, J.C., Ramanathan, A., Scedrov, A., Teague, V.: A probabilistic polynomial-time process calculus for the analysis of cryptographic protocols. Theor. Comput. Sci. **353**(1–3) (2006)

41. Müller-Quade, J., Unruh, D.: Long-term security and universal composability. In: Vadhan, S.P. (ed.) TCC 2007. LNCS, vol. 4392, pp. 41–60. Springer, Heidelberg (2007). https://doi.org/10.1007/978-3-540-70936-7_3

42. Ristenpart, T., Shacham, H., Shrimpton, T.: Careful with composition: limitations of the indifferentiability framework. In: Paterson, K.G. (ed.) EUROCRYPT 2011. LNCS, vol. 6632, pp. 487–506. Springer, Heidelberg (2011). https://doi.org/10.1007/978-3-642-20465-4_27

43. Rogaway, P.: Formalizing human ignorance. In: Nguyen, P.Q. (ed.) VIETCRYPT 2006. LNCS, vol. 4341, pp. 211–228. Springer, Heidelberg (2006). https://doi.org/10.1007/11958239_14

44. Rosulek, M.: The joy of cryptography. Online Draft (2018). http://web.engr.oregonstate.edu/~rosulekm/crypto/

45. Swamy, N., Hricu, C., Keller, C., Rastogi, A., Delignat-Lavaud, A., Forest, S., Bhargavan, K., Fournet, C., Strub, P.-Y., Kohlweiss, M., Zinzindohoue, J.-K., Zanella-Béguelin, S.: Dependent types and multi-monadic effects in F*. In: POPL (2016)

46. Syme, D., Granicz, A., Cisternino, A.: Expert F# 3.0. Springer, Heidelberg (2012). https://doi.org/10.1007/978-1-4302-4651-0

47. Tofte, M.: Essentials of standard ML modules. In: Launchbury, J., Meijer, E., Sheard, T. (eds.) AFP 1996. LNCS, vol. 1129, pp. 208–229. Springer, Heidelberg (1996). https://doi.org/10.1007/3-540-61628-4_8

48. van Leeuwen, J., Wiedermann, J.: Beyond the turing limit: evolving interactive systems. In: Pacholski, L., Ružička, P. (eds.) SOFSEM 2001. LNCS, vol. 2234, pp. 90–109. Springer, Heidelberg (2001). https://doi.org/10.1007/3-540-45627-9_8

49. Wikström, D.: Simplified universal composability framework. In: Kushilevitz, E., Malkin, T. (eds.) TCC 2016. LNCS, vol. 9562, pp. 566–595. Springer, Heidelberg (2016). https://doi.org/10.1007/978-3-662-49096-9_24

Security of the Blockchain Against Long Delay Attack

Puwen Wei[1(✉)], Quan Yuan[1(✉)], and Yuliang Zheng[2]

[1] Key Laboratory of Cryptologic Technology and Information Security,
Ministry of Education, Shandong University, Jinan, China
pwei@sdu.edu.cn, yuanquan_sdu@mail.sdu.edu.cn
[2] University of Alabama at Birmingham, Birmingham, USA
yzheng@uab.edu

Abstract. The consensus protocol underlying Bitcoin (the blockchain) works remarkably well in practice. However proving its security in a formal setting has been an elusive goal. A recent analytical result by Pass, Seeman and shelat indicates that an idealized blockchain is indeed secure against attacks in an asynchronous network where messages are maliciously delayed by at most $\Delta \ll 1/np$, with n being the number of miners and p the mining hardness. This paper improves upon the result by showing that if appropriate inconsistency tolerance is allowed the blockchain can withstand even more powerful external attacks in the honest miner setting. Specifically we prove that the blockchain is secure against long delay attacks with $\Delta \geq 1/np$ in an asynchronous network.

Keywords: Bitcoin · Blockchain · Delay · Random oracle

1 Introduction

Bitcoin introduced by Nakamoto [19] is the first cryptocurrency that allows a ledger to be maintained by the public in a decentralized manner. It has a number of attractive properties including decentralization and pseudonymity. At the core of Bitcoin is a consensus protocol, called the blockchain. The blockchain is a chain-structured ledger maintained by all the participants (or miners), where records (or blocks) can only be added by the miners to the end of the chain.

A key idea of Nakamoto's blockchain protocol to achieve consensus among distributed miners is the use of proof of work (POW), which requires the miners to solve a "cryptographic puzzle". Advantages of POW are two folds. First, the "cryptographic puzzle" makes it more difficult for an adversary to modify the block. Second, POW helps distributed miners to synchronize in a permissionless setting. While having low efficiency and high power consumption, the blockchain protocol based on POW is still the most successful one that gains peoples acceptance wildly in practice. The main concern over the blockchain protocol based on POW is security, which has not been proven formally until Garay, Kiayias, and Leonardas [10] provide a rigorous analysis of the blockchain protocol. They

T. Peyrin and S. Galbraith (Eds.): ASIACRYPT 2018, LNCS 11274, pp. 250–275, 2018.
https://doi.org/10.1007/978-3-030-03332-3_10

model the execution of the blockchain protocol by allowing the adversary to control a concrete percentage of computing power and also to interfere with communication among miners, whereby proving that two basic properties, which are common prefix and chain quality, hold for a blockchain built on POW. Considering the effect of delay, Pass, Seeman and shelat [22] prove the security of the blockchain protocol in an asynchronous network with a-priori bounded delay Δ, where the adversary can delay any message with at most Δ rounds. The security analysis in [22] holds for a relatively small delay only. Specifically the delay Δ should be significantly smaller than $1/np$, that is $\Delta \ll 1/np$, where n and p denote the number of miners and the mining hardness, respectively.

Networks delay is considered to be one of the most important threats to the security of a blockchain. As shown in [6], long delays lead to increased probabilities for forking, which may break the common prefix property. Pass, Seeman and shelat demonstrate a simple attack in a fully asynchronous setting where the adversary is allowed to schedule message delivery with a long delay relative to the mining hardness. What is worse, such attacks could be deployed even when all miners are honest, which means that the adversary does not need any hashing power [10].

In the real world, however, long delays, say $\Delta \geq 1/np$, could be caused not only by message propagation over a "bad" asynchronous network but also by malicious attacks. Instead of attempting to corrupt a sizable fraction of miners, it would be much easier for the adversary to disrupt communications among miners. Furthermore, it is also unpractical to require all the miners' chains to be consistent with the "main chain" due to the long delay.

In practice the adversary cannot delay messages successfully all the time. Consider the eclipse attack [14] that allow an adversary to control 32 IP addresses to monopolize all connections to and from a target bitcoin node with 85% probability. If the attack fails or the adversary loses the ability to intercept messages, blocks will be diffused to other miners at an exponentially fast rate. This naturally brings up a interesting question, that is

Is the blockchain protocol based on POW still secure in a real world asynchronous network, where long delay relative to the mining hardness, say $\Delta \geq 1/np$, is allowed?

Our contribution. In this paper, we focus on the effect of long delay, especially $\Delta \geq 1/np$, and give results that support a positive answer to the above question. Specifically, we propose a simplified model for the blockchain protocol based on POW, which captures an adversary's ability to deliver messages maliciously in the real world. We extend the definitions of chain growth and common prefix [10,11,22] to allow fractions of miners' chains to be inconsistent with the main chain. By analyzing the evolution of the main chain in a more subtle way, we prove that the common prefix property and the chain growth property still hold in our model. In addition, to illustrate the threat of long delay attack in our model, we present a concrete attack in which an adversary without any hash power may threaten the common prefix property of a blockchain protocol with certain parameters.

There are a number of subtle differences between our model and previous research in [10,11,22]. A detailed discussion follows.

- Long delay attack: In our model, the upper bound of delay can be large, say $\Delta \geq 1/np$, and the adversary can delay a message with probability $\alpha \in (0, 1]$, meaning that the adversary may not always disrupt communications successfully in practice. Previous works consider $\Delta \ll 1/np$ or $\Delta = 1$ and the adversary can always delay any message. Hence, our model is more general in capturing the adversary's ability to deliver messages maliciously.
- Common prefix for majority: We relax the requirements of common prefix and chain growth so that certain fractions of miners' chains are allowed to be inconsistent with the common prefix of the main chain. Previous definitions of common prefix require all the miners' chains be consistent with the common prefix of the main chain, which is a special case of our definition. We emphasize that such inconsistency tolerance is not only crucial to our proof but also necessary for the blockchain protocol to work in practice.
- Honest miners: Since we only focus on the effect of delay, we assume all the miners are honest. That is, all the miners follow the protocol honestly and the adversary neither corrupts any miners nor possesses any hash power. Hence, we only need to consider the common prefix property and the chain growth property. Previous works consider adversaries which can collect a fraction of the total hash power by means of corrupting miners and thus analyze chain quality. Additionally we impose restrictions on the miners' behavior: two consecutive blocks cannot be mined by the same miner. This restriction is reasonable in our honest miner setting, as in practice is unlikely that two consecutive blocks are mined by the same miner[1], especially when n is large whereas p is small.

In a large-scale blockchain protocol, it is hard for the adversary to collect enough computational power to mount an effective attack, where at least $1/3$ computational power of all miners is usually required. Therefore, we ignore the influence of the hash power of an adversary and instead focus on attacks by disrupting communications.

Main techniques. Informally, the common prefix property states that, in addition to the last T blocks, all the miners' chains should have the same prefix. In order to prove the common prefix property, [22] shows that there are enough "convergence opportunities" for the miners to synchronize the same chain, where the "convergence opportunities" depend on consecutive Δ rounds of "silence". Here, Δ rounds of "silence" means no honest miners mines a block during these Δ rounds. If $\Delta \ll 1/np$, it is likely that no block is mined during Δ rounds. However, the challenge is that, if $\Delta \geq 1/np$, at least one block is expected to be mined during those rounds, which will ruin the "convergence opportunities". So previous proof techniques cannot be applied when $\Delta \geq 1/np$. To solve this problem, we introduce an inconsistency tolerance parameter λ, which is inspired

---

[1] not the same mining pool.

by the fact that the common prefix property in the real world holds only for the majority miners. Therefore, we redefine the properties of chain growth rate and common prefix using $\lambda \in (\frac{1}{2}, 1]$, which captures to what extent the common prefix property holds. Our definitions are more general and allow us to exclude the "bad" miners during Δ rounds of silence. Furthermore, we introduce a powerful tool called $\mathsf{Tree_{MC}}$ to record the state of the main chains. Unlike the $\mathcal{F}_{tree}$ oracle in [22] which stores all the chains during the execution of the blockchain protocol, our $\mathsf{Tree_{MC}}$ only records the state of the main chain at the current round, which can capture the evolution of main chains in a subtle manner. Then, we show the relation between $\mathsf{Tree_{MC}}$ and the view of the real execution of blockchain protocol. Due to the good properties of $\mathsf{Tree_{MC}}$, we only need to focus on the analysis of $\mathsf{Tree_{MC}}$ instead of the original block chain protocol, which greatly simplified the analysis and security proof.

Related Work. Since the introduction of Bitcoin, a number of cryptocurrency, e.g., Litecoin, Zerocash [2] and Ethereum, have appeared, most of which are based on the idea of Bitcoin. Meanwhile, a series of works [3,6,8,9,12,15,21,23, 26–31] analyze the security of Bitcoin under different attack scenarios and investigate the conditions under which Bitcoin achieves a game-theoretic equilibrium. Eyal and Sirer [8] propose an attack strategy called "selfish mining", where the adversary only requires about 1/3 of the total mining power. Miller and LaViola [18] show the connection between bitcoin and probabilistic Byzantine agreement protocols. Heilman et al. [14] present eclipse attacks which allow an adversary controlling a sufficient number of IP addresses to "eclipse" a bitcoin node. As mentioned in [14], the attacker can eclipse a fraction of miners and launch N-confirmation double spending attacks without any mining power. In fact, such attacks can be extended to attacks on common prefix. For instance, the attacker can eclipse a fraction of miners in advance and launch the long delay attacks described in Sect. 7. Notice that the target block which the attacker intends to delay may be not mined by the eclipsed miners. In other words, a block can be delayed with some probability, which is the scenario captured by our model. Sompolinsky and Zohar [29] show that the bitcoin protocol with high throughput is more susceptible to double-spend attacks. In order to solve the above problem, [29] presents an algorithm called GHOST, which chooses the main chain by the heaviest subtree instead of the longest branch. Then, Natoli and Gramoli [20] propose the balance attack against POW blockchain systems, where the common prefix property can be broken by disrupting communications between subgroups of similar mining power.

Rigorous cryptographic analysis on blockchain protocol are initiated by Garay, Kiayias and Leonardas [10] and Pass, Seeman and shelat [22]. [10] abstracts the backbone protocol of Bitcoin and proves its security under the proposed model. Furthermore, [22] extends the model to an asynchronous network and shows the security of blockchain protocol with a bounded delay $\Delta \ll 1/np$. Kiayias and Panagiotakos [16] investigate the tradeoff between provable security and transaction processing speed. Then, Garay, Kiayias and Leonardas [11] analyze the security of blockchain protocol with variable difficulty. Pass and Shi [24] consider the sleepy model, where players can be either online or offline. Notice that it is difficult for the adversary to control large fractions of the total mining power in practice, and no such attacks has been observed to date. Hence, Badertscher et al. [1] investigates the reason why we can assume the majority of the mining power is honest or why the miners need to follow the protocol honestly. In order to overcome the problems induced by POW, such as large energy demands, another line of research focuses on the blockchain protocol based on proof of stake (POS), where the miner to issue the next block is decided by randomly selecting one of the miners proportionally to their stakes. For instance, Algorand [13], Snow White [4], Ouroboros/Ouroboros Praos [5,17], and Thunderella [25].

2   Preliminaries

In this section, we recall the blockchain protocol, following the notations of [10, 22].

2.1   Notation

Let B denote a block. A blockchain $C = \overrightarrow{B}$ consists of a sequence of ordered Bs and the length $|C|$ means the number of blocks in C. Let m denote the message contained in B. $\overrightarrow{m}$ denotes the messages in $\overrightarrow{B}$ correspondingly. We denote by C_i^r the chain of miner i at round r. $C^{\lceil k}$ denotes the chain C that removes the last k blocks, where k is a nonnegative integer. If $k \geq |C|$, $C^{\lceil k} = \varepsilon$. Let $C_1 \preceq C_2$ denotes that C_1 is a prefix of C_2. $\mathsf{B}(n,k)$ denotes the binomial distribution with n trials and success probability k. $H : \{0,1\}^* \rightarrow \{0,1\}^\kappa$ is a cryptographic hash function.

2.2   Blockchain Protocol

A blockchain protocol consists of two algorithms, which are Π^V and $\mathcal{C}$. Π^V is a stateful algorithm, receiving security parameter κ and maintaining a blockchain C. C is a sequence of block B, where $B = (h_{-1}, m, r, h)$. h_{-1} is a pointer to the previous block. m is the message from the environment. r is a nonce. h is the pointer to the current block such that $h = H(h_{-1}, m, r)$. The cryptographic hash function $H(\cdot)$ is modeled by a random oracle $\mathsf{H}(\cdot)$, which on inputs x outputs $H(x)$. Let $\mathsf{H.ver}(\cdot, \cdot)$ be an oracle which takes (x, y) as inputs and outputs 1 if $H(x) = y$ and 0 otherwise. The first block of a chain is called the genesis block $B_0 = (0, \perp, 0, H(0||\perp||0))$. The algorithm $\mathcal{C}$ takes C as input and outputs the corresponding sequence of messages $\overrightarrow{m}$ of C. That is, $\mathcal{C}(C) = \overrightarrow{m}$. V is an algorithm which checks the validity of $\overrightarrow{m}$. If $\overrightarrow{m}$ is valid, $V(\mathcal{C}(C))$ outputs 1. In the bitcoin protocol, m contains the transaction information and V is used to check the validity of transactions.

A block $B = (h_{-1}, m, r, h)$ is valid with respect to a predecessor block $B_{-1} = (h'_{-1}, m', r', h')$ only if following conditions hold:

- $h_{-1} = h'$,
- $h = H(h_{-1}, m, r) < D_p$, where D_p is the difficulty parameter.

If all blocks in C are valid and $V(\mathcal{C}(C)) = 1$, we say C is valid, where the corresponding validity check algorithm is called "chain-check" algorithm.

Suppose there are n miners, where $n = n(\kappa)$ is a polynomial function with κ. At each round, a miner receives a message m from the environment Z and runs Π^V to maintain a chain C as follows:

- If $V(\mathcal{C}(C)\|m) \neq 1$, proceed to the next step. Otherwise, pick $r \leftarrow \{0,1\}^\kappa$ randomly and compute h by querying H with (h_{-1}, m, r), where h_{-1} is the pointer of the last block of C. If $h < D_p$, set $C = CB$, where $B = (h_{-1}, m, r, h)$, and we say the miner succeeds in mining a new block B. The miner can query H at most q times before he succeeds. Then, broadcast the new chain C. In order to capture the attack that the adversary can disturb the communication among miners, C is considered as being delivered by the adversary.
- On receiving the chains delivered by the adversary, choose the longest and valid one, say C', where the validity of blocks is checked by querying H.ver. If $|C'| > |C|$, replace C by C'. Otherwise, go to the next round.

Note that under the random oracle model $H(\cdot)$ is modeled by a random oracle $H(\cdot)$ and a miner is allowed to query H for at most q times at each round, but can query H.ver for arbitrary times. p denotes the probability that a miner succeeds in mining a block at a round, where $p = 1 - (1 - \frac{D_p}{2^\kappa})^q \approx \frac{qD_p}{2^\kappa}$. We use p to describe the difficulty of mining in the following parts.

2.3 $\mathcal{F}_{tree}$ Model

In this section we recall the simplified blockchain protocol with access to $\mathcal{F}_{tree}$ oracle introduced by [22]. The $\mathcal{F}_{tree}$ oracle maintains a tree which contains messages of all valid chains and can answer two kinds of queries, Tree.extend and Tree.ver. When receiving query Tree.extend$((B_0, \ldots, B_{l-1}), B)$, it checks whether $(B_0, \ldots, B_{l-1})$ is a path of the tree, where the root of the tree is the genesis block B_0. If so, with probability p it extends this path with B and returns 1; Otherwise, return 0. When receiving Tree.ver$(B_0, \ldots, B_l)$, it returns 1 if $(B_0, \ldots, B_l)$ is a path of the tree; Otherwise, return 0. Here, a block B only contains message m, i.e., $B = (m)$. Then the random oracle in blockchain protocol is replaced with $\mathcal{F}_{tree}$ and the resulting protocol is called $(\Pi_{tree}, \mathcal{C}_{tree})$. The main differences between $(\Pi_{tree}, \mathcal{C}_{tree})$ and $(\Pi, \mathcal{C})$ are described as follows.

The protocol $(\Pi_{tree}, \mathcal{C}_{tree})$ is also directed by an environment $Z(1^\kappa)$. The environment activates n miners and sends each miner a message at each round. A miner receives a message m from the environment Z and runs Π_{tree} below:

- If $V_{tree}(\mathcal{C}_{tree}(C)\|m) \neq 1$, proceed to the next step. Otherwise, query $\mathcal{F}_{tree}$ with Tree.extend(C, m). If the oracle answers 1, a new block $B = (m)$ is mined. Set $C = CB$ and broadcast C.

– When receiving the chains delivered by the adversary, choose the longest and valid one, say C', where the validity of C' can be checked by querying Tree.ver(C'). If the oracle Tree.ver(C') returns 1, we say the chain is valid. If $|C'| > |C|$, set $C = C'$. Otherwise, go to the next round.

Under the $\mathcal{F}_{tree}$ model, a miner is allowed to query Tree.extend only once at each round, but can query Tree.ver for arbitrary times. Note that the miners described in Sect. 2.3 can query H at most q times at a round and the probability of successful mining at a round is p. Therefore those queries to H at a round are considered as one query to Tree.extend.

[22] shows that the security properties in $(\Pi_{tree}, \mathcal{C}_{tree})$ still hold in original protocol, while the analysis is much simpler in the $\mathcal{F}_{tree}$ model. For simplicity, we misuse $(\Pi, \mathcal{C})$ to denote the basic blockchain protocol in the $\mathcal{F}_{tree}$ model. Besides, the algorithm V_{tree} or V depends on the functionality of the concrete protocol. To simplify the description, we consider V which outputs 1 for all inputs. Hence, V is omitted in following parts.

3   Blockchain Model with Long Delays

Nakamoto's blockchain protocol is proved to be secure [22], where chains broadcasted by miners may suffer at most Δ-bounded delays such that $\Delta \ll 1/np$. As discussed in Sect. 1, on one hand, it is much easier for the adversary to disturb the communications rather than collect large computational power. On the other hand, if the adversary fails to delay the target chain, the chain will be diffused to other miners immediately. To capture such scenario, our modifications for the behavior of the adversary are as below:

Execution of adversary at round r:

– **Recieving.** On receiving the chains from miners, the adversary chooses which valid chains he wants to delay. But only with probability α the chosen one can be delayed. Those delayed chains are marked as "delayable". The other undelayed chains are marked as "undelayable". Then all the chains the adversary received together with their marks and the round r are saved in a list $\mathcal{T}$.
– **Distribution.** The adversary chooses which chains in $\mathcal{T}$ to be distributed and these chains will be received by all the miners at the next round. But the following two kinds of chains have to be distributed at the current round.
  • The chains marked as undelayable;
  • The chains having been marked as delayable for Δ rounds.

Note that if the adversary distributes more than one chains at a round, the adversary can adjust the order of these chains. For instance, the adversary can broadcast chains C_1 and C_2 in a way that (C_1, C_2) to miner i but (C_2, C_1) to miner j, where $|C_1| = |C_2|$. If C_1 and C_2 are longer than i and j's chains, then i accepts C_1 as his main chain while j accepts C_2. We emphasize that our model is in honest miner setting where the adversary does not corrupt any miners.

Remark. In practice, it is possible that some miners receive a block earlier than others due to the propagation delay in the bitcoin network. As shown in [6], the broadcast of a block follows an exponential behavior. Hence, once a block has been broadcasted to its neighbors, most miners will receive the block immediately and it is difficult for the adversary to delay anymore. It takes about 10 s for a broadcasted block to be known by almost all the miners [6,22]. In our model, if the adversary broadcasts a block, all the miners will receive it in the next round, where the time span of a round can be 10 s. Such time span is enough for the adversary to influence the miners' behavior. To capture the possible attacks, e.g., attacks on miner i and j described above, we allow the adversary can adjust the order of these chains, which is equivalent to the case that miner i received C_1 only.

Modification to blockchain protocol. We make additional restrictions on the miners' behavior in the blockchain protocol. That is, the miner cannot mine in a chain, the last block of which was mined by himself. In other words, the miner who has already mined a block will not execute the mining step of Π until he receives a new chain mined by other miners. The reason why we prevent consecutive blocks mined by the same miner is that such consecutive blocks may cause possible forks even in the honest miner setting. In addition, it is not likely that a miner (not the mining pool) can mine two consecutive blocks in practice due to the large number of miners n and the small difficulty parameter p. Hence, such a restriction is reasonable in our honest miner setting.

We emphasize that our restriction only applies to a single miner which is an independent communication node of the network and has a unit computational power. Hence, such a modification would lead to a slightly decline of the total mining power and we ignore such a mild change in the following proof for simplicity.

In our protocol, we say a miner is "being delayed" if his chain is being delayed by the adversary. Obviously, a miner being delayed will not mine a block until he accepts a new chain mined by others.

4 Properties of Our Blockchain Model

In this section we redefine the chain growth property and the common prefix property in our blockchain model.

4.1 Chain Growth

Previous definition of chain growth [22] considers the minimum increase of the length of all miners' chains during T rounds. In our model, we consider the length increase of the majority of miners' chains instead. Informally speaking, if the majority of chains, say, with fraction $\lambda > \frac{1}{2}$, grows by t blocks during consecutive rounds, we say the blockchain view grows by t blocks during these rounds with majority λ. In fact, the definition of chain growth in [22] is a special case of ours when $\lambda = 1$. It is, however, difficult to have $\lambda = 1$ in practice. Hence, our definition is more flexible in capturing the real scenario.

Let $\mathtt{view}(\Pi, \mathcal{C}, A, Z, \kappa)$ and $|\mathtt{view}(\Pi, \mathcal{C}, A, Z, \kappa)|$ denote the joint view of all miners and the number of rounds during the execution of $(\Pi, \mathcal{C})$, respectively.

Definition 1. *Given* $\mathtt{view}(\Pi, \mathcal{C}, A, Z, \kappa)$, *we say the blockchain grows by at least* t *blocks with majority* $\lambda \in (\frac{1}{2}, 1]$ *from round* r_1 *to* r_2, *if*

$$\Pr_{i,j}[|C_j^{r_2}| - |C_i^{r_1}| \geq t] \geq \lambda, \tag{1}$$

where the probability is taken over all the choice of $i, j \in [n]$.

Define $\mathtt{chain\text{-}increase}_{A,Z,\kappa}^{(\Pi,\mathcal{C})}(r_1, r_2, \lambda)$ *as the maximum value of* t *satisfying* (1). *That is,*

$$\mathtt{chain\text{-}increase}_{A,Z,\kappa}^{(\Pi,\mathcal{C})}(r_1, r_2, \lambda) = max\{t|\Pr_{i,j}[|C_j^{r_2}| - |C_i^{r_1}| \geq t] \geq \lambda\}.$$

Definition 2. *The blockchain protocol* $(\Pi, \mathcal{C})$ *has the chain growth rate* $g \in \mathbb{R}$ *with majority* $\lambda \in (\frac{1}{2}, 1]$, *if there exists some constant* c *and negligible functions* ϵ_1, ϵ_2 *such that for every* $\kappa \in \mathbb{N}, T \geq c\log(\kappa)$ *and every* $r \leq |\mathtt{view}(\Pi, \mathcal{C}, A, Z, \kappa)| - T$, *the following holds:*

$$\Pr[\mathtt{chain\text{-}increase}_{A,Z,\kappa}^{(\Pi,\mathcal{C})}(r, r + T, \lambda) \geq gT] \geq 1 - \epsilon_1(\kappa) - \epsilon_2(T), \tag{2}$$

where the probability is taken over the randomness of the protocol.

4.2   Common Prefix

Similarly, we can define common prefix as follows.

Definition 3. $\mathtt{common\text{-}prefix}_{A,Z,\kappa}^{(\Pi,\mathcal{C})}(r, k, \lambda) = 1$ *with majority* $\lambda \in (\frac{1}{2}, 1]$ *if the following holds:*

$$\Pr_{i,j}[(C_i^r \lceil k \preceq C_j^r) \wedge (C_j^r \lceil k \preceq C_i^r)] \geq \lambda, \tag{3}$$

where the probability is taken over all the choice of $i, j \in [n]$.

Definition 4. *A blockchain protocol* $(\Pi, \mathcal{C})$ *satisfies the common prefix property with parameter* $\lambda \in (\frac{1}{2}, 1]$, *if there exists some constant* c *and negligible function* ϵ_1 *and* ϵ_2 *such that for every* $\kappa \in \mathbb{N}, T \geq c\log(\kappa)$ *and every* $r \leq |\mathtt{view}(\Pi, \mathcal{C}, A, Z, \kappa)|$, *the following holds:*

$$\Pr[\mathtt{common\text{-}prefix}_{A,Z,\kappa}^{(\Pi,\mathcal{C})}(r, T, \lambda) = 1] \geq 1 - \epsilon_1(\kappa) - \epsilon_2(T), \tag{4}$$

where the probability is taken over the randomness of the protocol.

5   State of the Main Chain

In this section, we introduce a special tree to capture the evolution of the main chains.

5.1   Record the State of the Main Chain

During the execution of Π, miners will "reach agreement" on some chains at each round and those chains are called the main chains. Although the main chains may not be unique at each round, only one of those chains will be the prefix of the main chain after enough rounds. Since the evolution of the main chains is closely related to chain growth and common prefix, we introduce a special tree, denoted by $\mathsf{Tree_{MC}}$, to record the state of the main chains, where a node of the tree is a block of a chain. $\mathsf{Tree_{MC}}$ is initialized to the root B_0. Next, we show how to add and delete blocks at a round in $\mathsf{Tree_{MC}}$.

- **AddBlock:** When the adversary broadcasts a chain $C = (B_0, B_1, \ldots, B_l)$, and there exist a branch (or paths from root to leaves) C' in $\mathsf{Tree_{MC}}$ such that $C' = C^{\lfloor k}$ with the smallest k, extend C' with the last k ordered blocks of C. Note that the adversary is allowed to send more than one chain at a round. That means the same leaf node of $\mathsf{Tree_{MC}}$ may be extended with different branches simultaneously.
- **DeleteBlock:** At the end of a round (after the adversary finishes **Distribution**), suppose $\mathsf{Tree_{MC}}$ has the depth, say d. Delete "useless" blocks or forks so that only the branches Cs satisfying the following conditions remain.
  - $|C| = d$,
  - For any C' with depth d, the last block of C was added to $\mathsf{Tree_{MC}}$ no later than the last block of C'.

Once the adversary broadcast the chains, each miner will update his chain with the longer one, and no one will withhold the shorter chains or attempt to extend them. Hence, $\mathsf{Tree_{MC}}$ only records all the main chains of the undelayed miners at current round. But if a miner has a chain longer than the main chain but is delayed by the adversary, this delayed chain is not recorded in $\mathsf{Tree_{MC}}$.

5.2   Properties of $\mathsf{Tree_{MC}}$

Obviously, all of the branches on $\mathsf{Tree_{MC}}$ at the end of a round are of equal depth and the depth of $\mathsf{Tree_{MC}}$ never decreases. Other interesting properties of $\mathsf{Tree_{MC}}$ are shown below.

Lemma 1. *Properties of $\mathsf{Tree_{MC}}$.*

1. *If new blocks are successfully added to $\mathsf{Tree_{MC}}$ at the end of a round, then the depth of $\mathsf{Tree_{MC}}$ increases.*
2. *The depth of $\mathsf{Tree_{MC}}$ increases by at most 1 at each round.*
3. *If only one block is added to $\mathsf{Tree_{MC}}$ at the end of a round, then $\mathsf{Tree_{MC}}$ has only one branch and the depth increases by 1.*

Proof. 1. Suppose there are new blocks added to the $\mathsf{Tree_{MC}}$ while the depth remains unchanged. So those added blocks are useless and will be deleted at once due to **DeleteBlock**.

2. Without loss of generality, suppose the depth of Tree$_\text{MC}$ at round $r-1$ and r are d and $d+2$, respectively. If the $(d+2)$th block is mined by miner i, then $(d+1)$th block must be mined by a different miner, say miner j, due to the restriction that the same miner cannot mine two consecutive blocks. Hence, miner i received miner j's chain of length $d+1$ from the adversary. That means there exists a round r' such that $r' < r$ and the depth of Tree$_\text{MC}$ is $d+1$ at round r', which contradicts the fact that the depth of Tree$_\text{MC}$ is d at round $r-1$.

3. Suppose the depth of Tree$_\text{MC}$ is d at round r and only one block, say B, is successfully added at round $r+1$. Due to the first property, the depth increases to $d+1$. And the length of branches without B is still d. After **DeleteBlock**, the useless blocks of these branches will be deleted from the tree and only the branch with depth $d+1$ will remain.

5.3 Relation with the View of $(\Pi, \mathcal{C})$

Tree$_\text{MC}$ records the main chains known by all the miners at current round. But there are some chains at current round which are not recorded in Tree$_\text{MC}$ due to the adversarial delay. Hence, the actual view of the main chains of $(\Pi, \mathcal{C})$ may be different from Tree$_\text{MC}$. Fortunately, such difference in terms of chain growth and common prefix is negligible. Therefore, we can prove these properties of $(\Pi, \mathcal{C})$ by analyzing Tree$_\text{MC}$. The relations between Tree$_\text{MC}$ and the view of $(\Pi, \mathcal{C})$ are proven by the following lemmas. (Note that the following lemmas are all discussed after Tree$_\text{MC}$ finishes the step of **DeleteBlock**.)

Lemma 2. *Assume $1/2 < \lambda \le 1 - 8\alpha p\Delta$. Let m^r_{delay} be the number of being delayed miners at round r. There exists a polynomial function poly such that*

$$\Pr[m^r_{delay} > \frac{(1-\lambda)n}{4}] < e^{-poly(\kappa)}. \tag{5}$$

Proof. Consider the case that $r \ge \Delta$. If a miner i is being delayed at round r, that means i succeeded in mining a delayable block from round $r - \Delta + 1$ to round r. During these Δ rounds, there are $n\Delta$ independent events of mining, each of which is delayable with probability αp. So $m^r_{delay} \sim \mathsf{B}(n\Delta, \alpha p)$. According to the Chernoff bound, for any $\epsilon \ge 1$, we have

$$\Pr[m^r_{delay} > (1+\epsilon)\alpha np\Delta] < e^{\frac{-\epsilon\alpha np\Delta}{3}}. \tag{6}$$

Let $(1+\epsilon)\alpha np\Delta = \frac{(1-\lambda)n}{4}$ and $1/2 < \lambda \le 1 - 8\alpha p\Delta$. We have $\epsilon = \frac{1-\lambda}{4\alpha p\Delta} - 1 \ge 1$. Therefore,

$$\Pr[m^r_{delay} > \frac{(1-\lambda)n}{4}] < e^{\frac{-\epsilon(1-\lambda)n}{12(1+\epsilon)}} \le e^{\frac{-(1-\lambda)n}{24}}, \tag{7}$$

where the last inequality follows from $\frac{\epsilon}{1+\epsilon} \ge \frac{1}{2}$. Since $n = n(\kappa)$ is a polynomial function with κ, let $poly(\kappa) = \frac{(1-\lambda)n(\kappa)}{24}$. That completes the proof of Lemma 2.

We denote the event that $m_{delay}^r > \frac{(1-\lambda)n}{4}$ as **Over-delay** in the following parts.

Lemma 3. *Assume* $1/2 < \lambda \leq 1 - 8\alpha p \Delta$. *Let* d_{tree}^r *be the depth of* Tree_{MC} *at round* r. *We have*

$$\Pr[\text{chain-increase}_{A,Z,\kappa}^{(\Pi,\mathcal{C})}(r_1, r_2, \lambda) \geq d_{tree}^{r_2} - d_{tree}^{r_1}] \geq 1 - 2e^{-poly(\kappa)}. \tag{8}$$

Proof. If $|C_i^r| < d_{tree}^r$ which means there exists at least one chain of length d_{tree}^r distributed by the adversary and known to all the miners, miner i at the end of round r should have updated his state with the chain of length d_{tree}^r. That is, $|C_i^r| = d_{tree}^r$. So the event that $|C_i^r| < d_{tree}^r$ cannot happen.

If $|C_i^r| > d_{tree}^r$, which means C_i^r is being delayed by the adversary. Assuming that **Over-delay** doesn't happen at round r_1 and r_2 (with probability at least $1 - 2e^{-poly(\kappa)}$ due to Lemma 2), we have

$$\Pr_i[|C_i^r| \neq d_{tree}^r] = \frac{m_{delay}^r}{n} \leq \frac{1-\lambda}{4}. \tag{9}$$

Therefore,

$$\Pr_{i,j}[|C_j^{r_2}| - |C_i^{r_1}| \geq d_{tree}^{r_2} - d_{tree}^{r_1}]$$

$$\geq \Pr_{i,j}[|C_j^{r_2}| - |C_i^{r_1}| = d_{tree}^{r_2} - d_{tree}^{r_1}]$$

$$\geq 1 - \Pr_i[|C_i^{r_1}| \neq d_{tree}^{r_1}] - \Pr_j[|C_j^{r_2}| \neq d_{tree}^{r_2}]$$

$$\geq 1 - \frac{1-\lambda}{4} - \frac{1-\lambda}{4} > \lambda.$$

That means $\text{chain-increase}_{A,Z,\kappa}^{(\Pi,\mathcal{C})}(r_1, r_2, \lambda) \geq d_{tree}^{r_2} - d_{tree}^{r_1}$, which completes the proof of the Lemma 3.

Lemma 4. *Assume* $1/2 < \lambda \leq 1 - 8\alpha p \Delta$. *Let* d *be the depth of* Tree_{MC}. *If all the branches of* Tree_{MC} *at round* r *have a common prefix with length* $d - T$, *we have*

$$\Pr[\text{common-prefix}_{A,Z,\kappa}^{(\Pi,\mathcal{C})}(r, T, \lambda) = 1] \geq 1 - 2e^{-poly(\kappa)}. \tag{10}$$

Proof. Suppose all the branches of Tree_{MC} at round r have a common prefix with length $d - T$. For any two branches of Tree_{MC} at round r, say $C_{tree.1}^r$ and $C_{tree.2}^r$, we have $(C_{tree.1}^r \preceq^{\lfloor T} C_{tree.2}^r) \wedge (C_{tree.2}^r \preceq^{\lfloor T} C_{tree.1}^r)$. However, not every miner's view match with Tree_{MC}. Suppose C_i^r is not a branch of Tree_{MC} at round r, which is denoted by $C_i^r \not\subset \mathsf{Tree}_{MC}^r$. Consider the following two cases:

- Case 1: C_r^i is being delayed by the adversary at round r. Assume that **Over-delay** doesn't happen at round r. As is discussed in the proof of Lemma 3, the probability of this case is at most $\frac{1-\lambda}{4}$.

- Case 2: C_i^r is not being delayed by adversary at round r. Then $|C_i^r| = d_{tree}^r$. Suppose $C_i^r \not\subset \mathsf{Tree}_{MC}^r$. That is, C_i^r has been distributed by the adversary, which means the last block of C_i^r was added to Tree_{MC} due to **AddBlock** but then deleted due to **DeleteBlock** at round $r' \leq r$. Since $d_{tree}^{r'} \geq |C_i^r|$ and $d_{tree}^{r'} \leq d_{tree}^r$ due to Lemma 1, we have $d_{tree}^{r'} = |C_i^r| = d_{tree}^r$. Hence, there exists another branch C^* such that $|C_{tree}^*| = d_{tree}^r$ and C_{tree}^* is added to Tree_{MC} earlier than C_i^r. Let r^* denote the round at which C_{tree}^* is added. Since C_{tree}^* is distributed by the adversary at round r^* but the miner i didn't update his state with C_{tree}^*, $C_i^{r^*}$ must be no shorter than C_{tree}^*. Therefore, $|C_i^{r^*}| = |C_i^r| = d_{tree}^r$ and $C_i^{r^*} = C_i^r$. We thus conclude that C_i^r was created no later than r^* but was distributed at round $r' > r^*$. That means, miner i was being delayed at round r^*.

  Assuming that **Over-delay** doesn't happen at round r^*, the probability that miner i was being delayed at round r^* is at most $\frac{1-\lambda}{4}$ due to the proof of Lemma 3. So the probability of $C_i^r \not\subset \mathsf{Tree}_{MC}^r$ in this case is at most $\frac{1-\lambda}{4}$.

To sum up, on condition that **Over-delay** doesn't happen at round r^* and r (with probability at least $1 - 2e^{poly(\kappa)}$), the probability that C_i^r is not a branch of Tree_{MC} at round r is

$$\Pr_i[C_i^r \not\subset \mathsf{Tree}_{MC}^r]$$
$$= \Pr_i[C_i^r \not\subset \mathsf{Tree}_{MC}^r \wedge \text{Case 1}] + \Pr_i[C_i^r \not\subset \mathsf{Tree}_{MC}^r \wedge \text{Case 2}]$$
$$\leq \frac{m_{delay}^r}{n} + \frac{m_{delay}^{r^*}}{n}$$
$$\leq \frac{1-\lambda}{4} + \frac{1-\lambda}{4} = \frac{1-\lambda}{2}$$

Therefore,

$$\Pr_{i,j}[(C_i^{r\lceil T} \preceq C_j^r) \wedge (C_j^{r\lceil T} \preceq C_i^r)]$$
$$\geq \Pr_{i,j}[C_i^r \subset \mathsf{Tree}_{MC}^r \wedge C_j^r \subset \mathsf{Tree}_{MC}^r]$$
$$\geq 1 - \Pr_i[C_i^r \not\subset \mathsf{Tree}_{MC}^r] - \Pr_j[C_j^r \not\subset \mathsf{Tree}_{MC}^r]$$
$$\geq 1 - \frac{1-\lambda}{2} - \frac{1-\lambda}{2} = \lambda,$$

which completes the proof of Lemma 4.

6   Proofs of Security

In this section we analyze the chain growth property and the common prefix property of $(\Pi, \mathcal{C})$ using Tree_{MC}.

6.1   Chain Growth

Theorem 1 *(Chain growth). Assume $1/2 < \lambda \le 1 - 8\alpha p\Delta$. The blockchain protocol (Π, C) has the chain growth rate $g = \frac{(1-\delta)f}{1+fE[R^i_{delay}]}$ with majority λ, where $f = 1 - (1-p)^n$, $E[R^i_{delay}] = \frac{\alpha - \alpha\omega^{\Delta - 1}[\omega + \Delta(1-\omega^2)]}{1-\omega}$ and $\omega = 1 - (1-\alpha)f$.*

Proof. The aim of the adversary is to decrease the chain growth rate by delaying or scheduling the chain delivery. Due to Lemma 3, which shows the relation between the chain growth of (Π, C) and that of $\mathsf{Tree_{MC}}$, we only need to focus on the chain growth of $\mathsf{Tree_{MC}}$.

It seems that the adversary can use forks to distract the hashing power of miners in order to slow the chain growth rate. However, the forks does not help in breaking the chain growth property of $\mathsf{Tree_{MC}}$. More precisely, consider the rounds at which two consecutive blocks are added to $\mathsf{Tree_{MC}}$. Once a miner successfully mined a block B_1, which corresponds to chain C_1, the adversary can delay it with probability α for at most Δ rounds, and waits for the next block B'_1. If B_1 is delayable and the next block B'_1 corresponding to C'_1 is mined within Δ rounds, the adversary can generate a fork by broadcasting both chain C_1 and C'_1 simultaneously. Then B_1 and B'_1 can be added to $\mathsf{Tree_{MC}}$ such that B_1 is the neighbour of B'_1, and depth of $\mathsf{Tree_{MC}}$ grows by 1. Specifically, the adversary can broadcast C_1 to a set of miners, say S_1, and C'_1 to the remaining miners, say S'_1. Then miners in S_1 will accept chain C_1, while miners in S'_1 will accept C'_1. Let r_1 be the round at which B_1 and B'_1 are added to $\mathsf{Tree_{MC}}$ and r_2 be the round at which the next block B_2 is mined. Notice that $r_2 - r_1$ is not influenced by the number of forks which the adversary generated at round r_1, and only the number of the rounds of delays affect the chain growth rate of $\mathsf{Tree_{MC}}$.

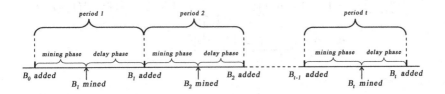

Fig. 1. The rounds during which t consecutive blocks are added to $\mathsf{Tree_{MC}}$

Consider t consecutive blocks in $\mathsf{Tree_{MC}}$ as shown in Fig. 1. Block B_0 is added to the tree at round r_0 and B_t is added at round r_t. We divide those rounds from r_0 to r_t into t periods, and each period consists of the rounds during which the depth of $\mathsf{Tree_{MC}}$ increases by 1.

Each period i consists of mining phase and delay phase. For each i, let B_i be the first block that mined in period i. The round at which block B_i is mined is the end of mining phase. Let R^i_{mine} and R^i_{delay} denotes the number of rounds of mining phase and delay phase of period i, respectively. Let $R_{mine} = \Sigma_{i=1}^{t} R_{mine}^{i}$ and $R_{delay} = \Sigma_{i=1}^{t} R_{delay}^{i}$. So $R_{mine} + R_{delay} = r_t - r_0$.

Next, we show how to compute R_{mine} and R_{delay}. Let $f = 1 - (1-p)^n$ be the probability that some miner succeeds in mining a block in a round. Since R_{mine}^{i}s are independent geometrically distributed variables such that $\Pr[R_{mine}^{i} = k] = (1-f)^{k-1}f$, the sum R_{mine} follows a negative binomial distribution $\mathsf{NB}(t, f)$. Due to Lemma 5 in Appendix A, we have

$$\Pr[R_{mine} \leq \frac{(1+\delta_1)t}{f}] \geq 1 - e^{-poly(\delta_1^2 t)}, \tag{11}$$

where $0 < \delta_1 < 1/2$.

In delay phase, if B_i is undelayable, it has to be added to $\mathsf{Tree_{MC}}$ at the current round and $R_{delay}^{i} = 0$. Otherwise, the adversary can delay the chain for at most Δ rounds, $R_{delay}^{i} \leq \Delta$. It is obvious that $R_{delay} \leq t\Delta$. To get a lower upper bound, we need to consider the event that a undelayable block is mined during each delay phase. Indeed, if an undelayable block is mined within Δ rounds since the beginning of a delay phase, the adversary has to add such block to $\mathsf{Tree_{MC}}$ and the delay phase is ended. Hence, the probability distribution of R_{delay}^{i} is defined as follows:

$$\Pr[R_{delay}^{i} = k] = \begin{cases} 1 - \alpha, & \text{if } k = 0, \\ \alpha(1 - (1-\alpha)f)^{k-1}(1-\alpha)f, & \text{if } 0 < k < \Delta, \\ \alpha(1 - (1-\alpha)f)^{k}, & \text{if } k = \Delta, \\ 0, & \text{otherwise.} \end{cases} \tag{12}$$

So we have

$$E[R_{delay}^{i}] = \alpha(1 - (1-\alpha)f)^{\Delta}\Delta + \sum_{k=1}^{\Delta-1} k\alpha(1 - (1-\alpha)f)^{k-1}(1-\alpha)f$$
$$= \frac{\alpha - \alpha\omega^{\Delta-1}[\omega + \Delta(1 - \omega^2)]}{1 - \omega},$$

where $\omega = 1 - (1-\alpha)f$.

Since R_{delay}^{i}s are independent random variables with the same distribution, the expectation $E[R_{delay}] = \sum_{i=1}^{t} E[R_{delay}^{i}] = tE[R_{delay}^{i}]$. Using the Chernoff bound, we get

$$\Pr[R_{delay} < (1+\delta_2)tE[R_{delay}^{i}]] > 1 - e^{-\frac{\delta_2^2 tE[R_{delay}^{i}]}{3}}, \quad \text{for } 0 \leq \delta_2 \leq 1. \tag{13}$$

So on the condition that (11) and (13) hold, the chain growth rate of $\mathsf{Tree_{MC}}$ is

$$g > \frac{t}{R_{mine} + R_{delay}} = \frac{t}{\frac{(1+\delta_1)t}{f} + (1+\delta_2)tE[R_{delay}^{i}]} = \frac{(1-\delta)f}{1 + fE[R_{delay}^{i}]}, \tag{14}$$

where δ is decided by picking sufficiently small δ_1 and δ_2.

Due to Lemma 3, the view of $(\Pi, \mathcal{C})$ has chain growth g with majority λ with probability at least $1 - 2e^{-poly(\kappa)}$ conditioned on that (11) and (13) hold. Therefore, given the view of $(\Pi, \mathcal{C})$, we have

$$\Pr[\text{chain-increase}_{A,Z,\kappa}^{(\Pi,\mathcal{C})}(r, r + T, \lambda) \geq gT]$$

$$\geq 1 - 2e^{-poly(\kappa)} - e^{-poly(\delta_1^2 T)} - e^{-\frac{\delta_2^2 T E[R_{delay}^i]}{3}},$$

which completes the proof of Theorem 1.

Remark. If $\alpha = 1$, then $E[R_{delay}^i] = \Delta$ and the chain growth rate is $\frac{(1-\delta)f}{1+f\Delta}$, which is the same as that of [22].

6.2   Common Prefix

Theorem 2 (*Common prefix*). *Assume* $0 < \alpha < 1 - np$ *and* $1/2 < \lambda \leq 1 - 8\alpha p\Delta$. *The blockchain protocol* $(\Pi, \mathcal{C})$ *satisfies the common prefix property with parameter* λ.

Proof. Due to Lemma 4, it remains to prove that $\mathsf{Tree}_{\mathsf{MC}}$ have the common prefix property. Suppose the adversary's goal is to break the common prefix of $\mathsf{Tree}_{\mathsf{MC}}$ with depth $d + T$. That is, the adversary aims to make the length of the common prefix of all branches in $\mathsf{Tree}_{\mathsf{MC}}$ at most $d - 1$.

Note that the depth of $\mathsf{Tree}_{\mathsf{MC}}$ can increase by 1 at most at each round due to Lemma 1. Therefore, in order to generate a fork in $\mathsf{Tree}_{\mathsf{MC}}$, the adversary has to broadcast more than one blocks in a round. If only one block is broadcasted, there will be only one branch in $\mathsf{Tree}_{\mathsf{MC}}$ according to Lemma 1 and the adversary fails to generate a fork.

In order to capture the attack for common prefix, we introduce the following game $\mathsf{Experiment}_{A,(\Pi,\mathcal{C})}^{\mathsf{COMM}}$, where the adversary generates a fork and tries to keep the branches of the fork as long as possible.

$\mathsf{Experiment}_{A,(\Pi,\mathcal{C})}^{\mathsf{COMM}}$: Run $(\Pi, \mathcal{C})$. Suppose that at current round r the depth of $\mathsf{Tree}_{\mathsf{MC}}$ is $d - 1$ and there is no blocks being delayed and no forks in $\mathsf{Tree}_{\mathsf{MC}}$. Then the adversary A tries to generate a fork and extend the length of forks as follows.

1. Wait for new blocks to be mined. If the new block or blocks are mined at some round r' such that $r' > r$.
   - If more than one block are mined in the same round r', A broadcasts the corresponding chains and goes to step 3. That means a fork is generated and recorded in $\mathsf{Tree}_{\mathsf{MC}}$.
   - If only one block, say B, is mined,
     - If B is delayable, A delays the corresponding chain, say C_1, and goes to step 2;
     - Otherwise, go to step 1.

2. A tries to delay C_1 as long as possible. During these rounds of delays, A tries to generate a fork by "collecting" new blocks. If no block have been mined during these rounds, A fails to generate a fork and goes to step 1. Otherwise, go to step 3.
3. A tries to keep the fork of $\mathsf{Tree_{MC}}$ as long as possible. If at least two branches of the fork are extended with T blocks, we say the adversary wins the common prefix game.

Since the adversary can always keep waiting and trying until a fork is created (in step 1 and step 2), the common prefix property is measured by the success probability of A in step 3.

Next, we consider a special event called **converge** which results in the failure of A. Suppose the depth of $\mathsf{Tree_{MC}}$ increases to l at round r. Let B^* be the first block mined after round r and let r^* denote the round at which B^* is mined. The event **converge** satisfies the following conditions.

1. Only one miner succeeds in mining at round r^*.
2. The chain C^* which B^* lies in is undelayable, or C^* is delayable while there is no new block mined in following Δ rounds.

Note that if the event **converge** happens in step 3, then the depth of $\mathsf{Tree_{MC}}$ increases by 1, e.g., from l to $l+1$.

When the depth of $\mathsf{Tree_{MC}}$ increases to l at round r, the chains of all the miners are of length l. (Notice that the $(l+1)$th block can be mined only if a chain of length l is distributed). Then, if only one miner succeeds in r^* and generates an undelayable chain C^*, C^* will be the unique chain in $\mathsf{Tree_{MC}}$ and A fails to extend the fork. If C^* is undelayable and there is no new block mined in following Δ rounds, A fails too.

Conditioned on that there exists some miner succeeding at round r^*, the probability of condition 1 is

$$\frac{np(1-p)^{n-1}}{1-(1-p)^n} > \frac{np(1-p)^{n-1}}{np} = (1-p)^{n-1} > 1 - np \tag{15}$$

The probability of condition 2 is

$$1 - \alpha + \alpha(1-p)^{n\Delta} > 1 - \alpha + \alpha(1 - np\Delta) = 1 - \alpha np\Delta \tag{16}$$

Therefore,

$$Pr[\textbf{converge}] > (1-np)(1-\alpha np\Delta) > 1 - np(1+\alpha\Delta) \tag{17}$$

The adversary can keep the fork for consecutive T blocks only if **converge** does not happen for consecutive T times, the probability of which is at most $(np(1+\alpha\Delta))^T$. So the probability that $\mathsf{Tree_{MC}}$ has a common prefix with depth $d-T$ is at least $1 - (np(1+\alpha\Delta))^T$.

If $\Delta \le 1/np$, considering the assumption $\alpha < 1 - np$, we have

$$np(1 + \alpha\Delta) < np(1 + \frac{1 - np}{np}) = 1 \qquad (18)$$

If $\Delta > 1/np$, the equality (16) can be replaced with $1-\alpha+\alpha(1 - p)^{n\Delta} > 1-\alpha$, and the probability that $\mathsf{Tree}_{\mathsf{MC}}$ has a common prefix with depth $d-T$ is at least $1 - (\alpha + np)^T$, where $\alpha + np < 1$.

To sum up, the probability that $\mathsf{Tree}_{\mathsf{MC}}$ has a common prefix path with depth $d-T$ is at least $1-negl(T)$, where $negl$ is a negligible function. Due to Lemma 4, the view of $(\Pi, \mathcal{C})$ satisfies $\mathtt{common\text{-}prefix}_{A,Z,\kappa}^{(\Pi,\mathcal{C})}(r, T, \lambda) = 1$ with probability at least $1 - 2e^{-poly(\kappa)}$. Therefore, given the view of $(\Pi, \mathcal{C})$, we have

$$\Pr[\mathtt{common\text{-}prefix}_{A,Z,\kappa}^{(\Pi,\mathcal{C})}(r, T, \lambda) = 1] \geq 1 - 2e^{-poly(\kappa)} - negl(T),$$

which completes the proof of Theorem 2.

7 Long Delay Attack on Common Prefix

7.1 Long Delay Attack

Note that Theorem 2 is an asymptotic result, which means the common prefix property can hold when T is large enough. To illustrate the threat of long delay attack comprehensively, we present a concrete attack on the common prefix of $\mathsf{Tree}_{\mathsf{MC}}$ when Δ and α are "too" large relative to a fixed T.

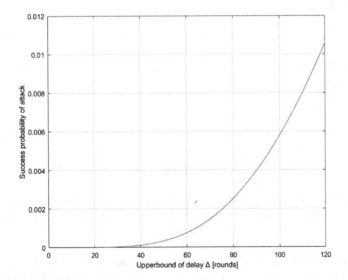

Fig. 2. For $\alpha = 0.8$ and $T = 6$, the success probability increases as Δ gets larger. In particular, the success probability grows much faster when $\Delta > 60$ (10 min). When $\Delta > 120$ (20 min), the success probability can reach about 1%.

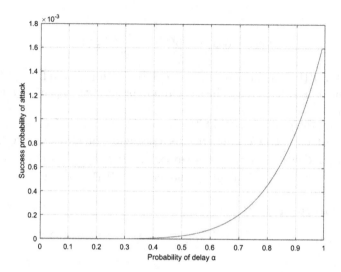

Fig. 3. For $\Delta = 60$ (10 min, the expected time of mining a block) and $T = 6$, the success probability increases as the probability of delay α get larger. As shown in the figure, the success probability increases much faster when $\alpha > 0.7$.

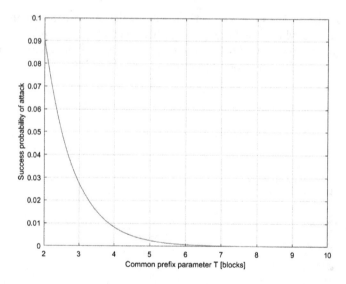

Fig. 4. For $\Delta = 60$ (10 min) and $\alpha = 0.8$, the success probability decreases as T gets larger. In particular, when $T \geq 6$, the success probability becomes extremely small.

Suppose that $\mathsf{Tree}_{\mathsf{MC}}$ has a fork with two branches[2] of depth 1, which lies in two chains, say chain A and chain B, respectively, and half of the miners

---

[2] Here the branch starts from the block where the fork begins and ends with the last block.

accepted chain A and the other half accepted chain B. Then the adversary aims to increase the length of the two branches by T. Note that once the adversary need to broadcast two chains, he distributes in a way that the number of miners which accept one chain equals to that of miners which accepts the other chain. More details of the attack and related analysis are described in Appendix B. The success probability of such attack is

$$(\frac{f}{4} + (\alpha + \frac{f(1-2\alpha)}{4})\frac{f(1-p_{next}^\Delta)}{2-2p_{next}})^T \tag{19}$$

where $p_{next} \approx \frac{(2-f(1-\alpha))(2-f)}{4}$.

For an experimental interpretation of the success probability of the attack, the parameters are set as follows: The time span of a round for full interaction is set to $10s$. Since the expected time to mine a block is about 10 min, the probability of all the miners succeeding in mining per round is about $f = 1/60$. Considering $n = 10^5$ miners in the network, we have $p \approx f/n \approx 1.67 \times 10^{-7}$. Let $\lambda = 99.8\%$, which satisfies the assumption $1/2 < \lambda \le 1 - 8\alpha p\Delta$ if $\Delta < 1.5 \times 10^3$ (about 4.2 h). In this case, the common prefix of $\mathsf{Tree_{MC}}$ is the same as that of $(\Pi, \mathcal{C})$ with probability at least 99.95% due to Lemma 4.

Given the above parameters, Figs. 2, 3 and 4 reflect the success probability of long delay attack when Δ, α and T varies. As shown in those figures, the adversary without any hash power may threaten the common prefix property of blockchain protocol especially when Δ and α are too large relative to the fixed T.

7.2 Balance Attack

Our attack is reminiscent of the balance attacks introduced by [20], since both attacks can create or maintain forks by splitting honest miners into subgroups of similar mining power. Main differences between the original balance attack in [20] and ours are as follows.

- The goal of the original balance attack is to make the target branch selected as the main chain, while the goal of ours is to maintain the forks for as long as possible.
- The attacker in the original balance attack requires a fraction, say 20%, of mining power to launch attack, while our attack as well as N-confirmation double spending attack in [14] does not require any mining power.
- The original balance attack disrupts the communication between subgroups by delaying messages and those isolated subgroups mine their own blockchains independently. Our attack delays the new block (or blockchain) as soon as it is successfully mined, e.g., the attacker "eclipses" the miner which mines a new block. Then the attacker delivers different blockchains to different subgroups once he obtains enough blockchains.

According to Theorem 5 of [20], we can evaluate the effectiveness of balance attack on bitcoin protocol. Table 1 shows the time of delays (in minutes) required by the original balance attack and ours, where we only consider the ideal case for the attacker of balance attack. More precisely, we assume that all the blocks mined in balance attack can be added to the main chain. For more details of balance attack, we refer to [20].

Table 1. Delays for balance attack and our long delay attack (minutes). $f = 1/60$ and $T = 6$. ϵ denotes the success probability of the attack. ρ denotes the fraction of mining power owned by the adversary in balance attack. α denotes the probability of delay in our attack. "-" denotes that the corresponding success probability cannot be achieved. For example, the maximum success probability of our attack is about 0.55 when $\alpha = 0.95$ and hence cannot reach 0.9.

Types of attack		Success probability		
		$\epsilon = 0.1$	$\epsilon = 0.5$	$\epsilon = 0.9$
Balance attack	$\rho = 0.1$	8055	11230	11920
	$\rho = 0.2$	1790	2495	4426
	$\rho = 0.3$	696	970	1724
Our attack	$\alpha = 0.85$	43.6	-	-
	$\alpha = 0.95$	26.6	78.4	-
	$\alpha = 1$	22.9	44.2	80.8

Although Table 1 shows that the balance attack requires longer delays than ours, we emphasize that it is not fair to say which attack is better. First, the goals are different. Second, the balance attack only considers the case that the attacker can always delay the message successfully, while our attack considers different probability of delay. Besides, the success probability estimation of balance attack on bitcoin, which is obtained by applying the result on GHOST [20] directly, is not tight and can be further improved.

Acknowledgements. We would like to thank the anonymous reviewers of ASI-ACRYPT 2018 for their insightful and helpful comments. We are also grateful to Siu Ming Yiu, Zhengyu Zhang, Yingnan Deng, Shichen Wu and Xianrui Qin for interesting discussions. Puwen Wei and Quan Yuan were supported by the National Natural Science Foundation of China (No. 61502276 and No. 61572293). Puwen Wei was also supported by the Chinese Major Program of National Cryptography Development Foundation (No. MMJJ2017012) and the Fundamental Research Funds of Shandong University (No. 2016JC029).

A   Chernoff Bound for Negative Binomial Distribution

Lemma 5. *Let $X_1, X_2, \ldots, X_k$ be independent random variables, such that for all $i \in [k]$ and integer $m \geq 1$, $Pr[X_i = m] = (1-p)^{m-1}p$. Let $X = \Sigma_{i=1}^k X_i$,* *the variable X is said to have a negative binomial distribution $NB(k, p)$, and for* $\delta \in (0, \frac{1}{2})$

$$\Pr[X \leq (1 - \delta)\frac{k}{p}] < e^{-poly(\delta^2 k)} \tag{20}$$

$$\Pr[X \geq (1 + \delta)\frac{k}{p}] < e^{-poly(\delta^2 k)} \tag{21}$$

Proof. Let $t = \frac{(1-\delta)k}{p}$ and $\epsilon = \frac{1}{1-\delta} - 1 \in (0, 1)$. Here, $k = \frac{pt}{1-\delta} = (1 + \epsilon)pt$. Let $Y_1, Y_2, \ldots, Y_{\lfloor t \rfloor}$ be independent random boolean variables, such that for all $i \in \{1, \ldots, \lfloor t \rfloor\}$, $\Pr[Y_i = 1] = p$. $Y = \Sigma_{i=1}^{\lfloor t \rfloor} Y_i$. Due to the Chernoff bound [7], we have

$$\Pr[Y \geq k] \leq \Pr[Y \geq (1 + \epsilon)p\lfloor t \rfloor] < e^{-\frac{\epsilon^2 p \lfloor t \rfloor}{3}} \tag{22}$$

Since

$$p\lfloor t \rfloor = pt - p(t - \lfloor t \rfloor) > pt - p = (1 - \delta)k - p \tag{23}$$

we have

$$\Pr[Y \geq k] < e^{-\frac{\epsilon^2}{3}((1-\delta)k-p)} < e^{-\frac{\delta^2 k}{3(1+\delta)} + \frac{\epsilon^2 p}{3}} < e^{-\frac{\delta^2 k}{3} + \frac{p}{3}} \tag{24}$$

Consider the event $Y \geq k$. If it happens, there are at least k successes in $\lfloor t \rfloor$ Bernoulli trials. In other words, it takes us at most $\lfloor t \rfloor$ experiments to achieve the kth successes. X_i is considered as the number of Bernoulli trials needed to get one success. So the event $Y \geq k$ is equivalent to the event $X \leq \lfloor t \rfloor$. Hence,

$$\Pr[X \leq t] = \Pr[X \leq \lfloor t \rfloor] = \Pr[Y \geq k] < e^{-\frac{\delta^2 k}{3} + \frac{p}{3}} \tag{25}$$

That completes the proof of inequality (20). Similarly, inequality (21) can be proved if $t = \frac{(1+\delta)k}{p}$ and $\epsilon = 1 - \frac{1}{1+\delta}$.

B   Long Delay Attack on Common Prefix

Suppose chain A and chain B are in $\mathsf{Tree_{MC}}$, such that chain A is similar to chain B except that only the last blocks are different. For convenience, let G_A and G_B denote the set of miners which accept chain A and chain B, respectively. The number of miners in group A equals to that of group B, i.e., $|G_A| = |G_B| = n/2$. Note that G_A or G_B is not fixed and will be changed due to the adversary delivery. Then the adversary waits for a new block. We say round r is successful if there is a new block mined at round r. Let $\gamma(n, p) = 1 - (1 - p)^n$. If p is small, we have $\gamma(n, p) \approx np$. Obviously, the probability that a round is successful is $f = \gamma(n, p)$. When a successful round appears, consider the following cases:

1. There is at least one block mined in each of the two branches. That means, chain A and chain B are extended at the same round. The adversary distributes the two chains in a way that the number of miners accepting chain A and the number of miners accepting chain B are equal. As a result, the

adversary succeeds in extending the length of the fork by 1. Since the probability of mining a block in one chain is $\gamma(\frac{n}{2}, p)$, the probability that this case happens is

$$\frac{\gamma(\frac{n}{2}, p) \cdot \gamma(\frac{n}{2}, p)}{\gamma(n, p)} \approx \frac{\frac{1}{4}n^2 p^2}{np} = \frac{np}{4} \tag{26}$$

2. There is at least one *undelayable* block mined in only one of the branches (without loss of generality, chain A) while no block mined in the another chain (chain B). In this case, the new chain A is broadcasted by the adversary, while the length of chain B remains the same. So the useless blocks in chain B is deleted due to **DeleteBlock** and the adversary fails to extend the fork. The probability of this case is

$$\frac{2\gamma(\frac{n}{2}, (1-\alpha)p)(1 - \gamma(\frac{n}{2}, p))}{\gamma(n, p)} \approx \frac{(1-\alpha)np(1 - \frac{np}{2})}{np} = \frac{(1-\alpha)(2 - np)}{2} \tag{27}$$

3. Otherwise, all the blocks mined at this round are delayable and in only one branch (without loss of generality, chain A). That means, the adversary neither succeeds nor fails at this round. The adversary can delay the new chain A and keep waiting for a new block in chain B in the following Δ rounds. Due to Eqs. (26) and (27), the probability that the adversary needs to delay the chain is

$$1 - \frac{np}{4} - \frac{(1-\alpha)(2 - np)}{2} = \alpha + \frac{np(1 - 2\alpha)}{4} \tag{28}$$

Then, the adversary keeps the chain A delayed and waits for a new block to be mined in chain B. At each of the following rounds, there are three cases to be discussed:

(a) If G_B succeeds in mining a block, the chain B can be extended and adversary distributes the delayed chain A and the new chain B in a way that $|G_A| = |G_B|$. As a result, the adversary succeeds in extending the length of chain A and chain B by 1. The probability of this case is $\gamma(\frac{n}{2}, p) \approx \frac{np}{2}$.

(b) If G_B does not succeed in mining a block while G_A mines an *undelayable* block. Then, the new chain A should be distributed, which means only chain A in Tree$_{MC}$ is extended. So the adversary fails.

(c) If G_A does not mine an undelayable block while G_B does not succeed in mining a block. The adversary checks whether the number of rounds for A being delayed exceeds Δ. If it exceeds Δ, the adversary has to broadcast chain A and fails. Otherwise, the adversary keeps chain A delayed and goes to the next round, where the probability of this event is

$$p_{next} = (1 - \gamma(\frac{n}{2}, (1-\alpha)p)) \cdot (1 - \gamma(\frac{n}{2}, p)) \approx \frac{(2 - np(1-\alpha))(2 - np)}{4}. \tag{29}$$

In a word, in case 3, the adversary can succeed with probability $\frac{np}{2}$ per round, or can go to the next round with probability p_{next}. Conditioned on case 3 happens at round r, the probability for the adversary succeeding at round $r+1$ is $\frac{np}{2}$ and the probability of success at round $r+2$ is $p_{next} \cdot \frac{np}{2}$. Similarly, conditioned on case 3 happens at round r, the probability of success at round $r+i$ is $p_{next}^{i-1} \cdot \frac{np}{2}$. Since the adversary only has Δ rounds for trying, the probability for adversary to succeed during those Δ rounds in case 3 is

$$\sum_{i=1}^{\Delta} p_{next}^{i-1} \cdot \frac{np}{2} = \frac{np(1 - p_{next}^{\Delta})}{2 - 2p_{next}}. \tag{30}$$

Considering case 1, 2 and 3, the probability of the adversary succeeding in increasing the length of branches by 1 for a successful round is

$$\frac{np}{4} + (\alpha + \frac{np(1 - 2\alpha)}{4})\frac{np(1 - p_{next}^{\Delta})}{2 - 2p_{next}}. \tag{31}$$

Then the adversary waits for another successful round and executes as described above.

We say the adversary's long delay attack is successful, if the adversary succeeds in increasing the length of the fork by 1 for consecutive T times. Therefore, the success probability of our long delay attack is

$$(\frac{f}{4} + (\alpha + \frac{f(1 - 2\alpha)}{4})\frac{f(1 - p_{next}^{\Delta})}{2 - 2p_{next}})^{T}. \tag{32}$$

where $np \approx f$.

References

1. Badertscher, C., Garay, J., Maurer, U., Tschudi, D., Zikas, V.: But why does it work? A rational protocol design treatment of bitcoin. In: Nielsen, J.B., Rijmen, V. (eds.) EUROCRYPT 2018. LNCS, vol. 10821, pp. 34–65. Springer, Cham (2018). https://doi.org/10.1007/978-3-319-78375-8_2
2. Ben-Sasson, E., et al.: Zerocash: decentralized anonymous payment from bitcoin. In: IEEE Symposium on Security and Privacy, pp. 459–474 (2014)
3. Carlsten, M., Kalodner, H.A., Weinberg, S.M., Narayanan, A.: On the instability of bitcoin without the block reward. In: ACM CCS 2016, pp. 154–167. ACM Press, New York (2016)
4. Daian, P., Pass, R., Shi, E.: Snow white: Provably secure proofs of stake. IACR Cryptology ePrint Archive, Report 2016/919 (2016)
5. David, B., Gaži, P., Kiayias, A., Russell, A.: Ouroboros praos: an adaptively-secure, semi-synchronous proof-of-stake blockchain. In: Nielsen, J.B., Rijmen, V. (eds.) EUROCRYPT 2018. LNCS, vol. 10821, pp. 66–98. Springer, Cham (2018). https://doi.org/10.1007/978-3-319-78375-8_3
6. Decker, C., Wattenhofer, R.: Information propagation in the bitcoin network. In: 13th IEEE International Conference on Peer-to-Peer Computing, pp. 1–10. IEEE Computer Society Press (2013)
7. Dubhashi, D.P., Panconesi, A.: Concentration of Measure for the Analysis of Randomized Algorithms. Cambridge University Press, Cambridge (2009)

8. Eyal, I., Sirer, E.G.: Majority is not enough: bitcoin mining is vulnerable. In: Christin, N., Safavi-Naini, R. (eds.) FC 2014. LNCS, vol. 8437, pp. 436–454. Springer, Heidelberg (2014). https://doi.org/10.1007/978-3-662-45472-5_28

9. Eyal, I., Sirer, E.G.: The miner's dilemma. In: 2015 IEEE Symposium on Security and Privacy, vol. 7, pp. 89–103. IEEE Computer Society Press (2015)

10. Garay, J., Kiayias, A., Leonardos, N.: The bitcoin backbone protocol: analysis and applications. In: Oswald, E., Fischlin, M. (eds.) EUROCRYPT 2015. LNCS, vol. 9057, pp. 281–310. Springer, Heidelberg (2015). https://doi.org/10.1007/978-3-662-46803-6_10

11. Garay, J., Kiayias, A., Leonardos, N.: The bitcoin backbone protocol with chains of variable difficulty. In: Katz, J., Shacham, H. (eds.) CRYPTO 2017. LNCS, vol. 10401, pp. 291–323. Springer, Cham (2017). https://doi.org/10.1007/978-3-319-63688-7_10

12. Gervais, A., Karame, G.O., Wust, K., Glykantzis, V., Ritzdorf, H., Capkun, S.: On the security and performance of proof of work blockchains. In: ACM CCS 2016, pp. 3–16. ACM Press (2016)

13. Gilad, Y., Hemo, R., Micali, S., Vlachos, G., Zeldovich, N.: Algorand: scaling byzantine agreements for cryptocurrencies. IACR Cryptology ePrint Archive, Report 2017/454 (2017)

14. Heilman, E., Kendler, A., Zohar, A., Goldberg, S.: Eclipse attacks on bitcoin peer-to-peer network. In: Jung, J. (ed.) 24th USENIX Security Symposium, pp. 129–144. USENIX Association (2015)

15. Kiayias, A., Koutsoupias, E., Kyropoulou, M., Tselekounis, Y.: Blockchain mining games. In: 2016 ACM Conference on Economics and Computation, pp. 365–382. ACM Press (2016)

16. Kiayias, A., Panagiotakos, G.: Speed-security tradeoffs in blockchain protocols. IACR Cryptology ePrint Archive: Report 2015/1019 (2016)

17. Kiayias, A., Russell, A., David, B., Oliynykov, R.: Ouroboros: a provably secure proof-of-stake blockchain protocol. In: Katz, J., Shacham, H. (eds.) CRYPTO 2017. LNCS, vol. 10401, pp. 357–388. Springer, Cham (2017). https://doi.org/10.1007/978-3-319-63688-7_12

18. Miller, A., LaViola, J.J.: Anonymous byzantine consensus from moderately-hard puzzles: a model of bitcoin. Technical report, CS-TR-14-01. University of Central Florida (2014)

19. Nakamoto, S.: Bitcoin: a peer-to-peer electronic cash system (2008)

20. Natoli, C., Gramoli, V.: The balance attack against proof-of-work blockchains: the R3 testbed as an example. Computing Research Repository (2016). arXiv:1612.09426

21. Nayak, K., Kumar, S., Miller, A., Shi, E.: Stubborn mining: generalizing selfish mining and combining with an eclipse attack. In: 2016 IEEE European Symposium on Security and Privacy, vol. 142, pp. 305–320. IEEE Computer Society Press (2016)

22. Pass, R., Seeman, L., Shelat, A.: Analysis of the blockchain protocol in asynchronous networks. In: Coron, J.-S., Nielsen, J.B. (eds.) EUROCRYPT 2017. LNCS, vol. 10211, pp. 643–673. Springer, Cham (2017). https://doi.org/10.1007/978-3-319-56614-6_22

23. Pass, R., Shi, E.: Fruitchains: a fair blockchain. In: ACM Symposium on Principles of Distributed Computing, pp. 315–324. ACM Press (2017)

24. Pass, R., Shi, E.: The sleepy model of consensus. In: Takagi, T., Peyrin, T. (eds.) ASIACRYPT 2017. LNCS, vol. 10625, pp. 380–409. Springer, Cham (2017). https://doi.org/10.1007/978-3-319-70697-9_14

25. Pass, R., Shi, E.: Thunderella: blockchains with optimistic instant confirmation. In: Nielsen, J.B., Rijmen, V. (eds.) EUROCRYPT 2018. LNCS, vol. 10821, pp. 3–33. Springer, Cham (2018). https://doi.org/10.1007/978-3-319-78375-8_1
26. Rosenfeld, M.: Analysis of bitcoin pooled mining reward systems. arXiv preprint arXiv:1112.4980 (2011)
27. Sapirshtein, A., Sompolinsky, Y., Zohar, A.: Optimal selfish mining strategies in bitcoin. In: Grosssklags, J., Preneel, B. (eds.) FC 2016. LNCS, vol. 9603, pp. 515–532. Springer, Heidelberg (2017). https://doi.org/10.1007/978-3-662-54970-4_30
28. Schrijvers, O., Bonneau, J., Boneh, D., Roughgarden, T.: Incentive compatibility of bitcoin mining pool reward functions. In: Grosssklags, J., Preneel, B. (eds.) FC 2016. LNCS, vol. 9603, pp. 477–498. Springer, Heidelberg (2017). https://doi.org/10.1007/978-3-662-54970-4_28
29. Sompolinsky, Y., Zohar, A.: Secure high-rate transaction processing in bitcoin. IACR Cryptology ePrint Archive: Report 2013/881 (2017)
30. Teutsch, J., Jain, S., Saxena, P.: When cryptocurrencies mine their own business. In: Grosssklags, J., Preneel, B. (eds.) FC 2016. LNCS, vol. 9603, pp. 499–514. Springer, Heidelberg (2017). https://doi.org/10.1007/978-3-662-54970-4_29
31. Zohar, A.: Bitcoin: under the hood. In: Communications of the ACM, vol. 58, pp. 104–113. ACM Press (2015)

Secret Sharing

Homomorphic Secret Sharing
for Low Degree Polynomials

Russell W. F. Lai$^{(\boxtimes)}$, Giulio Malavolta, and Dominique Schröder

Friedrich-Alexander-Universität Erlangen-Nürnberg, Erlangen, Germany
{russell.lai,malavolta}@cs.fau.de, dominique.schroeder@fau.de

Abstract. Homomorphic secret sharing (HSS) allows n clients to secret-share data to m servers, who can then homomorphically evaluate public functions over the shares. A natural application is outsourced computation over private data. In this work, we present the first plain-model homomorphic secret sharing scheme that supports the evaluation of polynomials with degree higher than 2. Our construction relies on any degree-k (multi-key) homomorphic encryption scheme and can evaluate degree-$((k + 1)m - 1)$ polynomials, for any polynomial number of inputs n and any sub-logarithmic (in the security parameter) number of servers m. At the heart of our work is a series of combinatorial arguments on how a polynomial can be split into several low-degree polynomials over the shares of the inputs, which we believe is of independent interest.

1 Introduction

Homomorphic secret sharing (HSS), introduced by Boyle, Gilboa, and Ishai [9], allows n clients to secret share the data x into the shares $x_1, \ldots, x_m$ which are distributed to m servers, who can then homomorphically evaluate public functions over the shares. The evaluation is done locally by each server, meaning that there exists a local evaluation algorithm $\mathsf{Eval}(f, x_j)$ that takes as input a description of the function f and a share x_j, and returns a value y_j. The result of the distributed computation can be re-constructed using the decoding algorithm $\mathsf{Dec}(y_1, \ldots, y_m)$, which returns the result $f(x)$. HSS schemes for meaningful classes of functions can be constructed under weak assumptions, such as decisional Diffie-Hellman (DDH) [9] or the security of Paillier encryption scheme [20]. A natural application of HSS is outsourced computation over private data.

1.1 Our Contribution

We propose a family of HSS schemes for polynomials from weak assumptions. More precisely, we show that:

Theorem 1 (Informal). *For all integers $k \geq 0$ and $m = O\left(\frac{\log \lambda}{\log \log \lambda}\right)$, if there exists a degree-k homomorphic public-key encryption scheme, then there exists an m-server homomorphic secret sharing for polynomials of degree $d = (k+1)m-1$.*

T. Peyrin and S. Galbraith (Eds.): ASIACRYPT 2018, LNCS 11274, pp. 279–309, 2018.
https://doi.org/10.1007/978-3-030-03332-3_11

Table 1. Comparison amongst existing HSS schemes for n clients, m servers and resilient against the corruption of t servers. "$n = *$" denotes unbounded number of clients.

	(n, m, t)	Functions	Assumptions
Shamir [30]	$(*, m, t)$	$\mathcal{R}_d$, $d = m - 1$	-
Benaloh [6]	$(*, m, m - 1)$	Affine	-
Information Theoretic PIR [18,31]	$(*, m, 1)$	Selection	-
Beimel et al. [5]	$(1, 3, 1)$	Depth 2 Boolean circuits	-
Computational PIR [13]	$(*, m, 1)$	Selection	Φ-Hiding
Function Secret Sharing [8,25]	$(1, m, m - 1)$	Point Function	OWF
Spooky Encryption [17]	$(*, m, m - 1)$	Circuits	LWE
Boyle et al. [9,10]	$(*, 2, 1)$	Branching Programs	DDH
Catalano and Fiore [15]	$(*, 2, 1)$	$\mathcal{R}_d$, $d = 2k$	k-HE
Sections 4 and 5	$(*, m, 1)$	$\mathcal{R}_d$, $d = (k + 1)m - 1$	k-HE

Our scheme is perfectly correct, assuming a perfectly correct homomorphic encryption scheme, and naturally generalizes to the multi-key and the threshold settings. Our construction is secure in the plain model, without the need for a public-key setup. Interestingly, when $k = 0$, i.e., the encryption scheme has no homomorphic properties, we recover the same functionality of Shamir secret sharing [30], i.e., the supported degree is $d = m - 1$. A comparison amongst existing HSS schemes is summarized in Table 1. Most of the known schemes are either limited to very restricted classes of functions (such as affine or point functions) or require assumptions from which we can instantiate fully homomorphic encryption (FHE), such as the learning with errors (LWE) assumption. Notable exceptions include the work of Catalano and Fiore [15] and the recent breakthrough result of Boyle, Gilboa, and Ishai [9]. The construction of Catalano and Fiore allows to efficiently outsource the computation of degree-$2k$ polynomials to 2 non-colluding servers, using only a degree-k homomorphic encryption scheme. Boyle et al. [9] proposed the first 2-server HSS scheme for branching programs (a superclass of NC1) assuming only the hardness of DDH. A shortcoming of this construction is that the correct result of the evaluation is recovered only with probability $\frac{1}{\text{poly}(\lambda)}$. Additionally, their multi-key variant assumes the existence of a public-key setup.

Our result directly improves over the work of Catalano and Fiore [15] in two ways. First, we increase the computable degree d from $d = 2k$ to $2k+1$. While this improvement seems small, it has significant consequences for small values of k: For example, for $k = 1$, we obtain a 2-server HSS for degree-3 polynomials, which can be bootstrapped to securely evaluate any function in P/poly [1] (assuming the existence of a PRG computable in NC1). In particular, it was shown [1] that any computation in P/poly can be probabilistically encoded by evaluating a set of polynomials of degree 3. The encoding can then be decoded in time proportional to the time complexity of the original computation. Furthermore, the encoding leaks nothing beyond the computation result.

Second, we generalize the scheme of Catalano and Fiore [15] for $m \geq 2$ servers, for any m which is sub-logarithmic in the security parameter. Increasing the number of supported servers allows us to relax the non-collusion assumption. We derive bounds for the maximum degree supported by the resulting scheme and characterize the requirements for determining the minimum number of servers needed for correct computation.

1.2 Applications

Our HSS can be applied directly to outsource the computation of low-degree polynomials on private data. Examples of particular interests include:

1. Privacy-preserving machine learning using shallow neural networks where highly non-linear activation functions are approximated by low-degree (*e.g.*, degree-6 [24]) polynomials to be evaluated on private data.
2. Computation of several statistical measures over private data, such as variance, skewness and higher moments.
3. A round-optimal m-server PIR which can be casted as the evaluation of the selection function (a degree d polynomial) over a private index and the entire database DB for a communication complexity dominated by a factor $\frac{|DB|}{2^d} + \mathsf{poly}(\lambda)$.

A recent work from Boyle et al. [11] describes how to generically bootstrap an additive 3-client 2-server HSS scheme for degree-3 polynomials (in the PKI model) into a round-optimal n-clients m-servers MPC protocol (in the PKI model) for any choice of n and m which are polynomial in the security parameter. Applying a similar transformation to our scheme we obtain a round-optimal n-clients m-servers *server-aided* MPC protocol in the plain model. Server-aided MPC [15,27,28] models real-life scenarios where clients outsource the burden of the computation to (non-colluding) cloud servers. In particular, such model allows the adversary to corrupt any strict subset of the servers *or* the output client, and an arbitrary number of input clients. Beyond being round-optimal, our MPC protocol has several interesting properties. First, it can be instantiated from any multi-key linearly homomorphic encryption (which can be constructed from the DDH assumption [14]). Additionally, our HSS scheme is perfectly correct and thus the transformation from HSS to MPC does not need to go through the probability amplification step of [10]. It also inherits the efficiency features of the transformation of Boyle et al. [11]: If $|f|$ is the size of the circuit computing f, then

- the computational efficiency is $|f| \cdot \mathsf{poly}(\lambda) \cdot n^3$ when $m = O(1)$ or $m = n$, and
- the output client complexity is bounded by $|f| \cdot \mathsf{poly}(\lambda) \cdot m$.

1.3   Our Techniques

We illustrate the basic ideas behind our HSS scheme with a simple example, where two servers wish to privately compute the function $f(x, y, z) = xyz$, for some values x, y, and z belonging to a ring R. The client computes a standard 2-out-of-2 Shamir's secret sharing of each input and arranges the shares into the following matrix:

$$T := \begin{bmatrix} x_1 & x_2 \\ y_1 & y_2 \\ z_1 & z_2 \end{bmatrix} \quad s.t. \ T \begin{bmatrix} 1 \\ 1 \end{bmatrix} = \begin{bmatrix} x \\ y \\ z \end{bmatrix}.$$

In the following, boxed shares are encrypted shares under a linearly homomorphic encryption scheme HE (assume for the moment under the same public key). The client then distributes the shares to the two servers (S_1, S_2) as follows:

$$S_1 \leftarrow \begin{bmatrix} \boxed{x_1} & x_2 \\ \boxed{y_1} & y_2 \\ \boxed{z_1} & z_2 \end{bmatrix} \qquad S_2 \leftarrow \begin{bmatrix} x_1 & \boxed{x_2} \\ y_1 & \boxed{y_2} \\ z_1 & \boxed{z_2} \end{bmatrix}$$

It is not hard to see that distributing the shares in that way does not reveal any information to either of the servers. This follows from the the semantic security of the encryption scheme because each server alone cannot recover the plain value of the original inputs. Now, we show how the two servers can jointly compute the function f over the inputs x, y, and z. Let us expand the product

$$xyz = (x_1 + x_2)(y_1 + y_2)(z_1 + z_2) = \sum_{i=1}^{2} \sum_{j=1}^{2} \sum_{\ell=1}^{2} x_i y_j z_\ell.$$

We now consider each term $x_i y_j z_\ell$ individually. By the pigeonhole principle, for each combination of indices $(i, j, \ell) \in \{1, 2\}^3$ there exists at least one server for which *at most* one of the entries is encrypted. As an example, $(1, 1, 2)$ is a "valid" set of indices for S_2, since it knows the plain values x_1 and y_1 and the encrypted share $\mathsf{HE.Enc(pk}, z_2)$. This implies that every monomial is computable by a server by treating the plaintext entries as a constant and multiplying them to the encrypted entry, e.g.,

$$\mathsf{HE.Enc(pk}, z_2)^{x_1 \cdot y_1} = \mathsf{HE.Enc(pk}, x_1 y_1 z_2).$$

This kind of operations is supported by the encryption scheme since it is linearly homomorphic. Let $\mathcal{I}_1 \subset \{1, 2\}^3$ be the set of valid indices for the server S_1, let $\mathcal{I}_2 := \{1, 2\}^3 \setminus \mathcal{I}_1$ be the set for S_2, and let m_i be the monomial indexed by the i-th set of indices. Exploiting the homomorphic properties of the encryption scheme each server computes

$$\mathsf{HE.Enc}\left(\mathsf{pk}, \sum_{i \in \mathcal{I}_1} m_i\right) \leftarrow S_1 \qquad \mathsf{HE.Enc}\left(\mathsf{pk}, \sum_{i \in \mathcal{I}_2} m_i\right) \leftarrow S_2$$

and sends the two ciphertext to the client. The client (who knows the secret key) can decrypt and sum the plaintexts up to recover the result of the computation: $\sum_{i \in \mathcal{I}_1} m_i + \sum_{i \in \mathcal{I}_2} m_i = \sum_{i=1}^{2} \sum_{j=1}^{2} \sum_{\ell=1}^{2} x_i y_j z_\ell = xyz$. Although the two plaintexts may contain some information of the intermediate values of the computation, this can be easily avoided by adding a dummy sum of two shares of 0. This immediately extends to the computation of any degree-3 polynomial.

Increasing the degree of the polynomial. The next observation is that, using the same principle, increasing the number of servers also increases the degree of the polynomial that can be computed. The inputs are shared across m servers with the same strategy and the view of each server looks as follows:

$$S_j \leftarrow \begin{bmatrix} x_1 \cdots x_{j-1} & \boxed{x_j} & x_{j+1} \cdots x_m \\ \vdots \ddots \vdots & \vdots & \vdots \ddots \vdots \\ z_1 \cdots z_{j-1} & \boxed{z_j} & z_{j+1} \cdots z_m \end{bmatrix}$$

Products are computed as before and a simple combinatorial argument shows that the maximum degree computable is $d = 2m - 1$. Extending to an arbitrary amount of servers introduces some subtlety in the splitting of monomials since now one combination of indices might be computable by more than one server. Thus one needs to take some extra care in the design of a suitable splitting function.

Furthermore, if we admit the existence of a homomorphic encryption scheme for degree-k polynomials, then the degree computable by each server increases even more since now k encrypted entry can be multiplied together locally. Our analysis shows that the degree increases to $d = (k + 1)m - 1$.

Extensions. We consider some natural extensions of our HSS scheme. In a multi-key HSS, clients can independently share their inputs such that servers can evaluate functions over an arbitrary set of shares. Since the shares from different clients are tied to different public keys, we need to upgrade the baseline homomorphic encryption scheme to a multi-key homomorphic encryption scheme. For completeness, we also explore the feasibility of increasing the corruption threshold t by increasing the amount of encrypted entries per server (and decreasing the maximum supported degree d).

1.4   Related Work

Similar techniques on splitting the evaluation of polynomials have been used in the context of simultaneous-message multiparty computation [2] and private information retrieval [4]. Barkol *et al.* [3] leveraged a similar observation to prove an upper bound on the degree of polynomials computable by any information theoretic secret sharing scheme. Another closely related work is by Franklin and Mohassel [21], who propose a two party computation protocol for degree-3 polynomials. However, their protocol is interactive and therefore does not imply a homomorphic secret sharing scheme.

2   Preliminaries

Notations. We denote by $\lambda \in \mathbb{N}$ the security parameter and by $\mathsf{poly}(\lambda)$ any function that is bounded by a polynomial in λ. We address any function that is *negligible* in the security parameter with $\mathsf{negl}(\lambda)$. An algorithm is PPT if it is modeled as a probabilistic Turing machine whose running time is bounded by some function $\mathsf{poly}(\lambda)$. Given a set S, we denote by $x \leftarrow S$ the sampling of an element uniformly at random in S and by $[n]$ we denote the set of integers $\{1, \ldots, n\}$. In the following we recall the definition of statistical distance.

Definition 1 (Statistical Distance). *Let X and Y be two random variables over a finite set $\mathcal{U}$. The statistical distance between X and Y is defined as*

$$\mathbb{SD}[X, Y] = \frac{1}{2} \sum_{u \in \mathcal{U}} |\Pr[X = u] - \Pr[Y = u]|.$$

2.1   Homomorphic Encryption

For conciseness, in the remaining of this section, we work with multivariate polynomials with the number of variables fixed to n. All results can be generalized to the case with unbounded number of variables. Formally, let R be a (finite) ring and $\mathcal{R} := R[X_1, \ldots, X_n]$ be the ring of n-variate polynomials over R. Let $\mathcal{R}_d := \{f \in \mathcal{R} : \deg(f) \leq d\}$ be a set of such polynomials of degree at most d. We recall the notion of homomorphic encryption, for which we assume that the message domain $\mathcal{M}$ of the scheme is a finite ring R that is publicly known and where it is possible to efficiently sample uniformly distributed elements (*e.g.*, [7,14,29], see [15] for a more comprehensive list).

Definition 2 (Homomorphic Encryption (HE)). *A public key homomorphic encryption scheme* $\mathsf{HE} = (\mathsf{KGen}, \mathsf{Enc}, \mathsf{Eval}, \mathsf{Dec})$ *over degree-d polynomials* $\mathcal{R}_d$, *consists of the following* PPT *algorithms:*

$\mathsf{KGen}(1^\lambda)$: *The* key generation *algorithm takes as input the security parameter λ and outputs the public key* pk *and the secret key* sk.
$\mathsf{Enc}(\mathsf{pk}, m)$: *The* encryption *algorithm takes as input the public key* pk *and the message $m \in \mathcal{M}$; it returns a ciphertext $c \in \mathcal{C}$.*
$\mathsf{Eval}(\mathsf{pk}, f, (c_1, \ldots, c_n))$: *The* evaluation *algorithm takes as input the public key* pk, *a polynomial $f \in \mathcal{R}_d$, and a vector of n ciphertexts $(c_1, \ldots, c_n) \in \mathcal{C}^n$; it returns a ciphertext $c \in \mathcal{C}$.*
$\mathsf{Dec}(\mathsf{sk}, c)$: *The* decryption *algorithm takes as input the private key* sk *and a ciphertext $c \in \mathcal{C}$; it returns a plaintext $m \in \mathcal{M}$.*

Correctness. A homomorphic encryption scheme has *decryption correctness* if for any $\lambda \in \mathbb{N}$, any $(\mathsf{pk}, \mathsf{sk}) \in \mathsf{KGen}(1^\lambda)$, and any message $m \in \mathcal{M}$, we have that

$$\Pr[\mathsf{Dec}(\mathsf{sk}, \mathsf{Enc}(\mathsf{pk}, m)) = m] \geq 1 - \mathsf{negl}(\lambda)$$

where the probability is taken over the random coins of Enc.

A homomorphic encryption scheme has *(2-hop) evaluation correctness* if for any $\lambda \in \mathbb{N}$, any $(\mathsf{pk}, \mathsf{sk}) \in \mathsf{KGen}(1^\lambda)$, any polynomials $f, f_1, \ldots, f_n \in \mathcal{R}$ such that $f(f_1, \ldots, f_n) \in \mathcal{R}_d$, any messages $m, m_i \in \mathcal{M}$ for $i \in [n]$ where $m = f(f_1(m_1, \ldots, m_n), \ldots, f_n(m_1, \ldots, m_n))$, we have that

$$\Pr\left[\mathsf{Dec}(\mathsf{sk}, c) = m : \begin{array}{l} \forall i \in [n], c_i \leftarrow \mathsf{Enc}(\mathsf{pk}, m_i), \\ c \leftarrow \mathsf{Eval}(\mathsf{pk}, f, (c_1, \ldots, c_n)) \end{array}\right] \geq 1 - \mathsf{negl}(\lambda)$$

where the probability is taken over the random coins of Enc and Eval. The scheme is *perfectly correct* if the above probabilities are exactly 1.

Compactness. We sometimes require a homomorphic encryption scheme to be *compact*. This imposes a bound on the size of the output of Eval: The size of the output (and consequently the running time of Dec) must be independent from the size of the evaluated polynomial (*e.g.*, when expressed as a circuit) [22].

Security. The security of a homomorphic encryption scheme is the standard notion of semantic security introduced by Goldwasser and Micali [26].

Definition 3 (Semantic Security). *A homomorphic encryption scheme* HE *is IND-CPA-secure (has indistinguishable messages under chosen plaintext attack) if for any* PPT *adversary* $\mathcal{A} = (\mathcal{A}_1, \mathcal{A}_2)$ *there exists a negligible function* $\mathsf{negl}(\lambda)$ *such that*

$$\Pr\left[b = b' : \begin{array}{l} (\mathsf{pk}, \mathsf{sk}) \leftarrow \mathsf{KGen}(1^\lambda), (m_0, m_1, \mathsf{state}) \leftarrow \mathcal{A}_1(\mathsf{pk}), \\ b \leftarrow \{0, 1\}, c \leftarrow \mathsf{Enc}(\mathsf{pk}, m_b), b' \leftarrow \mathcal{A}_1(\mathsf{state}, c) \end{array}\right] \leq \frac{1}{2} + \mathsf{negl}(\lambda)$$

where the probability is taken over the random coins of b, KGen, *and* Enc.

Circuit Privacy. In the context of homomorphic encryption, semantic security might be per se not sufficient to guarantee the secrecy of the encrypted messages. In particular, the output of Eval may still contain some information about the messages encrypted in the input ciphertexts. This leakage is ruled out by the notion of *circuit privacy* [12].

Definition 4 (Circuit Privacy). *A homomorphic encryption scheme* HE *is circuit-private with respect to a family of functions* $\mathcal{F}$, *if there exists a* PPT *simulator* $\mathcal{S}_{\mathsf{HE}}$ *and a negligible function* $\mathsf{negl}(\lambda)$ *such that for any* $\lambda \in \mathbb{N}$, *any* $(\mathsf{pk}, \mathsf{sk}) \in \mathsf{KGen}(1^\lambda)$, *any* $f \in \mathcal{F}$, *any vector of messages* $(m_1, \ldots m_n) \in \mathcal{M}^n$, *and any vector of ciphertexts* $(c_1, \ldots, c_n) \in \mathcal{C}^n$ *such that for all* $i \in \{1 \ldots t\} : c_i \in \mathsf{Enc}(\mathsf{pk}, m_i)$, *we have that*

$$\mathbb{SD}\left[\mathsf{Eval}(\mathsf{pk}, f, (c_1, \ldots, c_n)), \mathcal{S}_{\mathsf{HE}}(1^\lambda, \mathsf{pk}, f(m_1, \ldots, m_n))\right] \leq \mathsf{negl}(\lambda).$$

Multi-Key Homomorphic Encryption. The above definition of homomorphic encryption can be extended to the multi-client settings with minimal changes. To do so, we consider the scenario of n clients, each holding an independent key pair $(\mathsf{pk}_i, \mathsf{sk}_i)$: The key generation and encryption algorithms are unchanged whereas the evaluation and the decryption algorithms take as input vectors of public and secret keys, respectively, and are defined as $\mathsf{Eval}((\mathsf{pk}_1, \dots, \mathsf{pk}_n), f, (c_1, \dots, c_n))$ and $\mathsf{Dec}((\mathsf{sk}_1, \dots, \mathsf{sk}_n), c)$. The definitions of correctness and circuit privacy can easily be modified accordingly.

The (lifted) ElGamal encryption scheme [19] is an example of multi-key homomorphic encryption. Informally, given the ciphertexts $(g^r, h_1^r g^{m_1})$ and $(g^s, h_2^s g^{m_2})$ of m_1 and m_2 under the keys $h_1 = g^{x_1}$ and $h_2 = g^{x_2}$ respectively, one can compute $(g^r, g^s, h_1^r h_2^s g^{m_1+m_2})$ as a ciphertext of $m_1 + m_2$ under the combined key (h_1, h_2). The decryption of lifted ElGamal requires the computation of a discrete logarithm and therefore it is important that the evaluated message lies in a polynomial space. To overcome this limitation, one can use the variant of Castagnos and Laguillaumie [14].

3   Definition of Homomorphic Secret Sharing

We define a variant of homomorphic secret sharing [9] in the public-key setup model. Our variant considers three parties: one output client, many input clients, and many servers. The output client provides the setup, meaning that it generates a public and a secret key and it shares the public key among all participants. Furthermore, it also computes the final result. The input clients secret share their inputs as "input shares" to all servers. The servers homomorphically evaluate functions, in our case polynomials, over the input shares to obtain "output shares". These output shares are then sent to the output client, who uses its secret key to decode them.

The definition can be generalized to the multi-output- client (or multi-key) setting, where different parties receive the output of the computation. The definition can also be lifted to the plain model by simply removing the key generation algorithm and letting all public and secret keys inputs be empty strings.

Definition 5 (Homomorphic Secret Sharing (HSS)). *An n-input (1-output) m-server homomorphic secret sharing scheme for degree-d polynomials $\mathcal{R}_d$ (with public-key setup)* $\mathsf{HSS} = (\mathsf{KGen}, \mathsf{Share}, \mathsf{Eval}, \mathsf{Dec})$ *consists of the following* PPT *algorithms / protocols:*

$(\mathsf{pk}, \mathsf{sk}) \leftarrow \mathsf{KGen}(1^\lambda)$: *On input the security parameter* 1^λ, *the key generation algorithm outputs a public key* pk *and a secret key* sk.

$(s_{i,1}, \dots, s_{i,m}) \leftarrow \mathsf{Share}(\mathsf{pk}, i, x)$: *Given a public key* pk, *an input index* $i \in [n]$, *and an input* $x \in R$, *the sharing algorithm outputs a set of shares* $(s_{i,1}, \dots, s_{i,m})$.

$y_j \leftarrow \mathsf{Eval}(\mathsf{pk}, j, f, \{s_{i,j}\}_{i \in [n]})$: *The evaluation protocol is executed by a server* $\mathcal{S}_j$ *on inputs the public key* pk, *an index* j, *a degree-d polynomial* f, *and the corresponding tuple of shares* $(s_{i,j})_{i \in [n]}$. *Upon termination, the server* $\mathcal{S}_j$ *outputs the corresponding output share* y_j.

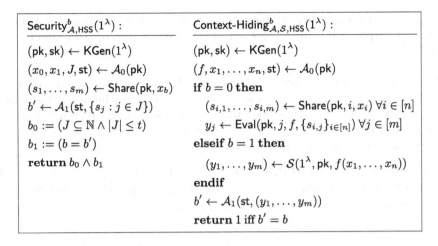

Fig. 1. Security experiments for $(*, m, t)$-HSS

$y \leftarrow \mathsf{Dec}(\mathsf{sk}, (y_1, \ldots, y_m))$: *On input a secret key* sk *and a tuple of output shares* $(y_1, \ldots, y_m)$, *the* decoding *algorithm outputs the result* y *of the evaluation.*

Correctness. An n-input m-server HSS scheme for degree-d polynomials $\mathcal{R}_d$ is *correct* if for any $\lambda \in \mathbb{N}$, any $m, n \in \mathsf{poly}(\lambda)$, any $(\mathsf{pk}, \mathsf{sk}) \in \mathsf{KGen}(1^\lambda)$, any $f \in \mathcal{R}_d$, any n-tuple of inputs $(x_1, \ldots, x_n) \in R^n$, it holds that

$$\Pr \begin{bmatrix} \mathsf{Dec}(\mathsf{sk}, (y_1, \ldots, y_m)) = f(x_1, \ldots, x_n) : \\ \forall i \in [n], (s_{i,1}, \ldots, s_{i,m}) \in \mathsf{Share}(\mathsf{pk}, i, x_i), \\ \forall j \in [m], y_j \in \mathsf{Eval}(\mathsf{pk}, j, f, \{s_{i,j}\}_{i \in [n]}) \end{bmatrix} \geq 1 - \mathsf{negl}(\lambda),$$

where the probability is taken over the random coins of Share and Eval. The scheme is *perfectly correct* if the above probability is exactly 1.

Security. The security of a HSS scheme guarantees that no information about the message is disclosed to any subset of servers of size at most t.

Definition 6 (Security). *An n-input m-server HSS scheme is t-secure if for any $\lambda \in \mathbb{N}$ there exists a negligible function* $\mathsf{negl}(\lambda)$ *such that for any* PPT *algorithm* $\mathcal{A} = (\mathcal{A}_0, \mathcal{A}_1)$,

$$\left| \Pr\left[\mathsf{Security}^0_{\mathcal{A}, \mathsf{HSS}} = 1\right] - \Pr\left[\mathsf{Security}^1_{\mathcal{A}, \mathsf{HSS}} = 1\right] \right| < \mathsf{negl}(\lambda)$$

where $\mathsf{Security}^b_{\mathcal{A}, \mathsf{HSS}}$ *is defined in Fig. 1 for* $b \in \{0, 1\}$.

For conciseness, we refer to an n-input, m-server, t-secure homomorphic secret sharing scheme as an (n, m, t)-HSS. If the number of inputs is unbounded, we denote it by $(*, m, t)$-HSS.

Robustness. An (n, m, t)-HSS scheme is *r-robust* if it suffices for the output client to collect output shares from any r out of m servers to recover the computation result.

Context Hiding. In the setting of outsourced computations, the party who decrypts may be different from the one who provides the inputs of the computation or determines the function to be computed. For this reason, Catalano and Fiore [15] introduced the notion of context-hiding, which assures that the decrypting party learns nothing beyond the output of the computation.

Definition 7 (Context Hiding). *A (n, m, t)-HSS scheme is context-hiding if for any $\lambda \in \mathbb{N}$ there exists a* PPT *simulator $\mathcal{S}$ and a negligible function* $\mathsf{negl}(\lambda)$ *such that for any* PPT *algorithm $\mathcal{A} = (\mathcal{A}_0, \mathcal{A}_1)$,*

$$\left| \Pr\left[\mathsf{Context\text{-}Hiding}^{b}_{\mathcal{A}, \mathcal{S}, \mathsf{HSS}} = 1 \right] - \Pr\left[\mathsf{Context\text{-}Hiding}^{b}_{\mathcal{A}, \mathcal{S}, \mathsf{HSS}} = 1 \right] \right| < \mathsf{negl}(\lambda)$$

where $\mathsf{Context\text{-}Hiding}^{b}_{\mathcal{A}, \mathcal{S}, \mathsf{HSS}}$ *is defined in Fig. 1 for $b \in \{0, 1\}$.*

Multi-Key HSS. Homomorphic secret sharing can be easily generalized to the multi-key/multi-input-client settings by extending the evaluation protocol so that all servers take as input all public keys of the participating output clients, and the decryption algorithm takes as input all of the corresponding secret keys. While the definition of security is unchanged and is required to hold for each secret key, the definitions of correctness, robustness, and context-hiding are extended accordingly.

4   Main Construction in the Public-Key Model

Let m and k be positive integers. We present a generic construction of an unbounded-input (1-output) m-server 1-secure homomorphic secret sharing $((*, m, 1)\text{-HSS})$ scheme HSS for degree-d polynomials $\mathcal{R}_d$ in the public-key model, where $d = (k+1)m - 1$. Our construction is generic and relies only a public key homomorphic encryption scheme HE for degree-k polynomials. We analyze the efficiency of our construction in Sect. 4.3 and show that it satisfies the security definitions for an HSS scheme in Sect. 4.4. For the sake of simplicity, we initially assume a public-key setup and we show how to upgrade it to the plain model in Sect. 5.

4.1   Construction

In the following we provide the reader with an intuitive description of our main construction and we refer to Fig. 2 for a formal description.

Key Generation. On input the security parameter, the output client generates the keys of the encryption HE scheme and publishes the public key.

Secret Sharing. To secret share a ring element $x_i \in R$, the input client samples random base secret shares $x_{i,j} \leftarrow R$ for $j \in [m]$ subject to the constraint that $\sum_{j \in [m]} x_{i,j} = x_i$. It then encrypts each share $x_{i,j}$ for $i \in [n]$, $j \in [m]$ as $\tilde{x}_{i,j}$. Similarly, base shares of 0 are randomly sampled as $(z_{i,1}, \ldots, z_{i,m}) \in R^m$ such that $\sum_{j \in [m]} z_{i,j} = 0$. For each $j' \in [m]$, the resulting j'-th secret share of $(x_1, \ldots, x_n)$ consists of all plaintext base shares $x_{i,j}$ for all $i \in [n]$ and $j \in [m] \setminus \{j'\}$, the encrypted base shares $\tilde{x}_{i,j'}$ for all $i \in [n]$, and the plain 0-shares $z_{i,j'}$ for all $i \in [n]$. The process of creating a share $s_{i,j'}$ is visualized below and formalized in Fig. 2.

$$0 \xrightarrow{\text{Base Share}} \begin{bmatrix} z_{i,1} & \cdots & z_{i,m} \end{bmatrix}$$

$$x_i \xrightarrow{\text{Base Share}} \begin{bmatrix} x_{i,1} & \cdots & x_{i,j'-1} & x_{i,j'} & x_{i,j'+1} & \cdots & x_{i,m} \end{bmatrix}$$

$$\xrightarrow{\text{HE.Enc}} \begin{bmatrix} x_{i,1} & \cdots & x_{i,j'-1} & \boxed{\tilde{x}_{i,j'}} & x_{i,j'+1} & \cdots & x_{i,m} & z_{i,j'} \end{bmatrix} := s_{i,j'}$$

Evaluation. Let $f \in \mathcal{R}_d$ be an n-variate polynomial of degree at most d for some $n \in \mathsf{poly}(\lambda)$. Without loss of generality, suppose the servers are to homomorphically evaluate f over x_i for $i \in [n]$ which have been secret shared as $(s_{i,1}, \ldots, s_{i,m})$ respectively[1]. To do so, $\mathcal{S}_j$ locally evaluates a function f_j over its shares $(s_{1,j}, \ldots, s_{n,j})$, to be explained below. We will construct (for each d) a function Split_d that splits f into some polynomials $g_1, \ldots, g_m$, with the following properties:

1. If $\sum_{j \in [m]} x_{i,j} = x_i$, then $f(x_1, \ldots, x_n) = \sum_{j \in [m]} g_j(x_{1,j}, \ldots, x_{n,j})$.
2. For all $i \in [n]$ and $j \in [m]$, fix $x_{i,j}$ such that $\sum_{j \in [m]} x_{i,j} = x_i$. Let $x_i^{-j} = (x_{i,1}, \ldots, x_{i,j-1}, x_{i,j+1}, \ldots, x_{i,m})$. Then for each $j \in [m]$, g_j is an n-variate polynomial over $(x_{1,j}, \ldots, x_{n,j})$ of degree at most k, whose coefficients are uniquely determined by f and $(x_1^{-j}, \ldots, x_n^{-j})$, denoted by $g_j = \mathsf{Split}_d(j, f, (x_1^{-j}, \ldots, x_n^{-j}))$.

Note that f and $(x_1^{-j}, \ldots, x_n^{-j})$ are known by server $\mathcal{S}_j$ in plaintext. Since the underlying encryption scheme supports degree k polynomials, $\mathcal{S}_j$ can evaluate $f_j = g_j + \sum_{i \in [n]} z_{i,j}$ over the encrypted base shares $(\tilde{x}_{1,j}, \ldots, \tilde{x}_{n,j})$ to obtain the output share y_j, which is a ciphertext encrypting $g_j(x_{1,j}, \ldots, x_{n,j}) + \sum_{i \in [n]} z_{i,j}$.

It remains to show how to construct the Split_d function. Let $f = f(X_1, \ldots, X_n)$ be a polynomial of degree d, write $f = \sum_w a_w M_w(X_1, \ldots, X_n)$, where M_w are monomials of some degree $c \leq d$, where c depends on w, with coefficients a_w. For each w, consider the monomial $M_w(X_1, \ldots, X_n) = X_{w_1} X_{w_2} \cdots X_{w_c}$ for some (possibly duplicating) indices $w_1, \ldots, w_c \in [n]$. Next, by defining a set of new variables $X_{i,j}$ for all $i \in [n]$ and $j \in [m]$ and substituting $X_i = \sum_{j \in [m]} X_{i,j}$, we can expand the monomial M_w as

---

[1] In general, i can be picked from any index set $I \subset \mathbb{N}$ of size n.

$$M_w(X_1, \ldots, X_n) = X_{w_1} X_{w_2} \cdots X_{w_c}$$

$$= \prod_{i \in \{w_1, \ldots, w_c\}} \left(\sum_{j=1}^{m} X_{i,j} \right)$$

$$= X_{w_1,1} \cdots X_{w_c,1} + \ldots + X_{w_1,m} \cdots X_{w_c,m}$$

$$= \sum_{e \in [m]^c} X_{w_1,e_1} \cdots X_{w_c,e_c}.$$

We now inspect the summand $X_{w_1,e_1} \cdots X_{w_c,e_c}$. Recall that $c \le d = (k+1)m-1$. By the (dual of) pigeonhole principle, any way of writing c as a sum of m non-negative integers must contain a summand which is at most k, where the "worst case" is $c = \underbrace{(k+1) + \ldots + (k+1)}_{m-1} + k$. In other words, for each summand $X_{w_1,e_1} \cdots X_{w_c,e_c}$, there exists an index $j \in \{e_1, \ldots, e_c\}$ which appears at most k times in the expression. Furthermore, such an index j can be chosen deterministically by a publicly known algorithm. For the moment, we will continue the description of the construction without specifying explicitly such an algorithm. In Sect. 4.3 we will give two explicit examples and analyze their efficiency.

With this observation in mind, we can rewrite each monomial M_w as

$$M_w(X_1, \ldots, X_n) = \sum_{e \in [m]^c} X_{w_1,e_1} \cdots X_{w_c,e_c}$$

$$= \sum_{j \in [m]} h_{w,j}[X_1^{-j}, \ldots, X_n^{-j}](X_{1,j}, \ldots, X_{n,j})$$

where $X_i^{-j} = (X_{i,1}, \ldots, X_{i,j-1}, X_{i,j+1}, \ldots, X_{i,n})$ is defined similar to x_i^{-j}, and each term $h_{w,j}[X_1^{-j}, \ldots, X_n^{-j}](X_{1,j}, \ldots, X_{n,j})$ is the sum over the subset of all summands with j being the chosen index as defined by the property above. Note that each $h_{w,j}$ can be interpreted as a degree-k (at most) polynomial over $X_{1,j}, \ldots, X_{n,j}$, with coefficients depending on $X_1^{-j}, \ldots, X_n^{-j}$.

Finally, we can rewrite the polynomial $f(X_1, \ldots, X_n)$ as

$$f(X_1, \ldots, X_n) = \sum_w a_w M_w = \sum_w a_w \sum_{j \in [n]} h_{w,j} = \sum_{j \in [m]} \sum_w a_w h_{w,j}.$$

Since each $h_{w,j}$ is a degree-k polynomial over $X_{1,j}, \ldots, X_{n,j}$, we can define $g_j := \sum_w a_w h_{w,j}$ which is a degree-k polynomial function over $X_{1,j}, \ldots, X_{n,j}$, with coefficients uniquely determined by f and $X_1^{-j}, \ldots, X_n^{-j}$. This completes the construction of the Split_d function.

Decoding. Let $f_{\mathsf{Add}}(Y_1, \ldots, Y_m) = Y_1 + \ldots + Y_m$. Since f_{Add} is of degree-1, its homomorphic evaluation is supported by HE. Thus, given the output shares $y_1, \ldots, y_m$ (which are HE ciphertexts), the output client can homomorphically evaluate f_{Add} over $y_1, \ldots, y_m$, which are ciphertexts encrypting $f_j(x_1^{-j}, \ldots, x_n^{-j})$ respectively. By the construction of f_j, the evaluation yields a ciphertext encrypting $f(x_1, \ldots, x_n)$, which can then be decrypted using sk.

Correctness. Note that by condition 2 of the Split_d algorithm the function g_j (and consequently f_j) is of degree at most k. Therefore the polynomial $f_{\text{Add}}(f_1, \ldots, f_m)$ is of degree at most k. By the evaluation correctness of HE, we have that

$$y = \mathsf{HE.Dec}(\mathsf{sk}, c) = \sum_{j \in [m]} g_j(x_{1,j}, \ldots, x_{n,j}) + \sum_{i \in [n]} \sum_{j \in [m]} z_{i,j}$$

except with negligible probability. By condition 1 of the Split_d algorithm and since for all $i \in [n]$ it holds that $\sum_{j \in [m]} z_{i,j} = 0$, we have that

$$y = \sum_{j \in [m]} g_j(x_{1,j}, \ldots, x_{n,j}) + \sum_{i \in [n]} \sum_{j \in [m]} z_{i,j}$$
$$= f(x_1, \ldots, x_n) + \sum_{i \in [n]} 0 = f(x_1, \ldots, x_n).$$

Note that if HE is perfectly correct, then HSS is also perfectly correct.

$(\mathsf{pk}, \mathsf{sk}) \leftarrow \mathsf{KGen}(1^\lambda)$

$(\mathsf{pk}, \mathsf{sk}) \leftarrow \mathsf{HE.KGen}(1^\lambda)$
return $(\mathsf{pk}, \mathsf{sk})$

$y \leftarrow \mathsf{Dec}(\mathsf{sk}, y_1, \ldots, y_m)$

$c \leftarrow \mathsf{HE.Eval}(\mathsf{pk}, f_{\text{Add}}, (y_1, \ldots, y_m))$
$y \leftarrow \mathsf{HE.Dec}(\mathsf{sk}, c)$
return y

$(s_{i,1}, \ldots, s_{i,m}) \leftarrow \mathsf{Share}(\mathsf{pk}, i, x_i)$

$(x_{i,1}, \ldots, x_{i,m}) \leftarrow R^m$ s.t. $\sum_{j \in [m]} x_{i,j} = x_i$

$(z_{i,1}, \ldots, z_{i,m}) \leftarrow R^m$ s.t. $\sum_{j \in [m]} z_{i,j} = 0$

$\tilde{x}_{i,j} \leftarrow \mathsf{HE.Enc}(\mathsf{pk}, x_{i,j})\ \forall j \in [m]$
$x_i^{-j} := (x_{i,1}, \ldots, x_{i,j-1}, x_{i,j+1}, \ldots, x_{i,m})$
$s_{i,j} := (x_i^{-j}, \tilde{x}_{i,j}, z_{i,j})$
return $(s_{i,1}, \ldots, s_{i,m})$

$y_j \leftarrow \mathsf{Eval}(j, f, (s_{1,j}, \ldots, s_{n,j}))$

parse $s_{i,j}$ **as** $(x_i^{-j}, \tilde{x}_{i,j}, z_{i,j})$

$f_j := \mathsf{Split}_d(j, f, (x_1^{-j}, \ldots, x_n^{-j})) + \sum_{i \in [n]} z_{i,j}$

$y_j \leftarrow \mathsf{HE.Eval}(\mathsf{pk}, f_j, (\tilde{x}_{1,j}, \ldots, \tilde{x}_{n,j}))$
return y_j

Fig. 2. Construction of a homomorphic secret sharing scheme HSS in the public-key setup model. (The functions f_{Add} and Split_d are defined in the text description.)

Remark 1 (The case $k = 0$). For completeness, we remark that the construction still works for the case of $k = 0$ (*i.e.*, HE is a public-key *non-homomorphic* encryption) for the most part, except that "homomorphic evaluations" (in the evaluation protocol and the decoding algorithm) are performed over the plaintext shares rather than ciphertexts. The ciphertexts can actually be discarded or not created in the first place.

4.2   Discussion

In the following we first argue that our techniques are "tight" with respect to the degree of the polynomial to be computed. Then we discuss some function-dependent optimizations that we can apply to improve the efficiency of our protocol.

On the upper bound of the supported degree d. In our construction, we showed that it is possible to support the evaluation of polynomials of degree at most $(k+1)m - 1$ using m servers. By a counting argument, we can show that $(k+1)m - 1$ is also the maximum possible supported degree of our construction. Suppose the n servers were to evaluate a degree $(k + 1)m$ polynomial f, then f contains a monomial $M_w = \sum_{j_1,\ldots,j_{c_w} \in [m]} X_{i_w,1,j_1} \cdots X_{i_w,c_w,j_{c_w}}$ of degree $(k+1)m$ which contains a summand $X_{i_w,1,j_1} \cdots X_{i_w,c_w,j_{c_w}}$ in which each $j \in \{j_1,\ldots,j_{c_w}\} = [m]$ appears exactly $k + 1$ times in the expression. Thus, it is impossible to write $M_w = \sum_{j \in [m]} h_{w,j}[X_{i_1}^{-j},\ldots,X_{i_c}^{-j}](X_{i_w,1,j},\ldots,X_{i_w,c_w,j})$ such that each $h_{w,j}$ is a polynomial of degree at most k. In fact, no matter how the indices j are chosen, there must exists $h_{w,j}$ which is of degree at least $k + 1$.

On computing polynomials with a subset of servers. A naïve usage of our HSS scheme requires one to query all of the m servers even when the degree of the polynomial is lower than d. In fact, a smaller number of servers could be used, with the following modification: Consider any subset $M \subseteq [m]$ and any ordering of its indices (say lexicographical). All base shares of each input $x_i = (x_{i,1},\ldots,x_{i,m})$ for m servers can be transformed into base shares for any set of $|M|$ servers by setting

$$x_i \overset{\text{Base Share}}{\to} \left[x_{i,j^*} + \sum_{j \notin M} x_{i,j}, \{x_{i,j}\}_{j \in M \setminus j^*} \right]$$

where j^* is the first element of M. This operation can be computed also homomorphically (when needed). Note that the resulting base share is a well-formed input for the set M. Additionally one needs to provide each server with all of the 0-shares $(z_{i,1},\ldots,z_{i,m})$ and apply the same transformation as described above. The resulting share $s_{i,j}$ is a correctly formed share for a set of $|M|$ servers. Note that this operation can be performed non-interactively by all servers belonging to M.

   In another perspective, one can view this as a mechanism for performing the evaluation (although for a lower degree polynomial) using only a subset of the servers of size r, *i.e.*, a r-robust HSS scheme. Using combinatorial arguments similar to those in Sect. 4.1, one can conclude that any size-r subset of the m servers is able to evaluate polynomials of degree $km + r - 1$.

On arithmetic circuits of the form $\sum \prod \sum$. In the construction of the Split_d function, we assume that the polynomial f to be evaluated is given in the fully expanded form. In general, the number of monomials in a fully expanded polynomial of degree d is exponential in d. It is therefore desirable if the Split_d function can handle representations of polynomials f which are not fully unrolled. In certain special cases, this might save an exponential factor (of the number of monomials and hence server computation complexity) in the degree of the polynomial.

Our observation is that in our construction, computing linear functions over the inputs is essentially "free": Given a linear function $\mathcal{L}(X_1, \ldots, X_n)$, and a set of shares $\{s_{i,j}\}_{i=1}^n = \{(x_i^{-j}, \tilde{x}_{i,j}, z_{i,j})\}_{i=1}^n$, each server $\mathcal{S}_j$ can locally compute $x'_{j'} = \mathcal{L}(x_{1,j'}, \ldots, x_{n,j'})$ for $j' \neq j$, and $\tilde{x}'_j = \mathsf{HE.Eval}(\mathsf{pk}, \mathcal{L}, (\tilde{x}_{1,j}, \ldots, \tilde{x}_{n,j}))$, which constitutes essentially the j-th share of the value $\mathcal{L}(x_1, \ldots, x_n)$.

With the above observation in mind, we notice that if f is given in the $(\sum \prod \sum)$-form $f = \sum_{w=1}^v a_w \prod_{i=1}^d \mathcal{L}_{w,i}(X_1, \ldots, X_n)$, i.e., the sum of products of d linear functions over $X_1, \ldots, X_n$, the servers can first locally evaluate the linear functions and treat the result as shares of additional inputs, then apply the Split_d function on these new inputs. Note that even if f consists of only one product of d linear functions, the fully expanded form of f would contain $(n+1)^d$ monomials in general. This class of functions may be of particular interest since there exists a generic efficient transformation [23], due to an observation by Ben-Or, from any multilinear symmetric polynomial to depth-3 $(\sum \prod \sum)$-arithmetic circuits.

4.3 Efficiency Analysis

We analyze the efficiency of the construction in terms of server communication and computation complexity. The client-server communication is that of one ciphertext and therefore is independent from the size of the function that is computed, under the assumption that the underlying encryption scheme is *compact*. The input and output clients computation complexity is dominated by m calls to the encryption algorithm and one decryption, respectively.

The complexity of server computation depends on the design of the Split_d functions. Below, we first analyze a simpler greedy design where the workload is distributed to the servers unevenly. Next, we analyze a fair design in which the workload of each server is identical. Surprisingly, the fair design seems to be worse than the greedy design in terms of computation complexity for $k > 1$.

We assume the polynomial f to be evaluated is given in the form $f = \sum_w a_w M_w(X_1, \ldots, X_n)$, where M_w are monomials of degree at most d. The efficiency analysis can be adapted easily to the setting where f is given as a sum of product of linear functions.

To bound the computation complexity of the servers, it is useful to use the following upper bounds, which can be verified straightforwardly:

$$\binom{n}{r_1,\ldots,r_m,n-r_1-\ldots-r_m} \leq \frac{(en)^{r_1+\ldots+r_m}}{r_1^{r_1}\cdot\ldots\cdot r_m^{r_m}} \tag{1}$$

$$\left(\frac{\alpha}{r}\right)^r \leq e^{\frac{\alpha}{e}} \tag{2}$$

where the multinomial coefficient $\binom{n}{r_1,\ldots,r_m,n-r_1-\ldots-r_m}$ denotes the number of ways to distribute n distinct objects into $m+1$ bins, with r_j objects in the j-th bin for $j \in [m]$, and $n - r_1 - \ldots - r_m$ objects in the last bin, and e is Euler's constant.

The Greedy Approach. One natural choice of Split_d is the greedy one: For each monomial $M_w = \prod_{i\in\{w_1,\ldots,w_c\}}\left(\sum_{j=1}^m x_{i,j}\right)$ in f, the first server (according to some fixed order) computes as many monomials in M_w as possible, then the second server computes as many monomials as possible except those which are already computed by the first server, and so on. We assume that each polynomial is given in the expanded form (as a sum of monomials). In turn, each monomial M_w is the product of several terms $X_{w_1}\cdots X_{w_c}$ for some $c \in [d]$, where each term X_i is shared as $X_i := x_{i,1} + \ldots + x_{i,m}$ for $i \in [n]$. This defines a circuit of depth 3 with $(n+1)$ sum gates.

As computing sums are essentially free, we analyze the computation complexity of each of the servers, in terms of the number of product gates of the arithmetic circuit evaluated. It is useful to consider the following matrix:

$$T := \begin{bmatrix} x_{w_1,1} & x_{w_1,2} & \cdots & x_{w_1,m} \\ x_{w_2,1} & x_{w_2,2} & \cdots & x_{w_2,m} \\ \vdots & \vdots & \ddots & \vdots \\ x_{w_c,1} & x_{w_c,2} & \cdots & x_{w_c,m} \end{bmatrix}.$$

All monomials in M_w can be obtained by multiplying c elements, such that each of which is chosen from a distinct row of T. The monomials that the first server can compute (homomorphically) consists of those obtained by multiplying at most k elements from the first column. One (efficient) way to compute the sum of these monomials is to first sum up the last $m - 1$ elements in each row i as $v_i = \sum_{j>1} x_{w_i,j}$, compute the products obtained by multiplying ℓ terms in $\{x_{w_1,1},\ldots,x_{w_c,1}\}$ and $(c-\ell)$ terms in $\{v_1,\ldots,v_c\}$ for $\ell \in \{0,\ldots,k\}$, and sum up all products. The circuit for computing the above consists of $\sum_{\ell=0}^k \binom{c}{\ell}$ product gates.

The second server computes all monomials obtained by multiplying at most k elements from the second column, except those already computed by the first server. A way to compute this is first sum up the last $m-2$ elements in each row i as $v_i = \sum_{j>2} x_{w_i,j}$, compute the products obtained by multiplying ℓ_1 terms in $\{x_{w_1,1},\ldots,x_{w_c,1}\}$, ℓ_2 terms in $\{x_{w_1,2},\ldots,x_{w_c,2}\}$, and $\ell_3 = (c-\ell_1-\ell_2)$ terms in $\{v_1,\ldots,v_c\}$ for $\ell_1 \in \{k+1,\ldots,c\}$ and $\ell_2 \in \{0,\ldots,k\}$ such that $\ell_1+\ell_2 \leq c$, and sum up all products. The number of product gates in the circuit for computing the above is given by

$$\sum_{\substack{\ell_1, \ell_2 : \\ \ell_1 + \ell_2 \leq c \\ \ell_1 \in \{k+1, \ldots, c\} \\ \ell_2 \in \{0, \ldots, k\}}} \binom{c}{\ell_1, \ell_2, c - \ell_1 - \ell_2}.$$

Proceeding this way, we can derive that the number of product gates in the circuit evaluated by the j-th server is given by

$$\sum_{\substack{\ell_1, \ldots, \ell_j : \\ \ell_1 + \ldots + \ell_j \leq c \\ \ell_1, \ldots, \ell_{j-1} \in \{k+1, \ldots, c\} \\ \ell_j \in \{0, \ldots, k\}}} \binom{c}{\ell_1, \ldots, \ell_j, c - \ell_1 - \ldots - \ell_j}$$

$$\leq \sum_{\substack{\ell_1, \ldots, \ell_j : \\ \ell_1 + \ldots + \ell_j \leq c \\ \ell_1, \ldots, \ell_{j-1} \in \{k+1, \ldots, c\} \\ \ell_j \in \{0, \ldots, k\}}} \frac{c^{\ell_1 + \ldots + \ell_j}}{\ell_1^{\ell_1} \ldots \ell_j^{\ell_j}}$$

$$= \sum_{\substack{\ell_1, \ldots, \ell_j : \\ \ell_1 + \ldots + \ell_j \leq c \\ \ell_1, \ldots, \ell_{j-1} \in \{k+1, \ldots, c\} \\ \ell_j \in \{0, \ldots, k\}}} \prod_{\ell \in \{\ell_1, \ldots, \ell_j\}} \left(\frac{c}{\ell}\right)^\ell$$

$$\leq (k+1)(c-k-1)^{j-1} j e^{c/e}$$
$$\leq (k+1)(c-k-1)^{m-1} m e^{c/e}$$
$$= O(m^m)$$
$$= O(2^{m \log m})$$

In order for the computation complexity of the servers to be polynomial, we set $m = O\left(\frac{\log \lambda}{\log \log \lambda}\right)$. Then, assuming f contains polynomially many monomials (or products of linear functions), the computation complexity of each server is bounded by

$$\mathsf{poly}(\lambda) \cdot O(2^{m \log m}) = O\left(2^{\frac{\log \lambda}{\log \log \lambda} \log\left(\frac{\log \lambda}{\log \log \lambda}\right)}\right) < O(2^{\log \lambda}) = \mathsf{poly}(\lambda)$$

The Fair Approach. Observe that in the greedy approach (the upper bound of) the workload of the j-th server increases as j increases, meaning that the distribution of work is unfair. This is undesirable since the overall computation time is determined by that of the slowest server. If the workload is distributed evenly, it might be possible that the workload of each server is lower than that of the slowest server in the greedy approach.

We denote by a vector $(\ell_1, \ldots, \ell_m)$ (where $\sum_{j \in [m]} \ell_j = d$) the classification of monomials obtainable by multiplying ℓ_j terms in the j-th column of T. For example, consider the case $k = 1$, $m = 3$, and $d = (k + 1)m - 1 = 5$. The monomial with classification $(1, 2, 2)$ can only be computed by the server with the first column encrypted, which is $\mathcal{S}_1$. Similarly, both $\mathcal{S}_1$ and $\mathcal{S}_2$ can compute monomials in the class $(0, 1, 4)$.

With the above observation in mind, we can design the Split_d function such that each server computes a weighted-sum of all monomials it can compute, where the monomials of a class that δ-many servers can compute are assigned the weight $1/\delta$ (assuming the message space R is also a field)[2]. The servers can thus group monomials of the same weight together, and try to reduce the number of multiplications as much as possible.

In the following, we describe one of the ways to group monomials, which is identical for all servers. Consider $\mathcal{S}_j$. To obtain the sum of all monomials which are only computable by $\mathcal{S}_j$, it chooses from each of the $m - 1$ columns besides its own (column j) $k + 1$ terms. This makes sure that no matter how the remaining k terms are chosen, the resulting monomials are only computable by $\mathcal{S}_j$. Due to the latter, it simply sum each of the remaining k rows where terms are not yet chosen, and multiply them to all $(k + 1)(m - 1)$ terms chosen in the beginning. Note that the number of ways to choose those $(k + 1)(m - 1)$ terms is given by

$$
S_1 := \binom{m-1}{m-1} \underbrace{\binom{c}{k+1,\ldots,k+1,k}}_{m-1}
$$

$$
\leq \sum_{\ell_1=0}^{k} \binom{m-1}{m-1} \underbrace{\binom{c}{k+1,\ldots,k+1,\ell_1,c-(k+1)(m-1)-\ell_1}}_{m-1},
$$

where inequality will be useful for the analysis later. Summing all S_1 polynomials obtained by the above procedures (and assigning weight 1 to them) covers all monomials that are only computable by $\mathcal{S}_j$.

Moving on, to obtain the sum of all monomials which are only computable by $\mathcal{S}_j$ and one other servers, $\mathcal{S}_j$ chooses $m-2$ columns out of the other $m-1$ columns, and chooses $k + 1$ terms each from these $m - 2$ columns. Let j' be the column which is not chosen. It then chooses ℓ_1 items from its own column (from the remaining rows), and ℓ_2 items from column j', such that $\ell_1, \ell_2 \in \{0, \ldots, k\}$. This ensures that both $\mathcal{S}_j$ and $\mathcal{S}_{j'}$ and no server else can compute these monomials. Next, it sums up the elements in each of the remaining rows in the $m - 2$ chosen columns, and multiplies each sum with the $(k+1)(m-2) + \ell_1 + \ell_2$ terms chosen before. Note that the number of ways to choose those $(k + 1)(m - 2) + \ell_1 + \ell_2$ terms is given by

$$
S_2 := \sum_{\ell_1,\ell_2=0}^{k} \binom{m-1}{m-2} \underbrace{\binom{c}{k+1,\ldots,k+1,\ell_1,\ell_2,c-(k+1)(m-2)-\ell_1-\ell_2}}_{m-2}.
$$

---

[2] In general, it suffices for the servers to assign weights which add up to 1.

Summing all S_2 polynomials obtained by the above procedures and assigning weight $1/2$ to them covers all monomials that are only computable by S_j and exactly one other server. Continue in this way, we conclude that the number of product gates for S_j is given by

$$S := \sum_{i=1}^{m-1} \sum_{\ell_1,\ldots,\ell_i=0}^{k} \binom{m-1}{m-i} \binom{c}{\underbrace{k+1,\ldots,k+1}_{m-i},\ell_1,\ldots,\ell_i, c-(k+1)(m-i)-\ell_1-\ldots-\ell_i}.$$

Using the inequality above, we have

$$\begin{aligned}
S &\le \sum_{i=1}^{m-1} \sum_{\ell_1,\ldots,\ell_i=0}^{k} \left(\frac{e(m-1)}{(m-i)}\right)^{m-i} \frac{(ec)^{(k+1)(m-i)+\ell_1+\ldots+\ell_i}}{(k+1)^{(k+1)(m-i)}\ell_1^{\ell_1}\cdot\ldots\cdot\ell_i^{\ell_i}} \\
&= \sum_{i=1}^{m-1} \left(\frac{e(m-1)}{(m-i)}\right)^{m-i} \frac{(ec)^{(k+1)(m-i)}}{(k+1)^{(k+1)(m-i)}} \sum_{\ell_1,\ldots,\ell_i=0}^{k} \prod_{\ell\in\{\ell_1,\ldots,\ell_i\}} \left(\frac{ec}{\ell}\right)^{\ell} \\
&= \sum_{i=1}^{m-1} \left(\frac{e(m-1)(ec)^{(k+1)}}{(m-i)(k+1)^{(k+1)}}\right)^{m-i} (k+1)i \left(\frac{ec}{\ell}\right)^{\ell} \\
&\le \frac{(k+1)m(m-1)}{2} \exp\left(\frac{(m-1)(ec)^{(k+1)}}{(k+1)^{(k+1)}}+c\right) \\
&\le O(2^{m^k}).
\end{aligned}$$

In order for the computation complexity of the servers to be polynomial, we set $m = O\left(\log^{1/k}\lambda\right)$. Then, assuming f contains polynomially many monomials (or products of linear functions), the computation complexity of each server is bounded by

$$\mathsf{poly}(\lambda)\cdot O(2^{m^k}) = O(2^{(\log^{1/k}\lambda)^k}) = O(2^{\log\lambda}) = \mathsf{poly}(\lambda).$$

Note that for the case $k = 1$, i.e., a linearly homomorphic encryption is used, we can set $m = O(\log\lambda)$, which is better than $m = O\left(\frac{\log\lambda}{\log\log\lambda}\right)$ set in the greedy approach.

4.4   Security Proof

We show that our construction is secure as per Definition 6 assuming HE is IND-CPA-secure. Furthermore, if HE is circuit-private, then our construction is context hiding.

Theorem 2. *Let* HE *be an IND-CPA-secure public key encryption scheme, then* HSS *constructed in Fig. 2 is a secure* $(*, m, 1)$*-HSS scheme in the public-key setup model.*

Proof. Suppose there exists an efficient adversary $\mathcal{A}$ which breaks the security of HSS with non-negligible probability, we show how to construct another efficient adversary $\mathcal{C}$ against the IND-CPA-security of HE.

$\mathcal{C}$ participates in the IND-CPA experiment of HE and receives pk which is forwarded to $\mathcal{A}$. The latter chooses $x_0^*, x_1^* \in R$, and an index $j^* \in [m]$. $\mathcal{C}$ samples $x_1, \ldots, x_{j^*-1}, x'_{j^*+1}, \ldots, x_m \leftarrow R$, and sets $x_{b,j^*} := x_b^* - \sum_{j \in [m] \setminus \{j^*\}}$ for $b \in \{0,1\}$. It then queries the challenge oracle of HE on (x_{0,j^*}, x_{1,j^*}), and receives in return $\tilde{x}_{j^*}$. Finally, it sends $s_{j^*} := (x_1, \ldots, x_{j^*-1}, \tilde{x}_{j^*}, x_{j^*+1}, \ldots, x_n)$ to $\mathcal{A}$. Eventually, $\mathcal{A}$ returns a bit b', which is forwarded by $\mathcal{C}$ to the IND-CPA experiment.

We analyze the success probability of $\mathcal{C}$ in breaking the IND-CPA-security of HE. By construction, if b is the bit chosen by the challenge oracle of HE, $\mathcal{C}$ simulates the $\mathsf{Security}^b_{\mathcal{A},\mathsf{HSS}}$ experiment for $\mathcal{A}$ faithfully, i.e., the view of $\mathcal{A}$ simulated by $\mathcal{C}$ is identical to that in $\mathsf{Security}^b_{\mathcal{A},\mathsf{HSS}}$. Therefore, the probability of $\mathcal{C}$ guessing b correctly is identical to that of $\mathcal{A}$ breaking the security of HSS. This concludes our proof. $\square$

Theorem 3. *Let* HE *be a circuit-private public key homomorphic encryption scheme, then* HSS *constructed in Fig. 2 is a context-hiding* $(*, m, 1)$-*HSS scheme in the public-key setup model.*

Proof. We first describe the simulator $\mathcal{S}$: On input the security parameter 1^λ, the public key pk, and the function output r, the simulator $\mathcal{S}$ samples some random $(r_1, \ldots, r_m)$ under the constraint that $\sum_{j \in [m]} r_j = r$ and executes $c_j \leftarrow \mathcal{S}_{\mathsf{HE}}(1^\lambda, \mathsf{pk}, r_j)$, for all $j \in [m]$, where $\mathcal{S}_{\mathsf{HE}}$ is the simulator of HE. The simulator $\mathcal{S}$ returns $(c_1, \ldots, c_m)$.

We analyze the distribution of the output of the simulator $\mathcal{S}$. Consider the output of the Eval algorithm, for all $j \in [m]$. By the circuit privacy of HE we have that:

$$
\begin{aligned}
y_j &= \mathsf{HE.Eval}(\mathsf{pk}, f_j, (\tilde{x}_{1,j}, \ldots, \tilde{x}_{n,j})) \\
&\approx \mathcal{S}_{\mathsf{HE}}\left(1^\lambda, \mathsf{pk}, f_j(x_{1,j}, \ldots, x_{n,j})\right) \\
&= \mathcal{S}_{\mathsf{HE}}\left(1^\lambda, \mathsf{pk}, g_j(x_{1,j}, \ldots, x_{n,j}) + \sum_{i \in [n]} z_{i,j}\right)
\end{aligned}
$$

where $\approx$ denotes statistical indistinguishability. Consider any subset $M \subseteq [m]$ of size $m-1$. Then for all $j \in M$ we have that:

$$
\begin{aligned}
y_j &\approx \mathcal{S}_{\mathsf{HE}}\left(1^\lambda, \mathsf{pk}, g_j(x_{1,j}, \ldots, x_{n,j}) + \sum_{i \in [n]} z_{i,j}\right) \\
&\approx \mathcal{S}_{\mathsf{HE}}\left(1^\lambda, \mathsf{pk}, r_j\right)
\end{aligned}
$$

for some $r_j \in R$ sampled uniformly at random, since there exists at least one (in fact all) $i \in [n]$ such that $z_{i,j}$ is sampled uniformly and independently in R. By the correctness of HSS it must be the case that for $j \notin M$:

$$
y_j \approx \mathcal{S}_{\mathsf{HE}}\left(1^\lambda, \mathsf{pk}, \sum_{j \in [m]} r_j - r\right)
$$

which is exactly the output of the simulator $\mathcal{S}$.   □

Multi-Use Context-Hiding. We point out that the standard definition of context-hiding takes into account only one execution of the Eval algorithms, whereas in certain scenarios it might be desirable to preserve context-hiding even when multiple functions are evaluated over the same shares. We propose a simple modification of our scheme that achieves the stronger version of the property: Instead of computing the shares for the value 0, the sharing algorithm initializes m keys for a certain pseudo-random function PRF $(\kappa_{i,1}, \ldots, \kappa_{i,m})$ and each server j is given $(\kappa_{i,j}, \kappa_{i,(j+1 \mod m)})$. Then, for all $j \in [m]$, the function f_j is defined as

$$f_j := \mathsf{Split}_d(j, f, (x_1^{-j}, \ldots, x_n^{-j})) + \sum_{i \in [n]} \mathsf{PRF}(\kappa_{i,j}, f) - \sum_{i \in [n]} \mathsf{PRF}(\kappa_{i,(j+1 \mod m)}, f).$$

The analysis follows, with minor modifications, along the lines of what discussed above.

5   Multi-key Construction in the Plain Model

In the following we show how to extend the scheme in Sect. 4 to the multi-key settings (in the public-key setup model) and how to turn it into a plain model scheme.

5.1   Intuition

First, we observe that the main construction in Sect. 4 can be naturally extended to the multi-key setting, where shares under different public keys are combined in the evaluation algorithm. In this context, it is useful to distinguish between *input* and *output* clients: The former provide the input data and share them to the same set of servers[3] whereas the latter decode the output of the computation. Note that these two sets of clients may intersect arbitrarily. We stress that the clients are not assumed to communicate with each other and can generate their input shares independently. Adapting our protocol to this setting is surprisingly simple: In a nutshell, it is sufficient to replace the homomorphic encryption scheme with the corresponding multi-key variant.

Next, we turn the multi-key construction into a plain model construction. The idea is to let the *input clients*, instead of the output clients, generate in the share algorithm a fresh pair of public and secret keys. They then secret share their data under the freshly generated public key as in the multi-key construction, and further secret share the fresh secret keys to all m servers using an m-out-of-m secret sharing scheme. The servers evaluate the shares as in the multi-key

---

[3] While sharing to different sets of servers is in general possible, it limits the class of polynomials that can be computed. Specifically, if there exists a server picked by client i but not client j, then any polynomial which contains a product of data contributed by both clients is not computable.

construction, and forward the output shares along with the shares of the secret keys to the output client. The latter recovers the secret keys and uses them to decode the output shares as in the multi-key construction.

5.2   Construction

Below, we describe briefly the modifications made to the construction in Sect. 4 to obtain a plain model scheme. A formal description is given in Fig. 3. Let m and k be positive integers. We present a generic construction of an unbounded-input (1-output) m-server 1-secure homomorphic secret sharing $((*, m, 1)$-HSS) scheme pHSS for degree-d polynomials $\mathcal{R}_d$ in the plain model, where $d = (k + 1)m - 1$, using only a public-key multi-key homomorphic encryption scheme HE for degree-k polynomials.

Key Generation. In the plain model, key generation is no longer needed.

Secret Sharing. An input client runs the key generation algorithm for a multi-key homomorphic encryption scheme to generate a public key and a secret key independent of other input clients. It then runs the same sharing algorithm (under the generated public key) to share its private data. It also secret-shares the secret key of the encryption scheme using an m-out-of-m secret sharing scheme. Finally, it appends the public key and the j-th share of the secret key to the j-th input share given to the j-th server.

Evaluation. The evaluation performed by the servers is almost identical, except that the evaluation algorithm of the multi-key homomorphic encryption scheme inputs ciphertexts encrypted under different pubic keys and outputs a ciphertext encrypted under the set of combined public keys. The shares of the secret keys remain untouched, and are forwarded to the output client along with the output of the homomorphic evaluation.

Decoding. The output client collects all shares of all secret keys, and recovers them. As in the previous construction, it homomorphically evaluates the output shares received from the servers and obtain a ciphertext encrypting the computation result. The only difference is that now the result is encrypted under a set of public keys. The output client thus uses all the recovered secret keys to decrypt the ciphertext and obtain the result.

The analyses of correctness, efficiency, and security are almost identical to those in Sect. 4. We thus state the formal results and omit the proofs.

Theorem 4. *Let* HE *be an IND-CPA-secure public-key encryption scheme, then* pHSS *constructed in Fig. 3 is a secure* $(*, m, 1)$-*HSS scheme in the plain model.*

Theorem 5. *Let* HE *be a circuit-private public-key multi-key homomorphic encryption scheme, then* pHSS *constructed in Fig. 3 is a context-hiding* $(*, m, 1)$-*HSS scheme in the plain model.*

$(s_{i,1},\ldots,s_{i,m}) \leftarrow \mathsf{Share}(i,x_i)$

$(\mathsf{pk}_i,\mathsf{sk}_i) \leftarrow \mathsf{HE.KGen}(1^\lambda)$
parse $\mathsf{sk}_i \in \{0,1\}^*$
$(x_{i,1},\ldots,x_{i,m}) \leftarrow R^m \; s.t. \sum_{j\in[m]} x_{i,j} = x_i$
$(z_{i,1},\ldots,z_{i,m}) \leftarrow R^m \; s.t. \sum_{j\in[m]} z_{i,j} = 0$
$(\mathsf{sk}_{i,1},\ldots,\mathsf{sk}_{i,m}) \leftarrow \{0,1\}^{m|\mathsf{sk}_i|} \; s.t. \oplus_{j\in[m]} \mathsf{sk}_{i,j} = \mathsf{sk}_i$
$\tilde{x}_{i,j} \leftarrow \mathsf{HE.Enc}(\mathsf{pk}_i, x_{i,j}) \; \forall j \in [m]$
$x_i^{-j} := (x_{i,1},\ldots,x_{i,j-1},x_{i,j+1},\ldots,x_{i,m})$
$s_{i,j} := (x_i^{-j}, \tilde{x}_{i,j}, z_{i,j}, \mathsf{pk}_i, \mathsf{sk}_{i,j})$
return $(s_{i,1},\ldots,s_{i,m})$

$y_j \leftarrow \mathsf{Eval}(j,f,(s_{1,j},\ldots,s_{n,j}))$

parse $s_{i,j}$ **as** $(x_i^{-j}, \tilde{x}_{i,j}, z_{i,j}, \mathsf{pk}_i, \mathsf{sk}_{i,j})$
$\mathsf{PK} := (\mathsf{pk}_1,\ldots,\mathsf{pk}_n)$
$f_j := \mathsf{Split}_d(j,f,(x_1^{-j},\ldots,x_n^{-j})) + \sum_{i\in[n]} z_{i,j}$
$y_j' \leftarrow \mathsf{HE.Eval}(\mathsf{PK}, f_j, (\tilde{x}_{1,j},\ldots,\tilde{x}_{n,j}))$
$y_j := (y_j', \mathsf{PK}, \mathsf{sk}_{1,j},\ldots,\mathsf{sk}_{n,j})$
return y_j

$y \leftarrow \mathsf{Dec}(y_1,\ldots,y_m)$

parse y_j **as** $(y_j', \mathsf{PK}, \mathsf{sk}_{1,j},\ldots,\mathsf{sk}_{n,j})$
$\mathsf{sk}_i := \oplus_{j\in[m]} \mathsf{sk}_{i,j}$
$c \leftarrow \mathsf{HE.Eval}(\mathsf{PK}, f_{\mathrm{Add}}, (y_1,\ldots,y_m))$
$y \leftarrow \mathsf{HE.Dec}((\mathsf{sk}_1,\ldots,\mathsf{sk}_n), c)$
return y

Fig. 3. Construction of a homomorphic secret sharing scheme pHSS in the plain model. (The functions f_{Add} and Split_d are defined in Sect. 4.1.)

6 Collusion-Resistance

The constructions in Sects. 4 and 5 are 1-secure, meaning that security is lost as soon as two servers collude. We outline how the construction can be upgraded to give a $(*,m,t)$-HSS scheme which tolerates $t > 1$ colluding servers, and investigate the effect on the supported degree d of the resulting secret sharing scheme.

Bounding the Number of Plaintext Base Shares. Unlike in the previous constructions, where we use an m-out-of-m secret sharing scheme to generate base shares of each input x_i, we now use a b-out-of-b secret sharing scheme instead, where b is a new independent variable. Suppose that for each x_i, a certain choice of p out of b base shares of x_i are given in plaintext to a server. In the previous constructions, $p = b - 1$. This means any two colluding servers collectively possess all base shares of x_i in plaintext, and hence are able to recover x_i. To tolerate t colluding servers, we must set p and b such that $b > tp$, so that any t colluding servers collectively possess at most $tp < b$ out of b base shares of each x_i in plaintext, and are thus unable to recover any x_i.

Bounding the Supported Degree of the Homomorphic Secret Sharing Scheme. Next, we analyze the supported degree d of the resulting HSS scheme, assuming an encryption scheme supporting degree k is used. Recall the matrix representation of the shares as defined in Sect. 4.3. The goal of the servers is to jointly compute (homomorphically) the product of the sums of each row, which can be rewritten as a sum of the products obtained by choosing one element from each row. A product of d-many rows (and therefore a degree d polynomial) is computable only if, for each monomial of such a product, there exists at least one server where at most k elements of such a monomial belong to the encrypted columns possessed by this server. A natural strategy to maximize the degree is to let the server possessing the highest number of plaintext columns to compute such a monomial. Let us rewrite $k = (b - p)u + v$, for some quotient u and remainder v. A "worst case" configuration is visualized as follows.

$$\overbrace{\underbrace{u, \ldots, u}_{b-p-v}, \underbrace{u + 1, \ldots, u + 1}_{v}}^{\text{Encrypted Columns, } k \text{ elements}}, \quad \overbrace{\underbrace{u + 1, \ldots, u + 1}_{p}}^{\text{Plaintext Columns, } d-k \text{ elements}}$$

The above means that u elements are chosen from each of the $b - p - v$ of the encrypted columns, and $u + 1$ elements are chosen from each of the remaining plaintext and encrypted columns. Consider shifting any element from a plaintext column to an encrypted column j^-. We argue that (after the shift) there exists a configuration of $b - p$ encrypted columns with at most k elements in the encrypted columns. Such a configuration is obtained as follows: Let j^+ be the plaintext column with the least amount of elements after the shift. We move j^- to the set of plaintext columns and j^+ to the set of encrypted columns. The numbers of plaintext and encrypted columns clearly do not change. Since j^- has at least $u + 1$ elements and j^+ has at most $u + 1$ elements, there is no positive gain in elements in the set of encrypted columns. Thus the new configuration has at most k elements in the encrypted columns, as the previous configuration does. This shows that the case constructed above is indeed the worst case. Assume for the moment that each monomial is computable by at least one server, then the supported degree cannot exceed

$$
\begin{aligned}
d &= bu + p + v \\
&= b\left(\frac{k - v}{b - p}\right) + p + v \\
&= \frac{bk}{b - p} + v\left(1 - \frac{b}{b - p}\right) + p \\
&= \frac{bk}{b - p} - v\left(\frac{p}{b - p}\right) + p.
\end{aligned}
$$

Depending on the value of v, which is uniquely determined by (k, b, p) and satisfies $0 \leq v < b - p$, the maximum supported degree lies within the range

$$k \cdot \frac{b}{b-p} < d \leq k \cdot \frac{b}{b-p} + p.$$

To maximize the above range, we can fix $p = \frac{b-1}{t}$, and have

$$k \cdot \frac{tb}{(t-1)b+1} < d \leq k \cdot \frac{tb}{(t-1)b+1} + \frac{b-1}{t}. \tag{3}$$

For consistency check, we can differentiate with respect to t. For the (non-trivial) case where $p \geq 1$, we have $1 \leq t \leq b - 1$, and hence

$$k < \frac{kb}{b-1} < d \leq (k+1)b - 1.$$

When no collusion is allowed, i.e., $t = 1$, we can set $b = m$ and recover the previous bound $d \leq (k+1)m - 1$. This bounds the maximum supported degree by $(k+1)m - 1$, regardless of how many servers are involved. The constructions in Sects. 4 and 5, show that this bound is actually achievable using m servers.

If a collusion of two servers is allowed, i.e., $t \geq 2$, we examine the bound given in Eq. 3. An interpretation is that the construction amplifies the supported degree of the base encryption scheme by roughly $t/(t-1)$ multiplicatively (by taking limit as the number of columns $b \to \infty$), then adds roughly $1/t$ degree per column.

Bounding the Minimum Number of Servers. It remains to show the condition for having each monomial computable by at least one server. Fix b, p, k and d. There must exists an integer δ such that $d \leq \delta \cdot k$. We argue that the number of servers m required is lower bounded by the solution of the following set cover problem.

From the set of all $\binom{b}{p}$ number of configurations of choosing p plaintext columns out of b columns in a secret share matrix, choose a subset satisfying the following properties: For any integer $s \in [b]$, any combination of s out of all b columns, any combination of $\lfloor s/\delta \rfloor$ out of these s columns, there exists at least one configuration (a secret share matrix) in the subset which has at most these $\lfloor s/\delta \rfloor$ columns (out of the s columns) encrypted. Each satisfying subset specifies a set of servers.

We argue that the above condition on m is both necessary and sufficient, i.e., the lower bound is tight. For the former, suppose that the condition is not satisfied, namely that there exists s, a combination of s columns, and a combination of $\lfloor s/\delta \rfloor$ out of these s columns, such that the secret share matrices of all servers have more than these $\lfloor s/\delta \rfloor$ columns encrypted. Consequently, no server is able to compute the monomial where all elements are contributed from these s/δ columns.

For the sufficiency, consider without loss of generality any degree d monomial, and denote the number of columns contributing elements to this monomial by

$s \in [b]$. Since $d \leq \delta \cdot k$, there must exist $\lfloor s/\delta \rfloor$ columns out of these s columns that are contributing at most k elements. By the condition specified above, there must exist a server whose secret share matrix has at most these $\lfloor s/\delta \rfloor$ columns encrypted (whereas the other $s - \lfloor s/\delta \rfloor$ are in plaintext). This server is thus able to compute the monomial.

Although the general set cover problem is NP-hard, the greedy algorithm is known to solve the general problem with (multiplicative) approximate factor $O(\log N)$ [16], where N is the number of elements to be covered.

Practically-Relevant Parameters. The above analysis does not give a close form for the number of servers m needed, for a fixed set of parameters (t, b, p, k, d). In the following, we investigate parameter settings which are most practically relevant. First, we restrict ourselves to use only encryption for affine functions, *i.e.*, $k = 1$. Next we consider the computation of polynomials of degree $d = 3$, since they are sufficient for the secure computation of any function via randomized encodings [1]. In order to compute degree-3 polynomials, we must have $p > 1^4$. We pick $p = 2$ and set $b = 2t + 1$, where $t > 1$. Using a greedy algorithm, it can be found that the number of servers needed for $t = 2, 3, 4$ are $m = 4, 9, 16$ respectively, which seems to suggest that $m \approx t^2$. If that is the case, the maximum tolerated ratio of colluding servers is $t/m \approx 1/t$, which gets worse as t grows. Therefore, a $(*, 4, 2)$-HSS for degree-3 polynomials from affine encryption seems to be the most interesting result in terms of collusion resistance.

7 Applications

We highlight several interesting applications of our HSS scheme.

7.1 Server-Aided Secure Evaluation of Low-Degree Polynomials

Server-aided secure computation is a natural application of HSS schemes. In this scenario, one or multiple input clients secret share their data to a set of servers. Later, the servers can homomorphically evaluate functions (*e.g.*, given by the input clients or other parties) on the shared data and send the result to an output client. The latter can efficiently recover the computation result, and due to the context-hiding property, without learning the original data and the function being evaluated beyond what is trivially revealed by the result. Using an HSS scheme in this scenario is particularly appealing since the client-server communication is succinct (independent of the size of the function evaluated) and the workload of the input and output clients is typically small.

When instantiated with linearly homomorphic encryption schemes such as ElGamal [19] or Paillier [29], our main construction allows input clients to outsource the computation of degree-d polynomials to m non-communicating

---

[4] If $p = 1$, then the best the Split_d function can do is to assign one element to the plaintext column and one element to one of the ciphertext columns, whose product is of degree 2.

servers, where $d = 2m - 1$ and $m = O(\log \lambda)$. Since Shamir secret sharing [30] allows to evaluate polynomials of degree $d = m - 1$ using $m = \mathsf{poly}(\lambda)$ servers, our result is more interesting when the number of servers, and hence the degree of the polynomials, are small. There are a few interesting scenarios where low-degree polynomials are evaluated over private data.

Moments: Moments are recurrent measures in statistics and physics to describe the shape of a set of points. The d-th moment is computable by a degree-d polynomials. The mean is the first row moment and the variance and the skewness are the second and third central moments, respectively. Notably, our scheme allows two servers to efficiently compute the third moment from standard assumptions whereas previous approaches with comparable efficiency [15] rely on bilinear maps.

Neural Networks: Multi-layered non-recurrent neural networks are arithmetic circuits consisting of gates computing non-linear functions. Previous work on privacy-preserving neural network evaluation [24] approximates these non-linear functions using low-degree polynomials, such that the modified neural network can be homomorphically evaluated using a fully homomorphic encryption [22] (FHE) scheme with a reasonable parameter. Suppose that the networks to be evaluated are shallow enough, then our constructions provide a relatively lightweight alternative to FHE for evaluating neural networks over private data.

Polynomials with Hidden Coefficients: Suppose the polynomial f of degree d to be evaluated is given also by the input clients, they can choose to hide the coefficients of the monomials in f by secret sharing them, and turning f into a new polynomial f' of degree $d+1$, where the coefficients in f become variables in f'. The clients can further hide the monomials appearing in f by secret sharing the (possibly zero) coefficients in f of all monomials of degree at most d. Note that although the number of such monomials is exponential in d, it is not an issue for a degree $d = O(\log \lambda)$ (when $k = 1$ and $m = O(\log \lambda)$) which is logarithmic in the security parameter.

m-Server PIR: Our HSS scheme for degree d polynomials can be easily converted into a (round-optimal) m-server PIR scheme as follows: Consider a set of m servers who store a copy of a database DB locally and let us split the database in 2^d equal chunks $(\mathsf{DB}_1, \ldots, \mathsf{DB}_{2^d})$, then, on input an index $i \in \{0,1\}^d$, the client shares i to the m servers with our HSS scheme. The servers evaluate the function

$$g(i) := \sum_{j=1}^{2^d} \mathsf{DB}_j (i = j) = \mathsf{DB}_i$$

and send the output of the computation to the client. Note that g is a polynomial of degree d with coefficients determined by DB, which is public. The communication complexity is dominated by the factor $\frac{|\mathsf{DB}|}{2^d} + \mathsf{poly}(\lambda)$ of the server-client message.

7.2 Round-Optimal Server-Aided Multiparty Computation in the Plain Model

A recent result by Boyle *et al.* [11] shows that an additive $(3, 2, 1)$-HSS schemes for degree-3 polynomials and a low-depth PRG imply a 2 round (n, m)-MPC protocols[5], where $n, m \in \mathsf{poly}(\lambda)$. Since the only $(3, 2, 1)$-HSS scheme from standard assumption was known to exist only in the PKI model [9], the resulting MPC protocol inherits the same setup assumption. Unfortunately the transformation assumes a linear reconstruction of the HSS, which is not satisfied by our scheme.

However, we can apply a similar transformation to our multi-client HSS scheme in Sect. 5 to obtain a 2 round (n, m)-MPC, where the adversary is allowed to corrupt any strict subset of the servers *or* the output client, and an arbitrary number of input clients. This corruption model has been introduced in the context of server-aided multiparty-computation [28]. We denote such a primitive by (n, m)-saMPC. Our scheme does not require a PKI and can be instantiated in the plain model. Moreover, since our HSS scheme is perfectly correct (assuming a perfectly correct homomorphic encryption scheme), we can avoid the probability amplification step in [10]. We briefly outline the steps of the transformation in the following.

Lemma 1. $(n, 2, 1)$-*HSS for degree 3 polynomials* $\implies$ $(n, 2, 1)$-*HSS for P/poly.*

This is a trivial implication using randomized encodings [1] and assuming the existence of a low-depth PRG.

Lemma 2. $(n, 2, 1)$-*HSS for P/poly* $\implies$ $(n, 3)$-*saMPC for P/poly.*

This is shown using the server-emulation technique described in [10], where the inputs of one server are secret shared among two new servers and its computation is emulated using the $(n, 2, 1)$-HSS. Note that the resulting $(n, 3)$-saMPC is resilient against the corruption of any strict subset of the 3 servers *or* the output client.

Lemma 3. $(n, 3)$-*saMPC for P/poly* $\implies$ (n, m)-*saMPC for degree 3 polynomials.*

This is shown using the following observation of [11]: Given a degree 3 polynomial $f(X_1, \ldots, X_n)$, then rewriting $X_j = \sum_{i=1}^{m} x_{j,i}$ we obtain another degree 3 polynomial $f(\sum_{i=1}^{m} x_{1,i}, \ldots, \sum_{i=1}^{m} x_{n,i})$. Each monomial is of the form $x_{1,i} x_{2,j} x_{2,k}$ and can be computed by the servers $(\mathcal{S}_i, \mathcal{S}_j, \mathcal{S}_k)$ with the $(n, 3)$-saMPC scheme. Padding each monomial with a blinding factor (such that all factors sum up to 0) gives us the final (n, m)-saMPC protocol for degree 3 polynomials.

Lemma 4. (n, m)-*saMPC for degree 3 polynomials* $\implies$ (n, m)-*saMPC for P/poly.*

---

[5] (n, m)-MPCs are n-client m-server MPCs which are secure against $m - 1$ corrupt server.

Follows by another application of randomized encodings.

Acknowledgements. This research is based upon work supported by the German research foundation (DFG) through the collaborative research center 1223, by the German Federal Ministry of Education and Research (BMBF) through the project PROMISE (16KIS0763), and by the state of Bavaria at the Nuremberg Campus of Technology (NCT). NCT is a research cooperation between the Friedrich-Alexander-Universität Erlangen-Nürnberg (FAU) and the Technische Hochschule Nürnberg Georg Simon Ohm (THN).

References

1. Applebaum, B., Ishai, Y., Kushilevitz, E.: Computationally private randomizing polynomials and their applications. Comput. Complex. **15**, 115–162 (2006)
2. Babai, L., Kimmel, P.G., Lokam, S.V.: Simultaneous messages vs. communication. In: Mayr, E.W., Puech, C. (eds.) STACS 1995. LNCS, vol. 900, pp. 361–372. Springer, Heidelberg (1995). https://doi.org/10.1007/3-540-59042-0_88
3. Barkol, O., Ishai, Y., Weinreb, E.: On d-multiplicative secret sharing. J. Cryptol. **23**(4), 580–593 (2010)
4. Beimel, A., Ishai, Y.: Information-theoretic private information retrieval: a unified construction. In: Orejas, F., Spirakis, P.G., van Leeuwen, J. (eds.) ICALP 2001. LNCS, vol. 2076, pp. 912–926. Springer, Heidelberg (2001). https://doi.org/10.1007/3-540-48224-5_74
5. Beimel, A., Ishai, Y., Kushilevitz, E., Orlov, I.: Share conversion and private information retrieval. In: Proceedings of the 27th Conference on Computational Complexity, CCC 2012, Porto, Portugal, 26–29 June 2012, pp. 258–268. IEEE Computer Society (2012)
6. Benaloh, J.C.: Secret sharing homomorphisms: keeping shares of a secret secret (extended abstract). In: Odlyzko, A.M. (ed.) CRYPTO 1986. LNCS, vol. 263, pp. 251–260. Springer, Heidelberg (1987). https://doi.org/10.1007/3-540-47721-7_19
7. Boneh, D., Goh, E.-J., Nissim, K.: Evaluating 2-DNF formulas on ciphertexts. In: Kilian, J. (ed.) TCC 2005. LNCS, vol. 3378, pp. 325–341. Springer, Heidelberg (2005). https://doi.org/10.1007/978-3-540-30576-7_18
8. Boyle, E., Gilboa, N., Ishai, Y.: Function secret sharing. In: Oswald, E., Fischlin, M. (eds.) EUROCRYPT 2015. LNCS, vol. 9057, pp. 337–367. Springer, Heidelberg (2015). https://doi.org/10.1007/978-3-662-46803-6_12
9. Boyle, E., Gilboa, N., Ishai, Y.: Breaking the circuit size barrier for secure computation under DDH. In: Robshaw, M., Katz, J. (eds.) CRYPTO 2016. LNCS, vol. 9814, pp. 509–539. Springer, Heidelberg (2016). https://doi.org/10.1007/978-3-662-53018-4_19
10. Boyle, E., Gilboa, N., Ishai, Y.: Group-based secure computation: optimizing rounds, communication, and computation. In: Coron, J.-S., Nielsen, J.B. (eds.) EUROCRYPT 2017. LNCS, vol. 10211, pp. 163–193. Springer, Cham (2017). https://doi.org/10.1007/978-3-319-56614-6_6
11. Boyle, E., Gilboa, N., Ishai, Y., Lin, H., Tessaro, S.: Foundations of homomorphic secret sharing. In: Innovations in Theoretical Computer Science, vol. 94. Schloss Dagstuhl-Leibniz-Zentrum fuer Informatik (2018)
12. Cachin, C., Camenisch, J., Kilian, J., Müller, J.: One-round secure computation and secure autonomous mobile agents. In: Montanari, U., Rolim, J.D.P., Welzl, E. (eds.) ICALP 2000. LNCS, vol. 1853, pp. 512–523. Springer, Heidelberg (2000). https://doi.org/10.1007/3-540-45022-X_43

13. Cachin, C., Micali, S., Stadler, M.: Computationally private information retrieval with polylogarithmic communication. In: Stern, J. (ed.) EUROCRYPT 1999. LNCS, vol. 1592, pp. 402–414. Springer, Heidelberg (1999). https://doi.org/10.1007/3-540-48910-X_28

14. Castagnos, G., Laguillaumie, F.: Linearly homomorphic encryption from DDH. In: Nyberg, K. (ed.) CT-RSA 2015. LNCS, vol. 9048, pp. 487–505. Springer, Cham (2015). https://doi.org/10.1007/978-3-319-16715-2_26

15. Catalano, D., Fiore, D.: Using linearly-homomorphic encryption to evaluate degree-2 functions on encrypted data. In: Ray, I., Li, N., Kruegel, C. (eds.) ACM CCS 15, Denver, CO, USA, 12–16 October, pp. 1518–1529. ACM Press (2015)

16. Chvatal, V.: A greedy heuristic for the set-covering problem. Math. Oper. Res. 4(3), 233–235 (1979)

17. Dodis, Y., Halevi, S., Rothblum, R.D., Wichs, D.: Spooky encryption and its applications. In: Robshaw, M., Katz, J. (eds.) CRYPTO 2016. LNCS, vol. 9816, pp. 93–122. Springer, Heidelberg (2016). https://doi.org/10.1007/978-3-662-53015-3_4

18. Efremenko, K.: 3-query locally decodable codes of subexponential length. In: Mitzenmacher, M. (ed.) 41st ACM STOC, Bethesda, MD, USA, 31 May–2 June, pp. 39–44 (2009). ACM Press (2009)

19. ElGamal, T.: A public key cryptosystem and a signature scheme based on discrete logarithms. In: Blakley, G.R., Chaum, D. (eds.) CRYPTO 1984. LNCS, vol. 196, pp. 10–18. Springer, Heidelberg (1985). https://doi.org/10.1007/3-540-39568-7_2

20. Fazio, N., Gennaro, R., Jafarikhah, T., Skeith, W.E.: Homomorphic secret sharing from paillier encryption. In: Okamoto, T., Yu, Y., Au, M.H., Li, Y. (eds.) ProvSec 2017. LNCS, vol. 10592, pp. 381–399. Springer, Cham (2017). https://doi.org/10.1007/978-3-319-68637-0_23

21. Franklin, M., Mohassel, P.: Efficient and secure evaluation of multivariate polynomials and applications. In: Zhou, J., Yung, M. (eds.) ACNS 2010. LNCS, vol. 6123, pp. 236–254. Springer, Heidelberg (2010). https://doi.org/10.1007/978-3-642-13708-2_15

22. Gentry, C.: Fully homomorphic encryption using ideal lattices. In: Mitzenmacher, M. (ed.) 41st ACM STOC, Bethesda, MD, USA, 31 May–2 June, pp. 169–178. ACM Press (2009)

23. Gentry, C., Halevi, S.: Fully homomorphic encryption without squashing using depth-3 arithmetic circuits. In: Ostrovsky, R. (ed.) 52nd FOCS, Palm Springs, CA, USA, 22–25 October, pp. 107–109. IEEE Computer Society Press (2011)

24. Gilad-Bachrach, R., Dowlin, N., Laine, K., Lauter, K., Naehrig, M., Wernsing, J.: Cryptonets: applying neural networks to encrypted data with high throughput and accuracy. In: International Conference on Machine Learning, pp. 201–210 (2016)

25. Gilboa, N., Ishai, Y.: Distributed point functions and their applications. In: Nguyen, P.Q., Oswald, E. (eds.) EUROCRYPT 2014. LNCS, vol. 8441, pp. 640–658. Springer, Heidelberg (2014). https://doi.org/10.1007/978-3-642-55220-5_35

26. Goldwasser, S., Micali, S.: Probabilistic encryption. J. Comput. Syst. Sci. 28(2), 270–299 (1984)

27. Kamara, S., Mohassel, P., Raykova, M.: Outsourcing multi-party computation. Cryptology ePrint Archive, Report 2011/272 (2011). http://eprint.iacr.org/2011/272

28. Kamara, S., Mohassel, P., Riva, B.: Salus: a system for server-aided secure function evaluation. In: Yu, T., Danezis, G., Gligor, V.D. (eds.) ACM CCS 12, Raleigh, NC, USA, 16–18 October, pages 797–808. ACM Press (2012)

29. Paillier, P.: Public-key cryptosystems based on composite degree residuosity classes. In: Stern, J. (ed.) EUROCRYPT 1999. LNCS, vol. 1592, pp. 223–238. Springer, Heidelberg (1999). https://doi.org/10.1007/3-540-48910-X_16
30. Shamir, A.: How to share a secret. Commun. Assoc. Comput. Mach. **22**(11), 612–613 (1979)
31. Yekhanin, S.: Towards 3-query locally decodable codes of subexponential length. In: Johnson, D.S., Feige, U. (eds.) 39th ACM STOC, San Diego, CA, USA, 11–13 June, pp. 266–274. ACM Press (2007)

Constructing Ideal Secret Sharing Schemes Based on Chinese Remainder Theorem

Yu Ning, Fuyou Miao[✉], Wenchao Huang, Keju Meng, Yan Xiong, and Xingfu Wang

School of Computer Science and Technology, University of Science and Technology of China, Hefei 230027, China
mfy@ustc.edu.cn

Abstract. Since (t, n)-threshold secret sharing (SS) was initially proposed by Shamir and Blakley separately in 1979, it has been widely used in many aspects. Later on, Asmuth and Bloom presented a (t, n)-threshold SS scheme based on the Chinese Remainder Theorem (CRT) for integers in 1983. However, compared with the most popular Shamir's thresholdtn SS scheme, existing CRT based schemes have a lower information rate, moreover, they are harder to construct due to the stringent condition on moduli. To overcome these shortcomings of CRT based schemes, (1) we first propose a generalized (t, n)-threshold SS scheme based on the CRT for polynomial ring over a finite field. We show that our scheme is ideal, i.e., it is perfect in security and has the information rate 1. Comparison show that our scheme has a better information rate and is easier to construct compared with the existing threshold SS schemes based on the CRT for integers. (2) We prove that Shamir's scheme, which is based on the Lagrange interpolation, is a special case of our scheme. Therefore, we establish the connection among threshold schemes based on the Lagrange interpolation, schemes based on the CRT for integers and our scheme. (3) As a natural extension of our threshold scheme, we present a weighted threshold SS scheme based on the CRT for polynomial rings, which inherits the above advantages of our threshold scheme over existing weighted schemes based on the CRT for integers.

Keywords: Threshold · Ideal secret sharing
Chinese Remainder Theorem · Polynomial ring

1 Introduction

Secret sharing (SS) was first introduced respectively by Shamir [29] and Blakley [4] in 1979 to construct robust key management schemes for cryptographic systems. Shamir's scheme is constructed based on the Lagrange interpolation

The original version of this chapter was revised: Two references were added. The correction to this chapter is available at https://doi.org/10.1007/978-3-030-03332-3_20

Supported partially by National NSF of China 61572454,61572453,61520106007 and National Key R&D Program of China 2018YFB0803400.

T. Peyrin and S. Galbraith (Eds.): ASIACRYPT 2018, LNCS 11274, pp. 310–331, 2018.
https://doi.org/10.1007/978-3-030-03332-3_12

polynomial, as a (t, n)-threshold SS scheme (i.e., (t, n)-SS), it divides a secret into n shares and distributes each share to one of n parties called shareholders; only t or more shareholders pooling their shares together can recover the secret while $t - 1$ or less shareholders cannot obtain any information about the secret. So far, many schemes [10, 18, 19, 27, 34] have been proposed based on Shamir's scheme. Later on, threshold schemes based on the Chinese Remainder Theorem (CRT) for integer ring were proposed by Mignotte [25] and Asmuth-Bloom [1].

Different from Shamir's scheme, Mignotte's scheme and Asmuth-Bloom's scheme illustrated a new method to construct (t, n)-threshold SS schemes using the CRT for integers. Both schemes are highly similar except that the latter improves the former in perfectness of security. Therefore, Asmuth-Bloom' scheme is our main concern among CRT based SS schemes in this paper. In nature, CRT-based schemes are capable of assigning shares of distinct size to different shareholders, this capability can in turn be used to implement new functionality, e.g., the weighted schemes of [15, 21, 35]. In constructing weighted SS schemes, CRT-based SS schemes allow a shareholder to possess only one share each. In contrast, Shamir's scheme needs to allocate trivially multiple shares to a shareholder, who has the weight more than 1. Moreover, the shareholder leaking any of its shares may cause the disclosure of the secret.

Asmuth-Bloom's scheme has become a popular and fundamental schemes. Based on the scheme, a lot of work [16–18, 22, 24] has been done to extend the original idea and meet different requirements of practical applications. One type of extension is to construct new access structures, e.g., the general access structure [18] and the multipartite scheme [16]. Another type of extension aims to improve functionality, e.g., the verifiable SS [17, 24] to prevent malicious action of dishonest shareholders and the proactive secret sharing for strengthening the security.

As we all know, Shamir's scheme is based on Lagrange interpolation and thus is easy to construct. Moreover, it is an ideal SS scheme, i.e., it is perfect in security and has the maximum information rate 1. Roughly speaking, information rate is the ratio of secret to share in size, which denotes the information efficiency of secret sharing. In comparison, the CRT-based Asmuth-Bloom's scheme, on one hand, is lower in information rate since each share is larger than the secret in size; on the other hand, it is difficult to construct because the scheme requires a series of pairwise coprime integers satisfying some stringent condition.

In a word, Shamir's scheme is ideal and easy to construct while Asmuth-Bloom's scheme is not ideal, hard to construct but more natural and neat in constructing weighted SS scheme. In this case, we are faced the following 2 questions,

– Is there any CRT-based SS scheme which is ideal as Shamir's scheme?
– If such a scheme exists, how to construct it in practice? and what is the connection in theory among Shamir' scheme, Asmuth-Bloom's scheme and the new scheme?

To answer the above questions, we need to study new CRT based schemes free from the above mentioned drawbacks in Asmuth-Bloom's scheme. To this end, this paper mainly focuses on constructing a generalized (t, n)-threshold SS scheme based on the CRT for the polynomial ring and further finds out the connection among these (t, n)-threshold SS schemes. Our contribution can be summarized as follows

- We propose a generalized (t, n)-threshold SS scheme based on the CRT for the polynomial ring over a finite field. Our scheme is perfect in security and has the information rate 1. Compared with Asmuth-Bloom's scheme, it is better in information rate, easier to construct and more computationally efficient. Therefore, our scheme can serve as a better substitution for Asmuth-Bloom's scheme. That is, existing schemes based on Asmuth-Bloom's scheme are allowed to base themselves on our scheme to overcome the above drawbacks inherited from Asmuth-Bloom's scheme.
- We show that Shamir's scheme is a special case of our scheme. As a result, we establish the connection among (t, n) threshold SS schemes based on Lagrange interpolation polynomial (the family of Shamir's scheme), CRT for integers (the family of Asmuth-Bloom's scheme) and CRT for polynomial rings (our proposed scheme).
- We present a weighted SS scheme based on the above proposed threshold scheme. Compared with [15, 21, 35], which are based on Asmuth-Bloom's scheme, our new weighted scheme enjoys advantages inherited from our (t, n) threshold SS scheme, which illustrates the power of our threshold scheme as a better base than Asmuth-Bloom's scheme.

The rest of this paper is organized as follows: Sect. 2 introduces some preliminaries about secret sharing and the CRT. In Sect. 3, we present our threshold scheme and compare it with Shamir's scheme and Asmuth-Bloom's scheme. Section 4 shows that Shamir's scheme is a special case of our threshold scheme. In Sect. 5, a weighted threshold scheme is given and compared with other existing CRT based schemes. Finally, Sect. 6 concludes our work.

2   Preliminaries

In this section, we introduce some fundamentals as a preliminary. Subsection 2.1 introduces some notations for convenience. In Subsect. 2.2, the CRT for different rings are discussed. Subsection 2.3 is devoted to some results on the irreducible polynomials in the polynomial ring over a finite field. We introduce some fundamental notions about secret sharing in Subsect. 2.4. Finally, Asmuth-Bloom's scheme and Shamir's scheme are reviewed in Subsects. 2.5 and 2.6 respectively.

2.1   Notation

Here, we introduce some notations that will be used all the way.

- Let $\mathbb{Z}$ denote the usual ring of integers. Let $n \in \mathbb{Z}$, $[n]$ denotes the set $\{1, 2, \ldots, n\}$ of n elements.

- Let $p \in \mathbb{Z}$ be a prime number, $\mathbb{F}_p$ denotes the finite field of p elements.
- Let R be some ring, for any $a, b \in R$, $\langle a \rangle$ denotes the principal ideal generated by a. Also, $a \mid b$ means that a divides b, that is, there is $c \in R$ such that $b = ac$.
- Let R be some ring, $R[x]$ denotes the univariate polynomial ring in the variable x over R. For any $f(x) \in R[x]$, $\deg(f(x))$ represents the degree of $f(x)$.
- Let I be an ideal of a ring R and $x, y \in R$, $x \equiv y \pmod{I}$ means that $x - y \in I$. If $I = \langle a \rangle$ is a principal ideal for some $a \in R$, it is also written as $x \equiv y \pmod{a}$.
- gcd denotes the greatest common divisor.
- Let S be a finite set, $|S|$ denotes the number of elements in S; 2^S denotes the power set of S, that is, 2^S contains all subsets of S as elements.

2.2   The Chinese Remainder Theorem (CRT)

In this subsection, we introduce the CRT for different rings, especially, for $\mathbb{Z}$ and $K[x]$ with K being a field. This subsection serves as the fundamental of Asmuth-Bloom's scheme and our proposed scheme.

The Asmuth-Bloom's scheme is based on the CRT for $\mathbb{Z}$. Actually, the CRT for $\mathbb{Z}$ can be generalized to any other ring as follows.

Theorem 1 (Theorem 2.1 of [23]). *Let $I_1, \ldots, I_n$ be ideals of a ring R such that $I_i + I_j = R$ for all $i, j \in [n], i \neq j$. Given elements $x_1, \ldots, x_n \in R$, there exists $x \in R$ such that*

$$x \equiv x_i \pmod{I_i} \text{ for all } i \in [n].$$

And x is unique in the sense that if y is another element satisfies all the congruences, then

$$x \equiv y \pmod{I_1 \cap I_2 \cdots \cap I_n}.$$

To have an intuitional understanding of this theorem, we can consider the case when $R = \mathbb{Z}$. Since $\mathbb{Z}$ is a principal ideal domain (PID), for all $i \in [n]$, $I_i = \langle m_i \rangle$ for some $m_i \in \mathbb{Z}$. The condition $I_i + I_j = R$ becomes that the linear combination of m_i and m_j with integer coefficients can represent any integer in $\mathbb{Z}$, specifically, can represent $1 \in \mathbb{Z}$, that is $\gcd(m_i, m_j) = 1$. Also, the congruence $x \equiv x_i \pmod{I_i}$ becomes $x \equiv x_i \pmod{m_i}$. In conclusion, by letting $R = \mathbb{Z}$, we have the following ordinary version of the CRT for $\mathbb{Z}$.

Theorem 2. *Let $m_1, \ldots, m_n \in \mathbb{Z}$ be pairwise coprime integers. Given integers $x_1, \ldots, x_n \in \mathbb{Z}$, there exists $x \in \mathbb{Z}$ such that*

$$x \equiv x_i \pmod{m_i} \text{ for all } i \in [n].$$

And x is unique in the sense that if y is another integer satisfies all the congruences, then

$$x \equiv y \pmod{\prod_{i=1}^{n} m_i}.$$

Note that the uniqueness also means that x is unique if we only consider numbers in the range $[0, \prod_{i=1}^{n} m_i - 1]$.

The reason that we can replace the ideals with the elements generating that ideal is that $\mathbb{Z}$ is a PID. It is well known that $K[x]$ is also a PID if K is a field. Similarly, we have the following CRT for the ring of polynomials over a field.

Theorem 3. *Let K be a field and $m_1(x), \ldots, m_n(x) \in K[x]$ be pairwise coprime polynomials. Given polynomials $f_1(x), \ldots, f_n(x) \in K[x]$, there exists $f(x)$ such that*

$$f(x) \equiv f_i(x) \pmod{m_i(x)} \text{ for all } i \in [n].$$

And $f(x)$ is unique in the sense that if $g(x)$ is another polynomial satisfies all the congruences, then

$$f(x) \equiv g(x) \pmod{\prod_{i=1}^{n} m_i(x)}.$$

Note that the uniqueness also means that $f(x)$ is unique if we only consider polynomials of degree less than $\deg(\prod_{i=1}^{n} m_i(x))$.

The above different versions of CRT (Theorems 1, 2, 3) does not give a concrete method of finding out the exact solution of a given system of congruences. For the most general case, it may be difficult to find such a method. But for Euclidean domains, we can explicitly write out and efficiently compute the solution as the following theorem states.

Theorem 4 (Generalized Algorithm 1.3.11 in [8]). *Let R be a Euclidean domain and $m_1, \ldots, m_n \in R$ be pairwise coprime elements. Given elements $x_1, \ldots, x_n \in R$ and a system of congruences*

$$x \equiv x_i \pmod{m_i} \text{ for all } i \in [n],$$

let $M = \prod_{i=1}^{n} m_i$, $M_i = M/m_i$ and $a_i \in R$ with $a_i M_i \equiv 1 \pmod{m_i}$, then,

$$x = \sum_{i=1}^{n} a_i M_i x_i$$

is a solution of the system of congruences.

2.3   Irreducible Polynomials over a Finite Field

In this subsection, we introduce some existing results about the number of irreducible polynomials and how to find irreducible polynomials in $\mathbb{F}_p[x]$. These results enable the practicality of our scheme.

Most results here are derived from the following theorem.

Theorem 5 (Theorem 1 in Chapter 26 of [7]). $x^{p^n} - x$ *is the product of all monic irreducible polynomials in $\mathbb{F}_p[x]$ of degree d, for all $d \mid n$.*

First, Theorem 5 shows a way to count the number of irreducible polynomials in $\mathbb{F}_p[x]$. Let $N(n,p)$ be the number of monic irreducible polynomials in $\mathbb{F}_p[x]$, by Theorem 5, considering the factorization of $x^{p^n} - x$ and counting the degree, it is clear that

$$p^n = \sum_{d|n} dN(d,p). \tag{1}$$

Applying the Mobius inversion formula to Expression 1 results in Theorem 6.

Theorem 6 (Theorem 7 in Chapter 26 of [7]). $N(n,p) = \frac{1}{n}\sum_{d|n} \mu(n/d)p^d$ *where μ is the Mobius function.*

Fixing p, $N(n,p)$ grows rapidly with respect to n, which can be seen in Table 1 and we have Theorem 7 to bound $N(n,p)$.

Theorem 7 (Theorem 19.12 of [31]). *For any prime number p, for all $n \geq 1$, we have*

$$\frac{p^n}{2n} \leq N(n,p) \leq \frac{p^n}{n} \text{ and } N(n,p) = \frac{p^n}{n} + \mathcal{O}(\frac{p^{n/2}}{n}).$$

Table 1. Number of irreducible polynomials

n	$N(n,p)$	$N(n,2)$	$N(n,3)$	$N(n,5)$	$N(n,7)$
1	p	2	3	5	7
2	$(p^2 - p)/2$	1	3	10	21
3	$(p^3 - p)/3$	2	8	40	112
4	$(p^4 - p^2)/4$	3	18	150	588
5	$(p^5 - p)/5$	6	48	624	3360
6	$(p^6 - p^2 - p^3 + p)/6$	9	116	2580	19544
7	$(p^7 - p)/7$	18	312	11160	117648
8	$(p^8 - p^4)/8$	30	810	48750	720300
9	$(p^9 - p^3)/9$	56	2184	217000	4483696
10	$(p^{10} - p^5 - p^2 + p)/10$	99	5880	976248	28245840

On the other hand, Theorem 5 also results in a primality testing algorithm in $\mathbb{F}_p[x]$. Suppose $f \in \mathbb{F}_p[x]$ is of degree d, if f is not irreducible, f has an irreducible divisor of degree at most $k = \lfloor \frac{d}{2} \rfloor$. Therefore, by Theorem 5, at least one term in Expression 2

$$\gcd(x^p - x, f), \gcd(x^{p^2} - x, f), \ldots, \gcd(x^{p^k} - x, f) \tag{2}$$

will return a non-trivial divisor of f. Thus, by checking each term in Expression 2, we can determine the primality of f as is in Algorithm 1.

With Algorithm 1, we have the probabilistic Algorithm 2 for finding irreducible polynomials of a given degree d in $\mathbb{F}_p[x]$.

Theorem 8 (Theorem 20.2 of [31]). *Algorithm 2 takes an expected number of $\mathcal{O}(d^3 \log d \log p)$ operations in $\mathbb{F}_p$.*

Input: $f(x) \in \mathbb{F}_p[x]$ of degree $d > 0$
Output: whether $f(x)$ is irreducible or not

$h \leftarrow x \bmod f$;
for $k \leftarrow 1$ **to** $\lfloor d/2 \rfloor$ **do**
$\quad\mid\quad h \leftarrow h^p \bmod f$;
$\quad\mid\quad$ **if** $\gcd(h - x, f) \neq 1$ **then**
$\quad\mid\quad\mid\quad$ **return** false;
$\quad\mid\quad$ **end**
end
return true;

Algorithm 1. Algorithm for Irreducible Polynomial Testing [29]

Input: the given degree d
Output: an irreducible polynomial of degree d

repeat
$\quad\mid\quad$ choose a polynomial f of degree d at random;
$\quad\mid\quad$ test whether f is irreducible using Algorithm 1;
until f *is irreducible*;
return f;

Algorithm 2. Generation Algorithm of Random Irreducible Polynomial [29]

2.4   Secret Sharing

Secret sharing was first introduced by Shamir [29] and Blakley [4] in 1979 to construct robust key management schemes for cryptographic systems. Nowadays, it has become a cryptographic primitive and is widely used in many applications, including multiparty computations [3,9], threshold cryptography [13,22] and generalized oblivious transfer [30,33] and so on.

In a secret sharing scheme, a dealer with a secret to share, a set $[n] = \{1, 2, \ldots, n\}$ of n parties and a collection $\Gamma \subseteq 2^{[n]}$ of authorized subsets are involved. In such a scheme, the dealer generates n shares and allocates each party a share such that

- any authorized subset of parties in Γ pooling their shares together can determine the secret
- any subset of parties not in Γ cannot get any information about the secret.

The collection Γ is called the access structure realized by the secret sharing scheme. It is reasonable to assume that if some subset of parties can recover the secret, with any other parties taking participant, they can still recover the secret. That is, if $A \subseteq [n]$ can recover the secret, then, for any $B \subseteq [n]$ with $A \subseteq B$, B is also able to recover the secret. Therefore, Γ has the following monotone property.

$$\forall A \in \Gamma, \forall B \subseteq [n], A \subseteq B \implies B \in \Gamma \tag{3}$$

And we use Expression 3 as the definition of access structure.

Definition 1 (Access Structure [2]). *Let $[n]$ denote a set of parties. A collection $\Gamma \subseteq 2^{[n]}$ is monotone if $\forall A \in \Gamma, \forall B \subseteq [n], A \subseteq B \implies B \in \Gamma$. An access structure is a monotone collection of subsets of $[n]$.*

Next, we introduce a mathematical model for secret sharing schemes and formalize the meaning of "determining the secret" and "cannot get any information about the secret".

Definition 2 (Perfect Secret Sharing Scheme [20]). *Suppose we have n parties $\{1, 2, \ldots, n\}$. For a monotone access structure $\Gamma \subseteq 2^{[n]}$, a perfect secret sharing scheme realizing Γ is a list of discrete random variables $(S, S_1, S_2, \ldots, S_n)$ over some finite sample space such that*

- *(correctness) - for any $A \in \Gamma$, $H(S \mid \{S_i \mid i \in A\}) = 0$*
- *(perfectness) - for any $B \subseteq [n]$ with $B \notin \Gamma$, $H(S \mid \{S_i \mid i \in B\}) = H(S)$*

where $H(\cdot)$ stands for the Shannon entropy and $H(\cdot \mid \cdot)$ denotes the conditional entropy.

Naturally, we have the information rate represented by the ratio of the length of the secret to that of shares, which is used to measure the efficiency of each party sharing the secret.

Definition 3 (Information Rate [20]). *The (worst-case) information rate of a secret sharing scheme $(S, S_1, \ldots, S_n)$ is*

$$\rho = \frac{H(S)}{max\{H(S_i) \mid i \in [n]\}}.$$

A lot of research has been carried out to study the bounds of the information rate for different kinds of access structures. In [6], it was shown that, in any perfect secret sharing scheme, $H(S) \leq H(S_i), i \in [n]$. Therefore, an upper bound for the information rate is $\rho \leq 1$. For a perfect scheme with information rate 1, its share size is at most as small as the secret and we call it an ideal scheme.

Threshold Access Structure: A fundamental case of secret sharing is the threshold case. The access structure realized by a (t, n)-threshold scheme is

$$\Gamma = \{A \subseteq [n] \mid |A| \geq t\}.$$

That is, only t or more parties can recover the secret while any $t - 1$ or less parties cannot gain any information about the secret.

Weighted Access Structure: The weighted threshold secret sharing is a direct generalization of the threshold case. In a weighted threshold case, a threshold t is set and each party is associated with a positive weight. Only subset of parties, whose sum of weights is larger than or equal to t, can recover the secret while parties, whose sum of weights is less than t, cannot gain any information about the secret. Formally, the access structure realized by a (t, n, ω)-weighted threshold scheme is

$$\Gamma = \{A \subseteq [n] \mid \sum_{i \in A} \omega(i) \geq t\}$$

where $\omega : [n] \to \mathbb{N}^+$ is the weight function and $\omega(i)$ is the weight of the i-th party. In [26], it was shown that weighted threshold access structures with a positive rational or real weight can always be converted to the same access structure with a weight of positive natural numbers. Therefore, we often only consider the weight as a positive natural number. Usually, we also require the condition that

$$\forall i \in [n], \omega(i) < t.$$

Otherwise, there is a party knowing the secret and there will be no sharing in some sense. Note that the weighted threshold case degenerates to the basic threshold case if

$$\forall i, j \in [n], \omega(i) = \omega(j).$$

2.5 Review of Asmuth-Bloom's Scheme [1]

In this subsection, we review Asmuth-Bloom's (t, n)-threshold SS scheme.

Share Distribution: The dealer selects integers m_0 and $m_1 < m_2 < \cdots < m_n$ satisfying Expressions 4 and 5.

$$\forall i, j \in [n] \cup \{0\}, i \neq j \implies \gcd(m_i, m_j) = 1 \tag{4}$$

$$m_0 \prod_{i=n-t+2}^{n} m_i < \prod_{i=1}^{t} m_i \tag{5}$$

The dealer then chooses the secret $s \in [0, m_0 - 1]$ and randomly selects an integer α such that

$$s + \alpha m_0 \in (\prod_{i=n-t+2}^{n} m_i, \prod_{i=1}^{t} m_i).$$

The share s_i for the i-th party would be

$$s_i = s + \alpha m_0 \bmod m_i$$

and is sent to the i-th party privately.

Secret Reconstruction: Suppose t parties $\{i_1, \ldots, i_t\} \subseteq [n]$ want to recover the secret. They pool their shares together and get the following system of congruences

$$\begin{cases} x \equiv s_{i_1} \pmod{m_{i_1}} \\ x \equiv s_{i_2} \pmod{m_{i_2}} \\ \cdots \cdots \\ x \equiv s_{i_t} \pmod{m_{i_t}} \end{cases}$$

By Theorems 4 and 2, they would get a unique solution x_0 in the range $[0, \prod_{k=1}^{t} m_{i_k} - 1]$. Since $s + \alpha m_0$ also satisfies this system of congruences and

$$s + \alpha m_0 < \prod_{i=1}^{t} m_i \leq \prod_{k=1}^{t} m_{i_k},$$

that is, $s + \alpha m_0$ is also in the range $[0, \prod_{k=1}^{t} m_{i_k} - 1]$. By the uniqueness, $s + \alpha m_0 = x_0$ and the secret can be recovered by computing $s = x_0 \bmod m_0$.

There are papers studying the perfectness or the information rate of Asmuth-Bloom's scheme. In [1], it is shown that the entropy of the secret in Asmuth-Bloom's scheme decreases "not too much" when $t - 1$ shares are known. In [14], it is advised to choose $m_0, m_1, \ldots, m_n$ being primes as close as possible and it is proved that $t - 2$ shares or less give no information on the secret for a (t, n)-threshold scheme. In [28], it is shown that Asmuth-Bloom's scheme with moduli being consecutive primes is asymptotically ideal. However, for fixed values of moduli, the scheme always has an lower information rate (less than 1), especially for not too large moduli.

2.6   Review of Shamir's Scheme [29]

In this subsection, we review Shamir's (t, n)-threshold SS scheme.

Share Distribution: The dealer selects a prime number p and randomly selects $t - 1$ elements $a_1, \ldots, a_{t-1}$ independently with a uniform distribution over $\mathbb{F}_p$. The secret is also some element s from $\mathbb{F}_p$. Then the dealer constructs a polynomial

$$f(x) = s + \sum_{i=1}^{t-1} a_i x^i \in \mathbb{F}_p[x]$$

and computes $s_i = f(i), i \in [n]$ as the private share of the i-th party. Finally, the dealer sends s_i to the i-th party in private.

Secret Reconstruction: Suppose t parties $\{i_1, \ldots, i_t\}$ want to recover the secret. They pool their shares together and get the following system of linear equations

$$\begin{bmatrix} 1 & i_1 & i_1^2 & \ldots & i_1^{t-1} \\ 1 & i_2 & i_2^2 & \ldots & i_2^{t-1} \\ \vdots & \vdots & \vdots & \vdots & \vdots \\ 1 & i_t & i_t^2 & \ldots & i_t^{t-1} \end{bmatrix} \begin{bmatrix} s \\ a_1 \\ a_2 \\ \vdots \\ a_{t-1} \end{bmatrix} = \begin{bmatrix} s_{i_1} \\ s_{i_2} \\ \vdots \\ s_{i_t} \end{bmatrix}$$

Since the coefficient matrix is a Vandermonde square matrix over the field $\mathbb{F}_p$ of size $t \times t$, it is invertible and this system of linear equations has a unique solution. Therefore, they can recover the secret s by solving this system of linear equations.

We have described this scheme from the point of view of solving systems of linear equations. Another way to recover the secret is based on the Lagrange interpolation (Theorem 7.15 of [31]). In this way, $f(x)$ can be written directly as

$$f(x) = \sum_{k=1}^{t} s_{i_k} \prod_{j=1,j\neq k}^{t} \frac{x - i_j}{i_k - i_j}$$

and the secret is

$$s = f(0) = \sum_{k=1}^{t} s_{i_k} \prod_{j=1,j\neq k}^{t} \frac{0 - i_j}{i_k - i_j}.$$

There are some works studying the perfectness or the information rate of Shamir's scheme [5,10,32]. We show in Sect. 4 that Shamir's scheme is a special case of our scheme and provide in Subsect. 3.2 a strict proof of the perfectness of our scheme, which also indicates that Shamir's scheme is perfect. Since the secret and the shares of Shamir's scheme are all selected in $\mathbb{F}_p$, its information rate is obviously 1. Thus, Shamir's scheme is ideal.

3   Threshold Scheme Based on CRT for Polynomial Ring over Finite Field

In this section, we first propose a (t, n)-threshold SS scheme based on the CRT for polynomial ring over finite field, and show that it can be ideal. Then, we show that Shamir's scheme is a special case of our scheme, revealing the connection among Shamir's scheme, Asmuth-Bloom's scheme and our scheme. Finally, we compare our scheme with the other two schemes.

3.1   The Scheme

In this subsection, we propose a (t, n)-threshold SS scheme. The scheme can be seen as the counterpart of Asmuth-Bloom's scheme for the polynomial ring over a finite field. It can also be regarded as a generalization of Shamir's scheme.

Share Distribution: The dealer chooses an integer $d_0 \geq 1$ and sets $m_0(x) = x^{d_0}$. The dealer chooses a prime integer p and pairwise coprime polynomials $m_i(x) \in \mathbb{F}_p[x], i \in [n]$. Let $d_i = \deg(m_i(x))$ for all $i \in [n]$. The polynomials must satisfy each of Expressions 6, 7 and 8.

$$\forall i \in [n], m_0(x) \text{ and } m_i(x) \text{ are coprime} \tag{6}$$

$$d_0 \leq d_1 \leq d_2 \leq \cdots \leq d_n \tag{7}$$

$$d_0 + \sum_{i=n-t+2}^{n} d_i \leq \sum_{i=1}^{t} d_i \tag{8}$$

The secret space is the set

$$\mathcal{S} = \{g(x) \in \mathbb{F}_p[x] \mid \deg(g) < d_0\},$$

i.e., all polynomials of degree at most $d_0 - 1$. Suppose that the dealer has picked his secret $s(x) \in \mathcal{S}$. Then, the dealer randomly chooses a polynomial $\alpha(x)$ from the set

$$\mathcal{A} = \{g(x) \in \mathbb{F}_p[x] \mid \deg(g) \leq (\sum\nolimits_{i=1}^{t} d_i) - d_0 - 1\}$$

and computes

$$f(x) = s(x) + \alpha(x)m_0(x) = s(x) + \alpha(x)x^{d_0}.$$

Let $d_\alpha = \deg(\alpha)$ and $d_f = \deg(f)$. It is clear that $d_f \leq \sum_{i=1}^{t} d_i - 1$. Finally, for each $i \in [n]$, the dealer computes $s_i(x) = f(x) \bmod m_i(x)$ as the share for the i-th party and sends $s_i(x)$ privately to the i-th party.

Share Reconstruction: If t parties $\{i_1, \ldots, i_t\} \subseteq [n]$ want to reconstruct the secret, they pool their private shares together and get the following system of congruences

$$\begin{cases} X(x) \equiv s_{i_1}(x) \pmod{m_{i_1}(x)} \\ X(x) \equiv s_{i_2}(x) \pmod{m_{i_2}(x)} \\ \ldots \\ X(x) \equiv s_{i_t}(x) \pmod{m_{i_t}(x)} \end{cases} \tag{9}$$

According to Theorems 4 and 3, they can solve Expression 9 and get a unique solution $X_0(x)$ among polynomials of degree less than $d = \sum_{j=1}^{t} d_{i_j}$. Let $\Pi = \prod_{j=1}^{t} m_{i_j}(x)$. It is clear that

$$d \geq \sum\nolimits_{j=1}^{t} d_j > \sum\nolimits_{j=1}^{t} d_j - 1 \geq d_f.$$

Since $f(x)$ also is a solution of the above system of congruences, by the uniqueness, $f(x) = X_0(x)$ and they can recover the secret by computing

$$s(x) = X_0(x) \bmod m_0(x) = X_0(x) \bmod x^{d_0}.$$

Before finishing this subsection, we would like to discuss some practical issues. In our scheme, the dealer is required to find a series of n pairwise coprime polynomials in $\mathbb{F}_p[x]$. In practice, it is convenient for the dealer to directly select distinct irreducible polynomials of specified degrees and these distinct irreducible polynomials with $m_0(x)$ are automatically pairwise coprime. By Theorem 7, we know that there are enough irreducible polynomials for this purpose in practice. Also, Algorithm 2 shows an efficient way to accomplish this job.

3.2   Security Analysis

In this subsection, we show that our scheme is perfect. The road map of the proof is as follows.

- First, Theorem 9 shows that coefficients of the computed $f(x)$ in the scheme regarded as random variables are independently identically distributed(i.i.d) of a uniform distribution over $\mathbb{F}_p$, if coefficients of both $s(x)$ and $\alpha(x)$ are i.i.d with respect to a uniform distribution over $\mathbb{F}_p$.
- Since $t-1$ parties together can eliminate some choices for $f(x)$, we must show that the number of choices for $f(x)$ left after the elimination is still greater than or equal to the number of choices for $s(x)$. Otherwise, the conditional probability distribution of $s(x)$ under the condition of knowing $t-1$ shares would not be a uniform distribution. And this part is completed in the proof of Theorem 10.
- However, what we get so far cannot imply that the conditional probability distribution of $s(x)$ is a uniform one, since Theorem 10 is only a necessary condition. Therefore, we need to study the correspondence between $s(x)$ and $f(x)$ under the relationship that $f(x) = s(x) + \alpha(x)x^{d_0}$. In particular, we show that after eliminating impossible choices for $f(x)$ with $t-1$ shares, the number of possible choices for $f(x)$ corresponding to a selected $s(x)$ is a constant. And this part is completed in the proof of Theorem 11.
- Finally, according to all the results above, we conclude that our scheme is perfect.

Theorem 9. *If the coefficients of $s(x)$ and $\alpha(x)$, regarded as random variables, are independently identically distributed(i.i.d) of a uniform distribution, then, the coefficients of $f(x)$, viewed as random variables, are also i.i.d with respect to a uniform distribution over $\mathbb{F}_p$.*

Proof. In the scheme, $f(x)$ is computed as

$$f(x) = s(x) + \alpha(x)m_0(x) = s(x) + \alpha(x)x^{d_0}$$

where the coefficients of $s(x)$ and $\alpha(x)$ are i.i.d with respect to a uniform distribution over $\mathbb{F}_p$. Since

- $f[i] = s[i]$ for $0 \leq i \leq d_0 - 1$
- $f[i] = \alpha[i - d_0]$ for $d_0 \leq i$

therefore, coefficients of f are i.i.d of a uniform distribution over $\mathbb{F}_p$.   □

To show that our scheme is perfect, it suffices to consider the worst case where the $t-1$ parties $\{n, n-1, \ldots, n-t+2\}$ with moduli of the highest degree pool their shares together and try to recover the secret. But they only get the following system of $t-1$ congruences

$$\begin{cases} X(x) \equiv s_n(x) \pmod{m_n(x)} \\ X(x) \equiv s_{n-1}(x) \pmod{m_{n-1}(x)} \\ \ldots \\ X(x) \equiv s_{n-t+2}(x) \pmod{m_{n-t+2}(x)} \end{cases} \quad (10)$$

By solving Expression 10, they can only find a unique solution $X_0(x) \in \mathbb{F}_p[x]$ among polynomials of degree less than $\sum_{i=n-t+2}^{n} d_i$. Since $f(x)$ also satisfies

Expression 10 and all the moduli are pairwise coprime, let $\Pi = \prod_{i=n-2+t}^{n} m_i(x)$, they know $f(x) \equiv X_0(x) \pmod{\Pi}$, that is,

$$s(x) + \alpha(x)x^{d_0} = f(x) = X_0(x) + k(x)\Pi \tag{11}$$

By Expression 11, $t-1$ parties can eliminate some choices of $f(x)$. We must consider how many possible $f(x)$ still satisfy this equation for given $X_0(x)$. That is, fixing $X_0(x)$, we need to find the cardinality of the set

$$F = \{g(x) \in \mathbb{F}_p[x] \mid \deg(g) \le \sum_{i=1}^{t} d_i - 1 \quad \text{and} \quad g \bmod \Pi = X_0(x)\}.$$

Let $d = \sum_{i=n-t+2}^{n} d_i$. Let $\delta = \sum_{i=1}^{t} d_i - d$. It is clear that $\delta \ge d_0$ by the selection of the parameters d_i during the scheme construction. We claim that $|F| = p^{\delta}$ as Theorem 10 states. Note that $|\mathcal{S}| = p^{d_0}$ and $|F| \ge |\mathcal{S}|$ for the secret space $\mathcal{S}$.

Theorem 10. $|F|$ is equal to p^{δ}.

Proof. Any element $g(x) \in F$ is of the form $g(x) = X_0(x) + k(x)\Pi$ with $\deg(g) \le \sum_{i=1}^{t} d_i - 1$. Therefore, one choice for $k(x)$ corresponds to one choice for $g(x) \in F$. Since $\deg(X_0) < \deg(\Pi)$, $\deg(g) = \deg(k) + \deg(\Pi)$. Therefore, $\deg(k) \le \sum_{i=1}^{t} d_i - 1 - \deg(\Pi)$. That is, $\deg(k) \le \delta - 1$. Therefore, the number of choices for $k(x)$ is p^{δ}. Hence, $|F| = p^{\delta}$. □

From Theorem 10, we can see that $t-1$ parties would know that the dealer must have selected one of the p^{δ} polynomials in F. And the probability that each polynomial is selected by the dealer is the same by Theorem 9.

Next, we study how these polynomials in F, modulo $m_0(x) = x^{d_0}$, map to the secret $s(x)$ to find out the conditional probability distribution of $s(x)$ regarded as a random variable.

Theorem 11. *Let*

$$\psi : F \to \mathcal{S}, g(x) \mapsto g(x) \bmod m_0(x).$$

For any $s(x) \in \mathcal{S}$, let

$$\psi^{-1}(s(x)) = \{g(x) \in F \mid \psi(g(x)) = s(x)\}.$$

Then, the following proposition holds.

$$\forall s_1(x), s_2(x) \in \mathcal{S}, |\psi^{-1}(s_1(x))| = |\psi^{-1}(s_2(x))|.$$

Proof. For any fixed $s(x) \in \mathcal{S}$, since $\psi^{-1}(s(x)) \subseteq F$, elements of $\psi^{-1}(s(x))$ is of the form $X_0(x) + k(x)\Pi$ with $\deg(k) \le \delta$ such that

$$X_0(x) + k(x)\Pi \equiv s(x) \pmod{m_0(x)}. \tag{12}$$

Therefore, to count the number of elements in $\psi^{-1}(s(x))$ is to count how many $k(x)$ with $\deg(k) \le \delta - 1$ satisfy Expression 12.
Subtracting $X_0(x)$ through Expression 12, we have

$$k(x)\Pi \equiv s(x) - X_0(x) \pmod{m_0(x)}.$$

Since $m_0(x)$ and Π are coprime in our scheme, Π has a multiplicative inverse modulo $m_0(x)$, then,

$$k(x) \equiv (s(x) - X_0(x))\Pi^{-1} \pmod{m_0(x)}.$$

Let $k_0(x) = (s(x) - X_0(x))\Pi^{-1} \bmod m_0(x)$. Then, any $k(x)$ satisfying Expression 12 is of the form $k(x) = k_0(x) + n(x)m_0(x)$ with $n(x) \in \mathbb{F}_p[x]$. Since $\deg(k_0) < \deg(m_0)$, $\deg(k) = \deg(n) + \deg(m_0)$. In addition, $\deg(k) \leq \delta - 1$, $\deg(n) \leq \delta - d_0 - 1$. Therefore, the number of such satisfiable $n(x)$ is $p^{\delta-d_0}$. Hence, $|\psi^{-1}(s(x))| = p^{\delta-d_0}$ is a constant.   □

So far, we have the foundation to discuss the conditional probability distribution of $s(x)$ under the condition that $t-1$ shares are known. It's clear that $t-1$ parties knowing $X_0(x)$ can determine the set F of all possible randomly selected $f(x)$, by Theorem 10, $|F| = p^{\delta}$. Over all the p^{δ} choices, by Theorem 11, only $p^{\delta-d_0}$ choices lead to the correct secret. Therefore, the conditional probability that $t-1$ parties can guess out the secret is $\frac{p^{\delta-d_0}}{p^{\delta}} = \frac{1}{p^{d_0}}$. That is,

$$\forall s_0(x) \in \mathcal{S}, \; Pr(s(x) = s_0(x) \mid X_0(x)) = \frac{1}{p^{d_0}} = Pr(s(x) = s_0(x)).$$

This implies that our scheme is perfect in security.

3.3 Information Rate

In this subsection, we discuss the information rate of our newly proposed scheme. In our scheme, the secret is a polynomial of degree at most $d_0 - 1$ and it takes d_0 elements in $\mathbb{F}_p$ to represent the secret. On the other hand, the n-th party holds the largest share which is a polynomial of degree at most $d_n - 1$ and consists of d_n elements in $\mathbb{F}_p$. Therefore, the information rate of our threshold scheme is $\frac{d_0}{d_n}$.

Note that our scheme does not require $d_0 < d_n$, instead, the dealer can select the modulus polynomials with the identical degree, i.e.,

$$d_0 = d_1 = \cdots = d_n. \tag{13}$$

In this case, the information rate is 1 and our scheme is an ideal one. By Theorem 7, we know that Expression 13 can be easily satisfied in practice and Algorithm 2 provides an efficient way.

3.4 Comparison

In this subsection, we compare our scheme with Asmuth-Bloom's scheme and Shamir's scheme. We show that our scheme has its advantage in some aspects, which encourages us to consider our scheme as a good base when designing new secret sharing schemes.

We start with the comparison with Asmuth-Bloom's scheme and our scheme enjoys the advantages in

– Perfectness and Information rate: From Subsect. 2.5, we know that Asmuth-Bloom's is neither perfect nor ideal. However, in Subsect. 3.2, we have shown that our scheme is perfect and in Subsect. 3.3, we have discussed that our scheme can reach information rate 1. Although, [28] has shown that Asmuth-Bloom's scheme is asymptotically ideal, it takes moduli of huge size to achieve this asymptotic property, which is not practical at all.

– Simplicity: During the construction of our scheme, the dealer only needs to find n distinct irreducible polynomials of degree d_0 with Algorithm 2 and these polynomials automatically satisfy the required conditions (Expressions 6, 7 and 8) of our scheme. However, Asmuth-Bloom's scheme failed to give an explicit way to find its moduli and to our knowledge, there is no such specialized algorithm. One candidate may be selecting consecutive prime numbers. But when the prime numbers are small, such consecutive prime numbers are not guaranteed to satisfy the required Expression 5. When the prime numbers are large, Expression 5 may be easier to satisfy, but it would be impractical if the number of secrets is small.

– Computing efficiency in certain cases: First, different from public key cryptosystems, where the private key related with the security level is usually large, the secret sharing schemes mentioned in this paper does not put its base on some intractable problem. Therefore, we usually do not put a restriction on the parameters related with security, but the parameters are determined considering both security level and practical needs. Now, suppose we are in the situation where we want to share a secret of huge size, e.g., a 2048 or larger bits key for the RSA cryptosystem, with Asmuth-Bloom's scheme, we may need to find prime moduli of this size (larger than 2^{2048}). However, it suffers from the fact that

  • to find a prime number or test the primality of numbers of such size takes a long time,

  • and the basic operations on numbers of such size is also time-consuming.

  In contrast, using our scheme with a proper d_0 selected (say $d_0 = 64$), a prime number around 2^{32} will handle this case without extremely huge numbers involved, thus, required computation can be completed efficiently.

  Another situation is when the secret can be expressed as a d_0 bit number. Then, by working in $\mathbb{F}_2[x]$, polynomial operations of our scheme can be implemented with bitwise operations to speed up.

When it comes to the comparison with Shamir's scheme, the above-mentioned advantages fade. Since Shamir's scheme is already ideal, our scheme can only draw with Shamir's scheme in perfectness and information rate. Shamir's scheme is also easy to construct, since the dealer only needs to find one prime number and the rest steps are clear. As for the last point, Shamir's scheme can also naturally work in the finite field of p^n elements to deal with the situation when the secret is of huge size and in the finite field of 2^{d_0} elements to enjoy the speed up of bitwise operations. Therefore, in all the aspects discussed, we can only say that our scheme draws with Shamir's scheme.

However, the important difference between Shamir's scheme and our scheme is that our scheme still preserves the structure of the CRT as Asmuth-Bloom's scheme does. That is,

- in Shamir's scheme, all parties are equal,
- while in our scheme, different parties can be easily assigned shares of different size to be distinguished from each other. Therefore, our scheme is more flexible than Shamir's scheme.

This may also be the reason why Asmuth-Bloom's scheme is significant even though Shamir's scheme behaves better than Asmuth-Bloom's scheme in perfectness, information rate and computing efficiency. In practice, schemes based on Asmuth-Bloom's scheme mostly take advantages of the property of CRT. For example,

- In the weighted scheme of [15], parties with larger weights are assigned larger moduli while parties with smaller weights are assigned smaller moduli. This can be easily achieved by the property of CRT.
- In the multilevel threshold scheme of [16], parties in different security levels are assigned moduli of different size to ensure different threshold for each level.

4   Shamir's Scheme as a Special Case of Our Scheme

As we know, Lagrange interpolation is closely related to CRT over polynomial ring [7].

In this section, we show that Shamir's scheme can be regarded as a special case of our scheme, indicating that Shamir's scheme, Asmuth-Bloom's scheme and our scheme are all tightly connected in essence.

To derive Shamir's scheme, we can select the parameters of our proposed scheme as follows.

- p is still a prime number
- let $d_0 = 1$ and $m_0(x) = x \in \mathbb{F}_p[x]$
- for all $i \in [n]$ let $m_i(x) = x - a_i \in \mathbb{F}_p[x]$ such that

$$\forall j, l \in [n], j \neq l \implies a_j \neq a_l$$

- let $s(x) = a_0 \in \mathbb{F}_p[x]$
- let $\alpha(x)$ be a random polynomial in $\{g(x) \in \mathbb{F}_p[x] \mid \deg(g(x)) \leq t - 2.\}$

It is easy to check that the above selection of parameters satisfies all the required conditions of our scheme. Then, $f(x) = s(x) + \alpha(x)m_0(x) = a_0 + \alpha(x)x$ is a random polynomial of degree at most $t - 1$ and the secret is exactly $s(x) = a_0 = f(0)$, which coincides with Shamir's scheme. The share for the i-th party would be $s_i(x) = (f(x) \bmod m_i(x)) = (f(x) \bmod (x - a_i)) = f(a_i)$, which also coincides with Shamir's scheme.

To see that $f(x) \pmod{x - a_i} = f(a_i)$, just divide $f(x)$ with $x - a_i$ and get $f(x) = (x - a_i)q(x) + r$ for some unique $q(x), r \in \mathbb{F}_p[x]$ with $\deg(r) < \deg(x - a_1) = 1$. Therefore, r is actually a constant in $\mathbb{F}_p[x]$. Then, replacing x with a_i in both side will result in $f(a_i) = r$, that is, $f(x) \pmod{x - a_i} = f(a_i)$.

In the secret reconstruction phase, for brevity of symbols, suppose t parties $\{1, 2, \ldots, t\}$ want to recover the secret. Pooling their shares together, they have the following system of congruences

$$\begin{cases} X(x) \equiv f(a_1) \pmod{x - a_1} \\ X(x) \equiv f(a_2) \pmod{x - a_2} \\ \cdots \\ X(x) \equiv f(a_t) \pmod{x - a_t} \end{cases} \tag{14}$$

Let

$$M(x) = \prod_{i=1}^{t} (x - a_i) \text{ and } M_j(x) = \frac{M(x)}{x - a_j} = \prod_{k=1, k \neq j}^{t} (x - a_k), \ j \in [t]$$

For all $i \in [t]$, since

$$M_i(x) \equiv M_i(a_i) \equiv \prod_{k=1, k \neq i}^{t} (a_i - a_k) \pmod{x - a_i}$$

and $\gcd(M_i(x), x - a_i) = 1$, we have

$$M_i^{-1}(x) \equiv (\prod_{k=1, k \neq i}^{t} (a_i - a_k))^{-1} \pmod{x - a_i}$$

Therefore, by Theorem 4, the solution of Expression 14 can be written as

$$\begin{aligned} X(x) &= \sum_{i=1}^{t} f(a_i) M_i(x) (M_i^{-1}(x) \pmod{x - a_i}) \\ &= \sum_{i=1}^{t} f(a_i) \prod_{k=1, k \neq i}^{t} (x - a_k)(\prod_{k=1, k \neq i}^{t} (a_i - a_k))^{-1} \\ &= \sum_{i=1}^{t} f(a_i) \prod_{k=1, k \neq i}^{t} \frac{x - a_k}{a_i - a_k} \end{aligned}$$

which coincides with the Lagrange interpolation polynomial for recovering the secret in Shamir's scheme.

5 A Weighted Threshold Secret Sharing Scheme

In this section, we propose a weighted secret sharing scheme based on our threshold scheme in Subsect. 3.1. The weighted scheme can also be seen as a counterpart of the scheme based on Asmuth-Bloom's scheme [15] for the polynomial ring over a finite field. By this weighted scheme, we illustrate that our scheme can serve as a better substitution for Asmuth-Bloom's scheme. Also, we recommend our threshold scheme for users who need some CRT based scheme as a base in the future. In Subsect. 5.1, we describe the weighted scheme. Then, in Subsect. 5.2, we discuss its security, information rate and comparison.

5.1 The Weighted Threshold Scheme

As is in Subsect. 2.4, the access structure realized by a (t, n, ω)-weighted threshold secret sharing scheme is of the form

$$\Gamma = \{A \subseteq [n] \mid \sum_{i \in A} \omega(i) \geq t\}$$

where ω is the weight function evaluated over $\mathbb{Z}$. For simplicity of notations, let $w_i = \omega(i)$ for all $i \in [n]$ and assume that

$$1 \le w_1 \le w_2 \le \cdots \le w_n < t.$$

Share Distribution: The dealer chooses a prime p and pairwise coprime polynomials $m_0(x) = x, m_1(x), \ldots, m_n(x) \in \mathbb{F}_p[x]$. Let

$$d_i = \deg(m_i) \text{ for all } i \in [n] \cup \{0\}.$$

The chosen polynomials must satisfy the condition that $\forall i \in [n], d_i = w_i$. The secret space is $\mathbb{F}_p$. Suppose that the dealer has picked his secret $s \in \mathbb{F}_p$. Then, the dealer randomly chooses a polynomial $\alpha(x)$ from the set

$$\mathcal{A} = \{g(x) \in \mathbb{F}_p[x] \mid \deg(g(x)) \le t - 2\}.$$

That is, $\alpha(x)$ is a polynomial of degree at most $t - 2$. Next, the dealer computes $f(x) = s + \alpha(x)m_0(x) = s + \alpha(x)x$. Let $d_f = \deg(f(x))$ and $d_\alpha = \deg(\alpha(x))$. It is clear that

$$d_f = d_\alpha + d_0 \le t - 2 + 1 = t - 1$$

Finally, the dealer computes

$$s_i(x) = f(x) \bmod m_i(x)$$

as the share of the i-th party and sends $s_i(x)$ privately to the i-th party.

Secret Reconstruction: If k parties $\{i_1, \ldots, i_k\} \subseteq [n]$ with

$$\sum_{j=1}^{k} \omega(i_j) \ge t$$

want to reconstruct the secret, they pool their private shares together and form the following system of congruences

$$\begin{cases} X(x) \equiv s_{i_1}(x) \pmod{m_{i_1}(x)} \\ X(x) \equiv s_{i_2}(x) \pmod{m_{i_2}(x)} \\ \cdots \\ X(x) \equiv s_{i_k}(x) \pmod{m_{i_k}(x)} \end{cases}$$

They can solve this system of congruences and get a solution $X_0(x) \in \mathbb{F}_p[x]$. By the CRT for polynomial rings over a field (Theorem 3), the solution is unique if only polynomials of degree less than $\sum_{j=1}^{k} d_{i_j}$ are considered. Since

$$\sum_{j=1}^{k} d_{i_j} \ge t > t - 1 \ge d_f$$

and $f(x)$ also is a solution of the above system of congruences, they have $f(x) = X_0(x)$. Then, the secret can be recovered by computing

$$s(x) = X_0(x) \bmod m_0(x).$$

5.2 Discussion of the Weighted Threshold Scheme

Since our weighted scheme can also be seen as a parameterization of our threshold scheme, we only briefly discuss the security and information rate of our weighted scheme in this subsection. Then, we compare it with the existing weighted scheme.

First, as a fundamental criterion, our weighted threshold scheme is perfect. This conclusion should be clear since the weighted scheme can be seen as a parameterization of our threshold scheme, except that, in the weighted scheme, one party with weight w is thought of as equivalent with w parties in the threshold scheme.

In our weighted scheme, the secret ranges over $\mathbb{F}_p$ while the largest share is the polynomial of degree $w_n - 1$ which consists of w_n coefficients in $\mathbb{F}_p$. Therefore, the information rate is $\frac{1}{w_n}$.

To our knowledge, there are several existing weighted threshold schemes based on the CRT for integers, like [21,35] and [15]. In [15], it is commented that

- Both schemes of [21] and [35] are not perfect while [15] is perfect.
- In the scheme of [21], the dealer needs to find out all minimal subsets of authorized access structure and then determines the modulus of each shareholder accordingly and it is a time-consuming process.
- The size of the CRT moduli and private shares of [15] is smaller than the moduli of [21] and [35].

Still, compared with the scheme of [15], our weighted scheme enjoys the following advantages in

- Information rate: Our information rate is $\frac{1}{w_n}$ while the information rate of the scheme of [15] is less than $\frac{1}{w_n}$.
- Simplicity: In the scheme of [15], the constraint on the modulus for each party is stricter than that in Asmuth-Bloom's scheme. As mentioned in Subsect. 3.4, to find such a series of moduli is not trivial and there's no specialized algorithm. But it is simpler to find the moduli of our scheme with Algorithm 2.
- Computing efficiency: Our weighted scheme still inherits the advantage of the computing efficiency in certain cases over the scheme based on the CRT for integers as mentioned in Subsect. 3.4.

6 Conclusion

Currently, existing CRT based (t, n)-threshold SS schemes are not ideal. Compared with Shamir's scheme, they have a lower information rate and are harder to construct. In this paper, we present the generalized (t, n)-threshold SS scheme based on the CRT for the ring of polynomials over a finite field. In particular, our scheme is perfect in security and has information rate 1. Moreover, we showed that Shamir's scheme is a special case of our threshold scheme and thus establish the connection among Shamir's scheme, Asmuth-Bloom's scheme and our proposed scheme. Finally, we present a weighted threshold scheme based on our threshold scheme. Comparison shows that our weighted scheme has great advantages over existing schemes based on Asmuth-Bloom's scheme, which enables our scheme to be a better substitution for Asmuth-Bloom's scheme.

References

1. Asmuth, C., Bloom, J.: A modular approach to key safeguarding. IEEE Trans. Inf. Theor. **29**(2), 208–210 (1983)
2. Beimel, A.: Secret-sharing schemes: a survey. In: Chee, Y.M., et al. (eds.) IWCC 2011. LNCS, vol. 6639, pp. 11–46. Springer, Heidelberg (2011). https://doi.org/10. 1007/978-3-642-20901-7_2
3. Ben-Or, M., Goldwasser, S., Wigderson, A.: Completeness theorems for non-cryptographic fault-tolerant distributed computation. In: Proceedings of the Twentieth Annual ACM Symposium On Theory Of Computing, pp. 1–10. ACM (1988)
4. Blakley, G.R., et al.: Safeguarding cryptographic keys. In: Proceedings of the National Computer Conference, vol. 48, pp. 313–317 (1979)
5. Brickell, E.F.: Some ideal secret sharing schemes. In: Quisquater, J.-J., Vandewalle, J. (eds.) EUROCRYPT 1989. LNCS, vol. 434, pp. 468–475. Springer, Heidelberg (1990). https://doi.org/10.1007/3-540-46885-4_45
6. Capocelli, R.M., De Santis, A., Gargano, L., Vaccaro, U.: On the size of shares for secret sharing schemes. J. Cryptol. **6**(3), 157–167 (1993)
7. Childs, L.N.: A Concrete Introduction to Higher Algebra. UTM. Springer, New York (2009). https://doi.org/10.1007/978-0-387-74725-5
8. Cohen, H.: A Course in Algorithmic Algebraic Number Theory, vol. 138. Springer, Heidelberg (1993). https://doi.org/10.1007/978-3-662-02945-9
9. Cramer, R., Damgård, I., Maurer, U.: General secure multi-party computation from any linear secret-sharing scheme. In: Preneel, B. (ed.) EUROCRYPT 2000. LNCS, vol. 1807, pp. 316–334. Springer, Heidelberg (2000). https://doi.org/10. 1007/3-540-45539-6_22
10. Fuyou, M., Yan, X., Xingfu, W., Badawy, M.: Randomized component and its application to (t, m, n)-group oriented secret sharing. IEEE Trans. Inf. Forensics Secur. **10**(5), 889–899 (2015)
11. Galibus, T., Matveev, G.: Generalized mignotte's sequences over polynomial rings. Electron. Notes Theor. Comput. Sci. **186**, 43–48 (2007). https://doi.org/10.1016/ j.entcs.2006.12.044
12. Galibus, T., Matveev, G., Shenets, N.: Some structural and security properties of the modular secret sharing. In: 10th International Symposium on Symbolic and Numeric Algorithms for Scientific Computing, pp. 197–200. IEEE Press, New York (2008). https://doi.org/10.1109/SYNASC.2008.14
13. Gennaro, R., Rabin, M.O., Rabin, T.: Simplified VSS and fast-track multiparty computations with applications to threshold cryptography. In: Proceedings of the Seventeenth Annual ACM Symposium on Principles Of Distributed Computing, pp. 101–111. ACM (1998)
14. Goldreich, O., Ron, D., Sudan, M.: Chinese remaindering with errors. In: Proceedings of the Thirty-first Annual ACM Symposium on Theory of Computing, pp. 225–234. ACM (1999)

15. Harn, L., Fuyou, M.: Weighted secret sharing based on the Chinese remainder theorem. Int. Netw. Secur., 1–7 (2013)
16. Harn, L., Fuyou, M.: Multilevel threshold secret sharing based on the Chinese remainder theorem. Inf. Process. Lett. **114**(9), 504–509 (2014)
17. Harn, L., Fuyou, M., Chang, C.C.: Verifiable secret sharing based on the chinese remainder theorem. Secur. Commun. Netw. **7**(6), 950–957 (2014)
18. Harn, L., Hsu, C., Zhang, M., He, T., Zhang, M.: Realizing secret sharing with general access structure. Inf. Sci. **367**, 209–220 (2016)
19. Harn, L., Lin, C.: Strong (n, t, n) verifiable secret sharing scheme. Inf. Sci. **180**(16), 3059–3064 (2010)
20. Iftene, S.: Secret sharing schemes with applications in security protocols. Sci. Ann. Cuza Univ. **16**, 63–96 (2006)
21. Iftene, S., Boureanu, I.C.: Weighted threshold secret sharing based on the Chinese remainder theorem. Sci. Ann. Cuza Univ. **15**(EPFL-ARTICLE-174320), 161–172 (2005)
22. Kaya, K., Selçuk, A.A.: Threshold cryptography based on Asmuth-Bloom secret sharing. Inf. Sci. **177**(19), 4148–4160 (2007)
23. Lang, S.: Algebra. Graduate Texts in Mathematics, vol. 211, 3rd edn. Springer, New York (2002). https://doi.org/10.1007/978-1-4613-0041-0. 1. ALL-ALL
24. Liu, Y., Harn, L., Chang, C.C.: A novel verifiable secret sharing mechanism using theory of numbers and a method for sharing secrets. Int. J. Commun. Syst. **28**(7), 1282–1292 (2015)
25. Mignotte, M.: How to share a secret. In: Beth, Thomas (ed.) EUROCRYPT 1982. LNCS, vol. 149, pp. 371–375. Springer, Heidelberg (1983). https://doi.org/10.1007/3-540-39466-4_27
26. Morillo, P., Padró, C., Sáez, G., Villar, J.L.: Weighted threshold secret sharing schemes. Inf. Process. Lett. **70**(5), 211–216 (1999)
27. Pang, L.J., Wang, Y.M.: A new (t, n) multi-secret sharing scheme based on Shamir's secret sharing. Appl. Math. Comput. **167**(2), 840–848 (2005)
28. Quisquater, M., Preneel, B., Vandewalle, J.: On the security of the threshold scheme based on the Chinese remainder theorem. In: Naccache, D., Paillier, P. (eds.) PKC 2002. LNCS, vol. 2274, pp. 199–210. Springer, Heidelberg (2002). https://doi.org/10.1007/3-540-45664-3_14
29. Shamir, A.: How to share a secret. Commun. ACM **22**(11), 612–613 (1979)
30. Shankar, B., Srinathan, K., Rangan, C.P.: Alternative protocols for generalized oblivious transfer. In: Rao, S., Chatterjee, M., Jayanti, P., Murthy, C.S.R., Saha, S.K. (eds.) ICDCN 2008. LNCS, vol. 4904, pp. 304–309. Springer, Heidelberg (2007). https://doi.org/10.1007/978-3-540-77444-0_31
31. Shoup, V.: A computational Introduction to Number Theory and Algebra. Cambridge University Press, Cambridge (2009)
32. Stinson, D.R.: An explication of secret sharing schemes. Des. Codes Cryptogr. **2**(4), 357–390 (1992)
33. Tassa, T.: Generalized oblivious transfer by secret sharing. Des. Codes Cryptogr. **58**(1), 11–21 (2011)
34. Yang, C.C., Chang, T.Y., Hwang, M.S.: A (t, n) multi-secret sharing scheme. Appl. Math. Comput. **151**(2), 483–490 (2004)
35. Zou, X., Maino, F., Bertino, E., Sui, Y., Wang, K., Li, F.: A new approach to weighted multi-secret sharing. In: 2011 Proceedings of 20th International Conference on Computer Communications and Networks, ICCCN, pp. 1–6. IEEE (2011)

Optimal Linear Multiparty Conditional Disclosure of Secrets Protocols

Amos Beimel$^{(\boxtimes)}$ and Naty Peter

Ben-Gurion University of the Negev, Be'er-Sheva, Israel
amos.beimel@gmail.com, naty@post.bgu.ac.il

Abstract. In a k-party CDS protocol, each party sends one message to a referee (without seeing the other messages) such that the referee will learn a secret held by the parties if and only if the inputs of the parties satisfy some condition (e.g., if the inputs are all equal). This simple primitive is used to construct attribute based encryption, symmetrically-private information retrieval, priced oblivious transfer, and secret-sharing schemes for any access structure. Motivated by these applications, CDS protocols have been recently studied in many papers.

In this work, we study linear CDS protocols, where each of the messages of the parties is a linear function of the secret and random elements taken from some finite field. Linearity is an important property of CDS protocols as many applications of CDS protocols required it.

Our main result is a construction of linear k-party CDS protocols for an arbitrary function $f : [N]^k \rightarrow \{0,1\}$ with messages of size $O(N^{(k-1)/2})$ (a similar result was independently and in parallel proven by Liu et al. [27]). By a lower bound of Beimel et al. [TCC 2017], this message size is optimal. We also consider functions with few inputs that return 1, and design more efficient CDS protocols for them.

CDS protocols can be used to construct secret-sharing schemes for uniform access structures, where for some k all sets of size less than k are unauthorized, all sets of size greater than k are authorized, and each set of size k can be either authorized or unauthorized. We show that our results imply that every k-uniform access structure with n parties can be realized by a linear secret-sharing scheme with share size $\min\left\{(O(n/k))^{(k-1)/2}, O(n \cdot 2^{n/2})\right\}$. Furthermore, the linear k-party CDS protocol with messages of size $O(N^{(k-1)/2})$ was recently used by Liu and Vaikuntanathan [STOC 2018] to construct a linear secret-sharing scheme with share size $O(2^{0.999n})$ for any n-party access structure.

Keywords: Secret-sharing schemes ·
Conditional disclosure of secrets protocols

The authors are supported by ISF grant 152/17 and by the Frankel center for computer science.

T. Peyrin and S. Galbraith (Eds.): ASIACRYPT 2018, LNCS 11274, pp. 332–362, 2018.
https://doi.org/10.1007/978-3-030-03332-3_13

1   Introduction

Conditional disclosure of secrets (CDS) protocols, introduced by Gertner, Ishai, Kushilevitz, and Malkin [20], is a cryptographic primitive related to secret-sharing that has many applications. In a CDS protocol, there are k parties, each one holds a private input x_i and the same secret s, and a referee that holds $x_1, \ldots, x_k$ but does know s. The goal is that the referee will learn s if and only if the inputs $x_1, \ldots, x_k$ satisfy some condition specified by a function f, i.e., $f(x_1, \ldots, x_k) = 1$. The challenge is that each party sends only one message to the referee (without seeing the other messages). This simple primitive is used to construct attribute based encryption [6,29], symmetrically-private information retrieval [20], priced oblivious transfer [1], secret-sharing for uniform access structures [3,13,14], and secret-sharing for general access structures [25]. Motivated by these applications, CDS protocols have been recently studied in many papers [3,4,10,12,14,19,22,26,27].

In this work, we study linear CDS protocols, where the messages of the parties are a linear function of the secret and random elements taken from some finite field. Equivalently, a CDS protocol is linear if the reconstruction of the secret by the referee from the messages is a linear mapping.[1] In many applications of CDS protocols, it is required that the protocol will be linear. For example, it was shown by Attrapadung [6] and Wee [29] that linear 2-party CDS protocols can be used to construct public-key (multi-user) attribute-based encryption. Furthermore, using a construction of Cramer et al. [16] and the construction of secret-sharing schemes of [25], linear k-party CDS protocols imply secure multiparty computation (MPC) protocols secure against Q2 adversarial structures.[2] The construction of Cramer et al. [16] requires a linear secret-sharing scheme, i.e., they must use a linear k-party CDS.

Linear CDS protocols can be used to construct linear secret-sharing schemes for uniform access structures, that is, access structures in which for some k all sets of size less than k are unauthorized, all sets of size greater than k are authorized, and each set of size k can be either authorized or unauthorized [3,12–14]. Very recently, Liu et al. [25] used the optimal linear k-party CDS protocols (constructed in our paper and in [27]) to construct linear secret-sharing schemes with share size $O(2^{0.999n})$ for any n-party access structure. They also used non-linear k-party CDS protocols to construct a non-linear secret-sharing scheme with share size $O(2^{0.994n})$ for any n-party access structure. These are the first major improvements in the share size of secret-sharing schemes for arbitrary access structures since the first constructions of [23], whose share size is 2^n.

CDS protocols share similarities with private simultaneous messages (PSM) protocols, a primitive introduced by Feige, Kilian, and Naor [18] for two-input functions, and generalized to k-input functions in [18,21]. In a PSM protocol,

---

[1] This equivalence is a special case of the equivalence for secret-sharing schemes. See [7] for discussion on equivalent definitions of linear secret-sharing schemes.

[2] An adversarial structure is Q2 if the union of any two sets that the adversary can control is not the entire set of parties.

there are k parties, each one holds a private input x_i; here the referee does not hold $x_1, \ldots, x_k$. The goal is that the referee will learn $f(x_1, \ldots, x_k)$, without learning any additional information on $x_1, \ldots, x_k$. As in CDS protocols, the challenge is that each party sends only one message to the referee (without seeing the other messages). Intuitively, compared to CDS, PSM is a stronger model, since in CDS the inputs are known to the referee and in PSM the referee should not learn any information about the inputs. A PSM protocol for a function f implies a CDS protocol for the function f [20]. PSM protocols for specific functions are used in the construction of CDS protocols in our work and in [27].

1.1   Our Results

Our first result is a construction of linear k-party CDS protocols for an arbitrary k-input function $f : [M] \times [N]^{k-1} \to \{0, 1\}$ with total message size $O(N^{(k-1)/2})$ for every $k > 2$ and integers M, N. Notice that the message size is independent of M, that is, the domain of inputs of one party can be very large without affecting the message size. For example, this property is useful for the index function where the size of the domain of the first party is $2^{N^{k-1}}$ and the size of the domains of the other parties in N. By [10], the size of the messages in linear CDS protocols for most k-input functions $f : [M] \times [N]^{k-1} \to \{0, 1\}$ is $\Omega(k^{-1} \cdot N^{(k-1)/2})$ (see details in Sect. 8), thus our construction is optimal (up to a factor of k). Previously, this result was only known for $k = 2$ [19] (for the case that $M = N$). For $k > 2$, in the best previously known linear CDS protocol the size of the messages was $O(N^k)$ [20].

Following [9,10,12], we also consider functions with few inputs that return 1. We consider k-input functions f such that $|f^{-1}(1)| \leq N^\gamma$ for some $0 < \gamma < (k+1)/2$ and construct a linear CDS protocol for them with message size $O(k^3 \cdot N^{\gamma(k-1)/(k+1)} \cdot \log N)$. The same result holds for functions such that $|f^{-1}(0)| \leq N^\gamma$. These results generalize the result of [11] that constructed a CDS protocol for 2-input functions f such that $|f^{-1}(1)| \leq N^\gamma$ for some constant $1 \leq \gamma < 2$ with message size $\tilde{O}(N^{\gamma/4})$. The results of [10] imply a lower bound of $\Omega(k^{-1} \cdot N^{\gamma(k-1)/2k})$ for the message size of linear CDS protocols for k-input functions. We do not know if our construction for k-input functions with few inputs that return 1 is optimal.

As discussed above, CDS protocols imply secret-sharing schemes for uniform access structures. Thus, our results imply the existence of linear secret-sharing schemes for uniform access structures as we next elaborate. Using a family of perfect hash functions and our CDS protocols, we show that every k-uniform access structure with n parties can be realized by a linear secret-sharing scheme with share size $O(k \cdot e^k \cdot \log n \cdot \lceil n/k \rceil^{(k-1)/2})$ (a similar transformation was presented in [3]; our transformation is more efficient). Furthermore, using a transformation of [14], every k-uniform access structure with n parties can be realized by a linear secret-sharing scheme with share size $O(n \cdot 2^{n/2})$; this protocol is more efficient when $k > 0.257n$. Finally, our results imply that every k-uniform access structure with n^γ minimal authorized sets of size k can be realized by a linear secret-sharing scheme in which the size of the share of each party is $O(k^4 \cdot e^k \cdot \log^2 n \cdot \lceil n/k \rceil^{\gamma(k-1)/(k+1)})$.

1.2   Our Technique

We use the following paradigm to design multiparty linear CDS protocols; this paradigm was implicitly used to design multiparty CDS protocols [27] and PSM protocols [14]. We start with a CDS protocol for a constant number of parties and use it to construct a CDS protocol for an arbitrary number of parties.

We demonstrate this idea by describing a linear k-party CDS protocol for a k-input function $f : [N]^k \to \{0, 1\}$ with complexity $O(N^{3k/4-1})$. Notice that for $k > 2$ this construction already improves the best previously known upper bound described in [20] of $O(N^k)$ for linear CDS protocols. For simplicity of the discussion, in this paragraph we only consider an even k (as explained in the technical section we also show how to handle odd values of k). Given the function f, we define a 2-input function $g : [N]^{k/2} \times [N]^{k/2} \to \{0, 1\}$, where $g((x_1, \ldots, x_{k/2}), (x_{k/2+1}, \ldots, x_k)) = f(x_1, \ldots, x_k)$. By [19], there is a linear 2-party CDS protocol for g with messages of size $O(N^{k/4})$. Denote the message of the first and second party in the CDS protocol for g by $m_1(x_1, \ldots, x_{k/2})$ and $m_2(x_{k/2+1}, \ldots, x_k)$, respectively (these messages are also a function of the common randomness of the CDS protocol). We construct a k-party CDS protocol for f, where the first $k/2$ parties (respectively, the last $k/2$ parties) use a $k/2$-party PSM protocol to compute $m_1(x_1, \ldots, x_{k/2})$ (respectively, $m_2(x_{k/2+1}, \ldots, x_k)$). The parties can use the PSM protocol of [18] to compute these functions; the complexity of the protocol is $O(N^{3k/4-1})$. The referee can reconstruct the messages $m_1(x_1, \ldots, x_{k/2})$ and $m_2(x_{k/2+1}, \ldots, x_k)$ and use the linear reconstruction function of the CDS protocol to reconstruct the secret. The problem is that the resulting CDS protocol is not linear since the PSM protocol of [18] is not linear. However, we can use the fact that in a CDS protocol the referee knows $x_1, \ldots, x_k$ and construct a simplified version of the protocol of [18] that is linear.

We use the above approach to design a linear k-party CDS protocol with messages of size $N^{(k-1)/2}$. We first construct a new linear 3-party CDS protocol for 3-input functions; this CDS protocol generalizes the linear 2-party CDS protocol of [19]. To construct a CDS protocol for a k-input function $f : [N]^k \to \{0, 1\}$ (for an odd k) we define a 3-input function $g : [N] \times [N]^{(k-1)/2} \times [N]^{(k-1)/2} \to \{0, 1\}$, where $g(x_1, (x_2, \ldots, x_{(k-1)/2}), (x_{(k+1)/2}, \ldots, x_k)) = f(x_1, \ldots, x_k)$; that is, we partition the parties to three sets, where the size of the first set is 1 and the sizes of the two other sets is $(k-1)/2$. We use our 3-party CDS protocol for g, and denote the messages in this protocol by m_1, m_2, m_3; in this protocol each message is of size at most $N^{(k-1)/2}$. We then show that m_2 and m_3 can be computed by efficient linear PSM protocols (where the referee knows the inputs $x_2, \ldots, x_{(k-1)/2}$ and $x_{(k+1)/2}, \ldots, x_k$, respectively).

To summarize our approach, one can start with any linear CDS protocol for a small number of parties and use a linear variant of the PSM protocol of [18], in which the parties send messages enabling the referee to compute the messages of the CDS protocol. However, this transformation does not necessary result in the most efficient protocol. To construct an optimal linear k-party CDS protocol, we design a specific 3-party CDS protocol, such that its messages can be computed by efficient linear PSM protocols.

Comparison to the protocol of [27]. In a work that was done independently and in parallel to our work, Liu et al. [27] have also constructed k-party linear CDS protocols for arbitrary k-input functions with total message size $O(k \cdot N^{(k-1)/2})$ for every $k > 2$. Their protocol is somewhat different than ours, however it uses very similar ideas. We apply some optimizations in our protocol, which reduces the total message size by a factor of k compared to the protocol of [27]. Furthermore, the protocol of [27] is only described for odd values of k (using our ideas it can be transformed to a protocol for even values of k).

1.3   Related Works

Gertner et al. [20] defined CDS protocols and used them to construct symmetrically-private information retrieval protocols. They gave some constructions of CDS protocols: (1) they showed that a PSM protocol for a function implies a CDS protocol for the same function, and (2) they showed that a span program (not necessarily monotone) computing a function f implies a linear CDS protocol for f. In particular, this gives a construction from formulas and branching programs. Their result implies that for every k-input function $f : [N]^k \to \{0,1\}$ there exist a linear CDS protocol with messages of size $O(N^k)$.

Beimel et al. [13] showed that for every 2-input function $f : [N] \times [N] \to \{0,1\}$ there exists a 2-party CDS protocol in which the size of the messages is $O(N^{1/2})$. Their protocol is not linear. Gay et al. [19] constructed a linear 2-party CDS protocol for arbitrary 2-input functions with the same message size of $O(N^{1/2})$. Following the above results, Liu et al. [26] have shown that every 2-input function has a non-linear 2-party CDS protocol with messages of size $2^{O(\sqrt{\log N \log \log N})}$. To construct this CDS protocol, they reduced it to a CDS protocol for the index function and constructed a CDS protocol for the index function based on the private information retrieval protocol of Dvir and Gopi [17]. Liu et al. [27] have generalized their results to k-input functions, designing a non-linear k-party CDS protocol with messages of size $2^{O(\sqrt{k \log N} \log(k \log N))}$.

Gay et al. [19] proved lower and upper bounds on the size of the messages in linear and non-linear 2-party CDS protocols for several functions with domain of size N. For example, they proved a lower bound of $\Omega(\sqrt{\log N})$ and a matching upper bound of $O(\sqrt{\log N})$ on the messages size of linear CDS protocols for the index function and a lower bound of $\Omega(\sqrt{\log N})$ and an upper bound of $O(\log N)$ on the messages size of linear CDS protocols for the disjointness function (which returns 1 if and only if the sets represented by the inputs are disjoint) and for the inner-product function. They also proved a lower bound of $\Omega(\log \log N)$ for any CDS protocol (possibly non-linear) for these functions. Applebaum et al. [4] proved a lower bound of $\Omega(\log N)$ for any CDS protocol (possibly non-linear) for some (non-explicit) function. Applebaum et al. [5] proved a lower bound of

$\log N - 3 - o(1)$ for any CDS protocol (possibly non-linear) for the inner product function. All the above lower bounds are for a one-bit secret.

Applebaum et al. [4] and Ambrona et al. [2] showed that if there is a linear 2-party CDS protocol for some function f with message size c and common random string with size r, then there is a linear CDS protocol for the complement function $\overline{f}$ in which the message size and the common random string size is linear in c and r. Applebaum et al. [4] also showed that if there is a 2-party CDS protocol (possibly non-linear) for some function f with message size c, common random string with size r, and an error of $2^{-\kappa}$ (in the reconstruction and in the privacy), then there is a CDS protocol for $\overline{f}$ in which the message size and the common random string size are polynomial in c, r, and κ.

Another result shown in [4] is that for every 2-input function there exists a linear CDS for secrets of ℓ bits, where ℓ is exponential in N^2, in which the size of the messages is $O(\ell \cdot \log N)$. This gives an amortized message size of $O(\log N)$ per each bit of the secret, much better than the message size of $2^{O(\sqrt{\log N \log \log N})}$ shown in [26]. Applebaum and Arkis [3] improved this result and extended it to k-input functions; they showed that for every function $f : [N]^k \to \{0,1\}$ there exists a multi-linear CDS protocol for secrets of ℓ bits, where ℓ is exponential in N^k, in which the size of each of the messages sent by the parties is 4ℓ.

CDS protocols are closely related to secret-sharing schemes for uniform access structures. Basically, k-party CDS protocols for functions $f : [N]^k \to \{0,1\}$ are equivalent to secret-sharing schemes for k-partite k-uniform access structures with $k \cdot N$ parties, where a k-uniform access structure is k-partite if there is a partition of the parties to k sets $V_1, \ldots, V_k$ such that every authorized set of size k contains exactly one party from each set V_i. Two-uniform access structures, called forbidden graph access structures, where first defined by Sun and Shieh [28], and where further studied in [3,10,12,13].

In particular, it was shown in [13] that there is a transformation from 2-party CDS protocols to secret-sharing schemes for 2-uniform access structures with n parties in which the share size is $O(\log n)$ times the message size in the CDS protocol; this transformation preserves linearity. Furthermore, if the size of the secret is increased, then the share size of the resulting scheme is only $O(1)$ times the message size in the CDS protocol; this transformation *does not* preserve linearity (for a linear CDS, the resulting scheme would be multi-linear). In [3], this transformation was generalized for any k, where the increase in the share size is $O(e^k \cdot \log n)$ if one wants to preserve linearity and $O(e^k)$ without preserving linearity. In this paper, we improve this transformation for short secrets, i.e., we transform k-party CDS protocols for a function *with domain of size n/k* to secret-sharing schemes for k-uniform access structures with n parties.

2 Preliminaries

2.1 Conditional Disclosure of Secrets Protocols

In this section we define k-party conditional disclosure of secrets (CDS) protocols, first presented in [20].

Definition 2.1 (Conditional Disclosure of Secrets Protocols – Syntax and Correctness). *Let* $f : X_1 \times \cdots \times X_k \to \{0,1\}$ *be some k-input function. A CDS protocol* $\mathcal{P}$ *for* f *with domain of secrets* S *consists of:*

- *A finite domain of common random strings* R, *and* k *finite message domains* $M_1, \ldots, M_k$.
- *Deterministic message computation functions* $\mathrm{ENC}_1, \ldots, \mathrm{ENC}_k$, *where* $\mathrm{ENC}_i : X_i \times S \times R \to M_i$ *for every* $i \in [k]$.
- *A deterministic reconstruction function* $\mathrm{DEC} : X_1 \times \cdots \times X_k \times M_1 \times \cdots \times M_k \to \{0,1\}$.

We say that a CDS protocol $\mathcal{P}$ *is correct (with respect to* f*) if for every* $(x_1, \ldots, x_k) \in X_1 \times \cdots \times X_k$ *for which* $f(x_1, \ldots, x_k) = 1$, *every secret* $s \in S$, *and every common random string* $r \in R$,

$$\mathrm{DEC}(x_1, \ldots, x_k, \mathrm{ENC}_1(x_1, s, r), \ldots, \mathrm{ENC}_k(x_k, s, r)) = s.$$

The total message size of a CDS protocol $\mathcal{P}$ *is the total size of the messages sent by the parties, i.e.,* $\sum_{i=1}^{k} \log |M_i|$.

We define the privacy of CDS protocols with a simulator, i.e., given $x_1, \ldots, x_k$ such that $f(x_1, \ldots, x_k) = 0$, we can simulate the messages sent by the parties by a simulator that has access only to $x_1, \ldots, x_k$, such that one cannot distinguish between the messages sent by the parties and the messages generated by the simulator. That is, a CDS protocol is private if everything that can be learned from it can be learned from $x_1, \ldots, x_k$ without knowing the secret.

Definition 2.2 (Conditional Disclosure of Secrets Protocols – Privacy). *We say that a CDS protocol* $\mathcal{P}$ *is private (with respect to* f*) if there exists a randomized function* SIM, *called the* simulator, *such that for every* $(x_1, \ldots, x_k) \in X_1 \times \cdots \times X_k$ *for which* $f(x_1, \ldots, x_k) = 0$, *every secret* $s \in S$, *and every* k *messages* $(m_1, \ldots, m_k) \in M_1 \times \cdots \times M_k$,

$$\Pr[\mathrm{SIM}(x_1, \ldots, x_k) = (m_1, \ldots, m_k)]$$
$$= \Pr[\mathrm{ENC}_1(x_1, s, r) = m_1, \ldots, \mathrm{ENC}_k(x_k, s, r) = m_k],$$

where the first probability is over the randomness of the simulator S *and the second probability is over the choice of* r *from* R *with uniform distribution.*

Informally, we say that a CDS protocol is linear if the reconstruction function of the referee is a linear function.

Definition 2.3 (Linear Conditional Disclosure of Secrets Protocols). *We say that a CDS protocol is linear over a finite field* $\mathbb{F}$ *if*

- $S = \mathbb{F}$,
- *There exists constants* $\ell, \ell_1, \ldots, \ell_k$ *such that* $R = \mathbb{F}^\ell$ *and* $M_i = \mathbb{F}^{\ell_i}$ *for every* $i \in [k]$, *and*

– *For every* $x_1, \ldots, x_k \in [N]$ *there exist field elements* $(\alpha_{i,j_i})_{i \in [k], j_i \in [\ell_i]} \in \mathbb{F}$ *such that*

$$\text{DEC}(x_1, \ldots, x_k, \text{ENC}_1(x_1, s, r), \ldots, \text{ENC}_k(x_k, s, r)) = \sum_{i \in [k], j_i \in [\ell_i]} \alpha_{i,j_i} m_{i,j_i},$$

where $\text{ENC}_i(x_i, s, r) = (m_{i,1}, \ldots, m_{i,\ell_i})$ *for every* $i \in [k]$.

Equivalently, we could have required that for every $i \in [k]$ and every $x_i \in X_i$ the function $\text{ENC}_i(x_i, s, r)$ is a linear function over $\mathbb{F}$ of the secret s and the field elements in $r = (r_1, \ldots, r_\ell)$ (see [7,24] for the equivalence).

2.2 Secret-Sharing Schemes

We next present the definition of secret-sharing schemes, similar to [8,15].

Definition 2.4 (Secret-Sharing Schemes). *Let* $P = \{P_1, \ldots, P_n\}$ *be a set of parties. A collection* $\Gamma \subseteq 2^P$ *is* monotone *if* $B \in \Gamma$ *and* $B \subseteq C$ *imply that* $C \in \Gamma$. *An* access structure *is a monotone collection* $\Gamma \subseteq 2^P$ *of non-empty subsets of* P. *Sets in* Γ *are called* authorized, *and sets not in* Γ *are called* unauthorized. *The family of minimal authorized subsets is denoted by* $\min \Gamma$.

A secret-sharing scheme $\Sigma = \langle \Pi, \mu \rangle$ *with domain of secrets* K *is a pair, where* μ *is a probability distribution on some finite set* R *called the set of random strings and* Π *is a mapping from* $K \times R$ *to a set of* n-tuples $K_1 \times K_2 \times \cdots \times K_n$, *where* K_j *is called the* domain of shares *of* P_j. *A dealer distributes a secret* $k \in K$ *according to* Σ *by first sampling a random string* $r \in R$ *according to* μ, *computing a vector of shares* $\Pi(k, r) = (s_1, \ldots, s_n)$, *and privately communicating each share* s_j *to party* P_j. *For a set* $A \subseteq P$, *we denote* $\Pi_A(k, r)$ *as the restriction of* $\Pi(k, r)$ *to its* A-entries *(i.e., the shares of the parties in* A).

Given a secret-sharing scheme, define the size of the secret *as* $\log |K|$, *the* share size *of party* P_j *as* $\log |K_j|$, *the* max share size *as* $\max_{1 \leq j \leq n} \log |K_j|$, *and the* total share size *as* $\sum_{j=1}^{n} \log |K_j|$.

Let K *be a finite set of secrets, where* $|K| \geq 2$. *A secret-sharing scheme* $\Sigma = \langle \Pi, \mu \rangle$ *with domain of secrets* K realizes *an access structure* Γ *if the following two requirements hold:*

CORRECTNESS. *The secret* k *can be reconstructed by any authorized set of parties. That is, for any set* $B = \{P_{i_1}, \ldots, P_{i_{|B|}}\} \in \Gamma$, *there exists a reconstruction function* $\text{Recon}_B : K_{i_1} \times \cdots \times K_{i_{|B|}} \to K$ *such that for every secret* $k \in K$ *and every random string* $r \in R$,

$$\text{Recon}_B \left(\Pi_B(k, r) \right) = k.$$

PRIVACY. *Every unauthorized set cannot learn anything about the secret from its shares. Formally, for any set* $T \notin \Gamma$, *every two secrets* $a, b \in K$, *and every possible vector of shares* $\langle s_j \rangle_{P_j \in T}$,

$$\Pr[\, \Pi_T(a, r) = \langle s_j \rangle_{P_j \in T} \,] = \Pr[\, \Pi_T(b, r) = \langle s_j \rangle_{P_j \in T} \,],$$

where the probability is over the choice of r *from* R *at random according to* μ.

A scheme is linear if the mapping that the dealer uses to generate the shares that are given to the parties is linear, as we formalize at the following definition.

Definition 2.5 (Linear Secret-Sharing Schemes). *Let* $\Sigma = \langle \Pi, \mu \rangle$ *be a secret-sharing scheme with domain of secrets K, where μ is a probability distribution on a set R and Π is a mapping from $K \times R$ to $K_1 \times K_2 \times \cdots \times K_n$. We say that Σ is a* linear secret-sharing scheme over a finite field $\mathbb{F}$ *if $K = \mathbb{F}$, the sets $R, K_1, \ldots, K_n$ are vector spaces over $\mathbb{F}$, Π is an $\mathbb{F}$-linear mapping, and μ is the uniform probability distribution over R.*

3 Linear CDS Protocols for 2 and 3 Parties

We present linear 2-party and 3-party CDS protocols. The 3-party CDS protocol will be used in Sect. 4 to construct k-party CDS protocols for $k > 3$. To avoid confusions, in this section we denote the parties by Alice, Bob, and Charlie.

3.1 A Linear 2-Party CDS Protocol

As a warm up, we first describe a linear 2-party CDS protocol for any 2-input function $f : [M] \times [N] \to \{0,1\}$ in which the total message size is N; i.e., the message size does not depend on M. This protocol is part of the protocol described in [19], and it is not the optimal protocol for 2 parties (in particular, by [19] there exist a linear 2-party CDS protocol for any 2-input function $f : [N] \times [N] \to \{0,1\}$ in which the message size is $O(N^{1/2})$).

In the CDS protocol, the parties, Alice and Bob, hold the inputs $x_1 \in [M]$ and $x_2 \in [N]$, respectively, and the common randomness is N uniform bits $r_1, \ldots, r_N$. We denote the secret by $s \in \{0,1\}$. Alice sends to the referee the bit

$$s \oplus \bigoplus_{i_2 \in [N], f(x_1, i_2) = 0} r_{i_2},$$

and Bob sends the bits $r_1, \ldots, r_{x_2-1}, r_{x_2+1}, \ldots, r_N$. The message size of the protocol is $1 + (N - 1) = N$.

The correctness of the above protocol follows from the fact that if $f(x_1, x_2) = 1$, then the bit r_{x_2} is not part of the exclusive-or of the bit that Alice sends. The referee gets all the bits $r_1, \ldots, r_N$ except for the bit r_{x_2}, and in particular all the bits among $r_1, \ldots, r_N$ that are part of the exclusive-or in $s \oplus \bigoplus_{i_2 \in [N], f(x_1, i_2) = 0} r_{i_2}$. Thus, the referee can reconstruct the secret. For the privacy, we observe that if $f(x_1, x_2) = 0$, then the bit r_{x_2} is part of the exclusive-or of the bit that Alice sends, and since the referee does not get this bit from Bob, then it cannot learn any information about the secret. Formally, a simulator independently chooses N uniform bits $s', r_1', \ldots, r_{N-1}'$ and outputs s' as the message of Alice and $r_1', \ldots, r_{N-1}'$ as the message of Bob.

Protocol $\mathcal{P}_3$

The secret: A bit $s \in \{0,1\}$.
Inputs: Alice, Bob, and Charlie hold the inputs $x_1 \in [M]$ and $x_2, x_3 \in [N]$, respectively.
Common randomness: The three parties hold the following random bits.

- $r_1, \ldots, r_N \in \{0,1\}$.
- $q_1, \ldots, q_N \in \{0,1\}$.

The protocol:

1. Alice sends to the referee the bits $s_{i_3} = s \oplus q_{i_3} \oplus \bigoplus_{i_2 \in [N], f(x_1, i_2, i_3) = 0} r_{i_2}$
   for every $i_3 \in [N]$.
2. Bob sends to the referee the bits $r_1, \ldots, r_{x_2-1}, r_{x_2+1}, \ldots, r_N$.
3. Charlie sends to the referee the bit q_{x_3}.
4. If $f(x_1, x_2, x_3) = 1$, the referee computes

$$s_{x_3} \oplus q_{x_3} \oplus \bigoplus_{i_2 \in [N], f(x_1, i_2, x_3) = 0} r_{i_2}.$$

Fig. 1. A linear 3-party CDS protocol $\mathcal{P}_3$ for a 3-input function $f : [M] \times [N] \times [N] \to \{0,1\}$.

3.2 A Linear 3-Party CDS Protocol

We adapt the above protocol and construct a linear 3-party CDS protocol $\mathcal{P}_3$ for any 3-input function $f : [M] \times [N] \times [N] \to \{0,1\}$ with message size $O(N)$ (again, the message size is independent of M).

Lemma 3.1. *Let $f : [M] \times [N] \times [N] \to \{0,1\}$ be a 3-input function. Then, there is a linear 3-party CDS protocol for f with total message size $O(N)$.*

Proof. The linear CDS protocol for f, denoted by $\mathcal{P}_3$, is described in Fig. 1. We start with an informal description of the protocol. The parties, Alice, Bob, and Charlie, hold the inputs $x_1 \in [M]$ and $x_2, x_3 \in [N]$, respectively. The common randomness is $2N$ bits $r_1, \ldots, r_N$ and $q_1, \ldots, q_N$, and the secret is $s \in \{0,1\}$.

For every possible value $i_3 \in [N]$ of the input of Charlie, Alice sends to the referee the bit $s_{i_3} = s \oplus q_{i_3} \oplus \bigoplus_{i_2 \in [N], f(x_1, i_2, i_3) = 0} r_{i_2}$ (i.e., the message that Alice sends in the 2-party CDS protocol, masked by q_{i_3}). Bob sends the bits $r_1, \ldots, r_{x_2-1}, r_{x_2+1}, \ldots, r_N$, and Charlie sends the bit q_{x_3}.

Next, we prove the correctness of $\mathcal{P}_3$. If $f(x_1, x_2, x_3) = 1$, then the bit r_{x_2} is not part of the exclusive-or in the bit s_{x_3} that Alice sends, since it contains only the bits r_{i_2} for which $f(x_1, i_2, x_3) = 0$. Thus, the referee, which gets the bit q_{x_3} and all the bits $r_1, \ldots, r_N$ except for the bit r_{x_2}, and in particular all the bits among $r_1, \ldots, r_N$ that are part of the exclusive-or in s_{x_3}, can reconstruct the secret s, as described in $\mathcal{P}_3$.

Now, we prove that $\mathcal{P}_3$ is private by constructing a simulator whose output is 3 messages, such that the distribution on the messages of $\mathcal{P}_3$ and the distribution on the messages of the simulator are the same. If $f(x_1, x_2, x_3) = 0$, then the bit r_{x_2} is part of the exclusive-or in the bit s_{x_3}, and, thus, the bit s_{x_3} is uniformly distributed given the messages of Bob and Charlie. Similarly, since the referee does not get the bits $q_1, \ldots, q_{x_3-1}, q_{x_3+1}, \ldots, q_N$, the distribution on the bits s_{i_3}, for every $i_3 \in [N]$ such that $i_3 \neq x_3$, is uniform. Hence, the simulator independently chooses $2N$ uniform bits $s'_1, \ldots, s'_N, r'_1, \ldots, r'_{N-1}, q'$ and outputs $s'_1, \ldots, s'_N$ as the message of Alice, $r'_1, \ldots, r'_{N-1}$ as the message of Bob, and q' as the message of Charlie.

Moreover, the protocol $\mathcal{P}_3$ is linear over $\mathbb{F}_2$, since for every $x_1 \in [M]$ and $x_2, x_3 \in [N]$ the reconstruction function of the referee is a linear combination of the bits in the messages it gets. Finally, Alice sends N bits, Bob sends $N - 1$ bits, and Charlie sends one bit, so the massage size of $\mathcal{P}_3$ is $N + (N - 1) + 1 = 2N$. □

4   Linear k-Party CDS Protocols

We use the protocol $\mathcal{P}_3$ to construct a k-party CDS protocol, for any integer k, using the approach described in the introduction. First, in Sect. 4.1, we show how to transform the 3-party CDS protocol $\mathcal{P}_3$ to a linear k-party CDS protocol $\mathcal{P}_k$ for any k-input function $f : [M] \times [N]^{k-1} \to \{0,1\}$, for an *odd* $k > 3$. Then, in Sect. 4.2, we show how we can adapt the transformation for an even $k > 3$.

4.1   A Linear k-Party CDS Protocol for an Odd k

Informal Description of the Protocol. We consider a k-input function $f : [M] \times [N]^{k-1} \to \{0,1\}$, for some odd k, and k parties $P_1, \ldots, P_k$ that hold the inputs $x_1 \in [M]$ and $x_2, \ldots, x_k \in [N]$, respectively. Let $k' = (k-1)/2$, $y_1 = x_1$, $y_2 = (x_2, \ldots, x_{k'+1})$, and $y_3 = (x_{k'+2}, \ldots, x_k)$, and define a 3-input function $g : [M] \times [N]^{k'} \times [N]^{k'} \to \{0,1\}$, where $g(x_1, (x_2, \ldots, x_{k'+1}), (x_{k'+2}, \ldots, x_k)) = f(x_1, \ldots, x_k)$. That is, we partition the parties into three sets, where the first set is $S_1 = \{P_1\}$, the second set is $S_2 = \{P_2, \ldots, P_{k'+1}\}$, and the third set is $S_3 = \{P_{k'+2}, \ldots, P_k\}$. Observe that $|S_2| = |S_3| = k'$.

We next describe a k-party CDS protocol $\mathcal{P}_k$ in which the parties $P_1, \ldots, P_k$ simulates the parties in the protocol $\mathcal{P}_3$ for the function g. In this simulation, party P_1 simulates Alice, the parties in S_2 simulate Bob, and the parties in S_3 simulate Charlie, as follows. We denote the simulated inputs in $\mathcal{P}_3$ by y_1, y_2, y_3 and use $h_2, h_3 \in [N]^{k'}$ as possible inputs of g in $\mathcal{P}_3$.

Simulating Alice. Party P_1 sends the bits $s_{h_3} = s \oplus q_{h_3} \oplus \bigoplus_{h_2 \in [N]^{k'}, f(x_1, h_2, h_3) = 0} r_{h_2}$, for every $h_3 = (i_{k'+2}, \ldots, i_k) \in [N]^{k'}$ (exactly as in $\mathcal{P}_3$).

Simulating Bob. The parties in S_2 should send the bits r_{h_2}, for every $h_2 = (i_2, \ldots, i_{k'+1}) \in [N]^{k'}$, except for $r_{y_2} = r_{x_2, \ldots, x_{k'+1}}$. To do so, every party $P_j \in S_2$ sends to the referee all the random bits r_{h_2} for every $h_2 = (i_2, \ldots, i_{k'+1}) \in [N]^{k'}$ such that $i_j \neq x_j$. Observe that $h_2 \neq (x_2, \ldots, x_{k'+1})$ if and only if $i_j \neq x_j$ for at least one j. Thus, the parties in S_2 send the bits that they should send.

Simulating Charlie. The parties in S_3 should send the bit q_{y_3}. To do so, we share every random bit q_{h_3}, for every $h_3 \in [N]^{k'}$, between the parties in S_3 using a k'-out-of-k' secret-sharing scheme. That is, for every $h_3 = (i_{k'+2}, \ldots, i_k) \in [N]^{k'}$, we choose k' random bits $q_{h_3}^{k'+2}, \ldots, q_{h_3}^{k}$ and define $q_{h_3} = q_{h_3}^{k'+2} \oplus \cdots \oplus q_{h_3}^{k}$. Every party $P_j \in S_3$ sends the bits $q_{h_3}^j$ for every $h_3 = (i_{k'+2}, \ldots, i_k) \in [N]^{k'}$ such that $i_j = x_j$. Thus, the referee can reconstruct the bit $q_{y_3} = q_{x_{k'+2}, \ldots, x_k}$, and cannot learn any information about the bits $(q_{h_3})_{h_3 \neq y_3}$.

As explained above, the referee in $\mathcal{P}_k$ can compute the messages in $\mathcal{P}_3$, and, thus, when $g(y_1, y_2, y_3) = 1$ (i.e., when $f(x_1, \ldots, x_k) = 1$), it can reconstruct the secret s. The message size of every party is at most $N^{k'} = N^{(k-1)/2}$, and the total massage size is $N^{k'} + k' \cdot N^{k'-1} \cdot (N-1) + k' \cdot N^{k'-1} = O(k \cdot N^{(k-1)/2})$.

Next, we show how to improve the total message size of the above protocol by a factor of k, by improving the simulations of Bob and Charlie by the parties in S_2 and S_3, respectively.

The improved simulation of the messages of Charlie is as follows. The common random string will contain bits $q_{i_j, \ldots, i_k}^j$, for every $j \in \{k'+2, \ldots, k\}$ and every $i_j, \ldots, i_k \in [N]$. First, let $q_{i_{k'+2}, \ldots, i_k} = \bigoplus_{j=k'+2}^{k} q_{i_j, \ldots, i_k}^j$, for every $i_{k'+2}, \ldots, i_k \in [N]$. Party P_j, for every $j \in \{k'+2, \ldots, k\}$, sends the random bits $q_{x_j, i_{j+1}, \ldots, i_k}^j$, for every $i_{j+1}, \ldots, i_k \in [N]$. The referee gets the bits $q_{x_{k'+2}, \ldots, x_k}^{k'+2}, q_{x_{k'+3}, \ldots, x_k}^{k'+3}, \ldots, q_{x_k}^{k}$, and thus can reconstruct $q_{x_{k'+2}, \ldots, x_k}$. We will show that all other bits $q_{i_{k'+2}, \ldots, i_k}$ remain random to the referee, and, thus, the privacy still holds.

The improved simulation of the messages of Bob is as follows. The common random string contains the bits $t_{i_j, \ldots, i_{k'+1}}$, for every $j \in \{3, \ldots, k'+1\}$ and every $i_j, \ldots, i_{k'+1} \in [N]$ (in addition to all previously mentioned bits). Party P_2 sends the random bits $r_{i_2, \ldots, i_{k'+1}}$, for every $i_2, i_3, \ldots, i_{k'+1} \in [N]$ such that $i_2 \neq x_2$ as before. In addition it also sends the bits $r_{x_2, i_3, \ldots, i_{k'+1}}$, for every $i_3, \ldots, i_{k'+1} \in [N]$, masked by random bits, that is, it sends $r_{x_2, i_3, \ldots, i_{k'+1}} \oplus t_{i_3, \ldots, i_{k'+1}}$, for every $i_3, \ldots, i_{k'+1} \in [N]$. Next, party P_3 sends all the bits $t_{i_3, \ldots, i_{k'+1}}$, for every $i_3, i_4, \ldots, i_{k'+1} \in [N]$ such that $i_3 \neq x_3$. Given those bits, the referee can learn all the bits $r_{i_2, i_3, \ldots, i_{k'+1}}$ for which $i_2 \neq x_2$, and all the bits $r_{i_2, i_3, \ldots, i_{k'+1}}$ for which $i_2 = x_2$ and $i_3 \neq x_3$. We continue in the same manner until we get to the party $P_{k'+1}$. That is, the party P_3 additionally sends the bits $t_{x_3, i_4 \ldots, i_{k'+1}} \oplus t_{i_4, \ldots, i_{k'+1}}$, for every $i_4, \ldots, i_{k'+1} \in [N]$, and so on. Finally, party $P_{k'+1}$ sends only the bits $t_{i_{k'+1}}$, for every $i_{k'+1} \in [N]$ such that $i_{k'+1} \neq x_{k'+1}$.

The referee will learn only the bit $q_{x_{k'+2}, x_{k'+3} \ldots, x_k}$ from the messages of the parties that simulate Charlie, and all the bits $r_{i_2, \ldots, i_{k'+1}}$, for every $i_2, \ldots, i_{k'+1} \in [N]$, except for $r_{x_2, \ldots, x_{k'+1}}$, from the messages of the parties that simulate Bob.

The size of the messages sent by parties $P_{k'+2}, \ldots, P_k$ is $N^{k'-1} + N^{k'-2} + \cdots + N + 1 < 2 \cdot N^{k'-1} = O(N^{(k-3)/2})$, and the size of the messages sent by parties $P_2, \ldots, P_{k'+1}$ is $N^{k'} + N^{k'-1} + \cdots + N^2 + N - 1 < 2 \cdot N^{k'} = O(N^{(k-1)/2})$.

Lemma 4.1. *Let $f : [M] \times [N]^{k-1} \to \{0,1\}$ be a k-input function, for some odd integer $k > 3$. Then, protocol $\mathcal{P}_k$, described in Fig. 2, is a linear k-party CDS protocol for f with total message size $O(N^{(k-1)/2})$.*

Proof. Recall that $k' = (k-1)/2$. We prove that protocol $\mathcal{P}_k$ is a CDS protocol for f with message size as in the lemma. Let $g : [M] \times [N]^{k'} \times [N]^{k'} \to \{0,1\}$ be the 3-input function where $g(x_1, (x_2, \ldots, x_{k'+1}), (x_{k'+2}, \ldots, x_k)) = f(x_1, \ldots, x_k)$. We first prove that in protocol $\mathcal{P}_k$, the referee can compute the messages that the referee gets in the protocol $\mathcal{P}_3$ for g, and, thus, it can compute s if $g(x_1, (x_2, \ldots, x_{k'+1}), (x_{k'+2}, \ldots, x_k)) = 1$, i.e., if $f(x_1, \ldots, x_k) = 1$. We then prove that if $f(x_1, \ldots, x_k) = 0$, then the messages in $\mathcal{P}_k$ can be simulated since they are uniformly distributed regardless of s.

CORRECTNESS. First, we show that the referee gets the bit $q_{x_{k'+2}, \ldots, x_k}$. Observe that the referee gets the bit $q^j_{x_j \ldots, x_k}$ from party P_j, for every $j \in \{k'+2, \ldots, k\}$. Thus, the referee can perform an exclusive-or between all these bits and reconstruct the bit $q_{x_{k'+2}, \ldots, x_k} = \bigoplus_{j=k'+2}^{k} q^j_{x_j, \ldots, x_k}$.

Second, we show that the referee gets all the bits $r_{i_2, \ldots, i_{k'+1}}$, for every $i_2, \ldots, i_{k'+1} \in [N]$, except for the bit $r_{x_2, \ldots, x_{k'+1}}$. Fix some $(i_2, \ldots, i_{k'+1}) \neq (x_2, \ldots, x_{k'+1})$, and let $\ell \in \{2, \ldots, k'+1\}$ be the first index for which $i_\ell \neq x_\ell$. If $\ell = 2$, then the referee gets the bit $r_{i_2, \ldots, i_{k'+1}}$ from party P_2. Otherwise, the referee gets the bit $r_{x_2, \ldots, x_{\ell-1}, i_\ell, \ldots i_{k'+1}} \oplus t_{x_3, \ldots, x_{\ell-1}, i_\ell, \ldots i_{k'+1}}$ from party P_2, and for every $j \in \{3, \ldots, \ell-1\}$, it gets the bit $t_{x_j, \ldots, x_{\ell-1}, i_\ell, \ldots i_{k'+1}} \oplus t_{x_{j+1}, \ldots, x_{\ell-1}, i_\ell, \ldots i_{k'+1}}$ from party P_j. Moreover, since $i_\ell \neq x_\ell$, the referee gets the bit $t_{i_\ell, \ldots i_{k'+1}}$ from party P_ℓ. Thus, the referee can perform an exclusive-or between all the above bits and reconstruct the bit $r_{i_2, \ldots, i_{k'+1}}$.

Using the above two facts, we prove the correctness of $\mathcal{P}_k$. The referee gets $s_{x_{k'+2}, \ldots, x_k}, (r_{i_2, \ldots, i_{k'+1}})_{(i_2, \ldots, i_{k'+1}) \neq (x_2, \ldots, x_{k'+1})}$, and $q_{x_{k'+2}, \ldots, x_k}$, i.e., the messages it would get in the protocol $\mathcal{P}_3$ for the function g. Hence, if $f(x_1, \ldots, x_k) = 1$, then $g(x_1, (x_2, \ldots, x_{k'+1}), (x_{k'+2}, \ldots, x_k)) = 1$ and the referee can reconstruct the secret s since it would have reconstructed it in $\mathcal{P}_3$, as described in $\mathcal{P}_k$.

PRIVACY. We prove that $\mathcal{P}_k$ is private by constructing a simulator. The simulator of $\mathcal{P}_k$ chooses independently uniform random bits as the messages sent by the parties. We show that the output of the simulator is distributed as the messages sent by the parties in the protocol $\mathcal{P}_k$ for $f(x_1, \ldots, x_k) = 0$, i.e., we show that in this case the messages in $\mathcal{P}_k$ are uniformly distributed.

First, the messages of parties $P_{k'+2}, \ldots, P_k$ contain random bits from the common randomness and each bit is only sent by one of the parties, thus, the messages sent by these parties are uniformly distributed. Next, the message of party $P_{k'+1}$ is uniformly distributed, since it contains the random bits $t_{i_{k'+1}}$, for every $i_{k'+1} \in [N]$ such that $i_{k'+1} \neq x_{k'+1}$. Given this message, the message of party $P_{k'}$ is uniformly distributed, since it contains the random bits $t_{i_{k'}, i_{k'+1}}$,

---

Protocol $\mathcal{P}_k$ for an Odd k

The secret: A bit $s \in \{0,1\}$.
Inputs: $P_1, \ldots, P_k$ hold the inputs $x_1 \in [M]$ and $x_2, \ldots, x_k \in [N]$, respectively.
Common randomness: Let $k' = (k-1)/2$. The k parties hold the following random bits.

- $r_{i_2,\ldots,i_{k'+1}} \in \{0,1\}$, for every $i_2, \ldots, i_{k'+1} \in [N]$.
- $t_{i_j,\ldots,i_{k'+1}} \in \{0,1\}$, for every $j \in \{3,\ldots,k'+1\}$ and $i_j, \ldots, i_{k'+1} \in [N]$.
- $q^j_{i_j,\ldots,i_k} \in \{0,1\}$, for every $j \in \{k'+2,\ldots,k\}$ and $i_j, \ldots, i_k \in [N]$.

The protocol:

1. Define $q_{i_{k'+2},\ldots,i_k} = \bigoplus_{j=k'+2}^{k} q^j_{i_j,\ldots,i_k}$ for every $i_{k'+2}, \ldots, i_k \in [N]$.
   (* SIMULATION OF ALICE *)
2. Party P_1 sends to the referee the bits

$$s_{i_{k'+2},\ldots,i_k} =$$

$$s \oplus q_{i_{k'+2},\ldots,i_k} \oplus \bigoplus_{i_2,\ldots,i_{k'+1} \in [N], f(x_1,i_2,\ldots,i_{k'+1},i_{k'+2},\ldots,i_k)=0} r_{i_2,\ldots,i_{k'+1}}$$

   for every $i_{k'+2}, \ldots, i_k \in [N]$.
   (* SIMULATION OF BOB *)
3. Party P_2 sends to the referee the bits $r_{i_2,\ldots,i_{k'+1}}$, for every $i_2, \ldots, i_{k'+1} \in [N]$ such that $i_2 \neq x_2$, and the bits $r_{x_2,i_3,\ldots,i_{k'+1}} \oplus t_{i_3,\ldots,i_{k'+1}}$, for every $i_3, \ldots, i_{k'+1} \in [N]$.
4. For every $j \in \{3,\ldots,k'\}$, party P_j sends to the referee the bits $t_{i_j,\ldots,i_{k'+1}}$, for every $i_j, \ldots, i_{k'+1} \in [N]$ such that $i_j \neq x_j$, and the bits $t_{x_j,i_{j+1},\ldots,i_{k'+1}} \oplus t_{i_{j+1},\ldots,i_{k'+1}}$, for every $i_{j+1}, \ldots, i_{k'+1} \in [N]$.
5. Party $P_{k'+1}$ sends to the referee the bits $t_{i_{k'+1}}$, for every $i_{k'+1} \in [N]$ such that $i_{k'+1} \neq x_{k'+1}$.
   (* SIMULATION OF CHARLIE *)
6. For every $j \in \{k'+2,\ldots,k\}$, party P_j sends to the referee the bits $q^j_{x_j,i_{j+1},\ldots,i_k}$, for every $i_{j+1}, \ldots, i_k \in [N]$.
   (* THE RECONSTRUCTION OF THE SECRET *)
7. If $f(x_1,\ldots,x_k) = 1$, the referee computes

$$s_{x_{k'+2},\ldots,x_k} \oplus q_{x_{k'+2},\ldots,x_k} \oplus$$

$$\bigoplus_{i_2,\ldots,i_{k'+1} \in [N], f(x_1,i_2,\ldots,i_{k'+1},x_{k'+2},\ldots,x_k)=0} r_{i_2,\ldots,i_{k'+1}}.$$

Fig. 2. A linear k-party CDS protocol $\mathcal{P}_k$ for a k-input function $f : [M] \times [N]^{k-1} \to \{0,1\}$, for an odd k.

for every $i_{k'}, i_{k'+1} \in [N]$ such that $i_{k'} \neq x_{k'}$, and the bits $t_{x_{k'},i_{k'+1}} \oplus t_{i_{k'+1}}$ which contains the random bit $t_{x_{k'},i_{k'+1}}$, for every $i_{k'+1} \in [N]$. We continue in the same manner, and conclude that given the messages of parties $P_3, \ldots, P_{k'+1}$, the message of party P_2 is uniformly distributed, since it contains the random bits $r_{i_2,\ldots,i_{k'+1}}$, for every $i_2, \ldots, i_{k'+1} \in [N]$ such that $i_2 \neq x_2$, and the bits $r_{x_2,i_3,\ldots,i_{k'+1}} \oplus t_{i_3,\ldots,i_{k'+1}}$, for every $i_3, \ldots, i_{k'+1} \in [N]$. Thus, the messages of parties $P_2, \ldots, P_{k'+1}$ are uniformly distributed. Note that the messages of $P_2, \ldots, P_{k'+1}$ and $P_{k'+2}, \ldots, P_k$ are independent.

We next argue that the message of P_1 is uniformly distributed given the messages of the other parties. We first prove that the bits $q_{i_{k'+2},\ldots,i_k}$, for every $(i_{k'+2}, \ldots, i_k) \neq (x_{k'+2}, \ldots, x_k)$, are uniformly distributed given the messages of $P_{k'+2}, \ldots, P_k$. Fix some $(i_{k'+2}, \ldots, i_k) \neq (x_{k'+2}, \ldots, x_k)$, and let $\ell \in \{k'+2, \ldots, k\}$ be the first index for which $i_\ell \neq x_\ell$, i.e., $(i_{k'+2}, \ldots, i_k) = (x_{k'+2}, \ldots, x_{\ell-1}, i_\ell, \ldots, i_k)$. Thus, the referee does not get the bit $q_{i_\ell,\ldots i_k}^\ell$ from party P_ℓ, and, thus, it cannot learn the bit $q_{i_{k'+2},\ldots,i_k}$, since $q_{i_\ell,\ldots i_k}^\ell$ is part of the exclusive-or in the bit $q_{i_{k'+2},\ldots,i_k}$. In the above argument, we used $q_{i_\ell,\ldots i_k}^\ell$ only for $q_{x_{k'+2},\ldots,x_{\ell-1},i_\ell,\ldots,i_k}$, thus, the set of bits $\{q_{i_{k'+2},\ldots,i_k}\}_{(i_{k'+2},\ldots,i_k) \neq (x_{k'+2},\ldots,x_k)}$ are uniformly distributed given the messages of $P_{k'+2}, \ldots, P_k$.

We next show that the referee does not learn the bit $r_{x_2,\ldots,x_{k'+1}}$. The referee gets the bit $r_{x_2,\ldots,x_{k'+1}} \oplus t_{x_3,\ldots,x_{k'+1}}$ from party P_2, and for every $j \in \{3, \ldots, k'\}$, it gets the bit $t_{x_j,\ldots,x_{k'+1}} \oplus t_{x_{j+1},\ldots,i_{k'+1}}$ from P_j. However, party $P_{k'+1}$ does not send to the referee the bit $t_{x_{k'+1}}$, so it cannot learn the bit $r_{x_2,\ldots,x_{k'+1}}$.

Now, we show that given the messages of parties $P_2, \ldots, P_k$, the message of party P_1 is uniformly distributed. Since $f(x_1, \ldots, x_k) = 0$, the bit $r_{x_{k'+2},\ldots,x_k}$ is part of the exclusive-or in the bit $s_{x_{k'+2},\ldots,x_k}$. As we have shown, the referee does not get $r_{x_{k'+2},\ldots,x_k}$, so the bit $s_{x_{k'+2},\ldots,x_k}$ is uniformly distributed. For every $(i_{k'+2}, \ldots, i_k) \neq (x_{k'+2}, \ldots, x_k)$, the bit $q_{i_{k'+2},\ldots,i_k}$ is part of the exclusive-or in the bit $s_{i_{k'+2},\ldots,i_k}$. As we have shown, the referee does not get $q_{i_{k'+2},\ldots,i_k}$, so the bit $s_{i_{k'+2},\ldots,i_k}$ is uniformly distributed. Thus, since for every $i_{k'+2}, \ldots, i_k \in [N]$ there is a unique random bit that is part of the exclusive-or in the bit $s_{i_{k'+2},\ldots,i_k}$ that cannot be learned by the referee, the bits $(s_{i_{k'+2},\ldots,i_k})_{i_{k'+2},\ldots,i_k \in [N]}$ are uniformly distributed and independent of each other and of the secret. Overall, the messages sent by the parties are uniformly distributed.

MESSAGE SIZE. The size of the message of party P_1 is $N^{k'}$, the sizes of the messages of parties $P_2, \ldots, P_{k'+1}$ are $N^{k'}, N^{k'-1}, \ldots, N^2, N-1$, respectively, and the sizes of the messages of parties $P_{k'+2}, \ldots, P_k$ are $N^{k'-1}, N^{k'-2}, \ldots, N, 1$, respectively. Thus, the total message size of $\mathcal{P}_k$ is $N^{k'} + (N^{k'} + \cdots + N - 1) + (N^{k'-1} + \cdots + 1) < N^{k'} + 2 \cdot N^{k'} + 2 \cdot N^{k'-1} = O(N^{(k-1)/2})$. $\square$

4.2 A Linear k-Party CDS Protocol for an Even k

Next, we adopt the CDS protocol $\mathcal{P}_k$ to even values of k. Given a k-input function $f : [M] \times [N]^{k-1} \to \{0, 1\}$, for an even k, and k parties $P_1, \ldots, P_k$ that hold the inputs $x_1 \in [M]$ and $x_2, \ldots, x_k \in [N]$, respectively, we define $k' = (k+2)/2$, $x_{k'} = (x_{k'}^1, x_{k'}^2)$, where $x_{k'}^1, x_{k'}^2 \in [N^{1/2}]$, and $y_1 = x_1, y_2 = (x_2, \ldots, x_{k'-1}, x_{k'}^1)$, and $y_3 = (x_{k'}^2, x_{k'+1}, \ldots, x_k)$. As before, we partition the parties into three sets S_1, S_2, S_3, but now we split the input of party $P_{k'}$, and it will be in both sets S_2, S_3, with half of its input in each of them. That is, $S_1 = \{P_1\}$, $S_2 = \{P_2, \ldots, P_{k'}\}$, and $S_3 = \{P_{k'}, \ldots, P_k\}$. The protocol for an even k is the same as the protocol for an odd k, where $P_{k'}$ participates in the simulations of Bob and Charlie, in which it uses $x_{k'}^1$ and $x_{k'}^2$, respectively.

The protocol $\mathcal{P}_k$ for an even k described in Fig. 3. The fact that now not all the inputs have the same size does not change the correctness and the privacy of the protocol. Moreover, the message size of protocol $\mathcal{P}_k$ for an even k is the same as in protocol $\mathcal{P}_k$ for an odd k.

The above explanation together with Lemma 4.1 implies the following result.

Theorem 4.2. *Let $f : [M] \times [N]^{k-1} \to \{0,1\}$ be a k-input function, for some integer $k > 2$. Then, there is a linear k-party CDS protocol for f with total message size $O(N^{(k-1)/2})$.*

5 Linear k-Party CDS Protocols for Unbalanced Functions

We show how to construct linear k-party CDS protocols for k-input functions with a small number of inputs that return 1 and for k-input functions with a small number of inputs that return 0. We start by constructing a k-party linear CDS protocol for k-input functions in which for every input x_k there are most d inputs $(x_1, \ldots, x_{k-1})$ such that $f(x_1, \ldots, x_{k-1}, x_k) = 1$. Next, we use this CDS protocol to construct a k-party linear CDS protocol for the desired functions.

First, let us present the following result from [10], which we are going to use in our basic construction.

Definition 5.1 (Degree of an Input). *Let $f : [M] \times [N]^{k-1} \to \{0,1\}$ be a k-input function. The degree of an input $x_k \in [N]$ is $|\{(x_1, \ldots, x_{k-1}) \in [M] \times [N]^{k-2} : f(x_1, \ldots, x_{k-1}, x_k) = 1\}|$.*

Claim 5.2 ([10]). *Let $f : [M] \times [N] \to \{0,1\}$ be a 2-input function in which the degree of every $x_2 \in [N]$ is at most $d \leq M$. Then, for a field $\mathbb{F}$ such that $|\mathbb{F}| \geq M$, there are M linear subspaces $V_1, \ldots, V_M \subseteq \mathbb{F}^{d+1}$ of dimension d and N vectors $\mathbf{z}_1, \ldots, \mathbf{z_N} \in \mathbb{F}^{d+1}$ such that for every $x_1 \in [M]$ and every $x_2 \in [N]$ it holds that $\mathbf{z_{x_2}} \in V_{x_1}$ if and only if $f(x_1, x_2) = 1$. Furthermore, for every $i \in [M]$, the basis of V_i is $\mathbf{v_1}, \ldots, \mathbf{v_d}$, where $\mathbf{v_j} = \mathbf{e_{j+1}} - i \cdot \mathbf{e_j}$ for every $j \in [d]$.*

These linear subspaces and vectors are used in [10] to construct the following linear 2-party CDS protocol for 2-input functions $f : [M] \times [N] \to \{0,1\}$ in which the degree of every $x_2 \in [N]$ is at most d. Alice and Bob, which hold the inputs $x_1 \in [M]$ and $x_2 \in [N]$, respectively, send the messages $\mathbf{v_1} \cdot \mathbf{r}, \ldots, \mathbf{v_d} \cdot \mathbf{r}$ and $s + \mathbf{z_{x_2}} \cdot \mathbf{r}$, respectively, where $s \in \mathbb{F}$ is the secret, $\mathbf{r} \in \mathbb{F}^{d+1}$ is the common randomness, and $\mathbf{v_1}, \ldots, \mathbf{v_d}$ are a basis of the linear subspace V_{x_1}. If $f(x_1, x_2) = 1$, then $\mathbf{z_{x_2}} \in V_{x_1}$ and there exist constants $u_1, \ldots, u_d$ such that $u_1 \cdot \mathbf{v_1} + \cdots + u_d \cdot \mathbf{v_d} = \mathbf{z_{x_2}}$.

Protocol $\mathcal{P}_k$ for an Even k

The secret: A bit $s \in \{0, 1\}$.

Inputs: $P_1, \ldots, P_k$ hold the inputs $x_1 \in [M]$ and $x_2, \ldots, x_k \in [N]$, respectively.

Common randomness: Let $k' = (k+2)/2$. The k parties hold the following random bits.

- $r_{i_2,\ldots,i_{k'-1},i^1_{k'}} \in \{0,1\}$, for every $i_2, \ldots, i_{k'-1} \in [N]$ and $i^1_{k'} \in [N^{1/2}]$.
- $t^j_{i_j,\ldots,i_{k'-1},i^1_{k'}} \in \{0,1\}$, for every $j \in \{3, \ldots, k'\}$, $i_j, \ldots, i_{k'-1} \in [N]$, and $i^1_{k'} \in [N^{1/2}]$.
- $q^{k'}_{i^2_{k'},i_{k'+1},\ldots,i_k} \in \{0,1\}$, for every $i^2_{k'} \in [N^{1/2}]$ and $i_{k'+1}, \ldots, i_k \in [N]$.
- $q^j_{i_j,\ldots,i_k} \in \{0,1\}$, for every $j \in \{k+1, \ldots, k\}$ and $i_j, \ldots, i_k \in [N]$.

The protocol:

1. Define $q_{i^2_{k'},i_{k'+1},\ldots,i_k} = q^{k'}_{i^2_{k'},i_{k'+1},\ldots,i_k} \oplus \bigoplus_{j=k'+1}^{k} q^j_{i_j,\ldots,i_k}$ for every $i^2_{k'} \in [N^{1/2}]$ and $i_{k'+1}, \ldots, i_k \in [N]$.
   (* SIMULATION OF ALICE *)

2. Party P_1 sends to the referee the bits

$$s_{i^2_{k'},i_{k'+1}\ldots,i_k} = s \oplus q_{i^2_{k'},i_{k'+1}\ldots,i_k} \oplus$$

$$\bigoplus_{i_2,\ldots,i_{k'-1}\in[N],i^1_{k'}\in[N^{1/2}],f(x_1,i_2,\ldots,i_{k'-1},i^1_{k'},i^2_{k'},i_{k'+1},\ldots,i_k)=0} r_{i_2,\ldots,i_{k'-1},i^1_{k'}}$$

for every $i^2_{k'} \in [N^{1/2}]$ and $i_{k'+1}, \ldots, i_k \in [N]$.
   (* SIMULATION OF BOB *)

3. Party P_2 sends to the referee the bits $r_{i_2,\ldots,i_{k'-1},i^1_{k'}}$, for every $i_2, \ldots, i_{k'-1} \in [N]$ such that $i_2 \neq x_2$ and $i^1_{k'} \in [N^{1/2}]$, and the bits $r_{x_2,i_3\ldots,i_{k'-1},i^1_{k'}} \oplus t_{i_3,\ldots,i_{k'-1},i^1_{k'}}$, for every $i_3, \ldots, i_{k'-1} \in [N]$ and $i^1_{k'} \in [N^{1/2}]$.

4. For every $j \in \{3, \ldots, k'-1\}$, party P_j sends to the referee the bits $t_{i_j,\ldots,i_{k'-1},i^1_{k'}}$, for every $i_j, \ldots, i_{k'-1} \in [N]$ such that $i_j \neq x_j$ and $i^1_{k'} \in [N^{1/2}]$, and the bits $t_{x_j,i_{j+1},\ldots,i_{k'-1},i^1_{k'}} \oplus t_{i_{j+1},\ldots,i_{k'-1},i^1_{k'}}$, for every $i_{j+1}, \ldots, i_{k'-1} \in [N]$ and $i^1_{k'} \in [N^{1/2}]$.

5. Party $P_{k'}$, which holds the input $x_{k'} = (x^1_{k'}, x^2_{k'})$, where $x^1_{k'}, x^2_{k'} \in [N^{1/2}]$, sends to the referee the bits $t_{i^1_{k'}}$, for every $i^1_{k'} \in [N^{1/2}]$ such that $i^1_{k'} \neq x^1_{k'}$.
   (* SIMULATION OF CHARLIE *)

6. Party $P_{k'}$ sends to the referee the bits $q^{k'}_{x^2_{k'},i_{k'+1},\ldots,i_k}$, for every $i_{k'+1}, \ldots, i_k \in [N]$.

7. For every $j \in \{k'+1, \ldots, k\}$, party P_j sends to the referee the bits $q^j_{x_j,i_{j+1},\ldots,i_k}$, for every $i_{j+1}, \ldots, i_k \in [N]$.
   (* THE RECONSTRUCTION OF THE SECRET *)

8. If $f(x_1, \ldots, x_k) = 1$, the referee computes

$$s_{x^2_{k'},x_{k'+1}\ldots,x_k} \oplus q_{x^2_{k'},x_{k'+1},\ldots,x_k} \oplus$$

$$\bigoplus_{i_2,\ldots,i_{k'-1}\in[N],i^1_{k'}\in[N^{1/2}],f(x_1,i_2,\ldots,i_{k'-1},i^1_{k'},x^2_{k'},x_{k'+1},\ldots,x_k)=0} r_{i_2,\ldots,i_{k'-1},i^1_{k'}}.$$

Fig. 3. A linear k-party CDS protocol $\mathcal{P}_k$ for a k-input function $f : [M] \times [N]^{k-1} \to \{0, 1\}$, for an even k.

Thus, the referee can compute $u_1 \cdot \mathbf{v_1} \cdot \mathbf{r} + \cdots + u_d \cdot \mathbf{v_d} \cdot \mathbf{r} = \mathbf{z_{x_2}} \cdot \mathbf{r}$ and unmask the secret s from the message $s + \mathbf{z_{x_2}} \cdot \mathbf{r}$. Otherwise, if $f(x_1, x_2) = 0$, it can be shown, given the messages of Alice, that the distribution on $\mathbf{z_{x_2}} \cdot \mathbf{r}$ is uniform, and, thus, the referee cannot reconstruct the secret. The total message size of this CDS protocol is $(d + 1) \log |\mathbb{F}|$ and the size of the secret is $\log |\mathbb{F}|$.

We show how to use these ideas to construct a linear k-party CDS protocol for k-input functions $f : [N]^k \to \{0, 1\}$ in which the degree of every input $x_k \in [N]$ of the last party is at most d, in which the message size of each party is $O(d \cdot k \cdot \log N)$. This result is non-trivial since we do not have any bound on the degree of the inputs of the first $k - 1$ parties.

In the following protocol we simulate the above 2-party CDS protocol for the 2-input function $g : [N]^{k-1} \times [N] \to \{0, 1\}$, where $g((x_1, \ldots, x_{k-1}), x_k) = f(x_1, \ldots, x_k)$. The first $k - 1$ parties simulate Alice and the kth party simulates Bob. For this simulation, we use properties of the basis of V_i as described in Claim 5.2. The protocol in [10] does not need to use these properties.

Lemma 5.3. *Let $f : [N]^k \to \{0, 1\}$ be a k-input function in which the degree of every $x_k \in [N]$ is at most $d \leq N^{k-1}$. Then, there is a linear k-party CDS protocol for f in which the message size of each of the first $k - 1$ parties is $O(d \cdot k \cdot \log N)$ and the message size of the last party is $O(k \cdot \log N)$.*

Proof. Let $\mathbb{F}$ be the smallest finite field with a prime number of elements such that $|\mathbb{F}| \geq N^{k-1}$, and define $g : [N]^{k-1} \times [N] \to \{0, 1\}$ as the 2-input function $g((x_1, \ldots, x_{k-1}), x_k) = f(x_1, \ldots, x_k)$, as above. Next, let $V_{1,\ldots,1}, \ldots, V_{N,\ldots,N} \subseteq \mathbb{F}^{d+1}$ and $\mathbf{z_1}, \ldots, \mathbf{z_N} \in \mathbb{F}^{d+1}$ be the N^{k-1} subspaces of dimension d and N vectors guarantied by Claim 5.2 for the function g. We represent the inputs of $P_1, \ldots, P_{k-1}$ as an element in $\{0, \ldots, N^{k-1} - 1\}$, i.e., $(x_1, \ldots, x_{k-1}) = (x_1 - 1)N^{k-2} + (x_2 - 1)N^{k-3} + \cdots + (x_{k-2} - 1)N + x_{k-1} - 1 \in \{0, \ldots, N^{k-1} - 1\}$. Thus, the ith vector in the basis of $V_{x_1, \ldots, x_{k-1}}$ is

$$\mathbf{v_i} = \mathbf{e_{i+1}} - (x_1, \ldots, x_{k-1}) \cdot \mathbf{e_i}$$
$$= \mathbf{e_{i+1}} - (x_1 - 1)N^{k-2} \cdot \mathbf{e_i} - \cdots - (x_{k-2} - 1)N \cdot \mathbf{e_i} - (x_{k-1} - 1) \cdot \mathbf{e_i},$$

that is, $\mathbf{v_i}$ is a sum of $k - 1$ vectors, where the jth vector is determined by x_j, i.e., the first vector is $\mathbf{v_{i,1}} = \mathbf{e_{i+1}} - (x_1 - 1)N^{k-2} \cdot \mathbf{e_i}$ and for every $j \in \{2, \ldots, k - 1\}$, the jth vector is $\mathbf{v_{i,j}} = -(x_j - 1)N^{k-j-1} \cdot \mathbf{e_i}$. To simulate Alice, parties $P_1, \ldots, P_{k-1}$ should send $\mathbf{v_i} \cdot \mathbf{r}$ for every $i \in [d]$. Since $\mathbf{v_i} = \sum_{j=1}^{k-1} \mathbf{v_{i,j}}$, where P_j knows $\mathbf{v_{i,j}}$, party P_j can send $\mathbf{v_{i,j}} \cdot \mathbf{r}$. However, this discloses additional information to the referee, so we need to mask the messages of the parties. Specifically, for every $j \in \{1, \ldots, k - 1\}$, the message of party P_j is $\mathbf{v_{1,j}} \cdot \mathbf{r} + r_1^j, \ldots, \mathbf{v_{d,j}} \cdot \mathbf{r} + r_d^j$, and the message of party P_k is $s + \mathbf{z_{x_k}} \cdot \mathbf{r}$, where $s \in \mathbb{F}$ is the secret and the common randomness is $\mathbf{r} \in \mathbb{F}^{d+1}$ and $r_i^j \in \mathbb{F}$, for every $j \in [k-1]$ and $i \in [d]$, such that $r_i^1 + \cdots + r_i^{k-1} = 0$ for every $i \in [d]$.

First, we prove the correctness of the protocol. If $f(x_1, \ldots, x_k) = 1$, then for every $i \in [d]$, the referee can compute $\mathbf{v_i} \cdot \mathbf{r} = \mathbf{v_{i,1}} \cdot \mathbf{r} + r_i^1 + \mathbf{v_{i,2}} \cdot \mathbf{r} + r_i^2 + \cdots + \mathbf{v_{i,k-1}} \cdot \mathbf{r} + r_i^{k-1}$ from the messages it gets. Next, since $\mathbf{z_{x_k}} \in V_{x_1, \ldots, x_{k-1}}$, there exist constants $u_1, \ldots, u_d$ such that $u_1 \cdot \mathbf{v_1} + \cdots + u_d \cdot \mathbf{v_d} = \mathbf{z_{x_k}}$. Thus, the referee can compute $u_1 \cdot \mathbf{v_1} \cdot \mathbf{r} + \cdots + u_d \cdot \mathbf{v_d} \cdot \mathbf{r} = \mathbf{z_{x_k}} \cdot \mathbf{r}$ and unmask the secret s from the message $s + \mathbf{z_{x_k}} \cdot \mathbf{r}$.

Now, we prove that the protocol is private, by constructing a simulator. The simulator independently chooses uniform random elements from $\mathbb{F}$ as the messages sent by the parties. We show that the messages sent by the parties in the protocol are uniformly distributed. Since the vectors $\mathbf{v_1}, \ldots, \mathbf{v_d}$ are independent, $\mathbf{v_1} \cdot \mathbf{r}, \ldots, \mathbf{v_d} \cdot \mathbf{r}$ are uniformly distributed. By [10], given the values $\mathbf{v_1} \cdot \mathbf{r}, \ldots, \mathbf{v_d} \cdot \mathbf{r}$, the message of party P_k is uniformly distributed when $g((x_1, \ldots, x_{k-1}), x_k) = 0$ (i.e., when $f(x_1, \ldots, x_k) = 0$). Furthermore, each of the messages of parties $P_1, \ldots, P_{k-1}$ contains d field elements, where the sum of the ith element from each of these messages is $\mathbf{v_i} \cdot \mathbf{r}$. Since we mask the messages, the messages of $P_1, \ldots, P_{k-2}$ are uniformly distributed, and the message of P_{k-1} is the random vector $(\mathbf{v_1} \cdot \mathbf{r}, \ldots, \mathbf{v_d} \cdot \mathbf{r})$ minus the messages of $P_1, \ldots, P_{k-2}$, that is, the message of P_{k-1} is uniformly distributed as well.

The protocol is linear, since the reconstruction function of the referee is a linear combination of the messages it gets. The total message size of the protocol is $(k-1) \cdot O(d \cdot k \cdot \log N) + O(k \cdot \log N) = O(k^2 \cdot d \cdot \log N)$.   □

Next, we show how to transform a k-party CDS protocol for such functions to a k-party CDS protocol for k-input functions with a small number of inputs that return 1. The transformation in Lemma 5.4 is general and can start from any k-party CDS protocol for functions where the degree of every $x_k \in [N]$ is bounded. Moreover, if we start with a linear k-party CDS protocol, then the resulting k-party CDS protocol is also linear.

Lemma 5.4. *Let $f : [N]^k \to \{0,1\}$ be a k-input function, in which there are at most N^γ inputs $(x_1, \ldots, x_k) \in [N]^k$ such that $f(x_1, \ldots, x_k) = 1$, for some $0 < \gamma < k$, and assume that for every k-input function $f' : [N]^k \to \{0,1\}$ such that the degree of every $x_k \in [N]$ is at most $d \leq N^{k-1}$ there is a k-party CDS protocol for f' with total message size c. Then, there is a k-party CDS protocol for f with total message size $k \cdot c + O((N^\gamma/d)^{(k-1)/2})$.*

Proof. Let S_i be the set of all the inputs $x_i \in [N]$ such that there are at most d inputs $(x_1, \ldots x_{i-1}, x_{i+1}, \ldots, x_k) \in [N]^{k-1}$ for which $f(x_1, \ldots, x_k) = 1$, for every $i \in [k]$. By our assumption, there is a CDS protocol with message size c for the restriction of f to the domain $[N]^{i-1} \times S_i \times [N]^{k-i}$, for every $i \in [k]$ (by reordering the parties, we can apply the assumption for every $i \in [k]$).

Next, the set $[N] \setminus S_i$ contains all the inputs $x_i \in [N]$ such that there are more than d inputs $(x_1, \ldots x_{i-1}, x_{i+1}, \ldots, x_k) \in [N]^{k-1}$ for which $f(x_1, \ldots, x_k) = 1$, and, thus, the number of inputs that return 1 of f is at least $|[N] \setminus S_i| \cdot d$. Therefore, $|[N] \setminus S_i| \leq N^\gamma/d$ for every $i \in [k]$. We use the protocol $\mathcal{P}_k$ of Theorem 4.2 to obtain a linear k-party CDS protocol with message size $O((N^\gamma/d)^{(k-1)/2})$ for the restriction of f to the domain $([N] \setminus S_1) \times ([N] \setminus S_2) \times \cdots \times ([N] \setminus S_k)$.

If $f(x_1, \ldots, x_k) = 1$, and $x_i \in S_i$ for at least one $i \in [k]$, then the referee can reconstruct the secret from the messages it gets from the CDS protocol for the restriction of f to the corresponding domain. If $x_i \in [N] \setminus S_i$ for every $i \in [k]$, then the referee can reconstruct the secret from the messages it gets from the CDS protocol of Theorem 4.2. Otherwise, if $f(x_1, \ldots, x_k) = 0$, then the referee cannot learn any information on the secret, which follows by the privacy of each of the independent CDS protocols we used.

Finally, if the CDS protocol with message size c we assume is linear, then the resulting protocol is linear, since in that case it is consist of independent linear protocols. The message size of the protocol is $k \cdot c + O((N^\gamma/d)^{(k-1)/2})$.   □

We use the above transformation and our basic linear k-party CDS protocol for inputs with bounded degree to construct a linear k-party CDS protocol for k-input functions with a small number of inputs that return 1.

Theorem 5.5. *Let $f : [N]^k \to \{0,1\}$ be a k-input function in which there are at most N^γ inputs $(x_1, \ldots, x_k) \in [N]^k$ such that $f(x_1, \ldots, x_k) = 1$, for some $0 < \gamma < (k+1)/2$. Then, there is a linear k-party CDS protocol for f with total message size $O(k^3 \cdot N^{\gamma(k-1)/(k+1)} \cdot \log N)$.*

Proof. By Lemma 5.3, for every k-input function $f' : [N]^k \to \{0,1\}$ such that the degree of every $x_k \in [N]$ is at most $d \le N^{k-1}$, there is a linear k-party CDS protocol for f' with total message size $O(k^2 \cdot d \cdot \log N)$. Thus, by Lemma 5.4, there is a linear k-party CDS protocol for f with total message size $O(k^3 \cdot d \cdot \log N + (N^\gamma/d)^{(k-1)/2})$. To minimize this expression, we require that $d = (N^\gamma/d)^{(k-1)/2}$, that is, $d = N^{\gamma(k-1)/(k+1)}$, and obtain a linear k-party CDS protocol with message size $O(k^3 \cdot d \cdot \log N) = O(k^3 \cdot N^{\gamma(k-1)/(k+1)} \cdot \log N)$.   □

By a small modification in the first protocol as in [10], the same results hold also for k-input functions with s small number of inputs that return 0.

Lemma 5.6. *Let $f : [N]^k \to \{0,1\}$ be a k-input function in which the degree of every $x_k \in [N]$ is at least $N^{k-1} - d$, for some $d \le N^{k-1}$. Then, there is a linear k-party CDS protocol for f in which the message size of each of the first $k-1$ parties is $O(d \cdot k \cdot \log N)$ and the message size of the last party is $O(k \cdot \log N)$.*

Theorem 5.7. *Let $f : [N]^k \to \{0,1\}$ be a k-input function in which there are at most N^γ inputs $(x_1, \ldots, x_k) \in [N]^k$ such that $f(x_1, \ldots, x_k) = 0$, for some $0 < \gamma < (k+1)/2$. Then, there is a linear k-party CDS protocol for f with total message size $O(k^3 \cdot N^{\gamma(k-1)/(k+1)} \cdot \log N)$.*

Note that the above results are not implied by the closure of CDS protocols to complement [2,4] since the randomness in the protocols of Lemma 5.3 and Theorem 5.5 is too big.

6   Linear k-Party CDS Protocols for Functions with Inputs of Different Sizes

We use the protocol $\mathcal{P}_k$ to construct linear k-party CDS protocols for k-input functions with inputs of different sizes; as in $\mathcal{P}_k$, the message size in these protocols is independent of the largest input size. In the following three protocols, we assume, by reordering the parties, that $\alpha_1 \ge \alpha_i$ for every $i \in \{2, \ldots, k\}$.

Theorem 6.1. *Let $f : [N^{\alpha_1}] \times [N^{\alpha_2}] \times \cdots \times [N^{\alpha_k}] \to \{0,1\}$ be a k-input function, for some integer $k > 2$ and real numbers $\alpha_1, \ldots, \alpha_k > 0$. Then, there is a linear k-party CDS protocol for f with total message size $O(2^{k/2} \cdot N^{\sum_{i=2}^k \alpha_i/2})$.*

Proof. We view f as a k'-input function $f' : [N^{\alpha_1}] \times \{0,1\}^{k'-1} \to \{0,1\}$, where $k' = 1 + \sum_{i=2}^k \lceil \alpha_i \log N \rceil \leq k + \log N \cdot \sum_{i=2}^k \alpha_i$, and

$$f'(x_1, x_{2,1}, \ldots, x_{2,\lceil \alpha_2 \log N \rceil}, \ldots, x_{k,1}, \ldots, x_{k,\lceil \alpha_k \log N \rceil})$$
$$= f(x_1, (x_{2,1}, \ldots, x_{2,\lceil \alpha_2 \log N \rceil}), \ldots, (x_{k,1}, \ldots, x_{k,\lceil \alpha_k \log N \rceil})).$$

We execute the linear k'-party CDS protocol $\mathcal{P}_{k'}$ promised by Theorem 4.2 for the k'-input function f', where party P_1 simulates the first party, party P_2 simulates the next $\lceil \alpha_2 \log N \rceil$ parties in the k'-party CDS protocol for f', party P_3 simulates the next $\lceil \alpha_3 \log N \rceil$ parties, and so on. Overall, since the message size of the protocol is independent of the size of the input of the first party, we get a linear k-party CDS protocol for the k-input function f with total message size $O(2^{(k'-1)/2}) = O(2^{(k+\log N \cdot \sum_{i=2}^k \alpha_i)/2}) = O(2^{k/2} \cdot N^{\sum_{i=2}^k \alpha_i/2})$. $\square$

We present alternative linear CDS protocols for k-input functions $f : [N^{\alpha_1}] \times [N^{\alpha_2}] \times \cdots \times [N^{\alpha_k}] \to \{0,1\}$, where for some parameters we remove the factor of $2^{k/2}$ of the above protocol. We start with a linear k-party CDS protocol for such k-input functions, for an odd k.

Theorem 6.2. *Let $f : [N^{\alpha_1}] \times [N^{\alpha_2}] \times \cdots \times [N^{\alpha_k}] \to \{0,1\}$ be a k-input function, for some odd integer $k > 2$ and real numbers $\alpha_1, \ldots, \alpha_k > 0$. Then, there is a linear k-party CDS protocol for f with total message size $O(\min_{S \subset \{2,\ldots,k\}, |S|=(k-1)/2} \{N^{\sum_{i \in S} \alpha_i} + N^{\sum_{i \in \{2,\ldots,k\} \setminus S} \alpha_i}\})$.*

Proof. Fix any set $S \subset \{2, \ldots, k\}$ such that $|S| = (k-1)/2$ and define $S_1 = \{P_j : j \in S\}$. By renaming the parties, we assume that $S_1 = \{P_2, \ldots, P_{(k+1)/2}\}$. We execute the linear k-party CDS protocol of Lemma 4.1 with the function f. Recall that in $\mathcal{P}_k$ party P_1 simulates Alice, the parties in $\{P_2, \ldots, P_{(k+1)/2}\}$ simulate Bob with an input from a domain of size $N^{\sum_{i \in S} \alpha_i}$, and the parties in $\{P_2, \ldots, P_k\} \setminus S_1 = \{P_{(k+3)/2}, \ldots, P_k\}$ simulate Charlie with an input from a domain of size $N^{\sum_{i \in \{2,\ldots,k\} \setminus S} \alpha_i}$. The message size of party P_1 is $N^{\sum_{i \in \{2,\ldots,k\} \setminus S} \alpha_i}$, the message size of parties $P_2, \ldots, P_{(k+1)/2}$ is less than $2 \cdot N^{\sum_{i \in S} \alpha_i}$, and the message size of parties $P_{(k+3)/2}, \ldots, P_k$ is less than $2 \cdot N^{\sum_{i \in \{2,\ldots,k\} \setminus S} \alpha_i}$. Thus, the total message size of the protocol is $O(N^{\sum_{i \in S} \alpha_i} + N^{\sum_{i \in \{2,\ldots,k\} \setminus S} \alpha_i})$. Since we can choose any set $S \subset \{2, \ldots, k\}$ of size $(k-1)/2$, the theorem follows. $\square$

In the above CDS protocol, either $\sum_{i \in S} \alpha_i$ or $\sum_{i \in \{2,\ldots,k\} \setminus S} \alpha_i$ is at least $\sum_{i=2}^k \alpha_i/2$. So, the total message size in the CDS protocol of Theorem 6.2 can be reduced by a factor of at most $2^{k/2}$ compared to the CDS protocol of Theorem 6.1 (for example, when $\sum_{i \in S} \alpha_i = \sum_{i \in \{2,\ldots,k\} \setminus S} \alpha_i = \sum_{i=2}^k \alpha_i/2$). However, there are cases for which the total message size of the CDS protocol of Theorem 6.1 will be smaller than the total message size of the CDS protocol of Theorem 6.2 (for example, when $\alpha_1, \alpha_2 \gg \sum_{i=3}^k \alpha_i$).

Similarly to Theorem 6.2, we can construct a linear k-party CDS protocol for k-input functions, for an even k. As this CDS protocol is similar to the previous CDS protocol, we omit its details.

Theorem 6.3. *Let* $f : [N^{\alpha_1}] \times [N^{\alpha_2}] \times \cdots \times [N^{\alpha_k}] \rightarrow \{0,1\}$ *be a k-input function, for some even integer $k > 2$ and real numbers $\alpha_1, \ldots, \alpha_k > 0$. Then, there is a linear k-party CDS protocol for f with total message size* $O(\min_{j \in \{2,\ldots,k\}, S \subset \{2,\ldots,k\}\setminus\{j\}, |S|=(k-2)/2} \{N^{\alpha_j/2 + \sum_{i \in S} \alpha_i} + N^{\alpha_j/2 + \sum_{i \in \{2,\ldots,k\}\setminus(S \cup \{j\})} \alpha_i}\})$.

7 Linear Secret-Sharing Schemes Realizing k-Uniform Access Structures

7.1 General k-Uniform Access Structures

Recall that an access structure is k-uniform if all sets of size less than k are unauthorized, all sets of size greater than k are authorized, and the access structure specifies which sets of size k are authorized. A k-uniform access structure is k-partite if the parties can be partitioned into k sets $V_1, \ldots, V_k$ such that each authorized set of size k contains exactly one party from each set V_i. Basically, k-party CDS protocols are equivalent to secret-sharing schemes realizing k-partite k-uniform access structures, see, e.g., [3, Lemma 4.2]. Furthermore, this equivalence preserves linearity. Thus, our results imply the following theorem.

Corollary 7.1. *Let Γ be a k-partite k-uniform access structure with partition $V_1, \ldots, V_k$, where $|V_i| = N$ for every $i \in [k]$. Then, there is a linear secret-sharing scheme realizing Γ in which the share size of every party is $O(N^{(k-1)/2})$.*

We next describe a secret-sharing scheme realizing k-uniform access structure (not necessarily k-partite). To obtain this result, we use a generic transformation from secret-sharing schemes realizing k-partite k-uniform access structures to secret-sharing schemes realizing k-uniform access structure (not necessarily k-partite). This transformation is similar to the transformation in [3], however, for short secrets our transformation is more efficient. The transformation uses a family of perfect hash functions.

Definition 7.2. *A set of functions $H = \{h_i : [n] \rightarrow [k] : i \in [\ell]\}$ is a family of perfect hash functions if for every set $A \subseteq [n]$ such that $|A| = k$ there exists at least one index $i \in [\ell]$ such that $|h_i(A)| = |\{h_i(a) : a \in A\}| = k$, i.e., h_i restricted to A is one-to-one.*

It is known that if we sample $\ell = O(k \cdot e^k \cdot \log n)$ random functions $h_i : [n] \rightarrow [k]$, then we get a family of perfect hash functions with high probability. In our transformation we need that the outputs of every h_i are evenly distributed. We next supply a simple proof that such a family of perfect hash functions exists.

Claim 7.3. *There exists a family of perfect hash functions* $H = \{h_i : [n] \to [k] : i \in [\ell]\}$, *where* $\ell = O(k \cdot e^k \cdot \log n)$, *such that for every* $i \in [\ell]$ *and every* $b \in [k]$ *it holds that*

$$|\{a \in [n] : h_i(a) = b\}| \leq \lceil n/k \rceil. \tag{1}$$

Proof. We prove the existence of H using the probabilistic method. We can assume that n/k is an integer (otherwise we add dummy elements to the domain). We choose ℓ functions h_i independently, where in each stage we choose a function satisfying (1) with uniform distribution.

First, we fix a set $A \in [n]$ of size k, and choose one function h satisfying (1) with uniform distribution. We give a lower bound on the probability that $|h(A)| = k$. We can view the choice of such a function h as the following process: Choose a random permutation $\pi : [n] \to [n]$ and define $h(a) = b$ if $(b - 1) \cdot n/k + 1 \leq \pi(a) \leq b \cdot n/k$ (e.g., all elements such that $\pi(a) \leq n/k$ are mapped to 1). Let $B = \pi(A) = \{\pi(a) : a \in A\}$. As π is a permutation chosen with uniform distribution, the set B is a uniformly distributed set of size k. Thus, the probability that $|h(A)| = k$ is the probability that a uniformly distributed set B of size k contains exactly one element from $(b - 1) \cdot n/k + 1, (b - 1) \cdot n/k + 2, \ldots, b \cdot n/k$, for every $b \in [k]$. The probability of the latter event is

$$\frac{(n/k)^k}{\binom{n}{k}} \geq \frac{(n/k)^k}{(e \cdot n/k)^k} = e^{-k}.$$

We choose $\ell = e^k \cdot (1 + k \cdot \ln n)$ functions $h_1, \ldots, h_\ell$ satisfying (1) independently with uniform distribution. Thus, the probability that every h_i is not one-to-one on a fixed A is at most $(1 - e^{-k})^{e^k \cdot (1 + k \cdot \ln n)} \leq e^{-(1 + k \cdot \ln n)} = 1/(e \cdot n^k) < 1/(e \cdot \binom{n}{k})$. By the union bound, the probability that there exits a set A of size k such that every h_i is not one-to-one on A is less than $1/e$. This implies that there exists a family of perfect hash functions H of size $\ell = O(k \cdot e^k \cdot \log n)$ such that all functions in H satisfy (1). $\qquad\square$

Next, we show how to transform a secret-sharing scheme realizing k-partite k-uniform access structures to a secret-sharing scheme realizing general k-uniform access structures. Moreover, if we start with a linear scheme, then the resulting scheme is also linear.

Lemma 7.4. *Let Γ be a k-uniform access structure with n parties. Assume that for every k-partite k-uniform access structure Γ' with partition $V_1, \ldots, V_k$, where $|V_i| \leq N$ for every $i \in [k]$, there is a secret-sharing scheme realizing Γ' in which the share size of every party is $c(k, N)$. Then, there is a secret-sharing scheme realizing Γ in which the share size of every party is $O(k \cdot e^k \cdot \log n \cdot c(k, \lceil n/k \rceil))$.*

Proof. Given a partition $\mathcal{V} = (V_1, \ldots, V_k)$ of the parties in Γ, we define the k-partite k-uniform access structure $\Gamma_\mathcal{V} \subset \Gamma$, where a set $A \in \Gamma$ is authorized in $\Gamma_\mathcal{V}$ if either $|A| > k$ or A contains exactly one party from each set V_i.

We use ℓ partitions $\mathcal{V}^1, \ldots, \mathcal{V}^\ell$ of the parties such that $\Gamma = \cup_{i=1}^\ell \Gamma_{\mathcal{V}^i}$ and realize each $\Gamma_{\mathcal{V}^i}$ independently. On one hand, every set $A \in \Gamma$ is authorized in at least one $\Gamma_{\mathcal{V}^i}$ so the parties in A can reconstruct the secret. On the other hand, every set $A \notin \Gamma$ is unauthorized in every $\Gamma_{\mathcal{V}^i}$ so the parties in A get no information on the secret. The share size of each party in the resulting scheme is ℓ times the size of the shares needed to realize $\Gamma_{\mathcal{V}^i}$.

We construct the ℓ partitions using the family of perfect hash functions $H = \{h_i : [n] \to [k] : i \in [\ell]\}$, for $\ell = O(k \cdot e^k \cdot \log n)$, guaranteed by Claim 7.3, where $\mathcal{V}^i = (h_i^{-1}(1), \ldots, h_i^{-1}(k))$. Using this family of perfect hash functions, every set in each partition is of size at most $\lceil n/k \rceil$. Moreover, by our assumption, there is a scheme realizing $\Gamma_{\mathcal{V}^i}$ in which the share size of every party is $c(k, \lceil n/k \rceil)$. This results in a scheme with share size $O(k \cdot e^k \cdot \log n \cdot c(k, \lceil n/k \rceil))$. $\qquad \square$

The above transformation combined with Corollary 7.1 immediately gives the following result.

Theorem 7.5. *Let Γ be a k-uniform access structure with n parties. Then, there is a linear secret-sharing scheme realizing Γ in which the share size of every party is $O(k \cdot e^k \cdot \log n \cdot \lceil n/k \rceil^{(k-1)/2})$.*

When $k > 0.257n$, the above scheme is less efficient than trivial scheme with share size 2^n. We can use a transformation of [14] showing that if every n-input function $f : \{0,1\}^n \to \{0,1\}$ has a CDS protocol with messages of size c, then any k-uniform access structure with n parties has a secret-sharing scheme with share size $O(c \cdot n)$. This transformation preserves linearity. Thus, our linear CDS protocol implies a linear secret-sharing scheme realizing every k-uniform access structure, in which the share size is independent of k.

Theorem 7.6. *Let Γ be a k-uniform access structure with n parties. Then, there is a linear secret-sharing scheme realizing Γ in which the share size of every party is $O(n \cdot 2^{n/2})$.*

7.2   Sparse and Dense k-Uniform Access Structures

By the equivalence between CDS and uniform access structures, we obtain results for sparse and dense k-partite k-uniform access structures, which follows from Theorems 5.5 and 5.7.

Corollary 7.7. *Let Γ be a k-partite k-uniform access structure with partition $V_1, \ldots, V_k$, where $|V_i| = N$ for every $i \in [k]$. If $|\{A \in \Gamma : |A| = k\}| \leq N^\gamma$ or $|\{A \in \Gamma : |A| = k\}| \geq N^k - N^\gamma$, for some $0 < \gamma < (k+1)/2$, then there is a linear secret-sharing scheme realizing Γ in which the share size of every party is $O(k^3 \cdot N^{\gamma(k-1)/(k+1)} \cdot \log N)$.*

Using the transformation in Lemma 7.4, we can generalize the above result to every sparse and dense k-uniform access structure (not necessarily k-partite).

Corollary 7.8. *Let Γ be a k-uniform access structure with n parties. If $|\{A \in \Gamma : |A| = k\}| \leq n^\gamma$ or $|\{A \in \Gamma : |A| = k\}| \geq \binom{n}{k} - n^\gamma$, for some $0 < \gamma < (k+1)/2$, then there is a linear secret-sharing scheme realizing Γ in which the share size of every party is $O(k^4 \cdot e^k \cdot \log^2 n \cdot \lceil n/k \rceil^{\gamma(k-1)/(k+1)})$.*

The above results should be compared to the trivial linear scheme realizing sparse k-uniform access structures with n parties, in which we share the secret independently for every minimal authorized set of size k; in this scheme the share size of every party is $O(n^\gamma)$.

8   Lower Bounds for Linear Schemes Realizing k-Uniform Access Structures

In this section, we use results of [10] to prove lower bounds on the size of the shares in linear secret-sharing schemes realizing k-uniform access structures and on the size of the messages in linear k-party CDS protocols.

8.1   Lower Bounds on the Size of One Share and Implications to CDS Protocols

First, we show lower bounds on the share size of at least one party in every linear secret-sharing scheme realizing general k-partite k-uniform access structures.

Before we start, we need some notations and a lemma from [10]. We say that the rank of an access structure Γ is r if the size of every minimal authorized set in Γ is at most r. Furthermore, we say that $\rho_q(\Gamma) \leq s$ if there exists a linear secret-sharing scheme over $\mathbb{F}_q$ realizing Γ such that each share in the scheme contains at most s field elements.

Lemma 8.1 ([10]). *For every prime power q and integers s, r, n such that $s > \log n$, the number of access structures Γ with n parties, rank r, and $\rho_q(\Gamma) \leq s$ is at most $2^{2rns^2 \cdot \log q}$.*

Theorem 8.2. *For most k-partite k-uniform access structures Γ with partition $V_1, \ldots, V_k$, where $|V_i| = N$ for every $i \in [k]$, the share size of at least one party for sharing a one-bit secret in every linear secret-sharing scheme realizing Γ is $\Omega(k^{-1} \cdot N^{(k-1)/2})$.*

Proof. If we share a one-bit secret using a linear secret-sharing scheme over $\mathbb{F}_q$ in which the largest share containing s field elements, then the size of the share of at least one party is $s \cdot \log q$. For the share size of every party to be less than $k^{-1} \cdot N^{(k-1)/2}$, it must be that $q \leq 2^{k^{-1} \cdot N^{(k-1)/2}}$ (otherwise, every share contains at least $k^{-1} \cdot N^{(k-1)/2}$ bits), and, furthermore, $s \cdot \log q \leq k^{-1} \cdot N^{(k-1)/2}$.

We next bound the number of k-partite k-uniform access structures Γ that can be realized by a secret-sharing scheme in which the share size of every party is at most θ. Recall that in k-uniform access structures all sets of size $k+1$ are authorized, that is, its rank is at most $k+1$.

By Lemma 8.1, the number of k-partite k-uniform access structures Γ with $k \cdot N$ parties and $\rho_q(\Gamma) \leq \theta / \log q$, is at most $2^{2(k+1) \cdot kN \cdot (\theta / \log q)^2 \cdot \log q} < 2^{2(k+1) \cdot kN \cdot \theta^2}$. Since we are counting linear schemes, we need to sum the number of the access structures that realized by linear schemes for every possible finite field (there are at most $2^{k-1} \cdot N^{(k-1)/2}$ such fields, because $q \leq 2^{k-1} \cdot N^{(k-1)/2}$). Consider the access structures that realized by linear schemes in which the size of the share of every party is $\theta < k^{-1} \cdot N^{(k-1)/2}$. The number of such access structures is at most $2^{k-1} \cdot N^{(k-1)/2} \cdot 2^{2(k+1) \cdot kN \cdot \theta^2} = 2^{k-1} \cdot N^{(k-1)/2} + 2(k+1) \cdot kN \cdot \theta^2}$.

On the other hand, the number of k-partite k-uniform access structures Γ, where the size of every part is N, is 2^{N^k}. Thus, if half of the k-partite k-uniform access structures Γ, where the size of every part is N, have linear secret-sharing schemes in which the share size of every party is at most θ, then $2^{k-1} \cdot N^{(k-1)/2} + 2(k+1) \cdot kN \cdot \theta^2} \geq \frac{1}{2} \cdot 2^{N^k}$, i.e., $k^{-1} \cdot N^{(k-1)/2} + 2(k+1) \cdot kN \cdot \theta^2 \geq N^k - 1$, so $\theta = \Omega(k^{-1} \cdot N^{(k-1)/2})$. $\square$

By [3, Lemma 4.2], we get the following corollary for k-party CDS protocols.

Corollary 8.3. *For most k-input functions $f : [N]^k \to \{0,1\}$, the message size of at least one party in every linear k-party CDS protocol for f is $\Omega(k^{-1} \cdot N^{(k-1)/2})$.*

As we show in Theorem 4.2, this bound is tight up to a factor of k.

Sparse and Dense k-Uniform Access Structures

Theorem 8.4. *Let $0 \leq \gamma \leq k$ be some real number. There exists a k-partite k-uniform access structure Γ with partition $V_1, \ldots, V_k$, where $|V_i| = N$ for every $i \in [k]$ and $|\{A \in \Gamma : |A| = k\}| \leq N^\gamma$, such that the share size of at least one party for sharing a one-bit secret in every linear secret-sharing scheme realizing Γ is $\Omega(k^{-1} \cdot N^{\gamma(k-1)/2k})$. Furthermore, there exists a k-partite k-uniform access structure Γ with partition $V_1, \ldots, V_k$, where $|V_i| = N$ for every $i \in [k]$ and $|\{A \in \Gamma : |A| = k\}| \geq N^k - N^\gamma$, such that the share size of at least one party for sharing a one-bit secret in every linear secret-sharing scheme realizing Γ is $\Omega(k^{-1} \cdot N^{\gamma(k-1)/2k})$.*

Proof. By Theorem 8.2, for every N there exists a k-partite k-uniform access structure Γ_N with N parties in every part such that the share size of at least one party for sharing a one-bit secret in every linear secret-sharing scheme realizing the access structure Γ_N is $\Omega(k^{-1} \cdot N^{(k-1)/2})$. We use this k-partite k-uniform access structure (with fewer parties) to construct a sparse k-partite k-uniform access structure Γ with N parties in every part. Let $V_1, \ldots, V_k$ be disjoint sets of parties of size N. For every $i \in [k]$, we fix an arbitrary set of parties $V_i' \subset V_i$ of size $N' = N^{\gamma/k}$, and construct the k-partite k-uniform access structure $\Gamma_{N'}$ with parties $V_1' \cup \cdots \cup V_k'$. We define Γ as the access structure with parties $V_1 \cup \cdots \cup V_k$ that contains all sets in $\Gamma_{N'}$ and all sets of size at least $k + 1$.

Since all minimal authorized sets of size k in Γ contain exactly one party from each V_i' (for every $i \in [k]$), the number of minimal authorized sets of size k is at most $(N')^k = (N^{\gamma/k})^k = N^\gamma$. The share size of at least one party for sharing a one-bit secret in every linear secret-sharing scheme realizing $\Gamma_{N'}$ (and, hence, Γ) is $\Omega(k^{-1} \cdot (N^{\gamma/k})^{(k-1)/2}) = \Omega(k^{-1} \cdot N^{\gamma(k-1)/2k}) = \Omega(k^{-1} \cdot N^{\gamma/2 - \gamma/2k})$.

To construct a dense k-partite k-uniform access structure with at least $N^k - N^\gamma$ minimal sets of size k that requires large shares in every linear scheme realizing it, we use a similar construction, however, we add all sets of size k with exactly k parties from different parts that contain at least one party in $V_i \setminus V_i'$ for some $i \in [k]$. Similar analysis implies that the resulting k-partite k-uniform access structure has at least $N^k - N^\gamma$ minimal authorized sets of size k and the share size of at least one party for sharing a one-bit secret in every linear scheme realizing this k-partite k-uniform access structure is $\Omega(k^{-1} \cdot N^{\gamma(k-1)/2k})$.   □

Again, by [3, Lemma 4.2], we get the following results.

Corollary 8.5. *Let $0 \le \gamma \le k$ be some real number. There exists a k-input function $f : [N]^k \to \{0,1\}$ such that $|\{(x_1, \ldots, x_k) : f(x_1, \ldots, x_k) = 1\}| \le N^\gamma$, in which the message size of at least one party in every linear k-party CDS protocol for f is $\Omega(k^{-1} \cdot N^{\gamma(k-1)/2k})$. Furthermore, there exists a k-input function $f : [N]^k \to \{0,1\}$ such that $|\{(x_1, \ldots, x_k) : f(x_1, \ldots, x_k) = 0\}| \le N^\gamma$, in which the message size of at least one party in every linear k-party CDS protocol for f is $\Omega(k^{-1} \cdot N^{\gamma(k-1)/2k})$.*

8.2 Lower Bounds on the Total Share Size

Next, we show lower bounds on the *total* share size in every linear secret-sharing scheme realizing k-uniform access structures.

Theorem 8.6. *For most k-uniform access structures Γ with n parties, the total share size for sharing a one-bit secret in every linear secret-sharing scheme realizing Γ is $\Omega(k^{-(k+3)/2} \cdot n^{(k+1)/2})$.*

Proof. If we share a one-bit secret using a linear secret-sharing scheme over $\mathbb{F}_q$ with shares containing S field elements, then the total share size is $S \cdot \log q$. For the total share size to be less than $k^{-(k+3)/2} \cdot n^{(k+1)/2}$, it must be that $q \le 2^{k^{-(k+3)/2} \cdot n^{(k-1)/2}}$ (otherwise, each share contains more than $k^{-(k+3)/2} \cdot n^{(k-1)/2}$ bits, and the total share size will be more than $k^{-(k+3)/2} \cdot n^{(k+1)/2}$), and, furthermore, $S \cdot \log q \le k^{-(k+3)/2} \cdot n^{(k+1)/2}$.

Denote the parties in Γ by P. First, we count the number of linear schemes realizing k-uniform access structures Γ over $\mathbb{F}_q$ with shares containing S field elements. Let B be the set of size at most n/k containing all the parties such that the share of each one of them containing more than $k \cdot S/n$ field elements. The set $P \setminus B$ contains all the parties such that the share of each one of them containing at most $k \cdot S/n$ field elements. We can add parties to B such that $|B| = n/k$, and the share of every party in $P \setminus B$ is still containing at most $k \cdot S/n$ field elements.

By Lemma 8.1, the number of k-uniform access structures over $\mathbb{F}_q$ with parties in $P \setminus B$ such that there exists linear schemes realizing them in which the share of every party containing at most $k \cdot S/n$ field elements is $2^{2(k+1) \cdot n(1-1/k) \cdot (kS/n)^2 \cdot \log q}$.

The number of sets with k parties that intersect B is the number of sets with k parties in P minus the number of sets with k parties contained in $P \setminus B$, i.e.,

$\binom{n}{k} - \binom{n(k-1)/k}{k} > (1 - (1-1/k)^k)\binom{n}{k}$. Moreover, the number of possible choices of the set B is $\binom{n}{n/k}$.

Thus, the number of k-uniform access structures Γ over $\mathbb{F}_q$ with linear schemes realizing them in which the shares containing S field elements is $\binom{n}{n/k} \cdot 2^{(1-(1-1/k)^k)\binom{n}{k}} \cdot 2^{2(k+1)\cdot n(1-1/k)\cdot(kS/n)^2 \cdot \log q} = \exp\left(O\left((1-(1-1/k)^k)\binom{n}{k} + \frac{k^3 \cdot S^2 \cdot \log q}{n}\right)\right)$.

Since we are counting linear schemes, we need to sum the number of the access structures that realized by linear schemes for every possible finite field (there are at most $2^{k^{-(k+3)/2} \cdot n^{(k-1)/2}}$ such fields, because $q \leq 2^{k^{-(k+3)/2} \cdot n^{(k-1)/2}}$). Consider the access structures that realized by linear schemes with total share size at most $S \cdot \log q = \Theta < k^{-(k+3)/2} \cdot n^{(k+1)/2}$ (so here $S = \Theta/\log q$). The number of such schemes is at most $\exp\left(O\left(k^{-(k+3)/2} \cdot n^{(k-1)/2} + (1-(1-1/k)^k)\binom{n}{k} + \frac{k^3 \cdot \Theta^2}{n}\right)\right)$.

Additionally, the number of k-uniform access structures Γ with n parties is $2^{\binom{n}{k}}$. Thus, if half of the k-uniform access structures Γ with n parties have linear secret-sharing schemes in which the share size of every party is at most Θ, then $\exp\left(O\left(k^{-(k+3)/2} \cdot n^{(k-1)/2} + (1-(1-1/k)^k)\binom{n}{k} + \frac{k^3 \cdot \Theta^2}{n}\right)\right) \geq \exp\left(\binom{n}{k} - 1\right)$, i.e., $\exp\left(O\left(k^{-(k+3)/2} \cdot n^{(k-1)/2} + \frac{k^3 \cdot \Theta^2}{n}\right)\right) \geq \exp\left(\Omega\left((1-1/k)^k\binom{n}{k}\right)\right) \geq \exp\left(\Omega\left(\frac{n^k}{k^k}\right)\right)$, so we get that $\Theta = \Omega(k^{-(k+3)/2} \cdot n^{(k+1)/2})$. □

As we show in Theorem 7.5, for a constant k this bound is tight up to a logarithmic factor.

Sparse and Dense k-Uniform Access Structures

Theorem 8.7. *Let $1 \leq \gamma \leq k$ be some real number. There exists a k-uniform access structure Γ with n parties and $|\{A \in \Gamma : |A| = k\}| \leq n^\gamma$, such that the total share size for sharing a one-bit secret in every linear secret-sharing scheme realizing Γ is $\Omega(k^{-(k+3)/2} \cdot n^{(\gamma+1)/2})$. Furthermore, there exists a k-uniform access structure Γ with n parties and $|\{A \in \Gamma : |A| = k\}| \geq \binom{n}{k} - n^\gamma$, such that the total share size for sharing a one-bit secret in every linear secret-sharing scheme realizing Γ is $\Omega(k^{-(k+3)/2} \cdot n^{(\gamma+1)/2})$.*

Proof. By Theorem 8.6, for every n there exists a k-uniform access structure with n parties such that the total share size for sharing a one-bit secret in every linear secret-sharing scheme realizing it is $\Omega(k^{-(k+3)/2} \cdot n^{(k+1)/2})$. Denote the parties in Γ by P. We use this k-uniform access structure (with fewer parties) to construct a sparse k-uniform access structure Γ with n parties. We partition the parties of P to $n' = n^{(k-\gamma)/(k-1)}$ disjoint sets of parties $V_1, \ldots, V_{n'}$, where $|V_i| = n/n' = n^{(\gamma-1)/(k-1)}$ for every $i \in [n']$. We construct a copy of a k-uniform access structure from Theorem 8.6 with $n/n' = n^{(\gamma-1)/(k-1)}$ parties among the parties of V_i, and denote this k-uniform access structure by Γ_i, for every $i \in [n']$. There are no authorized sets contain parties from different sets from $V_1, \ldots, V_{n'}$.

Since every authorized set in this construction contains parties from the same set V_i (for some $i \in [n']$), the number of authorized sets is at most $n' \cdot \binom{n/n'}{k} \leq n' \cdot (n/n')^k = n^{(k-\gamma)/(k-1)} \cdot (n^{(\gamma-1)/(k-1)})^k = n^{(k-\gamma+k\gamma-k)/(k-1)} = n^{\gamma(k-1)/(k-1)} = n^\gamma$. The total share size for sharing a one-bit secret in every linear secret-sharing scheme realizing Γ_i (for every $i \in [n']$) is $\Omega(k^{-(k+3)/2} \cdot (n^{(\gamma-1)/(k-1)})^{(k+1)/2}) = \Omega(k^{-(k+3)/2} \cdot n^{(\gamma-1)(k+1)/(2(k-1))}) = \Omega(k^{-(k+3)/2} \cdot n^{(k\gamma+\gamma-k-1)/(2(k-1))})$. Thus, the total share size for sharing a one-bit secret in every linear secret-sharing scheme realizing Γ is $n' \cdot \Omega(k^{-(k+3)/2} \cdot n^{(k\gamma+\gamma-k-1)/(2(k-1))}) = \Omega(k^{-(k+3)/2} \cdot n^{(k-\gamma)/(k-1)+(k\gamma+\gamma-k-1)/(2(k-1))}) = \Omega(k^{-(k+3)/2} \cdot n^{(k\gamma-\gamma+k-1)/(2(k-1))}) = \Omega(k^{-(k+3)/2} \cdot n^{(\gamma+1)(k-1)/(2(k-1))}) = \Omega(k^{-(k+3)/2} \cdot n^{(\gamma+1)/2})$.

To construct a dense k-uniform access structures with at least $\binom{n}{k} - n^\gamma$ authorizes sets that requires large shares in every linear scheme realizing it, we use a similar construction, however, we add all sets with exactly k parties, in which not all the paries are in the same set V_i, for some $i \in [n']$. Similar analysis implies that the resulting k-uniform access structure has at least $\binom{n}{k} - n^\gamma$ authorizes sets and the total share size for sharing a one-bit secret in every linear scheme realizing this k-uniform access structure is $\Omega(k^{-(k+3)/2} \cdot n^{(\gamma+1)/2})$.   □

References

1. Aiello, B., Ishai, Y., Reingold, O.: Priced oblivious transfer: how to sell digital goods. In: Pfitzmann, B. (ed.) EUROCRYPT 2001. LNCS, vol. 2045, pp. 119–135. Springer, Heidelberg (2001). https://doi.org/10.1007/3-540-44987-6_8

2. Ambrona, M., Barthe, G., Schmidt, B.: Generic transformations of predicate encodings: constructions and applications. In: Katz, J., Shacham, H. (eds.) CRYPTO 2017. LNCS, vol. 10401, pp. 36–66. Springer, Cham (2017). https://doi.org/10.1007/978-3-319-63688-7_2

3. Applebaum, B., Arkis, B.: Conditional disclosure of secrets and d-uniform secret sharing with constant information rate. Technical report, Electronic Colloquium on Computational Complexity (2017), to appear in TCC 2018. www.eccc.uni-trier.de/eccc/

4. Applebaum, B., Arkis, B., Raykov, P., Vasudevan, P.N.: Conditional disclosure of secrets: amplification, closure, amortization, lower-bounds, and separations. In: Katz, J., Shacham, H. (eds.) CRYPTO 2017. LNCS, vol. 10401, pp. 727–757. Springer, Cham (2017). https://doi.org/10.1007/978-3-319-63688-7_24

5. Applebaum, B., Holenstein, T., Mishra, M., Shayevitz, O.: The communication complexity of private simultaneous messages, revisited. In: Nielsen, J.B., Rijmen, V. (eds.) EUROCRYPT 2018. LNCS, vol. 10821, pp. 261–286. Springer, Cham (2018). https://doi.org/10.1007/978-3-319-78375-8_9

6. Attrapadung, N.: Dual system encryption via doubly selective security: framework, fully secure functional encryption for regular languages, and more. In: Nguyen, P.Q., Oswald, E. (eds.) EUROCRYPT 2014. LNCS, vol. 8441, pp. 557–577. Springer, Heidelberg (2014). https://doi.org/10.1007/978-3-642-55220-5_31

7. Beimel, A.: Secure schemes for secret sharing and key distribution. Ph.D. thesis, Technion (1996). www.cs.bgu.ac.il/~beimel/pub.html

8. Beimel, A., Chor, B.: Universally ideal secret-sharing schemes. IEEE Trans. Inf. Theory 40(3), 786–794 (1994)

9. Beimel, A., Farràs, O., Mintz, Y.: Secret-sharing schemes for very dense graphs. J. Cryptol. **29**(2), 336–362 (2016)
10. Beimel, A., Farràs, O., Mintz, Y., Peter, N.: Linear secret-sharing schemes for forbidden graph access structures. In: Kalai, Y., Reyzin, L. (eds.) TCC 2017. LNCS, vol. 10678, pp. 394–423. Springer, Cham (2017). https://doi.org/10.1007/978-3-319-70503-3_13
11. Beimel, A., Farràs, O., Mintz, Y., Peter, N.: Linear secret-sharing schemes for forbidden graph access structures. Technical report 2017/940, IACR Cryptology ePrint Archive (2017)
12. Beimel, A., Farràs, O., Peter, N.: Secret sharing schemes for dense forbidden graphs. In: Zikas, V., De Prisco, R. (eds.) SCN 2016. LNCS, vol. 9841, pp. 509–528. Springer, Cham (2016). https://doi.org/10.1007/978-3-319-44618-9_27
13. Beimel, A., Ishai, Y., Kumaresan, R., Kushilevitz, E.: On the cryptographic complexity of the worst functions. In: Lindell, Y. (ed.) TCC 2014. LNCS, vol. 8349, pp. 317–342. Springer, Heidelberg (2014). https://doi.org/10.1007/978-3-642-54242-8_14
14. Beimel, A., Kushilevitz, E., Nissim, P.: The complexity of multiparty PSM protocols and related models. In: Nielsen, J.B., Rijmen, V. (eds.) EUROCRYPT 2018. LNCS, vol. 10821, pp. 287–318. Springer, Cham (2018). https://doi.org/10.1007/978-3-319-78375-8_10
15. Chor, B., Kushilevitz, E.: Secret sharing over infinite domains. J. Cryptol. **6**(2), 87–96 (1993)
16. Cramer, R., Damgård, I., Maurer, U.: General secure multi-party computation from any linear secret-sharing scheme. In: Preneel, B. (ed.) EUROCRYPT 2000. LNCS, vol. 1807, pp. 316–334. Springer, Heidelberg (2000). https://doi.org/10.1007/3-540-45539-6_22
17. Dvir, Z., Gopi, S.: 2-server PIR with sub-polynomial communication. In: 47th STOC 2015, pp. 577–584 (2015)
18. Feige, U., Kilian, J., Naor, M.: A minimal model for secure computation. In: 26th STOC 1994, pp. 554–563 (1994)
19. Gay, R., Kerenidis, I., Wee, H.: Communication complexity of conditional disclosure of secrets and attribute-based encryption. In: Gennaro, R., Robshaw, M. (eds.) CRYPTO 2015. LNCS, vol. 9216, pp. 485–502. Springer, Heidelberg (2015). https://doi.org/10.1007/978-3-662-48000-7_24
20. Gertner, Y., Ishai, Y., Kushilevitz, E., Malkin, T.: Protecting data privacy in private information retrieval schemes. J. Comput. Syst. Sci. **60**(3), 592–629 (2000)
21. Ishai, Y., Kushilevitz, E.: Private simultaneous messages protocols with applications. In: 5th Israel Symposium on Theory of Computing and Systems, pp. 174–183 (1997)
22. Ishai, Y., Wee, H.: Partial garbling schemes and their applications. In: Esparza, J., Fraigniaud, P., Husfeldt, T., Koutsoupias, E. (eds.) ICALP 2014. LNCS, vol. 8572, pp. 650–662. Springer, Heidelberg (2014). https://doi.org/10.1007/978-3-662-43948-7_54
23. Ito, M., Saito, A., Nishizeki, T.: Secret sharing schemes realizing general access structure. In: Globecom 1987, pp. 99–102 (1987). Journal version: Multiple assignment scheme for sharing secret. J. Cryptol. **6**(1), 15–20 (1993)
24. Karchmer, M., Wigderson, A.: On span programs. In: 8th Structure in Complexity Theory, pp. 102–111 (1993)
25. Liu, T., Vaikuntanathan, V.: Breaking the circuit-size barrier in secret sharing. In: 50th STOC 2018, pp. 699–708 (2018)

26. Liu, T., Vaikuntanathan, V., Wee, H.: Conditional disclosure of secrets via non-linear reconstruction. In: Katz, J., Shacham, H. (eds.) CRYPTO 2017. LNCS, vol. 10401, pp. 758–790. Springer, Cham (2017). https://doi.org/10.1007/978-3-319-63688-7_25

27. Liu, T., Vaikuntanathan, V., Wee, H.: Towards breaking the exponential barrier for general secret sharing. In: Nielsen, J.B., Rijmen, V. (eds.) EUROCRYPT 2018. LNCS, vol. 10820, pp. 567–596. Springer, Cham (2018). https://doi.org/10.1007/978-3-319-78381-9_21

28. Sun, H., Shieh, S.: Secret sharing in graph-based prohibited structures. In: INFOCOM 1997, pp. 718–724 (1997)

29. Wee, H.: Dual system encryption via predicate encodings. In: Lindell, Y. (ed.) TCC 2014. LNCS, vol. 8349, pp. 616–637. Springer, Heidelberg (2014). https://doi.org/10.1007/978-3-642-54242-8_26

Isogeny-Based Cryptography

Towards Practical Key Exchange
from Ordinary Isogeny Graphs

Luca De Feo$^{1,4(\boxtimes)}$ (iD), Jean Kieffer^{2,3,4}, and Benjamin Smith^{4}

^{1} UVSQ, LMV, Université Paris Saclay, Versailles, France
`luca.de-feo@uvsq.fr`
^{2} École Normale Supérieure, Paris, France
`jean.kieffer.14@normalesup.org`
^{3} IMB - Institut de Mathématiques de Bordeaux, Inria Bordeaux - Sud-Ouest,
Talence, France
^{4} Inria and École polytechnique, Université Paris Saclay, Palaiseau, France
`smith@lix.polytechnique.fr`

Abstract. We revisit the ordinary isogeny-graph based cryptosystems of Couveignes and Rostovtsev–Stolbunov, long dismissed as impractical. We give algorithmic improvements that accelerate key exchange in this framework, and explore the problem of generating suitable system parameters for contemporary pre- and post-quantum security that take advantage of these new algorithms. We also prove the session-key security of this key exchange in the Canetti–Krawczyk model, and the IND-CPA security of the related public-key encryption scheme, under reasonable assumptions on the hardness of computing isogeny walks. Our systems admit efficient key-validation techniques that yield CCA-secure encryption, thus providing an important step towards efficient post-quantum non-interactive key exchange (NIKE).

Keywords: Post-quantum cryptography · Key exchange
Elliptic curves · Isogenies

1   Introduction

Isogeny-based protocols form one of the youngest and least-explored families of post-quantum candidate cryptosystems. The best-known isogeny-based protocol is Jao and De Feo's SIDH key exchange [36], from which the NIST candidate key-encapsulation mechanism SIKE was derived [4,53]. SIDH was itself inspired by earlier key-exchange constructions by Couveignes [19] and Rostovtsev and Stolbunov [57,61,62], which were widely considered unwieldy and impractical.

Indeed, the origins of isogeny-based cryptography can be traced back to Couveignes' "Hard Homogeneous Spaces" manuscript, that went unpublished for ten years before appearing in [19]. A *principal homogeneous space* (PHS) for a group G is a set X with an action of G on X such that for any $x, x' \in X$, there is a unique $g \in G$ such that $g \cdot x = x'$. Equivalently, the map $\varphi_x : g \mapsto g \cdot x$ is a bijection between G and X for any $x \in X$. Couveignes defines a *hard homogeneous*

© International Association for Cryptologic Research 2018
T. Peyrin and S. Galbraith (Eds.): ASIACRYPT 2018, LNCS 11274, pp. 365–394, 2018.
https://doi.org/10.1007/978-3-030-03332-3_14

space (HHS) to be a PHS where the action of G on X is efficiently computable, but inverting the isomorphism φ_x is computationally hard for any x.

Algorithm 1: Key generation for cryptosystems in an HHS X for a group G, with a fixed "base point" x_0 in X.

Input: ()
Output: A private-public keypair $(g, x) \in G \times X$ s.t. $x = g \cdot x_0$
1 **function** KeyGen()
2      $g \leftarrow \text{RANDOM}(G)$ // g is sampled uniformly at random from G
3      $x \leftarrow g \cdot x_0$
4   **return** (g, x)

Any HHS X for an *abelian* group G can be used to construct a key exchange based on the hardness of inverting φ_x, as shown in Algorithms 1 and 2. If Alice and Bob have keypairs (g_A, x_A) and (g_B, x_B), respectively, then the commutativity of G lets them derive a shared secret

$$\text{DH}(g_A, x_B) = g_A \cdot (g_B \cdot x_0) = g_B \cdot (g_A \cdot x_0) = \text{DH}(g_B, x_A).$$

The analogy with classic group-based Diffie–Hellman is evident.

Algorithm 2: Diffie–Hellman in an HHS X for a group G

Input: A private key $g_A \in G$ and a public key $x_B \in X$, each generated by calls to KeyGen
Output: A shared secret value $k \in X$
1 **function** DH(g_A, x_B)
2      $k \leftarrow g_A \cdot x_B$
3   **return** k

For example, if $X = \langle x \rangle$ is cyclic of order p and $G = (\mathbb{Z}/p\mathbb{Z})^*$ acts on $X \setminus \{1\}$ by $g \cdot x = x^g$, then inverting φ_x is the discrete logarithm problem (DLP) in X. But inverting φ_x for other homogeneous spaces may not be related to any DLP, and might resist attacks based on Shor's quantum algorithm. Similar ideas have occasionally appeared in the literature in different forms [40, 48].

Couveignes viewed HHS chiefly as a general framework encompassing various Diffie–Hellman-like systems. Nevertheless, he suggested using a specific HHS based on the theory of complex multiplication of elliptic curves, in a sense generalizing Buchmann and Williams' class-group-based Diffie–Hellman key exchange [10]. Independently, Rostovtsev and Stolbunov proposed in [57] a public key encryption scheme based on the same HHS. Later, Stolbunov [62] derived more protocols from this, including an interactive key exchange scheme similar to Algorithm 2. Rostovtsev and Stolbunov's proposal deviates from the HHS paradigm in the way random elements of G are sampled, as we will explain in Sect. 3. This makes the primitive less flexible, but also more practical.

Rostovtsev and Stolbunov advertised their cryptosystems as potential post-quantum candidates, leading Childs, Jao and Soukharev to introduce the first subexponential quantum algorithm capable of breaking them [13]. Hence, being already slow enough to be impractical in a classical security setting, their primitive appeared even more impractical in a quantum security setting.

But the Couveignes–Rostovtsev–Stolbunov primitive (CRS) has some important advantages over SIDH which make it worth pursuing. Unlike SIDH, CRS offers efficient and safe public key validation, making it suitable for non-interactive key exchange (NIKE). Further, CRS does not suffer from some of the potential cryptographic weaknesses that SIDH has, such as short paths and the publication of image points.

This paper aims to improve and modernize the CRS construction, borrowing techniques from SIDH and point-counting algorithms, to the point of making it usable in a post-quantum setting. Our main contributions are in Sects. 3, 4, where we present a new, more efficient way of computing the CRS group action, and in Sect. 5, where we give precise classic and quantum security estimates, formalize hardness assumptions, and sketch security proofs in stronger models than those previously considered. In Sect. 6 we present a proof-of-concept implementation and measure its performance. While the final result is far from competitive, we believe it constitutes progress towards a valid isogeny-based alternative to SIDH.

CSIDH. While preparing this paper we were informed of recent work by Castryck, Lange, Martindale, Panny, and Renes, introducing CSIDH, an efficient post-quantum primitive based on CRS [12]. Their work builds upon the ideas presented in Sects. 3, 4, using them in a different homogeneous space where they apply effortlessly. Their breakthrough confirms that, if anything, our techniques were a fundamental step towards the first practical post-quantum non-interactive key exchange protocol.

Side channel awareness. The algorithms we present here are not intended to provide any protection against basic side-channel attacks. Uniform and constant-time algorithms for arbitrary-degree isogeny computations are an interesting open problem, but they are beyond the scope of this work.

2   Isogenies and Complex Multiplication

We begin by recalling some basic facts on isogenies of elliptic curves over finite fields. For an in-depth introduction to these concepts, we refer the reader to [59]. For a general overview of isogenies and their use in cryptography, we suggest [21].

2.1   Isogenies Between Elliptic Curves

In what follows $\mathbb{F}_q$ is a finite field of characteristic p with q elements, and $\overline{\mathbb{F}}_q$ is its algebraic closure. Let E and E' be elliptic curves defined over $\mathbb{F}_q$. A homomorphism $\phi : E \rightarrow E'$ is an algebraic map sending 0_E to $0_{E'}$; it induces a group homomomorphism from $E(\overline{\mathbb{F}}_q)$ to $E'(\overline{\mathbb{F}}_q)$ [59, III.4]. An *endomorphism* is a homomorphism from a curve to itself. The endomorphisms of E form a ring $\mathrm{End}(E)$, with the group law on E for addition and composition for multiplication. The simplest examples of endomorphisms are the scalar multiplications $[m]$ (mapping P to the sum of m copies of P) and the *Frobenius* endomorphism

$$\pi : E \longrightarrow E,$$
$$(x, y) \longmapsto (x^q, y^q).$$

As an element of $\mathrm{End}(E)$, Frobenius satisfies a quadratic equation $\pi^2 + q = t\pi$. The integer t (the *trace*) fully determines the order of E as $\#E(\mathbb{F}_q) = q + 1 - t$. A curve is called *supersingular* if p divides t, *ordinary* otherwise.

An *isogeny* is a non-zero homomorphism of elliptic curves. The degree of an isogeny is its degree as an algebraic map, so for example the Frobenius endomorphism π has degree q, and the scalar multiplication $[m]$ has degree m^2. Isogenies of degree ℓ are called ℓ-*isogenies*. The kernel $\ker \phi$ of ϕ is the subgroup of $E(\overline{\mathbb{F}}_q)$ that is mapped to $0_{E'}$. An isogeny ϕ is *cyclic* if $\ker \phi$ is a cyclic group.

An *isomorphism* is an isogeny of degree 1. An *isomorphism class* of elliptic curves is fully determined by their common j-*invariant* in $\overline{\mathbb{F}}_q$. If any curve in the isomorphism class is defined over $\mathbb{F}_q$, then its j-invariant is in $\mathbb{F}_q$.

Any isogeny can be factored as a composition of a *separable* and a *purely inseparable* isogeny. *Purely inseparable* isogenies have trivial kernel, and degree a power of p. *Separable* isogenies include all isogenies of degree coprime to p. Up to isomorphism, separable isogenies are in one-to-one correspondence with their kernels: for any finite subgroup $G \subset E$ of order ℓ there is an elliptic curve E/G and an ℓ-isogeny $\phi : E \rightarrow E/G$ such that $\ker \phi = G$, and the curve and isogeny are unique up to isomorphism. In particular, if ϕ is separable then $\deg \phi = \# \ker \phi$. It is convenient to encode $\ker \phi$ as the polynomial whose roots are the x-coordinates of the points in $\ker \phi$, called the *kernel polynomial* of ϕ.

For any ℓ-isogeny $\phi : E \rightarrow E'$, there is a unique ℓ-isogeny $\hat{\phi} : E' \rightarrow E$ such that $\phi \circ \hat{\phi} = [\ell]$ on E' and $\hat{\phi} \circ \phi = [\ell]$ on E. We call $\hat{\phi}$ the *dual* of ϕ. This shows that being ℓ-*isogenous* is a symmetric relation, and that being isogenous is an equivalence relation. Further, a theorem of Tate states that two curves are isogenous over $\mathbb{F}_q$ if and only if they have the same number of points over $\mathbb{F}_q$.

2.2   Isogeny Graphs

Isogeny-based cryptosystems are based on *isogeny graphs*. These are (multi)-graphs whose vertices are elliptic curves up to isomorphism, and whose edges are isogenies between them (again up to isomorphism). The use of isogeny graphs for algorithmic applications goes back to Mestre and Oesterlé [49], followed notably by Kohel [41], and has been continued by many authors [26, 29, 31, 37, 50].

We write $E[\ell]$ for the subgroup of ℓ-torsion points of $E(\overline{\mathbb{F}}_q)$. If ℓ is coprime to p, then $E[\ell]$ is isomorphic to $(\mathbb{Z}/\ell\mathbb{Z})^2$. Furthermore, if ℓ is prime then $E[\ell]$ contains exactly $\ell + 1$ cyclic subgroups of order ℓ; it follows that, over $\overline{\mathbb{F}}_q$, there are exactly $\ell + 1$ distinct (non-isomorphic) separable ℓ-isogenies from E to other curves. Generically, a connected component of the ℓ-isogeny graph over $\overline{\mathbb{F}}_q$ will be an infinite $(\ell + 1)$-regular graph (a notable exception is the finite connected component of *supersingular* curves, used in SIDH and related protocols).

We now restrict to isogenies defined over $\mathbb{F}_q$. If E and E' are elliptic curves over $\mathbb{F}_q$, then an isogeny $\phi : E \to E'$ is defined over $\mathbb{F}_q$ (up to a twist of E') if and only if the Frobenius endomorphism π on E stabilizes $\ker \phi$. We emphasize that the points in $\ker \phi$ need not be defined over $\mathbb{F}_q$ themselves.

For the vertices of the $\mathbb{F}_q$-isogeny graph we use j-invariants, which classify elliptic curves up to $\overline{\mathbb{F}}_q$-isomorphism; but in the sequel we want to work up to $\mathbb{F}_q$-isomorphism, a stronger equivalence. If E and $\tilde{E}$ are not $\mathbb{F}_q$-isomorphic but $j(E) = j(\tilde{E})$, then $\tilde{E}$ is the *quadratic twist* of E (which is defined and unique up to $\mathbb{F}_q$-isomorphism).[1] When E is ordinary, its quadratic twist has a different cardinality (if $\#E(\mathbb{F}_q) = q + 1 - t$, then $\#\tilde{E}(\mathbb{F}_q) = q + 1 + t$), so E and $\tilde{E}$ are in different components of the isogeny graph. But every $\mathbb{F}_q$-isogeny $\phi : E \to E'$ corresponds to an $\mathbb{F}_q$-isogeny $\tilde{\phi} : \tilde{E} \to \tilde{E}'$ of the same degree between the quadratic twists. The component of the $\mathbb{F}_q$-isogeny graph containing an ordinary curve and the component containing its twist are thus isomorphic; we are therefore justified in identifying them, using j-invariants in $\mathbb{F}_q$ for vertices in the $\mathbb{F}_q$-graph.[2] This is not just a mathematical convenience: we will see in Sect. 3 below that switching between a curve and its twist often allows a useful optimization in isogeny computations.

If an isogeny ϕ is defined over $\mathbb{F}_q$ *and cyclic*, then π acts like a scalar on the points of $\ker \phi$. Thus, for any prime $\ell \neq p$, the number of outgoing ℓ-isogenies from E defined over $\mathbb{F}_q$ can be completely understood by looking at how π acts on $E[\ell]$. Since $E[\ell]$ is a $\mathbb{Z}/\ell\mathbb{Z}$-module of rank 2, the action of π is represented by a 2×2 matrix with entries in $\mathbb{Z}/\ell\mathbb{Z}$ and characteristic polynomial $X^2 - tX + q$ mod ℓ. We then have four possibilities:

(0) π has no eigenvalues in $\mathbb{Z}/\ell\mathbb{Z}$, i.e. $X^2 - tX + q$ is irreducible modulo ℓ; then E has no ℓ-isogenies.

(1.1) π has one eigenvalue of (geometric) multiplicity one, i.e. it is conjugate to a non-diagonal matrix $\left(\begin{smallmatrix} \lambda & * \\ 0 & \lambda \end{smallmatrix}\right)$; then there is one ℓ-isogeny from E.

(1.2) π has one eigenvalue of multiplicity two, i.e. it acts like a scalar matrix $\left(\begin{smallmatrix} \lambda & 0 \\ 0 & \lambda \end{smallmatrix}\right)$; then there are $\ell + 1$ isogenies of degree ℓ from E.

(2) π has two distinct eigenvalues, i.e. it is conjugate to a diagonal matrix $\left(\begin{smallmatrix} \lambda & 0 \\ 0 & \mu \end{smallmatrix}\right)$ with $\lambda \neq \mu$; then there are two ℓ-isogenies from E.

---

[1] There is a slight technicality here for j-invariants 0 and 1728, where non-quadratic twists may exist. We ignore these special cases because these curves never appear in our cryptosystem: the class groups of their endomorphism rings are trivial, and keyspaces of size 1 are of limited utility in cryptography.

[2] The situation is much more complicated for supersingular graphs, because the curve and its twist are in the same component of the graph; see [23, Sect. 2] for details.

The primes ℓ in Case (2) are called *Elkies primes* for E; these are the primes of most interest to us. Cases (1.x) are only possible if ℓ divides $\Delta_p i = t^2 - 4q$, the discriminant of the characteristic equation of π; for ordinary curves $\Delta_p i \neq 0$, so only a finite number of ℓ will fall in these cases, and they will be mostly irrelevant to our cryptosystem. We do not use any ℓ in Case (0).

Since all curves in the same isogeny class over $\mathbb{F}_q$ have the same number of points, they also have the same trace t and discriminant Δ_π. It follows that if ℓ is Elkies for some E in $\mathrm{Ell}_q(\mathcal{O})$, then it is Elkies for every curve in $\mathrm{Ell}_q(\mathcal{O})$.

Hence, if ℓ is an Elkies prime for a curve E, then the connected component of E in the ℓ-isogeny graph is a finite 2-regular graph—that is, a cycle. In the next subsection we describe a group action on this cycle, and determine its size.

2.3   Complex Multiplication

In this subsection we focus exclusively on ordinary elliptic curves. If E is an ordinary curve with Frobenius π, then $\mathrm{End}(E)$ is isomorphic to an *order*[3] in the quadratic imaginary field $\mathbb{Q}(\sqrt{\Delta_\pi})$ (see [59, III.9]). A curve whose endomorphism ring is isomorphic to an order $\mathcal{O}$ is said to have *complex multiplication* by $\mathcal{O}$. For a detailed treatment of the theory of complex multiplication, see [45,60].

The ring of integers $\mathcal{O}_K$ of $K = \mathbb{Q}(\sqrt{\Delta_\pi})$ is its *maximal order*: it contains any other order of K. Hence $\mathbb{Z}[\pi] \subset \mathrm{End}(E) \subset \mathcal{O}_K$, and there is only a finite number of possible choices for $\mathrm{End}(E)$. If we write $\Delta_\pi = d^2 \Delta_K$, where Δ_K is the discriminant[4] of $\mathcal{O}_K$, then the index $[\mathcal{O}_K : \mathrm{End}(E)]$ must divide $d = [\mathcal{O}_K : \mathbb{Z}[\pi]]$.

It turns out that isogenies allow us to navigate the various orders. If $\phi : E \to E'$ is an ℓ-isogeny, then one of the following holds [41, Prop. 21]:

- $\mathrm{End}(E) = \mathrm{End}(E')$, and then ϕ is said to be *horizontal*;
- $[\mathrm{End}(E) : \mathrm{End}(E')] = \ell$, and then ϕ is said to be *descending*;
- $[\mathrm{End}(E') : \mathrm{End}(E)] = \ell$, and then ϕ is said to be *ascending*.

Notice that the last two cases can only happen if ℓ divides $d^2 = \Delta_\pi / \Delta_K$, and thus correspond to Cases (1.x) in the previous subsection. If ℓ does not divide Δ_π, then ϕ is necessarily horizontal.

We now present a group action on the set of all curves up to isomorphism having complex multiplication by a fixed order $\mathcal{O}$; the key exchange protocol of Sect. 3 will be built on this action. Let $\mathfrak{a}$ be an invertible ideal in $\mathrm{End}(E) \simeq \mathcal{O}$ of norm prime to p, and define the $\mathfrak{a}$-*torsion* subgroup of E as

$$E[\mathfrak{a}] = \left\{ P \in E(\overline{\mathbb{F}}_q) \,\middle|\, \sigma(P) = 0 \text{ for all } \sigma \in \mathfrak{a} \right\}.$$

This subgroup is the kernel of a separable isogeny $\phi_\mathfrak{a}$.[5] The codomain $E/E[\mathfrak{a}]$ of $\phi_\mathfrak{a}$ is well-defined up to isomorphism and will be denoted $\mathfrak{a} \cdot E$. The isogeny $\phi_\mathfrak{a}$ is always horizontal—that is, $\mathrm{End}(\mathfrak{a} \cdot E) = \mathrm{End}(E)$—and its degree is the *norm* of $\mathfrak{a}$ as an ideal of $\mathrm{End}(E)$.

---

[3] An *order* is a subring which is a $\mathbb{Z}$-module of rank 2.

[4] Δ_K is a *fundamental discriminant*: $\Delta_K \equiv 0, 1 \pmod 4$, and Δ_K or $\frac{\Delta_K}{4}$ is squarefree.

[5] In fact, one can define $\phi_\mathfrak{a}$ for any invertible ideal $\mathfrak{a}$, but it is not always separable.

Let $\mathrm{Ell}_q(\mathcal{O})$ be the set of isomorphism classes over $\overline{\mathbb{F}}_q$ of curves with complex multiplication by $\mathcal{O}$, and assume it is non-empty. The construction above gives rise to an action of the group of fractional ideals of $\mathcal{O}$ on $\mathrm{Ell}_q(\mathcal{O})$. Furthermore, the principal ideals act trivially (the corresponding isogenies are endomorphisms), so this action induces an action of the *ideal class group* $\mathcal{C}(\mathcal{O})$ on $\mathrm{Ell}_q(\mathcal{O})$.

The main theorem of complex multiplication states that this action is *simply transitive*. In other terms, $\mathrm{Ell}_q(\mathcal{O})$ is a PHS under the group $\mathcal{C}(\mathcal{O})$: if we fix a curve E as base point, then we have a bijection

$$\mathcal{C}(\mathcal{O}) \longrightarrow \mathrm{Ell}_q(\mathcal{O})$$

Ideal class of $\mathfrak{a} \longmapsto$ Isomorphism class of $\mathfrak{a} \cdot E$.

The order of $\mathcal{C}(\mathcal{O})$ is called the *class number* of $\mathcal{O}$, and denoted by $h(\mathcal{O})$. An immediate consequence of the theorem is that $\# \mathrm{Ell}_q(\mathcal{O}) = h(\mathcal{O})$.

As before, we work with $\mathbb{F}_q$-isomorphism classes. Then $\mathrm{Ell}_q(\mathcal{O})$ decomposes into two isomorphic PHSes under $\mathcal{C}(\mathcal{O})$, each containing the quadratic twists of the curves in the other. We choose one of these two components, that we will also denote $\mathrm{Ell}_q(\mathcal{O})$ in the sequel. (The choice is equivalent to a choice of isomorphism $\mathrm{End}(E) \cong \mathcal{O}$, and thus to a choice of sign on the image of π in $\mathcal{O}$.)

Now let ℓ be an Elkies prime for $E \in \mathrm{Ell}_q(\mathcal{O})$. So far, we have seen that the connected component of E in the ℓ-isogeny graph is a cycle of horizontal isogenies. Complex multiplication tells us more. The restriction of the Frobenius to $E[\ell]$ has two eigenvalues $\lambda \neq \mu$, to which we associate the prime ideals $\mathfrak{a} = (\pi - \lambda, \ell)$ and $\hat{\mathfrak{a}} = (\pi - \mu, \ell)$, both of norm ℓ. We see then that $E[\mathfrak{a}]$ is the eigenspace of λ, defining an isogeny $\phi_{\mathfrak{a}}$ of degree ℓ. Furthermore $\mathfrak{a}\hat{\mathfrak{a}} = \hat{\mathfrak{a}}\mathfrak{a} = (\ell)$, implying that $\mathfrak{a}$ and $\hat{\mathfrak{a}}$ are the inverse of one another in $\mathcal{C}(\mathcal{O})$, thus the isogeny $\phi_{\hat{\mathfrak{a}}} : \mathfrak{a}\cdot E \to E$ of kernel $(\mathfrak{a}\cdot E)[\hat{\mathfrak{a}}]$ is the dual of $\phi_{\mathfrak{a}}$ (up to isomorphism).

The eigenvalues λ and μ define opposite directions on the ℓ-isogeny cycle, independent of the starting curve, as shown in Fig. 1. The size of the cycle is the order of $(\pi - \lambda, \ell)$ in $\mathcal{C}(\mathcal{O})$, thus partitioning $\mathrm{Ell}_q(\mathcal{O})$ into cycles of equal size.

3   Key Exchange from Isogeny Graphs

We would like to instantiate the key exchange protocol of Algorithm 2 with the PHS $X = \mathrm{Ell}_q(\mathcal{O})$ for the group $G = \mathcal{C}(\mathcal{O})$, for some well chosen order $\mathcal{O}$ in a quadratic imaginary field. However, given a generic element of $\mathcal{C}(\mathcal{O})$, the best algorithm [38] to evaluate its action on $\mathrm{Ell}_q(\mathcal{O})$ has subexponential complexity in q, making the protocol infeasible. The solution, following Couveignes [19], is to fix a set S of small prime ideals in $\mathcal{O}$, whose action on X can be computed efficiently, and such that compositions of elements of S cover the whole of G. The action of an arbitrary element of G is then the composition of a series of actions by small elements in S. As Rostovtsev and Stolbunov [57] observed, it is useful to visualise this decomposed action as a walk in an isogeny graph.

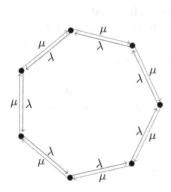
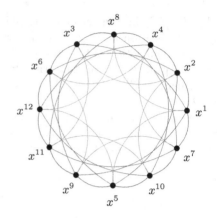

Fig. 1. An isogeny cycle for an Elkies prime ℓ, with edge directions associated with the Frobenius eigenvalues λ and μ.

Fig. 2. Undirected Schreier graph on $\langle x \rangle \setminus \{1\}$ where $x^{13} = 1$, acted upon by $(\mathbb{Z}/13\mathbb{Z})^*$, generated by $S = \{2,3,5\}$ (resp. blue, red and green edges). (Color figure online)

3.1 Walks in Isogeny Graphs

Let G be a group, X a PHS for G, and S a subset of G. The Schreier graph $\mathcal{G}(G, S, X)$ is the labelled directed graph whose vertex set is X, and where an edge labelled by $s \in S$ links x_1 to x_2 if and only if $s \cdot x_1 = x_2$. It is isomorphic to a Cayley graph for G. If S is symmetric (that is, $S^{-1} = S$), then we associate the same label to s and s^{-1}, making the graph undirected.

A *walk* in $\mathcal{G}(G, S, X)$ is a finite sequence $(s_1, \ldots, s_n)$ of *steps* in S. We define the action of this walk on X as

$$(s_1, \ldots, s_n) \cdot x = \Big(\prod_{i=1}^{n} s_i \Big) \cdot x.$$

In our application G is abelian, so the order of the steps s_i does not matter. We can use this action directly in the key exchange protocol of Algorithm 2, by simply taking private keys to be walks instead of elements in G.

Example 1. Figure 2 shows $\mathcal{G}(G, S, X)$ where $G = (\mathbb{Z}/13\mathbb{Z})^*$, $S = \{2,3,5\} \cup \{2^{-1}, 3^{-1}, 5^{-1}\}$, and $X = \langle x \rangle \setminus \{1\}$ is a cyclic group of order 13, minus its identity element. The action of G on X is exponentiation: $g \cdot x = x^g$. The action of 11, which takes x^k to x^{11k}, can be expressed using the walks $(2,5,5)$, or $(2^{-1}, 3^{-1})$, or $(3,5)$, for example. Note that 5 has order 4 modulo 13, thus partitioning $\langle x \rangle \setminus \{1\}$ into 3 cycles of length 4.

Returning to the world of isogenies, we now take

- $X = \mathrm{Ell}_q(\mathcal{O})$ as the vertex set, for some well-chosen q and $\mathcal{O}$; in particular we require $\mathcal{O}$ to be the maximal order (see Sect. 5).
- $G = \mathcal{C}(\mathcal{O})$ as the group acting on X;
- S a set of ideals, whose norms are small Elkies primes in $\mathcal{O}$.

The graph $\mathcal{G}(G, S, X)$ is thus an isogeny graph, composed of many isogeny cycles (one for the norm of each prime in S) superimposed on the vertex set $\text{Ell}_q(\mathcal{O})$. It is connected if S generates $\mathcal{C}(\mathcal{O})$. Walks in $\mathcal{G}(G, S, X)$ are called *isogeny walks*.

We compute the action of an ideal $\mathfrak{s}$ (a single *isogeny step*) on an $x \in \text{Ell}_q(\mathcal{O})$ by choosing a representative curve E with $x = j(E)$, and computing an isogeny $\phi_{\mathfrak{s}} : E \to E'$ from E corresponding to $\mathfrak{s}$; the resulting vertex is $\mathfrak{s} \cdot x = j(E')$. The action of an isogeny walk $(\mathfrak{s}_i)_i$ is then evaluated as the sequence of isogeny steps $\phi_{\mathfrak{s}_i}$. Algorithms for these operations are given in the next subsection.

Using this "smooth" representation of elements in $\mathcal{C}(\mathcal{O})$ as isogeny walks lets us avoid computing $\mathcal{C}(\mathcal{O})$ and $\text{Ell}_q(\mathcal{O})$, and avoid explicit ideal class arithmetic; only isogenies between elliptic curves are computed. In practice, we re-use the elliptic curve E' from one step as the E in the next; but we emphasize that when isogeny walks are used for Diffie–Hellman, the resulting public keys and shared secrets are not the final elliptic curves, but their j-invariants.

3.2   Computing Isogeny Walks

Since $\mathcal{C}(\mathcal{O})$ is commutative, we can break isogeny walks down into a succession of walks corresponding to powers of single primes $\mathfrak{s} = (\ell, \pi - \lambda)$; that is, repeated applications of the isogenies $\phi_{\mathfrak{s}}$. Depending on $\mathfrak{s}$, we will compute each sequence of $\phi_{\mathfrak{s}}$ using one of two different methods:

– Algorithm 5 (ELKIESWALK) uses Algorithm 3 (ELKIESFIRSTSTEP) followed by a series of calls to Algorithm 4 (ELKIESNEXTSTEP), both which use the *modular polynomial* $\Phi_\ell(X, Y)$. This approach works for any $\mathfrak{s}$.
– Algorithm 7 (VÉLUWALK) uses a series of calls to Algorithm 6 (VÉLUSTEP). This approach, which uses torsion points on E, can only be applied when λ satisfies certain properties.

Rostovtsev and Stolbunov only used analogues of Algorithms 3 and 4. The introduction of VÉLUSTEP, inspired by SIDH and related protocols (and now a key ingredient in the CSIDH protocol [12]), speeds up our protocol by a considerable factor; this is the main practical contribution of our work.

Elkies steps. Algorithms 3 and 4 compute single steps in the ℓ-isogeny graph. Their correctness follows from the definition of the modular polynomial Φ_ℓ: a cyclic ℓ-isogeny exists between two elliptic curves E and E' if and only if $\Phi_\ell(j(E), j(E')) = 0$ (see [58, Sect. 6] and [24, Sect. 3] for the relevant theory). One may use the classical modular polynomials here, or alternative, lower-degree modular polynomials (Atkin polynomials, for example) with minimal adaptation to the algorithms. In practice, Φ_ℓ is precomputed and stored: several publicly available databases exist (see [42] and [8,9,66], for example).

Given a j-invariant $j(E)$, we can compute its two neighbours in the ℓ-isogeny graph by evaluating $P(X) = \Phi_\ell(j(E), X)$ (a polynomial of degree $\ell + 1$), and then computing its two roots in $\mathbb{F}_q$. Using a Cantor–Zassenhaus-type algorithm, this costs $\tilde{O}(\ell \log q)$ $\mathbb{F}_q$-operations.

Algorithm 3: ELKIESFIRSTSTEP

Input: $E \in \mathrm{Ell}_q(\mathcal{O})$; (ℓ, λ) encoding $\mathfrak{s} = (\pi - \lambda, \ell)$
Output: $j(\mathfrak{s} \cdot E)$

1 $P \leftarrow \Phi_\ell(X, j(E))$
2 $\{j_1, j_2\} \leftarrow \mathrm{ROOTS}(P, \mathbb{F}_q)$
3 $K \leftarrow \mathrm{KERNELPOLYNOMIAL}(\mathrm{ISOGENY}(E, j_1, \ell))$ // e.g. BMSS algorithm [7]
4 $Q \leftarrow$ a nonzero point in K // e.g. $(x, y) \in E(\mathbb{F}_q[x, y]/(y^2 - f_E(x), K(x)))$
5 **if** $\pi(Q) = [\lambda]Q$ **then**
6 | **return** j_1
7 **else**
8 | **return** j_2

Algorithm 4: ELKIESNEXTSTEP

Input: (ℓ, λ) encoding $\mathfrak{s} = (\pi - \lambda, \ell)$; $(j_0, j_1) = (j(E), j(\mathfrak{s} \cdot E))$ for E in $\mathrm{Ell}_q(\mathcal{O})$
Output: $j(\mathfrak{s} \cdot \mathfrak{s} \cdot E)$

1 $P \leftarrow \Phi_\ell(X, j_1)/(X - j_0)$
2 $j_2 \leftarrow \mathrm{ROOT}(P, \mathbb{F}_q)$
                                      // It is unique
3 **return** j_2

Algorithm 5: ELKIESWALK

Input: $E \in \mathrm{Ell}_q(\mathcal{O})$; (ℓ, λ) encoding $\mathfrak{s} = (\pi - \lambda, \ell)$; $k \geq 1$
Output: $\mathfrak{s}^k \cdot E$

1 $j_0 \leftarrow j(E)$
2 $j_1 \leftarrow \mathrm{ELKIESFIRSTSTEP}(E, (\ell, \lambda))$
3 **for** $2 \leq i \leq k$ **do**
4 | $(j_0, j_1) \leftarrow (j_1, \mathrm{ELKIESNEXTSTEP}((\ell, \lambda), (j_0, j_1)))$
5 $E_R \leftarrow \mathrm{ELLIPTICCURVEFROMJINVARIANT}(j_1)$
6 **if** *not* $\mathrm{CHECKTRACE}(E_R, t)$ **then**
7 | $E_R \leftarrow \mathrm{QUADRATICTWIST}(E_R)$
8 **return** E_R

Algorithm 6: VÉLUSTEP

Input: $E \in \mathrm{Ell}_q(\mathcal{O})$; (ℓ, λ) encoding $\mathfrak{s} = (\pi - \lambda, \ell)$; $r > 0$; $C_r = \#E(\mathbb{F}_{q^r})$
Output: $\mathfrak{s} \cdot E$

1 **repeat**
2 | $P \leftarrow \mathrm{RANDOM}(E(\mathbb{F}_{q^r}))$
3 | $Q \leftarrow [C_r/\ell]P$
4 **until** $Q \neq 0_E$
5 $K \leftarrow \prod_{i=0}^{(\ell-1)/2}(X - x([i]Q))$ // Kernel polynomial of isogeny
6 $E_R \leftarrow \mathrm{ISOGENYFROMKERNEL}(E, K)$ // Apply Vélu's formulæ
7 **return** E_R

Algorithm 7: VÉLUWALK

Input: $E \in \mathrm{Ell}_q(\mathcal{O})$; (ℓ, λ) encoding $\mathfrak{s} = (\ell, \pi - \lambda)$; $k \geq 1$
Output: $\mathfrak{s}^k \cdot E$

1 $r \leftarrow \mathrm{ORDER}(\lambda, \ell)$ // Precompute and store for each (ℓ, λ)
2 $C_r \leftarrow \#E(\mathbb{F}_{q^r})$ // Precompute and store for each r
3 **for** $1 \leq i \leq k$ **do**
4 $\quad \lfloor \quad E \leftarrow \mathrm{V\acute{E}LUSTEP}(E, (\ell, \lambda), r, C_r)$

5 **return** E

We need to make sure we step towards the neighbour in the correct direction. If we have already made one such step, then this is easy: it suffices to avoid backtracking. Algorithm 4 (ELKIESNEXTSTEP) does this by removing the factor corresponding to the previous j-invariant in Line 4; this algorithm can be used for all but the first of the steps corresponding to $\mathfrak{s}$.

It remains to choose the right direction in the first step for $\mathfrak{s} = (\ell, \pi - \lambda)$. In Algorithm 3 we choose one of the two candidates for $\phi_{\mathfrak{s}}$ arbitrarily, and compute its kernel polynomial. This costs $\tilde{O}(\ell)$ $\mathbb{F}_q$-operations using the Bostan–Morain–Salvy–Schost algorithm [7] with asymptotically fast polynomial arithmetic. We then compute an element Q of $\ker \phi_{\mathfrak{s}}$ over an extension of $\mathbb{F}_q$ of degree at most $\frac{\ell-1}{2}$, then evaluate $\pi(Q)$ and $[\lambda]Q$. If they match, then we have chosen the right direction; otherwise we take the other root of $P(X)$.

Algorithm 5 (ELKIESWALK) combines these algorithms to compute the iterated action of $\mathfrak{s}$. Line 5 ensures that the curve returned is the the correct component of the ℓ-isogeny graph. Both ELKIESFIRSTSTEP and ELKIESNEXTSTEP cost $\tilde{O}(\ell \log q)$ $\mathbb{F}_q$-operations, dominated by the calculation of the roots of $P(X)$.

Vélu steps. For some ideals $\mathfrak{s} = (\ell, \pi - \lambda)$, we can completely avoid modular polynomials, and the costly computation of their roots, by constructing $\ker \phi_{\mathfrak{s}}$ directly from ℓ-torsion points. Let r be the order of λ modulo ℓ; then $\ker \phi_{\mathfrak{s}} \subseteq E(\mathbb{F}_{q^r})$. If r is not a multiple of the order of the other eigenvalue μ of π on $E[\ell]$, then $E[\ell](\mathbb{F}_{q^r}) = \ker \phi_{\mathfrak{s}}$. Algorithm 6 (VÉLUSTEP) exploits this fact to construct a generator Q of $\ker \phi_{\mathfrak{s}}$ by computing a point of order ℓ in $E(\mathbb{F}_{q^r})$. The roots of the kernel polynomial of $\phi_{\mathfrak{s}}$ $x(Q), \ldots, x([(\ell - 1)/2]Q)$. [6]

Constructing a point Q of order ℓ in $E(\mathbb{F}_{q^r})$ is straightforward: we take random points and multiply by the cofactor C_r/ℓ, where $C_r := \#E(\mathbb{F}_{q^r})$. Each trial succeeds with probability $1 - 1/\ell$. Note that C_r can be easily (pre)computed from the Frobenius trace t: if we write $C_r = q - t_r + 1$ for $r > 0$ (so $t_1 = t$) and $t_0 = 2$, then the t_r satisfy the recurrence $t_r = t \cdot t_{r-1} - q \cdot t_{r-2}$.

We compute the quotient curve in Line 6 with Vélu's formulæ [69] in $O(\ell)$ $\mathbb{F}_q$-operations. Since $\log C_r \simeq r \log q$, provided $\ell = O(\log q)$, the costly step in

---

[6] If the order of μ divides r, Algorithm 6 can be extended as follows: take $P \in E[\ell]$, and compute $\pi(P) - [\mu]P$; the result is either zero, or an eigenvector for μ. This is not necessary for any of the primes in our proposed parameters.

Algorithm 6 is the scalar multiplication at Line 3, which costs $\tilde{O}(r^2 \log q)$ $\mathbb{F}_q$-operations.

Comparing the costs. To summarize:

- Elkies steps cost $\tilde{O}(\ell \log q)$ $\mathbb{F}_q$-operations;
- Vélu steps cost $\tilde{O}(r^2 \log q)$ $\mathbb{F}_q$-operations, where r is the order of λ in $\mathbb{Z}/\ell\mathbb{Z}$.

In general $r = O(\ell)$, so Elkies steps should be preferred. However, when r is particularly small (and not a multiple of the order of the other eigenvalue), a factor of ℓ can be saved using Vélu steps. The value of r directly depends on λ, which is in turn determined by $\#E(\mathbb{F}_p) \bmod \ell$. Thus, we see that better STEP performances depend on the ability to find elliptic curves whose order satisfies congruence conditions modulo small primes. Unfortunately, we can only achieve this partially (see Sect. 4), so the most efficient solution is to use Vélu steps when we can, and Elkies steps for some other primes.

In practice, Algorithm 6 can be improved by using elliptic curve models with more efficient arithmetic. In our implementation (see Sect. 6), we used x-only arithmetic on Montgomery models [18,51], which also have convenient Vélu formulæ [17,56]. Note that we can also avoid computing y-coordinates in Algorithm 3 at Line 5 if $\lambda \neq \pm\mu$: this is the typical case for Elkies steps, and we used this optimization for all Elkies primes in our implementation.

Remark 1. Note that, in principle, Algorithm 6, can only be used to walk in one direction $\mathfrak{s}_\lambda = (\ell, \pi - \lambda)$, and not in the opposite one $\mathfrak{s}_\mu = (\ell, \pi - \mu)$. Indeed we have assumed that $E[\mathfrak{s}_\lambda]$ is in $E(\mathbb{F}_{q^r})$, while $E[\mathfrak{s}_\mu]$ is not. However, switching to a quadratic twist $\tilde{E}$ of E over $\mathbb{F}_{q^r}$ changes the sign of the Frobenius eigenvalues, thus it may happen that $\tilde{E}[\mathfrak{s}_{-\mu}]$ is in $\tilde{E}(\mathbb{F}_{q^r})$, while $\tilde{E}[\mathfrak{s}_{-\lambda}]$ is not. It is easy to force this behavior by asking that $p \equiv -1 \pmod{\ell}$, indeed then $\lambda = -1/\mu$.

For these eigenvalue pairs we can thus walk in both directions using Vélu steps at no additional cost, following either the direction λ on E, or the direction $-\mu$ on a twist. In Algorithm 6, only the curve order and the random point sampling need to be modified when using quadratic twists.

3.3   Sampling Isogeny Walks for Key Exchange

We now describe how keys are generated and exchanged in our protocol. Since the cost of the various isogeny walks depends on the ideals chosen, we will use adapted, or *skewed*, smooth representations when sampling elements in $\mathcal{C}(\mathcal{O})$ in order to minimize the total computational cost of a key exchange.

We take a (conjectural) generating set for $\mathcal{C}(\mathcal{O})$ consisting of ideals over a set S of small Elkies primes, which we partition into three sets according to the step algorithms to be used. We maintain three lists of tuples encoding these primes:

S_{VV} is a list of tuples (ℓ, λ, μ) such that the ideal $(\ell, \pi - \lambda)$ and its inverse $(\ell, \pi - \mu)$ are *both* amenable to VÉLUSTEP.

S_{VE} is a list of tuples (ℓ, λ) such that $(\ell, \pi - \lambda)$ is amenable to VÉLUSTEP but its inverse $(\ell, \pi - \mu)$ is *not*.
S_{EE} is a list of tuples (ℓ, λ, μ) such that *neither* $(\ell, \pi - \lambda)$ nor $(\ell, \pi - \mu)$ are amenable to VÉLUSTEP.

In S_{VV} and S_{EE}, the labelling of eigenvalues as λ and μ is fixed once and for all (that is, the tuples (ℓ, λ, μ) and (ℓ, μ, λ) do not both appear). This fixes directions in each of the ℓ-isogeny cycles. Looking back at Fig. 1, for ℓ associated with S_{EE} and S_{VV}, both directions in the ℓ-isogeny graph will be available for use in walks; for S_{VE}, only the Vélu direction will be used.

Each secret key in the cryptosystem is a walk in the isogeny graph. Since the class group $\mathcal{C}(\mathcal{O})$ is commutative, such a walk is determined by the multiplicities of the primes $\mathfrak{s}$ that appear in it. Algorithm 8 (KEYGEN) therefore encodes private-key walks as *exponent vectors*, with one integer exponent for each tuple in S_{VV}, S_{VE}, and S_{EE}. For a tuple (ℓ, λ, μ),

- a positive exponent k_ℓ indicates a walk of k_ℓ ℓ-isogeny steps in direction λ;
- a negative exponent $-k_\ell$ indicates k_ℓ ℓ-isogeny steps in direction μ.

For the tuples (ℓ, λ) in S_{VE}, where we do not use the slower μ-direction, we only allow non-negative exponents. We choose bounds M_ℓ on the absolute value of the exponents k_ℓ so as to minimize the total cost of computing isogeny walks, while maintaining a large keyspace. As a rule, the bounds will be much bigger for the primes in S_{VV} and S_{VE}, where Vélu steps can be applied.

The public keys are j-invariants in $\mathbb{F}_q$, so they can be stored in $\log_2 q$ bits; the private keys are also quite compact, but their precise size depends on the number of primes ℓ and the choice of exponent bounds M_ℓ, which is a problem we will return to in Sect. 6.

Algorithm 9 completes a Diffie–Hellman key exchange by applying a combination of Elkies and Vélu walks (Algorithms 5 and 7, respectively).

4 Public Parameter Selection

It is evident that the choice of public parameters has a heavy impact on the execution time: smaller Elkies primes, and smaller multiplicative orders of the Frobenius eigenvalues, will lead to better performance. Since all of this information is contained in the value of $\#E(\mathbb{F}_q)$, we now face the problem of constructing ordinary elliptic curves of prescribed order modulo small primes. Unfortunately, and in contrast with the supersingular case, no polynomial-time method to achieve this is known in general: the CM method [3, 64], which solves this problem when the corresponding class groups are small, is useless in our setting (see Sect. 5).

In this section we describe how to use the Schoof–Elkies–Atkin (SEA) point counting algorithm with early abort, combined with the use of certain modular curves, to construct curves whose order satisfies some constraints modulo small primes. This is faster than choosing curves at random and computing their orders completely until a convenient one is found, but it still does not allow us to use the full power of Algorithm VÉLUSTEP.

Algorithm 8: KEYGEN for cryptosystems in the isogeny graph on $\mathrm{Ell}_q(\mathcal{O})$ with walks based on S, and initial curve E_0. The ideal lists S_{EE}, S_{VV}, and S_{VE}, and the walk bounds M_ℓ, are system parameters.

Input: ()
Output: A secret key $(k_\ell)_{\ell \in S}$ and the corresponding public key $j(E)$
1 $E \leftarrow E_0$
2 **for** $(\ell, \lambda, \mu) \in S_{EE}$ **do**
3 $\quad$ $k_\ell \leftarrow \mathrm{RANDOM}([-M_\ell, M_\ell])$
4 $\quad$ **if** $k_\ell \geq 0$ **then** $\nu \leftarrow \lambda$
5 $\quad$ **else** $\nu \leftarrow \mu$
6 $\quad$ $E \leftarrow \mathrm{ELKIESWALK}(E, (\ell, \nu), |k_\ell|)$
7 **for** $(\ell, \lambda, \nu) \in S_{VV}$ **do**
8 $\quad$ $k_\ell \leftarrow \mathrm{RANDOM}([-M_\ell, M_\ell])$
9 $\quad$ **if** $k_\ell \geq 0$ **then** $\nu \leftarrow \lambda$
10 $\quad$ **else** $\nu \leftarrow \mu$
11 $\quad$ $E \leftarrow \mathrm{V\acute{E}LUWALK}(E, (\ell, \nu), |k_\ell|)$
12 **for** $(\ell, \lambda) \in S_{VE}$ **do**
13 $\quad$ $k_\ell \leftarrow \mathrm{RANDOM}([0, M_\ell])$
14 $\quad$ $E \leftarrow \mathrm{V\acute{E}LUWALK}(E, (\ell, \lambda), k_\ell)$
15 **return** $((k_\ell)_{\ell \in S}, j(E))$

Algorithm 9: DH for the isogeny graph on $\mathrm{Ell}_q(\mathcal{O})$ with primes in S. The ideal lists S_{EE}, S_{VV}, and S_{VE}, and the walk bounds M_ℓ, are system parameters. Public key validation is not included here, but (if desired) should be carried out as detailed in Sect. 5.4.

Input: A private key $k_A = (k_{A,\ell})_{\ell \in S}$ corresponding to a walk $(\mathfrak{s}_1, \ldots, \mathfrak{s}_n)$, and a public key $j_B = j(E_B)$ for $E_B \in \mathrm{Ell}_q(O)$
Output: A shared secret $j(\prod_{i=1}^n \mathfrak{s}_i \cdot E_B)$
1 $E \leftarrow \mathrm{ELLIPTICCURVEFROMJINVARIANT}(j_B)$
2 **if** *not* $\mathrm{CHECKTRACE}(E, t)$ **then**
3 $\quad$ $E \leftarrow \mathrm{QUADRATICTWIST}(E)$
4 **for** $(\ell, \lambda, \mu) \in S_{EE}$ **do**
5 $\quad$ **if** $k_{A,\ell} \geq 0$ **then** $\nu \leftarrow \lambda$
6 $\quad$ **else** $\nu \leftarrow \mu$
7 $\quad$ $E \leftarrow \mathrm{ELKIESWALK}(E, (\ell, \nu), |k_{A,\ell}|)$
8 **for** $(\ell, \lambda, \mu) \in S_{VV}$ **do**
9 $\quad$ **if** $k_{A,\ell} \geq 0$ **then** $\nu \leftarrow \lambda$
10 $\quad$ **else** $\nu \leftarrow \mu$
11 $\quad$ $E \leftarrow \mathrm{V\acute{E}LUWALK}(E, (\ell, \nu), |k_{A,\ell}|)$
12 **for** $(\ell, \lambda) \in S_{VE}$ **do**
13 $\quad$ $E \leftarrow \mathrm{V\acute{E}LUWALK}(E, (\ell, \lambda), k_{A,\ell})$
14 **return** $j(E)$

Early-abort SEA. The SEA algorithm [52,58] is the state-of-the-art point-counting algorithm for elliptic curves over large-characteristic finite fields. In order to compute $N = \#E(\mathbb{F}_p)$, it computes N modulo a series of small Elkies primes ℓ, before combining the results via the CRT to get the true value of N.

Cryptographers are usually interested in generating elliptic curves of prime or nearly prime order, and thus without small prime factors. While running SEA on random candidate curves, one immediately detects if $N \equiv 0 \pmod{\ell}$ for the small primes ℓ; if this happens then the SEA execution is aborted, and restarted with a new curve.

Here, the situation is the opposite: we *want* elliptic curves whose cardinality has many small prime divisors. To fix ideas, we choose the 512-bit prime

$$p := 7 \left(\prod_{2 \leq \ell \leq 380,\ \ell \text{ prime}} \ell \right) - 1 .$$

Then, according to Remark 1, Algorithm VÉLUSTEP can be used for ℓ-isogenies in both directions for any prime $\ell \leq 380$, as soon as the order of its eigenvalues is small enough. We now proceed as follows:

- Choose a smoothness bound B (we used $B = 13$).
- Pick elliptic curves E at random in $\mathbb{F}_p$, and use the SEA algorithm, aborting when any $\ell \leq B$ with $\#E(\mathbb{F}_p) \not\equiv 0 \pmod{\ell}$ is found.
- For each E which passed the tests above, complete the SEA algorithm to compute $\#E(\mathbb{F}_p)$, and estimate the key exchange running time using this curve as a public parameter (see Sect. 6).
- The "fastest" curves now give promising candidates for $\#E(\mathbb{F}_p)$.

In considering the efficiency of this procedure, it is important to remark that very few curves will pass the early-abort tests. The bound B should be chosen to balance the overall cost of the first few tests with that of the complete SEA algorithm for the curves which pass them. Therefore, its value is somewhat implementation-dependent.

Finding the maximal order. Once a "good" curve E has been computed, we want to find a curve E_0 having the same number of points, but whose endomorphism ring is maximal, and to ensure that its discriminant is a large integer. Therefore, we attempt to factor the discriminant Δ_π of $\mathbb{Z}[\pi]$: if it is squarefree, then E already has maximal endomorphism ring, and in general the square factors of Δ_π indicate which ascending isogenies have to be computed in order to find E_0.

Remark 2. Factoring random 512-bit integers is not hard in general, and discriminants of quadratic fields even tend to be slightly smoother than random integers.

If a discriminant fails to be completely factored, a conservative strategy would be to discard it, but ultimately undetected large prime-square factors do not present a security issue because computing the possible corresponding large-degree isogenies is intractable (see Sect. 5).

Using the modular curve $X_1(N)$. Since we are looking for curves with smooth cardinalities, another improvement to this procedure is available: instead of choosing elliptic curves uniformly at random, we pick random candidates using an equation for the modular curve $X_1(N)$ [65], which guarantees the existence of a rational N-torsion point on the sampled elliptic curve. This idea is used in the procedure of selecting elliptic curves in the Elliptic Curve Method for factoring [70,71]. In our implementation we used $N = 17$, and also incorporated the existence test in [54] for Montgomery models for the resulting elliptic curves.

Results. We implemented this search using the Sage computer algebra system. Our experiments were conducted on several machines running Intel Xeon E5520 processors at 2.27GHz. After 17,000 hours of CPU time, we found the Montgomery elliptic curve $E : y^2 = x^3 + Ax^2 + x$ over $\mathbb{F}_p$ with p as above, and

$$A = \frac{10861338504649280383859950140772947007703646408372831934324660566888732977789}{32142488253565145603672591944602210571423767689240032829444439469242521864171}.$$

The trace of Frobenius t of E is

$$-147189550172528104900422131912266898599387555512924231762107728432541952979290.$$

There is a rational ℓ-torsion point on E, or its quadratic twist, for each ℓ in

$$\{3, 5, 7, 11, 13, 17, 103, 523, 821, 947, 1723\};$$

each of these primes is Elkies. Furthermore, $\mathrm{End}(E)$ is the maximal order, and its discriminant is a 511-bit integer that has the following prime factorization:

$$-2^3 \cdot 20507 \cdot 67429 \cdot 11718238170290677 \cdot 12248034502305872059$$

$$\cdot 6088435818820474512946876275125472871 2569$$

$$\cdot 6849519768592643090516221124130048617189549148044406286079 4276603493.$$

In Sect. 6, we discuss the practical performance of our key-exchange protocol using these system parameters. Other proposals for parameters are given in [39].

5   Security

We now address the security of the CRS primitive, and derived protocols. Intuitively, these systems rely on two assumptions:

1. given two curves E and E' in $\mathrm{Ell}_q(\mathcal{O})$, it is hard to find a (smooth degree) isogeny $\phi : E \to E'$; and
2. the distribution on $\mathrm{Ell}_q(\mathcal{O})$ induced by the random walks sampled in Algorithm 8 is computationally undistinguishable from the uniform distribution.

We start by reviewing the known attacks for the first problem, both in the classical and the quantum setting. Then, we formalize security assumptions and give security proofs against passive adversaries. Finally, we discuss key validation and protection against active adversaries.

5.1 Classical Attacks

We start by addressing the following, more general, problem:

Problem 1. Given two ordinary elliptic curves E, E' defined over a finite field $\mathbb{F}_q$, such that $\#E(\mathbb{F}_q) = \#E'(\mathbb{F}_q)$, find an isogeny walk $(\phi_i)_{1 \leq i \leq n}$ such that $\phi_n \circ \cdots \circ \phi_1(E) = E'$.

The curves in Problem 1 are supposed to be sampled uniformly, though this is never exactly the case in practice. This problem was studied before the emergence of isogeny-based cryptography [28,29,31], because of its applications to conventional elliptic-curve cryptography [31,37,67]. The algorithm with the best asymptotic complexity is due to Galbraith, Hess and Smart [31]. It consists of three stages:

Stage 0. Use walks of *ascending* isogenies to reduce to the case where $\text{End}(E) \cong \text{End}(E')$ is the maximal order.
Stage 1. Start two random walks of horizontal isogenies from E and E'; detect the moment when they collide using a Pollard-rho type of algorithm.
Stage 2. Reduce the size of the obtained walk using index-calculus techniques.

To understand Stage 0, recall that all isogenous elliptic curves have the same order, and thus the same trace t of the Frobenius endomorphism π. We know that $\text{End}(E)$ is contained in the ring of integers $\mathcal{O}_K$ of $K = \mathbb{Q}(\sqrt{\Delta_\pi})$, where $\Delta_\pi = t^2 - 4q$ is the Frobenius discriminant. As before we write $\Delta_\pi = d^2 \Delta_K$, where Δ_K is the discriminant of $\mathcal{O}_K$; then for any $\ell \mid d$, the ℓ-isogeny graph of E contains *ascending* and *descending* ℓ-isogenies; these graphs are referred to as *volcanoes* [26] (see Fig. 3). Ascending isogenies go from curves with smaller endomorphism rings to curves with larger ones, and take us to a curve with $\text{End}(E) \simeq \mathcal{O}_K$ in $O(\log d)$ steps; they can be computed efficiently using the algorithms of [22,26,35,41]. Assuming[7] all prime factors of d are in $O(\log q)$, we can therefore compute Stage 0 in time polynomial in $\log q$.

The set $\text{Ell}_q(\mathcal{O}_K)$ has the smallest size among all sets $\text{Ell}_q(\mathcal{O})$ for $\mathcal{O} \subset \mathcal{O}_K$, so it is always interesting to reduce to it. This justifies using curves with maximal endomorphism ring in the definition of the protocol in Sect. 3. When Δ_π is square-free, $\mathbb{Z}[\pi]$ is the maximal order, and the condition is automatically true.

The collision search in Stage 1 relies on the birthday paradox, and has a complexity of $O(\sqrt{h(\mathcal{O}_K)})$.

It is known that, on average, $h(\mathcal{O}_K) \approx 0.461 \cdots \sqrt{|\Delta_K|}$ (see [15, 5.10]), and, assuming the extended Riemann hypothesis, we even have a lower bound (see [47])

$$h(\mathcal{O}_K) \geq 0.147 \cdots \frac{(1 + o(1))\sqrt{|\Delta_K|}}{\log \log |\Delta_K|}.$$

Since $\Delta_K \sim q$, we expect Stage 1 to take time $O(q^{1/4})$, which justifies a choice of q four times as large as the security parameter. Unfortunately, class numbers

---

[7] This is typical for isogeny-based protocols. No counter-example has ever been constructed.

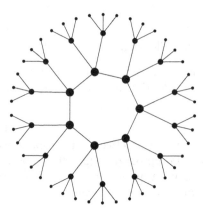

Fig. 3. 3-isogeny graph (*volcano*) containing the curve with $j(E) = 607$ over $\mathbb{F}_{6007}$. A larger vertex denotes a larger endomorphism ring.

are notoriously difficult to compute, the current record being for a discriminant of 300 bits [5]. Computing class numbers for ~ 500-bit discriminants seems to be expensive, albeit feasible; thus, we can only rely on these heuristic arguments to justify the security of our proposed parameters.

The horizontal isogeny produced by Stage 1 is represented by an ideal constructed as a product of exponentially many small ideals. Stage 2 converts this into a sequence of small ideals of length polynomial in $\log q$. Its complexity is bounded by that of Stage 1, so it has no impact on our security estimates.

Remark 3. The Cohen–Lenstra heuristic [16] predicts that the odd part of $\mathcal{C}(\mathcal{O}_K)$ is cyclic with overwhelming probability, and other heuristics [33] indicate that $h(\mathcal{O}_K)$ is likely to have a large prime factor. However, since there is no known way in which the group structure of $\mathcal{C}(\mathcal{O}_K)$ can affect the security of our protocol, we can disregard this matter. No link between the group structure of $E(\mathbb{F}_q)$ itself and the security is known, either.

5.2   Quantum Attacks

On a quantum computer, an attack with better asymptotic complexity is given by Childs, Jao and Soukharev in [13]. It consists of two algorithms:

1. A (classical) algorithm that takes as input an elliptic curve $E \in \mathrm{Ell}_q(\mathcal{O})$ and an ideal $\mathfrak{a} \in \mathcal{C}(\mathcal{O})$, and outputs the curve $\mathfrak{a} \cdot E$;
2. A generic quantum algorithm for the dihedral hidden subgroup problem (dHSP), based upon previous work of Kuperberg [43,44] and Regev [55].

The ideal evaluation algorithm has sub-exponential complexity $L_q(\frac{1}{2}, \frac{\sqrt{3}}{2})$. However, after a subexponential-time classical precomputation, any adversary can know the exact class group structure; in that case, this ideal evaluation step could possibly be performed in polynomial time (and non-negligible success probability) using LLL-based methods, as discussed in [63] and [19, Sect. 5].

The dHSP algorithm uses the ideal evaluation algorithm as a (quantum) black box, the number of queries depending on the variant. Childs–Jao–Soukharev gave two versions of this algorithm, Kuperberg's [43] and Regev's [55]. However, both are superseded by Kuperberg's recent work [44]: his new algorithm solves the dHSP in any abelian group of order N using $2^{O(\sqrt{\log N})}$ quantum queries and classical space, but only $O(\log N)$ quantum space. Given this estimate, we expect the bit size of q to grow at worst like the square of the security parameter.

Unfortunately, the analysis of Kuperberg's new algorithm is only asymptotic, and limited to N of a special form; it cannot be directly used to draw conclusions on concrete cryptographic parameters at this stage, especially since the value of the constant hidden by the $O()$ in the exponent is unclear. Thus, it is hard to estimate the impact of this attack at concrete security levels such as those required by NIST [53].

Nevertheless, we remark that the first version of Kuperberg's algorithm, as described in [55, Algorithm 5.1 and Remark 5.2] requires $O(2^{3\sqrt{\log N}} \log N)$ black-box queries and $\sim 2^{3\sqrt{\log N}}$ qubits of memory. Although the quantum memory requirements of this algorithm are rather high, we will take its query complexity as a crude lower bound for the complexity of Kuperberg's newer algorithm in the general case. Of course, this assumption is only heuristic, and should be validated by further study of quantum dHSP solvers; at present time, unfortunately, no precise statement can be made.

Table 1 thus proposes various parameter sizes, with associated numbers of quantum queries based on the observations above; we also indicate the estimated time to (classically) precompute the class group structure according to [5].[8] Whenever the quantum query complexity alone is enough to put a parameter in one of NIST's security categories [53], we indicate it in the table. We believe that using query complexity alone is a very conservative choice, and should give more than enough confidence in the post-quantum security properties of our scheme.

The system parameters we proposed in Sect. 4 correspond to the first line of Table 1, thus offering at least 56-bit quantum and 128-bit classical security.

5.3   Security Proofs

We now formalize the assumptions needed to prove the security of the key exchange protocol, and other derived protocols such as PKEs and KEMs, in various models. Given the similarity with the classical Diffie–Hellman protocol on a cyclic group, our assumptions are mostly modeled on those used in that context. Here we are essentially following the lead of Couveignes [19] and Stolbunov [62,63]. However, we take their analyses a step further by explicitly modeling the hardness of distinguishing random walks on Cayley graphs from

---

[8] Computing the class group structure is an instance of the hidden subgroup problem, and thus can be solved in quantum polynomial time by Shor's algorithm.

Table 1. Suggested parameter sizes and associated classical security, class group computation time, and query complexity, using the heuristic estimations of Sect. 5.2.

$\log \Delta_K$	$\log h(\mathcal{O}_K)$	classical security	$L_{|\Delta_K|}(1/2,1)$	quantum queries	NIST category
512	256	2^{128}	$2^{56.6}$	$> 2^{56}$	
688	344	2^{172}	$2^{67.0}$	$> 2^{64}$	1
768	384	2^{192}	$2^{71.4}$	$> 2^{67}$	1
1024	512	2^{256}	$2^{84.2}$	$> 2^{76}$	1
1656	828	2^{414}	$2^{110.8}$	$> 2^{96}$	3
3068	1534	2^{767}	$2^{156.9}$	$> 2^{128}$	5

the uniform distribution: this yields stronger proofs and a better separation of security concerns.

For the rest of this section q is a prime power, $\mathcal{O}$ is an order in a quadratic imaginary field with discriminant $\Delta \sim q$, $\mathcal{C}(\mathcal{O})$ is the class group of $\mathcal{O}$, $\mathrm{Ell}_q(\mathcal{O})$ is the (non-empty) set of elliptic curves with complex multiplication by $\mathcal{O}$, and E_0 is a fixed curve in $\mathrm{Ell}_q(\mathcal{O})$. Finally, S is a set of ideals of $\mathcal{O}$ with norm polynomial in $\log q$, and σ is a probability distribution on the set S^* of isogeny walks (i.e. finite sequences of elements in S) used to sample secrets in the key exchange protocol. We write $x \overset{\sigma}{\in} X$ for an element taken from a set X according to σ, and $x \overset{R}{\in} X$ for an element taken according to the uniform distribution.

Our security proofs use four distributions on $\mathrm{Ell}_q(\mathcal{O})^3$:

$$\mathcal{G}_{q,\Delta} := \left\{ (\mathfrak{a}{\cdot}E_0, \mathfrak{b}{\cdot}E_0, \mathfrak{a}\mathfrak{b}{\cdot}E_0) \,\middle|\, \mathfrak{a}, \mathfrak{b} \overset{R}{\in} \mathcal{C}(\mathcal{O}) \right\},$$

$$\mathcal{W}_{q,\Delta,\sigma} := \left\{ ((\mathfrak{a}_i)_i{\cdot}E_0, (\mathfrak{b}_j)_j{\cdot}E_0, (\mathfrak{a}_i)_i{\cdot}(\mathfrak{b}_j)_j{\cdot}E_0) \,\middle|\, (\mathfrak{a}_i)_i, (\mathfrak{b}_j)_j \overset{\sigma}{\in} S^* \right\},$$

$$\mathcal{R}_{q,\Delta,\sigma} := \left\{ ((\mathfrak{a}_i)_i{\cdot}E_0, (\mathfrak{b}_i)_i{\cdot}E_0, E') \,\middle|\, (\mathfrak{a}_i)_i, (\mathfrak{b}_i)_i \overset{\sigma}{\in} S^*, \ E' \overset{R}{\in} \mathrm{Ell}_q(\mathcal{O}) \right\},$$

$$\mathcal{U}_{q,\Delta} := \left\{ (E_a, E_b, E_{ab}) \,\middle|\, E_a, E_b, E_{ab} \overset{R}{\in} \mathrm{Ell}_q(\mathcal{O}) \right\}.$$

The assumption needed to prove security of the protocols is the hardness of a problem analogous to the classic Decisional Diffie–Hellman (DDH) problem.

Definition 1 (Isogeny Walk DDH (IW-DDH)). *Given a triplet of curves* (E_a, E_b, E_{ab}) *sampled with probability* $\frac{1}{2}$ *from* $\mathcal{R}_{q,\Delta,\sigma}$ *and* $\frac{1}{2}$ *from* $\mathcal{W}_{q,\Delta,\sigma}$, *decide from which it was sampled.*

We split this problem into two finer-grained problems. The first is that of distinguishing between commutative squares sampled uniformly at random and commutative squares sampled from the distribution σ.

Definition 2 (Isogeny Walk Distinguishing (IWD)). *Given a triplet of curves* (E_a, E_b, E_{ab}) *sampled with probability* $\frac{1}{2}$ *from* $\mathcal{W}_{q,\Delta,\sigma}$ *and* $\frac{1}{2}$ *from* $\mathcal{G}_{q,\Delta}$, *decide from which it was sampled.*

The second problem is a group-action analogue of DDH. It also appears in [19] under the name *vectorization*, and in [62,63] under the name DDHAP.

Definition 3 (Class Group Action DDH (CGA-DDH)). *Given a triplet of curves* (E_a, E_b, E_{ab}) *sampled with probability* $\frac{1}{2}$ *from* $\mathcal{G}_{q,\Delta}$ *and* $\frac{1}{2}$ *from* $\mathcal{U}_{q,\Delta}$, *decide from which it was sampled.*

We want to prove the security of protocols based on the primitive of Sect. 3 under the CGA-DDH and IWD assumptions combined. To do this we give a lemma showing that CGA-DDH and IWD together imply IW-DDH. The technique is straightforward: we use an IW-DDH oracle to solve both the CGA-DDH and IWD problems, showing that at least one of the two must be solvable with non-negligible advantage. The only technical difficulty is that we need an efficient way to simulate the uniform distribution on $\text{Ell}_q(\mathcal{O})$; for this, we use another Cayley graph on $\text{Ell}_q(\mathcal{O})$, with a potentially larger edge set, that is proven in [37] to be an expander under the generalized Riemann hypothesis (GRH).

We let $\text{Adv}^A_{\text{IW-DDH}}$ be the *advantage* of an adversary A against IW-DDH, defined as the probability that A answers correctly, minus $1/2$:

$$2\text{Adv}^A_{\text{IW-DDH}} = \Pr\left[A(\mathcal{R}_{q,\Delta,\sigma}) = 1\right] - \Pr\left[A(\mathcal{W}_{q,\Delta,\sigma}) = 1\right].$$

We define $\text{Adv}^A_{\text{CGA-DDH}}$ and $\text{Adv}^A_{\text{IWD}}$ similarly. Switching answers if needed, we can assume all advantages are positive. We let $\text{Adv}_X(t)$ denote the maximum of Adv^A_X over all adversaries using at most t resources (running time, queries, etc.).

Lemma 1. *Assuming GRH, for q large enough and for any bound t on running time, and for any $\epsilon > 0$,*

$$\text{Adv}_{IW\text{-}DDH}(t) \le 2\text{Adv}_{IWD}(t + \text{poly}(\log q, \log \epsilon)) + \text{Adv}_{CGA\text{-}DDH}(t) + \epsilon.$$

Proof (Sketch). We start with an adversary A for IW-DDH, and we construct two simulators S and T for CGA-DDH and IWD respectively.

- The simulator S simply passes its inputs to A, and returns A's response.
- The simulator T receives a triplet (E_a, E_b, E_{ab}) taken from $\mathcal{G}_{q,\Delta}$ or $\mathcal{W}_{q,\Delta,\sigma}$, and flips a coin to decide which of the two following actions it will do:
  - forward (E_a, E_b, E_{ab}) to A, and return the bit given by A; or
  - generate a random curve $E_c \in \text{Ell}_q(\mathcal{O})$, forward (E_a, E_b, E_c) to A, and return the opposite bit to the one given by A.

The curve E_c must be sampled from a distribution close to uniform for the simulator T to work. The only way at our disposal to sample E_c uniformly would be to sample a uniform $\mathfrak{c} \in \mathcal{C}(\mathcal{O})$ and take $E_c = \mathfrak{c} \cdot E_0$, but this would be too costly. Instead we use [37, Theorem 1.5], combined with standard results about random walks in expander graphs (for instance, an easy adaptation of the proof of [37, Lemma 2.1]), to sample E_c so that any curve in $\text{Ell}_q(\mathcal{O})$ is taken with probability between $(1 - \epsilon)/h(\mathcal{O})$ and $(1 + \epsilon)/h(\mathcal{O})$, using only $\text{poly}(\log q, \log \epsilon)$ operations.

We can consider this sampling as follows: with probability $1 - \epsilon$, sample E_c uniformly, and with probability ϵ sample it from an unknown distribution.

Now, if T forwarded (E_a, E_b, E_{ab}) untouched, then we immediately get

$$2\mathsf{Adv}_{\mathrm{IWD}}^{T} = \mathsf{Adv}_{\mathrm{IW\text{-}DDH}}^{A} - \mathsf{Adv}_{\mathrm{CGA\text{-}DDH}}^{S};$$

if T forwarded (E_a, E_b, E_c), then we get

$$2\mathsf{Adv}_{\mathrm{IWD}}^{T} \geq \mathsf{Adv}_{\mathrm{IW\text{-}DDH}}^{A} - (1 - \epsilon)\mathsf{Adv}_{\mathrm{CGA\text{-}DDH}}^{S} - \epsilon.$$

Averaging over the two outcomes concludes the proof. ☐

Finally, we define an isogeny-walk analogue of the classic Computational Diffie–Hellman (CDH) problem for groups. Using the same techniques as above, we can prove the security of the relevant protocols based only on CGA-CDH and IWD, without the generalized Riemann hypothesis.

Definition 4 (Class Group Action CDH (CGA-CDH)). *Given $E_a = \mathfrak{a}{\cdot}E_0$ and $E_b = \mathfrak{b}{\cdot}E_0$ with $\mathfrak{a}, \mathfrak{b} \overset{R}{\in} \mathcal{C}(\mathcal{O})$, compute the curve $E_{ab} = \mathfrak{a}\mathfrak{b}{\cdot}E_0$.*

Stolbunov proved the security of HHS Diffie–Hellman under the equivalent of CGA-DDH [62]. Repeating the same steps, we can prove the following theorem.

Theorem 1. *If the CGA-DDH and IWD assumptions hold, assuming GRH, the key-agreement protocol defined by Algorithms 8 and 9 is session-key secure in the authenticated-links adversarial model of Canetti and Krawczyk [11].*

Similarly, we can prove the IND-CPA security of the hashed ElGamal protocol derived from Algorithm 8 by replicating the techniques of e.g. [30, Sect. 20.4.11].

Theorem 2. *Assuming CGA-CDH and IWD, the hashed ElGamal protocol derived from Algorithms 8 and 9 is IND-CPA secure in the random oracle model.*

A heuristic discussion of the IWD assumption. From its very definition, the IWD problem depends on the probability distribution σ we use to sample random walks in the isogeny graph. In this paragraph, we provide heuristic arguments suggesting that the IWD instances generated by Algorithm 9 are hard, provided

1. the keyspace size is at least $\sqrt{|\Delta_K|}$, and
2. S is *not too small*, i.e. the number of isogeny degrees used is in $\Omega(\log q)$.

Proving rapid mixing of isogeny walks with such parameters seems out of reach at present, even under number-theoretic hypotheses such as GRH. The best results available, like [37, Theorem 1.5] (used in the proof of Lemma 1), typically require isogeny degrees in $\Omega((\log q)^B)$ for some $B > 2$, and fully random walks that are not, for example, skewed towards smaller-degree isogenies.

However, numerical evidence suggests that these theoretical results are too weak. In [37, 7.2], it is asked whether an analogue of the previous theorem would be true with the sole constraint $B > 1$. In [31, Sect. 3], it is mentioned that many fewer split primes are needed to walk in the isogeny graph than theoretically expected. Practical evidence also suggests that the rapid mixing properties are not lost with skewed random walks: such walks are used in [28] to accelerate an algorithm solving Problem 1. We believe that these experiments can bring some evidence in favor of relying on the IWD assumptions with more aggressive parameters than those provided by GRH, although further investigation is required.

5.4   Key Validation and Active Security

Modern practice in cryptography mandates the use of stronger security notions than IND-CPA. From the DLP assumption, it is easy to construct protocols with strong security against active adversaries. For example, it is well-known that the hashed ElGamal KEM achieves IND-CCA security in the random oracle model under various assumptions [1,2,20].

All of these constructions crucially rely on *key validation*: that is, Alice must verify that the public data sent by Bob defines valid protocol data (e.g., valid elements of a cyclic group), or abort if this is not the case. Failure to perform key validation may result in catastrophic attacks, such as small subgroup [46], invalid point [6], and invalid curve attacks [14].

In our context, key validation amounts to verifying that the curve sent by Bob really is an element of $\mathrm{Ell}_q(\mathcal{O}_K)$. Failure to do so exposes Alice to an *invalid graph attack*, where Bob forces Alice onto an isogeny class with much smaller discriminant, or different Elkies primes, and learns something on Alice's secret.

Fortunately, key validation is relatively easy for protocols based on the CRS primitive. All we need to check is that the received j-invariant corresponds to a curve with the right order, and with maximal endomorphism ring.

Verifying the curve order. Since we already know the trace t of the Frobenius endomorphism of all curves in $\mathrm{Ell}_q(\mathcal{O})$, we only need to check that the given E has order $q + 1 - t$. Assuming that E is cyclic, or contains a cyclic group of order larger than $4\sqrt{q}$, a very efficient randomized algorithm consists in taking a random point P and verifying that it has the expected order. This task is easy if the factorization of $q + 1 - t$ is known.

Concretely, the curve given in Sect. 4 has order

$$N = 2^2 \cdot 3^2 \cdot 5 \cdot 7 \cdot 11 \cdot 13^2 \cdot 17 \cdot 103 \cdot 523 \cdot 821 \cdot 1174286389 \cdot (\text{432-bit prime}),$$

and its group structure is $\mathbb{Z}/2\mathbb{Z} \times \mathbb{Z}/\frac{N}{2}\mathbb{Z}$. To check that a curve is in the same isogeny class, we repeatedly take random points until we find one of order $N/2$.

Verifying the endomorphism ring level. The curve order verification proves that $\mathrm{End}(E)$ is contained between $\mathbb{Z}[\pi]$ and $\mathcal{O}_K$. We have already seen that there is only a finite number of possible rings: their indices in $\mathcal{O}_K$ must divide d where $d^2 = \Delta_\pi/\Delta_K$. Ascending and descending isogenies connect curves with different endomorphism rings, thus we are left with the problem of verifying that E is on the crater of any ℓ-volcano for $\ell \mid d$. Assuming no large prime divides d, this check can be accomplished efficiently by performing random walks in the volcanoes, as described in [41, Sect. 4.2] or [26]. Note that if we choose Δ_π square-free, then the only possible endomorphism ring is $\mathcal{O}_K$, and there is nothing to be done.

Concretely, for the curve of Sect. 4 we have $\Delta_\pi / \Delta_K = 2^2$, so there are exactly two possible endomorphism rings. Looking at the action of the Frobenius endomorphism, we see that $\mathrm{End}(E) = \mathcal{O}_K$ if and only if $E[2] \simeq (\mathbb{Z}/2\mathbb{Z})^2$.

Example 2. Let p and $\mathcal{O}$ be as in Sect. 4. Suppose we are given the value

$$\alpha = \frac{67746537624003763704733620725115945552778190049699052959500793811735672493775}{18737748913882816398715695086623890791069381771311397884649111333755665289025}$$

in $\mathbb{F}_p$. It is claimed that α is in $\mathrm{Ell}_p(\mathcal{O})$; that is, it is a valid public key for the system with parameters defined in Sect. 4. Following the discussion above, to validate α as a public key, it suffices to exhibit a curve with j-invariant α, full rational 2-torsion, and a point of order $N/2$. Using standard formulæ, we find that the two $\mathbb{F}_p$-isomorphism classes of elliptic curves with j-invariant α are represented by the Montgomery curve $E_\alpha/\mathbb{F}_p : y^2 = x(x^2 + Ax + 1)$ with

$$A = \frac{41938099794353656685283683753335350833889799939411549418804218343694887415884}{66125999279694898695485836446054238175461312078403116671641017301728201394907}$$

and its quadratic twist E'_α. Checking the 2-torsion first, we have $E_\alpha[2](\mathbb{F}_p) \cong E'_\alpha[2](\mathbb{F}_p) \cong (\mathbb{Z}/2\mathbb{Z})^2$, because $A^2 - 4$ is a square in $\mathbb{F}_p$. Trying points on E_α, we find that $(23, \sqrt{23(23^2 + 23A + 1)})$ in $E_\alpha(\mathbb{F}_p)$ has exact order $N/2$. We conclude that $\mathrm{End}(E_\alpha) = \mathcal{O}$, so α is a valid public key. (In fact, E_α is connected to the initial curve by a single 3-isogeny step.)

Consequences for cryptographic constructions. Since both of the checks above can be done much more efficiently than evaluating a single isogeny walk, we conclude that key validation is not only possible, but highly efficient for protocols based on the CRS construction. This stands in stark contrast to the case of SIDH, where key validation is known to be problematic [32], and even conjectured to be as hard as breaking the system [68].

Thanks to this efficient key validation, we can obtain CCA-secure encryption from the CRS action without resorting to generic transforms such as Fujisaki–Okamoto [27], unlike the case of SIKE [4,34]. This in turn enables applications such as non-interactive key exchange, for which no practical post-quantum scheme was known prior to [12].

6   Experimental Results

In order to demonstrate that our protocol is usable at standard security levels, we implemented it in the Julia programming language. This proof of concept also allowed us to estimate isogeny step costs, which we needed to generate the initial curve in Sect. 4. We developed several Julia packages[9], built upon the

---

[9] The main code is available at https://github.com/defeo/hhs-keyex/, and the additional dependencies at https://github.com/defeo/EllipticCurves.jl/ and https://github.com/defeo/ClassPolynomials.jl/.

computer algebra package Nemo [25]. Experiments were conducted using Julia 0.6 and Nemo 0.7.3 on Linux, with an Intel Core i7-5600U cpu at 2.60 GHz.

Consider the time to compute one step for an ideal $\mathfrak{s} = (\ell, \pi - \lambda)$. Using Elkies steps, this is approximately the cost of finding the roots of the modular polynomial: roughly $0.017 \cdot \ell$ seconds in our implementation. Using Vélu steps, the cost is approximately that of one scalar multiplication in $E(\mathbb{F}_{q^r})$; timings for the extension degrees r relevant to our parameters appear in Table 2.

Table 2. Timings for computing scalar multiplications in $E(\mathbb{F}_{p^r})$, the dominant operation in VÉLUSTEP (Algorithm 6), as a function of the extension degree r.

r	1	3	4	5	7	8	9
time (s)	0.02	0.10	0.15	0.24	0.8	1.15	1.3

Using this data, finding efficient walk length bounds M_ℓ offering a sufficient keyspace size is easily seen to be an integer optimization problem. We used the following heuristic procedure to find a satisfactory solution. Given a time bound T, let KEYSPACESIZE(T) be the keyspace size obtained when each M_ℓ is the greatest such that the *total time spent on ℓ-isogenies* is less than T. Then, if n is the (classical) security parameter, we look for the *least* T such that KEYSPACESIZE(T) $\geq 2^{2n}$ (according to Sect. 5), using binary search. While the M_ℓ we obtain are most likely not the best possible, intuitively the outcome is not too far from optimal.

In this way, we obtain a proposal for the walk length bounds M_ℓ to be used in Algorithm 8 along with the curve found in Sect. 4, to achieve 128-bit classical security. Table 3 lists the isogeny degrees amenable to Algorithm 6, each with the corresponding extension degree r (a star denotes that the twisted curve allows us to use both directions in the isogeny graph, as in Remark 1). Table 4 lists other primes for which we apply Algorithm 5.

Table 3. Primes ℓ amenable to Algorithm 6 (VÉLUSTEP) for our candidate isogeny graph, with corresponding extension degrees r and proposed walk length bounds M_ℓ.

r	M_ℓ	ℓ	r	M_ℓ	ℓ	r	M_ℓ	ℓ
1*	409	3, 5, 7, 11, 13, 17, 103	4	54	1013, 1181	8	7	881
1	409	523, 821, 947, 1723	5	34	31*, 61*, 1321	9	6	37*, 1693
3	81	19*, 661	7	10	29*, 71*, 547			

Using these parameters, we perform one isogeny walk in approximately 520 s. These timings are *worst-case*: the number of isogeny steps is taken to be exactly M_ℓ for each ℓ. This is about as fast as Stolbunov's largest parameter [62], which is for a prime of 428 bits and a keyspace of only 216 bits.

Table 4. Primes ℓ amenable to Algorithm 5 (ELKIESWALK) for our candidate isogeny graph, with proposed walk length bounds M_ℓ.

M_ℓ	ℓ	M_ℓ	ℓ	M_ℓ	ℓ
20	23	6	73	2	157, 163, 167, 191, 193, 197, 223, 229
11	41	5	89	1	241, 251, 257, 277, 283, 293, 307
10	43	4	107, 109, 113	1	317, 349, 359
9	47	3	131, 151		

We stress that our implementation is *not* optimised. General gains in field arithmetic aside, optimised code could easily beat our proof-of-concept implementation at critical points of our algorithms, such as the root finding steps in Algorithms 3 and 4.

For comparison, without Algorithm 6 the total isogeny walk time would exceed 2000 seconds. Our ideas thus yield an improvement by a factor of over 4 over the original protocol. A longer search for efficient public parameters would bring further improvement.

7   Conclusion

We have shown that the Couveignes–Rostovtsev–Stolbunov framework can be improved to become practical at standard pre- and post-quantum security levels; even more so if an optimized C implementation is made. The main obstacle to better performance is the difficulty of generating optimal system parameters: even with a lot of computational power, we cannot expect to produce ordinary curve parameters that allow us to use *only* Vélu steps. In this regard, the CSIDH protocol [12], which overcomes this problem using supersingular curves instead of ordinary ones, is promising.

One particularly nice feature of our protocol is its highly efficient key validation, which opens a lot of cryptographic doors. However, side-channel-resistant implementations remain an interesting problem for future work.

Acknowledgments. We would like to thank Wouter Castryck, Tanja Lange, Chloe Martindale, Lorenz Panny, and Joost Renes for sharing a draft of their paper with us, and Alexandre Gélin and François Morain for fruitful discussions. De Feo acknowledges the support of the French *Programme d'Investissements d'Avenir* under the national project RISQ n° P141580-3069086/DOS0044212.

References

1. Abdalla, M., Bellare, M., Rogaway, P.: DHAES: an encryption scheme based on the Diffie-Hellman problem. Cryptology ePrint Archive, Report 1999/007 (1999), https://eprint.iacr.org/1999/007

2. Abdalla, M., Bellare, M., Rogaway, P.: The oracle diffie-hellman assumptions and an analysis of DHIES. In: Naccache, D. (ed.) CT-RSA 2001. LNCS, vol. 2020, pp. 143–158. Springer, Heidelberg (2001). https://doi.org/10.1007/3-540-45353-9_12
3. Atkin, A.O.L., Morain, F.: Elliptic curves and primality proving. Math. Comp. **61**(203), 29–68 (1993). https://doi.org/10.2307/2152935
4. Azarderakhsh, R., et al.: Supersingular Isogeny Key Encapsulation (2017). http://sike.org
5. Biasse, J.F., Jacobson, M.J., Silvester, A.K.: Security estimates for quadratic field based cryptosystems. In: Steinfeld, R., Hawkes, P. (eds.) Information Security and Privacy, pp. 233–247. Springer, Berlin, Heidelberg (2010). https://doi.org/10.1007/978-3-642-14081-5_15
6. Biehl, I., Meyer, B., Müller, V.: Differential fault attacks on elliptic curve cryptosystems. In: Bellare, Mihir (ed.) CRYPTO 2000. LNCS, vol. 1880, pp. 131–146. Springer, Heidelberg (2000). https://doi.org/10.1007/3-540-44598-6_8
7. Bostan, A., Morain, F., Salvy, B., Schost, É.: Fast algorithms for computing isogenies between elliptic curves. Math. Comput. **77**(263), 1755–1778 (2008). https://doi.org/10.1090/S0025-5718-08-02066-8
8. Bröker, R., Lauter, K.E., Sutherland, A.V.: Modular polynomials via isogeny volcanoes. Math. Comput. **81**(278), 1201–1231 (2012). https://doi.org/10.1090/S0025-5718-2011-02508-1
9. Bruinier, J.H., Ono, K., Sutherland, A.V.: Class polynomials for nonholomorphic modular functions. J. Num. Theory **161**, 204–229 (2016). https://doi.org/10.1016/j.jnt.2015.07.002
10. Buchmann, J., Williams, H.C.: A key-exchange system based on imaginary quadratic fields. J. Crypt. **1**(2), 107–118 (1988). https://doi.org/10.1007/BF02351719
11. Canetti, R., Krawczyk, H.: Analysis of key-exchange protocols and their use for building secure channels. In: Pfitzmann, B. (ed.) EUROCRYPT 2001. LNCS, vol. 2045, pp. 453–474. Springer, Heidelberg (2001). https://doi.org/10.1007/3-540-44987-6_28
12. Castryck, W., Lange, T., Martindale, C., Panny, L., Renes, J.: CSIDH: an efficient post-quantum commutative group action. In: Galbraith, S.D., Peyrin, T. (eds.) ASIACRYPT 2018, LNCS, vol. 11274, pp. 380–411. Springer (2018)
13. Childs, A., Jao, D., Soukharev, V.: Constructing elliptic curve isogenies in quantum subexponential time. J. Math. Crypto. **8**(1), 1–29 (2014)
14. Ciet, M., Joye, M.: Elliptic curve cryptosystems in the presence of permanent and transient faults. Des. Codes Crypt. **36**(1), 33–43 (2005). https://doi.org/10.1007/s10623-003-1160-8
15. Cohen, H.: A Course in Computational Algebraic Number Theory. Springer, New York (1993). https://doi.org/10.1007/978-3-662-02945-9
16. Cohen, H., Lenstra, H.W.: Heuristics on class groups of number fields. In: Jager, H. (ed.) Number Theory Noordwijkerhout 1983, pp. 33–62. Springer, Heidelberg (1984). https://doi.org/10.1007/BFb0099440
17. Costello, C., Hisil, H.: A simple and compact algorithm for SIDH with arbitrary degree isogenies. In: Takagi, T., Peyrin, T. (eds.) Advances in Cryptology - ASIACRYPT 2017, ASIACRYPT 2017. Lecture Notes in Computer Science, vol. 10625. Springer, Heidelberg (2017). https://doi.org/10.1007/978-3-319-70697-9_11
18. Costello, C., Smith, B.: Montgomery curves and their arithmetic. J. Crypt. Eng. **8**(3), 227–240 (2017). https://doi.org/10.1007/s13389-017-0157-6. hal.inria.fr/hal-01483768

19. Couveignes, J.M.: Hard homogeneous spaces. Cryptology ePrint Archive, Report 2006/291 (2006). https://eprint.iacr.org/2006/291

20. Cramer, R., Shoup, V.: Design and analysis of practical public-key encryption schemes secure against adaptive chosen ciphertext attack. SIAM J. Comput. **33**(1), 167–226 (2003). https://doi.org/10.1137/S0097539702403773

21. De Feo, L.: Mathematics of isogeny based cryptography. CoRR abs/1711.04062 (2017). http://arxiv.org/abs/1711.04062

22. De Feo, L., Hugounenq, C., Plût, J., Schost, É.: Explicit isogenies in quadratic time in any characteristic. LMS J. Comput. Math. **19**(A), 267–282 (2016)

23. Delfs, C., Galbraith, S.D.: Computing isogenies between supersingular elliptic curves over $\mathbb{F}_p$. Des. Codes Cryptography **78**(2), 425–440 (2016). https://doi.org/10.1007/s10623-014-0010-1

24. Serre, J.-P.: A Course in Arithmetic. GTM, vol. 7. Springer, New York (1973). https://doi.org/10.1007/978-1-4684-9884-4

25. Fieker, C., Hart, W., Hofmann, T., Johansson, F.: Nemo/Hecke: computer algebra and number theory packages for the Julia programming language. In: Proceedings of the 2017 ACM on International Symposium on Symbolic and Algebraic Computation, ISSAC 2017, pp. 157–164. ACM, New York, (2017). https://doi.org/10.1145/3087604.3087611

26. Fouquet, M., Morain, F.: Isogeny volcanoes and the SEA algorithm. In: Fieker, C., Kohel, D.R. (eds.) Algorithmic Number Theory, ANTS 2002. Lecture Notes in Computer Science, vol. 2369. Springer, Heidelberg (2002). https://doi.org/10.1007/3-540-45455-1_23

27. Fujisaki, E., Okamoto, T.: Secure integration of asymmetric and symmetric encryption schemes. In: Wiener, M. (ed.) CRYPTO 1999. LNCS, vol. 1666, pp. 537–554. Springer, Heidelberg (1999). https://doi.org/10.1007/3-540-48405-1_34

28. Galbraith, S., Stolbunov, A.: Improved algorithm for the isogeny problem for ordinary elliptic curves. Appl. Algebra Eng. Commun. Comput. **24**(2), 107–131 (2013). https://doi.org/10.1007/s00200-013-0185-0

29. Galbraith, S.D.: Constructing isogenies between elliptic curves over finite fields. LMS J. Comput. Math. **2**, 118–138 (1999). https://doi.org/10.1112/S1461157000000097

30. Galbraith, S.D.: Mathematics of public key cryptography. Cambridge University Press, Cambridge (2012). https://www.math.auckland.ac.nz/sgal018/crypto-book/crypto-book.html

31. Galbraith, S.D., Hess, F., Smart, N.P.: Extending the GHS weil descent attack. In: Knudsen, L.R. (ed.) EUROCRYPT 2002. LNCS, vol. 2332, pp. 29–44. Springer, Heidelberg (2002). https://doi.org/10.1007/3-540-46035-7_3

32. Galbraith, S.D., Petit, C., Shani, B., Ti, Y.B.: On the security of supersingular isogeny cryptosystems. In: Cheon, J.H., Takagi, T. (eds.) ASIACRYPT 2016. LNCS, vol. 10031, pp. 63–91. Springer, Heidelberg (2016). https://doi.org/10.1007/978-3-662-53887-6_3

33. Hamdy, S., Möller, B.: Security of cryptosystems based on class groups of imaginary quadratic orders. In: Okamoto, T. (ed.) ASIACRYPT 2000. LNCS, vol. 1976, pp. 234–247. Springer, Heidelberg (2000). https://doi.org/10.1007/3-540-44448-3_18

34. Hofheinz, D., Hövelmanns, K., Kiltz, E.: A modular analysis of the fujisaki-okamoto transformation. In: Kalai, Y., Reyzin, L. (eds.) TCC 2017. LNCS, vol. 10677, pp. 341–371. Springer, Cham (2017). https://doi.org/10.1007/978-3-319-70500-2_12

35. Ionica, S., Joux, A.: Pairing the volcano. Math. Comput. **82**(281), 581–603 (2013)

36. Jao, D., De Feo, L.: Towards quantum-resistant cryptosystems from supersingular elliptic curve isogenies. In: Yang, B.Y. (ed.) Post-Quantum Cryptography, PQCrypto 2011. Lecture Notes in Computer Science, vol. 7071. Springer, Heidelberg (2011). https://doi.org/10.1007/978-3-642-25405-5_2
37. Jao, D., Miller, S.D., Venkatesan, R.: Expander graphs based on GRH with an application to elliptic curve cryptography. J. Number Theory **129**(6), 1491–1504 (2009). https://doi.org/10.1016/j.jnt.2008.11.006
38. Jao, D., Soukharev, V.: A subexponential algorithm for evaluating large degree isogenies. In: Hanrot, G., Morain, F., Thomé, E. (eds.) Algorithmic Number Theory, ANTS 2010. Lecture Notes in Computer Science, vol. 6197. Springer, Heidelberg (2010). https://doi.org/10.1007/978-3-642-14518-6_19
39. Kieffer, J.: Étude et accélération du protocole d'échange de clés de Couveignes-Rostovtsev-Stolbunov. Master's thesis, Inria Saclay & Université Paris VI (2017)
40. Ko, K.H., Lee, S.J., Cheon, J.H., Han, J.W., Kang, J., Park, C.: New public-key cryptosystem using braid groups. In: Bellare, M. (ed.) CRYPTO 2000. LNCS, vol. 1880, pp. 166–183. Springer, Heidelberg (2000). https://doi.org/10.1007/3-540-44598-6_10
41. Kohel, D.R.: Endomorphism rings of elliptic curves over finite fields. Ph.D. thesis, University of California at Berkley (1996)
42. Kohel, D.R.: Echidna databases (2018). http://iml.univ-mrs.fr/~kohel/dbs/
43. Kuperberg, G.: A subexponential-time quantum algorithm for the dihedral hidden subgroup problem. SIAM J. Comput. **35**(1), 170–188 (2005)
44. Kuperberg, G.: Another subexponential-time quantum algorithm for the dihedral hidden subgroup problem. In: Severini, S., Brandao, F. (eds.) 8th Conference on the Theory of Quantum Computation, Communication and Cryptography (TQC 2013), Leibniz International Proceedings in Informatics (LIPIcs), vol. 22, pp. 20–34. Schloss Dagstuhl-Leibniz-Zentrum fuer Informatik, Dagstuhl, Germany (2013). https://doi.org/10.4230/LIPIcs.TQC.2013.20, http://drops.dagstuhl.de/opus/volltexte/2013/4321
45. Lang, S.: Elliptic Functions Graduate Texts in Mathematics. Springer, New York (1987). https://doi.org/10.1007/978-1-4612-4752-4
46. Lim, C.H., Lee, P.J.: A key recovery attack on discrete log-based schemes using a prime order subgroup. In: Kaliski, B.S. (ed.) CRYPTO 1997. LNCS, vol. 1294, pp. 249–263. Springer, Heidelberg (1997). https://doi.org/10.1007/BFb0052240
47. Littlewood, J.E.: On the class-number of the corpus $p(\sqrt{k})$. Proc. London Math. Soc. **2**(1), 358–372 (1928)
48. Maze, G., Monico, C., Rosenthal, J.: Public key cryptography based on semigroup actions. Adv. Math. Commun. **1**(4), 489–507 (2007). https://doi.org/10.3934/amc.2007.1.489
49. Mestre, J.: La méthode des graphes. Exemples et applications. In: Proceedings of the International Conference on Class Numbers and Fundamental Units of Algebraic Number Fields (Katata), pp. 217–242 (1986)
50. Miret, J.M., Moreno, R., Sadornil, D., Tena, J., Valls, M.: An algorithm to compute volcanoes of 2-isogenies of elliptic curves over finite fields. Appli. Math. Comput. **176**(2), 739–750 (2006)
51. Montgomery, P.L.: Speeding the pollard and elliptic curve methods of factorization. Math. comput. **48**(177), 243–264 (1987)
52. Morain, F.: Calcul du nombre de points sur une courbe elliptique dans un corps fini: aspects algorithmiques. J. Théor. Nombres Bordeaux **7**(1), 255–282 (1995). http://jtnb.cedram.org/item?id=JTNB_1995__7_1_255_0, les Dix-huitièmes Journées Arithmétiques, Bordeaux (1993)

53. National institute of standards and technology: announcing request for nominations for public-key post-quantum cryptographic algorithms (2016). https://www.federalregister.gov/d/2016-30615

54. Okeya, K., Kurumatani, H., Sakurai, K.: Elliptic curves with the montgomery-form and their cryptographic applications. In: Imai, H., Zheng, Y. (eds.) Public Key Cryptography, PKC 2000. Lecture Notes in Computer Science, vol. 1751. Springer, Heidelberg (2000). https://doi.org/10.1007/978-3-540-46588-1_17

55. Regev, O.: A subexponential time algorithm for the dihedral hidden subgroup problem with polynomial space June 2004. arXiv:quant-ph/0406151. http://arxiv.org/abs/quant-ph/0406151

56. Renes, J.: Computing isogenies between montgomery curves using the action of (0, 0). In: Lange, T., Steinwandt, R. (eds.) PQCrypto 2018. LNCS, vol. 10786, pp. 229–247. Springer, Cham (2018). https://doi.org/10.1007/978-3-319-79063-3_11

57. Rostovtsev, A., Stolbunov, A.: Public-key cryptosystem based on isogenies. Cryptology ePrint Archive, Report 2006/145 April 2006. http://eprint.iacr.org/2006/145/

58. Schoof, R.: Counting points on elliptic curves over finite fields. J. de Théorie des Nombres de Bordeaux **7**(1), 219–254 (1995)

59. Silverman, J.H.: The Arithmetic of Elliptic Curves. GTM, vol. 106. Springer, New York (2009). https://doi.org/10.1007/978-0-387-09494-6

60. Silverman, J.H.: Advanced Topics in the Arithmetic of Elliptic Curves Graduate Texts in Mathematics. Springer, New York (1994)

61. Stolbunov, A.: Reductionist security arguments for public-key cryptographic schemes based on group action. In: Mjølsnes, S.F., (ed.) Norsk informasjonssikkerhetskonferanse (NISK) (2009)

62. Stolbunov, A.: Constructing public-key cryptographic schemes based on class group action on a set of isogenous elliptic curves. Adv. Math. Commun. **4**(2), 215–235 (2010)

63. Stolbunov, A.: Cryptographic schemes based on isogenies (2012)

64. Sutherland, A.V.: Accelerating the CM method. LMS J. Comput. Math. **15**, 172–204 (2012). https://doi.org/10.1112/S1461157012001015

65. Sutherland, A.V.: Constructing elliptic curves over finite fields with prescribed torsion. Math. Comput. **81**, 1131–1147 (2012)

66. Sutherland, A.V.: Modular polynomials (2018). https://math.mit.edu/~drew/ClassicalModPolys.html

67. Teske, E.: An elliptic curve trapdoor system. J. Crypt. **19**(1), 115–133 (2006). https://doi.org/10.1007/s00145-004-0328-3

68. Urbanik, D., Jao, D.: SoK: The problem landscape of SIDH. Cryptology ePrint Archive, Report 2018/336 (2018). https://doi.org/10.1145/3197507.3197516, https://eprint.iacr.org/2018/336

69. Vélu, J.: Isogénies entre courbes elliptiques. C. R. Acad. Sci. Paris Sér. A-B 273, A238–A241 (1971)

70. Zimmermann, P., Dodson, B.: 20 years of ECM. In: Hess, F., Pauli, S., Pohst, M. (eds.) Algorithmic Number Theory, ANTS 2006. Lecture Notes in Computer Science, vol. 4076, pp. 525–542. Springer, Heidelberg (2006). https://doi.org/10.1007/11792086_37

71. Zimmermann, P., et al.: GMP-ECM software (2018). http://ecm.gforge.inria.fr/

CSIDH: An Efficient Post-Quantum Commutative Group Action

Wouter Castryck[1], Tanja Lange[2], Chloe Martindale[2], Lorenz Panny[2], and Joost Renes[3]

[1] Department of Mathematics, imec-COSIC, KU Leuven, Leuven, Belgium
`wouter.castryck@esat.kuleuven.be`
[2] Department of Mathematics and Computer Science,
Eindhoven University of Technology, Eindhoven, The Netherlands
`tanja@hyperelliptic.org`, `chloemartindale@gmail.com`, `lorenz@yx7.cc`
[3] Digital Security Group, Radboud Universiteit, Nijmegen, The Netherlands
`j.renes@cs.ru.nl`

Abstract. We propose an efficient commutative group action suitable for non-interactive key exchange in a post-quantum setting. Our construction follows the layout of the Couveignes–Rostovtsev–Stolbunov cryptosystem, but we apply it to supersingular elliptic curves defined over a large prime field $\mathbb{F}_p$, rather than to ordinary elliptic curves. The Diffie–Hellman scheme resulting from the group action allows for public-key validation at very little cost, runs reasonably fast in practice, and has public keys of only 64 bytes at a conjectured AES-128 security level, matching NIST's post-quantum security category I.

Keywords: Post-quantum cryptography · Class-group action Isogeny-based cryptography · Non-interactive key exchange Key confirmation

1 Introduction

During the past five to ten years, elliptic-curve cryptography (ECC) has taken over public-key cryptography on the internet and in security applications. Many protocols such as Signal (https://signal.org) or TLS 1.3 rely on the small key sizes and efficient computations to achieve forward secrecy, often meaning that keys are used only once. However, it is also important to notice that security does

Author list in alphabetical order; See https://www.ams.org/profession/leaders/culture/CultureStatement04.pdf. This work was supported in part by the Commission of the European Communities through the Horizon 2020 program under project number 643161 (ECRYPT-NET), 645622 (PQCRYPTO), 645421 (ECRYPT-CSA), and CHIST-ERA USEIT (NWO project 651.002.004); the Technology Foundation STW (project 13499 – TYPHOON) from the Dutch government; and the Research Foundation - Flanders (FWO) through the WOG Coding Theory and Cryptography. The first listed author is affiliated on a free basis with the Department of Mathematics, Ghent University. Date of this document: 2018.09.07.

T. Peyrin and S. Galbraith (Eds.): ASIACRYPT 2018, LNCS 11274, pp. 395–427, 2018.
https://doi.org/10.1007/978-3-030-03332-3_15

not break down if keys are reused. Indeed, some implementations of TLS, such as Microsoft's SChannel, reuse keys for some fixed amount of time rather than for one connection [2]. Google's QUIC (https://chromium.org/quic) relies on servers keeping their keys fixed for a while to achieve quick session resumption. Several more examples are given by Freire, Hofheinz, Kiltz, and Paterson in their paper [25] formalizing non-interactive key exchange. Some applications require this functionality and for many it provides significant savings in terms of roundtrips or implementation complexity. Finding a post-quantum system that permits non-interactive key exchange while still offering decent performance is considered an open problem. Our paper presents a solution to this problem.

Isogeny-based cryptography is a relatively new kind of elliptic-curve cryptography, whose security relies on (various incarnations of) the problem of finding an explicit isogeny between two given isogenous elliptic curves over a finite field $\mathbb{F}_q$. One of the main selling points is that quantum computers do not seem to make the isogeny-finding problem substantially easier. This contrasts with regular elliptic-curve cryptography, which is based on the discrete-logarithm problem in a group and therefore falls prey to a polynomial-time quantum algorithm designed by Shor in 1994 [57].

The first proposal of an isogeny-based cryptosystem was made by Couveignes in 1997 [17]. It described a non-interactive key exchange protocol where the space of public keys equals the set of $\mathbb{F}_q$-isomorphism classes of ordinary elliptic curves over $\mathbb{F}_q$ whose endomorphism ring is a given order $\mathcal{O}$ in an imaginary quadratic field and whose trace of Frobenius has a prescribed value. It is well-known that the ideal-class group $\mathrm{cl}(\mathcal{O})$ acts freely and transitively on this set through the application of isogenies. Couveignes' central observation was that the commutativity of $\mathrm{cl}(\mathcal{O})$ naturally allows for a key-exchange protocol in the style of Diffie and Hellman [23]. His work was only circulated privately and thus not picked up by the community; the corresponding paper [17] was never formally published and posted on ePrint only in 2006. The method was eventually independently rediscovered by Rostovtsev and Stolbunov in 2004 (in Stolbunov's master's thesis [60] and published on ePrint as [54] in 2006). In 2010, Childs, Jao and Soukharev [12] showed that breaking the Couveignes–Rostovtsev–Stolbunov scheme amounts to solving an instance of the abelian hidden-shift problem, for which quantum algorithms with a time complexity of $L_q[1/2]$ are known to exist; see [43,52]. While this may be tolerable (e.g., classical subexponential factorization methods have not ended the widespread use of RSA), a much bigger concern is that the scheme is unacceptably slow: despite recent clever speed-ups due to De Feo, Kieffer, and Smith [21,41], several minutes are needed for a single key exchange at a presumed classical security level of 128 bits. Nevertheless, in view of its conceptual simplicity, compactness, and flexibility, it seems a shame to discard the Couveignes–Rostovtsev–Stolbunov scheme.

The attack due to Childs–Jao–Soukharev strongly relies on the fact that $\mathrm{cl}(\mathcal{O})$ is commutative, hence indirectly on the fact that $\mathcal{O}$ is commutative. This led Jao and De Feo [38] to consider the use of supersingular elliptic curves, whose full ring of endomorphisms is an order in a quaternion algebra; in particular it is non-commutative. Their resulting (interactive) key-agreement scheme, which nowadays goes under the name "Supersingular Isogeny Diffie–Hellman" (SIDH), has attracted almost the entire focus of isogeny-based cryptography over the past six years. The current state-of-the-art implementation is SIKE [37], which was recently submitted to the NIST competition on post-quantum cryptography [48].

It should be stressed that SIDH is *not* the Couveignes–Rostovtsev–Stolbunov scheme in which one substitutes supersingular elliptic curves for ordinary elliptic curves; in fact SIDH is much more reminiscent of a cryptographic hash function from 2006 due to Charles, Goren, and Lauter [11]. SIDH's public keys consist of the codomain of a secret isogeny and the image points of certain public points under that isogeny. Galbraith, Petit, Shani, and Ti showed in [29] that SIDH keys succumb to active attacks and thus should not be reused, unless combined with a CCA transform such as the Fujisaki–Okamoto transform [26].

In this paper we show that adapting the Couveignes–Rostovtsev–Stolbunov scheme to supersingular elliptic curves is possible, provided that one restricts to supersingular elliptic curves defined over a prime field $\mathbb{F}_p$. Instead of the full ring of endomorphisms, which is non-commutative, one should consider the subring of $\mathbb{F}_p$-rational endomorphisms, which is again an order $\mathcal{O}$ in an imaginary quadratic field. As before $\mathrm{cl}(\mathcal{O})$ acts via isogenies on the set of $\mathbb{F}_p$-isomorphism classes of elliptic curves whose $\mathbb{F}_p$-rational endomorphism ring is isomorphic to $\mathcal{O}$ and whose trace of Frobenius has a prescribed value; in fact if $p \geq 5$ then there is only one option for this value, namely 0, in contrast with the ordinary case. See e.g. [70, Theorem 4.5], with further details to be found in [8,22] and in Sect. 3 of this paper. Starting from these observations, the desired adaptation of the Couveignes–Rostovtsev–Stolbunov scheme almost unrolls itself; the details can be found in Sect. 4. We call the resulting scheme CSIDH, where the C stands for "commutative".[1]

While this fails to address Jao and De Feo's initial motivation for using supersingular elliptic curves, which was to avoid the $L_q[1/2]$ quantum attack due to Childs–Jao–Soukharev, we show that CSIDH eliminates the main problem of the Couveignes–Rostovtsev–Stolbunov scheme, namely its inefficiency. Indeed, in Sect. 8 we will report on a proof-of-concept implementation which carries out a non-interactive key exchange at a presumed classical security level of 128 bits and a conjectured post-quantum security level of 64 bits in about 80 ms, while using key sizes of only 64 bytes. This is over 2000 times faster[2] than the current state-of-the-art instantiation of the Couveignes–Rostovtsev–Stolbunov scheme by De Feo, Kieffer and Smith [21,41], which itself presents many new ideas and speedups to even achieve that speed.

For comparison, we remark that SIDH, which is the NIST submission with the smallest combined key and ciphertext length, uses public keys and ciphertexts of over 300 bytes each. More precisely SIKE's version p503 uses uncompressed keys of 378 bytes long [37] for achieving CCA security. The optimized SIKE

---

[1] Since this work was started while being very close to a well-known large body of salt water, we pronounce CSIDH as ['siːˌsaɪd] rather than spelling out all the letters.

[2] This speed-up is explained in part by comparing our own C implementation to the **sage** implementation of De Feo–Kieffer–Smith.

implementation is about ten times faster than our proof-of-concept C implementation, but even at 80 ms, CSIDH is practical.

Another major advantage of CSIDH is that we can efficiently validate public keys, making it possible to reuse a key without the need for transformations to confirm that the other party's key was honestly generated.

Finally we note that just like the original Couveignes–Rostovtsev–Stolbunov scheme, CSIDH relies purely on the isogeny-finding problem; no extra points are sent that could potentially harm security, as argued in [50].

To summarize, CSIDH is a new cryptographic primitive that can serve as a drop-in replacement for the (EC)DH key-exchange protocol while maintaining security against quantum computers. It provides a *non-interactive* (static–static) key exchange with full public-key validation. The speed is practical while the public-key size is the smallest for key exchange or KEM in the portfolio of post-quantum cryptography. This makes CSIDH particularly attractive in the common scenario of prioritizing bandwidth over computational effort. In addition, CSIDH is compatible with 0-RTT protocols such as QUIC.

Why supersingular? To understand where the main speed-up comes from, it suffices to record that De Feo–Kieffer–Smith had the idea of choosing a field of characteristic p, where p is congruent to -1 modulo all small odd primes ℓ up to a given bound. They then look for an ordinary elliptic curve $E/\mathbb{F}_p$ such that $\#E(\mathbb{F}_p)$ is congruent to 0 modulo as many of these ℓ's as possible, i.e., such that points of order ℓ exist over $\mathbb{F}_p$. These properties ensure that $\ell\mathcal{O}$ decomposes as a product of two prime ideals $\mathfrak{l} = (\ell, \pi - 1)$ and $\bar{\mathfrak{l}} = (\ell, \pi + 1)$, where π denotes the Frobenius endomorphism. For such primes the action of the corresponding ideal classes $[\mathfrak{l}]$ and $[\bar{\mathfrak{l}}] = [\mathfrak{l}]^{-1}$ can be computed efficiently through an application of Vélu-type formulae to E (resp. its quadratic twist E^t), the reason being that only $\mathbb{F}_p$-rational points are involved. If this works for enough primes ℓ, we can expect that a generic element of $\mathrm{cl}(\mathcal{O})$ can be written as a product of small integral powers of such $[\mathfrak{l}]$, so that the class-group action can be computed efficiently. However, finding an ordinary elliptic curve $E/\mathbb{F}_p$ such that $\#E(\mathbb{F}_p)$ is congruent to 0 modulo many small primes ℓ is hard, and the main focus of De Feo–Kieffer–Smith is on speeding up this search. In the end it is only practical to enforce this for 7 primes, thus they cannot take full advantage of the idea.

However, in the supersingular case the property $\#E(\mathbb{F}_p) = p+1$ implies that $\#E(\mathbb{F}_p)$ is congruent to 0 modulo *all* primes $\ell \mid p + 1$ that we started from in building p! Concretely, our proof-of-concept implementation uses 74 small odd primes, corresponding to prime ideals $\mathfrak{l}_1, \mathfrak{l}_2, \ldots, \mathfrak{l}_{74}$ for which we heuristically expect that almost all elements of our 256-bit size class group can be written as $[\mathfrak{l}_1]^{e_1}[\mathfrak{l}_2]^{e_2} \cdots [\mathfrak{l}_{74}]^{e_{74}}$, where the exponents e_i are taken from the range $\{-5, \ldots, 5\}$; indeed, one verifies that $\log{(2 \cdot 5 + 1)^{74}} \approx 255.9979$. The action of such an element can be computed as the composition of at most $5 \cdot 74 = 370$ easy isogeny evaluations. This should be compared to using 7 small primes, where the same approach would require exponents in a range of length about $2^{256/7} \approx 2^{36}$, in view of which De Feo–Kieffer–Smith also resort to other primes with less beneficial properties, requiring to work in extensions of $\mathbb{F}_p$.

The use of supersingular elliptic curves over $\mathbb{F}_p$ has various other advantages. For instance, their trace of Frobenius t is 0, so that the absolute value of the discriminant $|t^2 - 4p| = 4p$ is as large as possible. As a consequence, generically the size of the class group $cl(\mathcal{O})$ is close to its maximal possible value for a fixed choice of p. Conversely, this implies that for a fixed security level we can make a close-to-minimal choice for p, which directly affects the key size. Note that this contrasts with the CM construction from [9], which could in principle be used to construct ordinary elliptic curves having many points of small order, but whose endomorphism rings have very small class groups, ruling them out for the Couveignes–Rostovtsev–Stolbunov key exchange.

To explain why key validation works, note that we work over $\mathbb{F}_p$ with $p \equiv 3$ (mod 8) and start from the curve $E_0 \colon y^2 = x^3 + x$ with $\mathbb{F}_p$-rational endomorphism ring $\mathcal{O} = \mathbb{Z}[\pi]$. As it turns out, all Montgomery curves $E_A \colon y^2 = x^3 + Ax^2 + x$ over $\mathbb{F}_p$ that are supersingular appear in the $cl(\mathcal{O})$-orbit of E_0. Moreover their $\mathbb{F}_p$-isomorphism class is uniquely determined by A. So all one needs to do upon receiving a candidate public key $y^2 = x^3 + Ax^2 + x$ is check for supersingularity, which is an easy task; see Sect. 5. The combination of large size of $cl(\mathcal{O})$ and representation by a single $\mathbb{F}_p$-element A explains the small key size of 64 bytes.

1.1 One-Way Group Actions

Although non-interactive key exchange is the main application of our primitive, it is actually more general: It is (conjecturally) an instance of Couveignes' *hard homogeneous spaces* [17], ultimately nothing but a finite commutative group action for which some operations are easy to compute while others are hard. Such group actions were first formalized and studied by Brassard and Yung [7]. We summarize Couveignes' definition:

Definition 1. *A hard homogeneous space consists of a finite commutative group G acting freely and transitively on some set X.*
The following tasks are required to be easy (e.g., polynomial-time):

- *Compute the group operations in G.*
- *Sample randomly from G with (close to) uniform distribution.*
- *Decide validity and equality of a representation of elements of X.*
- *Compute the action of a group element $g \in G$ on some $x \in X$.*

The following problems are required to be hard (e.g., not polynomial-time):

- *Given $x, x' \in X$, find $g \in G$ such that $g * x = x'$.*
- *Given $x, x', y \in X$ such that $x' = g * x$, find $y' = g * y$.*

Any such primitive immediately implies a natural Diffie–Hellman protocol: Alice and Bob's private keys are random elements a, b of G, their public keys are $a * x_0$ resp. $b * x_0$, where $x_0 \in X$ is a public fixed element, and the shared secret is $b * (a * x_0) = a * (b * x_0)$. The private keys are protected by the difficulty of the first hard problem above, while the shared secret is protected by the second problem. Note that traditional Diffie–Hellman on a cyclic group C is an instance of this, where X is the set of generators of C and G is the multiplicative group $(\mathbb{Z}/\#C)^*$ acting by exponentiation.

1.2 Notation and Terminology

We stress that throughout this paper, we consider two elliptic curves defined over the same field identical whenever they are isomorphic *over that field*. Note that we do *not* identify curves that are only isomorphic over some extension field, as opposed to what is done in SIDH, for instance. In the same vein, for an elliptic curve E defined over a finite field $\mathbb{F}_p$, we let $\mathrm{End}_p(E)$ be the subring of the endomorphism ring $\mathrm{End}(E)$ consisting of endomorphisms defined over $\mathbb{F}_p$.[3] This subring is always isomorphic to an order in an imaginary quadratic number field. Conversely, for a given order $\mathcal{O}$ in an imaginary quadratic field and an element $\pi \in \mathcal{O}$, we let $\mathcal{E}\ell\ell_p(\mathcal{O}, \pi)$ denote the set of elliptic curves E defined over $\mathbb{F}_p$ with $\mathrm{End}_p(E) \cong \mathcal{O}$ such that π corresponds to the $\mathbb{F}_p$-Frobenius endomorphism of E. In particular, this implies that $\varphi \circ \beta = \beta \circ \varphi$ for all $\mathbb{F}_p$-isogenies φ between two curves in $\mathcal{E}\ell\ell_p(\mathcal{O}, \pi)$ and all $\beta \in \mathcal{O}$ interpreted as endomorphisms.
Ideals are always assumed to be non-zero.
The notation "log" refers to the base-2 logarithm.

Acknowledgements. This project started during a research retreat on post-quantum cryptography, organized by the European PQCRYPTO and ECRYPT-CSA projects in Tenerife from 29 January until 1 February 2018. We would like to thank Jeffrey Burdges, whose quest for a flexible post-quantum key exchange protocol made us look for speed-ups of the Couveignes–Rostovtsev–Stolbunov scheme. We are grateful to Luca De Feo, Jean Kieffer, and Ben Smith for sharing a draft of their paper in preparation, and to Daniel J. Bernstein, Luca De Feo, Jeroen Demeyer, Léo Ducas, Steven Galbraith, David Jao, and Fré Vercauteren for helpful feedback.

2 Isogeny Graphs

Good mixing properties of the underlying isogeny graph are relevant for the security of isogeny-based cryptosystems. Just as in the original Couveignes–Rostovtsev–Stolbunov cryptosystem, in our case this graph is obtained by taking the union of several large subgraphs (each being a union of large isomorphic cycle graphs) on the same vertex set, one for each prime ℓ under consideration; see Fig. 1 for a (small) example. Such a graph is the *Schreier graph* associated with our class-group action and the chosen generators. We refer to the lecture notes of De Feo [19, Sect. 14.1] for more background and to [40] for a discussion of its rapid mixing properties. One point of view on this is that one can quickly move between distant nodes in the subgraph corresponding to one generator by switching to the subgraph corresponding to another generator. This thereby replaces the square-and-multiply algorithm in exponentiation-based cryptosystems (such as classical Diffie–Hellman).

The goal of this section is to analyze the structure of the individual cycles.

---

[3] This constraint only makes a difference for supersingular curves: in the ordinary case, all endomorphisms are defined over the base field.

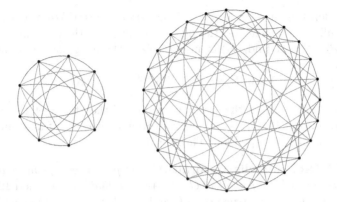

Fig. 1. Union of the supersingular ℓ-isogeny graphs for $\ell \in \{3, 5, 7\}$ over $\mathbb{F}_{419}$. CSIDH makes use of the larger component, corresponding to curves whose ring of $\mathbb{F}_{419}$-rational endomorphisms is isomorphic to $\mathbb{Z}[\sqrt{-419}]$.

Definition 2. *For a field k and a prime $\ell \nmid \operatorname{char} k$, the k-rational ℓ-isogeny graph $G_{k,\ell}$ is defined as having all the elliptic curves defined over k as its vertices, and having a directed edge (E_1, E_2) for each k-rational ℓ-isogeny from E_1 to E_2.*[4]

Remark 3. A priori $G_{k,\ell}$ is a directed graph, but given two elliptic curves E_1 and E_2 whose j-invariants are not in $\{0, 1728\}$, there are exactly as many edges (E_2, E_1) as (E_1, E_2), obtained by taking dual isogenies. Annoyingly, the nodes with j-invariants 0 and 1728 are more complicated, since these are exactly the curves with extra automorphisms: an elliptic curve E in $G_{k,\ell}$ has fewer incoming than outgoing edges if and only if either $j(E) = 0$ and $\sqrt{-3} \in k$, or if $j(E) = 1728$ and $\sqrt{-1} \in k$. Throughout this paper, we will assume for simplicity that $\sqrt{-3}, \sqrt{-1} \notin k$, so that neither of these automorphisms are defined over k and we may view $G_{k,\ell}$ as an undirected graph. In the case of a finite prime field $k = \mathbb{F}_p$, it suffices to restrict to $p \equiv 11 \pmod{12}$, which will be satisfied in the class of instantiations we suggest.

If $k = \mathbb{F}_q$ is a finite field, then $G_{k,\ell}$ is a finite graph that is the disjoint union of ordinary connected components and supersingular connected components. The ordinary components were studied in Kohel's PhD thesis [42]. Due to their regular structure, these components later became known as *isogeny volcanoes*.

In general (e.g. over non-prime fields), the supersingular components may bear no similarity at all to the volcanoes of the ordinary case. Traditionally, following Pizer [51], one instead studies the unique supersingular component of $G_{k,\ell}$ where $k = \overline{\mathbb{F}}_q$, which turns out to be a finite $(\ell+1)$-regular Ramanujan graph and forms the basis for the SIDH protocol.

However, Delfs and Galbraith [22] showed that if $k = \mathbb{F}_p$ is a finite prime field, then all connected components are volcanoes, even in the supersingular case

---

[4] Due to our convention of identifying k-isomorphic curves, we also identify isogenies if they are k-isomorphic, i.e., equal up to post-composition with a k-isomorphism.

(where the depth is at most 1 at $\ell = 2$ and 0 otherwise). We present a special case of a unified statement, restricting our attention to the cases in which $G_{\mathbb{F}_p,\ell}$ is a cycle. Recall that $\mathrm{End}_p(E)$ is an order $\mathcal{O}$ in the imaginary quadratic field

$$\mathrm{End}_p(E) \otimes_{\mathbb{Z}} \mathbb{Q} \cong \mathbb{Q}(\sqrt{t^2 - 4p}) = K,$$

where $|t| \leq 2\sqrt{p}$ denotes the (absolute value of the) trace of the Frobenius endomorphism, and that two curves are isogenous over $\mathbb{F}_p$ if and only if their traces of Frobenius are equal [66, Theorem 1].

Theorem 4 (Kohel, Delfs–Galbraith). *Let $p \geq 5$ be a prime number and let V be a connected component of $G_{\mathbb{F}_p,\ell}$. Assume that $p \equiv 11 \pmod{12}$ or that V contains no curve with j-invariant 0 or 1728. Let t be the trace of Frobenius common to all vertices in V, and let K be as above. Assume that $\ell \nmid t^2 - 4p$.*

    Then all elliptic curves in V have the same $\mathbb{F}_p$-rational endomorphism ring $\mathcal{O} \subseteq K$, and $\mathcal{O}$ is locally maximal at ℓ. Moreover if $t^2 - 4p$ is a (non-zero) square modulo ℓ, then V is a cycle whose length equals the order of $[\mathfrak{l}]$ in $\mathrm{cl}(\mathcal{O})$, where $\mathfrak{l}$ is a prime ideal dividing $\ell\mathcal{O}$. If not, then V consists of a single vertex and no edges.

Proof. In the case of an ordinary component this is just a special case of [65, Theorem 7]. In the case of a supersingular component this follows from the proof of [22, Theorem 2.7]. (In both cases, we could alternatively (re)prove this theorem by proving that an ℓ-isogeny can only change the conductor of the endomorphism ring of an elliptic curve locally at ℓ and applying Theorem 7.) □

    In the ordinary case a curve and its quadratic twist can never appear in the same component because they have a different trace of Frobenius. This is the main difference with the supersingular case, where this possibility is not excluded. To avoid confusion, we clarify that by the quadratic twist of a given elliptic curve $E \colon y^2 = f(x)$ over $\mathbb{F}_p$ we mean the curve $E^t \colon dy^2 = f(x)$, where $d \in \mathbb{F}_p^*$ is any non-square. If $p \equiv 3 \pmod{4}$ and $j(E) = 1728$ then this may deviate from what some readers are used to, because in this case E^t and E are $\mathbb{F}_p$-isomorphic. Note that such a curve is necessarily supersingular.

Remark 5. In fact, if $p \equiv 3 \bmod 4$ then there are two non-isomorphic curves over $\mathbb{F}_p$ with j-invariant 1728, namely $y^2 = x^3 - x$ and $y^2 = x^3 + x$, whose endomorphism rings are the full ring of integers $\mathbb{Z}[(1 + \sqrt{-p})/2]$ and the order $\mathbb{Z}[\sqrt{-p}]$ of conductor 2 respectively. The connected component of each curve is "symmetric": if E is n steps along $G_{\mathbb{F}_p,\ell}$ in one direction from a curve of j-invariant 1728 then the curve that is n steps in the other direction is the quadratic twist of E. In the case of $G_{\mathbb{F}_{83},3}$ we can see this in Fig. 2, which is taken from [22, Fig. 8].

    It is also interesting to observe that the symmetry around $j = 1728$ confirms the known fact that the class numbers of $\mathbb{Z}[(1 + \sqrt{-p})/2]$ and $\mathbb{Z}[\sqrt{-p}]$ are odd, at least in the case that $p \equiv 3 \pmod{4}$; see [47].

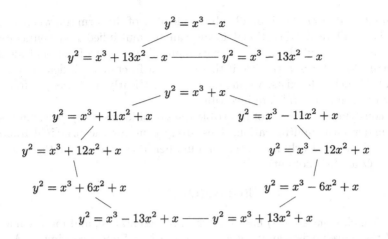

Fig. 2. The two supersingular components of $G_{\mathbb{F}_{83},3}$. The curves in the top component have $\mathbb{F}_p$-rational endomorphism ring $\mathbb{Z}[(1+\sqrt{-83})/2]$, while those in the lower component correspond to $\mathbb{Z}[\sqrt{-83}]$. Running clockwise through these components corresponds to the repeated action of $[(3, \pi - 1)]$.

3 The Class-Group Action

It is well-known that the ideal-class group of an imaginary quadratic order $\mathcal{O}$ acts freely via isogenies on the set of elliptic curves with $\mathbb{F}_p$-rational endomorphism ring $\mathcal{O}$. Using this group action on a set of ordinary elliptic curves for cryptographic purposes was first put forward by Couveignes [17] and independently rediscovered later by Rostovtsev and Stolbunov [54,60]. Our suggestion is to use the equivalent of their construction in the supersingular setting, thus the following discussion covers both cases at once. For concreteness, we focus on prime fields with $p \geq 5$ and point out that the ordinary (but not the supersingular) case generalizes to all finite fields. We recall the following standard lemma:

Lemma 6. *Let $E/\mathbb{F}_p$ be an elliptic curve and G a finite $\mathbb{F}_p$-rational (i.e., stable under the action of the $\mathbb{F}_p$-Frobenius) subgroup of E. Then there exists an elliptic curve $E'/\mathbb{F}_p$ and a separable isogeny $\varphi \colon E \to E'$ defined over $\mathbb{F}_p$ with kernel G. The codomain E' and isogeny φ are unique up to $\mathbb{F}_p$-isomorphism.*[5]

Proof. [59, Proposition III.4.12, Remark III.4.13.2, and Exercise III.3.13e]. □

The ideal-class group. We recall the definitions and basic properties of class groups of quadratic orders that will be needed in the following. This section is based on [18, Sect. 7]. Let K be a quadratic number field and $\mathcal{O} \subseteq K$ an order (that is, a subring which is a free $\mathbb{Z}$-module of rank 2). The *norm* of an $\mathcal{O}$-ideal $\mathfrak{a} \subseteq \mathcal{O}$ is defined as $N(\mathfrak{a}) = |\mathcal{O}/\mathfrak{a}|$; it is equal to $\gcd(\{N(\alpha) \mid \alpha \in \mathfrak{a}\})$. Norms are multiplicative: $N(\mathfrak{a}\mathfrak{b}) = N(\mathfrak{a})N(\mathfrak{b})$.

---

[5] This statement remains true in vast generality, but we only need this special case.

A *fractional ideal* of $\mathcal{O}$ is an $\mathcal{O}$-submodule of K of the form $\alpha\mathfrak{a}$, where $\alpha \in K^*$ and $\mathfrak{a}$ is an $\mathcal{O}$-ideal.[6] Fractional ideals can be multiplied and conjugated in the evident way, and the norm extends multiplicatively to fractional ideals. A fractional $\mathcal{O}$-ideal $\mathfrak{a}$ is *invertible* if there exists a fractional $\mathcal{O}$-ideal $\mathfrak{b}$ such that $\mathfrak{ab} = \mathcal{O}$. If such a $\mathfrak{b}$ exists, we define $\mathfrak{a}^{-1} = \mathfrak{b}$. Clearly all *principal* fractional ideals $\alpha\mathcal{O}$, where $\alpha \in K^*$, are invertible.

By construction, the set of invertible fractional ideals $I(\mathcal{O})$ forms an abelian group under ideal multiplication. This group contains the principal fractional ideals $P(\mathcal{O})$ as a (clearly normal) subgroup, hence we may define the *ideal-class group* of $\mathcal{O}$ as the quotient

$$\mathrm{cl}(\mathcal{O}) = I(\mathcal{O})/P(\mathcal{O}).$$

Every ideal class $[\mathfrak{a}] \in \mathrm{cl}(\mathcal{O})$ has an integral representative, and for any non-zero $M \in \mathbb{Z}$ there even exists an integral representative of norm coprime to M.

There is a unique *maximal order* of K with respect to inclusion called the ring of integers and denoted $\mathcal{O}_K$. The *conductor* of $\mathcal{O}$ (in $\mathcal{O}_K$) is the index $f = [\mathcal{O}_K : \mathcal{O}]$. Away from the conductor, ideals are well-behaved; every $\mathcal{O}$-ideal of norm coprime to the conductor is invertible and factors uniquely into prime ideals.

The class-group action. Fix a prime $p \geq 5$ and an (ordinary or supersingular) elliptic curve E defined over $\mathbb{F}_p$. The Frobenius endomorphism π of E satisfies a characteristic equation

$$\pi^2 - t\pi + p = 0$$

in $\mathrm{End}_p(E)$, where $t \in \mathbb{Z}$ is the trace of Frobenius. The curve E is supersingular if and only if $t = 0$. The $\mathbb{F}_p$-rational endomorphism ring $\mathrm{End}_p(E)$ is an order $\mathcal{O}$ in the imaginary quadratic field $K = \mathcal{O} \otimes_{\mathbb{Z}} \mathbb{Q} \cong \mathbb{Q}(\sqrt{\Delta})$, where $\Delta = t^2 - 4p$. We note that $\mathcal{O}$ always contains the Frobenius endomorphism π, and hence the order $\mathbb{Z}[\pi]$.

Any invertible ideal $\mathfrak{a}$ of $\mathcal{O}$ splits into a product of $\mathcal{O}$-ideals as $(\pi\mathcal{O})^r\mathfrak{a}_s$, where $\mathfrak{a}_s \nsubseteq \pi\mathcal{O}$. This defines an elliptic curve $E/\mathfrak{a}$ and an isogeny

$$\varphi_{\mathfrak{a}} : E \to E/\mathfrak{a}$$

of degree $N(\mathfrak{a})$ as follows [70]: the separable part of $\varphi_{\mathfrak{a}}$ has kernel $\bigcap_{\alpha \in \mathfrak{a}_s} \ker \alpha$, and the purely inseparable part consists of r iterations of Frobenius. The isogeny $\varphi_{\mathfrak{a}}$ and codomain $E/\mathfrak{a}$ are both defined over $\mathbb{F}_p$ and are unique up to $\mathbb{F}_p$-isomorphism (by Lemma 6), justifying the notation $E/\mathfrak{a}$. Multiplication of ideals corresponds to the composition of isogenies. Since principal ideals correspond to endomorphisms, two ideals lead to the same codomain if and only if they are equal up to multiplication by a principal fractional ideal. Moreover, every $\mathbb{F}_p$-isogeny

---

[6] Note that the use of the word "ideal" is inconsistent in the literature. We make the convention that "ideal" without qualification refers to an *integral* $\mathcal{O}$-ideal (i.e., an ideal in the sense of ring theory), while fractional ideals are clearly named as such.

ψ between curves in $\mathscr{E}\!\ell_p(\mathcal{O}, \pi)$ comes from an invertible $\mathcal{O}$-ideal in this way, and the ideal $\mathfrak{a}_s$ can be recovered from ψ as $\mathfrak{a}_s = \{\alpha \in \mathcal{O} \mid \ker \alpha \supseteq \ker \psi\}$. In other words:

Theorem 7. *Let $\mathcal{O}$ be an order in an imaginary quadratic field and $\pi \in \mathcal{O}$ such that $\mathscr{E}\!\ell_p(\mathcal{O}, \pi)$ is non-empty. Then the ideal-class group $\mathrm{cl}(\mathcal{O})$ acts freely and transitively on the set $\mathscr{E}\!\ell_p(\mathcal{O}, \pi)$ via the map*

$$\mathrm{cl}(\mathcal{O}) \times \mathscr{E}\!\ell_p(\mathcal{O}, \pi) \longrightarrow \mathscr{E}\!\ell_p(\mathcal{O}, \pi)$$
$$([\mathfrak{a}], E) \longmapsto E/\mathfrak{a},$$

in which $\mathfrak{a}$ is chosen as an integral representative.

Proof. See [70, Theorem 4.5]. Erratum: [55, Theorem 4.5]. □

To emphasize the fact that we are dealing with a group action, we will from now on write $[\mathfrak{a}] * E$ or simply $[\mathfrak{a}]E$ for the curve $E/\mathfrak{a}$ defined above.

The structure of the class group. The class group $\mathrm{cl}(\mathcal{O})$ is a finite abelian group whose cardinality is asymptotically [58]

$$\#\mathrm{cl}(\mathcal{O}) \approx \sqrt{|\Delta|}.$$

More precise heuristics actually predict that $\#\mathrm{cl}(\mathcal{O})$ grows a little bit faster than $\sqrt{|\Delta|}$, but the ratio is logarithmically bounded so we content ourselves with the above estimate. The exact structure of the class group can be computed in subexponential time $L_{|\Delta|}[1/2; \sqrt{2} + o(1)]$ using an algorithm of Hafner and McCurley [33]. Unfortunately, this requires too much computation for the sizes of Δ we are working with, but there are convincing heuristics concerning the properties of the class group we need. See Sect. 7.1 for these arguments. If the absolute value $|t|$ of the trace of Frobenius is "not too big", the discriminant Δ is about the size of p, hence by the above approximation we may assume $\#\mathrm{cl}(\mathcal{O}) \approx \sqrt{p}$. This holds in particular when E is supersingular, where $t = 0$, hence $|\Delta| = 4p$.

We are interested in primes ℓ that split in $\mathcal{O}$, i.e., such that there exist (necessarily conjugate) distinct prime ideals $\mathfrak{l}, \bar{\mathfrak{l}}$ of $\mathcal{O}$ with $\ell\mathcal{O} = \mathfrak{l}\bar{\mathfrak{l}}$. Such ℓ are known as *Elkies primes* in the point-counting literature. The ideal $\mathfrak{l}$ is generated as $\mathfrak{l} = (\ell, \pi - \lambda)$, where $\lambda \in \mathbb{Z}/\ell$ is an eigenvalue of the Frobenius endomorphism π on the ℓ-torsion, and its conjugate is $\bar{\mathfrak{l}} = (\ell, \pi - p/\lambda)$, where by abuse of notation p/λ denotes any integral representative of that quotient modulo ℓ. Note that ℓ splits in $\mathcal{O}$ if and only if Δ is a non-zero square modulo ℓ.

Computing the group action. Any element of the class group can be represented as a product of small prime ideals [10, Propositions 9.5.2 and 9.5.3], hence we describe how to compute $[\mathfrak{l}]E$ for a prime ideal $\mathfrak{l} = (\ell, \pi - \lambda)$. There are (at least) the following ways to proceed, which vary in efficiency depending on the circumstances [21,41]:

- Find $\mathbb{F}_p$-rational roots of the modular polynomial $\Phi_\ell(j(E), y)$ to determine the two j-invariants of possible codomains (i.e., up to four non-isomorphic curves, though in the ordinary case wrong twists can easily be ruled out); compute the kernel polynomials [42] $\chi \in \mathbb{F}_p[x]$ for the corresponding isogenies (if they exist); if $(x^p, y^p) = [\lambda](x, y)$ modulo χ and the curve equation, then the codomain was correct, else another choice is correct.
- Factor the ℓth division polynomial $\psi_\ell(E)$ over $\mathbb{F}_p$; collect irreducible factors with the right Frobenius eigenvalues (as above); use Kohel's algorithm [42, Sect. 2.4] to compute the codomain.
- Find a basis of the ℓ-torsion—possibly over an extension field—and compute the eigenspaces of Frobenius; apply Vélu's formulas [69] to a basis point of the correct eigenspace to compute the codomain.

As observed in [21,41], the last method is the fastest if the necessary extension fields are small. The optimal case is $\lambda = 1$; in that case, the curve has a rational point defined over the base field $\mathbb{F}_p$. If in addition $p/\lambda = -1$, the other eigenspace of Frobenius modulo ℓ is defined over $\mathbb{F}_{p^2}$, so both codomains can easily be computed using Vélu's formulas over an at most quadratic extension (but in fact, a good choice of curve model allows for pure prime field computations, see Sect. 8; alternatively one could switch to the quadratic twist). Note that if $p \equiv -1 \pmod{\ell}$, then $\lambda = 1$ automatically implies $p/\lambda = -1$.

Much of De Feo–Kieffer–Smith's work [21,41] is devoted to finding an ordinary elliptic curve E with many small Elkies primes ℓ such that both E and its quadratic twist E^t have an $\mathbb{F}_p$-rational ℓ-torsion point. Despite considerable effort leading to various improvements, the results are discouraging. With the best parameters found within $17\,000\,\text{h}$ of CPU time, evaluating one class-group action still requires several minutes of computation to complete. This suggests that without new ideas, the original Couveignes–Rostovtsev–Stolbunov scheme will not become anything close to practical in the foreseeable future.

4   Construction and Design Choices

In this section, we discuss the construction of our proposed group action and justify our design decisions. For algorithmic details, see Sect. 8. Notice that the main obstacle to performance in the Couveignes–Rostovtsev–Stolbunov scheme— constructing a curve with highly composite order—becomes trivial when using supersingular curves instead of ordinary curves, since for $p \geq 5$ any supersingular elliptic curve over $\mathbb{F}_p$ has exactly $p + 1$ rational points.

The cryptographic group action described below is a straightforward implementation of this construction. Note that we require $p \equiv 3 \pmod 4$ so that we can easily write down a supersingular elliptic curve over $\mathbb{F}_p$ and so that an implementation may use curves in Montgomery form. It turns out that this choice is also beneficial for other reasons. In principle, this constraint is not necessary for the theory to work, although the structure of the isogeny graph changes slightly (see [22] and Remark 3 for details).

Parameters. Fix a large prime p of the form $4 \cdot \ell_1 \cdots \ell_n - 1$, where the ℓ_i are small distinct odd primes. Fix the elliptic curve $E_0 \colon y^2 = x^3 + x$ over $\mathbb{F}_p$; it is supersingular since $p \equiv 3 \pmod 4$. The Frobenius endomorphism π satisfies $\pi^2 = -p$, so its $\mathbb{F}_p$-rational endomorphism ring is an order in the imaginary quadratic field $\mathbb{Q}(\sqrt{-p})$. More precisely, Proposition 8 (below) shows $\mathrm{End}_p(E_0) = \mathbb{Z}[\pi]$, which has conductor 2.

Rational Elkies primes. By Theorem 4, the choices made above imply that the ℓ_i-isogeny graph is a disjoint union of cycles. Moreover, since $\pi^2 - 1 \equiv 0 \pmod{\ell_i}$ the ideals $\ell_i \mathcal{O}$ split as $\ell_i \mathcal{O} = \mathfrak{l}_i \overline{\mathfrak{l}_i}$, where $\mathfrak{l}_i = (\ell_i, \pi - 1)$ and $\overline{\mathfrak{l}_i} = (\ell_i, \pi + 1)$. In other words, *all* the ℓ_i are Elkies primes. In particular, we can use any one of the three algorithms described at the end of Sect. 3 to walk along the cycles.

Furthermore, the kernel of $\varphi_{\mathfrak{l}_i}$ is the intersection of the kernels of the scalar multiplication $[\ell_i]$ and the endomorphism $\pi - 1$. That is, it is the subgroup generated by a point P of order ℓ_i which lies in the kernel of $\pi - 1$ or, in other words, is defined over $\mathbb{F}_p$. Similarly, the kernel of $\varphi_{\overline{\mathfrak{l}_i}}$ is generated by a point Q of order ℓ_i that is defined over $\mathbb{F}_{p^2}$ but not $\mathbb{F}_p$ and such that $\pi(Q) = -Q$. This greatly simplifies and accelerates the implementation, since it allows performing all computations over the base field (see Sect. 8 for details).

Sampling from the class group. Ideally,[7] we would like to know the exact structure of the ideal-class group $\mathrm{cl}(\mathcal{O})$ to be able to sample elements uniformly at random. However, such a computation is currently not feasible for the size of discriminant we need, hence we resort to heuristic arguments. Assuming that the $\mathfrak{l}_i$ do not have very small order and are "evenly distributed" in the class group, we can expect ideals of the form $\mathfrak{l}_1^{e_1} \mathfrak{l}_2^{e_2} \cdots \mathfrak{l}_n^{e_n}$ for small e_i to lie in the same class only very occasionally. For efficiency reasons, it is desirable to sample the exponents e_i from a short range centered around zero, say $\{-m, \ldots, m\}$ for some integer m. We will argue in Sect. 7.1 that choosing m such that $2m + 1 \geq \sqrt[n]{\#\mathrm{cl}(\mathcal{O})}$ is sufficient. Since the prime ideals $\mathfrak{l}_i$ are fixed global parameters, the ideal $\prod_i \mathfrak{l}_i^{e_i}$ may simply be represented as a vector $(e_1, \ldots, e_n)$.

Evaluating the class-group action. Computing the action of an ideal class represented by $\prod_i \mathfrak{l}_i^{e_i}$ on an elliptic curve E proceeds as outlined in Sect. 3. Since $\pi^2 = -p \equiv 1 \pmod{\ell_i}$, we are now in the favourable situation that the eigenvalues of Frobenius on *all* ℓ_i-torsion subgroups are $+1$ and -1. Hence we can efficiently compute the action of $\mathfrak{l}_i$ (resp. $\overline{\mathfrak{l}_i}$) by finding an $\mathbb{F}_p$-rational point (resp. $\mathbb{F}_{p^2}$-rational with Frobenius eigenvalue -1) of order ℓ_i and applying Vélu-type formulas. This step could simply be repeated for each ideal $\mathfrak{l}_i^{\pm 1}$ whose action is to be evaluated, but see Sect. 8 for a more efficient method.

---

[7] No pun intended.

5   Representing and Validating $\mathbb{F}_p$-isomorphism Classes

A major unsolved problem of SIDH is its lack of public-key validation, i.e., the inability to verify that a public key was honestly generated. This shortcoming leads to polynomial-time active attacks [29] on static variants for which countermeasures are expensive. For example, the actively secure variant SIKE [37] applies a transformation proposed by Hofheinz, Hövelmanns, and Kiltz [36] which is similar to the Fujisaki–Okamoto transform [26], essentially doubling the running time on the recipient's side compared to an ephemeral key exchange.

The following proposition tackles this problem for our family of CSIDH instantiations. Moreover, it shows that the Montgomery coefficient forms a unique representative for the $\mathbb{F}_p$-isomorphism class resulting from the group action, hence may serve as a shared secret without taking j-invariants.

Proposition 8. *Let $p \geq 5$ be a prime such that $p \equiv 3$ (mod 8), and let $E/\mathbb{F}_p$ be a supersingular elliptic curve. Then $\mathrm{End}_p(E) = \mathbb{Z}[\pi]$ if and only if there exists $A \in \mathbb{F}_p$ such that E is $\mathbb{F}_p$-isomorphic to the curve $E_A\colon y^2 = x^3 + Ax^2 + x$. Moreover, if such an A exists then it is unique.*

Proof. First suppose that E is isomorphic over $\mathbb{F}_p$ to E_A for some $A \in \mathbb{F}_p$. If E_A has full $\mathbb{F}_p$-rational 2-torsion, then Table 1 of [16] shows that either E_A or its quadratic twist must have order divisible by 8. However, both have cardinality $p + 1 \equiv 4$ (mod 8). Hence E_A can only have one $\mathbb{F}_p$-rational point of order 2. With Theorem 2.7 of [22], we can conclude $\mathrm{End}_p(E) = \mathrm{End}_p(E_A) = \mathbb{Z}[\pi]$.

Now assume that $\mathrm{End}_p(E) = \mathbb{Z}[\pi]$. By Theorem 7, the class group $\mathrm{cl}(\mathbb{Z}[\pi])$ acts transitively on $\mathcal{E}\ell\ell_p(\mathbb{Z}[\pi], \pi)$, so in particular there exists $[\mathfrak{a}] \in \mathrm{cl}(\mathbb{Z}[\pi])$ such that $[\mathfrak{a}]E_0 = E$, where $E_0\colon y^2 = x^3 + x$. Choosing a representative $\mathfrak{a}$ that has norm coprime to $2p$ yields a separable $\mathbb{F}_p$-isogeny $\varphi_\mathfrak{a}\colon E_0 \to E$ of odd degree. Thus, by [53, Proposition 1] there exists an $A \in \mathbb{F}_p$ and a separable isogeny $\psi\colon E_0 \to E_A\colon y^2 = x^3 + Ax^2 + x$ defined over $\mathbb{F}_p$ such that $\ker \psi = \ker \varphi_\mathfrak{a}$. As isogenies defined over $\mathbb{F}_p$ with given kernel are unique up to post-composition with $\mathbb{F}_p$-isomorphisms (Lemma 6), we conclude that E is $\mathbb{F}_p$-isomorphic to E_A.

Finally, let $B \in \mathbb{F}_p$ such that $E_A \cong E_B\colon Y^2 = X^3 + BX^2 + X$. Then by [59, Proposition III.3.1(b)] there exist $u \in \mathbb{F}_p^*$ and $r, s, t \in \mathbb{F}_p$ such that

$$x = u^2 X + r, \quad y = u^3 Y + su^2 X + t.$$

Substituting this into the curve equation for E_A and subtracting the equation of E_B (scaled by u^6) equals zero in the function field and thus leads to a linear relation over $\mathbb{F}_p$ between the functions 1, X, X^2, Y, and XY. Writing ∞ for the point at infinity of E_B, it follows from Riemann–Roch [59, Theorem 5.4] that $\mathcal{L}(5(\infty))$ is a 5-dimensional $\mathbb{F}_p$-vector space with basis $\{1, X, Y, X^2, XY\}$. Hence the obtained linear relation must be trivial, and a straightforward computation yields the relations

$$s = t = 0, \qquad\qquad 3r^2 + 2Ar + 1 = u^4,$$
$$3r + A = Bu^2, \qquad\qquad r^3 + Ar^2 + r = 0.$$

But since E_A only has a single $\mathbb{F}_p$-rational point of order 2, the only $r \in \mathbb{F}_p$ such that $r^3 + Ar^2 + r = 0$ is simply $r = 0$. In that case $u^4 = 1$, and hence $u = \pm 1$ since $p \equiv 3 \pmod 8$. In particular, $u^2 = 1$ and thus $A = B$.   □

Therefore, by choosing public keys to consist of a Montgomery coefficient $A \in \mathbb{F}_p$, Proposition 8 guarantees that A represents a curve in the correct isogeny class $\mathcal{E}\ell\ell_p(\mathcal{O}, \pi)$, where $\pi = \sqrt{-p}$ and $\mathcal{O} = \mathbb{Z}[\pi]$, under the assumption that it is smooth (i.e. $A \notin \{\pm 2\}$) and supersingular.

Verifying supersingularity. As $p \geq 5$, an elliptic curve E defined over $\mathbb{F}_p$ is supersingular if and only if $\#E(\mathbb{F}_p) = p + 1$ [59, Exercise 5.10]. In general, proving that an elliptic curve has a given order N is easy if the factorization of N is known; exhibiting a subgroup (or in particular, a single point) whose order d is a divisor of N greater than $4\sqrt{p}$ implies the order must be correct. Indeed, the condition $d > 4\sqrt{p}$ implies that there exists only one multiple of d in the Hasse interval $[p + 1 - 2\sqrt{p}; p + 1 + 2\sqrt{p}]$ [35]. This multiple must be the group order by Lagrange's theorem.

Now note that a random point generally has very large order d. In our case $E(\mathbb{F}_p) \cong \mathbb{Z}/4 \times \prod_{i=1}^{n} \mathbb{Z}/\ell_i$, so that $\ell_i \mid d$ with probability $(\ell_i - 1)/\ell_i$. Ignoring the even part, this shows that the expected order is lower bounded by

$$\prod_{i=1}^{n} \left(\ell_i - 1 + \frac{1}{\ell_i} \right).$$

This product is about the same size as p, and it is easily seen that a random point will with overwhelming probability have order (much) greater than $4\sqrt{p}$. This observation leads to a straightforward verification method, see Algorithm 1.[8]

Algorithm 1. Verifying supersingularity.

Input: An elliptic curve $E/\mathbb{F}_p$, where $p = 4 \cdot \ell_1 \cdots \ell_n - 1$.
Output: *supersingular* or *ordinary*.

Randomly pick a point $P \in E(\mathbb{F}_p)$ and set $d \leftarrow 1$.
for each ℓ_i **do**
  Set $Q_i \leftarrow [(p+1)/\ell_i]P$.
  If $[\ell_i]Q_i \neq \infty$ **then return** *ordinary*.   // since $\#E(\mathbb{F}_p) \nmid p + 1$
  If $Q_i \neq \infty$ **then set** $d \leftarrow \ell_i \cdot d$.   // since $\ell_i \mid \text{ord } P$
  If $d > 4\sqrt{p}$ **then return** *supersingular*.

If the condition $d > 4\sqrt{p}$ does not hold at the end of Algorithm 1, the point P had too small order to prove $\#E(\mathbb{F}_p) = p + 1$. In this case one may retry with a new random point P (although this outcome has negligible probability and

---

[8] The same idea gives rise to a simpler Monte Carlo algorithm which does not require the factorization of $p + 1$ but has a chance of false positives [64, Sect. 2.3].

could just be ignored). There is no possibility of wrongly classifying an ordinary curve as supersingular.

Note moreover that if x-only Montgomery arithmetic is used (as we suggest) and the point P is obtained by choosing a random x-coordinate in $\mathbb{F}_p$, there is no need to differentiate between points defined over $\mathbb{F}_p$ and $\mathbb{F}_{p^2}$; any x-coordinate in $\mathbb{F}_p$ works. Indeed, any point that has an x-coordinate in $\mathbb{F}_p$ but is only defined over $\mathbb{F}_{p^2}$ corresponds to an $\mathbb{F}_p$-rational point on the quadratic twist, which is supersingular if and only if the original curve is supersingular.

There are more optimized variants of this algorithm; the bulk of the work are the scalar multiplications required to compute the points $Q_i = [(p+1)/\ell_i]P$. Since they are all multiples of P with shared factors, one may more efficiently compute all Q_i at the same time using a divide-and-conquer strategy (at the expense of higher memory usage). See Sect. 8, and in particular Algorithm 3, for details.

6   Non-interactive Key Exchange

Starting from the class-group action on supersingular elliptic curves and the parameter choices outlined in Sects. 3 and 4, one obtains the following non-interactive key-exchange protocol.

Setup. Global parameters of the scheme are a large prime $p = 4 \cdot \ell_1 \cdots \ell_n - 1$, where the ℓ_i are small distinct odd primes, and the supersingular elliptic curve $E_0 : y^2 = x^3 + x$ over $\mathbb{F}_p$ with endomorphism ring $\mathcal{O} = \mathbb{Z}[\pi]$.

Key generation. The private key is an n-tuple $(e_1, \ldots, e_n)$ of integers, each sampled randomly from a range $\{-m, \ldots, m\}$. These integers represent the ideal class $[\mathfrak{a}] = [\mathfrak{l}_1^{e_1} \cdots \mathfrak{l}_n^{e_n}] \in \mathrm{cl}(\mathcal{O})$, where $\mathfrak{l}_i = (\ell_i, \pi - 1)$. The public key is the Montgomery coefficient $A \in \mathbb{F}_p$ of the elliptic curve $[\mathfrak{a}]E_0 : y^2 = x^3 + Ax^2 + x$ obtained by applying the action of $[\mathfrak{a}]$ to the curve E_0.

Key exchange. Suppose Alice and Bob have key pairs $([\mathfrak{a}], A)$ and $([\mathfrak{b}], B)$. Upon receiving Bob's public key $B \in \mathbb{F}_p \setminus \{\pm 2\}$, Alice verifies that the elliptic curve $E_B : y^2 = x^3 + Bx^2 + x$ is indeed in $\mathcal{E}\ell\ell_p(\mathcal{O}, \pi)$ using Algorithm 1. She then applies the action of her secret key $[\mathfrak{a}]$ to E_B to compute the curve $[\mathfrak{a}]E_B = [\mathfrak{a}][\mathfrak{b}]E_0$. Bob proceeds analogously with his own secret $[\mathfrak{b}]$ and Alice's public key A to compute the curve $[\mathfrak{b}]E_A = [\mathfrak{b}][\mathfrak{a}]E_0$. The shared secret is the Montgomery coefficient S of the common secret curve $[\mathfrak{a}][\mathfrak{b}]E_0 = [\mathfrak{b}][\mathfrak{a}]E_0$ written in the form $y^2 = x^3 + Sx^2 + x$, which is the same for Alice and Bob due to the commutativity of $\mathrm{cl}(\mathcal{O})$ and Proposition 8.

Remark 9. Besides key exchange, we expect that our cryptographic group action will have several other applications, given the resemblance with traditional Diffie–Hellman and the ease of verifying the correctness of public keys. We refer to previous papers on group actions for a number of suggestions in this direction, in particular Brassard–Yung [7], Couveignes [17, Sect. 4], and Stolbunov [61]. We highlight the following 1-bit identification scheme, which in our case uses a key pair $([\mathfrak{a}], A)$ as above. One randomly samples an element $[\mathfrak{b}] \in \mathrm{cl}(\mathcal{O})$ and commits to a curve $E' = [\mathfrak{b}]E_0$. Depending on a challenge bit b, one then releases either $[\mathfrak{b}]$ or $[\mathfrak{c}] := [\mathfrak{b}][\mathfrak{a}]^{-1}$, as depicted in Fig. 3. As already pointed out in Stolbunov's PhD thesis [62, Sect. 2.B], this can be turned into a signature scheme by repeated application of the 1-bit protocol and by applying the Fiat–Shamir [24] or Unruh [68] transformation. However, we point out that it is not immediately clear how to represent $[\mathfrak{c}]$ in a way that is efficiently computable and leaks no information about the secret key $[\mathfrak{a}]$. We leave a resolution of this issue for future research, but mention that a related problem was recently tackled by Galbraith, Petit and Silva [30] who studied a similar triangular identification protocol in the context of SIDH.[9]

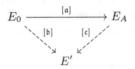

Fig. 3. A 1-bit identification protocol.

7 Security

The central problem of our new primitive is the following analogue to the classical discrete-logarithm problem.

Problem 10 (Key recovery). Given two supersingular elliptic curves E, E' defined over $\mathbb{F}_p$ with the same $\mathbb{F}_p$-rational endomorphism ring $\mathcal{O}$, find an ideal $\mathfrak{a}$ of $\mathcal{O}$ such that $[\mathfrak{a}]E = E'$. This ideal must be represented in such a way that the action of $[\mathfrak{a}]$ on a curve can be evaluated efficiently, for instance $\mathfrak{a}$ could be given as a product of ideals of small norm.

Note that just like in the classical group-based scenario, security notions of Diffie–Hellman schemes built from our primitive rely on slightly different hardness assumptions (cf. Sect. 1.1) that are straightforward translations of the computational and decisional Diffie–Hellman problems. However, continuing the analogy with the classical case, and since we are not aware of any ideas to attack the key exchange without recovering one of the keys, we will assume in the following analysis that the best approach to breaking the key-exchange protocol is to solve Problem 10.

We point out that the "inverse Diffie-Hellman problem" is easy in the context of CSIDH: given $[\mathfrak{a}]E_0$ we can compute $[\mathfrak{a}]^{-1}E_0$ by mere quadratic twisting; see Remark 5. This contrasts with the classical group-based setting [28, Sect. 21.1].

---

[9] The "square" SIDH counterparts of this protocol, as considered in [20, 30, 71], are not meaningful in the case of a commutative group action.

Note that just like identifying a point (x, y) with its inverse $(x, -y)$ in an ECDLP setting, this implies a security loss of one bit under some attacks: An attacker may consider the curves $[\mathfrak{a}]E$ and $[\mathfrak{a}]^{-1}E$ identical, which reduces the search space by half.

No torsion-point images. One of the most worrying properties of SIDH seems to be that Alice and Bob publish the images of known points under their secret isogenies along with the codomain curve, i.e., a public key is of the form $(E', \varphi(P), \varphi(Q))$ where $\varphi \colon E \to E'$ is a secret isogeny and $P, Q \in E$ are publicly known points. Although thus far nobody has succeeded in making use of this extra information to break the original scheme, Petit presented an attack using these points when overstretched, highly asymmetric parameters are used [50]. The Couveignes–Rostovtsev–Stolbunov scheme, and consequently our new scheme CSIDH, does not transmit such additional points—a public key consists of *only* an elliptic curve. Thus we are confident that a potential future attack against SIDH based on these torsion points would not apply to CSIDH.

Chosen-ciphertext attacks. As explained in Sect. 5, the CSIDH group action features efficient public-key validation. This implies it can be used without applying a CCA transform such as the Fujisaki–Okamoto transform [26], thus enabling efficient non-interactive key exchange and other applications in a post-quantum world.

7.1   Classical Security

We begin by considering classical attacks.

Exhaustive key search. The most obvious approach to attack any cryptosystem is to simply search through all possible keys. In the following, we will argue that our construction provides sufficient protection against key search attacks, including dumb brute force and (less naïvely) a meet-in-the-middle approach.

As explained in Sect. 4, a private key of our scheme consists of an exponent vector $(e_1, \ldots, e_n)$ where each e_i is in the range $\{-m, \ldots, m\}$, representing the ideal class $[\mathfrak{l}_1^{e_1} \mathfrak{l}_2^{e_2} \cdots \mathfrak{l}_n^{e_n}] \in \mathrm{cl}(\mathcal{O})$. There may (and typically will) be multiple such vectors that represent the same ideal class and thus form equivalent private keys. However, we argue (heuristically) that the number of *short* representations per ideal class is small. Here and in the following, "short" means that all e_i are in the range $\{-m, \ldots, m\}$. The maximum number of such short representations immediately yields the min-entropy[10] of our sampling method, which measures the amount of work a brute-force attacker has to do while conducting an exhaustive search for the key.

---

[10] The min-entropy of a random variable is the negative logarithm of the probability of the most likely outcome.

We assume in the following discussion that $\mathrm{cl}(\mathcal{O})$ is "almost cyclic" in the sense that it has a very large cyclic component, say of order N not much smaller than $\#\mathrm{cl}(\mathcal{O})$. According to a heuristic of Cohen and Lenstra, this is true with high probability for a "random" imaginary quadratic field [13, Sect. 9.I], and this conjecture is in line with our own experimental evidence. So suppose

$$\rho\colon \mathrm{cl}(\mathcal{O}) \twoheadrightarrow (\mathbb{Z}/N, +)$$

is a surjective group homomorphism (which may be thought of as a projection to the large cyclic subgroup followed by an isomorphism) and define $\alpha_i = \rho([\mathfrak{l}_i])$. We may assume that $\alpha_1 = 1$; this can be done without loss of generality whenever at least one of the $[\mathfrak{l}_i]$ has order N in the class group. For some fixed $[\mathfrak{a}] \in \mathrm{cl}(\mathcal{O})$, any short representation $[\mathfrak{l}_1^{e_1} \mathfrak{l}_2^{e_2} \cdots \mathfrak{l}_n^{e_n}] = [\mathfrak{a}]$ yields a short solution to the linear congruence

$$e_1 + e_2\alpha_2 + \cdots + e_n\alpha_n \equiv \rho([\mathfrak{a}]) \pmod{N},$$

so counting solutions to this congruence gives an upper bound on the number of short representations of $[\mathfrak{a}]$. These solutions are exactly the points in some shifted version (i.e., a coset) of the integer lattice spanned by the rows of the matrix

$$L = \begin{pmatrix} N & 0 & 0 & \cdots & 0 \\ -\alpha_2 & 1 & 0 & \cdots & 0 \\ -\alpha_3 & 0 & 1 & \cdots & 0 \\ \vdots & \vdots & \vdots & \ddots & \vdots \\ -\alpha_n & 0 & 0 & \cdots & 1 \end{pmatrix},$$

so by applying the Gaussian heuristic [49, Chap. 2, Definition 8] one expects

$$\mathrm{vol}\,[-m; m]^n \,/ \det L = (2m+1)^n/N$$

short solutions. Since we assumed $\mathrm{cl}(\mathcal{O})$ to be almost cyclic, this ratio is not much bigger than $(2m+1)^n/\#\mathrm{cl}(\mathcal{O})$, which is not very large for our choice of m as small as possible with $(2m+1)^n \geq \#\mathrm{cl}(\mathcal{O})$.

As a result, we expect the complexity of a brute-force search to be around $2^{\log \sqrt{p} - \varepsilon}$ for some positive ε that is small relative to $\log \sqrt{p}$. To verify our claims, we performed computer experiments with many choices of p of up to 40 bits (essentially brute-forcing the number of representations for all elements) and found no counterexamples to the heuristic result that our sampling method loses only a few bits of brute-force security compared to uniform sampling from the class group. For our sizes of p, the min-entropy was no more than 4 bits less than that of a perfectly uniform distribution on the class group (i.e. $\varepsilon \leq 4$). Of course this loss factor may grow in some way with bigger choices of p (a plot of the data points for small sizes suggests an entropy loss proportional to $\log \log p$), but we see no indication for it to explode beyond a few handfuls of bits, as long as we find m and n so that $(2m+1)^n$ is not much larger than $\#\mathrm{cl}(\mathcal{O})$.

Meet-in-the-middle key search. Since a private key trivially decomposes into a product of two smooth ideals drawn from smaller sets (e.g. splitting $[\mathfrak{l}_1^{e_1} \mathfrak{l}_2^{e_2} \cdots \mathfrak{l}_n^{e_n}]$ as $[\mathfrak{l}_1^{e_1} \cdots \mathfrak{l}_\nu^{e_\nu}] \cdot [\mathfrak{l}_{\nu+1}^{e_{\nu+1}} \cdots \mathfrak{l}_n^{e_n}]$ for some $\nu \in \{1, \dots, n\}$), the usual time-memory trade-offs à la baby-step giant-step [56] with an optimal time complexity of $O(\sqrt{\#\mathrm{cl}(\mathcal{O})}) \approx O(\sqrt[4]{p})$ apply.[11] Another interpretation of this algorithm is finding a path between two nodes in the underlying isogeny graph by constructing a breadth-first tree starting from each of them, each using a certain subset of the edges, and looking for a collision. Details, including a memoryless variation of this concept, can be found in Delfs and Galbraith's paper [22], and for the ordinary case in [27].

Remark 11. The algorithms mentioned thus far scale exponentially in the size of the key space, hence they are asymptotically more expensive than the quantum attacks outlined below which is subexponential in the class-group size. This implies one could possibly balance the costs of the different attacks and use a key space smaller than $\#\mathrm{cl}(\mathcal{O})$ without any loss of security (unless the key space is chosen particularly badly, e.g., as a subgroup), which leads to improved performance. We leave a more thorough analysis of this idea for future work.

Pohlig–Hellman-style attacks. Notice that the set $\mathcal{E}\ell\ell_p(\mathcal{O}, \pi)$ we are acting on does not form a group with efficiently computable operations (that are compatible with the action of $\mathrm{cl}(\mathcal{O})$). Thus there seems to be no way to apply Pohlig–Hellman-style algorithms making use of the decomposition of finite abelian groups. In fact, the Pohlig–Hellman algorithm relies on efficiently computable homomorphisms to proper subgroups, which in the setting at hand would correspond to an efficient algorithm that "projects" a given curve to the orbit of E_0 under a *sub*group action. Therefore, we believe the structure of the class group to be largely irrelevant (assuming it is big enough); in particular, we do not require it to have a large prime-order subgroup.

7.2 Quantum Security

We now discuss the state of quantum algorithms to solve Problem 10.

Grover's algorithm and claw finding. Applying Grover search [32] via claw finding as described in [38] is fully applicable to CSIDH as well, leading to an attack on Problem 10 in $O(\sqrt[6]{p})$ calls to a quantum oracle that computes our group action. The idea is to split the search space for collisions into a classical $O(\sqrt[6]{p})$ target part and a $O(\sqrt[3]{p})$ search part on which a quantum search is applied. Our choices of p that lead to classical security are also immediately large enough to imply quantum security against this attack (cf. [48, Sect. 4.A.5 in Call

---

[11] Strictly speaking, the complexity depends on the size of the subset one samples private keys from, rather than the size of the class group, but as was argued before, these are approximately equal for our choice of m and n.

for Proposals]). That is, the number of queries to our quantum oracle necessary to solve Problem 10 is larger than the number of quantum queries to an AES oracle needed to retrieve the key of the corresponding AES instantiation via Grover's algorithm. For example, an AES-128 key can be recovered with approximately 2^{64} (quantum) oracle queries, which requires us to set $p > 2^{384}$. However, p is much larger than that (see Table 1) due to the existence of subexponential quantum attacks.

The abelian hidden-shift problem. A crucial result by Kuperberg [43] is an algorithm to solve the hidden-shift problem with time, query and space complexity $2^{O(\sqrt{\log N})}$ in an abelian group H of order N. He also showed that any abelian hidden-shift problem reduces to a dihedral hidden-subgroup problem on a different but closely related oracle. A subsequent alternative algorithm by Regev [52] achieves polynomial quantum space complexity with an asymptotically worse time and query complexity of $2^{O(\sqrt{\log N \log \log N})}$. A follow-up algorithm by Kuperberg [44] uses $2^{O(\sqrt{\log N})}$ time, queries and classical space, but only $O(\log N)$ quantum space. All these algorithms have subexponential time and space complexity.

Attacking the isogeny problem. The relevance of these quantum algorithms to Problem 10 has been observed by Childs–Jao–Soukharev [12] in the ordinary case and by Biasse–Jao–Sankar [4] in the supersingular setting. By defining functions $f_0, f_1 \colon \mathrm{cl}(\mathcal{O}) \to \mathcal{Ell}_p(\mathcal{O}, \pi)$ as $f_0 \colon [\mathfrak{b}] \mapsto [\mathfrak{b}]E$ and $f_1 \colon [\mathfrak{b}] \mapsto [\mathfrak{b}]E' = [\mathfrak{b}][\mathfrak{a}]E$, the problem can be viewed as an abelian hidden-shift problem with respect to f_0 and f_1. We note that each query requires evaluating the functions f_i on arbitrary ideal classes (i.e. without being given a representative that is a product of ideals of small prime norm) which is non-trivial. However, Childs–Jao–Soukharev show this can be done in subexponential time and space [12, Sect. 4].

Subexponential vs. practical. An important remark about all these quantum algorithms is that they do not immediately lead to estimates for runtime and memory requirements on concrete instantiations with $H = \mathrm{cl}(\mathcal{O})$. Although the algorithms by Kuperberg and Regev are shown to have subexponential complexity in the limit, this asymptotic behavior is not enough to understand the space and time complexity on actual (small) instances. For example, Kuperberg's first paper [43, Theorem 3.1] mentions $O(2^{3\sqrt{\log N}})$ oracle queries to achieve a non-negligible success probability when N is a power of a small integer. It also presents a second algorithm that runs in $\tilde{O}(3^{\sqrt{2\log_3 N}}) = O(2^{1.8\sqrt{\log N}})$ [43, Theorem 5.1]. His algorithms handle arbitrary group structures but he does not work out more exact counts for those. Of course, this does not contradict the time complexity of $2^{O(\sqrt{\log N})}$ as stated above, but for a concrete security analysis the hidden constants certainly matter a lot and ignoring the O typically underestimates the security. Childs–Jao–Soukharev [12, Theorem 5.2] prove a query complexity of

$$L_N\left[1/2, \sqrt{2}\right] = \exp\left[\left(\sqrt{2} + o(1)\right)\sqrt{\ln N \ln \ln N}\right], \tag{1}$$

where $N = \#\mathrm{cl}(\mathcal{O})$, for using Regev's algorithm for solving the hidden-shift problem. This estimates only the query complexity, so does not include the cost of queries to the quantum oracle (i.e. the isogeny oracle). Childs–Jao–Soukharev present two algorithms to compute the isogeny oracle, the fastest of which is due to Bisson [5]. In [12, Remark 4.8] Childs–Jao–Soukharev give an upper bound of

$$L_p[1/2, 1/\sqrt{2}] = \exp\left[\left(1/\sqrt{2} + o(1)\right)\sqrt{\ln p \ln \ln p}\right] \tag{2}$$

on the running time of Bisson's algorithm.

Remark 12. Childs–Jao–Soukharev compute the total cost for computing the secret isogeny in [12, Remark 5.5] to be $L_p[1/2, 3/\sqrt{2}]$ (using Regev and Bisson's algorithms, requiring only polynomial space). They appear to obtain this by setting $N = p$ when multiplying (1) and (2), but as $N \sim \sqrt{p}$ this is an overestimation and should be $L_p[1/2, 1 + 1/\sqrt{2}]$. Either way, this is the largest asymptotic complexity of the estimates. Also, Galbraith and Vercauteren [31] point out this algorithm actually has superpolynomial space complexity due to the high memory usage of the isogeny oracle in [12], but see [39].

Childs–Jao–Soukharev additionally compute the total time $L_p[1/2, 1/\sqrt{2}]$ for computing the secret isogeny combining Kuperberg [43] and Bisson. This requires superpolynomial storage (also before considering the memory usage of the oracle). Note that in this combination the costs of the oracle computation dominate asymptotically.

It is important to mention that asymptotically worse algorithms may provide practical improvements on our "small" instances over either of the algorithms studied by Childs–Jao–Soukharev: For example, Couveignes [17, Sect. 5] provides heuristic arguments that one can find smooth representatives of ideal classes by computing the class-group structure (which can be done in polynomial time on a quantum computer [34]) and applying a lattice-basis-reduction algorithm such as LLL [45] to its lattice of relations. This might be more efficient than using Childs–Jao–Soukharev's subexponential oracle. However, note that this method makes evaluating the oracle several times harder for the attacker than for legitimate users, thus immediately giving a few additional bits of security, since users only evaluate the action of very smooth ideals by construction. We believe further research in this direction is necessary and important, since it will directly impact the cost of an attack, but we consider a detailed analysis of all these algorithms and possible trade-offs to be beyond the scope of this work.[12]

Remark 13. After we posted a first version of this paper on the Cryptology ePrint Archive, there were three independent attempts at assessing the security of CSIDH.

---

[12] The page margins are certainly too narrow to contain such an analysis.

Biasse, Iezzi, and Jacobson [3] work out some more details of the attack ideas mentioned above for Regev's algorithm. They focus on the class-group-computation part of the oracle and they work out how to represent random elements of the class group as a product of small prime ideals. Their analysis is purely asymptotic and an assessment of the actual cost on specific instances is explicitly left for future work.

Bonnetain and Schrottenloher [6] determine (quantum) query complexities for breaking CSIDH under the assumption that the quantum memory can be made very large, which implies that Kuperberg's faster algorithms would be applicable. They estimate the number of oracle queries as $(5\pi^2/4)2^{1.8\sqrt{\log N}}$. The 1.8 appears to approximate the $\sqrt{2\log 3}$ in Kuperberg [43, Theorem 5.1]. They state $2^{1.8\sqrt{\log N}+2.3}$ for the number of qubits.

While we ignored Kuperberg's algorithm due to the large memory costs, they take the stance that "the most time-efficient version is relevant", and so do not ignore this algorithm. For small N the number of qubits stated in [6] might be possible, which makes Kuperberg's algorithm indeed relevant for these sizes. However, this also highlights the high cost of computing the oracle, which Childs–Jao–Soukharev placed at $L_p[1/2, 1/\sqrt{2}]$. Bonnetain and Schrottenloher investigate the oracle computation using Couveignes' LLL idea and improve it using better lattice basis reduction.

The current version of Bonnetain–Schrottenloher [6] also presents concrete estimates for the attack costs for our parameter sets, but unfortunately this version ignores most of the cost of evaluating isogenies. For example: (1) Algorithm 2 in our paper makes heavy use of input-dependent branches, which is impossible in superposition [39, Sect. 4]; (2) [6] skips finding points of order ℓ_i which are needed as the kernel of the ℓ_i isogeny; (3) [6] applies a result for multiplication costs in $\mathbb{F}_{2^n}$ to multiplications in $\mathbb{F}_p$. We analyzed the (significantly higher) cost of a quantum oracle for isogeny evaluation and conclude that the current estimates of Bonnetain–Schrottenloher do *not* imply that the 512-bit parameters stated below are broken under NIST level 1.

Jao, LeGrow, Leonardi, and Ruiz-Lopez recently made a preprint [39] of their MathCrypt paper available to us. They address the issue of superpolynomial space in the oracle computation identified by Galbraith and Vercauteren (stated above) and give a new algorithm for finding short representations of elements. Their paper focuses on the asymptotic analysis of the oracle step so that they achieve overall polynomial quantum space, but does not obtain any concrete cost estimates.

7.3   Instantiations

Finally we present estimates for some sizes of p.

Security estimates. As explained in Sect. 7.1, the best classical attack has query complexity $O(\sqrt[4]{p})$, and the number of queries has been worked out for different quantum attacks. We consider [12] in combination with Regev and Kuperberg ($L_p[1/2, 3/\sqrt{2}]$ and $L_p[1/2, 1/\sqrt{2}]$, respectively) as well as the pure query complexity of Regev's and Kuperberg's algorithms ($L_N[1/2, \sqrt{2}]$, $O(2^{3\sqrt{\log N}})$, and $O(2^{1.8\sqrt{\log N}})$, respectively). We summarize the resulting attack complexities, ignoring the memory costs and without restricting the maximum depth of quantum circuits, for some sizes of p in Table 1. We note again that we expect these complexities to be subject to more careful analysis, taking into account the implicit constants, the (in-)feasibility of long sequential quantum operations, and the large memory requirement. We also include the recent estimates on the query complexity and full attack complexity by Bonnetain and Schrottenloher [6].

We point out a recent analysis [1] which shows that the classical attack on SIDH (which is the same for CSIDH) is likely slower in practice than current parameter estimates assumed, which is due to the huge memory requirements of the searches. Similarly, the cost of the quantum attacks is significantly higher than just the query complexity times the cost of the group action because evaluating the oracle in superposition is significantly more expensive than a regular group action.

Table 1. Estimated attack complexities ignoring limits on depth. The three rightmost columns state costs for the complete attack; the others state classical and quantum query complexities. All numbers are rounded to whole bits and use $N = \#\mathrm{cl}(\mathcal{O}) = \sqrt{p}$, $o(1) = 0$, and all hidden O-constants 1, except for numbers taken from [6].

CSIDH-$\log p$	Classical $\log \sqrt[4]{p}$	Regev [52] $\log L_N[1/2, \sqrt{2}]$	Kuperberg [43] $3\sqrt{\log N}$	Kuperberg [43] $1.8\sqrt{\log N}$	Table 7 in [6]	[12]-Regev $\log L_p[1/2, 3/\sqrt{2}]$	[12]-Kuperberg $\log L_p[1/2, 1/\sqrt{2}]$	Table 8 in [6]
CSIDH-512	128	62	48	29	32.5	139	47	71
CSIDH-1024	256	94	68	41	44.5	209	70	88
CSIDH-1792	448	129	90	54	57.5	288	96	104

Recall that public keys consist of a single element $A \in \mathbb{F}_p$, which may be represented using $\lceil \log p \rceil$ bits. A private key is represented as a list of n integers in $\{-m, \dots, m\}$, where m was chosen such that $n \log(2m + 1) \approx \log \sqrt{p}$, hence it may be stored using roughly $(\log p)/2$ bits. Therefore the rows of Table 1 correspond to public key sizes of 64, 128, and 224 bytes, and private keys are approximately half that size when encoded optimally.

Security levels. We approximate security levels as proposed by NIST for the post-quantum standardization effort [48, Sect. 4.A.5]. That is, the k-bit security level means that the required effort for the best attacks is at least as large as that needed for a key-retrieval attack on a block cipher with a k-bit key (e.g. AES-k for $k \in \{128, 192, 256\}$). In other words, under the assumption that the attacks query an oracle on a circuit at least as costly as AES, we should have a query complexity of at least 2^{k-1} resp. $\sqrt{2^k}$ to a classical resp. quantum oracle. NIST further restricts the power of the quantum computation to circuits of maximum depth 2^{40} up to 2^{96}, meaning that theoretically optimal tradeoffs (such as the formulas in Table 1 above) might not be possible for cryptographic sizes.

The parameters for CSIDH-log p were chosen to match the query complexity of Regev's attack on the hidden-shift problem (see the third column in Table 1) for roughly $2^{k/2}$, which should match NIST levels 1-3 as the group action computation has depth at least as large as AES.

Some other algorithms give lower estimates which makes it necessary to evaluate the exact cost of the oracle queries or compute the lower-order terms in the complexity. The analysis in [6, Table 8] states lower overall costs compared to AES. While this is a signficant improvement, we believe that this does not affect our security claim when accounting precisely for the actual cost of oracle queries, as stated above. Our preliminary analysis shows costs of more than 2^{50} qubit operations for evaluating the oracle for $\log p = 512$, where [6] assumes 2^{37}. This means that the NIST levels are reached even with the low query numbers in [6]. More analysis is certainly needed and it is unclear whether that will result in larger or smaller choices of p.

Note that adjusting parameters only involves changing the prime p (and a few numbers derived from it) and is therefore very simple, should it turn out that our initial estimates are insufficient.

8   Implementation

In this section, we outline our most important tricks to make the system easier to implement or the code faster. As pointed out earlier, the crucial step is to use a field of size $4 \cdot \ell_1 \cdots \ell_n - 1$, where the ℓ_i are small distinct odd primes; this implies that all ℓ_i are Elkies primes for a supersingular elliptic curve over $\mathbb{F}_p$ and that the action of ideals $(\ell_i, \pi \pm 1)$ can be computed efficiently using $\mathbb{F}_p$-rational points. See Sect. 4 for these design decisions. The following section focuses on lower-level implementation details.

Montgomery curves. The condition $p + 1 \equiv 4 \pmod 8$ implies that all curves in $\mathcal{E}\ell\ell_p(\mathbb{Z}[\pi], \pi)$ can be put in the form $y^2 = x^3 + Ax^2 + x$ (cf. Proposition 8) for some $A \in \mathbb{F}_p$ via an $\mathbb{F}_p$-isomorphism. This is commonly referred to as the Montgomery form [46] of an elliptic curve and is popular due to the very efficient arithmetic on its x-line. This extends well to computations of isogenies on the x-line, as was first shown by Costello–Longa–Naehrig [15, Sect. 3]. Our implementation uses exactly the same formulas for operations on curves. For isogeny computations on Montgomery curves we use a projectivized variant (to avoid almost all inversions) of the formulas from Costello–Hisil [14] and Renes [53]. This can be done as follows.

For a fixed prime $\ell \geq 3$, a point P of order ℓ, and an integer $k \in \{1, \ldots, \ell-1\}$, let $(X_k : Z_k)$ be the projectivized x-coordinate of $[k]P$. Then by defining $c_i \in \mathbb{F}_p$ such that

$$\prod_{i=1}^{\ell-1}(Z_i w + X_i) = \sum_{i=0}^{\ell-1} c_i w^i$$

as polynomials in w, we observe that

$$(\tau(A - 3\sigma) : 1) = \left(A c_0 c_{\ell-1} - 3(c_0 c_{\ell-2} - c_1 c_{\ell-1}) : c_{\ell-1}^2\right),$$

where

$$\tau = \prod_{i=1}^{\ell-1} \frac{X_i}{Z_i}, \quad \sigma = \sum_{i=1}^{\ell-1} \left(\frac{X_i}{Z_i} - \frac{Z_i}{X_i}\right)$$

and A is the Montgomery coefficient of the domain curve. By noticing that $x([k]P) = x([\ell-k]P)$ for all $k \in \{1, \ldots, (\ell-1)/2\}$ we can reduce the computation needed by about half. That is, we can compute $(\tau(A-3\sigma) : 1)$ iteratively in about $5\ell\mathbf{M} + \ell\mathbf{S}$ operations[13], noting that $\tau(A - 3\sigma)$ is the Montgomery coefficient of the codomain curve of an isogeny with kernel $\langle P \rangle$ [53, Proposition 1]. If necessary, a single division at the end of the computation suffices to obtain an affine curve constant. We refer to the implementation for more details.

Note that for a given prime ℓ, we could reduce the number of field operations by finding an appropriate representative of the isogeny formulas modulo (a factor of) the ℓ-division polynomial ψ_ℓ (as done in [15] for 3- and 4-isogenies). Although this would allow for a more efficient implementation, we do not pursue this now for the sake of simplicity.

Rational points. Recall that the goal is to evaluate the action of (the class of) an ideal $\mathfrak{l}_1^{e_1} \cdots \mathfrak{l}_n^{e_n}$ on a curve $E \in \mathcal{E}\!\ell\ell_p(\mathbb{Z}[\pi], \pi)$, where each $\mathfrak{l}_i = (\ell_i, \pi - 1)$ is a prime ideal of small odd norm ℓ_i and the e_i are integers in a short range $\{-m, \ldots, m\}$. We assume E is given in the form $E_A : y^2 = x^3 + Ax^2 + x$.

The obvious way to do this is to consider each factor $\mathfrak{l}_i^{\pm 1}$ in this product and to find the abscissa of a point P of order ℓ_i on E, which (depending on the sign) is defined over $\mathbb{F}_p$ or $\mathbb{F}_{p^2} \setminus \mathbb{F}_p$. This exists by our choice of p and ℓ_i (cf. Sect. 4). Finding such an abscissa amounts to sampling a random $\mathbb{F}_p$-rational x-coordinate, checking whether $x^3 + Ax^2 + x$ is a square or not (for $\mathfrak{l}_i^{+1}$ resp. $\mathfrak{l}_i^{-1}$) in $\mathbb{F}_p$ (and resampling if it was wrong), followed by a multiplication by $(p+1)/\ell_i$ and repeating from the start if the result is ∞. The kernel of the isogeny given by $\mathfrak{l}_i^{\pm 1}$ is then $\langle P \rangle$, so the isogeny may be computed using Vélu-type formulas. Repeating this procedure for all $\mathfrak{l}_i^{\pm 1}$ gives the result.

However, fixing a sign before sampling a random point effectively means wasting about half of all random points, including an ultimately useless square test. Moreover, deciding on a prime ℓ_i before sampling a point and doing the cofactor multiplication wastes another proportion of the points, including both

---

[13] Here $\mathbf{M}$ and $\mathbf{S}$ denote a multiplication and squaring in $\mathbb{F}_p$.

an ultimately useless square test and a scalar multiplication. Both of these issues can be remedied by not fixing an ℓ_i before sampling a point, but instead taking *any* x-coordinate, determining the smallest field of definition (i.e. $\mathbb{F}_p$ or $\mathbb{F}_{p^2}$) of the corresponding point, and then performing whatever isogeny computations are possible using that point (based on its field of definition and order). The steps are detailed in Algorithm 2.

Algorithm 2. Evaluating the class-group action.

Input: $A \in \mathbb{F}_p$ and a list of integers $(e_1, \ldots, e_n)$.
Output: B such that $[\mathfrak{l}_1^{e_1} \cdots \mathfrak{l}_n^{e_n}]E_A = E_B$ (where $E_B : y^2 = x^3 + Bx^2 + x$).

While some $e_i \neq 0$ **do**
     Sample a random $x \in \mathbb{F}_p$.
     Set $s \leftarrow +1$ if $x^3 + Ax^2 + x$ is a square in $\mathbb{F}_p$, else $s \leftarrow -1$.
     Let $S = \{i \mid e_i \neq 0, \operatorname{sign}(e_i) = s\}$. **If** $S = \emptyset$ **then** start over with a new x.
     Let $k \leftarrow \prod_{i \in S} \ell_i$ and compute $Q \leftarrow [(p+1)/k]P$.
     For each $i \in S$ **do**
         Compute $R \leftarrow [k/\ell_i]Q$. **If** $R = \infty$ **then** skip this i.
         Compute an isogeny $\varphi : E_A \to E_B : y^2 = x^3 + Bx^2 + x$ with $\ker \varphi = R$.
         Set $A \leftarrow B$, $Q \leftarrow \varphi(Q)$, $k \leftarrow k/\ell_i$, and finally $e_i \leftarrow e_i - s$.
Return A.

Due to the commutativity of $\mathrm{cl}(\mathcal{O})$, and since we only decrease (the absolute value of) each e_i once we successfully applied the action of $\mathfrak{l}_i^{\pm 1}$ to the current curve, this algorithm indeed computes the action of $[\mathfrak{l}_1^{e_1} \mathfrak{l}_2^{e_2} \cdots \mathfrak{l}_n^{e_n}]$.

Remark 14. Since the probability that a random point has order divisible by ℓ_i (and hence leads to an isogeny step in Algorithm 2) grows with ℓ_i, the isogeny steps for big ℓ_i are typically completed before those for small ℓ_i. Hence it may make sense to sample the exponents e_i for ideals $\mathfrak{l}_i$ from different ranges depending on the size of ℓ_i, or to not include any very small ℓ_i in the factorization of $p + 1$ at all to reduce the expected number of repetitions of the loop above. Note moreover that doing so may also improve the performance of straightforward constant-time adaptions of our algorithms, since it yields stronger upper bounds on the maximum number of required loop iterations (at the expense of slightly higher cost per isogeny computation). Varying the choice of the ℓ_i can also lead to performance improvements if the resulting prime p has lower Hamming weight. Finding such a p is a significant computational effort but needs to be done only once; all users can use the same finite field.

Remark 15. Algorithm 2 is obviously strongly variable-time when implemented naïvely. Indeed, the number of points computed in the isogeny formulas is linear in the degree, hence the iteration counts of certain loops in our implementation are very directly related to the private key. We note that it would not be very hard to create a constant-time implementation based on this algorithm by always performing the maximal required number of iterations in each loop and only storing the results that were actually needed (using constant-time conditional instructions), although this incurs quite a bit of useless computation, leading to a doubling of the number of curve operations on average. We leave the design of optimized constant-time algorithms for future work.

Public-key validation. Recall that the public-key validation method outlined in Sect. 5 essentially consists of computing $[(p+1)/\ell_i]P$ for each i, where P is a random point on E. Performing this computation in the straightforward way is simple and effective. On the other hand, a divide-and-conquer approach, such as the following recursive algorithm, yields better speeds at the expense of slightly higher memory usage. Note that Algorithm 3 only operates on public data, hence need not be constant-time in a side-channel resistant implementation.

Algorithm 3. Batch cofactor multiplication. [63, Algorithm 7.3]

Input: An elliptic-curve point P and positive integers $(k_1, \ldots, k_n)$.
Output: The points $(Q_1, \ldots, Q_n)$, where $Q_i = \big[\prod_{j \neq i} k_j\big]P$.
If $n = 1$ then return (P).   // base case
Set $m \leftarrow \lceil n/2 \rceil$ and let $u \leftarrow \prod_{i=1}^m k_i$, $v \leftarrow \prod_{i=m+1}^n k_i$.
Compute $L \leftarrow [v]P$ and $R \leftarrow [u]P$.
Recurse with input $L, (k_1, \ldots, k_m)$ giving $(Q_1, \ldots, Q_m)$.   // left half
Recurse with input $R, (k_{m+1}, \ldots, k_n)$ giving $(Q_{m+1}, \ldots, Q_n)$.   // right half
Return $(Q_1, \ldots, Q_n)$.

This routine can be used for verifying that an elliptic curve $E/\mathbb{F}_p$ is supersingular as follows: Pick a random point $P \in E(\mathbb{F}_p)$ and run Algorithm 3 on input $[4]P$ and $(\ell_1, \ldots, \ell_n)$ to obtain the points $Q_i = [(p+1)/\ell_i]P$. Then continue like in Algorithm 1 to verify that E is supersingular using these precomputed points.

In practice, it is not necessary to run Algorithm 3 as a black-box function until it returns all the points $Q_1, \ldots, Q_n$: The order checking in Algorithm 1 can be performed as soon as a new point Q_i becomes available, i.e., in the base case of Algorithm 3. This reduces the memory usage (since the points Q_i can be discarded immediately after use) and increases the speed (since the algorithm terminates as soon as enough information was obtained) of public-key validation using Algorithms 1 and 3. We note that the improved performance of this algorithm compared to Algorithm 1 alone essentially comes from a time-space trade-off, hence the memory usage is higher (cf. Sect. 8.1). On severely memory-constrained devices one may instead opt for the naïve algorithm, which requires less space but is slower.

8.1   Performance Results

On top of a minimal implementation in the sage computer algebra system [67] for demonstrative purposes, we created a somewhat optimized proof-of-concept implementation of the CSIDH group action for a particular 512-bit prime p.

While this implementation features 512-bit field arithmetic written in assembly (for Intel Skylake processors), it also contains generic C code supporting other field sizes and can therefore easily be ported to other computer architectures or parameter sets if desired.[14]

The prime p is chosen as $p = 4 \cdot \ell_1 \cdots \ell_{74} - 1$ where ℓ_1 through ℓ_{73} are the smallest 73 odd primes and $\ell_{74} = 587$ is the smallest prime distinct from the other ℓ_i that renders p prime. This parameter choice implies that public keys have a size of 64 bytes. Private keys are stored in 37 bytes for simplicity, but an optimal encoding would reduce this to only 32 bytes. Table 2 summarizes performance numbers for our proof-of-concept implementation. Note that private-key generation is not listed as it only consists of sampling n random integers in a small range $\{-m, \ldots, m\}$, which has negligible cost.

Table 2. Performance numbers of our proof-of-concept implementation, averaged over 10 000 runs on an Intel Skylake i5 processor clocked at 3.5 GHz.

	Clock cycles	Wall-clock time	Stack memory
Key validation	$5.5 \cdot 10^6$ cc	2.1 ms	4 368 bytes
Group action	$106 \cdot 10^6$ cc	40.8 ms	2 464 bytes

We emphasize that both our implementations are intended as a proof of concept and unfit for production use; in particular, they are explicitly *not side-channel resistant* and may contain any number of bugs. We leave the design of hardened and more optimized implementations for future work.

References

1. Adj, G., Cervantes-Vázquez, D., Chi-Domínguez, J.-J., Menezes, A., Rodríguez-Henríquez, F.: On the cost of computing isogenies between supersingular elliptic curves. In: SAC 2018 (2018)
2. Bernstein, D.J., van Gastel, B., Janssen, W., Lange, T., Schwabe, P., Smetsers, S.: TweetNaCl: a crypto library in 100 tweets. In: Aranha, D.F., Menezes, A. (eds.) LATINCRYPT 2014. LNCS, vol. 8895, pp. 64–83. Springer, Cham (2015). https://doi.org/10.1007/978-3-319-16295-9_4
3. Biasse, J.-F., Iezzi, A., Jacobson Jr., M.J.: A note on the security of CSIDH (2018). https://arxiv.org/abs/1806.03656. To be published at Kangacrypt 2018
4. Biasse, J.-F., Jao, D., Sankar, A.: A quantum algorithm for computing isogenies between supersingular elliptic curves. In: Meier, W., Mukhopadhyay, D. (eds.) INDOCRYPT 2014. LNCS, vol. 8885, pp. 428–442. Springer, Cham (2014). https://doi.org/10.1007/978-3-319-13039-2_25
5. Bisson, G.: Computing endomorphism rings of elliptic curves under the GRH. J. Math. Cryptol. **5**(2), 101–114 (2012)

---

[14] All our code is published in the public domain and is available for download at https://yx7.cc/code/csidh/csidh-latest.tar.xz.

6. Bonnetain, X., Schrottenloher, A.: Quantum security analysis of CSIDH and ordinary isogeny-based schemes. IACR Cryptology ePrint Archive 2018/537, version 20180621:135910 (2018). https://eprint.iacr.org/2018/537/20180621:135910

7. Brassard, G., Yung, M.: One-way group actions. In: Menezes, A.J., Vanstone, S.A. (eds.) CRYPTO 1990. LNCS, vol. 537, pp. 94–107. Springer, Heidelberg (1991). https://doi.org/10.1007/3-540-38424-3_7

8. Bröker, R.: A p-adic algorithm to compute the Hilbert class polynomial. Math. Comput. **77**(264), 2417–2435 (2008)

9. Bröker, R., Stevenhagen, P.: Efficient CM-constructions of elliptic curves over finite fields. Math. Comput. **76**(260), 2161–2179 (2007)

10. Buchmann, J., Vollmer, U.: Binary Quadratic Forms: An Algorithmic Approach. Algorithms and Computation in Mathematics, vol. 20. Springer, Heidelberg (2007). https://doi.org/10.1007/978-3-540-46368-9

11. Charles, D.X., Lauter, K.E., Goren, E.Z.: Cryptographic hash functions from expander graphs. J. Cryptol. **22**(1), 93–113 (2009)

12. Childs, A.M., Jao, D., Soukharev, V.: Constructing elliptic curve isogenies in quantum subexponential time. J. Math. Cryptol. **8**(1), 1–29 (2014)

13. Cohen, H., Lenstra Jr., H.W.: Heuristics on class groups of number fields. In: Jager, H. (ed.) Number Theory Noordwijkerhout 1983. LNM, vol. 1068, pp. 33–62. Springer, Heidelberg (1984)

14. Costello, C., Hisil, H.: A simple and compact algorithm for SIDH with arbitrary degree isogenies. In: Takagi, T., Peyrin, T. (eds.) ASIACRYPT 2017. LNCS, vol. 10625, pp. 303–329. Springer, Cham (2017). https://doi.org/10.1007/978-3-319-70697-9_11

15. Costello, C., Longa, P., Naehrig, M.: Efficient algorithms for supersingular isogeny Diffie-Hellman. In: Robshaw, M., Katz, J. (eds.) CRYPTO 2016. LNCS, vol. 9814, pp. 572–601. Springer, Heidelberg (2016). https://doi.org/10.1007/978-3-662-53018-4_21

16. Costello, C., Smith, B.: Montgomery curves and their arithmetic: the case of large characteristic fields. IACR Cryptology ePrint Archive 2017/212 (2017). https://ia.cr/2017/212

17. Couveignes, J.-M.: Hard homogeneous spaces. IACR Cryptology ePrint Archive 2006/291 (2006). https://ia.cr/2006/291

18. Cox, D.A.: Primes of the Form $x^2 + ny^2$: Fermat, Class Field Theory, and Complex Multiplication. Pure and Applied Mathematics, 2nd edn. Wiley, Hoboken (2013)

19. De Feo, L.: Mathematics of isogeny based cryptography (2017). https://arxiv.org/abs/1711.04062

20. De Feo, L., Jao, D., Plût, J.: Towards quantum-resistant cryptosystems from supersingular elliptic curve isogenies. J. Math. Cryptol. **8**(3), 209–247 (2014)

21. De Feo, L., Kieffer, J., Smith, B.: Towards practical key exchange from ordinary isogeny graphs. In: Galbraith, S.D., Peyrin, T. (eds.) ASIACRYPT 2018, LNCS, vol. 11274, pp. xx–yy. Springer, Heidelberg (2018)

22. Delfs, C., Galbraith, S.D.: Computing isogenies between supersingular elliptic curves over $\mathbb{F}_p$. Des. Codes Cryptogr. **78**(2), 425–440 (2016)

23. Diffie, W., Hellman, M.E.: New directions in cryptography. IEEE Trans. Inf. Theory **22**(6), 644–654 (1976)

24. Fiat, A., Shamir, A.: How to prove yourself: practical solutions to identification and signature problems. In: Odlyzko, A.M. (ed.) CRYPTO 1986. LNCS, vol. 263, pp. 186–194. Springer, Heidelberg (1987). https://doi.org/10.1007/3-540-47721-7_12

25. Freire, E.S.V., Hofheinz, D., Kiltz, E., Paterson, K.G.: Non-interactive key exchange. In: Kurosawa, K., Hanaoka, G. (eds.) PKC 2013. LNCS, vol. 7778, pp. 254–271. Springer, Heidelberg (2013). https://doi.org/10.1007/978-3-642-36362-7_17
26. Fujisaki, E., Okamoto, T.: Secure integration of asymmetric and symmetric encryption schemes. In: Wiener, M. (ed.) CRYPTO 1999. LNCS, vol. 1666, pp. 537–554. Springer, Heidelberg (1999). https://doi.org/10.1007/3-540-48405-1_34
27. Galbraith, S.D.: Constructing isogenies between elliptic curves over finite fields. LMS J. Computat. Math. **2**, 118–138 (1999)
28. Galbraith, S.D.: Mathematics of Public-Key Cryptography. Cambridge University Press, Cambridge (2012)
29. Galbraith, S.D., Petit, C., Shani, B., Ti, Y.B.: On the security of supersingular isogeny cryptosystems. In: Cheon, J.H., Takagi, T. (eds.) ASIACRYPT 2016. LNCS, vol. 10031, pp. 63–91. Springer, Heidelberg (2016). https://doi.org/10.1007/978-3-662-53887-6_3
30. Galbraith, S.D., Petit, C., Silva, J.: Identification protocols and signature schemes based on supersingular isogeny problems. In: Takagi, T., Peyrin, T. (eds.) ASIACRYPT 2017. LNCS, vol. 10624, pp. 3–33. Springer, Cham (2017). https://doi.org/10.1007/978-3-319-70694-8_1
31. Galbraith, S.D., Vercauteren, F.: Computational problems in supersingular elliptic curve isogenies. Quant. Inf. Process. 17. IACR Cryptology ePrint Archive 2017/774 (2018). https://ia.cr/2017/774
32. Grover, L.K.: A fast quantum mechanical algorithm for database search. In: STOC, pp. 212–219. ACM (1996)
33. Hafner, J.L., McCurley, K.S.: A rigorous subexponential algorithm for computation of class groups. J. Am. Math. Soc. **2**(4), 837–850 (1989)
34. Hallgren, S.: Fast quantum algorithms for computing the unit group and class group of a number field. In: STOC, pp. 468–474. ACM (2005)
35. Hasse, H.: Zur Theorie der abstrakten elliptischen Funktionenkörper III. Die Struktur des Meromorphismenrings. Die Riemannsche Vermutung. J. für die reine und angewandte Mathematik **175**, 193–208 (1936)
36. Hofheinz, D., Hövelmanns, K., Kiltz, E.: A Modular analysis of the Fujisaki-Okamoto transformation. In: Kalai, Y., Reyzin, L. (eds.) TCC 2017. LNCS, vol. 10677, pp. 341–371. Springer, Cham (2017). https://doi.org/10.1007/978-3-319-70500-2_12
37. Jao, D., Azarderakhsh, R., Campagna, M., Costello, C., De Feo, L., Hess, B., Jalali, A., Koziel, B., LaMacchia, B., Longa, P., Naehrig, M., Renes, J., Soukharev, V., Urbanik, D.: SIKE. Submission to [48]. http://sike.org
38. Jao, D., De Feo, L.: Towards quantum-resistant cryptosystems from supersingular elliptic curve isogenies. In: Yang, B.-Y. (ed.) PQCrypto 2011. LNCS, vol. 7071, pp. 19–34. Springer, Heidelberg (2011). https://doi.org/10.1007/978-3-642-25405-5_2
39. Jao, D., LeGrow, J., Leonardi, C., Ruiz-Lopez, L.: A subexponential-time, polynomial quantum space algorithm for inverting the CM group action. In: MathCrypt 2018 (2018, to appear)
40. Jao, D., Miller, S.D., Venkatesan, R.: Expander graphs based on GRH with an application to elliptic curve cryptography. J. Number Theory **129**(6), 1491–1504 (2009)
41. Kieffer, J.: Étude et accélération du protocole d'échange de clés de Couveignes-Rostovtsev-Stolbunov. Mémoire du Master 2, Université Paris VI (2017). https://arxiv.org/abs/1804.10128

42. Kohel, D.: Endomorphism rings of elliptic curves over finite fields. Ph.D. thesis, University of California at Berkeley (1996)

43. Kuperberg, G.: A subexponential-time quantum algorithm for the dihedral hidden subgroup problem. SIAM J. Comput. **35**(1), 170–188 (2005)

44. Kuperberg, G.: Another subexponential-time quantum algorithm for the dihedral hidden subgroup problem. In: TQC, LIPIcs, vol. 22, pp. 20–34. Schloss Dagstuhl - Leibniz-Zentrum für Informatik (2013)

45. Lenstra Jr., H.W., Lenstra, A.K., Lovász, L.: Factoring polynomials with rational coefficients. Math. Ann. **261**, 515–534 (1982)

46. Montgomery, P.L.: Speeding the Pollard and elliptic curve methods of factorization. Math. Comput. **48**(177), 243–264 (1987)

47. Mordell, L.J.: The congruence $(p - 1/2)! \equiv \pm 1$ (mod p). Am. Math. Mon. **68**(2), 145–146 (1961)

48. National Institute of Standards and Technology: Post-quantum Cryptography Standardization, December 2016. https://csrc.nist.gov/Projects/Post-Quantum-Cryptography/Post-Quantum-Cryptography-Standardization

49. Nguyen, P.Q., Vallée, B. (eds.): The LLL Algorithm. Springer, Heidelberg (2010). https://doi.org/10.1007/978-3-642-02295-1

50. Petit, C.: Faster algorithms for isogeny problems using torsion point images. In: Takagi, T., Peyrin, T. (eds.) ASIACRYPT 2017. LNCS, vol. 10625, pp. 330–353. Springer, Cham (2017). https://doi.org/10.1007/978-3-319-70697-9_12

51. Pizer, A.K.: Ramanujan graphs and Hecke operators. Bull. Am. Math. Soc. (N.S.) **23**(1), 127–137 (1990)

52. Regev, O.: A subexponential time algorithm for the dihedral hidden subgroup problem with polynomial space (2004). https://arxiv.org/abs/quant-ph/0406151

53. Renes, J.: Computing isogenies between Montgomery curves using the action of (0, 0). In: Lange, T., Steinwandt, R. (eds.) PQCrypto 2018. LNCS, vol. 10786, pp. 229–247. Springer, Cham (2018). https://doi.org/10.1007/978-3-319-79063-3_11

54. Rostovtsev, A., Stolbunov, A.: Public-key cryptosystem based on isogenies. IACR Cryptology ePrint Archive 2006/145 (2006). https://ia.cr/2006/145

55. Schoof, R.: Nonsingular plane cubic curves over finite fields. J. Comb. Theory Ser. A **46**(2), 183–211 (1987)

56. Shanks, D.: Class number, a theory of factorization, and genera. In: Proceedings of Symposia in Pure Mathematics, vol. 20, pp. 415–440 (1971)

57. Shor, P.W.: Polynomial-time algorithms for prime factorization and discrete logarithms on a quantum computer. SIAM J. Comput. **26**(5), 1484–1509 (1997)

58. Siegel, C.: Über die Classenzahl quadratischer Zahlkörper. Acta Arithmetica **1**(1), 83–86 (1935)

59. Silverman, J.H.: The Arithmetic of Elliptic Curves. Graduate Texts in Mathematics, vol. 106, 2nd edn. Springer, New York (2009). https://doi.org/10.1007/978-0-387-09494-6

60. Stolbunov, A.: Public-key encryption based on cycles of isogenous elliptic curves. Master's thesis, Saint-Petersburg State Polytechnical University (2004). (in Russian)

61. Stolbunov, A.: Constructing public-key cryptographic schemes based on class group action on a set of isogenous elliptic curves. Adv. Math. Commun. **4**(2), 215–235 (2010)

62. Stolbunov, A.: Cryptographic schemes based on isogenies. Ph.D. thesis, Norwegian University of Science and Technology (2011)

63. Sutherland, A.V.: Order computations in generic groups. Ph.D. thesis, Massachusetts Institute of Technology (2007). https://groups.csail.mit.edu/cis/theses/sutherland-phd.pdf

64. Sutherland, A.V.: Identifying supersingular elliptic curves. LMS J. Comput. Math. **15**, 317–325 (2012)

65. Sutherland, A.V.: Isogeny volcanoes. In: ANTS X. Open Book Series, vol. 1, pp. 507–530. MSP (2012). https://arxiv.org/abs/1208.5370

66. Tate, J.: Endomorphisms of abelian varieties over finite fields. Inventiones Mathematicae **2**(2), 134–144 (1966)

67. The Sage Developers: SageMath, The Sage Mathematics Software System, Version 8.1 (2018). https://sagemath.org

68. Unruh, D.: Quantum proofs of knowledge. In: Pointcheval, D., Johansson, T. (eds.) EUROCRYPT 2012. LNCS, vol. 7237, pp. 135–152. Springer, Heidelberg (2012). https://doi.org/10.1007/978-3-642-29011-4_10

69. Vélu, J.: Isogénies entre courbes elliptiques. Comptes Rendus de l'Académie des Sciences de Paris **273**, 238–241 (1971)

70. Waterhouse, W.C.: Abelian varieties over finite fields. Annales scientifiques de l'École Normale Supérieure **2**, 521–560 (1969)

71. Yoo, Y., Azarderakhsh, R., Jalali, A., Jao, D., Soukharev, V.: A post-quantum digital signature scheme based on supersingular isogenies. In: Kiayias, A. (ed.) FC 2017. LNCS, vol. 10322, pp. 163–181. Springer, Cham (2017). https://doi.org/10.1007/978-3-319-70972-7_9

Computing Supersingular Isogenies
on Kummer Surfaces

Craig Costello[✉]

Microsoft Research, Redmond, USA
craigco@microsoft.com

Abstract. We apply Scholten's construction to give explicit isogenies between the Weil restriction of supersingular Montgomery curves with full rational 2-torsion over $\mathbb{F}_{p^2}$ and corresponding abelian surfaces over $\mathbb{F}_p$. Subsequently, we show that isogeny-based public key cryptography can exploit the fast Kummer surface arithmetic that arises from the theory of theta functions. In particular, we show that chains of 2-isogenies between elliptic curves can instead be computed as chains of Richelot $(2, 2)$-isogenies between Kummer surfaces. This gives rise to new possibilities for efficient supersingular isogeny-based cryptography.

Keywords: Supersingular isogenies · SIDH · Kummer surface Richelot isogeny · Scholten's construction

1 Introduction

Public key cryptography based on supersingular isogenies is gaining increased popularity due to its conjectured quantum-resistance. In November 2017, an actively secure key encapsulation mechanism called SIKE [22], which is based on Jao and De Feo's supersingular isogeny Diffie-Hellman (SIDH) protocol [16,23], was submitted to NIST in response to their call for quantum-resistant public key solutions [34]. When compared to other proposals of quantum-resistant key encapsulation mechanisms, SIKE currently offers an interesting bandwidth versus performance trade-off; its keys are appreciably smaller than its code- and lattice-based counterparts, but the times required for encapsulation and decapsulation are significantly higher. This performance drawback of supersingular isogeny-based cryptography is the main practical motivation for this paper.

This Work. 15 years ago, Scholten [31] showed that if E is an elliptic curve defined over a quadratic extension field L of a non-binary field K, and if its entire 2-torsion is L-rational, then a genus-2 curve C can be constructed over K such that its Jacobian J_C is isogenous to the Weil restriction $\mathrm{Res}_K^L(E)$. Fortuitously, supersingular isogeny-based cryptography currently uses elliptic curves that precisely meet these requirements. In particular, state-of-the-art implementations (e.g., [14,15]) of SIDH fix a large prime field $K = \mathbb{F}_p$ with $p = 2^i 3^j - 1$ for

© International Association for Cryptologic Research 2018
T. Peyrin and S. Galbraith (Eds.): ASIACRYPT 2018, LNCS 11274, pp. 428–456, 2018.
https://doi.org/10.1007/978-3-030-03332-3_16

$i > j > 100$, construct $L = \mathbb{F}_{p^2}$, and work in the supersingular isogeny class of elliptic curves over $\mathbb{F}_{p^2}$ whose group structures are all isomorphic to $\mathbb{Z}_{p+1} \times \mathbb{Z}_{p+1}$. This necessarily means that all curves in the supersingular isogeny class have full rational 2-torsion, can be written in Montgomery form, and that for any such curve $E/\mathbb{F}_{p^2}$, Scholten's construction can be used to write down the curve $C/\mathbb{F}_p$ whose Jacobian J_C is isogenous to the Weil restriction of E with respect to $\mathbb{F}_{p^2}/\mathbb{F}_p$.

In Proposition 1 we use Scholten's construction to write down a curve whose Jacobian is isogenous to the Weil restriction of any supersingular curve that satisfies the above requirements. Although the existence of this isogeny is guaranteed by his construction, Scholten does not provide the isogeny itself, and as is pointed out in [6, Sect. 2], the construction does not guarantee that this isogeny is efficiently computable. In our supersingular setting, however, we are able to derive simple explicit isogenies between the two varieties; these turn out to be dual $(2,2)$-isogenies whose compositions are, by definition, the multiplication-by-2 morphism on the corresponding varieties.

The application of Scholten's construction and the derivation of the explicit maps above allows us to study SIDH computations on abelian surfaces over $\mathbb{F}_p$, rather than on elliptic curves over $\mathbb{F}_{p^2}$. In particular, rather than using Vélu's formulas [35] to compute secret 2e-isogenies as chains of 2- and/or 4-isogenies on elliptic curves over $\mathbb{F}_{p^2}$ [16], we show that the same secret isogenies can instead be computed as a chain of $(2,2)$-isogenies on Jacobian varieties over $\mathbb{F}_p$. While computing isogenies on higher genus abelian varieties is, in general, much more complicated than Vélu's formulas for elliptic curve isogenies, the special case of $(2,2)$-isogenies between genus-2 Jacobians dates back to the works of Richelot [29,30] from almost two centuries ago. Subsequently, the computation of *Richelot isogenies* is already well-documented in the literature (cf. [10,33]), and this allows us to tailor the explicit formulas to our scenario of computing chains of $(2,2)$-isogenies on supersingular Jacobians.

Crucial to the efficacy of this work is that we are able to compute $(2,2)$-isogenies on the Kummer surfaces associated to supersingular Jacobians, rather than in the full Jacobian groups. This allows us to leverage the fast Kummer surface arithmetic arising from the classical theory of theta functions, which was first proposed for computational purposes by the Chudnovsky brothers [12], and which was brought to life in cryptography by Gaudry [19]. In his article [19, Remark 3.5], Gaudry points out that the fast (pseudo-)doublings on Kummer surfaces are the result of pushing points back and forth through a $(2,2)$-isogenous variety, i.e., that the corresponding $(2,2)$-isogenies split the multiplication-by-2 map on the associated Kummer surface. This observation plays a key role in deriving efficient isogenies on fast Kummer surfaces.

Related Work. This paper relies on the results of several authors:-

– The construction in Scholten's unpublished manuscript [31] is at the heart of this work. It gives rise to Proposition 1 which paves the way for the rest of the paper.

- In 2014, Bernstein and Lange [6] revived Scholten's work when they proposed using his construction in the context of (hyper)elliptic curve cryptography (H)ECC to convert keys back and forth between elliptic and hyperelliptic curves, in such a way so as to exploit advantageous properties of both settings. They were also the first to explicitly derive instances of the isogenies alluded to by Scholten, and to show that they can be efficient enough to be used in online cryptographic computations. The setting considered in [6] has the advantage of having a single elliptic-and-hyperelliptic curve pair that is fixed once-and-for-all (meaning the back-and-forth maps also remain fixed), while in our scenario we will need general-purpose maps that can handle any supersingular Montgomery curves efficiently at runtime. However, in the supersingular setting, we have the advantage that our Jacobians have a fixed embedding degree of $k = 2$, and we can therefore exploit the existence of an efficiently computable *trace map*; this allows us to derive much simpler back-and-forth isogenies than those presented in [6].

- Renes and Smith [28] recently introduced qDSA: the quotient digital signature algorithm. In order to instantiate their scheme on fast Kummer surfaces, they deconstructed the pseudo-doubling map into the explicit $(2,2)$-isogenies alluded to by Gaudry [19, Remark 3.5]; this deconstruction (depicted in [28, Fig. 1]) plays a key role in this paper. Indeed, it was their explicit treatment of *the dual Kummer surface* and subsequent illustration of simple $(2,2)$-isogenies between fast Kummer surfaces that, in part, inspired the present work.

- Being able to study Kummer surface arithmetic as a viable alternative in the supersingular isogeny landscape is made easier by virtue of the fact that state-of-the-art SIDH implementations already work entirely in the Kummer variety, $E/\{\pm\}$, of a given supersingular elliptic curve E. In their article introducing SIDH, Jao and De Feo [23] showed that, in addition to its widely known application of computing scalar multiplications, fast Montgomery x-only style arithmetic [25] could also be used to push points through isogenies. In more recent work, Costello, Longa and Naehrig [14] exploited a similar optimisation when computing the isogenous curves in SIDH, observing that isogeny arithmetic is twist-agnostic in SIDH in a similar fashion to point arithmetic being twist-agnostic in Bernstein's Curve25519 ECC software [3]. Subsequently, in the SIKE proposal [22], all elliptic curve points are only ever represented up to sign and all elliptic curves are only ever represented up to quadratic twist. Ultimately, this means that when we move to genus 2, we are able to work in the pre-existing SIDH infrastructure and replace abelian surfaces with Kummer surfaces and points on abelian surfaces with points on these Kummer surfaces.

- One significant hurdle to overcome in order to exploit fast isogenies on our Kummer surfaces it that *the* $(2,2)$-isogeny that splits pseudo-doublings[1] corresponds to a special kernel, and in SIDH computations we need isogenies that

---

[1] By definition, every $(2,2)$-isogeny will give the multiplication-by-2 map when composed with its dual, but here we are referring to the specific $(2,2)$-isogeny alluded to in [19, Remark 3.5], and made explicit by the dualising procedure in [28, Fig. 1].

work identically for general kernel elements, or at least identically for all of the kernel elements that can arise in a large-degree supersingular isogeny routine. This was achieved in the elliptic curve case by De Feo, Jao and Plût [16], who use an isomorphism to move the *general* Montgomery 2-torsion point $(\alpha, 0)$ with $\alpha \neq 0$ to the special 2-torsion point $(0, 0)$. However, in our case, the kernels of Richelot isogenies are non-cyclic, and finding the isomorphism to move general kernels to special kernels is less obvious. Our overcoming this hurdle on Jacobians (see Sect. 4) is aided by the use of *quadratic splittings* introduced by Smith in his treatment of Richelot kernels [33, Chap. 8], and our overcoming this hurdle on fast Kummer surfaces (see Sect. 5) employs the technique of [16, Sect. 4.3.2], which uses higher order torsion points (lying above the kernel) to avoid square root computations.

Roadmap. Section 2 provides background and sets notation. Section 3 defines the abelian surfaces corresponding to supersingular Montgomery curves (by way of Proposition 1), and gives the back-and-forth maps between these two objects. Section 4 then studies $(2, 2)$-isogenies on supersingular abelian surfaces and, in particular, it shows how to replace even-power elliptic curve isogenies defined over $\mathbb{F}_{p^2}$ with chains of $(2, 2)$-isogenies inside full Jacobians defined over $\mathbb{F}_p$. This lays the foundations to move to Kummer surfaces in Sect. 5, where the $(2, 2)$-isogenies simplify and become much faster. Implications for isogeny-based cryptography are discussed in Sect. 6.

There are many constants, variables and formulas in this work, so the risk of typographical error is high. Thus, for readers wanting to verify or replicate this work, illustrative Magma source files can be found at

https://www.microsoft.com/en-us/download/details.aspx?id=57309.

Before going any further, we stress that this paper in no way changes the security picture of isogeny-based cryptography, and that using Kummer surfaces over $\mathbb{F}_p$ instead of elliptic curves over $\mathbb{F}_{p^2}$ can be viewed as a mere implementation choice. The efficient back-and-forth maps in Sect. 3 show that any conceivable hard problem that can be posed in one setting can be efficiently ported over to the other setting.

2   Preliminaries

This section gives the necessary background for the remainder of the paper. We start with a brief summary of some jargon for non-experts. An *abelian variety* is a general term for a projective algebraic variety that possesses an algebraic group law. When we quotient an abelian variety by the map that takes elements to their inverses, we get the associated *Kummer variety*. There are two examples that are relevant in this paper. An *elliptic curve* is an abelian variety of dimension 1, and its quotient by $\{\pm 1\}$ gives the associated *Kummer line*; if E is a short Weierstrass or Montgomery curve, then a geometric point $P \in E$ can be parameterised on the Kummer line $E/\{\pm 1\}$ by its x-coordinate, $x(P)$, which is why it is often called the x-line. An *abelian surface* is an abelian variety of dimension 2, and all such instances in this work occur as Jacobian groups of genus-2 hyperelliptic curves; if C is a genus-2 curve and J_C is its Jacobian, then the quotient $J_C/\{\pm 1\}$ is called a *Kummer surface*.

Supersingular Montgomery Curves. State-of-the-art SIDH implementations (cf. [14, 15]) currently employ large prime fields of the form $p = 2^i 3^j - 1$ with $i > j > 100$, so that, over $\mathbb{F}_{p^2}$, the supersingular isogeny class consists entirely of curves whose abelian group structure is isomorphic to $\mathbb{Z}_{p+1} \times \mathbb{Z}_{p+1}$. This necessarily means that all of the curves in the isogeny class have full $\mathbb{F}_{p^2}$-rational 2-torsion, and moreover, that they can be written in Montgomery form over $\mathbb{F}_{p^2}$ as $By^2 = x^3 + Ax^2 + x$. Rather than parameterising Montgomery curves in this way, we will make an arbitrary choice of one of the two rational 2-torsion points $(\alpha, 0)$ with $\alpha \notin \{-1, 0, 1\}$ (the other is $(1/\alpha, 0)$), and from hereon will use E_α to denote the curve

$$E_\alpha/K: y^2 = x(x - \alpha)(x - 1/\alpha), \tag{1}$$

the j-invariant of which is

$$j(E_\alpha) = 256 \frac{(\alpha^4 - \alpha^2 + 1)^3}{\alpha^4(\alpha^2 - 1)^2}.$$

Note that the j-invariant is the same for E_α as it is for the curve $\delta y^2 = x(x - \alpha)(x - 1/\alpha)$; this is because δ only helps fix the quadratic twist, i.e., only fixes the curve up to $\bar{K}$-isomorphism. As mentioned in Sect. 1, point and isogeny arithmetic is independent of δ, so our curves need only be defined up to twist.

Throughout the paper we will often be making implicit use of the following result, which is essentially due to Auer and Top [1].

Lemma 1. *If $E_\alpha/\mathbb{F}_{p^2}: y^2 = x(x - \alpha)(x - 1/\alpha)$ is supersingular, then $\alpha \in (\mathbb{F}_{p^2}^\times)^2$, and $\alpha^2 - 1 \in (\mathbb{F}_{p^2}^\times)^8$.*

Proof. The group structure of E_α implies that at least one of the three 2-torsion points $(0, 0)$, $(\alpha, 0)$ and $(1/\alpha, 0)$ must be in $[2]E(\mathbb{F}_{p^2})$, so $\alpha \in (\mathbb{F}_{p^2}^\times)^2$ by [1, Lemma 2.1]. Thus, there exists $\epsilon \in \mathbb{F}_{p^2}$ such that $\epsilon^2 = -\alpha^3$, and it follows that E is isomorphic over $\mathbb{F}_{p^2}$ to the curve $\tilde{E}: y^2 = x(x - 1)(x + \alpha^2 - 1)$ via $(x, y) \mapsto (-\alpha x + 1, \epsilon y)$. Applying [1, Proposition 3.1] yields that $\alpha^2 - 1 \in (\mathbb{F}_{p^2}^\times)^8$. □

Abelian Surfaces. Over a field K of characteristic not 2, every genus-2 curve is birationally equivalent to a curve of the form $C: y^2 = f(x)$, where $f(x) \in K[x]$ is of degree 6 and has no repeated factors. In this work we will only encounter such curves where $f(x)$ splits completely in $K[x]$, so we will often be writing them in the form

$$C/K: y^2 = (x - z_1)(x - z_2)(x - z_3)(x - z_4)(x - z_5)(x - z_6), \tag{2}$$

where $z_i \in K$ for $i \in \{1, \ldots, 6\}$, and where we write y^2 instead of δy^2 for the same reason as for the elliptic curve case above.

Denote the difference $z_i - z_j$ by (ij). Following Igusa [21, p. 620], define the quantities

$$I_2 := \sum (12)^2 (34)^2 (56)^2,$$

$$I_4 := \sum (12)^2 (23)^2 (31)^2 (45)^2 (56)^2 (64)^2,$$

$$I_6 := \sum (12)^2 (23)^2 (31)^2 (45)^2 (56)^2 (64)^2 (14)^2 (25)^2 (36)^2,$$

$$I_{10} := \prod (12)^2, \tag{3}$$

where the sums and product above run over all of the distinct expressions obtained by permuting the index set $\{1, \ldots, 6\}$. The invariants I_2, I_4, I_6, and I_{10} are called the *Igusa-Clebsch invariants*, and they play an analogous role to the j-invariant of an elliptic curve: two curves C and C', with respective Igusa-Clebsch invariants (I_2, I_4, I_6, I_{10}) and $(I_2', I_4', I_6', I_{10}')$, are isomorphic over $\bar{K}$ if and only if

$$(I_2 : I_4 : I_6 : I_{10}) = (I_2' : I_4' : I_6' : I_{10}') \in \mathbb{P}(2, 4, 6, 10)(\bar{K}),$$

i.e., if and only if there exists a $\lambda \in \bar{K}^\times$ such that

$$(I_2', I_4', I_6', I_{10}') = (\lambda^2 I_2, \lambda^4 I_4, \lambda^6 I_6, \lambda^{10} I_{10}).$$

Observe that, as in the elliptic curve case, the invariants here are independent of δ, i.e., are twist-independent. For $a, b, c, d \in K$ with $ad \neq bc$ and $e \in K^\times$, the map

$$\kappa_{(a,b,c,d)} : \quad C \to C', \quad (x, y) \mapsto \left(\frac{ax + b}{cx + d}, \frac{ey}{(cx + d)^3} \right) \tag{4}$$

is a K-rational isomorphism to the curve C'. Up to isomorphism and quadratic twist, and by abuse of notation, we can write C' as $C' \colon y^2 = \prod_{i=1}^{6} (x - z_i')$, where $z_i' = (az_i + b)/(cz_i + d)$. Let $\{\ell_0, \ell_1, \ell_\infty, \ell_\lambda, \ell_\mu, \ell_\nu\} = \{z_1, \ldots, z_6\}$ be some relabeling of the roots of the sextic in (2). Setting

$$a = \ell_1 - \ell_\infty, \quad b = \ell_0(\ell_\infty - \ell_1), \quad c = \ell_1 - \ell_0, \quad \text{and} \quad d = \ell_\infty(\ell_0 - \ell_1)$$

in (4) yields a map $\kappa_{(a,b,c,d)} \colon C \to C_{\lambda,\mu,\nu}$, where

$$C_{\lambda,\mu,\nu} \colon y^2 = x(x - 1)(x - \lambda)(x - \mu)(x - \nu)$$

is the so-called *Rosenhain form* of C. Under $\kappa_{(a,b,c,d)}$, the points $(\ell_\lambda, 0)$, $(\ell_\mu, 0)$ and $(\ell_\nu, 0)$ on C are respectively sent to $(\lambda, 0)$, $(\mu, 0)$ and $(\nu, 0)$ on $C_{\lambda,\mu,\nu}$, while the points $(\ell_0, 0)$, $(\ell_1, 0)$ and $(\ell_\infty, 0)$ are respectively sent to $(0, 0)$, $(1, 0)$, and *the point at infinity on $C_{\lambda,\mu,\nu}$*. There are $6! = 720$ possible relabelings of the six z_i, and as such there are 720 possible (ordered) triples (λ, μ, ν) of *Rosenhain invariants*. In this work we can identify the Jacobian variety, J_C, of the curve C/K with the degree zero divisor class group of C, i.e., with $\mathrm{Pic}^0_K(C) = \mathrm{Div}^0_K(C)/\mathrm{Prin}_K(C)$ (cf. [18, Sect. 7.8]). In this way a point in the *affine part* of J_C (see [18, p. 204]) is represented using the *Mumford representation* of the corresponding divisor $D \in \mathrm{Pic}^0_K(C)$; if D is reduced and non-zero, then the effective component of the support of D either contains 1 or 2 (not necessarily unique) $\bar{K}$-rational points on C. In the first (so-called *degenerate*) case, if (x_1, y_1) is the only such point (and its multiplicity is 1) in the support of D, then $(x_1, y_1) \in C(K)$, and its Mumford representation is $(x - x_1, y_1) \in K[x] \times K[x]$. In the general case, when (x_1, y_1) and (x_2, y_2) with $x_1 \neq x_2$ are the two $\bar{K}$-rational points on C in $\mathrm{supp}(D)$, then the corresponding Mumford representation is

$$(x^2 + u_1 x + u_0, v_1 x + v_0) \in K[x] \times K[x],$$

where

$$u_1 = -x_1 - x_2, \quad u_0 = x_1 x_2, \quad v_1 = \frac{y_2 - y_1}{x_2 - x_1}, \quad \text{and} \quad v_0 = \frac{y_1 x_2 - x_1 y_2}{x_2 - x_1}. \quad (5)$$

Note that, in general, the Mumford representation of a point in $J_C(K)$ can always be written in $K[x] \times K[x]$, but this does not imply that the underlying points on $C(\bar{K})$ are K-rational.

If $(x^2 + u_1 x + u_0, v_1 x + v_0)$ is a generic point in J_C, then the map $\kappa_{(a,b,c,d)} : C \to C'$ in (4) induces a map between their Jacobians, where, for elements with $\ell_1 = c^2 u_0 - c d u_1 + d^2$ and $\ell_2 = ad - bc$ such that $\ell_1 \ell_2 \neq 0$, we have $(x^2 + u_1 x + u_0, v_1 x + v_0) \mapsto (x^2 + u_1' x + u_0', v_1' x + v_0')$, with

$$u_1' = \ell_1^{-1} \left((ad + bc)u_1 - 2acu_0 - 2bd\right), \qquad u_0' = \ell_1^{-1} \left(a^2 u_0 - abu_1 + b^2\right),$$

$$v_0' = -e(\ell_1^2 \ell_2)^{-1} \Big(ac^2(u_0 u_1 v_1 - u_1^2 v_0 + u_0 v_0) - c(2ad + bc)(u_0 v_1 - u_1 v_0)$$

$$- d(ad + 2bc)v_0 + bd^2 v_1\Big), \qquad (6)$$

$$\text{and} \qquad v_1' = e(\ell_1^2 \ell_2)^{-1} \left(c^2(cu_1 - 3d)(u_0 v_1 - u_1 v_0) + cv_0(c^2 u_0 - 3d^2) + d^3 v_1\right).$$

Weil Restriction of Scalars. The Weil restriction of scalars is the process of re-writing a system of equations over a finite extension L/K as a system of equations in more variables over K – we refer to [18, Sect. 5.7] for a more general discussion. In this work it can be considered as merely a formality to increase dimension so that speaking of isogenies makes sense. The Weil restriction of our one-dimensional varieties $E_\alpha/\mathbb{F}_{p^2}$ (with respect to the extension $\mathbb{F}_{p^2} = \mathbb{F}_p(i)$ with $i^2 + 1$) is the two-dimensional variety

$$W_\alpha := \mathrm{Res}^{\mathbb{F}_{p^2}}_{\mathbb{F}_p} (E_\alpha) = V\Big(W_0(x_0, x_1, y_0, y_1), W_1(x_0, x_1, y_0, y_1)\Big),$$

where

$$W_0 = (\alpha_0^2 + \alpha_1^2)\left(\alpha_0(x_0^2 - x_1^2) - 2\alpha_1 x_0 x_1 + \delta_0(y_0^2 - y_1^2) - 2y_0 y_1 \delta_1 - x_0(x_0^2 - 3x_1^2 + 1)\right)$$
$$+ \alpha_0(x_0^2 - x_1^2) + 2\alpha_1 x_0 x_1 \qquad \text{and}$$

$$W_1 = (\alpha_0^2 + \alpha_1^2)\left(\alpha_1(x_0^2 - x_1^2) + 2\alpha_0 x_0 x_1 + \delta_1(y_0^2 - y_1^2) + 2y_0 y_1 \delta_0 - x_1(3x_0^2 - x_1^2 + 1)\right)$$
$$+ \alpha_1(x_1^2 - x_0^2) + 2\alpha_0 x_0 x_1$$

are obtained by putting $x = x_0 + x_1 \cdot i$, $y = y_0 + y_1 \cdot i$ as well as $\alpha = \alpha_0 + \alpha_1 \cdot i$ and $\delta = \delta_0 + \delta_1 \cdot i$ (with $x_0, x_1, y_0, y_1, \alpha_0, \alpha_1, \delta_0, \delta_1 \in \mathbb{F}_p$) into (1). In terms of dimension, it now makes sense to speak of isogenies between W_α and the two-dimensional abelian surfaces described in the next section.

We make the disclaimer that oftentimes we will speak loosely and refer to isogenies and maps between E_α, intermediate curves, and abelian surfaces, but that from hereon it should be clear that, technically speaking, these maps are only well-defined when speaking of the corresponding Weil restrictions of these elliptic curves with respect to $\mathbb{F}_{p^2}/\mathbb{F}_p$.

Power-of-2 Elliptic Curve Isogenies in SIDH. Understanding how 2^e-isogenies are computed in SIDH is key in understanding the directions we take in Sects. 4 and 5. Recall the three 2-torsion points on E_α as $(0,0)$, $(\alpha, 0)$ and $(1/\alpha, 0)$; in general, each of these corresponds to a different 2-isogeny emanating from E_α. Following [16, Sect. 4.3.2] and [27, Sect. 4.2], when the kernel is generated by the special point $(0,0)$, applying Vélu's formulas [35] to write down the isogeny allows us to (re)write the image curve in Montgomery form[2]. However, when the kernel is generated by one of the other two points, direct application of Vélu's formulas makes writing the image curve in Montgomery form much less obvious. This was achieved in [16,27] by using an isomorphism to move these two kernel points to $(0,0)$ on an isomorphic curve (which differs depending whether the kernel is $\langle(\alpha, 0)\rangle$ or $\langle(1/\alpha, 0)\rangle$), prior to invoking Vélu.

In our case we follow an analogous path. From the work in [28], we have a very simple Kummer surface isogeny that corresponds to a special kernel O, and we use an isomorphism to move our two more general kernels, Υ and $\tilde{\Upsilon}$, prior to applying the isogeny (see Sects. 4 and 5 for the definitions of O, Υ and $\tilde{\Upsilon}$).

We point out that this analogue is not a coincidence, and is made concrete in Lemma 2. Moreover, just like in the elliptic curve case where $(0,0)$ cannot arise as the kernel of a repeated isogeny in SIDH (because it gives rise to the dual isogeny – see [16]), in our case it is O that corresponds to the dual so our kernel will, with the possible exception of the very first $(2,2)$-isogeny, only ever correspond to Υ and $\tilde{\Upsilon}$.

3   Abelian Surfaces Isogenous to Supersingular Montgomery Curves

This section links supersingular Montgomery curves defined over $\mathbb{F}_{p^2}$ with abelian surfaces defined over $\mathbb{F}_p$. We start with Proposition 1, which writes down the genus-2 curve $C_\alpha/\mathbb{F}_p$ arising from Scholten's construction; its proof is postponed until after we have derived the back-and-forth $(2,2)$-isogenies between the given Weil restriction and abelian surface. We point out that the exposition

---

[2] The importance of the codomain curve sharing the same form as the domain curve is a result of our need to repeat many small isogeny computations (which we want to be as efficient and uniform as possible).

below is simplified by assuming[3] $p \equiv 3 \bmod 4$ so that $\mathbb{F}_{p^2} = \mathbb{F}_p(i)$ with $i^2 + 1 = 0$, but treating the complimentary or general case is analogous. The only impactful restriction made in addition to Scholten's requirements is that of supersingularity. As mentioned in Sect. 1, this gives rise to simpler maps than those in [6] by way of the trace map, but several of our intermediate steps may still be useful beyond the supersingular scenario.

Proposition 1. *Let $p \equiv 3 \bmod 4$, let $\mathbb{F}_{p^2} = \mathbb{F}_p(i)$ with $i^2 + 1 = 0$, and let*

$$E_\alpha/\mathbb{F}_{p^2} : y^2 = x(x - \alpha)(x - 1/\alpha)$$

be supersingular with $\alpha \notin \mathbb{F}_p$. Write $\alpha = \alpha_0 + \alpha_1 \cdot i$ with $\alpha_0, \alpha_1 \in \mathbb{F}_p$. The Weil restriction of scalars of $E_\alpha(\mathbb{F}_{p^2})$ with respect to $\mathbb{F}_{p^2}/\mathbb{F}_p$ is $(2,2)$-isogenous to the Jacobian, J_{C_α}, of

$$C_\alpha/\mathbb{F}_p : y^2 = f_1(x)f_2(x)f_3(x), \tag{7}$$

where

$$f_1(x) = x^2 + \frac{2\alpha_0}{\alpha_1} \cdot x - 1,$$

$$f_2(x) = x^2 - \frac{2\alpha_0}{\alpha_1} \cdot x - 1, \qquad and$$

$$f_3(x) = x^2 - \frac{2\alpha_0(\alpha_0^2 + \alpha_1^2 - 1)}{\alpha_1(\alpha_0^2 + \alpha_1^2 + 1)} \cdot x - 1.$$

Remark 1 (Singular quadratic splittings and split Jacobians). We immediately point out that the $f_i(x)$ in Proposition 1 are linearly dependent; namely, $f_3(x) = 1/(N+1) \cdot f_1(x) + N/(N+1) \cdot f_2(x)$, where $N = N_{\mathbb{F}_{p^2}/\mathbb{F}_p}(\alpha) = \alpha_0^2 + \alpha_1^2$. Oftentimes in the literature, this is referred to as the *singular* scenario, where the Jacobian of C_α is reducible, or *split* (e.g., [10, Theorem 14.1.1(ii)] and [33, Proposition 8.3.1]). However, we stress that those results do not necessarily imply that this splitting occurs over $\mathbb{F}_p$; Cassels and Flynn assume that they are working in the algebraic closure [10, p. 154] and Smith's construction of the linear polynomials on [33, p. 119] also requires a field extension in the general case. Indeed, if all of the elliptic curves in our isogeny graph were $(2,2)$-isogenous to a Jacobian that is split over $\mathbb{F}_p$, this would have serious implications on the quantum security of SIDH (see [11]). We conjecture that the Jacobian of C_α only splits over $\mathbb{F}_p$ when the j-invariant of E_α is itself defined over $\mathbb{F}_p$, and note that adhering to the constructions in [10] and [33] (over the algebraic closure) yields an isogeny between $J_{C_\alpha}(\mathbb{F}_{p^2})$ and $E_\alpha^2(\mathbb{F}_{p^2})$, which manifests J_{C_α} being supersingular [26, Theorem 4.2].

---

[3] In the current landscape of isogeny-based cryptography, the assumption of $p \equiv 3 \bmod 4$ is standard [14–16, 22].

Fixing Roots of the Sextic. Following Lemma 1, let $\gamma, \beta \in \mathbb{F}_{p^2}$ be such that

$$\gamma^2 = \alpha \qquad \text{and} \qquad \beta^2 = (\alpha^2 - 1)/\alpha, \tag{8}$$

and write $\beta = \beta_0 + \beta_1 \cdot i$ and $\gamma = \gamma_0 + \gamma_1 \cdot i$ for $\beta_0, \beta_1, \gamma_0, \gamma_1 \in \mathbb{F}_p$. The curve $C_\alpha/\mathbb{F}_p$ from Proposition 1 will henceforth be written as

$$C_\alpha/\mathbb{F}_p : y^2 = (x - z_1)(x - z_2)(x - z_3)(x - z_4)(x - z_5)(x - z_6),$$

where

$$z_1 := \frac{\beta_0}{\beta_1}, \quad z_2 := \frac{\gamma_0}{\gamma_1}, \quad z_3 := -\frac{\gamma_0}{\gamma_1}, \quad z_4 := -\frac{\beta_1}{\beta_0}, \quad z_5 := -\frac{\gamma_1}{\gamma_0}, \quad z_6 := \frac{\gamma_1}{\gamma_0}, \tag{9}$$

and where we note at once that

$$z_3 = -z_2, \quad z_4 = -1/z_1, \quad z_5 = -1/z_2, \quad \text{and} \quad z_6 = 1/z_2.$$

Furthermore, observe that any combination of the choices of roots for γ and β in (8) gives rise to the same values of the z_i in (9).

Mapping from $E_\alpha(\mathbb{F}_{p^2})$ to $J_{C_\alpha}(\mathbb{F}_p)$. The $(2,2)$-isogeny from (the Weil restriction of) $E_\alpha(\mathbb{F}_{p^2})$ to the Jacobian $J_{C_\alpha}(\mathbb{F}_p)$ will be derived as the composition of maps between intermediate curves. We start by defining the curve

$$\tilde{E}_\alpha/\mathbb{F}_{p^2} : y^2 = (x - r_1)(x - r_2)(x - r_3),$$

with

$$r_1 := (\alpha - 1/\alpha)^{p-1}, \qquad r_2 := \alpha^{p-1}, \qquad \text{and} \qquad r_3 := 1/\alpha^{p-1}.$$

Fix $\hat{\beta}$ such that $\hat{\beta}^2 = r_3 - r_2$ (it is easy to see that $\hat{\beta}$ always exists over $\mathbb{F}_{p^2}$), and define an isomorphism between E_α and $\tilde{E}_\alpha$ as

$$\psi : E_\alpha \to \tilde{E}_\alpha, \quad (x, y) \mapsto \left((\hat{\beta}/\beta)^2 \cdot x + r_1, \, (\hat{\beta}/\beta)^3 \cdot y \right).$$

Following [31, Lemma 2.1], define $\tilde{C}_\alpha/\mathbb{F}_{p^2}$ as the hyperelliptic curve

$$\tilde{C}_\alpha/\mathbb{F}_{p^2} : y^2 = (x^2 - r_1)(x^2 - r_2)(x^2 - r_3),$$

where we have the map

$$\omega : \tilde{C}_\alpha \to \tilde{E}_\alpha, \quad (x, y) \mapsto (x^2, y).$$

Observing that r_1, r_2 and r_3 are all square in $\mathbb{F}_{p^2}$, let W be the set of x-coordinates of the six Weierstrass points of $\tilde{C}_\alpha$. A key step in Scholten's construction is to choose a map ϕ that, restricted to x-coordinates, leaves $\phi(W)$ invariant under the action of Galois. With $\mathbb{F}_{p^2} = \mathbb{F}_p(i)$, our choice is

$$\phi : \tilde{C}_\alpha(\mathbb{F}_{p^2}) \to C_\alpha(\mathbb{F}_{p^2}),$$

$$(x, y) \mapsto \left(-i \cdot \frac{x - 1}{x + 1}, \, \frac{y}{w} \left(1 - \frac{x - 1}{x + 1} \right)^3 \right),$$

where $w := r_3(1 - r_1)(r_2 - 1)^2$ and C_α is the curve from Proposition 1. An important observation here is that C_α is defined over $\mathbb{F}_p$, while $\tilde{C}_\alpha$ is defined over $\mathbb{F}_{p^2}$, and the map ϕ is between the $\mathbb{F}_{p^2}$-rational points on these curves.

Composing the image of the *pullback* ω^* (see [18, Definition 8.3.1]) with ϕ (which is extended linearly into $J_{C_\alpha}(\mathbb{F}_{p^2})$ via the Abel-Jacobi map as in (5)), induces the map

$$\rho\colon \tilde{E}_\alpha(\mathbb{F}_{p^2}) \to J_{C_\alpha}(\mathbb{F}_{p^2}),$$
$$(\tilde{x}, \tilde{y}) \mapsto (x^2 + u_1 x + u_0, v_1 + v_0),$$

where

$$u_1 = 2i \cdot \left(\frac{\tilde{x}+1}{\tilde{x}-1}\right), \quad u_0 = -1, \quad v_1 = -4i \cdot \frac{\tilde{y}(\tilde{x}+3)}{w(\tilde{x}-1)^2}, \quad v_0 = \frac{4\tilde{y}}{w(\tilde{x}-1)}.$$

Since J_{C_α} is defined over $\mathbb{F}_p$ and is supersingular with embedding degree $k = 2$, we can use the *trace map* $\mathcal{T}$ to move elements from $J_{C_\alpha}(\mathbb{F}_{p^2})$ into $J_{C_\alpha}(\mathbb{F}_p)$, i.e.,

$$\mathcal{T}\colon \quad J_{C_\alpha}(\mathbb{F}_{p^2}) \to J_{C_\alpha}(\mathbb{F}_p),$$
$$P \mapsto \sum_{\sigma \in \mathrm{Gal}(\mathbb{F}_{p^2}/\mathbb{F}_p)} \sigma(P),$$

which for generic elements in $J_{C_\alpha}(\mathbb{F}_{p^2})$, becomes

$$\mathcal{T}\colon (x^2 + u_1 x + u_0, v_1 x + v_0) \mapsto (x^2 + u_1 x + u_0, v_1 x + v_0) \oplus_J (x^2 + u_1^p x + u_0^p, v_1^p x + v_0^p),$$

where $\oplus_J$ denotes the addition law in $J_{C_\alpha}(\mathbb{F}_{p^2})$, explicit formulas for which are in [20, Sect. 5].

Finally, we can now define the map from (the Weil restriction of) $E_\alpha(\mathbb{F}_{p^2})$ to $J_{C_\alpha}(\mathbb{F}_p)$ as

$$\eta\colon E_\alpha(\mathbb{F}_{p^2}) \to J_{C_\alpha}(\mathbb{F}_p),$$
$$P \mapsto (\mathcal{T} \circ \rho \circ \psi)(P).$$

Mapping from $J_{C_\alpha}(\mathbb{F}_p)$ to $E_\alpha(\mathbb{F}_{p^2})$. We start by writing down ϕ^{-1}, the inverse of ϕ, as

$$\phi^{-1}\colon C_\alpha(\mathbb{F}_{p^2}) \to \tilde{C}_\alpha(\mathbb{F}_{p^2}),$$
$$(x, y) \mapsto \left(-\frac{x-i}{x+i}, \; -i \cdot \frac{yw}{(x+i)^3}\right).$$

Extending ϕ^{-1} linearly to $\mathrm{Div}_{\overline{\mathbb{F}}_p}(C_\alpha)$ (and recalling our identification of $J_{C_\alpha}(K)$ and $\mathrm{Pic}_K^0(C_\alpha)$ – see Sect. 2) induces a map $\hat{\rho}$, defined for generic elements in the affine part of $J_{C_\alpha}(\mathbb{F}_p)$ as

$$\hat{\rho}\colon J_{C_\alpha}(\mathbb{F}_p) \to \tilde{E}_\alpha(\mathbb{F}_{p^2}) \times \tilde{E}_\alpha(\mathbb{F}_{p^2}),$$
$$P \mapsto \left((\omega \circ \phi^{-1})(x_1, y_1), (\omega \circ \phi^{-1})(x_2, y_2)\right),$$

where the Mumford representation of $P \in J_{C_\alpha}(\mathbb{F}_p)$ is exactly as in (5), with $(x_1, y_1), (x_2, y_2) \in C_\alpha(\mathbb{F}_{p^2})$.

We can now define the full map from $J_{C_\alpha}(\mathbb{F}_p)$ to $E_\alpha(\mathbb{F}_{p^2})$ as

$$\hat{\eta} \colon J_{C_\alpha}(\mathbb{F}_p) \to E_\alpha(\mathbb{F}_{p^2}),$$
$$P \mapsto \left(\psi^{-1} \circ \oplus_{\tilde{E}} \circ \hat{\rho} \right)(P),$$

where $\oplus_{\tilde{E}} \colon \tilde{E}_\alpha \times \tilde{E}_\alpha \to \tilde{E}_\alpha$ is the addition law on $\tilde{E}_\alpha$, and the inverse of the isomorphism ψ is

$$\psi^{-1} \colon \tilde{E}_\alpha \to E_\alpha, \quad (x, y) \mapsto \left((\beta/\hat{\beta})^2 \cdot (x - r_1), (\beta/\hat{\beta})^3 \cdot y \right).$$

Kernels and Group Structures. Let $\mathcal{O}_{E_\alpha}$ be the point at infinity on E_α. The kernel of the map $\eta \colon E_\alpha(\mathbb{F}_{p^2}) \to J_{C_\alpha}(\mathbb{F}_p)$ is

$$\ker(\eta) = E_\alpha[2] = \{\mathcal{O}_{E_\alpha}, (0, 0), (\alpha, 0), (1/\alpha, 0)\},$$

which is isomorphic to $\mathbb{Z}_2 \times \mathbb{Z}_2$.

Let $\mathcal{O}_J$ be the identity in J_{C_α}. The kernel of the map $\hat{\eta} \colon J_{C_\alpha}(\mathbb{F}_p) \to E_\alpha(\mathbb{F}_{p^2})$ is

$$\ker(\hat{\eta}) = \{\mathcal{O}_J, ((x - z_1)(x - z_4), 0), ((x - z_3)(x - z_6), 0), ((x - z_2)(x - z_5), 0)\},$$

a maximal 2-Weil isotropic subgroup of $J_{C_\alpha}[2]$, which is also isomorphic to $\mathbb{Z}_2 \times \mathbb{Z}_2$. It is readily verified that, up to isomorphism, we have $(\hat{\eta} \circ \eta) = [2]_{E_\alpha}$, where $[2]_{E_\alpha}$ is the multiplication-by-2 map on E_α. Similarly, up to isomorphism, we have $(\eta \circ \hat{\eta}) = [2]_J$, where $[2]_J$ is the multiplication-by-2 map on J_{C_α}. Thus, η and $\hat{\eta}$ are the (unique, up to isomorphism) dual isogenies of one another.

As abelian groups, we have

$$E_\alpha(\mathbb{F}_{p^2}) \cong \mathbb{Z}_{p+1} \times \mathbb{Z}_{p+1},$$

and

$$J_{C_\alpha}(\mathbb{F}_p) \cong \mathbb{Z}_2 \times \mathbb{Z}_2 \times \mathbb{Z}_{\frac{p+1}{2}} \times \mathbb{Z}_{\frac{p+1}{2}}. \tag{10}$$

Proof (of Proposition 1). This follows from [31]. E_α is isomorphic to $\tilde{E}_\alpha$ under ψ (indeed, $\tilde{E}_\alpha$ is a monic version of the second curve in [31, Lemma 3.1], when E_α is the first). Thus, under $\omega \colon (x, y) \mapsto (x^2, y)$, $\tilde{E}_\alpha$ and J_{C_α} have the same L-polynomial and are therefore isogenous [31, Lemma 2.1]. It remains to show that η is a $(2, 2)$-isogeny, which is an immediate consequence of $\ker(\omega^*) \subseteq \tilde{E}_\alpha[2]$ [18, Exercise 10.5.2] and the definition of ρ. $\square$

4   Richelot Isogenies on Supersingular Abelian Surfaces

This section studies Richelot $(2, 2)$-isogenies whose domain is the Jacobian, J_{C_α}, of the curve C_α defined in Proposition 1. This lays the foundations for the following section, where we will study these isogenies as they are pushed down onto a corresponding Kummer surface $\mathcal{K}_\alpha = J_{C_\alpha}/\{\pm 1\}$. Readers should rest assured that, as is usual in the genus-2 landscape, the situation looks much more complicated on the full Jacobian (e.g., in (13)) than it does once we move to a well-specified Kummer surface.

In general, there are 15 Richelot isogenies emanating from J_{C_α}, but we will be restricting our focus to the three that correspond to the 2-isogenies on E_α.

Kernels of (2, 2)-Isogenies as Quadratic splittings. Recall the labeling of the roots $z_1, \ldots, z_6 \in \mathbb{F}_p$ of the sextic $f(x) \in \mathbb{F}_p[x]$ in (9). As an abelian group, the 2-torsion of J_{C_α}, $J_{C_\alpha}[2]$, is isomorphic to $(\mathbb{Z}/2\mathbb{Z})^4$; it consists of the zero element, $\mathcal{O}_J$, together with the 15 points whose Mumford representations are $((x - z_i)(x - z_j), 0)$, where $i, j \in \{1, \ldots 6\}$ and $i \neq j$. We will use $G_{i,j}$ to denote the quadratic polynomial $(x - z_i)(x - z_j) \in \mathbb{F}_p[x]$ and write $P_{i,j} \in J_{C_\alpha}[2]$ for the non-zero 2-torsion point whose Mumford representation is $P_{i,j} = (G_{i,j}, 0)$.

Following [33, Sect. 8.1], kernels of (2, 2)-isogenies are called (2, 2)-*subgroups*, and these correspond to the maximal 2-Weil isotropic subgroups of $J_{C_\alpha}[2]$. Smith [33, Sect. 8.2] formalises this connection by introducing *quadratic splittings*. In our case, a quadratic splitting is simply a choice of factorisation of the sextic polynomial $f(x)$ in Proposition 1 into three quadratic factors in $\mathbb{F}_p[x]$; one such choice was already illustrated in (7). Henceforth, for any $\{i, j, k, l, m, n\} = \{1, 2, 3, 4, 5, 6\}$, we use the notation $(G_{i,j}, G_{k,l}, G_{m,n}) \in \mathbb{F}_p[x]^3$ to denote the corresponding quadratic splitting of $f(x) = G_{i,j} \cdot G_{k,l} \cdot G_{m,n}$. There are 15 choices of splittings, and each corresponds to a unique (2, 2)-subgroup: the quadratic splitting $(G_{i,j}, G_{k,l}, G_{m,n})$ corresponds to the (2, 2)-subgroup of $J_{C_\alpha}[2]$ generated by any two of the three points in $\{P_{i,j}, P_{k,l}, P_{m,n}\}$ (the third point is the sum of the other two). In this way, we see that (2, 2)-subgroups are isomorphic to $(\mathbb{Z}/2\mathbb{Z})^2$.

(2, 2)-Subgroups Corresponding to the Montgomery 2-Torsion. Out of the 15 possible splittings described above, there are three splittings we are interested in; those where the subsequent (2, 2)-isogenies on J_{C_α} correspond to the three 2-isogenies on E_α. We make these splittings concrete in the following lemma.

Lemma 2. *Let $E_{\hat{\alpha}}/\mathbb{F}_{p^2}$, $E_{\alpha'}/\mathbb{F}_{p^2}$ and $E_{\alpha''}/\mathbb{F}_{p^2}$ be three Montgomery curves that are respectively $\mathbb{F}_{p^2}$-isomorphic to $E_\alpha/\langle(0,0)\rangle$, $E_\alpha/\langle(\alpha,0)\rangle$, and $E_\alpha/\langle(1/\alpha,0)\rangle$, and let $C_{\hat{\alpha}}/\mathbb{F}_p$, $C_{\alpha'}/\mathbb{F}_p$ and $C_{\alpha''}/\mathbb{F}_p$ be the corresponding hyperelliptic curves (as in Proposition 1). Furthermore, fix the three quadratic splittings O, Υ, and $\tilde{\Upsilon}$, as*

$$
\begin{aligned}
O = (O_1, O_2, O_3) &:= (G_{2,3}, G_{5,6}, G_{1,4}), \\
\Upsilon = (\Upsilon_1, \Upsilon_2, \Upsilon_3) &:= (G_{4,5}, G_{1,2}, G_{3,6}), \qquad \text{and} \\
\tilde{\Upsilon} = (\tilde{\Upsilon}_1, \tilde{\Upsilon}_2, \tilde{\Upsilon}_3) &:= (G_{1,6}, G_{3,4}, G_{2,5}).
\end{aligned}
$$

Then, up to isomorphism, the image curves C_O, C_Υ and $C_{\tilde{\Upsilon}}$ of the Richelot $(2,2)$-isogenies (with respective kernels corresponding to O, Υ and $\tilde{\Upsilon}$) are such that

$$C_O = C_{\hat{\alpha}}, \qquad \text{and} \qquad \{C_\Upsilon, C_{\tilde{\Upsilon}}\} = \{C_{\alpha'}, C_{\alpha''}\}.$$

Proof. Direct substitution of (9) gives

$$O_1 = x^2 - \frac{\gamma_0^2}{\gamma_1^2}, \qquad O_2 = x^2 - \frac{\gamma_1^2}{\gamma_0^2}, \qquad O_3 = x^2 + \left(\frac{\beta_1^2 - \beta_0^2}{\beta_0\beta_1}\right)x - 1, \quad (11)$$

$$\Upsilon_1 = x^2 + \left(\frac{\beta_1\gamma_0 + \gamma_1\beta_0}{\beta_0\gamma_0}\right)x + \frac{\beta_1\gamma_1}{\beta_0\gamma_0}, \quad \Upsilon_2 = x^2 - \left(\frac{\beta_0\gamma_1 + \gamma_0\beta_1}{\beta_1\gamma_1}\right)x + \frac{\beta_0\gamma_0}{\beta_1\gamma_1}, \quad \Upsilon_3 = x^2 + \left(\frac{\gamma_0^2 - \gamma_1^2}{\gamma_0\gamma_1}\right)x - 1,$$

and

$$\tilde{\Upsilon}_1 = x^2 - \left(\frac{\beta_0\gamma_0 + \gamma_1\beta_1}{\beta_1\gamma_0}\right)x + \frac{\beta_0\gamma_1}{\beta_1\gamma_0}, \quad \tilde{\Upsilon}_2 = x^2 + \left(\frac{\beta_0\gamma_0 + \gamma_1\beta_1}{\beta_0\gamma_1}\right)x + \frac{\beta_1\gamma_0}{\beta_0\gamma_1}, \quad \tilde{\Upsilon}_3 = x^2 + \left(\frac{\gamma_1^2 - \gamma_0^2}{\gamma_0\gamma_1}\right)x - 1.$$

In each case, if the splitting is written as

$$S = \left(x^2 + g_{1,1}x + g_{1,0}, x^2 + g_{2,1}x + g_{2,0}, x^2 + g_{3,1}x + g_{3,0}\right),$$

then the curve with the corresponding $(2,2)$-isogenous Jacobian (cf. [10, Sect. 9.2]) is isomorphic to

$$C_S : y^2 = h(x) = h_1(x)h_2(x)h_3(x),$$

where

$$h_1(x) = (g_{1,1} - g_{2,1})x^2 + 2\left(g_{1,0} - g_{2,0}\right)x + g_{1,0}g_{2,1} - g_{2,0}g_{1,1},$$
$$h_2(x) = (g_{2,1} - g_{3,1})x^2 + 2\left(g_{2,0} - g_{3,0}\right)x + g_{2,0}g_{3,1} - g_{3,0}g_{2,1}, \qquad \text{and}$$
$$h_3(x) = (g_{3,1} - g_{1,1})x^2 + 2\left(g_{3,0} - g_{1,0}\right)x + g_{3,0}g_{1,1} - g_{1,0}g_{3,1}. \qquad (12)$$

Now, following Sect. 2, and using (8), we first write $\hat{\alpha} = (\alpha + 1)/(1 - \alpha)$, $\alpha' = 2\alpha(\alpha + \beta\gamma) - 1$ and $\alpha'' = (2 - \alpha^2 + 2\beta\gamma \cdot i)/\alpha^2$, and then write each of these constants in terms of its two $\mathbb{F}_p$ components (under the basis $\{1, i\}$ for $\mathbb{F}_{p^2}/\mathbb{F}_p$ as usual). We can then apply Proposition 1 to write down $C_{\hat{\alpha}}$, $C_{\alpha'}$ and $C_{\alpha''}$. Using (3), lengthy but straightforward calculations show that the result follows from comparing the Igusa-Clebsch invariants of these three curves to those of the curves C_O, C_Υ and $C_{\tilde{\Upsilon}}$ obtained above. $\square$

The explicit Richelot isogeny corresponding to O. Equation (12) writes down the curve whose Jacobian is $(2,2)$-isogenous to that of a given genus-2 curve; here the prescribed kernel can be any $(2,2)$-subgroup. To fully describe the isogeny, we also need to write down explicit formulas for pushing points in the domain Jacobian through the corresponding isogeny, which is the purpose of this subsection. However, we first note that we will only be needing explicit formulas for the special case when the kernel subgroup corresponds to a quadratic splitting of the form of O in (11). To compute isogenies when the splitting is of the form of Υ and/or $\tilde{\Upsilon}$, we will be (pre)composing the isogeny described in this subsection with the isomorphisms (that transform these splittings into splittings of the form of O) in the next subsection. For reasons analogous to Montgomery 2-isogenies in the elliptic curve case (see Sect. 2), proceeding in this way makes life easier when we move down to the Kummer surface in Sect. 5.

Bost and Mestre [8] derive explicit $(2,2)$-isogenies from *Richelot correspondences* [33, Definition 8.4.7]. In general, correspondences are divisors on the product $C \times C'$ of the two curves C and C', and the theory of correspondences relates such divisors to homomorphisms between their Jacobians (see [33, Chap. 3]). In this paper we focus on the particular case of the Richelot correspondence

$$V_O := V \begin{pmatrix} O_1(x_1)O_1'(x_2) + O_2(x_1)O_2'(x_2), \\ y_1 y_2 - O_1(x_1)O_1'(x_2)(x_1 - x_2) \end{pmatrix}$$

on $C_\alpha \times C_O$. With O_1 and O_2 as in (11), and with O_1' and O_2' as their derivatives, we get

$$V_O = V \begin{pmatrix} 4x_2(x_1^2 - 2\alpha_0^2/\alpha_1^2 - 1), \\ \alpha_1^2 y_1 y_2 + 2x_2(4\alpha_0^2 + 4\alpha_0\gamma_1^2 + \alpha_1^2(1 - x_1^2))(x_1 - x_2) \end{pmatrix}.$$

Following [33, Sect. 3.3], and viewing V_O as a curve on $C_\alpha \times C_O$, we make use of the coverings

$$\pi_1^{V_O} : V_O \to C_\alpha, \quad ((x_1, y_1), (x_2, y_2)) \mapsto (x_1, y_1)$$

and

$$\pi_2^{V_O} : V_O \to C_O, \quad ((x_1, y_1), (x_2, y_2)) \mapsto (x_2, y_2),$$

and compose the pullback $\pi_1^{V_O*}$ with the pushforward $\pi_{2*}^{V_O}$ to obtain[4] the induced isogeny

$$\varphi_O : \quad J_{C_\alpha} \to J_{C_O},$$

defined on general elements of J_{C_α} as

$$\varphi_O : \quad (x^2 + u_1 x + u_0, v_1 x + v_0) \mapsto (x^2 + u_1' x + u_0', v_1' x + v_0'), \qquad (13)$$

where

$$u_1' = -\frac{\alpha_1(u_1^2 - 1)(N + 1)}{\alpha_0(N - 1)}, \quad u_0' = u_1^2, \quad v_0' = 2M \cdot \frac{u_1(\alpha_0(N - 1) - u_1\alpha_1(N + 1))}{v_1\alpha_1(N + 1)},$$

and

$$v_1' = 2M \cdot \frac{(\alpha_1 u_1(N + 1))^2 - (N^2 - 1)\alpha_1\alpha_0 u_1 - N(N + 2\alpha_0 + 1)(N - 2\alpha_0 + 1)}{\alpha_0\alpha_1(N^2 - 1)v_1},$$

---

[4] Those unfamiliar with these maps can view this process informally as follows: for a fixed (x_1, y_1), take the image as the divisor sum of the (in this case) two points, P and Q, whose coordinates satisfy the resulting equations in (x_2, y_2). This gives a map $(x_1, y_1) \mapsto (P) + (Q)$ between $\mathrm{Div}(C_\alpha)$ and $\mathrm{Div}(C_O)$ that can be extended (linearly) to give a map from $\mathrm{Pic}^0(C_\alpha)$ to $\mathrm{Pic}^0(C_O)$, and then from J_{C_α} to J_{C_O}.

with $N = \alpha_0^2 + \alpha_1^2$ and $M = (u_1^2 - 2\alpha_0/\alpha_1 u_1 - 1)(u_1^2 + 2\alpha_0/\alpha_1 u_1 - 1)$, and with

$$C_O: y^2 = \epsilon_0 x \left(x^2 - \epsilon_1 x - 1\right) \left(x^2 - \epsilon_2 x - 1\right),$$

where $\epsilon_0 = \frac{4\alpha_0(N-1)}{\alpha_1(N+1)}$, $\epsilon_1 = \frac{2\alpha_0(N+1)+4N}{\alpha_1(N-1)}$ and $\epsilon_2 = \frac{2\alpha_0(N+1)-4N}{\alpha_1(N-1)}$.

Isomorphisms of (2,2)-kernels. As mentioned in Sect. 2, we follow a similar path to that which was taken in the elliptic curve case and precompose the isogeny described above with isomorphisms that transform the $(2,2)$-kernels Υ and $\tilde{\Upsilon}$ to be of the same form as O, but on an isomorphic curve.

Our situation is more complicated than the elliptic curve case because our kernels are non-cyclic, meaning that they cannot be defined using a single point in the Jacobian. But, in the scenario of chained $(2,2)$-isogeny computations on supersingular abelian surfaces, we are able to overcome this and still use individual 2-torsion points $P_{i,j}$ to distinguish between the three kernel splittings O, Υ, and $\tilde{\Upsilon}$. If n is the even integer $(p+1)/4$, and if $\mathcal{O}_J$ is the identity on J_{C_α}, then $[n]J_{C_\alpha}$ is a $(2,2)$-subgroup (see (10)), and in our case is always one of

$$[n]J_{C_\alpha} = \{\mathcal{O}_J,\ (O_1, 0),\ (\Upsilon_1, 0),\ (\tilde{\Upsilon}_1, 0)\},$$

or

$$[n]J_{C_\alpha} = \{\mathcal{O}_J,\ (O_2, 0),\ (\Upsilon_2, 0),\ (\tilde{\Upsilon}_2, 0)\}.$$

In either case, if P is a point of exact order 2^ℓ with $\ell > 1$ in J_{C_α}, then we see that $[2^{\ell-1}]P \neq \mathcal{O}_J$ reveals which of the three splittings O, Υ or $\tilde{\Upsilon}$, corresponds to our $(2,2)$-kernel. Moreover, as discussed at the end of Sect. 2, in SIDH our kernel will always correspond to one of Υ or $\tilde{\Upsilon}$, since O generates the dual of the previous isogeny.

Our task is now to define an isomorphism that moves the kernels Υ and $\tilde{\Upsilon}$ into a kernel of the same form as O, but on an isomorphic curve. For a given point $P = (x^2 + u_1 x + u_0, v_1 x + v_0)$ in J_{C_α}, we define

$$\xi_P: \quad J_{C_\alpha} \to J_{C'_\alpha}$$

as the isomorphism of Jacobians corresponding to $\kappa_{a,b,c,d}: C_\alpha \to C'_\alpha$ from (4), with

$$d = 1, \qquad c = -\frac{u_0 - 1 + \sqrt{(u_0 - 1)^2 + u_1^2}}{u_1},$$

$$b = -\frac{\sqrt{-u_1(2c(u_0 - 1) - u_1)}}{u_1}, \qquad \text{and} \quad a = -b\frac{2u_0 + cu_1}{2c + u_1}. \qquad (14)$$

When $P = (x^2 + u_1 x + u_0, 0)$ is a 2-torsion point, the induced isomorphism of Jacobians in (6) simplifies significantly. Straightforward calculations reveal that, when P corresponds to the quadratic splitting Υ (i.e., when $P \in \{\Upsilon_1, \Upsilon_2\}$), we have

$$\{\ \xi_{(\Upsilon_1,0)}((\Upsilon_1,0)),\ \xi_{(\Upsilon_1,0)}((\Upsilon_2,0))\ \} = \{\ \xi_{(\Upsilon_2,0)}((\Upsilon_1,0)),\ \xi_{(\Upsilon_2,0)}((\Upsilon_2,0))\}$$

$$= \{\ ((x^2 - \gamma_0'^2/\gamma_1'^2), 0),\ ((x^2 - \gamma_1'^2/\gamma_0'^2), 0)\ \},$$

and

$$\xi_{(\Upsilon_1,0)}((\Upsilon_3,0)) = \xi_{(\Upsilon_2,0)}((\Upsilon_3,0)) = \left(x^2 + \left(\frac{\beta_1'^2 - \beta_0'^2}{\beta_0'\beta_1'}\right)x - 1, 0\right),$$

for some $\gamma_0', \gamma_1', \beta_0', \beta_1' \in \mathbb{F}_p$ such that $\beta' = \beta_0' + \beta_1' \cdot i \in \mathbb{F}_{p^2}$ and $\gamma' = \gamma_0' + \gamma_1' \cdot i \in \mathbb{F}_{p^2}$ satisfy $\gamma'^2 \beta'^2 = \gamma'^4 - 1$, which comes from the relation in (8). Thus, the $(2,2)$-subgroup corresponding to the splitting Υ on J_{C_α} is isomorphic (via either $\xi_{(\Upsilon_1,0)}$ or $\xi_{(\Upsilon_2,0)}$) to the splitting

$$O' = \left(x^2 - \gamma_0'^2/\gamma_1'^2, \quad x^2 - \gamma_1'^2/\gamma_0'^2, \quad x^2 + (\beta_1'^2 - \beta_0'^2)/(\beta_0'\beta_1')x - 1\right)$$

on $J_{C_\alpha'}$.

Crucially, the analogous statements apply when the point P corresponds to the quadratic splitting $\tilde{\Upsilon}$ (i.e., when $P \in \{\tilde{\Upsilon}_1, \tilde{\Upsilon}_2\}$), with the only difference being different values of $\gamma_0', \gamma_1', \beta_0', \beta_1' \in \mathbb{F}_p$ and a different (but still isomorphic) image curve $J_{C_\alpha'}$.

Finally, we fix

$$\varphi_P := (\varphi_O \circ \xi_P)$$

as the $(2,2)$-isogeny of Jacobians whose kernel is the $(2,2)$-subgroup corresponding to Υ if $P \in \{(\Upsilon_1, 0), (\Upsilon_2, 0)\}$, or corresponding to $\tilde{\Upsilon}$ if $P \in \{(\tilde{\Upsilon}_1, 0), (\tilde{\Upsilon}_2, 0)\}$. It is important to point out that φ_P is computed in the same way regardless of whether P corresponds to Υ or to $\tilde{\Upsilon}$.

To summarise, we have so far derived all of the ingredients necessary to replace chained 2-isogenies on elliptic curves over $\mathbb{F}_{p^2}$ with chained $(2,2)$-isogenies on Jacobians over $\mathbb{F}_p$. However, the combination of a relatively inefficient φ_P and point doublings in the full Jacobian is what prompts us to now push this arithmetic down onto the corresponding fast Kummer surfaces.

Remark 2. It is not surprising that the isomorphism in (14) that transforms the $(2,2)$-kernels Υ and $\tilde{\Upsilon}$ into a kernel of the form of O (but on an isomorphic curve) seems to require square roots. Indeed, De Feo, Jao and Plût [16] encountered the same problem in their treatment of 2-isogenies between Montgomery curves, but noticed that the square roots were related to rational functions of torsion elements lying above their kernels, so were able to use these higher order points to avoid square roots and efficiently chain together 2-isogenies in the SIDH framework. We employ this same technique in the next section to avoid square roots during Kummer isogeny computations, and claim that (if there was any practical motivation to sort out these details) the square roots in (14) could also be circumvented by using points of order 4 lying above $P \in J_{C_\alpha}$. Indeed, the functions of u_0 and u_1 in (14) being squares in $\mathbb{F}_p$ is undoubtedly related to their being the output of a point doubling in J_{C_α}. Finally, we point out that in the case of 2-isogenies on Montgomery elliptic curves, Renes [27, Sect. 4] recently removed the need for any higher order points, giving explicit formulas that depend only on the kernel element of order 2.

5   Richelot Isogenies on Supersingular Kummer Surfaces

The efficacy of this work relies on our being able to push φ_P down onto specific choices of Kummer surfaces.

Supersingular Kummer Surfaces. Following the initial works of the Chudnovskys [12] and of Gaudry [19], a number of authors have exploited the fast Kummer surface arithmetic in the context of modern HECC (cf. [4,5,7]). We draw on the applicable techniques from that line of work in this paper, and in particular adopt the Chudnovskys' [12] *squared Kummer surface* approach that was first exploited in high-speed HECC by Bernstein [4] and for fast factorisation by Cosset [13].

Choices of notations and parameterisations of Kummer surfaces have varied in the literature (see [28, Table 1]). We will aim to stick to that used in [28], but warn that our supersingular Kummer surfaces are special and will be defined as such. Kummer surfaces and their arithmetic are defined by fixing four fundamental theta constants, and the special squared Kummer surfaces used in this paper work entirely with their squares, denoted μ_1, μ_2, μ_3 and μ_4.

Following [7, Sect. 5.2], the μ_i can be computed from the Rosenhain form $C_{\lambda,\mu,\nu}$ of the associated genus-2 curve, as

$$\mu_4 = 1, \qquad \mu_3 = \sqrt{\frac{\lambda\mu}{\nu}}, \qquad \mu_2 = \sqrt{\frac{\mu(\mu-1)(\lambda-\nu)}{\nu(\nu-1)(\lambda-\mu)}}, \qquad \mu_1 = \mu_2\mu_3\frac{\nu}{\mu}. \quad (15)$$

In the supersingular scenario, with the sextic form of genus-2 curves as in (9), we will fix the transformation to Rosenhain form that sends the point $(z_1, 0)$ to $(0,0)$, the point $(z_2, 0)$ to $(1,0)$, the point $(z_4, 0)$ to the unique point at infinity, the point $(z_3, 0)$ to $(\lambda, 0)$, the point $(z_6, 0)$ to $(\mu, 0)$, and the point $(z_5, 0)$ to $(\nu, 0)$. We achieve this by taking $a = z_2 - z_4$, $b = -az_1$, $c = z_2 - z_1$ and $d = -cz_4$, i.e.,

$$\kappa_{(a,b,c,d)} \colon C_\alpha \to C_{\lambda,\mu,\nu}$$

$$(x,y) \mapsto \left(\left(\frac{\beta_0\gamma_0 + \beta_1\gamma_1}{\gamma_0\beta_1 - \gamma_1\beta_0} \right) \cdot \left(\frac{\beta_1 x - \beta_0}{\beta_0 x + \beta_1} \right) \,,\; ey \cdot \left(\frac{\beta_0\beta_1\gamma_1}{(\beta_1\gamma_0 - \beta_0\gamma_1)(\beta_0 x + \beta_1)} \right)^3 \right),$$

with $e^2 = ac(a-c)(a-\nu c)(a-\mu c)(a-\lambda c)$, and where

$$\lambda := -\frac{(\beta_0\gamma_1 + \beta_1\gamma_0)(\beta_0\gamma_0 + \beta_1\gamma_1)}{(\beta_0\gamma_0 - \beta_1\gamma_1)(\beta_0\gamma_1 - \beta_1\gamma_0)}, \quad \mu := \frac{(\beta_0\gamma_0 + \beta_1\gamma_1)(\beta_0\gamma_0 - \beta_1\gamma_1)}{(\beta_0\gamma_1 + \beta_1\gamma_0)(\beta_0\gamma_1 - \beta_1\gamma_0)}, \quad \nu := -\frac{(\beta_0\gamma_0 + \beta_1\gamma_1)^2}{(\beta_0\gamma_1 - \beta_1\gamma_0)^2}.$$

Thus, we see that $\nu = \lambda\mu$, meaning that (15) simplifies to

$$\mu_4 := 1, \qquad \mu_3 := 1, \qquad \mu_2 := \left(\frac{\gamma_0^2 - \gamma_1^2}{\gamma_0^2 + \gamma_1^2} \right) / \sqrt{\lambda}, \qquad \mu_1 := \left(\frac{\gamma_0^2 - \gamma_1^2}{\gamma_0^2 + \gamma_1^2} \right) \cdot \sqrt{\lambda}.$$

Previous works in the realm of high-speed HECC do not have $\mu_3 = 1$ in addition to $\mu_4 = 1$ (because the chances of finding a secure such Kummer surface over a given field are very small), which is why we stated above that our Kummer surfaces are special. One bonus of having $\mu_3 = 1$ is a simplified description of the Kummer surface, and for a fixed[5] Kummer surface of this form, another is more efficient arithmetic for the pseudo-group operations.

Our special squared Kummer surface, $\mathcal{K}^{\mathrm{Sqr}}$, is defined as

$$\mathcal{K}^{\mathrm{Sqr}}: \qquad F \cdot X_1 X_2 X_3 X_4 =$$
$$\left(X_1^2 + X_2^2 + X_3^2 + X_4^2 - G(X_1 + X_2)(X_3 + X_4) - H(X_1 X_2 + X_3 X_4) \right)^2,$$

where

$$F := 4\mu_1\mu_2 \frac{(\mu_1 + \mu_2 + 2)^2(\mu_1 + \mu_2 - 2)^2}{(\mu_1\mu_2 - 1)^2}, \quad G := \mu_1 + \mu_2, \quad \text{and} \quad H := \frac{\mu_1^2 + \mu_2^2 - 2}{\mu_1\mu_2 - 1}.$$

Elements on $\mathcal{K}^{\mathrm{Sqr}}$ are projective points $(X_1: X_2: X_3: X_4) \in \mathbb{P}^3$ satisfying this equation, and the zero element is $\mathcal{O}_\mathcal{K} = (\mu_1: \mu_2: 1: 1)$.

Let τ and $\tilde{\tau}$ be the roots of $x^2 - Gx + 1$ in $\mathbb{F}_p[x]$, and observe that $\tau \cdot \tilde{\tau} = 1$. On $\mathcal{K}^{\mathrm{Sqr}}$, the three $(2,2)$-subgroups corresponding to those defined in Sect. 4 are

$$O = (\mathcal{O}_\mathcal{K}, O_1, O_2, O_3) = \Big((\mu_1: \mu_2: 1: 1), (1: 1: \mu_1: \mu_2), (1: 1: \mu_2: \mu_1), (\mu_2: \mu_1: 1: 1) \Big),$$

$$\Upsilon = (\mathcal{O}_\mathcal{K}, \Upsilon_1, \Upsilon_2, \Upsilon_3) = \Big((\mu_1: \mu_2: 1: 1), (1: 0: 0: \tau), (1: 0: \tau: 0), (\mu_1 - \tau: \mu_2 - \tau: 0: 0) \Big),$$

$$\tilde{\Upsilon} = (\mathcal{O}_\mathcal{K}, \tilde{\Upsilon}_1, \tilde{\Upsilon}_2, \tilde{\Upsilon}_3) = \Big((\mu_1: \mu_2: 1: 1), (1: 0: 0: \tilde{\tau}), (1: 0: \tilde{\tau}: 0), (\mu_1 - \tilde{\tau}: \mu_2 - \tilde{\tau}: 0: 0) \Big).$$

$$(16)$$

Pseudo-doublings and φ_O on $\mathcal{K}^{\mathrm{Sqr}}$. Our $(2,2)$-isogenies and pseudo-doublings on $\mathcal{K}^{\mathrm{Sqr}}$ will be comprised of three sub-operations. Define $\mathcal{H}: \mathbb{P}^3 \to \mathbb{P}^3$ as the 4-way Hadamard transform in $\mathbb{P}^3$, i.e.,

$$\mathcal{H}: (\ell_1: \ell_2: \ell_3: \ell_4) \mapsto (\ell_1 + \ell_2 + \ell_3 + \ell_4: \ell_1 + \ell_2 - \ell_3 - \ell_4: \ell_1 - \ell_2 + \ell_3 - \ell_4: \ell_1 - \ell_2 - \ell_3 + \ell_4),$$

together with the coordinate squaring operation $\mathcal{S}: \mathbb{P}^3 \to \mathbb{P}^3$, as

$$\mathcal{S}: \quad (\ell_1: \ell_2: \ell_3: \ell_4) \mapsto (\ell_1^2: \ell_2^2: \ell_3^2: \ell_4^2),$$

and the coordinate scaling operation $\mathcal{C}_{(d_1: d_2: d_3: d_4)}: \mathbb{P}^3 \to \mathbb{P}^3$, as

$$\mathcal{C}_{(d_1: d_2: d_3: d_4)}: \quad (\ell_1: \ell_2: \ell_3: \ell_4) \mapsto (\ell_1/d_1: \ell_2/d_2: \ell_3/d_3: \ell_4/d_4)$$
$$= (\pi_1\ell_1: \pi_2\ell_2: \pi_3\ell_3: \pi_4\ell_4),$$

where $\pi_i = d_1 d_2 d_3 d_4 / d_i$ for $i \in \{1, 2, 3, 4\}$. It follows that $\mathcal{H}$ requires at most 8 field additions, $\mathcal{S}$ requires at most 4 field squarings, and $\mathcal{C}_{(d_1: d_2: d_3: d_4)}$ requires at most 10 field multiplications if the π_i are not precomputed, and at most 4 field multiplications if they are.

---

[5] When we move from Kummer to Kummer in SIDH, we will not be normalising μ_3 and μ_4, so the only savings that remain are those that arise from $\mu_3 = \mu_4$.

Following [28, Sect. 4], define the dual squared Kummer surface as

$$\hat{\mathcal{K}}_O^{\mathrm{Sqr}}: \qquad \hat{F} \cdot X_1 X_2 X_3 X_4 =$$

$$\left(X_1^2 + X_2^2 + X_3^3 + X_4^2 - \hat{G}(X_1 + X_2)(X_3 + X_4) - \hat{H}(X_1 X_2 + X_3 X_4) \right)^2,$$

where

$$\hat{F} := 64\mu_1^2 \mu_2^2 \frac{(\mu_1 + \mu_2 + 2)(\mu_1 + \mu_2 - 2)}{(\mu_1\mu_2 - 1)^2(\mu_1 - \mu_2)^2}, \quad \hat{G} := 2\left(\frac{\mu_1 + \mu_2}{\mu_1 - \mu_2}\right), \quad \text{and} \quad \hat{H} := 2\left(\frac{\mu_1\mu_2 + 1}{\mu_1\mu_2 - 1}\right).$$

In the previous section we derived formulas for computing φ_O in the full Jacobian – see (13). The corresponding isogeny on the Kummer surface is defined (with abuse of notation) as

$$\varphi_O: \quad \mathcal{K}^{\mathrm{Sqr}} \to \hat{\mathcal{K}}_O^{\mathrm{Sqr}},$$

$$P \mapsto \left(\mathcal{C}_{(\hat{\mu}_1 : \hat{\mu}_2 : \hat{\mu}_3 : \hat{\mu}_4)} \circ \mathcal{S} \circ \mathcal{H}\right)(P),$$

where $\hat{\mu}_1 := (\mu_1 + \mu_2 + 2)/2$, $\hat{\mu}_2 := (\mu_1 + \mu_2 - 2)/2$, and $\hat{\mu}_3 := \hat{\mu}_4 := (\mu_1 - \mu_2)/2$.

For the pseudo-doubling map, we compose φ_O with its dual, $\hat{\varphi}_O: \hat{\mathcal{K}}^{\mathrm{Sqr}} \to \mathcal{K}^{\mathrm{Sqr}}$, which simply replaces $\mathcal{C}_{(\hat{\mu}_1 : \hat{\mu}_2 : \hat{\mu}_3 : \hat{\mu}_4)}$ with $\mathcal{C}_{(\mu_1 : \mu_2 : \mu_3 : \mu_4)}$. The kernel of φ_O is the $(2,2)$-subgroup O in (16), and the kernel of $\hat{\varphi}_O$ is the $(2,2)$-subgroup consisting of $(\hat{\mu}_1 : \hat{\mu}_2 : \hat{\mu}_3 : \hat{\mu}_4)$, $(\hat{\mu}_2 : \hat{\mu}_1 : \hat{\mu}_4 : \hat{\mu}_3)$, $(\hat{\mu}_3 : \hat{\mu}_4 : \hat{\mu}_1 : \hat{\mu}_2)$, and $(\hat{\mu}_4 : \hat{\mu}_3 : \hat{\mu}_2 : \hat{\mu}_1)$.

Isomorphisms and φ_P on $\mathcal{K}^{\mathrm{Sqr}}$. We now turn to defining the $(2,2)$-isogenies whose kernels are Υ and $\tilde{\Upsilon}$ in (16).

Observe that there is a subtle difference between our description φ_O and $\hat{\varphi}_O$ above, and those described in the journey around the hexagon in [28, Fig. 1]. We define φ_O as $\varphi_O = \left(\mathcal{C}_{(\hat{\mu}_1 : \hat{\mu}_2 : \hat{\mu}_3 : \hat{\mu}_4)} \circ \mathcal{S} \circ \mathcal{H}\right)$, swapping the order of the scaling and squaring morphisms in [28, Fig. 1], which instead takes $\varphi_O = \left(\mathcal{S} \circ \mathcal{C}_{(\hat{\nu}_1 : \hat{\nu}_2 : \hat{\nu}_3 : \hat{\nu}_4)} \circ \mathcal{H}\right)$, where $\hat{\nu}_i^2 = \hat{\mu}_i$ for $i = 1, 2, 3, 4$ (this is analogous for $\hat{\varphi}_O$, but with $\nu_i^2 = \mu_i$). In their intended application to HECC, this ordering makes no difference, since the (presumably $\mathbb{F}_p$-rational) ν_i and $\hat{\nu}_i$ are always fixed public parameters. In our case, however, all of the Kummer parameters change each time we compute an isogeny, and the ordering here turns out to be crucial; we will never be computing the ν_i or $\hat{\nu}_i$ (or, at least, not in time for their use in the pseudo-doublings that typically take place prior to the following isogeny computation in the SIDH framework).

Nevertheless, viewing the first two steps from $\mathcal{K}^{\mathrm{Sqr}}$ around the hexagon exactly as in [28, Fig. 1] aids our derivation of the isomorphisms. The first step is the Hadamard isomorphism, which moves us from $\mathcal{K}^{\mathrm{Sqr}}$ to $\mathcal{K}^{\mathrm{Int}}$, and the next step is the scaling isomorphism $\mathcal{C}_{(\hat{\nu}_1 : \hat{\nu}_2 : \hat{\nu}_3 : \hat{\nu}_4)}$, which takes us from $\mathcal{K}^{\mathrm{Int}}$ to $\hat{\mathcal{K}}_O^{\mathrm{Can}}$; here $\mathcal{K}^{\mathrm{Int}}$ is exactly as in [28] and $\hat{\mathcal{K}}_O^{\mathrm{Can}}$ corresponds to $\hat{\mathcal{K}}^{\mathrm{Can}}$ in [28]. Writing O^{Can} as the image of O under $\mathcal{C}_O \circ \mathcal{H}$ with $\mathcal{C}_O := \mathcal{C}_{(\hat{\nu}_1 : \hat{\nu}_2 : \hat{\nu}_3 : \hat{\nu}_4)}$, and similarly for Υ and $\tilde{\Upsilon}$, reveals that

$$O^{\mathrm{Can}} = \Big((a:b:c:d),\, (a:-b:c:-d),\, (a:-b:-c:d),\, (a:b:-c:-d) \Big),$$

$$\Upsilon^{\mathrm{Can}} = \Big((a:b:c:d),\, (d:c:b:a),\, (c:d:a:b),\, (b:a:d:c) \Big),\ \text{and}$$

$$\tilde{\Upsilon}^{\mathrm{Can}} = \Big((a:b:c:d),\, (d:-c:-b:a),\, (c:-d:a:-b),\, (b:a:-d:-c) \Big),$$

$$\tag{17}$$

where $(a:b:c:d) = (\hat{\nu}_1 : \hat{\nu}_2 : \hat{\nu}_3 : \hat{\nu}_4)$ is the neutral element on $\hat{\mathcal{K}}_O^{\mathrm{Can}}$. Note that $\hat{\mathcal{K}}^{\mathrm{Can}}$ is the Kummer surface used by Gaudry, which is why the points in (17) match up with those in [19, Sect. 3.4].

We now proceed analogously to the treatment in Sect. 4. When Υ^{Can} is the intended $(2,2)$-kernel, we seek an isomorphism that will transform Υ^{Can} into a $(2,2)$-subgroup whose four elements *act* like the four elements in O^{Can}, but on an isomorphic surface. At the same time, this isomorphism should also transform the two subgroups in $\{O^{\mathrm{Can}}, \tilde{\Upsilon}^{\mathrm{Can}}\}$ into two subgroups whose elements act like those in the two subgroups in $\{\Upsilon^{\mathrm{Can}}, \tilde{\Upsilon}^{\mathrm{Can}}\}$, but on an isomorphic surface. Here the term 'act' refers to the action of translation by the 2-torsion elements of the corresponding Kummer surfaces. In the case of the 2-torsion on $\hat{\mathcal{K}}_O^{\mathrm{Can}}$, these actions (explained in [19, Sect. 3.4]) are extremely simple: for example, translating $(x:y:z:t) \in \hat{\mathcal{K}}_O^{\mathrm{Can}}$ by the element $(c:-d:a:-b)$ gives the point $(y: - x: t: - z)$.

We observe that when the $(2,2)$-kernel is Υ^{Can}, its image under the Hadamard transform satisfies these constraints, but when the $(2,2)$-kernel is $\tilde{\Upsilon}^{\mathrm{Can}}$, we need to use a modified transform $\tilde{\mathcal{H}} : (x:y:z:t) \mapsto \mathcal{H}(-x:y:z:t)$. Looking closer, and using the relationship $\tau\tilde{\tau} = 1$ in (16), we see that we can instead replace the scaling $\mathcal{C}_O$ with scalings $\mathcal{C}_\Upsilon$ and $\mathcal{C}_{\tilde{\Upsilon}}$ that depend on the subgroup at hand, and to follow both by the original Hadamard transform $\mathcal{H}$.

Importantly, the function for computing the constants for the coordinate scalings $\mathcal{C}_\Upsilon$ and $\mathcal{C}_{\tilde{\Upsilon}}$ is independent of which subgroup we are in; the values of the torsion elements are what changes the values of the scaling constants, which is crucial for obtaining a uniform isogeny algorithm. As alluded to above, to avoid the computation of square roots, the formulas for computing the scaling constants also take as input a point of order 4 on $\mathcal{K}^{\mathrm{Sqr}}$.

Let $Q \in \mathcal{K}^{\mathrm{Sqr}}$ be a point of order 4 such that $P = [2]Q \in \{\Upsilon, \tilde{\Upsilon}\}$; writing $Q' = \mathcal{H}(Q) = (Q'_1 : Q'_2 : Q'_3 : Q'_4)$ and $P' = \mathcal{H}(P) = (P'_1 : P'_2 : P'_3 : P'_4)$, then the coordinate scaling is

$$\mathcal{C}_{Q,P} : (X_1 : X_2 : X_3 : X_4) \mapsto (\pi_1 X_1 : \pi_2 X_2 : \pi_3 X_3 : \pi_4 X_4),$$

where

$$\pi_1 = P'_2 Q'_4, \qquad \pi_2 = P'_1 Q'_4, \qquad \text{and} \qquad \pi_3 = \pi_4 = P'_2 Q'_1,$$

when $P \in \{\Upsilon_1, \tilde{\Upsilon}_1\}$ (such that its last coordinate is non-zero), and where

$$\pi_1 = P'_2 Q'_3, \qquad \pi_2 = P'_1 Q'_3, \qquad \text{and} \qquad \pi_3 = \pi_4 = P'_2 Q'_1,$$

when $P \in \{\Upsilon_2, \tilde{\Upsilon}_2\}$ (such that its second to last coordinate is non-zero).

In our target application of chained $(2,2)$-isogenies in the SIDH framework, the 2-torsion points that represent our $(2,2)$-kernels are either always of the form of Υ_1 and $\tilde{\Upsilon}_1$, or they are always of the form of Υ_2 and $\tilde{\Upsilon}_2$. Thus, the function that computes the scaling constants can be determined at setup and fixed once-and-for-all in an implementation.

Let $\mathcal{G} \in \{\Upsilon, \tilde{\Upsilon}\}$ and let $P \in \mathcal{G}$ with $P = [2]Q$. We can now define the full $(2,2)$-isogeny with $(2,2)$-kernel $\mathcal{G}$ as

$$\varphi_P: \quad \mathcal{K}^{\mathrm{Sqr}} \to \mathcal{K}^{\mathrm{Sqr}}/\mathcal{G},$$
$$R \mapsto (\mathcal{S} \circ \mathcal{H} \circ \mathcal{C}_{Q,P} \circ \mathcal{H})(R). \tag{18}$$

Note that all four elements of the $(2,2)$-kernel $\mathcal{G}$ map to the neutral element $(\mu_1': \mu_2': 1: 1)$ on $\mathcal{K}^{\mathrm{Sqr}}/\mathcal{G}$.

In Fig. 1 we summarise the situation by making use of [28, Fig. 1]. The arrows in the middle comprise half of their hexagon; this corresponds to φ_O, whose kernel is the subgroup O. Note that our SIDH-style computations will never compute this isogeny, and that we will always be taking either the top or bottom path, depending on whether our $(2,2)$-kernel is Υ or $\tilde{\Upsilon}$.

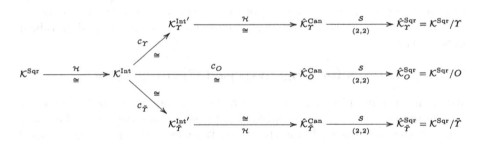

Fig. 1. An illustration of the two $(2,2)$-isogenies corresponding to the subgroups Υ and $\tilde{\Upsilon}$, based on the diagram in [28, Fig. 1]. Here $\mathcal{C}_\Upsilon$ is used to denote $\mathcal{C}_{Q,P}$ when $P \in \Upsilon$, and $\mathcal{C}_{\tilde{\Upsilon}}$ is used to indicate $\mathcal{C}_{Q,P}$ when $P \in \tilde{\Upsilon}$.

We point out that our use of the 4-torsion point Q above the 2-torsion point P means that we must modify the computational strategy to account for this; we refer to [16, Sect. 4.3.2], where this was done when 8-torsion points lying above 2-torsion kernel elements were incorporated into the computational *strategies*.

Operation Counts. Even though our Kummer surfaces are defined by the projective tuple $(\mu_1: \mu_2: 1: 1)$, once we move into an SIDH computation (where we avoid inversions in the main loop), we cannot expect the surface constants to be normalised in this fashion, so in our context all multiplications by constants are counted as generic multiplications (the analogue in the elliptic curve case was treating the Montgomery coefficient in $\mathbb{P}^1$ – see [14]). In the HECC context, pseudo-doublings on fast Kummer surfaces incur 6 multiplications by curve constants, but this is because 2 of the constants were normalised; in our case, pseudo-doublings incur 4 multiplications during each of the scalings $\mathcal{D}_{(\mu_1 : \mu_2 : \mu_3 : \mu_4)}$ and $\mathcal{D}_{(\hat{\mu}_1 : \hat{\mu}_2 : \hat{\mu}_3 : \hat{\mu}_4)}$. This brings the operation count for a pseudo-doubling to 8 multiplications, 8 squarings, and 16 additions, and the operation count for pushing a point through a $(2,2)$-isogeny to 4 multiplications, 4 squarings, and 16 additions. Note that both of these counts are obtained by assuming that the inverted constants in the coordinate scalings have been precomputed during the computation of the $(2,2)$-isogenous Kummer surface.

It therefore remains to tally the operations required to compute the isogenous Kummer surface constants. Firstly, we point out that an optimised implementation does not actually need to compute or use the constants F, G and H defining the surface, since these are not used directly in the pseudo-group law computations. The only constants needed are those in the two coordinate scalings that occur during pseudo-doublings; we obtain these by pushing any kernel point through the $(2,2)$-isogeny to get the squared theta constants $(\mu_1' : \mu_2' : \mu_3' : \mu_4')$ that define the image surface, a further 6 multiplications to obtain a projective tuple equivalent to $(1/\mu_1' : 1/\mu_2' : 1/\mu_3' : 1/\mu_4')$, and then 8 more additions and 6 more multiplications to compute a projective tuple whose coordinates are projectively equivalent to the inverses of the coordinates of $\mathcal{H}(\mu_1' : \mu_2' : \mu_3' : \mu_4')$. In total, the computation of the set of isogenous surface constants requires 19 multiplications, 4 squarings, and 28 additions. These counts are used in Table 1 in the next section.

6   Implications for Isogeny-Based Cryptography

We discuss potential implications and practical considerations of the Kummer surface approach in the realm of SIDH. The takeaway message is that this paper is a first step towards exploring the use of Kummer surfaces in isogeny-based cryptography, and that more work needs to be done to determine whether they will be utilised in real-world implementations. For example, it is possible that our approach to computing the isogeny φ_P is sub-optimal, and that faster methods will be discovered, or that there are more specialised parameterisations of supersingular Kummer surfaces that provide even faster arithmetic.

Efficiency of (2,2)-Isogenies in SIDH. In Table 1, we compare $(2,2)$-isogenies on Kummer surfaces with 2-isogenies on elliptic curves, by comparing the operation counts for isolated operations in both scenarios. On the elliptic curve side, the current state-of-the-art implementations actually use repeated 4-isogenies as they are slightly faster [14, 16, 27], so to take this into account we simply double the relevant operation counts for the $(2,2)$-isogenies reported above (recall from Lemma 2 that our $(2,2)$-isogenies correspond to 2-isogenies on the elliptic curves). Operation counts for the relevant 4-isogeny operations in the elliptic curve case are exactly as in the optimised version of the SIKE implementation [22], and for the relevant 2-isogeny operations are exactly as in [27, Table 1].

We use **M**, **S** and **A** to denote multiplications, squarings and additions in $\mathbb{F}_{p^2}$, and use **m**, **s** and **a** to denote the same respective operations in $\mathbb{F}_p$. It is common to approximate the former in terms of the latter by assuming Karatsuba-like routines for $\mathbb{F}_{p^2}$ operations, but this can be rather crude. To give a fairer comparison, we benchmarked these field operations directly using v3.0 of Microsoft's SIDH library[6]: on a 3.4GHz Intel i7-6700 (Skylake) architecture, and over the 751-bit prime from [14], this benchmarking reported **M** = 1004 cycles, **S** = 763 cycles, and **A** = 80 cycles, while **m** = 349 cycles and **a** = 43 cycles. The current library does not have a tailored squaring routine over $\mathbb{F}_p$, because the routines for $\mathbb{F}_{p^2}$ operations never call $\mathbb{F}_p$ squarings as a subroutine. Thus, we give two cycle count approximations for the Kummer case: one that assumes **s** = **m** (i.e., that the $\mathbb{F}_p$ multiplication routine is called to compute squarings), and one that assumes **s** = 0.8**m**, a common ratio used to approximate the speedup obtained by optimising tailored field squarings. We note that using cycle counts instead of Karatsuba approximations favours the elliptic curve setting over this work. For example, when using the above clock cycles as units, we have **M** < 3**m**, but a common approximation is that **M** $\approx$ 3**m** + 5**a** $\gg$ 3**m**.

Table 1. Field arithmetic required for the three main isolated operations on one side of the SIDH framework, comparing chained 2-isogenies on Montgomery curves over $\mathbb{F}_{p^2}$ (previous work) with chained Richelot isogenies on Kummer surfaces over $\mathbb{F}_p$ (this work). Further explanation in text.

Operation	chained 2-isogenies on Montgomery curves over $\mathbb{F}_{p^2}$ (previous work)				chained $(2,2)$-isogenies on Kummer surfaces over $\mathbb{F}_p$ (this work)				
	M	S	A	$\approx$ cycles	m	s	a	$\approx$ cycles	
								s = m	s = 0.8 m
doubling	4	2	4	5862	8	8	16	6272	5714
2-isog. curve	-	2	1	2088	19	4	28	9231	8952
2-isog. point	4	0	4	4336	4	4	16	3480	3200
quadrupling	8	4	8	11724	16	16	32	12544	11427
4-isog. curve	-	4	5	3452	38	8	56	18462	17903
4-isog. point	6	2	6	8030	8	8	32	6960	6401

The approximations in Table 1 suggest that the Kummer surface approach of computing Richelot isogenies over $\mathbb{F}_p$ will be competitive with the previous approaches that apply Vélu's formulas to the x-line of Montgomery elliptic curves over $\mathbb{F}_{p^2}$. The main operations of interest are 'quadrupling' and '4-isog. point', since these costs and their ratios are what determines the optimal strategy

---

[6] See https://github.com/Microsoft/PQCrypto-SIDH.

(see [16]), and they are computed many more times than the '4-isog. curve' operation. Moreover, doubling the $(2, 2)$-isogeny operation counts is only accurate in the case of the point operations; in terms of the curve operations, we would not need to compute the full set of the surface constants of the intermediate curve in back-to-back $(2, 2)$-isogenies, so a more careful approach to computing the image curve in this case would likely lead to counts close to half of those in this row (on our side). One caveat worth mentioning is that the special Kummer surfaces in this work will also have a fast ladder for computing scalar multiplications, as well as a fast three-point ladder that is typically used before any isogenies are computed in the SIDH framework.

Of course, the only way to determine if the Kummer approach can outperform the elliptic curve approach is to present an optimised implementation of Kummer surface isogenies within the SIDH framework, e.g., one that factors in the cost ratios of pseudo-doublings and $(2, 2)$-isogenies to derive optimal strategies for the full SIDH isogeny computation – see [16, Sect. 4.2]. We leave such an implementation as future work (perhaps until the motivation is heightened by odd-power Kummer isogenies that can be used on the other side of the SIDH protocol, as we discuss below), but also mention that Kummer arithmetic is especially amenable to aggressive vectorised implementations (see [5]).

Utilising Kummer Surfaces in Practice. We discuss two potential options for taking advantage of Kummer surface arithmetic in the SIDH framework, and the practical considerations of each. The first option is that the public parameters and wire transmissions are as usual, i.e., using (points on) elliptic curves, but that Kummer arithmetic is internally preferred by at least one party. The second assumes that Kummer arithmetic is preferred everywhere, and that the SIDH framework is defined to facilitate this.

Option 1 – Kummer arithmetic in private. Suppose Alice wants to compute her secret isogenies on Kummer surfaces while engaging in an SIDH protocol that is specified entirely using elliptic curves. In terms of the public parameters, her easiest option would be to convert them (offline and once-and-for-all) into Kummer parameters by first using the map $\eta: E_\alpha \to J_{C_\alpha}$ in Sect. 3, and then applying the usual maps from J_{C_α} to $\mathcal{K}^{\mathrm{Sqr}}$. While this process seems complicated at a first glance, a closer inspection of these maps reveals that an optimised conversion in this direction would only require a few dozen field multiplications; the x-coordinates of three co-linear points on E_α (see [14,22]) are all Alice needs to compute the corresponding Kummer surface and the three Kummer points required to kick-start her computations. Indeed, the only additional information she needs to convert Bob's public key down to the Kummer domain is the initial 2-torsion point $(\alpha, 0)$ (assuming Bob sends her information for the curve coefficient instead), and this requires at most one square root in $\mathbb{F}_{p^2}$, which is not a deal-breaker.

In the other direction, after computing her public key or shared secret on $\mathcal{K}^{\mathrm{Sqr}}$, Alice needs to lift this information back up to E_α in order to comply with Bob. The maps lifting from $\mathcal{K}^{\mathrm{Sqr}}$ back up to $J_{C_{\lambda,\mu,\nu}}$ are naturally more complicated than their inverses [13,19], but again the SIDH x-only framework simplifies the process significantly; we can recover the x-coordinate on E_α given only the values of u_1, u_0 and v_0^2 (corresponding to the Mumford coordinates of a point in J_{C_α}), and we can lift up from $\mathcal{K}$ to these values without any square roots – see [19, Sect. 4.3].

In any case, equipped with the efficient maps in Sect. 3, we do not see any theoretical or practical obstacle preventing Alice from complying, should the efficiency of the Kummer warrant a small conversion overhead at either or both sides of the main isogeny computation.

Option 2 – Kummer arithmetic everywhere. If both sides of the SIDH protocol eventually warrant Kummer arithmetic (see below), then defining the public parameters to facilitate this is easy. The main issues we foresee involve maintaining the size of the public keys in the compressed setting.

Firstly, in the uncompressed scenario, transmitting elliptic curves and Kummer surfaces in the current framework has the same cost; Montgomery curves are specified up to twist with one element in $\mathbb{F}_{p^2}$, and our supersingular Kummer surfaces are completely specified by two elements of $\mathbb{F}_p$ (μ_1 and μ_2). Unambiguously specifying points on Montgomery curves amounts to sending one element of $\mathbb{F}_{p^2}$ and a sign bit; on the Kummer side, the elegant techniques in [28, Sect. 6] show that Kummer points can be specified by two elements of $\mathbb{F}_p$ and two sign bits, meaning we lose at most one bit per group element. Rather than sending any curve coefficients over the wire, recent works (including the SIKE proposal [22]) have instead specified public keys as three co-linear Montgomery x-coordinates, from which the underlying Montgomery curve can be recovered on the other side [14]. We have not yet investigated this analogue in the Kummer surface setting, but even if it does not work in a straightforward way, reverting back to the original form of public keys (from [16]) adds at most 4 bits to the public key sizes. To summarise, we would lose at most a few bits to specify uncompressed SIDH entirely using Kummer surfaces.

In terms of the shared secret, both parties would eventually arrive at a fast supersingular Kummer surface specified by $(\mu_1 : \mu_2 : 1 : 1)$. While we have yet to investigate convenient Kummer surface invariants that could act as the shared secret, we remark that empirical evidence seems to suggest that the approach of computing λ, μ and $\nu = \lambda\mu$ from (15) and normalising the Igusa-Clebsch invariants in $\mathbb{P}(2, 4, 6, 10)(\mathbb{F}_p)$ makes the SIDH protocol commute. We leave further investigation into appropriate invariants as future work.

In terms of optimal compression of public keys, applying the techniques in [2] directly to the Kummer setting seems less straightforward, but again we cannot see any reason preventing this possibility[7]. This too needs further investigation, but we point out that as a fallback, we could of course always map the problem of compression back to the elliptic curve setting (moving back to the first option above), and specify the compressed public keys accordingly.

---

[7] In recent years Kummer surfaces have been shown to be more cryptographically versatile [24,28] than originally thought [32].

Of course, there are several other possibilities that lie somewhere between the two options above, e.g., where the two parties send information in such a way that the overall cost of the protocol is minimised.

Beyond (2,2)-Isogenies. The case for the Kummer approach in supersingular isogeny-based cryptography would be much stronger if it were able to be applied efficiently for both parties. There has been some explicit work done in the case of $(3,3)$- and $(5,5)$-isogenies (cf. [9,17]), but those situations appear much more complicated than the case of Richelot isogenies, and we leave their investigation as future work. One hope in this direction is the possibility of pushing odd degree ℓ-isogeny maps from the elliptic curve setting to the Kummer setting by way of the maps in Sect. 3. This was difficult in the case of 2-isogenies because the maps themselves are $(2,2)$-isogenies (e.g., their kernel is the 2-torsion on E_α), but in the case of odd degree isogenies there is nothing obvious preventing this approach.

Acknowledgements. Big thanks to Joost Renes for his help in ironing out some kinks on the Kummer surfaces, to Michael Naehrig for several helpful discussions during the preparation of this work, and to the anonymous reviewers for their useful comments.

References

1. Auer, R., Top, J.: Legendre elliptic curves over finite fields. J. Number Theor. **95**(2), 303–312 (2002)
2. Azarderakhsh, R., Jao, D., Kalach, K., Koziel, B., Leonardi, C.: Key compression for isogeny-based cryptosystems. In: Emura, K., Hanaoka, G., Zhang, R. (eds.) Proceedings of the 3rd ACM International Workshop on ASIA Public-Key Cryptography, AsiaPKC@AsiaCCS, Xi'an, China, 30 May – 03 June 2016, pp. 1–10. ACM (2016)
3. Bernstein, D.J.: Curve25519: new Diffie-Hellman speed records. In: Yung, M., Dodis, Y., Kiayias, A., Malkin, T. (eds.) PKC 2006. LNCS, vol. 3958, pp. 207–228. Springer, Heidelberg (2006). https://doi.org/10.1007/11745853_14
4. Bernstein, D.J.: Elliptic vs. Hyperelliptic, part I. Talk at ECC, September 2006. (http://cr.yp.to/talks/2006.09.20/slides.pdf)
5. Bernstein, D.J., Chuengsatiansup, C., Lange, T., Schwabe, P.: Kummer strikes back: new DH speed records. In: Sarkar, P., Iwata, T. (eds.) ASIACRYPT 2014. LNCS, vol. 8873, pp. 317–337. Springer, Heidelberg (2014). https://doi.org/10.1007/978-3-662-45611-8_17
6. Bernstein, D.J., Lange, T.: Hyper-and-elliptic-curve cryptography. LMS J. Comput. Math. **17**(A), 181–202 (2014)
7. Bos, J.W., Costello, C., Hisil, H., Lauter, K.E.: Fast cryptography in genus 2. J. Cryptol. **29**(1), 28–60 (2016)
8. Bost, J.-B., Mestre, J.-F.: Moyenne arithmético-géométrique et périodes des courbes de genre 1 et 2. Gaz. Math. **38**, 36–64 (1988)
9. Bruin, N., Flynn, E.V., Testa, D.: Descent via $(3,3)$-isogeny on Jacobians of genus 2 curves. Acta Arithmetica **165**, 201–223 (2014)
10. Cassels, J.W.S., Flynn, E.V.: Prolegomena to a Middlebrow Arithmetic of Curves of Genus 2, vol. 230. Cambridge University Press, Cambridge (1996)

11. Childs, A.M., Jao, D., Soukharev, V.: Constructing elliptic curve isogenies in quantum subexponential time. J. Math. Cryptol. **8**(1), 1–29 (2014)
12. Chudnovsky, D.V., Chudnovsky, G.V.: Sequences of numbers generated by addition in formal groups and new primality and factorization tests. Adv. Appl. Math. **7**(4), 385–434 (1986)
13. Cosset, R.: Factorization with genus 2 curves. Math. Comput. **79**(270), 1191–1208 (2010)
14. Costello, C., Longa, P., Naehrig, M.: Efficient algorithms for supersingular isogeny Diffie-Hellman. In: Robshaw, M., Katz, J. (eds.) CRYPTO 2016. LNCS, vol. 9814, pp. 572–601. Springer, Heidelberg (2016). https://doi.org/10.1007/978-3-662-53018-4_21
15. Faz-Hernández, A., López, J., Ochoa-Jiménez, E., Rodríguez-Henríquez, F.: A faster software implementation of the supersingular isogeny Diffie-Hellman key exchange protocol. IEEE Trans. Comput. **67**(11), 1622–1636 (2017)
16. De Feo, L., Jao, D., Plût, J.: Towards quantum-resistant cryptosystems from supersingular elliptic curve isogenies. J. Math. Cryptol. **8**(3), 209–247 (2014)
17. Flynn, E.V.: Descent via (5, 5)-isogeny on Jacobians of genus 2 curves. J. Number Theor. **153**, 270–282 (2015)
18. Galbraith, S.D.: Mathematics of Public Key Cryptography. Cambridge University Press, Cambridge (2012)
19. Gaudry, P.: Fast genus 2 arithmetic based on Theta functions. J. Math. Cryptol. **1**(3), 243–265 (2007)
20. Hisil, H., Costello, C.: Jacobian coordinates on genus 2 curves. J. Cryptol. **30**(2), 572–600 (2017)
21. Igusa, J.: Arithmetic variety of moduli for genus two. Ann. Math. 612–649 (1960)
22. Jao, D., et al.: SIKE: Supersingular Isogeny Key Encapsulation (2017). sike.org/
23. Jao, D., De Feo, L.: Towards quantum-resistant cryptosystems from supersingular elliptic curve isogenies. In: Yang, B.-Y. (ed.) PQCrypto 2011. LNCS, vol. 7071, pp. 19–34. Springer, Heidelberg (2011). https://doi.org/10.1007/978-3-642-25405-5_2
24. Lubicz, D., Robert, D.: Arithmetic on abelian and Kummer varieties. Finite Fields Appl. **39**, 130–158 (2016)
25. Montgomery, P.L.: Speeding the Pollard and elliptic curve methods of factorization. Math. Comput. **48**(177), 243–264 (1987)
26. Oort, F.: Subvarieties of moduli spaces. Inventiones Mathematicae **24**(2), 95–119 (1974)
27. Renes, J.: Computing isogenies between montgomery curves using the action of (0, 0). In: Lange, T., Steinwandt, R. (eds.) PQCrypto 2018. LNCS, vol. 10786, pp. 229–247. Springer, Cham (2018). https://doi.org/10.1007/978-3-319-79063-3_11
28. Renes, J., Smith, B.: qDSA: small and secure digital signatures with curve-based Diffie-Hellman key pairs. In: Takagi, T., Peyrin, T. (eds.) ASIACRYPT 2017. LNCS, vol. 10625, pp. 273–302. Springer, Cham (2017). https://doi.org/10.1007/978-3-319-70697-9_10
29. Richelot, F.: Essai sur une methode generale pour determiner la valuer des integrales ultra-elliptiques, fondee sur des transformations remarquables des ce transcendantes. CR Acad. Sci. Paris **2**, 622–627 (1836)
30. Richelot, F.: De transformatione integralium Abelianorum primi ordinis commentatio. J. für die reine und angewandte Mathematik **16**, 221–284 (1837)
31. Scholten, J.: Weil restriction of an elliptic curve over a quadratic extension (2003). http://citeseerx.ist.psu.edu/viewdoc/download?doi=10.1.1.118.7987&rep=rep1&type=pdf

32. Smart, N.P., Siksek, S.: A fast Diffie-Hellman protocol in genus 2. J. Cryptol. **12**(1), 67–73 (1999)
33. Smith, B.A.: Explicit endomorphisms and correspondences. Ph.D. thesis, University of Sydney (2005)
34. The National Institute of Standards and Technology (NIST): Submission requirements and evaluation criteria for the post-quantum cryptography standardization process, December 2016
35. Vélu, J.: Isogénies entre courbes elliptiques. CR Acad. Sci. Paris Sér. AB **273**, A238–A241 (1971)

Foundations

Robustly Reusable Fuzzy Extractor
from Standard Assumptions

Yunhua Wen[1] and Shengli Liu[1,2,3(✉)]

[1] Department of Computer Science and Engineering, Shanghai Jiao Tong University,
Shanghai 200240, China
{happyle8,slliu}@sjtu.edu.cn
[2] State Key Laboratory of Cryptology, P.O. Box 5159, Beijing 100878, China
[3] Westone Cryptologic Research Center, Beijing 100070, China

Abstract. A fuzzy extractor (FE) aims at deriving and reproducing
(almost) uniform cryptographic keys from noisy non-uniform sources.
To reproduce an identical key R from subsequent readings of a noisy
source, it is necessary to eliminate the noises from those readings. To
this end, a public helper string P, together with the key R, is produced
from the first reading of the source during the initial enrollment phase.

In this paper, we consider computational fuzzy extractor. We formalize *robustly reusable fuzzy extractor* (rrFE) which considers *reusability*
and *robustness* simultaneously in the Common Reference String (CRS)
model. Reusability of rrFE deals with source reuse. It guarantees that
the key R output by fuzzy extractor is pseudo-random even if the initial
enrollment is applied to the same source several times, generating multiple public helper strings and keys (P_i, R_i). Robustness of rrFE deals
with active probabilistic polynomial-time adversaries, who may manip-
ulate the public helper string P_i to affect the reproduction of R_i. Any
modification of P_i by the adversary will be detected by the robustness
of rrFE.

- We show how to construct an rrFE from a Symmetric Key Encapsulation Mechanism (SKEM), a Secure Sketch (SS), an Extractor
  (Ext), and a Lossy Algebraic Filter (LAF). We characterize the key-
  shift security notion of SKEM and the homomorphic properties of
  SS, Ext and LAF, which enable our construction of rrFE to achieve
  both reusability and robustness.
- We present an instantiation of SKEM from the DDH assumption.
  Combined with the LAF by Hofheinz (EuroCrypt 2013), homomorphic SS and Ext, we obtain the first rrFE based on standard assumptions.

Keywords: Fuzzy extractor · Reusability · Robustness
Standard assumptions

1 Introduction

Uniformly distributed keys are pivots of cryptographic primitives. However, it
is not easy for us to create, memorize and safely store random keys. In practice,

© International Association for Cryptologic Research 2018
T. Peyrin and S. Galbraith (Eds.): ASIACRYPT 2018, LNCS 11274, pp. 459–489, 2018.
https://doi.org/10.1007/978-3-030-03332-3_17

there are plenty of noisy sources, which possess high entropy and provide similar but not identical reading at each enrollment. Such sources include biometrics like fingerprint, iris, face and voice [9,17,19,20], Physical Unclonable Functions [21,23] and quantum sources [3,16]. How to make use of these noisy sources to derive uniform and reproducible keys for cryptographic applications is exactly the concern of Fuzzy Extractors [12].

Fuzzy extractor. A fuzzy extractor FE consists of a pair of algorithms (Gen, Rep). It works as follows. The generation algorithm Gen takes as input a reading w of some source and outputs a public helper string P and an extracted key R. The reproduction algorithm Rep takes as input the public helper string P and a reading w' of the same source (w' is a noisy version of w). It reproduces R if w and w' are close enough. The security of fuzzy extractor requires that R is statistically (or computationally) indistinguishable from a uniform one, even conditioned on the public helper string P.

With a fuzzy extractor FE, one may invoke Gen to generate a random key R and a public helper string P from a noisy source, then he stores the helper string P (publicly), and uses the key R in a cryptographic application. Note that it is not necessary for the user to store R. Whenever key R is needed again, he just re-reads the (noisy) source and invokes Rep to reproduce R with the help of P.

However, there are two limitations of FE, leading to two issues.

- The extracted key R is (pseudo)random under the assumption that no more than a single extraction is performed on the noisy source by Gen. In reality, biometric information, like fingerprint or iris, is unique and cannot be changed or created. One may hope that the same source is enrolled multiple times by Gen to generate different keys $R_1, R_2, \ldots, R_\rho$ for different applications. But no security guarantee can be provided for any R_i if $\rho \geq 2$.
- The security notion of FE only considers passive adversary and says nothing about active attacks. If the public helper string P is modified by an active adversary, then the reproduction algorithm Rep may generate a wrong key $\widetilde{R}$. In this case, one might not realize that $\widetilde{R}$ is a wrong one, and it may lead to unbearable economic loss.

The first issue can be resolved by reusable FE and the second by robust FE.

Reusable Fuzzy Extractor. Reusable Fuzzy Extractor aims to address the first issue. It allows of multiple extractions from the same source, i.e., apply Gen to correlated readings $w, w_1, \ldots, w_\rho$ of a source to obtain keys and public helper strings (P, R) $\{P_i, R_i\}_{i \in \{1,2,\ldots,\rho\}}$. Define $[\rho] := \{1, 2, \ldots, \rho\}$. *Reusability* of FE asks for pseudorandomness of R, even conditioned on $\{P_i, R_i\}_{i \in [\rho]}$ and P.

The concept of reusable FE was first proposed by Boyen [4], who presented two reusable FE constructions with outsider security and insider security respectively. Outsider security considers the pseudorandomness of R even if the adversary is able to adaptively choose δ_i and see P_i (but not R_i), where $(P_i, R_i) \leftarrow \text{Gen}(w + \delta_i)$. It can be regarded as weak reusability in the sense that the adversary sees only $\{P_i\}_{i \in [\rho]}$. Insider security is stronger by allowing the adversary to obtain not only $\{P_i\}_{i \in [\rho]}$ but also $\tilde{R}_i \leftarrow \mathsf{Rep}(\tilde{P}_i, w + \tilde{\delta}_i)$ where $\tilde{P}_i$ and $\tilde{\delta}_i$ are chosen by the adversary. However, the construction for insider security in [4] relies on the random oracle model. Meanwhile, the perturbation δ_i in the reusable FE constructions [4] is very special and independent of w, no matter for outsider security or insider security. Apon et al. [2] adapted the FE proposed by Fuller et al. [14] to obtain a weakly reusable FE. They also gave a reusable FE based on the LWE assumption. Their security model is similar to [4] but has no special requirements on δ_i except that $\mathsf{dis}(\delta_i) \leq t$. However, just like [14] their reusable FE can only tolerate a logarithmic fraction of errors. With the same security model, a reusable FE tolerating linear fraction of errors from the LWE assumption was proposed in [24].

Canetti et al. [6] constructed a reusable FE for Hamming distance. The security model of their reusable FE makes no assumption about how repeating readings are correlated, but their construction only tolerates sub-linear fraction of errors. Moreover, their construction of FE has to rely on a powerful tool named "digital locker". Up to now, digital locker can only be instantiated with a hash function modeled as random oracle or constructed from the non-standard strong vector DDH assumption. Following the line of constructing reusable FE from digital locker, Alamelou et al. [1] constructed a reusable FE for both the set difference metric and Hamming distance. Their construction tolerates linear fraction of errors but requires that noisy secrets distributions have enough entropy in each symbol of a large alphabet.

Recently, Wen et al. [26] proposed a reusable FE from the DDH assumption which can tolerate linear fraction of errors. But a strong requirement is imposed on the input distribution: any differences between two distinct inputs should not leak too much information of the source w.

As far as we know, the available works on reusable FE follow three lines according to the correlations among source readings w_i's. The first line considers arbitrary correlations among w_i's and has to rely on non-standard assumptions or random oracle. The second line imposes strong requirements on the source, i.e., any differences between two distinct inputs should not leak too much information of the source w_i. The third line considers δ_i ($= w_i - w$) controlled by adversaries. See Fig. 1. The related works are also summarized in Table 1.

Robust Fuzzy Extractor. Robust Fuzzy Extractor aims to address the second issue. *Robustness* of FE requires that any modification of P by an adversary will be detected. Boyen et al. [5] introduced the concept of robust FE, and proposed a general way of converting a FE to a robust one. In their approach, a hash function is employed and modeled as a random oracle. Dodis et al. [10] strengthened robustness to *post-application robustness*, which guarantees that the FE will detect any modification of P by adversary who also sees R. Later, robust FE was slightly improved in [18]. Nevertheless, it was shown in [13] that in the information theoretic setting, it is impossible to construct a robust FE if the entropy rate of W is less than half in the plain model. Cramer et al. [7] broke this barrier by building a robust FE in the Common Reference String (CRS) model. Recall that CRS can be hardwired or hardcoded into the system

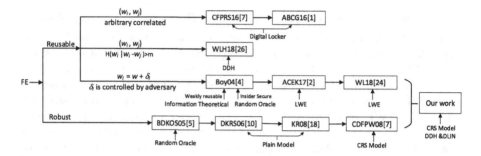

Fig. 1. Related works about reusable FE and robust FE. $H(w_i|w_i - w_j)$ is the average min-entropy of w_i conditioned on $w_i - w_j$.

so that CRS can be observed but not modified by adversaries. See Fig. 1 and Table 1 for related works of robust FE.

We stress that up to now there is no work ever considering robustness of reusable FE or reusability of robust FE in the standard model, since designing reusable FE or robust FE alone is already an uneasy task.

Table 1. Comparison with known FE schemes. "Robustness?" asks whether the scheme achieves robustness; "Reusability?" asks whether the scheme achieves reusability; "Standard Assumption ?" asks whether the scheme is based on standard assumptions. "Linear Errors?" asks whether the scheme can correct linear fraction of errors. "–" represents the scheme is an information theoretical one.

FE Schemes	Robustness?	Reusability?	Standard Assumption?	Linear Errors?
FMR13 [14]	✗	✗	✔	✗
DRS04 [12], Boy04 [4]	✗	weak	–	✔
CFPRS16 [6]	✗	✔	✗	✗
Boy04 [4] ABCG16 [1]	✗	✔	✗	✔
ACEK17 [2]	✗	✔	✔	✗
BDKOS05 [5]	✔	✗	✗	✔
DKRS06 [10], KR08 [18], CDFPW08 [7]	✔	✗	–	✔
WL18 [24], WLH18 [26]	✗	✔	✔	✔
Ours	✔	✔	✔	✔

1.1 Our Contributions

We consider how to construct fuzzy extractors satisfying reusability and robustness simultaneously based on standard assumptions in the CRS model.

- We formalize *robustly reusable fuzzy extractor* (rrFE) whose security notions include both *reusability* and post-application *robustness* in the computational setting.

- We propose a general construction of rrFE from a Symmetric Key Encapsulation Mechanism (SKEM), a Secure Sketch (SS), an Extractor (Ext), and a Lossy Algebraic Filter (LAF) in the CRS model.
    • We characterize the required security notion of SKEM and the homomorphic properties of SS, Ext and LAF, which enable the construction of rrFE to achieve both reusability ad robustness.
    • SKEM is a primitive similar to Key Encapsulation Mechanism (KEM), but the encapsulation and decapsulation make use of the same secret key. We define Key-Shift (KS) security for SKEM, which says that the encapsulated key is pseudorandom, even if the adversary sees multiple encapsulations under shifted secret keys where the shifts are designated by the adversary. We present an instantiation of SKEM and prove its KS-security from the DDH assumption.
- We obtain the first rrFE tolerating linear fraction of errors based on standard assumptions by instantiating SKEM, LAF, SS and Ext. More precisely, SKEM is built from the DDH assumption and LAF by Hofheinz (EuroCrypt 2013) is based on the DLIN assumption.

Our construction is the first FE possessing both reusability and robustness. Meanwhile, our construction is able to tolerate a linear fraction of errors. However, we do not assume arbitrary correlations between different readings of w. Instead, we assume that the shifts between different readings are controlled by the adversary in the security model, just like [2]. Our work can be regarded as a step forward from the the third and fourth branches in Fig. 1.

Table 1 compares our rrFE with the available reusable FE and robust FE.

1.2 Our Approach

Our work stems from the traditional *sketch-and-extract* paradigm [11] due to Dodis et al. First, we review the traditional *sketch-and-extract* paradigm [11]. Then we introduce a new primitive called Symmetric Key Encapsulation Mechanism (SKEM) and define for it a so-called *Key-Shift* security. We also recall the definition of Lossy Algebraic Filter (LAF) introduced by Hofheinz [15]. Equipped with SKEM and LAF, we show how to construct a *robustly reusable Fuzzy Extractor* (rrFE) from SS, Ext, SKEM and LAF. Finally, we describe the high level idea of why our construction of rrFE achieves both reusability and robustness.

The Sketch-and-Extract Paradigm. In [11], Dodis et al. proposed a paradigm of constructing FE from secure sketch and extractor.

Secure Sketch (SS) is used for removing noises from fuzzy inputs. An SS scheme consists of a pair of algorithms SS = (SS.Gen, SS.Rec). Algorithm SS.Gen on input w outputs a sketch s; algorithm SS.Rec on input s and w' recovers w as long as w and w' are close enough. For SS, it is required that W still has enough entropy conditioned on s.

An extractor Ext distills an almost uniform key R from the non-uniform random variable W of enough entropy, with the help of a random seed i_{ext}.

The sketch-and-extract construction of FE = (Gen, Rep) [11] works as follows.

- Gen(w, i_{ext}): Set $P := (\text{SS.Gen}(w), i_{ext})$, $R := \text{Ext}(w, i_{ext})$. Output (P, R).
- Rep$(w', P = (s, i_{ext}))$: Recover $w := \text{SS.Rec}(w', s)$ and output $R := \text{Ext}(w, i_{ext})$.

Symmetric Key Encapsulation Mechanism. For reusability, we introduce a technical tool called *symmetric key encapsulation mechanism* (SKEM). It is similar to Key Encapsulation Mechanism (KEM) [8], except that the encapsulation and decapsulation algorithms share the same secret key sk.

- Encapsulation algorithm SKEM.Enc takes as input the secret key sk, and outputs a ciphertext c and an encapsulated key $k \in \mathcal{K}$.
- Decapsulation algorithm SKEM.Dec recovers the key k, on input c and sk.

The requirement for SKEM is *key-shift* security. That is, $(c, k) \leftarrow \text{SKEM.Enc}(sk)$ is computationally indistinguishable from (c, u), where u is uniformly chosen from $\mathcal{K}$, even if the adversary has an access to a key-shift encapsulation oracle SKEM.Enc$(sk + \Delta_i)$, where Δ_i is chosen by the adversary adaptively.

Lossy Algebraic Filter. For robustness, we introduce a technical tool named lossy algebraic filter (LAF) by Hofheinz [15]. It is a family of functions indexed by a public key F_{pk} and a tag tag. A tag is lossy, injective or neither. A function from that family takes a vector $X = (X_i)_{i=1}^{n} \in \mathbb{Z}_p^n$ as input. If tag is an injective tag, then the function $\text{LAF}_{F_{pk}, \text{tag}}(\cdot)$ is an injective function. If tag is lossy, then the function is *lossy* in the sense that the value only depends on a linear combination of $\sum_{i=1}^{n} u_i X_i \in \mathbb{Z}_p$ (instead of the whole X), where the coefficients $\{u_i\}_{i \in [n]}$ are independent of the lossy tag and depend only on the public key. In particular, evaluating the same input X under multiple lossy tags with respect to a common public key only reveals the same linear combination $\sum_{i=1}^{n} u_i X_i \in \mathbb{Z}_p$, thus leaking at most $\log p$ bits of information about X. It is required that there are many lossy tags and with a trapdoor one can efficiently sample a lossy tag. Additionally, LAF has two more properties named *evasiveness* and *indistinguishability*. Evasiveness demands that without the trapdoor, any PPT adversary can hardly find a new non-injective tag even given many lossy tags; indistinguishability demands that it is hard to distinguish lossy tags from random tags for all PPT adversaries.

Our Construction. Our rrFE stems from the basic "sketch-and-extract" FE [11], but an SKEM and an LAF are integrated to this basic FE to achieve reusability and robustness. The construction is shown in Fig. 2.

In our construction, the reading w of a source plays two roles, one is for extraction(reproduction) of R ($\tilde{R}$), the other is for authentication (verification). We stress that $\text{LAF}_{F_{pk}, \text{tag}}(w)$ can be regarded as a message authentication code (MAC)[1], where w is the authentication key, tag is the message, and the output of LAF is just the authenticator σ.

---

[1] The traditional MAC does not apply in the scenario of robust fuzzy extractor: the adversary can arbitrarily modify the public helper string P, so the key of the MAC is modified accordingly. As a result, the message and the authentication key are not independent anymore.

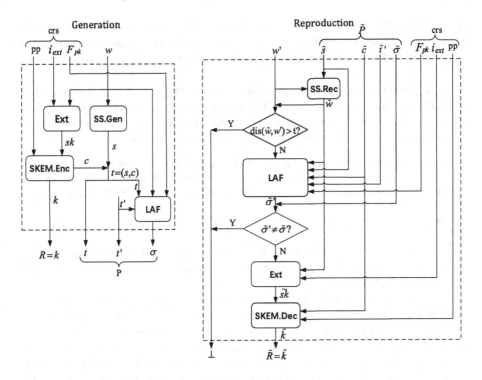

Fig. 2. Construction of robustly reusable fuzzy extractor.

Below describes how the generation algorithm of our rrFE works.

- The common reference string crs consists of the public parameter pp of SKEM, the random seed i_{ext} of Ext, and the public key F_{pk} of LAF.
- The reading w of a source is fed not only to SS and Ext, but also to LAF. This results in a sketch s from SS.Gen, a secret key sk from Ext, and an authenticator σ from LAF.
- We do not take the output sk of Ext as the final extracted key. Instead, the output sk of Ext serves as the secret key of SKEM.Enc, which in turn outputs a ciphertext c and an encapsulated key k. This encapsulated key k is served as the final extracted key $R := k$.
- The evaluation of LAF on w under tag $\mathsf{tag} = (s, c, t')$ results in an authenticator σ, where t' is randomly chosen. The public helper string is set as $P := (s, c, t', \sigma)$.

Given the public helper string $\widetilde{P} = (\widetilde{s}, \widetilde{c}, \widetilde{t}', \widetilde{\sigma})$ and a reading w', the reproduction algorithm of our rrFE will return the reproduced key $\widetilde{R} :=$ SKEM.Dec(Ext($\widetilde{w}, i_{ext}), \widetilde{c}$) only if the distance of $\widetilde{w} :=$ SS.Rec($w', \widetilde{s}$) and w' is no more than a predetermined threshold t and the computed authenticator $\widetilde{\sigma}' :=$ LAF$_{F_{pk}, (\widetilde{s}, \widetilde{c}, \widetilde{t}')}(\widetilde{w})$ is identical to the authenticator $\widetilde{\sigma}$ contained in $\widetilde{P}$.

Reusability. Reusability says that the extracted key R is pseudorandom even if the PPT adversary knows $P = (s, c, t, \sigma)$ and can adaptively asks the generation oracle with shift δ_i to get multiple $\{P_i = (s_i, c_i, t'_i, \sigma_i), R_i\}_{i \in [\rho]}$ where $(P_i, R_i) \leftarrow$ Gen$(w + \delta_i)$.

To achieve reusability, we require that the underlying building blocks SS, Ext and LAF are homomorphic and SKEM is key-shift secure. Recall that i_{ext} and F_{pk} are parts of crs so they are independent of each other and distributed as designed. The high level idea of proving reusability is as follows.

1. By the homomorphic property of SS, Ext and LAF, we have
   - $s_i := \text{SS.Gen}(w_i) = \text{SS.Gen}(w + \delta_i) = \text{SS.Gen}(w) + \text{SS.Gen}(\delta_i) = s + \text{SS.Gen}(\delta_i)$;
   - $sk_i = \text{Ext}(w_i, i_{\text{ext}}) = \text{Ext}(w + \delta_i, i_{\text{ext}}) = \text{Ext}(w, i_{\text{ext}}) + \text{Ext}(\delta_i, i_{\text{ext}}) = sk + \text{Ext}(\delta_i, i_{\text{ext}})$;
   - $\sigma_i := \text{LAF}_{F_{pk}, \text{tag}_i}(w + \delta_i) = \text{LAF}_{F_{pk}, \text{tag}_i}(w) + \text{LAF}_{F_{pk}, \text{tag}_i}(\delta_i) = \sigma + \text{LAF}_{F_{pk}, \text{tag}_i}(\delta_i)$.

   Observe that the knowledge of SS.Gen(w), Ext(w) and $\{\text{LAF}_{F_{pk}, \text{tag}_i}(w)\}_{i \in [\rho]}$ suffices for the challenger to simulate the whole view of the adversary in the reusability experiment.
2. By the indistinguishability property of LAF, $\{\text{tag}_i\}_{i \in [\rho]}$ can be replaced with lossy tags. Now the challenger can use SS.Gen(w), Ext(w) and $\mathcal{S} := \{\text{LAF}_{F_{pk}, \text{tag}}(w)$ for all lossy tags$\}$ to simulate the view of the adversary.
3. By the lossiness of LAF, the information of W leaked by $\mathcal{S}$ is at most $\log p$ bits. By the security of SS, the information of W leaked by SS.Gen(w) is also bounded. Meanwhile, SS.Gen(w) and set $\mathcal{S}$ are independent of i_{ext} due to the independence between (W, F_{pk}) and i_{ext} (note that the lossy tag space is determined by F_{pk}). Consequently, $sk := \text{Ext}(w, i_{ext})$ is almost uniform conditioned on SS.Gen(w) and $\mathcal{S}$.
4. Observe that $(c_i, k_i) \leftarrow \text{SKEM.Enc}(sk_i)$ can be regarded as encapsulations under shifted key $sk_i := sk + \text{Ext}(\delta_i)$. With a uniform sk (conditioned on SS.Gen(w) and $\mathcal{S}$), the KS-security of SKEM makes sure that $R := k$ is pseudorandom given P and $\{P_i = (s_i, c_i, t'_i, \sigma_i), R_i = k_i\}_{i \in [\rho]}$, where $(c, k) \leftarrow \text{SKEM.Enc}(sk)$.

Robustness. Robustness states that even if the PPT adversary can adaptively asks the generation oracle with shift δ_i to get $(P_i, R_i) \leftarrow$ Gen$(w + \delta_i)$, it is still hard to forge a fresh valid $\tilde{P}$.

Following 1, 2 and 3 of the above analysis for reusability, the view of adversary in the robustness experiment can be simulated with the knowledge of SS.Gen(w) and $\mathcal{S}$. Note that the SS.Gen(w) and set $\mathcal{S}$ only leak bounded information of W. Consequently, even if the adversary sees $\{P_i, R_i\}_{i \in [\rho]}$, there is still enough entropy left in W. By the *evasiveness* of LAF, the forged tag $\widetilde{\text{tag}} = (\tilde{s}, \tilde{c}, \tilde{t}')$ contained in $\tilde{P} = (\tilde{s}, \tilde{c}, \tilde{t}', \tilde{\sigma})$ must be injective, hence $\text{LAF}_{F_{pk}, \widetilde{\text{tag}}}(\cdot)$ is an injective function. Consequently, the entropy of W is intactly transferred to $\tilde{\sigma}' := \text{LAF}_{F_{pk}, \widetilde{\text{tag}}}(\tilde{w})$ and the forged authenticator $\tilde{\sigma}$ hits the value of $\tilde{\sigma}'$ with negligible probability.

2   Preliminaries

Let λ be the security parameter. We write PPT short for probabilistic polynomial-time. Let $[\rho]$ denote set $\{1, 2 \cdots, \rho\}$. Let $\lceil x \rceil$ denote the smallest integer that is not smaller than x. If X is a distribution, $x \leftarrow X$ denotes sampling x according to distribution X; if X is a set, $x \leftarrow_{\$} X$ denotes choosing x from X uniformly. For a set X, let $|X|$ denote the size of X. Let $\overbrace{xxx}^{y}$ and $\underbrace{xxx}_{y}$ denote $y := xxx$. For a primitive XX and a security notion YY, by $\mathsf{Exp}_{\mathsf{XX},\mathcal{A}}^{\mathsf{YY}}(\cdot) \Rightarrow 1$, we mean that the security experiment outputs 1 after interacting with an adversary $\mathcal{A}$; by $\mathsf{Adv}_{\mathsf{XX},\mathcal{A}}^{\mathsf{YY}}(1^{\lambda})$, we denote the advantage of a PPT adversary $\mathcal{A}$ and define $\mathsf{Adv}_{\mathsf{XX}}^{\mathsf{YY}}(1^{\lambda}) := \max_{\mathsf{PPT}\mathcal{A}} \mathsf{Adv}_{\mathsf{XX},\mathcal{A}}^{\mathsf{YY}}(1^{\lambda})$. Our security proof will proceed by a sequence of games. By $a \overset{\mathsf{G}}{=} b$ we mean that a equals b or is computed as b in game G. By $\mathsf{G}^{\mathcal{A}} \Rightarrow b$, we mean that game G outputs b after interacting with $\mathcal{A}$.

2.1   Metric Spaces

A metric space is a set $\mathcal{M}$ with a distance function $\mathsf{dis}: \mathcal{M} \times \mathcal{M} \mapsto [0, \infty)$. We usually consider multi-dimensional metric spaces of form $\mathcal{M} = \mathcal{F}^{n}$ for some alphabet $\mathcal{F}$ (usually a finite filed $\mathbb{F}_{p}$) equipped with the Hamming distance. For any two element $w, w' \in \mathcal{M}$, the Hamming distance $\mathsf{dis}(w, w')$ is the number of coordinates in which they differ. For an element $w \in \mathcal{M}$, let $\mathsf{dis}(w) := \mathsf{dis}(w, 0)$.

2.2   Min-Entropy, Statistical Distance and Extractor

Definition 1 (Min-Entropy). *For a random variable X, the* min-entropy *of X is defined by $H_{\infty}(X) = -\log(\max_{x} \Pr[X = x])$. The* average min-entropy *of X given Y is defined by $\widetilde{H}_{\infty}(X|Y) = -\log[\mathbb{E}_{y \leftarrow Y}(\max_{x} \Pr[X = x|Y = y])]$.*

Obviously, for a deterministic function f and a randomized function g with the random coins R independent of X, we have that

$$\widetilde{H}_{\infty}(X \mid Y, f(Y)) = \widetilde{H}_{\infty}(X \mid Y). \tag{1}$$

$$\widetilde{H}_{\infty}(X \mid Y, g(Y, R)) = \widetilde{H}_{\infty}(X \mid Y). \tag{2}$$

Lemma 1. [11] *If Y takes at most 2^{λ} possible values, then $\widetilde{H}_{\infty}(X \mid Y) \geq \widetilde{H}_{\infty}(X) - \lambda$.*

Definition 2 (Statistical Distance). *For two random variables X and Y over a set $\mathcal{M}$, the* statistical distance *of X and Y is given by $\mathbf{SD}(X, Y) = \frac{1}{2}\sum_{w \in \mathcal{M}} |\Pr[X = w] - \Pr[Y = w]|$. If $\mathbf{SD}(X, Y) \leq \varepsilon$, X and Y are called ε-statistically indistinguishable, denoted by $X \overset{\varepsilon}{\approx} Y$.*

Lemma 2. [22] *Let* $\mathcal{M}_1$ *and* $\mathcal{M}_2$ *be finite sets,* X *and* Y *be random variables over* $\mathcal{M}_1$, *and* $f\colon \mathcal{M}_1 \mapsto \mathcal{M}_2$ *be a function. Then* $\mathbf{SD}(f(X), f(Y)) \leq \mathbf{SD}(X, Y)$.

Definition 3 (Average-Case Strong Extractor [11]**).** *We call a function* $\mathsf{Ext}\colon \mathcal{M} \times \mathcal{I} \mapsto \mathcal{SK}$ *an average-case* $(\mathcal{M}, m, \mathcal{SK}, \varepsilon)$-*strong extractor with seed space* $\mathcal{I}$, *if for all pairs of random variables* (X, Y) *such that* $X \in \mathcal{M}$ *and* $\widetilde{H}_\infty(X \mid Y) \geq m$, *we have*

$$(\mathsf{Ext}(X, I), I, Y) \stackrel{\varepsilon}{\approx} (U, I, Y), \tag{3}$$

where I *and* U *are uniformly distributed over* $\mathcal{I}$ *and* $\mathcal{SK}$, *respectively.*

2.3 Secure Sketch

Definition 4 (Secure Sketch [11]**).** *An* $(m, \hat{m}, t)$-*secure sketch (SS)* $\mathsf{SS} = (\mathsf{SS.Gen}, \mathsf{SS.Rec})$ *for metric space* $\mathcal{M}$ *with distance function* dis, *consists of a pair of PPT algorithms and satisfies correctness and security.*

- $\mathsf{SS.Gen}$ *on input* $w \in \mathcal{M}$, *outputs a sketch* s.
- $\mathsf{SS.Rec}$ *takes as input* $w' \in \mathcal{M}$ *and a sketch* s, *and outputs* $\tilde{w}$.

Correctness. $\forall w \in \mathcal{M}$, *if* $\mathsf{dis}(w, w') \leq \mathsf{t}$, *then* $\mathsf{SS.Rec}(w', \mathsf{SS.Gen}(w)) = w$.
Security. *For any random variable* W *over* $\mathcal{M}$ *with min-entropy* m, *we have* $\widetilde{H}_\infty(W \mid \mathsf{SS.Gen}(W)) \geq \hat{m}$.

Lemma 3. [5]. *Let* $\mathsf{SS} = (\mathsf{SS.Gen}, \mathsf{SS.Rec})$ *be an* $(m, \hat{m}, t)$-*SS for* $\mathcal{M}$, *if* W_0, W_1 *are two random variables over* $\mathcal{M}$ *satisfying* $\mathsf{dis}(W_0, W_1) \leq \mathsf{t}$, *then for any variable* Y, *we have* $\widetilde{H}_\infty(W_1 \mid (\mathsf{SS.Gen}(W_0), Y)) \geq \widetilde{H}_\infty(W_0 \mid (\mathsf{SS.Gen}(W_0), Y))$.

2.4 Lossy Algebraic Filter

Our construction of robustly reusable fuzzy extractor relies on a technical tool, named lossy algebraic filter which is proposed by Hofheinz [15].

Definition 5 (Lossy Algebraic Filter). *An* $(l_{\mathsf{LAF}}, \mathsf{n})$-*lossy algebraic filter* $\mathsf{LAF} = (\mathsf{FGen}, \mathsf{FEval}, \mathsf{FTag})$ *consists of three PPT algorithms.*

- **Key generation.** $\mathsf{FGen}(1^\lambda)$ outputs a public key F_{pk} together with a trapdoor F_{td}, i.e., $(F_{pk}, F_{td}) \leftarrow \mathsf{FGen}(1^\lambda)$. The public key F_{pk} contains an l_{LAF}-bit prime p and defines a tag space $\mathcal{T}_{\mathsf{tag}} = \{0, 1\}^* \times \mathcal{T}'$, a lossy tag space $\mathcal{T}_{lossy} \subseteq \mathcal{T}_{\mathsf{tag}}$ and an injective tag space $\mathcal{T}_{inj} \subseteq \mathcal{T}_{\mathsf{tag}}$. A tag $\mathsf{tag} = (t, t') \in \mathcal{T}_{\mathsf{tag}}$ consists of a core tag $t' \in \mathcal{T}'$ and an auxiliary tag $t \in \{0, 1\}^*$. F_{td} is a trapdoor that allows of sampling lossy tags.
- **Evaluation.** FEval takes as input the public key F_{pk}, a tag $\mathsf{tag} = (t, t')$, and $X = (X_i)_{i=1}^{\mathsf{n}} \in \mathbb{Z}_p^{\mathsf{n}}$, and outputs $\mathsf{LAF}_{F_{pk}, \mathsf{tag}}(X)$, i.e., $\mathsf{LAF}_{F_{pk}, \mathsf{tag}}(X) = \mathsf{FEval}(F_{pk}, \mathsf{tag}, X)$.
- **Lossy tag generation.** FTag takes as input the trapdoor F_{td} and an auxiliary tag t, and returns a core tag t', i.e., $t' \leftarrow \mathsf{FTag}(F_{td}, t)$, such that $\mathsf{tag} = (t, t')$ is a lossy tag.

We require the following:

- **Lossiness.** If tag $\in \mathcal{T}_{inj}$, then the function $\mathsf{LAF}_{F_{pk},\mathsf{tag}}(\cdot)$ is injective. If tag $\in \mathcal{T}_{lossy}$, then $\mathsf{LAF}_{F_{pk},\mathsf{tag}}(X)$ depends only on $\sum_{i=1}^{n} u_i X_i \mod p$ for $u_i \in \mathbb{Z}_p$ that only depends on F_{pk}.

- **Indistinguishability.** For all PPT adversaries, it is hard to distinguish lossy tags from random tags. Formally,

$$\mathsf{Adv}_{\mathsf{LAF},\mathcal{A}}^{\mathsf{ind}}(1^\lambda) := \left| \Pr\left[\mathcal{A}(1^\lambda, F_{pk})^{\mathsf{FTag}(F_{td},\cdot)} = 1 \right] - \Pr\left[\mathcal{A}(1^\lambda, F_{pk})^{\mathcal{O}_{\mathcal{T}'}(\cdot)} = 1 \right] \right|$$

is negligible for all PPT adversary $\mathcal{A}$, where $(F_{pk}, F_{td}) \leftarrow \mathsf{FTag}(1^\lambda)$ and $\mathcal{O}_{\mathcal{T}'}(\cdot)$ is the oracle that ignores its input and samples a random core tag t'.

- **Evasiveness.** For all PPT adversaries, without the trapdoor, non-injective tags are hard to find, even given multiple lossy tags. More precisely,

$$\mathsf{Adv}_{\mathsf{LAF},\mathcal{A}}^{\mathsf{eva}}(1^\lambda) := \Pr\left[\mathsf{tag} \notin \mathcal{T}_{inj} \mid \mathsf{tag} \leftarrow \mathcal{A}(1^\lambda, F_{pk})^{\mathsf{FTag}(F_{td},\cdot)} \right]$$

is negligible for all PPT admissible adversary $\mathcal{A}$ where $(F_{pk}, F_{td}) \leftarrow \mathsf{FGen}(1^\lambda)$. We call $\mathcal{A}$ is admissible if $\mathcal{A}$ never outputs a tag obtained from its oracle.

Remark 1. If $\mathsf{tag} = (t, t')$, we use $\mathsf{FEval}(F_{pk}, t, t', X)$ to denote $\mathsf{FEval}(F_{pk}, \mathsf{tag}, X)$.

Remark 2. Let us consider multiple, say m, evaluations of LAF of the same $X = (X_1, X_2, \ldots, X_n)$ under a fixed public key F_{pk} but different tags (t_j, t'_j). According to the lossiness property of LAF, each evaluation of $\mathsf{FEval}(F_{pk}, t_j, t'_j, X)$ is completely determined by $\sum_{i=1}^{n} u_i X_i$ and (t_j, t'_j), so there exists a function f such that $\mathsf{FEval}(F_{pk}, t_j, t'_j, X) = f\left(\sum_{i=1}^{n} u_i X_i, (t_j, t'_j) \right)$. Suppose that F_{pk} is independent of X. As long as tags $\{(t_j, t'_j)\}_{j \in [\mathsf{m}]}$ are independent of X or are (randomized) functions of $\sum_{i=1}^{n} u_i X_i$, we have

$$\widetilde{H}_\infty \left(X \middle| \{\mathsf{FEval}(F_{pk}, t_j, t'_j, X)\}_{j \in [\mathsf{m}]} \right) = \widetilde{H}_\infty \left(X \middle| \left\{ f\left(\sum_{i=1}^{n} u_i X_i, (t_j, t'_j) \right) \right\}_{j \in [\mathsf{m}]} \right)$$

$$\geq \widetilde{H}_\infty \left(X \middle| \sum_{i=1}^{n} u_i X_i \right) \geq \widetilde{H}_\infty(X) - \log p, \tag{4}$$

where the last but one step is due to Eq. (2) and the last step is by Lemma 1.

2.5 Homomorphic Properties

We assume that the domains and codomains of Ext, SS and LAF are groups with operation "+" (we abuse "+" for different group operations for simplicity). Now we characterize homomorphic properties of Ext, SS and LAF.

Definition 6 (Homomorphic Average-Case Strong Extractor). *An average-case $(\mathcal{M}, m, \mathcal{SK}, \varepsilon)$-strong extractor* $\mathsf{Ext} : \mathcal{M} \times \mathcal{I} \to \mathcal{SK}$ *is homomorphic if for all $w_1, w_2 \in \mathcal{M}$, all $i_{\mathsf{ext}} \in \mathcal{I}$, we have* $\mathsf{Ext}(w_1 + w_2, i_{\mathsf{ext}}) = \mathsf{Ext}(w_1, i_{\mathsf{ext}}) + \mathsf{Ext}(w_2, i_{\mathsf{ext}})$.

It was shown in [11], universal hash functions are average-case strong extractors. In particular, $\mathsf{Ext}(x, i)\colon \mathbb{Z}_q^{l+1} \times \mathbb{Z}_q^l \to \mathbb{Z}_q$ defined by

$$\mathsf{Ext}(x, i) := x_0 + i_1 x_1 + \cdots + i_l x_l \tag{5}$$

is an average-case strong $(\mathbb{Z}_q^{l+1}, m, \mathbb{Z}_q, \varepsilon)$-extractor with $\log q \le m + 2 \log \varepsilon$, as shown in [22]. Obviously, it is homomorphic.

Definition 7 (Homomorphic Secure Sketch). *A secure sketch is homomorphic if for all $w_1, w_2 \in \mathcal{M}$, $\mathsf{SS.Gen}(w_1 + w_2) = \mathsf{SS.Gen}(w_1) + \mathsf{SS.Gen}(w_2)$.*

The syndrome-based secure sketch [12] is homomorphic (see the full version [25]).

Definition 8 (Homomorphic Lossy Algebraic Filter). *We call an $(l_{\mathsf{LAF}}, \mathsf{n})$-LAF with domain $\mathbb{Z}_p^{\mathsf{n}}$ is homomorphic if for all $(F_{pk}, F_{td}) \leftarrow \mathsf{FGen}(1^\lambda)$, all $\mathsf{tag} \in \mathcal{T}_{\mathsf{tag}}$ and all $w_1, w_2 \in \mathbb{Z}_p^{\mathsf{n}}$, the following holds $\mathsf{FEval}(F_{pk}, \mathsf{tag}, w_1 + w_2) = \mathsf{FEval}(F_{pk}, \mathsf{tag}, w_1) + \mathsf{FEval}(F_{pk}, \mathsf{tag}, w_2)$.*

The LAF constructed from the DLIN assumption in [15] is homomorphic. See the full version [25] for the specific construction of homomorphic LAF.

2.6 Decisional Diffie-Hellman Assumption

Definition 9 (Decisional Diffie-Hellman Assumption). *The decisional Diffie-Hellman assumption holds w.r.t. a group generation algorithm $\mathcal{IG}$, if*

$$\mathsf{Adv}^{\mathsf{DDH}}_{\mathcal{IG}, \mathcal{A}}(1^\lambda) := |\Pr[\mathcal{A}((\mathbb{G}, q, g), g^x, g^y, g^z) = 1] - \Pr[\mathcal{A}((\mathbb{G}, q, g), g^x, g^y, g^{xy}) = 1]|$$

is negligible for all PPT adversary $\mathcal{A}$, where $(\mathbb{G}, q, g) \leftarrow \mathcal{IG}(1^\lambda)$, $\mathbb{G}$ is a cyclic group of order q with generator g and $x, y, z \leftarrow_s \mathbb{Z}_q$.

3   Symmetric Key Encapsulate Mechanism

3.1   Definition of SKEM

In this section, we propose a new primitive called *symmetric key encapsulate mechanism* (SKEM). It is one of the core technical tools in our rrFE.

Definition 10 (Symmetric Key Encapsulate Mechanism). *A symmetric key encapsulate mechanism $\mathsf{SKEM} = (\mathsf{SKEM.Init}, \mathsf{SKEM.Enc}, \mathsf{SKEM.Dec})$ consists of a triple of PPT algorithms.*

- $\mathsf{SKEM.Init}$ *takes as input the security parameter 1^λ and outputs public parameter pp which implicitly defines the secret key space $\mathcal{SK}$, encapsulated key space $\mathcal{K}$ and ciphertext space, i.e., $\mathsf{pp} \leftarrow \mathsf{SKEM.Init}(1^\lambda)$.*
- $\mathsf{SKEM.Enc}$ *takes as input pp and the secret key sk, and outputs a ciphertext c and an encapsulated key $k \in \mathcal{K}$, i.e., $(c, k) \leftarrow \mathsf{SKEM.Enc}(\mathsf{pp}, sk)$.*

- SKEM.Dec *takes as input* pp, *the secret key* sk *and a ciphertext* c, *and outputs* $k \in \mathcal{K}$, *i.e.*, $k \leftarrow$ SKEM.Dec(pp, sk, c).

The correctness of SKEM is that for all pp $\leftarrow$ SKEM.Init(1^λ), $sk \in \mathcal{SK}$, $(c, k) \leftarrow$ SKEM.Enc(pp, sk), $k' \leftarrow$ SKEM.Dec(pp, sk, c), we have $k' = k$.

We require pseudorandomness of the encapsulated key under key-shift attack. Roughly speaking, the encapsulated key is pseudorandom even if the adversary observes multiple encapsulations under shifted secret key where the shift Δ_i is designated by the adversary adaptively. The formal definition is given below.

Definition 11 (KS-Security of SKEM). *A* SKEM SKEM = (SKEM.Init, SKEM.Enc, SKEM.Dec) *is Key-Shift (KS) secure if for all PPT adversary* $\mathcal{A}$,

$$\mathsf{Adv}^{\mathsf{ks}}_{\mathsf{SKEM},\mathcal{A}}(1^\lambda) := |\Pr[\mathsf{Exp}^{\mathsf{ks}}_{\mathsf{SKEM},\mathcal{A}}(1) \Rightarrow 1] - \Pr[\mathsf{Exp}^{\mathsf{ks}}_{\mathsf{SKEM},\mathcal{A}}(0) \Rightarrow 1]|$$

is negligible. Here $\mathsf{Exp}^{\mathsf{ks}}_{\mathsf{SKEM},\mathcal{A}}(\beta)$, $\beta \in \{0, 1\}$, *is an experiment played between an adversary* $\mathcal{A}$ *and a challenger* $\mathcal{C}$ *as follows.*
$\mathsf{Exp}^{\mathsf{ks}}_{\mathsf{SKEM},\mathcal{A}}(\beta)$:

- $\mathcal{C}$ *invokes* pp $\leftarrow$ SKEM.Init(1^λ), *samples* $sk \leftarrow_s \mathcal{SK}$ *and returns* pp *to* $\mathcal{A}$.
- *Challenge: Challenger* $\mathcal{C}$ *invokes* $(c, k) \leftarrow$ SKEM.Enc(pp, sk). *If* $\beta = 0$, *it resets* k *with* $k \leftarrow_s \mathcal{K}$. *Finally it returns* (c, k) *to* $\mathcal{A}$.
- *During the whole experiment,* $\mathcal{A}$ *may adaptively make encapsulation oracle queries of the following form:*
  - $\mathcal{A}$ *submits a shift* $\Delta_i \in \mathcal{SK}$ *to challenger* $\mathcal{C}$.
  - $\mathcal{C}$ *invokes* $(c_i, k_i) \leftarrow$ SKEM.Enc(pp, $sk + \Delta_i$), *and returns* (c_i, k_i) *to* $\mathcal{A}$.
- *As long as* $\mathcal{A}$ *outputs a guessing bit* β', *the experiment outputs* β'.

3.2 Construction of Symmetric Key Encapsulate Mechanism

We instantiate a KS-secure SKEM from the DDH assumption, and the construction is given in Fig. 3.

SKEM.Init(1^λ):	SKEM.Enc(pp, sk): // $sk \in \mathcal{SK}$	
$(\mathbb{G}, q, g) \leftarrow \mathcal{IG}(1^\lambda)$.	$r \leftarrow_s \mathbb{Z}_q$.	SKEM.Dec(pp, sk, c):
pp := $(\mathbb{G}, q, g)$.	$c = g^r$.	$k = c^{sk}$.
$\mathcal{SK} := \mathbb{Z}_q$.	$k = c^{sk}$.	Return k.
$\mathcal{K} := \mathbb{G}$.	Return (c, k).	
Return pp.		

Fig. 3. Construction of SKEM with KS-security from the DDH assumption.

Theorem 1. *If the DDH assumption holds with respect to* $\mathcal{IG}$, *then* SKEM *constructed in Fig. 3 is KS-secure. More precisely, for any PPT adversary* $\mathcal{A}$,

$$\mathsf{Adv}^{\mathsf{ks}}_{\mathsf{SKEM},\mathcal{A}}(1^\lambda) \leq \mathsf{Adv}^{\mathsf{DDH}}_{\mathcal{IG}}(1^\lambda).$$

Proof. Suppose that there exists a PPT adversary $\mathcal{A}$ who has advantage ϵ in the key-shift attack of SKEM in Fig. 3, then we can construct a PPT algorithm $\mathcal{B}$ with the same advantage ϵ in solving the DDH problem.

Given $(\mathbb{G}, q, g, g^x, g^y, g^d)$, where x, y are uniformly and independently chosen from $\mathbb{Z}_q$, algorithm $\mathcal{B}$ simulates an environment for $\mathcal{A}$ as follows.

- Algorithm $\mathcal{B}$ returns $\mathsf{pp} = (\mathbb{G}, q, g)$ to $\mathcal{A}$ and implicitly sets $sk := x$.
- Algorithm $\mathcal{B}$ returns (g^y, g^d) to $\mathcal{A}$.
- When adversary $\mathcal{A}$ makes an encapsulation query with $\Delta_i \in \mathbb{Z}_p$, algorithm $\mathcal{B}$ uniformly chooses $y_i \leftarrow \mathbb{Z}_q$ and sets $c_i := g^{y_i}$, $k_i := (g^x g^{\Delta_i})^{y_i}$ and returns (c_i, k_i) to $\mathcal{A}$.
- When adversary $\mathcal{A}$ returns a bit β', algorithm $\mathcal{B}$ returns β' to its own challenger.

Obviously, $\mathcal{B}$ simulates answers to the encapsulation queries for $\mathcal{A}$ perfectly. For the challenge,

- If $d = xy$, then $\mathcal{B}$ perfectly simulates $\mathsf{Exp}^{\mathsf{ks}}_{\mathsf{SKEM},\mathcal{A}}(1)$ for $\mathcal{A}$.
- If $d = z$, where $z \leftarrow_\$ \mathbb{Z}_q$, then $\mathcal{B}$ perfectly simulates $\mathsf{Exp}^{\mathsf{ks}}_{\mathsf{SKEM},\mathcal{A}}(0)$ for $\mathcal{A}$.

Consequently,

$$\mathsf{Adv}^{\mathsf{DDH}}_{\mathcal{IG},\mathcal{B}}(1^\lambda) = \Pr[\mathcal{B}((\mathbb{G}, q, g), g^x, g^y, g^{xy}) = 1] - \Pr[\mathcal{B}((\mathbb{G}, q, g), g^x, g^y, g^z) = 1]$$
$$= |\Pr[\mathsf{Exp}^{\mathsf{ks}}_{\mathsf{SKEM},\mathcal{A}}(1) \Rightarrow 1] - \Pr[\mathsf{Exp}^{\mathsf{ks}}_{\mathsf{SKEM},\mathcal{A}}(0) \Rightarrow 1]| = \mathsf{Adv}^{\mathsf{ks}}_{\mathsf{SKEM},\mathcal{A}}(1^\lambda).$$

This completes the proof of Theorem 1. ∎

4   Robustly Reusable Fuzzy Extractor

In this section, we define robustly reusable fuzzy extractor (rrFE) and present a construction of rrFE in the CRS model.

4.1   Definition of Robustly Reusable Fuzzy Extractor

First, we recall the definition of fuzzy extractor presented in [7].

Definition 12 (Fuzzy Extractor). *An $(\mathcal{M}, m, \mathcal{R}, \mathsf{t}, \varepsilon)$-fuzzy extractor FE for metric space $\mathcal{M}$ consists of three PPT algorithms* (Init, Gen, Rep),

- Init *on input security parameter 1^λ outputs common reference string* crs, *i.e.,* crs $\leftarrow$ Init(1^λ).
- Gen *on input the common reference string* crs *and $w \in \mathcal{M}$, outputs a public helper string P and an extracted string $R \in \mathcal{R}$, i.e., $(P, R) \leftarrow$ Gen(crs, w).*
- Rep *takes as input the common reference string* crs, *public helper string P and $w' \in \mathcal{M}$, and outputs an extracted string R or $\bot$, i.e., $R/\bot \leftarrow$ Rep(crs, P, w').*

It satisfies the following properties.

Correctness. *If* $\mathrm{dis}(w, w') \leq t$, *then for any* $\mathrm{crs} \leftarrow \mathrm{Init}(1^\lambda)$, $(P, R) \leftarrow \mathrm{Gen}(\mathrm{crs}, w)$ *and* $R' \leftarrow \mathrm{Rep}(\mathrm{crs}, P, w')$, *it holds that* $R' = R$.

Privacy. *For any distribution W over metric space $\mathcal{M}$ with $H_\infty(W) \geq m$, any PPT adversary $\mathcal{A}$, it holds that*

$$\mathsf{Adv}^{\mathsf{ind}}_{\mathsf{FE}, \mathcal{A}}(1^\lambda) := |\Pr[\mathcal{A}(\mathrm{crs}, P, R) = 1] - \Pr[\mathcal{A}(\mathrm{crs}, P, U) = 1]| \leq \varepsilon,$$

where $\mathrm{crs} \leftarrow \mathrm{Init}(1^\lambda)$, $(P, R) \leftarrow \mathrm{Gen}(\mathrm{crs}, W)$ *and* $U \leftarrow_\$ \mathcal{R}$.

A fuzzy extractor is reusable if its privacy is retained even if the same noisy source is reused multiple times. We follow the definition of reusability of fuzzy extractor from [2] (which is called "strong reusability" in [2]).

Definition 13 (Reusable Fuzzy Extractor). *A fuzzy extractor* $\mathsf{rFE} = (\mathsf{Init},$ $\mathsf{Gen}, \mathsf{Rep})$ *is an* $(\mathcal{M}, m, \mathcal{R}, t, \varepsilon_1)$-*reusable fuzzy extractor if it is a fuzzy extractor with ε_1-reusability. An $(\mathcal{M}, m, \mathcal{R}, t, \varepsilon_1)$-fuzzy extractor is ε_1-reusable, if for any distribution W over metric space $\mathcal{M}$ with $H_\infty(W) \geq m$, for any PPT adversary $\mathcal{A}$, it holds that*

$$\mathsf{Adv}^{\mathsf{reu}}_{\mathsf{rFE}, \mathcal{A}}(1^\lambda) := |\Pr[\mathsf{Exp}^{\mathsf{reu}}_{\mathsf{rFE}, \mathcal{A}}(1) \Rightarrow 1] - \Pr[\mathsf{Exp}^{\mathsf{reu}}_{\mathsf{rFE}, \mathcal{A}}(0) \Rightarrow 1]| \leq \varepsilon_1,$$

where $\mathsf{Exp}^{\mathsf{reu}}_{\mathsf{rFE}, \mathcal{A}}(\beta)$, $\beta \in \{0, 1\}$, *describes the reusability experiment played between an adversary $\mathcal{A}$ and a challenger $\mathcal{C}$.*

$\underline{\mathsf{Exp}^{\mathsf{reu}}_{\mathsf{rFE}, \mathcal{A}}(\beta)} :$ // $\beta \in \{0, 1\}$

1. *Challenger $\mathcal{C}$ invokes* $\mathrm{crs} \leftarrow \mathrm{Init}(1^\lambda)$ *and returns* crs *to $\mathcal{A}$.*
2. *$\mathcal{C}$ samples* $w \leftarrow W$ *and invokes* $(P, R) \leftarrow \mathrm{Gen}(\mathrm{crs}, w)$. *If $\beta = 1$, return (P, R) to $\mathcal{A}$; otherwise, it chooses* $U \leftarrow_\$ \mathcal{R}$ *and returns (P, U) to $\mathcal{A}$.*
3. *$\mathcal{A}$ may adaptively make queries of the following form:*
   - *$\mathcal{A}$ submits a shift* $\delta_i \in \mathcal{M}$ *satisfying* $\mathrm{dis}(\delta_i) \leq t$ *to $\mathcal{C}$.*
   - *$\mathcal{C}$ invokes* $(P_i, R_i) \leftarrow \mathrm{Gen}(\mathrm{crs}, w + \delta_i)$, *and returns (P_i, R_i) to $\mathcal{A}$.*
4. *As long as $\mathcal{A}$ outputs a guessing bit β', the experiment outputs β'.*

Robust fuzzy extractor guarantees that any modification of the public helper string by a PPT adversary will be detected. Now, combining the definition of reusability in [2] and robustness of fuzzy extractor in [7], we give the definition of robustly reusable fuzzy extractor.

Definition 14 (Robustness of Reusable Fuzzy Extractor). *Let* $\mathsf{rrFE} = (\mathsf{Init}, \mathsf{Gen}, \mathsf{Rep})$ *be an* $(\mathcal{M}, m, \mathcal{R}, t, \varepsilon_1)$-*reusable fuzzy extractor. We say rrFE is ε_2-robust if for any distribution W over metric space $\mathcal{M}$ with $H_\infty(W) \geq m$, for any PPT adversary $\mathcal{A}$, it holds that*

$$\mathsf{Adv}^{\mathsf{rob}}_{\mathsf{rrFE}, \mathcal{A}}(1^\lambda) := \Pr[\mathsf{Exp}^{\mathsf{rob}}_{\mathsf{rrFE}, \mathcal{A}}(1^\lambda) \Rightarrow 1] \leq \varepsilon_2,$$

where $\mathsf{Exp}^{\mathsf{rob}}_{\mathsf{rrFE}, \mathcal{A}}(1^\lambda)$ *describes the robustness experiment played between an adversary $\mathcal{A}$ and a challenger $\mathcal{C}$.*

$\mathsf{Exp}^{\mathsf{rob}}_{\mathsf{rrFE},\mathcal{A}}(1^\lambda):$

1. *Challenger* $\mathcal{C}$ *invokes* $\mathsf{crs} \leftarrow \mathsf{Init}(1^\lambda)$, *and returns* crs *to* $\mathcal{A}$.
2. $\mathcal{C}$ *samples* $w \leftarrow W$, *invokes* $(P, R) \leftarrow \mathsf{Gen}(\mathsf{crs}, w)$ *and returns* (P, R) *to* $\mathcal{A}$.
3. $\mathcal{A}$ *may adaptively make queries of the following form:*
   - $\mathcal{A}$ *submits a shift* $\delta_i \in \mathcal{M}$ *satisfying* $\mathsf{dis}(\delta_i) \leq \mathsf{t}$ *to challenger* $\mathcal{C}$.
   - $\mathcal{C}$ *invokes* $(P_i, R_i) \leftarrow \mathsf{Gen}(\mathsf{crs}, w + \delta_i)$, *and returns* (P_i, R_i) *to* $\mathcal{A}$.
4. $\mathcal{A}$ *submits its forgery* $(\widetilde{P}, \widetilde{\delta})$ *to* $\mathcal{C}$. $\mathcal{A}$ *wins if* $\mathsf{dis}(\widetilde{\delta}) \leq \mathsf{t}$, $\widetilde{P}$ *is fresh (i.e.,* $\widetilde{P}$ *is different from* P *and those* P_i*) and* $\mathsf{Rep}(\mathsf{crs}, \widetilde{P}, w + \widetilde{\delta}) \neq \bot$. *The experiment outputs 1 if* $\mathcal{A}$ *wins and 0 otherwise.*

Definition 15 (Robustly Reusable Fuzzy Extractor). *An* $(\mathcal{M}, m, \mathcal{R},$ $\mathsf{t}, \varepsilon_1, \varepsilon_2)$-*robustly reusable fuzzy extractor* (rrFE) *is an* $(\mathcal{M}, m, \mathcal{R}, \mathsf{t}, \varepsilon_1)$-*reusable fuzzy extractor with* ε_2-*robustness.*

Remark 3. In the robustness experiment, the adversary submits not only $\widetilde{P}$, but also the shift $\widetilde{\delta}$. In the previous works, such as [8], the authors considered two perturbation styles: (1) the shift is independent of W; (2) the shift can arbitrarily depend on W. In our definition, the shift is controlled by the adversary, and it just sits in the middle of the two styles. The reason we adopt such a definition is to make the perturbation style consistent with that in the reusability experiment.

4.2 Construction of Robustly Reusable Fuzzy Extractor

Figure 4 illustrates our construction of robustly reusable FE rrFE $=$ (Init, Gen, Rep) for metric space $\mathcal{M}$, which makes use of the following building blocks:

- A key-shift secure symmetric key encapsulation mechanism SKEM $=$ (SKEM.Init, SKEM.Enc, SKEM.Dec). Let its secret key space be $\mathcal{SK}$ and encapsulation key space be $\mathcal{K}$.
- A homomorphic average-case $(\mathcal{M}, \hat{m}, \mathcal{SK}, \varepsilon_{\mathsf{ext}})$-strong extractor Ext.
- A homomorphic $(m - \lceil \log p \rceil, \hat{m}, 2\mathsf{t})$-secure sketch SS $=$ (SS.Gen, SS.Rec) for metric space $\mathcal{M}$ with $\hat{m} - \lceil \log p \rceil \geq \omega(\log \lambda)$.
- A homomorphic $(l_{\mathsf{LAF}}, \mathsf{n})$-lossy algebraic filter LAF $=$ (FGen, FEval, FTag) with domain $\mathbb{Z}_p^{\mathsf{n}}$, $l_{\mathsf{LAF}} = \lceil \log p \rceil$, and tag space $\{0, 1\}^* \times \mathcal{T}'$. We assume that any $w \in \mathcal{M}$ can be explained as an element in $\mathbb{Z}_p^{\mathsf{n}}$.

The correctness of the fuzzy extractor follows from the correctness of the underlying SS and SKEM.

Theorem 2. *If the underlying* SKEM *is key-shift secure with secret key space* $\mathcal{SK}$ *and encapsulation key space* $\mathcal{K}$, Ext *is a homomorphic average-case* $(\mathcal{M}, \hat{m},$ $\mathcal{SK}, \varepsilon_{\mathsf{ext}})$-*strong extractor,* SS *is a homomorphic* $(m - \lceil \log p \rceil, \hat{m}, 2\mathsf{t})$-*secure sketch for metric space* $\mathcal{M}$ *with* $\hat{m} - \lceil \log p \rceil \geq \omega(\log \lambda)$, *and* LAF *is a homomorphic* $(l_{\mathsf{LAF}}, \mathsf{n})$-*lossy algebraic filter with domain* $\mathbb{Z}_p^{\mathsf{n}}$ *and* $l_{\mathsf{LAF}} = \lceil \log p \rceil$, *and every element in* $\mathcal{M}$ *can be explained as an element in* $\mathbb{Z}_p^{\mathsf{n}}$, *then the fuzzy extractor*

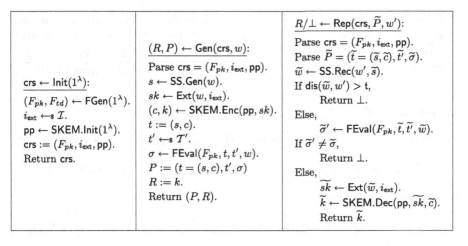

Fig. 4. Construction of robustly reusable fuzzy extractor rrFE.

rrFE *in Fig. 4 is an* $(\mathcal{M}, m, \mathcal{K}, \mathsf{t}, \varepsilon_1, \varepsilon_2)$-*robustly reusable fuzzy extractor, where* $\varepsilon_1 = 2\mathsf{Adv}_{\mathsf{LAF}}^{\mathsf{ind}}(1^\lambda) + 2\varepsilon_{\mathsf{ext}} + \mathsf{Adv}_{\mathsf{SKEM}}^{\mathsf{ks}}(1^\lambda)$ *and* $\varepsilon_2 = \mathsf{Adv}_{\mathsf{LAF}}^{\mathsf{ind}}(1^\lambda) + \varepsilon_{\mathsf{ext}} + \mathsf{Adv}_{\mathsf{LAF}}^{\mathsf{eva}}(1^\lambda) + 2^{-\omega(\log \lambda)}$.

Proof. All we have to do is to show that rrFE is ε_1-reusable and ε_2-robust, which are proved in Theorems 3 and 4 respectively.

Theorem 3. *Given the building blocks specified in Theorem 2, the fuzzy extractor* rrFE *in Fig. 4 is* ε_1-*reusable, where* $\varepsilon_1 = 2\mathsf{Adv}_{\mathsf{LAF}}^{\mathsf{ind}}(1^\lambda) + 2\varepsilon_{\mathsf{ext}} + \mathsf{Adv}_{\mathsf{SKEM}}^{\mathsf{ks}}(1^\lambda)$.

Proof. We will prove this theorem by a sequence of games. The changes from Game G_j to Game G_{j+1} are underlined.

Game G_0: It is exactly experiment $\mathsf{Exp}_{\mathsf{rFE}, \mathcal{A}}^{\mathsf{reu}}(1)$. More precisely,

1. Challenger $\mathcal{C}$ invokes $(F_{pk}, F_{td}) \leftarrow \mathsf{FGen}(1^\lambda)$ and $\mathsf{pp} \leftarrow \mathsf{SKEM.Init}(1^\lambda)$, samples a seed $i_{\mathsf{ext}} \leftarrow_\$ \mathcal{I}$, sets $\mathsf{crs} = (F_{pk}, i_{\mathsf{ext}}, \mathsf{pp})$, and returns crs to $\mathcal{A}$.
2. $\mathcal{C}$ samples $w \leftarrow W$, invokes $s \leftarrow \mathsf{SS.Gen}(w)$, $sk \leftarrow \mathsf{Ext}(w, i_{\mathsf{ext}})$, $(c, k) \leftarrow \mathsf{SKEM.Enc}(\mathsf{pp}, sk)$, sets $t := (s, c)$, samples $t' \leftarrow_\$ T'$, computes $\sigma \leftarrow \mathsf{FEval}(F_{pk}, t, t', w)$, sets $P := (s, c, t', \sigma)$, $R := k$, and returns (P, R) to $\mathcal{A}$.
3. Upon receiving a shift $\delta_i \in \mathcal{M}$ from $\mathcal{A}$ with $\mathsf{dis}(\delta_i) \leq \mathsf{t}$, challenger $\mathcal{C}$ invokes $s_i \leftarrow \mathsf{SS.Gen}(w + \delta_i)$, $sk_i \leftarrow \mathsf{Ext}(w + \delta_i, i_{\mathsf{ext}})$, $(c_i, k_i) \leftarrow \mathsf{SKEM.Enc}(\mathsf{pp}, sk_i)$, sets $t_i := (s_i, c_i)$, samples $t'_i \leftarrow_\$ T'$, invokes $\sigma_i \leftarrow \mathsf{FEval}(F_{pk}, t_i, t'_i, w + \delta_i)$, sets $P_i := (s_i, c_i, t'_i, \sigma_i)$, $R_i := k_i$, and returns (P_i, R_i) to $\mathcal{A}$.
4. If $\mathcal{A}$ outputs a bit β', the game outputs β'.

Obviously,

$$\Pr[\mathsf{Exp}_{\mathsf{rFE}, \mathcal{A}}^{\mathsf{reu}}(1) \Rightarrow 1] = \Pr[\mathsf{G}_0^{\mathcal{A}} \Rightarrow 1]. \tag{6}$$

Game G_1: It is the same as G_0, except for conceptual changes of generating (P_i, R_i). More precisely,

3. Upon receiving a shift $\delta_i \in \mathcal{M}$ from $\mathcal{A}$ with $\mathsf{dis}(\delta_i) \leq t$, challenger $\mathcal{C}$ computes $\underline{s_i := s + \mathsf{SS.Gen}(\delta_i)}$, $\underline{sk_i := sk + \mathsf{Ext}(\delta_i, i_{\mathsf{ext}})}$, $(c_i, k_i) \leftarrow \mathsf{SKEM.Enc}(\mathsf{pp}, sk_i)$, sets $t_i := (s_i, c_i)$, samples $t'_i \leftarrow_\$ \mathcal{T}'$, computes $\sigma_i := \mathsf{FEval}(F_{pk}, t_i, t'_i, w) + \underline{\mathsf{FEval}(F_{pk}, t_i, t'_i, \delta_i)}$, sets $P_i := (s_i, c_i, t'_i, \sigma_i)$, $R_i := \overline{k_i}$, and returns (P_i, R_i) to $\mathcal{A}$.

Lemma 4. $\Pr[\mathsf{G}_0^{\mathcal{A}} \Rightarrow 1] = \Pr[\mathsf{G}_1^{\mathcal{A}} \Rightarrow 1]$.

Proof. By the homomorphic property of the deterministic secure sketch, we have:

$$s_i \stackrel{\mathsf{G}_0}{=} \mathsf{SS.Gen}(w + \delta_i) = \mathsf{SS.Gen}(w) + \mathsf{SS.Gen}(\delta_i) = s + \mathsf{SS.Gen}(\delta_i) \stackrel{\mathsf{G}_1}{=} s_i.$$

By the homomorphic property of Ext, we have:

$$sk_i \stackrel{\mathsf{G}_0}{=} \mathsf{Ext}(w + \delta_i, i_{\mathsf{ext}}) = \mathsf{Ext}(w, i_{\mathsf{ext}}) + \mathsf{Ext}(\delta_i, i_{\mathsf{ext}}) = sk + \mathsf{Ext}(\delta_i, i_{\mathsf{ext}}) \stackrel{\mathsf{G}_1}{=} sk_i.$$

Similarly, by the homomorphic property of LAF, we have:

$$\sigma_i \stackrel{\mathsf{G}_0}{=} \mathsf{FEval}(F_{pk}, t_i, t'_i, w + \delta_i) = \mathsf{FEval}(F_{pk}, t_i, t'_i, w) + \mathsf{FEval}(F_{pk}, t_i, t'_i, \delta_i) \stackrel{\mathsf{G}_1}{=} \sigma_i.$$

Thus the changes are just conceptual, and Lemma 4 follows. ∎

Game G_2: It is the same as G_1, except that the core tags t', t'_i are not uniformly chosen any more. Now they are generated by FTag in G_2. More precisely,

2. Challenger $\mathcal{C}$ samples $w \leftarrow W$, computes $s \leftarrow \mathsf{SS.Gen}(w)$, $sk \leftarrow \mathsf{Ext}(w, i_{\mathsf{ext}})$, $(c, k) \leftarrow \mathsf{SKEM.Enc}(\mathsf{pp}, sk)$, sets $t := (s, c)$, $\underline{\text{generates } t' \leftarrow \mathsf{FTag}(F_{td}, t)}$, computes $\sigma \leftarrow \mathsf{FEval}(F_{pk}, t, t', w)$, sets $P := (s, c, t', \sigma)$, $R := k$, and returns (P, R) to $\mathcal{A}$.

3. Upon receiving a shift $\delta_i \in \mathcal{M}$ from $\mathcal{A}$ with $\mathsf{dis}(\delta_i) \leq t$, challenger $\mathcal{C}$ computes $s_i := s + \mathsf{SS.Gen}(\delta_i)$, $sk_i := sk + \mathsf{Ext}(\delta_i, i_{\mathsf{ext}})$, $(c_i, k_i) \leftarrow \mathsf{SKEM.Enc}(\mathsf{pp}, sk_i)$, sets $t_i := (s_i, c_i)$, $\underline{\text{generates } t'_i \leftarrow \mathsf{FTag}(F_{td}, t_i)}$, computes $\sigma_i := \mathsf{FEval}(F_{pk}, t_i, t'_i, w) + \mathsf{FEval}(F_{pk}, t_i, t'_i, \delta_i)$, sets $P_i := (s_i, c_i, t'_i, \sigma_i)$, $R_i := k_i$, and returns (P_i, R_i) to $\mathcal{A}$.

Lemma 5. $|\Pr[\mathsf{G}_1^{\mathcal{A}} \Rightarrow 1] - \Pr[\mathsf{G}_2^{\mathcal{A}} \Rightarrow 1]| \leq \mathsf{Adv}_{\mathsf{LAF}}^{\mathsf{ind}}(1^\lambda)$.

Proof. Assume there exists a PPT adversary $\mathcal{A}$ such that $|\Pr[\mathsf{G}_1^{\mathcal{A}} \Rightarrow 1] - \Pr[\mathsf{G}_2^{\mathcal{A}} \Rightarrow 1]| = \epsilon$. We construct a PPT algorithm $\mathcal{B}$ who, given F_{pk}, can distinguish oracle $\mathsf{FTag}(F_{td}, \cdot)$ from oracle $\mathcal{O}_{\mathcal{T}'}(\cdot)$ with advantage ϵ. Algorithm $\mathcal{B}$ simulates an environment for $\mathcal{A}$ as follows:

– Given F_{pk}, algorithm $\mathcal{B}$ invokes $\mathsf{pp} \leftarrow \mathsf{SKEM.Init}(1^\lambda)$, samples a seed $i_{\mathsf{ext}} \leftarrow_\$ \mathcal{I}$, sets $\mathsf{crs} := (F_{pk}, i_{\mathsf{ext}}, \mathsf{pp})$, and returns crs to $\mathcal{A}$.
– Algorithm $\mathcal{B}$ samples $w \leftarrow W$, computes $s \leftarrow \mathsf{SS.Gen}(w)$, $sk \leftarrow \mathsf{Ext}(w, i_{\mathsf{ext}})$, $(c, k) \leftarrow \mathsf{SKEM.Enc}(\mathsf{pp}, sk)$ and sets $t := (s, c)$.
    – $\mathcal{B}$ queries its own oracle with $t = (s, c)$, and the oracle replies $\mathcal{B}$ with t'. After receiving t' from its oracle, $\mathcal{B}$ invokes $\sigma \leftarrow \mathsf{FEval}(F_{pk}, t, t', w)$, sets $P := (t = (s, c), t', \sigma)$, $R := k$, and returns (P, R) to $\mathcal{A}$.

- Upon receiving a shift $\delta_i \in \mathcal{M}$ from $\mathcal{A}$ with $\mathsf{dis}(\delta_i) \leq t$, algorithm $\mathcal{B}$ computes $s_i := s + \mathsf{SS.Gen}(\delta_i)$, $sk_i := sk + \mathsf{Ext}(\delta_i, i_{\mathsf{ext}})$, $(c_i, k_i) \leftarrow \mathsf{SKEM.Enc}(pp, sk_i)$ and sets $t_i = (s_i, c_i)$.
   - $\mathcal{B}$ queries its oracle with $t_i := (s_i, c_i)$, and the oracle replies $\mathcal{B}$ with t_i'. After receiving t_i' from its oracle, $\mathcal{B}$ computes $\sigma_i := \mathsf{FEval}(F_{pk}, t_i, t_i', w) + \mathsf{FEval}(F_{pk}, t_i, t_i', \delta_i)$, sets $P_i := (s_i, c_i, t_i', \sigma_i)$, $R_i := k_i$, and returns (P_i, R_i) to $\mathcal{A}$.
- When $\mathcal{A}$ outputs a bit β', algorithm $\mathcal{B}$ returns β'.

Observe that if the oracle to which $\mathcal{B}$ has access is $\mathsf{FTag}(F_{td}, \cdot)$, then $\mathcal{B}$ perfectly simulates G_2 for $\mathcal{A}$; otherwise it perfectly simulates G_1 for $\mathcal{A}$. Thus

$$\mathsf{Adv}^{\mathsf{ind}}_{\mathsf{LAF}, \mathcal{B}}(1^\lambda) = |\Pr[\mathsf{G}_1^{\mathcal{A}} \Rightarrow 1] - \Pr[\mathsf{G}_2^{\mathcal{A}} \Rightarrow 1]|.$$

This completes the proof of Lemma 5.   ∎

Game G_3: It is the same as G_2, except that sk is changed to a uniform one. More precisely,

2. Challenger $\mathcal{C}$ samples $w \leftarrow W$, computes $s \leftarrow \mathsf{SS.Gen}(w)$, $\underline{\text{samples } \widehat{sk} \leftarrow_{\$} \mathcal{SK}}$, computes $(c, k) \leftarrow \mathsf{SKEM.Enc}(pp, \widehat{sk})$, sets $t := (s, c)$, generates $t' \leftarrow \mathsf{FTag}(F_{td}, t)$, computes $\sigma \leftarrow \mathsf{FEval}(F_{pk}, t, t', w)$, sets $P := (s, c, t', \sigma)$, $R := k$, and returns (P, R) to $\mathcal{A}$.

3. Upon receiving a shift $\delta_i \in \mathcal{M}$ from $\mathcal{A}$ with $\mathsf{dis}(\delta_i) \leq t$, challenger $\mathcal{C}$ computes $s_i := s + \mathsf{SS.Gen}(\delta_i)$, $sk_i := \underline{\widehat{sk}} + \mathsf{Ext}(\delta_i, i_{\mathsf{ext}})$, $(c_i, k_i) \leftarrow \mathsf{SKEM.Enc}(pp, sk_i)$, sets $t_i := (s_i, c_i)$, generates $t_i' \leftarrow \mathsf{FTag}(F_{td}, t_i)$, computes $\sigma_i := \mathsf{FEval}(F_{pk}, t_i, t_i', w) + \mathsf{FEval}(F_{pk}, t_i, t_i', \delta_i)$, sets $P_i := (s_i, c_i, t_i', \sigma_i)$, $R_i := k_i$, and returns (P_i, R_i) to $\mathcal{A}$.

Lemma 6. $|\Pr[\mathsf{G}_2^{\mathcal{A}} \Rightarrow 1] - \Pr[\mathsf{G}_3^{\mathcal{A}} \Rightarrow 1]| \leq \varepsilon_{\mathsf{ext}}$.

Proof. Assume that $\mathcal{A}$ makes ρ queries to the challenger. The only difference between G_2 and G_3 is that $sk \leftarrow \mathsf{Ext}(w, i_{\mathsf{ext}})$ in G_2 is changed to $\widehat{sk} \leftarrow_{\$} \mathcal{SK}$ in G_3. We will show that the views of adversary $\mathcal{A}$ in G_2 and G_3 are statistically indistinguishable.

Since F_{pk}, F_{td} and pp are independent of W, we have

$$\widetilde{H}_\infty(W \mid (F_{pk}, F_{td}, pp)) = \widetilde{H}_\infty(W) \geq m. \tag{7}$$

Define $\mathcal{S} := \{\sigma \mid \sigma = \mathsf{FEval}(F_{pk}, t, t', W) \land \mathsf{tag} = (t, t') \in \mathcal{T}_{lossy}\}$, which collects all function values w.r.t. the same W and the same F_{pk} but under all possible lossy tags. By the lossiness of LAF, $\mathcal{S}$ only reveals $\log p$ bits information of W (see Remark 2). According to Lemma 1 and Eq. (7), we have

$$\widetilde{H}_\infty(W \mid (F_{pk}, F_{td}, pp, \mathcal{S})) \geq \widetilde{H}_\infty(W \mid (F_{pk}, F_{td}, pp)) - \log p \geq m - \log p. \tag{8}$$

Since SS is a $(m - \log p, \hat{m}, 2t)$-secure sketch, we have

$$\widetilde{H}_\infty(W \mid (s = \mathsf{SS.Gen}(W), F_{pk}, F_{td}, pp, \mathcal{S})) \geq \hat{m}.$$

Define AuxiliaryInput $:=$ $(s = \mathsf{SS.Gen}(W), F_{pk}, F_{td}, \mathsf{pp}, \mathcal{S})$. Obviously AuxiliaryInput is independent of i_{ext}. According to Eq. (3), the average-case $(\mathcal{M}, \hat{m}, \mathcal{SK}, \varepsilon_{\mathsf{ext}})$-strong extractor Ext implies

$$\Big(\underbrace{sk, i_{\mathsf{ext}}, (s = \mathsf{SS.Gen}(W), F_{pk}, F_{td}, \mathsf{pp}, \mathcal{S})}_{\text{AuxiliaryInput}} \Big) \overset{\varepsilon_{\mathsf{ext}}}{\approx} \Big(\underbrace{\widehat{sk}, i_{\mathsf{ext}}, (s = \mathsf{SS.Gen}(W), F_{pk}, F_{td}, \mathsf{pp}, \mathcal{S})}_{\text{AuxiliaryInput}} \Big), (9)$$

where $sk := \mathsf{Ext}(W, i_{\mathsf{ext}})$ and $\widehat{sk} \leftarrow_\$ \mathcal{SK}$. Since $\mathsf{crs} = (F_{pk}, i_{\mathsf{ext}}, \mathsf{pp})$, Eq. (9) implies

$$\Big(\underbrace{sk, s = \mathsf{SS.Gen}(W), \mathsf{crs}, F_{td}, \mathcal{S}}_{\Omega} \Big) \overset{\varepsilon_{\mathsf{ext}}}{\approx} \Big(\underbrace{\widehat{sk}, s = \mathsf{SS.Gen}(W), \mathsf{crs}, F_{td}, \mathcal{S}}_{\Xi} \Big). \tag{10}$$

Let w be a specific value taken by random variable W.

Recall that $P = (s, c, t', \sigma)$ and $R = k$, where $s \leftarrow \mathsf{SS.Gen}(w)$, $(c, k) \leftarrow \mathsf{SKEM.Enc}(\mathsf{pp}, sk)$, $t := (s, c)$, $t' \leftarrow \mathsf{FTag}(F_{td}, t)$, $\sigma \leftarrow \mathsf{FEval}(F_{pk}, t, t', w)$. Obviously, (P, R) can be regarded as an output of some randomized function on input Ω.

Define $\widehat{P} := (s, \widehat{c}, \widehat{t'}, \widehat{\sigma})$ and $\widehat{R} := \widehat{k}$, where $s \leftarrow \mathsf{SS.Gen}(w)$, $(\widehat{c}, \widehat{k}) \leftarrow \mathsf{SKEM.Enc}(\mathsf{pp}, \widehat{sk})$, $\widehat{t} = (s, \widehat{c})$, $\widehat{t'} \leftarrow \mathsf{FTag}(F_{td}, \widehat{t})$, $\widehat{\sigma} \leftarrow \mathsf{FEval}(F_{pk}, \widehat{t}, \widehat{t'}, w)$. In other words, $(\widehat{P}, \widehat{R})$ is the helper string and the extracted string generated with the random key $\widehat{sk}$. Then $(\widehat{P}, \widehat{R})$ can be regarded as an output of the same randomized function on input Ξ as that for (P, R).

According to Lemma 2, Formula (10) implies

$$\Big(\underbrace{\overbrace{sk := \mathsf{Ext}(W, i_{\mathsf{ext}}), s = \mathsf{SS.Gen}(W), \mathsf{crs}, F_{td}, \mathcal{S}}^{\Omega}, P, R}_{\Omega_0} \Big) \overset{\varepsilon_{\mathsf{ext}}}{\approx} \Big(\underbrace{\overbrace{\widehat{sk} \leftarrow_\$ \mathcal{SK}, s = \mathsf{SS.Gen}(W), \mathsf{crs}, F_{td}, \mathcal{S}}^{\Xi}, \widehat{P}, \widehat{R}}_{\Xi_0} \Big),$$

in short,

$$\Big(\underbrace{\Omega, P, R}_{\Omega_0} \Big) \overset{\varepsilon_{\mathsf{ext}}}{\approx} \Big(\underbrace{\Xi, \widehat{P}, \widehat{R}}_{\Xi_0} \Big). \tag{11}$$

Before $\mathcal{A}$ submits its first query δ_1 in G_2, its view is described by $\langle \mathsf{crs}, P, R \rangle$. Obviously, δ_1 can be computed by some randomized function of $\langle \mathsf{crs}, P, R \rangle$ (the function is determined by $\mathcal{A}$'s strategy). Naturally, it can be regarded as an output of some randomized function on input Ω_0.

Similarly, the first query $\widehat{\delta}_1$ of $\mathcal{A}$ in G_3 is determined by the same randomized function of its view $\langle \mathsf{crs}, \widehat{P}, \widehat{R} \rangle$, hence it can also be regarded as an output of the same randomized function of Ξ_0.

By Lemma 2 again, Formula (11) implies

$$\Big(\underbrace{\Omega, P, R, \delta_1}_{\Omega_0'} \Big) \overset{\varepsilon_{\mathsf{ext}}}{\approx} \Big(\underbrace{\Xi, \widehat{P}, \widehat{R}, \widehat{\delta}_1}_{\Xi_0'} \Big). \tag{12}$$

Recall that $P_1 := (s_1, c_1, t_1', \sigma_1)$, $R_1 := k_1$, where $s_1 = s + \mathsf{SS.Gen}(\delta_1)$, $sk_1 = sk + \mathsf{Ext}(\delta_1, i_{\mathsf{ext}})$, $(c_1, k_1) \leftarrow \mathsf{SKEM.Enc}(\mathsf{pp}, sk_1)$, $t_1 = (s_1, c_1)$, $t_1' \leftarrow \mathsf{FTag}(F_{td}, t_1)$

$\sigma_1 = \mathsf{FEval}(F_{pk}, t_1, t_1', w) + \mathsf{FEval}(F_{pk}, t_1, t_1', \delta_1)$. Note that (t_1, t_1') is a lossy tag, hence $\mathsf{FEval}(F_{pk}, t_1, t_1', w) \in \mathcal{S}$. Obviously, P_1 and R_1 can be determined by some randomized function of Ω_0'.

Define $\widehat{P_1} := (\widehat{s_1}, \widehat{c_1}, \widehat{t_1'}, \widehat{\sigma_1})$, $\widehat{R_1} := \widehat{k_1}$, where $\widehat{s_1} = s + \mathsf{SS.Gen}(\widehat{\delta_1})$, $\widehat{sk_1} = \widehat{sk} + \mathsf{Ext}(\widehat{\delta_1}, i_{\text{ext}})$, $(\widehat{c_1}, \widehat{k_1}) \leftarrow \mathsf{SKEM.Enc}(pp, \widehat{sk_1})$, $\widehat{t_1} = (\widehat{s_1}, \widehat{c_1})$, $\widehat{t_1'} \leftarrow \mathsf{FTag}(F_{td}, \widehat{t_1})$ $\widehat{\sigma_1} = \mathsf{FEval}(F_{pk}, \widehat{t_1}, \widehat{t_1'}, w) + \mathsf{FEval}(F_{pk}, \widehat{t_1}, \widehat{t_1'}, \widehat{\delta_1})$. Similarly, $\widehat{P_1}$ and $\widehat{R_1}$ can be determined by the same randomized function of of Ξ_0'.

Applying Lemma 2 once more, Formula (12) implies

$$\left(\underbrace{\overbrace{\Omega, P, R, \delta_1, P_1, R_1}^{\Omega_0'}}_{\Omega_1} \right) \stackrel{\varepsilon_{\text{ext}}}{\approx} \left(\underbrace{\overbrace{\Xi, \widehat{P}, \widehat{R}, \widehat{\delta_1}, \widehat{P_1}, \widehat{R_1}}^{\Xi_0'}}_{\Xi_1} \right). \tag{13}$$

By induction on $i \in [\rho]$, we have that

$$\left(\underbrace{\Omega, P, R, \{\delta_i, P_i, R_i\}_{i \in [\rho]}}_{\Omega_\rho} \right) \stackrel{\varepsilon_{\text{ext}}}{\approx} \left(\underbrace{\Xi, \widehat{P}, \widehat{R}, \{\widehat{\delta_i}, \widehat{P_i}, \widehat{R_i}\}_{i \in [\rho]}}_{\Xi_\rho} \right). \tag{14}$$

More precisely,

$$\left(\underbrace{sk := \mathsf{Ext}(W, i_{\text{ext}}), s = \mathsf{SS.Gen}(W), \overbrace{crs, F_{td}, \mathcal{S}, P, R, \{\delta_i, P_i, R_i\}_{i \in [\rho]}}^{\Omega}}_{\Omega_\rho} \right) \stackrel{\varepsilon_{\text{ext}}}{\approx}$$

$$\left(\underbrace{sk := \mathsf{Ext}(W, i_{\text{ext}}), s = \mathsf{SS.Gen}(W), \overbrace{crs, F_{td}, \mathcal{S}, \widehat{P}, \widehat{R}, \{\widehat{\delta_i}, \widehat{P_i}, \widehat{R_i}\}_{i \in [\rho]}}^{\Xi}}_{\Xi_\rho} \right). \tag{15}$$

(15) implies $\left(\underbrace{crs, P, R, \{\delta_i, P_i, R_i\}_{i \in [\rho]}}_{\Omega_\rho^*} \right) \stackrel{\varepsilon_{\text{ext}}}{\approx} \left(\underbrace{crs, \widehat{P}, \widehat{R}, \{\widehat{\delta_i}, \widehat{P_i}, \widehat{R_i}\}_{i \in [\rho]}}_{\Xi_\rho^*} \right).$ (16)

Observe that Ω_ρ^* is just the whole view of $\mathcal{A}$ in G_2, and Ξ_ρ^* is the whole view of $\mathcal{A}$ in G_3. The statistical distance of Ω_ρ^* and Ξ_ρ^* is smaller than ε_{ext}. As a consequence, we have $|\Pr[\mathsf{G}_2^{\mathcal{A}} \Rightarrow 1] - \Pr[\mathsf{G}_3^{\mathcal{A}} \Rightarrow 1]| \leq \varepsilon_{\text{ext}}$. ∎

Game G_4: It is the same as G_3, except that R is uniformly chosen from $\mathcal{K}$ instead of being output by SKEM. More precisely,

2. Challenger $\mathcal{C}$ samples $w \leftarrow W$, computes $s \leftarrow \mathsf{SS.Gen}(w)$, samples $\widehat{sk} \leftarrow_\$ \mathcal{SK}$, computes $(c, k) \leftarrow \mathsf{SKEM.Enc}(pp, \widehat{sk})$, sets $t := (s, c)$, generates $t' \leftarrow \mathsf{FTag}(F_{td}, t)$, computes $\sigma \leftarrow \mathsf{FEval}(F_{pk}, t, t', w)$, sets $P := (s, c, t', \sigma)$, <u>samples $R \leftarrow_\$ \mathcal{K}$</u>, and returns (P, R) to $\mathcal{A}$.

Lemma 7. $|\Pr[\mathsf{G}_3^{\mathcal{A}} \Rightarrow 1] - \Pr[\mathsf{G}_4^{\mathcal{A}} \Rightarrow 1]| \leq \mathsf{Adv}_{\mathsf{SKEM}}^{\mathsf{ks}}(1^\lambda)$.

Proof. Assume there exists a PPT adversary $\mathcal{A}$ such that $|\Pr[G_3^{\mathcal{A}} \Rightarrow 1] - \Pr[G_4^{\mathcal{A}} \Rightarrow 1]| = \epsilon$. We construct a PPT algorithm $\mathcal{B}$ who can implement the key-shift attack with the same advantage ϵ. Algorithm $\mathcal{B}$ simulates an environment for $\mathcal{A}$ as follows:

- After receiving pp from its own challenger, algorithm $\mathcal{B}$ invokes $(F_{pk}, F_{td}) \leftarrow$ FGen(1^λ), samples a seed $i_{ext} \leftarrow_\$ \mathcal{I}$, sets crs $= (F_{pk}, i_{ext}, pp)$, and returns crs to $\mathcal{A}$.
- Algorithm $\mathcal{B}$ samples $w \leftarrow W$, computes $s \leftarrow$ SS.Gen(w), asks the *challenge* oracle of SKEM to get (c, k). Then $\mathcal{B}$ sets $t := (s, c)$, generates $t' \leftarrow$ FTag(F_{td}, t), computes $\sigma \leftarrow$ FEval(F_{pk}, t, t', w), sets $P := (t = (s, c), t', \sigma)$, $R := k$, and returns (P, R) to $\mathcal{A}$.
- Upon receiving a shift $\delta_i \in \mathcal{M}$ queried from $\mathcal{A}$ with dis$(\delta_i) \leq t$, algorithm $\mathcal{B}$ computes $s_i := s + $ SS.Gen(δ_i), $\Delta_i :=$ Ext(δ_i, i_{ext}), asks its *encapsulation* oracle with Δ_i to obtain (c_i, k_i), where $(c_i, k_i) \leftarrow$ SKEM.Enc$(pp, sk + \Delta_i)$. Then $\mathcal{B}$ sets $t_i := (s_i, c_i)$, generates $t_i' \leftarrow$ FTag(F_{td}, t_i), computes $\sigma_i :=$ FEval$(F_{pk}, t_i, t_i', w) + $ FEval $(F_{pk}, t_i, t_i', \delta_i)$, sets $P_i := (s_i, c_i, t_i', \sigma_i)$, $R_i := k_i$, and returns (P_i, R_i) to $\mathcal{A}$.
- When $\mathcal{A}$ outputs a bit β', algorithm $\mathcal{B}$ outputs β' to its own challenger.

Note that if (c, k) is generated by $(c, k) \leftarrow$ SKEM.Enc(pp, sk), then algorithm $\mathcal{B}$ perfectly simulates G_3 for $\mathcal{A}$; otherwise k is uniformly chosen from $\mathcal{K}$, then algorithm $\mathcal{B}$ perfectly simulates G_4 for $\mathcal{A}$. Hence $\mathcal{B}$ shares exactly the same advantage with $\mathcal{A}$. Thus $\mathsf{Adv}_{\mathsf{SKEM}, \mathcal{B}}^{\mathsf{mrka}}(1^\lambda) = |\Pr[G_3^{\mathcal{A}} \Rightarrow 1] - \Pr[G_4^{\mathcal{A}} \Rightarrow 1]| \leq \mathsf{Adv}_{\mathsf{SKEM}}^{\mathsf{mrka}}(1^\lambda)$. This completes the proof of Lemma 7. ∎

Game G_5: It is the same as G_4, except that the generation of $\widehat{sk}$ is changed back to $sk \leftarrow$ Ext(w, i_{ext}). More precisely,

2. Challenger $\mathcal{C}$ samples $w \leftarrow W$, computes $s \leftarrow$ SS.Gen(w), $\underline{sk \leftarrow \text{Ext}(w, i_{ext})}$, $(c, k) \leftarrow$ SKEM.Enc$(pp, \underline{sk})$, sets $t := (s, c)$, generates $t' \leftarrow \overline{\text{FTag}(F_{td}, t)}$, computes $\sigma \leftarrow$ FEval(F_{pk}, t, t', w), sets $P := (s, c, t', \sigma)$, samples $R \leftarrow_\$ \mathcal{K}$, and returns (P, R) to $\mathcal{A}$.

3. Upon receiving a shift $\delta_i \in \mathcal{M}$ from $\mathcal{A}$ with dis$(\delta_i) \leq t$, challenger $\mathcal{C}$ computes $s_i := s + $ SS.Gen(δ_i), $sk_i := \underline{sk} + $ Ext(δ_i, i_{ext}), $(c_i, k_i) \leftarrow$ SKEM.Enc(pp, sk_i), sets $t_i := (s_i, c_i)$, generates $t_i' \leftarrow$ FTag(F_{td}, t_i), computes $\sigma_i :=$ FEval$(F_{pk}, t_i, t_i', w) + $ FEval$(F_{pk}, t_i, t_i', \delta_i)$, sets $P_i := (s_i, c_i, t_i', \sigma_i)$, $R_i := k_i$, and returns (P_i, R_i) to $\mathcal{A}$.

Lemma 8. $|\Pr[G_4^{\mathcal{A}} \Rightarrow 1] - \Pr[G_5^{\mathcal{A}} \Rightarrow 1]| \leq \varepsilon_{ext}$.

Proof. The proof is similar to the proof of Lemma 6, since the changes from G_4 to G_5 is symmetric to that from G_2 to G_3. We omit the proof here. ∎

Game G_6: It is the same as G_5, except that the core tags are changed back to random tags. More precisely,

2. C samples $w \leftarrow W$, computes $s \leftarrow \mathsf{SS.Gen}(w)$, $sk \leftarrow \mathsf{Ext}(w, i_{\mathsf{ext}})$, $(c, k) \leftarrow \mathsf{SKEM.Enc}(\mathsf{pp}, sk)$, sets $t := (s, c)$, samples $t' \leftarrow_\$ T'$, computes $\sigma \leftarrow \mathsf{FEval}(F_{pk}, t, t', w)$, sets $P := (s, c, t', \sigma)$, samples $R \leftarrow_\$ \mathcal{K}$, and returns (P, R) to $\mathcal{A}$.
3. Upon receiving a shift $\delta_i \in \mathcal{M}$ from $\mathcal{A}$ with $\mathsf{dis}(\delta_i) \leq \mathsf{t}$, C computes $s_i := s + \mathsf{SS.Gen}(\delta_i)$, $sk_i := sk + \mathsf{Ext}(\delta_i, i_{\mathsf{ext}})$, $(c_i, k_i) \leftarrow \mathsf{SKEM.Enc}(\mathsf{pp}, sk_i)$, sets $t_i := (s_i, c_i)$, samples $t'_i \leftarrow_\$ T'$, computes $\sigma_i := \mathsf{FEval}(F_{pk}, t_i, t'_i, w) + \mathsf{FEval}(F_{pk}, t_i, t'_i, \delta_i)$, sets $P_i := (s_i, c_i, t'_i, \sigma_i)$, $R_i := k_i$, and returns (P_i, R_i) to $\mathcal{A}$.

Lemma 9. $|\Pr[\mathsf{G}_5^{\mathcal{A}} \Rightarrow 1] - \Pr[\mathsf{G}_6^{\mathcal{A}} \Rightarrow 1]| \leq \mathsf{Adv}_{\mathsf{LAF}}^{\mathsf{ind}}(1^\lambda).$

Proof. The proof is similar to the proof of Lemma 5, since the changes from G_5 to G_6 is symmetric to that from G_1 to G_2. We omit the proof here. ∎

Game G_7: It is the same as G_6, except for conceptual changes of generating (P_i, R_i). More precisely,

3. Upon receiving a shift $\delta_i \in \mathcal{M}$ from $\mathcal{A}$ with $\mathsf{dis}(\delta_i) \leq \mathsf{t}$, challenger C computes $s_i \leftarrow \mathsf{SS.Gen}(w + \delta_i)$, $sk_i \leftarrow \mathsf{Ext}(w + \delta_i, i_{\mathsf{ext}})$, $(c_i, k_i) \leftarrow \mathsf{SKEM.Enc}(\mathsf{pp}, sk_i)$, sets $t_i := (s_i, c_i)$, samples $t'_i \leftarrow_\$ T'$, computes $\sigma_i \leftarrow \mathsf{FEval}(F_{pk}, t_i, t'_i, w + \delta_i)$, sets $P_i := (s_i, c_i, t'_i, \sigma_i)$, $R_i := k_i$, and returns (P_i, R_i) to $\mathcal{A}$.

Lemma 10. $\Pr[\mathsf{G}_6^{\mathcal{A}} \Rightarrow 1] = \Pr[\mathsf{G}_7^{\mathcal{A}} \Rightarrow 1].$

Proof. The proof is identical to the proof of Lemma 4, since the changes from G_6 to G_7 is symmetric to that from G_0 to G_1. We omit the proof here. ∎

Note that G_7 is identical to experiment $\mathsf{Exp}_{\mathsf{rFE}, \mathcal{A}}^{\mathsf{reu}}(0)$. Thus

$$\Pr[\mathsf{Exp}_{\mathsf{rFE}, \mathcal{A}}^{\mathsf{reu}}(0) \Rightarrow 1] = \Pr[\mathsf{G}_7 \Rightarrow 1]. \tag{17}$$

Taking all things together, by Eq. (6), Lemmas 4–10 and Eq. (17), we have that

$$\mathsf{Adv}_{\mathsf{rFE}, \mathcal{A}}^{\mathsf{reu}} \leq 2\mathsf{Adv}_{\mathsf{LAF}}^{\mathsf{ind}}(1^\lambda) + 2\varepsilon_{\mathsf{ext}} + \mathsf{Adv}_{\mathsf{SKEM}}^{\mathsf{ks}}(1^\lambda).$$

This completes the proof of Theorem 3. ∎

Theorem 4. *Given the building blocks specified in Theorem 2, the fuzzy extractor rrFE in Fig. 4 is ε_2-robust, where $\varepsilon_2 = \mathsf{Adv}_{\mathsf{LAF}}^{\mathsf{ind}}(1^\lambda) + \varepsilon_{\mathsf{ext}} + \mathsf{Adv}_{\mathsf{LAF}}^{\mathsf{eva}}(1^\lambda) + 2^{-\omega(\log \lambda)}$.*

Proof. Similar to the proof of reusability, we will prove this theorem by a sequence of games again. The changes from Game G_j to adjacent Game G_{j+1} are underlined. Let win_j denote the event that adversary $\mathcal{A}$ wins in G_j. G_j outputs 1 if $\mathcal{A}$ wins and 0 otherwise. Obviously, $\Pr[\mathsf{win}_j] = \Pr[\mathsf{G}_j^{\mathcal{A}} \Rightarrow 1]$.

Game G_0: It is identical to the robustness experiment $\mathsf{Exp}_{\mathsf{rrFE}, \mathcal{A}}^{\mathsf{rob}}(1^\lambda)$.

1. Challenger C invokes $(F_{pk}, F_{td}) \leftarrow \mathsf{FGen}(1^\lambda)$ and $\mathsf{pp} \leftarrow \mathsf{SKEM.Init}(1^\lambda)$, samples a seed $i_{\mathsf{ext}} \leftarrow_\$ \mathcal{I}$, sets $\mathsf{crs} = (F_{pk}, i_{\mathsf{ext}}, \mathsf{pp})$, and returns crs to $\mathcal{A}$.

2. Challenger $\mathcal{C}$ samples $w \leftarrow W$, computes $s \leftarrow \mathsf{SS.Gen}(w)$, $sk \leftarrow \mathsf{Ext}(w, i_{\mathsf{ext}})$, $(c, k) \leftarrow \mathsf{SKEM.Enc}(pp, sk)$, sets $t := (s, c)$, samples $t' \leftarrow_{\!\!\$} T'$, computes $\sigma \leftarrow \mathsf{FEval}(F_{pk}, t, t', w)$, sets $P := (t = (s, c), t', \sigma)$, $R := k$, and returns (P, R) to $\mathcal{A}$.

3. Upon receiving a shift $\delta_i \in \mathcal{M}$ from $\mathcal{A}$ with $\mathsf{dis}(\delta_i) \leq t$, challenger $\mathcal{C}$ computes $s_i \leftarrow \mathsf{SS.Gen}(w + \delta_i)$, $sk_i \leftarrow \mathsf{Ext}(w + \delta_i, i_{\mathsf{ext}})$, $(c_i, k_i) \leftarrow \mathsf{SKEM.Enc}(pp, sk_i)$, sets $t_i := (s_i, c_i)$, samples $t'_i \leftarrow_{\!\!\$} T'$, computes $\sigma_i \leftarrow \mathsf{FEval}(F_{pk}, t_i, t'_i, w + \delta_i)$, sets $P_i := (t_i = (s_i, c_i), t'_i, \sigma_i)$, $R_i := k_i$, and returns (P_i, R_i) to $\mathcal{A}$.

4. $\mathcal{A}$ submits to $\mathcal{C}$ its forgery $(\widetilde{P}, \widetilde{\delta})$ with $\widetilde{P} = (\widetilde{t} = (\widetilde{s}, \widetilde{c}), \widetilde{t}', \widetilde{\sigma})$. $\mathcal{A}$ wins if $\mathsf{dis}(\widetilde{\delta}) \leq t$, $\widetilde{P}$ is fresh and $\mathsf{Rep}(crs, \widetilde{P}, w + \widetilde{\delta}) \neq \perp$. Recall that $\mathsf{Rep}(crs, \widetilde{P}, w + \widetilde{\delta}) \neq \perp$ if and only if $\mathsf{dis}(\widetilde{w}, w + \widetilde{\delta}) \leq t$ and $\widetilde{\sigma}' = \widetilde{\sigma}$ holds, where $\widetilde{w} \leftarrow \mathsf{SS.Rec}(w + \widetilde{\delta}, \widetilde{s})$ and $\widetilde{\sigma}' \leftarrow \mathsf{FEval}(F_{pk}, \widetilde{t}, \widetilde{t}', \widetilde{w})$. The game outputs 1 if $\mathcal{A}$ wins and 0 otherwise.

Obviously,

$$\Pr[\mathsf{G}_0^{\mathcal{A}} \Rightarrow 1] = \Pr[\mathsf{Exp}_{\mathsf{rrFE}, \mathcal{A}}^{\mathsf{rob}}(1^\lambda) \Rightarrow 1]. \tag{18}$$

Game G_1: It is the same as G_0, except for conceptual changes of generating (P_i, R_i). More precisely,

3. Upon receiving a shift $\delta_i \in \mathcal{M}$ from $\mathcal{A}$ with $\mathsf{dis}(\delta_i) \leq t$, challenger $\mathcal{C}$ computes $\underline{s_i := s + \mathsf{SS.Gen}(\delta_i)}$, $\underline{sk_i := sk + \mathsf{Ext}(\delta_i, i_{\mathsf{ext}})}$, $(c_i, k_i) \leftarrow \mathsf{SKEM.Enc}(pp, sk_i)$, sets $t_i := (s_i, c_i)$, samples $t'_i \leftarrow_{\!\!\$} T'$, computes $\underline{\sigma_i \leftarrow \mathsf{FEval}(F_{pk}, t_i, t'_i, w) + }$ $\underline{\mathsf{FEval}(F_{pk}, t_i, t'_i, \delta_i)}$, sets $P_i := (t_i = (s_i, c_i), t'_i, \sigma_i)$, $R_i := k_i$, and returns (P_i, R_i) to $\mathcal{A}$.

Lemma 11. $\Pr[\mathsf{G}_0^{\mathcal{A}} \Rightarrow 1] = \Pr[\mathsf{G}_1^{\mathcal{A}} \Rightarrow 1]$.

Proof. The changes are just conceptual by the homomorphic properties of SS, Ext, LAF. Similar to the proof of Lemma 4, Lemma 11 follows. ∎

Game G_2: It is the same as G_1, except that the core tags t', t'_i are not uniformly chosen any more. Now they are generated by FTag in G_2. More precisely,

2. Challenger $\mathcal{C}$ samples $w \leftarrow W$, computes $s \leftarrow \mathsf{SS.Gen}(w)$, $sk \leftarrow \mathsf{Ext}(w, i_{\mathsf{ext}})$, $(c, k) \leftarrow \mathsf{SKEM.Enc}(pp, sk)$, sets $t := (s, c)$, $\underline{\text{generates } t' \leftarrow \mathsf{FTag}(F_{td}, t)}$, computes $\sigma \leftarrow \mathsf{FEval}(F_{pk}, t, t', w)$, sets $P := (s, c, t', \sigma)$, $R := k$, and returns (P, R) to $\mathcal{A}$.

3. Upon receiving a shift $\delta_i \in \mathcal{M}$ from $\mathcal{A}$ with $\mathsf{dis}(\delta_i) \leq t$, challenger $\mathcal{C}$ computes $s_i := s + \mathsf{SS.Gen}(\delta_i)$, $sk_i := sk + \mathsf{Ext}(\delta_i, i_{\mathsf{ext}})$, $(c_i, k_i) \leftarrow \mathsf{SKEM.Enc}(pp, sk_i)$, sets $t_i := (s_i, c_i)$, $\underline{\text{generates } t'_i \leftarrow \mathsf{FTag}(F_{td}, t_i)}$, computes $\sigma_i := \mathsf{FEval}(F_{pk}, t_i, t'_i, w) + \mathsf{FEval}(F_{pk}, t_i, t'_i, \delta_i)$, sets $P_i := (s_i, c_i, t'_i, \sigma_i)$, $R_i := k_i$, and returns (P_i, R_i) to $\mathcal{A}$.

Lemma 12. $|\Pr[\mathsf{G}_1^{\mathcal{A}} \Rightarrow 1] - \Pr[\mathsf{G}_2^{\mathcal{A}} \Rightarrow 1]| \leq \mathsf{Adv}_{\mathsf{LAF}}^{\mathsf{ind}}(1^\lambda)$.

Proof. The proof is similar to that of Lemma 5 (the difference is the output strategy of algorithm $\mathcal{B}$). Assume there exists a PPT adversary $\mathcal{A}$ such that $|\Pr[\mathsf{G}_1^{\mathcal{A}} \Rightarrow 1] - \Pr[\mathsf{G}_2^{\mathcal{A}} \Rightarrow 1]| = \epsilon$. We construct a PPT algorithm $\mathcal{B}$ who, given F_{pk}, can distinguish oracle $\mathsf{FTag}(F_{td}, \cdot)$ from oracle $\mathcal{O}_{T'}(\cdot)$ with advantage ϵ. Algorithm $\mathcal{B}$ simulates an environment for $\mathcal{A}$ as follows:

- Given F_{pk}, algorithm $\mathcal{B}$ invokes pp $\leftarrow$ SKEM.Init(1^λ), samples a seed $i_{\text{ext}} \leftarrow_\$ \mathcal{I}$, sets crs $= (F_{pk}, i_{\text{ext}}, \text{pp})$, and returns crs to $\mathcal{A}$.
- Algorithm $\mathcal{B}$ samples $w \leftarrow W$, computes $s \leftarrow$ SS.Gen(w), $sk \leftarrow$ Ext(w, i_{ext}), $(c, k) \leftarrow$ SKEM.Enc(pp, sk), sets $t := (s, c)$ and queries its oracle with t to obtain t'. After receiving t' from its oracle, $\mathcal{B}$ computes $\sigma \leftarrow$ FEval(F_{pk}, t, t', w), sets $P := (t = (s, c), t', \sigma)$, $R := k$, and gives (P, R) to $\mathcal{A}$.
- Upon receiving a shift $\delta_i \in \mathcal{M}$ from $\mathcal{A}$ with dis(δ_i) $\leq$ t, algorithm $\mathcal{B}$ computes $s_i := s +$ SS.Gen(δ_i), $sk_i := sk +$ Ext(δ_i, i_{ext}), $(c_i, k_i) \leftarrow$ SKEM.Enc(pp, sk_i), sets $t_i := (s_i, c_i)$ and queries its oracle with t_i to obtain t'_i. After receiving t'_i from its oracle, $\mathcal{B}$ computes $\sigma_i := $ FEval(F_{pk}, t_i, t'_i, w) + FEval $(F_{pk}, t_i, t'_i, \delta_i)$, sets $P_i := (s_i, c_i, t'_i, \sigma_i)$, $R_i := k_i$, and returns (P_i, R_i) to $\mathcal{A}$.
- When $\mathcal{A}$ submits its forgery $(\widetilde{P} = (\widetilde{s}, \widetilde{c}, \widetilde{t}', \widetilde{\sigma}), \widetilde{\delta})$, algorithm $\mathcal{B}$ checks whether $\mathcal{A}$ wins. $\mathcal{B}$ returns 1 if $\mathcal{A}$ wins; otherwise, it returns 0.

Recall that $\mathcal{A}$ wins means that conditions dis($\widetilde{\delta}$) $\leq$ t, $\widetilde{P}$ is fresh and Rep(crs, $\widetilde{P}, w + \widetilde{\delta}$) $\neq \perp$ are satisfied. These conditions can be efficiently checked by $\mathcal{B}$. Moreover, if the oracle to which $\mathcal{B}$ has access is FTag($F_{td}, \cdot$), then $\mathcal{B}$ perfectly simulates G_2 for $\mathcal{A}$; otherwise it perfectly simulates G_1 for $\mathcal{A}$. Thus

$$\mathsf{Adv}^{\text{ind}}_{\mathsf{LAF},\mathcal{B}}(1^\lambda) = \big| \Pr[\text{win}_1] - \Pr[\text{win}_2] \big| = \big| \Pr[\mathsf{G}_1^{\mathcal{A}} \Rightarrow 1] - \Pr[\mathsf{G}_2^{\mathcal{A}} \Rightarrow 1] \big|.$$

This completes the proof of Lemma 12. $\blacksquare$

Game G_3: It is the same as G_2, except that sk is changed to a uniform one. More precisely,

2. Challenger $\mathcal{C}$ samples $w \leftarrow W$, computes $s \leftarrow$ SS.Gen(w), samples $\widehat{sk} \leftarrow_\$ \mathcal{SK}$, computes $(c, k) \leftarrow$ SKEM.Enc(pp, $\widehat{sk}$), sets $t := (s, c)$, generates $t' \leftarrow$ FTag(F_{td}, t), computes $\sigma \leftarrow$ FEval(F_{pk}, t, t', w), sets $P := (s, c, t', \sigma)$, $R := k$, and returns (P, R) to $\mathcal{A}$.
3. Upon receiving a shift $\delta_i \in \mathcal{M}$ from $\mathcal{A}$ with dis(δ_i) $\leq$ t, challenger $\mathcal{C}$ computes $s_i := s +$ SS.Gen(δ_i), $sk_i := \widehat{sk} +$ Ext(δ_i, i_{ext}), $(c_i, k_i) \leftarrow$ SKEM.Enc(pp, sk_i), sets $t_i = (s_i, c_i)$, generates $t'_i \leftarrow$ FTag(F_{td}, t_i), computes $\sigma_i :=$ FEval(F_{pk}, t_i, t'_i, w) + FEval($F_{pk}, t_i, t'_i, \delta_i$), sets $P_i := (s_i, c_i, t'_i, \sigma_i)$, $R_i := k_i$, and returns (P_i, R_i) to $\mathcal{A}$.

Lemma 13. $\big| \Pr[\mathsf{G}_2^{\mathcal{A}} \Rightarrow 1] - \Pr[\mathsf{G}_3^{\mathcal{A}} \Rightarrow 1] \big| \leq \varepsilon_{\text{ext}}.$

Proof. The only difference between G_2 and G_3 is that $sk \leftarrow$ Ext(w, i_{ext}) in G_2 is changed to $\widehat{sk} \leftarrow_\$ \mathcal{SK}$ in G_3. The proof is exactly the same as that of Lemma 6.

Assume that $\mathcal{A}$ makes ρ queries to the challenger before submitting its forgery $(\widetilde{P}, \widetilde{\delta})$. Following similar arguments as those in the proof Lemma 6, we can show that the views of adversary $\mathcal{A}$ before submitting the forgery in G_2 and G_3 are statistically indistinguishable, i.e.,

$$\Big(\underbrace{\mathsf{crs}, P, R, \{\delta_i, P_i, R_i\}_{i \in [\rho]}}_{\Omega^*_\rho} \Big) \overset{\varepsilon_{\text{ext}}}{\approx} \Big(\underbrace{\mathsf{crs}, \widehat{P}, \widehat{R}, \{\widehat{\delta}_i, \widehat{P}_i, \widehat{R}_i\}_{i \in [\rho]}}_{\Xi^*_\rho} \Big). \tag{19}$$

Here Ω_ρ^* summerizes the view of $\mathcal{A}$ in G_2, and Ξ_ρ^* the view of $\mathcal{A}$ in G_3 before $\mathcal{A}$ submits its forgery. The statistical distance of Ω_ρ^* and Ξ_ρ^* is smaller than ε_{ext}. As a consequence,

$$\left| \Pr[\text{win}_2] - \Pr[\text{win}_3] \right| = \left| \Pr[G_2^{\mathcal{A}} \Rightarrow 1] - \Pr[G_3^{\mathcal{A}} \Rightarrow 1] \right| \leq \varepsilon_{\text{ext}}.$$

∎

Lemma 14. $\Pr[\text{win}_3] \leq \mathsf{Adv}_{\mathsf{LAF}}^{\mathsf{eva}}(1^\lambda) + 2^{-\omega(\log \lambda)}$.

Proof. Let bad denote the event that $\mathcal{A}$'s forgery $\widetilde{P} = (\widetilde{t}, \widetilde{t'}, \widetilde{\sigma})$ contains a non-injective tag, i.e., $(\widetilde{t}, \widetilde{t'}) \notin \mathcal{T}_{inj}$. We have

$$\Pr[\text{win}_3] = \Pr[\text{win}_3 \wedge \text{bad}] + \Pr[\text{win}_3 \wedge \neg\text{bad}]. \tag{20}$$

Thus it suffices to prove the following two claims.

Claim. $\Pr[\text{win}_3 \wedge \text{bad}] \leq \mathsf{Adv}_{\mathsf{LAF}}^{\mathsf{eva}}(1^\lambda)$.

Proof. If there exists a PPT adversary $\mathcal{A}$ whose forgery makes $\text{win}_3 \wedge \text{bad}$ happen in G_3, we can construct a PPT algorithm $\mathcal{B}$ attacking on LAF's evasiveness. Given F_{pk} and a lossy tag generation oracle $\mathsf{FTag}(F_{td}, \cdot)$, $\mathcal{B}$ aims to output a new lossy tag. To this end, $\mathcal{B}$ simulates G_3 for $\mathcal{A}$ as follows:

- After receiving F_{pk} from its own challenger, $\mathcal{B}$ invokes $\mathsf{pp} \leftarrow \mathsf{SKEM.Init}(1^\lambda)$, samples a seed $i_{\mathsf{ext}} \leftarrow_\$ \mathcal{I}$, sets $\mathsf{crs} = (F_{pk}, i_{\mathsf{ext}}, \mathsf{pp})$, and returns crs to $\mathcal{A}$.
- $\mathcal{B}$ samples $w \leftarrow W$, computes $s \leftarrow \mathsf{SS.Gen}(w)$, samples $\widehat{sk} \leftarrow_\$ \mathcal{SK}$, computes $(c, k) \leftarrow \mathsf{SKEM.Enc}(\mathsf{pp}, \widehat{sk})$, and sets $t := (s, c)$.
  - $\mathcal{B}$ asks its own lossy tag generation oracle $\mathsf{FTag}(F_{td}, \cdot)$ with $t = (s, c)$ and obtains t' from the oracle. Obviously the oracle generates t' by $t' \leftarrow \mathsf{FTag}(F_{td}, t)$.

  $\mathcal{B}$ computes $\sigma \leftarrow \mathsf{FEval}(F_{pk}, t, t', w)$, sets $P := (s, c, t', \sigma)$ and $R := k$, and returns (P, R) to $\mathcal{A}$.

- Upon receiving a shift $\delta_i \in \mathcal{M}$ from $\mathcal{A}$ with $\mathsf{dis}(\delta_i) \leq t$, $\mathcal{B}$ computes $s_i := s + \mathsf{SS.Gen}(\delta_i)$, $sk_i := \widehat{sk} + \mathsf{Ext}(\delta_i, i_{\mathsf{ext}})$, $(c_i, k_i) \leftarrow \mathsf{SKEM.Enc}(\mathsf{pp}, sk_i)$ and sets $t_i := (s_i, c_i)$.
  - $\mathcal{B}$ asks its own lossy tag generation oracle $\mathsf{FTag}(F_{td}, \cdot)$ with $t_i = (s_i, c_i)$ and obtains t_i' from the oracle. Obviously the oracle generates t_i' by $t_i' \leftarrow \mathsf{FTag}(F_{td}, t_i)$.

  $\mathcal{B}$ computes $\sigma_i := \mathsf{FEval}(F_{pk}, t_i, t_i', w) + \mathsf{FEval}(F_{pk}, t_i, t_i', \delta_i)$, sets $P_i := (s_i, c_i, t_i', \sigma_i)$ and $R_i := k_i$, and returns (P_i, R_i) to $\mathcal{A}$.

- When $\mathcal{A}$ outputs its forgery $\left(\widetilde{P} = (\widetilde{t} = (\widetilde{s}, \widetilde{c}), \widetilde{t'}, \widetilde{\sigma}), \ \widetilde{\delta} \right)$, $\mathcal{B}$ returns the tag $(\widetilde{t}, \widetilde{t'})$ to it own challenger.

Note that $\mathcal{B}$ perfectly simulates G_3 for $\mathcal{A}$, since its oracle generates lossy tags with $\mathsf{FTag}(F_{td}, t_i)$.

If event $\mathsf{win}_3 \wedge \mathsf{bad}$ occurs, the forged helper string $\widetilde{P}$ must be fresh, i.e., $\widetilde{P} \neq P$ and $\widetilde{P} \neq P_i$ for $i \in [\rho]$. Define freshT as the event that the forged tag $(\widetilde{t}, \widetilde{t'})$ is a fresh one, i.e., $(\widetilde{t}, \widetilde{t'}) \neq (t, t')$ and $(\widetilde{t}, \widetilde{t'}) \neq (t_i, t_i')$ for all $i \in [\rho]$. Clearly,

$$\Pr[\mathsf{win}_3 \wedge \mathsf{bad}] = \underbrace{\Pr[\mathsf{win}_3 \wedge \mathsf{bad} \wedge \neg\mathsf{freshT}]}_{\text{Case 1}} + \underbrace{\Pr[\mathsf{win}_3 \wedge \mathsf{bad} \wedge \mathsf{freshT}]}_{\text{Case 2}}. \qquad (21)$$

Case 1. In this case, freshT does not happen. Then we have $(\widetilde{t}, \widetilde{t'}) = (t, t')$ or $(\widetilde{t}, \widetilde{t'}) = (t_i, t_i')$ for some $i \in [\rho]$. With loss of generality, we assume that $(\widetilde{t}, \widetilde{t'}) = (t_i, t_i')$. Clearly $\widetilde{t} = t_i$ implies $\widetilde{s} = s_i$. Note that $\mathsf{dis}(\delta_i) \leq \mathsf{t}$ and $\mathsf{dis}(\widetilde{\delta}) \leq \mathsf{t}$, thus $\mathsf{dis}(w + \widetilde{\delta}, w + \delta_i) \leq \mathsf{dis}(w + \widetilde{\delta}, w) + \mathsf{dis}(w, w + \delta_i) \leq 2\mathsf{t}$. By the correctness of $(m - \lceil \log p \rceil, \hat{m}, 2\mathsf{t})$-secure sketch SS, we have $\widetilde{w} = w + \delta_i$, where $\widetilde{w} \leftarrow \mathsf{SS.Rec}(w + \widetilde{\delta}, s_i)$ and $s_i \leftarrow \mathsf{SS.Gen}(w + \delta_i)$. As a result,

$$\widetilde{\sigma}' = \mathsf{FEval}(\widetilde{t}, \widetilde{t'}, \widetilde{w}) = \mathsf{FEval}(t_i, t_i', w + \delta_i) = \sigma_i.$$

If win_3 occurs, then $\widetilde{\sigma} = \widetilde{\sigma}'$ must hold. This implies $\widetilde{P} = (\widetilde{t}, \widetilde{t'}, \widetilde{\sigma}) = (t_i, t_i', \sigma_i) = P_i$. This contradicts to the requirement of win_3 that $\widetilde{P}$ is fresh. Thus we have

$$\Pr[\mathsf{win}_3 \wedge \mathsf{bad} \wedge \neg\mathsf{freshT}] = 0. \qquad (22)$$

Case 2. If both bad and freshT occur, then the forged tag $(\widetilde{t}, \widetilde{t'})$ is a fresh non-injective tag. Observe that $\mathcal{B}$ perfectly simulates G_3 for $\mathcal{A}$, then $\mathcal{B}$ succeeds in outputting a fresh non-injective tag, as long as $\mathsf{bad} \wedge \mathsf{freshT}$ occurs. Consequently,

$$\Pr[\mathsf{win}_3 \wedge \mathsf{bad} \wedge \mathsf{freshT}] \leq \Pr[\mathsf{bad} \wedge \mathsf{freshT}] = \mathsf{Adv}_{\mathsf{LAF}, \mathcal{B}}^{\mathsf{eva}}(1^\lambda). \qquad (23)$$

Combining (21), (22) and (23) together, we have

$$\Pr[\mathsf{win}_3 \wedge \mathsf{bad}] \leq \mathsf{Adv}_{\mathsf{LAF}, \mathcal{B}}^{\mathsf{eva}}(1^\lambda).$$

∎

Claim. $\Pr[\mathsf{win}_3 | \neg\mathsf{bad}] \leq 2^{-\omega(\log \lambda)}$.

Proof. In G_3, adversary $\mathcal{A}$ interacts with the challenger and presents its forgery $(\widetilde{P}, \widetilde{\delta})$ at the end. Define $\mathcal{A}$'s view before it submits its forgery as

$$\boxed{\mathsf{view}} := \left(\mathsf{crs}, P, R, \{\delta_i, P_i, R_i\}_{i \in [\rho]}\right) = \left(\mathsf{crs}, (s, c, t', \sigma), k, \{\delta_i, (s_i, c_i, t_i', \sigma_i), k_i\}_{i \in [\rho]}\right).$$

Given the forgery $(\widetilde{P} = (\widetilde{s}, \widetilde{c}, \widetilde{t'}, \widetilde{\sigma}), \widetilde{\delta})$, $\mathcal{A}$ wins if $\mathsf{Rep}(\mathsf{crs}, \widetilde{P}, w + \widetilde{\delta}) \neq \perp$, $\widetilde{P}$ is fresh and $\mathsf{dis}(\widetilde{\delta}) \leq \mathsf{t}$. In the mean time, $\mathsf{Rep}(\mathsf{crs}, \widetilde{P}, w + \widetilde{\delta}) \neq \perp$ if and only if $\mathsf{dis}(\widetilde{w}, w + \widetilde{\delta}) \leq \mathsf{t}$ and $\widetilde{\sigma} = \widetilde{\sigma}'$ hold, where $\widetilde{w} \leftarrow \mathsf{SS.Rec}(w + \widetilde{\delta}, \widetilde{s})$ and $\widetilde{\sigma}' \leftarrow \mathsf{FEval}(F_{pk}, \widetilde{t}, \widetilde{t'}, \widetilde{w})$. Therefore,

$$\Pr\left[\text{win}_3 \wedge \neg\text{bad}\right] = \Pr\left[\begin{array}{c} \widetilde{P} \text{ is fresh } \wedge \text{ dis}(\widetilde{\delta}) \leq t \wedge \\ \text{dis}(\widetilde{w}, w + \widetilde{\delta}) \leq t \wedge \widetilde{\sigma} = \widetilde{\sigma}' \wedge \neg\text{bad} \end{array} \middle| G_3\right]$$
$$\leq \Pr\left[\text{dis}(\widetilde{w}, w + \widetilde{\delta}) \leq t \wedge \widetilde{\sigma} = \widetilde{\sigma}' \wedge \neg\text{bad} \middle| G_3\right].$$

Now that bad does not occur, then the tag $\widetilde{\text{tag}} = (\widetilde{t} = (\widetilde{s}, \widetilde{c}), \widetilde{t}')$ contained in $\widetilde{P}$ must be an injective tag. Thus $\text{LAF}_{F_{pk}, (t, t')}(\cdot)$ is injective and entropy preserving. This means $\widetilde{\sigma}' := \text{FEval}(F_{pk}, \widetilde{t}, \widetilde{t}', \widetilde{W})$ has the same entropy as $\widetilde{W}$. Consequently, it will be hard for adversary $\mathcal{A}$ to forge a valid $\widetilde{\sigma}$ (i.e., $\widetilde{\sigma} = \widetilde{\sigma}'$) if $\widetilde{W}$ has enough min-entropy conditioned on $\mathcal{A}$'s view in G_3.

The outline of the proof is as follows.

- First, we prove that if $\text{dis}(\widetilde{w}, w + \widetilde{\delta}) \leq t$, then

$$\widetilde{H}_\infty(\widetilde{W} \mid \boxed{\text{view}}) \geq \widetilde{H}_\infty(W \mid \boxed{\text{view}}). \tag{24}$$

- Next, we show that

$$\widetilde{H}_\infty(W \mid \boxed{\text{view}}) \geq \omega(\log \lambda). \tag{25}$$

- Formulas (24) and (25) give $\widetilde{H}_\infty(\widetilde{W} \mid \boxed{\text{view}}) \geq \omega(\log \lambda)$. If the event bad does not happen, $(\widetilde{t}, \widetilde{t}')$ must be an injective tag, hence $\text{LAF}_{F_{pk}, (\widetilde{t}, \widetilde{t}')}(\cdot)$ is an injective function, and $\widetilde{\sigma}' = \text{FEval}(F_{pk}, \widetilde{t}, \widetilde{t}', \widetilde{W})$ preserves the entropy of $\widetilde{W}$. So we have

$$\Pr[\text{win}_3 | \neg\text{bad}] \leq \Pr\left[\text{dis}(\widetilde{w}, w + \widetilde{\delta}) \leq t \wedge \widetilde{\sigma} = \widetilde{\sigma}' \wedge \neg\text{bad} \middle| G_3\right] \leq 2^{-\omega(\log \lambda)}.$$

It remains to prove (24) and (25).

Proof of (24). Define the random variable $\widetilde{W} := \text{SS.Rec}(\widetilde{s}, W + \widetilde{\delta})$, where W is the random variable in the robustness game. Let $w, \widetilde{w}$ denote the values taken by the random variables $W, \widetilde{W}$, respectively. If $\mathcal{A}$ wins, then $\text{dis}(w + \widetilde{\delta}, \widetilde{w}) \leq t$. By Lemma 3, we have

$$\widetilde{H}_\infty\left(\widetilde{W} \mid \left(\text{SS.Gen}(W + \widetilde{\delta}), \boxed{\text{view}}, \widetilde{\delta}\right)\right) \geq \widetilde{H}_\infty\left(W + \widetilde{\delta} \mid \left(\text{SS.Gen}(W + \widetilde{\delta}), \boxed{\text{view}}, \widetilde{\delta}\right)\right). \tag{26}$$

Note that $\text{SS.Gen}(W + \widetilde{\delta}) = \text{SS.Gen}(W) + \text{SS.Gen}(\widetilde{\delta})$. The sketch $s = \text{SS.Gen}(W)$ belongs to $\boxed{\text{view}}$, so $\text{SS.Gen}(W + \widetilde{\delta})$ can be computed from $\boxed{\text{view}}$ and $\widetilde{\delta}$. As a result, according to Eq. (1),

$$\widetilde{H}_\infty\left(W + \widetilde{\delta} \mid \left(\text{SS.Gen}(W + \widetilde{\delta}), \boxed{\text{view}}, \widetilde{\delta}\right)\right) = \widetilde{H}_\infty\left(W + \widetilde{\delta} \mid \left(\boxed{\text{view}}, \widetilde{\delta}\right)\right). \tag{27}$$

Note that $\tilde{\delta}$ is determined by $\mathcal{A}$ after seeing $\boxed{\text{view}}$, therefore, it can be further eliminated from the condition because of Eq. (2), and we have

$$\tilde{H}_\infty \left(W \mid \left(\boxed{\text{view}}, \tilde{\delta} \right) \right) = \tilde{H}_\infty \left(W \mid \boxed{\text{view}} \right). \tag{28}$$

With Eqs. (27) and (28), we have

$$\tilde{H}_\infty \left(W + \tilde{\delta} \mid \left(\mathsf{SS.Gen}(W + \tilde{\delta}), \boxed{\text{view}}, \tilde{\delta} \right) \right) = \tilde{H}_\infty \left(W \mid \boxed{\text{view}} \right). \tag{29}$$

Similarly, we have

$$\tilde{H}_\infty \left(\widetilde{W} \mid \left(\mathsf{SS.Gen}(W + \tilde{\delta}), \boxed{\text{view}}, \tilde{\delta} \right) \right) = \tilde{H}_\infty \left(\widetilde{W} \mid \boxed{\text{view}} \right). \tag{30}$$

Combining (26), (29) and (30), we have

$$\tilde{H}_\infty \left(\widetilde{W} \mid \boxed{\text{view}} \right) \geq \tilde{H}_\infty \left(W \mid \boxed{\text{view}} \right). \tag{31}$$

Proof of (25). The general idea of the proof is that we will, step by step, show that the view of adversary can be perfectly simulated by a simulator with $\mathcal{S}$ and s, where $\mathcal{S} := \{\sigma \mid \sigma = \mathsf{FEval}(F_{pk}, t, t', W) \wedge \mathsf{tag} = (t, t') \in \mathcal{T}_{lossy}\}$ and $s = \mathsf{SS.Gen}(W)$. By the lossiness of LAF, the information of W leaked by $\mathcal{S}$ is at most $\log p$ bits. By the fact that SS is a $(m - \lceil \log p \rceil, \hat{m}, 2t)$-secure sketch and the fact that $\hat{m} - \lceil \log p \rceil \geq \omega(\log \lambda)$, we have that $\tilde{H}_\infty(W \mid \boxed{\text{view}}) \geq \omega(\log \lambda)$. Details can be found in the full version [25]. ∎

Taking all things together, by Eq. (18) and Lemmas 11–14, it follows that

$$\mathsf{Adv}^{\mathsf{rob}}_{\mathsf{rrFE}, \mathcal{A}} \leq \mathsf{Adv}^{\mathsf{ind}}_{\mathsf{LAF}}(1^\lambda) + \varepsilon_{\mathsf{ext}} + \mathsf{Adv}^{\mathsf{eva}}_{\mathsf{LAF}}(1^\lambda) + 2^{-\omega(\log \lambda)}.$$

∎

Corollary 1. *If* SS *is instantiated by a syndrome-based secure sketch,* Ext *is instantiated as Eq. (5),* LAF *is instantiated with the scheme in [15], and* SKEM *is instantiated with the scheme shown in Fig. 3, then the construction in Fig. 4 results in a robustly reusable fuzzy extractor based on the DLIN assumption and the DDH assumption.*

Remark 4. Since there exist efficient linear error correcting codes which can correct linear fraction of errors, the syndrome-based secure sketch is able to correct linear fraction of errors as well, so is our robustly reusable fuzzy extractor.

Acknowledgements. We would like to thank the reviewers for their valuable comments. The authors are supported by the National Natural Science Foundation of China (NSFC No. 61672346).

References

1. Alamélou, Q., et al.: Pseudoentropic isometries: a new framework for fuzzy extractor reusability. In: Kim, J., Ahn, G., Kim, S., Kim, Y., López, J., Kim, T. (eds.) AsiaCCS 2018, pp. 673–684. ACM (2018). http://doi.acm.org/10.1145/3196494. 3196530
2. Apon, D., Cho, C., Eldefrawy, K., Katz, J.: Efficient, reusable fuzzy extractors from LWE. In: Dolev, S., Lodha, S. (eds.) CSCML 2017. LNCS, vol. 10332, pp. 1–18. Springer, Cham (2017). https://doi.org/10.1007/978-3-319-60080-2_1
3. Bennett, C.H., DiVincenzo, D.P.: Quantum information and computation. Nature **404**(6775), 247–255 (2000)
4. Boyen, X.: Reusable cryptographic fuzzy extractors. In: Atluri, V., Pfitzmann, B., McDaniel, P.D. (eds.) CCS 2004, pp. 82–91. ACM (2004). http://doi.acm.org/10. 1145/1030083.1030096
5. Boyen, X., Dodis, Y., Katz, J., Ostrovsky, R., Smith, A.: Secure remote authentication using biometric data. In: Cramer, R. (ed.) EUROCRYPT 2005. LNCS, vol. 3494, pp. 147–163. Springer, Heidelberg (2005). https://doi.org/10.1007/ 11426639_9
6. Canetti, R., Fuller, B., Paneth, O., Reyzin, L., Smith, A.: Reusable fuzzy extractors for low-entropy distributions. In: Fischlin, M., Coron, J.-S. (eds.) EUROCRYPT 2016. LNCS, vol. 9665, pp. 117–146. Springer, Heidelberg (2016). https://doi.org/ 10.1007/978-3-662-49890-3_5
7. Cramer, R., Dodis, Y., Fehr, S., Padró, C., Wichs, D.: Detection of algebraic manipulation with applications to robust secret sharing and fuzzy extractors. In: Smart, N. (ed.) EUROCRYPT 2008. LNCS, vol. 4965, pp. 471–488. Springer, Heidelberg (2008). https://doi.org/10.1007/978-3-540-78967-3_27
8. Cramer, R., Shoup, V.: Design and analysis of practical public-key encryption schemes secure against adaptive chosen ciphertext attack. SIAM J. Comput. **33**(1), 167–226 (2003). https://doi.org/10.1137/S0097539702403773
9. Daugman, J.: How iris recognition works. IEEE Trans. Circuits Syst. Video Techn. **14**(1), 21–30 (2004). https://doi.org/10.1109/TCSVT.2003.818350
10. Dodis, Y., Katz, J., Reyzin, L., Smith, A.: Robust fuzzy extractors and authenticated key agreement from close secrets. In: Dwork, C. (ed.) CRYPTO 2006. LNCS, vol. 4117, pp. 232–250. Springer, Heidelberg (2006). https://doi.org/10. 1007/11818175_14
11. Dodis, Y., Ostrovsky, R., Reyzin, L., Smith, A.D.: Fuzzy extractors: How to generate strong keys from biometrics and other noisy data. SIAM J. Comput. **38**(1), 97–139 (2008). https://doi.org/10.1137/060651380
12. Dodis, Y., Reyzin, L., Smith, A.: Fuzzy extractors: how to generate strong keys from biometrics and other noisy data. In: Cachin, C., Camenisch, J.L. (eds.) EUROCRYPT 2004. LNCS, vol. 3027, pp. 523–540. Springer, Heidelberg (2004). https://doi.org/10.1007/978-3-540-24676-3_31
13. Dodis, Y., Wichs, D.: Non-malleable extractors and symmetric key cryptography from weak secrets. In: Mitzenmacher, M. (ed.) STOC 2009, pp. 601–610. ACM (2009). http://doi.acm.org/10.1145/1536414.1536496
14. Fuller, B., Meng, X., Reyzin, L.: Computational fuzzy extractors. In: Sako, K., Sarkar, P. (eds.) ASIACRYPT 2013. LNCS, vol. 8269, pp. 174–193. Springer, Heidelberg (2013). https://doi.org/10.1007/978-3-642-42033-7_10

15. Hofheinz, D.: Circular chosen-ciphertext security with compact ciphertexts. In: Johansson, T., Nguyen, P.Q. (eds.) EUROCRYPT 2013. LNCS, vol. 7881, pp. 520–536. Springer, Heidelberg (2013). https://doi.org/10.1007/978-3-642-38348-9_31

16. Imamog, A., et al.: Quantum information processing using quantum dot spins and cavity QED. Phys. Rev. Lett. **83**(20), 4204 (1999)

17. Jain, A.K., Ross, A., Prabhakar, S.: An introduction to biometric recognition. IEEE Trans. Circuits Syst. Video Techn. **14**(1), 4–20 (2004). https://doi.org/10.1109/TCSVT.2003.818349

18. Kanukurthi, B., Reyzin, L.: An improved robust fuzzy extractor. In: Ostrovsky, R., De Prisco, R., Visconti, I. (eds.) SCN 2008. LNCS, vol. 5229, pp. 156–171. Springer, Heidelberg (2008). https://doi.org/10.1007/978-3-540-85855-3_11

19. Li, S.Z., Jain, A.K. (eds.): Handbook of Face Recognition, 2nd edn. Springer, Heidelberg (2011). https://doi.org/10.1007/978-0-85729-932-1

20. Marasco, E., Ross, A.: A survey on antispoofing schemes for fingerprint recognition systems. ACM Comput. Surv. **47**(2), 28:1–28:36 (2014). https://doi.org/10.1145/2617756

21. Rührmair, U., Sehnke, F., Sölter, J., Dror, G., Devadas, S., Schmidhuber, J.: Modeling attacks on physical unclonable functions. In: Al-Shaer, E., Keromytis, A.D., Shmatikov, V. (eds.) CCS 2010, pp. 237–249. ACM (2010). http://doi.acm.org/10.1145/1866307.1866335

22. Shoup, V.: A Computational Introduction to Number Theory and Algebra. Cambridge University Press, Cambridge (2006)

23. Suh, G.E., Devadas, S.: Physical unclonable functions for device authentication and secret key generation. In: DAC 2007, pp. 9–14. IEEE (2007). http://doi.acm.org/10.1145/1278480.1278484

24. Wen, Y., Liu, S.: Reusable fuzzy extractor from LWE. In: Susilo, W., Yang, G. (eds.) ACISP 2018. LNCS, vol. 10946, pp. 13–27. Springer, Cham (2018). https://doi.org/10.1007/978-3-319-93638-3_2

25. Wen, Y., Liu, S.: Robustly reusable fuzzy extractor from standard assumptions. Cryptology ePrint Archive, Report 2018/818 (2018). https://eprint.iacr.org/2018/818

26. Wen, Y., Liu, S., Han, S.: Reusable fuzzy extractor from the decisional Diffie-Hellman assumption. Des. Codes Cryptogr. **86**, 2495–2512 (2018). https://doi.org/10.1007/s10623-018-0459-4

Simple and More Efficient PRFs with Tight Security from LWE and Matrix-DDH

Tibor Jager[1][(✉)], Rafael Kurek[1], and Jiaxin Pan[2]

[1] Paderborn University, Paderborn, Germany
{tibor.jager,rafael.kurek}@upb.de
[2] Karlsruhe Institute of Technology, Karlsruhe, Germany
jiaxin.pan@kit.edu

Abstract. We construct efficient and tightly secure pseudorandom functions (PRFs) with only logarithmic security loss and short secret keys. This yields very simple and efficient variants of well-known constructions, including those of Naor-Reingold (FOCS 1997) and Lewko-Waters (ACM CCS 2009). Most importantly, in combination with the construction of Banerjee, Peikert and Rosen (EUROCRYPT 2012) we obtain the currently most efficient LWE-based PRF from a weak LWE-assumption with a much smaller modulus than the original construction. In comparison to the only previous construction with this property, which is due to Döttling and Schröder (CRYPTO 2015), we use a modulus of similar size, but only a *single* instance of the underlying PRF, instead of $\lambda \cdot \omega(\log \lambda)$ parallel instances, where λ is the security parameter. Like Döttling and Schröder, our security proof is only almost back-box, due to the fact that the number of queries made by the adversary and its advantage must be known *a-priori*.

Technically, we introduce *all-prefix* universal hash functions (APUHFs), which are hash functions that are (almost-)universal, even if *any* prefix of the output is considered. We give simple and very efficient constructions of APUHFs, and show how they can be combined with the augmented cascade of Boneh *et al.* (ACM CCS 2010) to obtain our results. Along the way, we develop a new and more direct way to prove security of PRFs based on the augmented cascade.

Keywords: Pseudorandom functions · LWE · MDDH
Augmented cascade · Tight security

1 Introduction

A pseudorandom function (PRF) is a function $F : \mathcal{K} \times \mathcal{D} \rightarrow \mathcal{G}$ with the following security property. For random $k \xleftarrow{\$} \mathcal{K}$, the function $F(k, \cdot)$ is computationally

The first and second authors were supported by DFG grant JA 2445/1-1. The third author was supported by DFG grant HO 4534/4-1.

T. Peyrin and S. Galbraith (Eds.): ASIACRYPT 2018, LNCS 11274, pp. 490–518, 2018.
https://doi.org/10.1007/978-3-030-03332-3_18

indistinguishable from a random function $R(\cdot)$, given oracle access to either $F(k, \cdot)$ or $R(\cdot)$. PRFs are a foundational cryptographic primitive with countless applications, see [Gol01, Bel06, BG90, GGM84, Kra10] for example. While PRFs can be constructed generically from one-way functions (via pseudorandom generators) [GGM86], this generic construction is rather inefficient. Therefore we seek to construct efficient PRFs from as-weak-as-possible assumptions and with tight security proof.

Tight security. In a cryptographic security proof, we often consider an adversary $\mathcal{A}$ against a primitive like a PRF, and describe a reduction $\mathcal{B}$ that runs $\mathcal{A}$ as a subroutine to break some computational problem which is assumed to be hard. Let $(t_{\mathcal{A}}, \epsilon_{\mathcal{A}})$ and $(t_{\mathcal{B}}, \epsilon_{\mathcal{B}})$ denote the running time and success probability of $\mathcal{A}$ and $\mathcal{B}$, respectively. Then we say that the reduction $\mathcal{B}$ *loses* a factor ℓ, if

$$\frac{t_{\mathcal{B}}}{\epsilon_{\mathcal{B}}} \geq \ell \cdot \frac{t_{\mathcal{A}}}{\epsilon_{\mathcal{A}}}$$

A reduction is usually considered "efficient", if ℓ is bounded by a polynomial in the security parameter. We say that a reduction is "tight", if ℓ is small. Our goal is to construct reductions $\mathcal{B}$ such that ℓ is as small as possible. Ideally we would like to have $\ell = O(1)$ constant, but there are many examples of cryptographic constructions and primitives where this is impossible to achieve [Cor02, KK12, HJK12, LW14, BJLS16].

State of the art. Many constructions of efficient number-theoretic PRFs, including the very general Matrix-DDH-based construction of [EHK+17] (with the well-known algebraic constructions of Naor-Reingold [NR97] and Lewko-Waters [LW09] as special cases), as well as the LWE-based PRF of Banerjee, Peikert, and Rosen [BPR12], can in retrospect be seen as concrete instantiations of the *augmented cascade* framework of Boneh et al. [BMR10]. For these constructions, the size of the secret key and the loss in the security proof grow linearly[1] with the length n of the function input. Thus, efficiency and security both depend on the size of the input space. In order to extend the input space to $\{0,1\}^*$, one can generically apply a collision-resistant hash function $H : \{0,1\}^* \rightarrow \{0,1\}^n$, where $n = 2\lambda$ and λ denotes the security parameter, to the input before processing it in the PRF. This yields secret keys consisting of $n = O(\lambda)$ elements (where the concrete type of elements depends on the particular instantiation of the augmented cascade) and a security loss of $\ell = n = O(\lambda)$.

Contributions. We introduce *all-prefix universal hash functions* (APUHFs) as a special type of hash functions that are universal, even if the output of the hash function is truncated. We also describe a very simple and efficient construction, which is based on the hash function of Dietzfelbinger et al. [DHKP97], as well as a generic construction from pairwise independent hash functions with range $\{0,1\}^n$ for some $n \in \mathbb{N}$.

---

[1] As common in the literature, we count the number of elements here, not their bit size that increases with the security parameter.

Then we show that by combining the augmented cascade with an APUHF, we are able to significantly improve both the asymptotic size of secret keys and the security loss of these constructions. Specifically, we achieve keys consisting of only a slightly super-logarithmic number of elements $m = \omega(\log \lambda)$ and an only logarithmic security loss $O(\log \lambda)$. Both the number of elements in the secret key and tightness are *independent* of the input size n, except for the key of the APUHF, which consists of n bits when instantiated with the APUHF of Dietzfelbinger *et al.* [DHKP97]. Based on this generic result, we then obtain simple variants of algebraic PRFs based on a large class of Matrix-DDH assumptions [EHK+17], which include the PRFs of Naor and Reingold [NR97] and its generalization by Lewko and Waters [LW09] as special cases.

Furthermore, we obtain a simple variant of the PRF of Banerjee, Peikert and Rosen [BPR12] (BPR). This PRF is based on the learning-with-errors (LWE) assumption [Reg05], and has the property that the required size of the LWE modulus depends on the length of the PRF input. More precisely, the lower bound on the LWE modulus p is exponential in the input length $n = \Theta(\lambda)$. We observe this in almost all the well-known LWE-based PRFs such as [BLMR13,BP14]. In order to improve efficiency and to base security on a weaker LWE assumption, it is thus desirable to make p as small as possible. We show that simply encoding the PRF input with an APUHF before processing it in the original BPR construction makes it possible to reduce the lower bound on the LWE modulus p from exponential to only slightly super-polynomial in the security parameter, which yields a weaker assumption and a significant efficiency improvement (see Sect. 5.2 for details). Furthermore, even for an arbitrary polynomially-bounded input size n, our construction requires to store only $m = \omega(\log \lambda)$ matrices, independent of the size n of the input space $\{0, 1\}^n$, plus a single bitstring of length n when instantiated with the APUHF of Dietzfelbinger *et al.* [DHKP97]. In contrast, the original construction from [BPR12] requires $\Theta(n)$ matrices.

A similar improvement of the LWE modulus p was achieved by a different BPR variant due to Döttling and Schröder in [DS15], via a technique called *on-the-fly adaptation*. However, their construction requires to run $\lambda \cdot \omega(\log \lambda)$ copies of the BPR PRF in parallel, while ours requires only a single copy plus an APUHF. Thus, our approach is significantly more efficient, and also more direct, as it essentially corresponds to the original BPR function, except that an APUHF is applied to the input. This simplicity gives not only a useful conceptual perspective on the construction of tightly secure PRFs, but it also makes schemes easier to implement securely.

Another advantage of our approach is that the resulting PRF construction is extremely simple. It is essentially identical to the augmented cascade from [BMR10], except that an APUHF h is applied to the input before it is processed by the PRF. More precisely, let $\hat{F}^m$ be a PRF that is constructed from an m-fold application of an underlying function F via the augmented cascade construction from [BMR10]. Then our construction $\hat{F}(K, x)$ has the form

$$\hat{F}(K, x) := \hat{F}^m(s, h(x))$$

where the key of our new function is a tuple $K = (s, h)$ consisting of a random key s for the augmented cascade construction and a random function $h \xleftarrow{\$} \mathcal{H}$ from a family $\mathcal{H} = \{h : \{0,1\}^n \rightarrow \{0,1\}^m\}$ of APUHFs.

We remark that we require an additional property called *perfect one-time security* ("1-uniformity") of the underlying function F of the augmented cascade, and thus technically our variant of [BMR10] is slightly less general. However, this is a minor restriction, as we show that this property is satisfied by all known instantiations of the augmented cascade. Furthermore, our security proof assumes that the reduction "knows" sufficiently close approximations of the number of queries Q and the advantage $\epsilon_{\mathcal{A}}$ of the adversary. Thus, the proof shows how such non-black-box knowledge can be used to achieve more efficient PRFs with short keys and very tight security from weaker assumptions.

Technical approach. Technically, our argument is inspired by the construction of adaptively-secure PRFs from non-adaptively secure ones by Berman and Haitner [BH12]. Essentially, an augmented cascade PRF with m-bit input is a function $\hat{F}^m : S^m \times K \times \{0,1\}^m \rightarrow K$ with key space $S^m \times K$. In the sequel, let $(s_1, \ldots, s_m, k) \in S^m \times K$ be a key for $\hat{F}^m$ and $h : \{0,1\}^n \rightarrow \{0,1\}^m$. For a string $a \in \{0,1\}^m$ we write $a_{v:w}$ to denote the substring $(a_v, \ldots, a_w) \in \{0,1\}^{w-v+1}$ of a. Let j be an integer with $j \leq m$ (we will explain later how to choose j in a suitable way).

We start from the observation that, for each $j \in \{1, \ldots, m\}$, we can implement an augmented cascade PRF $\hat{F}^m$ equivalently as a two-step algorithm, which proceeds as follows.

1. In the first step, the function $\hat{F}^m$ processes only the first j bits $h(x)_{1:j} \in \{0,1\}^j$ of $h(x)$, to compute an intermediate value k_x that depends only on the first j bits of $h(x)$:

$$k_x = \hat{F}^j((s_1, ..., s_j), k, h(x)_{1:j})$$

2. Then the remaining $m - j$ bits are processed, starting from k_x, by computing

$$y = \hat{F}^{m-j}((s_{j+1}, ..., s_m), k_x, h(x)_{j+1:m})$$

The resulting function is identical to the function $\hat{F}^m$, so this is merely a specific way to implement $\hat{F}^m$, which will be particularly useful to describe our approach.

To explain how we prove security, let $x^{(1)}, \ldots, x^{(Q)}$ denote the sequence of pairwise distinct oracle queries issued by the adversary in the PRF security experiment, and suppose for now that it holds $h(x^{(u)})_{1:j} \neq h(x^{(v)})_{1:j}$ for $u \neq v$. Our goal is to show that then the security of $\hat{F}^m$ is implied by the security of $\hat{F}^j$, which is a PRF with shorter input. Intuitively, this holds due to the following two-step argument.

1. We replace $\hat{F}^j$ with a random function R, which is computationally indistinguishable thanks to the security of $\hat{F}^j$. Note that now the intermediate value $k_x = R(h(x)_{1:j})$ is an independent random value for each oracle query made by the adversary, because we assume $h(x^{(u)})_{1:j} \neq h(x^{(v)})_{1:j}$ for $u \neq v$.

2. Next we argue that now also $\hat{F}^m$ is distributed exactly like a random function. We achieve this by identifying an additional property required from $\hat{F}^{m-j}$ that we call *perfect one-time security*. This property guarantees that

$$\Pr_{k_x \overset{\$}{\leftarrow} K} \left[\hat{F}^{m-j}((s_{j+1}, ..., s_m), k_x, h(x)_{j+1:m}) = y \right] = \frac{1}{|K|}$$

for all $(s_{j+1}, ..., s_m), h(x)_{j+1:m}, y) \in S^{m-j} \times \{0,1\}^{m-j} \times K$. This is sufficient to show that indeed now the function

$$\hat{F}^{m-j}((s_{j+1}, ..., s_m), R(h(x)_{1:j}), h(x)_{j+1:m})$$

is a random function, because we have $h(x^{(u)})_{1:j} \neq h(x^{(v)})_{1:j}$ for $u \neq v$.

It remains to ensure that $h(x^{(u)})_{1:j} \neq h(x^{(v)})_{1:j}$ holds for all $u \neq v$ with "sufficiently large" probability and for some "sufficiently small" value of j. Here we use the all-prefix universal hash function, in combination with an argument which on a high level follows similar proofs from [BH12] and [DS15]. The main difference is that we use the all-prefix universality to argue that setting $j := \lceil \log(2Q^2/\epsilon_{\mathcal{A}}) \rceil = O(\log \lambda)$, where Q is the number of oracle queries made by the adversary in the PRF security experiment and $\epsilon_{\mathcal{A}}$ is its advantage, is sufficient to guarantee that $h(x^{(u)})_{1:j} \neq h(x^{(v)})_{1:j}$ holds with sufficiently large probability for all $u \neq v$.

Note that we have $j = O(\log \lambda)$, so that we only have to require security of a "short-input" augmented cascade $\hat{F}^j$ with $j = O(\log \lambda)$. For our algebraic instantiations based on Matrix-DDH problems, this yields tightness with a security loss of only $O(\log \lambda)$. For our application to the LWE-based PRF of Banerjee, Peikert and Rosen [BPR12], this yields that we have to require only a weaker LWE assumption. Furthermore, since we need only that $m \geq j$ holds for all possible values of j, and we have $j = \lceil \log(2Q^2/\epsilon_{\mathcal{A}}) \rceil = O(\log \lambda)$, it is sufficient to set $m = \omega(\log \lambda)$ slightly super-logarithmic, which yields short secret keys and efficient evaluation for all instantiations.

Our proof technique, in particular the perfect one-time security property, can also be seen as an alternative and more direct way of proving the augmented cascade construction secure, while Boneh et al. used the somewhat more complex q-parallel security of the underlying PRF.

Why all-prefix *universal hash functions?* We stress that we need an *all-prefix* universal hash function, which works for any possible prefix length j. This is necessary to make the construction and the security proof independent of particular values Q and $\epsilon_{\mathcal{A}}$ of a particular adversary, because j depends on these values via the definition $j = \lceil \log(2Q^2/\epsilon_{\mathcal{A}}) \rceil$. *All-prefix* universality guarantees basically that a suitable value of j exists for any efficient adversary. This is also required to achieve tightness. See Sect. 4.7 for further discussion.

More related work. There were several other works about the domain extension of PRFs. The first one is due to Levin [Lev87]. It shows that larger inputs can be hashed with a universal hash function if the underlying PRF has a sufficiently large domain. Otherwise it is vulnerable to the so called "birthday attack". The framework of Jain, Pietrzak, and Tentes [JPT12] works for small domains, but has a rather lossy security proof and is not very efficient, as it needs $\mathcal{O}(\log q)$ invocations of the underlying pseudo-random generator (PRG), where q is the upper bound of queries to the PRF. Additionally, as the authors already mention, it seems not to work for number-theoretic PRFs like the Naor-Reingold PRF. It was revisited by Chandran and Garg [CG14]. Bernam *et al.* show how to circumvent the "birthday attack" using Cuckoo Hashing [BHKN13] via two invocations of the original PRF.

2 Preliminaries

Let $\lambda \in \mathbb{N}$ denote a security parameter. All our results are in the asymptotic setting, that is, we view all expressions involving λ as functions in λ. This includes the running time $t_{\mathcal{A}} = t_{\mathcal{A}}(\lambda)$ and success probability $\epsilon_{\mathcal{A}} = \epsilon_{\mathcal{A}}(\lambda)$ of adversaries, even though we occasionally omit λ in this case to simplify our notation. Similarly, all algorithms implicitly receive the security parameter 1^{λ} as their first input. We say that an algorithm is *efficient*, if it runs in (probabilistic) polynomial time in λ.

Notation. If A is a finite set, then we write $a \xleftarrow{\$} A$ to denote the action of sampling a uniformly random element a from A. If A is a probabilistic algorithm, then $a \xleftarrow{\$} A(x)$ denotes the action of running $A(x)$ on input x with uniform coins and output a. For $v, w \in \mathbb{N}$ and $v < w$, we write $[\![v, w]\!] := \{v, \ldots, w\} \subset \mathbb{N}$ to denote the interval of positive integers from v to w, and set $[\![w]\!] := \{1, \ldots, w\} \subset \mathbb{N}$. For a bit string $a = (a_1, \ldots, a_n) \in \{0,1\}^n$ and $v, w \in [\![n]\!]$ with $v \leq w$, we write $a_{v:w}$ to denote the substring $(a_v, \ldots, a_w)$ of a, and a_i to denote the i-th bit a_i.

2.1 Pseudorandom Functions

Let $\mathcal{K}, \mathcal{D}$ be sets such that there is an efficient algorithm that samples uniformly random elements $k \xleftarrow{\$} \mathcal{K}$. Let $F : \mathcal{K} \times \mathcal{D} \rightarrow \mathcal{G}$ be an efficiently computable function. For an adversary $\mathcal{A}$ define the following security experiment $\mathsf{Exp}_{\mathcal{A},F}^{\mathsf{prf}}(\lambda)$.

1. The experiment generates a random key $k \xleftarrow{\$} \mathcal{K}$ and tosses a coin $b \xleftarrow{\$} \{0,1\}$.
2. The experiment provides adversary $\mathcal{A}^{\mathcal{O}}(1^{\lambda})$ with an oracle $\mathcal{O}$ which takes as input $x \in \mathcal{D}$ and responds as follows.

$$\mathcal{O}(x) = \begin{cases} F(k, x) & \text{if } b = 1 \\ R(x) & \text{if } b = 0 \end{cases}$$

where $R : \mathcal{D} \rightarrow \mathcal{G}$ is a random function. When the adversary terminates and outputs a bit b', then the experiment outputs 1 if $b = b'$, and 0 otherwise.

Let $x_1, \ldots, x_Q \in \mathcal{D}$ be the sequence of queries issued by $\mathcal{A}$ throughout the security experiment. We assume that we always have $Q \geq 1$, as otherwise the output of $\mathcal{A}$ is independent of b. Furthermore, we assume that $\mathcal{A}$ never issues the same query twice. More precisely, we assume $x_u \neq x_v$ for $u \neq v$. This is without loss of generality, since both $F(k, \cdot)$ and $R(\cdot)$ are deterministic functions.

Definition 1. *We say that adversary $\mathcal{A}$ $(t_{\mathcal{A}}, \epsilon_{\mathcal{A}}, Q)$-breaks the pseudorandomness of F, if $\mathcal{A}$ runs in time $t_{\mathcal{A}}$, issues Q queries in the PRF security experiment, and*

$$\Pr\left[\mathsf{Exp}^{\mathsf{prf}}_{\mathcal{A}, F}(\lambda) = 1\right] \geq 1/2 + \epsilon_{\mathcal{A}}$$

2.2   (Almost-)Universal Hash Functions

Let us first recall the standard definition of universal hash functions.

Definition 2 ([CW79]). *A family $\mathcal{H}$ of hash functions mapping finite set $\{0, 1\}^n$ to finite set $\{0, 1\}^m$ is* universal, *if for all $x, x' \in \{0, 1\}^n$ with $x \neq x'$ holds that*

$$\Pr_{h \xleftarrow{\$} \mathcal{H}} [h(x) = h(x')] \leq 2^{-m}.$$

We will also consider *almost-universal* hash functions, as defined below.

Definition 3. *A family $\mathcal{H}$ of hash functions mapping finite set $\{0, 1\}^n$ to finite set $\{0, 1\}^m$ is* almost-universal, *if for all $x, x' \in \{0, 1\}^n$ with $x \neq x'$ holds that*

$$\Pr_{h \xleftarrow{\$} \mathcal{H}} [h(x) = h(x')] \leq 2^{-m+1}.$$

Universal and almost-universal hash functions can be constructed efficiently and without additional complexity assumptions, see e.g. [CW79, DHKP97, IKOS08].

3   All-Prefix Universal Hash Functions

In this section, we define all-prefix almost universal hash functions and describe two constructions. The first one is based on the almost-universal hash function of Dietzfelbinger *et al.* [DHKP97], and yields an all-prefix almost-universal hash function. The second one is based on pairwise independent hash functions with suitable range, and yields an all-prefix universal hash function.

3.1   Definitions

Recall that for a bit string $a = (a_1, \ldots, a_n) \in \{0, 1\}^n$ and $v, w \in [\![n]\!]$ with $v \leq w$, we write $a_{v:w} := (a_v, \ldots, a_w)$.

Definition 4. *Let $\mathcal{H}$ be a family of hash functions mapping $\{0, 1\}^n$ to $\{0, 1\}^m$. We say that $\mathcal{H}$ is a family of* all-prefix universal *hash functions, if for all $x, x' \in \{0, 1\}^n$ with $x \neq x'$ and all $w \in [\![m]\!]$ holds that*

$$\Pr_{h \xleftarrow{\$} \mathcal{H}} [h(x)_{1:w} = h(x')_{1:w}] \leq 2^{-w}.$$

Note that all-prefix universality essentially means that for all prefixes of length w the truncation of h to its first w bits $h(x)_{1:w}$ is a universal hash function. We also define the slightly weaker notion of all-prefix *almost*-universality.

Definition 5. *Let $\mathcal{H}$ be a family of hash functions mapping $\{0,1\}^n$ to $\{0,1\}^m$. We say that $\mathcal{H}$ is a family of all-prefix almost-universal hash functions (APUHFs), if for all $x, x' \in \{0,1\}^n$ with $x \neq x'$ and all $w \in [\![m]\!]$ holds that*

$$\Pr_{h \xleftarrow{\$} \mathcal{H}} [h(x)_{1:w} = h(x')_{1:w}] \leq 2^{-w+1}.$$

3.2 First Construction (Almost-Universal)

We construct a simple and efficient APUHF family based on the almost-universal hash function of Dietzfelbinger *et al.* [DHKP97], which is defined as follows. Let $m, n \in \mathbb{N}$ with $m \leq n$. Let

$$\mathcal{H}_{n,m} := \{h_a : a \in [\![2^n - 1]\!] \text{ and } a \text{ is odd}\} \tag{1}$$

be the family of hash functions, which for $x \in \mathbb{Z}_{2^n}$ is defined as

$$h_a(x) := (ax \bmod 2^n) \operatorname{div} 2^{n-m}, \tag{2}$$

Before we prove that this function is all-prefix almost-universal, we first state the following lemma of Dietzfelbinger *et al.* [DHKP97].

Lemma 1 ([DHKP97]). *Let n and m be positive integers with $m \in [\![n]\!]$. If $x, y \in \mathbb{Z}_{2^n}$ are distinct and $h_a \in \mathcal{H}_{n,m}$ is chosen at random, then*

$$\Pr[h_a(x) = h_a(y)] \leq 2^{-m+1}$$

Thus, $\mathcal{H}_{n,m}$ is a family of almost-universal hash functions in the sense of Definition 3.

All-prefix almost-universality of $\mathcal{H}_{n,m}$. Now we prove that the hash function family $\mathcal{H}_{n,m}$ of Dietzfelbinger *et al.* [DHKP97] is not only almost-universal, but also satisfies the stronger property of *all-prefix* almost-universality.

Theorem 1. *$\mathcal{H}_{n,m}$ is a family of all-prefix almost-universal hash functions in the sense of Definition 5.*

Proof. Let ω, m, n be any positive integers with $\omega \leq m \leq n$. Note that if $h_a(\cdot)$ is a function in $\mathcal{H}_{n,m}$ then $h_a(\cdot)_{1:\omega}$ is a function in $\mathcal{H}_{n,\omega}$. Further note that Lemma 1 holds for all $\omega \in [\![n]\!]$, which proves the claim. $\square$

In the sequel, we will sometimes write h instead of h_a, when it is clear from the context that h is be chosen uniformly random from $\mathcal{H}_{n,m}$.

3.3   Second Construction (Universal)

While the almost-universal construction from Sect. 3.2 is already sufficient for all our applications, it is natural to ask whether also all-prefix *universal* hash functions (not almost-universal) can be constructed. We will show that each pairwise-independent family of hash functions with range $\{0,1\}^n$ is also a family of all-prefix universal hash functions. To this end, let us first recall the notion of pairwise independent hash functions.

Definition 6. *Let $\mathcal{H}$ be a family of hash functions with domain $\{0,1\}^n$ and range $\{0,1\}^m$. We say that $\mathcal{H}$ is* pairwise independent, *if for all $x, x' \in \{0,1\}^n$ with $x \neq x'$ and all $y, z \in \{0,1\}^m$ holds that*

$$\Pr_{h \xleftarrow{\$} \mathcal{H}} [h(x) = y \wedge h(x') = z] = 2^{-2m}.$$

We first show that pairwise independence implies all-prefix pairwise independence, which is defined below. Then we show that this implies all-prefix universality.

Let us write x_i to denote the i-th bit of the bit string x.

Definition 7. *Let $\mathcal{H}$ be a family of hash functions mapping $\{0,1\}^n$ to $\{0,1\}^m$. We say that $\mathcal{H}$ is* all-prefix pairwise independent, *if for all $x, x' \in \{0,1\}^n$ with $x \neq x'$ and all $y, z' \in \{0,1\}^m$ holds that*

$$\Pr_{h \xleftarrow{\$} \mathcal{H}} [h(x)_{1:w} = y_{1:w} \wedge h(x')_{1:w} = z_{1:w}] = 2^{-2w}$$

for all $w \in [\![m]\!]$.

Lemma 2. *If $\mathcal{H}$ is pairwise independent, then it is also all-prefix pairwise independent.*

Proof. We have

$$\Pr_{h \xleftarrow{\$} \mathcal{H}} [h(x)_{1:j} = y_{1:j} \wedge h(x')_{1:j} = z_{1:j}]$$

$$= \Pr_{h \xleftarrow{\$} \mathcal{H}} \left[\left(\bigcup_{y' \in \{0,1\}^{m-j}} h(x) = (y_{1:j} \parallel y') \right) \wedge \left(\bigcup_{z' \in \{0,1\}^{m-j}} h(x') = (z_{1:j} \parallel z') \right) \right]$$

$$= \sum_{y' \in \{0,1\}^{m-j}} \sum_{z' \in \{0,1\}^{m-j}} \Pr_{h \xleftarrow{\$} \mathcal{H}} [h(x) = (y_{1:j} \parallel y') \wedge h(x') = (z_{1:j} \parallel z')]$$

$$= \sum_{y' \in \{0,1\}^{m-j}} \sum_{z' \in \{0,1\}^{m-j}} \frac{1}{2^{2m}} = \frac{2^{m-j} \cdot 2^{m-j}}{2^{2m}} = \frac{1}{2^{2j}}.$$

$\square$

Now it remains to show that all-prefix pairwise independence implies all-prefix universality.

Lemma 3. *If $\mathcal{H}$ is all-prefix pairwise independent, then it is also all-prefix universal.*

Proof. It holds that

$$\Pr_{h \xleftarrow{\$} \mathcal{H}} [h(x)_{1:j} = h(x')_{1:j}] = \sum_{y_{1:j} \in \{0,1\}^j} \Pr_{h \xleftarrow{\$} \mathcal{H}} [h(x)_{1:j} = y_{1:j} \wedge h(x')_{1:j} = y_{1:j}] \quad (3)$$

$$= \sum_{y_{1:j} \in \{0,1\}^j} \frac{1}{2^{2j}} = \frac{1}{2^j},$$

where (3) holds because of Lemma 2. $\qquad\qquad\square$

Example instantiation. Let $n \in \mathbb{N}$ and let

$$\mathcal{H}_n := \{h_{a,b} : a, b \in \{0,1\}^n\}$$

be the family of hash functions

$$h_{a,b} : GF(2^n) \to GF(2^n); x \mapsto ax + b,$$

where the arithmetic operations are in $GF(2^n)$. Since it is well-known that $\mathcal{H}_n$ is pairwise independent we leave the following theorem without proof.

Theorem 2. *$\mathcal{H}_n$ is a family of all-prefix universal hash functions.*

Note that in the explicit construction of $GF(2^n)$ the choice of the irreducible polynomial has big impact on the efficiency of the arithmetic operations.

4   Augmented Cascade PRFs with Tighter Security

In this section, we show that APUHFs enable the instantiation of augmented cascade PRFs [BMR10] with shorter keys of slightly super-logarithmic size $\omega(\log \lambda)$. The security proof loses only a factor $O(\log \lambda)$, independent of the input size of the PRF, assuming that (reasonably close bounds) on the number of queries Q and the success probability $1/2 + \epsilon_{\mathcal{A}}$ of the PRF adversary $\mathcal{A}$ are known *a priori*. In contrast, the loss of the previous security proof of [BMR10] is linear in the input size of the PRF (which is usually linear in λ), but does not assume any *a priori* knowledge about $\mathcal{A}$.

4.1   Augmented Cascade PRFs

Boneh *et al.* [BMR10] showed how to construct a PRF

$$\hat{F}^m : (S^m \times K) \times X^m \to K$$

with key space $(S^m \times K)$ and input space X from an augmented cascade of functions

$$F : (S \times K) \times X \to K$$

The augmented cascade construction is described in Fig. 1. Boneh *et al.* [BMR10] prove that $\hat{F}^m$ is a secure PRF, if F is *parallel secure* in the following sense.

> **Input:** Key $(s_1, ..., s_m, k_0) \in S^m \times K$ and $(x_1, ..., x_m) \in X^m$
> For $i = 1, ..., m$:
> $k_i \leftarrow F((s_i, k_{i-1}), x_i)$
> Return k_m.

Fig. 1. Definition of function $\hat{F}^m$ of Boneh *et al.* [BMR10].

Definition 8 ([BMR10]). *For a function $F : (S \times K) \times X \to K$ define $F^{(Q)}$ as the function*

$$F^{(Q)} : (S \times K^Q) \times (X \times [\![Q]\!]) \to K \qquad ((s, k_1, ..., k_q), (x, i)) \mapsto F((s, k_i), x).$$

We say that $\mathcal{A}$ $(t_{\mathcal{A}}, \epsilon_{\mathcal{A}}, Q)$-breaks the Q-parallel security of $F : (S \times K) \times X \to K$, if it $(t_{\mathcal{A}}, \epsilon_{\mathcal{A}}, Q)$-breaks the pseudorandomness of $F^{(Q)}$ in the sense of Definition 1.

Theorem 3 ([BMR10]). *From each adversary $\mathcal{A}$ that $(t_{\mathcal{A}}, \epsilon_{\mathcal{A}}, Q)$-breaks the pseudorandomness of $\hat{F}^m$, one can construct an adversary $\mathcal{B}$ that $(t_{\mathcal{B}}, \epsilon_{\mathcal{B}}, Q)$-breaks the Q-parallel security of $F^{(Q)}$ with*

$$t_{\mathcal{B}} = \Theta(t_{\mathcal{A}}) \qquad and \qquad \epsilon_{\mathcal{B}} \geq \frac{\epsilon_{\mathcal{A}}}{m}$$

Note that the security loss of this construction is linear in the length m of the input of function $\hat{F}^m$.

4.2   The Augmented Cascade with Encoded Input

We consider augmented cascade PRFs which are almost identical to the construction of Boneh *et al.* [BMR10], except that we apply an all-prefix almost-universal hash function to the input before processing it in the augmented cascade, and show that this enables a tighter security proof. We consider the special case with input space $X = \{0, 1\}$, which encompasses the MDDH-based construction of Escala *et al.* [EHK+17] and thus includes in particular both the instantiations of Naor-Reingold [NR97] and Lewko-Waters [LW09].

Let $\mathcal{H}_{n,m}$ be a family of all-prefix almost-universal hash functions according to Definition 5, and let $F : (S \times K) \times \{0, 1\} \to K$ be a function. We define the corresponding augmented cascade PRF with $\mathcal{H}_{n,m}$-encoded input as the function

$$\hat{F}^{\mathcal{H}_{n,m}} : S^m \times K \times \mathcal{H}_{n,m} \times \{0, 1\}^n \to K$$

$$((s_1, ..., s_m), k, h, x) \mapsto \hat{F}^m((s_1, ..., s_m), k, h(x)) \qquad (4)$$

where $\hat{F}^m$ is the augmented cascade construction of Boneh *et al.* [BMR10], applied to F as described in Fig. 1.

Remark 1. Note that evaluating the PRF requires only m recursions in the augmented cascade, and that, accordingly, the secret key consists of only m elements and the description of h, while the input size can be any polynomial number of n bits, with possibly $n \gg m$. We will later show that it suffices to set $m = \omega(\log \lambda)$ slightly super-logarithmic, thanks to the input encoding with an all-prefix almost-universal hash function. Also the security loss of this construction is only $O(\log \lambda)$ and independent of the size of the input n.

4.3   Preparation for the Security Proof

In this section we describe a few technical observations which will simplify the security proof. Furthermore, we define *perfect one-time security* as an additional property of a function $F(s, x, k)$, which will also be required for the proof. We will argue later that the Matrix-DDH-based instantiations of the augmented cascade of [EHK+17], including the functions of Naor-Reingold [NR97] and Lewko-Waters [LW09], all satisfy this additional notion. Moreover, we will show that the LWE-based PRF of [BPR12] can be viewed as an augmented cascade and it is perfectly one-time secure.

An observation about the augmented cascade. The following observation will be useful to follow the security proof more easily. Suppose we want to compute

$$z = \hat{F}^m((s_1, ..., s_m), k, h(x))$$

then, due to the recursive definition of $\hat{F}^m$, we can equivalently proceed in the following two steps.

1. Let $i \in [\![m]\!]$. We first process the first i bits $h(x)_{1:i}$ of $h(x)$ with $(s_1, \ldots, s_i, k)$, and compute and "intermediate key" k_x as

$$k_x := \hat{F}^i((s_1, \ldots, s_i), k, h(x)_{1:i})$$

2. Then we process the remaining $m-i$ bits $h(x)_{i+1:m}$ of $h(x)$ with the remaining key elements $(s_{i+1}, \ldots, s_m, k_x)$ by computing

$$z = \hat{F}^{m-i}((s_{i+1}, ..., s_m), k_x, h(x)_{i+1:m})$$

We formulate this observation as a lemma.

Lemma 4. *For all $i \in [\![m]\!]$, we have*

$$\hat{F}^m((s_1, ..., s_m), k, h(x)) = \hat{F}^{m-i}((s_{i+1}, ..., s_m), k_x, h(x)_{i+1:m})$$

where $k_x := \hat{F}^i((s_1, \ldots, s_i), k, h(x)_{1:i})$.

Perfect One-Time Security. We will furthermore require an additional security property of F, which we call *perfect one-time security*, and show that this property is satisfied by all instantiations of function F considered in this section. We demand that $F(s, x, k)$ is identically distributed to a random function $R(x)$, if it is only evaluated once. This must hold over the uniformly random choice $k \xleftarrow{\$} K$, and for any $s \in S$ and $x \in \{0, 1\}$.

Definition 9. *We say that a function* $F : S \times K \times \{0,1\}^m \to K$ *is* perfectly one-time secure, *if*

$$\Pr_{k \xleftarrow{\$} K} [F(s,k,x) = k'] = \frac{1}{|K|}$$

for all $(s, x, k') \in S \times \{0,1\}^m \times K$.

Perfect one-time security basically guarantees uniformity of the hash function, if it is evaluated only once ("1-uniformity").

The following lemma follows directly from Definition 9. It will be useful to prove security of our variant of the augmented cascade.

Lemma 5. *Let* $m \in \mathbb{N}$ *and* $F : S \times K \times \{0,1\} \to K$ *be perfectly one-time secure. Then the augmented cascade* $\hat{F}^m$ *constructed from* F *is also perfectly one-time secure. That is*

$$\Pr_{k \xleftarrow{\$} K} \left[\hat{F}^m((s_1, ..., s_m), k, x) = k' \right] = \frac{1}{|K|}$$

for all $((s_1, ..., s_m), k', x) \in S^m \times K \times \{0,1\}^m$.

Proof. For a uniformly random chosen k it holds that $\Pr[F(s_1, k, x_1) = k_1] = \frac{1}{|K|}$ for all $(s_1, k, x_1) \in S \times K \times \{0,1\}$ because of the perfect one-time security of F. Thus the input for the second iteration stays uniformly random. Due to the recursive construction executing all the following iterations will keep this distribution, which gives us the perfect one-time security of $\hat{F}^m$.   □

4.4   Security Proof

Now we are ready to prove the following theorem.

Theorem 4. *Let* $m = \omega(\log \lambda)$ *be (slightly) super-logarithmic,* $\mathcal{H}_{n,m}$ *be a family of all-prefix almost universal hash functions and* F *be perfectly one-time secure.*
From each adversary $\mathcal{A}$ *that* $(t_\mathcal{A}, \epsilon_\mathcal{A}, Q)$-*breaks the pseudorandomness of* $\hat{F}^{\mathcal{H}_{n,m}}$ *with* $Q/\epsilon_\mathcal{A} = \mathsf{poly}(\lambda)$ *for some polynomial* poly, *we can construct an adversary* $\mathcal{B}$ *that* $(t_\mathcal{B}, \epsilon_\mathcal{B}, Q)$-*breaks the pseudorandomness of* $\hat{F}^j$, *where*

$$j = O(\log \lambda) \qquad and \qquad t_\mathcal{B} = \Theta(t_\mathcal{A}) \qquad and \qquad \epsilon_\mathcal{B} \geq \epsilon_\mathcal{A}/2$$

Proof. In the sequel let $j = j(\lambda)$ be defined such that

$$j := \lceil \log(2Q^2/\epsilon_\mathcal{A}) \rceil \tag{5}$$

Observe that we have $j(\lambda) \leq m(\lambda)$ for sufficiently large λ, because the fact that we have $Q/\epsilon_\mathcal{A} = \mathsf{poly}(\lambda)$ for some polynomial poly and $j < \log(2Q^2/\epsilon_\mathcal{A}) + 1$ together yield that $j = O(\log \lambda)$, while we have $m = \omega(\log \lambda)$.

Remark 2. Note that although we have $j = O(\log(2Q^2/\epsilon_\mathcal{A})) = O(\log \lambda)$, the constant hidden in the big-O notation depends on the adversary.

We describe a sequence of games, where Game 0 is the original PRF security experiment, and in the last game the probability that the experiment outputs 1 is $1/2$, such that no adversary can have any advantage. Let X_i denote the event that the experiment outputs 1 in Game i, and let $\mathcal{O}_i$ denote the oracle provided by the experiment in Game i.

Game 0. This is the original security experiment. In particular, we have

$$\mathcal{O}_0(x) = \begin{cases} \hat{F}^{\mathcal{H}_{n,m}}((s_1, ..., s_m), k, h, x) & \text{if } b = 1 \\ R(x) & \text{if } b = 0 \end{cases}$$

where R is a random function. Therefore, by definition, it holds that

$$\Pr[X_0] = 1/2 + \epsilon_{\mathcal{A}}$$

Game 1. We change the way how the oracle implements function $\hat{F}^{\mathcal{H}_{n,m}}$. That is, we modify the behaviour of $\mathcal{O}_1$ in case $b = 1$, while in case $b = 0$ oracle $\mathcal{O}_1$ proceeds identical to $\mathcal{O}_0$. Recall that

$$\hat{F}^{\mathcal{H}_{n,m}}((s_1, ..., s_m), k, h, x) = \hat{F}^m((s_1, ..., s_m), k, h(x))$$

$\mathcal{O}_1$ implements this function in a specific way. Using the observation from Lemma 4, it computes $\hat{F}^m((s_1, ..., s_m), k, h(x))$ in two steps:

1. $k_x := \hat{F}^j((s_1, \ldots, s_j), k, h(x)_{1:j})$,
2. $z := \hat{F}^{m-j}((s_{j+1}, ..., s_m), k_x, h(x)_{j+1:m})$,

where j is as defined above, and we use that $j \le m$. By Lemma 4, this is just a specific way to implement function $\hat{F}^m$, so the change is purely conceptual and we have

$$\Pr[X_1] = \Pr[X_0]$$

Game 2. This game is identical to Game 1, except that we replace the function $\hat{F}^m$ implemented by oracle $\mathcal{O}_1$ *partially* with a random function. More precisely, oracle $\mathcal{O}_2$ chooses a second random function $R_j : \{0,1\}^j \to K$. If $b = 1$, then it computes $z = \mathcal{O}_2(x)$ as

1. $k_x := R_j(h(x)_{1:j})$
2. $z := \hat{F}^{m-j}((s_{j+1}, ..., s_m), k_x, h(x)_{j+1:m})$

If $b = 0$, then it proceeds exactly like $\mathcal{O}_1$. The proof of the following lemma is postponed to Sect. 4.5.

Lemma 6. *From each $\mathcal{A}$ that runs in time $t_{\mathcal{A}}$ and issues Q oracle queries one can construct an adversary $\mathcal{B}$ that $(t_{\mathcal{B}}, \epsilon_{\mathcal{B}}, Q)$-breaks the pseudorandomness of $\hat{F}^j$ where*

$$t_{\mathcal{B}} = \Theta(t_{\mathcal{A}}) \quad and \quad \epsilon_{\mathcal{B}} = |\Pr[X_1] - \Pr[X_2]| \tag{6}$$

Game 3. This game is identical to Game 2, but $\mathcal{O}_3$ performs an additional check. Whenever $\mathcal{A}$ makes an oracle query x, $\mathcal{O}_3$ checks whether there has been a previous oracle query x' such that

$$h(x)_{1:j} = h(x')_{1:j}$$

If this holds, then $\mathcal{O}_3$ raises event coll, and the experiment outputs a random bit and terminates. Note that the check is always performed, for both values $b \in \{0, 1\}$. Since both games are identical until coll, we have

$$|\Pr[X_2] - \Pr[X_3]| \leq \Pr[\text{coll}]$$

Again, the proof of the following lemma is postponed, to Sect. 4.6.

Lemma 7. *If F is perfectly one-time secure, then* $\Pr[\text{coll}] \leq \epsilon_{\mathcal{A}}/2$ *and* $\Pr[X_3 \mid \overline{\text{coll}}] = 1/2$.

We finish the proof of Theorem 4 before we prove Lemmas 6 and 7. We have

$$\Pr[X_3] = \Pr[X_3 \mid \text{coll}] \cdot \Pr[\text{coll}] + \Pr[X_3 \mid \overline{\text{coll}}] \cdot (1 - \Pr[\text{coll}]) \qquad (7)$$

Recall that X_3 denotes the probability that the experiment outputs 1, which happens if and only if $\mathcal{A}$ outputs b' with $b = b'$. By construction of the experiment, we abort and output a random bit in Game 3, if coll occurs. In combination with Lemma 7 we thus get

$$\Pr[X_3 \mid \text{coll}] = \Pr[X_3 \mid \overline{\text{coll}}] = 1/2$$

Plugging this into (7) yields

$$\Pr[X_3] = 1/2 \cdot \Pr[\text{coll}] + 1/2 \cdot (1 - \Pr[\text{coll}]) = 1/2 \qquad (8)$$

Lower bound on $\epsilon_{\mathcal{B}}$. Finally, using (8), the bounds from Lemmas 6 and 7, and the fact that $\Pr[X_0] = \Pr[X_1]$, we obtain a lower bound on $\epsilon_{\mathcal{B}}$:

$$1/2 + \epsilon_{\mathcal{A}} = \Pr[X_0] = \Pr[X_1] \leq \Pr[X_2] + \epsilon_{\mathcal{B}} \leq 1/2 + \epsilon_{\mathcal{A}}/2 + \epsilon_{\mathcal{B}}$$
$$\Longleftrightarrow \quad \epsilon_{\mathcal{B}} \geq \epsilon_{\mathcal{A}}/2$$

Furthermore, by Lemma 6, algorithm $\mathcal{B}$ runs in time $t_{\mathcal{B}} = \Theta(t_{\mathcal{A}})$ and issues Q oracle queries. $\qquad\square$

4.5   Proof of Lemma 6

Adversary $\mathcal{B}$ plays the pseudorandomness security experiment with function $\hat{F}^j$. Let $\mathcal{O}$ denote the PRF oracle provided to $\mathcal{B}$ in this game. $\mathcal{B}$ runs $\mathcal{A}$ as a subroutine by simulating the security experiment as follows.

Initialization. $\mathcal{B}$ samples a bit $b \xleftarrow{\$} \{0, 1\}$, a hash function $h \leftarrow \mathcal{H}_{n,m}$, and picks $(s_{j+1}, ..., s_m)$, where $s_i \leftarrow S$ for all $i \in [\![j + 1, m]\!]$.

Handling of oracle queries. Whenever $\mathcal{A}$ queries $x \in \{0,1\}^n$, $\mathcal{B}$ proceeds as follows.

- If $b = 0$, then $\mathcal{B}$ proceeds exactly like the original experiment. That is, it responds with $R(x)$, where $R : \{0,1\}^n \to K$ is a random function.
- If $b = 1$, then $\mathcal{B}$ computes $h(x)$ and queries $\mathcal{O}$ to obtain $k_x := \mathcal{O}(h(x)_{1:j})$. Then it computes

$$z := \hat{F}^{m-j}((s_{j+1}, ..., s_m), k_x, h(x)_{j+1:m})$$

and returns z to $\mathcal{A}$.

Finalization. Finally, when $\mathcal{A}$ terminates, then $\mathcal{B}$ outputs whatever $\mathcal{A}$ outputs, and terminates.

Analysis of $\mathcal{B}$. Note that the running time of $\mathcal{B}$ is essentially identical to the running time of $\mathcal{A}$ plus a minor number of additional operations, thus we have $t_{\mathcal{B}} = \Theta(t_{\mathcal{A}})$. If $\mathcal{O}(x) = \hat{F}^j((s_1, ..., s_j, k), h(x)_{1:j})$, then by Lemma 4 it holds that $z = \hat{F}^m((s_1, ..., s_m, k), h(x))$. Thus, the view of $\mathcal{A}$ is identical to Game 1. If $\mathcal{O}(x)$ implements a random function, then its view is identical to Game 2. This yields the claim.

4.6   Proof of Lemma 7

In order to show that $\Pr[\mathsf{coll}] \leq \epsilon_{\mathcal{A}}/2$, we prove that all queries of $\mathcal{A}$ are independent of h, regardless of $b = 0$ or $b = 1$, until coll occurs. This allows us to derive an upper bound on coll. Consider the sequence of queries $x_1, ..., x_Q$ made by $\mathcal{A}$. Recall that we assume $x_u \neq x_v$ for $u \neq v$ without loss of generality.

The case $b = 0$. In this case, $\mathcal{O}_3(x_i)$ is a random function $R(x_i)$, and therefore all information observed by $\mathcal{A}$ is independent of h, until coll occurs. Thus, the view of $\mathcal{A}$ is equivalent to a world in which the experiment does not choose h at the beginning, but only after $\mathcal{A}$ has made all queries, and only then computes $h(x_i)_{1:j}$ for all $i \in [\![Q]\!]$ and outputs a random bit if a collision occurred. By the almost-universality, we thus obtain that

$$\Pr[\mathsf{coll} \mid b = 0] \leq \sum_{i=2}^{Q} \frac{i-1}{2^{j-1}} \leq \frac{Q^2}{2^j} \leq \frac{Q^2 \epsilon_{\mathcal{A}}}{2Q^2} = \frac{\epsilon_{\mathcal{A}}}{2}.$$

Note that we use here that $j \geq \log(2Q^2/\epsilon_{\mathcal{A}})$, which holds due to the definition of j in (5).

The case $b = 1$. We may assume without loss of generality that $Q > 0$, as otherwise $\mathcal{A}$ receives no information about b and thus we would have $\epsilon_{\mathcal{A}} = 0$. Consider the first query $\mathcal{O}_3(x_1)$ of $\mathcal{A}$. The oracle proceeds as follows. At first it computes $k_{x_1} := R_j(h(x_1)_{1:j})$. Since R_j is a random function, this value is independent of h. In the next step it computes $z_1 := \hat{F}^{m-j}((s_{j+1}, ..., s_m), k_{x_1}, h(x_1)_{j+1:m})$, which is still uniformly random. To see this, note that the perfect one-time security of F guarantees perfect one-time security of $\hat{F}^{m-j}$ as shown in Lemma 5. Thus $\mathcal{A}$ gains no information about h at this point and the next query cannot be adaptive with regard to h.

Now if $\mathcal{A}$ queries $\mathcal{O}_3(x_2)$, then the experiment will evaluate the random functions R_j on a different position than in the first query, unless

$$h(x_1)_{1:j} = h(x_2)_{1:j} \tag{9}$$

Due to the fact that the response to x_1 was independent of h and the almost-universality of h, (9) happens with probability at most $1/2^{j-1}$. Therefore, again by the perfect one-time security of F, $\mathcal{A}$ receives another uniformly random value z_2, which is independent of h, except with probability at most $1/2^{j-1}$. Continuing this argument inductively over all Q queries of $\mathcal{A}$, we see that on its i-th query $\mathcal{A}$ will receive a random response which is independent of h, except with probability $(i-1)/2^{j-1}$, provided that all previous responses were independent of h. A union bound now yields

$$\Pr\left[\mathsf{coll} \mid b = 1\right] \leq \sum_{i=2}^{Q} \frac{i-1}{2^{j-1}} \leq \frac{Q^2}{2^j} \leq \frac{Q^2 \epsilon_{\mathcal{A}}}{2Q^2} = \frac{\epsilon_{\mathcal{A}}}{2}.$$

It remains to show that $\Pr\left[X_3 \mid \overline{\mathsf{coll}}\right] = 1/2$. Let us consider the case $b = 1$. If $\overline{\mathsf{coll}}$ occurs, then there are no collisions, such that the oracle calls random function R_j on always different inputs, each time receiving an independent, uniformly random value. Applying the perfect one-time security of $\hat{F}^{m-j}$ again, the response of the oracle to each query is therefore uniformly distributed and independent of all other queries. Thus, provided that no collision occurs, the view in case $b = 1$ is perfectly indistinguishable from the case $b = 0$, which yields the claim.

4.7   On the Necessity of the *"all-prefix"* Property

One may ask at this point whether the *"all-prefix"* property is really necessary, or whether it is possible to use a standard universal hash function with fixed output space $\{0, 1\}^j$ instead.

Let us explain why the *"all-prefix"* property is not only sufficient, but also necessary. Recall that j depends on the particular values of Q and $\epsilon_{\mathcal{A}}$ of a particular given adversary, via the definition $j = \lceil \log(2Q^2/\epsilon_{\mathcal{A}}) \rceil$ in (5). One may wonder why we set j so precisely, depending on the given adversary, rather than simply choosing j sufficiently large such that it would work for *any* efficient adversary.

The purpose of this precise choice is because we have to find the right balance between two properties that we need to obtain *tight* security:

1. On the one hand, we need j to be sufficiently large, such that the probability of a collision of (the j-bit prefix of) the universal hash function is sufficiently unlikely.

2. On the other hand, we have to keep j short enough, in order to get a tight reduction.

This is why we make the value j dependent on the given adversary, specifically on the particular values of Q and $\epsilon_{\mathcal{A}}$. We stress that we do this *only in the security proof*, but not in the PRF *construction* itself. That is, we do not simply fix j to be the largest value of j such that the collision probability is sufficiently small for any adversary, because then for certain adversaries j could be "too large" such that the reduction would not be tight. Similarly, if we used a standard universal hash function with output length j, then this would also fix j to some specific value in the *construction* of the PRF, and thus would again make the PRF construction only tightly secure for certain adversaries that match this particular choice of j, but not necessarily for all efficient adversaries.

For example using a standard UHF with $m = \omega(\log \lambda)$ is sufficient to bound the collision probability, but this yields only super-logarithmic tightness, and thus would be worse than in the construction of Döttling and Schröder [DS15], while with an APUHF we achieve logarithmic tightness.

Hence, the important new feature that *all-prefix* universality provides is that it guarantees that a suitable choice of j exists for *any* efficient adversary. This makes the construction independent of a particular class of adversaries that match a certain fixed value of j, while at the same time it ensures that the security proof depends *tightly* on the particularly given adversary. Hence, using an APUHF instead of a standard universal hash function is not just sufficient, but also necessary in order to capture all efficient adversaries and to keep the security proof tight.

We note that Döttling and Schröder [DS15] also use multiple instances of the underlying pseudorandom function, with increasing security, in order to achieve tightness. Essentially, we replace these multiple instances with a single instance, in combination with an all-prefix universal hash function. From an abstract high-level perspective, in our approach each prefix implicitly corresponds to one PRF instance of [DS15]. This makes our construction significantly more efficient.

5 Applications

5.1 Efficient and Tightly-Secure PRF from Matrix Diffie-Hellman Assumptions

We recall the definition of the matrix Diffie-Hellman (MDDH) assumption and the pseudorandom function (PRF) from [EHK+17]. We consider a variant where an all-prefix almost-universal hash function is applied to the input before it is processed by the PRF. We note that the MDDH assumption generalizes the Decisional Diffie-Hellman (DDH) and Decisional d-Linear (d-LIN) assumptions, and, moreover, it gives us a framework to analyze the algebraic structure behind the Diffie-Hellman-based cryptographic primitives. Thus, our results can be carried on to the Naor-Reingold PRF (based on the DDH assumption) [NR97] and the Lewko-Waters PRF (based on the d-LIN assumption) [LW09].

Notations and the MDDH *Assumption.* Let $\mathcal{G} := (\mathbb{G}, P, q)$ be a description of an additive group $\mathbb{G}$ with random generator P and prime order q. Following the "implicit notation" of [EHK+13], we write $[a]$ shorthand for aP. More generally, for a matrix $\mathbf{A} = (a_{ij}) \in \mathbb{Z}_q^{n \times m}$, we define $[\mathbf{A}]_s$ as the implicit representation of $\mathbf{A}$ in $\mathbb{G}$:

$$[\mathbf{A}] := \begin{pmatrix} a_{11}P \; \dots \; a_{1m}P \\ a_{n1}P \; \dots \; a_{nm}P \end{pmatrix} \in \mathbb{G}^{n \times m}$$

Let us first recall the definition of the matrix Diffie-Hellman (MDDH) problem [EHK+13, EHK+17].

Definition 10 (Matrix distribution). *Let $\ell, d \in \mathbb{N}$ and $\ell > d$. We call $\mathcal{D}_{\ell,d}$ a matrix distribution if it outputs matrices in $\mathbb{Z}_q^{\ell \times d}$ of full rank d in polynomial time, namely, it is efficiently samplable. We define $\mathcal{D}_d := \mathcal{D}_{d+1,d}$.*

Without loss of generality, we assume the first d rows of $\mathbf{A} \xleftarrow{\$} \mathcal{D}_{\ell,d}$ form a full-rank and invertible matrix, and we denote it by $\overline{\mathbf{A}}$ and the rest $\ell - d$ rows by $\underline{\mathbf{A}}$.

Definition 11 (Transformation matrix). *Let $\mathcal{D}_{\ell,d}$ be a matrix distribution and $\mathbf{A}$ be a matrix from it. The transformation matrix of $\mathbf{A}$ is defined as $\mathbf{T} := \underline{\mathbf{A}} \cdot \overline{\mathbf{A}}^{-1} \in \mathbb{Z}_q^{(\ell-d) \times d}$.*

The $\mathcal{D}_{\ell,d}$-MDDH problem is to distinguish the two distributions $([\mathbf{A}], [\mathbf{Aw}])$ and $([\mathbf{A}], [\mathbf{u}])$ where $\mathbf{A} \xleftarrow{\$} \mathcal{D}_{\ell,d}$, $\mathbf{w} \xleftarrow{\$} \mathbb{Z}_q^d$ and $\mathbf{u} \xleftarrow{\$} \mathbb{Z}_q^\ell$.

Definition 12 ($\mathcal{D}_{\ell,d}$-Matrix Diffie-Hellman assumption, $\mathcal{D}_{\ell,d}$-MDDH). *Let $\mathcal{D}_{\ell,d}$ be a matrix distribution. We say that adversary $\mathcal{A}$ $(t_\mathcal{A}, \epsilon_\mathcal{A})$-breaks the $\mathcal{D}_{\ell,d}$-Matrix Diffie-Hellman ($\mathcal{D}_{\ell,d}$-MDDH) assumption in group $\mathbb{G}$, if $\mathcal{A}$ runs in time $t_\mathcal{A}$ and*

$$|\Pr[\mathcal{A}(\mathcal{G}, [\mathbf{A}], [\mathbf{Aw}]) = 1] - \Pr[\mathcal{A}(\mathcal{G}, [\mathbf{A}], [\mathbf{u}]) = 1]| \geq \epsilon_\mathcal{A},$$

where the probability is taken over $\mathbf{A} \xleftarrow{\$} \mathcal{D}_{\ell,d}, \mathbf{w} \xleftarrow{\$} \mathbb{Z}_q^d, \mathbf{u} \xleftarrow{\$} \mathbb{Z}_q^\ell$.

Examples of $\mathcal{D}_{\ell,d}$-MDDH. [EHK+13, EHK+17] define distributions $\mathcal{L}_d$, $\mathcal{C}_d$, $\mathcal{SC}_d$, $\mathcal{IL}_d$, and $\mathcal{U}_d$ which corresponds to the d-Linear, d-Cascade, d-Symmetric-Cascade, d-Incremental-Linear, and d-Uniform assumption, respectively. All these assumptions are proven secure in the generic group model [EHK+13, EHK+17] and form a hierarchy of increasingly weaker assumptions.

A simple example is the $\mathcal{L}_1$-MDDH assumption for $d = 1$, which is the DDH assumption: Choose $a, w, z \xleftarrow{\$} \mathbb{Z}_q$, and the DDH assumption states that the following two distributions are computationally indistinguishable:

$$([1, a, w, aw]) \approx_c ([1, a, w, z]).$$

This can be represented via the $\mathcal{L}_1$-MDDH assumption which states the following two distributions are computationally indistinguishable:

$$([\begin{smallmatrix} a \\ 1 \end{smallmatrix}], [\begin{smallmatrix} aw \\ w \end{smallmatrix}]) =: ([\mathbf{A}], [\mathbf{A}w]) \approx_c ([\mathbf{A}], [\mathbf{u}]) := ([\begin{smallmatrix} a \\ 1 \end{smallmatrix}], [\begin{smallmatrix} z \\ w \end{smallmatrix}]).$$

For $d = 1$ the transformation matrix $\mathbf{T}$ contains only one element, and for $\mathcal{L}_1$-MDDH the corresponding transformation matrix is $\mathbf{T} = \frac{1}{a}$.

We give more examples of matrix distributions from [EHK+13, EHK+17] for $d = 2$ in Appendix A.

The PRF construction of [EHK+17] *and its security.* Let $\mathcal{G} := (\mathbb{G}, P, q)$ be a description of an additive group $\mathbb{G}$ with random generator P and prime order q. Let $\mathcal{D}_{\ell,d}$ be a matrix distribution and we assume that $(\ell - d)$ divides d and define $t := d/(\ell - d)$.

Following the approach of Sect. 5.3 of [EHK+17], we choose a random vector $\mathbf{h} \xleftarrow{\$} \mathbb{Z}_q^d$, and, for $i = 1, ..., m$ and $j = 1, ..., t$, we choose $\mathbf{A}_{i,j} \xleftarrow{\$} \mathcal{D}_{\ell,d}$ and compute transformation matrices $\hat{\mathbf{T}}_{i,j} := \underline{\mathbf{A}}_{i,j} \overline{\mathbf{A}}_{i,j}^{-1} \in \mathbb{Z}_q^{(\ell-d) \times d}$ and define the aggregated transformation matrices

$$\mathbf{T}_i := \begin{pmatrix} \hat{\mathbf{T}}_{i,1} \\ \vdots \\ \hat{\mathbf{T}}_{i,t} \end{pmatrix} \in \mathbb{Z}_q^{d \times d},$$

and $\mathbf{S} := (\mathbf{T}_1, ..., \mathbf{T}_m)$. Here, for $i \in \{1, ..., m\}$, we require that $\mathbf{T}_i$ has full rank. We note that this requirement can be satisfied by all the matrix distributions described in [EHK+17] with overwhelming probability. This implies the distribution of our $\mathbf{T}_i$'s is statistically close to that in [EHK+17], up to a negligibly small statistical distance of $1/(q-1)$. Thus, their security results can be applied here.

Now let $S := \mathbb{Z}_q^{d \times d}$, $K := \mathbb{G}^d$, and $X := \{0,1\}$. The basis of the PRF construction from [EHK+17] is the function $F_{\text{MDDH}} : S \times K \times X \to K$ defined as

$$F_{\text{MDDH}}(\mathbf{T}, [\mathbf{h}], x) := \begin{cases} [\mathbf{h}] & \text{if } x = 0 \\ [\mathbf{T} \cdot \mathbf{h}] & \text{if } x = 1 \end{cases} \tag{10}$$

By applying the augmented cascade of Boneh *et al.* [BMR10] (Fig. 1) to F_{MDDH}, Escala *et al.* [EHK+17] obtain their PRF F_{MDDH}^m with key space $(\mathbb{Z}_q^{(d \times d)})^m \times \mathbb{G}^d$ and domain $\{0,1\}^m$:

$$F_{\text{MDDH}}^m : (\mathbb{Z}_q^{(d \times d)})^m \times \mathbb{G}^d \times \{0,1\}^m \to \mathbb{G}$$

$$F_{\text{MDDH}}^m(\mathbf{S}, [\mathbf{h}], x) := \left[\left(\prod_{i:x_i=1} \mathbf{T}_i \right) \cdot \mathbf{h} \right] \tag{11}$$

where $\mathbf{S} := (\mathbf{T}_1, ..., \mathbf{T}_m)$. The following theorem was proven in [EHK+13, EHK+17].

Theorem 5 ([EHK+17, Theorem 12]). *From each adversary $\mathcal{A}$ that $(t_\mathcal{A}, \epsilon_\mathcal{A}, Q)$-breaks the security of F^m_{MDDH} with input space $\{0,1\}^m$ we can construct an adversary $\mathcal{B}$ that $(t_\mathcal{B}, \epsilon_\mathcal{B})$-breaks the $\mathcal{D}_{\ell,d}$-MDDH assumption in $\mathbb{G}$ with*

$$t_\mathcal{B} = \Theta(t_\mathcal{A}) \qquad \text{and} \qquad \epsilon_\mathcal{B} \geq \frac{\epsilon_\mathcal{A}}{dm}$$

Note that d is a constant, so that the security loss is linear in the size m of the input space.

Our construction. By additionally encoding the input with an APUHF as described in (4), we finally obtain the function $F^{\mathcal{H}_{n,m}}_{\text{MDDH}} : S^m \times K \times \mathcal{H}_{n,m} \times \{0,1\}^n \to K$ as

$$F^{\mathcal{H}_{n,m}}_{\text{MDDH}}(\mathbf{S}, [\mathbf{h}], h, x) = F^m_{\text{MDDH}}(\mathbf{S}, [\mathbf{h}], h(x)) = \left[\left(\prod_{i:h(x)_i = 1}^{m} \mathbf{T}_i \right) \cdot \mathbf{h} \right] \tag{12}$$

In order to apply Theorem 4 to show that this particular instance of the augmented cascade with encoded input is a secure PRF with key space $S^m \times K \times \mathcal{H}_{n,m}$ and domain $\{0,1\}^n$, we merely have to prove that function F_{MDDH} is perfectly one-time secure.

Lemma 8. *Function F_{MDDH} from (10) is perfectly one-time secure.*

Proof. We have to show that

$$\Pr_{[\mathbf{h}] \xleftarrow{\$} \mathbb{G}^d} [F_{\text{MDDH}}(\mathbf{T}, [\mathbf{h}], x) = [\mathbf{h}']] = \frac{1}{|\mathbb{G}|^d}.$$

for all $(\mathbf{T}, x, [\mathbf{h}']) \in S \times \{0,1\} \times \mathbb{G}^d$.

If $x = 0$ then $F_{\text{MDDH}}(\mathbf{T}, [\mathbf{h}], 0) = [\mathbf{h}]$, which is a random vector in $\mathbb{G}^d$ by definition. If $x = 1$ then $F_{\text{MDDH}}(\mathbf{T}, [\mathbf{h}], 1) = [\mathbf{Th}]$, which is again a random vector, due to the fact that $\mathbf{T}$ is a full-rank matrix. $\qquad \square$

By combining Theorem 4 with Theorem 5 we now obtain the following result, which shows that setting $m = \omega(\log \lambda)$ is sufficient to achieve tight security.

Theorem 6. *Let $m = \omega(\log \lambda)$ be (slightly) super-logarithmic and $\mathcal{H}_{n,m}$ be a family of all-prefix almost universal hash functions. From each adversary $\mathcal{A}$ that $(t_\mathcal{A}, \epsilon_\mathcal{A}, Q)$-breaks the security of $F^{\mathcal{H}_{n,m}}_{MDDH}$ with $Q/\epsilon_\mathcal{A} = \text{poly}(\lambda)$ for some polynomial poly we can construct an adversary $\mathcal{B}'$ that $(t'_\mathcal{B}, \epsilon'_\mathcal{B})$-breaks the $\mathcal{D}_{\ell,d}$-MDDH assumption in $\mathbb{G}$ with*

$$t'_\mathcal{B} = \Theta(t_\mathcal{A}) \qquad \text{and} \qquad \epsilon'_\mathcal{B} \geq \frac{\epsilon_\mathcal{A}}{2dj}$$

where $j = O(\log \lambda)$.

Proof. Theorem 4 shows that from each adversary $\mathcal{A}$ that $(t_{\mathcal{A}}, \epsilon_{\mathcal{A}}, q)$-breaks the pseudorandomness of $F_{\text{MDDH}}^{\mathcal{H}_{n,m}}$ with $Q/\epsilon_{\mathcal{A}} = \text{poly}(\lambda)$ for some polynomial poly, we can construct an adversary $\mathcal{B}$ that $(t_{\mathcal{B}}, \epsilon_{\mathcal{B}}, Q)$-breaks the pseudorandomness of the function F_{MDDH}^j with input space $\{0,1\}^j$, where

$$j = O(\log \lambda) \qquad \text{and} \qquad t_{\mathcal{B}} = \Theta(t_{\mathcal{A}}) \qquad \text{and} \qquad \epsilon_{\mathcal{B}} \geq \epsilon_{\mathcal{A}}/2$$

Theorem 5 in turn shows that from each adversary $\mathcal{B}$ that $(t_{\mathcal{B}}, \epsilon_{\mathcal{B}}, Q)$-breaks the security of F_{MDDH}^j we can construct an adversary $\mathcal{B}'$ that $(t'_{\mathcal{B}}, \epsilon'_{\mathcal{B}})$-breaks the $\mathcal{D}_{\ell,d}$-MDDH assumption in $\mathbb{G}$ with

$$t'_{\mathcal{B}} = \Theta(t_{\mathcal{B}}) \qquad \text{and} \qquad \epsilon'_{\mathcal{B}} \geq \frac{\epsilon_{\mathcal{B}}}{dj} \geq \frac{\epsilon_{\mathcal{A}}}{2dj}$$

which yields the claim. $\qquad\qquad\qquad\qquad\qquad\qquad\qquad\qquad\qquad\qquad\qquad\qquad\quad\square$

Comparison to the DDH-based PRF of [NR97]. One particularly interesting instantiation of F_{MDDH}^m is based on the $\mathcal{L}_1$-MDDH assumption, which is an improvement over the famous Naor-Reingold construction based on the DDH (namely, $\mathcal{L}_1$-MDDH) assumption from [NR97]. In F_{MDDH}^m, we sample $\mathbf{A}_i$ from $\mathcal{D}_{\ell,d}$ and then compute the aggregated transformation matrices $\mathbf{T}_i$. For the $\mathcal{L}_1$ distribution, we can equivalently pick random elements T_i from $\mathbb{Z}_q$.

Let $\mathbb{G}$ be a group of prime order q, $S := \mathbb{Z}_q$, $K := \mathbb{G}$, $X := \{0,1\}^n$ and $m = \omega(\log \lambda)$ as above. Then we choose $T_1, \ldots, T_m, a \overset{\$}{\leftarrow} \mathbb{Z}_q$ and obtain a PRF with domain $\{0,1\}^n$ as

$$F_{\text{DDH}}^{\mathcal{H}_{n,m}}(\mathbf{S}, [a], h, x) = \left[\left(\prod_{i:h(x)_i=1}^{m} T_i \right) \cdot a \right].$$

Note that the resulting PRF is identical to the original Naor-Reingold function [NR97], except that an APUHF h is applied to the input x before it is processed in the Naor-Reingold construction. For the original construction from [NR97] both the size of the secret key and the tightness loss of the security proof (based on the DDH assumption in $\mathbb{G}$) are *linear* in the bit-length of the function input. We show that merely by encoding the input with an APUHF one can obtain shorter secret keys of size $m = \omega(\log \lambda)$ and with security loss $O(\log \lambda)$ (based on the same assumption as [NR97]), even for input size $n \gg m$.

Comparison to the Matrix-DDH PRF of [DS15]. Döttling and Schröder [DS15] also described a variant of the Matrix-DDH-based PRF of [EHK+13]. Their PRF is the function

$$F_{\text{MDDH}}^{\text{DS15}}(\mathbf{S}, [\mathbf{h}], x) := \left[\left(\prod_{j=1}^{m} (\mathbf{T}_i + x^{2^j} \cdot \mathbf{I}) \right) \cdot \mathbf{h} \right] \tag{13}$$

where $\mathbf{S}$, $[\mathbf{h}]$, and m are as in our construction, and $x \in \mathbb{Z}_q$. Thus, in comparison, our construction from (12) uses the same value of m, but is somewhat simpler that (13) and also slightly more efficient to evaluate. In particular, the computation of the terms of the form $(x^{2^j} \cdot \mathbf{I})$ is replaced with a single evaluation of the APUHF h. Another difference is that the domain of their function is restricted to $x \in \mathbb{Z}_q$, while in our case $x \in \{0,1\}^n$ can be any bit string of polynomially-bounded length $n = n(\lambda)$.

5.2   More Efficient LWE-Based PRFs

We recall the learning with error (LWE) assumption. Then we apply our results to the LWE-based PRF from Banerjee, Peikert and Rosen [BPR12].

Definition 13 (Learning With Errors assumption, LWE). *Let p be a modulus, N be a positive integer, and $\chi_\alpha := D_{\mathbb{Z}_p, \alpha}$ be a Gaussian distribution with noise parameter α. Let $\mathbf{h} \xleftarrow{\$} \mathbb{Z}_p^N$ be a random vector. We say that adversary $\mathcal{A}$ $(t_{\mathcal{A}}, \epsilon_{\mathcal{A}})$-breaks the $LWE_{p,N,\alpha}$ assumption if it runs in time $t_{\mathcal{A}}$ and*

$$| \Pr[\mathcal{A}(\mathbf{h}, \mathbf{h}^\top \mathbf{s} + e) = 1] - \Pr[\mathcal{A}(\mathbf{h}, u) = 1]| \geq \epsilon_{\mathcal{A}},$$

where $\mathbf{h} \xleftarrow{\$} \mathbb{Z}_p^N$, $\mathbf{s} \xleftarrow{\$} \mathbb{Z}_p^N$, $e \xleftarrow{\$} \chi_\alpha$ and $u \xleftarrow{\$} \mathbb{Z}_p$.

Let $\lfloor \cdot \rceil$ be the rounding function, which rounds a real number to the largest integer which does not exceed it. Let $p \geq q$. For an element $h \in \mathbb{Z}_p$, we define the rounding function $\lfloor \cdot \rceil_q : \mathbb{Z}_p \to \mathbb{Z}_q$ as $\lfloor h \rceil_q := \lfloor (q/p)h \rceil$, and for a vector $\mathbf{h} \in \mathbb{Z}_p^N$, the rounding function $\lfloor \mathbf{h} \rceil_q$ is defined component-wise.

The PRF construction of [BPR12] *and its security.* Let $S := \chi_\alpha^{N \times N}$ and $K := \mathbb{Z}_p^N$, and $X := \{0,1\}$. We assume that $\mathbf{S} \in S$ has full rank. The basis of the PRF of [BPR12] is the function $F_{\mathrm{LWE}} : S \times K \times X \to K$,

$$F_{\mathrm{LWE}}(\mathbf{S}, \mathbf{h}, x) := \begin{cases} \mathbf{h} & \text{if } x = 0 \\ \mathbf{S} \cdot \mathbf{h} & \text{if } x = 1 \end{cases} \tag{14}$$

We apply a slightly different augmented cascade transformation in Fig. 1 to obtain the PRF of [BPR12] with key space $(\chi_\alpha^{(N \times N)})^m \times \mathbb{Z}_p^N$ and domain $\{0,1\}^m$:

$$F_{\mathrm{LWE}}^m : (\chi_\alpha^{(N \times N)})^m \times \mathbb{Z}_p^N \times \{0,1\}^m \to \mathbb{Z}_q$$

$$F_{\mathrm{LWE}}^m(\mathbf{S}, \mathbf{h}, x) := \left\lfloor \left(\prod_{i:x_i=1}^{m} \mathbf{S}_i \right) \cdot \mathbf{h} \right\rceil_q \tag{15}$$

where $\mathbf{S} := (\mathbf{S}_1, ..., \mathbf{S}_m)$ and $\mathbf{h} \xleftarrow{\$} \mathbb{Z}_p^N$. Different to Fig. 1, we apply the rounding function on the output of Fig. 1.

Theorem 7 ([BPR12, Theorem 5.2]). *Let $\chi_\alpha = D_{\mathbb{Z}, \alpha}$ be a Gaussian distribution with parameter $\alpha > 0$, let m be a positive integer that denotes the length of* *message inputs. Define* $B := m(C\alpha\sqrt{N})^m$ *for a suitable universal constant* C. *Let* p, q *be two moduli such that* $p > q \cdot B \cdot N^{\omega(1)}$.

From each adversary $\mathcal{A}$ *that* $(t_\mathcal{A}, \epsilon_\mathcal{A}, Q)$-*breaks the security of* F_{LWE}^m *with input space* $\{0, 1\}^m$ *(for an arbitrary positive integer* m) *we can construct an adversary* $\mathcal{B}$ *that* $(t_\mathcal{B}, \epsilon_\mathcal{B})$-*breaks the* $LWE_{p,N,\alpha}$ *assumption with*

$$t_\mathcal{B} = \Theta(t_\mathcal{A}) \qquad and \qquad \epsilon_\mathcal{B} \geq \frac{\epsilon_\mathcal{A}}{m \cdot N}$$

Note that B is an important parameter, since it determines the size of the LWE modulus p and contains the expensive term $N^{m/2}$, which is exponential in m. Thus, a smaller m can give us a smaller p, which in turn yields a weaker LWE assumption and a much more efficient PRF. In the following, we apply our results to F_{LWE}^m to reduce m from polynomial to logarithmic in security parameter λ.

Our construction. By additionally encoding the input with an APUHF as described in (4), we finally obtain $F_{\mathrm{LWE}}^{\mathcal{H}_{n,m}} : (\chi_\alpha^{(N \times N)})^m \times \mathbb{Z}_p^N \times \mathcal{H}_{n,m} \times \{0,1\}^m \to \mathbb{Z}_q^N$ as

$$F_{\mathrm{LWE}}^m(\mathbf{S}, \mathbf{h}, h(x)) := \left\lfloor \left(\prod_{i:h(x)_i=1}^m \mathbf{S}_i \right) \cdot \mathbf{h} \right\rceil_q \qquad (16)$$

In order to apply Theorem 4 to show that this particular instance of the augmented cascade with encoded input is a secure PRF with key space $S^m \times K \times \mathcal{H}_{n,m}$ and domain $\{0,1\}^n$, we have to prove that function F_{LWE} is perfectly one-time secure.

Lemma 9. *Function* F_{LWE} *from (14) is perfectly one-time secure.*

Proof. We have to show that

$$\Pr_{\mathbf{h} \overset{\$}{\leftarrow} \mathbb{Z}_p} [F_{\mathrm{LWE}}(\mathbf{S}, \mathbf{h}, x) = \mathbf{h}'] = \frac{1}{p^N}.$$

for all $(\mathbf{S}, x, \mathbf{h}') \in S \times \{0, 1\} \times \mathbb{Z}_p^N$.

If $x = 0$ then $F_{\mathrm{LWE}}(\mathbf{S}, \mathbf{h}, 0) = \mathbf{h}$, which is a random vector in $\mathbb{Z}_p^N$ by definition. If $x = 1$ then $F_{\mathrm{LWE}}(\mathbf{S}, \mathbf{h}, 1) = \mathbf{S} \cdot \mathbf{h}$, which is again a random vector, due to the fact that $\mathbf{S}$ is a full-rank matrix. $\square$

We recall the following useful notations and corollary for the proof of Theorem 8 given below. We define an error sampling function $E : \{0,1\}^j \to \mathbb{Z}^N$ and for $x \in \{0,1\}^j$ and $j \in \llbracket m \rrbracket$ we define the randomized version of F_{LWE}^j as $\tilde{F}_{\mathrm{LWE}}^j(x) = \left(\prod_{i:x_i=1}^j \mathbf{S}_i \right) \cdot \mathbf{h} + E(x)$. The proof of Theorem 5.2 and Lemma 5.5 in [BPR12] show that $\tilde{F}_{\mathrm{LWE}}^j$ is pseudorandom based on the decisional LWE assumption and it holds that $F_{\mathrm{LWE}}^m(x) = \left\lfloor \left(\prod_{i>j \wedge x_i=1}^m \mathbf{S}_i \right) \cdot \tilde{F}_{\mathrm{LWE}}^j(x) \right\rceil_q$, except with negligible probability. We summarize this in the following corollary.

Corollary 1. *Let all the parameters be defined as in Theorem 7. There exists an efficiently randomized error sampling function $E : \{0,1\}^j \to \mathbb{Z}^N$, such that, from each adversary $\mathcal{A}$ that $(t_{\mathcal{A}}, \epsilon_{\mathcal{A}}, Q)$-breaks the security of $\tilde{F}^j_{LWE}(x) = \left(\prod^j_{i:x_i=1} \mathbf{S}_i\right) \cdot \mathbf{h} + E(x)$ with input $x \in \{0,1\}^j$ (for $j \in [\![m]\!]$) we can construct an adversary $\mathcal{B}$ that $(t_{\mathcal{B}}, \epsilon_{\mathcal{B}})$-breaks the $LWE_{p,N,\alpha}$ assumption with*

$$t_{\mathcal{B}} = \Theta(t_{\mathcal{A}}) \qquad and \qquad \epsilon_{\mathcal{B}} \geq \frac{\epsilon_{\mathcal{A}}}{m \cdot N}.$$

Moreover, except with probability $2^{-\Omega(N)}$, we have

$$F^m_{LWE}(x) = \left\lfloor \left(\prod^m_{i>j \wedge x_i=1} \mathbf{S}_i\right) \cdot \tilde{F}^j_{LWE}(x) \right\rceil_q.$$

Theorem 8. *Let $m = \omega(\log \lambda)$ be (slightly) super-logarithmic and $\mathcal{H}_{n,m}$ be a family of all-prefix almost universal hash functions. Let $\chi_\alpha = D_{\mathbb{Z},\alpha}$ be a Gaussian distribution with parameter $\alpha > 0$, let m be a positive integer denotes the length of message inputs. Define $B := m(C\alpha\sqrt{N})^m$ for a suitable universal constant C. Let p, q be two moduli such that $p > q \cdot B \cdot N^{\omega(1)}$.*

From each adversary $\mathcal{A}$ that $(t_{\mathcal{A}}, \epsilon_{\mathcal{A}}, Q)$-breaks the security of $F^{\mathcal{H}_{n,m}}_{LWE}$ with $Q/\epsilon_{\mathcal{A}} = \text{poly}(\lambda)$ for some polynomial poly we can construct an adversary $\mathcal{B}'$ that $(t'_{\mathcal{B}}, \epsilon'_{\mathcal{B}})$-breaks the $LWE_{p,N,\alpha}$ assumption with

$$t'_{\mathcal{B}} = \Theta(t_{\mathcal{A}}) \qquad and \qquad \epsilon'_{\mathcal{B}} \geq \frac{\epsilon_{\mathcal{A}}}{2j \cdot N} - 2^{-\Omega(N)}$$

where $j = O(\log \lambda)$.

Proof. The proof is the same as the one for Theorem 4. The only difference is between Games 1 and 2. Here we do one intermediate game transition Game 1':
We simulate $\mathcal{O}_1(x)$ by returning $F^m_{\text{LWE}}(x) = \left\lfloor \left(\prod^m_{i>j \wedge x_i=1} \mathbf{S}_i\right) \cdot \tilde{F}^j_{\text{LWE}}(x) \right\rceil_q$ and $\mathcal{O}_0$ by returning a random vector in $\mathbb{Z}^N_q$.

By the second statement of Corollary 1, the difference between Games 1 and 1' is bounded by the statistical difference $2^{-\Omega(N)}$. Moreover, the difference between Games 1' and 2 is bounded by the security of $\tilde{F}^j_{\text{LWE}}$. By the first statement of Corollary 1 we can conclude the proof. $\square$

Comparison to the LWE PRF of [DS15]. Döttling and Schröder [DS15] describe a different variant of the BPR PRF. Their approach is to instantiate their Construction 1 with the BPR PRF and then obtain the following function

$$F^{\text{DS15}}_{\text{LWE}}(K, \mathbf{h}, x) = \bigoplus^L_{i=1} \bigoplus^\lambda_{j=1} F^{2^i}_{\text{LWE}}(\mathbf{S}, \mathbf{h}, \text{Bin}(j)\|H_{2^i,j}(x))$$

where $L = \omega(\log \lambda)$, for each $j \in [\![\lambda]\!]$ the function $H_{2^i,j} : \{0,1\}^n \to \{0,1\}^{i+1}$ is chosen from a suitable universal hash function family with range $\{0,1\}^{i+1}$, and $\mathbf{S}$ is chosen the same as ours.

Compared with $F_{\text{LWE}}^{\text{DS15}}$, our variant has shorter secret keys: instead of having $L \cdot \lambda$ many hash functions, we only have a single one. In terms of computation efficiency, instead of running H_i and F_{LWE}^i for $L \cdot \lambda$ times, we only run the hash function and F_{LWE}^m once.

6   Conclusion

We have introduced all-prefix (almost-)universal hash functions (APUHFs) as a tool to generically improve the augmented cascade construction of pseudorandom functions by Boneh, Montgomery, and Raghunathan [BMR10]. By generically applying an APUHF to the function input before processing it in the augmented cascade, we are able to reduce both the key size and the tightness of the security proof by one order of magnitude. We gave simple and very efficient constructions of such a function families, based on the almost-universal hash function family of Dietzfelbinger et al. [DHKP97], which can be evaluated by essentially a single modular multiplication, and generically on pairwise-independent hash functions.

For the instantiation based on Matrix-DDH assumptions of [EHK+13], which includes the classical constructions of Naor-Reingold [NR97] and the Lewko-Waters [LW09] as special cases, this yields asymptotically short keys consisting of only $\omega(\log \lambda)$ elements, and tight security with loss only $O(\log \lambda)$. These parameters are similar to the respective constructions of Döttling and Schröder [DS15], but our instantiation is conceptually much simpler and slightly more efficient.

For the LWE-based instantiation based of Banerjee, Peikert and Rosen [BPR12] (BPR), we are able to reduce the required size of the LWE modulus p from exponential to super-polynomial in the security parameter, which significantly improves efficiency and allows to prove security under a weaker LWE assumption. Again, the latter is similar to a result from [DS15], but we replace their relatively expensive generic construction, which requires to run $\lambda \cdot \omega(\log \lambda)$ instances of the BPR function in parallel, with a *single* instance plus an all-prefix almost-universal hash function.

We believe that APUHFs may have many further applications in cryptography beyond pseudorandom functions. This may include, for example, constructions of more efficient cryptosystems with tight provable security, such as digital signatures or public-key encryption schemes. In particular constructions using arguments similar to pseudorandom functions based on the augmented cascade, such as [CW13, GHKW16], seem to be promising targets.

Acknowledgements. We would like to thank all anonymous reviewers for their helpful comments.

A   Further Examples of Matrix Distributions

Let us recall some further examples for matrix distributions from [EHK+13, EHK+17] for completeness and self-containedness.

$$\mathcal{L}_2 : \mathbf{A} = \begin{pmatrix} a_1 & 0 \\ 0 & a_2 \\ 1 & 1 \end{pmatrix}, \quad \mathcal{C}_2 : \mathbf{A} = \begin{pmatrix} a_1 & 0 \\ 1 & a_2 \\ 0 & 1 \end{pmatrix}, \quad \mathcal{IL}_2 : \mathbf{A} = \begin{pmatrix} a_1 & 0 \\ 0 & a_1+1 \\ 1 & 1 \end{pmatrix},$$

$$\mathcal{SC}_2 : \mathbf{A} = \begin{pmatrix} a_1 & 0 \\ 1 & a_1 \\ 0 & 1 \end{pmatrix}, \quad \mathcal{U}_2 : \mathbf{A} = \begin{pmatrix} a_1 & a_2 \\ a_3 & a_4 \\ a_5 & a_6 \end{pmatrix},$$

where $a_1, \ldots, a_6 \xleftarrow{\$} \mathbb{Z}_q$. The corresponding transformation matrices are as follow,

$$\mathcal{L}_2 : \mathbf{T} = (\frac{1}{a_1}, \frac{1}{a_2}), \quad \mathcal{C}_2 : \mathbf{T} = (\pm\frac{1}{a_1 a_2}, \mp\frac{1}{a_2}), \quad \mathcal{IL}_2 : \mathbf{T} = (\frac{1}{a_1}, \frac{1}{a_1 + 1})$$

$$\mathcal{SC}_2 : \mathbf{T} = (\pm\frac{1}{a_1^2}, \mp\frac{1}{a_1}), \quad \mathcal{U}_2 : \mathbf{T} = (\frac{a_4 a_5 - a_3 a_6}{a_1 a_4 - a_2 a_3}, \frac{a_1 a_6 - a_2 a_5}{a_1 a_4 - a_2 a_3}).$$

The advantage of $\mathcal{SC}_d$ and $\mathcal{IL}_d$ is that they can be represented by one group element and have the same security guarantee as the d-Linear assumption.

References

[Bel06] Bellare, M.: New proofs for NMAC and HMAC: security without collision-resistance. In: Dwork, C. (ed.) CRYPTO 2006. LNCS, vol. 4117, pp. 602–619. Springer, Heidelberg (2006). https://doi.org/10.1007/11818175_36

[BG90] Bellare, M., Goldwasser, S.: New paradigms for digital signatures and message authentication based on non-interactive zero knowledge proofs. In: Brassard, G. (ed.) CRYPTO 1989. LNCS, vol. 435, pp. 194–211. Springer, New York (1990). https://doi.org/10.1007/0-387-34805-0_19

[BH12] Berman, I., Haitner, I.: From non-adaptive to adaptive pseudorandom functions. In: Cramer, R. (ed.) TCC 2012. LNCS, vol. 7194, pp. 357–368. Springer, Heidelberg (2012). https://doi.org/10.1007/978-3-642-28914-9_20

[BHKN13] Berman, I., Haitner, I., Komargodski, I., Naor, M.: Hardness preserving reductions via Cuckoo hashing. In: Sahai, A. (ed.) TCC 2013. LNCS, vol. 7785, pp. 40–59. Springer, Heidelberg (2013). https://doi.org/10.1007/978-3-642-36594-2_3

[BJLS16] Bader, C., Jager, T., Li, Y., Schäge, S.: On the impossibility of tight cryptographic reductions. In: Fischlin, M., Coron, J.-S. (eds.) EUROCRYPT 2016, Part II. LNCS, vol. 9666, pp. 273–304. Springer, Heidelberg (2016). https://doi.org/10.1007/978-3-662-49896-5_10

[BLMR13] Boneh, D., Lewi, K., Montgomery, H., Raghunathan, A.: Key homomorphic PRFs and their applications. In: Canetti, R., Garay, J.A. (eds.) CRYPTO 2013, Part I. LNCS, vol. 8042, pp. 410–428. Springer, Heidelberg (2013). https://doi.org/10.1007/978-3-642-40041-4_23

[BMR10] Boneh, D., Montgomery, H.W., Raghunathan, A.: Algebraic pseudorandom functions with improved efficiency from the augmented cascade. In: Al-Shaer, E., Keromytis, A.D., Shmatikov, V. (eds.) ACM CCS 2010, pp. 131–140. ACM Press, October 2010

[BP14] Banerjee, A., Peikert, C.: New and improved key-homomorphic pseudorandom functions. In: Garay, J.A., Gennaro, R. (eds.) CRYPTO 2014, Part I. LNCS, vol. 8616, pp. 353–370. Springer, Heidelberg (2014). https://doi.org/10.1007/978-3-662-44371-2_20

[BPR12] Banerjee, A., Peikert, C., Rosen, A.: Pseudorandom functions and lattices. In: Pointcheval, D., Johansson, T. (eds.) EUROCRYPT 2012. LNCS, vol. 7237, pp. 719–737. Springer, Heidelberg (2012). https://doi.org/10.1007/978-3-642-29011-4_42

[CG14] Chandran, N., Garg, S.: Balancing output length and query bound in hardness preserving constructions of pseudorandom functions. In: Meier, W., Mukhopadhyay, D. (eds.) INDOCRYPT 2014. LNCS, vol. 8885, pp. 89–103. Springer, Cham (2014). https://doi.org/10.1007/978-3-319-13039-2_6

[Cor02] Coron, J.-S.: Optimal security proofs for PSS and other signature schemes. In: Knudsen, L.R. (ed.) EUROCRYPT 2002. LNCS, vol. 2332, pp. 272–287. Springer, Heidelberg (2002). https://doi.org/10.1007/3-540-46035-7_18

[CW79] Carter, L., Wegman, M.N.: Universal classes of hash functions. J. Comput. Syst. Sci. 18(2), 143–154 (1979)

[CW13] Chen, J., Wee, H.: Fully, (almost) tightly secure IBE and dual system groups. In: Canetti, R., Garay, J.A. (eds.) CRYPTO 2013, Part II. LNCS, vol. 8043, pp. 435–460. Springer, Heidelberg (2013). https://doi.org/10.1007/978-3-642-40084-1_25

[DHKP97] Dietzfelbinger, M., Hagerup, T., Katajainen, J., Penttonen, M.: A reliable randomized algorithm for the closest-pair problem. J. Algorithms 25(1), 19–51 (1997)

[DS15] Döttling, N., Schröder, D.: Efficient pseudorandom functions via on-the-fly adaptation. In: Gennaro, R., Robshaw, M. (eds.) CRYPTO 2015, Part I. LNCS, vol. 9215, pp. 329–350. Springer, Heidelberg (2015). https://doi.org/10.1007/978-3-662-47989-6_16

[EHK+13] Escala, A., Herold, G., Kiltz, E., Ràfols, C., Villar, J.: An algebraic framework for Diffie-Hellman assumptions. In: Canetti, R., Garay, J.A. (eds.) CRYPTO 2013, Part II. LNCS, vol. 8043, pp. 129–147. Springer, Heidelberg (2013). https://doi.org/10.1007/978-3-642-40084-1_8

[EHK+17] Escala, A., Herold, G., Kiltz, E., Ràfols, C., Villar, J.: An algebraic framework for Diffie-Hellman assumptions. J. Cryptol. 30(1), 242–288 (2017)

[GGM84] Goldreich, O., Goldwasser, S., Micali, S.: On the cryptographic applications of random functions (extended abstract). In: Blakley, G.R., Chaum, D. (eds.) CRYPTO 1984. LNCS, vol. 196, pp. 276–288. Springer, Heidelberg (1985). https://doi.org/10.1007/3-540-39568-7_22

[GGM86] Goldreich, O., Goldwasser, S., Micali, S.: How to construct random functions. J. ACM 33(4), 792–807 (1986)

[GHKW16] Gay, R., Hofheinz, D., Kiltz, E., Wee, H.: Tightly CCA-secure encryption without pairings. In: Fischlin, M., Coron, J.-S. (eds.) EUROCRYPT 2016, Part I. LNCS, vol. 9665, pp. 1–27. Springer, Heidelberg (2016). https://doi.org/10.1007/978-3-662-49890-3_1

[Gol01] Goldreich, O.: Foundations of Cryptography: Basic Tools, vol. 1. Cambridge University Press, Cambridge (2001)

[HJK12] Hofheinz, D., Jager, T., Knapp, E.: Waters signatures with optimal security reduction. In: Fischlin, M., Buchmann, J., Manulis, M. (eds.) PKC 2012. LNCS, vol. 7293, pp. 66–83. Springer, Heidelberg (2012). https://doi.org/10.1007/978-3-642-30057-8_5

[IKOS08] Ishai, Y., Kushilevitz, E., Ostrovsky, R., Sahai, A.: Cryptography with constant computational overhead. In: Ladner, R.E., Dwork, C. (eds.) 40th ACM STOC, pp. 433–442. ACM Press, May 2008

[JPT12] Jain, A., Pietrzak, K., Tentes, A.: Hardness preserving constructions of pseudorandom functions. In: Cramer, R. (ed.) TCC 2012. LNCS, vol. 7194, pp. 369–382. Springer, Heidelberg (2012). https://doi.org/10.1007/978-3-642-28914-9_21

[KK12] Kakvi, S.A., Kiltz, E.: Optimal security proofs for full domain hash, revisited. In: Pointcheval, D., Johansson, T. (eds.) EUROCRYPT 2012. LNCS, vol. 7237, pp. 537–553. Springer, Heidelberg (2012). https://doi.org/10.1007/978-3-642-29011-4_32

[Kra10] Krawczyk, H.: Cryptographic extraction and key derivation: the HKDF scheme. In: Rabin, T. (ed.) CRYPTO 2010. LNCS, vol. 6223, pp. 631–648. Springer, Heidelberg (2010). https://doi.org/10.1007/978-3-642-14623-7_34

[Lev87] Levin, L.A.: One way functions and pseudorandom generators. Combinatorica **7**(4), 357–363 (1987)

[LW09] Lewko, A.B., Waters, B.: Efficient pseudorandom functions from the decisional linear assumption and weaker variants. In: Al-Shaer, E., Jha, S., Keromytis, A.D. (eds.) ACM CCS 2009, pp. 112–120. ACM Press, November 2009

[LW14] Lewko, A.B., Waters, B.: Why proving HIBE systems secure is difficult. In: Nguyen, P.Q., Oswald, E. (eds.) EUROCRYPT 2014. LNCS, vol. 8441, pp. 58–76. Springer, Heidelberg (2014). https://doi.org/10.1007/978-3-642-55220-5_4

[NR97] Naor, M., Reingold, O.: Number-theoretic constructions of efficient pseudorandom functions. In: 38th FOCS, pp. 458–467. IEEE Computer Society Press, October 1997

[Reg05] Regev, O.: On lattices, learning with errors, random linear codes, and cryptography. In: Gabow, H.N., Fagin, R. (eds.) 37th ACM STOC, pp. 84–93. ACM Press, May 2005

Simulatable Channels: Extended Security that is Universally Composable and Easier to Prove

Jean Paul Degabriele$^{(\boxtimes)}$ and Marc Fischlin

Cryptoplexity, Technische Universität Darmstadt, Darmstadt, Germany
{jeanpaul.degabriele,marc.fischlin}@cryptoplexity.de
http://www.cryptoplexity.de

Abstract. Ever since the foundational work of Goldwasser and Micali, simulation has proven to be a powerful and versatile construct for formulating security in various areas of cryptography. However security definitions based on simulation are generally harder to work with than game based definitions, often resulting in more complicated proofs. In this work we challenge this viewpoint by proposing new simulation-based security definitions for secure channels that in many cases lead to simpler proofs of security. We are particularly interested in definitions of secure channels which reflect real-world requirements, such as, protecting against the replay and reordering of ciphertexts, accounting for leakage from the decryption of invalid ciphertexts, and retaining security in the presence of ciphertext fragmentation. Furthermore we show that our proposed notion of channel simulatability implies a secure channel functionality that is universally composable. To the best of our knowledge, we are the first to study universally composable secure channels supporting these extended security goals. We conclude, by showing that the Dropbear implementation of SSH-CTR is channel simulatable in the presence of ciphertext fragmentation, and therefore also realises a universally composable secure channel. This is intended, in part, to highlight the merits of our approach over prior ones in admitting simpler security proofs in comparable settings.

Keywords: Secure channels · Ciphertext fragmentation
Universal composability · SSH · Subtle authenticated encryption

1 Introduction

Over the years, several security notions for symmetric encryption have been proposed in the cryptographic literature. In [8] Bellare *et al.* studied four notions of confidentiality: semantic security, find-then-guess security, left-or-right security, and real-or-random security, and showed them to be all equivalent. Another notion, used in [1], demands indistinguishability between encryptions of real messages and encryptions of some fixed message of the same length. This is known

© International Association for Cryptologic Research 2018
T. Peyrin and S. Galbraith (Eds.): ASIACRYPT 2018, LNCS 11274, pp. 519–550, 2018.
https://doi.org/10.1007/978-3-030-03332-3_19

to be equivalent to the other four definitions and indeed we will make extensive use of it in this work. Perhaps the most popular notion of confidentiality today is indistinguishability from random bits, often denoted as IND\$-CPA, which was put forward in [27,28]. This requires ciphertexts to be indistinguishable from random strings of the same length. In [27] Rogaway gave a number of reasons why he prefers this notion over all others, arguing that it is stronger, easier to prove, yielding more versatile objects, and being conceptually simpler. Indeed these are likely to be the reasons to which this notion owes its popularity.

In our view, however, the aspect that makes IND\$-CPA fundamentally different from all other notions is that it requires the encryption of real messages to be indistinguishable from something computed without any knowledge of the secret key. Thus, at its core is the idea that encryption be *simulatable*, where in this specific case the simulator is required to be of a specific type. The all-in-one notion of authenticated encryption introduced in [29], requiring indistinguishability of the encryption from $\$(\cdot)$ and of the decryption from $\perp(\cdot)$, can be similarly viewed as requiring that both processes be simulatable. It is then natural to ask if there is something special about these two specific simulators, or if they can be generalised further.

It turns out that a more general formulation is possible, and this is exactly what we set out to explore in this work. As we shall see, formulating security this way requires some care in order to guarantee the level of security that we expect. In this respect, we identify some necessary restrictions that need to be imposed on the simulators in order to meet their intended goal. We also establish relations between the notions that we propose and also uncover certain interesting connections, for instance, if (and only if) encryption can be simulated by a *stateless* algorithm, then the encryption is key private. In addition, our security notions have the added nice feature that, unlike other security definitions, there are no prohibited queries that the adversary is not allowed to make.

Beyond being of theoretical interest, there is also a more pragmatic reason motivating our study of these security notions. We are primarily interested in symmetric encryption with advanced properties such as protecting against replay and reordering of ciphertexts, maintaining security in the presence of inadvertent leakage from invalid ciphertexts, and supporting ciphertext fragmentation. Such properties are particularly relevant to the security of encryption schemes that are deployed in practice. A number of prior works [2,5,6,9,11,12,20,21,26] have provided treatments of symmetric encryption with such properties, some of which are rather intricate. We believe that our corresponding security definitions, based on simulation, can help to tame this complexity. For instance, most works treat chosen ciphertext security and ciphertext integrity separately. One reason for this is that the all-in-one notion of authenticated encryption does not lend itself well to these extended settings. In particular, indistinguishability from random strings is too strong a requirement. In practice ciphertexts will be encoded or prepended with additional fields that render them easy to distinguish. In the presence of ciphertext fragmentation [2,11,26], this is particularly hard to achieve since it implies that ciphertext boundaries should remain hidden.

However, because decryption can now process ciphertexts in a bit-by-bit fashion, ciphertext boundaries are implicitly demarcated by the point at which decryption returns an output. Another complication is that the combination of chosen plaintext security and ciphertext integrity, embodied by the all-in-one notion, no longer implies chosen ciphertext security for schemes which may return more than one error message [12]. Our notion of *channel simulatability with Integrity*, which can be viewed as a generalisation of the all-in-one notion of Rogaway and Shrimpton, overcomes all these limitations. Another reason why our notions are easier to work with is that they bring the security goal closer to the starting point. Our goal in a security proof will now be to transform the scheme into a simulated one, but because the structure that this simulator needs to satisfy is very loose, it will normally require fewer and simpler steps.

Yet another perk of channel simulatability, is that it also guarantees universal composability. More precisely, we show that a scheme being channel simulatable with integrity implies that it realises a universally composable secure channel. In particular, it is universally composable even when leakage from invalid ciphertexts and ciphertext fragmentation are taken into account. Moreover, channel simulatability is conceptually much simpler and easier to use than the universal composability framework.

We conclude by presenting a proof that the Dropbear SSH-CTR implementation satisfies channel simulatability with integrity. In a recent measurement study [2] it was found that Dropbear is the most ubiquitous SSH implementation on the Internet, with counter mode being the preferred choice of ciphersuite – hence our choice to analyse this scheme. The security of SSH-CTR, in the case of OpenSSH, was analysed by Paterson and Watson in [26]. While the difference between the two implementations is not major and their treatment did take ciphertext fragmentation and multiple errors into account, their security model had some limitations which were pointed out and addressed in [2,11]. Furthermore, our treatment guarantees universal composability, which is not known to be implied by any of the prior works. However, we mostly intend this result to serve as testament to the simplicity of our approach and invite the reader to contrast our proof with that in [26].

2   Preliminaries

We start by surveying some prior related works, which we will later build upon.

Leakage from Invalid Ciphertexts. In most padding-oracle attacks, such as [4,16,17], information is leaked to the adversary during the decryption of invalid ciphertexts rather than valid ones. Consequently such attacks are not captured by the usual security models where invalid ciphertexts invariably generate the same error symbol. This motivated Boldyreva *et al.* to revisit the theory of authenticated encryption in the case where distinguishable error symbols may be returned [12]. In [5] Andreeva *et al.* set out to model the case where the decrypted plaintext, or part thereof, becomes available to the adversary – known as Release of Unverified Plaintext (RUP) security. This work employs a syntax where decryption is split into two algorithms, decryption and verification. Combined with the correctness requirement, this has the undesirable consequence that their security model does not capture padding-oracle attacks, since the padding cannot form part of the released plaintext. Yet in [5] RUP security was in part motivated by the need to protect against such attacks. A related notion, called Robust Authenticated Encryption (RAE), was put forward in [21] in which the adversary also gets access to a plaintext string even if the ciphertext was deemed invalid. RAE is formulated rather differently however, here a scheme is required to be indistinguishable from a randomly-sampled injection with variable expansion augmented with a leakage simulator. This renders RAE a relatively strict security notion, attainable only by a limited set of schemes that generally require two pass encryption and decryption. The above security notions were unified in [6], for the case of nonce-based encryption, under the name Subtle Authenticated Encryption. Here a nonce-based scheme is augmented with a leakage function, to model the information leaked from the decryption of invalid ciphertexts, due to the scheme's implementation. The usual nonce-based security notions are then augmented by additionally providing the adversary with oracle access to the leakage function. We adopt a syntax similar to Subtle AE, adapted to the secure channel setting. Consequently our security notions do capture leakage from invalid ciphertexts.

Ciphertext Fragmentation. Secure channels realised over TCP/IP need to be able to decrypt ciphertexts that may be fragmented in an arbitrary way. The mechanisms needed to support ciphertext fragmentation have been exploited to break confidentiality in the secure channel realisations of SSH [3] and IPsec [17] which employ CBC encryption. These attacks exposed a limitation of our security models, notably the affected secure channel realisation in SSH was proven secure in [9] in a model which did not account for ciphertext fragmentation. To amend this Paterson and Watson [26] proposed a model which accounted for ciphertext fragmentation and used it to show that when SSH is instantiated with counter mode encryption it is secure in this extended security model. The proposed security definition, however, was closely tied to the SSH design and suffered from a number of other issues which limited its applicability and generality. These issues were addressed in [11] which studied ciphertext fragmentation more generally and introduced the related security notions of boundary hiding and resilience to denial of service. In [20] Fischlin et al. consider an extended setting where in addition to supporting ciphertext fragmentation, encryption takes as input a stream of data (rather than atomic messages) which it may fragment arbitrarily and encrypt separately. Recently in [2] Albrecht et al. did a measurement study of SSH deployment and then used the framework of [11] to analyse the security of three newly introduced ciphersuites in OpenSSH. In this work we propose simulation-based security definitions supporting ciphertext fragmentation, following the approach used in [2,11].

2.1 Notation

Unless otherwise stated, an algorithm may be randomised. An adversary is an algorithm. For any adversary $\mathcal{A}$ and algorithms $\mathcal{X}, \mathcal{Y}, \ldots$ we use $\mathcal{A}^{\mathcal{X}(\cdot), \mathcal{Y}(\cdot), \cdots} \Rightarrow z$ to denote the process of running $\mathcal{A}$ with fresh coins and oracle access to algorithms $\mathcal{X}, \mathcal{Y}, \ldots$ and returning an output z. By convention the running time of an adversary refers to the sum of its actual running time and the size of its description. We generically refer to the resources of an adversary as any subset of the following quantities: its running time, the number of queries that it makes to its oracles, and the total length (in bits) of its oracle queries. If $\mathcal{S}$ is a set then $|\mathcal{S}|$ denotes its size, and $y \twoheadleftarrow \mathcal{S}$ denotes the process of selecting an element from $\mathcal{S}$ uniformly at random and assigning it to y.

We use % to denote the integer modulo operation. For a bit b and a positive integer n, we denote by b^n the string composed of b repeated n times. With $\{0,1\}^n$ we denote the set of all binary strings of length n, and $\{0,1\}^*$ denotes the set of all binary strings of finite length. The empty string is represented by ε. For any two strings u and v, $|u|$ and $|u|_B$ denote the length of u in bits and bytes, respectively, $u \| v$ denotes their concatenation, $u \oplus v$ denotes their bitwise XOR, $u \preceq v$ denotes the prefix predicate which assumes the value true if and only if there exists $w \in \{0,1\}^*$ such that $v = u \| w$. We use $u[i,j]$ to denote the substring of u from bit i to bit j inclusive, where the indexes start at 1 and $*$ points to the end of the string. Similarly, $u[i,j]_B$ denotes the substring from byte i to byte j. If i is a non-negative integer, then $\langle i \rangle_\ell$ denotes the unsigned ℓ-bit canonical binary representation of i. Accordingly, $\langle \cdot \rangle^{-1}$ represents the inverse mapping which maps strings of any length to $\mathbb{N}$. We use $\{0,1\}^{**}$ to denote the set of all string sequences.

In every experiment where an adversary interacts with an encryption oracle (real or simulated), we assume that a transcript is maintained of its queries and responses. More specifically, a transcript T is an ordered list of message-ciphertext pairs (m, c), where each entry corresponds to an encryption query. We endow this list with a next() method which returns its entries, one entry per call, in the same order in which they were created – similarly to a queue. Other times, we will treat T as a set and test whether a specific pair (m, c) is in T. When present in an experiment, the sync flag is initially set to true.

It is often convenient to write distinguishing advantages in a compact form. That is, given an adversary $\mathcal{A}$ which interacts with oracles $\mathcal{X}_1, \mathcal{X}_2$ or with oracles $\mathcal{Z}_1, \mathcal{Z}_2$, we write

$$\underset{\mathcal{A}}{\Delta} \begin{bmatrix} \mathcal{X}_1, \mathcal{X}_2 \\ \mathcal{Z}_1, \mathcal{Z}_2 \end{bmatrix} := \left| \mathrm{Prob} \left[\mathcal{A}^{\mathcal{X}_1, \mathcal{X}_2} \Rightarrow 1 \right] - \mathrm{Prob} \left[\mathcal{A}^{\mathcal{Z}_1, \mathcal{Z}_2} \Rightarrow 1 \right] \right|.$$

According to this notation we can for example apply the triangle inequality

$$\left| \mathrm{Prob} \left[\mathcal{A}^{\mathcal{X}_1, \mathcal{X}_2} \Rightarrow 1 \right] - \mathrm{Prob} \left[\mathcal{A}^{\mathcal{Z}_1, \mathcal{Z}_2} \Rightarrow 1 \right] \right|$$
$$\leq \left| \mathrm{Prob} \left[\mathcal{A}^{\mathcal{X}_1, \mathcal{X}_2} \Rightarrow 1 \right] - \mathrm{Prob} \left[\mathcal{A}^{\mathcal{Y}_1, \mathcal{Y}_2} \Rightarrow 1 \right] \right|$$
$$+ \left| \mathrm{Prob} \left[\mathcal{A}^{\mathcal{Y}_1, \mathcal{Y}_2} \Rightarrow 1 \right] - \mathrm{Prob} \left[\mathcal{A}^{\mathcal{Z}_1, \mathcal{Z}_2} \Rightarrow 1 \right] \right|$$

and write

$$\Delta_{\mathcal{A}} \begin{bmatrix} \mathcal{X}_1, \mathcal{X}_2 \\ \mathcal{Z}_1, \mathcal{Z}_2 \end{bmatrix} \leq \Delta_{\mathcal{A}} \begin{bmatrix} \mathcal{X}_1, \mathcal{X}_2 \\ \mathcal{Y}_1, \mathcal{Y}_2 \end{bmatrix} + \Delta_{\mathcal{A}} \begin{bmatrix} \mathcal{Y}_1, \mathcal{Y}_2 \\ \mathcal{Z}_1, \mathcal{Z}_2 \end{bmatrix}.$$

Similarly, if an adversary $\mathcal{A}'$ simulates oracles $\mathcal{X}_2$ resp. $\mathcal{Z}_2$ to $\mathcal{A}$ through some other oracles $\mathcal{X}_2'$ resp. $\mathcal{Z}_2'$ by modifying the answers, e.g., if $\mathcal{X}_2$ and $\mathcal{Z}_2$ output truncated answers of $\mathcal{X}_2'$ and $\mathcal{Z}_2'$, but otherwise executes $\mathcal{A}$, then we can write

$$\Delta_{\mathcal{A}} \begin{bmatrix} \mathcal{X}_1, \mathcal{X}_2 \\ \mathcal{Z}_1, \mathcal{Z}_2 \end{bmatrix} \leq \Delta_{\mathcal{A}} \begin{bmatrix} \mathcal{X}_1, \mathcal{X}_2' \\ \mathcal{Z}_1, \mathcal{Z}_2' \end{bmatrix}.$$

Note that, strictly speaking, the right hand side considers adversary $\mathcal{A}'$, but since this adversary only adapts the oracle replies we take this already into account by using the other oracles in the notation. Moreover, in all cases, $\mathcal{A}'$ will consume the same resources as $\mathcal{A}$, except for a small overhead in its running time to adapt the oracle queries and responses. Since this overhead is usually minor in comparison to the overall running time, we ignore it.

Syntax. We consider two types of symmetric encryption, atomic encryption [8,9] and encryption supporting ciphertext fragmentation [2,11]. In both cases we allow invalid ciphertexts to leak information to the adversary, as in *Subtle AE* [6]. However, in contrast to *Subtle AE* our focus is on symmetric channels rather than nonce-based symmetric encryption. We view the latter as a stepping stone to building the former, and we believe that the utility of our security definitions manifests itself when considering symmetric encryption with more complex functionalities than nonce-based encryption.

An *atomic symmetric encryption scheme* $\mathcal{SE} = (\mathcal{K}, \mathcal{E}, \mathcal{D})$ is a triple of algorithms:

- The randomised key generation algorithm $\mathcal{K}$ returns a secret key K. We will slightly abuse notation and use $\mathcal{K}$ to also identify the key space associated to the key generation algorithm.
- The encryption algorithm $\mathcal{E} : \mathcal{K} \times \{0,1\}^* \to \{0,1\}^*$, may be randomised, stateful or both. It takes as input the secret key $K \in \mathcal{K}$, a plaintext message $m \in \{0,1\}^*$, and returns a ciphertext in $\{0,1\}^*$. For stateful versions it may update its internal state when executed.
- The decryption algorithm $\mathcal{D} : \mathcal{K} \times \{0,1\}^* \to (\{\top, \bot\} \times \{0,1\}^*)$ is deterministic and may be stateful. It takes the secret key K, a ciphertext $c \in \{0,1\}^*$, to return a tuple (v, m) such that $v \in \{\top, \bot\}$ indicates the validity of the corresponding ciphertext and m is a binary string representing a message or some leakage. It may update its state upon execution.

Note that decryption may either return $(\top, m)$, indicating that the ciphertext was valid and decrypts to the message $m \in \{0,1\}^*$, or $(\bot, m)$, indicating that the ciphertext was invalid where $m \in \{0,1\}^*$ may represent an error message, some internal value, or some other form of leakage. The leakage-free setting is modeled by returning $(\bot, \varepsilon)$ in response to an invalid ciphertext.

We further require that an atomic encryption scheme satisfies the following standard correctness condition. We write $c_1, \ldots, c_n \leftarrow \mathcal{E}_K(m_1, \ldots, m_n)$ as shorthand to denote the sequence of encryption operations $c_1 \leftarrow \mathcal{E}_K(m_1), c_2 \leftarrow \mathcal{E}_K(m_2), \ldots, c_n \leftarrow \mathcal{E}_K(m_n)$. Similarly, $(v_1, m_1'), \ldots, (v_n, m_n') \leftarrow \mathcal{D}_K(c_1, \ldots, c_n)$ denotes the analogous sequence of decryption operations.

Definition 1 (Atomic Correctness). *For all keys K output by $\mathcal{K}$ and all message sequences $m_1, \ldots, m_n \in \{0, 1\}^{**}$, if $c_1, \ldots, c_n \leftarrow \mathcal{E}_K(m_1, \ldots, m_n)$ and $(v_1, m_1'), \ldots, (v_n, m_n') \leftarrow \mathcal{D}_K(c_1, \ldots, c_n)$, then for all $1 \leq i \leq n$ it holds that $v_i = \top$ and $m_i' = m_i$.*

We only require decryption to recover the honestly generated messages when ciphertexts are decrypted in the same order as they were produced. This slightly weaker correctness requirement allows us to cater for schemes with a stateful decryption algorithm.

A *symmetric encryption scheme supporting ciphertext fragmentation* $\mathcal{SE} = (\mathcal{K}, \mathcal{E}, \mathcal{D})$ is a triple of algorithms, where $\mathcal{K}$ and $\mathcal{E}$ act as before. The deterministic and possibly stateful decryption algorithm $\mathcal{D} : \mathcal{K} \times \{0, 1\}^* \to (\{\top, \bot\} \times \{0, 1\}^*)^*$, this time, takes as input the secret key K and a ciphertext fragment $f \in \{0, 1\}^*$, and returns a sequence of one or more tuples (v, m) or the empty string. Here $v \in \{\top, \bot\}$ indicates whether the corresponding ciphertext part is valid or not, and m is a binary string representing the recovered message (when $v = \top$) or leakage from an invalid ciphertext (when $v = \bot$).

In contrast to the atomic case, decryption may now return more than one tuple. This is because a ciphertext fragment could be composed of a concatenation of ciphertexts in which case a tuple is returned for each ciphertext. Alternatively, a ciphertext fragment may not contain sufficient information to recover the message or even determine its validity, in which case decryption returns no output. Accordingly, we will generally denote the process of decrypting a ciphertext fragment by $(v_1, m_1') \ldots (v_\ell, m_\ell') \leftarrow \mathcal{D}_K(f)$, where a single output and no output are indicated by $\ell = 1$ and $\ell = 0$ respectively. Note also that in order to support ciphertext fragmentation decryption must necessarily be stateful.

For schemes supporting ciphertext fragmentation we also require a stronger correctness condition. Namely, decryption should recover the original sequence of messages even when the ciphertexts returned by the encryption algorithm are concatenated together, optionally appended with an arbitrary string, and the result is arbitrarily fragmented into substrings which are individually submitted for decryption in their original order. This is stated formally below, using analogous notation for composite encryption and decryption operations as before.

Definition 2 (Correctness Under Ciphertext Fragmentation). *For all keys K output by $\mathcal{K}$, all message sequences $m_1, \ldots, m_n \in \{0, 1\}^{**}$, and all ciphertext fragment sequences $f_1, \ldots, f_k \in \{0, 1\}^{**}$, if $c_1, \ldots, c_n \leftarrow \mathcal{E}_K(m_1, \ldots, m_n)$ and $(v_1, m_1') \ldots (v_\ell, m_\ell') \leftarrow \mathcal{D}_K(f_1, \ldots, f_k)$, where $c_1 \parallel \ldots \parallel c_n \preceq f_1 \parallel \ldots \parallel f_k$, then it holds that $m_i' = m_i$ and $v_i = \top$ for all $1 \leq i \leq n$.*

A Note on Our Choice of Syntax. Our syntax for schemes supporting ciphertext fragmentation differs from that used in [2,11] in three main ways. The most significant difference is that our syntax is more restrictive about how decryption should behave. The syntax in [2,11] allows decryption to return a message in separate chunks, similarly to online decryption [22]. Moreover, what chunk of the message is returned, and when, may vary from scheme to scheme for a given sequence of ciphertext fragments. The only requirement is that the concatenation of the outputs be an encoding of the original sequence of messages. In our case, we ultimately want to relate our security notion to an ideal functionality in the UC framework. Specifying such a functionality forces us to choose a concrete output behaviour for decryption. We opted for a functionality where the message is returned all at once, which is how protocols like TLS and SSH behave in practice. This choice is reflected in our syntax, which allows for slightly simpler security definitions. We encounter a similar issue if we try to extend encryption to take a stream as its input [20]. We would again be forced to decide on a specific functionality regarding how the plaintext stream is to be fragmented. The most natural and common choice in practice, is to separately encrypt each message fragment as soon as it is input to the encryption algorithm. In turn this would yield a syntax that is equivalent to the one we already have.

The other two differences, however, are merely cosmetic. Instead of decryption returning error symbols from some set $\{\perp_1, \perp_2, \dots\}$, decryption now returns $\perp$ together with a string. Clearly this is without loss of generality, as the former case can be easily be mapped to the latter. Thirdly, due to the differences we just described, the end of message symbol (¶), previously used to delineate message boundaries in the decryption output, becomes redundant in our setting and we therefore drop it.

One notable exception that is not captured by our syntax is the InterMAC scheme, described in [11], which does exhibit an online decryption behaviour. It should be possible to formulate a different ideal functionality, that reflects Inter-MAC's behaviour, and replicate our general approach for that setting. However, we do not pursue that direction in this work.

2.2 Security Without Simulation

For atomic encryption schemes we consider two types of security, *plain* and *stateful*. The plain notions of confidentiality and integrity are IND-CCA and INT-CTXT, which correspond to the similarly named notions from Bellare and Namprempre [10] extended to the (stronger) *subtle* security setting of [6], where subtleties refer to leakage from different error messages or release of unverified plaintexts. Note that subtle security follows directly from our extended syntax rather than any specific alteration in the security definitions. Stateful notions of confidentiality (IND-sfCCA) and integrity (INT-sfCTXT) were introduced in [9] to additionally protect against the replay and reordering of ciphertexts. Again, through our choice of syntax, we here extend these stateful notions to the subtle setting. We emphasize that our syntax of atomic encryption schemes requires neither encryption nor decryption to be stateful. However the decryption algorithm must be stateful in order for a scheme to satisfy stateful security – hence the name. For schemes supporting ciphertext fragmentation the confidentiality and integrity analogues are IND-sfCFA and INT-sfCFRG from [2,11] which we here adapt to our syntax. In all three cases, the weaker IND-CPA notion is the usual one since it is unaffected by subtle security, stateful security, or ciphertext fragmentation.

Dec(c')	sfDec(c')	cfDec(f)
$(v, m') \leftarrow \mathcal{D}_K(c')$	$(v, m') \leftarrow \mathcal{D}_K(c')$	$(v_1, m'_1) \ldots (v_\ell, m'_\ell) \leftarrow \mathcal{D}_K(f)$
if $\exists\, m$ s.t. $(m, c') \in$ T	if sync	$F \leftarrow F \,\|\, f; j \leftarrow 1$
$\quad (v, m') \leftarrow (\varepsilon, \varepsilon)$	$\quad (m, c) \leftarrow$ T.next()	while sync $\wedge\, j \leq \ell$
return (v, m')	$\quad$ if $c' = c$	$\quad$ if T $= []$
	$\qquad (v, m') \leftarrow (\varepsilon, \varepsilon)$	$\qquad$ sync $\leftarrow$ false
	$\quad$ else	$\quad$ else
	$\qquad$ sync $\leftarrow$ false	$\qquad (m, c) \leftarrow$ T.next()
	return (v, m')	$\qquad C \leftarrow C \,\|\, c$
		$\qquad$ if $C \preceq F$
		$\qquad\quad j \leftarrow j + 1$
		$\qquad$ else
		$\qquad\quad$ sync $\leftarrow$ false
		return $(v_j, m'_j) \ldots (v_\ell, m'_\ell)$

Fig. 1. Decryption oracles for defining IND-CCA, IND-sfCCA, IND-sfCFA, INT-CTXT, INT-sfCTXT, and INT-sfCFRG security. T is a live transcript of the adversary's queries to its encryption oracle containing message-ciphertext pairs.

Definition 3 (Confidentiality). *Let* $\mathcal{SE} = (\mathcal{K}, \mathcal{E}, \mathcal{D})$ *be an atomic symmetric encryption scheme. Let algorithms* Dec *and* sfDec *be as specified in Fig. 1, then for any adversary* $\mathcal{A}$ *we define the corresponding* IND-CCA *and* IND-sfCCA *advantages as:*

$$\mathsf{Adv}^{\text{ind-cca}}_{\mathcal{SE}}(\mathcal{A}) = \left| \Pr\left[\mathcal{A}^{\mathcal{E}_K(\cdot), \text{Dec}(\cdot)} \Rightarrow 1 \right] - \Pr\left[\mathcal{A}^{\mathcal{E}_K(0^{|\cdot|}), \text{Dec}(\cdot)} \Rightarrow 1 \right] \right|,$$

and

$$\mathsf{Adv}^{\text{ind-sfcca}}_{\mathcal{SE}}(\mathcal{A}) = \left| \Pr\left[\mathcal{A}^{\mathcal{E}_K(\cdot), \text{sfDec}(\cdot)} \Rightarrow 1 \right] - \Pr\left[\mathcal{A}^{\mathcal{E}_K(0^{|\cdot|}), \text{sfDec}(\cdot)} \Rightarrow 1 \right] \right|,$$

where in both cases the probabilities are over $K \leftarrow \mathcal{K}$ *and the algorithms' coin tosses. Alternatively, if* $\mathcal{SE}$ *is a symmetric encryption scheme supporting ciphertext fragmentation, then for any adversary* $\mathcal{A}$ *the corresponding* IND-sfCFA *advantage is given by:*

$$\mathsf{Adv}^{\text{ind-sfcfa}}_{\mathcal{SE}}(\mathcal{A}) = \left| \Pr\left[\mathcal{A}^{\mathcal{E}_K(\cdot), \text{cfDec}(\cdot)} \Rightarrow 1 \right] - \Pr\left[\mathcal{A}^{\mathcal{E}_K(0^{|\cdot|}), \text{cfDec}(\cdot)} \Rightarrow 1 \right] \right|,$$

where cfDec *is as specified in Fig. 1. A scheme* $\mathcal{SE}$ *is said to be* $(\epsilon, \mathcal{R}_\mathcal{A})$-NN *secure, for* NN $\in$ {IND-CCA, IND-sfCCA, IND-sfCFA}, *if for any adversary* $\mathcal{A}$ *with resources at most* $\mathcal{R}_\mathcal{A}$, *its* NN *advantage is bounded by* ϵ.

In the above definition, $\mathcal{E}_K(0^{|\cdot|})$ is an oracle that on input m returns an encryption of $0^{|m|}$. This formulation of confidentiality is equivalent (up to a small constant factor in the advantages) to the more popular left-or-right and real-or-random formulations.

Definition 4 (Ciphertext Integrity). *Let* $\mathcal{SE} = (\mathcal{K}, \mathcal{E}, \mathcal{D})$ *be an atomic symmetric encryption scheme. Let algorithms* Dec *and* sfDec *be as specified in Fig. 1 and* FORGE *denote the event that the decryption oracle returns a pair* (v, m') *where* $v = \top$. *Then for any adversary* $\mathcal{A}$ *the corresponding* INT-CTXT *and* INT-sfCTXT *advantages are defined as:*

$$\mathsf{Adv}^{\mathsf{int\text{-}ctxt}}_{\mathcal{SE}}(\mathcal{A}) = \Pr\left[K \leftarrow \mathcal{K}, \mathcal{A}^{\mathcal{E}_K(\cdot), \mathsf{Dec}(\cdot)} : \mathsf{FORGE} \right],$$

and

$$\mathsf{Adv}^{\mathsf{int\text{-}sfctxt}}_{\mathcal{SE}}(\mathcal{A}) = \Pr\left[K \leftarrow \mathcal{K}, \mathcal{A}^{\mathcal{E}_K(\cdot), \mathsf{sfDec}(\cdot)} : \mathsf{FORGE} \right].$$

Alternatively, if $\mathcal{SE}$ *is a symmetric encryption scheme supporting ciphertext fragmentation, let algorithm* cfDec *be as specified in Fig. 1 and* FORGE *denote the event that the decryption oracle return an output* $(v_1, m'_1), \ldots, (v_\ell, m'_\ell)$ *where* $v_i = \top$ *for some* $1 \leq i \leq \ell$. *Then for any adversary* $\mathcal{A}$ *the corresponding* INT-sfCFRG *advantage is given by:*

$$\mathsf{Adv}^{\mathsf{int\text{-}sfcfrg}}_{\mathcal{SE}}(\mathcal{A}) = \Pr\left[K \leftarrow \mathcal{K}, \mathcal{A}^{\mathcal{E}_K(\cdot), \mathsf{cfDec}(\cdot)} : \mathsf{FORGE} \right],$$

where cfDec *is as specified in Fig. 1. A scheme* $\mathcal{SE}$ *is said to be* $(\epsilon, \mathcal{R}_\mathcal{A})$-NN *secure, for* NN $\in$ {INT-CTXT, INT-sfCTXT, INT-sfCFRG}, *if for any adversary* $\mathcal{A}$ *with resources at most* $\mathcal{R}_\mathcal{A}$, *its* NN *advantage is bounded by* ϵ.

In Sect. 3 we establish a relation between encryption simulatability and key privacy. Key privacy was considered in [1,19] for *stateless* symmetric encryption and then covered more extensively in [7] for the case of public-key encryption. Our definition of key-privacy roughly follows the definitions used in [1,19] but we adapt them to cater for stateful schemes. Roughly speaking, the prior definitions would give the adversary access to two encryption oracles and it would then have to distinguish whether the two oracles use the same key or not. Counter mode encryption would not satisfy this definition since an adversary can easily detect two encryptions under the same key and counter value. However counter mode is meant to be used in a way that never re-uses the same counter value (as even confidentiality would fail in that case) and such a situation should never arise in practice. Accordingly we progress the state of the two encryption oracles simultaneously, by encrypting every message by both instances and return to the adversary only one ciphertext which it is allowed to select via an extra bit b given to the oracle. This is stated more formally below.

Definition 5 (Key Privacy). *Let $\mathcal{SE} = (\mathcal{K}, \mathcal{E}, \mathcal{D})$ be a symmetric encryption scheme, atomic or supporting ciphertext fragmentation. Let $\langle \mathcal{O}_0(\cdot), \mathcal{O}_1(\cdot) \rangle(b, m)$ be the exclusive oracle combination described in Fig. 2, then for any adversary $\mathcal{A}$ we define its* KP-CPA *advantage as:*

$$\mathsf{Adv}^{\mathsf{kp\text{-}cpa}}_{\mathcal{SE}}(\mathcal{A}) = \left| \Pr\left[\mathcal{A}^{\langle \mathcal{E}_K(\cdot), \mathcal{E}_{\bar{K}}(\cdot) \rangle(\cdot, \cdot)} \Rightarrow 1 \right] - \Pr\left[\mathcal{A}^{\langle \mathcal{E}_K(\cdot), \mathcal{E}_K(\cdot) \rangle(\cdot, \cdot)} \Rightarrow 1 \right] \right|,$$

where the probabilities are over the choice of $K, \bar{K} \leftarrow \mathcal{K}$ resp. $K \leftarrow \mathcal{K}$, and the algorithms' coin tosses. A scheme $\mathcal{SE}$ is said to be $(\epsilon, \mathcal{R}_\mathcal{A})$-KP-CPA secure, if for any adversary $\mathcal{A}$ with resources at most $\mathcal{R}_\mathcal{A}$, its KP-CPA advantage is bounded by ϵ.

$$\langle \mathcal{O}_0(\cdot), \mathcal{O}_1(\cdot) \rangle(b, m)$$

$c_0 \leftarrow \mathcal{O}_0(m)$
$c_1 \leftarrow \mathcal{O}_1(m)$
return c_b

Fig. 2. Exclusive oracle combination used in the KP-CPA security definition.

3   Encryption Simulatability

3.1   Defining Encryption Simulatability

As observed in the introduction, IND\$-CPA security stands out from other definitions of confidentiality in that it employs an encryption oracle ($\$(\cdot)$) that does not make use of the encryption key. In particular, we might ask what is special about it that if encryption is indistinguishable from it, then confidentiality is guaranteed? The absence of the encryption key suggests a notion of encryption simulatability and that perhaps pseudorandomness is not really necessary. Indeed this turns out to be the case, but we are still missing one ingredient. The simulator needs to emulate encryption without any knowledge of the message contents except its length. Otherwise the scheme $m \leftarrow \mathcal{E}_K(m)$ would be trivially simulatable but is clearly insecure. A formal definition of encryption simulatability is given below.

Definition 6 (Encryption Simulatability). *Let $\mathcal{SE} = (\mathcal{K}, \mathcal{E}, \mathcal{D})$ be a symmetric encryption scheme, either atomic or supporting ciphertext fragmentation. For an adversary $\mathcal{A}$ and a simulator $\mathcal{S}$ we define the corresponding* ES *advantage as:*

$$\mathsf{Adv}^{\mathsf{es}}_{\mathcal{SE}}(\mathcal{A}, \mathcal{S}) = \Pr\left[K \leftarrow \mathcal{K} : \mathcal{A}^{\mathcal{E}_K(\cdot)} \Rightarrow 1 \right] - \Pr\left[K \leftarrow \mathcal{K} : \mathcal{A}^{\mathcal{S}(|\cdot|)} \Rightarrow 1 \right]$$

The scheme $\mathcal{SE}$ is said to be $(\epsilon, \mathcal{R}_S, \mathcal{R}_A)$-ES secure if there exists a randomised and possibly stateful simulator S, requiring at most $\mathcal{R}_S$ resources per query, such that for any adversary $\mathcal{A}$, requiring at most $\mathcal{R}_A$ resources, its respective advantage $\mathsf{Adv}^{es}_{\mathcal{SE}}(\mathcal{A}, S)$ is bounded by ϵ.

The presence of a simulator in our definition is perhaps reminiscent of other simulation-based security definitions, such as semantic security and even zero knowledge. Intuitively, encryption simulatability says that interacting with the encryption algorithm should convey no knowledge of the key or the message contents. There are some important differences however. In contrast to semantic security, here the simulator is emulating the encryption algorithm rather than the adversary. The simulator cannot depend on the adversary either, due to the reversed order of quantifiers. Finally, contrary to the case of zero knowledge, here the simulator is not allowed to rewind the adversary.

3.2   Understanding Encryption Simulatability

We motivated ES as a generalisation of IND\$-CPA, and indeed from the definition it follows straight away that IND\$-CPA implies ES for any length-regular scheme. Showing that the reverse implication does not hold, i.e., ES $\not\Longrightarrow$ IND\$-CPA is also straightforward, e.g., if the ciphertext contains redundant 0-bits. Despite the differences we mentioned previously, between semantic security (equivalently IND-CPA) and ES, the two notions turn out to be equivalent. In essence, for any IND-CPA symmetric encryption scheme there exists a *stateful* encryption simulator which samples a fresh key at the beginning and runs the encryption algorithm on that key and a fixed message of the length indicated in its input. This is stated more formally together with the reverse implication in Theorem 1.

Theorem 1 (IND-CPA $\Longleftrightarrow$ ES). *Let $\mathcal{SE} = (\mathcal{K}, \mathcal{E}, \mathcal{D})$ be a symmetric encryption scheme.*

(a) Then for any encryption simulator S it holds that:

$$\mathsf{Adv}^{\mathsf{ind\text{-}cpa}}_{\mathcal{SE}}(\mathcal{A}) \leq 2 \cdot \mathsf{Adv}^{es}_{\mathcal{SE}}(\mathcal{A}, S).$$

(b) Furthermore, there exists a stateful encryption simulator $\bar{S}(\ell)$, which on its first input runs $\bar{K} \twoheadleftarrow \mathcal{K}$ once and responds to every query with $\mathcal{E}_{\bar{K}}(0^\ell)$, such that:

$$\mathsf{Adv}^{es}_{\mathcal{SE}}(\mathcal{A}, \bar{S}) \leq \mathsf{Adv}^{\mathsf{ind\text{-}cpa}}_{\mathcal{SE}}(\mathcal{A}).$$

Proof. For any adversary $\mathcal{A}$ its IND-CPA advantage given by:

$$\mathsf{Adv}^{\mathsf{ind\text{-}cpa}}_{\mathcal{SE}}(\mathcal{A}) = \mathop{\Delta}_{\mathcal{A}} \begin{bmatrix} \mathcal{E}_K(\cdot) \\ \mathcal{E}_K(0^{|\cdot|}) \end{bmatrix}.$$

By the triangle inequality we obtain:

$$\leq \mathop{\Delta}_{\mathcal{A}} \begin{bmatrix} \mathcal{E}_K(\cdot) \\ S(|\cdot|) \end{bmatrix} + \mathop{\Delta}_{\mathcal{A}} \begin{bmatrix} S(|\cdot|) \\ \mathcal{E}_K(0^{|\cdot|}) \end{bmatrix}.$$

Now the first distinguishing game is exactly the ES game, whereas the second game can be reduced to the ES game. In particular, any query m can be simulated by querying $0^{|m|}$ in the ES game, since $|0^{|m|}| = |m|$. Thus it follows that:

$$\mathsf{Adv}_{\mathcal{SE}}^{\mathsf{ind\text{-}cpa}}(\mathcal{A}) \leq 2 \cdot \mathsf{Adv}_{\mathcal{SE}}^{\mathsf{es}}(\mathcal{A}, \mathcal{S}).$$

This proves the first part of the theorem, we now prove the other direction. For the given simulator $\bar{\mathcal{S}}$ and any adversary $\mathcal{A}$ we have that:

$$\mathsf{Adv}_{\mathcal{SE}}^{\mathsf{es}}(\mathcal{A}, \bar{\mathcal{S}}) = \mathop{\Delta}_{\mathcal{A}} \begin{bmatrix} \mathcal{E}_K(\cdot) \\ \mathcal{E}_{\bar{K}}(0^{|\cdot|}) \end{bmatrix}.$$

Applying the triangle inequality we obtain:

$$\leq \mathop{\Delta}_{\mathcal{A}} \begin{bmatrix} \mathcal{E}_K(\cdot) \\ \mathcal{E}_K(0^{|\cdot|}) \end{bmatrix} + \mathop{\Delta}_{\mathcal{A}} \begin{bmatrix} \mathcal{E}_K(0^{|\cdot|}) \\ \mathcal{E}_{\bar{K}}(0^{|\cdot|}) \end{bmatrix}.$$

Now note that the first term is exactly the IND-CPA advantage, whereas the second term is zero because the two oracles are distributional identical, i.e. for any sequence of queries they yield identically distributed responses (over the choice of the key and potentially the randomness of the encryption scheme). Thus, the result follows:

$$\mathsf{Adv}_{\mathcal{SE}}^{\mathsf{es}}(\mathcal{A}, \bar{\mathcal{S}}) \leq \mathsf{Adv}_{\mathcal{SE}}^{\mathsf{ind\text{-}cpa}}(\mathcal{A}) + 0.$$

$\square$

One could also consider chosen-ciphertext extensions of encryption simulatability (ES-ATK for ATK $\in \{\mathsf{CCA}, \mathsf{sfCCA}, \mathsf{CFA}\}$) by additionally providing the adversary with access to the corresponding decryption oracle from Fig. 1. While the first implication extends to these settings, i.e. ES-ATK $\implies$ IND-ATK, the implication in the other direction does not! The reason can be seen in the above proof for the IND-CPA case. In the final step of the proof the second advantage term in the proof is no longer zero when a decryption oracle is available. To see why, consider an IND-CCA scheme where every ciphertext is valid, i.e. decrypts to some string [18]. Now modify this scheme such that it uses two keys, one used for encryption and decryption and the other is appended to the ciphertexts during encryption. Decryption now checks whether the correct key is appended to the ciphertext, if so it proceeds to decrypt the rest of the ciphertext and returns an error otherwise. The resulting scheme is still IND-CCA secure but a simulator can only guess the right key with negligible probability. An adversary can distinguish the two cases by modifying the part of the ciphertext which is not the key and observe whether its decryption returns a string or an error message. This separation extends easily to the sfCCA and CFA settings. Thus the equivalence between encryption simulatability and semantic security does not extend to the chosen-ciphertext setting.

Interestingly, if we further require that the simulator be stateless, meaning that it maintains no state and uses independent coins in each call, then encryption simulatability additionally guarantees key privacy. The implication holds for schemes which are either stateless or whose state progression is independent of the coins used, which is usually the case in practice, e.g., if a counter is incremented for each call.

Theorem 2 (ES $\wedge$ **Stateless**($\mathcal{S}$) $\implies$ KP-CPA). *Let $\mathcal{SE} = (\mathcal{K}, \mathcal{E}, \mathcal{D})$ be a symmetric encryption scheme such that $\mathcal{E}$ uses fresh coins on each call, and is either stateless or it progresses its state independently of its coins. Then for a stateless simulator $\mathcal{S}$ using fresh coins on every query and any adversary $\mathcal{A}$, it holds that:*

$$\mathsf{Adv}_{\mathcal{SE}}^{\mathsf{kp\text{-}cpa}}(\mathcal{A}) \leq 3 \cdot \mathsf{Adv}_{\mathcal{SE}}^{\mathsf{es}}(\mathcal{A}, \mathcal{S}).$$

Proof. For any adversary $\mathcal{A}$ the KP-CPA advantage is given by:

$$\mathsf{Adv}_{\mathcal{SE}}^{\mathsf{kp\text{-}cpa}}(\mathcal{A}) = \underset{\mathcal{A}}{\Delta} \begin{bmatrix} \langle \mathcal{E}_K(\cdot), \mathcal{E}_{\bar{K}}(\cdot) \rangle (\cdot, \cdot) \\ \langle \mathcal{E}_K(\cdot), \mathcal{E}_K(\cdot) \rangle (\cdot, \cdot) \end{bmatrix}.$$

By the triangle inequality, for any encryption simulator $\mathcal{S}$ we have that:

$$\leq \underset{\mathcal{A}}{\Delta} \begin{bmatrix} \langle \mathcal{E}_K(\cdot), \mathcal{E}_{\bar{K}}(\cdot) \rangle (\cdot, \cdot) \\ \langle \mathcal{E}_K(\cdot), \mathcal{S}(|\cdot|) \rangle (\cdot, \cdot) \end{bmatrix} + \underset{\mathcal{A}}{\Delta} \begin{bmatrix} \langle \mathcal{E}_K(\cdot), \mathcal{S}(|\cdot|) \rangle (\cdot, \cdot) \\ \langle \mathcal{S}(|\cdot|), \mathcal{S}(|\cdot|) \rangle (\cdot, \cdot) \end{bmatrix}$$
$$+ \underset{\mathcal{A}}{\Delta} \begin{bmatrix} \langle \mathcal{S}(|\cdot|), \mathcal{S}(|\cdot|) \rangle (\cdot, \cdot) \\ \langle \mathcal{E}_K(\cdot), \mathcal{E}_K(\cdot) \rangle (\cdot, \cdot) \end{bmatrix}.$$

Each of the above terms can be reduced to the encryption simulatability game. In the first term the reduction (playing against $\mathcal{E}_{\bar{K}}(\cdot)$ or $\mathcal{S}(|\cdot|)$) simulates the first oracle $\mathcal{E}_K(\cdot)$ by sampling an independent encryption key K. In the second term the reduction simulates the second oracle by running its own copy of the simulator. The third reduction is where we require the simulator to be stateless and the encryption algorithm to have a state progression that is independent of its coins. The reduction uses one instance of the simulator to emulate two independent ones, which is only possible if the simulator answers each query independently. Similarly for encryption, if the state progression depends only on the key and the message sequence, then both instances of the left and right oracle will progress through the same sequence of states and can therefore be emulated via a single instance. Thus we obtain:

$$\mathsf{Adv}_{\mathcal{SE}}^{\mathsf{kp\text{-}cpa}}(\mathcal{A}) \leq \underset{\mathcal{A}}{\Delta} \begin{bmatrix} \mathcal{E}_{\bar{K}}(\cdot) \\ \mathcal{S}(|\cdot|) \end{bmatrix} + \underset{\mathcal{A}}{\Delta} \begin{bmatrix} \mathcal{E}_K(\cdot) \\ \mathcal{S}(|\cdot|) \end{bmatrix} + \underset{\mathcal{A}}{\Delta} \begin{bmatrix} \mathcal{S}(|\cdot|) \\ \mathcal{E}_K(\cdot) \end{bmatrix} \leq 3 \cdot \mathsf{Adv}_{\mathcal{SE}}^{\mathsf{es}}(\mathcal{A}, \mathcal{S}).$$

$\square$

We emphasise that the above implication necessitates that the simulator be stateless. That is, if the simulator is allowed to be stateful then ES does not imply KP-CPA. In particular, a scheme may leak a fixed portion of its key in its ciphertexts and still be IND-CPA secure. Then by Theorem 1 the scheme has a *stateful* encryption simulator, but clearly the scheme is not key private.

A Length-Hiding Variant. Our definition of encryption simulatability could be extended to offer a limited form of length hiding by replacing the length function $|\cdot|$ with a rounding length function $\lceil\cdot\rceil$. This would partition the message space into intervals according to the message length. Then messages of differing lengths but wich fall within the same interval would map to the same input to the simulator. Intuitively, the simulator can now only leak the length interval that the message belongs to but not its precise length. This security notion nicely captures the intended protection against traffic analysis offered by practical schemes which pad messages up to a multiple of the block length or some larger value.

4   Decryption Simulatability

It also makes sense to consider an analogous security notion where decryption is required to be simulatable. Although not stated explicitly, security proofs often involve either simulating part of the decryption oracle or employ a specific type of simulator. Indeed ciphertext integrity can be viewed as requiring the existence of a specific type of decryption simulator—one which returns $\bot$ to every query. Error predictability [20] and leakage simulation [6] are two other examples where parts of the decryption algorithm is simulated. The notion we propose is a generalisation of these ideas, adapted to the channel setting, where we require the whole decryption algorithm to be simulatable. It also allows us to argue about the chosen ciphertext security of schemes which do not provide ciphertext integrity, such as the schemes proposed in [18], where any string constitutes a valid ciphertext but it will decrypt to a random-looking message.

4.1   Defining Decryption Simulatability

When defining decryption simulatability it makes sense to also give the adversary access to the encryption algorithm. Then simulation of decryption requests is only possible if as usual we prohibit the adversary from forwarding the ciphertexts it obtains from the encryption oracle. In this particular case, however, we have an alternative option. We can lift these restrictions from the adversary and instead give the decryption simulator access to a live transcript of the encryption queries. Intuitively, this information is already known to the adversary and should result in an equivalent security notion. However, as it turns out, this intuition is not quite correct. We need to restrict the simulator's access to the transcript in order for security to be preserved.

To see why, consider the classical example where we alter a scheme by appending a redundant bit to the ciphertext during encryption and ignore this bit during decryption. This modification renders the scheme malleable and thereby fails to be IND-CCA even if the underlying scheme is. However the resulting scheme does have a decryption simulator if it is given unrestricted access to the encryption transcript. In particular, the decryption simulator could use the transcript to simulate the decryption of ciphertexts which are not in the transcript. More concretely, let us assume that the underlying scheme is IND-CPA secure and provides ciphertext integrity. Now, if the encryption of m returned $c\|0$ and the adversary queries $c\|1$, the simulator can, through the available transcript, detect that this is a mauled ciphertext and return m as its response. Alternatively, if the ciphertext is unrelated to a prior encryption query, the simulator returns $\perp$. Thus, if we were to allow unrestricted access to the transcript, the resulting notion of decryption simulatability would not suffice to reduce IND-CCA security to IND-CPA security.

To overcome this limitation we will wrap the simulator S with a *fixed* wrapper algorithm that has access to the transcript and possibly overwrites the outputs of S. Specifically, the wrapper will detect whether a ciphertext corresponds to a prior encryption query and replace the output of S with the message in the transcript, unnoticeable for the simulator. Equivalently, the resulting algorithm can be viewed as a composite decryption simulator where the wrapper component has access to the transcript but its functionality is fixed and S has no access to the transcript but its functionality is unrestricted and may depend on the scheme. We consider three different wrappers V, W, and Z, described in Fig. 3, each yielding a different notion of decryption simulatability. The first, denoted by DS, is plain decryption simulatability and is intended for atomic schemes. Stateful decryption simulatability (SDS) corresponds to the stateful family of security notions which additionally protect against replay and reordering. Fragmented decryption simulatability (FDS) is intended for schemes supporting ciphertext fragmentation.

Definition 7 (Decryption Simulatability). *Let $\mathcal{SE} = (\mathcal{K}, \mathcal{E}, \mathcal{D})$ be an atomic symmetric encryption scheme. For an adversary $\mathcal{A}$ and a decryption simulator S we define the corresponding* DS *and* SDS *advantages as:*

$$\mathsf{Adv}^{\mathsf{ds}}_{\mathcal{SE}}(\mathcal{A}, S) = \Pr\left[\mathcal{A}^{\mathcal{E}_K(\cdot), \mathcal{D}_K(\cdot)} \Rightarrow 1 \right] - \Pr\left[\mathcal{A}^{\mathcal{E}_K(\cdot), \mathsf{V}[S](\cdot)} \Rightarrow 1 \right],$$

and

$$\mathsf{Adv}^{\mathsf{sds}}_{\mathcal{SE}}(\mathcal{A}, S) = \Pr\left[\mathcal{A}^{\mathcal{E}_K(\cdot), \mathcal{D}_K(\cdot)} \Rightarrow 1 \right] - \Pr\left[\mathcal{A}^{\mathcal{E}_K(\cdot), \mathsf{W}[S](\cdot)} \Rightarrow 1 \right].$$

where the probabilities are over $K \leftarrow \mathcal{K}$ and the algorithms' coin tosses. Alternatively, if $\mathcal{SE}$ is a symmetric encryption scheme supporting ciphertext fragmentation, its corresponding FDS *advantage is given by:*

$$\mathsf{Adv}^{\mathsf{fds}}_{\mathcal{SE}}(\mathcal{A}, S) = \Pr\left[\mathcal{A}^{\mathcal{E}_K(\cdot), \mathcal{D}_K(\cdot)} \Rightarrow 1 \right] - \Pr\left[\mathcal{A}^{\mathcal{E}_K(\cdot), \mathsf{Z}[S](\cdot)} \Rightarrow 1 \right].$$

A scheme $\mathcal{SE}$ is said to be $(\epsilon, \mathcal{R}_S, \mathcal{R}_\mathcal{A})$-NN secure, for NN $\in \{\mathsf{DS}, \mathsf{SDS}, \mathsf{FDS}\}$, *if there exists a randomised and possibly stateful simulator S, requiring at most $\mathcal{R}_S$ resources per query, such that for any adversary $\mathcal{A}$, requiring at most $\mathcal{R}_\mathcal{A}$ resources, its respective advantage $\mathsf{Adv}^{\mathsf{nn}}_{\mathcal{SE}}(\mathcal{A}, S)$ is bounded by ϵ.*

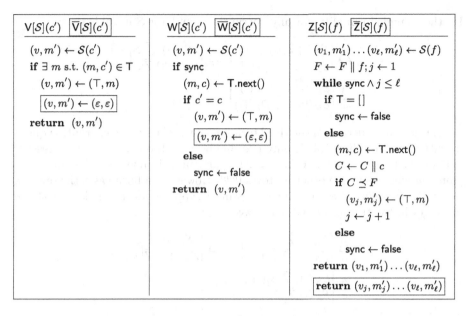

Fig. 3. The V and W wrappers for an atomic decryption simulator and the Z wrapper for the decryption simulator supporting ciphertext fragmentation, used to define decryption simulatability and channel simulatability. In all three cases the boxed code is omitted. In the suppressing variants $\overline{V}$, $\overline{W}$, and $\overline{Z}$ the boxed lines of code replace the lines above them. T is a live transcript of the adversary's queries to the encryption oracle and is not accessible to S. Note that $(\varepsilon, \varepsilon)$ represents the empty string.

4.2 Decryption Simulatability and Chosen-Ciphertext Security

The next theorem states that, as intended, decryption simulatability suffices to reduce chosen ciphertext security to chosen plaintext security. We here state the theorem for the case of schemes supporting ciphertext fragmentation but analogous results hold for atomic schemes in the plain security setting (IND-CPA $\wedge$ DS $\implies$ IND-CCA) as well as the stateful security setting (IND-CPA $\wedge$ SDS $\implies$ IND-sfCCA).

Theorem 3 (IND-CPA $\wedge$ FDS $\implies$ IND-sfCFA). *Let* $\mathcal{SE} = (\mathcal{K}, \mathcal{E}, \mathcal{D})$ *be a symmetric encryption scheme supporting ciphertext fragmentation. Then for any adversary* $\mathcal{A}$ *and any decryption simulator* S *it holds that:*

$$\mathsf{Adv}_{\mathcal{SE}}^{\text{ind-sfcfa}}(\mathcal{A}) \leq \mathsf{Adv}_{\mathcal{SE}}^{\text{ind-cpa}}(\mathcal{A}) + 2 \cdot \mathsf{Adv}_{\mathcal{SE}}^{\text{fds}}(\mathcal{A}, S).$$

Proof. Observe that the decryption oracle $\mathsf{cfDec}(\cdot)$ in Fig. 1 is identical to $\overline{Z}[\mathcal{D}_K](\cdot)$, where $\overline{Z}$ is described in Fig. 3. Then, for any adversary $\mathcal{A}$ its IND-sfCFA advantage is given by:

$$\mathsf{Adv}_{\mathcal{SE}}^{\text{ind-sfcfa}}(\mathcal{A}) = \underset{\mathcal{A}}{\Delta} \begin{bmatrix} \mathcal{E}_K(\cdot) \,, \overline{Z}[\mathcal{D}_K](\cdot) \\ \mathcal{E}_K(0^{|\cdot|}), \overline{Z}[\mathcal{D}_K](\cdot) \end{bmatrix}.$$

By the triangle inequality, for any decryption simulator $\mathcal{S}$ it holds that:

$$\leq \mathop{\Delta}_{\mathcal{A}} \begin{bmatrix} \mathcal{E}_K(\cdot),\overline{Z}[\mathcal{D}_K](\cdot) \\ \mathcal{E}_K(\cdot), \ \overline{Z}[\mathcal{S}](\cdot) \end{bmatrix} + \mathop{\Delta}_{\mathcal{A}} \begin{bmatrix} \mathcal{E}_K(\cdot) \ ,\overline{Z}[\mathcal{S}](\cdot) \\ \mathcal{E}_K(0^{|\cdot|}),\overline{Z}[\mathcal{S}](\cdot) \end{bmatrix}$$
$$+ \mathop{\Delta}_{\mathcal{A}} \begin{bmatrix} \mathcal{E}_K(0^{|\cdot|}), \ \overline{Z}[\mathcal{S}](\cdot) \\ \mathcal{E}_K(0^{|\cdot|}),\overline{Z}[\mathcal{D}_K](\cdot) \end{bmatrix}.$$

By means of a reduction on the third term we now replace every encryption query m with $0^{|m|}$. Note how this is only possible because the wrapper is suppressing and would not be possible otherwise. In particular, in one case the transcript stores m whereas in the other it stores $0^{|m|}$. However, in both cases the oracle's behaviour is identical since the suppressing wrapper does not make use of the messages in the transcript. We now have that:

$$\leq \mathop{\Delta}_{\mathcal{A}} \begin{bmatrix} \mathcal{E}_K(\cdot),\overline{Z}[\mathcal{D}_K](\cdot) \\ \mathcal{E}_K(\cdot), \ \overline{Z}[\mathcal{S}](\cdot) \end{bmatrix} + \mathop{\Delta}_{\mathcal{A}} \begin{bmatrix} \mathcal{E}_K(\cdot) \ ,\overline{Z}[\mathcal{S}](\cdot) \\ \mathcal{E}_K(0^{|\cdot|}),\overline{Z}[\mathcal{S}](\cdot) \end{bmatrix}$$
$$+ \mathop{\Delta}_{\mathcal{A}} \begin{bmatrix} \mathcal{E}_K(\cdot), \ \overline{Z}[\mathcal{S}](\cdot) \\ \mathcal{E}_K(\cdot),\overline{Z}[\mathcal{D}_K](\cdot) \end{bmatrix}.$$

We now reduce the first and third terms to the FDS game. We employ a straightforward reduction that applies $\overline{Z}$ to the decryption oracle, and observe that applying $\overline{Z}$ after Z is equivalent to applying $\overline{Z}$ directly. This means we can simulate $\overline{Z}[\mathcal{D}_K]$ resp. $\overline{Z}[\mathcal{S}]$ through $Z[\mathcal{D}_K]$ and $Z[\mathcal{S}]$, and we can then also take advantage of $Z[\mathcal{D}_K] = \mathcal{D}_K$. Regarding the second term, it can be reduced to IND-CPA by running a local copy of the decryption simulator and wrapper. This yields:

$$\leq \mathop{\Delta}_{\mathcal{A}} \begin{bmatrix} \mathcal{E}_K(\cdot),\mathcal{D}_K(\cdot) \\ \mathcal{E}_K(\cdot),Z[\mathcal{S}](\cdot) \end{bmatrix} + \mathop{\Delta}_{\mathcal{A}} \begin{bmatrix} \mathcal{E}_K(\cdot) \\ \mathcal{E}_K(0^{|\cdot|}) \end{bmatrix} + \mathop{\Delta}_{\mathcal{A}} \begin{bmatrix} \mathcal{E}_K(\cdot),Z[\mathcal{S}](\cdot) \\ \mathcal{E}_K(\cdot), \mathcal{D}_K(\cdot) \end{bmatrix},$$
$$= \mathsf{Adv}_{\mathcal{SE}}^{\mathsf{fds}}(\mathcal{A},\mathcal{S}) + \mathsf{Adv}_{\mathcal{SE}}^{\mathsf{ind\text{-}cpa}}(\mathcal{A}) + \mathsf{Adv}_{\mathcal{SE}}^{\mathsf{fds}}(\mathcal{A},\mathcal{S}).$$

$$\square$$

Note that chosen ciphertext security does not imply decryption simulatability, i.e. IND-CCA $\not\Longrightarrow$ DS. To show this separation we can use again the same counterexample that we used in the discussion following Theorem 1. That is, a scheme can leak part of the key in its ciphertext and still be IND-CCA secure. Then decryption can behave differently, by returning a string or an error message, depending on whether a ciphertext contains the right key or not. Now, since a decryption simulator does not know the key, it cannot successfully emulate this behaviour and is therefore not DS secure. However, for the case of encryption simulatability the implication is valid, that is, ES-CCA $\Longrightarrow$ DS. In particular, we can simulate decryption by running the algorithm on an independently sampled key. Thus, if encryption is simulatable to an adversary with oracle access to decryption, it follows that decryption is simulatable to an adversary with oracle access to encryption. Analogous relations hold for stateful security and schemes supporting ciphertext fragmentation. Below we state more formally, with proof, the relation for the fragmentation setting.

Theorem 4 (ES-sfCFA $\implies$ FDS). *Let $\mathcal{SE} = (\mathcal{K}, \mathcal{E}, \mathcal{D})$ be a symmetric encryption scheme supporting ciphertext fragmentation. Then there exists a stateful decryption simulator $\mathcal{S}_D(c)$, which on its first input runs $\bar{K} \twoheadleftarrow \mathcal{K}$ and responds to every query using $\mathcal{D}_{\bar{K}}(c)$, such that for any encryption simulator $\mathcal{S}_E$ it holds that:*

$$\mathsf{Adv}_{\mathcal{SE}}^{\mathsf{fds}}(\mathcal{A}, \mathcal{S}_D) \leq 2 \cdot \mathsf{Adv}_{\mathcal{SE}}^{\mathsf{es\text{-}sfcfa}}(\mathcal{A}, \mathcal{S}_E).$$

Proof. For the given simulator $\mathcal{S}_D$, which decrypts under a freshly chosen key $\bar{K}$, and any adversary $\mathcal{A}$ the FDS advantage is given by:

$$\mathsf{Adv}_{\mathcal{SE}}^{\mathsf{fds}}(\mathcal{A}, \mathcal{S}_D) = \mathop{\Delta}_{\mathcal{A}} \begin{bmatrix} \mathcal{E}_K(\cdot), & \mathcal{D}_K(\cdot) \\ \mathcal{E}_K(\cdot), \mathsf{Z}[\mathcal{S}_D](\cdot) \end{bmatrix} = \mathop{\Delta}_{\mathcal{A}} \begin{bmatrix} \mathcal{E}_K(\cdot), & \mathcal{D}_K(\cdot) \\ \mathcal{E}_K(\cdot), \mathsf{Z}[\mathcal{D}_{\bar{K}}](\cdot) \end{bmatrix}.$$

By the triangle inequality, for any encryption simulator $\mathcal{S}_E$ it holds that:

$$\leq \mathop{\Delta}_{\mathcal{A}} \begin{bmatrix} \mathcal{E}_K(\cdot), & \mathcal{D}_K(\cdot) \\ \mathcal{S}_E(|\cdot|), \mathsf{Z}[\mathcal{D}_K](\cdot) \end{bmatrix} + \mathop{\Delta}_{\mathcal{A}} \begin{bmatrix} \mathcal{S}_E(|\cdot|), \mathsf{Z}[\mathcal{D}_K](\cdot) \\ \mathcal{E}_K(\cdot), \mathsf{Z}[\mathcal{D}_{\bar{K}}](\cdot) \end{bmatrix}.$$

By the correctness of the scheme, we can replace $\mathcal{D}_K(\cdot)$ by $\mathsf{Z}[\mathcal{D}_K](\cdot)$ in the upper row of the first term. With respect to the second term we drop the decryption oracle since it can be simulated locally by sampling an independent key and maintaining a local transcript for simulating the wrapper. We thus have:

$$\leq \mathop{\Delta}_{\mathcal{A}} \begin{bmatrix} \mathcal{E}_K(\cdot), \mathsf{Z}[\mathcal{D}_K](\cdot) \\ \mathcal{S}_E(|\cdot|), \mathsf{Z}[\mathcal{D}_K](\cdot) \end{bmatrix} + \mathop{\Delta}_{\mathcal{A}} \begin{bmatrix} \mathcal{S}_E(|\cdot|) \\ \mathcal{E}_K(\cdot) \end{bmatrix}.$$

The first term can now be reduced to a similar game employing a suppressing wrapper since the suppressed queries can be answered by maintaining a local copy of the transcript. Therefore:

$$= \mathop{\Delta}_{\mathcal{A}} \begin{bmatrix} \mathcal{E}_K(\cdot), \bar{\mathsf{Z}}[\mathcal{D}_K](\cdot) \\ \mathcal{S}_E(|\cdot|), \bar{\mathsf{Z}}[\mathcal{D}_K](\cdot) \end{bmatrix} + \mathop{\Delta}_{\mathcal{A}} \begin{bmatrix} \mathcal{S}_E(|\cdot|) \\ \mathcal{E}_K(\cdot) \end{bmatrix},$$

and the result now follows

$$= \mathsf{Adv}_{\mathcal{SE}}^{\mathsf{es\text{-}sfcfa}}(\mathcal{A}, \mathcal{S}_E) + \mathsf{Adv}_{\mathcal{SE}}^{\mathsf{es}}(\mathcal{A}, \mathcal{S}_E).$$

$\square$

4.3 Decryption Simulatability and Ciphertext Integrity

Informally, decryption simulatability says that access to the decryption algorithm is of no use to an adversary, thereby allowing us to reduce chosen ciphertext security to chosen plaintext security. However, by itself, this does not guarantee ciphertext integrity. Luckily, we only need to impose a minor additional requirement on the simulator for it to cover ciphertext integrity. Essentially, the requirement is that the simulator always returns an error for mauled ciphertexts. It then follows that the real decryption algorithm can only deviate from this behaviour with negligible probability. In our definition we conveniently make use of the suppressing variants of the wrapper algorithms, from Fig. 3, in order to filter out any ciphertexts that were obtained from the encryption oracle.

Definition 8 (Decryption Simulatability with Integrity). *Let* $\mathcal{SE} = (\mathcal{K}, \mathcal{E}, \mathcal{D})$ *be an atomic symmetric encryption scheme. Then* $\mathcal{SE}$ *is said to be* $(\epsilon, \mathcal{R}_\mathcal{S}, \mathcal{R}_\mathcal{A})$*-DS-I or* $(\epsilon, \mathcal{R}_\mathcal{S}, \mathcal{R}_\mathcal{A})$*-SDS-I secure, if it is respectively* $(\epsilon, \mathcal{R}_\mathcal{S}, \mathcal{R}_\mathcal{A})$*-DS or* $(\epsilon, \mathcal{R}_\mathcal{S}, \mathcal{R}_\mathcal{A})$*-SDS secure, and, in addition, the corresponding simulator* $\mathcal{S}$ *augmented with* $\overline{\mathsf{V}}$ *or* $\overline{\mathsf{W}}$ *respectively never (with probability zero) outputs a pair* (v, m') *where* $v = \top$.

Similarly, if $\mathcal{SE}$ *is a symmetric encryption scheme supporting ciphertext fragmentation it is said to be* $(\epsilon, \mathcal{R}_\mathcal{S}, \mathcal{R}_\mathcal{A})$*-FDS-I secure if it is* $(\epsilon, \mathcal{R}_\mathcal{S}, \mathcal{R}_\mathcal{A})$*-FDS secure and its corresponding simulator* $\mathcal{S}$ *is such that* $\overline{\mathsf{Z}}[\mathcal{S}]$ *never (with probability zero) returns an output* $(v_1, m'_1), \ldots, (v_\ell, m'_\ell)$ *where* $v_i = \top$ *for some* $1 \leq i \leq \ell$.

Informally, the above says that the simulator will never return a valid output for a ciphertext that is not in the transcript (DS-I) or once the queries become out of sync (SDS-I and FDS-I). Note that such a property can be verified simply by inspecting the code of the simulator. Thus no additional steps may be required to prove ciphertext integrity if the decryption simulator already satisfies this condition.

The following theorem says that decryption simulatability with integrity implies the usual notions of ciphertext integrity. We prove this only for schemes supporting ciphertext fragmentation, but analogous theorems and proofs hold for the atomic setting, i.e. DS-I $\implies$ INT-CTXT and SDS-I $\implies$ INT-sfCTXT.

Theorem 5 (FDS-I $\implies$ INT-sfCFRG). *Let* $\mathcal{SE} = (\mathcal{K}, \mathcal{E}, \mathcal{D})$ *be a symmetric encryption scheme supporting ciphertext fragmentation and let* $\mathcal{S}$ *be a decryption simulator such that it is* $(\epsilon, \mathcal{R}_\mathcal{S}, \mathcal{R}_\mathcal{A})$*-FDS-I secure. Then* $\mathcal{SE}$ *is* $(\epsilon, \mathcal{R}_\mathcal{A})$*-INT-sfCFRG secure.*

Proof. Note that $\mathsf{cfDec}(\cdot)$ is identical to $\overline{\mathsf{Z}}[\mathcal{D}_K](\cdot)$. Hence for any simulator $\mathcal{S}$ and any adversary $\mathcal{A}$ with at most $\mathcal{R}_\mathcal{A}$ resources, we have that:

$$\underset{\mathcal{A}}{\Delta} \begin{bmatrix} \mathcal{E}_K(\cdot), \mathsf{cfDec}(\cdot) \\ \mathcal{E}_K(\cdot), \overline{\mathsf{Z}}[\mathcal{S}](\cdot) \end{bmatrix} = \underset{\mathcal{A}}{\Delta} \begin{bmatrix} \mathcal{E}_K(\cdot), \overline{\mathsf{Z}}[\mathcal{D}_K](\cdot) \\ \mathcal{E}_K(\cdot), \overline{\mathsf{Z}}[\mathcal{S}](\cdot) \end{bmatrix}.$$

Then, by a straightforward reduction that applies $\overline{\mathsf{Z}}$ to the decryption oracle and observing that $\overline{\mathsf{Z}}[\mathsf{Z}[\mathcal{S}]](\cdot)$ is identical to $\overline{\mathsf{Z}}[\mathcal{S}](\cdot)$, it follows that:

$$\leq \underset{\mathcal{A}}{\Delta} \begin{bmatrix} \mathcal{E}_K(\cdot), \mathcal{D}_K(\cdot) \\ \mathcal{E}_K(\cdot), \mathsf{Z}[\mathcal{S}](\cdot) \end{bmatrix},$$

$$= \mathsf{Adv}_{\mathcal{SE}}^{\mathsf{fds}}(\mathcal{A}, \mathcal{S}).$$

From the above relation it then follows that:

$$\mathsf{Adv}^{\mathsf{int\text{-}sfcfrg}}_{\mathcal{SE}}(\mathcal{A}) = \Pr\left[K \twoheadleftarrow \mathcal{K}, \mathcal{A}^{\mathcal{E}_K(\cdot),\mathsf{cfDec}(\cdot)} : \mathsf{FORGE} \right],$$

$$\leq \Pr\left[\mathcal{A}^{\mathcal{E}_K(\cdot),\overline{\mathcal{Z}}[\mathcal{S}](\cdot)} : \mathsf{FORGE} \right] + \mathsf{Adv}^{\mathsf{fds}}_{\mathcal{SE}}(\mathcal{A},\mathcal{S}).$$

Now since $\mathcal{SE}$ is $(\epsilon, \mathcal{R}_{\mathcal{S}}, \mathcal{R}_{\mathcal{A}})$-FDS-I secure, there exists a simulator such that the first term is zero and the second term is bounded by ϵ, thus:

$$\leq \epsilon.$$

Comparing DS to Prior Notions. We are not the first to consider notions requiring the decryption algorithm to be simulatable. Two notable cases are the works of Andreeva *et al.* [5] and that of Hoang, Krovetz, and Rogaway [21]. Below is a comparison of our notion with these

Inspired by plaintext awareness the authors of [5] propose two security notions called PA1 and PA2, which involve an *extractor* algorithm that essentially acts as a decryption simulator. Their first notion, PA1, roughly corresponds to a notion of decryption simulatability where the simulator has unrestricted access to the transcript. As we described in Sect. 4.1, such a formulation would not suffice to guarantee chosen-ciphertext security and results in a weaker notion. Accordingly, the authors put forward PA2 where the extractor no longer has access to the transcript and the adversary is prohibited from querying ciphertext to the extractor that it obtains from its encryption oracle. We note, however, that a our notions and relations are not directly comparable to those in [5] since their work assumes a different syntax. Apart from being nonce-based and requiring encryption to be deterministic, their syntax splits decryption into separate decryption and verification algorithms. This choice of syntax has important consequences, where for instance, their resulting IND-CCA notion is weaker than the traditional one, see [6].

A decryption simulator also appears in the definition of Robust Authenticated Encryption (RAE) from [21]. RAE security requires that a (nonce-based) encryption scheme be indistinguishable from an idealised scheme where encryption is a randomly-sampled injection, and decryption can be viewed as answering its queries either by looking up the transcript or via a simulator. That is, the idealised decryption oracle in RAE essentially behaves as our combination of a decryption simulator and wrapper algorithm. Note that in RAE the decryption simulator appears in conjunction with an ideal encryption oracle, whereas in DS it appears in conjunction with the real encryption algorithm. As such, RAE is perhaps more akin to ES ∧ DS (discussed in Sect. 5.1). Indeed, RAE security could be viewed as a special case of ES ∧ DS (translated to the nonce-based setting), where the encryption simulator is further restricted to be a pseudorandom injection.

5 Channel Simulatability

We can now go a step further and require that both encryption and decryption be simulatable.

5.1 Defining Channel Simulatability

A natural formulation is to require that there exist an encryption simulator $\mathcal{S}_E$ and a decryption simulator $\mathcal{S}_D$ such that no adversary can distinguish between unrestricted oracle access to $\mathcal{E}_K(\cdot)$ and $\mathcal{D}_K(\cdot)$ or $\mathcal{S}_E(|\cdot|)$ and $\mathsf{V}[\mathcal{S}_D](\cdot)$. Such a notion turns out to be equivalent to ES $\wedge$ DS, i.e. the requirement that a scheme satisfy both simulatability notions ES and DS. This notion can be viewed as a stronger analogue of IND-CCA security. Indeed, because decryption simulatability reduces IND-CCA security to IND-CPA security and encryption simulatability implies IND-CPA, it follows that ES $\wedge$ DS $\implies$ IND-CCA. Similarly ES $\wedge$ DS-I, where decryption simulatability also ensures integrity, can be viewed as an analogue and a generalisation of the combined authenticated encryption security notion from [29]. Clearly, all of the above also holds for stateful security (ES $\wedge$ SDS-I) and for schemes supporting ciphertext fragmentation (ES $\wedge$ FDS-I).

We believe these notions are appealing for a number of reasons. On an intuitive level, these notions say that an adversary's computational abilities are not any better when it is given oracle access to the channel, since it can be simulated. That is, the ability to choose the messages that get encrypted, replay, reorder and fragment ciphertexts arbitrarily, and observe the output of the decryption algorithm (possibly augmented with additional leakage such as error messages and the release of unverified plaintext) are of no help to the adversary. Moreover, there are no prohibited or suppressed queries, as is the case with all CCA and authenticated encryption type of definitions. Being single-game definitions, they are also easier to prove than their two-game counterparts used in [2,9,11,20,26]. Further backing to the claim that these notions are easier to prove can be found in Sect. 7. Finally, as we will show later on, any scheme that meets these notions realises a universally composable secure channel. Thus our notions guarantee composability under extended security requirements, such as the presence of leakage from invalid ciphertexts [5,6,12,21], protection against replay and reordering [9], and security in the presence of ciphertext fragmentation [2,11,20,26].

However the above formulation, requiring separate simulators, has some limitations. For instance the schemes used in SSH, which include an encrypted length field as part of their ciphertext – see Sect. 7 or [2,26], cannot meet this notion. In particular, because a ciphertext may be delivered as multiple fragments, the length field is used by the decryption algorithm to determine the total length of the ciphertext and accordingly at which point to verify the MAC tag. As such the decryption simulator needs to be able to predict, both for in-sync and out-of-sync ciphertexts, after how many bytes it should return an output. Note that the contents of length field are known to the adversary and any inconsistency between the real scheme and the simulated one would allow it to distinguish the two. At the same time, the encryption simulator cannot leak this information anywhere in the ciphertext, except through its size, as otherwise it would either not constitute a good simulator, or the encryption used to protect the length field in the real scheme is insecure. Consequently, for the schemes used in SSH there can exist no pair of simulators that satisfy the security definition outlined above.

In the case of SSH-CTR this issue can be overcome by allowing the simulators to share a random tape that they can then use to one-time-pad the length field. In general, the more freedom we give the simulators to share resources and communicate the easier it becomes to satisfy such a security notion. We therefore lift all such restrictions by replacing the two simulators with a single simulator having separate interfaces for encryption and decryption, $\mathcal{S}(\mathsf{e}, \cdot)$ and $\mathcal{S}(\mathsf{d}, \cdot)$. The resulting notion, which we call channel simulatability (CS) is stated more formally in Defintion 9 and in Defintion 10. Note that ES $\wedge$ DS $\implies$ CS since two separate simulators can easily be combined into one, but the converse is not true. While it is easy to see that channel simulatability retains the appealing properties that we mentioned earlier, the SSH example we just described separates it from ES $\wedge$ DS. We must therefore make sure that channel simulatability still offers an adequate level of security. We assert this in Theorems 6 and 10, where we prove that it guarantees chosen ciphertext security and integrity. The results are stated for schemes supporting ciphertext fragmentation but analogous results hold in the atomic setting for plain and stateful security. In Sect. 6 we show that channel simulatability implies UC-realising the secure channel ideal functionality. By transitivity, it follows that ES $\wedge$ DS also guarantees universal composability.

Definition 9 (Channel Simulatability). *Let $\mathcal{SE} = (\mathcal{K}, \mathcal{E}, \mathcal{D})$ be a symmetric encryption scheme. For any adversary $\mathcal{A}$ and a channel simulator $\mathcal{S}$ we define the corresponding* CS *and* SCS *advantages as:*

$$\mathsf{Adv}^{\mathsf{cs}}_{\mathcal{SE}}(\mathcal{A}, \mathcal{S}) = \Pr\left[\mathcal{A}^{\mathcal{E}_K(\cdot), \mathcal{D}_K(\cdot)} \Rightarrow 1 \right] - \Pr\left[\mathcal{A}^{\mathcal{S}(\mathsf{e}, |\cdot|), \mathsf{V}[\mathcal{S}](\mathsf{d}, \cdot)} \Rightarrow 1 \right],$$

and,

$$\mathsf{Adv}^{\mathsf{scs}}_{\mathcal{SE}}(\mathcal{A}, \mathcal{S}) = \Pr\left[\mathcal{A}^{\mathcal{E}_K(\cdot), \mathcal{D}_K(\cdot)} \Rightarrow 1 \right] - \Pr\left[\mathcal{A}^{\mathcal{S}(\mathsf{e}, |\cdot|), \mathsf{W}[\mathcal{S}](\mathsf{d}, \cdot)} \Rightarrow 1 \right],$$

where the probabilities are over $K \leftarrow \mathcal{K}$ and the algorithms' coin tosses. Alternatively, if $\mathcal{SE}$ is a symmetric encryption scheme supporting ciphertext fragmentation, its corresponding FCS *advantage is given by:*

$$\mathsf{Adv}^{\mathsf{fcs}}_{\mathcal{SE}}(\mathcal{A}, \mathcal{S}) = \Pr\left[\mathcal{A}^{\mathcal{E}_K(\cdot), \mathcal{D}_K(\cdot)} \Rightarrow 1 \right] - \Pr\left[\mathcal{A}^{\mathcal{S}(\mathsf{e}, |\cdot|), \mathsf{Z}[\mathcal{S}](\mathsf{d}, \cdot)} \Rightarrow 1 \right].$$

A scheme $\mathcal{SE}$ is said to be $(\epsilon, \mathcal{R}_\mathcal{S}, \mathcal{R}_\mathcal{A})$-NN secure, for NN $\in \{$CS, SCS, FCS$\}$, *if there exists a randomised and possibly stateful simulator $\mathcal{S}$ such that every query of the form $\mathcal{S}(\mathsf{e}, \cdot)$ or $\mathcal{S}(\mathsf{d}, \cdot)$ requires at most $\mathcal{R}_\mathcal{S}$ resources, and for any adversary $\mathcal{A}$, requiring at most $\mathcal{R}_\mathcal{A}$ resources, its respective advantage $\mathsf{Adv}^{\mathsf{nn}}_{\mathcal{SE}}(\mathcal{A}, \mathcal{S})$ is bounded by ϵ.*

Theorem 6 (FCS $\implies$ IND-sfCFA). *Let $\mathcal{SE} = (\mathcal{K}, \mathcal{E}, \mathcal{D})$ be a symmetric encryption scheme supporting ciphertext fragmentation. Then for any adversary $\mathcal{A}$ and any channel simulator $\mathcal{S}$ it holds that:*

$$\mathsf{Adv}^{\mathsf{ind\text{-}sfcfa}}_{\mathcal{SE}}(\mathcal{A}) \leq 2 \cdot \mathsf{Adv}^{\mathsf{fcs}}_{\mathcal{SE}}(\mathcal{A}, \mathcal{S}).$$

Proof. Observing that $\mathsf{cfDec}(\cdot)$ is identical to $\overline{\mathsf{Z}}[\mathcal{D}_K](\cdot)$, it follows that for any adversary $\mathcal{A}$:

$$\mathsf{Adv}_{\mathcal{SE}}^{\text{ind-sfcfa}}(\mathcal{A}) = \underset{\mathcal{A}}{\Delta}\left[\begin{matrix}\mathcal{E}_K(\cdot) \ ,\overline{\mathsf{Z}}[\mathcal{D}_K](\cdot)\\ \mathcal{E}_K(0^{|\cdot|}),\overline{\mathsf{Z}}[\mathcal{D}_K](\cdot)\end{matrix}\right].$$

By the triangle inequality, for any channel simulator $\mathcal{S}$ it follows that:

$$\leq \underset{\mathcal{A}}{\Delta}\left[\begin{matrix}\mathcal{E}_K(\cdot) \ ,\overline{\mathsf{Z}}[\mathcal{D}_K](\cdot)\\ \mathcal{S}(\mathsf{e},|\cdot|),\overline{\mathsf{Z}}[\mathcal{S}](\mathsf{d},\cdot)\end{matrix}\right] + \underset{\mathcal{A}}{\Delta}\left[\begin{matrix}\mathcal{S}(\mathsf{e},|\cdot|),\overline{\mathsf{Z}}[\mathcal{S}](\mathsf{d},\cdot)\\ \mathcal{E}_K(0^{|\cdot|}),\overline{\mathsf{Z}}[\mathcal{D}_K](\cdot)\end{matrix}\right].$$

In the second term, since the wrapper is suppressing, we can replace every encryption query m with $0^{|m|}$, reducing it to:

$$\leq \underset{\mathcal{A}}{\Delta}\left[\begin{matrix}\mathcal{E}_K(\cdot) \ ,\overline{\mathsf{Z}}[\mathcal{D}_K](\cdot)\\ \mathcal{S}(\mathsf{e},|\cdot|),\overline{\mathsf{Z}}[\mathcal{S}](\mathsf{d},\cdot)\end{matrix}\right] + \underset{\mathcal{A}}{\Delta}\left[\begin{matrix}\mathcal{S}(\mathsf{e},|\cdot|),\overline{\mathsf{Z}}[\mathcal{S}](\mathsf{d},\cdot)\\ \mathcal{E}_K(\cdot) \ ,\overline{\mathsf{Z}}[\mathcal{D}_K](\cdot)\end{matrix}\right].$$

Through a straightforward reduction that applies $\overline{\mathsf{Z}}$ to the decryption oracle and observing that applying $\overline{\mathsf{Z}}$ after Z is equivalent to applying $\overline{\mathsf{Z}}$ directly, we obtain:

$$\leq \underset{\mathcal{A}}{\Delta}\left[\begin{matrix}\mathcal{E}_K(\cdot) \ ,\mathsf{Z}[\mathcal{D}_K](\cdot)\\ \mathcal{S}(\mathsf{e},|\cdot|),\mathsf{Z}[\mathcal{S}](\mathsf{d},\cdot)\end{matrix}\right] + \underset{\mathcal{A}}{\Delta}\left[\begin{matrix}\mathcal{S}(\mathsf{e},|\cdot|),\mathsf{Z}[\mathcal{S}](\mathsf{d},\cdot)\\ \mathcal{E}_K(\cdot) \ ,\mathsf{Z}[\mathcal{D}_K](\cdot)\end{matrix}\right],$$

and the result follows

$$= \quad \mathsf{Adv}_{\mathcal{SE}}^{\text{fcs}}(\mathcal{A},\mathcal{S}) \quad + \quad \mathsf{Adv}_{\mathcal{SE}}^{\text{fcs}}(\mathcal{A},\mathcal{S}).$$

$\square$

5.2   Channel Simulatability with Integrity

Just like decryption simulatability, channel simulatability can easily be extended to guarantee ciphertext integrity by additionally requiring an easily verifiable property from the channel simulator. Informally, we require that, by design, the simulator never return a valid output for a ciphertext that is not in the transcript (CS-I) or once the queries become out of sync (SCS-I and FCS-I).

Definition 10 (Channel Simulatability with Integrity). *Let $\mathcal{SE} = (\mathcal{K},\mathcal{E},\mathcal{D})$ be an atomic symmetric encryption scheme. Then $\mathcal{SE}$ is said to be $(\epsilon,\mathcal{R}_{\mathcal{S}},\mathcal{R}_{\mathcal{A}})$-CS-I or $(\epsilon,\mathcal{R}_{\mathcal{S}},\mathcal{R}_{\mathcal{A}})$-SCS-I secure, if it is respectively $(\epsilon,\mathcal{R}_{\mathcal{S}},\mathcal{R}_{\mathcal{A}})$-CS or $(\epsilon,\mathcal{R}_{\mathcal{S}},\mathcal{R}_{\mathcal{A}})$-SCS secure, and, in addition, the corresponding channel simulator $\mathcal{S}$ is such that $\overline{\mathsf{V}}[\mathcal{S}](\mathsf{d},\cdot)$, or respectively $\overline{\mathsf{W}}[\mathcal{S}](\mathsf{d},\cdot)$, never (with probability zero) outputs a pair (v,m') where $v = \top$.*

Similarly, if $\mathcal{SE}$ is a symmetric encryption scheme supporting ciphertext fragmentation it is said to be $(\epsilon,\mathcal{R}_{\mathcal{S}},\mathcal{R}_{\mathcal{A}})$-FCS-I secure if it is $(\epsilon,\mathcal{R}_{\mathcal{S}},\mathcal{R}_{\mathcal{A}})$-FCS secure and its corresponding simulator $\mathcal{S}$ is such that $\overline{\mathsf{Z}}[\mathcal{S}](\mathsf{d},\cdot)$ never (with probability zero) returns an output $(v_1,m'_1),\ldots,(v_\ell,m'_\ell)$ where $v_i = \top$ for some $1 \leq i \leq \ell$.

The theorem below states that channel simulatability with integrity implies the respective notion of ciphertext integrity. The theorem is stated for the case of ciphertext fragmentation, but analogous results hold for the atomic schemes. Its proof is similar to that of Theorem 5 with some minor adaptations. A proof can be found in the full version of this paper.

Theorem 7 (FCS-I $\implies$ INT-sfCFRG). *Let* $\mathcal{SE} = (\mathcal{K}, \mathcal{E}, \mathcal{D})$ *be a symmetric encryption scheme supporting ciphertext fragmentation and let* S *be a channel simulator such that it is* $(\epsilon, \mathcal{R}_S, \mathcal{R}_{\mathcal{A}})$-FCS-I *secure. Then* $\mathcal{SE}$ *is* $(\epsilon, \mathcal{R}_{\mathcal{A}})$-INT-sfCFRG *secure.*

6   Simulatable Channels and Universal Composability

In this section we show that any scheme satisfying channel simulatability with integrity realises a universally composable channel.

6.1   UC Framework

The universal composition framework [13] is a simulation-based security notion for a protocol π implementing some ideal functionality $\mathcal{F}$. The approach requires that for any adversary $\mathcal{A}_{\mathrm{UC}}$ attacking a real protocol π between parties $P_1, P_2, \ldots$ there exists an ideal-model adversary $\mathcal{S}_{\mathrm{UC}}$ (or, simulator) interacting in a world where all parties are connected to the ideal functionality $\mathcal{F}$. The only task of the parties in this ideal world is to forward their inputs to $\mathcal{F}$ and output the responses of $\mathcal{F}$. The communication with the ideal functionality is not visible to other parties and cannot be tampered with.

We give here only an informal introduction to the model and refer to [13] for the details. The UC model is different from other simulation-based notions in that it uses an interactive distinguisher to decide in which of the two worlds the execution takes place. This interactive distinguisher is called the environment $\mathcal{E}_{\mathrm{UC}}$, since it represents other potentially ongoing protocols and thereby ensures composability. The environment determines the input of the parties, learns their outputs, and can interact with the (real or ideal) adversary. To distinguish inputs for different sessions, the UC model assumes that globally unique and publicly known session identifiers sid are assigned to each protocol execution.

Let $\mathsf{REAL}_{\mathcal{A}_{\mathrm{UC}}, \mathcal{E}_{\mathrm{UC}}, \pi}(n)$ be the random variable denoting the environment's output in a real-world execution, where $\mathcal{A}_{\mathrm{UC}}$ interacts with the protocol π for security parameter n, and $\mathsf{IDEAL}_{\mathcal{S}_{\mathrm{UC}}, \mathcal{E}_{\mathrm{UC}}, \mathcal{F}}(n)$ be the corresponding random variable when interacting with $\mathcal{S}_{\mathrm{UC}}$ in the ideal world. We say that a protocol π *securely realises* $\mathcal{F}$ if for any probabilistic polynomial time (PPT) adversary $\mathcal{A}_{\mathrm{UC}}$ there exists a PPT simulator $\mathcal{S}_{\mathrm{UC}}$ such that for any PPT environment $\mathcal{E}_{\mathrm{UC}}$ the random variables $\mathsf{REAL}_{\mathcal{A}_{\mathrm{UC}}, \mathcal{E}_{\mathrm{UC}}, \pi}$ and $\mathsf{IDEAL}_{\mathcal{S}_{\mathrm{UC}}, \mathcal{E}_{\mathrm{UC}}, \mathcal{F}}$ are computationally indistinguishable. For concrete security one would measure the difference in the output distributions exactly. By viewing a potential distinguisher of the environment's output as part of the environment itself, we can equivalently assume that the environment only outputs a bit to indicate which world it is in.

A secure channel functionality has been given in [15]. It consists of a stage in which the channel between two parties P_i and P_j is established. Once this is done, party P_i can securely transmit messages m to the other party. This is performed by sending m to the secure channel functionality. The functionality then informs the adversary about a transmission, but keeps the actual message m secret. Only the length $|m|$ of the message is revealed to the adversary. The adversary can then decide when to deliver the next message to the receiving party P_j.

We adapt this secure channel functionality to the unidirectional setting, i.e., only party P_i sends messages, and it is a single-instance functionality, i.e., it only allows to establish a single channel. The UC composition theorem allows to extend this simple form of a channel to more complex constructions. The resulting secure channel functionality is described in Fig. 4.

Functionality $\mathcal{F}_{SC}$

1. Upon receiving a command $(\mathtt{EstCh}, sid, P_i, P_j)$ from P_i send $(\mathtt{EstCh}, sid, P_i, P_j)$ to the adversary and (delayed) to P_j. Store $(\mathtt{EstCh}, sid, P_i, P_j)$ and ignore all further establishment requests. Create an empty queue $\mathcal{Q}$ for $(\mathtt{EstCh}, sid, P_i, P_j)$
2. Upon receiving a command $(\mathtt{Send}, sid, m)$ from P_i check if there is a stored entry $(\mathtt{EstCh}, sid, P_i, P_j)$. If not, ignore the message. Else send $(\mathtt{Sent}, sid, |m|)$ to the adversary and enqueue $\mathcal{Q}.\mathsf{enq}(m)$ in the queue.
3. Upon receiving a command $(\mathtt{Deliver}, sid)$ from the adversary, check if $\mathcal{Q}$ is empty; if so, ignore the message. Else dequeue the next message $m \leftarrow \mathcal{Q}.\mathsf{deq}()$ and send $(\mathtt{Sent}, sid, m)$ to P_j.

Fig. 4. Ideal functionality for a secure channel (with static corruptions).

6.2 Simulatable Channels with Integrity are Universally Composable

Here we show that simulatable channels (with integrity) are also universally composable. The necessity of the integrity property stems from the definition of the ideal channel functionality: The UC adversary can only demand to deliver messages which have been actually inserted into the channel; it cannot make the receiving party output further messages. In contrast, simulatable channels without integrity in principle allow the simulator to output other messages as well. Put differently, the secure channel functionality stipulates integrity by construction.

We are, of course, faced with the problem that the two parties need to share a key in the symmetric setting, without having a way to communicate securely yet. Previous solutions [14] assumed that the keys are established by running a suitable key exchange protocol first. To abstract out this step, we design our protocol π_{SC} in the hybrid setting where an ideal functionality $\mathcal{F}_{KE}$ establishes a shared key between the two parties. That is, π_{SC} may call the ideal functionality $\mathcal{F}_{KE}$, shown in Fig. 5, as part of the protocol steps. We parameterise this functionality by a key generation algorithm $\mathcal{K}$ to describe the underlying distribution over keys. The concrete implementation of the key establishment protocol is a matter of choice, but the UC framework says that any protocol realising $\mathcal{F}_{KE}$ securely, can then be composed with our protocol π_{SC} to yield a secure, fully implemented protocol for $\mathcal{F}_{SC}$. We assume that the session identifier sid' of the sub procedure has a one-to-one correspondence with the session identifier sid of the calling protocol, e.g., are given by $sid\|0$ and $sid\|1$.

Functionality $\mathcal{F}_{KE}^{\mathcal{K}}$

1. Upon receiving a command (EstKey, sid', P_i, P_j) from P_i, check that there is no entry for sid' yet. If so, pick a random key $K \leftarrow \mathcal{K}$ and send (EstKey, sid', P_i, P_j) to the adversary and the (delayed-output) messages (EstKey, sid', P_i, P_j, K) to P_i and P_j.

Fig. 5. Ideal functionality for key establishment (with static corruptions).

Construction 8. *Let $\mathcal{SE} = (\mathcal{K}, \mathcal{E}, \mathcal{D})$ be an encryption scheme. Define the protocol π_{SC} in the $\mathcal{F}_{KE}^{\mathcal{K}}$-hybrid model follows:*

- *On input (EstCh, sid, P_i, P_j) to P_i make a call (EstKey, sid', P_i, P_j) to $\mathcal{F}_{KE}^{\mathcal{K}}$.*
- *On input (EstKey, sid', P_i, P_j, K) from $\mathcal{F}_{KE}^{\mathcal{K}}$ to P_i or P_j store (sid, P_i, P_j, K).*
- *On input (Send, sid, m) to P_i check for an entry (sid, P_i, P_j, K). If found, compute $c \leftarrow \mathcal{E}(K, m)$, and possibly update the state, and send (sid, c) to P_j.*
- *On input (sid, f) check for an entry (sid, P_i, P_j, K). If found, compute the sequence $(v_1, m_1), \ldots, (v_\ell, m_\ell) \leftarrow \mathcal{D}(K, f)$, possibly updating the state, and for each $v_i = \top$ output (Sent, sid, m_i) (in this order).*

We state our theorem with respect to the stateful fragmentation notion FCS-I. The result also transfers straightforwardly to the stateless and stateful atomic cases CS-I and SCS-I.

Theorem 9. *If $\mathcal{SE} = (\mathcal{K}, \mathcal{E}, \mathcal{D})$ supports fragmentation and is channel simulatable with integrity (FCS-I) then the protocol π_{SC} securely realises $\mathcal{F}_{SC}$ in the $\mathcal{F}_{KE}^{\mathcal{K}}$-hybrid model.*

The idea is to turn the channel simulator S, embedded into a wrapper Z, into a UC simulator $\mathcal{S}_{UC}$, interacting with the channel functionality $\mathcal{F}_{SC}$ instead. The reduction then shows that any UC environment $\mathcal{E}_{UC}$ (in combination with a fixed but sufficiently general UC dummy adversary $\tilde{\mathcal{A}}_{UC}$) against this UC simulator can be transformed into a channel simulatability adversary $\mathcal{A}$. Note that the order of quantifiers is important here: the UC simulator $\mathcal{S}_{UC}$ works for any environment $\mathcal{E}_{UC}$ just as the channel simulator S works for any channel

alg. SSH-CTR-$\mathcal{E}_K(m)$	alg. SSH-CTR-$\mathcal{D}_K(f)$
1 : **parse** K as (K_e, K_m, IV)	1 : **parse** K as (K_e, K_m, IV)
2 : **if** e-seqnr $= 0$	2 : **if** d-seqnr $= 0 \wedge \alpha = \varepsilon$
3 : e-ctr $\leftarrow IV$ // initialise on first call	3 : d-ctr $\leftarrow IV$ // initialise on first call
4 : mlen $\leftarrow |m|_B$	4 : **if** closed
5 : // calculate padding length	5 : out $\leftarrow (\bot, \mathsf{CONN\_CLOSED})$; **break**
6 : padlen $\leftarrow$ blocksize $- (5 + \text{mlen})\%$blocksize	6 : $\alpha \leftarrow \alpha \parallel f$; out $\leftarrow \varepsilon$ // update buffer and reset output
7 : **if** padlen < 4	7 : **while** (true) // process buffer (α)
8 : padlen $\leftarrow$ padlen $+$ blocksize	8 : **if** $|\alpha|_B <$ blocksize
9 : // encode the message	9 : **break** // first ciphertext block is incomplete
10 : pad $\leftarrow \{0, 1\}^{\text{padlen} \cdot 8}$	10 : // decrypt first ciphertext block
11 : len $\leftarrow 1 + \text{mlen} + \text{padlen}$	11 : ptxt$' \leftarrow \alpha[1, \text{blocksize}] \oplus \mathsf{BC}(K_e, \text{d-ctr})$
12 : ptxt $\leftarrow \langle \text{len} \rangle_{32} \parallel \langle \text{padlen} \rangle_8 \parallel m \parallel \text{pad}$	12 : d-ctr $\leftarrow$ d-ctr $+ 1$
13 : // encrypt and mac	13 : clen $\leftarrow (\text{ptxt}'[1, 32])^{-1} + 4 + \text{macsize}$
14 : $\tau \leftarrow \mathsf{MAC}(K_m, \langle \text{e-seqnr} \rangle_{32} \parallel \text{ptxt})$	14 : inRange $\leftarrow (16 + \text{macsize} \le \text{clen} \le 35000)$
15 : $z \leftarrow \varepsilon$	15 : isMult $\leftarrow ((\text{clen} - \text{macsize})\%$blocksize $\ne 0)$
16 : **while** $|z| < |\text{ptxt}|$	16 : **if** $\neg$inRange $\vee$ isMult // validate length
17 : $z \leftarrow z \parallel \mathsf{BC}(K_e, \text{e-ctr})$	17 : out $\leftarrow$ out $\parallel (\bot, \mathsf{INVALID\_LENGTH})$
18 : e-ctr $\leftarrow$ e-ctr $+ 1$	18 : closed $\leftarrow$ true; **break**
19 : $c \leftarrow (\text{ptxt} \oplus z) \parallel \tau$	19 : **if** $|\alpha|_B <$ clen
20 : e-seqnr $\leftarrow$ e-seqnr $+ 1$	20 : **break** // wait to complete ciphertext
21 : **return** c	21 : $z \leftarrow \varepsilon$ // decrypt and verify mac
	22 : **while** $|z| < (\text{clen} - \text{blocksize} - \text{macsize})$
	23 : $z \leftarrow z \parallel \mathsf{BC}(K_e, \text{e-ctr})$
	24 : d-ctr $\leftarrow$ d-ctr $+ 1$
	25 : $z \leftarrow z[1, \text{clen} - \text{blocksize} - \text{macsize}]$ // trim
	26 : ptxt$' \leftarrow$ ptxt$' \parallel z \oplus \alpha[\text{blocksize} + 1, \text{clen} - \text{macsize}]_B$
	27 : $\tau' \leftarrow \alpha[\text{clen} - \text{macsize} + 1, \text{clen}]_B$
	28 : $\alpha \leftarrow \alpha[\text{clen} + 1, *]_B$ // remove decrypted ciphertext
	29 : **if** $\tau' \ne \mathsf{MAC}(K_m, \langle \text{d-seqnr} \rangle_{32} \parallel \text{ptxt}')$
	30 : out $\leftarrow$ out $\parallel (\bot, \mathsf{INVALID\_MAC})$
	31 : closed $\leftarrow$ true; **break**
	32 : padlen $\leftarrow \langle \text{ptxt}'[5, 5]_B \rangle^{-1}$ // validate padding length
	33 : mlen$' \leftarrow$ clen $-$ padlen $- 4 - 1 -$ macsize
	34 : **if** $(\text{mlen}' > 32789) \vee (\text{mlen}' < 1)$
	35 : out $\leftarrow$ out $\parallel (\bot, \mathsf{INVALID\_PAD\_LENGTH})$
	36 : closed $\leftarrow$ true; **break**
	37 : $m' \leftarrow$ ptxt$'[6, \text{clen} - \text{macsize} - \text{padlen}]_B$
	38 : out $\leftarrow$ out $\parallel (\top, m')$
	39 : d-seqnr $\leftarrow$ d-seqnr $+ 1$
	40 : **return** out

Fig. 6. The SSH-CTR scheme as implemented in Dropbear.

adversary $\mathcal{A}$. Integrity of the channel ensures that the simulation of the UC simulator $\mathcal{S}_{\mathrm{UC}}$ is sound. The proof appears in the full version of this paper.

Unfortunately, we cannot show that universal composability implies channel simulatability (with or without integrity). The reason is that ciphertexts may carry redundancy, e.g., an extra bit appended to the ciphertext $c \parallel 0$, which still allows a UC simulator to detect an altered but valid ciphertext, say, $c \parallel 1$, and to ask the ideal functionality to forward the next message in the queue. Our channel simulator, on the other hand, does not know the message encapsulated in $c\|0$ and the wrapper would not reveal it either.

6.3   Other Work on Composable Secure Channels

In [23], Küsters and Tuengerthal consider two ideal functionalities, one for encryption and one for authenticated encryption and present matching protocols which realise these functionalities iff the underlying symmetric encryption schemes respectively satisfy IND-CCA and IND-CPA ∧ INT-CTXT. These results are limited to atomic and single-error encryption schemes. More importantly, however, the ideal functionalities considered therein are significantly different from that in [15] (and consequently also to ours): They consider the stronger notion of adaptive corruptions and thus have to deal with the committing property of encryption schemes. At the same time, their composition, in an intermediate step, uses an encryption scheme with full key reveals, such that the problem of key cycles —the environment asking for circular encryptions of a key under that key— must be taken care of. In contrast, [15] and we here work with the common notion of secret keys.

   An alternative formulation of secure channels can be found in [24,25], in the language of Maurer's Constructive Cryptography framework. We believe that an analogue of Theorem 9 should also hold for the Constuctive Cryptography framework. That is, any scheme that is channel simulatable with integrity (CS-I/SCS-I/FCS-I) can be used to convert an insecure channel into a secure channel.

7   Dropbear's SSH-CTR Implementation is FCS-I Secure

Dropbear is an SSH distribution intended specifically for resource-constrained devices such as embedded systems. In a measurement study performed in early 2016 [2] it was found to be the most widely deployed SSH implementation on the Internet. Owing to its minimalist design it only implements a handful of ciphersuites. Following the attack from [3] which affected CBC encryption, it added support for counter mode encryption and set this as the default. The study from [2] identified counter-mode encryption as the preferred choice for more than 90% of the Dropbear servers.

   The SSH-CTR scheme described in Fig. 6 is an accurate representation of SSH's symmetric encryption using counter mode that we extracted from Dropbear's open source code. Throughout it is assumed that compression is disabled. At various points during decryption a ciphertext may be deemed to be invalid resulting in the connection being torn down. We model this by setting a closed flag at which point all subsequent calls to the decryption algorithm will return an error of the form ($\perp$, CONN_CLOSED). Dropbear does not return specific error messages prior to closing a connection, however we adopt a conservative approach and return distinct error messages for every decryption failure that results in a connection tear-down. This only serves to strengthen our security result, since security will hold even if an adversary can distinguish these events through timing information or some other means.

We next show that SSH-CTR is FCS-I secure. To prove this, we need to transform the scheme, through a sequence of game hops, into a pair of algorithms such that (a) both algorithm do not make use of the key, (b) encryption does not make use of the message contents, and (c) decryption only returns error messages for out-of-sync ciphertexts. This is easier than it sounds, in particular by the point where we switch from a block cipher and MAC to their idealised forms (i.e. random functions) we have already eliminated the key. We then only need a couple of simple probabilistic arguments to reach our goal. The advantage of channel simulatability is that we can focus on specific portions of the code without having to worry about its functionality as a whole. For example, we do not have to worry about the parts of the code which handle the reconstruction of ciphertexts and validating of the length field. Indeed if the scheme made use of a nonce-based AEAD scheme, such as GCM, we would only need one game hop to prove channel simulatability.

Below is a formal statement of the security theorem. Its proof can be found in the full version of this paper

Theorem 10 (SSH-CTR is FCS-I secure). *Let* SSH-CTR *be the encryption scheme supporting ciphertext fragmentation, composed of a blockcipher* BC *and a MAC algorithm* MAC, *described in Fig. 6. Then there exists a simulator* S *such that for any* FCS-I *adversary* $\mathcal{A}_{fcs}$ *attempting to distinguish* S *from* SSH-CTR, *running in time* t, *making at most* q_e *encryption queries totalling* μ_e *bits, and at most* q_d *decryption queries totalling* μ_d *bits, it holds that:*

$$\mathsf{Adv}^{\mathsf{fcs}}_{\mathsf{SSH\text{-}CTR}}(\mathcal{A}_{\mathsf{fcs}}) \leq \mathsf{Adv}^{\mathsf{prf}}_{\mathsf{BC}}(t', q_f) + \frac{q_f^2}{2^{\mathsf{blocksize}+1}} + \mathsf{Adv}^{\mathsf{prf}}_{\mathsf{MAC}}(t', q_m) + 2^{-\mathsf{macsize}},$$

where $q_f = \lceil \frac{\mu_e + 40q_e}{\mathsf{blocksize}} \rceil + q_e + \lceil \frac{\mu_d + 40q_d}{\mathsf{blocksize}} \rceil + q_d$, $q_m = q_e + q_d$, *and* $t' \approx t$.
Furthermore, S *is such that* $\overline{Z}[S](\mathsf{d}, \cdot)$ *never returns an output* $(v_1, m'_1), \ldots,$ (v_ℓ, m'_ℓ) *where* $v_i = \top$ *for some* $1 \leq i \leq \ell$.

References

1. Abadi, M., Rogaway, P.: Reconciling two views of cryptography (the computational soundness of formal encryption). J. Cryptol. **20**(3), 395 (2007)
2. Albrecht, M.R., Degabriele, J.P., Hansen, T.B., Paterson, K.G.: A surfeit of SSH cipher suites. In: Weippl, E.R., Katzenbeisser, S., Kruegel, C., Myers, A.C., Halevi, S. (eds.) ACM CCS 2016, pp. 1480–1491. ACM Press, October 2016
3. Albrecht, M.R., Paterson, K.G., Watson, G.J.: Plaintext recovery attacks against SSH. In: 2009 IEEE Symposium on Security and Privacy, pp. 16–26. IEEE Computer Society Press, May 2009
4. AlFardan, N.J., Paterson, K.G.: Lucky thirteen: breaking the TLS and DTLS record protocols. In: 2013 IEEE Symposium on Security and Privacy, pp. 526–540. IEEE Computer Society Press, May 2013

5. Andreeva, E., Bogdanov, A., Luykx, A., Mennink, B., Mouha, N., Yasuda, K.: How to securely release unverified plaintext in authenticated encryption. In: Sarkar, P., Iwata, T. (eds.) ASIACRYPT 2014. LNCS, vol. 8873, pp. 105–125. Springer, Heidelberg (2014). https://doi.org/10.1007/978-3-662-45611-8_6

6. Barwell, G., Page, D., Stam, M.: Rogue decryption failures: reconciling AE robustness notions. In: Groth, J. (ed.) IMACC 2015. LNCS, vol. 9496, pp. 94–111. Springer, Cham (2015). https://doi.org/10.1007/978-3-319-27239-9_6

7. Bellare, M., Boldyreva, A., Desai, A., Pointcheval, D.: Key-privacy in public-key encryption. In: Boyd, C. (ed.) ASIACRYPT 2001. LNCS, vol. 2248, pp. 566–582. Springer, Heidelberg (2001). https://doi.org/10.1007/3-540-45682-1_33

8. Bellare, M., Desai, A., Jokipii, E., Rogaway, P.: A concrete security treatment of symmetric encryption. In: 38th FOCS, pp. 394–403. IEEE Computer Society Press, October 1997

9. Bellare, M., Kohno, T., Namprempre, C.: Authenticated encryption in SSH: provably fixing the SSH binary packet protocol. In: Atluri, V. (ed.) ACM CCS 2002, pp. 1–11. ACM Press, November 2002

10. Bellare, M., Namprempre, C.: Authenticated encryption: relations among notions and analysis of the generic composition paradigm. In: Okamoto, T. (ed.) ASIACRYPT 2000. LNCS, vol. 1976, pp. 531–545. Springer, Heidelberg (2000). https://doi.org/10.1007/3-540-44448-3_41

11. Boldyreva, A., Degabriele, J.P., Paterson, K.G., Stam, M.: Security of symmetric encryption in the presence of ciphertext fragmentation. In: Pointcheval, D., Johansson, T. (eds.) EUROCRYPT 2012. LNCS, vol. 7237, pp. 682–699. Springer, Heidelberg (2012). https://doi.org/10.1007/978-3-642-29011-4_40

12. Boldyreva, A., Degabriele, J.P., Paterson, K.G., Stam, M.: On symmetric encryption with distinguishable decryption failures. In: Moriai, S. (ed.) FSE 2013. LNCS, vol. 8424, pp. 367–390. Springer, Heidelberg (2014). https://doi.org/10.1007/978-3-662-43933-3_19

13. Canetti, R.: Universally composable security: a new paradigm for cryptographic protocols. In: 42nd FOCS, pp. 136–145. IEEE Computer Society Press, October 2001

14. Canetti, R., Krawczyk, H.: Analysis of key-exchange protocols and their use for building secure channels. In: Pfitzmann, B. (ed.) EUROCRYPT 2001. LNCS, vol. 2045, pp. 453–474. Springer, Heidelberg (2001). https://doi.org/10.1007/3-540-44987-6_28

15. Canetti, R., Krawczyk, H.: Universally composable notions of key exchange and secure channels. In: Knudsen, L.R. (ed.) EUROCRYPT 2002. LNCS, vol. 2332, pp. 337–351. Springer, Heidelberg (2002). https://doi.org/10.1007/3-540-46035-7_22

16. Canvel, B., Hiltgen, A.P., Vaudenay, S., Vuagnoux, M.: Password interception in a SSL/TLS channel. In: Boneh, D. (ed.) CRYPTO 2003. LNCS, vol. 2729, pp. 583–599. Springer, Heidelberg (2003). https://doi.org/10.1007/978-3-540-45146-4_34

17. Degabriele, J.P., Paterson, K.G.: On the (in)security of IPsec in MAC-then-encrypt configurations. In: Al-Shaer, E., Keromytis, A.D., Shmatikov, V. (eds.) ACM CCS 2010, pp. 493–504. ACM Press, October 2010

18. Desai, A.: New paradigms for constructing symmetric encryption schemes secure against chosen-ciphertext attack. In: Bellare, M. (ed.) CRYPTO 2000. LNCS, vol. 1880, pp. 394–412. Springer, Heidelberg (2000). https://doi.org/10.1007/3-540-44598-6_25

19. Fischlin, M.: Pseudorandom function tribe ensembles based on one-way permutations: improvements and applications. In: Stern, J. (ed.) EUROCRYPT 1999. LNCS, vol. 1592, pp. 432–445. Springer, Heidelberg (1999). https://doi.org/10.1007/3-540-48910-X_30

20. Fischlin, M., Günther, F., Marson, G.A., Paterson, K.G.: Data is a stream: security of stream-based channels. In: Gennaro, R., Robshaw, M.J.B. (eds.) CRYPTO 2015. LNCS, vol. 9216, pp. 545–564. Springer, Heidelberg (2015). https://doi.org/10.1007/978-3-662-48000-7_27

21. Hoang, V.T., Krovetz, T., Rogaway, P.: Robust authenticated-encryption AEZ and the problem that it solves. In: Oswald, E., Fischlin, M. (eds.) EUROCRYPT 2015. LNCS, vol. 9056, pp. 15–44. Springer, Heidelberg (2015). https://doi.org/10.1007/978-3-662-46800-5_2

22. Hoang, V.T., Reyhanitabar, R., Rogaway, P., Vizár, D.: Online authenticated-encryption and its nonce-reuse misuse-resistance. In: Gennaro, R., Robshaw, M.J.B. (eds.) CRYPTO 2015. LNCS, vol. 9215, pp. 493–517. Springer, Heidelberg (2015). https://doi.org/10.1007/978-3-662-47989-6_24

23. Küsters, R., Tuengerthal, M.: Universally composable symmetric encryption. In: Proceedings of the 22nd IEEE Computer Security Foundations Symposium, CSF 2009, Port Jefferson, New York, USA, 8–10 July 2009, pp. 293–307. IEEE Computer Society (2009). https://doi.org/10.1109/CSF.2009.18

24. Maurer, U., Rüedlinger, A., Tackmann, B.: Confidentiality and integrity: a constructive perspective. In: Cramer, R. (ed.) TCC 2012. LNCS, vol. 7194, pp. 209–229. Springer, Heidelberg (2012). https://doi.org/10.1007/978-3-642-28914-9_12

25. Maurer, U., Tackmann, B.: On the soundness of authenticate-then-encrypt: formalizing the malleability of symmetric encryption. In: Al-Shaer, E., Keromytis, A.D., Shmatikov, V. (eds.) ACM CCS 2010, pp. 505–515. ACM Press, October 2010

26. Paterson, K.G., Watson, G.J.: Plaintext-dependent decryption: a formal security treatment of SSH-CTR. In: Gilbert, H. (ed.) EUROCRYPT 2010. LNCS, vol. 6110, pp. 345–361. Springer, Heidelberg (2010). https://doi.org/10.1007/978-3-642-13190-5_18

27. Rogaway, P.: Nonce-based symmetric encryption. In: Roy, B.K., Meier, W. (eds.) FSE 2004. LNCS, vol. 3017, pp. 348–358. Springer, Heidelberg (2004). https://doi.org/10.1007/978-3-540-25937-4_22

28. Rogaway, P., Bellare, M., Black, J., Krovetz, T.: OCB: a block-cipher mode of operation for efficient authenticated encryption. In: ACM CCS 2001, pp. 196–205. ACM Press, November 2001

29. Rogaway, P., Shrimpton, T.: A provable-security treatment of the key-wrap problem. In: Vaudenay, S. (ed.) EUROCRYPT 2006. LNCS, vol. 4004, pp. 373–390. Springer, Heidelberg (2006). https://doi.org/10.1007/11761679_23

Correction to: Constructing Ideal Secret Sharing Schemes Based on Chinese Remainder Theorem

Yu Ning, Fuyou Miao, Wenchao Huang, Keju Meng, Yan Xiong, and Xingfu Wang

Correction to:
Chapter "Constructing Ideal Secret Sharing Schemes Based on Chinese Remainder Theorem" in: T. Peyrin and S. Galbraith (Eds.): *Advances in Cryptology – ASIACRYPT 2018*, **LNCS 11274,**
https://doi.org/10.1007/978-3-030-03332-3_12

Two references to papers by T. Galibus et al. have been added to this paper because these publications, published in 2007 and 2008, contain results mentioned in the present paper. The authors of the present paper were unaware of these publications and obtained their results independently.

The updated version of this chapter can be found at
https://doi.org/10.1007/978-3-030-03332-3_12

Author Index

Printed in the United States
By Bookmasters